AMERICAN FOREIGN POLICY IN THE NUCLEAR AGE

AMERICAN FOREIGN POLICY IN THE NUCLEAR AGE

Third Edition

CECIL V. CRABB, Jr.
Louisiana State University

Harper & Row, Publishers
New York, Evanston, San Francisco, London

AMERICAN FOREIGN POLICY IN THE NUCLEAR AGE, Third
Edition

Standard Book Number: 06–041382–4

Library of Congress Catalog Card Number: 71–168366

CONTENTS

PREFACE

The third edition of this book, a thorough revision, retains the basic organizational structure—early chapters focusing upon the conduct of American foreign relations and later chapters dealing with substantive policy issues and problems. Experience has shown this to be a useful delineation of the subject-matter, allowing maximum flexibility in meeting the needs of instructors and students.

This edition has been revised to delete dated material, to incorporate the findings of recent studies, to introduce questions of current concern to students of American foreign policy, and to stimulate greater interest in a topic whose contemporary relevance can hardly be overemphasized.

Informational aspects of foreign affairs and economic techniques of foreign policy have been combined in Chapter 14; disarmament proceedings and American participation in the United Nations have been consolidated in Chapter 15. Other noteworthy changes are as follows: In Chapter 1, greater attention has been devoted to the impact of domestic needs and problems upon the foreign policy of the United States, especially as these limit the allocation of resources available for diplomatic purposes. American versus Soviet economic competition is dealt with and projections of each nation's economic prospects for the 1970s and beyond are included.

The treatment of the roles of the President and of the State Department in the foreign policy process (Chapter 3) highlights two recent concerns of many citizens: the powers of the President (vis-à-vis Congress or public opinion) in external affairs, particularly as regards the chief executive's authority to employ the armed forces for foreign policy objectives; and the role of the State Department in the management of foreign relations. Recent criticism of the State Department's performance is considered and an attempt made to answer the question: Why has the State Department apparently lost its once unchallenged position as the governmental agency that is clearly "in charge" of America's relations with other countries?

In Chapter 4 national security policy is analyzed, with particular reference to many of the "lessons" taught by the Vietnam War and the influence exercised by the Military–Industrial Complex on foreign policy and other aspects of national life.

A reexamination of the role of Congress in foreign relations has been underway in recent years. In Chapter 5, attention is directed to the experience afforded by the Vietnam conflict, as well as to other issues (like the presence of American troops in Western Europe), bringing the issue of legislative influence into sharp relief.

In the contemporary period, few questions are perhaps more salient—and often productive of more emotionalism and misinformation—than the role of public opinion in the foreign policy process. A new case study dealing with the impact of public opinion on American foreign policy toward Communist China down to the early 1970s has been added to Chapter 7, and references are made to the role of public sentiment during the prolonged national debate over the Vietnam War.

Two chapters deal directly with Soviet–American relations. A new frame of reference for understanding the origins and escalation of the Cold War down to the early postwar period—the conflicting viewpoints of "revisionist" and "orthodox" interpretations of the conflict—has been provided in Chapter 8. In Chapter 9, significant trends in Soviet foreign policy in the post-Khrushchev era are identified and appraised.

Chapters 10 through 13 deal with American foreign policy toward the major geographic regions of the world: with Western Europe—the impact of recent developments upon the future of NATO, and the continuing evolution of the European Economic Community; toward the Middle East—emphasizing the ongoing Arab–Israeli controversy and its implications for the United States, and Soviet Russia's growing "presence" and the conflict between revolutionary and evolutionary models of political and economic development in the region; with Black Africa—the region of lowest American involvement.

Chapter 12 concentrates upon one of the most

difficult and frustrating dimensions of American foreign policy: relations among the nations of the Western Hemisphere—the mixed results achieved thus far with the Alliance for Progress; the overall economic prospect for the Latin American nations; and major causes of ongoing political instability throughout Latin America, including forces producing both right-wing and left-wing political movements and regimes.

Chapter 13, focusing upon American foreign policy toward postwar Asia, required extensive revision in the light of the Vietnam conflict, the beginning of a "thaw" in long frozen Sino–American relations, and the emergence of Japan as the third-ranking industrial power in the world. One of the most important modifications in postwar American foreign policy—the Nixon Doctrine—receives detailed attention.

The final chapter presents a perennial and extremely difficult subject—the philosophical foundations underlying American foreign policy. The viewpoints of "realists" and of "idealists" are given in terms of their applicability for the kinds of choices confronting American policy-makers and citizens.

A conscious effort has been made in this book to present evidence and divergent points of view as objectively as possible, in full knowledge that total objectivity is unattainable (perhaps even undesirable). (Foreign policy discussions in the United States have not lacked polemical and doctrinaire utterances, slogans and simplistic formulas, distortions, emotionalism, and sometimes evident ignorance of pertinent background information.) Here, the basic goal has been to enhance student *understanding* of American foreign relations, not to reenforce prejudices, present fashionable points of view, or supply indictments.

On the basis of experience in the classroom, I am convinced that greater student (and of course overall citizen) enlightenment with respect to the complexities of foreign policy decision-making is an imperative need. I am no less convinced that it can be acquired only as the result of a willingness to examine the issues confronting policy-makers calmly, rationally, and with a receptive mind. On controversial issues (like the origins and causes of the Cold War), I never ask students to "agree" with my interpretation or any other particular point of view. I do expect that they will familiarize themselves with diverse interpretations, that they demonstrate a willingness to examine contrary viewpoints fairly, that they endeavor to learn *new* facts and gain *new* insights, and that in the end they reevaluate their own positions in the light of their educational experiences. It is my hope that this new edition will contribute in some useful way to that educational process in which every mature citizen ought to be unendingly engaged, and that it will provide at least one worthwhile "in-put" in creating a foundation of involved and intelligent citizen opinion upon which successful American foreign policy must necessarily be based.

ACKNOWLEDGMENTS

More than most writers, the author of a textbook is heavily dependent upon the contributions of others. As with the two earlier editions, this one is a product of my teaching and research interests in the fields of American foreign policy and international relations. I am happy to acknowledge my indebtedness to literally hundreds of scholars and commentators on these subjects who continue to enhance my insight significantly.

The assistance provided by the LSU Library staff has been indispensable. Special thanks are owed to Miss Edith M. Sims (Head, Social Science Division), Mrs. Marion T. Reid (Head, Order Department), and Mr. Jimmie H. Hoover (Head, Government Documents Division) for their willing and capable cooperation.

The secretaries of the Political Science Department, Miss Josephine Scurria and Mrs. Sue Kearns, have provided essential assistance in typing successive drafts of the chapters, and in preparing and typing the Bibliography and the Index. They have patiently endured the inevitable disruptions and delays in the office routine caused by my prolonged involvement in writing and research.

As my Graduate Assistant, Mrs. Barbara Manner performed many useful chores necessary in the revision, particularly in connection with preparation of the Bibliography. Her contribution is gratefully acknowledged.

More than they know, my students have contributed to this revision. For the stimulation provided by the dialogue with them, as well as for their criticisms of earlier editions, I am extremely grateful.

As always, I am deeply indebted to my versatile, gifted, and understanding wife, Harriet. In addition to the other demands on her time, she has had to endure the burden of "another book"; and she has done so with outstanding grace and fortitude. For this edition, as for earlier ones, she has served as "critic in residence"; her comments have invariably been pertinent and useful. Now, as in the past, she deserves to be listed as a co-author.

I am most deeply indebted to my parents, to whom this book is fondly dedicated.

Acknowledging the contributions of friends, colleagues, and students, I have no wish to involve them in responsibility for errors of fact or judgment which may be found here. All such errors are mine alone, and I bear fully responsibility for them.

—C.V.C., Jr.

AMERICAN FOREIGN POLICY IN THE NUCLEAR AGE

One
FOUNDATIONS OF AMERICAN FOREIGN POLICY

Reduced to its most fundamental ingredients, foreign policy consists of two elements: national objectives to be achieved and means for achieving them. The interaction between national goals and the resources for attaining them is the perennial subject of statecraft. In its ingredients the foreign policy of all nations, great and small, is the same.

To say that foreign policy consists essentially of ends and means, however, is a statement that misleads by its very simplicity. Its breadth does not reveal the obvious differences in national goals and the methods used by various countries for attaining them. No one can doubt, for instance, that the foreign policies of the United States and the Soviet Union today are at antipodes in many respects. Similarly, in recent history sharp divergencies have existed between the policies of Israel and the Arab states, India and Pakistan, China and Japan, Germany and France. Let us begin by looking at the goals of American foreign policy.

THE NATURE OF FOREIGN POLICY GOALS

General Characteristics of External Goals

Like all nations, the United States confronts certain problems related to the role of goals in the foreign policy process. Let us ask the question at the outset, "What precisely is meant by the term foreign policy goals?" In general a nation's foreign policy goals are those objectives it seeks to achieve in its relationships with other nations and with international agencies like the United Nations, in pursuit of which it is prepared to commit its resources.

Two important elements are thus present in our definition. First, it is assumed that nations *have* goals to which they are committed in external affairs. In foreign affairs, as in all other political relationships, the supposition (which of course may not always be true) is that political activity is *purposive and rational.* Nations, we must assume, do not normally "react" to external stimuli, like some lower forms of animal life. If the President attends a new summit conference, or if the United

States sells modern jet aircraft to Israel, or if Washington engages in diplomatic discussions with Hanoi—if America does these and many other things in foreign affairs, its behavior is designed to achieve some consciously chosen objective. Sometimes, of course, the rationale of national policy may not be evident; the reasons behind policy decisions may be deliberately concealed by policy-makers or they may be imperfectly understood by the public. Nevertheless, national purposes presumably explain American conduct in global affairs, else policy has degenerated into inertia or aimless and emotional activity.

No less important is the second element in our definition of goals: the requirement that the aims *be supported by national resources.* This prerequisite enables us to differentiate between actual foreign policy objectives and what might variously be designated hopes, aspirations, visions, pious dreams, fantasies, and the like—developments which many citizens might desire, but for which they are unprepared seriously to utilize their resources. Thus, the postwar reconstruction of Western Europe was a major *goal* of American foreign policy; its attainment was supported by the expenditure of several billion dollars, by considerable time and energy spent by both Americans and Europeans, and by various other means. By contrast, the "liberation" of Eastern Europe from Communist control cannot properly be considered a goal of postwar American foreign policy, since the United States has consistently *refused* to commit either its armed forces or significant funds to its realization, even when Moscow has imposed its will by military means upon countries like Hungary and Czechoslovakia. In recent years, it might be questioned whether the elimination of racial discrimination in countries like South Africa and Southern Rhodesia is really a goal of American foreign policy; officials in Washington normally have been prepared to do little more than make periodic "gestures" to achieve this aim. Another borderline case in recent diplomatic experience is promoting the idea of "equality" within the NATO alliance. Whether successive administrations in Washington have been genuinely committed to this objective is open to question, despite official statements from time to time endorsing equality. In such cases, the commitment of national resources has been too small to entitle these purposes to be ranked as important goals of American foreign policy.

Goal Formulation and Selection

How are national goals formulated and identified? What group of officials assumes this responsibility? Few questions related to the foreign policy process are more complex. Even today, it must be conceded that students of government can give very few authoritative answers to them; it might be difficult for foreign policy officials themselves to answer them satisfactorily. One reason for this state of affairs is that the problem of goal formulation and identification has almost infinite ramifications into many spheres of national life. To cite but one example, policy-makers who are seeking to formulate a set of goals concerning American relations with Europe in the 1970s are compelled to understand, and to take into account, a multitude of influences. There is, for example, the residue of traditional American "isolationist" attitudes toward Europe. There is America's decisive intervention in two world wars, in which Europe was the principal theater. There is awareness of Great Britain's decline as a first-rank power, of France's aspirations to greatness in the contemporary world, and of West Germany's restiveness under the restrictions imposed by the Allies. There is the matter of Soviet Russia's goals in Europe and its probable intentions in the years ahead. Above all perhaps, there is the question of the total resources available to American policy-makers and of Western Europe's proper claim upon these resources, vis-à-vis Africa, Asia, and other areas. Such considerations—and the list above is far from exhaustive—are among the dominant influences combining to produce a more or less clear conception among American officials of what the United States is seeking to accomplish in its relations with the European community. Complex as it is, the process of formulating goals must be carried on, unless the American response to problems in the external environment is to be purely episodic and irrational. Even when goals are formulated, complaints are apt to be voiced by critics of current policy that they are vague, contradictory, and otherwise unsatisfactory.

As every reader of the daily newspaper is aware, some of the most heated controversies within the United States throughout the postwar period have revolved around the fundamental goals of national policy. During the second half of the 1960s, for example, there was considerable domestic dissension surrounding the Vietnam War. Among criticisms directed at America's involvement in Vietnam were the accusations: (1) that the goals of the United States in Southeast Asia were unclear and ambiguous; (2) that American policy objectives (even when they were clear) were unsatisfactory, possibly because they were unattainable or self-defeating or incompatible with the nation's highest moral–ethical standards; (3) that American goals in Vietnam were—in juxtaposition to objectives in other parts of the world—contradictory and mutually antagonistic; and (4) that a "credibility gap" of massive proportions existed between the goals *proclaimed* by American policy-makers and the *actual behavior* of the United States in Southeast Asia, the latter being strikingly at variance with the former.[1]

The Korean War (1950–1953) presented a somewhat different example of the same fundamental problem. In that situation, much of the public dissatisfaction surrounding American policy arose from the fact that the United States in fact professed *several goals,* some of which seemed incompatible with others. During the Korean conflict, policy-makers tended frequently to shift from one avowed objective to another. The general public (which may have had some difficulty understanding even the *initial* goal of American military intervention) simply could not, and did not, comprehend these rapid policy shifts. The consequence was, and perhaps still is, widespread disagreement about whether America "won" or "lost" the war in Korea, and about precisely what was won or lost as a result of the fighting and the truce settlement.[2]

These examples underscore several key facts about foreign policy goals. When initial objectives are not altogether clear, perhaps even to the officials involved, tension and controversy are engendered in the foreign policy process, especially within democratic societies. Moreover, even when initial goals are clear, in an external environment characterized by rapid change, *goals can never be static and inflexible.* They must continually be examined and re-examined, and national policy must be modified accordingly. The Vietnam controversy focuses attention upon another key aspect of the problem of national goals. Despite our earlier emphasis upon goal formulation as a rational and deliberate process, it is nonetheless true that nations can, and not infrequently do, find their goals largely selected *for them* by outside events. It is perhaps always true in some measure that a combination of past policies, circumstances abroad, influential domestic factors (such as public opinion or the state of the economy at home), internal political considerations, and past and present miscalculations limit the choices available to policy-makers, sometimes severely. Several officials involved in the Vietnam conflict, for example, have testified that no American policy-maker really wanted or rationally "decided" to undertake a massive national military commitment in Southeast Asia. This was perhaps never a policy decision arrived at consciously and intentionally. Instead, America's heavy involvement in Vietnam came about as a result of a series of small, often seemingly insignificant steps, taken over a period of many months under three different American Presidents. As a consequence of these steps, America ultimately found itself bearing primary responsibility for the peace and security of South Vietnam—even while some American officials were disclaiming any real desire to assume such a commitment.* Similarly, no high-level American official after 1958 deliberately chose to antagonize French President Charles de Gaulle or precipitate a crisis within the NATO alliance. Nevertheless (to the French mind, at least) this seemed the inevitable result of the pursuit of certain goals (like the nonproliferation of nuclear weapons) generating tensions in Franco–American relations. As a general principle, it is not at all unusual for a great power to discover that pursuit of one set of goals prejudices the attainment of another set applicable in other parts of the world or dealing with different issues.

Critics of American foreign policy in recent years have complained about another dimension of the problem of national goals. They have contended, sometimes with considerable justification, that the foreign policy objectives of the United States appeared internally inconsistent and contradictory. Perhaps more in democracies than other states, the problem of achieving and maintaining *consistency* among a variety of foreign policy objectives is indeed formidable. As a democracy, for example, the United States is identified with promotion of the democratic ideology outside its own borders—an objective that has been more or less prominent in such diverse undertakings as military intervention in Southeast Asia, the provision of economic assistance to other countries, and the operations of the United States Information Agency (USIA). Yet it is also true that for many years, the United States has extended economic and military aid to authoritarian (in some instances, totalitarian) regimes throughout the "third world"; it has provided both economic and military aid to the Marxist government of Yugoslavia, as well as economic aid to Communist-ruled Poland; it has maintained cordial relations with General Franco's government in Spain, with monarchies in Saudi Arabia and Iran, and with

military juntas in several countries like Ghana, Jordan, Pakistan, and South Korea. Such behavior supplies what many Americans regard as distressing examples of the patent "inconsistency" of the nation's foreign policy.

Viewed in its global range, the foreign policy of the United States is indeed perhaps characterized *more by inconsistency than consistency.* Almost never does the United States (or any other nation, for that matter) adopt a single, clear principle of foreign relations to which it adheres with little or no deviation from one region to another or from one major external issue to another. As we shall emphasize in Chapter 2, *pragmatism* is a uniquely American approach to most internal and external policy questions; eclecticism—or the principle of "one problem at a time"—is also a singularly American trait. The American tradition has not normally favored rigid "ideological" principles or concepts for the solution of internal and external problems. Its peculiar attachment to pragmatism aside, the United States is far from being alone in trying to evolve an internally consistent foreign policy. A careful examination of the Russian, or French, or Indian diplomatic record might reveal equal (sometimes even more glaring) policy inconsistencies. This fact suggests that the problem is, to a large degree, inherent in the foreign policy process itself, although certain influences may make it unusually difficult for the United States.

The behavior of human societies at all political levels is characterized by the existence of *multiple goals,* many of which are mutually exclusive. Studies have shown that in democracies—where the role of public opinion is often decisive in national policy formulation—citizens customarily pursue divergent objectives; they seldom understand how these objectives relate to one another; and least of all are they normally conscious of the fact that pursuit of one goal may render achievement of another goal impossible. Thus, in foreign affairs, American citizens expect officials to protect national security interests abroad, but they also desire a reduction in the level of taxes or elimination of the draft to secure military manpower. Or, Americans favor participation in the United Nations, but they resist moves designed to give the UN any real voice in, or control over, the policy decisions of their own country. Again, citizens may be concerned about America's tarnished image abroad, while they also favor some unilateral national action against Communist influence in Latin America which would further tarnish the national image. Or, they want to resolve tensions with France, while remaining obdurate about changing any of the major policies that alienate French opinion.*

---

*The Vietnam conflict is discussed in detail in Chapter 13. For explanations of how the American commitment in that country grew by what one commentator describes as "incremental" decisions, see Roger Hilsman, *To Move a Nation* (Garden City, N.Y.: Doubleday, 1967), pp. 413–541. See also Theodore C. Sorensen, *Kennedy* (New York: Harper & Row, 1965), pp. 509–667; and Arthur M. Schlesinger, Jr., *A Thousand Days* (Boston: Houghton Mifflin, 1965), pp. 320–343, 532–551.

*Such incongruities in public attitudes are discussed more fully in Chapter 7

Inconsistency among national goals can arise from a different source: the necessity to adapt foreign policy to what are often highly varied circumstances in the outside world. For a great power—which, by definition, has commitments in all regions of the globe—this necessity perhaps makes some incompatibility among national objectives unavoidable. Consider again the promotion of democracy as a goal of American foreign policy. Given even the best of intentions, it is very difficult for national policy-makers to avoid some inconsistencies in their encouragement of democracy. For it is a fact that some societies simply do not share America's faith in democracy (at least, not in a form that is recognizable by Western liberal democratic standards); there is no evidence that some societies really desire democracy. In such cases, an American policy of energetically promoting democracy could well alienate a society with which the United States desires friendly relations. Even if another society accepts the democratic ideal, its idea of what that concept means can vary fundamentally from that of America. New definitions of the term—like "African democracy" or "Arab democracy" or "guided democracy"—have appeared in the postwar era with the emergence of the new Afro–Asian nations. As we shall see in future chapters, the main ingredients in terms like "African democracy" are often at variance with the essentials of democracy as defined in the West. In turn, the African conception of democracy may differ from the Latin American version. Even within a single region like the Middle East, divergent definitions of democracy can be found. Algeria's conception of it, for example, contrasts in many respects with Syria's or Egypt's, not to mention Lebanon's. Confronted with these realities, American policy-makers are almost compelled to adopt seemingly inconsistent policy goals. A policy that clearly "encourages" democracy in one region or country may inhibit it in another. In almost all cases (and critics of American policy have seldom understood this) a frontal assault by the United States on "nondemocratic" governments, even by methods short of military force, might well produce a tendency *against democracy* and toward *even greater authoritarianism* within the society concerned—if for no other reason than that the concept of democracy is identified with *an alien power* that is trying to control the nation's political destiny. Illogical as it appears, therefore, sometimes the best way for the United States to encourage democracy in foreign societies is by appearing to *discourage* it. More concretely, the most effective approach the United States can often take (and one it has followed in recent years toward Yugoslavia, Spain, Pakistan, Thailand, Paraguay, and other countries where democracy seems conspicuously absent) is to maintain reasonably cordial relations with incumbent governments, in the hope that in time an evolution toward more democratic political institutions and processes will gradually occur. On the assumption that American influence over such countries may, under optimum circumstances, be minimal, this has often proved the most satisfactory resolution of a difficult problem, in spite of its apparent contravention of America's avowed democratic principles.

The Problem of Goal Priorities

Another important dimension of the problem of goals in the foreign policy process is the matter of establishing some kind of hierarchy, or order of priority, among multiple national objectives. All foreign policy goals are obviously not of equal importance or urgency. Some require one combination of circumstances for their realization, while others may require a very different one. Certain goals may be important to one group of officials, governmental agencies, or citizens, while other goals are less important. It is not unlikely, for example, that even among the members of the National Security Council, the highest committee within the government dealing with foreign affairs, no two lists of goals would be identical.

That some scale of priorities among foreign policy goals is mandatory is dictated by one of the elements in our earlier definition of "goals": They are objectives in pursuit of which a nation is prepared to *commit its resources*. This very fact makes creation of some kind of de facto or explicit hierarchy among various goals inescapable. The United States is of course the wealthiest, and perhaps most powerful, nation known in world history. America's abundant wealth does not, however, alter the fact that its foreign policy goals must be supported by *a finite quantity or increment of national resources*. The resources available to American policy-makers may be vast, but they are not infinite. Hence, resources must be apportioned among numerous competing foreign policy objectives. This being true, officials are always compelled to decide which goals are most important and most urgent. Whatever total increment of national resources they may have available in a given year, they must divide this increment among several goals, which we may designate A, B, C, D, E, etc. This situation requires that officials decide that C is perhaps currently a goal of very high priority, while E is of perhaps secondary priority, and A may be deferred indefinitely. More specifically, officials may conclude that assisting a threatened military ally is more urgent than promoting the economic advancement of Africa, no matter how much they endorse the latter aim in principle. Or, they may decide that correcting the American balance of payments deficit is more essential than eliminating trade barriers for products of the developing nations. They may conclude that sending modern jet fighter planes to Israel makes a more vital contribution to national security than cultivating Arab good will. Or, they may be convinced that American economic assistance may be more constructively utilized at the present time by Iran than by Tanzania.

Whatever priorities may be determined in any given year, the main point is that some kind of hierarchy among goals is *always* required for the purpose of allocating a finite increment of national resources. The ordering of goals of course can seldom remain fixed for long; conditions in the external environment—together with influences like the demands of the public at home, the results of new political elections, and changes in the kinds and magnitudes of resources available to policy-makers—compel a constant re-evaluation of goals and their relative important. A sudden crisis abroad, for example, can, and not infrequently does, demand a reappraisal of national objectives and a reallocation of the resources available to policy officials. In the light of experience, officials may also conclude that some goals are unrealistic; circumstances abroad may convince them that their attainment is no longer possible. For a variety of reasons, then, the rank ordering of goals may, and normally does, undergo significant change over the course of time.

One further general point about the hierarchy of foreign policy goals needs to be mentioned. As often as not, the order of priority among them *is implicit rather than explicit.* As we have noted, different individuals—not excluding high-level government officials themselves—often have conflicting ideas concerning which objectives in foreign relations are important and urgent, and which are not. Sometimes such disagreement is to be found even among the President's closest foreign policy advisers, not to speak of the members of Congress and of public groups. Under such conditions, where would one find a definitive list, setting forth the goals of American foreign policy and ranking them on some kind of hierarchical basis? The answer is that *many* such lists exist, and they may not agree in every respect. The President or the Secretary of State may articulate the major goals of American foreign policy in public speeches. A member of the Senate Foreign Relations Committee in Congress may do the same thing. The Joint Chiefs of Staff may have their own list, for the purpose of planning strategic policy. The federal budget—allocating revenues for specific purposes—might qualify as another such list. (Many lists would of course be "classified" and hence unavailable to the citizen.) Nevertheless, some major goals of foreign policy may still be left implicit and unarticulated. Thus, although it may never be stated publicly or embodied in a treaty, the United States unquestionably has a stake in

the maintenance of the territorial inviolability of the Republic of India. Washington would also unquestionably view a resurgence of Communist parties in Western Europe as affecting its security adversely. America does not normally wish to antagonize the Afro–Asian majority in the UN General Assembly. Nor would the United States be indifferent to the eruption of hostilities between Persian Gulf states like Iran and Saudi Arabia. No statement of foreign policy goals can possibly cover every foreseeable and unforeseeable contingency in global affairs; nor can it serve, with perfect consistency, as a guide to national policy in a world characterized by constant change and crises.

Specific Policy Goals

Any list of specific foreign policy goals must, as we have emphasized, be tentative and, to a substantial degree, subjective. Bearing in mind that allowances must always be made for time and circumstances, we may examine three categories of foreign policy goals pursued by the United States.

Highest priority of course must be accorded those goals—sometimes referred to as a nation's "vital interests,"*— directly relating to preservation of national security. Self-preservation is pehaps the first law of statecraft. Thus, there exists a group of objectives all of which contribute to protection of the security interests of the nation. These include the defense of national boundaries and territories. For a great power with global commitments, this category also encompasses defense of military allies and friends, and creation and maintenance of conditions abroad—perhaps by such means as encouragement of political stability, support for orderly political change, and promotion of economic advancement in developing nations—designed to enhance national security and well-being.

Next on the list is a category of *secondary goals.* These consist of objectives, adherence to which is desirable as long as national security is not impaired. In the recent period, American goals in this category have been: <u>peace</u>, <u>nonintervention</u> in the internal affairs of other nations, observance and extension of <u>international law</u>, support for <u>collective security</u>, development of economically

---

*Nomenclature in reference to foreign policy goals is far from precise. When we discuss the views of one influential group of commentators on American foreign policy (the so-called "realists," in Chapter 16), the term "national interest" is employed. All foreign policy goals are presumably in the "national interest," in the sense that they seek to achieve some worthwhile national purpose, else they would not be goals of foreign policy. "Vital interests" refer to those policies of the nation related most intimately to its survival. For the United States, for example, preservation of the security of a NATO ally would be among its vital interests.

backward countries, and respect for human rights.

Finally, there is a group of objectives which, according to our earlier definition, do not perhaps really qualify as "goals" at all. They are more properly called hopes, aspirations, visions, or dreams, since the United States is normally unprepared to commit its resources to their fulfillment. These include: the elimination of poverty on a worldwide basis, extension of democracy to other countries,* winning or retaining the friendship of all nations, liberation of Eastern Europe and other Marxist-controlled areas from Communist domination, substantial reduction of global armaments, conversion of the United Nations into an effective instrument for international peace-keeping, and adherence to the highest ethical standards in international affairs. Any of the items on this list might in time *become* a goal of American foreign policy. To date, however, they have enjoyed very low priority.

In conclusion, it is necessary to emphasize two points about the goals of American foreign policy. First, the selection and ranking of national objectives is always *a dynamic process*: It goes on continuously, and a particular goal may be shifted from one category to the next—or dropped altogether—over the course of time. Second, the precise meaning of any particular goal may also change and be susceptible to widely varying interpretations among officials and citizens alike. Consider a "vital interest" like defending the territorial integrity of the United States. Few would deny that this is a paramount goal of national policy; it is one of the few such goals that remains fairly constant. Even such a fundamental objective as this, however, can elicit heated debate inside and outside the government in terms of such issues as the nature of a particular threat posed to the United States, the magnitude of the danger involved, the imminence of the threat, and the identification of those aspects of American life that are directly jeopardized. Controversy over such questions, for example, was implicit in much of the discord surrounding America's involvement in the Vietnam conflict in the late 1960s. Soviet construction of an antiballistic missile system likewise evoked dissent among policymakers and students of American foreign policy over *whether* American security was jeopardized and, if so, precisely *how* it was affected.

Nonetheless, it remains true, as the discerning reader will have concluded, that some of the most difficult questions affecting American foreign policy are more concerned with *the means* used to achieve national objectives than with the goals

*In our earlier discussion, we *assumed* that the promotion of democracy was a major foreign policy goal of the United States. In reality, it is doubtful that this is the case, since America is rarely prepared to use its resources for that end.

themselves. How a nation goes about trying to attain its goals can, in many important respects, influence its relations with the outside world even more crucially than its declared aims. For good or ill, other countries often judge a nation more by the methods it employs than by its avowed commitment to certain commendable purposes. We turn therefore to a consideration of the second major element in the foreign policy of any nation: the means of national policy.

THE MEANS OF FOREIGN POLICY

Earlier we suggested that there were two elements in the foreign policy of any nation: objectives and means for reaching them. Let us now look at the means by which nations try to reach their goals in foreign affairs. This leads us directly to one of the most important and complex subjects basic to interstate relations: national power. *Power is the ability of a nation to influence the actions of other countries in a manner favorable to itself.* Its most fundamental aim is preservation of national security. Americans are not accustomed to discussing international questions in the language of "power politics." Indeed, they have tended to believe that power politics could be eliminated altogether. But Americans are very accustomed to discussing the *reality* of power. They devote considerable time and energy to learning "how to win friends and influence people," how to get a promotion, how to put across a sales contract, and how to pass or defeat legislation in which they are interested. These are all efforts to exercise power. On a limited scale, such efforts resemble in many ways power politics on the international level.

The Manifestations of Power

One significant difference between power as exercised by individuals within the state and by nations within the world community resides in the role of force and coercion. Normally within a state, especially within a democratic state, force plays a relatively insignificant role in interpersonal and intergroup relationships. The government monopolizes force, using it to prevent violations of its laws when all other methods of restraint have failed. But in international affairs, force and coercion are used (or the threat of their use is invoked) frequently by all members of the world community. In its most extreme manifestation, the use of force takes the form of war. On its most primitive level, national power is the capacity to preserve the identity of the nation by military force, construed broadly to include propaganda, economic coercion, and other modern methods of warfare. That is why the power of a nation is often judged solely—and when solely, then erroneously—by the strength of its armed forces. Every other goal of foreign policy—the ability of the United States, let us say, to preserve advantageous trade relations with the outside world, or to contribute to the advancement of economically backward countries, or to propagate democratic ideology—presupposes the continued existence of the nation. This is the *sine qua non* of all national policy, foreign or domestic.

Though military strength is a central element in a nation's power, it is by no means the only element, nor is it always the most important one in the day-to-day conduct of international affairs. The free world alliance against the Communist bloc, for example, is not held together because of the overwhelming military superiority of the United States over its members. The cement of this alliance is to be found much more in recognition of a common danger, geographical proximity, ideological affinity, and a sense of common purpose. Decisions emerging from the alliance are a result more of persuasion than of coercion by the dominant nations within it.

Manifestly, there are limits to the usefulness of military power. It cannot be used to compel other nations, such as Burma in the postwar period, to accept American economic and technical assistance. Respect for American military strength has not always forced other nations, such as India, Egypt, or Ghana, to accept the American position on issues dividing the Communist and non-Communist worlds. Nor does the mere existence of great military power prevent the growth of Communist influence in areas like Southeast Asia or Latin America. In other words, *force is not always relevant to certain kinds of foreign policy situations.* Remembering the definition—that power is *influence*—the improper use of force may in fact result in lessened, rather than in increased, influence over the actions of other countries.

Power thus has many manifestations. Some of the more important of these are: persuasion and friendship, propaganda, economic aid (leading sometimes to economic coercion), ideological penetration, moral suasion, and public opinion. There is no necessity to examine these manifestations of power here. That can better be done in future chapters, when we discuss American foreign policy toward specific international problems. At this stage, we must take note of some of the general characteristics of power.

The Relativity of Power

A basic fact to be grasped about the concept is that *power is always relative.* We observed earlier that national security is a dynamic, not a static, concept. This circumstance stems largely from the relativity of power. When we ask, "What is the power of the United States in world affairs?" we are trying to solve an equation containing an al-

most infinite number of variables. No two experts from the State Department, the Pentagon, or other governmental agencies would answer this question in exactly the same way, because no final and completely authoritative answer is ever possible. The variables in the problem derive from the four important respects in which power is relative.

Power is relative with respect to time. The power of the United States has undergone a profound transformation within the past fifty years. This change has resulted principally from two facts: proven ability to wage war successfully, and the decision to play a more active role in world affairs, which has demanded that the United States develop and use some of its tremendous potential power during time of peace. Furthermore, America's power today is far vaster than it was immediately after World War II, when its armed forces had been stripped to skeleton strength, and before it had begun to develop nuclear weapons in large quantities.

The fact that power is relative to time is highlighted by the distinction between *potential* power and power *in being.* If it is asked, "What is the power of the United States and the NATO community to defend Western Europe from a possible Communist attack?" a major consideration would be the amount of time available to the free world to bring its military forces to bear in defense. Throughout the postwar period the United States has possessed great power in being. Yet the existing power of the United States is only a fraction of its potential power.

Power is relative to the problem toward which it is directed. When we evaluate national power, we must always think in terms of power to reach certain specified objectives, to achieve concrete goals. America's power to defend its shores from aggression may be entirely different from its capacity to deal with Communist influences in Asia, to maintain friendly relations with Egypt, to raise living standards in Iran, or to prevent excessive use of the veto in the United Nations. Success in foreign affairs demands skill in using appropriate weapons and skill in dealing with diverse global problems.

The power of one country is relative to that of other countries. The ability of the United States to influence the course of world events will almost invariably require comparative judgments about power. Knowing that the United States at any given time possessed 5 or 25 or 50 hydrogen bombs would tell us little or nothing of significance about American power. Such weapons might have little relevance to the problem under consideration. But even if they did, we could still not settle the issue until we asked, "What is the power of the United States *relative to the power of other countries* that are actively concerned with the problem at hand?" The issue of relative power has come into clear focus in recent years because of the steady accretion in Soviet nuclear and missile technology. In the immediate postwar period, the United States had a monopoly on nuclear weapons. In this one category its power was therefore infinitely greater than the Soviet Union's. Gradually, the U.S.S.R. began to acquire nuclear weapons, along with effective methods of delivery. The Kremlin's rate of production for such weapons grew much faster than the American rate. If we assume that, by the early 1970s, the free world coalition had a two-to-one lead over the Communist bloc in nuclear striking power, its relative position vis-à-vis the Communist bloc had deteriorated greatly—so much so in fact that "nuclear parity"—in the sense of the ability of each side totally to devastate the other—had been largely reached between the two camps. Both sides were equal, or nearly so, in the capacity to achieve objectives requiring reliance upon nuclear weapons.

The same principle of course holds for nonmilitary types of power, although differentials of strength are much more difficult, if not virtually impossible, to measure with precision. What is the relative power of the United States and India to persuade the masses throughout Asia to support a given course of action in foreign affairs? What is the respective influence of countries such as France and Egypt in determining Arab attitudes toward the free world coalition? How much power does the United States possess to gain widespread acceptance of its policies within the NATO alliance? In international affairs, there is power and countervailing power, American push and Soviet or Indian or Egyptian pull. To decide what the power of a nation is, it is necessary to identify all the forces that are operative in any given international issue.

Power is relative to the country by which it is applied. Suppose, for purposes of illustration, that we measure the relative power of countries by looking *only* at their military forces. What kind of evaluation is possible? No matter what the statistics show, the effective military power of two countries is never exactly comparable. This would be true, even if it could be shown—and in reality of course it could not—that the military strengths of two nations were exactly equal. Why is it not possible to think that "ten divisions are ten divisions," irrespective of the country to which they belong?

Ignoring for the moment the fact that the divisions of two countries will differ markedly in firepower, number of troops, leadership, and many other respects, we may note that ten Russian divisions would be more easily available to the Kremlin for crushing the Hungarian Revolt than would ten American divisions to Washington for dealing with anti-American demonstrations in Egypt of Japan. Few limitations exist on the Kremlin's ability to use troops for such purposes. Governmental leaders of the United States, on the other hand, must operate within a constitutional framework of civilian control over the military establishment and within a historical tradition which emphasizes nonintervention in the internal affairs of other countries. Public contention in the United States over the Vietnam conflict during the 1960s also underscored the power exercised by vocal minorities, who often objected to the use of American force in Vietnam per se and who protested vigorously against the use of certain weapons (like napalm and bombs) against the enemy.

The mere possession of power, therefore, along with an even greater potential power, is no guarantee that a nation will exert a decisive influence in global affairs. Totalitarian regimes are often free to use all the resources at their command for diplomatic purposes. However, democratic nations usually limit, sometimes severely, the means available to policy-makers for the achievement of foreign policy objectives.

THE INGREDIENTS OF AMERICAN POWER

The major elements that combine to make up the power of a nation are: geography, economic and technological resources, population, military forces, ideology, and national character.

Geographical Determinants of American Power

Because they are the most permanent elements in a nation's power, and because they underlie other kinds of power, geographical attributes have been held by leading scholars to be the most fundamental in determining a nation's role in world affairs. "Power," the noted geographer Nicholas J. Spykman once wrote, "is in the last instance the ability to wage successful war, and in geography lie the clues to the problems of military and political strategy." He concludes that geography "is the most fundamental factor in the foreign policy of states because it is the most permanent."[3]

The modern student of international relations would probably be inclined to question the preeminent role of geography. Today, a strong technological–scientific base might be viewed as the *sine qua non* of national power. It is true that geographical determinants of power may have less permanence than Spykman's statement suggests. Canals have been dug to connect important waterways; deserts have been made at least semiarable; desalinization programs can provide vast quantities of fresh water at relatively low cost; air conditioning can mitigate the heat of the tropics; nuclear energy can provide a source of power where other sources are unavailable; in the age of jet airplanes and missiles, the importance of seemingly permanent geographical barriers (like the English Channel) can be minimized. Consequently, it would be a mistake to regard geographical factors as fixed and unyielding before the efforts of man or to view them as immutable "givens" in the power equation of a particular nation. There is a danger—amply illustrated during the Nazi era in prewar Germany—of slipping into a kind of geographical determinism, popularly called "geopolitics." Thus, German geopoliticians endeavored to prove that geographical forces compelled Germany to embark upon its *Drang Nach Osten* (drive to the east) and perhaps even gave it a mandate to conquer Europe and the entire world.

Keeping these qualifications in mind, let us examine the salient geographical facts about American power, starting with climate. The United States is in the temperate zone, the zone in which great nations have invariably been situated. Scholars since antiquity have sought to establish a correlation between national greatness and climate.[4] That no precise correlation is possible is now conceded. Nevertheless, it seems that climatic extremes militate against a nation's becoming a great power in world affairs. Most of the United States escapes both extreme tropical heat and Arctic cold. Another climatic factor conducive to energetic life is moderate variation in temperature, rainfall, humidity, and wind velocities. The United States escapes the stultifying effect of uniform climatic conditions for long periods. These facts are of cardinal importance for American economic pursuits, especially agriculture, and undoubtedly have some significance in shaping the character and outlook of the American people.[5]

No one ingredient in the power of a nation is likely to be so basic as its geographical location. Location determines the pattern of relations between a nation and other countries. It is crucial in national defense. The presence or absence of "natural frontiers," as Poland has discovered throughout its history, can decide whether or not national security can be preserved. Location is crucial in trade and commerce. Britain and Japan —small islands off the coasts of Europe and Asia— became great nations because of their ability to use the oceans as highways of commerce. Even the cultural and ideological influence exerted by a nation may depend on its location. Greek and Roman thought infused the European world because of the proximity of these nations to the European hinterland and the consequent ease of communication.

Long imbued with the idea of Western "hemispheric solidarity," Americans have difficulty appreciating the objective facts about their geographical relationship with the rest of the world. Having expanded over a continent which contains few natural land barriers, the people of the United States have traditionally thought in continental terms. They have tended to believe that land connects and that water divides. They have overlooked the fact that land can present formidable barriers, and that oceans may cease to be obstacles to contact between nations. In the twentieth century travel is often easier by sea or air than by land. Freight can be hauled much more cheaply by water than by land. Military forces can often be transported more conveniently by sea or air than by land.

Widespread reliance by Americans upon the Mercator map projection is also responsible for distorted notions about geographic relationships. Every map distorts global relationships to some degree. The peculiarity of the Mercator projection is that it suggests that the United States *is* geographically isolated, except from Canada and Latin America. Vast ocean distances seem to divide the United States from Europe and Asia. The accessibility of polar routes, first by airplanes and now by submarine, does not emerge. The Western Hemisphere appears to be a geographically compact unit, with the other great land areas of the earth scattered along its fringes. Such "ship thoughts," as George T. Renner has labeled them, have largely dominated American thinking about foreign affairs throughout the nation's history.[6]

The only realistic perspective from which the salient facts about America's relationships with the rest of the world become apparent is the global one. More than at any other stage in history, the globe, not the map, needs to be the constant source of reference for every student of foreign policy. Once Americans adopt the perspective of the globe—thereby comprehending relationships that are obscured by flat map projections—they will understand several basic facts about their country's geographical location. One is that America is not isolated, nor has it ever been isolated to the degree imagined in the nation's folklore. The United States is not safely protected by two expansive oceans and by Arctic wastelands to the north. Arbitrary divisions of the globe into hemispheres by lines running north and south possess virtually no military or strategic validity. An almost infinite number of hemispheres can be projected on the globe, including of course those dividing the world along an east–west axis, or those created by lines running at an acute angle to the equator. And, as S. W. Boggs has observed, if hemispheres were projected embracing the United States, they could be drawn in such a way that there would be "no human being anywhere on earth" who did not "live in some hemisphere that includes *all* of the United States." Every major area of culture in the world is part of some imaginable "American hemisphere." [7]

Global thinking facilitates a proper understanding of the distances between the United States and other countries. Americans are inclined to view the Western Hemisphere as the immediate backyard of the United States. A typical expression of this misconception was Wisconsin Governor Philip LaFollette's warning to Americans during World War II to beware lest they fight "not in this hemisphere where we can be supreme, but . . . with expeditionary forces four thousand miles away in Europe and six thousand miles away in Asia."[8]

Few Americans are psychologically prepared to believe that Europe is the closest neighbor of the United States, excluding Canada, Mexico, and the Caribbean countries. Few Americans today would look upon a trip from Washington, D.C., to San Francisco (about 2300 miles) as a particularly lengthy journey, especially if it were made by a transcontinental jet airplane. Yet this is approximately the distance by air from Chicago to the southern tip of Greenland, to the Arctic Circle, or the Beaufort Sea north of Alaska and east of Soviet Siberia; from San Francisco to the Bering Sea adjacent to Siberia; from Denver to the Beaufort Sea and Baffin Island in the northeastern Arctic Ocean; from Cleveland to the Arctic Circle and the North Atlantic west of Greenland; and from Boston to Iceland. In the Western Hemisphere, this is also about the distance from New York to the Panama Canal—a distance farther than the mileage by plane or ship from the "bulge" of Africa at Dakar to the closest point in South America.

The erroneous assumptions underlying Governor LaFollette's statement quoted earlier are highlighted by the fact that from Madison, Wisconsin, it is farther to Brazil than to Benghazi in North Africa; about equidistant to Ankara, Turkey, and Buenos Aires, Argentina; closer to every major European capital than to Buenos Aires (and only one, Athens, is as far as Rio de Janeiro); closer to Gibraltar than to Bolivia, Argentina, Chile, Paraguay, and Uruguay (and it is closer by sea to Gibraltar from the nearest American port than from Miami to the nearest point in South America); closer to Manchuria than to Buenos Aires.[9] New York City is 3700 miles from Gibraltar, about 3000 miles less than the distance to Buenos Aires and nearly 1800 miles less than the distance to Rio de Janeiro. Washington, D.C., is closer to Berlin than to Rio de Janeiro; Chicago closer to many points in Russia than to many Latin American countries; Boston closer to Moscow than to half the countries in Latin America.[10]

These facts possess added significance in an age of supersonic, long-range aircraft and guided missiles capable of being launched from remote sites and of traversing the shortest distances to selected targets. Ocean expanses, Arctic wastelands, deserts, and the like, present no obstacles to airplanes and missiles. To appreciate the impact these technological advances have had upon America's relation with the outside world, let us imagine that an enemy wished to attack this country. Both the

United States and the Soviet Union posses intermediate-range (1500-mile) guided missiles. Utilizing missile sites in eastern Germany, Soviet Russia could bring the whole of Western Europe, including Iceland and Spain, plus the coastal fringe areas of North Africa, within its range. From bases in Bulgaria, an intermediate-range missile attack could be launched against practically any point in the Mediterranean Sea, including about half of Algeria, most Libya, all of Egypt, and about one-third of Iran. An arc drawn with a 1500-mile radius centered upon New York City would extend into waters north of Newfoundland, into the central Atlantic, southward through Haiti and the Dominican Republic. An enemy submarine firing a 1500-mile missile, submerged 500 miles in the Atlantic east of New York City, could bring most of the United States east of the Mississippi River within its range. The same submarine submerged 500 miles off the coast of California would command a field of fire embraced by an arc extending from the northern tip of Idaho, east to Colorado, and southeast to the Arizona–New Mexico boundary. Similarly, a submarine submerged in the Gulf of Mexico 500 miles south of New Orleans could fire an intermediate-range missile at Philadelphia in the northeast, Detroit in the north, Omaha in the northwest, and Pueblo, Colorado, in the west.

The United States and Soviet Russia also possess long-range guided missiles. These weapons nullify any remaining vestige of protection afforded the United States by its geographical location. The arc formed by a radius of 5000 miles centered on Moscow includes Alaska, sweeps through northern Oregon, passes through the north central and midwestern portions of the United States and embraces most of the eastern and Atlantic seaboard area, excluding only the extreme southern portions of the country. This means that the industrial heartland of the United States would be within range of missiles launched from behind the Iron Curtain.

Translating these data into general strategic terms, we may say that today almost every point in the United States is within range of an enemy armed with submarine- or ship-launched intermediate-range missiles or of aircraft with round-trip range of 3000 to 4000 miles. When missiles with a 5000-mile range are envisioned, no point in the United States or the Western Hemisphere remains outside the field of fire of enemy missiles. These facts demonstrate forcefully that any thought of hemispheric isolation or noninvolvement by the United States in global affairs is a dangerous fiction.

If the concept of hemispheres must be retained in the study of international affairs, a much more meaningful term would be "Northern Hemisphere." America's presence in the "North Atlantic quarter-sphere" Hartshorne has written, "is the most important aspect of our location, now as in the past."[11] This zone includes Europe, North America, the greater portion of the Soviet Union, and the connecting and intervening oceans. With the exception of Japan, it embraces all the great military powers known to modern history.[12]

Geographical facts and concepts have a vital bearing upon every goal of American foreign policy. They have, for example, largely determined the nation's response to the Communist challenge since World War II. The American concept of containment has rested upon the premise that enemy control over the great land mass of Europe and Asia—roughly coterminous with what the eminent geographer Sir Halford Mackinder called the "world island"—would give an adversary a well-nigh impregnable position from which to extend it influence to other nations and regions. From Eurasia, an aggressor could soon overrun the Near and Middle East, the fringe lands of the Far East, and Africa. If an enemy succeeded in consolidating its hold upon these areas, it would then be able to isolate the United States from its major allies by cutting sea communication–transportation routes at key points, by imposing an economic blockade, and perhaps by penetrating South America politically and militarily. The huge Eurasian land mass contains two-thirds of the land area of the earth, five-sixths of its population, and a large proportion of its natural resources. Its possession in enemy hands would place the United States in a militarily and economically vulnerable position, such that it could not, in all likelihood, continue to maintain its independence.[13]

The United States consequently has no choice about playing an active role in global affairs. That decision has been foreordained by the facts of geography and the economic–strategic corollaries deriving from those facts. The only real alternatives relate to the kind of role it will play. Will its policies be based upon realities? Or will they be based upon stereotypes and misconceptions concerning the nation's relationships with other important countries? The first alternative is, of course, no guarantee of success in the diplomatic field, but it is clearly a *sine qua non* of successful policy. The second, on the other hand, could jeopardize the continued existence of the United States as a great and independent power.

Economic and Technological Determinants of American Power

Since World War I it has become apparent that a nation's power—especially its capacity to wage war—is determined largely by its economic base. Without the ability to equip military forces, and to keep them supplied with materials of war for long periods, a nation cannot protect its security or its vital interests. Creation of a firm economic foundation to support its foreign policy, therefore, demands that a nation possess or have unimpeded access to important industrial raw materials.

In over-all terms, the United States has achieved the highest standard of living of any nation known to world history. Moreover, as we shall see, the gap between the wealth of the United States and that of most other nations is, in nearly all cases, *widening* in favor of the American society. In this sense, although the term has numerous (and often ambiguous) connotations, it may accurately be said that America is the most "underdeveloped" society on the globe, when that concept refers to an *economic potential* capable of realization within a reasonable period in the future.

By the usual economic indicators, America's economic power is vast and continues to expand at an impressive rate. In 1960, for example, the American gross national product—the total of all goods and services produced in the country during a given year—exceeded $500 billion; in 1966, it was $743 billion; by the end of the 1960s, it was *some $1 trillion*. By the end of the 1960s also, the annual economic growth rate for the American economy (which registered 5.5 percent annual growth in 1966) exceeded the growth rates achieved by any other industrialized nation, including the Soviet Union, Japan, and the members of the European Common Market. For a twenty-year period (1948–1968), the United States increased its annual productive output by an increment that exceeded the entire annual output of the Soviet Union. The manufacturing capacity of American industry doubled from 1951 to 1967; during this fifteen-year interval, the United States added as much to its industrial plant as it built during the first 150 years of its existence as a nation.

Another highly significant economic indictor is the *rate of productivity*. In the early stages of American industrialization (1850–1889), output per man-hour grew at an average annual rate of 1.5 percent; between World Wars I and II, it reached an average of 2.1 percent annually; after World War II, it averaged 3.2 percent each year; and by the late 1960s, economists predicted that it would continue to grow at the rate of approximately 3 percent annually in the future. One estimate held that, by the 1980s, output per man-hour in American industry would double in terms of the productivity achieved in the late 1960s.

In the production of specific commodities, America has remained at, or near, the front rank among the industrialized nations. By the late 1960s, the United States manufactured around 135 million tons of steel annually, despite a rising level of steel imports. It produced over 15 million tons of anthracite and bituminous coal, at a price that was perhaps the most competitive on the world market. It was among the largest producers of important metals like copper, lead, zinc, and primary aluminum. In 1966, America produced and refined over 3 million barrels of oil—a quantity equal to about five-sixths of the entire yearly output of the oil-rich Middle East and more than twice the oil production for all of Latin America.

While a strong industrial base is normally regarded as a fundamental prerequisite for great-power status, the productive record of American agriculture is also significant for two reasons. First, the agricultural revolution historically preceded, and in many respects made possible, the industrial revolution in the United States. Today, the continued expansion of American agricultural production still plays a vital part in the achievement of high industrial output. Second, agricultural productivity is important in its own right, as many emerging nations have perhaps discovered belatedly. A mounting "world food crisis," which began to manifest itself in the mid-1960s, increasingly required that the United States not only feed its own growing population, but also alleviate famine conditions and food shortages in countries like India and Egypt. During the second half of the twentieth century, it appeared that America was one of the few nations on the globe capable of feeding itself, while also producing surpluses available to feed hungry populations throughout the world.

Few people are aware that, by many standards, agriculture has been and remains the most productive sector of the American economy. The number of farms in the United States grew only from 2.7 million in 1870 to 3.2 million in 1964. The percentage of Americans employed on farms, meanwhile, declined by some 60 percent during the period 1915–1966. By the latter date, the United States was predominantly an urban (or suburban) society. Yet farm output in America continued to climb steadily—from a base of 100 in 1950 to 225 in 1966 (vis-à-vis an increase from 100 to 145 in nonfarm production over the same period). Some 50 million acres of cropland were "retired" from production from 1950 to 1967. Despite that fact, during this same interval corn production rose from 2.7 billion to 4.5 billion bushels; wheat production climbed from 1 billion to 1.4 billion bushels; and beef output expanded from 10 billion to 18.5 billion pounds. Since 1947, farm output in America has been increasing at an over-all average rate of 6.1 percent annually. Even if economists expected this productive rate to decline slightly in the years ahead, the United States would, in all probability, still remain the most efficient producer of many agricultural commodities in the world for decades to come.

Another important area of economic activity is trade. In the twentieth century, the United States has been the largest trading nation in the world. By 1966, for example, it was exporting goods and services valued at more than $30 billion annually.

It also provided the world's largest market for imports. So competitive were American-made goods in the world market that nearly all other nations (not excluding the members of the European Common Market) raised barriers of one kind or another against American exports. Similarly, American investments in other countries rose from $12 billion to $50 billion from 1952 to 1967. American automobile manufacturers largely dominated the British market, while American industrial giants (like IBM and General Electric) established a commanding position on the European continent in producing computers.

As we have noted, the same—or even higher—economic growth rates for most sectors of the American economy have been forecast for the 1970s and beyond. A Labor Department projection in the late 1960s (assuming an annual unemployment rate of 3 to 4 percent) forecast that in the years ahead over-all American productivity would grow at an average annual rate of 3.2 percent (an even higher average than was obtained for the postwar period as a whole). Yet it also predicted that the average number of hours per week worked by Americans would continue to decline, the labor force would expand by 1.9 to 2 percent annually, and the United States would maintain an over-all average economic growth rate of 4.3 percent annually. Other studies anticipated that the industrial capacity of the United States would double by the late 1980s; agricultural production (unless sharply cut back by governmental policies) would continue to increase; and real family income in America would continue to grow, with more and more families (comprising some 25 percent of the total in 1965) earning over $10,000 annually.[14]

Soviet–American Economic Competition

These data about the United States become more meaningful if we compare the economic capacities of America with those of its principal diplomatic opponent, the Soviet Union. Under Premier Nikita Khrushchev (who was ousted in 1964), Soviet policy-makers boasted of their ability and intention to surpass the United States economically. Rising productivity under Marxism, Khrushchev once asserted, would be the "battering ram" with which the citadel of world capitalism would finally be destroyed. In the post-Khrushchev era, less and less was heard of this theme outside Moscow—and for good reason. Major economic indicators left little doubt that Soviet Russia was failing to "surpass" the United States in productivity; in many important respects, in fact, America was *gaining ground* on its rival in the arena of economic competition. One commentator in the late 1960s, for example, estimated over-all Soviet economic strength at roughly one-half of American strength. He noted that the growth rates in

GNP for both countries either favored America or were approximately equal. Even if the rates were equal, the differential between the economic might of America and that of the Soviet Union would still widen to Russia's detriment.* Moreover, the civilian consumption level of Soviet society was less than one-third the level prevailing in the United States in the 1960s; in mid-decade, per capita after-tax personal income in the Soviet Union was approximately one-fourth the income achieved in the United States (and in fact lagged behind the levels achieved in East Germany and Czechoslovakia). Moreover, the Soviet worker was believed to be about one-third as productive as his counterpart in the United States.

Although Soviet economic output had risen substantially in the half-century since the Bolshevik Revolution, in the production of specific commodities, the United States continued to hold an impressive lead. In steel manufacturing—the one industry Moscow's planners had always regarded as crucial in the competition with America—in the late 1960s, the United States produced nearly 134 million tons annually, versus 99 million tons for the Soviet Union. America generated almost 1.3 billion kwh. of electricity each year, while Russia generated 545 million kwh. In coal output, Russia was slightly ahead of America, with 586 million tons mined in the former, as against 545 million tons for the latter. In petroleum products, America refined 404 million tons of oil annually, while Russia refined 265 million tons. In automobile production, the United States had a wide lead, producing 8.5 million vehicles annually, against Russia's output of only 235,000. According to Soviet officials themselves, Russian industry surpassed American only in the production of commodities like coal, metal-cutting tools, cement, and granulated sugar.

Experience with the new Soviet Five-Year Plan promulgated for 1966–1970 confirmed Russia's inability to forge rapidly ahead. The goals postulated in the plan (adopted after the overthrow of Premier Khrushchev) involved a sharp curtailment of earlier Soviet objectives and reflected a realization in Moscow that earlier, more ambitious goals were unlikely to be achieved in the near future. The relatively modest targets projected in this new plan indicated that, even by the 1980s, Soviet society would still not reach the level of consumer abundance promised for many years by the Communist hierarchy. If Russian officials can ever fulfill their promise of giving Soviet citizens the highest standard of living in the world, this result is most improbable (assuming normal American growth rates) before 2000 A.D.* That the Soviet economy continued to experience problems was highlighted by the fact that, within a year after the announcement of this new plan, many of the goals projected for the five years after 1966 were curtailed, particularly in industrial enterprises like electric power generation, chemicals, steel, automobiles, and natural gas.

The Soviet determination to overtake America economically confronted a number of massive obstacles. One of these was the chronically uncertain condition of Russian agriculture, which had been generally depressed since 1917. If accelerating agricultural production was pivotal in American economic advancement, the opposite is true for the Soviet Union. In that country, disappointing farm yields have crippled industrial progress and posed a recurrent challenge for Soviet policymakers which, to date, they have had minimum success in meeting. Despite intensive efforts by Premier Khrushchev and his successors to raise agricultural output, Russia continues to lag far beyond the United States in the production of key farm commodities. In 1967, for example, the U.S.S.R. had some 38 million farmers, while the United States had some 4 million. Yet, beginning in the mid-1960s, Russia was compelled to make large purchases of wheat abroad, some from the United States. Russia was unable to feed its own population of some 235 million people, not to speak of making any significant contribution to the relief of famine conditions in India, Egypt, and other countries. Moscow had to import as much grain as India and China together! Although its agricultural acreage was more than double the total for America, Soviet grain production was just over half that achieved by American farmers. Premier Khrushchev had depended upon a highly publicized "virgin lands" program to open new acreage for Soviet agriculture and solve the nation's long-standing agricultural problems. After a short period of initial gains, the over-all result of this scheme proved highly disappointing. By the late 1960s, Soviet officials had turned to a more modest, long-term project to apply proven methods (many copied from the United States) for raising agricultural yields. Russian production may well benefit from this slow and unspectacular ap-

*Writing in 1967, Edwin L. Dale, Jr., cited the following hypothetical example: If the American economy currently stands at a level of 100 and the Soviet economy at a level of 50, amd the former grows by 5 percent annually, while the latter grows at 8 percent annually (a figure much above the *actual* Soviet growth rate), in five years' time, the United States will be at a level of 125, while the Soviet Union will be at a level of 70. See Edwin L. Dale, Jr., "The U.S. Economic Giant Keeps Growing," *The New York Times Magazine* (March 19, 1967), pp. 31, 135–152.

*Major targets for the 1966–1970 plan called for raising Soviet national income by 38–41 percent for the five-year period; increasing over-all industrial output by 50 percent; and elevating agricultural production—for a half-century, the most vulnerable point in the Soviet economy—by 25 percent. As in other Soviet plans, heavy industry was accorded priority over consumer-goods production, although the latter received higher priority than before.

proach, although it stands in rather sharp contrast to the announced Marxist objective of carrying out an "agricultural revolution."

Many obstacles hindered Soviet economic improvement. These included a continuing high commitment of industrial output to military and defense requirements and the evident Soviet determination to equal or surpass the United States in space technology and exploration—an endeavor which unquestionably strained Soviet resources. Both of these spheres demanded a considerably higher percentage of the Soviet GNP than comparable programs took from the American GNP. Moreover, Soviet citizens, along with many countries inporting goods from Moscow, complained of the inferior quality of Russian-made goods. Waste and inefficiency characterized at least some sectors of Soviet enterprise. In the late 1960s, also, Soviet industry was disrupted by the introduction of the "Liberman profit system" (the concept of "market socialism," named for a prominent Soviet economist, Evsei Liberman). Designed to correct many of the ills afflicting Soviet production, this semicapitalist approach might in time prove highly effective, just as the liberalized use of "private plots" induced Soviet farmers to increase their yields because they increased their own profits. In the short run, however, the system of market socialism encountered opposition from hard-line Marxists within the U.S.S.R.

In brief, the evidence indicates rather conclusively that the Soviet Union neither has overtaken the United States economically, nor is on the verge of doing so except in a few isolated goods. If projected American and Soviet growth rates are reasonably accurate, America is likely to retain its economic superiority for an indefinite period.[15]

Population as a Determinant of National Power

Throughout history, students of international affairs have been aware of the intimate connection between population and national power. This relationship is as complex as it is far-reaching in its implications. Military strength, economic productivity, scientific and technological know-how, national morale, the long-range goals of a society— all of these are functions of the size and character of the nation's population. Size of population is crucial in determining national power. Yet mere size alone cannot guarantee a nation great-power status. If this were the case, global affairs would be controlled by heavily populated countries like India and China, which between them possess nearly 40 percent of the total population of the world. Lacking another key ingredient in national power—adequate land and other resources requisite for a fairly high standard of living and a broad industrial base—the hundreds of millions of people living in these countries may constitute more

of a drain upon the power of the nation than an addition to it. The equation of national power contains many variables, and it is the relationship among these variables that largely determines whether nations will be weak or strong. Consequently, to decide whether a nation is "over-populated," "underpopulated," or possesses an "optimum" population, consideration must be given to the capacity of the nation to support its people. Nevertheless, in recent history nations have been powerful only when they have possessed reasonably large populations. Perhaps the figure 50 million people could be taken as an approximate lower limit for nations that aspire to become great powers.

By 1965, the United States contained 194 million people; the estimated population for 1970 was 208 million; and by 1975, the projection was 218 million. In addition to growth throughout its history, the United States also underwent a highly significant shift in the composition of its population. A predominantly rural society for most of its existence, America in the late 1960s had some 70 percent of its population classified as "urban" (or suburban).

Throughout American history the rate of population growth has been phenomenal. The population quadrupled in the first half of the nineteenth century; trebled during the last half; and has more than doubled since 1900. There has been an uneven growth during each decade, but the trend of the population curve has been steadily upward. The large population expansion during World War II and throughout the postwar era surprised many demographers. Many had come to regard the United States as a country possessing a relatively stable population, compared with the rapid growth witnessed in regions like Africa, Asia, and Latin America. The census of 1950 revealed that they had underestimated the total population of the country by 5 percent, which entailed an error of 41 percent in predicting the *growth* of the population over the preceding decade. Consequently, in recent years demographers have become more cautious in predicting population trends. Now they normally make several predictions, utilizing different sets of assumptions concerning possible changes in the birth rate, death rate, median marriage age of the population, immigration, and related factors. If, for example, "high estimates" of future birth rates prove to be correct, the United States may continue to experience a population growth rate of more than 1.5 percent annually, as it did from 1945 to 1961. But if, as many demographers expect, a decline in the birth rate occurs in the late 1960s and early 1970s, then the American population will grow only 1 percent annually, an average rate among the industrialized nations of the world.

Other salient characteristics of the present and expected population of the United States may be alluded to briefly. The "median age" of the American people, for example, is declining—that is, the percentage within the total population of the 20–29 and 30–34 year "age groups" is rising appreciably. Conversely, the number of youth (up to 20 years) is growing more slowly; the age category of 35–44 years is in fact expected to show a net decrease in 1964–1975, while the segment of the population classified as "elderly" (65 years and older) is growing at about half the rate of the 20–29 age group.

The increasing "youthfulness' of the American population has significant implications for many spheres of national life. Economically, there is no dearth of young people (and presumably new ideas) in the labor force and production. From a military–strategic standpoint, there is no shortage of manpower (although in the light of the internal dissension over Vietnam, there may of course be a reluctance on the part of young people to serve in the armed forces). Governmental and private economists, on the other hand, will be challenged to maintain a prosperous economic system, capable of absorbing large increments of new workers each year.* Another important population trend is the fact that during the 1970s, the percentage of women in the 20–24 year age bracket will increase, providing the basis perhaps for another "baby boom" in the mid-1970s. Moreover, geographically the American population has shifted. The West coast, the Mountain states, and the South Atlantic states have gained, and will continue to gain, population faster than the country as a whole; New England, the Middle Atlantic states, and the West North Central states will probably fall behind the national average in population increase.

Our interest in American demographic tendencies is confined to their implications for foreign policy. On that point, perhaps the most relevant considerations emerging from our brief survey are that America's population is continuing to expand at a normal (or perhaps slightly higher than normal) rate for an industrial nation; that America's economic capacity is sufficiently great so that a growing population can be supported with a constantly rising standard of living (with the latter climbing more rapidly than nearly all other nations in the world); that demographic projections indicate ample population resources to meet anticipated economic and military needs; and that for the bulk of the American society—if not for

*One study divides the population into two categories: consumers and producers. The former are those age groups either too young or too old to work; the latter are those groups in their normal working years (21–65). On this basis in 1965, 51 percent of all Americans were producers. In the mid-1970s, this proportion is expected to rise to around 53 percent—and to continue to increase. See Lawrence A. Mayer, "Why the U.S. Population Isn't Exploding," *Fortune* 75 (April, 1967), 162–166, 186–192.

certain groups in the ghettos or isolated geographic pockets like Appalachia—medical, nutritional, and educational standards will continue to rise. In brief, in nearly all respects, population affords an element of *strength* for the United States and a vital element in its power to influence external events favorably.[16]

The Limits of American Power

According to nearly any reasonably objective criterion, the power of the United States is vast, if not overwhelming. In some respects, it is becoming greater year by year. America's economic system has been productive enough, for example, to support a massive national commitment in Vietnam for several years. Yet by 1966, this commitment in Southeast Asia involved only some 8 percent of annual gross national product, as contrasted with the 14 percent of the GNP that was devoted to the Korean War. American resources have also been abundant enough to permit the United States to extend approximately $130 billion in various kinds of foreign assistance to other countries since World War II. Militarily, the American arsenal contains a great variety of nuclear and conventional weapons powerful enough to devastate potential enemies, perhaps with a severalfold margin of "overkill." In more intangible aspects of power, despite a rising level of public "protests," riots, demonstrations, and the like, America has remained the oldest, and in some respects perhaps most stable, democratic system in the world, with a substantial majority of Americans committed on most public issues to moderate positions and programs. That American power is impressive is indisputable, even by the nation's enemies.

Although few commentators doubted that the United States possessed a vast reservoir of resources for achieving its foreign policy goals, by the 1960s, it was also evident that limits existed to the power of even the strongest nation ever known. American power was vast; but it was finite. Great power was still not equivalent to omnipotence or infinite power. A few years after World War II, the astute Scotsman, D. W. Brogan, referred to "the illusion of American omnipotence." This was the idea, which Brogan encountered widely in America, that there was literally no problem or issue or challenge facing America in international relations that could not be solved. Americans, Brogan was convinced, too often overlooked the distinction between vast power and infinite power. Much the same theme was expressed by critics of the Vietnam War several years later. Thus, Senator J. William Fulbright (Democrat of Arkansas), the articulate chairman of the Senate Foreign Relations Committee, referred to the "arrogance" of American power. Fulbright meant by this that too many Americans, not excluding high government officials, believed the United States was capable of achieving any foreign policy goal imaginable. Fulbright seriously questioned whether it really lay within the capacity of even the United States to "go into a small, alien, undeveloped Asian nation and create stability where there is chaos, the will to fight where there is defeatism, democracy where there is no tradition of it, and honest government where corruption is almost a way of life." Fulbright lamented that Americans lacked

an appreciation of the dimensions of our own power, we fail to understand our enormous and disruptive impact on the world; we fail to understand that no matter how good our intentions . . . other nations are alarmed by the very existence of such great power, which, whatever its benevolence, cannot help but remind them of their own helplessness before it.[17]

Such criticism might well be overdrawn. After due allowance has been made, however, it remains true—as the Vietnam conflict during the 1960s reminded Americans almost daily—that the United States has confronted a frustrating paradox in the application of its power in the external environment. The paradox arose from the fact that during the very era when the power of the nation was unparalleled, the United States in some respects encountered *more resistance to the achievement of its foreign policy goals than in earlier periods!* At a time when America had unrivaled power, public (and often even official) dissatisfaction with the results of applying that power abroad was also at a peak.

This paradox had a number of interesting implications. Initially, its existence raised the fundamental question of whether the concept of "national power" itself, as invoked by political scientists for many years, might not be defective and misleading. According to traditional conceptions of power, the United States *should* be more successful than ever in the realization of its external objectives.

The paradox also raised questions about how the United States has *used* its vast power. Perhaps a partial explanation of the paradox lay in *a failure of national strategies* for responding to the multitude of problems in global affairs. For international issues like the population explosion or internal strains within the NATO alliance or the volatile Arab–Israeli dispute, it is highly possible that American policy-makers have not yet been able to formulate strategies which effectively utilize America's abundant resources to achieve satisfactory solutions.

Conditions in the postwar external environment also contributed to the paradox. One such condition was the proliferation in the sheer *number* of nations with which the United States maintained relations. By the late 1960s, for example,

the United Nations had grown to over 120 members (vis-à-vis 51 charter members in 1945). Among some 51 existing territories still classified as political dependencies, it is reasonable to expect further expansion in the number of independent nations, although at a much slower rate than occurred during the late 1950s and 1960s. This trend meant that *the number of claimants upon American resources has multiplied dramatically since World War II.*

Moreover, the expansion in the number of independent states came about primarily among societies *whose internal needs were almost limitless,* insofar as their requirements for outside assistance were concerned. Even if the United States increased its annual foreign aid allocation severalfold, the total available to needy societies would still be inadequate in the view of the recipients and insufficient to accomplish many of America's stated policy goals.

Programs like foreign aid remind us of another condition inhibiting America's ability to achieve its objectives overseas. A *fundamental change in the basic concerns of foreign policy* has occurred during the recent period. In eighteenth-century Europe, for example, the great powers were preoccupied chiefly with wars of conquest, territorial annexations and boundary adjustments, dynastic rivalries, colonial competition, the control of trade routes, and the like. Such concerns have not entirely disappeared from contemporary international relations, but in general their importance has declined. Today, the relationships among nations tend to revolve around a different set of issues and problems involving a very wide range of issues which were not normally important in diplomatic relationship before World War II.

This change in the nature of the issues central to international relations has taken place both horizontally and vertically. Horizontally, it has entailed a steady *widening* of the compass of foreign policy to include a broad spectrum of subjects often ignored by policy-makers in an earlier age. Today, for example, besides their traditional interest in protecting the security of the United States, strengthening defensive alliances, and carrying on routine diplomatic business, American officials are keenly interested in promoting the economic advancement of Afro–Asian societies; encouraging political stability (and, hopefully, democracy) throughout much of the world; forging constructive relations with regional organizations like the European Common Market or the Organization of African Unity; preventing (or curbing) tribal, ethnic, and linguistic rivalries that impair national unity in countries like India or Nigeria; endeavoring to secure favorable terms of trade for the emerging nations; enhancing respect for human rights in the Soviet Union or the Republic of South Africa; and trying to make the

United Nations a viable international organization.

Vertically, the realm of foreign policy has also expanded. Increasingly, great powers today not only endeavor to influence government leaders in other countries; to an unparalleled extent, they also seek *to influence private citizens and groups within other societies.* Many programs sponsored by the United States—such as foreign aid, the activities of the United States Information Agency (USIA), and efforts to check the population explosion—seek to induce the individual citizen or family to act in a way which beneficially affects American foreign policy. In no previous era have foreign policy officials so routinely gone "over the heads" of governments, so to speak, in their efforts to affect the behavior of citizens and groups directly; occasionally (as in earlier American propaganda to Communist China), an effort is made by one government to discredit a regime in the minds of its citizens or to induce public behavior that is contrary to the policies of the regime itself. This kind of vertical expansion in the compass of foreign policy means that America now seeks to apply its power to countless millions of people, instead of a few hundred governmental leaders, among the nations of the world. This fact sets additional limits upon the ability of the United States to apply its power successfully abroad.

A related limitation upon American power as applied in external affairs stems from what might be called the *radical nature of prevalent foreign policy goals.* If the number of people America seeks to influence has multiplied spectacularly, the demands made upon these millions of people by the United States have also broadened. Take the Alliance for Progress, formulated by the United States in 1961 to launch Latin America upon the path of modernization and self-sustaining economic growth. The Alliance for Progress was sometimes described as a "controlled revolution" or a "revolution in freedom." Such phrases were not inappropriate, since the program contemplated nothing less than pervasive and far-reaching changes in life styles, patterns of social organization, economic institutions and processes, political systems and modes—in short, in nearly every sphere of human experience in Latin America. That the program consistently fell short of reaching its proclaimed goals was perhaps ordained from the beginning, given the fact that the goals themselves anticipated that millions of citizens in Latin America would abandon ancient customs and learn new behavior, all within a decade! The United States expected to sponsor a successful "revolution in freedom," while scrupulously observing a principle which its American neighbors had long insisted be kept at the forefront of hemispheric relations: the concept of "nonintervention" in the internal affairs of other countries. Even if a formula could be found for reconciling these two somewhat antithetical ideas, successful implementation of the "revolution in freedom" taxed the ingenuity of the United States to the utmost in its attempt to apply its vast power effectively upon the Brazilian peasant, the Indian citizen of Bolivia, and the Venezuelan oil worker.

Finally, the inability of the United States to achieve many of its important foreign policy goals suggests that, in the present context of international affairs, a kind of Newtonian law may well operate when a great power seeks to effect basic changes in foreign societies. Under some circumstances, the "action" of the United States may produce a massive "reaction," which may well be inherent in the very process of using American power. Thus, in the attempt to solve one set of problems, new—and often more difficult—problems are created for American policy-makers.

The attempt by the United States to encourage political and economic modernization throughout the developing world affords numerous examples of this Newtonian phenomenon. A number of "actions" by the United States—economic and technical assistance programs, efforts to elevate living standards, and attempts to curb population expansion—may in time begin to launch a society along the path of modernization. In the process, however, modernization itself gives rise to a host of novel, and often unexpected, problems. Traditional family ties are disrupted; tribal and ethnic bonds are weakened; rural unemployment rises when mechanized and scientific agricultural techniques begin to raise farm output; and rural overpopulation accelerates mass migration to already overcrowded cities, producing new slums. Politically, such actions can, and not infrequently do, create unanticipated problems for the United States.

To the extent that American power is responsible for encouraging modernization in primitive societies, then the United States may contribute to future political instability, extremism, and turmoil within these countries. Quiescent masses living in age-old poverty do not normally provide the ingredients of a revolutionary situation. It is only when individuals and groups become deeply dissatisfied with their condition—a frame of mind normally occurring *after their conditions have begun to improve*—that political upheaval erupts and begins to attract a mass following. Dissident political groups are then apt to criticize the incumbent government because the pace of change is too slow or because the benefits accruing from modernization are not shared equitably throughout the society. Under these conditions, political discontent can accelerate for another reason: to the extent that American aid is successfully utilized, this very fact can make it more difficult than ever for the incumbent regime to retain the loyalty of its citizens. Symbolically (if not actually), reliance upon American assistance may compromise a government's claim to genuine independence and may raise questions in the minds of its citizens about the degree of foreign influence upon national decision-making. As a matter of political survival, foreign political leaders must continually "prove" their devotion to national sovereignty, perhaps by periodically denouncing America and other countries providing them with needed assistance. Similarly, extensive American aid to another country may also in time create a kind of obligation for the United States to support the government in power; because of intimate association with it, the United States becomes somehow "responsible" for the behavior of a foreign government receiving its assistance, no matter how unpopular or repressive the regime may be.

On the basis of postwar experience, the evidence seems rather persuasive that the application of vast power in a diverse and frequently turbulent external environment often generates as may problems as it solves. If the United States succeeds in making the Indian villager dissatisfied with his traditionally primitive existence—a necessary early step in the modernization process—the chances are that it will also make him politically restless, impatient with the process of slow and "orderly" change, and possibly receptive to some kind of authoritarian (even totalitarian) approach which promises to accelerate the pace of change. As often as not, the United States is blamed because progress is too slow, because the volume of American aid is inadequate, or because evident inequalities still exist within the society concerned. This syndrome is not untypical of the kind of reaction American foreign policy has engendered in other countries since World War II or of the kind of difficult challenge which American policy-makers must continually face.

NOTES

1. For public criticisms of American goals in Vietnam, see the selections included in Marcus G. Raskin and Bernard B. Fall, *The Viet-Nam Reader* (New York: Random House, 1965); criticisms of American policy in Southeast Asia are also contained in Marvin E. Gettleman, *Vietnam: History, Documents, and Opinions on a Major World Crisis* (Greenwich, Conn.: Fawcett Publications, 1965); and the spectrum of opinion on Vietnam is well represented in the lenghty compilation by Wesley R. Fishel, *Vietnam: Anatomy of a Conflict* (Itasca, Ill.: F. E. Peacock, 1968).
2. The problem of shifting American goals in the Korean War is examined in Matthew B. Ridgway, *The Korean War* (New York: Popular Library, 1967), *passim;* and John W. Spanier, *The Truman–MacArthur Contro-*

versy and the Korean War (Cambridge, Mass.: Belknap Press of Harvard University, 1959), pp. 84–104.
3. Nicholas J. Spykman, *America's Strategy in World Politics* (New York: Harcourt Brace Jovanovich, 1942), p. 41.
4. Sir Ernest Barker, *National Character* (London: Methuen, 1948), pp. 70–71.
5. *Ibid.*, pp. 70–74.
6. George T. Renner, "Air Age Geography," *Harper's Magazine* 187 (June, 1943), 38.
7. S. Whittemore Boggs, "Global Relations of the United States," *Department of State Bulletin* 30 (June 14, 1954), 908.
8. Eugene Staley, "The Myth of the Continents," *Foreign Affairs* 19 (April, 1941), 485.
9. *Ibid.*, pp. 485–486.
10. Renner, *op. cit.*, p. 39.
11. Richard Hartshorne, "Where in the World Are We?" *Journal of Geography* 52 (December, 1953), 388.
12. *Ibid.*, pp. 388–393.
13. See G. F. Hudson, "America and the World-Island," *Twentieth Century* 158 (July, 1955), 35–44, for an application of Mackinder's ideas to the cold war. The geographical implications of Axis strategy in World War II are discussed in Spykman, *op. cit.*, pp. 320–453.
14. Data on American economic growth is drawn from *The New York Times* (January 20, January 23, August 8, July 4, and December 16, 1966; January 22, 1967; February 4, 1968; January 6 and 13, 1969); Gilbert Burck, "The Still-Bright Promise of Productivity," *Fortune* 78 (October, 1968), 134–137, 218, 223; Edwin L. Dale, Jr., "The U.S. Economic Giant Keeps Growing," *New York Times Magazine* (March 19, 1967) pp. 31, 135–152; William Bowen, "The U.S. Economy Enters a New Era," *Fortune* 75 (March, 1967), 111–115, 246.
15. Our discussion of the economic problems and prospects of the Soviet Union is based upon data provided in Charles J. V. Murphy, "Khrushchev's Paper Bear," *Fortune* (December, 1964), 115, 224–230; Edward Crankshaw, "The Farmer Frustrates Khrushchev," *New York Times Magazine* (September 20, 1964), pp. 17, 110–114; Allen B. Ballard, "Private Plot vs. Collective Farm," *The New York Times Magazine* (June 13, 1965), pp. 14–15, 69–74; Howard Rausch, "Russia's Economic Reformation," *The Reporter* 37 (November 16, 1967), 33–35; and *The New York Times* (January 3 and 17, March 11, 1965; January 2, February 3 and 21, March 13, July 31, and November 25, 1966; January 30, April 17, June 18, July 23, October 10, 22, and 29, 1967; January 15, February 19, and March 31, 1968). Good background studies are Alec Nove, *The Soviet Economy: An Introduction*, rev. ed. (New York: Praeger, 1966); A. Bergson and S. Kuznets, *Economic Trends in the Soviet Union* (Cambridge, Mass.: Harvard University Press, 1963); J. P. Cole, *Geography of the U.S.S.R.*

(Baltimore: Penguin, 1967); and Peter Wiles, "The Pursuit of Affluence: The Economic Record," in Samuel Hendel and Randolph L. Braham, eds., *The U.S.S.R. After 50 Years: Promise and Reality* (New York: Knopf, 1967).

16. Data on American population trends and projections are taken from Lawrence A. Mayer, "Why the U.S. Population Isn't Exploding," *Fortune* 75 (April, 1967), 162–166, 186–192; *The New York Times* (January 17, 1966).

17. Senator J. William Fulbright, *The Arrogance of Power* (New York: Random House, 1966), pp. 15, 21.

Two
AMERICA LOOKS AT THE WORLD:
A Study in National Character

By the usual criteria used for determing national power—the total wealth of the nation, the size and quality of the population, the level of industrialization, the strength of the nation's armed forces —the United States is entitled to be designated a great power. According to many standards, indeed, it is the greatest nation in the history of the world. Yet by the 1970s, it had become apparent that the *results* achieved by applying American power in various regions of the world were far from satisfying to millions of citizens within the United States, not to speak of countless foreigners. The popular discontent surrounding the Vietnam War provided a graphic illustration of this phenomenon. After expending untold billions of dollars and sustaining more casualties than had been experienced in the Korean War, officials of the Johnson and Nixon administrations were severely challenged to demonstrate what this massive commitment of men and resources had actually achieved, in terms of fulfilling the purposes of the United States abroad or safeguarding vital diplomatic interests. A case could be made for the idea that America's involvement in Vietnam *was* justifiable on several grounds. However, we are not concerned with the pros and cons of the debate over Vietnam at this stage.* Our interest is confined to emphasizing the existence of an evident disparity between what America expected to achieve and what it in fact accomplished as a result of its large-scale commitment in Southeast Asia.

This dichotomy no doubt could be explained by reference to several factors, such as America's lack of experience in counter-insurgency warfare, the ineptitude of the government in South Vietnam, the Asian aversion to colonialism, and various tactical and strategic conditions favoring the Communist forces over those of South Vietnam and the United States. But the explanation which concerns us here relates to the popular attitudes, basic assumptions, unarticulated premises, and often quite unconscious viewpoints displayed by Americans toward the external environment.

Better than any other case that might be cited from recent American diplomatic experience, the Vietnam problem illustrates the often crucial role played by what (for want of a more precise term) we may call "national character" in the foreign policy process. As a result of their historical conditioning in internal and external affairs, Americans have acquired certain deeply ingrained viewpoints and propensties affecting their approach to foreign relations. For the most part, the principal elements in this outlook are derived from domestic and foreign experience *before World War II.* Yet increasingly since 1945, Americans have discovered that their psychological frame of reference in approaching the outside world does not fit the realities confronting their policy-makers in unfamiliar regions like the Middle East, sub-Saharan Africa, or east Asia. The tensions generated by the conflict between America's perception of the world and existing realities in areas like Southeast Asia accounted in no small measure for the dissension surrounding public discussion of the Vietnam issue. Speaking more broadly, the "crisis of confidence" which many Americans experienced toward America's role in foreign affairs was partially attributable to the cluster of mental images and habits of mind which they brought to bear upon the external environment.

THE CONCEPT OF NATIONAL CHARACTER

What is meant by the "national character" of a society? What factors determine how a particular nation will react to events abroad? The question that Winston Churchill defiantly addressed to the Nazi government early in World War II—"What kind of people do they think we are?"—is at once a necessary inquiry in any study of foreign policy and an inordinately complex one. As Henry Steele Commager observed, Hitler failed so completely to comprehend the importance of national character that the Nazi bid for world domination ended in catastrophe. His failure was

*The Vietnam conflict as a problem in recent American foreign policy is discussed in Chapter 13.

fundamental and pervasive. . . . He failed to realize, as throughout history tyrants have failed to realize, that a people's character is, in the last analysis, the most important thing about them. . . . For material things cannot in themselves achieve something. They count only where there is a will to use them, and whether they count for weal or for woe depends upon the way that they are used.[1]

When we ask: "What is the national character of the American people?" we shall focus upon the characteristics they have traditionally exhibited as they looked out upon the world. We want to establish the psychological perspective or frame of reference within which they have customarily approached foreign policy. We are searching for what an eminent English scholar, Sir Ernest Barker, called the "sum of acquired tendencies" and the "expectable action" of a nation. He elaborated this idea by saying:

Each nation lives in a set of ideas (and of emotions associated with the ideas and even with the very words used to express the ideas), which is peculiar to itself. . . . Any man who has to act between nations . . . is bound to understand, to the best of his power, the peculiarities of each national fund of ideas. He must realize that there are as many atmospheres, and as many characters, as there are nations. . . . Nations are realities; and their characters—the set of their minds, and the atmosphere of their ideas—are as real as they are.[2]

Put more simply, we are asking, "Are there certain habits of mind that we can identify as distinctive elements in the American approach to foreign relations?"* Many authorities agree that there are. Before we attempt to delineate them, however, certain reservations should be considered.

Pitfalls in the Study of National Character

In the first place, some authorities deny the existence of national character altogether. They believe that attempts to discuss it entail nothing more than impressionism and hasty generalization which scientific methodology cannot support.[3] While their admonitions have some validity, most students agree that the subject is important, that it permits investigation and that we can learn something about it, however tentative and qualified our conclusions must sometimes be.

*As our discussion of the role of public opinion in the foreign policy process (Chapter 7) emphasizes, public viewpoints in the United States are far from monolithic —perhaps less so in the 1970s than ever. The differences between the attitudes of ordinary citizens and those of the "informed" or "elite" public are often marked. Here, however, our focus is upon the viewpoints displayed by the average citizen toward the outside world.

Second, it is imperative that we avoid stereotyped thinking in dealing with the concept of national character. All of us are familiar with stereotypes in this field. "The Germans are inherently militaristic and expansionist." The inference follows that peace with Germany is an illusion. "The French are decadent, immoral, and unreliable." Hence, they make very poor allies. "The Latin Americans are ignorant and proud, politically immature, mercurial, and easily misled." Hence, they need guidance by the United States in solving their problems. Such sweeping characterizations are largely false, and the inferences drawn from them are equally false. Sometimes there is a germ of truth in such stereotypes— enough to make them widely accepted. Similarly, by choosing certain episodes in American diplomatic history one could also find enough evidence to make credulous people believe that the United States is imperialistic, money-loving, war-mongering, fickle, and xenophobic. These examples illustrate an important point in the study of national character: Nations should be characterized by traits which are in accord with the over-all pattern of the nation's history and ethos and which represent, as nearly as possible typical behavior of the people described.

In the third place, it must be recognized that many of the traits of national character delineated in this chapter constitute subconscious premises growing out of historical experience, rather than explicit and clearly thought-out popular attitudes on matters of public policy. For this reason, inconsistencies persist among diverse traits of national character. To cite an example dealt with at length at a later stage: Americans in the past have exhibited a dogmatic attachment to "principle" in international affairs, while at the same time remaining devoted to expediency and trial-and-error methods in coping with many of their domestic problems. Yet such inconsistencies are seldom perceived by the average American, chiefly perhaps because he infrequently questions the basic values and beliefs that shape his attitudes toward problems at home and abroad.

A final warning concerns the danger of regarding national character as something fixed and unalterable. The character of neither individuals nor nations is cast in a permanent mold. Sir Ernest Barker wrote: ". . . There is no such thing as a given and ineluctable national character, which stamps and makes the members of a nation, and is their individual and collective destiny. Character is not a destiny to each nation. Each nation makes its character and its destiny."[4] The proper analogy to illustrate national character is an organism—evolving, adapting to influences about it, learning from mistakes, ever-changing.

With these admonitions in mind, let us examine more closely the leading attributes of American national character.

AMERICAN ATTITUDES TOWARD POWER

Down to the postwar period, no feature of the approach of the American people to foreign relations was more pronounced and had more important consequences for foreign policy than their attitude toward power conflicts and, specifically, toward war. Throughout most of their history, the American people have deprecated the role of power in international affairs. They have looked upon conflict as abnormal, transitory, and avoidable. Hostilities have existed among nations, not because their vital interests sometimes clashed, but because of "misunderstandings." These, it was believed, could be eliminated by a variety of means: agreements to denounce war "as an instrument of national policy," as in the Kellogg–Briand Pact of 1928; pledges to reduce armaments; solemn oaths to respect the territorial integrity of small countries; ratification of the charter of an international organization; resounding declarations of high principle, such as the Fourteen Points or the Four Freedoms; faith in the "moral opinion of mankind" to deter aggressors; and belief that international student exchange programs and "good-will missions" will reduce tensions, as the nations "get to know each other better." The keynote of American life, according to many historians, was the word *consensus.* As the "melting pot" of the world, the American society was successfully engaged in assimilating minorities, in erasing significant differences between rich and poor, in demonstrating the viability of the two-party political system, in overcoming the divisive influence of sectionalism—in brief, in creating a unified nation in which the differences that periodically destroyed the unity of the Old World were unknown and, many Americans believed, inconceivable.*

Few writers have stressed the American misunderstanding of the fundamental role of power as frequently, and as pointedly, as Walter Lippmann. Lippmann feels that our approach to foreign relations has been filled with "stereotyped prejudices and sacred cows and wishful conceptions," to the extent that we are often incapable of formulating workable policies. Our basic weakness is a failure to recognize, "to admit, to take as the premise of our thinking, the fact that rivalry and strife and conflict among states, communities, and factions are the normal condition of mankind."[5]

Such habits of thought stem from a variety of influences in the nation's history. From America's own internal experience, the people have taken the view that fundamental human conflicts did not exist, or if they did, that they could be quickly resolved, because down to the 1960s remarkably few such conflicts in fact did persist. Marxist ideology notwithstanding, the United States perhaps approximates more nearly than any other country the "classless society."[6] Until recent years, conflicts of all kinds—economic, religious, ethnic, racial—produced relatively little enduring strife, compared with the Old World and the newer nations of Asia and Africa. America has never experienced prolonged and irreconcilable divisions among its people. Throughout most of their history, Americans somehow learned to channel existing differences into nonviolent avenues, to smooth them out, to make them seem secondary to the task of creating upon a continent the "American way of life." This has been done (or Americans *believed* it was being done) by providing unparalleled opportunities for material advancement; by steadily trying to offer equal opportunities for all in ever-widening spheres of national life; by de-emphasizing doctrinal and ideological differences in favor of immediate and attainable goals for human betterment; by listening to the demands of dissatisfied groups and, in time, meeting most of them; by insisting upon fair play in economic, social, and political life. Our experience has built in us the conviction that perseverance and will power can solve all problems.

Consequences for American Security

The consequences of America's attitude toward the role of power conflicts have been far-reaching and decisive. It has heavily colored the nation's appraisal of the basis of its security. From superficial examinations of their own history, Americans have believed that their security could be explained by a variety of factors, none of which had anything to do with power. There was first the evident fact of geographical separation from Europe and Asia which, before the air age, did provide a substantial degree of military protection. Then there was the fact that the United States had repeatedly warned other countries to stay out of the Western Hemisphere—and, with few exceptions, the warning had been heeded. There was also the belief that if America chose to ignore the Old World, the Old World would respond by ignoring America. The illusion persisted that no vital interests connected the Old and New

---

*Here, as elsewhere in this chapter, it is important to distinguish between what Americans thought they were doing and what they were in fact accomplishing. As events during the 1960s and 1970s made abundantly clear, the degree of "consensus" in American life—particularly in regard to the nation's largest minority, its black citizens— has no doubt been considerably exaggerated, both in popular folklore and by reputable historians. Among the latter, by the late 1960s a group of "revisionists" were attacking the traditional emphasis upon consensus in interpreting America's experience; according to this view, such interpretations merely perpetuated "the establishment" and glossed over many fundamental defects of the American society.

Worlds, that America could be secure no matter what transpired in Europe. From the time of the Monroe Doctrine in 1823 to World War II, the United States acted as though its security were a natural right; as though changes in the European balance of power could not affect it; and as though power played an inconsequential if not altogether negligible, role in international relations. Walter Lippmann has written that for over a hundred years

The idealistic objections to preparedness to strategic precautions, and to alliances came to dominate American thinking. . . . The objections flourished, and became a national ideology, owing to the historical accident that in that period Asia was dormant, Europe divided, and Britain's command of the sea unchallenged. As a result, we never had to meet our obligations in this hemisphere and in the Pacific, and we enjoyed a security which in fact we took almost no measures to sustain.[7]

Because the American mythology before World War II traditionally de-emphasized power, the United States lived off an unrecognized and unacknowledged inheritance: the British fleet ruled the seas, and the quarrels of Europe kept aggressors otherwise occupied.

A corollary of the American failure to accept the role of power has been the failure to understand that, in the successful management of foreign affairs, assets must equal or exceed liabilities. While it is true that power cannot be calculated with great precision, a rough kind of equilibrium must be maintained between a nation's foreign commitments and its ability to protect them. Bankruptcy, Walter Lippmann has argued, is the only word to describe American foreign policy at crucial intervals in history. American foreign policy was bankrupt for the same reason that we speak of a bankrupt business: Obligations were assumed greater than the nation's resources, at least greater than the resources available to the nation's leaders at any given time. The art of conducting foreign policy successfully, Lippmann has contended, "consists in bringing into balance, with a comfortable surplus of power in reserve, the nation's commitments and the nation's power."[8]

In almost any period in American history since 1900, evidence of bankruptcy can be found. The American acquisition of the Philippines after the war with Spain was, in the words of the diplomatic historian Samuel F. Bemis, "The Great Aberration." It was an aberration because annexation of these islands entailed responsibilities whose implications most Americans did not begin to understand. Yet even after some of the consequences of extending America's boundaries thousands of miles into the Pacific—to the very doorstep of Japan—finally became apparent, the United States

was still unwilling to take the necessary steps to protect its commitments there.[9]

From World War I to World War II this pattern of bankruptcy was repeated on an even broader and more ominous scale. At the very time when threats to its commitments were growing, especially in the Orient, America was *reducing* its military power. Not until 1941 did the American people begin to understand that America's refusal to use its power in behalf of its vital interests was in itself a policy. No nation, especially a powerful nation, can escape having an influence in world affairs. Unwittingly, unconsciously, and to its own great detriment, America cast its vote in this period on the side of destroying the military security of the Atlantic community, of turning over the military approaches of the Western Hemisphere to would-be conquerors, of giving Japan a free hand in the Pacific—in summary, of doing everything possible to insure bankruptcy in foreign affairs.

Much the same form of bankruptcy characterized American foreign and defense policy immediately after World War II. The United States emerged from this contest as in many respects the acknowledged "leader" of the Allied coalition. Although Britain, France, and Nationalist China were given the honorary status of great powers, in reality the Big Two—the United States and the Soviet Union—became the arbiters of the postwar world. In the West, American power overshadowed that of all other countries combined; behind the Iron Curtain, Soviet Russia's power was perhaps even more decisive. Soviet policy-makers understood the fundamental changes in the distribution of global power which had been brought about by World War II; as their moves in Eastern Europe made clear, they grasped the intimate connection between the possession of power and the ability to achieve important political objectives. In the main, American policy-makers, however, did not understand this connection; and the American people appeared even more oblivious to it. The result was that, within a few months after the end of World War II, America's military might disintegrated (while Russia's remained largely intact), leaving the United States little more than its nuclear arsenal with which to support its foreign policy and national defense goals. When Communist forces attacked South Korea (on June 25, 1950), America once again embarked upon a program of rapid military mobilization and preparedness.

America's traditional deprecation of power—which has led to situations affecting its security adversely—has had a momentous effect upon popular and official attitudes toward foreign relations. The Japanese victory at Pearl Harbor (December 7, 1941) was a military disaster for the United States. Correctly or not, many Americans attributed the intrusion of Communist power in regions like Eastern Europe and China after World War II to America's lack of power adequate to contain this expansionism. The Communist attempt to gain control over South Korea, many Americans were convinced, grew out of a conviction in Moscow and other Marxist capitals that the free world was too weak to prevent this incursion. In the light of these developments in their recent diplomatic experience, small wonder that many Americans were prone to swing to the opposite extreme in their viewpoints toward the role of power in international relations. Owing to the lessons learned from World War II, the communization of Eastern Europe and China, and the Korean conflict, Americans no longer needed to be taught that adequate <u>national</u> <u>power</u> was the foundation upon which successful foreign policy had to be based. From the early 1950s onward, defense spending climbed steadily; America was determined to allow no "missile gap" to develop favoring the Soviet Union; through a series of military pacts, the United States acquired over forty military allies, involving several hundred foreign military installations (some in neutralist countries). As the leader of the "free world," the United States was determined to prevent any new Communist encroachments against weak countries. In the popular description, America had become "the <u>policeman of the world</u>," intervening to preserve order and guarantee security in such far-flung settings as Latin America, Lebanon, Southeast Asia, and Korea. Under these circumstances, many commentators believed, the American society now suffered from a different, but no less serious, disorder: the "arrogance of power," or the inclination to believe that the vast economic and military might of the United States was sufficient to achieve *any* goal to which the American government was committed. Conversely, Americans too often seemed indifferent to the *disruptive effects* accompanying the use of their power in regions like Latin America or Southeast Asia, where U.S. involvement in the destiny of other societies was itself productive of tensions and upheavals. We shall discuss this last problem at greater length at a later stage.

Wars Are Aberrations

Another corollary of America's failure to comprehend the role of power in international politics can be found in its attitudes toward the causes and consequences of war. As we shall see more fully in Chapter 4, the nineteenth century Prussian General Carl Maria von Clausewitz taught that war is but the continuation of policy by other means. Hence the cliché that the United States has never lost a war nor won a peace means that the American people have lacked a clear understanding of the political issues leading to and growing out of

armed conflict among nations; their policies for dealing with such issues have, therefore, more often than not been feeble and ineffective. Regarding wars as aberrations (which, from a moral-ethical viewpoint they may certainly be), Americans were unprepared psychologically to accept the Clausewitzian idea that wars are an alternative method for settling political disputes among nations. Accordingly, they evinced minimum awareness of both why they were involved in hostilities and what political issues were likely to follow. The popular American slogan during the 1920s—"Back to normalcy!"—more or less accurately describes the American state of mind about every military contest in which the United States has been engaged, not excluding in many respects the Vietnam War. A belief that America (and, for that matter, the entire international community) could return to the *status quo ante bellum* has been a persistent theme in the diplomatic history of the United States.

This mentality is well illustrated by the revisionism that has characterized historical writing and literature following virtually every war in which the United States has been engaged.* Recurrent themes in revisionist writings have been that responsibility for hostilities rested on both sides, and often more on the American side than on the enemy's; that the United States had no vital interests at stake and hence was under no necessity to fight; and that the American people had been deluded by a variety of influences—propaganda, munitions makers, Wall Street, political leaders and, most recently, the military-industrial complex—into believing that their security demanded recourse to arms.[10] Revisionism, writes Dexter Perkins, has tried to convince the citizenry that "every war in which this country has been engaged was really quite unnecessary or immoral or both; and that it behooves us in the future to pursue policies very different from those pursued in the past." Behind such thinking, he continues, often lies "the assumption that the will to avoid war is sufficient to prevent war."[11] Water Lippmann has made this point even more forcefully. Writing in 1940, he explained the blindness of Americans toward the Axis dictators by referring to "a falsification of American history." The American people had been

. . . miseducated by a swarm of innocent but ignorant historians, by reckless demagogues, and by foreign interests, into believing that America entered the other war because of British propaganda, loans of the bankers, the machinations of President Wilson's advisers, and drummed-up patriotic ecstasy. The people have been told to believe that anyone who challenges this explanation of 1917 and insists that America was defending

*For a detailed treatment of revisionist interpretations of the cold war, see Chapter 8.

American vital interests is himself a victim or an agent of British propaganda.[12]

Largely because the United States was attacked at Pearl Harbor, considerably less revisionist or "disillusionist" literature appeared with regard to World War II. Yet, even before 1941, right-wing critics of the Roosevelt administration—supported in rare instances by eminent American historians—were convinced that President Roosevelt deliberately maneuvered Japan into striking the first blow in a conflict which Roosevelt and his advisers believed to be inevitable. However, this viewpoint received little popular following in the United States; nor was it supported by the great majority of American historians.[13] The same could be said of the Korean War. The main source of public dissatisfaction with regard to that conflict centered upon the Truman administration's determination to keep the war *limited;* little or no public disaffection could be found with the fact of America's involvement in the security of South Korea, either in the early 1950s or afterwards. As in World War II, the Communist attack against a recognized military frontier (the 38th Parallel) convinced the United States, along with a majority of the United Nations, that a clear case of "aggression" had occured against a defenseless nation.

America's involvement in the Vietnam War, after the United States began to assume the major burden of the war effort in the early 1960s, in time evoked what may well have been the most intense popular disenchantment with a foreign military commitment in American history. Led by intellectuals, the opposition to the Vietnam War became a crescendo of disillusionment and dismay; and while this wave of disaffection may not have been the only force affecting such decisions, it clearly was one factor compelling Presidents Lyndon B. Johnson and Richard M. Nixon to de-escalate America's military presence in Southeast Asia. Opponents of the war in Vietnam denounced the conflict as "immoral," as "criminal," as "stupid"—to mention only some of the milder epithets used. The military presence of the United States in Southeast Asia was explained by critics on several grounds—such as the desire to maintain right-wing military elites in power or opposition to Asian nationalism or a determination to protect America's economic stake in the region— none of which usually had anything to do with the underlying security interests of the United States regionally or globally. Opponents of the Vietnam War were disinclined to put any credence in the so-called "domino theory," the crux of which was that if Indochina passed under Marxist control, then much of Asia would succumb ("like a row of falling dominoes") to Communist domination. The SEATO treaty was regarded as symbolizing American "pactitis" during the 1950s: Not only

was it ineffectual but, critics contended, it actually promoted instability within the region. In brief, for many citizens opposing the war in Vietnam there existed *no valid security justification* for America's involvement in Southeast Asia; and the invalid reasons related primarily to compulsions arising from "the arrogance of American power."

Whether such explanations were defensible or not does not concern us at this stage. Our interest is limited to emphasizing the rather remarkable fact that, for a significant number of critics of America's behavior, *the power considerations at stake in the conflict seemed strangely irrelevant.* Opposition to America's commitments in Southeast Asia stemmed mainly from moral, ethical, or psychological revulsions; from concern about how the Vietnam conflict affected America's "image" throughout the world; from aversion to the behavior of the ruling political elite in Saigon; and (most crucially, perhaps, for a majority of Americans) from a conviction that the United States was incapable of "winning" the contest militarily and politically without incurring a prohibitive cost. Many of these doubts rested upon persuasive evidence. But a singular feature of the antiwar sentiment within the American society was the extent to which it paralleled various "disillusionment" and "revisionist" interpretations of World War I: Only rarely did critics address themselves to the larger strategic issues involved and to the political consequences which could almost certainly be expected to follow the precipitous withdrawal of American power from Southeast Asia. Their contemptuous dismissal of the "domino theory" served merely as one indication of many Americans' relative indifference to this dimension of the problem, and their more general condemnation of America's role as the "policeman of the world" strongly implied a lack of interest in the strategic aspects of national policy. Few critics of America's involvement in Vietnam offered any *alternative* strategy for achieving America's diplomatic goals of protecting its security interests in Asia; indeed, among this group, a goodly number opposing the policies of the Johnson and Nixon administrations appeared unwilling to concede that the United States even *had* such interests on the Asian (and, inferentially, the Latin America, African, or Middle Eastern) scene. Policy-makers or citizens favoring the nation's behavior in Southeast Asia who suggested otherwise were apt to be denounced as spokesmen for the military-industrial complex.

Still another behavior characteristic associated with prevalent American misconceptions about the role of national power in international affairs has been the tendency throughout much of the nation's history to identify threats to national security *with specific countries or individuals.* From World War I to the present day, Americans have exhibited a propensity for *objectifying* their problems and frustrations. In World War I, millions of Americans were convinced that Kaiser Wilhelm's Germany epitomized the threat to the security of the United States and its allies; the logical corollary of this reasoning was that, after a radical change of regimes in Germany, the threat would disappear. It seldom occurred to Americans that it was *Germany's behavior* in threatening the military equilibrium of Europe which endangered world peace; that this behavior could (and of course did) become even more ominous under an entirely different system of government; or that the same threat could (and in fact did) arise at a later stage from countries other than Germany. Less than a generation later, the "Axis dictators" of World War II played much the same role in American mythology. Their defeat would not only bring the war to a victorious conclusion; it would open a new era in which mankind would enjoy the Four Freedoms (such as freedom from want and from fear) throughout the world. Only a small minority of Americans (and the distinguished diplomatic official George F. Kennan was among this group) publicly doubted this roseate assumption. As in World War II, Kennan and a handful of other Americans tried (with no conspicuous success) to convince the nation that the Axis powers threatened America primarily for strategic and military reasons, rather than because of political and ideological differences. It followed, and postwar events quickly confirmed the view, that another powerful country like Soviet Russia could pose similarly grave threat to the security of the United States and its allies.

The era of cold war witnessed a comparable tendency among Americans to identify the challenges confronting them abroad with a particular system of government or political movement. For several years after World War II, it was "Stalin's Russia" which endangered world peace and stability; and (after Mao Tse-tung's revolutionary movement gained control of China) it later became "international Communism" which threatened international security. For many Americans, every incidence of political turmoil or armed conflict anywhere in the world—from the latest revolution in Latin America, to a border conflict in Africa, to the Arab–Israeli dispute, to political turbulence in Southeast Asia—could be attributed to the machinations of international Communism, whose headquarters was in the Kremlin. It was heretical (and is still far from a popular notion) to suggest that the disruption of the Marxist monolith, which has resulted chiefly from the Sino–Soviet dispute, could be even more inimical to the security of the non-Communist world than the earlier condition of largely unchallenged Soviet hegemony.

The tendency we are describing here, it is important to point out, was not displayed merely by conservatively oriented or right-wing political elements within American society or by citizens whose understanding of international affairs was primitive. Intellectuals may be prone to suppose that stereotyped thinking about the outside world is confined to such groups. But if it was not clear earlier, the period of the Vietnam War provided ample evidence that intellectuals themselves are often no less prone to objectify the problems plaguing America abroad; according to such reasoning (or nonreasoning), once the particular evils identified were eliminated, America would enter a new era of diplomatic success. Ironically, for many Americans who had become extremely disdainful of concepts like "international Communism," the *real* source of America's difficulties abroad was clear: It was right-wing (usually military) dictatorships, whose internal and external policies were anathema and whose very existence threatened regional or global peace. Supposedly kept in power by the so-called military–industrial complex within the United States, these governments (whose numbers seemed to increase every year) posed the most formidable barrier to the achievement of American objectives overseas. On this premise, the cure for the malaise afflicting the nation's foreign relations was equally obvious: In every region (possibly excepting Western Europe), the United States ought unequivocally to *support revolutions* against indigenous governments, thereby identifying itself with the "forces of change" in other societies.[14] That many societies outside the West had (or thought they had) experienced their revolution already; or that the peoples in these countries often evinced no notable desire for revolutionary change; or that there appeared to be no viable alternative to rule by military elements or other elitist groups in a number of these countries; or that the officials of the incumbent government were already committed to programs of change and modernization, often against great odds; or that America's overt sponsorship of an opposition political force would be an almost certain death sentence for it; or that a new revolutionary regime could (and many times in the past has) become exploitive and self-serving —such aspects of the problem almost never received attention from those calling upon the United States to get on the "right side" of revolutionary movements abroad.

A variation on this same theme was prominent in domestic criticism of the Vietnam War. This was the idea that the central defect of American foreign policy was its failure to endorse and actively support Asian nationalism. Once America recitified this mistake, Asia would presumably become stabilized and the problems facing the West in that region would quickly be surmounted. Proponents of this view revealed little or no awareness of the fact that nationalism can produce conflict, no less than harmony, among nations. In Asia as in other regions, some nationalist movements may be conducive to peace and stability, while others are not. Nor was there any realization that so many varieties of nationalism have existed in modern history as to make this prescription for America all but worthless.

America Reacts to Power

The unwillingness of many Americans to recognize the reality of power in world affairs, in the face of conflicts and tensions among nations, has resulted in several behavior patterns characteristic of the American approach to foreign relations. One of these patterns has been periodic retreat into an illusory isolationism. When it became clear after World War I that power rivalries were as deeply embedded in international relationships as before, America's reaction was to retire from the field and "let Europe stew in its own juice." Similarly after World War II, with apparently little thought concerning the consequences of its actions, the United States brought its troops home from overseas and demobilized its armed forces.

Paradoxically, widespread public misapprehension about the centrality of power in global relationships has also led to popular viewpoints and national policies that are diametrically opposed to isolationism. For example, Americans have shown an affinity for policies whose evident purpose was to make a frontal assault upon the problem of international conflicts in the hope of eliminating them altogether, much as medical science would concentrate its energies and skill to eliminate an epidemic. This pattern of behavior is illustrated by the eagerness many Americans display in embracing slogans and in participating in verbal crusades. Significant numbers of Americans expected that World War I was "the war to end wars" and that victory would "make the world safe for democracy." Two decades later, the conviction prevailed widely that once the Axis was defeated, the goal of "One World" would be achieved, perhaps by establishing the United Nations or by instituting the "Four Freedoms." As cooperation among the wartime Allies withered in the face of rising cold war tensions, basically the same mentality was displayed by the tendency of many Americans to think that reiteration of the determination to "stand firm" in the face of Communist threats and intonation of militant phrases like "massive retaliation" would go far toward preserving national security. Paradoxical as it seems, the "doves" and "hawks" during the Vietnam War had several things in common—the principal one being perhaps an ultimate desire to liquidate America's commitment in Southeast Asia rapidly, to reduce its responsibilities in that area of the world, and to permit the nation to concentrate upon the solution of *internal* problems. The methods advocated by both groups were of course very different; but their underlying goals were remarkably parallel.

People Are Good; Rulers Are Bad

America's failure to appreciate the role of power is also reflected in the contrast it often draws between peoples and their rulers. Throughout its history the United States has had a profound suspicion of political authority.[15] It has embraced Jefferson's dictum that "that government is best which governs least," and it has clung to this credo even while the powers of government on all levels were being expanded.

Americans have periodically sought to explain the presence of conflict in global affairs by distinguishing between the unfriendly acts of governmental leaders and the supposedly peaceful inclinations of ordinary citizens. Admittedly, this distinction can be used advantageously as a diplomatic technique to encourage a rift between an unfriendly government and its people, in the hope that the leaders can thereby be overthrown or induced to modify their policies. President Wilson undoubtedly was motivated by this hope when he repeatedly distinguished between the leaders and citizens of Imperial Germany. The Allies, he said, had no quarrel with the "German people" but only with their misguided rulers. During World War II, President Roosevelt took the same position toward the political hierarchies of Germany and Italy and, to a lesser degree, Japan. The people of these countries, it was widely believed, had been seduced by their rulers into paths of military conquest. After World War II, much the same attitude could be discerned in America's relationships with Soviet Russia and Red China. Political orators proclaimed that the common people throughout the Communist empire were essentially peace-loving and that they yearned for deliverance from their Communist masters.

Distinctions between peoples and their leaders, nevertheless, rest upon questionable assumptions. For one thing, they often naïvely presuppose that rulers can govern without reference to the wishes of their subjects. For another thing, they fail to account for the continuity between a nation's foreign policy goals and its historic goals and needs as a society. Third, citizens of other countries often actively share the goals of their leaders or, at a minimum, are relatively indifferent to foreign policy questions. Finally, even if the rulers of a country often do not receive explicit public approval for their policies, public opinion will oftentimes support them once the issue of patriotism infuses disputes with foreign nations. It is open to serious question, for example, whether many of the issues dividing Russia and the West today would melt away if Russia adopted democratic political institutions. Similarly, it is doubtful whether a liberalization of the Communist regime in China would appreciably alter that country's determination to become and remain the dominant power in the Orient.

MORALISM: THE SHADOW

A second discernible trait in American national character is the emphasis placed upon moralism in relations with other countries. Moralism is not the same as morality, although both derive from a common etymological root. Morality has to do with the substance of behavior. It is conduct in accordance with a predetermined code of behavior, and throughout Christendom this refers to behavior sanctioned by the Christian faith. Moralism, as used here, is concerned with appearances, with the concepts and language employed in foreign relations, with the symbols used, and with the way that ends and means are visualized and expressed publicly. Moralism is not so much moral behavior but public recognition that such behavior is expected and is being carried out by one's own country. Thus it is possible for a nation devoted to moralism to be in fact moral, immoral, or amoral, however the case may be, in its actual conduct. Later in the chapter we shall have more to say about morality in American foreign relations. Now we are interested in the questions, "What forms has moralism taken in American foreign policy? What are its tangible evidences?"

American Conceptions of "Manifest Destiny"

Americans have always drawn a significant contrast between their own territorial expansion and expansion by other countires. They have deprecated expansionism as a goal of foreign policy —even while in the midst of expanding. Denouncing the British empire and applauding its dissolution; condemning Germany's territorial ambitions; castigating Soviet Russia's aggrandizements; and in the Korean and Vietnam conflicts, going to war to vindicate the principle that aggression cannot be condoned—these ideas have formed dominant themes in successive periods of American diplomatic history.

Toward their own experience of expansionism, Americans have taken a somewhat different view. Seemingly irresistible pressure—Americans called it "Manifest Destiny"—propelled American dominion westward to the Pacific and, after that, outward to the Caribbean and Pacific islands. Believing that this process had nothing in common with ordinary expansionism—soon forgetting that many great Indian tribes were almost exterminated in the process and the remainder confined to almost barren reservations—America looked upon westward expansion as a God-given

right. As Ray A. Billington, a historian of westward expansion, observed concerning the Mexican War:

Every patriot who clamored for Mexico's provinces would indignantly deny any desire to exploit a neighbor's territory. The righteous but ill-informed people of that day sincerely believed their democratic institutions were of such magnificent perfection that no boundaries could contain them. Surely a benevolent Creator did not intend such blessing for the few—expansion was a divinely ordered means of extending enlightenment to despot-ridden masses in near-by countries. This was not imperialism, but enforced salvation. So the average American reasoned in the 1840s when the spirit of manifest destiny was in the air.[16]

Or, as a congressman from Massachusetts sardonically observed in the 1840s, Manifest Destiny was opening "a new chapter in the law of nations or rather, in the special laws of our own country, for I suppose the right of a manifest destiny to spread will not be admitted to exist in any other nation except the universal Yankee nation."[17]

The "Arrogance of American Power"

A closely related behavior pattern which many commentators believe has increasingly characterized American postwar foreign policy, is exemplification of what Senator J. William Fulbright described as the "arrogance of American power."[18] As we have already observed, American society has never really grasped the concept of national power or explicitly accepted its central role in international relations. Americans do not find the idea of power psychologically congenial; it is perhaps too suggestive of the Machiavellianism of the Old World or of the behavior identified with Hitler's Germany or Stalin's Russia. Yet by the postwar period, the United States was acknowledged to be one of the Super-Powers of the contemporary world; the disparity between American and Soviet (not to mention American and French, or American and Chinese) power was vast and, by most standards, widening to America's favor. It had become a truism to say that the power of the United States had preserved the security of the non-Communist world since the Second World War. But commonplace as the idea was, there was no denying its basic correctness. The fact that the United Nations had survived various constitutional, financial, and other crises since 1946 could be attributed in no small measure to American power. Europe was also heavily indebted to American power for its postwar recovery and its phenomenal economic progress in the years which followed. Insofar as the developing nations had been able to take at least the initial steps toward modernization, most of them had benefited from American power. (As we shall see in Chapter 14, one of the interesting points which critics of American diplomatic behavior in the contemporary period tend to overlook is that nearly all of these nations have repeatedly called for *an expansion* of American power within their societies, in the form of greatly increased economic and technical assistance. Their complaint tends to be that *too little American power* is directed toward the solution of their problems! Needless to say, Latin American, African, Arab, and Asian societies concurrently desire to avoid any corresponding growth in American influence or domination over them.)

Recent critics who have complained about the "arrogance of American power" are surely correct in one respect: Since 1900, but especially since World War II, Americans have been insensitive to the impact of the power of the United States upon other societies. Finding the very concept of national power unpalatable, postwar Americans have been unable to comprehend several facts related to their own role as a great power. One of these is that, intentional or not, massive American involvement in the affairs of other countries can be *a highly disruptive force*, shattering traditional ways of life and modes of thought. The mere presence of several hundred American diplomatic and propaganda officials, aid technicians, and other representatives of the United States—together with the infusion of American funds and military equipment into the society involved—can set in motion forces, many of whose consequences are neither anticipated nor desired by the United States or the host country. The prolonged "exposure" of a foreign society to the American way of life (and in this respect, Hollywood's products play a crucial role) can have a profound and lasting impact. Simply because of the range and nature of America's worldwide commitments in the recent period, the power of the United States has unquestionably been a devastating force in many foreign societies. As an agent producing change, American power has quite possibly brought about more rapid and more radical innovations than Soviet or Chinese Communism, or any other force with which it might be compared. Whether deriving from "arrogance" or not, American power has been—and probably remains—the most potent instrument for change witnessed in the contemporary world.

For the most part, the American people have been oblivious to this reality. Their attitudes toward the outside world reflect little recognition that the United States has extended its power into every quarter of the globe, sometimes with what can only be called revolutionary results. However much they may denounce Western colonialism (or "neo-colonialism"), societies outside the West have been profoundly influenced by the United States. And although they may admit the "need"

for radical change in the abstract, such societies are seldom grateful to outsiders for introducing it or for setting in motion forces which bring economic dislocations, political upheavals, and social tensions in their wake.

"No Compromise with Principle"

Historically, no nation has placed so much emphasis upon "principle" in dealing with other countries as the United States. "No compromise with principle!" is a perennial slogan of the American people. Before virtually every international conference in recent history, America's leaders have devoted an inordinate amount of time and energy to giving public assurances that principle would not be abandoned. In their attitudes toward such negotiations, certain groups within the United States have come dangerously close to equating the very process of negotiation and diplomacy with "appeasement" and abandonment of principle in international affairs. The tendency of vocal groups and individuals within the United States to make such an identification has placed formidable obstacles in the path of a flexible and imaginative American foreign policy and often compelled officials to spend as much time reassuring critics as endeavoring to achieve the nation's goals in the outside world.*

This emphasis, one might even say fixation, upon principle has its roots deep in the nation's past. The diplomatic historian Dexter Perkins has shown that it underlay America's failure to reach an accord with Great Britain after the Revolution

---

*Sir Anthony Eden, a British statesman who openly opposed Chamberlain's appeasement policies in the late 1930s, has stated that it was the fault of those policies that they cherished "the illusion that to buy a little time, even at the expense of the security of any ally . . . was to contribute to peace, whereas it was in truth a surrender to the threat of force, laying the paving stones to war." The test of whether a proposal in international affairs constitutes appeasement, he has emphasized, is whether it will "serve only to relax tension for a while, or whether it is in the true interests of lasting peace." A government must, therefore, "consider whether its decision gives peace, not just for an hour or a day or two, but in its children's time. That is the difference between appeasement and peace" *The New York Times* (September 29, 1963). Admittedly, the difference between legitimate peace proposals and appeasement remains cloudy and involves judgments that will not always command universal agreement. Synonyms for appeasement listed by Webster—to pacify, quiet, calm, sooth, allay—suggest that the idea is basic to human relationships and is central to efforts aimed at resolving differences among nations by peaceful means. As we shall see in our analysis of "revisionist" interpretations of the cold war (Chapter 8), the "appeasement analogy" has been a prominent feature of the orthodox viewpoint toward American relations with the Soviet Union and other Marxist nations. Repulsed by the appeasement diplomacy at the Munich Conference, many Americans have tended to regard any attempt to reduce tensions with the Soviet Union or Red China as morally reprehensible and politically disastrous.

and, against its own true diplomatic interests, America's affinity for the French cause during the Napoleonic period.[19] The Monroe Doctrine in 1823 literally resounded with principles. In this period and in later ones, America identified itself with revolutionary causes abroad. In the mid-nineteenth century, for example, American enthusiasm for European revolutionary causes threatened to precipitate several diplomatic incidents between the United States and European governments.

At no time did the American insistence upon principle emerge so clearly as during World War I, when it lay at the root of our quarrel with Germany and, by contrast, our long-suffering endurance of repeated British provocations. The Allies were fighting for freedom and democracy; for freedom of the seas (even while they denied it to us); for self-determination and independence from monarchial and totalitarian rule; for the rights of small nations; and for international integrity. What did the Central Powers, especially Germany, stand for? They represented militarism and authoritarian rule within, expansionism and calloused opportunism without. They were breakers of treaties, violators of innocent nations, and, perhaps most heinous of all, contemptuous of the ordinary standards of decency and morality expected of nations in the Western community. American principles and German behavior (at least America's image of it) were at antipodes. It was this fact which more than any other finally drew the United States into World War I.

Principle again pervaded the American attitude toward dictators in the interwar period. In the eyes of many Americans, the most serious indictment of, and great cause for concern about, Japanese or German or Italian diplomatic conduct was that these countries were flagrantly violating international agreements like the Kellogg–Briand Pact and the Covenant of the League of Nations, or that their conduct was at variance with the conventions, understandings, and rules of comity that normally governed relations among civilized societies. Americans often tended to condemn the Axis dictators much more because they regarded treaties as "scraps of paper" or because their pledged word was contradicted with impunity than because the Axis powers posed a growing military and economic threat to the security of the North Atlantic community.[20]

Turning to the postwar period, we find evidences of moralism toward a number of important international issues. Soviet Russia's exploitation of the Eastern European satellites, for instance, was viewed as a calculated and willful violation of the agreements reached at Yalta and Potsdam concerning the treatment to be accorded conquered and liberated nations. So great was America's aversion to Soviet machinations in this area that the United States sometimes took a keener interest in events there—in a zone where it had in fact very few vital interests—than in many other areas, such as Southeast Asia or the Middle East, where its own diplomatic interests were more direct and fundamental. Similarly, moral principle has been invoked repeatedly in defense of America's attitude toward Red China. The vast majority of Americans have felt that Red China cannot be permitted to "shoot its way into the United Nations" and that it must prove "by deeds and not words" that it is ready to become a peace-loving member of the family of nations before American recognition of the Communist regime can even be contemplated. More generally, the language customarily used by Americans to describe contemporary international relations —in which the United States is the leader of the "free world" or the cold war is a contest between "freedom and tyranny"—also reflects the kind of moralism to which we have alluded.

Some Consequences of Moralism

America's affinity for moralism has had both positive and negative aspects. On the positive side, it may be said that no other course accords with American experience and ideology. If Americans invoke principle more than most countries, it may be because the American people are conscious of how often principle is lacking in international affairs. If they insist upon a "decent respect for the opinions of mankind," it is because of a deep conviction that mankind is tired of Machiavellianism, that it yearns for an international order in which justice, enforced by law, prevails. In common with all reformers, Americans tend to concentrate upon the ultimate goal without gazing down at the pitfalls in the path of its attainment. If they are forever exhorting other nations and calling them to repentance, it is because they are so impressed with the need for charting new paths.

To foreigners, Americans must resemble nothing so much as the Puritan: motivated by high ideals, austere, unshakable in his conviction that goodness will triumph in the end—but at the same time impatient with wrong-doing, sanctimonious, and at times insufferably self-righteous.

This tendency toward moralism in relations with other countries also of course poses a number of problems for the United States. Many of these were exemplified by Secretary of State John Foster Dulles during the Eisenhower administration. Dulles was a deeply religious man who possessed a strong sense of moral and ethical conviction; with a keen intellect, a lawyer's training, and a passionate devotion to the country's welfare, Dulles had impressive qualifications for his office. His achievements while Secretary of State were perhaps more noteworthy than many of his detractors (particularly in the Democratic Party) have been willing to concede.* Yet Dulles also exhibited many of the qualities which we have identified with moralism. He was supremely confident of the correctness of his own point of view, often impatient with those who disagreed with him, inclined to intimidate subordinates or officials from other countires with whom he dealt, lacking in empathy and understanding of the viewpoints and problems of other societies, and prone to conceive of the cold war as a contest pitting the forces of evil (Soviet Russia and the forces of "international Communism") against those of righteousness (America and the "free world"). His widely quoted denunciation of neutralism as "immoral" alienated governments and citizens throughout the Afro–Asian world, and some of his actions (such as revoking American aid to Egypt for building the Aswan Dam in 1956) won little admiration for the United States. Much as they respected Dulles' intellectual powers and his devotion to the service of the United States, few foreigners felt genuine affection for him. More than any other high-ranking American official since World War II, Dulles epitomized the moralistic shortcomings of the nation's approach to foreign relations.

A moralistic frame of mind toward the outside world has led Americans in recent years to postulate total extremes and mutually exclusive alternatives in their approach to vexatious and complex global issues. In the cold war, other nations "are either with us or against us"; all countries must "choose" whether they support freedom or tyranny. General MacArthur's dictum during the Korean conflict—"In war there is no substitute for victory"—struck a responsive chord with millions of Americans. That this principle afforded little useful guidance for conducting the affairs of the nation in the new era of *limited war* or nuclear stalemate was not an idea which the American society found congenial.[21] Firmly convinced of the goodness of their cause, Americans find it difficult to understand why it does not triumph speedily and decisively. "The illusion of American omnipotence," the perceptive Scotsman D. W. Brogan wrote, lies in the belief that "any situation which distresses or endangers the United States can only exist because some Americans have been fools or knaves." Large numbers of Americans, Brogan observed, "have yet to learn that the world cannot be altered overnight by a speech or a platform."[22]

Although pragmatism and trial-and-error methods have characterized their approach to problems with American society, Americans have found it difficult to accept *partial solutions* to age-old problems disturbing the peace and security of the international community. Their usual expectation is that such problems will be "solved" within a relatively short time and that the tensions between nations will be "eliminated" by some dramatic development like an East–West summit conference or a new nonaggression treaty. For reasons that are not altogether apparent, Americans have been slow to apply a lesson that emerges from their own experience with countless internal problems, like divorce, delinquency, alcoholism, traffic accidents, crime, poverty, and many other issues. This is that few problems in human affairs are ever "solved" in a final sense. They are ameliorated, softened, mitigated, made endurable, adjusted to, outlived—but seldom eliminated. Another lesson which experience with concerns of this kind teaches is that they seldom yield before a dogged insistence upon principle, accompanied by short-lived and passionate crusades. Instead, progress in dealing with them is made as a result of patient understanding and an awareness that, if principle is present at all, it is likely to be present in some degree on both sides.

MORALITY: THE SUBSTANCE

The American people have been outstandingly moralistic in their foreign affairs. Have they at the same time been more than ordinarily moral? What is their record in practicing the ideals they have professed and have tried to impose on others? In broad outline, the answer is that throughout most of their diplomatic history American citizens have placed a high value on moral behavior for themselves and for other countries as well.

The American Attitude Toward War

If we are to judge by the number of wars, both major and minor, in which the United Stated has engaged, the record does not indicate that the nation has been conspicuously peace-loving. From the Revolution to the Vietnam conflict, there have been nine major wars and in between a host of small-scale ones. Reviewing this record, Dexter Perkins comments that "it does not seem to be a strikingly pacific one, at least not utterly out of line with the history of other nations." He adds also that we must keep in mind that territorial acquisitions—for which many other countries are forced to wage war—came to Americans primarily through purchase and negotiation.[23]

But the number of wars in which the United States has been engaged proves little or nothing

*For a highly laudatory account of Secretary Dulles' role in American foreign policy, see Eleanor Lansing Dulles, *American Foreign Policy in the Making* (New York: Harper & Row, 1968). For a more balanced treatment, highlighting both Dulles' accomplishments and weaknesses as Secretary of State, see Richard Goold-Adams, *John Foster Dulles: A Reappraisal* (New York: Appleton-Century-Crofts, 1962).

about the extent of morality in its foreign policy. America has fought only one, the Mexican War, which could even remotely be construed as a war for territorial aggrandizement, and even then it compensated Mexico for the territory taken. America has traditionally been slow to anger. It has never gone to war over a "diplomatic incident." In its two greatest wars it has endured repeated provocations and has devoted months to seeking peaceful solutions before finally and reluctantly drawing the sword. This fact alone, of course, does not prove superior morality on the part of the American society; in part, the explanation derives from an overwhelming preoccupation with domestic pursuits and from a widespread inability to perceive the connection between events in Europe and national security. Nevertheless, the United States has probably been as unwarlike as any great power in history. In the vast majority of instances, only repeated provocations have forced the nation to enter military conflicts.

Moreover, the terms imposed upon vanquished nations have not, in the main, been severe. To the contrary, the United States has been on balance a magnanimous victor. In both world wars, American influence was cast against the idea of a "harsh peace" for defeated enemies. With rare exceptions, vindictiveness has not been a characteristic of the American mind. It may occasionally have been a passing phase, but it soon gave way to a sincere desire to help rehabilitate conquered nations, to aid them in re-entering the family of nations. Postwar American aid to Germany and Japan furnish outstanding examples of this trait. In the more recent Vietnam conflict, American officials have several times indicated their readiness to cooperate with North Vietnam to develop the resources of the Mekong River Valley for regional use.

We have already alluded to America's reluctance to annex foreign territories as a result of war. The United States has of course done so, but usually because, as in the Spanish–American War, there appeared no other alternative. Moreover, it has repeatedly refused to take reparations and indemnities. A classic case was the Boxer Rebellion (1900), when indemnities paid to the United States were set aside for the future education of Chinese students in America.

Is America "Imperialistic"?

America's territorial expansion raises the question, "Can the United States fairly be accused of being imperialistic?" The answer depends in large part upon how imperialism is defined. If it signifies the acquisition of foreign territory primarily for the exploitation and advantage of the mother country, only one judgment on American foreign policy is possible. It has been remarkably nonim-

perialistic. However, if imperialism is defined as meaning chiefly the exercise of American power —primarily economic and military power—over other countries (or what is sometimes called today *neo-imperialism*), then the verdict is more debatable.

As Dexter Perkins insists, a fundamental distinction must be maintained between expansionism and imperialism.[24] The United States— beginning as a weak country along the fringes of the Atlantic Ocean and becoming within 150 years one of two super-powers—has expanded more than any country in recent history, with the possible exception of Russia under tsarist and Communist rule. Most of America's territory was acquired by purchase or negotiation. That taken by conquest—by some interpretations, Florida, the territory acquired after the Mexican War, the Philippines, and the Panama Canal region—was later compensated for by the United States. Admittedly, this account ignores the fact that most of the continental United States was in fact taken by conquest from its original inhabitants, the Indian tribes. And, parenthetically, it also ignores the fact that in dealing with the Indians the United States was guilty of violating practically every moral precept it has tried to follow toward other countries.

American domination over foreign territories, Perkins holds, has "always been rule with an uneasy conscience."[25] Toward the vast continental land mass at home, one principle was consistently followed throughout America history: Whenever the frontier lands were ready for statehood, they were admitted to the Union on an equal plane with the older states. (The most recent cases were Alaska and Hawaii, which entered the Union in 1959.) Toward colonial societies a somewhat different but closely related principle has prevailed: They were to be tutored in the art of self-government and prepared for ultimate independence.

American administration of possessions and dependencies overseas has almost invariably led to marked improvement in their national life. Living standards have been elevated; modern sanitary practices introduced; education fostered and made available to ever-growing numbers; with greater or lesser success, democratic political ideas and practices have been instilled in the society concerned.* After reviewing America's re-

---

*By the late 1960s, many of these considerations had come sharply to the fore in American–Filipino relations. The United States granted independence to the Philippines on July 4, 1946; after that time, military, economic, and cultural relations between the two nations remained close. Officials in both countries acknowledged that many of these ties were necessary and mutually beneficial; yet they also were aware that the massive American "presence" in the Philippines sometimes caused frictions and animosities. An earlier political insurgency (led by the "Huks") had been overcome by the Philippine government in the 1950s; but by the 1970s new signs of political turbulence had appeared. Among

cord as a colonial power, Dexter Perkins concluded that "in the moderation which ought to go with strength, the United States has played and is playing a creditable role."[26]

What America has done with its dependent territories, however, may not be as significant as what it has not done. For, as Herbert Feis has emphasized, few countries in history have voluntarily foregone so many opportunities to engage in territorial aggrandizement and to subordinate weaker societies as the United States.[27] Historically, the United States has refused to join with other strong countries in parceling out colonies and delineating spheres of influence. Much of the tension which developed between the United States and Japan during the 1930s could be traced to the former's unwillingness to divide the Orient into American and Japanese spheres of influence. Similarly, the Roosevelt administration repeatedly rejected the idea that the United States and the Soviet Union ought to "divide the world" (or even regions like Europe) between them. Wisely or unwisely (and many students of the cold war believe the latter), Washington refused to engage in the kind of sphere-of-influence diplomacy which had long been characteristic of the Old World, and which had, in the view of many Americans, contributed to two global wars in the twentieth century.

Could it be said that this traditional behavior pattern governed American foreign policy in the postwar period? Critics who denounced the "arrogance of American power" and other commentators were doubtful. Citing America's worldwide military commitments and foreign bases, and its various interventions since World War II (in Greece, in Korea, in Lebanon, in the Dominican Republic, in Southeast Asia, and less graphically perhaps in other areas) some students of American foreign policy maintained that the United States only opposed spheres of influence controlled by *other countries* (particularly Communist countries). Although it rejected the idea of spheres of influence in principle, the reality was that—in regions like the Caribbean and South America, Oceania and Southeast Asia, and per-

haps Western Europe and the Mediterranean—the United States had expanded its own power perceptibly, so much in some instances as to exercise an almost *exclusive* military or economic influence. There was undeniably some validity to this accusation. Americans did not like the basic concept of spheres of influence or related ideas (like "satellites" or "client states"); such language was almost never employed by leaders or citizens of the United States, except to describe the relationship of Nazi Germany or Communist Russia with weaker countries. But this fact of course did not signify that America lacked its own spheres of influence. The classic example has perhaps been the relationship between the United States and Latin America, a subject analyzed more fully in Chapter 12.

Meanwhile, several points need to be made before we leave the question of America's so-called "imperialistic" tendencies since World War II. The United States, as we have previously underscored, *is* a Great Power; as such, it has worldwide responsibilities and commitments, which require it to use its vast power under widely differing circumstances around the globe. And as we have already emphasized, the use of this power under some conditions can be, and not infrequently is, a traumatic experience both for America and for the other country (or countries) involved. An appropriate analogy might be to the construction of a large dam, the effect of which is to "upset the balance of nature" within the area affected. The dam, let us assume, is a worthwhile and desirable project—one which will ultimately be advantageous to the society concerned. But the effect of building the dam is still destabilizing: It may have various adverse short- and long-run consequences which the society neither desired nor predicted. So it has been with the exercise of American power. In some instances (unlike the case of the dam), it may be true that the basic *purpose* for which American power is applied can be legitimately questioned. Yet even when this is not the case, the very exercise of power by the United States can be unsettling, resembling the process of imperialism.

It should also be observed that the kind of "mirror image" reasoning in which some recent students of American foreign policy have engaged—e.g., Soviet Russia has its satellites in Eastern Europe, while the United States has its clients in Latin America (or Southeast Asia)—is more plausible than convincing. There is a deceptive symmetry to such logic that makes it appealing, especially to Americans who oppose the nation's involvement in Southeast Asia or some other region. However, it has several fundamental defects. It tends to obscure, for example, the *political* dimension of America's relations with Latin America vis-à-vis Russia's relations with Eastern Europe. In whatever degree it may

some political groups, anti-Americanism was a popular slogan. With an average annual income of only $200 per person, the Philippines suffered acutely from problems like widespread poverty, the unequal distribution of wealth, inadequate health and educational services, the lack of meaningful land reform, and over-all economic backwardness. America's extensive military involvement in the country was both financially rewarding and socially and politically disruptive, furnishing political agitators with a visible symbol of discontent. More than ever, officials in Manila became concerned with the country's "identity" and its "independence" from its powerful mentor. For general background, see David T. Sternberg, "The Philippines: Contour and Perspective," *Foreign Affairs* 44 (April, 1966), 501–511. For discussions of more recent events, see *The New York Times* (January 3, 6, and 28, 1969; March 12, 1970).

be appropriate to speak of Latin America as a "sphere of influence" of the United States (and ever since the Monroe Doctrine was enunciated in 1823, that interpretation could perhaps be drawn), several facts about inter-American relations since World War II are noteworthy. Communism has remained the system of government prevailing in Cuba; the United States has made no significant effort to change that fact since the early 1960s. Almost every month, some change of political regime occurs in Latin America; not infrequently, the diplomatic and economic interests of the United States in the region are adversely affected. The Organization of American States is far from being a pliable instrument of United States foreign policy; there is simply no comparison between the role of the United States in it and Soviet Russia's domination of the Warsaw Pact. Overt interventions by the United States in the political affairs of Latin America since World War II (in contrast to the preceding half-century) have been *exceptional and episodic.* Neither Guatemala, the Dominican Republic, nor any other Latin American republic has been placed under permanent American military occupation or political domination. When the Rockefeller Study Group visited Latin America in the late 1960s, it discovered that the universal lament throughout the region was *neglect by the United States* of its needs. Most Latin American societies have repeatedly asked for *expanded* economic assistance, loans, and private investment from the United States; they have also sought larger military aid programs—a request which American policy-makers in recent years have in most cases denied.[28] Although these distinctions might conceivably be regarded as differences in degree from Soviet Russia's role in Eastern Europe, they are nonetheless fundamental. Without being oblivious to the many grievances which Latin Americans bear toward the "North American colossus," it is still possible to say that the relationship between the United States and its hemispheric neighbors lacks most of the characteristics of both classical "imperialism" and its more recent versions as symbolized by Russia's dominance of Eastern Europe or Chinese hegemony over Tibet.

America and Militarism

A conspicuous theme among critics of America's involvement in the Vietnam War was that the United States had fallen increasingly under the influence of the military–industrial complex and that its policies in Southeast Asia and elsewhere were largely dictated by the vested interests of that group.[29] We shall reserve fuller discussion of that question for Chapter 4. Meanwhile, we may note that this sentiment reflected a deep-seated skepticism in the American ethos concerning the role of the military establishment in national life. Whatever the precise influence of the military–industrial complex in the contemporary period, the American historical tradition runs counter to the idea that military elements ought to play anything approaching an autonomous role in policy-making. Until very recent times, Americans have opposed the idea of a large standing army (and perhaps still oppose it, even if they concede its necessity). They have preferred voluntary recruitment over conscription as a method of raising military manpower requirements. In several articles, the American Constitution affirms the principle of military subordination to civilian authority—a concept which was underscored by President Truman's unceremonious dismissal of General Douglas MacArthur in 1951. To date, the dangers depicted in popular novels like *Seven Days in May*—where in America, as in many other nations in the contemporary world, a military junta planned to depose the civilian government—have been altogether remote. (In the contemporary period, the greater danger may well be the opposite: that disaffected civilian groups will blame military leaders for mistakes made by the President and his civilian advisers)

The American aversion to military service was graphically illustrated by the rapidity with which the United States demobilized its armed forces at the end of both major wars. Once the Allies had defeated the Axis powers, it would be charitable to say that the United States "demobilized"; it would be more accurate to say that its armed strength disintegrated—to the point of imperiling the security of Western Europe and other regions vital to American security. Only as the United States became painfully aware of the implications of Communist expansionism—conveyed most forcefully perhaps by the Communist attack against South Korea in 1950—did Americans prepare to rebuild their military strength to the level required of a great power.

Although the American tradition has been antimilitaristic, it has not been *antimilitary.* The distinction is fundamental. Throughout their history, Americans have feared and distrusted the substance of military power, but they have applauded and glorified many of its trappings. Every parade includes one or more military units, together with a number of civilian organizations whose uniforms, music, march steps, and the like are drawn from military sources. No other country has so many military academies for the training of its youth—schools, it must be emphasized, which place the building of disciplined minds and bodies, and the encouragement of approved behavior, above the creation of a military elite dedicated to bringing the nation glory through conquest. America has gone a long way toward finding a substitute for militarism: It lies, in large part, in glorifying many of the superficial aspects of military life, while at the same time rejecting its substance.[30]

In the second half of the twentieth century, however, a number of commentators were apprehensive that the American society had abandoned its long-standing skepticism toward the military establishment. Sociologists like C. Wright Mills were convinced that, without even being conscious of the process, Americans had permitted the Pentagon, in concert with industrial and labor groups dependent upon defense contracts for their economic survival, to dominate governmental decision-making. America's involvement in the Vietnam War, along with the apparent unwillingness of national policy-makers for several years to liquidate that commitment, was cited as proof of growing military influence upon American life. Without anticipating our discussion in Chapter 4, we may make a few brief observations at this point. The first is that such assertions rest upon what has to be viewed, according to the most charitable interpretation, as indirect and circumstantial evidence. That there has been an enormous growth in the military budget of the United States and in defense spending since the Korean War is incontestable. Whether the conclusion follows that this is tantamount to an increase in the *political influence* of the military–industrial complex—to the point of subverting the principle of civilian supremacy in the American government—is a moot question. It is conceivable (and critics of the military–industrial complex have offered no very convincing evidence to disprove the contention) that the growth in the size and financial resources available to the armed forces came about as a result of a series of decisions deliberately made by *civilian authorities,* in the belief that American diplomatic and security interests demanded this step. While America's military elite perhaps did not oppose this tendency, and indeed doubtless favored it, there are few grounds for believing that they in any sense "dictated" it or otherwise exceeded constitutional bounds in expressing their opinions. Second, it was one of America's most distinguished wartime military leaders, and later President, Dwight D. Eisenhower, who cautioned the nation against the influence exercised by the military–industrial complex. This seems a highly significant fact: Among other things, it indicates that high-ranking members of the military elite themselves subscribe to the principle of civilian supremacy; that they are convinced of its central importance for the future of American democracy; that they are alert to tendencies which might undermine it; and that they are as determined as other Americans to maintain the concept in the face of threats to its viability. It is a remarkable fact that one of the most influential members of the military–industrial complex since World War II should (long before sociologists and critics of the Vietnam

War discovered the danger) alert the nation to the need for vigilance against militaristic tendencies in American life. Third, it is not surprising perhaps that the size and budget of the military establishment has grown in recent years; given America's worldwide military and diplomatic commitments, that was perhaps inevitable. What was outstanding, in terms of the the American traditions we are discussing here, was the willingness of the American people and their leaders to be actively concerned about the matter, to reassert their characteristic insistence upon greater civilian authority in decision-making, and to seek new methods for curbing military influence throughout the society. Coupled with these tendencies was another, which could only be called extraordinary for a society in which military elements and their allies in business and labor supposedly dominated policy-making: This was the willingness of military leaders to cooperate with, and to accept, new civilian-imposed limitations upon their role.

"A Moral Equivalent for War"

The great American philosopher William James urged the nation to find a moral equivalent for war—some concept or activity that would elicit the same sense of dedication to a higher cause, the same spirit of sacrifice, the same passionate ardor that Americans had demonstrated during time of war. From the time of the Jay Treaty with England in 1794, the United States has been in the forefront of nations seeking alternatives to force for settling international disputes. For example, it has time and again favored the arbitration of boundary and territorial disputes.[31] It has followed the same course toward controversies over neutral rights, such as occurred with Britain over the "Alabama claims" during 1866–1872, and over violations of American neutral rights during World Wars I and II.[32] It has sponsored and joined efforts to institutionalize arbitration, as when it accepted the Hague conventions of 1899 and 1907, and when it sponsored the Bryan arbitration treaties in the early 1900s.[33]

In seeking a moral equivalent to war, it has taken the lead in establishing international organizations for dealing with threats to the peace. True, it refused to join the League of Nations. Nevertheless, it supported the League in a number of ways during the years that followed; and during the 1930s it cast its moral, though never its military, influence behind the League's efforts to deal with repeated aggressions by the Axis states. During World War II it very early took the initiative in planning for a new international security organization to preserve world peace. Since the war, few countries have been more conscious of the necessity for strengthening the United Nations than the United States. As much as any other country, and more than most, America has worked to establish the UN upon a firm foundation and to endow it with enough power to deal effectively with international threats. In the case of major international and regional crises in the recent period—the Korean War, the Middle Eastern conflicts of 1956 and 1967, the Congo crisis in 1960, and the Cuban crisis in 1962—the United States was in the forefront of states calling for collective action to prevent or curb military hostilities. In the two most recent crises threatening international peace—the Vietnam conflict and the continuing dispute between Israel and the Arab states—the United States has repeatedly expressed its willingness to participate in, or to encourage, negotiations among the parties concerned. Similarly, although the record of the last half-century offered little hope of success, the United States continued to believe that it was possible to arrive at an international agreement limiting national armaments.

This record is not intended to suggest that the United States is totally averse to unilateral decision-making in its foreign relations, that it is prepared to "turn over" external policy-making to the United Nations, the Organization of American States, and other multilateral agencies, or that (vague as it is) the concept of "national interest" is lacking from American foreign policy. Still, the American record in trying to discover "a moral equivalent to war" is creditable. Insofar as the international community continues to seek nonviolent methods for resolving differences among nations, the reason must be attributed in large part to American diplomatic initiatives.

ISOLATIONISM IN WORD AND DEED

Isolationism has pervaded the American approach to foreign relations since the earliest days of the republic. America's pattern of isolationist thought is well illustrated by its foreign policies during the 1920s and 1930s. What is not so widely recognized is that isolationism goes much deeper than merely the desire to avoid foreign entanglements. It is above all a habit of mind, a cluster of national attitudes, a feeling of spiritual separation from other countries, especially Europe, with roots penetrating deeply into the nation's heritage and experience.

Isolationism, as Albert K. Weinberg has aptly put it, is "not a theory of American foreign policy. Isolationism is a theory about a theory of American foreign policy."[34] It is more than a doctrine advanced to explain the objective facts of America's geographical relationship with the rest of the world. Instead, it is supposed to explain *what the American people believe to be the proper relationship between themselves and other countries.* Isolationist thinking permeates the American cultural experience, its philosophy, and what may be called more generally "the American way of life." It is basically a conviction that Americans are different from other people; that they do not look to foreigners for guidance but that foreigners should look to them; that their national destiny is to serve as a beacon to pilot all mankind into new paths of greatness—but that all this should be done primarily by precept and example.

The Roots of American Isolationism

The influences that have contributed to isolationist thinking are many and complex. Here we can do no more than allude to some of the more important ones.[35] The desire for separation from the vicissitudes of Europe brought settlers to the New World. The wish to begin life anew, to leave behind the turmoil, the hopelessness, the bigotry of the Old World—these ambitions brought the religious dissenter, the peasant, the adventuresome aristocrat, the skilled artisan, the speculator, and the felon to American shores. From all walks of life they came, and with one objective: to find a new birth, as it were, in a far-off continent.

The Revolution cut the political ties with England, and as the years passed, Americans came to believe more firmly than ever in their uniqueness. Presidents Washington and Jefferson both cautioned their countrymen that America and Europe had different interests and advised that America's best course was to concentrate on keeping these interests distinct. Very early in the nation's history, isolationism became the underlying principle of foreign policy. One pretext after another, for example, was found to justify America's refusal to honor the French alliance during the Napoleonic wars. Against the wishes of many citizens, especially those in New England, the nation was finally drawn into a war against England in 1812. But within a little over a decade, President Monroe in 1823 asserted that the United States had but one objective in its relations with the Old World. A free translation of Monroe's admonitions would be that America wanted the European countries to mind their own business and, if they must persist in power struggles, to keep them out of the Western Hemisphere. Owing to an underlying identity of interests between the United States and Great Britain—an identity that did not become widely recognized until the post-World War II period—the United States, shielded by the British navy, experienced remarkably few challenges to the Monroe Doctrine during the course of almost a century.

America Looks Inward

From the Monroe Doctrine until World War II the American people were profoundly isolationist; isolationism may in fact still be the preferred foreign policy position of the American people. We must regard participation in World War I as an interlude. Its politico–strategic significance generally passed unnoticed within the United States. Historically, the energies, thoughts, and ambitions of the American people have been directed inward. Americans possessed a continent to populate and to incorporate within the boundaries of their country. They were feverishly creating out of their seemingly unlimited resources vast wealth and expanding opportunities for all. The political intrigues and conflicts witnessed on the continent of Europe held no appeal compared with the challenge of creating the "American way of life." Passionately dedicated to the belief that human progress was limitless, the American people were tackling many of the formidable problems older civilizations had been unable to solve and, in most instances at least, they were solving them reasonably well: problems of unemployment, of unequal distribution of land, of racial and national minorities, of religious liberty, of illiteracy, of political oppression, of the pressure of population upon food supply, of the equitable distribution of wealth, and of hereditary rights. And if it became apparent in the second half of the twentieth century that America's solutions to these and other problems left some groups unsatisfied, the United States still had a better record of success in coping with such issues than almost any other society on the globe.

Isolationism thus derived as much from the dominant concern of the American society with domestic affairs as it did from a deliberate rejection of foreign entanglements. The achievement of virtually every goal associated with the "American dream" demanded that internal interests receive primary attention. This fact prompted one of the nation's leading historians, Charles A. Beard, to prefer the term "continentalism," instead of isolationism, to characterize the nation's historic orientation in foreign policy. Elaborating Beard's idea, a contemporary American observer, Max Lerner,* has written: "It was not so much a question of cutting America off from the world as it was of rounding out and fully exploiting the part of the world that was America."[36]

*Lerner's comprehensive study, *America as a Civilization*, affords many insights into the American mentality toward foreign affairs. His discussion of isolationism is particularly illuminating. Lerner calls attention to the kinship existing between two seemingly antithetical schools of thought in foreign affairs, isolationism and interventionism. The isolationist wants to reduce the nation's foreign commitments and follow a go-it-alone philosophy in foreign relations. By contrast, the interventionist advocates greater reliance upon military power in dealing with threats to security, and urges the nation to undertake diplomatic offensives to achieve goals like the liberation of the Communist satellite countries or the defeat of Communism in Korea and Southeast Asia. Despite the marked dissimilarities in their methods, Lerner contends, their underlying goal is basi-

America Is the "New Society"

What then were the elements in this new society, this "American way of life"? We shall leave its dominant theme—belief in the perfectibility of man and his institutions—for consideration later in the chapter. There was intense pride in the accomplishments of the American people. A penetrating foreign observer, D. W. Brogan, has written admiringly: "To have created a free government, over a continental area, without making a sacrifice of adequate efficiency or of liberty is the American achievement. It is a unique achievement in world history."[37]

Then too there was the theme of cultural separation that pervaded American literature during the nineteenth century. Listen to James Russell Lowell in "A Fable for Critics":

> Forget Europe wholly,
> your veins throb with blood,
> To which the dull current
> in hers is but mud; . . .
> O my friends, thank your god
> if you have one, that he
> Twixt the Old World and you
> sets a gulf of a sea; . . .
> To your own New-World instincts
> contrive to be true, . . .[38]

This was a dominant strain of New World literature throughout the greater part of the nineteenth and twentieth centuries. American writers were fully mindful of their great dependence upon a common English and European literary heritage. But now they wanted a literature distinctly American, one that would express the nation's hopes and ideals in a way that European writers never could. This uniquely American flavor made Walt Whitman America's outstanding poet. "I Hear America Singing" may not have been his greatest poem, but it expressed better than most his abiding ambition: to chronicle in song the American way of life, to point to both its achievements and its unsolved problems, and to show the world that America was well on the way toward building a society based upon the principle of the brotherhood of man.

> Thou, too, sail on, O Ship of State!
> Sail on, O Union, strong and great!
> Humanity with all its fears,
> With all the hopes of future years,
> Is hanging breathless on thy fate!

cally the same: to create conditions throughout the world that will permit the United States once again to focus its energies on domestic affairs, with minimum involvement in foreign affairs. Both schools operate upon the assumpton that the nation's destiny continues to be, as in the past, preoccupation with the American way of life, see *ibid.*, pp. 881–907, *passim.* Insistence by critics of the Vietnam War that the United States give first priority to internal problems is thus but a recent variation upon a very old theme.

These familiar lines from Henry Wadsworth Longfellow ("The Building of the Ship," 1849) point to another consequence of the belief that America was the new society. America's example, it was thought, would be sufficient for other nations to take hope and, by tugging at their own bootstraps, as the American people had done, to raise themselves to new levels of human attainment. The United States, as Hans Kohn put it, has been the "universal nation" in two senses. First, American institutions, philosophies, and accomplishments have mirrored the hopes of mankind.* Second, for over a century, America's doors were open to receive the stranger and to provide him every opportunity for making the American dream come true.[39] This part of the American dream had been expressed by Jefferson in 1817, when he wrote that America's mission was

to consecrate a sanctuary for those whom the misrule of Europe may compel to seek happiness in other climes. This refuge once known will produce reaction on the happiness even of those who remain there, by warning their taskmasters that when the evils of Egyptian oppression become heavier than those of the abandonment of country, another Canaan is open where their subjects will be received as brothers. . . .[40]

Emerson was convinced that "Our whole history appears like a last effort of the Divine Providence in behalf of the human race. . . ."[41] And in 1839, John Louis O'Sullivan wrote an article entitled "The Great Nation of Futurity," the theme of which was that

Our national birth was the beginning of a new history, the formation and progress of an untried political system, which separates us from the past and connects us with the future only; so far as regards the entire development of the rights of man, in moral, political and national life, we may confidently assume that our country is destined to be the great nation of futurity.[42]

Experience at home and overseas since World War II has no doubt offered several persuasive reasons for questioning whether America was ordained by Providence to redeem the rest of the world by precept and example. Outside the West, the "American model" of national life appeared

*In the contemporary period, there might well be a tendency to regard such a claim by the United States as hopelessly provincial and egocentric, stemming from an earlier age of American innocence. It is interesting to note, however, that this idea is the theme of a recent book on America's role in world affairs. The author's basic thesis is that, much as they might fear American power or dislike certain particular American actions in foreign affairs, other nations are powerfully affected by American science and technology—perhaps the most crucial force affecting their future. See Zbigniew Brzezinski, *Between Two Ages: America's Role in the Technetronic Era* (New York: Viking, 1970).

inappropriate for most nations, the great majority of which lacked America's vast resources. Yet it remained difficult for many citizens of the United States (and sentiment within Congress consistently reflected this view) to understand why other societies could not emulate American experience, by evolving rapidly from an agrarian, "frontier" society into a modern industrialized state. That few countries had been able to do so— or showed any reasonable prospect of doing so in the near future—was widely interpreted in the United States as a sign that they were variously indolent, without sufficient motivation, lacking in initiative, or willfully ignorant. Such reservations posed a serious obstacle to any contemplated expansion of American foreign aid programs, especially on Capitol Hill.

Some Consequences of Isolationist Thought

The way in which isolationist thought has shaped American foreign relations is a subject too vast to engage our attention here. We shall take note of it in future chapters in our discussion of American relations with Europe, Asia, and other important regions. But we can at least point to several specific corollaries of America's isolationist mentality.

A familiar maxim of American foreign relations down to the post-World War II era was avoidance of "foreign entanglements," in order to preserve freedom of action at home. If America was to regenerate the world by its example, it must remain free to save itself—a theme which has been revived by critics of the nation's involvement in the Vietnam conflict. "Nonintervention" was another watchword: America demanded that the Old World keep out of the New and, in turn, the United States would forego intervention in the affairs of other regions (Latin America of course always excepted). Moreover, until the recent period, the United States usually refused joint action with other countries. The Monroe Doctrine was proclaimed unilaterally even though Britain had initially suggested it. The United States refused to join the League of Nations. Toward the dictators in the 1930s it usually preferred to play a lone hand. Not until the postwar years has the United States been willing to engage in joint action for long periods of time.

The great awakening which came in American national consciousness only after World War II was the realization that the United States was not isolated from the world and never had been. It might pretend that it was; it might delude itself into thinking that by will power alone the nation could avoid entanglement in the destiny of the world. But this mythology, the nation discovered through painful experience, courted national disaster. Other nations did not regard the United States as isolated. Other nations were very much interested in what America would do with its massive power. Other nations would not accept the view that America could remain aloof from political developments around the globe. After World War II the American people had at last come to see, if at times only dimly, that disengagement was possible only for a minor power, a decadent power, or a country that deliberately chose to imperil its own future security. But if there was to be involvement, what kind of involvement was it to be? What ought to be its objectives? What were the proper means to attain them? Even after conflicts like the wars in Korea and Vietnam, such questions remained pertinent and often extremely difficult.

"Neo-Isolationism" After Vietnam

A quarter-century after the end of Word War II—with the United States encountering widespread criticism for trying to serve as "the policeman of the world"—it might seem curiously irrelevant even to raise the question of whether a revival of isolationist sentiment among the American people is a realistic prospect. Indiscriminate "interventionism," rather than indifference toward events abroad, many critics are convinced, has been the principal malaise of American foreign policy in recent years; the "illusion of American omnipotence" is the captivating fantasy to which the American people seem peculiarly susceptible. Admittedly, it difficult to conceive of the possibility (much less the probability) that the United States will ever forsake its position as a great power and withdraw into its earlier isolationist cocoon. If for no other reason, modern science and technology rule out such diplomatic atavism. Even if the American republic were really as isolated from the world as its traditional mentality toward foreign affairs supposed, modern communications and transportation systems have effectively transcended geographic barriers sealing it off from other countries. Enemy missiles, for example, could strike the United States in less than thirty minutes after they were launched (in considerably less time, if they were fired from enemy submarines). In addition, with many of its own raw materials being depleted, the United States is more dependent than ever upon outside sources; maintenance of the American standard of living requires the nation to carry on a high volume of foreign trade. Although some retrenchment in American overseas responsibilities can be expected to follow the Vietnam War, the United States will also retain important treaty obligations in Europe, in the Western Hemisphere, and even in parts of Asia. Given these realities, a reversion to the pre-World War II type of American isolationism seems unimaginable. Whatever their frustrations and aversions to global responsibilites in the contemporary period, and their growing concern about acute domestic problems, the Ameri-

can people cannot by an act of will alter the fact that the United States is a great power; as such, it is required to bear certain obligations which accompany that role.

Yet by the 1970s it was clear that some retrenchment in America's overseas involvement would be a hallmark of foreign policy after the Vietnam War. Recognizing that the term is sometimes derogatory, this new stance might properly be called "neo-isolationism" (the preferred term had come to be a policy of "low profile" or "low visibility" in several parts of the world). By whatever term it is described, this new policy unquestionably bears some similarity to America's traditional isolationist position—both in terms of the forces producing it and in terms of its meaning for America's relations with other countries. After the experience in Vietnam, the United States would abandon (or sharply limit) the kind of indiscriminate interventionist strategy that had characterized American foreign policy during the 1950s and 1960s. Under the "Nixon Doctrine,"* the United States proposed to undertake no new treaty commitments and it sought (in regions like Europe, as well as Asia) to induce friendly governments and allies to assume a greater responsibility for their own defense. Sub-Saharan Africa remained an area of residual interest and involvement for the United States; and by the early 1970s, Washington was endeavoring to re-define its goals and methods for dealing with Latin America, one motivation being to reduce its involvement in problems existing in that region.† At the same time, as the Nixon Doctrine emphasized, America recognized the existence of numerous treaty obligations; it proposed to honor its security commitments to other countries; it was not willing to assume that Communist or other threats to international peace and stability had disappeared; it did not believe a high level of defense spending and preparedness could be safely dispensed with; nor was it prepared to reduce its own armed strength without equivalent Soviet (and perhaps Chinese) concessions. As in the period before World War II, by the 1970s the American society had become deeply preoccupied with *domestic* questions. Most Americans seemed convinced that some reordering of national priorities was required to redress the balance between the allocation of resources to internal and external policy needs. Increasingly, America's influence abroad was determined in some degree by its success in promoting racial justice and equality, in eliminat-

---

*The Nixon Doctrine was President Richard M. Nixon's redefinition of American foreign policy toward Asia (and inferentially, toward other regions) during the closing stages of the Vietnam War. It is discussed more fully in Chapter 13.
†The reformulation of American foreign policy toward Latin America in the late 1960s and early 1970s is treated at greater length in Chapter 12.

ing (or reducing) poverty, and in attacking acute environmental problems. Improving the quality of American life was clearly an overdue step if the United States wanted to maintain its leadership abroad.

Many lessons could perhaps be drawn from the agony of the Vietnam War. Not the least of these was the fact that the conflict provided an object lesson in "the illusion of American omnipotence." Although he perhaps did not always follow his own precept, President John F. Kennedy had cautioned his countrymen that

the United States is neither omnipotent nor omniscient . . . that we cannot impose our will upon the other 94 percent of mankind—that we cannot right every wrong or reverse each adversity—and that therefore there cannot be an American solution to every world problem.[43]

If "interventionists" and "hawks" clearly needed to heed Kennedy's admonition, the same could also be said for many citizens who complained about "the arrogance of American power" and who condemned the nation's involvement in the Vietnam War. The latter group was fully mindful of the limits of American power in Southeast Asia. Yet many critics often appeared oblivious to such limitations in other settings—like the Middle East and sub-Saharan Africa—and to the alternatives available to the United States in responding to military *coups* in Greece, Latin America, and elsewhere. Ironically, some Americans prone to remind policy-makers daily of the "futility" or the "stupidity" of trying to guarantee the security of South Vietnam or Cambodia were equally forthright in urging Washington to "protect" Israel against almost 100 million Arabs, to spearhead a "confrontation" with South Africa, or to do something (and the specific steps advocated were seldom made clear) about the problem of military dictatorship in Greece. And while they called for a concerted attack by the federal government upon domestic problems, entailing the expenditure of many billions of dollars over a period of several decades, they also urged the United States to spearhead a new worldwide campaign to eliminate poverty. After its frustrations in Vietnam, American society seemed totally unprepared to assume such new international responsibilities.

By the 1970s, the United States had already carried out a substantial military withdrawal from Southeat Asia; further staged evacuations were scheduled for the months ahead. Some reduction of American forces NATO also seemed likely in the future, as did a scaling down of Americans forces in South Korea. Toward nearly all regions, American military aid programs had been cut back; the national defense budget was being pared (at least moderately); and the Nixon ad-

ministration had accepted the idea that, if it could feasibly be done, the United States ought to meet its military manpower needs by reliance upon volunteers. This movement away from a strategy of active interventionism abroad rested perhaps on two fundamental realizations shared broadly by the American people and their leaders. The first was recognition of the fact that, in terms of its goals abroad, the United States had become overextended; its "vital interests" had been defined too broadly, without sufficient attention to national capabilities and priorities. Former Under Secretary of State George Ball likens the American frame of mind before and during the Vietnam War to the biblical idea that the Almighty watches the fall of every sparrow:[44] for some twenty years before the 1970s, successive administrations in Washington were prone to regard the fall of any incumbent government, any political upheaval, or any conflict between two or more nations throughout the world as involving its own security and well-being, particularly when the assumption was that such disturbances had their origins in the machinations of "international Communism." Events in Vietnam—as well as along the Arab–Israeli frontier, in independent Africa, and even in Latin America—amply demonstrated that the United States (lacking the Almighty's qualities of omnipotence, omniscience, and omnipresence) should not and could not concern itself directly with every untoward development in the international community. One meaning of the doctirne of "low profile" was that the United States had to re-establish *a new order of priorites* for employing its vast power at home and abroad.

Second, the strategy of "low profile" reflected a twofold awareness that American power is, in the last analysis, *finite* and that its use under many circumstance abroad *exacts an excessive cost from the American society itself.* American power is limited quantitatively and qualitatively. Not even a super-power like the United States is able to specify and indefinitely preserve systems of government for Latin America and all other regions of the world; in spite of its great wealth and military strength, the United States is unable to prevent Arab nations from having friendly relations with the Soviet Union or smaller Asian states from normalizing their relations with Red China; it is unable to inhibit even its closest allies in Europe from independently seeking a *détente* with the Soviet Union; and there may even be instances in which it is impossible for the United States to protect other countries from a military threat arising from outside their own borders. Even where the problem is not the adequacy of America's power, there is the other inhibition upon its use: the growing comprehension of the fact that an extraordinarily high price may have to be paid for applying that power successfully overseas. It is conceivable, for example, that—by stationing its own armed forces along the Arab–Israeli frontier —America might more or less guarantee the security of Israel in the face of Arab animosity. But the risks would be enormous: A direct Soviet–American confrontation could occur in the Middle East; Arab alienation from America would be total and, for many years, irreparable; Israel itself would probably come to resent any American restraints upon its policy-making; and this kind of military commitment could drain the United States of funds, manpower, and morale for an indefinite period—all without laying the basis for a lasting settlement of the Arab–Israeli controversy.

Whether correctly designated as neo-isolationism or called by some other label, the post-Vietnam War era of American foreign policy will unquestionably witness a number of significant changes in the nation's international role.[45] As always, the precise circumstances arising abroad will dictate in large measure the specific nature of the American response. Yet, as a generalization, it can be predicted that American foreign policy will exhibit several of the characteristics associated with the earlier isolationist position. Difficult as it might be to document satisfactorily, it would not be amiss to say that the American people remain devoted to many of the assumptions and viewpoints upon which their isolationist approach has long rested. A point which many critics of recent American foreign policy have ignored altogether or too lightly dismissed is that, for the vast majority of Americans, the nation's global commitments are *unwanted and resented burdens*, assumed more out of necessity than out of deliberate preference. Complaints about "the arrogance of American power" to the contrary, there is very little evidence in American diplomatic experience since World War II that the vast majority of Americans desire or enjoy or otherwise really want to serve as the "policeman of the world" in international relations. Viewed in the long time-span of history, their traditional frame of mind has been in the main antithetical to such a strategy. And if circumstances permitted it (and most citizens reluctantly agree that they do not), the majority of Americans would probably choose to revert to their earlier, more comfortable, and less psychologically enervating isolationist existence.

THE THEME OF PROGRESS AND HOPE

We have reserved discussion of what is perhaps the most characteristically American attitude toward foreign and domestic affairs—the theme of progress and hope—for consideration last. To some degree this state of mind has infused all the other qualities we have identified as associated with the American approach to foreign relations.

The changes accompanying American foreign policy in the post-Vietnam War era derive in some measure from a waning of the American people's traditional confidence (not to say certainty) concerning two interrelated beliefs: that problems disturbing the security and tranquility of human society *could be solved;* and that, even though other countries might have difficulty finding the required solutions, America would succeed. Throughout the history of the United States, progress and the "American way of life" have been synonymous terms.

The American belief in progress has impressed nearly every foreign visitor to the United States. One described America as "the land of perfectionism. The American knew that nothing was impossible, in his brave new world, and history confirmed his intuition. Progress was not, to him, a mere philosophical ideal but a commonplace of experience, and he could not understand why foreigners should see vulgar realities where he saw visions."[46] Lord Bryce found that, in America, "Men seem to live in the future rather than in the present. Not that they fail to work while it is called today, but that they see the country not merely as it *is* but as it *will be,* twenty, thirty, fifty, a hundred years hence, when the seedlings they have planted shall have grown to forest trees."[47] A more recent writer has stated that when he looked at America he saw "a people who, by everlastingly tugging at their own bootstraps, have raised themselves to a new peak of economic welfare."[48] Contrasting the attitude of Americans toward world affairs in the postwar period with that exhibited by Europeans, D. W. Brogan concluded: "Probably the only people in the world who now have the historical sense of inevitable victory are the Americans."[49]

The Wellsprings of Optimism

What explains this undeniable optimism, this belief in the limitless possibilities for the advancement of mankind? Let us answer the question by asking another, "What *other* credo could possibly accord with America's philosophical and religious heritage, its material advancement, and the total pattern of its history?" Optimism and hope have ever pervaded American thought, because in no other country in the world has there been so much ground for optimism and hope. If it was believed that the lot of mankind could be infinitely improved, that was because America had demonstrated it. When the Seabees chose their motto during World War II—"The difficult we do at once, the impossible takes a little longer"—they were expressing a great national creed.

The eminent American historian Frederick Jackson Turner believed that no influence was more important in instilling optimism than the frontier. As Ray A. Billington has phrased the

Turner thesis: ". . . No one force did more to Americanize the nation's people and institutions than the repeated rebirth of civilization around the western edge of settlement during the three centuries required to occupy the continent."[50] An American orator in the nineteenth century, Edward Everett, commented that "the wheel of fortune is in constant revolution, and the poor, in one generation, furnish the rich of the next."[51] When Horace Greeley advised "Go West, young man!" he was in effect expressing the national conviction that a new start was always possible, that by will power alone an individual could leave his past behind and carve out a new future for himself and his posterity.

The closing of the frontier was a milestone in the nation's history, but not as important as is sometimes supposed. After 1900, new frontiers beckoned: Disease must be wiped out; corruption must be eradicated from American political life; industry must be compelled to operate within a context of the public interest; depressions must be prevented and protection afforded against unemployment; wealth must be distributed more equitably; religious, racial, ethnic, and social barriers must be torn down; education must be made available to all; and new paths must be blazed in the one area which seemed most persistently to defy man's best efforts—the conduct of international affairs.

Underneath the conviction that mankind could and must improve itself lay firm philosophical and theological foundations. One was the religious heritage of Calvinism, with its emphasis upon predestination. An important part of this belief was that material blessings were an outward symbol of salvation. As the American dream unfolded, it was easy for this belief to become corrupted into the view that material blessings *were* salvation. If faith could move mountains, then the moving of mountains, must surely be a sign of superior faith! Material progress and the view that America had been predestined by Divine Providence to lead in the spiritual regeneration of the world were the warp and woof of the New World's credo.[52]

From Enlightenment philosophy America took a belief in the perfectibility of man and his institutions. The Enlightenment philosophers had believed passionately in the inherent goodness of man as he was led by reason. Two political upheavals—the French and the American Revolutions—had tried to prove them right. Both tried to create the "new society." One failed and the other succeeded; but somehow, Americans fixed their attention only on their own success. Scornful of religious dogmas emphasizing natural depravity and "the fall" of man, fiercely devoted to the scientific study of nature, clinging doggedly to the conviction that "all men are created equal" and that they possess equal rights, Enlightenment philosophers and their intellectual descendants

never doubted that good would conquer evil, if man would make the necessary effort.

America, says the anthropologist Geoffrey Gorer, has always been a materialistic nation—not merely in the narrow sense of wishing to possess material goods and judging success by their acquisition, but in a much deeper sense. It has been materialistic because it has believed profoundly that personality, character, human qualities, and actions can all be manipulated in the same way that man utilizes machines to create better products and achieve a higher standard of living. If matter is subordinate to the will, so is human character and personality.[53] "The power of positive thinking" can remove problems and eliminate barriers to human progress. As D. W. Brogan has phrased it: "Many, very many Americans . . . find it inconceivable that an American policy, announced and carried out by the American government, acting with the support of the American people, does not immediately succeed."[54]

Some Consequences of the American Dream

Optimism and almost boundless confidence in man's ability—and possibly even more important, his desire—to imporve his lot are reflected in a variety of attitudes and actions characteristic of the American people. We have already referred to the historically naïve belief that military force and "power politics" can and must be eliminated from the sphere of international relations. Until recent years it was difficult for many Americans to believe that other countries might plan and carry out aggression, exploit weaker nations, willfully violate treaties, and embark upon programs of aggrandizement. America has ever thought that good intentions could prevent war, especially if they were committed to paper and statesmen pledged the sacred honor of the nation to abide by them. The main thing, America has traditionally believed, is agreement on broad principles—justice, democracy, freedom, self-determination, peace—coupled with the trust that the good will of reasonable men will translate these into specific courses of action beneficial to all.[55] There is a close parallel, D. W. Brogan has observed, "between the optimism that led to the enactment of prohibition and the optimism which welcomed that international Volstead Act, the Kellogg Pact. In that optimism there was a strong element of the old-time religion, of belief in the old evangelical mass conversion. Hundreds and thousands had renounced the world, the flesh, and the devil . . . why should not the nations renounce mutual murder?"[56]

Not infrequently, the ingrained optimism characteristic of the American approach to foreign relations, has infused a new breath of hope into seemingly fruitless international negotiations. In many instances, like disarmament negotiations or reliance upon the United Nations or efforts to resolve the Arab–Israel dispute, American diplomatic initiative has been largely responsible for maintaining the quest for global peace and security. Despite many setbacks in achieving their foreign policy goals, Americans as a whole have never been prone to accept the view that mankind was fated forever to witness violent clashes of rival national ambitions, which in the nuclear age might imperil civilization itself.

Yet America's buoyant optimism has also tended to breed utopian expectations about the nation's role in the global scene. Projecting their own domestic experiences into this realm, Americans have traditionally held bright visions and idealistic goals for the world community. When these had little immediate effect upon an often unreceptive and intractable international environment, in time large segments of the American society were prone to retreat into a kind of crestfallen and disillusioned isolationism. Such habits of mind, for example, have long been conspicuous in connection with the foreign aid program. Distressed by the meager results sometimes achieved with such aid, and chagrined that it did not always guarantee a pro-Western orientation on the part of the recipient countries, individuals and groups within the American society tended to oppose foreign aid per se or to urge that it be reduced drastically. President Kennedy warned his countrymen in the early 1960s that "we cannot remake the world simply by our command."[57] As time passed —and as the evidence accumulated that American foreign aid programs were not promoting progress and stability throughout the world— natural American optimism gave way to pessimism and cynicism. Temperamentally, it was very difficult for Americans to accept the idea that progress outside the West might require generations or that for several decades Afro–Asian societies might experience more *retrogression* than advancement.

Optimism is closely tied up with another American trait: a preference for expediency and pragmatism, and rejection of doctrinaire blueprints for remaking society. America's acknowledged material prosperity is an eloquent testimonial to ingenuity, improvisation, and experimentation. The quest for wealth at home has been accompanied by an easy tolerance of differing opinions, so long as these did not interfere with material progress.[58] Relatively few Americans have been struck by the contradiction between pragmatism at home and the great emphasis upon "principle" often manifested in the nation's relationships with foreign countries. Lewis Galantière has written: "We are not doctrinaire, we have no dogmas to exalt; we are empiricists, and our defects are revealed when we are compelled to shift rapidly from the short to the long view. We leave ourselves free to act as seems rationally requisite or emotionally satisfying in any present situation."[59]

America's nonideological approach to internal and external problems—its concentration upon solving "one problem at a time" by trial-and-error methods—has much to recommend it. As we have emphasized, no other point of view would perhaps be consonant with the mainstream of American history and the lessons of American experience. Today, as in the past, the vast majority of Americans remains devoted to nondoctrinaire solutions and programs; as we shall see in Chapter 7 in our discussion of public opinion, the preponderance of the American people reject extremist solutions (as in the Vietnam War), preferring a "moderate" or middle-of-the-road position on most national issues. The kind of de-ideologization (or decline of global interest in doctrinal and philosophical disputes) witnessed behind the Iron Curtain and in Western Europe in recent years is a phenomenon that has long been characteristic of the American society; considerable evidence exists for believing that other societies have come to share America's viewpoint in this regard. And this process has unquestionably played some part in the reduction of Soviet–American tensions since the 1950s, in lessening the risks of nuclear war, and even in making possible some instances (such as concerted Soviet–American peace initiatives in the Middle East, or the willingness of both countries to assist India and several other needy countries) of collaboration between Washington and Moscow on behalf of a common goal. To cite a different type of example, the kind of eclecticism displayed by many newly independent African nations—whose programs represent an ideological *mélange*, strongly colored by their own traditions and experiences— is not fundamentally different from America's traditional pragmatism and constant inprovisation.

Yet the belief that any problem can be resolved to the satisfaction of Americans on the basis of trial-and-error methods, can and often does create genuine difficulties for the United States in foreign affairs, difficulties which were enhanced after the nation became one of the two super-powers on the global scene. This conviction almost inescapably fosters an "involvement mentality" on the part of Americans: Others may have been unable to solve a variety of knotty international problems, but this very fact sometimes becomes a challenge to Americans to "try their hand" at a solution, in the expectation that success will soon be forthcoming. This assurance undoubtedly characterized the American attitude toward the thorny Palestine question during the 1940s. The key to that conundrum had eluded the Zionists, the Arabs, and the British since World War I; but, as we shall see more fully in Chapter 11, Americans were supremely confident of their own ability to produce a solution. (In fact, of course, their endorsement of the "partition" proposal did nothing of the kind.) Similarly, most Afro–Asian and Latin American countries have had great difficulty overcoming their traditional backwardness; but many Americans were sanguine that, with advice and assistance from the United States, they could be brought quickly to the "take-off stage" of national development. The phrase which Americans used to describe such societies—the *developing nations*—betrayed their underlying optimism. And since it was widely assumed (but seldom proved) that political turmoil was a function of economic and social backwardness, Americans expected the process of "modernization" to impart political stability, encourage democracy, and reduce global and regional tensions. Even today, Americans find it difficult to believe that many of their expectations related to the modernization process outside the West may be at worst utopian and at best only partly correct. In a region like Latin America, for example, it was simply inconceivable to citizens of the United States that in many societies elites and masses alike *showed no strong desire for change*, or at least did not seem willing to undertake the steps needed to achieve it. Or in another setting countless Americans found it inexplicable that many Afro–Asian countries (South Vietnam being a well-known instance, although India, Indonesia, and several other countries could equally well be cited) were not unduly troubled by the existence of widespread corruption throughout their societies.

America's draining and frustrating involvement in the Vietnam War afforded numerous lessons to policy-makers and citizens alike. A cogent one lay in the shortcomings of a totally pragmatic approach to external problems. By a process of step-by-step, ever-expanding commitments (some commentators referred to it as "incrementalism"), the United States gradually assumed the main burden for the security of South Vietnam and a substantial part of the responsibility for the defense of Cambodia and Laos.[60] Without consciously and deliberately doing so, the nation violated one of the strategic axioms which had been central to its defense planning for several decades —avoidance of a land war on the Asian continent. In the end, as the result of a series of discrete steps (often intended at the time to achieve quite limited objectives) the United States found itself in a situation in which *all* the military and political alternatives were unpalatable, and in which even the most appealing offered only a limited hope of gain for the United States. One conclusion which emerged strikingly from the Vietnam experience was that policy-making based upon eclecticism perhaps has as many drawbacks as adherence to rigid ideological or dogmatic decision-making.

Although it may be the most graphic example, America's involvement in the Vietnam conflict was not the only experience whose impact upon traditional American optimism was likely to be profound. We have already mentioned declining hopes for the rapid economic advancement of the Afro–Asian and Latin American nations. Much the same sanguine frame of mind accompanied American efforts, beginning seriously in the early 1960s, to bring the global population explosion under control; again, results to date have been disappointing to Americans interested in the problem—not to say potentially disastrous for several developing societies. Although it has numerous achievements to its credit (as we shall see in Chapter 15), the United Nations has also fallen considerably short of American expectations as an instrument for international peace and security. In various direct and subtle ways, by the 1970s it was apparent that the United States had moved away from overt reliance upon the United Nations to resolve major international issues. American optimism concerning the ability of the United States to "contain" expansive Communism— especially by creating a network of interlocking alliance systems designed to protect against Communist thrusts into other countries—had also declined. Contemporary Asia and the Middle East exemplified the defects of this strategy.

Despite these major and minor setbacks abroad, Americans had discovered perhaps even stronger reasons to re-examine their customary optimism because of developments in *domestic policy*. A leading tenet of the old isolationist doctrine had been the idea that within its own borders the United States could create a New World, exemplifying many of the higher aspirations of mankind; as we have already noted, in many important respects American experience vindicated this confidence. For millions of citizens, the "American dream" became a substantial reality. Yet it proved highly disconcerting to the majority of American citizens to discover that for several minorities (blacks, Mexican–Americans, Indians, and Puerto Ricans especially) the opportunities afforded by life in the United States had been largely elusive and unattainable. Even more traumatic for most Americans perhaps was the realization that substantial numbers of students and young people had "dropped out" of traditional American society; that campus upheavals stemmed in part from student alienation; and, possibly most distressing of all, that some groups (with students and minority elements assuming a leading role) actually favored revolutionary and violent methods for restructuring the American society. Every reader of the daily headlines is familiar with examples of these tendencies. Collectively, they represented perhaps the most eloquent opposition in American history to the kind of optimistic consensus which many historians claimed (and this view too was under heavy attack) had united the American society since its birth as a nation.[61]

Our interest in such far-reaching and fascinating developments must be confined to their foreign policy implications. We have already referred to one likely consequence of these disruptive tendencies: a revival of a neo-isolationist mentality among the American people. Other implications may be mentioned briefly. To a degree unprecedented in the postwar period, the solution of urgent domestic problems is likely to take priority over most foreign policy concerns. (In the early 1970s, the cutback in the space budget and in the allocations for national defense were examples.) Policy-makers have more often than usual been required to take into account the *domestic repercussions* of foreign policy ventures, particularly those entailing major financial or military commitments for prolonged periods overseas. At the same time, as President Nixon's limited intervention in Cambodia in 1970 illustrated, this restriction does not necessarily *prohibit* reliance upon force to achieve external goals, although it may limit the magnitude and duration of such commitments. The changing domestic milieu in which national policy is made also creates a number of difficulties for government officals. For example, they have been forced to tell needy societies abroad that—although America's gross national product approximates $1 trillion annually—the United States cannot "afford" to increase its foreign assistance or even perhaps to maintain it at the levels reached in the recent past. Several smaller American military allies (South Korea was a case in point) have been left in doubt about the firmness of America's military commitment to their security; after Vietnam, even West Germany may have legitimate grounds on which to question the reliability of its NATO guarantees. Countries like Israel, India, and Indonesia, with which the United States had no formal defense obligations, may be even more prone to question how much support the United States will give them in a crisis. In over-all terms, it will be very difficult for policy-makers to convince their counterparts in other countries that American society has not turned inward, directing its energies and resources mainly toward the solution of its own problems, while losing interest in the well-being of societies outside the West. Perhaps most fundamentally, one lesson which militarily vulnerable societies are apt to draw from the Vietnam episode is that the United States *has not yet evolved an effective limited war strategy* and that given the existing frame of mind of the American people, *it is not likely to evolve one in the near future.* Because of Vietnam, involvement in limited war is per se a discredited and unpopular idea, with which Americans are likely to associate burdensome obligations abroad and widespread discontent at home. Granted that the Vietnam conflict affords many good reasons for such conclusions, the fact remains that policy-makers may be forced to choose between two unappealing alternatives:

total war or acquiescence to some threat to vital American diplomatic and military interest. It is not an enviable position within which to make sound national policies.

That the usually sanguine attitudes of American toward foreign and domestic problems has been modified in the light of events in the second half of the twentieth century seems indisputable. Faith in progress has been subjected to a succession of setbacks and sobering realizations—most poignantly perhaps with respect to America's own internal affairs. America's "age of innocence" as a nation has come to an end; if it were not apparent earlier, events during the 1960s and 1970s underscored the fact that few problems in the internal or external environment yielded in the face of fatuous optimism or statements of good intentions. To this extent, America's trauma in Vietnam, coupled with its ongoing internal turmoil, may be a beneficial development for foreign relations, compelling citizens and officials to assess the challenges confronting the nation more realistically and to adopt less expansive and more attainable goals.

A belief in progress, in the perfectability (or at least the substantial improvement) of human institutions, and in the promise of the future have always been deeply embedded American characteristics. The contemporary period is by no means the only episode in the nation's history which has severely challenged this viewpoint. More than once, Americans have lived through "the times that tried men's souls"; although few young people have experienced them, the American society has witnessed several periods of adversity, generating widespread conviction that the "American dream" had to be abandoned. Somehow, America's characteristic optimism has survived these tribulations. For nearly two centuries, the American belief in progress and hope has had a way of outliving its detractors at home and overseas. Even agonizing experiences like the Vietnam conflict, it seems reasonable to suppose, will not change it fundamentally. Unjustified as their optimism may have been from time to time, Americans probably will continue to accept the idea that progress remains both desirable and possible, for their own society as well as for other countries in the family of nations.

NOTES

1. Henry S. Commager, ed., *America in Perspective* (New York: Random House, 1947), p. xi.
2. Ernest Barker, *National Character* (London: Methuen, 1948), p. xi
3. Boyd C. Shafer, *Nationalism: Myth and Reality* (New York: Harcourt Brace Jovanovich,

1955). Boyd contends that there is no such thing as national character, and he cites the views of other commentators to support his thesis.

4. Barker, *op. cit.*, p. 7
5. Quoted in D. W. Brogan, *The American Problem* (London: Hamish Hamilton, 1944), p. 18.
6. Hans Kohn, *American Nationalism: An Interpretive Essay* (New York: Macmillan, 1957), pp. 140–150. This is one of the most illuminating treatments of American nationalism available.
7. Walter Lippmann, U.S. *Foreign Policy: Shield of the Republic* (Boston: Little, Brown, 1943), p. 49.
8. *Ibid.*, p. 9.
9. See Samuel Flagg Bemis, *A Diplomatic History of the United States*, rev. ed. (New York: Holt, Rinehart and Winston, 1942), pp. 463–479.
10. Cushing Stout, "The Twentieth Century Enlightment," *American Political Science Review* **XLIX** (June, 1955), 335–337.
11. Dexter Perkins, "American Wars and Critical Historians," *Yale Review* **40** (Summer, 1951), 686, 695.
12. Kohn, *op. cit.*, p. 219.
13. For an illuminating discussion of the nature and impact of revisionist interpretations of recent American diplomacy, see Arthur Schlesinger, Jr., "Origins of the Cold War," *Foreign Affairs* **46** (October, 1967), 22–53.
14. For a recent critique of American foreign policy exemplifying this point of view, see Richard J. Barnet, *Intervention and Revolution: America's Confrontation with Insurgent Movements Around the World* (New York: World Publishing, 1968).
15. Geoffrey Gorer, *The American People* (New York: Norton, 1948), pp. 30–39, 227–229. A provocative study of American character by a cultural anthropologist, even if the explanations offered sometimes seem highly oversimplified.
16. Quoted in Kohn, *op cit.*, p. 181.
17. Quoted in *ibid.*, p. 183.
18. This theme is elaborated fully in Senator J. William Fulbright's book, *The Arrogance of Power* (New York: Random House, 1966).
19. Dexter Perkins, *The American Approach to Foreign Policy* (Cambridge, Mass.: Harvard University Press, 1952), pp. 68–70.
20. *Ibid.*, pp. 69–75.
21. An illuminating analysis of traditional American attitudes is Walter Lippmann, "The Rivalry of Nations," *The Atlantic Monthly* **181** (February, 1948), 19–26. For a recent study of the impact of the Korean War upon American viewpoints, see David Rees, *Korea: The Limited War* (Baltimore: Penguin, 1964).
22. D. W. Brogan, "The Illusion of American Omnipotence," *Harper's Magazine* **205** (December, 1952), 21, 28. The intervening years have done little to change the force of Brogan's perceptive observations about American attitudes in global affairs.

23. Perkins, *The American Approach to Foreign Policy, op. cit.*, p. 84.
24. *Ibid.*, pp. 30–31.
25. *Ibid.*, p. 32.
26. *Ibid.*, p. 45.
27. Herbert Feis, "Is the United States Imperialistic?" *Yale Review* **41** (Autumn, 1951), pp. 13–24.
28. See *The New York Times, The Rockefeller Report on the Americas* (Chicago: Quadrangle, 1969).
29. For discussions of the nature and impact of the military–industrial complex, see George Thayer, *The War Business* (New York: Avon Books, 1969); Erwin Knoll and Judith N. McFadden, eds., *American Militarism: 1970* (New York: Viking, 1969); and Ralph Lapp, *The Weapons Culture* (Baltimore: Penguin, 1969).
30. Brogan, *The American Problem, op. cit.*, pp. 62–65; Gorer, *op. cit.*, pp. 30–39.
31. Julius W. Pratt, *A History of United States Foreign Policy* (Englewood Cliffs, N.J.: Prentice-Hall, 1955), pp. 143–154, 201–218, 247–352, 458–460. An interestingly written and scholarly one-volume account of American foreign relations.
32. *Ibid.*, pp. 315–319; 466–482; 634–645.
33. *Ibid.*, pp. 451–456.
34. Albert K. Weinberg, "The Historical Meaning of the American Doctrine of Isolation," *American Political Science Review* **34** (April, 1940), 539.
35. For more detailed discussion of the sources of isolationist thought, see Max Beloff, "The Foundations of American Policy," *The Spectator* (London) **194** (February 25 and March 4, 1955), 210–211 and 247–249, respectively; Gorer, *op. cit.*, pp. 224–237; Lippmann, *U.S. Foreign Policy: Shield of the Republic, op. cit.*, and Weinberg, *op. cit.*
36. Max Lerner, *America as a Civilization* (New York: Simon and Schuster, 1957), p. 888.
37. Brogan, *The American Problem, op. cit.*, p. 101.
38. Cited in Kohn, *op. cit.*, p. 69.
39. *Ibid.*, p. 139.
40. *Ibid.*, p. 138.
41. Quoted in *ibid.*, p. 140.
42. Quoted in *ibid.*, pp. 152–153.
43. Quoted in Theodore Sorensen, *Kennedy* (New York: Harper & Row, 1965), p. 511.
44. See George W. Ball, *The Discipline of Powers: Essentials of a Modern World Structure* (Boston: Little, Brown, 1968), p. 233. While he refers specifically to recent American relations with the developing nations, we have applied his metaphor to the broad range of the nation's foreign policy.
45. For an illuminating series of essays dealing with many of these changes in American foreign policy in the post-Vietnam War period, see Abdul A. Said, ed., *America's World Role in the '70s* (Englewood Cliffs, N.J.: Prentice-Hall, 1970).
46. Commager, *op. cit.*, p. xix
47. Quoted in Ernest L. Klein, *Our Appointment*

with Destiny (New York: Farrar, Straus & Giroux, 1952), p. 97.

48. Quoted in *ibid.*, pp. 8–9.
49. Brogan, "The Illusion of American Omnipotence," *op. cit.*, p. 22.
50. Kohn, *op. cit.*, p. 21.
51. Quoted in *ibid.*, p. 18.
52. Ralph Barton Perry, *Characteristically American* (New York: Knopf, 1949), pp. 93–105. In this volume a distinguished American philosopher examines his society's character, with particular attention to its philosophical and religious roots.
53. Gorer, *op. cit.*, pp. 137–224.
54. Brogan, "The Illusion of American Omnipotence," *op. cit.*, pp. 25–26.
55. Perkins, *The American Approach to Foreign Policy, op. cit.*, p. 111.
56. Brogan, *The American Problem, op. cit.*, pp. 62–63.
57. *The New York Times* (September 27, 1963).
58. Gerald W. Johnson, *Our English Heritage* (Philadelphia: Lippincott, 1949), pp. 44–45.
59. Lewis Galantière, "America Today: A Free-Hand Sketch," *Foreign Affairs* **28** (July, 1950), 532.
60. This is the term employed by the former State Department official Roger Hilsman, in his *To Move a Nation: The Politics of Foreign Policy in the Administration of John F. Kennedy* (Garden City, N.Y.: Doubleday, 1967), pp. 413–541.
61. By the late 1960s, one of the oldest themes of American historical writing—the idea that, to a degree surpassing any other society in history, Americans shared a broad national consensus about political, economic, and social affairs—was under sharp attack. For essays illustrating this debate among historians, see Herbert J. Bass, ed., *The State of American History* (Chicago: Quadrangle, 1970).

Three
THE WHITE HOUSE AND THE STATE DEPARTMENT

THE PRESIDENCY AT THE VORTEX OF WORLD AFFAIRS

Over a half-century ago, President Woodrow Wilson said that the Spanish–American War and its aftermath had "greatly increased power and opportunity for constructive statesmanship given the President by the plunge into international politics and into the administration of distant dependencies. . . ." After World War II, President Harry S. Truman declared: "I make American foreign policy. . . ." The American presidency, said Truman, "is the greatest office in the history of the world."[1]

These comments underscore a fact that is one of the most important realities confronting the student of American foreign policy. The management of foreign affairs, President Thomas Jefferson once declared, was "executive altogether." Even today, the Chief Executive does not enjoy a monopoly upon the levers of power which influence the nation's role outside its own borders. Yet, both in constitutional theory and in practice, his role has become sufficiently powerful to justify entitling a recent study of the presidency as *The President as World Leader*.[2] This evolution in the President's role was highlighted by President Lyndon Johnson's experience in the period immediately following the tragic death of President John F. Kennedy. Among the former's most urgent problems was reassuring foreign governments that there would be no disruption or significant change in America's international commitments. During his first week in office, President Johnson met with over 90 representatives of foreign countries to assure them that "they need have no fear or doubt" about the constancy of American foreign policy.[3]

The change in national policy as a result of America's emergence from the long era of isolationism had many significant repercussions—none perhaps more noteworthy than that of strengthening the President's position at the pinnacle of the foreign policy process and placing the White House at the vortex of change in global affairs. Today, it would be no exaggeration to say, an incumbent President exercises powers exceeding those of most kings, emperors, and world conquerors throughout history. For, as we observed in Chapter 1, if the United States is not omnipotent, it is nonetheless powerful enough to influence decisively the lives of countless millions of citizens inside and outside its own borders. Whether mankind will escape the perils of the nuclear age; whether Indian villagers will begin to discern some gradual improvement in their standard of living; whether the concept of "Atlantic unity" will be translated into successful programs of cooperation; whether the United Nations will be able to finance its expanding activities; whether Berliners will be able to preserve their freedom in the face of relentless Communist pressure—in these and innumerable other instances the outcome will be determined in no small measure by decisions made by the Chief Executive of the United States.

Every President, as we shall see in this chapter and the one that follows, has advisers; some of these may occasionally seek to contest his claim to leadership in the foreign policy field. Moreover, as we shall emphasize in Chapter 5, Congress has always possessed certain prerogatives in foreign affairs. Many of its powers have also been augmented as a result of America's emergence as a global leader. Despite these trends, the power of the President in foreign relations has unquestionably grown *more rapidly* than the power of rivals in Congress or elsewhere. As Richard P. Longaker has expressed it, the President's international responsibilities have become more and more "institutionalized," through treaty obligations, American membership in the United Nations and regional associations like the Organization of American States, and the impact abroad of such problems as racial conflicts in the United States.[4]

What are the constitutional sources of the President's authority in foreign affairs? What are the principal techniques of leadership available to him? What conditions in international affairs since

World War II have combined to enhance his position in the foreign policy process? By contrast, what forces even now inhibit and limit presidential power, preventing the emergence of a "presidential dictatorship" in the United States? These are among the basic questions to be discussed in our analysis of the President's role in foreign policy.

Constitutional Appearance and Reality

At the outset, the student of American foreign relations must be cognizant of the distinction between constitutional *appearance* and *reality*. Perhaps even more than in domestic affairs, he must be mindful that constitutional theories, provisions, grants of power, and the like, must always be understood in terms of the context within which they were presented, the evolution in their meaning throughout American history, and the court decisions interpreting relevant principles of constitutional law. Chapter 5 calls attention to the fact, for example, that while the power of Congress to "declare war" (Art. I, Sec. 8) meant one thing to the Founding Fathers, conditions prevailing throughout American history and particularly since World War II have given this provision a very different meaning.

In any discussion of the powers of the national government in foreign relations, two constitutional principles are fundamental. One is the idea that the national government exercises only "delegated powers" or—in the light of the Supreme Court's classic decision in *McCulloch* v. *Maryland* (1819)[5]—those powers which may logically be *implied* to carry out its delegated powers. Whether granted outright or implied, the powers of the national government, according to this doctrine, are conferred upon it by the Constitution of the United States. This idea, the Supreme Court declared in *United States* v. *Curtiss–Wright Export Corporation* (1936), was subject to drastic modification when applied to foreign relations:

The broad statement that the Federal government can exercise no powers except those specifically enumerated in the Constitution and such implied powers as are necessary and proper to carry into effect the enumerated powers, is categorically true only in respect of our internal affairs.[6]

The powers of the national government in foreign affairs, the Court held, "did not depend upon the affirmative grants of the Constitution." If they had not been enumerated in the Constitution, they would have belonged to the national government "as necessary concomitants of nationality."[7] That is, they would have been among the prerogatives of the national government because the United States is a nation and a member of the family of nations.

Similarly, the constitutional doctrine of "separation of powers" is largely inapplicable to the sphere of foreign relations. The theory that the powers of the national government are divided (as American folklore has it) among three "equal and coordinate" branches of the government has always possessed less validity, even in domestic affairs, then many Americans imagined. In the same case of *United States* v. *Curtiss–Wright* the Supreme Court also dealt with this concept. Its judgment was that the participation by Congress and the courts in the control of foreign relations was "significantly limited," whereas the powers of the Chief Executive were vast. It concluded:

In this vast external realm, with its important, complicated, delicate and manifold problems, the President alone has the power to speak or listen as a representative of the nation. He *makes* treaties with the advice and consent of the Senate; but he alone negotiates. Into the field of negotiation the Senate cannot intrude and Congress itself is powerless to invade it. . . .

The Supreme Court referred to the "plenary and exclusive power of the President as the sole organ of the Federal government in the field of international relations. . . ."[8]

The Supreme Court and Foreign Affairs

Applying such *dicta* to its own approach to constitutional and legal issues involving foreign affairs, the Supreme Court has been most reluctant to intrude into the conduct of foreign policy. We may dispose of the Supreme Court's role in American foreign relations by saying that in the vast majority of cases, its decisions have tended to follow one of two directions. In a number of important decisions the Court has, as we have seen, upheld the idea of broad discretionary power for the Chief Executive. Decisions of the Supreme Court, therefore, constitute a significant force adding to the President's powers in foreign relations. In other cases, the Supreme Court has designated certain controversies in foreign affairs as "political questions," falling outside its jurisdiction. Does the President have the power to "recognize" another government, like Bolshevik Russia, Communist China, or some new regime among the developing nations? Can he send American armed forces abroad, to Greece, Korea, Vietnam, or other areas, without a congressional declaration of war? What are the recognized boundaries of Israel and adjacent Arab states? Which of two contending political factions is the proper "government" of another country? Have the actions of another state rendered the terms of a treaty between it and the United States inoperative? These and kindred questions arising in foreign affairs are political issues, not properly susceptible of resolution by resort to the courts.* In most instances, the result of the Supreme Court's refusal to decide foreign policy issues on the grounds that they are "political questions" is to leave the President's prerogatives in foreign policy unfettered by judicial restraints. Whatever limitations exist upon the President's powers, that is to say, are found largely outside the legal realm.

For convenience, we may divide the President's powers in foreign relations into three categories: those specifically designated in the Constitution; those which have evolved through usage and tradition, especially as the United States has responded to crises abroad; and a special category called war or "emergency" powers. These categories are to some extent artificial; a particular technique of presidential leadership may conceivably embrace more than one of them, while another may not fit unambiguously into any. With these admonitions in mind, let us examine each category more fully.

THE PRESIDENT'S CONSTITUTIONAL POWERS

The Treaty-Making Process

The Constitution provides that the President "shall have power, by and with the advice and

---

*A landmark case in this connection is *Stewart* v. *Kahn*, 11 Wallace 493 (1871), in which Justice Swayne stated: "The measures to be taken in carrying on war and to suppress insurrection are not defined. The decision of all questions rests wholly in the discretion of those to whom the substantial powers involved are confided by the Constitution." Again, in the case of *United States* v. *Belmont*, 301 U.S. 324 (1937), the Court said that "who is the sovereign of a territory is not a judicial question, but one the determination of which by the political departments conclusively binds the courts. . . ."

In law, it needs to be observed, "political questions" do not denote issues which are politically controversial, although of course they may well be so. Rather, they are questions which are essentially *nonjudiciable:* They are not capable of determination or resolution by legal processes. Thus in the contemporary era, the question of whether the President may send troops to Vietnam—an issue heavily emphasized by critics of American involvement in that conflict—is a "political question' to be resolved by the executive and legislative branches of the government. Such controversies, in other words, cannot properly be called "cases" within the meaning of Article III, Section 2, giving the national courts jurisdiction over "all Cases, in Law and Equity, arising under this Constitution, the Laws of the United States, and Treaties made, or which shall be made, under their Authority. . . ." Questions of this kind may be *politically controversial* within the country; they may evoke strong feelings among different groups of citizens; they may present difficult moral and ethical choices; they may even affect the survival of certain individuals called into military service. But none of these qualities makes them "cases" within the Court's interpretation of constitutional principles.

consent of the Senate, to make treaties, provided two-thirds of the Senators present concur . . ." (ART. II, Sec. 2). It is worth noting that Article VI of the Constitution places "all Treaties made, or which shall be made, under the Authority of the United States" on the same level with the Constitution itself and "the Laws of the United States"; all three are to be regarded as "the supreme Law of the Land. . . ." Article I, Section 10 of the Constitution alludes to another kind of international agreement or compact, when it states that "No State shall, without the Consent of Congress, . . . enter into any Agreement or Compact with another State, or with a foreign Power. . . ."

Implicitly, then, the Constitution of the United States recognizes two categories of international agreements. The first is *treaties*, in the making of which the President and the Senate are given responsibilities. The second is *agreements or compacts*, the nature of which is undefined in the Constitution. Nor does the Constitution prescribe how they are made, as it does with treaties. Reference to this latter category, however, strongly suggests that the Founding Fathers were familiar with international agreements that were less formal and explicit than treaties, and that they expected the United States to engage in such agreements with other countries.

The treaty process between the United States and other governments involves two stages: negotiation of the treaty and its ratification by the nations concerned. The constitutional requirement for ratification is clearly set forth. Treaties become the "law of the land" only when two-thirds of the members of the Senate present approve them. Even then, treaty agreements do not enter into force until the President has proclaimed them as ratified. A President may (and sometimes has) refused to proclaim a treaty even after it has been ratified by the Senate.

Much greater controversy, however, has surrounded the process of *treaty negotiation:* that is, the process by which the representatives of the United States secure agreement with officials of other countries upon the terms of the treaty, as signified by their willingness to sign the document. The Constitution states that the President makes treaties with the "advice" of the Senate. What does this provision mean? How does the Senate give its advice? At what point in the treaty-making process is this advice rendered? To what degree is the Senate's advice binding upon the President and his subordinates? Such questions have produced endless argument throughout American history.* Broadly speaking, there are

---

*For examples, consult: Cecil V. Crabb, Jr., *Bipartisan Foreign Policy: Myth or Reality* (New York: Harper & Row, 1957), chap. 1; D. F. Fleming, *The Treaty Veto of*

two schools of thought concerning the problem. The theory most frequently asserted within the Senate, and by advocates of greater legislative influence in foreign policy, is that the President is obliged to seek the "advice" of the upper chamber *from the earliest stages of negotiation* with foreign governments. According to this view, the Senate serves as a kind of advisory council to the President in reaching agreements with other nations. The second school of thought—the view espoused by successive Presidents and advocates of vigorous executive leadership in foreign affairs—is that senatorial "advice and consent" are in fact tantamount to the same thing. The President seeks the "advice" of the Senate when he requests its "consent" to a treaty already prepared and signed by executive officials.

Whatever the merits of the argument—the Founding Fathers probably held the first theory—there can be no doubt about which view has predominated. Throughout the entire process of treaty-making the President retains the initiative. Tradition and precedent have reduced the Senate's role largely to deciding whether treaties shall or shall not be ratified. The executive branch negotiates them, signs them in the name of the United States, presents them to the Senate for approval, and, after they are ratified, proclaims them as law. The Senate may refuse to ratify them, in which case the President has other means of achieving agreements with other nations. Moreover, the chief executive may refuse to accept amendments affixed by the Senate; he may withdraw the treaty from consideration by the Senate at any time; and he may even refuse to proclaim a treaty after it has been ratified, if he feels its terms no longer accord with the national interest.

Over two-thirds of all treaties submitted to the Senate between the years 1789 and 1963 were approved unconditionally; only 15 (or 1.1 percent of the total) were rejected. Some 27 percent of all treaties submitted during this period were either approved with amendments and reservations, or withdrawn with no action taken on them.[9] At the same time, it is also true that occasionally the Senate relies upon its power to ratify treaties to assert its will vigorously. Senate amendments and reservations attached to the Treaty of Versailles were unacceptable to President Wilson, with the result that the United States did not join the League of Nations. In the more recent period, the Senate expressed some apprehension about the nuclear test-ban treaty submitted to it by President Kennedy in 1963. It ratified the treaty only after receiving assurances from the President that this agreement would not deter America from main-taining an adequate system of national defense and that, if amendments in the treaty were needed, they would not be added without the Senate's concurrence.[10]

Such examples, however, must be viewed as exceptional. So passive has the Senate's role become in the treaty-making process that even senators themselves have cautioned that body against attempts to intrude into the President's direction of foreign affairs by construing the "advice and consent" clause broadly. Thus the highly respected Senator Arthur H. Vandenberg (Republican of Michigan) told his colleagues in 1948:

I think the Senate is entitled, at any time it pleases, to use the advice clause of the Constitution to tell the Executive what it thinks concerning foreign affairs. But I think it would be a tragic and unfortunate thing if the habit ever became general or too contagious because I respectfully submit, . . . only in those instances in which the Senate can be sure of a complete command of all the essential information prerequisite to an intelligent decision, should it take the terrific chance of muddying the international waters by some sort of premature and ill-advised expression of its advice to the Executive.[11]

The President's Use of Executive Agreements

Treaties, as we have noted, are only the most formal agreements reached among governments. The Constitution evidently contemplated that other kinds of agreements would be utilized in foreign affairs. In time, these came to be called "executive agreements"—formal and informal understandings among heads of state binding them to take a certain course of action. Such agreements may and do cover a great range of activities—from routine business like international mail delivery, rules governing quarantine procedures, and regulations dealing with civil aviation—to diplomatic and political issues whose subject matter may be as important as a treaty—like the wartime agreements among the Allies dealing with the future of Eastern Europe, or the mutual reduction of tariff rates, or the participation of American armed forces in UN peace-keeping operations.

George Washington negotiated an executive agreement in 1792 providing for reciprocal mail delivery. Although other Presidents utilized executive agreements over the years that followed, Franklin D. Roosevelt raised them to a new pinnacle of importance as a technique of executive control over foreign relations. A well-known example is the "Destroyer Deal" made between FDR and Prime Minister Churchill in 1940, exchanging fifty obsolete destroyers for British bases in the Western Hemisphere. The following year FDR was granted authority by Congress to enter into

---

the American Senate (New York: Putnam, 1930); W. Stull Holt, *Treaties Defeated by the Senate* (Baltimore: Johns Hopkins, 1933).

agreements with the nation's allies for the provision of lend-lease assistance. During the war, Allied conferences at Casablanca, Tehran, Yalta, and Potsdam resulted in a host of agreements concerning military strategy and postwar political settlements. None of these was submitted to the Senate for approval. Surveying diplomatic experience during the first half of the twentieth century, one commentator found that almost half of the international commitments made by the United States were in the form of executive agreements. In more recent years they "have outnumbered treaties by perhaps ten to one."[12]

Although treaties and executive agreements may be legally distinguished on several grounds (the latter, for example, are not included by the Constitution as part of the "supreme law of the land"), in practice the differences between them are of concern chiefly to lawyers. For the ordinary citizen and governmental officials, both are binding. In some instances, treaties clearly anticipate that the heads of state of the signatory countries will later arrive at agreements giving effect to their terms, as in the case of the reciprocal trade program undertaken under the Roosevelt administration during the 1930s. Executive agreements made under this program superseded tariff provisions earlier determined by Congress. While legislators from time to time denounce the President's reliance upon executive agreements as an instrument of foreign policy, Congress not infrequently approves such agreements later*—as when an executive agreement made in 1845 for the annexation of Texas was later confirmed by a joint resolution of Congress, and when Congress similarly approved an executive agreement in 1898 by which the President annexed Hawaii. More recently, Congress belatedly approved an agreement between the United States and Canada when it enacted the St. Lawrence Seaway Act in 1954, making possible this important venture in Canadian–American cooperation.[13]

Concluding our discussion of executive agreements, we may note the views of Bernard Schwartz on the use and validity of such agreements as a technique of presidential leadership in foreign affairs:

The will of the nation in the external sphere may be expressed through other acts than treaties and such acts do not have to be ratified by the President by and with the advice and consent of the Senate in order to be valid and binding. The President himself may, as the sole organ of the nation in foreign relations, enter into executive agreements which are binding obligations of the United States.[14]

Authority over the Military Establishment

In the transition of the United States, from the isolationist period to the postwar era of global leadership, few changes have been more outstanding than the role of military force in achieving foreign policy objectives. Before World War II, to be sure, the United States relied upon its armed services from time to time in its foreign relations. In the annexation of Texas in the 1940s, in Admiral Perry's "opening" of Japan to the outside world in 1854, in various interventions carried out in Latin America—in these and other instances, military force was employed for achieving some foreign policy goal.

In degree at least, the postwar era differs from earlier ones in regard to the relationship between foreign policy and military power. For the first time in history, the United States must maintain a large and highly varied *peacetime military establishment*, along with a large contingent of "ready reserves." Many of these forces are stationed overseas, in Europe, in the Mediterranean, in East Asia, in the skies, and submerged in oceans around the world. The armed forces must be maintained in an advanced state of readiness to deal with diverse crises in Berlin, or in the Middle East, or in the Caribbean. They must be capable of *rapid and effective deployment* to protect the North American continent from attack, or to preserve the security of West Germany, or to bolster the defenses of an Asian ally. In an age of accelerating technology, the military establishment must be *constantly modernized* and equipped with the latest weapons to counter the threat posed by well-armed enemies.

But perhaps the most salient contrast with the prewar period lies in the challenge posed to the United States by the concept of "limited war." Beginning with the decision of the United States to defend Greece in 1947, the nation has been presented with a series of crises which fall under the category of limited wars, in which military measures must be very closely concerted with the political, economic, psychological, and cultural components of policy to produce an over-all strategy capable of attaining national objectives.

Given the greatly enhanced role of armed force in external affairs in the contemporary period, it follows that control over the military establishment is an extremely influential technique of leadership in the foreign policy field. Yet at intervals throughout the postwar period—when American forces were sent to Europe in 1950–1951, when President Truman ordered the armed forces to defend South Korea in 1950, and on fre-

*This phenomenon provides another difference between treaties and executive agreements: The former must be ratified by two-thirds *of the Senate;* executive agreements (when they are approved by the legislature at all) are approved by a majority of Congress as a whole.

quent occasions after America began to expand its military commitment in Vietnam after 1960—controversy has erupted within the United States over the use of armed forces abroad. Critics of America's involvement in the Vietnam War, for example, were especially vocal in their assertion that use of American troops in that conflict was "illegal," since there had been no "declaration of war" by Congress.*

Article II, Section 2, of the American Constitution designates the President as "Commander-in-Chief of the Army and Navy. . . ." As with the treaty power, Congress also possesses important prerogatives over the military establishment, such as the duty to provide for the army and navy, to regulate its size, to equip and support it, and to declare war. Theoretically, this fact places substantial limits upon the President's control of foreign relations, because success in foreign affairs is heavily dependent upon military strength.

Assuming then that Congress has provided for adequate military force, what agency of the government shall determine its use for foreign policy ends? By virtue of its powers in this field, and especially its power to declare war, can Congress instruct the President in the use of the military establishment in times of peace of war? Is the President limited in the use he can make of armed forces to the extent that he must not risk war without the consent of Congress?

The answer to all these questions is negative.[15] Once the armed forces have come into being and their character (e.g., their size, the proportion of ground, naval, and air forces to the whole) has been determined by Congress, the President alone utilizes them in behalf of national policy. It is difficult to unravel the exact intention of the Founding Fathers when they gave Congress the power to "declare war." In their era, wars usually were "declared" formally, often weeks or months before hostilities actually began. Legislators could therefore safely debate the wisdom of going to war.

Today, such deliberation has been rendered impossible by technological developments. The radar warning system maintained by the United States and Canada, for example, would give officials in the two capitals approximately *thirty minutes'* warning of an impending missile attack against North America! To appreciate the military consequences of a sudden attack upon a nation's defenses, it is necessary only to realize that Israel's destruction of Arab air forces in 1967 tipped the military scales decisively in its favor in the early stages of this "third round" in the Arab–Israeli conflict. Speed in committing the armed forces is,

therefore, essential in protecting national security. Conversely, speed in ascertaining that the deployment of military force by other countries does *not* pose a threat to American security (as the President might determine by using the "hot line" communications link with the Kremlin) is no less vital. A recent student of the presidency has concluded that

. . . when it comes to action risking war, technology has modified the Constitution: the President perforce becomes the only man in such a system capable of exercising judgment under the extraordinary limits now imposed by secrecy, complexity, and time.[16]

Modern technology may have placed a greater premium than ever upon presidential control over the armed forces. Yet the principle that the powers of the Chief Executive as Commander-in-Chief may be used to commit the armed forces in defense of the nation has been invoked many times throughout American history. As it does for many other precedents involving executive power, Lincoln's administration affords numerous examples. After his inauguration, President Lincoln took a variety of steps to protect the Union against the secession movement. One of these was his "blockade" of southern ports, without the approval of Congress. Under international law, a blockade is normally regarded as an act of war; yet there had been no "declaration of war" by Congress, nor did the national government admit the existence of a state of war between North and South. In *The Prize Cases* (1863), the Supreme Court held that "the President is not only authorized but bound to resist force, by force. He does not initiate the war, but is bound to accept the challenge without waiting for any special legislative authority. And whether the hostile party be a foreign invader, or States organized in rebellion, it is none the less a war, although the declaration of it be *'unilateral.' "* War, said the Court, "may exist without a declaration on either side." When the threat to national integrity arose, the Court asserted, "The President was bound to meet it in the shape it presented itself, without waiting for Congress to baptize it with a name. . . ." The Court took note of the fact that, by various legislative enactments, Congress subsequently legitimatized many of Lincoln's actions during the Civil War.[17] As early as the Civil War, defense of the nation was thus recognized as a presidential obligation, requiring the Chief Executive to react swiftly and decisively to threats to national security. Nearly a century later, President Eisenhower declared that "hanging ought to be the fate of any President who failed to act instantly to protect the American people against a sudden attack in this atomic age."[18]

---

*It is noteworthy that this contention found no support in the Supreme Court or lesser courts. The issue of the legality of American involvement in Vietnam was another "political question," the merits of which the courts consistently refused to decide.

The threat posed by the secession of the southern states, or the danger of a nuclear attack against the United States itself in the modern era, it might be objected, pose very different issues from the President's use of armed forces in settings like Greece, or Korea, or Vietnam, or the Dominican Republic, ostensibly for the purpose of safeguarding American security. Critics of American involvement in Vietnam, for example, have contested the idea that national security is really concerned in events in Southeast Asia. Even if it is, they maintain, the American military buildup in that region per se endangers national security, by adding to the risk of a war with the Soviet Union or Communist China. Much the same point was made in 1951 when President Truman sent American troops to Europe and when he committed armed forces to the defense of South Korea.

In controversies of this kind, two questions are really at stake. One is the *power or authority* of the President to use the armed forces for foreign policy ends. On this point, the weight of precedent and of relevant court decisions is clearly on the side of presidential authority. When President Eisenhower asked Congress to pass the "Eisenhower Doctrine" in 1957, authorizing employment of the armed forces to protect American interests in the Middle East, or when President Johnson made basically the same request in the Tonkin Gulf episode in 1964 in Vietnam, both Presidents underscored the idea that they did not *need* such legislative authorization. Congress's action did not really add anything to the President's constitutional powers, but legislative approval furnished an impressive indication of *broad national unity* in dealing with external crises. Early in American history, President Jefferson had sent naval units against the Barbary pirates; at the end of the nineteenth century, President McKinley committed American troops in China during the "Boxer Rebellion." President Kennedy took the nation, and perhaps the whole world, to the "brink of war" in 1962 when he placed the armed services on maximum alert and ordered the navy to intercept Soviet ships carrying missiles to Cuba. In 1965 President Johnson sent the marines into the Dominican Republic to stabilize that country. In the light of such precedents, the power of the Chief Executive to employ the armed forces abroad in behalf of foreign policy goals hardly seems contestable.

The *wisdom* of employing armed forces abroad —and the extent to which such a commitment actually enhances national security—is of course a different question. During the Vietnam conflict, for example, many Americans who did not question the right of the President to expand military commitments abroad had doubts about the advisability of doing so or challenged the assertion of executive policy-makers that the security of Vietnam was vital to the security of the United States

itself. On the theory that in a democracy, the people ultimately determine public policy, many citizens—supported by influential congressmen and public groups—castigated the Southeast Asian policies of the Kennedy and Johnson administrations.

When the issue is whether using armed force contributes to achieving some American foreign policy objective, the problem may be analyzed as a short-run and a long-run phenomenon. In the short run, Presidents Kennedy and Johnson disagreed with their critics; the latter possessed few effective techniques for preventing a steady American military escalation in Southeast Asia. Even critics of the war in Congress showed little disposition to vote against military appropriations requested by the White House or otherwise to deny the President the military strength he requested for use in Asia. In the long run, of course, continuing criticism of American policy in Vietnam unquestionably had an impact upon executive policy-makers. President Johnson's decision early in 1968 not to seek re-election was prompted substantially by recurrent criticisms of his Vietnam policy and the contention it fostered throughout the United States. To some undetermined extent, the decision of the United States to inaugurate a "bombing halt" in North Vietnam in 1968, as a first step towards undertaking peace talks with representatives of North Vietnam and the Viet Cong, was also an outgrowth of popular dissatisfaction with events in Asia.*

In a most indirect way—by subjecting their leaders to the test of re-election periodically and by exercising their freedom to choose new leaders who espouse different policies—it may be said that the electorate determines the policies of the government. It should also be remembered, however, that elections in the United States seldom constitute "mandates" for successful candidates; or if they do, the precise mandates such candidates possess is far from clear. If, by some interpretations, President Nixon's election in 1968 constituted a "repudiation" of the policies of the Johnson administration, it was also true that: (1) President Nixon and the Republican Party were in general more "hawkish" in terms of their reliance upon armed forces than the outgoing Johnson administration; (2) Nixon's campaign speeches and early statements as President offered no indication of a radical change in American foreign policy in Southeast Asia; and (3) early in 1969,

*Public criticism of American policy in Vietnam, it ought to be remembered, was by no means unanimous in its views of what the United States ought to do. Such criticism was far from unified, for example, in demanding an American withdrawal from Vietnam; some segments of American opinion clearly favored a tougher, or more "hawkish" stand in dealing with the threat. President Johnson was also influenced by, and had to take account of, this segment of opinion.

President Nixon made a point of stating publicly that his administration was *not bound* to employ the same weapons or tactics used by the United States earlier in Vietnam—that is, under Nixon, the United States would at least consider using new weapons and tactics, if the Vietnam contest erupted anew.

Maintenance of Diplomatic Relations with Other Governments

By the end of the 1960s, the United States still had not "recognized" Communist China, after more than twenty years of Communist rule on the mainland. Brazil—regarded earlier in the postwar period as a good prospect for stable democracy in Latin America—was ruled by a military junta, as was Argentina, the other South American giant. In Africa, Nigeria was torn by civil war between the national government and the secessionist Republic of Biafra. Following a new eruption of military conflict in the Middle East in 1967, the boundaries of the state of Israel, and correspondingly of Syria, Jordan, and Egypt, were in dispute. Tension continued to inflame relations between Cambodia, on one hand, and Thailand and South Vietnam, on the other, growing out of a long-standing border dispute among them. Southern Rhodesia, governed by its white minority, had declared its "independence" from Great Britain; curiously enough, most Afro–Asian states refused to recognize its right to throw off colonial control.

In terms of the foreign policy process in the United States, such diverse issues had a common theme: They all involved the "recognition" of other governments by America and the maintenance of harmonious diplomatic relations with them. What group actually constitutes the government of another state? What are a nation's proper boundaries? Is a country like Southern Rhodesia an independent nation, or is it still a colonial dependency? What American official decides if and when to recognize a government overseas or, conversely, to withdraw such recognition? In all cases, the answer is the same. The Constitution, said President Grant in 1877, "has indicated the President as the agency to represent the national sovereignty, and to receive all official communications" from other governments.[19]

The President's exclusive authority to "recognize" other governments is conferred by Article II, Section 3 of the Constitution, empowering him to "receive Ambassadors and other public Ministers. . . ." Ambassadors, ministers, and other official representatives from foreign countries are accredited to the President; for this purpose, only one branch of the American government exists—the executive branch.

Foreign diplomats are accredited to the President of the United States. Official communications from other governments are addressed to him or his subordinates. Long-standing diplomatic protocol prohibits foreign governments from having any official contact with other leaders or institutions within the American government or from appealing to public groups over the head of the President, upon pain of having diplomats violating this rule declared *persona non grata*, thereby requiring them to leave the country. On occasion, flagrant departure from this rule has led to strained diplomatic relations between the United States and foreign countries, as exemplified by tensions growing out of Imperial Germany's propaganda activities in the United States prior to the country's entry into World War I.*

If part of the process of recognition of one government by another entails receiving ambassadors from abroad, the other involves sending America's own ambassadors, ministers, or lesser officials to foreign countries. Normal diplomatic intercourse assumes an exchange of officials between the countries. With regard to this latter process, the Constitution (Art. II, Sec. 2) stipulates that the President "shall nominate, and by and with the Advice and Consent of the Senate, shall appoint Ambassadors, and other public Ministers and Consuls. . . ." Greater attention will be devoted to the Senate's prerogatives under this article in Chapter 5. At this point, it is sufficient to observe that, in contrast to the President's power to receive officials from abroad, the Senate must concur in the selection of diplomatic officials to represent the United States overseas or to serve in high diplomatic positions in Washington. Such positions as Secretary of State, Under Secretary of State, Assistant Secretary of State, ambassador, and minister must receive senatorial confirmation.

Yet, as with the Senate's prerogatives in the treaty process, forceful Presidents throughout American history have discovered various techniques of bypassing senatorial control. They may rely upon "personal representatives" who may or may not already hold governmental positions. The chief spokesman for American foreign policy during the Wilson administration was Colonel Edward M. House, who performed many diplomatic

---

*Severance of diplomatic relations does not of course always presage war—even less so today than in the past. It is, however, an indication of strain or tension in relations between nations, as when Egypt severed relations with the United States during the Middle East crisis of 1967 or when the United States during the 1960s severed relations for a brief period with nations governed by military juntas in Latin America. A less extreme form of such tension occurs when the United States "calls home" its ambassador from a country like the Soviet Union for "consultations" that may last several weeks or months, leaving the embassy in charge of a lesser official (a *chargé d'affaires*). An initial refusal to establish diplomatic relations, as in the case of the United States and Communist China, also of course signifies hostility between the countries concerned.

functions at home and abroad, with minimum liaison with the State Department. Franklin D. Roosevelt leaned heavily upon Harry Hopkins, so much so that ultimately Hopkins was referred to in the press as "Roosevelt's personal foreign office." In the early months of World War II, Hopkins played a decisive role in cementing closer Anglo–American relations, a process made possible in part by his prolonged residence at Prime Minister Churchill's home.[20] Then, too, Presidents may make "interim appointments" in the diplomatic field when the Senate is not in session. Even if the Senate ultimately refuses to confirm the individual so appointed, he may have already performed important duties, as was the case with Philip Jessup, President Truman's appointee to the American delegation to the United Nations in 1951.[21]

Vigorous claims have been asserted periodically throughout American history that the Senate's power of confirmation gives that body the right to determine the substance of American foreign policy by specifying the duties that appointees are to carry out. Occasionally, the Senate will rely upon its power to confirm appointments to express its displeasure at the general direction of American foreign policy.* In the main, however, after more than 150 years, the Senate's power to influence foreign policy decisively by scrutinizing presidential appointments remains peripheral. Determined and imaginative Presidents are seldom deterred from carrying out policies they believe to be in the national interest, even when they encounter opposition in the Senate.

If the recognition power must be counted among the influential techniques by which the President controls foreign policy, it may be asked, "What is the basis upon which a President normally decides to recognize another government?" In very general terms, the answer is when such recognition promotes the diplomatic interests of the United States, as the Chief Executive interprets them. Admittedly such an answer offers very little guidance for understanding presidential action or inaction. One factor which nearly always influences presidential decisions is *international law.* A leading authority has said this concerning the problem of recognition.

---

*Normally, the Senate raises no objection to the President's diplomatic appointments. An exception occurred under President Eisenhower, when he nominated Charles E. Bohlen as American Ambassador to the U.S.S.R. Bohlen was suspect in the eyes of many Republican senators because he was, in their view, "too soft" on Communism. Ultimately, under the leadership of Senator Robert A. Taft (Republican of Ohio), the Senate confirmed Bohlen's nomination; but Taft sent word to the White House that he did not want any more officials like Bohlen nominated! See Dwight D. Eisenhower, *Mandate for Change* (Garden City, N.Y.: Doubleday, 1963), pp. 212–213.

Actually the subject of recognition is one of the most difficult branches of international law, not merely from the point of view of exposition of principles, but also intrinsically by reason of the many difficult questions which continually arise in practice.

The concept of recognition in international law, he adds, "can be presented less as a collection of clearly defined rules or principles than as a body of fluid, inconsistent, and unsystematic State practice."[22]

It is neither possible nor necessary, in limited space, to enter into a discussion of the legal complexities involved in the matter of recognition of one state by another. Our purpose is served by observing that: (1) Certain criteria exist in international law which states must traditionally satisfy before they are entitled to recognition;* (2) even when nations invoke these criteria, considerable flexibility exists for them to interpret the extent to which particular states have met them; (3) some states give greater weight to certain criteria than to others in their recognition policy; and (4) as Stark notes, "there is an irresistible tendency in recognizing States to use legal principles as a convenient camouflage for political decisions."[23] While there exists an impressive corpus of international law dealing with recognition, in other words, nations are usually inclined to base their decisions in particular cases upon nonlegal or *political* considerations.

Such political considerations are apt to vary greatly from one case to another, making it very difficult to generalize about why America *has* recognized Communist states in Eastern Europe and *has not* recognized Red China; or why the United States *withdraws* recognition from a Latin American government after military groups seize power and *maintains recognition* of General Franco's regime in Spain; or why Washington *recognizes* one rival faction contending for power in the Congo and *does not recognize* other factions (some of which may be recognized by other nations); or why it recognized the government of Israel *within minutes* after its creation in 1947, but refused to recognize the government of Soviet Russia for some *sixteen years* after the Bolshevik Revolution. As the last category of cases suggests, the *timing* of recognition is often important; prompt recognition indicates, for example, that the United States is hopeful of harmonious relations with the government so recognized. Tardy recognition usually indicates some

---

*Major international law criteria are: that the government seeking recognition *must in fact govern,* without serious opposition to its rule; it must be reasonably stable and have a future beyond a few days or weeks; it must indicate its willingness to discharge its international obligations to other countries; and (if it applies for UN membership), it must theoretically be a "peace-loving nation."

question in the mind of American policy-makers about a government's political coloration or the likely course of its relations with the United States. Implicit in the power of the President to recognize other governments is the idea that the Chief Executive is *the sole channel of communication* between the United States and other nations. Theoretically, no contacts or negotiations with officials of another country may be carried on without the President's permission. This principle was embodied in the Logan Act, passed in 1799, prohibiting communications by private citizens with officials of other countries (in this case, France), without the President's authorization. In practice, no one has ever been prosecuted for violating the Logan Act. In the postwar period, its spirit (if not its letter) has been violated on numerous occasions—often by congressmen, who discuss foreign policy questions with officials of other nations during trips abroad.[24] During the Vietnam War in the late 1960s, several groups of Americans visited North Vietnam and discussed various aspects of the conflict in Southeast Asia with spokesmen for Ho Chi Minh's government. Occasionally, even the President himself authorizes a private citizen to carry out important negotiations, as when President Kennedy permitted private contacts with Castro's government in Cuba, following the "Bay of Pigs" episode.*

•HISTORICAL–TRADITIONAL TECHNIQUES OF PRESIDENTIAL LEADERSHIP

Let us look next at certain important techniques of presidential diplomatic leadership that are largely an outgrowth of history and tradition. Some of these techniques are not mentioned, except perhaps by indirection, in the Constitution. Yet many of them have become well-nigh permanent features of the American constitutional system.

The President's Control over Information

Wise decisions in foreign policy, as in any field, require the continuous collection and evaluation of information pertinent to the problems at hand. It follows, therefore, that executive leadership in foreign relations flows naturally from the ability of the executive branch to gather such information and, when national security demands it, to preserve its confidential character. Through the intelligence activities of the State Department, the Central Intelligence Agency, the military establishment, and other agencies, the President is in a

*The "Bay of Pigs" episode arose out of an attempt by anti-Castro Cuban refugees, aided by agencies of the American government, to overthrow the government of Cuba in the spring of 1961. It is discussed more fully in Chapter 12.

unique position to know more about external developments than any other individual or group within the government.

Very early in American history, Congress recognized the necessity to give the Chief Executive and his advisers wide discretionary powers to gather information and to keep it confidential. Alone among the executive departments, the Department of State has always been regarded by Congress as solely accountable to the President. This principle also governs legislative relations with the Central Intelligence Agency and the National Security Council. Other executive agencies may from time to time be *required* to furnish records and data for the guidance of Congress. In regard to the State Department and other agencies concerned with national security problems, however, Congress can only *request* the President to supply desired information when such a step is "not incompatible with the public interest."[25] The right—even the constitutional duty—of the Chief Executive to withhold confidential information bearing upon national security has been affirmed again and again throughout American history, not alone by the President but by the Supreme Court as well.

Any President has available to him the informational resources of what has come to be called the "intelligence community"—a group of cooperating intelligence agencies in the national government, including the Central Intelligence Agency (CIA), National Security Agency (NSA),† the Defense Intelligence Agency (which coordinates the intelligence operations of army, navy, and air force intelligence), the Bureau of Intelligence and Research in the Department of State, and the Federal Bureau of Investigation (FBI). From these principal sources, and under the supervision of the U.S. Intelligence Board,** a "National Intelli-

*The case of *United States ex. rel. Touhy* v. *Ragen*, 95 L. Ed. 417, illustrates the Supreme Court's historic viewpoints on the matter of executive secrecy. This case also contains a lengthy annotation on court decisions dealing with this issue.

Reviewing prevailing legal opinion on this matter, one authoritative study concludes that unauthorized citizens have "no enforceable legal right to inspect any federal non-judicial records." Its over-all finding is that "the opportunity of the people to know depends upon the favorable exercise of official grace or indulgence of 'discretion.' " Harold L. Cross, *The People's Right to Know* (New York: Columbia University Press, 1953), p. 197.

†NSA is among the newest, and most covert, intelligence agencies of the government; its principal responsibility is international communications, especially learning everything possible about the codes and ciphers of other countries. The U.S. Navy ship *Pueblo*, captured by North Korea early in 1968, was engaged in a mission for NSA. The ship was apparently collecting information on North Korean radar and communications systems.

**The U.S. Intelligence Board consists of representatives of the major agencies engaged in intelligence; its chairman is the Director of the CIA.

gence Estimate" is prepared for the guidance of the President and the National Security Council on significant developments abroad affecting American foreign policy. These and other intelligence reports are produced periodically or whenever some crisis abroad indicates the need for a new intelligence analysis.[26] In addition, a President has access to countless telegrams and longer reports coming into the State Department, the U.S. Information Agency, the Agency for International Development, and other executive departments, on events and conditions abroad having implications for American foreign policy. The result is that no other individual or group can rival the Chief Executive in his access to relevant information, much of which he is entitled to keep confidential if he feels its disclosure would prejudice national security.*

It should not be imagined that Presidents have always acquired the power to collect and preserve the confidential character of information in the face of legislative opposition. Congress itself has done much to strengthen the President's hand in this regard, by enacting severe penalties for disclosing classified information dealing with national security or for releasing without permission information collected by agencies like the CIA or the Department of Defense.[27] In most instances, legislators realize that release of such information to 100 senators and 435 representatives would be tantamount to releasing it to the world. Legislators are perhaps also restrained in attempting to contest the President's pre-eminent position in this regard by recalling an episode which occurred just before World War II. Informed by President Roosevelt and Secretary of State Cordell Hull that war was imminent in Europe, Senator William E. Borah (an avowed isolationist) replied: "I have sources in Europe that I regard as more reliable than those of the State Department." In this case, if not in all such cases, reliance upon Senator Borah's information could have been disastrous for the United States.[28]

A recurrent theme among critics of postwar American foreign policy consists of complaints about the "wall of secrecy" surrounding the operations of the executive branch. During the period of the Vietnam War, much the same idea was present in the accusation that a "credibility gap" characterized the Johnson administration's poli-

cies in Southeast Asia. News media discovered a considerable discrepancy between what the Johnson administration *said* it was doing in Southeast Asia and what it was *in fact* doing. Newsmen periodically lamented that "management of the news" by officials of the American government kept them from learning the facts and from reporting them to the American people.

While Presidents throughout recent history have been confronted with this charge—President Kennedy, for example, was viewed by some reporters as an expert in the art of "news management"[29]—more than any other twentieth-century occupant of the White House, President Johnson was criticized for his attempts to conceal, control, and manipulate information. Ironically, President Johnson sometimes devoted more time to talking with newsmen (usually in small informal groups) than his predecessors; yet to the end of his term, he faced the accusation that a credibility gap existed in the conduct of his administration at home and abroad.

For a nation with major international responsibilities and commitments, few problems are more difficult than striking and maintaining a satisfactory balance between the two opposing tendencies inherent in the problem of "news management." Two fundamental principles—each perfectly defensible and legitimate in its own right—are perpetually in conflict. One is the public's right to know what its chosen leaders are doing, to be kept informed of the policies and behavior of its own government—particularly with regard to steps entailing the risk of nuclear devastation. The Wilsonian principle of "open covenants, openly arrived at" has become deeply embedded in the fabric of American democracy; an even earlier and perhaps more sacrosanct principle is the concept of "freedom of the press," guaranteed in Amendment I of the Constitution. Government operations surrounded by secrecy are widely viewed as the hallmarks of a totalitarian regime.

The other principle, however, is no less important and relevant for a nation exercising global leadership. This is that a premature disclosure of information might jeopardize national security, by alerting the nation's enemies to impending developments, by compromising strategies and programs that depend upon surprise for their success, and by giving an opponent time to evolve effective counter-strategies. Few Americans, for example, would contest the right of a President to withhold information dealing with military strategy. As in General Douglas MacArthur's brilliant amphibious landing at Inchon during the Korean War, surprise can be a vital ingredient in success.

On a more restricted basis perhaps, the same principle can be applied to the diplomatic sphere. More than ever before, military and diplomatic

---

*From time to time, the President or his subordinates are requested by Congress to release information bearing upon national policy. During a controversial Senate investigation of the army in 1954 instigated by Senator Joseph McCarthy (Republican of Wisconsin), for example, President Eisenhower instructed Secretary of Defense Charles E. Wilson to refuse McCarthy's demands for executive records. The student is urged to read the letter from the President to Mr. Wilson of May 17, 1954, on this matter. The letter is reproduced in Dwight D. Eisenhower, *Mandate for Change* (Garden City, N.Y.: Doubleday, 1963) pp. 597–598.

moves must be *carefully coordinated* to achieve national objectives. Surprise may affect the outcome of diplomatic, fully as much as military, undertakings. A classic case is provided by the Kennedy administration's diplomacy during the Cuban missile crisis of 1962. President Kennedy's response to the efforts of Havana and Moscow to implant Soviet missiles in Cuba has been widely cited as a case study in smoothly coordinated and successful national policy. From the time the administration initially discovered the presence of enemy missiles in Cuba, however, until President Kennedy disclosed this fact, along with his decisions for dealing with it, to the American people on October 22, 1962, *the utmost secrecy surrounded the government's consideration of this problem.* Not only were extraordinary steps taken to prevent "leaks" to newsmen; none but a handful of the President's closest advisers was aware of the threat and of President Kennedy's planned response to it. Very few members of the State Department were cognizant that the United States was in the midst of one of the most dangerous confrontations in its history, in which the risk of nuclear war was extremely high.

The success of the Kennedy administration's diplomacy in bringing about the removal of Soviet missiles from Cuba was heavily dependent upon keeping Havana and Moscow in ignorance of the facts that Washington knew the missiles were there and that it was prepared to employ force, if necessary, to secure their removal from the hemisphere. If the Cuban missile crisis emerged as a victory for American policy-makers—particularly in brightening the nation's image as a country that used its power wisely and cautiously, but decisively—part of the explanation lay in the ability of the President and his advisers to catch Communist officials off guard, to expose their provocative activities before world opinion, and to present them with a series of American moves to which they had no predetermined response.

The conflict between these two contrary principles, it may safely be predicted, will continue. Incumbent Presidents will be criticized for inhibiting freedom of the press and for concealing their policies behind a "wall of secrecy." For their part, Presidents and their advisers—charged constitutionally with the preservation of national security—may also be expected to resort to news suppression and distortion whenever they think the welfare of the nation demands it. As always, compromise is likely to leave many advocates of each principle unreconciled.

The President and Public Opinion

"The biggest problem facing any President," former President Truman once declared, "is to sell the American people on a policy. They have to be led forward.... That's the biggest challenge every President faces, and one which he cannot escape." In the same vein, early in 1919, President Wilson stated at the Paris Peace Conference: ". . . we are not representatives of governments, but representatives of people. It will not suffice to satisfy governmental circles anywhere. It is necessary that we should satisfy the opinion of mankind."[30]

Among the techniques available to the Chief Executive for controlling foreign relations, in the contemporary period none perhaps surpasses his role in influencing, shaping, and leading public opinion. As with the President's power to utilize the armed forces, modern technology has greatly strengthened executive power vis-à-vis legislative power, or competition from private individuals and groups, in this respect. The President of the United States is the most "newsworthy" individual in the nation, if not in the world. Hardly a radio or television news program is presented which lacks some reference to the President's viewpoints or activities. When he wishes to address the nation, the President can preempt radio and TV time, at a period of his own selection, to present his views to the American people; when he travels within the United States or outside it, he is invariably accompanied by reporters and commentators representing all the major news media. With "live" TV coverage, the President's words—together with his expression and tone of voice in speaking them—can be communicated almost instantaneously throughout the world, where they are analyzed carefully by officials in nearly every government. A President's power over public opinion—together with another technique of presidential leadership we shall discuss presently, his power *to commit the nation* to a given course of action—gives the Chief Executive a formidable advantage over those seeking to contest his leadership.

A President possesses numerous methods for influencing public opinion. President Franklin D. Roosevelt, for example, utilized his highly effective speech-making ability: His radio "fireside chats" with the American people were employed repeatedly, and with telling effect, to rally public support behind his policies.[31] FDR also held press conferences, but these were often designed to keep the President informed about conditions in the government and the nation as much as they were to inform the American people. President Truman relied upon his numerous appointments —often as many as 95 weekly—to familiarize himself with public thinking. Beginning with FDR, Presidents have been routinely kept informed of the trend of opinion in mail received by the White House; occasionally, they read and answer some of the thousands of letters received weekly. Truman, Eisenhower, and other postwar Presidents have also from time to time sent their agents on trips to "take the pulse" of the public and report their findings. Conversations with legislators, together with reports submitted by executive officials who regularly deal with senators and representatives, also provide the President with viewpoints outside the circle of his immediate advisers. The Bureau of Public Affairs in the Department of State regularly prepares studies of public opinion, as expressed in newspapers, magazines and other publications; in the results of public opinion polls; in the resolutions passed by various organizations within the United States; and in mail received by the State Department.[32] President John F. Kennedy excelled in keeping the presidency at the forefront of national consciousness. One technique he utilized heavily was granting exclusive interviews to reporters and writers, who were free to quote his views, but not to attribute them directly to him. President Kennedy was also criticized (often by members of the press themselves) for practicing "social flattery," by bringing small groups of editors to the White House for intimate dicussions.[33]

Early in 1969, President Richard Nixon toured Europe. As always, his trip was massively covered (even before he left the United States) by the news media, which frequently interrupted their regular programs to present highlights of the President's visit. Described by the White House primarily as an opportunity for the new President to gain a better understanding of Europe's views, Nixon's tour was no less important in affording the President a chance *to influence European opinion favorably*, especially at a time when America's image was badly tarnished because of the Vietnam War. President Nixon often took occasion to greet the crowds along his route, to talk with representatives of various political parties and citizen groups, and generally to impress European opinion favorably.

President Nixon's trip to Europe underlined a point made earlier in this chapter. The Chief Executive is an *international*, as well as a national, *leader.* He seeks to influence, and is influenced by, opinion in other countries. As the strongest member of a far-flung alliance system, the United States cannot afford to be indifferent to currents of public thinking which affect the alliance collectively or the welfare of nations within it. Accordingly, Presidents in recent years have been compelled to give more attention than ever to viewpoints prevailing overseas.[34]

Our discussion emphasizes two aspects of the President's relationship to public opinion which are discussed more fully in Chapter 7: the role of public opinion in influencing national policy, and the unequalled position of the President in influencing public opinion. As our later discussion will show, these two processes impinge heavily upon each other. If a President is clearly limited by what public opinion will accept or support, it is no less true that resourceful Presidents can, and do, generate public support for policies they be-

lieve to be in the national interest. And in the cultivation of a favorable environment of public opinion, the President has an advantage which none of his rivals can match.*

The President as Legislative Leader

According to the principle of separation of powers, the President should not have anything to do with legislation. It is doubtful that even the Founding Fathers believed in rigid adherence to this principle, and it certainly has never been strictly observed in American governmental practice. In many ways, the President is the foremost legislator in the government.

Today, three-fourths or more of all bills enacted by Congress originate in the executive branch of the government. A former assistant to President Johnson has said (paraphrasing the President's own words) ". . . no person in his respective department could ever be any more important than the head of the congressional relations activity." In the view of this White House assistant, "Nothing has a greater priority in the President's view than the legislative program. . . ."[35] In the Kennedy administration, some 40 officials in the executive branch dealt with what was called "legislative liaison."[36]

Nearly all of the great legislative enactments affecting American foreign relations in the postwar period—the Greek-Turkish Aid Program, the Marshall Plan, the China Aid Bill, the Point Four Program and the various programs of foreign assistance (like the Alliance for Progress) which followed it, the provision of military assistance to other nations, the support of American military involvement in the Korean and Vietnam Wars, agreements with other countries for reciprocal tariff reductions, and America's cultural and informational programs—have had their origin in the executive branch. And after their initiation, executive officials have, at critical junctures, pressed for their adoption by Congress. Conversely, executive officials engaged in "legislative liaison"

---

*The experience of President Johnson—who was compelled to give up his plans for re-election because of adverse opinion concerning the war in Vietnam—might be cited in contradiction to the above assertion. Widely regarded as a master of "news manipulation," President Johnson perhaps faced the most hostile exhibition of public discontent witnessed by any Chief Executive in recent history. Indeed, the experience of the Johnson administration might indicate the existence of a point of diminishing returns in any President's attempt to control news output. Two points can be made, however, about this example. First, the phenomenon may be accounted for in part because President Johnson and his principal advisers were *not overly skillful* in using the resources available to them for influencing public opinion. Second, public disaffection about the Vietnam War may have been so deep among some segments of public opinion as to be *largely impervious* to efforts made by the administration to change it.

have sought to *prevent* congressional enactment of bills deemed by the White House to be inimical to America's interests abroad, such as efforts to cut off aid to Yugoslavia, or to prohibit assistance to any nation trading with North Vietnam, or to place barriers in the way of the President's use of armed forces abroad. When such restrictions upon executive policy-making could not be prevented, they could be (and often were) largely vitiated by inclusion of a provision permitting the President to waive the restriction when he believed circumstances warranted such action.

The scope of present-day global commitments of the United States has drawn Congress more than ever into the foreign policy process. But it has also drawn the executive as never before into the *legislative* process, requiring it as in other spheres of foreign policy, to provide the direction and initiative needed for framing legislation bearing upon external affairs. In fact, the *legislative record* of an administration may well be viewed by the electorate as the standard by which its success is judged.

The President as a Political Leader

Adequate discussion of the political role of the President would require a volume. The most we can do here is take for granted his pre-eminent political position and suggest some of the consequences of this position for foreign affairs. Historically, one of the President's most effective means for influencing the actions of legislators has been the patronage he has had to distribute to the party faithful, in the form of appointments to the federal service. No President in recent history has surpassed FDR in the skillful way he utilized this weapon.[37] Since the New Deal, the importance of patronage has declined, because more jobs have been placed under civil service regulations.

In addition, the President plays an influential role in national elections. Every national candidate who is a member of the President's party desires to have his "endorsement" in a political campaign. The regularity with which candidates seek to "ride the President's coattails" is a well-known phenomenon in American political history, as illustrated by President Eisenhower's success in carrying a number of Republican candidates into office with him by his victories in 1952 and 1956.

Members of Congress do not follow a party line slavishly in their legislative actions. Still, they prefer, when possible, to work in close harmony with their party leaders, because such a course pays tangible political benefits. The party in power tries to establish a record which will generate wide voter appeal. Such a record can be created only if the party, led by the President, works in close harmony to produce it.

Power to Commit the Nation

Following the disastrous Bay of Pigs invasion of Cuba in 1961, President Kennedy observed that he had listened fully to the advice of his advisers in this instance—and that the advice he received had been wrong. Nevertheless, as President, he alone assumed full responsibility for this ill-fated undertaking.[38] This event thus illustrated a power that has more and more come to be exercised decisively by the Chief Executive in his response to rapidly changing circumstances abroad: the ability *to commit the nation* to a specified course of action which Congress or other agencies of government are all but powerless to change. Virtually every major undertaking in foreign affairs at some stage requires legislative support, thereby giving Congress an influence in foreign relations today transcending its influence in earlier eras. Yet the power of the President to commit the nation to particular policies and diplomatic moves can, at least in the short run, largely negate Congress' newly found power in the foreign policy field.

Postwar diplomatic experience is replete with examples. Take the Greek–Turkish Aid Program of 1947. After President Truman announced dramatically on March 12 that "it must be the policy of the United States to support free people who are resisting subjection by armed minorities or outside pressures, . . ." what choice did Congress have but to agree and subsequently to vote the funds required to translate these words into effective policy for saving Greece from Communist domination? The answer was provided by a *St. Louis Post Dispatch* editorial on the President's speech: "Congress may ponder and debate but the President's address has committed the nation to all-out diplomatic action just as a declaration of a shooting war must necessarily follow when the President asks for it."[39]

Yet the most forceful example of presidential initiative in making national commitments binding upon the United States is provided by the Vietnam War. From the time President Kennedy, early in his administration, began to send American forces to participate directly in this conflict, until cease-fire negotiations (again, undertaken solely by presidential directive) were begun in 1969, a series of national commitments in Southeast Asia followed. During the mid-1960s, the Vietnam contest had largely become "an American war," although in time the government of South Vietnam gradually assumed a larger reponsibility for national security.* It is true that on August 10, 1964, the Gulf of Tonkin Resolution was approved, authorizing President Johnson to "take all necessary measures to repel any armed attack against the forces of the United States and to pre-

---

*The Vietnam War, as a problem in recent American foreign policy, is discussed at length in Chapter 13.

vent further aggression" in Southeast Asia.* Yet it should also be noted that a substantial American troop buildup had occurred in Vietnam *before* Congress approved this resolution; that President Johnson, as well as Presidents before him, took the position that he did not *need* such legislative authorization before making commitments overseas involving the use of military force; and that, even though considerable sentiment later existed in Congress against American involvement in the Vietnam crisis, no concerted move was taken to repeal the resolution or to repudiate the President's public commitments. It was especially significant that, as Congress debated the President's military budget each year thereafter, the tendency invariably was for the legislative branch to provide the funds required to support commitments in Southeast Asia made by the White House.

Judging from the experience in Vietnam, the President's power to commit the nation to a specified course of action had clearly emerged as one of the most influential techniques available to the White House for controlling (critics would say, dominating) the foreign policy process. Whatever their own assessment of White House policies in Vietnam and other settings, legislators were often extremely loath to disavow presidential commitments, if for no other reason than that they did not want to be held accountable politically for the consequences! By the end of the 1960s, even members of Congress realized that Presidents could present them with a *fait accompli* which was very difficult to change. Thus, influential legislators supported moves seeking to prevent such commitments by the executive branch, without the participation of Congress. The Senate Majority Leader, Senator Mike Mansfield (Democrat of Montana) declared in mid-1967 that the President should make no commitment in the latest crisis in the Middle East without consulting Congress.[40] Senator J. William Fulbright (Democrat of Arkansas), chairman of the Foreign Relations Committee, went even further: He urged Congress to pass a resolution inhibiting the President from making *any* commitment overseas without the approval of Congress. Senator Fulbright was convinced that for some twenty-five years, the executive branch "has indeed acted and then sought to justify its intervention by dubious references to equally dubious prior commitments."[41] Late in 1967, the Senate Foreign Relations Committee itself approved a resolution requiring "affirmative action by Congress" before the President committed American forces abroad, except to repel an attack upon the United States

or to protect American citizens or property overseas.[42] Although in no way binding upon the executive branch, this resolution signified recognition by an influential legislative committee that once the President had made a commitment abroad, there was little Congress could do to alter that fact.*

In spite of such legislative uneasiness, it can be predicted with reasonable assurance that in the future, few Presidents will be deterred from using their power to commit the nation overseas, whenever they believe the security and diplomatic interests of the United States demand it.

THE PRESIDENT'S EMERGENCY POWERS

Immediately after the Civil War, the Supreme Court declared that "the government, within the Constitution, has all the powers granted to it which are necessary to preserve its existence. . . ."† This doctrine has been repeatedly affirmed, as in 1934 when the Court held that "the war power of the Federal Government . . . *is a power to wage war successfully.* . . ."** From the Civil War onward, national crises have called for the exercise of sweeping governmental powers, powers which many students have thought were unknown to the original Constitution. The point of principal concern to us is that exercise of these powers has entailed a vast expansion in executive authority to deal with national crises.

The emergency powers of the President derive primarily from two constitutional sources: his designation as Commander-in-Chief (Art. II, Sec. 2); and his obligation to "take care that the laws be faithfully executed" (Art. II, Sec. 3). Together these two clauses constitute the so-called "war powers" of the executive. Besides this constitutional source, Congress within the last half-century has added to the President's power to deal with national emergencies. Relying both upon his authority as Commander-in-Chief and legislative authority given him for coping with emergency conditions, Franklin D. Roosevelt created numerous new governmental agencies during World War II and made them responsible solely to himself, often bypassing established executive departments. In an executive order issued on February

---

*See H. J. Res. 1145, adopted unanimously by the House and by a vote of 88 to 2 by the Senate, as reproduced in Council on Foreign Relations, *Documents on American Foreign Relations: 1964* (New York: Harper & Row, 1965), pp. 216–217.

*This attempt by the Senate Foreign Relations Committee to curtail executive power, it ought to be observed, left major loopholes for executive initiative. For example, both the American military intervention in Lebanon in 1957 under President Eisenhower, and the intervention in the Dominican Republic in 1965 under President Johnson, were undertaken for the ostensible purpose of protecting American lives and property (although it is doubtful that this was in fact their real goal).

†*Ex parte Milligan*, 4 Wallace 2 (1886).

***Home Building and Loan Association* v. *Blaisdell*, 290 U.S. 398 (1934). Italics inserted.

19, 1942, Roosevelt directed his military commanders to bar American citizens of Japanese ancestry from occupying designated areas on the West coast; this order was subsequently incorporated into an act of Congress.[43] When President Truman, on December 16, 1950, proclaimed "the existence of a national emergency," according to the noted constitutional commentator Edward S. Corwin, he activated over sixty statutes or portions of statutes that become applicable during periods characterized as "a condition of emergency" or "in time of war or national emergency." In most cases, the President determines when such conditions prevail. His determination will, in turn, greatly enlarge his own powers, in part by removing limitations existing upon them during normal times.[44]

Lincoln was the first President to claim broad executive powers for dealing with a national crisis. During the spring and summer of 1861, Lincoln took many steps which, up to that time, had been thought to lie largely or exclusively within the domain of Congress. He ordered a blockade of southern ports in the absence of a "declaration of war" and directed that ships violating the blockade be confiscated. He increased the size of the army and navy; called out the militia; closed the post office to treasonable correspondence; expended funds from the treasury without legislative authorization; and suspended the writ of habeas corpus. During the course of the Civil War, Lincoln also freed the slaves on his own authority and drew up plans for the "reconstruction" of the South that contemplated little, if any, active participation by Congress. Collectively, these actions asserted "for the President, for the first time in our history, an initiative of indefinite scope in meeting the domestic aspects of a war emergency."[45]

Lincoln's dynamic conception of presidential emergency power has become firmly incorporated into the nation's constitutional fabric. Speaking for the Supreme Court in the Neagle case,* Justice Miller in 1890 asked whether the President was limited "to the enforcement of acts of Congress or of treaties of the United States according to their *express terms.* . . ." He answered in the negative, holding that in the discharge of his constitutional obligation to take care that the laws be faithfully executed, the President also was required to include "the rights, duties and obligations growing out of the Constitution itself, our international relations, and all the protection implied by the nature of the government under the Constitution." In the spirit of this idea, President Wilson armed American merchant shipping, in spite of the fact that Congress refused to pass a law giving him such authority.[46] The power of Presidents to take such steps was justified by Solicitor

General John W. Davis in 1914 by his assertion that "in ways short of making laws or disobeying them, the Executive may be under a grave constitutional duty to act for the national protection in situations not covered by the acts of Congress, and in which, even, it may not be said that his action is the direct expression of any particular one of the independent powers which are granted to him specifically by the Constitution."[47]

What then are the limitations upon the emergency powers of the President? One stems from the limitations imposed upon President Truman by the Supreme Court in the steel seizure case,* in which the Court was reiterating long-standing precedent: When Congress has specified the means by which the President is to cope with emergencies, then the President is obligated to follow the procedure prescribed by law. Moreover, the President cannot take action that is plainly denied him by constitutional prohibitions, although admittedly Presidents in recent years have sometimes taken an extremely elastic view of constitutional provisions designed to keep governmental power within clearly defined channels.†

We may conclude our discussion of the President's role in foreign relations by asking what effective checks or limitations exist with respect to executive power in this field. The weight of our discussion thus far is that *in the short term,* very few such limitations exist. It is extraordinarily difficult for Congress, or interested citizen groups, to prevent a President from taking those steps he is convinced are essential for national security or needed to achieve some major diplomatic goal. Over *the long term,* flagrant abuse of executive authority could still subject a President to impeachment, to political defeat, to a refusal by Congress to provide funds for his programs, and to other forms of restraint. When crises arise abroad, however—and these appear to have increased appreciably in the contemporary era—such restrictions are seldom operative. In a crisis-ridden world, the President's own conscience, his adherence to the values of American society, and his attachment to constitutional principles; his desire to create and maintain some kind of national consensus behind his policies; his preoccupation with his own "place in history"; his necessity to preserve maximum rapport with NATO and the other alliance systems within which the United States is the leading member—these are likely to prove the most effective barriers to unilateral and whimsical presidential leadership.

*135 U.S. 1 (1890).

Youngstown Company v. *Sawyer,* 343 U.S. 579 (1952).
†See, for example, the case of *Korematsu* v. *United States,* 323 U.S. 214 (1944), in which the Supreme Court dealt with President Roosevelt's treatment of Japanese-Americans, many of whom were citizens, during World War II.

Presidential Advisers and Foreign Affairs

The expansion of the powers and activities of the federal government since the New Deal is symbolized by the emergence of the presidency as the center of leadership in national decision-making. This tendency in turn has been mirrored by the growth in size and influence of *the White House staff* in all spheres of policy-making—so much so in recent years as to elicit complaints among established executive departments that the President's advisers were usurping their functions. During the early 1960s, for example, the lament was frequently heard in Washington that "Bundy's State Department" had become the real locus of effective decision-making on foreign policy issues.*

As we have already observed, the Chief Executive's dependence upon his own intimate advisers to assist him in reaching decisions is no new phenomenon. Throughout the postwar period, Presidents have used White House advisers, as well as their friends and confidences outside the government, to aid them in reaching important decisions affecting national security and foreign policy. Few individuals have been more influential in this regard than Clark Clifford, a prominent Washington attorney who has served as an official and unofficial adviser to several Presidents. In the Truman administration, Clifford played a key role in the President's decision to "recognize" the new state of Israel in May, 1948, in the face of strong State Department objections. Earlier, Clifford also was in large part responsible for President Truman's adoption of the "containment" strategy for dealing with Communist expansionism; Clifford urged the President to conceive of containment primarily in *military terms.*† Curiously enough, several years later, as an adviser to President John-

son, it was Clifford who successfully counseled the President to de-escalate the level of military involvement in the Vietnam War and to strive for a *political* solution of that frustrating conflict.

Although he was the most "staff-oriented" President in recent experience, Eisenhower reposed great confidence in his Secretary of State, John Foster Dulles; Dulles tolerated little interference by White House aides in his capacity as principal foreign policy adviser. This situation changed abruptly under President John F. Kennedy. During his administration, the White House staff consistently exercised more influence upon the policy-making process than it had under any other recent American President. Kennedy was intensely interested in foreign affairs; after the disastrous "Bay of Pigs" episode in 1961, he became disillusioned with the "experts" in the State and Defense Departments and in the CIA; increasingly, he turned to his personal aides and confidants for advice in policy-making. Presidential assistants like Theodore Sorensen (Kennedy's chief speech writer) and McGeorge Bundy (his aide in charge of national security and foreign policy issues) were sometimes even more influential than members of the Cabinet in resolving policy questions. Kennedy's aversion to the State Department was well known; more than once, high-ranking State Department officials complained about "interference" in their responsibilities by White House aides. Relations with Latin America were a case in point. One of Kennedy's chief assistants, Richard Goodwin, was instrumental in coining the term "Alliance for Progress"; Goodwin was convinced (again with little evident enthusiasm in the State Department) that radical changes were needed in relations between the United States and Latin America. Owing in large part to his influence, President Kennedy committed the United States to this new program.

Although President Johnson enlarged the size of the White House staff (he had ten or so "special assistants," each of whom had a small staff), the influence of the State and Defense Departments in decision-making revived during his administration. Secretary of State Dean Rusk and Secretary of Defense Robert McNamara became his administration's principal foreign policy advisers and spokesmen. Despite (or, to some extent perhaps, because of) public disenchantment with Rusk's performance, the President continued to depend heavily upon him for advice in dealing with external problems; the President's White House aides concentrated their attention primarily upon domestic policy issues. After President Richard M. Nixon took office in 1968, the role of White House assistants in decision-making once again was enhanced. The new Secretary of State, William P. Rogers, was relatively inexperienced in diplomacy. By contrast, Nixon's chief aide for national security and foreign policy questions, Dr.

---

*McGeorge Bundy was President John F. Kennedy's chief White House aide for national security and foreign policy questions. Bundy and other top advisers were assigned to the White House Office, which was one of several agencies (along with the Council of Economic Advisers, the National Security Council, the Central Intelligence Agency, and a number of others) comprising the Executive Office of the President.

†For more detailed discussions of Clark Clifford's role in the foreign policies of successive administrations in Washington, see Patrick Anderson, *The President's Men* (Garden City, N.Y.: Doubleday, 1969), pp. 134–159. Former Secretary of State Dean Acheson has corroborated Clifford's influence upon such undertakings as the Truman Doctrine and the Point Four Program. See his *Present at the Creation* (New York: Norton, 1969), pp. 22, 254, 265, 717. Although he does not identify him specifically, it was presumably Clifford who converted George Kennan's initially *limited* program of aid to Greece in 1947 into the sweeping Truman Doctrine, which depended upon a *global program* of military aid for deterring Communist expansionism. See George F. Kennan, *Memoirs (1925–1950)* (New York: Bantam, 1967), pp. 330–341. Yet for frequent allusions to Clifford's role in de-escalating the Vietnam conflict, see Townsend Hoopes, *The Limits of Intervention* (New York: McKay, 1969), *passim.*

Henry Kissinger, was a recognized authority on international relations. Highly intelligent, well-informed, and forceful, Kissinger presented his ideas capably and persuasively; within a few months, he had become in some respects the most influential member of President Nixon's team with regard to defense and foreign policy. Although there was no evidence that President Nixon had "abandoned" the State and Defense Departments as major sources for advice, Kissinger's role in decision-making was obviously noteworthy. He was known, for example, to have played a prominent part in President Nixon's decision to send American troops into Cambodia in the spring of 1970.

The enhanced influence of the White House staff in the foreign policy process undeniably has certain advantages. Greater reliance upon his personal advisers inside and outside the government provides a Chief Executive with another source of ideas, thereby reducing his "dependence" upon established (and often parochial) executive departments. President Kennedy especially believed that his White Houses aides served as a reservoir of *new and creative ideas*, which furnished a needed antidote to the kind of stale, ponderous, and bureaucratically rigid deliberations characteristic of the State Department. Kennedy and other postwar Presidents have looked to their assistants to present them with a full range of policy options and to provide them with careful evaluations of proposals submitted by established governmental agencies. Too often, perhaps, the State or Defense Departments have failed to consider such dimensions of a policy as its domestic political implications or the reaction of public opinion—aspects toward which no President can afford to be totally indifferent.

Yet the growing role of the White House staff in decision-making has certain more or less obvious drawbacks. It can, and sometimes has, made the foreign policy process unduly complex; it introduces another "layer" of officialdom between the President and the operating departments of the government; it perhaps inevitably encourages divisiveness and competition among White House aides, on the one hand, and Cabinet officers and their subordinates, on the other, for "the ear" of the President; it impairs the morale (and possibly the performance) of the State Department— thereby *perpetuating* many of the problems within that agency about which Presidents have complained in recent years; it makes it more difficult than ever to *coordinate* policy-making within the executive branch and to achieve *unified* decisions; and, for the citizen, it compounds the already difficult problem of determining precisely who is *responsible* for key foreign policy decisions. Yet, after all of these drawbacks have been listed, it may be safely predicted that presidential reliance upon the White House Staff has become

a permanent feature of the policy-making process within the United States.*

THE DEPARTMENT OF STATE: ITS FUNCTION AND ORGANIZATION

A few days after he assumed office, President Richard Nixon stated that his new Secretary of State, William P. Rogers, had been designated the President's "principal foreign policy adviser"; Secretary Rogers had been given "clear authority" by the President in overseeing the operations of all governmental agencies abroad. By 1969, this number included some 30,000 non-State Department officials, assigned to 118 American embassies overseas. In the same period, in announcing a reorganization in the responsibilities of the National Security Council,† President Nixon asserted that the Department of State would play a "central and dynamic" role in this agency's deliberations.[48]

These developments directed attention to several problems we shall analyze in the remainder of this chapter and in the following one. One of these is the role of the State Department in the foreign policy process—a role that has evinced a number of interesting amd significant tendencies in recent years. Another is the proliferation of governmental agencies concerned with foreign relations and the extent to which the coordination of their diverse activities and interests presents a continuing challenge. Still another is the relationship between national security policy and foreign policy, which entails integrating two closely related governmental activities successfully. Let us examine initially the place of the State Department in the foreign policy process.

The Challenge of New Obligations

In 1924, Congress passed the Rogers Act, which for the first time established the Foreign Service as a "professional" corps of diplomatic officials ap-

*Our discussion of the role of the White House staff in formulating national security and foreign policy relies heavily upon the informative treatment by Patrick Anderson, *The President's Men* (Garden City, N.Y.: Doubleday, 1969). Clark Clifford's influential role in the Truman administration is discussed on pp. 134–159; President Kennedy's heavy reliance upon White House aides is analyzed on pp. 233–360. For a more scholarly account of the role of the White House staff in national security policy, see Keith C. Clark and Laurence J. Legere, eds., *The President and the Management of National Security* (New York: Praeger, 1969), pp. 55–115. President Nixon's reliance upon White House aide Dr. Henry Kissinger is highlighted in the discussion of his decision to invade Cambodia in *Newsweek* **LXXV** (May 25, 1970), 29–32.

†The National Security Council, created in 1947, is the highest committee in the national government for dealing with problems of defense and security policy. It is discussed more fully in Chapter 4.

pointed on the basis of merit, rather than political influence or other criteria. An experienced Foreign Service officer has referred to life in the State Department during the 1920s, when messengers delivered communications within the State Department "at unhurried intervals." In that period:

The coding apparatus belonged to another era; correspondence moved at the speed of molasses; nobody bothered to put the papers away or lock the safe at lunchtime; security-consciousness was nonexistent. Critics were to say that in 1914 the Department was about ready to cope with the Spanish–American War; that in 1939 it was prepared for World War I.[49]

To carry the figure further, we might add that by 1970 critics might concede that the State Department was prepared for the responsibilities of World War II!

It is instructive to contrast the changes in the Department of State and the Foreign Service during the half-century following enactment of the Rogers Act. Although still one of the smallest among the executive departments (only the Labor Department was smaller), by the 1960s the State Department had close to 25,000 employees at home and abroad; 278 diplomatic outposts overseas reported to the department; its budget approached $.5 billion annually; its top echelon consisted of a Secretary of State, two Under Secretaries, and 16 Assistant Secretaries; some 3750 career Foreign Service officers manned its diplomatic posts abroad, with three-fourths of America's ambassadors being chosen from the Foreign Service; and the volume of messages flowing into, and out of, the State Department totaled some 3000 cablegrams daily, or around 20 million words a month during the late 1960s. Besides its own responsibilities, the Department of State was required, as we have suggested, to oversee and coordinate the activities of a growing number of other governmental agencies whose involvement in foreign affairs had mushroomed during the postwar era.* Some 44 agencies of the American government, for example, had representatives in the London embassy! Among 700 civilians assigned to New Delhi, India, by the United States in 1964, only 100 of these were assigned to the State Department.[50]

As long as isolationism remained the keynote of America's foreign relations, State Department duties consisted chiefly of routine consular business, furnishing information about and promoting foreign trade, protecting American lives and property in other countries, and performing ceremonial functions. Since World War II, the United States has become actively involved in an expanding range of global activities; the organizational structure of the State Department, together with the attendant involvement of numerous other executive agencies in foreign affairs, reflects the nation's new role. During the 1930s, for instance, national defense and foreign policy took approximately 35–40 percent of the federal budget; today, they take 75–80 percent. Along with a quantitative increase in State Department business has gone a fundamental change in its *character*. A noteworthy trend since World War II has been the extent to which the economic, social, cultural, and informational aspects of foreign policy have assumed unprecedented importance. Judged by the number of employees involved in these activities, they appear in some instances to eclipse the *political* aspects of America's relations with the outside world.

Basic Organizational Structure

In common with other executive departments, since World War II the State Department has experienced a great proliferation among its internal units. The Hoover Commission in 1948 found that the department contained 94 separate units, with 25 officials reporting directly to the Secretary of State. After thorough study, a basic reorganization plan was proposed which, if it did not cut down drastically on the size of the department, at least brought some semblance of order out of the administrative jungle previously prevailing.[51]

The basic organizational pattern of the State Department conforms to the same hierarchial structure typical of most governmental agencies. The Secretary of State—considered the "ranking" member of the President's Cabinet—is of course in charge of the department; and by presidential directive, as we observed earlier, he is technically in charge of the entire span of America's relations with other countries, under the authority of the President. Directly below the Secretary of State are two Under Secretaries (whose responsibilities are sometimes divided between political and economic affairs) and two Deputy Under Secretaries (one for political affairs and the other for administration). Below these officials are some 16 Assistant Secretaries, who are in charge of the principal bureaus of the State Department.

The organizational pattern of the Department

---

*Although they possess considerable operating autonomy, it should be noted that agencies like the U.S. Information Agency (USIA), the Agency for International Development (AID), the Peace Corps, and the Arms Control and Disarmament Agency are engaged in functions bearing directly upon American foreign policy. For policy directives, these agencies are responsible to the State Department.

*Easy as it is to "assign" such responsibilities to the Secretary of State, it has sometimes proved very difficult in practice to enforce the assignment, as we shall see. Meanwhile, we may point out that technically all speeches by governmental officials dealing with foreign policy must be "cleared" with the State Department; the State Department alone negotiates with other governments; and as head of the American "country team," the American ambassador in another country reports to the Department of State.

of State is an outgrowth of two somewhat contradictory organizational principles. Traditionally, and perhaps even today, the dominant organizational concept has been *geographic;* by many criteria, the core of the State Department consists of the five geographic bureaus—Europe, Inter-American affairs, Africa, the Far East, and Near Eastern–South Asian affairs—plus the Bureau of International Organization Affairs, which deals with the United Nations. Within each bureau, a "country desk" staffed by one or more officers is responsible for American relations with each nation within the region. The "chain of command" for a country like Brazil, for example, extends upward from the American embassy and consulates within Brazil, to the "Brazilian desk" in the Bureau of Inter-American Affairs; important policy questions are referred upward to the Assistant Secretary of State for Inter-American Affairs, to an Under Secretary (or a Deputy Under Secretary), to the Secretary of State himself, and possibly to the White House. Normally, policy directives move in reverse order, ultimately reaching American diplomatic and consular installations in the field. In general, a high level of expertise is available to the State Department among the officers assigned to the country desks, many of whom are Foreign Service officers who have had first-hand experience in the countries for which they are responsible.

Superimposed upon the traditional geographical organizational structure of the State Department is a pattern of *functional* bureaus and offices, engaged in activities which cut across geographical lines and may be of interest to several of the geographical bureaus. Thus the Bureau of Economic Affairs deals with problems that may be (with suitable variations) common to all major geographical areas; from an early stage, the Legal Adviser of the State Department is involved in treaty agreements between the United States and other countries; the Bureau of Public Affairs is concerned with both communicating information about American foreign policy to public opinion and relaying public reaction on foreign policy to appropriate officials within the State Department; the Bureau of Intelligence and Research prepares studies and reports useful to all agencies within the State Department, as well as other departments having access to information supplied by the "intelligence community."

Brief mention may be made of several postwar innovations in the State Department's structure. The position of Counselor (created in the period 1907–1919) was re-established in 1937. Among this official's major responsibilities is heading the Policy Planning Council, which was established after World War II to function (somewhat like a military staff) as a long-range planning agency in foreign relations. The best-known Counselor in the recent period was George F. Kennan, a distinguished historian and recognized authority on the

Soviet Union; Kennan was largely responsible for providing the theoretical foundations for America's postwar policy of containment.

As a result of the Hoover Commission's investigations and recommendations, the Office of Congressional Relations was established after World War II to facilitate the State Department's harmonious and continous liaison with Congress. Working closely with legislative specialists in the White House, this office seeks to generate support on "the Hill" for legislation related to foreign affairs. In addition, it answers congressional inquiries on foreign policy and provides assistance in arranging trips abroad for legislative committees.

Reflecting the new emphasis upon nonpolitical aspects of foreign policy, the Bureau of Educational and Cultural Affairs administers overseas educational and cultural programs (in close cooperation with the U.S. Information Agency); student and faculty exchange programs (such as those carried on under the Fulbright Program) are also under its supervision.

Special mention needs to be made of another bureau within the State Department, established after the creation of the United Nations in 1945: the Bureau of International Organization Affairs. Its primary responsibility is to serve as a link between the State Department in Washington and the American mission to the United Nations in New York. Accredited to the United Nations, the American ambassador to the UN holds a position very different, in several fundamental respects, from those of ambassadors to nations with which the United States maintains relations. This difference is suggested by former UN Ambassador Stevenson's comment that "In a sense, a U.S. Ambassador to the U.N. is a U.N. Ambassador to the U.S."[52] Since the individuals holding this position (like Henry Cabot Lodge, Jr., Adlai Stevenson, and Arthur Goldberg) have often been influential figures in their own right, and have sometimes sat on the President's Cabinet, the problem of assuring smoothly coordinated policy between the State Department and the UN mission in New York has sometimes posed difficulties. For certain international issues, at any rate, the latter may be the most important diplomatic establishment maintained by the United States.*

---

*The United Nations is not, however, the only international organization to which the United States sends a mission. Smaller ones include the mission to the UN Economic Committee for Europe (ECE), the International Labor Organization, the World Health Organization, and the UN Conference on Trade and Development (UNCTAD). Although it tends to exaggerate the extent to which the UN mission is free of State Department control, a recent study focuses upon the operation of the mission and upon the problems confronted in coordinating policy between it and the Department of State. See Arnold Beichman, *The "Other" State Department* (New York: Basic Books, 1968).

The Foreign Service: Role and Duties

The Foreign Service as it exists today owes its origin to the Rogers Act of 1924, when Congress spelled out requirements for entry into the diplomatic service and set up a basic organizational structure for it. For the first time, the principle was accepted that appointment to the Foreign Service and advancement within it ought to be on the basis of merit, rather than political connections, social class, or other considerations. Since 1924, successful applicants for the diplomatic corps have been required to pass a difficult battery of written and oral examinations, as well as to continue their education and training after they have been appointed.[53]

After passage of the Rogers Act, the Foreign Service expanded from some 600 officers to around 4000 by the mid-1960s. Several classifications exist within the Foreign Service, ranging from career ambassador and career minister (the highest and second highest appointments, respectively) to the Foreign Service staff, whose duties consist chiefly of providing stenographic, clerical, custodial, and other services. The nucleus of America's diplomatic corps, however, is provided by the Foreign Service officers, who are assigned major responsibility for representing the United States abroad. Collectively, this group provides the President, the Secretary of State and other high-ranking policymakers with a pool of extremely able, well-educated, informed public servants, whose judgment is often relied upon heavily by their superiors. Most Foreign Service officers over the years acquire experience in posts both overseas and in the United States (mainly in Washington, D.C.). After serving in a particular assignment abroad, for example, a Foreign Service may be "rotated" back to Washington, where he will be assigned to the bureau within the State Department dealing with the country in which he has served. Advancement within the Foreign Service is governed by the principle: "up—or out." The performance of Foreign Service officers is evaluated at frequent intervals; they must be promoted regularly or they are discharged (or "retired") from the service. Foreign Service officers may reach Class 1, and in a few cases, the position of career minister or career ambassador (although vis-à-vis the number of Class 1 Foreign Service officers, the number of ministerial and ambassadorial appointments is limited). While some ministerial and ambassadorial appointments are still made outside the Foreign Service (particularly for posts like London and Paris, where the American ambassador must of necessity have a substantial outside income to supplement his salary and expense account), some three-fourths of all American ambassadors today are appointed by the President from the Foreign Service.

Organization and Reorganization

The postwar period has witnessed a number of major and minor reorganizations of the Foreign Service to correct long-standing deficiencies and to enable the service to respond more effectively to the challenges confronting the United States in world affairs. Immediately after World War II, several considerations—the shift in the State Department's duties, evident organizational duplication throughout the executive branch, a decline in enlistments in the diplomatic corps—dictated a sweeping modification in existing organizational patterns. Guided chiefly by the State Department's own recommendations, Congress in 1946 enacted the Foreign Service Act.

This new act did not contemplate sweeping changes in the Foreign Service. In the language of Congress, it attempted merely to "improve, strengthen, and expand" the existing corps. Salary scales for each officer grade were raised sharply; the number of grades was reduced; allowances, promotions, leaves, and retirement benefits were liberalized. The objective was to make the service a more attractive career, and give it a better competitive position among other governmental agencies and with private industry. As we have noted, the principle of "promotion-up, or selection-out" governed an officer's continuance in the service. A Foreign Service Institute was also established in Washington to train successful applicants for the service and to provide periodic in-service and language training for officers already on the job. Moreover, the Act of 1946 set up a "career service" (called the Foreign Service staff) for clerical and secretarial employees. Primarily designed to grant this group attractive salaries and job security rights, it also served to overcome their feeling of inferiority in traditionally being excluded from the Foreign Service.

During the late 1940s and 1950s, the morale and efficiency of the Foreign Service were impaired by several developments. Instigated by Senator Joseph McCarthy (Republican of Wisconsin), attacks were widely made upon the loyalty and reliability of the Foreign Service, some of whose members were accused of what were tantamount to treasonable activities. The charges were almost never substantiated. Early in his tenure as Secretary of State, John Foster Dulles made a speech to State Department officials in which he pointedly demanded "positive loyalty" from his subordinates; intentional or not, the implication was that American diplomatic officials were lacking in loyalty to their superiors or to the United States.[54] Along with declining morale, recruitment into the Foreign Service during this period dropped sharply.

At length, the Eisenhower administration appointed a Public Committee on Personnel, headed by Dr. Henry M. Wriston of Brown University, to investigate the Foreign Service and submit recommendations for its improvement. The process of "Wristonization" which followed brought far-reaching changes (if morale within the service did not notably improve).* As a result of the committee's findings, many State Department officials (who had hitherto been under Civil Service) were integrated into the Foreign Service. Foreign Service officers were "rotated" more frequently between Washington and posts abroad. Entrance requirements into the service were liberalized and delays in processing applications reduced. Some 1200 members of the "staff corps" were also brought into the Foreign Service. In-service training was provided for experienced members of the corps, and greater emphasis was placed upon the acquisition of language skills by diplomatic personnel.[55]

Late in 1964, President Johnson approved another modification in the Foreign Service, when he directed that officials of the United States Information Agency (USIA) be included in the Foreign Service of the United States. Some 900 USIA officials were immediately given Foreign Service officer status. This development led to speculation that in time officials of the Agency for International Development (AID) would be accorded similar status.[56] Then in 1968, the Foreign Service (having grown to some 8,200 officers) undertook an experimental program to draw larger numbers of blacks, Spanish–Americans, and members of other minority groups into its ranks.[57]

"Open Season" on the Department of State

Writing in 1969, an experienced State Department official observed:

Recommendations for fundamental reforms in the organization and administration of foreign affairs have been made by high-level committees and task forces on the average of every two years since World War II. Despite the near unanimity of diagnosis, little has been done to deal with the

serious problems uncovered; they are still with us, unsolved and debilitating.[58]

Responding to the challenge of widening American responsibilities and commitments in global affairs, the State Department has grown in size and complexity since World War II. Concurrently, there has been a significant escalation in the volume of *criticism* directed at the department, both in Washington and overseas. By the late 1960s, it would be fair to say, discontent with the State Department pervaded public and legislative attitudes. As the agency charged with primary responsibility for American foreign relations —and as the department at the center of what was often called the "foreign affairs complex"—the State Department encountered detractors on all sides, and sometimes within its own ranks. Denunciations of the agency almost became *de rigueur* in any serious discussion of American foreign relations.

Although it would be impossible to list all of the articles in the lengthy indictment which critics presented, we may at least take note of the diversity of such criticisms. During the Vietnam War, for example, Secretary of State Rusk and his principal subordinates were reluctant to accept outside speaking engagements, for fear that their presence would trigger some new "demonstration" against American foreign policy. More than any other group within the government, leading State Department officials were held accountable for events in Vietnam. When President Kennedy took office in 1963, he was warned by Adlai Stevenson that he would find the State Department a great force for "inertia." Later, President Kennedy himself referred to the department as a "bowl of jelly"; as we have seen he relied increasingly on his personal aides in making foreign policy. One of Kennedy's White House assistants, Theodore C. Sorensen, has written that President Kennedy

was discouraged with the State Department almost as soon as he took office. He felt that it too often seemed to have a built-in inertia which deadened initiative and that its tendency toward excessive delay obscured determination. It spoke with too many voices and too little vigor. It was never clear to the President (and this continued to be true, even after the personnel changes) who was in charge, who was clearly delegated to do what, and why his own policy line seemed consistently to be altered or evaded. The top State Department team . . . reflected an abundance of talent ironically unmatched by production.[59]

Diplomatic officials themselves have not been reluctant to criticize the State Department and Foreign Service. Former Under Secretary of State George Ball termed the Department of State a "fudge factory"; his successor, Under Secretary

---

*Several recommendations made by the Wriston Committee were not carried out. A leading one (also proposed by other groups and individuals from time to time) was for establishment of a Foreign Service Academy similar to the military academies, for training American diplomatic officials. This recommendation encountered opposition from a variety of sources. Many congressmen opposed it, both as a needless expenditure and because of a possible conflict between adherence to the principle of academic freedom at such an institution and the necessity to "support" the foreign policy of the United States. Former Secretary of State Dean Acheson also rejected the idea as "based on wholly false assumptions"; he urged that better use be made, in training future Foreign Service officers, of the existing Foreign Service Institute, the military war colleges, and private academic institutions. He also believed that a possible conflict between academic freedom and support for the policies of the United States would exist. See *The New York Times* (June 3, 1963, and January 21, 1964).

Nicholas Katzenbach, believed that a complete overhaul of the department was needed. As only one instance of bureaucratic complexity and inefficiency, Katzenbach discovered that a single outgoing cablegram dealing with milk exports required 29 separate signatures within the department for "clearance" before it could be sent![60] Even Secretary of State Dean Rusk joined the chorus of critics, declaring:

When I read a telegram coming in in the morning, it poses a very specific question, and the moment I read it I know myself what the answer must be. But that telegram goes on its appointed course into the bureau, and through the office down to the desk. If it doesn't go down there somebody feels that he is being deprived of his participation in a matter of his responsibility.

Then it goes from the action officer back up through the department to me a week or 10 days later, and if it isn't the answer that I knew had to be the answer, then I change it at that point, having taken into account the advice that came from below. But usually it is the answer that everybody would know has to be the answer.[61]

Retired Foreign Service officers are also numbered among the State Department's more outspoken detractors. A former career ambassador, Mr. Ellis Briggs, noted that 700 State Department officials worked for Secretary of State Charles Evans Hughes, while some 7000 worked for Secretary of State Rusk. These officials, he continued, "make so much work for each other that they have little time to think"; a total of some 4000 Foreign Service officers is "an overabundance of manpower" and a "personnel inundation" which seldom produces "substantive accomplishment." Briggs noted also that nine words—"In charge of relations with the other American Republics"—sufficed in earlier years to describe the duties of the Bureau of Inter-American Affairs; in 1964, it took a 25-page pamphlet to describe the responsibilities of the bureau (now shared with similar bureaus in the Agency for International Development and in the Alliance for Progress).[62] Another experienced Foreign Service officer, Henry S. Villard, has referred to the "Alice in Wonderland" quality of the State Department's bureaucratic structure. In "today's labyrinthine Department," which tends to "befuddle even the inmates," thousands of officials "slip into or out of cubicles behind a nightmare row of numbered doors, or mill around the cafeteria at lunchtime— bureaucracy uncontrolled and, one fears, uncontrollable." When the department wishes to communicate with one of its embassies, "those who must be consulted are infinite in their jurisdictional duties"; and when other governmental agencies must also be consulted "it may be weeks before the final product is dispatched." Villard is particularly sharp in his denunciation of the "committee system" within the State Department— characterized by one wit as "the unwilling called by the unfit to do what was unnecessary."[63]

The charges made by present-day critics of the State Department and the "foreign affairs complex" generally, may be summarized as follows: (1) The Department of State is a large (and still growing), unwieldy, diffuse, and bewildering bureaucracy; (2) its internal and overseas operations are characterized by all the evils traditionally associated with a ponderous and labyrinthine organizational structure—delay, meaningless routine and "paper shuffling," deep-seated provincialism, a determined resistance to change, jealous attachment to its established "prerogatives" vis-à-vis other agencies; (3) perhaps the most persistent criticism of the American diplomatic establishment, *it constitutes an elite* which is ingrown, hostile to outsiders, supremely confident in its own judgment, skeptical of the viewpoints of outsiders, and unrepresentative of American society; (4) thus far, the State Department has successfully defied numerous attempts to reform it and to correct organizational defects, with the result that it remains in many respects an ineffectual instrument of American foreign policy; and (5), in what may well rank as the most serious allegation on the bill of particulars, the *results produced abroad* by a State Department that remains ill-equipped to manage its global responsibilities, *have often been confused and self-defeating, unresponsive to many of the real problems confronting the United States in international relations, and occasionally even inimical to America's own interests.* In brief, the State Department has not exhibited the kind of imaginative and effective leadership role required of the foreign office of the most powerful nation in world history.

The evidence of State Department malfunctioning, organizational defects, and generally poor performance has been widely documented in too many cases, and has been supported by too many well-qualified observers, to be ignored or dismissed lightly. When even members of the nation's own diplomatic elite lend their voices to the chorus of critics, we may safely conclude that some problems are very serious, and that some reforms are urgently needed. Not even President Kennedy could discover who was "in charge" of the State Department (the implication being that his own Secretary of State was not). Secretary of State Dean Rusk repeatedly complained about the problem of "layering" within the department—that is, the seemingly endless multiplication of committees and organizational units (a process that went on in other agencies concerned with foreign policy as well), which had to be "consulted" before decisions could be reached. Still another all-too-familiar lament is the State Department's addiction to pragmatism, its *ad hoc* approach to problems in the external sphere, and its inability or unwillingness to evolve a reasonably clear and consistent set of *principles* to guide American foreign policy. Former Under Secretary of State George Ball has written that

.. we can easily fall into a mindless and automatic pattern of dealing with problems always for the short term, unless, quite self-consciously, we develop a satisfactory conceptual frame work in which to fit the jagged edges of our day-to-day decisions. Great as it is, our power is finite, and we need a clear frame of reference to tell us how we can use it best. . . .[64]

The kind of "clear frame of reference" for decision-making that Ball advocates, however, has been one of the most conspicuously absent ingredients of postwar American foreign policy.

Criticisms of the Diplomatic Establishment in Perspective

It would be foolhardy to deny the cogency of many criticisms directed at the national diplomatic establishment. By the early 1970s, many of the problems—like "layering" or the dearth of imaginative ideas emanating from the Department of State—may well have become more acute.

Yet, it is no less true that many criticisms aimed at the Department of State are misdirected. Some stem from a simplistic understanding of the foreign policy process and the global context within which it must operate. Other criticisms may represent little more than popular or legislative frustration at conditions in the outside world. And still other complaints stem from discontent over particular episodes (like America's involvement in the Vietnam War) which many Americans resent and often cannot understand. It is clearly necessary, therefore, to evaluate such criticisms *in perspective*.

A starting point is the recognition that, both constitutionally and often actually, *the President determines American foreign policy*. To be sure, the State Department is his leading instrument for that purpose; it is charged by the President with over-all responsibility for management in the foreign policy field. But it must be noted that, to an increasing degree (as we shall see more fully in Chapter 4), other agencies also play a part, occasionally a major part, in the foreign policy process. When and how a President uses the State Department is largely a decision he alone makes. It is, of course, reasonable to suppose that the Chief Executive will rely upon the State Department to the extent that he believes it to be an *effective* instrument of national policy. The very fact that

Presidents have "bypassed" the department may be impressive evidence that they had doubts on this score. Nevertheless, there has also been a tendency in the postwar period for Presidents to involve themselves actively and directly in foreign policy, in part because of the gravity of the problems in this realm and because of their far-reaching implications.*

We need to be mindful of the fact also that a number of forces have combined to produce a kind of built-in and deeply embedded skepticism in the American mind toward the State Department, and especially toward the Foreign Service. The historical American aversion to the diplomatic quarrels and intrigues of the Old World; the conviction that diplomats usually came from, and were closely associated with, royalty and the upper classes; the Jacksonian tradition of the Common Man—a corollary of which was that that any citizen was competent to fill any governmental position; America's emphasis upon democracy and egalitarianism; a deep distrust of *all government*—but particularly positions filled *by appointment*, rather than election—which America inherited from the Enlightenment philosophers; popular dissatisfaction with what many citizens believed diplomats achieved (or did not achieve) after World Wars I and II; perhaps a nostalgic yearning for the simpler and more pristine era of isolationism—all of these have produced a frame of mind in the United States which tends to be congenitally hostile to diplomatic officials and diplomatic activities. More often than not, these are identified with unwanted international responsibilities, with the use of resources abroad rather than at home, and with seemingly endless problems.

While all agencies of the American government somewhat are affected by this state of mind, the State Department is uniquely vulnerable. It is usually very difficult for the average American to see any correlation between what the State Department is doing in France, India, or Ghana *and his own welfare*. American money and other resources are flowing out of the United States. But what, many citizens ask, is flowing back in return? In contrast to the Agriculture or Labor Departments, for example, the State Department has *no domestic constituents*. If this assertion overstates the case, perhaps it would be more accurate to say that the State Department has a superabundance of "negative constituents": groups whose view-

---

*In this connection, it needs to be remembered that all top-level State Department officials—down through, and including, the rank of Assistant Secretary of State—*are presidential appointees*. In making such appointments, a President may or they may not obtain the approval of the Secretary of State. In other words, there is no assurance that the latter can select his own principal subordinates or that they will have views which accord with his own

points are likely to be vocally expressed when their interests are endangered by State Department action or inaction. Pro-Zionist groups can be counted upon to react strongly to American policies deemed inimical to Israel; German–Americans have criticized the State Department's approach to Germany; mothers, students, and peace organizations castigate the State Department because young men must be called into the armed services. Very few groups (e.g., the Council on Foreign Relations, the Foreign Policy Association, the Brookings Institution, the American Association for the United Nations) normally support the State Department or answer its critics. Even these groups suffer many of the same disabilities besetting the State Department itself: They are "elitist" organizations, composed of well-educated and well-informed citizens, professionals, and the like, who have neither the mass political strength of farmers and workers nor the rapport with Congress needed to strengthen the State Department's position on Capitol Hill. Almost never do citizen groups testify before Congress to *commend* the State Department's activities in Africa or to ask for a *larger* budgetary appropriation for diplomatic activities.

The State Department has been, and remains, highly vulnerable to public and legislative discontent for another reason—one which may in some measure be a fault of foreign policy officials themselves, but which is in most cases inherent in America's massive involvement in the world outside its borders. This is the *continuing gap between public expectations and State Department accomplishments.* That the gap is wide can hardly be doubted. And without denying the need for improved accomplishments by American diplomatic officials, it remains true that the best-organized and best-administered foreign office in the world would have difficulty bridging the gulf between what many Americans genuinely desire to achieve abroad and what the State Department can realistically be expected to accomplish in an unstable external environment.

Whether in terms of rapid economic, social, and political progress in countries receiving American foreign assistance; or agreement with American policies by the nation's military allies; or the growth of democratic principles and practices in Latin America; or the elimination of corruption in societies where it has long been indigenous—many Americans demand evidence from the State Department of prompt and significant progress abroad. When it is not forthcoming—or when the State Department is forced to concede that many external problems are *more critical* than they were a decade ago—doubts about what the diplomatic establishment is really achieving naturally multiply. Completely honest responses to problems of this kind—such as, *"Some* developing nations are *slowly* making progress" or "Anti-

American sentiment in the Arab world is *less than might be expected*" or "The chances of nuclear war are *somewhat reduced* vis-á-vis ten years ago" —generate little positive enthusiasm with the public or on Capitol Hill. Nor does the fact that Congress (often citing adverse popular opinion) is unwilling to *expend the funds* needed to achieve the more utopian goals of many Americans protect the State Department from public resentment.

Finally, note must be taken of a recent phenomenon affecting the State Department's public image. Until the 1960s, the one group within the American society which could usually be counted upon to defend the State Department from its critics was America's *intellectual elite.* Many well-educated citizens belonged to organizations like the Council on Foreign Relations, the Foreign Policy Association, and other groups actively concerned with American foreign relations and were well informed about them. If mass opinion in the United States was chronically suspicious of diplomats and generally uninformed about foreign policy questions, this *stratum* of society normally understood the intricacy of such issues and comprehended many of the difficulties under which the State Department labored.

The Vietnam conflict, however, produced a fundamental change in this situation: Now the State Department was increasingly attacked *by intellectuals* in the United States and outside it. Some of the sharpest criticism directed against it came from informed citizens. Opposition to the war in Vietnam and the "alienation" of the intellectuals from the administration of President Johnson doubtless played a role in this change. Yet other, perhaps more enduring, forces were also at work. Some intellectuals—a number of whom at least helped formulate American policy toward Southeast Asia under the Kennedy administration —were expressing frustration at their own inability to transform the world. Some may have become disillusioned because the "new approach" to global problems adopted under President Kennedy did not somehow produce a noticeable improvement in America's position abroad or solve long-standing international problems. America became more deeply involved in Vietnam than ever; democracy seemed more remote in Latin America than before; Sino–American relations did not notably improve; France continued to follow its own course within the Western community; many developing nations fell *further behind* in their economic development than they were in the mid-1950s. Other intellectuals (revealing an attitude that had once supported the American isolationist policy) became convinced that *domestic affairs* ought to have first claim upon national resources. Significant too has been a change in the traditional opinions of many political "liberals," who once exhibited great confidence in the ability of *government* to resolve human problems; by the late 1960s, some liberal groups had become deeply suspicious of "establishments" like the State Department. Some intellectuals may also have become conscious of antithetical demands which not infrequently characterized their own approach to foreign relations. Thus, intellectuals were often prone simultaneously to condemn the State Department for not "doing something" about corruption in South Vietnam or other settings, and for "intervening" in the internal affairs of other societies! Or, the State Department was excoriated concurrently for its failure to exercise a restraining influence in the latest Middle East crisis, while it was blamed for its refusal to supply Israel with the latest jet aircraft!

Discontent with the State Department, it seems safe to predict, will survive the Vietnam conflict. For it is, perhaps above all, a reflection of pervasive public anxiety about conditions outside the United States and an outgrowth of popular resentment on the part of many Americans that they must carry burdens and responsibilities they do not want, and yet cannot delegate to others.

NOTES

1. President Wilson's views are cited in Sidney Warren, *The President as World Leader* (New York: McGraw-Hill, 1967), p. 78; for Truman's views, see Louis W. Koenig, *The Chief Executive*, rev. ed. (New York: Harcourt Brace Jovanovich, 1968), p. 209.
2. Warren, *op. cit.*
3. For President Johnson's views, see Sidney Warren, ed., *The American President* (Englewood Cliffs, N.J.: Prentice-Hall, 1967), pp. 53–54.
4. Richard P. Longaker, "The President as International Leader," in Donald B. Johnson and Jack L. Walker, eds., *The Dynamics of the American Presidency* (New York: John Wiley, 1964), p. 303.
5. See McCulloch v. Maryland, 4 Wheaton 316 (1819). The student is urged to become familiar with legal citation. After the name of the case, the first number refers to the *volume* number; Wheaton was one of the *compilers* of Supreme Court decisions in the nineteenth century; the next number is the *page number* on which the case begins; and the date is of course in the year in which the decision was rendered. After 1882, the name of the compiler was no longer used; the *United States Reports* became the official record of Supreme Court decisions. This series was often cited as follows: *United States* v. *Belmont*, 301 U.S. 324 (1937).
6. See United States v. Curtiss–Wright Export Corporation, 299 U.S. 304 (1936).
7. *Idem.*
8. *Idem.* Italics in original.
9. See the study in *The New York Times* (August 25, 1963), as cited in Joseph E. Kallenbach, *The American Chief Executive* (New York: Harper & Row, 1966), p. 506.
10. See Koenig, *op. cit.*, p. 211.
11. Quoted in Cecil V. Crabb, Jr., *Bipartisan Foreign Policy: Myth or Reality?* (New York: Harper & Row, 1957), p. 16.
12. William L. Langer, "The Mechanism of American Foreign Policy," *International Affairs* 24 (July, 1948), 322.
13. See Kallenbach, *op. cit.*, p. 503.
14. Bernard Schwartz, *A Commentary on the Constitution of the United States* (New York: Macmillan, 1963), Part I, p. 143. For a lengthy analysis of the constitutional distinction between treaties and executive agreements, along with frequent citations of precedents, see *ibid.*, pp. 117–159.
15. For detailed documentation, see Charles Fairman, "The President as Commander-in-Chief," in *The Presidency in Transition* (a symposium) (Gainesville, Fla.: University of Florida Press, 1949); Clinton Rossiter, *The Supreme Court and the Commander in Chief* (Ithaca: Cornell University Press, 1951), pp. 11–25; Edward S. Corwin, *Total War and the Constitution* (New York: Knopf, 1947), pp. 7–33.
16. Richard E. Neustadt, *Presidential Power: The Politics of Leadership* (New York: John Wiley, 1960), p. 199.
17. *The Prize Cases*, 2 Black 635 (1863). Italics in original.
18. Eisenhower's comment is quoted in Edward S. Corwin and Louis W. Koenig, *The President Today* (New York: New York University Press, 1956), p. 48.
19. Edward S. Corwin, *The President's Control of Foreign Relations* (Princeton, N.J.: Princeton University Press, 1917), p. 44.
20. Hopkins' diplomatic activities are described in Robert E. Sherwood, *Roosevelt and Hopkins*, vol. I (New York: Bantam, 1948), pp. 283, 285, 305, 328, 536.
21. *The New York Times* (October 23, 1951).
22. J. G. Starke, *An Introduction to International Law*, 5th ed. (London: Butterworths, 1963), p. 120.
23. *Ibid.*, p. 121.
24. Kallenbach, *op. cit.*, pp. 492–493.
25. See Corwin, *op. cit.*, p. 177.
26. Burton M. Sapin, *The Making of United States Foreign Policy* (Washington, D.C.: Brookings Institution, 1966), pp. 305–309.
27. Elias Huzar, "Reorganization for National Security," *Journal of Politics* 12 (February, 1950), 149.
28. Senator Borah's views are quoted in Warren, *The President as World Leader, op. cit.*, p. 200. In a more recent instance, a senator's information proved much more reliable. Thus, for many weeks prior to the Cuban missile crisis late in 1962, Senator Kenneth Keating (Republican of New York) alerted the Kennedy administration and the nation at large to Soviet machinations in Cuba. See

Theodore C. Sorensen, *Kennedy* (New York: Harper & Row, 1965), pp. 667–718; and Arthur M. Schlesinger, Jr., *A Thousand Days* (Boston: Houghton Mifflin, 1965), pp. 800–801, 834, 836.

29. For discussions of President Kennedy's approach to the problem of news management see Harold W. Chase and Allen H. Lerman, eds., *Kennedy and the Press* (New York: Thomas Y. Crowell, 1965), p. x; and Johnson and Walker, *op. cit.*, pp. 284–290.

30. For Truman's views, see Warren, *The President as World Leader, op. cit.* p. 97; Wilson's views are cited in Koenig, *op cit.*, p. 184.

31. Wilfred E. Binkley, *President and Congress* (New York: Knopf, 1947), p. 250.

32. The activities of the State Department's Bureau of Public Affairs are described in Smith Simpson, *Anatomy of the State Department* (Boston: Houghton Mifflin, 1967), pp. 184–205.

33. See, for example, Koenig, *op. cit.*, pp. 199–204, for a discussion of "the art of news management." Experienced reporters have complained about the tendency of recent Presidents to "use" the press for their own ends. See the views of Arthur Krock in *ibid.*, p. 199; and those of Roscoe Drummond in David E. Haight and Larry D. Johnston, *The President: Roles and Powers* (Skokie, Ill.: Rand McNally, 1965), pp. 275–281. A detailed treatment of the role of the press as it relates specifically to foreign affairs is James Reston, *The Artillery of the Press: Its Influence on American Foreign Policy* (New York: Harper & Row, 1967).

34. For example, see the discussion of President Kennedy's activities directed at influencing foreign opinion, in Koenig, *op. cit.*, pp. 225–226.

35. See the views of Lawrence O'Brien, as cited in Warren, *The American President, op. cit.*, p. 136.

36. *Ibid.*, p. 135.

37. Binkley, *op. cit.*, p. 246.

38. *Documents on American Foreign Relations: 1962* (New York: Harper & Row, 1963), pp. 47–48.

39. Quoted in *The New York Times* (March 13, 1947).

40. *The New York Times* (June 5, 1967).

41. *The New York Times* (August 1, 1967).

42. *The New York Times* (November 17, 1967).

43. Edward S. Corwin, *The Constitution of the United States of America* (Washington, D.C.: Legislative Reference Service, Library of Congress, 1953), pp. 393–395.

44. *Ibid.*, pp. 81–82.

45. Edward S. Corwin, *Total War and the Constitution* (New York: Knopf, 1947), p. 19.

46. Corwin, *The Constitution of the United States of America, op. cit.*, p. 493.

47. *Ibid.*, p. 496.

48. *The New York Times* (February 8, 1969).

49. Henry S. Villard, *Affairs at State* (New York: Thomas Y. Crowell, 1965), pp. xi, 60.

50. See *The New York Times* (August 13, 1967); and *Time Magazine* **86** (October 15, 1965), 34–35.

51. James L. McCamy, *The Administration of American Foreign Affairs* (New York: Knopf, 1950), pp. 70–73.

52. Quoted in Arnold Beichman, *The "Other" State Department* (New York: Basic Books, 1968), p. 14.

53. The principles guiding the operation of the Foreign Service down to the postwar era are described and appraised in Alona E. Evans, "The Re-Organization of the American Foreign Service," *International Affairs* **24** (April, 1948), 206–217. For a more detailed account, focusing upon the period before World War II, consult Warren F. Ilchman, *Professional Diplomacy in the United States, 1779–1939* (Chicago: University of Chicago Press, 1961).

54. For a discussion of Dulles' concept of "positive loyalty" by the members of the State Department, see Richard Goold-Adams, *John Foster Dulles: A Reappraisal* (New York: Appleton-Century-Crofts, 1952), p. 57.

55. The Wriston Committee's findings are embodied in its report, *Toward a Stronger Foreign Service* (Washington, D.C.: U.S. Government Printing Office, 1954).

56. *The New York Times* (October 9, 1964).

57. *The New York Times* (March 24, 1968).

58. Lannon Walker, "Our Foreign Affairs Machinery: Time for an Overhaul," *Foreign Affairs*, **47** (January, 1969), 309.

59. Sorensen, *op. cit*, p. 287.

60. The views of Ball and Katzenbach are cited in *Newsweek* **69** (January 16, 1967), 22–23.

61. Rusk's views are cited at length in *The New York Times* (June 29, 1964).

62. Ellis Briggs, *Farewell to Foggy Bottom* (New York: McKay, 1964), pp. 9–10. As these excerpts suggest, Briggs' views are acerbic and candid; his memoirs illuminate many aspects of the Foreign Service and American foreign policy generally.

63. Villard, *op. cit.*, pp. 22–23. More balanced than Briggs' account, Villard's treatment of the State Department and Foreign Service is also highly enlightening.

64. George W. Ball, *The Discipline of Power* (Boston: Little, Brown, 1968), p. 343.

Four
NATIONAL SECURITY AND
POLICY COORDINATION

Postwar American foreign policy has witnessed a number of fundamental departures from the earlier isolationist tradition. Among these new trends, few are more striking than *the growing interrelationship between military and political components of national policy* in behalf of what has come to be called *national security policy.* We shall attempt to define this sometimes elusive term at a later stage. Meanwhile, it would contribute to more intelligent understanding of the concept if we take note of certain tendencies and forces that have brought national security policy to the forefront and have shaped official and unofficial American attitudes toward it.

THE POSTWAR CONTEXT

The growing American concern with national security policy, it must be remembered, took place within a context characterized by two important, but rather contradictory, tendencies. These tendencies are still present within the American society; the tension between them is responsible in no small measure for ambivalent public (and occasionally official) attitudes toward the role of military power in the foreign policy process. Two examples in the late 1960s—the public debate over the Vietnam War and the controversy over the proposed antiballistic missile (ABM) system—indicated that the hiatus between these two ideas had not disappeared from the internal setting of national policy. One of these tendencies is *the deep-seated American commitment to the principle of civilian control over the armed forces.* Derived from the colonial and Revolutionary War experiences, this principle was reflected in such constitutional provisions as Article I, Section 8, which gave Congress the power to provide for the army and navy (and prohibited even Congress from making military appropriations for longer than two years*), and Article II, Section 2, designating the President as the Commander-in-

Chief of the armed forces. As we observed in Chapter 3, the latter power has become one of the President's most potent instruments for determining and controlling foreign relations. Although the determination of military strategy is normally entrusted to the nation's high-ranking military commanders, during World War II President Roosevelt immersed himself actively in the determination of strategy, such as the decision to give Europe priority over the Pacific theater, the policy of "unconditional surrender" toward the Axis powers, and the determination to secure Soviet entry into the war against the Japanese empire.* Similarly, during the Korean War, the principle of ultimate civilian supremacy was vividly upheld, when President Harry Truman dismissed one of America's most popular military leaders, General Douglas MacArthur, because of growing divergencies between them on a variety of military and political issues. Although Truman's action precipitated a public furor, and led to a congressional investigation of MacArthur's dismissal, in time most Americans understood that a Chief Executive cannot tolerate insubordination (or even the appearance of it) on the part of a theater commander. Any course other than MacArthur's dismissal would have seriously eroded the constitutional safeguard against undue military influence in national policy-making.[1]

After nearly two centuries as an independent

---

*After the Japanese attack on Pearl Harbor on December 7, 1941, one commentator has written, President Roosevelt "asserted his leadership so effectively that virtually every major political and military decision bore the personal mark of Franklin D. Roosevelt. He completely dominated the policy-making scene." On military questions, FDR often did not consult the civilian heads of the War and Navy Departments, but worked closely with the military Chiefs of Staff, "with whom he shared a remarkable identity of views." As a rule, FDR "consulted his intimate advisers and then reached his own conclusions." The process by which FDR arrived at the policy of "unconditional surrender" for the Axis nations is especially interesting and illuminating. See the discussion of President Roosevelt's wartime leadership in Sidney Warren, *The President as World Leader* (New York: McGraw-Hill, 1964), pp. 235–282.

---

*In practice, Congress appropriates funds for the military services on an *annual* basis.

nation, the United States remains as devoted as ever to the concept of civilian supremacy in policy-making. Indeed, as we shall see, one theme expressed by critics of American foreign policy during the late 1960s was that the power exercised by the "military–industrial complex" in American society endangered this vital constitutional principle.

A second, and equally influential, tendency has also affected the context of national security policy. This has been the pre-World War II, wartime, and postwar experience of the United States in protecting its vital interests and endeavoring to achieve its foreign policy goals. The over-all result of this tendency has been to highlight the fact that *for too many years America neglected the problem of national security policy;* only in the postwar era could it be said that policy-makers accorded this dimension of national policy the importance and urgency it demanded.

Examples of this neglect abound in recent diplomatic experience. President Franklin D. Roosevelt's rising apprehension about Japanese expansionism in Asia—coupled with his determination to resist further Japanese demands—was not accompanied by the military buildup in the Pacific needed to support a policy of "firm" opposition to Tokyo's demands. The military disaster at Pearl Harbor on December 7, 1941, taught several lessons to policy-makers in the United States, one of which surely was the overdue necessity of coordinating military and political components of national policy. Similarly, during World War II, military and political decisions too often remained separated, with the former frequently taking precedence over the latter. As a rule, President Roosevelt favored deferring political questions until victory over the Axis powers had been achieved. The American attitude on this issue was succinctly expressed by General Omar N. Bradley, Commander of the First Army in Europe, who wrote after the war: "As soldiers we looked naïvely on this British inclination to *complicate the war* with political foresight and nonmilitary objectives."[2] Adherence to this viewpoint by high-ranking American officials (while British, Soviet, and French officials continually kept political considerations at the forefront of their wartime strategies) meant that in a number of crucial wartime decisions—such as those affecting Berlin and Germany as a whole, Eastern Europe, the stability and future of China, the economic and political viability of Korea—Washington failed to understand the intimate relationship between military and political moves or the extent to which each conditions and determines the other.

Military leaders, however, were not alone in failing to comprehend the intimate connection between the political and military elements of national policy. For many months after the war, the State Department was genuinely reluctant to assume responsibility for formulating policies toward "occupied" countries like Germany, Japan, and Austria. The demilitarization and democratization of Japan—along with radical transformations in that country's economic and social structures—were carried out by American military authorities under General Douglas MacArthur. Nor was the State Department prepared until 1949 to take responsibility for West Germany.[3] If military leaders had tended to be indifferent to political questions while the war was in progress, civilian leaders revealed a curious reluctance and unpreparedness to deal with major political problems once the war was over.

A New Concern for National Security Policy

As "Allied unity" evaporated in the tensions generated by the cold war between Soviet Russia and the United States, traditional American indifference to the problem of national security policy gradually began to change. The Communist adversary, America finally became aware, had always placed a high premium upon the need to concert military and political moves; Marxist regimes in Eastern Europe, for example, were created by Moscow's skillful blending of military and political decisions during and after the war. The victory of Communism in China likewise testified to Marxist skill in unifying *all* components of policy—military force, terror, propaganda, economic instruments (like land reform), guerrilla tactics, organizational skill—to achieve victory in the face of adverse military odds.

Passage of the National Security Act of 1947, introducing far-reaching changes in the philosophy and machinery of national security policy in the United States, reflected belated American realization that this problem had been too long neglected. Over the years that followed, the relationship between military and civilian policy-making achieved a prominence it had never attained earlier. After the Korean War in 1950, the United States created a large peacetime military establishment, available to support its diplomatic interests throughout the world. By the end of the 1960s, America had 432 military bases overseas; it had treaty commitments to defend some 42 other nations; in 1967, the American military budget was approximately equal to the *entire gross national product of Latin America;* between 1947 and 1969, the members of NATO collectively expended over *$1 trillion* for defense; the Pentagon (which by 1969 spent all revenues raised by the income tax on individual Americans) had become by all odds the largest single American "business establishment" and employer in the United States; in the mid-1960s, the Pentagon's total inventory of real estate, equipment, and parts was close to $140 billion; while the American military establishment was the largest sponsor of "research" activies in the world.[4] Besides obvious military tasks like defending the United States from attack, defending the nation's allies, and meeting military threats in settings like Korea and Vietnam, the armed forces of the United States had steadily acquired new responsibilities. These included formulating and directing arms-aid programs to other nations; engaging in "civic action" programs in selected countries involving health measures, construction schemes, and educational ventures under military auspices; and evolving effective antiguerrilla strategies, which required the development of skills by military groups in understanding propaganda campaigns, social conflicts, economic problems, educational programs and other issues not traditionally central to military concern.[5]

One index of the extent to which political and military decisions impinge upon one another is the use of military contingents for avowedly diplomatic purposes. The United States Navy has long been accustomed to such a role. Beginning with the Spanish–American War, American naval officers were trained to discharge diplomatic functions; "showing the flag" close to trouble spots around the world has been, and remains, a primary assignment of the navy. Writing in the late 1960s, one commentator pointed out that American naval forces within the past decade had been used in many instances—to transport American troops to Lebanon in 1956, to supply beleaguered Quemoy, to execute a "show of force" off Santo Domingo in the early 1960s, to interdict Soviet ships bound for Cuba in 1962—all without firing a single shot.[6]

Perhaps the best way of underscoring the central importance of national security policy, however, is to examine briefly the principal challenges confronting the United States abroad, noting particularly the degree to which they involve both political and military considerations. In its relations with Western Europe, for example, the United States is deeply concerned with the cohesion of NATO, with the security of Berlin and West Germany, with the Soviet Union's continued intervention in Eastern Europe, and with the difficult question of nuclear proliferation as illustrated by the French atomic *force de frappe*. In the Middle East, the ongoing Arab–Israeli conflict, the buildup of Soviet naval strength in the Mediterranean, Moscow's arms-aid programs to Arab nations, and the security of regional oil supplies create recurrent anxieties in Washington. In Asia, the Korean and Vietnam Wars testify to deep American military involvement in the problem of regional security. Other developments—like the tensions between Pakistan and India, Red China's expansionism in the Himalayan region, insurgent movements in Thailand and the Philippines, new threats to South Korea by North Korea, and public dissatisfaction within Japan because of Tokyo's de-

fense links with the United States—have compelled the United States to formulate responses involving the close integration of military and political elements. To the south in Latin America, the United States has been preoccupied with insurgent movements supported by Castro's Cuba, the Soviet Union, and (to lesser extent) Red China; it confronted a Soviet attempt in 1962 to install offensive missiles in the Western Hemisphere; it has witnessed innumerable political *coups* carried out by military elites in Latin America (some of whom were trained in the United States); it has sought to establish a "peace force" under the auspices of the Organization of American States, as an alternative to U.S. intervention and it has wrestled with the difficult question of whether to supply modern armaments to Latin American governments. On the level of the United Nations, the recurrent issues of disarmament, of UN "peace-keeping" operations in crisis areas like the Congo, Cyprus, and the Middle East, and of the challenge of making the UN relevant to violent conflicts like the Vietnam War, also involve the merger of political and military aspects of national policy.

"National Security Policy" and Its Corollaries

Thus far, we have used the term "national security policy" without defining it. At this point, let us examine the concept and take note of some of its important corollaries and implications.

National security policy may be defined *as the integration of military and political decisions to produce a unified strategy designed to protect the vital interests of the state and to achieve its foreign policy goals.* Thus, national security policy is a synthesis of military and political elements.* Neither of these two dimensions of national policy is of course new. What is new about the postwar emphasis upon national security policy is the attempt to *unify and concert* these two key areas, so that military decisions *are compatible with and support political goals.* Conversely, the concept of national security policy suggests that in formulating political objectives, civilian policy-makers will consider carefully the *military resources* available to the nation for achieving alternative goals. If military leaders are required at all times to recognize that the commitment of armed force is not an end in itself, civilian leaders are no less obliged to remember that the adoption of national goals, without carefully studying military needs and resources, can be futile, if not disastrous.

---

*As used here and in most discussions of national security policy, the term "political" is given a broad connotation—to include economic, psychological, cultural, and other aspects of national policy. It is evident, for example, that America's "dollar crisis" affects national security policy, as does its success in creating and preserving a favorable "national image" abroad.

Much of the present-day emphasis upon national security policy can be traced to certain military thinkers and strategists of the eighteenth and nineteenth centuries. Outstanding among these was the Prussian General Carl von Clausewitz, whom we mentioned in Chapter 2. Clausewitz's often-quoted dictum—"War is the continuation of politics by other means"—focused attention upon the key relationship between military and political elements which lies at the heart of national security policy. Hans Rothfels has summarized Clausewitz's thought by saying that "War is only part of a social totality; it differs from the whole only by its specific means. . . . For political aims are the end and war is the means, and the means can never be conceived without the end." According to Clausewitz, "State policy first is the 'womb in which war develops.' Policy therefore determines the main lines along which war is to move."[7] It is interesting to observe that Clausewitz distinguished between two kinds of military conflicts and that his classification is clearly relevant to wars and lesser acts of violence today. First, Clausewitz identified what Rothfels calls "war to overthrow the enemy"; in our age, this is known as "total war," the object of which (as in World War II) is the "unconditional surrender" of the adversary. The nuclear balance of terror has made the great powers extremely cautious about acts of violence likely to lead to general nuclear war, which might entail mutual annihilation.

Second, Clausewitz also devoted considerable attention to that category of violent encounters that has become more frequent in the contemporary period and that has sometimes posed a difficult challenge to American policy-makers, *limited war.* Such wars have as their aim something less than the total defeat of the adversary. In our age, these more limited ends encompass such objectives as defeating insurgent movements, teaching an enemy that "aggression does not pay," or compelling an opponent to cease his attempt to conquer another nation. Clausewitz emphasized the idea that limited war, even more than total war, involved the intimate association between military and political strategy. The aim of limited war, according to a modern student of Clausewitz, "is to stop the infringement upon our interests."[9] Another contemporary student of military strategy has highlighted what he calls the growing "indecisiveness" of modern war; in the nuclear age, war is less capable than ever of "realizing the aims of those who have resorted to it deliberately."[10] More than any other Western society, the American people perhaps would benefit from a careful study of Clausewitz's ideas on the relationship between war and politics, particularly as it applies to limited encounters like Korea and Vietnam.

Clausewitz's dictum that "War is the continuation of politics by other means" also suggests that the military and political realms constitute *a continuum.* Except when militarism per se actuates national policy, the application of armed force always takes place within a *political context* and in behalf of *political goals.* This continuum in turn may be thought of in three reasonably distinct, if closely related, stages. The first consists of the period of political conflict, tension, and hostility that ultimately leads to war. The prolonged and increasingly hostile controversies among the European powers over the twenty or so years preceding World War I come to mind. The inability of nations to resolve these political controversies by nonviolent methods finally led to armed conflict. The war was fought, that is to say, to achieve political objectives that could be realized in no other way.

The second stage is the period of the war itself. After hostilities have erupted, as Clausewitz himself conceded, there is sometimes a tendency (and, as we have noted, World War II affords numerous examples) for the political goals to become eclipsed by military decisions and exigencies. Even though political issues may have produced war, once the conflict begins it is not unusual for these issues to recede, while questions of *military* strategy come to the forefront. Experience has shown that this is especially likely under conditions of general (or total) war, where the "unconditional surrender" of the enemy is the stated objective. As in World War II, it is easy for officials and citizens alike to lose sight of such questions as, "What political considerations are at stake in the war with the Axis powers?" or "What political conditions will reduce the probability of new military hostilities, once the war has ended?" Furthermore, during this second stage, it is easy to overlook the fact that military decisions during the war *will sharply limit future political alternatives.* Thus, when the United States (for persuasive reasons of military strategy) rejected the British proposal to invade Europe through the Balkans, it greatly restricted Anglo–American influence over events in Soviet-occupied Eastern Europe, both as the war ended and in the months that followed. Similarly, the decision of the Allied forces under General Dwight D. Eisenhower to "pull back" from Berlin—and to leave this vital city for liberation by the Soviet Red Army—contributed substantially to Berlin's acute vulnerability in the postwar period.

The third stage is the postwar phase, when presumably military considerations are no longer dominant and political issues again move to the fore. The normal sequence of events is for a war to be terminated initially by a cease-fire or armistice agreement, followed by a peace conference which drafts a treaty among the belligerents. Theoretically (if not always actually), the peace treaty reflects agreement among the nations involved upon outstanding political questions, and restores some degree of "normalization" in relations among them. In some measure, the cold war that has characterized international relations since World War II is an outgrowth of the fact that it has been impossible to agree upon a peace treaty for Germany. As a consequence, the "German problem" remains in some respects the crux and symbol of Soviet–American animosity. Similarly, no peace treaty followed the cease-fire agreement ending the Korean conflict in 1953. Although cease-fire negotiations are under way in Paris seeking to end the war in Vietnam, there seems little prospect that this conflict will be formally terminated by a peace treaty. For both the Korean and Vietnam conflicts, therefore, many of the underlying political sources of tension remain unresolved.

Considerable attention has been devoted to the concept of national security policy, and to Clausewitz's ideas about the relationship between military and political strategy, because this subject has received insufficient attention by Americans. Yet one of the inescapable implications of the "revolution in American foreign policy" that occurred after World War II was the necessity of keeping the relationship between these two key aspects of national policy at the center of defense and political decision-making. As we shall see in our discussion of national defense reorganization, *military* policy-makers sometimes understood the relationship between war and politics better than their civilian counterparts.

THE MILITARY ROLE IN FOREIGN POLICY

Prewar and Wartime Patterns

Before World War II, civilian and military policy-makers tended, with some exceptions, to operate in separate realms. Even worse, the two principal branches of the armed services—the army and the navy—made little effort to arrive at unified military strategy or to concert their military moves. One student of American military policy has found that during the McKinley–Roosevelt–Taft period, for example, there was no evidence of any communication "from a Secretary of State, asking for a military cost accounting before some diplomatic stroke." Before the 1930s, liaison among the Secretaries of State, War (or Army), and Navy was more often than not by letter.[11] America's unpreparedness for Japan's attack against Pearl Harbor at the end of 1941 could be attributed in part to lack of coordination between army and navy intelligence activities, as well as to the gulf separating political and military decision-making. After the United States entered the war, one commentator has declared, Secretary of State Hull virtually abdicated his control over foreign

policy, saying: "I have washed my hands of it and it is now in the hands of . . . the Army and Navy. . . ."[12] Even when civilian leaders recognized the need for considering political questions during the war, this assignment was often entrusted to the President's personal representatives, who reported directly to the White House, bypassing the State Department.[13] Relying upon various *ad hoc* and makeshift arrangements, the military services were able to coordinate their activities reasonably well during the war, in part because President Roosevelt himself often made many important strategic decisions. Even so, divergent assessments by the army and navy concerning conditions in Japan (with FDR accepting the more pessimistic, but inaccurate, army estimates about Japanese military might) were crucial in a wartime decision which had fateful political consequences. This was America's insistence that Soviet Russia enter the conflict with Japan once the war in Europe had been won. Although Moscow might have obtained a number of them by its own power, the United States made several concessions (such as agreeing to recognize traditional Russian rights in Manchuria) to gain this military end.[14]

During the war, the emergence of the United States Air Force imparted urgency to the problem of according this service parity within the defense organization with the army and navy. However, even the experience of World War II, it is fair to say, created no significant sentiment within the military establishment in favor of a totally unified defense organization. If anything, the war may have made each service more conscious than ever of its "identity" and strengthened the conviction that complete unification of the armed forces was *not* necessary to achieve victory. Yet by the end of the war, civilian policy-makers had become persuaded that major changes were required in the policy machinery and processes related to national security. As our treatment has suggested, two overriding problems existed: the necessity to create greater unity of effort among the military services, and the need to merge political and military decisions more effectively.

Defense Reorganization in 1947

Although President Truman sent a plan for defense reorganization to Congress late in 1945, it was well over a year later that Congress finally passed the National Security Act of 1947. Several times in the years that followed, this act was amended; the defense reorganization plan of 1958, for example, vastly increased the powers available to the Secretary of Defense to achieve a unified approach to national security. Without attempting a detailed chronological presentation of postwar defense reorganization, let us note certain major stages and developments.[15]

As is true of most questions of public policy, the National Security Act of 1947 emerged as a compromise. It was an attempt to accommodate and conciliate the viewpoints of a wide variety of official and public groups. Some of these (particularly military pressure groups like the Navy League and the Associations of the United States Army) wanted little or no change in existing arrangements. Ranged against them were extreme critics of the status quo, who pointed to catastrophes like Pearl Harbor as the price that could be paid for continuing provincialism and separatism within the military services. On Capitol Hill, a diversity of viewpoints also prevailed. Perhaps the most influential opinion, held by Representative Carl Vinson, powerful chairman of the House Armed Services Committee, was that America must resist creating anything resembling a "Prussian general staff," and must not concentrate too much power in the hands of even a civilian official, making him a kind of "defense Czar."[16]

The result of this interplay of conflicting forces was the National Security Act of 1947, which largely set the pattern for many years thereafter in American defense organization. Attempting to steer a middle course between too much and too little change, the act in effect created a kind of "federation" among the military services, leaving them substantial de facto autonomy within a newly established Department of Defense, headed by a civilian Secretary of Defense. This official's powers, however, remained circumscribed; possessing little authority and virtually no staff, vis-à-vis that of the separate services, the office was initially weak. Yet the principle of a single defense department, headed by a civilian secretary, was established in the months following World War II. Two decades later, as a result of continuing changes in defense organization, the Secretary of Defense had become one of the most powerful members of the President's Cabinet.

Another major innovation introduced by the National Security Act of 1947 was creation of a National Security Council. As its name implied, its function was to serve as the highest-level mechanism or committee in the government for recommending national security policy to the President. It is important to note that individuals and agencies other than the National Security Council might, and did, advise the President; the Chief Executive was free to use NSC and other advisory organs as he saw fit. NSC was deliberately created as a *small* agency, to facilitate discussion and reasonably prompt decision-making. Its "statutory members" were (in 1969): the President, the Vice President, the Secretary of State, the Secretary of Defense, the Director of the Office of Emergency Preparedness, and the President's Special Assistant on national security affairs. Ever since its creation, however, Presidents have "invited" other high-ranking government officials (such as the director of the Central Intelligence Agency, the director of the U.S. Information Agency, and the Secretary of the Treasury) to attend NSC meetings when problems affecting their particular responsibilities were under discussion.*

Another significant innovation made by the National Security Act of 1947 was creation of the Joint Chiefs of Staff (JCS). Consisting of the military heads of the army, navy, and air force, and (when its interests are affected by strategic planning, which is most of the time) the commandant of the marine corps, the JCS were expected to provide unified defense planning and to serve, individually and collectively, as the President's principal military advisers. The JCS mechanism, as we have noted, reflected the continued existence of *separate* military services; each member of JCS served as *operational commander* of his respective service arm (a realm which the civilian Secretary of Defense was prohibited from entering). This ambivalent position for each member of the JCS gave rise to the doctrine of the "two hats": *Individually,* the Joint Chiefs were responsible for the operations involving their services, while *collectively* they were responsible for formulating *national* defense strategy and making policy recommendations to civilian leaders. If this concept of defense reorganization was untidy and left many logical inconsistencies, as critics often pointed out, it nevertheless remained the guiding principle for planning military strategy for more than two decades. And if a number of problems remained after 1947, requiring changes in the JCS and many other levels of the defense structure, it could at least be said that in both the Korean and Vietnamese Wars, rivalries and lack of cooperation among the military services posed no significant obstacles to civilian policy-makers.

Ongoing Changes in National Security Policy

Experience after 1947 demonstrated that the creation of machinery and procedures designed to produce a unified national security policy was an ongoing challenge. The National Security Act of 1947 had been a compromise, fully satisfying few public officials or students of national security policy. In addition, the rapid pace of civilian and military technology—along with new develop-

*In addition to the statutory members, other agencies of government may and do participate in NSC deliberations, both by having their representatives present at NSC meetings and by participating in studies prepared for the Council. Early in President Nixon's administration, for example, a detailed study of American foreign aid was prepared for the NSC. Known as National Security Memo No. 4, this study was written by officials of the State, Defense, and Treasury Departments, joined by officials from the Export–Import Bank, the Council of Economic Advisers, and the Agency for International Development. See *The New York Times* (May 27, 1969).

ments in global affairs, like limited wars and insurrections against established governments—gave momentum to proposals for modifications in policy machinery. New weapons like "tactical" nuclear armaments, helicopters, and long-range guided missiles, posed recurrent problems in terms of where they "fit" into the traditional military services. More than any armed conflict in which the United States had been involved, the Vietnam War placed a premium upon the intimate coordination of the military, political, economic, and psychological instruments of national policy. During some phases of this contest, it was evident that such coordination was conspicuously absent.

Another force compelling policy-makers and interested citizen groups to restudy the mechanism for formulating national security policy was the *rising costs of military hardware and related space technology.* By the 1960s, it was not uncommon for the Department of Defense to be confronted with a five- to tenfold disparity between the "estimated" cost of new weapons and their actual cost! Such financial pressures gave rise to demands by high-ranking executive and legislative leaders that security planners give greater attention to "cost effectiveness" and efficiency in the expenditure of funds.

Beginning in the early 1960s, another development gave impetus to the movement for reform and innovation in policy-making affecting national security. This was the series of hearings carried out by the Subcommittee on National Security Policy of the Senate Committee on Government Operations; headed by Senator Henry Jackson (Democrat of Washington), this group produced a series of illuminating reports on the subject and focused attention upon a number of unsolved problems.[17]

In 1967, General Earle G. Wheeler, chairman of the Joint Chiefs of Staff, cited three major goals which successful national security planning sought to achieve.[18] These objectives provide a convenient framework within which to discuss changes in the formulation and administration of national security policy in the postwar era.*

---

*Although our discussion of national defense organization will not focus upon chronological developments, it might be useful here to identify briefly the major stages through which reorganization movements have passed. The National Security Act of 1947 created essentially a "federation" among the military services, leaving them substantial power vis-à-vis the new Secretary of Defense. Within a few months, the powers of the Secretary of Defense were augmented when he was given an independent staff, along with an Under Secretary of Defense as his chief deputy. At the same time, a nonvoting chairman was appointed to preside over the Joint Chiefs of Staff, and the Joint Staff was itself enlarged. The Hoover Commission's study of the organization of the executive branch in 1949 elicited further modifications in defense organization, in the direction of strengthening the authority of the Secretary of Defense, although he was still prohibited from encroaching on the "combat functions"

1. Successful national security policy requires the existence of *machinery and procedures for translating over-all military strategy into unified military action.* Successful blending of the military and political components of national security policy, that is to say, presupposes a high level of agreement within the government on the *military strategy* needed to protect the security of the United States, as well as on methods for *unifying military efforts* on the basis of the agreed-upon strategy.

While Congress, many citizen groups, and military officials themselves, have rejected the idea of setting up a Prussian-style "general staff" in the United States, it was envisioned that the Joint Chiefs of Staff would afford a mechanism for achieving much greater unity in military planning by the services than had prevailed earlier. Initially, the JCS were given a small staff—called the Joint Staff—to assist them in over-all strategic planning; over the years that followed, the Joint Staff grew in size, to reach over 400 officers by the mid-1960s. To a large degree, this growth reflected the increasing *complexity* of issues confronting the nation's highest military leaders—problems like the cohesion of alliance systems, the expanded involvement of the military services in activities like "civic action" and antiguerrilla warfare, disarmament negotiations, and efforts to prevent the proliferation of nuclear weap-

---

of the separate services, whose indentities remained intact.

Major changes were introduced in 1953: Several new Assistant Secretaries of Defense were created and given responsibilities for "functional areas" in defense activities (e.g., supply, manpower, personnel), although these new officials served as advisers only to the Secretary of Defense and were not in the military chain of command; concurrently, an effort was made to strengthen the role of the Joint Chiefs of Staff as national military advisers, by divorcing them from operational responsibilities for their respective service arms.

The last major statutory reorganization occurred in 1958. It was prompted by recurrent disagreement and "split papers" among the Joint Chiefs and continuing intraservice rivalries during the Eisenhower administration. Under this act, the Secretary of Defense was permitted to exercise his authority *directly upon unified military commands;* he could, for example, transfer weapons from one military service to another and centralize military research. In effect, the Secretary of Defense could now define the roles and missions of the separate services, thereby bringing about substantial de facto unification of the armed forces. This act endeavored to make the Joint Chiefs of Staff concerned primarily with national strategic planning; the operational responsibility of each member of JCS in his respective service arm was further reduced; all combat forces were now included in a "unified command," embracing elements of army, navy, and air force contingents. See Major John F. McMahon, Jr., "Streamlining the Joint Chiefs of Staff," *Military Review* **XLIX** (January, 1969), 36–47; Gene M. Lyons, "The New Civil-Military Relations," in Andrew M. Scott and Raymond H. Dawson, eds., *Readings in the Making of American Foreign Policy* (New York: Macmillan, 1965), pp. 411–420.

ons throughout the international community.[19]

In pursuing the twofold objective of more unified strategic planning and greater coordination among military activities, the Joint Chiefs became increasingly occupied with the preparation of long-range, detailed projections of America's strategic needs and of the resources available for meeting them. In making such projections, the JCS were required to take political, economic, and other relevant factors into account in determining national military strategy. After such strategy had been formulated and agreed upon, the specific needs of the military services were determined; these needs were in turn reflected in the budgetary requests submitted by the Department of Defense to the White House, and ultimately to Congress.*

As for the goal of more effective coordination among the services in military action, several noteworthy developments occurred after 1947. The National Security Act of 1947, we need to recall, anticipated that each member of the Joint Chiefs would wear "two hats": one as the *operational commander* of his service, and the other as a *national staff officer* who was supposed to formulate military strategy for the country as a whole. That these two roles were, from the beginning, somewhat antithetical seems undeniable. Nor was this ambivalence completely eliminated by the various modifications in national defense structure in the years that followed. As long as each chief remained the head of his respective military arm, some tension between these two contrary assignments would perhaps always exist.

Yet since 1947, there has also unquestionably been less emphasis upon each chief's capacity as commandant of his service, and a heightened emphasis upon his role as a national military planner. Writing in 1969, for example, one observer found that the Joint Chiefs exercised their greatest influence, not as service commanders, but in determining "the strategic disposition and employ-

ment of our combined armed forces deployed throughout the world."[20] By the 1970s, the armed forces of the United States remained divided into the three services—the air force, the army, and the navy (with the marine corps as part of the navy). Yet considerable de facto unification of the services had been achieved. If the military forces of the United States were still not "integrated" into a single service, the Korean War, the Vietnam War, and several lesser conflicts demonstrated that a very high level of *operational unification* existed; since World War II, interservice rivalries have posed no significant barrier to the ability of the United States to achieve its military and security objectives abroad.

An impressive level of operational unity was achieved during the incumbency of Robert McNamara as Secretary of Defense (1962–1968). In that period, the device of "unified commands" was employed to promote closer cooperation among the service arms in behalf of national objectives. As early as 1953, a new defense reorganization plan had substantially reduced the responsibility of the Joint Chiefs of Staff for issuing operational orders to the separate services. In 1958 the military roles of the individual services were "reduced" to organizing, training, and equipping forces which would be employed by one of the "unified commands" established to protect or achieve various national security objectives. In time all the *combat forces* of the United States were included in one of these unified commands. Thus, all American combat forces in Western Europe have as their principal objective the defense of the West from a Soviet attack; these forces are, therefore, commanded by the Commander-in-Chief, United States Forces in Europe (CINCEUR). In this theater, the Supreme Allied Commander, Europe (SACEUR) has always been an American officer who directs American, as well as all other NATO, forces.

Functional, as well as geographical, military unification has also been carried out, particularly in regard to new weapons whose use cuts across traditional service lines. An example is the Strike Command (STRICOM), set up to be quickly available for use by commanders of unified forces overseas or to achieve American goals in remote areas. STRICOM consists of elements of the army's "strategic reserve," squadrons available from the Tactical Air Command, and airlift units for transportation. Functional unification was also vigorously pushed under Secretary McNamara for noncombatant units and activities within the armed forces. A Defense Intelligence Agency (DIA) was created to coordinate the separate intelligence operations carried out by the army, navy, and air force; DIA reported to the Secretary of Defense through the Joint Chiefs. Encountering pressure from Congress and public groups to reduce costs, the Secretary of Defense also pro-

---

*One example of such a projection was the Joint Strategic Objectives Plan (JSOP), which served as what one commentator called "the starting point in the development of the annual military budget." The JSOP consisted of two parts: First there was a projection of the *military strategy* which the United States needed to adopt to defend the nation and its allies and to protect its diplomatic vital interests; second, JSOP recommended the *major military forces* required to carry out this strategy. The nature of the forces needed, that is to say, was a function of the strategy contemplated. In such plans, the Joint Chiefs customarily made projections from five to seven years ahead. This meant that they needed to try to answer questions like, "What will the Soviet Union's military potential be like?" and "What will be the capacity of the NATO allies to defend themselves?" from five to seven years in the future. For more detailed treatment of such strategic projections, see Lt. Col. George S. Jones III, "Strategic Planning," *Military Review* XLVII (September, 1967), 14–20; and Major John F. MacMahon, Jr., "Streamlining the Joint Chiefs of Staff," *Ibid.* XLIX (January, 1969), 42–43.

posed a Defense Supply Agency; DSA was to apply principles of centralized management to the acquisition of supplies common to the three services, thereby in theory reducing costs and increasing efficiency.[21]

The effect of creating unified commands was that, as one authority has expressed it, the army, air force, and navy became "divorced totally from the operational chain of command—except for one link—the service chief." Operational orders were now issued from the Joint Chiefs of Staff *directly* to a unified command, where they were relayed to the military forces (like naval units) assigned responsibility for executing them. Unified commanders thus look to the JCS for "instantaneous, timely, and effective direction and advice."[22]

By the 1970s, then, although the separate military services retained their existence, a substantial degree of de facto military unification had been achieved. The Joint Chiefs had been given an expanding responsibility for national defense planning, while their operational duties in the services they headed had been correspondingly reduced.

2. A second major objective of national security policy, according to General Earle G. Wheeler, is *facilitating the extension of professional military advice to civilian policy-makers.* Once military leaders have agreed upon the strategy needed to protect national security, channels and procedures are required for conveying this viewpoint to the President and his advisers within the executive branch. The National Security Act of 1947, we noted earlier, set up the National Security Council to serve as a high-level coordinating mechanism to achieve this purpose. After 1947, other changes broadened the scope of military-political coordination and provided new procedures for continous liaison at many levels of government.

A former director of the Joint Chiefs of Staff, General Andrew Goodpaster, has observed that the Chiefs convey their advice to civilian officials both *formally* and *informally.* Formally, the National Security Council has served since 1947 as the highest-level committee within the American government for promoting the kind of merger between military and political viewpoints demanded to safeguard and promote national security. As a rule, the chairman of the Joint Chiefs expresses the viewpoints of the military establishment on issues considered by the NSC; occasionally, when the Chiefs themselves hold divided opinions, each member of JCS may present the views of his service at NSC meetings.* Although their view are solicited regularly, the Joint Chiefs of Staff are *not members* of the National

Security Council. By law, only the civilian Secretary of Defense is entitled to participate in NSC deliberations; yet the Joint Chiefs may be, and are, invited to do so. Moreover, the President is always at liberty to consult the Joint Chiefs, as a group or individually, without recourse to the National Security Council.

Since its establishment, the National Security Council has had a checkered history.[23] Noting that the NSC had in time become "a well-established part of the governmental machinery" and that the White House had "endorsed, supported and fully utilized" this channel for coordinating national security policy, one student also emphasized that the council had "evolved continuously" since 1947.[24] That evolutionary process, it is safe to say, will continue—if for no other reason than that every incumbent President in the postwar period has used the council differently and has left his own imprint upon it. Until the Korean War in 1950, for example, President Truman did not attend NSC meetings regularly, on the theory that in his absence his advisers would feel less constraint about expressing their opinions freely. Truman also wanted to preserve his own ultimate freedom to decide national security policy, upon the basis of the recommendations made to him by the council.[25]

As a result of his military background, President Eisenhower brought a different perspective to bear in the formulation of national security policy. Valuing careful and prolonged staff work, Eisenhower utilized the NSC heavily; during his administration, elaborate procedures were established within the council to achieve a twofold purpose: to coordinate civilian and military viewpoints in the stage of national security policy *formulation* and (to correct faults that had shown up during the Truman administration) to assure carefully supervised *"follow-up" and implementation of proposals* that had received the President's approval.[26]

President John F. Kennedy—who felt that he had been poorly advised by civilian and military "experts" alike early in his administration, before the disastrous Bay of Pigs episode—was much less staff-oriented than his predecessor. Kennedy preferred to consult his advisers individually or in small groups. He was also prone to create *ad hoc* advisory committees, as specific issues arose which required a presidential decision. An example was the *ad hoc* committee (later called the "Executive Committee of the National Security Council"*) assembled to advise the president

---

*Such divisions of opinion among the Joint Chiefs have, however, become less frequent than they were during the 1950s.

*This committee consisted of Secretary of State Dean Rusk and four other high-ranking State Department officials, Secretary of Defense Robert McNamara, two other civilian advisers from the Defense Department, General Maxwell Taylor (chairman of the Joint Chiefs), CIA Director John McCone, Attorney General Robert Kennedy, Secretary of the Treasury Douglas Dillon, and

when evidence was discovered late in 1962 that the Soviet Union was installing offensive missile sites in Cuba. It was only *after* the President had largely decided how the United States would respond to this threat—by imposing a blockade (or "quarantine") against Cuba, with an implicit threat of more forceful measures if this failed—that the National Security Council was called into session![27]

President Johnson's use of the National Security Council contained elements of both Eisenhower's and Kennedy's approaches. Like President Eisenhower, Johnson met regularly with the NSC, solicited a wide range of opinions from its members, and generally availed himself of the kind of regularized procedures for bringing his political and military advisers together that the council afforded. Yet under Johnson, the NSC did *not* have the organizational complexity and elaborate structure it possed in the Eisenhower period. Like President Kennedy, Johnson also depended upon *ad hoc* committees, White House aides, and individuals outside the government to provide him with advice on national security problems. Criticized severely during the Vietnam War because of undue "military influence" alleged to be present during his administration, President Johnson repeatedly stated that, in the last analysis, the President determined national security policy. Johnson, for example, personally selected targets in North Vietnam to be bombed by the United States Air Force; any "escalation" in hostilities in Vietnam was a result of his personal decision.[28]

A few months after he assumed office in 1969, as we have mentioned, President Richard M. Nixon announced that Secretary of State William Rogers would serve as his spokesman, and that the State Department would coordinate all governmental activities in foreign affairs. At the same time, President Nixon also designated the National Security Council as the proper organ for considering national security problems and for making recommendations to the President. Directed by White House assistant, Dr. Henry Kissinger, a wide-ranging series of studies for the National Security Council was undertaken in the early months of Nixon's presidency. These developments presaged a "revitalization" of the NSC. As is always the case when governmental agencies jockey for influence in decision-making, the *personalities* of leading officials—the President, the Secretary of State, the Secretary of Defense, White House aides—played a key role in the outcome. Early indications were that, given an inexperienced Secretary of State and a President keenly interested in foreign affairs, the National

Security Council would probably play a more decisive role than it had under Presidents Kennedy and Johnson, but that it still would not reach the pinnacle it had attained under Eisenhower.[29]

Two other formal devices for facilitating the exchange of viewpoints between military and civilian policy-makers may be mentioned briefly. One of these is the Office of International Security Affairs, in the Department of Defense (ISA). As set forth in a directive from the Department of Defense on May 20, 1961. the Assistant Secretary of Defense for National Security Affairs serves as the "principal staff assistant" to the Secretary of Defense for national security problems. Heading an office consisting of civilian and military officials, the Assistant Secretary for ISA has the general responsibility for relating military interests and programs to over-all American foreign policy goals.* More specifically, ISA is the Defense Department's link with the Department of State. With both regional and functional units, the internal organization of ISA largely parallels the structure of the State Department itself. Thus, the director of ISA's Latin American directorate, for example, deals with his opposite number in the State Department's Bureau of Inter-American Affairs, to assure continuity in American foreign policy toward that region.

Several programs in which the Defense Department is involved come under ISA's jurisdiction. These include the provision of arms-aid to other countries through the Military Assistance Program (MAP); problems arising out of the treatment of prisoners of war, as in the Vietnam conflict; the operations of Military Assistance Advisory Groups (MAGS) which the United States sends to other countries when requested to do so, perhaps to train military forces abroad or to work with another country in antiguerrilla campaigns; efforts by the United States to gain acceptance of an antiproliferation agreement, inhibiting the spread of nuclear weapons; and issues affecting the cohesiveness of NATO, Soviet intervention in

---

two presidential assistants—McGeorge Bundy and Theodore Sorensen. Later, USIA Deputy Director Donald Wilson was included in the deliberations. See Theodore C. Sorensen, *Kennedy* (New York: Harper & Row, 1965), pp. 674–675.

---

*Our discussion of ISA in the Department of Defense provides a natural occasion for emphasising a distinction that has largely been left implicit thus far in the discussion of national security policy. Confusion may very easily arise between the closely related terms, "national security policy" and "foreign policy." How precisely do they differ? The thrust of our discussion so far is that *the former is a constituent part of the latter.* Foreign policy is the broader and more inclusive concept; it *includes* national security policy, but it may (and nearly always does) include other factors not directly related to national security (such, perhaps, as cultural and educational relations with other countries, economic aid programs and tariff negotiations, or many aspects of American diplomacy in the United Nations). Put differently, in principle (if not always in practice), foreign policy goals *determine* national security policy. The Joint Chiefs of Staff, for example, plan military strategy on the basis of America's objectives in world affairs, as determined by civilian policy-makers.

Eastern Europe, and the growing Soviet naval threat in the Mediterranean area. ISA has proved extremely useful to the State Department in permitting this agency to communicate its viewpoints to civilian and military officials in the Department of Defense.[30]

Another formal channel of communication between civilian and military officials involved in national security policy was the *Senior Interdepartmental Group*, established early in 1966 by President Johnson. Believing that some more systematic approach to coordinating national security policy was needed than President Kennedy's reliance upon *ad hoc* committees, Johnson established a new high-level interdepartmental committee, chaired by the Under Secretary of State. The President's directive designated SIG to serve as a "focal point for decisions and actions on overseas interdepartmental matters which are referred to it by the Secretary of State or by an Assistant Secretary of State, or raised by the action of an individual member." Endeavoring to avoid many of the pitfalls endemic in the committee system, President Johnson gave the Under Secretary of State the right to "decide all matters" after discussion by SIG; other members of the committee, however, had a right to appeal the decision to higher authority. Besides the State Department, other agencies represented on SIG were the Department of Defense (represented by the Deputy Secretary of Defense); the directors of the Agency for International Development (AID), the United States Information Agency (USIA), and the Central Intelligence Agency (CIA); the chairman of the Joint Chiefs of Staff; and the Special Assistant to the President for National Security Affairs. When issues arose affecting their interests and responsibilities, other agencies of the government were invited to the committee's meetings.[31]

Since World War II, numerous *informal* methods for promoting cooperation and an exchange of viewpoints among agencies involved in national security policy have also evolved. One of these is State Department participation in the budget-making process in the Department of Defense. Earlier it was noted that the defense budget contains long-range projections of national strategy which are in turn functions of analyses of political and military developments likely to affect the security of the United States. Before its budget recommendations are put in final form, therefore, the Pentagon solicits the views of the State Department in an effort to assure that projected military force levels are those required to achieve the objectives of the United States abroad.

Mention might also be made of the extent to which the training of military officers in all the armed services increasingly entails emphasis upon *political* subjects and issues closely related to defense planning. At the United States Military Academy and Naval Academy, and at service colleges where senior commanders and staff officers are trained (like the Air War College), the armed services follow curriculums which are heavily infused with political content.

Still another informal technique of coordination is the State–Defense Department Officer Exchange Program, inaugurated early in 1961. The purpose of the program, in the words of Secretary of State Christian A. Herter, was "the continuing development of personnel in both departments who share understanding and perspective in the gray area where foreign policy and military policy come in contact or overlap." Under this program, a Foreign Service officer may be assigned to the Pentagon for a period of two years, or he may attend one of the military service colleges. In the Pentagon, this officer might be given responsibilities in ISA, where he could be asked to write a study on the future of the North Atlantic alliance system. Similarly, a navy captain billeted for a two-year tour of duty at the State Department might be asked to prepare a study dealing with the implications of the Sixth Fleet's proposed visit to various Mediterranean ports. After eight years, both the Secretary of State and the Secretary of Defense expressed their belief that this exchange program was of great value and should be continued. Thus, Secretary of State William P. Rogers found that it was "a substantial success"; that it had "increased the base of personnel experienced in dealing with politico–military problems"; and that it had also "contributed to the improvement of State–Defense relationships."

A somewhat different approach involves the assignment of State Department officials as Political Advisers to military commands overseas. As a consultant to the American commander, the Political Adviser familiarizes him with political, economic, and other relevant implications of military decisions affecting American relations with other countries. Attached to such offices as the Commander-in-Chief, Pacific (CINCPAC), or of the Commander, Military Airlift Command (MAC), these Political Advisers have also facilitated intimate State–Defense Department cooperation.[32]

The combination of these formal and informal techniques of coordination has gone far toward erasing the old distinction between "military" and "political" questions and merging these two essential ingredients into a cohesive national security policy. This is not to say that all problems in formulating and executing national security policy have been solved. A later portion of the chapter will call attention to ongoing issues in this regard. But it does indicate recognition among all the major agencies of government concerned that a unified national approach to security issues is indispensable and that continual attention must be devoted to achieving the desired synthesis of military and political components.

3. A third principle of successful national

security policy—in some respects, its most essential requirement—*is preservation of civilian supremacy in policy-making.* The Founding Fathers regarded this concept as vital to the preservation of the republic; it is no less basic as the United States approaches its second century. Indeed, with the weapons controlled by military establishments today, and with the economic power that is in their hands, both the need of adhering to the precept, and the difficulty of doing so, may be greater than ever. When the defense sector is by all odds the largest category in the national budget; when military commanders control weapons powerful enough to devastate the planet and make parts of it uninhabitable; when, by the late 1960s, some 3.5 million men and women were in active service (and another 1 million in the active reserves); when some military leaders obviously chafe under restrictions imposed upon them by civilian authorities during the Vietnam War; when the public is expressing apprehension about the power exercised by the "military–industrial complex" in American life; when, in one instance after another, military elements have overthrown civilian rulers in other countries, often on the theory that they are the "custodians" of national welfare—in this setting, it is imperative that the concept of ultimate civilian leadership be strengthened and that methods for exerting effective civilian control be continually improved.

The National Security Act of 1947 and its later modifications did not ignore this requirement. The National Security Council was and remains a civilian-dominated advisory agency. When President Nixon asserted early in 1969 that, in reinvigorating the NSC, he would retain final responsibility for deciding policy, he was reiterating a principle emphasized many times by Presidents since World War II. Only rarely in recent history—and the outstanding case was General Douglas MacArthur during the Korean War—have American military commanders contested the idea of civilian control. Indeed, members of the military elite sometimes appear to understand many of the implications of the principle of civilian supremacy better than some civilian groups! During crises like the Vietnam conflict, the President perhaps encountered as much dissatisfaction from civilians for "shackling" the military as he did from the Pentagon itself. Although there are clearly no grounds for complacency, the fact is that at no time in American history has there existed a serious danger of military *coup d'état* against civilian authority. In practice, there is as least as much danger from a contrary tendency: that civilian officials may infringe too heavily upon matters of military strategy and tactics or other fields lying outside the realm of their competence and training.

In recent years, two figures—President John F. Kennedy and Secretary of Defense Robert McNamara—symbolized the dominant role of civilian leadership over the military establishment. Poorly advised by the Joint Chiefs of Staff concerning the Bay of Pigs undertaking, as we have mentioned, President Kennedy remained forever skeptical about the advice he received from generals and admirals. It was significant, for example, that Kennedy rejected the advice of the Joint Chiefs that the United States immediately employ force to eliminate Soviet missile sites from Cuba in 1962. It is no less noteworthy that—even in what was perhaps the most dangerous confrontation between the United States and the Soviet Union, involving the possibility of a global nuclear war—President Kennedy's military advisers did not seriously contest his right to decide national policy. Once the President had made his decision, the armed forces of the United States executed his orders promptly and effectively. Similarly, much as the "high brass" may have chafed under restrictions upon military activity imposed by the White House in Vietnam, there was little or no evidence that they refused to abide by White House directives. When military officers could not reconcile themselves to the President's decisions, they could resign, retire, or be relieved of command. As private citizens, they could (and sometimes did) express their viewpoints on any public issue.

In upholding the concept of civilian supremacy in national security policy, Secretary of Defense Robert McNamara's impress was especially strong. From 1961 until his retirement in 1968, McNamara did more than any incumbent in that office to assure civilian control over the Pentagon and to initiate new procedures calculated to strengthen that control. As we noted earlier, McNamara was compelled to accept certain realities, such as the existence of three separate military services, continued competition among them for available funds, and even fears on Capitol Hill that he would become an all-powerful "defense Czar."

Within these limitations, however, McNamara accomplished a great deal in defense reorganization and in maintaining civilian control. During his tenure, the powers of his office were greatly expanded. Securing congressional approval when needed, McNamara made the civilian-dominated office of the Secretary of Defense the hub of Pentagon activities—if not sometimes of national security policy itself. McNamara's advisers (popularly called his "Whiz Kids") immersed themselves actively in every sphere of defense, from logistics to military strategy. Relying upon computer-based cost effectiveness studies and other evaluations, McNamara was instrumental in setting up eight unified military commands, in allocating combat functions to these new commands, in standardizing much military procurement, in closing down obsolete military bases at home and abroad, in determining budgetary allocations for the armed forces and in rigorously questioning ideas (like the navy's need for new aircraft carriers) long held by military commanders and their supporters in Congress, and in communicating advice to the White House which was known to be at variance with the opinions held by military commanders. The combination of McNamara's intellectual brilliance, his energy and drive, his devotion to the ideal of civilian supremacy—along with an obvious reluctance or inability by his counterpart in the State Department to exert that department's views with equal effectiveness—dictated that McNamara function as perhaps the dominant Cabinet officer under Presidents Kennedy and Johnson.[33] Significantly, it was only after his departure from the government that fears were widely expressed that the "military–industrial complex" was exercising an overriding influence upon national policy-making. While McNamara was Secretary of Defense, the opposite complaint tended to be voiced, by many civilians as well as military leaders: that the Secretary of Defense and his "Whiz Kids" too often ventured into areas like military strategy which were beyond their competence, and that the computer was rapidly superceding the highly trained, experienced military professional in defense planning. A not unrelated lament (repeatedly heard on Capitol Hill) was that in the interest of a "unified" approach to national security planning, McNamara was "gagging" the Joint Chiefs of Staff and was imposing a spurious unity in the Pentagon. Secretary McNamara's civilian managers were criticized by the House Armed Services Committee in 1968 for relying too heavily upon those "who lack actual military experience and a frame of reference which can best be gained by long immersion in military matters over a period of years."[34]

Thus, throughout the postwar period, the constitutional principle of civilian supremacy in national policy-making has not been in serious jeopardy. American military commanders continue to regard the concept as central to national security planning, as when General Matthew B. Ridgway advocated an "intimate day-to-day collaboration among military and civilian leaders, wherein the civilian leaders propose the *ends* that must be achieved and the military leaders supply their estimate of how much can be attained by military *means* and how those means may be best employed."[35]

The CIA and Other Intelligence Agencies

A noteworthy innovation of the National Security Act of 1947 was the establishment of the Central Intelligence Agency as a separate organ, accountable to the National Security Council and ultimately to the President. The CIA grew out of the widespread conviction that existing intelligence operations were inadequate, fragmented, uncoordinated, and generally incapable of making the kind of contribution required to safeguard the interests of the United States in its new role as a great power. Correctly or not, many Americans attributed the military disaster at Pearl Harbor to an *intelligence failure.* Nor, they felt, had the American people and their leaders been sufficiently warned about the wartime and postwar goals of the Soviet Union in regions like Eastern Europe, where Russian and American diplomatic objectives quickly came into conflict.

By their very nature, intelligence operations tend to be surrounded by a veil of secrecy. The purpose of intelligence activities would be defeated if they became known to actual or potential enemies (sometimes even to friends and allies); no less vitally, the clandestine sources relied upon by the CIA and other intelligence units would be jeopardized by public disclosure. Such realities mean of course that any discussion of the role of intelligence agencies in the process of national decision-making must, to a substantial degree, be speculative. Certain facts about the CIA and related agencies are public knowledge. It is incontestable, for example, that the CIA exists (although even the fact of its existence was denied by government officials for many years after 1947). Nor is it open to question that the CIA's personnel and budget have grown substantially since its creation. One former official of the Kennedy administration has estimated total expenditures for all intelligence operations as approximating $2 billion annually, with the CIA receiving the lion's share. Over the years, the size of the CIA grew steadily—by the early 1960s the agency "had almost as many officers abroad engaged in intelligence activities as the State Department had for the whole range of its activities." Moreover, the CIA's personnel tended to be capable, dedicated, and (in contrast to the prevailing stereotype about its personnel) infused with enthusiasm and *new ideas.** Very quickly, the CIA became an influential organ of the American government, exercising an important role in national security and foreign policy. Even President Harry Truman expressed concern about the growth in its influence; by the late 1960s and early 1970s, many critics of American foreign policy were certain that the CIA had become in effect the real "power structure" in foreign affairs,

---

*See the informative discussion of the role of intelligence agencies in national policy-making in Roger Hilsman, *To Move a Nation: The Politics of Foreign Policy in the Administration of John F. Kennedy* (Garden City, N.Y.: Doubleday, 1967), pp. 63–91. Hilsman, formerly the head of the State Department's Bureau of Intelligence Research, has presented a provocative and balanced discussion of what is often a highly controversial issue, too often discussed in polemical terms.

eclipsing the influence of the State Department and the National Security Council.

As its title suggests, the CIA serves as the *central* intelligence agency of the American government; it supervises and directs the activities of what has come to be called the "intelligence community," whose members both carry on intelligence operations independently within their own spheres and cooperate in joint intelligence ventures. Although he is not a statutory member of the National Security Council, the director of the CIA frequently attends its meetings in an advisory capacity; he and his principal subordinates are of course also available to advise the President on intelligence matters. A major responsibility of the CIA, drawing upon the resources of the intelligence community, is preparation of documents like the National Intelligence Estimates (NIE's) and other reports regularly submitted to the White House. NIE's provide the President and his principal advisers with the intelligence community's summary and evaluation of important events and crises overseas likely to affect American foreign policy, such as a new violent eruption in the Middle East or tendencies in the Sino–Soviet dispute. Other documents (like the National Intelligence Surveys) consist of comprehensive catalogs of information about different countries, analyzing such subjects as their governmental and political processes, their economic conditions and prospects, and other topics relevant to the formulation of American foreign policy.*

The concept of "intelligence" as a component of national security and foreign policy may be variously defined, and the process of intelligence involves several different, if closely related, functions. Broadly speaking, the function of intelligence is to provide policy-makers with *reliable information*, together with an *evaluation or analysis* of such information, as a basis for decision-making. In addition, intelligence involves miscellaneous functions which are difficult to categorize. Thwarting the espionage efforts of an enemy ("counter-espionage" activities); preventing the assassination of a governmental leader friendly to the United States; furnishing supplies to a revolutionary movement against a regime which is unfriendly to America; fostering popular suspicion of Soviet Russia or Communist China in African countries; endeavoring to win good will toward the West in labor unions or youth movements abroad—these are merely some of the enterprises which the CIA and other American intelligence agencies have been engaged in in recent years. Such activities are almost always *covert intelligence operations*. Disclosure of the CIA's role in them can, and not infrequently does, cancel out any gains for America in undertaking them at all. Although they tend to be among the better-known and more publicized activities carried on by intelligence agencies, however, such operations tend to be a relatively minor part of the intelligence community's over-all responsibilities. The primary duty of the CIA and related agencies, as we have said, consists of gathering and evaluating information needed by American policy-makers for making sound decisions affecting national security and foreign affairs.

Such information may be (and usually is) derived from both *overt* (or open) and *covert* (or clandestine) sources. For most issues affecting national security and foreign policy, the former category yields much more information than the latter. The most valuable "intelligence" source available to the CIA may well be the Library of Congress! Despite the romantic mythology surrounding intelligence work, in reality it often consists of painstaking examination of literally hundreds of foreign periodicals and journals, newspapers, technical reports, and the like (most of which are fairly readily available to ordinary citizens); from such sources, the bulk of information incorporated into intelligence reports is collected. What kind of progress is the Soviet Union making in overcoming its agricultural problems? Have Moscow or Peking recently made some new technological breakthrough that might threaten the security of the United States? How stable are the Communist regimes in the smaller Marxist nations? Are fundamental changes to be expected in the foreign policy of Communist China after Mao Tse-tung's death? What is the real extent of Soviet "influence" or "control" over the government of Egypt? What are the prospects for political stability in Brazil? The Library of Congress is apt to yield more information on such question than are the CIA's agents abroad. A major CIA enterprise involves *biographical research*, the importance of which has risen significantly during an era of rapid and pervasive political change. Many of the leaders of Afro–Asian nationalist move-

---

*Besides the CIA, the "intelligence community" consists of the *Federal Bureau of Investigation* (FBI), which concentrates upon intelligence operations within the United States; the *National Security Agency* (considered perhaps the most "supersecret" of all intelligence operations), which specializes in communications intelligence, such as cryptography and the "breaking" of diplomatic and military codes; a *Defense Intelligence Agency* (DIA), established in 1961 in the Pentagon to coordinate the military intelligence activities carried on by the army, navy, and air force (military attachés stationed in American diplomatic installations abroad, for example, send their reports to the Pentagon); the *Bureau of Intelligence and Research* in the State Department; and the intelligence operations conducted by the Atomic Energy Commission (which are concerned with the military aspects of nuclear and thermonuclear power). Individually, these agencies carry on separate, often highly specialized, intelligence functions; under CIA direction, they often collaborate in joint intelligence operations; normally they "pool" their resources in the preparation of such reports as the National Intelligence Estimates.

ments, for example, have died, retired, or been forced from office. Who are the "rising" members of Indonesia's or Ghana's or Iraq's political elite? What are their social and education backgrounds? What are their viewpoints toward the United States, the Soviet Union, and other countries? If a successful revolution erupts in Ethiopia, what groups are likely to spearhead it, and what will be their new program at home and abroad? Again, in biographical research, public sources provide the preponderance of information available to intelligence agencies.

The intelligence process has of course traditionally depended also upon covert sources of information. "Cloak-and-dagger" operations, secret agents, informers, and the like sometimes provide data needed by decision-makers which is available from no other source. Totalitarian governments especially tend to be highly secretive about activities normally publicized widely in the American society. In all probability, intelligence officials in Moscow or Peking need to make minimum use of secret agents to keep track of America's progress in space technology; 90 percent or more of what they wish to know is available in American newspapers, journals, and scientific publications. These countries, however, tend to be highly secretive about their space programs. Indeed, outside the West (in the Arab world, for instance, almost any information bearing upon military or foreign policy tends to be "classified") obstacles are often deliberately placed in the path of foreigners seeking to obtain such information. While the general public (misled often by popular novelists) tends to exaggerate the role of covert sources in intelligence operations, it remains true that information supplied by such sources does supply the missing pieces of the puzzle needed by intelligence officials to acquire a complete picture of the problem with which they are working. It is difficult to think, for example, of a substitute for the information provided to the Kennedy administration by the U-2's and other reconnaissance aircraft which photographed Soviet missile installations in Cuba during the early 1960s.

Even more difficult than intelligence-gathering, however, is the accurate *evaluation* of information collected. Facts, in the popular phrase, may "speak for themselves"; but the task of the intelligence expert is to ascertain what they are saying! More often than not, equally well-informed individuals can and do differ as to the *meaning* of factual data. Aerial photographs, let us agree, provide documentary evidence that the Soviet Union is ringing Moscow and other major Russian cities with antiballistic missile defenses. What precisely are the implications of this fact for the security and diplomatic interests of the United States? Does it indicate that Moscow has decided to "escalate" the arms race, perhaps reflecting a conviction in the Kremlin that disarmament dis-

cussions are foredoomed to failure? Does it instead indicate merely Soviet Russia's "defensive" reaction to ongoing American progress in space and missile technology? These and other interpretations are possible. Intelligence officials must *interpret and analyze* the information collected, indicating at least *alternative conclusions* which might be drawn from their data. The President and his principal advisers can then decide upon the most likely interpretation and can make national decisions accordingly.

In practice, of course, the line separating intelligence functions from policy-making tends to be less distinct than we have drawn it here, to the point sometimes of disappearing entirely. Theoretically, intelligence agencies do not *make* national security and foreign policy; they supply the information and analyses upon which such policies are made by higher authorities. Yet it is also true that the nature and accuracy of the information furnished to the President and the National Security Council are key factors in determining the decision ultimately made. A President may give considerable weight to how CIA officials evaluate the information collected, accepting their estimate that X is more likely to happen than W, Y, or Z. Conversely (as occurred after President Kennedy became disillusioned with the CIA after the ill-fated Bay of Pigs invasion of Cuba in 1961), a Chief Executive may be predisposed *against* CIA evaluations, reasoning that he has been "misled" by intelligence officials too often in the past. The precise role which intelligence agencies actually play in the decision-making process is thus likely to vary according to the influence of several major factors: the personality, preferences, and decision-making "style" of the President; the degree of confidence he reposes in the agencies belonging to the intelligence community (which may, in turn, depend upon the kind of advice rendered to him in the past); the kinds of issues—and the *urgency of the issues*—confronting the United States during any given time interval; the effectiveness of other agencies (like the State Department or the U.S. Information Agency) in providing persuasive alternative policy recommendations to the White House; and the conception of their roles held by the director of the CIA and other intelligence officials.

Although the collection and evaluation of information are the primary responsibilities of the CIA and other members of the intelligence community, these agencies are also engaged in a variety of other operations aimed at strengthening national security and promoting the diplomatic interests of the United States. "The wall of secrecy" customarily surrounding these activities poses a real barrier to accurate knowledge concerning the role and nature of CIA involvement in specific episodes abroad. The full story of the CIA's part in the American-encouraged movement to oust Iranian Premier Mossadegh in the early 1950s is still not known to outsiders. (Mossadegh threatened to cut off Iran's oil supplies to the West and to permit Soviet Russia to expand its position in the Persian Gulf area.) Similarly, the CIA was also involved in the successful American attempt (discussed more fully in Chapter 12) to overthrow the pro-Communist regime of Jacobo Arbenz in Guatemala in 1954; anti-Marxists groups which invaded Guatemala from Honduras were equipped with American-supplied weapons. Separatist tendencies in Indonesia during the 1950s, weakening the government of President Sukarno, were also fostered by the CIA. During the 1960s and early 1970s, the CIA was massively involved in Southeast Asia. For several years, the CIA had carried on anti-Communist programs in Laos and Cambodia; informed observers were convinced that the agency maintained a large and influential "presence" in South Vietnam, where it conducted various clandestine operations related to the Vietnam War. These and other newsworthy examples illustrate the range and nature of overseas CIA operations in recent years.

Had the CIA gotten "out of control," to the point perhaps of determining American foreign policy in some settings? Did its activities exceed constitutional and statutory authority, making it a kind of "state within a state," whose operations were really impervious to control by the President, Congress, or other higher authorities? With regard to national security and foreign policy, was the CIA the real "power structure" of the American government and the epicenter of influence within the military–industrial complex? Could the decline of America's influence in regions like Latin America or Africa, or the inability of the United States to achieve its objectives in Southeast Asia, be attributed to CIA machinations in other countries? Satisfactory answers to such questions were not easy to acquire. As in intelligence operations themselves, it was often easier to secure agreement on many (although by no means all) of the salient facts than to arrive at a consensus on what the facts proved. The substantial growth in the size and budgetary allocations of the CIA and other members of the intelligence community during the postwar period, for example, was undeniable. The CIA's involvement in Southeast Asia in recent years also seemed beyond dispute. Nor could it be seriously questioned that the CIA had played a significant role in episodes like the U-2 crisis of 1960 and the abortive Bay of Pigs invasion of Cuba in 1961; in these and several other less publicized incidents, the United States has suffered clear diplomatic defeats.*

Much more open to question, however, was the matter of what such examples really proved about the role of the CIA in the formulation and execution of national policy and the adequacy of the controls established to keep it and other intelligence agencies within their proper bounds. Clearly, the more extreme criticisms directed against the CIA have been misplaced. By nature, intelligence agencies can, in a democracy, easily become targets for criticism which ought rightfully to be directed at the nation's civilian leaders and the policies they espouse. In the American setting, the CIA and other intelligence agencies will thus perhaps always experience difficulty in maintaining a good "public image," especially with certain segments of the public like intellectuals and political liberals. To many Americans, intelligence activities are inherently suspect, if not ethically abhorrent. Intelligence activities per se (especially espionage and counter-espionage operations) appear to be at variance with the American tradition, with the concept of "fair play," and with the values which Americans identify with the New World vis-à-vis the diplomatic connivings of the Old World. Moreover, the CIA is vulnerable to public criticism, because of the very nature of its operations. The agency's "failures" can be, and frequently are, exposed to public scrutiny and ridicule. Its successes, however, do not and cannot receive the same degree of publicity. The Soviet government, for example, derived maximum propaganda advantage from exposing the CIA's role in the U-2 affair. But neither the agency itself, nor foreign governments concerned, are likely to inform the world that the CIA has contributed to preventing a coup against a government friendly to the West, or that because of CIA efforts the President has been informed ahead of time of an important change in Soviet foreign policy, or that the CIA has successfully taken steps to lessen Chinese influence in East Africa. Among other reasons, the CIA is inhibited from engaging in such publicity because of the necessity to protect its sources and to prevent its future operations from becoming compromised.

From the beginning, the CIA has been subjected to restraints imposed by constitutional and statutory authority. By law, the director of the CIA and other intelligence officials are clearly subordinate to the President and the National Security Council; the agency has no independent authority to determine American foreign policy or to engage in activities without presidential approval. Although the extent of its actual supervision is unknown, a congressional CIA "watchdog committee" also oversees the agency's operations;

---

*For a more detailed discussion of the U-2 crisis of 1960, which stemmed from American overflights of Soviet territory by high-flying reconnaissance aircraft, see the author's *Nations in a Multipolar World* (New York: Harper & Row, 1968), pp. 102–105; the Bay of Pigs invasion is treated at greater length in Chapter 12.

the director of the CIA and his subordinates are periodically interrogated on Capitol Hill (although seldom in public sessions). From time to time also, the President appoints a committee, consisting of prominent citizens, to report to him on CIA performance and to make recommendations for improvements in the intelligence field. Not infrequently, administrative and personnel changes result from such reports. Controls, therefore, plainly exist to keep the activities of the CIA consonant with the over-all purposes of American foreign and defense policies and to guard against usurpation by intelligence agencies.

How effective are these restraints? Again, it is necessary to reiterate the difficulty of answering this question with assurance. Outsiders are not privy to the meetings of the National Security Council or the sessions on Capitol Hill at which CIA officials are questioned. From the evidence available, it seems clear that intelligence estimates have sometimes been faulty as in the Bay of Pigs episode. On some occasions, the CIA has badly misjudged the diplomatic consequences of exposure (as in the U-2 affair), a failure in which other executive officials have also shared. In still other instances, the underlying *wisdom or rationale* of national policy could legitimately be questioned (as in Laos or Cambodia). In common with all governmental agencies, the CIA is no doubt from time to time afflicted with bureaucratic confusion and delay, with an impulse toward "empire-building," with a desire to maximize its own prestige and influence, and with an exaggerated idea of its own mission. The influence exercised by the CIA will be a function to some extent of the "countervailing power" brought to bear in the policy-making councils by the President himself, the White House staff, the State Department, and other agencies involved in the foreign policy process. In some periods, the CIA may have exercised a disproportionate influence in policy-making because of a problem discussed in Chapter 3: the existence of a vacuum growing out of the unwillingness or inability of the State Department to discharge its proper responsibilities.

Yet after these realities have been acknowledged, the judgment of many experienced public officials and commentators is that the United States possesses *a highly effective* intelligence establishment—in some respects, the best in the contemporary world. Considering its relatively brief existence, the CIA has learned much (in some periods perhaps painfully) since World War II. It has conducted its operations with greater skill and finesse over the years. In the light of the unique problems accompanying the operation of an intelligence network within a democratic society, the restraints upon the CIA and other agencies belonging to the intelligence community appear to have worked reasonably well. Exposés

and well-publicized incidents of American intelligence failures to the contrary, there seems to be very little reliable evidence that CIA officials have endeavored to usurp authority, that they have sought to "subvert" American foreign policy, or that in anything more than isolated instances they have abused the power and secrecy accompanying the agency's role. More often than not, perhaps, the real "failures" of the CIA have been *defects of national policy itself*, for which the President and his chief advisers—and, behind them, Congress and the public—bear the major responsibility.

Two contrary dangers exist with respect to the operations of intelligence agencies. One is that, without constant vigilance and effective safeguards, they may get "out of bounds," exercising powers assigned to other agencies or to their superiors; the secrecy surrounding their activities makes this a problem that must be controlled by continued scrutiny and awareness of the dangers involved. The other hazard—exemplified by many of the CIA's critics and by groups disaffected with American foreign policy—is that the CIA becomes the target of emotionalism and polemical denunciations, the symbol of everything that is "wrong" with the diplomacy of the United States. In recent years, political liberals have been prone to depict the CIA in much the same terms that many Americans visualized "international Communism" during the 1940s and 1950s—as a gigantic conspiracy, accounting for the inability of the United States to achieve its foreign policy goals. The complexity of foreign policy issues—coupled with the continued hiatus between what Americans would like to accomplish, and what they are able to achieve overseas—provides a fertile ground for demonological accounts of policy failures. In the long run, however, this tendency could prove as subversive of democracy and the American way of life—and could pose as many obstacles to the fulfillment of national purposes abroad—as the failure of intelligence agencies to confine their activities to proper channels.*

*Our discussion of the role of intelligence agencies in national security and foreign policy relies heavily upon Hilsman, *op. cit.*, pp. 63–91; Allan W. Dulles, *The Craft of Intelligence* (New York: Harper & Row, 1963); and Curton M. Sapin, *The Making of United States Foreign Policy* (Washington, D.C.: Brookings Institution, 1966), pp. 287–328. For a more general treatment of the question, see Harry H. Ransom, *Central Intelligence and National Security* (Cambridge, Mass.: Harvard University Press, 1958); a more dated account is Sherman Kent, *Strategic Intelligence* (Princeton, N.J.: Princeton University Press, 1949). For a discussion of the process whereby the State Department permitted the CIA to assume functions formerly performed by the former, see Dean Acheson, *Present at the Creation* (New York: Norton, 1969), pp. 157–163. Several "inside" accounts and exposés of the CIA of greater or less reliability are: David Wise and Thomas B. Ross, *The Invisible Government*

Research Organizations and "Think Tanks"

A striking development in the postwar period has been the extent to which research, study, and debate with regard to issues affecting national security have become "institutionalized" within the military establishment or carried out under Pentagon auspices. The Defense Department, one commentator has observed, may indeed "be the largest debating and research society in the world." In addition, it utilizes the services of a broad range of consultants, consisting of individuals, groups, and business concerns who advise it on aspects of national defense policy.*

Many of the larger universities in the United States have "institutes" or other organizations which conduct research for the armed forces. A number of private business concerns—like the Hudson Institute and the Rand Corporation—specialize in defense analysis and military research projects. The Rand Corporation is perhaps the best-known and most prestigious of these organizations. Heavily supported by air force research grants, this concern has attracted a large and able staff of experts whose studies and reports have affected postwar defense policy momentously. Rand Corporation studies, for example, were instrumental in such developments as the use of space satellites for weather forecasting and military reconnaisance; adoption of the "fail-safe" system used by the air force for preventing an accidental nuclear war; in-flight refueling tech-

niques which greatly extended the range of American long-range bombers; the concept of "second strike capacity" and other ideas central to the strategy of nuclear deterrence; and various ideas and suggestions related to disarmament negotiations.

The Pentagon's reliance upon civilian experts has been in large part responsible for the infusion of new and imaginative ideas into defense planning throughout the postwar period. Insofar as America's armed forces have succeeded in avoiding the rigidities and ossified thinking associated with the "military mind" in recent years—and in some (although certainly not all) respects, the Pentagon has been a remarkably adaptable institution in an age of rapid scientific–technological change—civilian consultants are in no small measure responsible. The exchange of ideas between civilian and military experts has no doubt benefited both—most of all perhaps, the latter. The *willingness* of the armed services to utilize the intellectual resources of the nation, and their apparent readiness to adopt ideas emanating from civilian sources, serve as an antidote to military provincialism and prevent the kind of "alienation" between the two groups that has sometimes fragmented other societies.

At the same time, a group of critics includes civilian consultants and "think tanks" like the Rand Corporation as prominent parts of the military–industrial complex, whose power now extends into nearly every sphere of American life. Student protests in recent years have been directed against military research projects carried out by universities. Experts in the Rand Corporation and the Hudson Institute, some critics assert, have basically *accepted* the militarization of American society and the extension of American power throughout the world; the studies issued by such organizations merely provide the armed services with more effective means for exerting their power and furnish them with a persuasive rationale for costly new weapons programs. In its crudest terms, such criticism alleges that these consultants have no genuine interest in *resolving* international tensions or in *reducing* worldwide military budgets. To the contrary, like all groups belonging to the military–industrial complex, they have a direct stake in perpetuating large-scale military spending, in fostering rapid weapons obsolescence, and in maintaining the armed forces of the United States at a high level of military "readiness"—all at the expense of socially constructive domestic programs. Some of these civilian research organizations (and the Rand Corporation is specifically excluded from the indictment), C. W. Borklund has observed, have been prone to tell "the military customer what he wants to hear to support his own preconceived conviction." We shall discuss the problem of the military–industrial complex at a later stage. It is

(New York: Random House, 1964); Lyman B. Kirkpatrick, *The Real CIA* (New York: Macmillan, 1967); Andrew Tully, *CIA: The Inside Story* (New York: Morrow, 1962); and Paul W. Blackstock, *The Strategy of Subversion: Manipulating the Politics of Other Nations* (Chicago: Quadrangle, 1964). For detailed appraisals of the role of the CIA in specific crises abroad, see David Wise and Thomas B. Ross, *The U-2 Affair* (New York: Random House, 1961); and Klaus Knorr, "Failures in National Estimates: The Case of the Cuban Missiles," *World Politics* 16 (April, 1964), 455–467. Additional information and insight on the role of the CIA, especially in Southeast Asia, are provided in *The New York Times* (April 25, 26, 27, 28, and 29, 1966); and *Time Magazine* 89 (February 24, 1967), 13–17.

*See William W. Kaufmann, *The McNamara Strategy* (New York: Harper & Row, 1964), pp. 291–293. Our discussion of the role of civilian consultants in national security policy also relies upon Sapin, *op. cit.*, pp. 314–315; C. W. Borklund, *The Department of Defense* (New York: Praeger, 1969), pp. 169, 239; and Laurence I. Radway, *Foreign Policy and National Defense* (Glenview, Ill.: Scott, Foresman, 1969), pp. 124–125. For examples of the kinds of studies produced by "think tanks," see Bernard Brodie, *Strategy in the Missile Age* (Princeton, N.J.: Princeton University Press, 1959), and John J. Johnson, *The Role of the Military in Underdeveloped Countries* (Princeton, N.J.: Princeton University Press, 1962) —both books published under the auspices of the Rand Corporation; and Herman Kahn and Andrew J. Wiener, *The Year 2000: A Framework for Speculation on the Next Thirty-Three Years* (New York: Macmillan, 1967), and Frank E. Ambruster, *et al.*, *Can We Win in Vietnam?* (New York: Praeger, 1968)—both published under the auspices of the Hudson Institute.

sufficient here to note that some indictments of this kind undoubtedly have merit. Yet the larger conclusion often drawn from them—that the Pentagon has somehow subverted civilian agencies or "bought" the kind of advice military leaders really want—rests on very dubious evidence. Abuses aside, the Defense Department's reliance upon outside civilian consultants is perhaps crucial in preserving the kind of civilian–military balance required for the survival of democratic government.

RECURRENT PROBLEMS IN NATIONAL SECURITY POLICY

If postwar experience with national security policy affords a reliable guide, one idea would seem to be beyond dispute: many of the questions surrounding national security are *persistent issues*, likely to confront officials and citizens for many years to come. At no point in the past could it be said that most of these questions had been finally "resolved"; nor was there any reasonable expectation that definitive solutions would be found in the future. To the contrary, there is every reason to suppose that the over-all problem of national security policy may become *more difficult* and *more complex* with the passage of time. This result seems assured by several forces. The nuclear balance of terror permits (if it does not in some ways encourage) the use of limited forms of violence in international relations. Ongoing technological and scientific progress continues to render old weapons, strategies, tactics, and the like, obsolete, and to require new organizational and procedural methods for their effective utilization. Meanwhile, the rising costs of modern armaments pose difficult choices for policy-makers, both in terms of how much ought to be spent for national security and how the funds ought to be allocated among the military services. These questions must in turn be answered against a background of massive *domestic* needs and considerable resistance by citizens to higher taxes.

In the concluding section of this chapter we shall focus upon three basic problems associated with national security policy. All of them tend to be recurrent, and some of them may well become more formidable than ever as the attempt is made to merge political and military components into a unified and successful national security policy for the United States.

The Military–Industrial Complex

The first problem is posed by the existence and, according to some accounts, the growing influence at all levels of American society, of what is termed the military–industrial complex. By the 1970s, many government officials and citizens

alike had become apprehensive about the extent to which the armed services had become a powerful economic force within the United States. Even more crucially, to its critics, the military–industrial complex seemed to have steadily expanded its influence over national policy, usurping the role constitutionally assigned to civilian policymakers and undermining traditional safeguards against undue military pressure in governmental decision-making. Some legislators even questioned whether Congress itself had not become a "captive of the military" in making defense appropriations or in approving measures demanded by the Pentagon for conducting the war in Southeast Asia. Other students of American government were concerned about the extent to which the Pentagon "controlled" the White House and the degree to which the military voice drowned out the voices of the President's other advisers. The scientific community—particularly scientific research programs—they felt, had been substantially infiltrated by, and oriented toward, military activities. To critics of recent American foreign policy like Senator J. William Fulbright (Democrat of Arkansas), the military–industrial complex played a key role in America's "arrogance" abroad and explained the tendency of policy-makers to depend upon military force in responding to nationalist movements and insurgencies overseas. It was no less responsible, critics asserted, for Washington's preference for military juntas over revolutionary regimes in other countries and for an official inclination to favor the status quo over radical change in societies abroad. America's "neglect" of urgent internal problems could also be attributed in some measure to the influence of the military–industrial complex. The Pentagon's perennial demand for new and better weapons, its insistence upon constant additions to the nation's nuclear stockpile (already large enough to devastate the planet several times), its urge to supply large quantities of armaments to other governments—such propensities meant that the United States was unable to expend the funds needed for the elimination of poverty or the provision of really adequate educational facilities for a growing population. In brief, the over-all influence of the military–industrial complex was cast, critics charged, in a direction contrary to the highest ethical and humanitarian aspirations of the American society.

On the basis of many criteria, it would be difficult to refute a number of the allegations made concerning the role and influence of the military–industrial complex upon American life. Since World War II, the United States has undeniably experienced a vast buildup in its military strength; by the 1970s, it had acquired perhaps the most potent military arsenal known to world history. Throughout the postwar era, defense spending climbed steadily—to some $80 billion annually by

1970, or close to one-half of the total national budget. In the two decades from 1947 to 1967, the United States and its NATO allies expended over $1 trillion on their defense budgets, or some five times the entire federal budget of the United States in 1970! By the end of the 1960s, the Pentagon was spending around 5 percent of the nation's gross national product; about two-thirds of all federal tax revenues were expended for defense; this exceeded the sum total spent by all units of government (federal, state, and local) for programs like health, education, old-age assistance, and housing; well over one-third of America's blue-collar and professional workers received their wages and salaries from defense production. It was estimated that all federal revenues derived from income taxes on individuals were spent by governmental agencies within the military–industrial complex! Moreover, the commitments and influence of this group were worldwide. The United States had more than forty military allies, and was deeply involved in the security of several other countries (like India). To defend its overseas commitments, America maintained some 429 *major* overseas bases and military installations, along with 2972 minor ones.* The United States maintained close to 150 bases in Japan alone. Around 1 million members of the armed forces were required to staff and operate these installations; and between $4 and $5 billion were needed annually to keep the bases operational; this expenditure constituted a drain of some $2.5 billion on America's acute balance-of-payments problems. Extending from Greenland to the Panama Canal Zone, and from the Azores to Guam, these American military installations involved the United States in the domestic political, military, and economic affairs of many nations. Even in countries which did not contain American military installations, but were near strategic bases, political movements, insurgencies, and other developments might create a threat to American interests. Some critics of recent American foreign policy charged that, by its very military "presence," the United States inescapably intervened in the affairs of countries like Spain, Turkey, and Thailand.[36] In some societies (Vietnam and Thailand were prominent examples), America's military presence was in many respects a devastating force—disrupting ancient ways of life, customs, and institutions; creating economic and financial dislocations; generating popular resentment; and generally negating official claims in Washington that America had no desire to intervene in the domestic affairs of other nations. Determined to preserve its military position in strategic areas around the world, the United States appeared to cast the weight of its influence in behalf of preserving the political status quo and of cooperating with regimes whose outstanding characteristic seemed a readiness to accept American aid—especially military aid—which was often used to maintain them in power.

Critics claimed that, in both its domestic and foreign manifestations, the influence of the military–industrial complex was extremely difficult to counteract. Not only did it wield enormous military and economic power; the Pentagon alone expended some $4 million a year and employed 340 "legislative specialists" in attempts to generate public and legislative support for its policies. In addition, a large number of retired military officers were employed by civilian defense establishments for the purposes of acquiring lucrative contracts from the Pentagon and gaining congressional approval of large defense appropriations.[37]

By many standards, therefore, the military–industrial complex constituted a potent (some commentators said a decisive) influence in American society. By the 1970s, fears were widely expressed that it represented, in the literal sense of the word, a *subversive* force, undermining traditional American values and constitutional safeguards, and exercising a dominant role in determining national policy.

How legitimate were these apprehensions? With all the economic and military power at its disposal, did the military–industrial complex *really* control national policy? Could the Johnson administration's decisions in Vietnam, or the Nixon administration's decision to construct an antiballistic missile system be attributed to the influence of this group? In these and other cases, what convincing evidence existed that spokesmen for the military–industrial complex had imposed their viewpoints upon the President, his principal civilian advisers, and Congress?

In evaluating such questions, a starting point perhaps is the recognition that much the same complaint that is expressed about the role of the military–industrial complex today was heard in earlier eras of American history. A notable case occurred after World War I. During the 1920s and 1930s, the "merchants of death" and the "munitions makers" were accused of having engineered America's entry into the war and producing many of the popular frustrations growing out of that involvement. Among this group of critics, the assumption was that the United States had no legitimate reason to become embroiled in this global conflict; it had no interests to protect and its own security was in no way involved. The logical inference was, therefore, that its participation was a result of successful machinations by the "munitions makers," whose profits would be greatly enhanced by American belligerency. This was a dominant theme, at any rate, of much of the "disil-

*This total, it ought to be noted, represented the number of American bases still operating overseas after President John F. Kennedy closed some 60 bases during his administration.

lusionist literature" of the interwar period. In the end, no reputable historian accepted this theory or found any creditable evidence to support it. But for many Americans, it was easier to accept a demonological explanation of why America entered World War I, and why it failed to achieve many of its goals in the negotiations which followed, than it was to undertake an objective analysis of the complex issues involved or to accept many of the implications of America's "rise to world power" after 1900. With some Americans, a belief in evil spirits became a substitute for rational thought; and when this occurred, large numbers of citizens deceived themselves grievously about the origins and consequences of World War I.

Unfortunately, demonology is not a tendency confined to bygone eras. Today, when they are faced with difficult challenges—like waging a successful antiguerrilla campaign, or formulating a national policy toward governments experiencing revolutionary political change—Americans are perhaps no less tempted to attribute policy inadequacies or failures to demonic forces. The contemporary international environment, much more than the interwar period, is in many respects hostile to the achievement of goals or purposes deemed important by Americans, like the promotion of democracy on a global basis, *evolutionary* political change, encouragement of political stability in vital regions, and rapid economic advancement for developing societies. Thus critics assert—but seldom convincingly prove—that, save for the machinations of the military–industrial complex, America would have escaped involvement in the Vietnam conflict; or it would have genuinely harmonious relations with most societies in the "third world"; or its global image would be untarnished; or it would be progressing steadily toward the solution of numerous pressing domestic problems.

Without discounting the power available to the military–industrial complex, thus far it appears that its dominant role in the governmental decision-making process is more *potential* than actual. Nearly all major decisions in Vietnam, for example, were made by *civilian* leaders like Presidents Kennedy and Johnson who in turn relied heavily upon the advice of civilians such as Defense Secretary Robert McNamara and Secretary of State Dean Rusk. As we observed earlier, President Johnson personally selected bombing targets in North Vietnam; he placed military commanders under strict orders not to escalate hostilities without his approval.[38] Earlier, in 1962, President Kennedy rejected the advice of his military advisers, who favored immediate military strikes against Soviet missile sites in Cuba. Early in his administration, President Nixon also rejected the recommendations made by many military spokesmen, who favored an extensive and costly antiballistic missile system for the United States. President Nixon's decision followed neither the viewpoints of this group nor the wishes of those who were against any ABM system. As far as the evidence indicates, in these cases important policy decisions were *still being made ultimately by civilian leaders.* Quite properly, of course, the President and subordinate civilian officials consulted their military advisers about issues affecting national security. But the military viewpoint remained where it ideally should remain—"on tap, but never on top." Some critics of recent American foreign policy unquestionably find it psychologically easier to blame the military–industrial complex for policy failures than to place the blame where it rightfully belongs—upon a failure in *civilian* leadership.

In evaluating the danger posed by the military–industrial complex, care must also be exercised in recognizing an assumption usually implicit in the concept, along with kindred ones like the "military mind." The assumption is that military viewpoints are *monolithic.* Thus, the idea of the military–industrial complex often evokes the image of a unified military elite, whose innate tendency is to rely upon armed force for the solution of human problems and whose impulse is to impose its viewpoints upon the policy process. One former State Department official, however, has said that the modern American military establishment "gives every indication, in fact, of having become a remarkable *community of minds.*"[39] Another former military officer, who later held a high position in the State Department, has similarly described the American military establishment as amorphous and loosely organized; the power of entities like the military–industrial complex as "more potential than structured."[40] An experienced Defense Department official, Robert A. Lovett, called attention to the fact that since World War II, the impact of the scientific revolutions upon military technology has produced an "increasing intermingling of military and civilian personnel and the blurring of lines between civil and military activities." His view was that alleged military efforts to dominate the policy-making process were a "strawman issue," since no American military leader with whom he was acquainted contested the principle of over-all civilian supremacy.[41] Other commentators have identified forces within the American government which tend to assign an often unwanted "political role" to military elements. More perhaps than any other force, Congress itself often compels military leaders to participate in political controversies (like the size and nature of the defense budget), which civilian officials ought properly to resolve.[42]

The growth in America's international commitments since World War II, together with the spiraling cost of modern armaments, have enhanced the position of the military–industrial complex in many spheres of American life, as well as in foreign societies. At the end of his administration, one of the nation's most respected wartime military leaders, President Dwight D. Eisenhower, cautioned about the dangers involved in this phenomenon.[43] The warning lost none of its cogency in the years that followed. Yet to date, there is no persuasive evidence that the military–industrial complex has in fact impaired constitutional safeguards against undue military influence or that it has usurped the role of civilian policy-makers. Exaggerating the threat posed by this group may well impede understanding of the complex problems besetting the United States in national security policy and in foreign affairs generally. It may be tempting, for example, to place the onus for America's frustrating involvement in Vietnam, or its failure to solve the problem of urban ghettoes, upon the influence exercised by the military–industrial complex. Such a demonological explanation, as we have noted, is often easier (and perhaps more psychologically satisfying) than efforts to comprehend why civilian policy-makers were misled at many points in the Vietnam conflict, why "limited war" situations generally impose great demands upon the United States, why political instability seems chronic among the emerging nations, or why it is proving more difficult than ever for the United States to employ its vast power overseas to achieve goals congenial to Americans.

The Problem of Role Definition by Civilian Leaders

Reference to the political role of military leaders suggests a second persistent problem in national security policy: the redefinition of an appropriate role for *civilian* officials. If the concept of civilian supremacy remains a cardinal doctrine of the American constitutional system, it can be meaningfully applied only when both military and civilian policy-makers have a reasonably clear understanding of the role both should play in national security policy. When the international environment is in a state of flux—and when technological changes rapidly outmode existing weapons and strategic doctrines—the problem of role definition by both groups admits of no easy or permanent solution. Evidence exists for believing that in the main military officials have been aware of this challenge and have responded to it more effectively than their civilian counterparts. To a substantial degree, apprehensions about the influence of the military–industrial complex on national policy have arisen because of failures by the State Department and other civilian agencies to accept the responsibilities demanded by a strict adherence to the principle of civilian supremacy in policy-making.

A number of examples from recent American experience might be cited. Mention has already been made of the State Department's reluctance to assume obligations for administering Germany and Japan after the Axis defeat in 1945. For a considerable period, the Pentagon administered both countries—and in the process made a number of inherently *political* decisions affecting the future of both nations. In the Korean and Vietnamese Wars, other examples occurred. Significant dissatisfaction existed within Congress and the electorate concerning American involvement in both conflicts. Without oversimplifying these complex, and in several respects *very different*, cases of limited war, it would not be inaccurate to say that much of the public discontent in the United States stemmed from a failure *by civilian leaders to define American objectives clearly and consistently*. Why was it necessary for the United States to intervene in Korea in 1950? Was the object to "halt aggression" against South Korea? Was it to defeat North Korea militarily? Was it more ambitious goals like unifying the Korean Peninsula politically or perhaps teaching *all* aggressors that reliance upon armed force in dealing with their neighbors "does not pay"? The fact is that at various times throughout the Korean conflict, the Truman administration espoused one or more of these goals, depending upon the military situation within Korea itself. Not unexpectedly, ambitious goals were enunciated when United Nations forces were experiencing military success; more limited goals were advocated when the reverse was true. Small wonder that military commanders like General Douglas MacArthur had difficulty understanding the rationale of intervention in Korea; citizens lacking MacArthur's experience and insight were perhaps even more confused.[44]

An even greater degree of uncertainty and ambiguity over national goals marked America's involvement in the Vietnam War. Time and again, critics questioned the basic purposes which guided American conduct in the war; and they had fundamental questions also about America's large role in Asian affairs. In no small part, the "credibility gap" which critics attributed to the Johnson administration related directly to alleged confusion over *why* the United States was involved in the conflict in Southeast Asia and what it proposed to achieve as a result of this involvement. Was the aim merely the protection of South Vietnam from military aggression or internal insurrection? Was it to keep the regime in Saigon in power against *all* internal forces hostile to it? Was it to "teach North Vietnam" (and possibly Red China) the lesson that "aggression does not pay"? Was it to create and maintain a "democracy" in South Vietnam? Was it perhaps to maintain a permanent American "presence" in the region, a new "sphere of influence"? Was the U.S. interested primarily in the security of nearby Asian states, which might collapse (like a row of dominoes), if South Vietnam succumbed to Communism? Or, was it heavily committed in Vietnam mainly to protect its own national security and diplomatic interests? After the early 1960s, when the American commitment in Vietnam expanded rapidly, such questions evoked sharp disagreement—not only among critics of American policy in Asia, but often among executive policy-makers themselves. The "credibility gap" existing over *why* the United States found itself involved in hostilities in Southeast Asia understandably engendered skepticism on Capitol Hill and among public groups concerning *whether* the United States ought to be engaged in the conflict at all or what its massive intervention had achieved. Ambiguity and uncertainty over national goals in Vietnam inevitably placed American military leaders in an untenable position. For the adoption of a set of goals obviously required certain military commitments and strategies. Most crucially, perhaps, answers to the question of whether the United States was achieving its objectives in Southeast Asia were heavily conditioned by what the goals were and whether they could be achieved at all.

Different as the Korean and Vietnamese conflicts were, the point common to both contests was that successful national policy required civilian leaders to define America's objectives clearly and consistently—a requirement which in turn presupposes that goals be selected that can be achieved by the military establishment and other agencies involved in national security policy.

Conversely, successful policy-making in national security affairs can also be endangered when civilian leaders forget another admonition: *Civilians are not trained military professionals.* The constitutional principle of military subordination to civilian authority does not mean—as some competent students of the problem feared it meant when McNamara was Secretary of Defense —that civilian officials substitute their judgments on military questions for those of the Joint Chiefs of Staff. Adherence to the principle of *ultimate* civilian supremacy, in other words, need not imply derogation of the legitimate role in national policy-making of the trained professional military officer.

Civilian agencies of government can also do more, it seems clear, to make more effective use of existing mechanisms and procedures available for exchanging viewpoints among civilian and military groups involved in national security policy. Earlier in this chapter, the officer "exchange program" between the State and Defense Departments was discussed. Several commentators have pointed out that thus far the State Department's use of this program has been minimal and half-hearted. Officials from that department assigned for a tour of duty with the Pentagon have not infrequently found that when they returned to the Department of State,

little or no use was made of their experiences.[45]

Finally, if fears exist about a growing "military influence" in national police, one reason is to be found in a problem we have already referred to in Chapter 3 and in this chapter: the inability or unwillingness of civilian agencies, notably the State Department, *to assert its role energetically and capably in the decision-making process.* In both the Korean and Vietnam Wars, for example, military spokesmen gained considerable influence in policy-making, in large part because the Secretary of State and other high-ranking civilian officials often were not forceful in asserting their views.

Perhaps it is never (and never will be) possible to achieve and maintain an ideal balance between the influence exercised by the civilian and military components of national policy. For one thing, the impact of powerful personalities is likely to vary from one era to another and to give one side a greater impact in any given policy decision. The interplay of forces on any international issue is affected by the nature of America's involvement in the question, by the selection of individuals engaged in policy-making toward it, by the manner and degree to which the President utilizes his advisers, by the extent to which various agencies of government feel deeply involved in the matter and demand to be consulted, by the time available in which a decision must be made, and by a great variety of other influences tending to tilt the balance in one direction or another. By the 1970s, for example, it was evident that the policy-making environment was considerably *less* favorable than previously for military policy officials; apprehensions about the machinations of the military–industrial complex were widespread and often crucial in shaping congressional attitudes toward the Pentagon. In this respect, the public "mood" clearly favored a more dominant role for civilian policy-makers. It might also safely be predicted, however, that in time this mood would probably *change;* past experience indicated that in due course a similar reaction could limit the influence of *civilian* policy-makers! It seems evident that if the concept of civilian supremacy is to remain dynamic and relevant, then civilian policy-makers must be prepared to assert their ideas forcefully and capably in the highest councils of government. Above all, they must be prepared to offer *viable alternatives* to proposals championed by military officials in order to prevent the creation of a policy vacuum which military leaders may fill because no other group involved in policy-making is ready to take the responsibility for safeguarding national security.

Role Definition for Military Leaders

Much that has already been said about civilian role definition applies to military leaders. For the latter, the cardinal principle is continued adherence to the doctrine of civilian supremacy in the formulation of national policy. This, in turn, dictates constant awareness that *the armed forces of the United States are essentially instruments of national policy,* never its masters.

Experience since World War II suggests that, in the main, American military leaders continue to subscribe to this concept and to regard it as central to the American constitutional system. This fact, to be sure, offers no guarantee that military leaders will always accord the principle a high place. From the time of ancient Sparta to the present era, military elites have been tempted to seize power or to become the de facto behind-the-scenes decision-makers. In innumerable cases in the postwar period, military groups abroad have seized (or attempted to seize) control of the government, often on the grounds that they possessed a mandate to "protect" society from inept civilian leaders. The extent to which the concept of civilian supremacy remains at the forefront within the United States will probably depend upon many factors—not the least of which surely will be continued recognition by military officials themselves of its fundamental importance, coupled with their determination to secure compliance with it at all levels of the armed forces.

Other problems continue to impair a sound and effective role by the military establishment in national policy-making. A matter of ongoing concern is the existence of continued intraservice rivalries and jealousies, especially as new weapons are developed. While major and minor Defense Department reorganizations since World War II have mitigated the problem, they have not eliminated it. As in the past, the army, navy, and air force (and on some issues, the marine corps) continue to exert their service "interests" in approaching issues like the development and assignment of new weapons, estimates of Soviet or Chinese military strength (and its strategic implications for the United States), and most notably military appropriations.* And, as always, these "service viewpoints" have their champions among influential public groups and legislators who have become identified with a particular service arm.[46] Bureaucratic inertia, attachment to old modes of thought and strategies, resistance to innovations—these qualities traditionally associated with the "military mind" have in no sense disappeared altogether as a result of Pentagon reforms in the postwar era. For many years, for example, the navy was reluctant to adopt the often novel proposals of Captain (now Admiral) Hyman Rickover dealing with the application of nuclear power to naval vessels, particularly submarines. In the early 1960s, despite President Kennedy's personal interest in the matter, the "high brass" in the Pentagon displayed very little enthusiasm for training the armed forces in antiguerrilla warfare; experience in Vietnam showed that the United States still had a great deal to learn about coping with guerrilla-led insurgencies.[47] And during the Vietnam War, despite steadily mounting evidence to the contrary, air force officials repeatedly insisted upon the effectiveness of "strategic bombing" as a method of achieving American political and military objectives in Southeast Asia.

In the future, as in the past, the military establishment can be counted upon to overestimate national defense requirements and to disregard the extent to which other needs (like antipoverty programs or the problem of the urban ghettoes or the improvement of education) are also legitimate claims against always finite federal revenues. In one respect, of course, this tendency is normal, and within prescribed limits, beneficial. In the nuclear age, military strategists have the awesome responsibility of safeguarding national security in a highly *insecure* global environment. More than at any other stage of history, major miscalculations about an enemy's intentions or his capabilities could be catastrophic, not only for the United States but for much of the world. Moreover, the nuclear era has witnessed a fundamental change in the basic purposes of military strategy. Today, if not in earlier periods, the dominant objective of American military strategy is *to deter war.* If deterrence fails, the *next* aim is to win the ensuing conflict at minimum cost to the United States.* America's great nuclear stockpile,

---

*Some commentators, it should be noted, believe that within limits, intraservice rivalries and competition are basically healthy developments, since they promote somewhat the same kind of "pluralism" among the armed services that exists within the American society generally. The continued existence of separate "service viewpoints" perhaps guarantees that all sides of a question affecting national security are aired; that a forced "conformity" is not imposed upon the nation's highest military officials; and that diversity of viewpoints within the military establishment affords one check against the emergence of a monolithic "officer caste" or highly provincial "military mind" among the nation's armed forces. For one expression of this view, see Burton M. Sapin, *The Making of United States Foreign Policy* (Washington, D.C.: Brookings Institution, 1966), p. 146.

*The statement that deterrence or *prevention of war* is the dominant goal of American military strategists may come as a novel idea, particularly to those whose minds are conditioned by the role of military force in the *pre-atomic era.* Yet General Earle G. Wheeler, former chairman of the Joint Chiefs of Staff, has said that the basic aim "of a global strategy is the melding of foreign policy and military capabilities in such a manner as to preclude war or, if entered into, give maximum assurance of victory." See Wheeler's views as cited in Craig Powell, "Policy, Power Mesh in Formula of Global Strategy," *Armed Forces Management* 14 (June, 1968), 43; and Lt. Col. George S. Jones III, "Strategic Planning," *Military Review* XLVII (September, 1967), 14–15. The emphasis upon deterrence as the leading goal of military strategy today of course reflects a fact that has become increasingly clear to all students of warfare

for example, has been infinitely more useful to the United States *as a deterrent force* than as a weapon of war that was, or could be, used against an enemy. A by-product of successful deterrence has been to shift violent conflicts away from global nuclear engagements toward "limited" wars fought with so-called "conventional" weapons (whose firepower, we should note, has steadily escalated in the postwar period). It would, therefore, be more accurate perhaps to say that the goal of American strategy is to *prevent* certain wars (global nuclear ones) and to win certain other kinds of military conflicts (those fought with conventional weapons). Experience in both Korea and Vietnam indicated that American strategists had been considerably more successful in achieving the former objective than in attaining the latter one.

If military elites traditionally tend to exaggerate in estimating the "defense needs" of the nation—in that they almost invariably "overinsure" against external threats, or they assume that because another nation *can* threaten American interests it *will in fact* do so—successful deterrence, as well as victory in limited encounters, require both that America *be* strong and that its enemies *know* it is militarily prepared to defend its security interests. Within these parameters, there is naturally room for disagreement about "how much preparedness is enough," about the nature and quantity of new weapons required, and about the total increment of the federal budget that can be allocated to the sphere of national defense. Civilian policy-makers tend to be pulled by two conflicting forces. One is the usually "inflated" budgetary demands submitted by the Pentagon. The other is the still vivid recollection of the lesson learned as a result of Pearl Harbor and the Korean War: that military unpreparedness may, in the long run, turn out to be even *more costly* in American lives and resources than providing the funds necessary to keep the defense establishment up to date and in a condition of military readiness.

Nevertheless, the fact remains that military officials still play an essentially subordinate role in determining national policy. The nuclear era has not altered the relationship which General Matthew B. Ridgway described as a process in which the civilian leaders propose the *ends* that much

___

since World War I: The traditional distinction between "victors" and "vanquished" in a military conflict—particularly one fought with nuclear weapons—has very little relevence. One student of national strategy cites four basic goals: (1) to deter a nuclear attack against the United States, initiated either by design or accident; (2) if deterrence fails, to limit damage to the nation and to obtain the best "war outcome" possible; (3) to deter aggression against America's principal allies and to defend them if deterrence fails; and (4) to aid in the defense of other allies and nations in the free world. See Jones, *op. cit.*, p. 15.

be achieved and the military leaders supply their estimate of how much can be attained by military *means* and how those means may be best employed.[48]

NOTES

1. The Truman–MacArthur controversy is discussed in detail in General Matthew B. Ridgway, *The Korean War* (New York: Popular Library, 1967), pp. 223–237. Commenting on the lessons of this episode, General Ridgway has written that the military officer "should not be the one to set the political objectives our military effort seeks to attain".
2. General Omar N. Bradley, *A Soldier's Story* (New York: Holt, Rinehart and Winston, 1951), p. 536.
3. Smith Simpson, *Anatomy of the State Department* (Boston: Houghton Mifflin, 1967), p. 77.
4. William W. Kaufmann, *The McNamara Strategy* (New York: Harper & Row, 1964), p. 194.
5. For more detailed appraisals of "civic action" and other paramilitary activities by American agencies, see Major Laun C. Smith, Jr., "Military Civic Action in Central America," *Military Review* XLIX (January, 1969), 64–71; and Edward B. Glick, "Military Civic Action: Thorny Art of the Peacekeepers," *Army* 17 (September, 1967), 67–71.
6. The navy's key role in various diplomatic undertakings in American history is discussed in Simpson, *op. cit.*, pp. 72–74; the army's diplomatic role is dealt with in Colonel William D. Neale, "Warriors in Striped Pants," *Army* 17 (June, 1967), 55–62; and for projections of the future military role in diplomacy, see J. I. Coffey, "Toward the Navy of the Future," *Military Affairs* XXXI (Spring, 1967), 17–26.
7. Quoted in Hans Rothfels, "Clausewitz," in Edward M. Earle, ed., *Makers of Modern Strategy* (New York: Atheneum, 1966), p. 106. A valuable recent study of Clausewitz's thought is Roger A. Leonard, ed., *Clausewitz on War* (New York: Capricorn Books, 1967).
8. For Clausewitz's ideas on limited war, see Rothfels, *op. cit.*, pp. 106–113.
9. See William D. Franklin, "Clausewitz on Limited War," *Military Review* XLVII (June, 1967), 25.
10. Brian Bond, "The Indecisiveness of Modern War," *Military Review* XLVII (December, 1967), 46.
11. For prewar precedents and practices involving liaison among the military services, see Ernest R. May, "The Development of Political–Military Consultation in the United States," *Political Sciences Quarterly* 70 (June, 1955), 161–181.
12. Hull's views are cited in Neale, *op. cit.*, p. 55
13. An outstanding case was Roosevelt's appointment of Robert Murphy to various political assignments during World War II; frequently, FDR directed Murphy to report directly to

him, bypassing the State Department altogether. See Robert Murphy, *Diplomat Among Warriors* (New York: Pyramid Books, 1965), *passim*, but especially Murphy's account of the North African campaign, pp. 82–211.

14. Military pressure upon President Roosevelt to have the Soviet Union enter World War II against Japan is discussed in James F. Byrnes, *Speaking Frankly* (New York: Harper & Row, 1947), pp. 42–45; and Sidney Warren, *The President as World Leader* (New York: McGraw-Hill, 1964), pp. 252, 261–262.

15. Detailed discussions of postwar governmental reorganizations and modifications bearing upon national security policy may be found in Timothy W. Stanley, *American Defense and National Security* (Washington, D.C.: Public Affairs Press, 1956): General James M. Gavin has discussed many of the problems of national security organization in his book *War and Peace in the Space Age* (New York: Harper & Row, 1958); another useful account is William R. Kintner, *Forging a New Sword* (New York: Harper & Row, 1958); an illuminating study of individuals and groups shaping postwar American defense strategy is Arthur Herzog, *The War–Peace Establishment* (New York: Harper & Row, 1965); a recent study of national defense organization is C. W. Borklund, *The Department of Defense* (New York: Praeger, 1968).

16. For two appraisals of the influence of this key legislator upon postwar defense reorganization, see John C. Ries, "Congressman Vinson and the 'Deputy' to the JCS Chairman," *Military Affairs* 30 (Spring, 1966), 16–25; and Russell Baker, "Again Vinson Mounts the Ramparts," *The New York Times Magazine* (May 4, 1958), pp. 13, 78.

17. The "Jackson Subcommittee"—officially named the Subcommittee on National Security and International Operations of the Senate Committee on Government Operations—has published a wealth of data available to the student of national security policy. These are in the form of hearings conducted by the committee, memoranda and staff studies, collections of relevant readings, and bibliographies.

18. General Wheeler's views are cited at length in Craig Powell, "Civilian–Military Rapport Reaches a New Maturity in the Defense Arena," *Armed Forces Management* 14 (December, 1967), 44–50. Both the author of the article and General Wheeler take a basically sanguine view of how postwar changes in national security organization have worked out. For a considerably less optimistic view, focusing upon the Joint Chiefs of Staff, see Major John F. McMahon, Jr., "Streamlining the Joint Chiefs of Staff," *Military Review* XLIX (January, 1969), 36–47.

19. For statistical and other evidence of the extent to which the responsibilities assigned to the Joint Chiefs of Staff have multiplied in the postwar era, see McMahon, *op. cit.*, p. 42.

20. *Ibid.*, p. 38.

21. Detailed discussions of progress toward military unification in the postwar period are available in Burton M. Sapin, *The Making of United States Foreign Policy* (Washington, D.C.: Brookings Institution, 1966), pp. 142–147; and William D. Kaufmann, *The McNamara Strategy* (New York: Harper & Row, 1964), pp. 190–203.

22. McMahon, *op. cit.*, pp. 41–43.

23. The "Jackson Subcommittee" has published numerous studies focusing upon the National Security Council since its establishment. A convenient history of the agency down to the 1960s, showing changes in its internal structure and its operating procedures, is provided in Senate Government Operations Committee, *Organizational History of the National Security Council*, 86th Congress, 2nd Session, 1960. Shortly after the Nixon administration took office, the committee issued a new report entitled *The National Security Council: New Role and Structure*, 91st Congress, 1st Session, 1969.

24. See Senate Government Operations Committee, *Organizational History of the National Security Council, op. cit.*, p. 1.

25. *Ibid.*, p. 5.

26. For a detailed discussion of the operation of the National Security Council under President Eisenhower, see Robert Cutler, "The Development of the National Security Council," *Foreign Affairs* 34 (April, 1956), 441–458.

27. President Kennedy's use of the National Security Council during the Cuban missile crisis is discussed in Theodore C. Sorensen, *Kennedy* (New York: Harper & Row, 1965), p. 693.

28. See Powell, *op. cit.*, p. 48; and Roland Evans and Robert Novak, *Lyndon B. Johnson: The Exercise of Power* (New York: New American Library, 1968), p. 564. These latter authors contend that the President's civilian advisers, fully as much as civilian officials, often urged him to expand the war in Vietnam (*ibid.*, p. 560).

29. President Nixon's views concerning the proper role of the National Security Council are cited at length in Senate Government Operations Committee, *The National Security Council: New Role and Structure, op. cit.*, pp. 1–3; and "Who's Making Foreign Policy for the United States?" *U.S. News and World Report* LXVI (April 7, 1969), 45–46.

30. A fuller discussion of the role of ISA in the Defense Department is provided in Sapin, *op. cit.*, pp. 158–163, 179.

31. For discussions of the evolution and role of the SIG, see Simpson, *op. cit.*, pp. 66–69.

32. For a recent assessment of the State–Defense Department exchange program, see Senate Government Operations Committee, *The State–Defense Department Officer Exchange Program: Analysis and Assessment*, 91st Congress, 1st Session, 1969; Secretary Rogers' evaluation is included on pp. 5–7. An informa-

tive secondary source is Lt. Col. Billy W. Byrd, "The State-Defense Department Officer Exchange Program," *Military Review* XLVIII (April, 1968), 41–46. The use of political advisers as a liaison technique is discussed and evaluated in Senate Government Operations Committee, *Political Advisers to U.S. Military Commanders: Analysis and Assessment*, 91st Congress, 1st Session, 1969. For comments by military commanders on the value of the program, see pp. 15–16.

33. A comprehensive analysis of McNamara's impact upon the Defense Department is provided in Kaufmann, *op. cit., passim.* Briefer (and often more critical) studies are Hanson W. Baldwin, "How the Military Rate McNamara's Performance," *The Reporter* 38 (April 18, 1968), 15–18; Jack Raymond, "Mr. McNamara Remodels the Pentagon," *Ibid.* 26 (January 18, 1962), 31–35; and Joseph Kraft, "McNamara and His Enemies," *Harper's Magazine* 223 (August, 1961), 41–48.

34. Criticisms of Secretary McNamara, involving his alleged "gagging" of the Joint Chiefs of Staff and "disregarding" of the views of professional military officers, were expressed in a report by the House Armed Services Committee, as cited in McMahon, *op. cit.,* p. 37.

35. Matthew B. Ridgway, *The Korean War* (New York: Popular Library, 1967), p. 7. Italics in original.

36. A highly critical (not to say at times, polemical) treatment of the impact of American military involvement in a foreign country is Louis E. Lomax, *Thailand: The War That Is, The War That Will Be* (New York: Random House, 1967).

37. The impact of the military–industrial complex is a theme that has become pervasive in recent studies of American foreign policy, especially by critics of the Vietnam War. A detailed discussion of this theme, particularly with reference to American policy toward the "third world," is Richard J. Barnet, *Intervention and Revolution: America's Confrontation with Insurgent Movements Around the World* (Cleveland, Ohio: World Publishing, 1968), *passim.* Another author finds America's "destiny" to lead a new "Roman Age," in which the dominating impulse is "Caesarism." See Amaury de Riencourt, *The Coming Caesars* (New York: Capricorn Books, 1964), especially pp. 292–343. For detailed information on the scope and nature of American military activities at home and abroad, see *Time Magazine* 93 (April 11, 1969), 16–26, and *The New York Times,* (April 9, 1969).

38. *Time Magazine,* 93 (April 11, 1969), 23. For President Johnson's careful "restraint" of military activities during the Vietnam war, and his conviction that the strongest pressure upon the White House came from hawkish groups, see Eric F. Goldman, *The Tragedy of Lyndon Johnson* (New York: Dell Publishing Co., 1968), pp. 466–494.

39. Simpson, *op. cit.,* p. 88. Italics inserted.

40. Roger Hilsman, *To Move a Nation* (Garden City, N.Y.: Doubleday, 1967), 559.

41. See the views of Robert A. Lovett, as cited in Andrew M. Scott and Raymond H. Dawson, *Readings in the Making of American Foreign Policy* (New York: Macmillan, 1965), p. 410.

42. See the views of Gene M. Lyons, in *ibid.,* p. 412.

43. For President Eisenhower's views on the military–industrial complex, see Dwight D. Eisenhower, *Waging Peace* (Garden City, N.Y.: Doubleday, 1965), pp. 614–616. Based upon a lifetime of close association with military groups and business heavily engaged in defense production, Eisenhower was convinced that this group could become an overpowering influence in American life "unless watched by an alert citzenry"; the tendency was for "powerful lobbies" representing the special interests of this group to "spring up to argue for even larger munitions expenditures. And the web of special interest grows." *Ibid.,* p. 615.

44. For discussions of the problems of goals and the public's understanding of them during the Korean War, see Ridgway, *op. cit.,* pp. 223–247; and John W. Spanier, *The Truman–MacArthur Controversy and the Korean War* (Cambridge, Mass.: Belknap Press of Harvard University, 1959), pp. 257–277.

45. Criticisms of the State Department's lack of interest in the "exchange program" with the Defense Department are expressed by a former State Department official. See Simpson, *op. cit.,* pp. 71, 82.

46. An illuminating discussion of public relations and lobbying activities by military agencies, and by public groups identified with them, is contained in R. Joseph Monsen, Jr., and Mark W. Cannon, *The Makers of Public Policy: American Power Groups and Their Ideologies* (New York: McGraw-Hill, 1965), pp. 258–308.

47. President Kennedy's efforts to persuade the military services to strengthen their anti-guerrilla warfare activities are described in Sorensen, *op. cit.,* pp. 631–633. Sorensen says that the responsibility for this assignment rested with the Pentagon; in fact, it "rested" there so long that eventually President Kennedy became something of an expert on antiguerrilla warfare himself, finally compelling reluctant generals to set up the Special Forces ("Green Berets") that were finally dispatched to Vietnam.

48. Ridgway, *op. cit.,* p. 7.

Five
CONGRESS AND FOREIGN RELATIONS

A leading student of American national government has written that "no important policy, domestic or foreign, can be pursued for long by even the most forceful President unless Congress comes to his support with laws and money."[1] Another commentator has said concerning the role of Congress in foreign relations: "The authority of Congress in foreign policy appears to be increasing as the boundaries of foreign and domestic policy become more and more obscure, and as the dollar cost of foreign policy programs requires Congressional authorization."[2] In an era in which the tendency, in one nation after another, is clearly *against* congressional or parliamentary influence in national policy-making, these statements underscore the fact that the American Congress still enjoys vast powers. Thus, one study finds that among all legislative bodies throughout the world, the Congress of the United States alone is "still capable of initiating legislation."[3] Moreover, the late 1960s and early 1970s witnessed forceful assertions of legislative leadership on Capitol Hill, particularly concerning national commitments made by executive policy-makers that might eventually entail billions of dollars in expenditures and perhaps even the loss of American lives. A feeling has been prevalent among senators and representatives that Congress must "recover" its power to determine national policy in the vital realm of foreign relations.

THE SCOPE OF LEGISLATIVE INVOLVEMENT

Virtually all of the important postwar foreign policy programs of the United States have entailed congressional participation at one or more stages. Beginning with the Greek–Turkish Aid Program early in 1947 (which signified America's formal abandonment of isolationism), the United States has dispensed over $130 billion in various forms of military, economic, and techical assistance to foreign countries. These foreign aid mea-

sures required initial legislative approval, along with annual appropriations for their implementation. America's worldwide network of security treaties—including the Rio Treaty of hemispheric defense in 1947, the North Atlantic Treaty (NATO) in 1952, the Southeast Asia Treaty (SEATO) in 1955, and other bilateral and multilateral defense agreements—needed the consent of the Senate. Informational and cultural programs —like the Fulbright–Hays Act of 1961, subsidizing educational exchange between the United States and other countries—required legislative sanction and annual appropriations for their continued operation. One of the most successful postwar foreign aid programs, the Peace Corps, was set up by act of Congress in 1961. America's program for disposing of its agricultural surpluses abroad (which was called the "Food for Peace" program after 1966) had to be authorized by Congress. Periodically, the legislative branch has approved major and minor governmental reorganization plans affecting the State Department, the Defense Department, and other agencies involved in foreign affairs. America's participation in the United Nations is based upon the Senate's ratification of the UN Charter on August 8, 1945, and upon congressional passage of the UN Participation Act on September 28, 1945; in 1962, when the UN was experiencing an acute financial crisis, Congress authorized a loan to the international organization. Several important international financial institutions—like the Export–Import Bank, the International Monetary Fund, and the International Bank for Reconstruction and Development—depend upon Congress for a substantial amount of their operating funds. Despite a significant degree of antiwar sentiment on Capitol Hill, America's massive involvement in the Vietnam conflict had some legislative authority, since it was based upon a congressional resolution made on August 10, 1964 (the Tonkin Gulf Resolution), empowering the President to protect American security interests in Southeast Asia. More or less comparable legislative resolutions had been passed earlier when crises confronted the United States in Berlin, the Formosa Straits, the Middle East, and Cuba.*

Cutting across these and other specific instances of congressional action in recent American foreign policy has been the power and influence of Congress *as a mirror of national sentiment.* As President Johnson discovered with regard to the Vietnam War, without reasonably unified congressional support for major national commitments, it is very difficult, if not impossible, for executive policy-makers to plan and carry out successful foreign policy programs. This is true even when (as during the Vietnam War) Congress usually votes the funds needed by the military establishment and is content to let the President and his military advisers determine national strategy. Evident and recurrent legislative misgivings about the course of events in Vietnam unquestionably weakened the authority and prestige of the Johnson administration at home and abroad—a fact which loomed large in President Johnson's determination not to seek reelection in 1968.

Still another index of legislative activity in the foreign policy field is the extent to which a growing number of congressional committees are directly or indirectly concerned with issues impinging upon foreign relations. During the 1960s, for example, with regard to a single important program—the provision of military aid to other countries—the Secretary of State and the Secretary of Defense were normally compelled to maintain close liaison with *ten* separate committees or subcommittees of Congress. Occasionally, specific questions related to national security concerned as many as *twenty-five* legislative committees and subcommittees! Nine congressional committees or subcommittees have been involved in recent years in the problem of the organization of the State Department. Foreign aid programs customarily fell within the jurisdictions of five congressional committees and sometimes, depending upon the novelty and complexity of the program, as many as *thirty* committees and subcommittees were involved.[4]

The House Foreign Affairs Committee in 1965

A somewhat different perspective is gained on Congress' recent role American foreign relations by focusing upon the activities of the House Foreign Affairs Committee during a single year, 1965. The emergence of this committee as an important force in the foreign policy process is itself a noteworthy development in the postwar period.

Before World War II, the House Foreign Affairs Committee was considered one of the *least* desirable assignments in the lower chamber, chiefly because foreign relations were deemed much less important than domestic affairs and because the role of the House vis-à-vis the Senate in this sphere was considered tangential. While even now, the House Foreign Affairs Committee is not regarded as being among the most prestigious units within the House (even on foreign policy issues), it is nevertheless influential; it has grown steadily in size since World War II; its staff has greatly expanded; and, because of its elaborate system of subcommittees, many of its members have become extremely well informed on at least some aspects of American foreign relations.

In 1965, the House Foreign Affairs Committee had 36 members—24 Democrats and 12 Republicans.* It had a staff of 17 members. It had 9 standing subcommittees, dealing with the following issues:

Far East and Pacific
National Security and Scientific Developments
Europe
State Department and Foreign Operations
Inter-American Affairs
Africa
Near East
International Organizations and Movements
Foreign Economic Policy

In addition, in 1965 a special Subcommittee for Review of Foreign Aid Programs was established.

During that year, the House Foreign Affairs Committee had 196 bills and joint resolutions dealing with foreign policy issues referred to it, along with 412 simple or concurrent resolutions.† Like all congressional committees, the House Foreign Affairs Committee considered only a small fraction of the bills and resolutions submitted to it, and it approved an even smaller number of these. The committee carefully considered 25 bills and joint resolutions; it reported 20 of these favorably to the full House. All the bills and joint resolutions endorsed by the committee were passed by the House, and 16 of them eventually were enacted into law.

---

*A later section of the chapter will call attention to differences among these resolutions and will analyze the question of whether the President really "needed" the approval of Congress to protect American security and diplomatic interests in these areas.

*Like all congressional committees, the size of the House Foreign Affairs Committee varied from one legislative session to the next, as did the ratio of members from each major party on the committee. As a rule, this ratio reflected the balance between Democrats and Republicans within the House as a whole. The chairmen of the major legislative committees were of course members of the majority party, with chairmanship being determined normally by seniority on the committee.

†Resolutions adopted by the House or Senate, or concurrent resolutions adopted by both, express the sense of one or both legislative chambers on some particular issue. They are thus merely expressions of legislative opinion, as distinct from enactments which (when signed by the President) become laws.

In carrying out its responsibilities during 1965, the House Foreign Affairs Committee held 335 hearings (both public and "executive" or secret). It published over 3000 pages of printed testimony taken during hearings. Over 300 witnesses testified before the committee and its subcommittees, and some 64 different reports were issued, totaling almost 1000 pages.

Major substantive legislation approved by the committee, and subsequently approved by Congress as a whole, included: authorization for the foreign assistance program; amendments to the Arms Control and Disarmament Act; amendments to the Peace Corps Act; further amendments to the Foreign Service Act of 1946 (which had already been modified several times); a resolution expressing congressional sentiment with regard to persecution of minorities within Soviet Russia; and a resolution expressing legislative opposition to Communist expansionism within the Western Hemisphere.[5]

The Senate Foreign Relations Committee

For any given year, comparable data could be cited to illustrate the activities of the Senate Foreign Relations Committee. The concerns and procedures of the two committees are roughly parallel. Yet some interesting and important differences exist. Established in 1816, the Senate Foreign Relations Committee is one of the oldest standing committees in Congress. It is considered the "ranking" committee of the United States Senate, since it appeared first on the list of that chamber's committees. Since the Senate has certain prerogatives in foreign affairs which the House does not possess—chiefly, the power to consent to treaties and to confirm executive appointments—the Senate Foreign Relations Committee has always been more prestigious than its House counterpart. Studies have revealed that in the postwar period, it has been the most "sought after" committee assignment within the Senate.[6] The Senate Foreign Relations Committee, it is important to note, is *not* generally regarded as the most influential within the upper house; several Senate committees rank ahead of it by that criterion. But senators tend to view it as the most desirable committee assignment—perhaps because of the vital subject matter it deals with, or because membership affords an opportunity to become directly involved in the foreign policy process, or because the members *hope* to make the committee much more influential than it is in shaping both executive and legislative attitudes on foreign policy issues.

In any case, the size of the committee had expanded from 5 members in 1816 to 19 by 1965; by the late 1960s, the committee had a staff of 26 persons employed on a full-time basis. Beginning in 1950, the committee set up a system of consultative subcommittees, in most respects comparable to the subcommittee system prevailing within the House Foreign Affairs Committee. However, traditionally the entire committee considers legislation, treaties, and nominations coming within its jurisdiction.* By the end of the 1960s, as we shall see in greater detail at a later stage, members of the Senate Foreign Relations Committee were at the forefront of those legislators demanding a "reassertion" of Congress' powers in the foreign policy field.†

*In contrast to the House Foreign Affairs Committee, in other words, the SFRC's subcommittees are intended primarily to facilitate "consultation" with the executive branch. A publication of the committee states that the subcommittees were established "primarily for consultation and not for consideration of legislative matters." See Senate Foreign Relations Committee, *Background Information on the Committee on Foreign Relations,* 90th Congress, 2nd Session, 1968, p. 16.

†This tendency, it is worth noting, may have derived in part from a realization that the influence of the Senate Foreign Relations Committee itself perhaps declined significantly during the 1960s. Although remaining a highly desirable assignment in the Senate, the committee has nonetheless lost the eminent position it held during the late 1940s and 1950s, when it was clearly the dominant group on Capitol Hill with respect to foreign policy issues.

A number of forces accounted for the phenomenon. The personality of the chairman—in recent years, Senator J. William Fulbright (Democrat of Arkansas)—has had an impact upon both the committee's function and its effectiveness. As a result of the Dominican crisis in 1965, Fulbright "broke" with his old friend, President (former senator) Lyndon B. Johnson; from that point on, relations between the committee and executive policy-makers remained tense and distant. The Vietnam conflict also tended to fragment the committee; disagreements between "hawks" and "doves" impaired its internal unity. One member said in 1967 that the committee had "19 men on it, and they represent 21½ different viewpoints"!

Moreover, under Fulbright, the committee largely abandoned the earlier pattern whereby it collaborated intimately with executive officials to formulate programs like the Marshall Plan and NATO. By the mid-1960s, the committee had emerged as what one commentator called "a nationally known institution of articulate dissent" on foreign policy issues. On some questions (like American involvement in Vietnam and the Dominican Republic), it looked upon itself as the "conscience" of the nation, whose primary duty was to "confront" executive officials with the consequences of their behavior. The "education" of public opinion—with the clear goal of bringing about *changes* in American foreign policy—was also high on the committee's list of priorities. Rather than formulating legislation, it conceived of its main mission as calling attention to anomalies and failures in national policy and, by using its investigative powers, bringing these to the forefront of public concern. If the committee's influence with the executive branch had undeniably decreased, it was perhaps more influential than ever with public opinion (particularly intellectuals and other "opinion makers"). See Marvin Kalb, "Doves, Hawks and Flutterers in the Foreign Relations Committee," *The New York Times Magazine* (November 19, 1967), pp. 56–82; Joseph Kraft, "The Dean Rusk Show," *ibid.* (March 24, 1968), pp. 34–35, 130–140. For studies of this committee before and right after World War II, see David N. Farnsworth, *The Senate Committee on Foreign Relations* (Urbana,

The Variety of Legislative "Involvement" in Foreign Affairs

Besides the two committees of Congress exercising responsibility for measures falling directly in the realm of foreign relations, a significant postwar trend has been *the proliferation of committees within Congress whose jurisdiction extends to foreign policy issues.* As the traditional line between "domestic" and "foreign" policy questions has become increasingly eroded, it would be fair to say that nearly *all* committees of Congress have become to some degree concerned with foreign affairs. The Joint Committee on Atomic Energy, for example, plays a key role in national policy relating to the development of nuclear weapons, the construction of an antiballistic missile system, and the problem of "nuclear sharing" within the NATO alliance. The Agriculture Committee of the House and Senate is directly involved in programs of commodity disposal abroad. The two committees on the armed services must "authorize" the defense budget—the largest single expenditure of the national government. Since all bills for "raising revenue" must originate in the House of Representatives, the House Ways and Means Committee is concerned with tariff legislation—a key area in determining American relations with the European Common Market or with the emerging nations. The Senate Committee on Government Operations for several years has carried on an investigation of executive agencies engaged in formulating security policy, such as the State Department and the National Security Council. Indeed, it would be difficult to think of an important congressional committee whose activities did not impinge in some way upon foreign relations.

If this tendency is clear evidence of legislative involvement and concern with developments outside America's borders, it is also a factor clearly hindering an *effective* legislative role in foreign relations. Most students of the legislative process are agreed that Congress has little chance of reasserting its role in foreign policy (and, even in some aspects, in domestic policy) unless and until it is willing to institute reforms that will counteract the centrifugal forces which tend to destroy unified behavior.

With this general background, let us analyze Congress' role in American foreign policy by concentrating upon three topics: the formal and constitutional powers of Congress in foreign relations; informal and extra-constitutional techniques of legislative influence; and the problem involved in a "reassertion" of legislative influence in the foreign policy field.

Ill.: University of Illinois Press, 1961); and the same author's "A Comparison of the Senate and Its Foreign Relations Committee on Selected Roll-Call Votes," *Western Political Quarterly* 14 (March, 1961), 168–175.

CONSTITUTIONAL POWERS OF CONGRESS IN FOREIGN AFFAIRS

Senate Ratification of Treaties

The Constitution (Art. II, Sec. 2) provides that the President "shall have Power, by and with the Advice and Consent of the Senate, to make Treaties, provided two thirds of the Senators present concur. . . ." The Senate's power to ratify treaties is one of the upper chamber's prerogatives that is not shared with the House of Representatives.[*] From the beginning of the republic, therefore, the Senate was assigned an important role in the foreign policy process—a fact which even today gives that body a degree of prestige and a sense of involvement in foreign policy issues that differentiates it from the House. In some measure, recent efforts by leading senators to recapture legislative prerogatives in foreign relations have stemmed from a conviction that the American Constitution envisioned a forceful legislative role in determining national policy overseas.

In an earlier era (particularly when the United States was devoted to an "isolationist" policy), treaties were considered a vital dimension of the nation's relationships with foreign governments. It is significant that Article VI of the Constitution provides that the Constitution itself, laws made in pursuance of it, and "all Treaties made, or which shall be made, under the authority of the United States, shall be the supreme Law of the Land. . . ." Treaties, that is to say, were placed on a par with the Constitution and statutes in the American constitutional system. An echo of this same idea is found in Article III, Section 2, dealing with the federal judiciary: The power of the judiciary is extended to cases arising under the Constitution, the laws of the United States, "and Treaties made, or which shall be made" under the authority of the Constitution and the laws of the land.

In exercising its power of "advice and consent" to treaties, the Senate has several alternatives which, at the risk of some oversimplification, may be reduced to three courses: (1) It may *accept* a treaty without change, as submitted by the President, whose agents have negotiated the agreement with the governments concerned; (2) it may *modify* the treaty—by inserting amendments, reservations, understandings, declarations, interpretations, and the like—the result of which is to make the treaty an essentially different instru-

[*]Although it has become commonplace to refer to the power of the Senate to "ratify" treaties, it ought to be noted that technically a treaty is not officially "ratified" by the United States until it has been signed by the President. As our treatment of the treaty process will emphasize, even if the Senate approves a treaty by a two-thirds vote, the President can still "withdraw" it or refuse to proclaim it.

ment from the agreement submitted by the President; or (3) it may *reject* the treaty outright, by the failure of two-thirds of the Senate to vote in favor of its ratification.

On the basis of the Senate's disposition of treaties throughout American history, statistically the chances are very high that the Senate will *approve* unconditionally treaties submitted to it by the executive branch. One study found, for example, that from 1789 to 1963, the Senate approved without change 944 treaties, or 69 percent of those submitted to it. The only major treaty agreements which have been rejected by the Senate in recent years concerned American adherence to the International Court of Justice in 1935 and the St. Lawrence Seaway proposal, which was rejected the year before.[7]

Treaties which are not accepted are likely to be changed in some way to meet Senate objections. Several options are available to the Senate. It may approve a treaty subject to an "interpretation and understanding" of one or more of its provisions; thus the Statute of the International Atomic Energy Agency was approved by the Senate on the condition that any amendment to it would also require the advice and consent of the Senate. The Senate may also attach one or more *reservations* to a treaty. The Senate attached numerous such reservations to the Treaty of Versailles, making that agreement unacceptable to President Wilson. After World War II, when the United States accepted the jurisdiction of the International Court of Justice, a Senate reservation inserted an "optional clause" into this agreement, specifying that the jurisdiction of the Court did not extend to matters essentially within the domestic jurisdiction of the United States, as determined by the U.S. itself. Unlike an "interpretation and understanding," a Senate-instigated reservation actually *changes the contractual obligations* of the United States with other countries signatory to the treaty and (if the treaty is to become binding) must be acceptable to them. A somewhat different change is an *amendment* to a treaty which may be insisted upon by the Senate. The most formal kind of change, an amendment must be acceptable to the President and to the other signatory countries, since it actually modifies the provisions of the treaty itself. Treaties to which the Senate has affixed amendments must, therefore, be renegotiated before they become binding.

In the period 1789–1963, the Senate made modifications of one kind or another in some 252 treaties, or just over 18 percent of those submitted to it by the President. Statistically, the chances are thus around one in five that a treaty will be altered in some way when the President seeks the advice and consent of the Senate.[8]

The postwar emphasis upon "bipartisan" cooperation in foreign affairs has meant, as we shall see more fully in Chapter 6, that in practice a high degree of unity normally characterizes executive–Senate relationships throughout the process of treaty-making. For important treaties (like the North American Treaty in 1949), it is not uncommon for influential senators to be consulted at an early stage, even before executive officials engage in discussions with other governments. Similarly, the peace treaty with Japan in 1951 was agreed upon after continued consultation between John Foster Dulles, who was serving as a special consultant to the Truman administration, and the Senate.[9] The impetus for the NATO treaty in fact came from Senator Arthur H. Vandenberg (Republican of Michigan), who sponsored the Vandenberg Resolution in the Senate proposing that a western security pact be negotiated. It has also become standard practice for Presidents to appoint senators as part of the negotiating team which agrees to a treaty with other countries; senators who serve in this role normally become champions of the agreement when it is sent to Capitol Hill for approval.

Part of the discontent evident in the Senate, and throughout Congress generally, with the "decline" of legislative influence in foreign affairs could be attributed in part to a realization that its role in the treaty-making process allowed the Senate minimal opportunity to shape American relations with other countries. This was true for two fundamental reasons. One was the decline in importance of treaties per se. Although the Founding Fathers unquestionably viewed treaty commitments as a vital realm of foreign relations, modern diplomatic history has de-emphasized their importance. Today, issues arising out of the nontreaty relationships of the United States are at least as crucial, and sometimes more so, than those related to the nation's treaty commitments. Not infrequently since World War II, as in the case of South Korea, America has protected its vital interests in a region and *after it has done so* formalized these interests by embodying them in a security treaty. In other cases (as in the American decision to supply arms-aid to India in 1962), major national commitments have been assumed even when there was no treaty relationship with a particular nation and no prospect of such a treaty.

The second reason why the Senate has been unable to affect foreign policy decisively by giving its advice and consent to treaties is even more influential. This is the great enhancement of the power of the President in foreign relations over the course of American history. The President's dominant position in the foreign policy process was discussed at length in Chapter 3. There, it was pointed out that an influential instrument of presidential leadership is *the executive agreement.* Only in very rare instances would Senate refusal to consent to a treaty preclude a President from reaching some kind of *de facto* agreement with other heads of state. For most purposes (if not always constitutionally), executive agreements are comparable to treaties. They can and do obligate the United States to assume certain responsibilities in foreign relations; as we observed in our earlier discussion, some executive agreements (like trade agreements) are made under legislative authority. In other cases, Congress later appropriates the funds required to carry out the terms of an executive agreement with other governments. Unlike treaties, however, such agreements do not require the advice and consent of the Senate; in certain cases (such as the Yalta Agreement early in 1945), they may be kept secret. The President and his subordinates, however, may regard such agreements as equivalent in all essential respects to more formal treaty undertakings.

In brief, the President dominates the treaty-making process. Officials within the executive branch usually make the decision to enter into negotiations with other governments. The President's agents negotiate the treaty and ultimately sign it in behalf of the United States. The President submits the treaty to the Senate for ratification. His "legislative specialists" devote considerable time and energy to mustering a two-thirds Senate vote in favor of the treaty. At any time, the President may "withdraw" the treaty from the Senate, if he no longer believes that the agreement serves the national interest. If the Senate consents to the treaty, the President must sign it as the last stage in the ratification process. Occasionally in the past, the President has refused to proclaim a treaty even after it has received two-thirds Senate approval, in which case the treaty dies. Moreover, the President may submit treaties to the Senate in reasonable confidence that, even without Senate approval, he may rely upon an executive agreement to secure the kind of international commitment he desires.

The real impact of the Senate's role in treaty-making, therefore, clearly does not lie in the likelihood that it will *reject* treaties submitted to it, or even that it will alter treaties radically. It lies rather in the opportunity to express its viewpoints; to prevail upon executive officials to modify objectionable provisions to avoid disunity within the government; and to focus public attention upon the important global commitments that are embodied in treaties.

Senate Confirmation of Appointments

A second prerogative belonging to the Senate alone, as specified in Article II, Section 2, of the Constitution, is the power to "confirm" presidential appointments. Since our interest is confined to foreign affairs, this power entails Senate confirmation of ambassadors, ministers, and consuls; appointments to, and promotions within, the Foreign Service; and appointments to high policy positions (from the level of Assistant Secretary upward) in agencies like the State Department, the U.S. Information Agency, the Agency for International Development, the Peace Corps, and the U.S. Arms Control and Disarmament Agency. Senate confirmation is also required for both civilian and military appointments to policy-making positions in the Defense Department, as well as for high-level promotions within the armed services.

That the exercise of its power to confirm appointments has become a time-consuming business is indicated by the fact that in the mid-1960s, the Senate Foreign Relations Committee scrutinized nearly 2800 appointments (of which close to 2600 were Foreign Service officers). Beginning in in the early 1950s, the committee decided to examine *all* appointees to high foreign policy positions; and in 1957, it inaugurated the practice of selectively examining several candidates who were entering the Foreign Service, in order to satisfy itself concerning the caliber of new diplomatic personnel.[10]

In the early period of American history, the Senate was prone to use its powers of confirmation to pass upon the establishment of diplomatic missions abroad. This occurred for example in 1809, when the Senate refused to approve an exchange of ministers between the United States and Russia.[11] The confirmation power has also been used to influence the treaty-making process, as when the Senate refused for some time to confirm negotiators who were to settle outstanding differences with Great Britain in Washington's administration. Bitter and prolonged wrangling ensued between the President and Senate before the highly controversial Jay Treaty, signed in 1794, could even be negotiated. Under Cleveland, the upper chamber rejected a fisheries agreement with Britain, because the President had sent negotiators who had not received Senate confirmation. The dispute over confirmation, however, may have been a pretext for defeating a treaty which many senators, particularly those from New England, opposed anyway.[12]

In the postwar period, along with other legislative prerogatives in the foreign policy field, the power of confirmation has received renewed emphasis. Two examples may be cited to illustrate the point. First, when the United States joined the United Nations, the Senate successfully insisted upon the right to confirm the appointments of highranking diplomatic personnel assigned to both existing and future UN agencies. Second, when Congress approved the Greek–Turkish aid bill in 1947, it added a proviso that the Senate must confirm the appointments of any high officials sent to oversee the administration of foreign aid in other countries. The following year, Congress also specified that the roving ambassador to supervise administration of the Marshall Plan should be confirmed by the Senate.[13]

In Chapter 3, it was noted that Presidents may use two techniques for circumventing senatorial control over their appointments. One of these is the power to rely upon "personal representatives" for diplomatic missions (thereby also sometimes bypassing the State Department and regular diplomatic personnel abroad). Harry Hopkins served in such a capacity many times for President Franklin D. Roosevelt. In the postwar period, W. Averell Harriman was sent abroad as the personal representative of successive Presidents. Such agents (many of whom already hold government positions) do not require senatorial confirmation.

Or, if the President finds the Senate opposed to a nominee, he may make an "interim appointment" after Congress has adjourned. The President is then required, however, to submit the candidate's name to the Senate within 40 days after the next session of Congress opens. A celebrated case of an "interim appointment" occurred in 1951, when President Truman named Philip Jessup as a member of the U.S. delegation to the United Nations. Many senators opposed Jessup's nomination because of his identification with left-wing causes. Although the Senate refused to confirm his appointment, President Truman gave Jessup an "interim appointment" which permitted him to serve on the delegation for several months.

Among all legislative prerogatives in foreign affairs, the Senate's power to confirm appointments perhaps gives that body less influence over the substance and direction of foreign policy than any other technique available to it. As a rule, the Senate is content to let an incumbent President "pick his team"; it is aware that any Chief Executive needs subordinates and advisers in whom he has confidence. Conversely, Presidents rarely appoint individuals to high positions of responsibility if there is substantial question about their qualifications. In the last analysis, Presidents can always rely upon officials who already hold office, upon "personal representatives," and upon "interim appointments" to circumvent Senate control.

Congressional Control over Appropriations

In the prolonged contest between the monarchy and Parliament in England—resulting ultimately in a victory by the legislature over the Crown—the "power of the purse" proved the decisive weapon in Parliament's triumph. Ever since this crucial encounter, legislative control over money has emerged as perhaps the most influential prerogative of national parliaments. As national security and foreign policy programs require ever-larger appropriations—approximating $100 billion by the early 1970s—Congress is afforded an unprecedented opportunity to influence foreign relations through its control of the purse strings.

More than any other leverage at its disposal, the power to appropriate money gives Congress a central role in nearly all aspects of American foreign relations. The national defense budget, foreign aid programs, American contributions to the United Nations, the Peace Corps, the operations of the U.S. Information Agency, the provision of military assistance to other countries, educational and cultural exchange programs, the maintenance of adequate diplomatic representation abroad, American participation in a vast number of international conferences—all such activities require funds for their operation. Legislative approval of them, coupled with congressional willingness to appropriate required funds, is thus indispensable for their continuous and successful operation.

The appropriations process is significant for another reason. The Constitution gives the Senate two prerogatives in foreign relations—the right to give its advice and consent to treaties, and the right to confirm executive appointments—which are denied to the House of Representatives. These Senate powers unquestionably give the upper chamber a feeling of involvement and prestige with regard to foreign policy issues that is lacking in the House. By contrast, the House has certain special prerogatives of its own, which to a large extent counterbalance the Senate's unique position. Article I, Section 7, of the Constitution provides: "All Bills for raising Revenue shall originate in the House of Representatives. . . ." Although this provision specifies only *revenue* bills—that is, bills levying taxes or tariffs—long-standing custom within Congress has extended this constitutional requirement to *spending measures* (or appropriations bills) as well. As the "popular chamber," in which the "will of the people" is presumably most accurately expressed, the House of Representatives has come to rely heavily upon its prerogatives in the appropriations process to influence both domestic and foreign policy. Particularly in the latter sphere (where its members unquestionably suffer some feeling of inferiority vis-à-vis the Senate), it uses control of the purse strings to exert its viewpoints, sometimes in the face of both senatorial and presidential opposition.

The student of American foreign policy must be reminded of a fact which he perhaps learned in a high-school civics course or a college course on American government. Federal programs entailing the expenditure of money must, in effect, go through Congress twice. They must first be "authorized" by Congress. Normally, in this stage, bills originating in the Senate dealing with foreign relations are referred to the Foreign Relations Committee; the Foreign Affairs Committee deals with such bills in the House. Each chamber must "authorize" the program in question, usually after a conference committee (consisting of both senators and representatives) agrees upon an identical bill.

Programs requiring funds for their implementation (nearly *all* programs in foreign affairs) must then go through the stage of "appropriations," in which funds are allocated for them. Programs that have been "authorized" by Congress are thus scrutinized by each chamber a second time. A separate appropriations bill is required for each major program; this bill is referred to the Appropriations Committees of the House and Senate. Again, each chamber must pass the appropriations measure (normally producing an identical version after a conference committee session) before statutory authority exists for executive officials to expend funds for national defense or for foreign aid or to pay America's contribution to the United Nations.

Theoretically, this cumbersome two-stage process is justified by the idea that the "authorization" stage is concerned solely with the *merits* of the program. Does national security require the development of a new weapons system, like the antiballistic missile? Does it promote some American diplomatic interest to increase foreign assistance to India? Would the United States benefit from paying additional funds to the United Nations for extraordinary peace-keeping activities? In principle, the "authorization" stage permits Congress to examine such questions from the perspective of their necessity or desirability on the grounds of national policy.

In theory, the appropriations stage is concerned with a very different consideration: Can the nation afford a particular program, along with all others already "authorized" by Congress, when all of them collectively entail expenditures totaling many billions of dollars? The two Appropriations Committees, that is to say, seek to arrive at some kind of equilibrium between the projections of anticipated federal revenues and total expenditures, so that the latter do not substantially exceed the former. Implicit in this process is the idea that these two committees establish some sense of *priority* among programs that have been "authorized" and for which funds must be found. Nearly always in any legislative session, the total of funds authorized exceeds anticipated government revenues. The Appropriations Committees thus have the difficult task of deciding that some authorized programs are more urgent than others, or that parts of a particular program (like foreign aid) are less essential than others. In either case, because the impulse to spend more money than is available is nearly always prevalent within Congress, the usual tendency of the House and the Senate Appropriations Committees (especially the former) is to *cut* appropriations below the level authorized earlier. For a variety of reasons we shall

allude to below, foreign policy programs often lend themselves to such legislative budget-paring better than domestic policy measures.

The theoretical justification given above for this intricate and time-consuming sequence of authorization and appropriation has in fact largely become an anachronism. Competent students of congressional behavior are convinced that key legislative committees seldom observe theoretical guidelines governing their activities. In a host of areas—national defense, State Department operations at home and abroad, foreign aid and military assistance, cultural and informational exchange programs—the two Appropriations Committees (especially the House committee) *do* pass judgment on the merits of programs, *do* attempt to influence the substance of policy, and *do* attempt to substitute their judgment for that of both the Senate Foreign Relations Committee and House Foreign Affairs Committee, on the one hand, and the executive branch, on the other hand, regarding important foreign policy issues. Similarly, the Senate Foreign Relations and House Foreign Affairs Committees also evaluate programs like foreign aid in terms of whether the nation can "afford" them and whether expanding aid to Latin America is more indispensable than spending federal funds on antipoverty programs at home. In reality, the crucial legislative hurdle for many undertakings in foreign affairs has become the House Appropriations Committee. As we shall see, its members tend to be much less receptive to presidential leadership and suggestion than either the Senate Appropriations Committee or the two committees charged with "authorizing" foreign policy programs.

On the basis of postwar experience, it is possible to forecast a kind of cycle or natural rhythm when Congress acts on a program like foreign aid.* Months of preparation within the executive branch are required to compile the foreign aid budget (during which time budgetary requests are carefully screened by the Bureau of the Budget) before it is submitted to Congress. Let us assume that for the coming fiscal year, the President requests a total of $2.5 billion for assistance to other countries. After the bill has been introduced in each chamber, the foreign aid "authorization" bill is considered by the Senate Foreign Relations and House Foreign Affairs Committees;

*It is not implied that the cycle identified above necessarily applies to other major spending programs, like the national defense budget. Each program is in some measure unique, in terms of legislative attitudes toward, and treatment of, it. Since the late 1950s, foreign aid has been a candidate for massive appropriations cuts on Capitol Hill, more so than the defense budget— the largest single item in the federal budget. By the early 1970s, however, it seemed likely that Congress was prepared to scrutinize some aspects of military appropriations as carefully and critically as it has examined foreign aid programs.

both committees will probably hold hearings and conduct selective investigations into some aspects of the foreign aid program. Ultimately each committee, and after that each chamber, will authorize the expenditure of some amount for foreign aid. Let us suppose that, after a conference committee has reached a compromise, both houses accept a foreign aid authorization measure totaling $2.2 billion. Experience has indicated that in the authorization phase, the funds are likely to be cut slightly, but not drastically, below the President's request.

The $2.2 billion authorization for foreign aid must now be considered by Congress as an "appropriations" measure, in which funds are made available to finance the program. Invoking its constitutional and traditional prerogatives over revenue bills, the House takes the initiative in this process. After the bill is introduced in the House, it is referred to the House of Appropriations Committee; the full committee in turn refers it to the proper subcommittee—in this case, the Subcommittee on Foreign Operations.* In due course,

this subcommittee "reports" its recommendations to the full Appropriations Committee, which nearly always endorses the report submitted to it. In turn, the Appropriations Committee "reports" the foreign aid appropriations bill to the House. Again, customarily the House of Representatives accepts this key committee's report with little or no change.

Throughout the postwar period, this has been the stage at which foreign aid programs usually encountered massive legislative opposition. It is a safe prediction that substantial reductions will be made every year in the foreign aid program by the Subcommittee on Foreign Operations and that these reductions will be accepted by the full committee and by the House itself. If $2.2 billion is initially authorized for foreign aid, we can reasonably predict that the House of Representatives will appropriate only $1.7 billion for the program.

Once the House has completed action on the appropriations for foreign aid (and characteristically this may be rather late in the legislative session), the Senate must act on the bill. Tradition, together with the nature of the Senate as a legislative body, decree that the upper chamber's role in the appropriations process differs fundamentally from that of the House. In dealing with appropriations, the Senate—in practice, the Senate Appropriations Committee—serves as an "appeals" body, before which executive officials plead for a "restoration" of at least some of the budgetary items eliminated, or pared, by the House.*

---

*Earlier, the statement was made that consideration of the foreign aid bill by the House Appropriations Committee (in practice by its Subcommittee on Foreign Operations) was the crucial stage in determining the scope and nature of the foreign aid program in any given year. One commentator has asserted that the chairman of this powerful subcommittee (for many years Representative Otto E. Passman, Democrat of Louisiana) exercised more influence over the fate of the program than did the chairman of the House Foreign Affairs Committee. See Richard F. Fenno, Jr., "The Internal Distribution of Influence: The House," in David Truman, ed., *The Congress and America's Future* (Englewood Cliffs, N.J.: Prentice-Hall, 1965), p. 55.

What factors account for the vast power exercised by this committee? Several may be identified. The first is the unique position of the House in regard to *all* money bills (both raising and spending revenues). Historically, such bills have come to be regarded as the special province of the house vis-à-vis the Senate. With 435 members (versus only 100 in the Senate), the house is able to apportion work among its committees in a way that permits representatives to become greater "specialists" in their subject matter than senators; the latter often are compelled to rely upon their staffs for expert advice. The House Appropriations Committee has some 50 members, making it the largest committee in the lower chamber. Assignment to the committee is highly coveted, since the committee is one of the most prestigious on Capitol Hill. More than most, this committee tends to be a "law unto itself." It meets in secret and almost never divulges its internal debates or votes; once agreement is reached within the committee (and its subcommittees), members unite to support its recommendations against critics, both within the House itself and outside it. Routinely, the full House accepts the committee's recommendations with little or no change.

Members of the House Appropriations Committee and its subcommittee view themselves as primarily "custodians" of the federal treasury against various claimants, whose demands (in the committee view, at least) are always inflated. One member of the committee likened budget requests submitted to it to the process of buying an automobile: Agencies had an "asking price" which the committee almost never accepted! Invariably, the committee "trims the fat" from budget rec-

ommendations it considers—and with some programs (like foreign aid) massive cuts are normal.

The House Appropriations Committee has consistently refused to accept any move—like making two- or three-year foreign aid appropriations—that would tend to weaken its control over spending or deny it an opportunity to review expenditures *annually*.

The role of the House Appropriations Committee in the legislative process is discussed in detail in Richard F. Fenno, Jr., "The House Appropriations Committee as a Political System," *American Political Science Review* LVI (June, 1962), 310–324; Nelson W. Polsby, *Congress and the Presidency* (Englewood Cliffs, N.J.: Prentice-Hall, 1964), pp. 91–96; Lewis A. Dexter, "Congressmen and the Making of Military Policy," in Robert L. Peabody and Nelson W. Polsby, eds., *New Perspectives on the House of Representatives* (Skokie, Ill.: Rand McNally, 1963), pp. 305–325; and Aaron Wildavsky, *The Politics of the Budgetary Process* (Boston: Little, Brown, 1964), pp. 47–61.

*The House of Representatives, especially its powerful Appropriations Committee, cherishes and carefully safeguards its traditional prerogatives in dealing with money bills. Unlike members of the smaller Senate, representatives on the House Appropriations Committee serve on no other major House committee; membership on the latter is considered a full-time job, and the committee is regarded as the "hardest working" on Capitol Hill. Its members are expected to become "specialists" on the subject matter coming before the subcommittee to which they are assigned. With less time to devote to their committee duties, members of the Senate Appropriations Committee are able to give programs like foreign aid and national defense much less detailed scrutiny than they receive in the House. Moreover, in

This dialogue, found in testimony before the Senate Appropriations Committee in 1967, illustrates the Senate's role. The witness was a State Department official, Mr. Joseph F. Friedkin, who was being interrogated by the chairman of the committee, Senator John McClellan (Democrat of Arkansas):

Senator McClellan: . . . The 1968 estimate [submitted in the President's budget] is $2,760,000. The House allowed $2.5 million, a reduction of $260,000, and you are requesting that the full amount be restored.
You may proceed and tell us why it should be restored. . . .
Mr. Friedkin: Yes, sir. Mr. Chairman and members of the committee, I do appreciate this opportunity to appear before you to appeal for the restoration of the House reduction of $260,000. . . .[14]

Normally, the executive branch can count upon some "restoration" by the Senate of House-instigated reductions in the foreign aid budget. Because the Senate has historically been more involved in foreign policy than the House, or because in the postwar period senators have often cooperated closely with executive officials in foreign relations, or because their six-year terms give senators more political security than is true of representatives, or because senators believe they have a mandate to restrain overzealous budget-paring in the House—for many such reasons, the Senate normally approves a higher foreign aid budget than was passed in the House. Let us assume that the Senate approved a foreign aid appropriation of $2.0 billion.

The differing appropriations bills voted by the House and Senate must be reconciled by a conference committee consisting of members from the two Appropriations Committees. Since such conference committees meet in closed (or secret) session, little is actually known about the process whereby such agreement is reached. From the evidence available, however, it appears that the committee concentrates its attention upon disputed items in the bill in a search for a consensus. There is a tendency for House and Senate conferees to "trade" items in the bill—that is, the House members will agree to an item strongly supported by Senate members, and *vice versa* until agreement is reached between them. Ultimately, the conference committee will arrive at the necessary compromises and will report an identical bill to both the House and Senate. As a rule, this conference report tends to "split the difference" between the appropriations bills voted earlier by each chamber. Since conference reports are unamendable, each chamber usually accepts the agreement worked out by the committee. (Rarely, however, one chamber may vote to send the report to the committee a second time for further changes.)

If the House approved an appropriation of $1.7 billion and the Senate $2.0 billion, the conference committee might arrive at the figure of $1.85 billion as a reasonable compromise. Thus, after many months of preparation in the executive branch, and several additional months of legislative deliberation, the President's foreign aid request of $2.5 billion for assistance to other countries has been reduced to a congressional appropriation of $1.85 billion.[15]

The Appropriations Process and the Defense Budget

Our treatment of the appropriations process thus far has suggested that legislative disposition of a program like foreign aid may be markedly different from its disposition of other programs like national defense. Without reproducing the entire cycle of the legislative process with regard to military appropriations, let us take note briefly of certain behavior patterns Congress has traditionally displayed in providing funds for the armed forces.

The President, Elias Huzar observed, was designated Commander-in-Chief of the military forces, but he "was to command only those forces which Congress put at his disposal. . . ."[16] And General Omar Bradley stated before a congressional committee in 1949 that: "Under our form of government, the military policy of the United States is shaped by the Congress not by the armed forces . . . because . . . Congress controls the appropriations which in the final analysis . . . control the military policy. . . ."[17]

The founders counted heavily upon the power of the purse to guard against military usurpation and to assure that the armed forces would always be utilized in the public interest. Thus the Constitution gives Congress the power to raise and support the military forces of the nation and specified that Congress may not make any military appropriation for longer than two years. In practice, Congress makes annual appropriations, thereby assuring itself an opportunity to review national defense policy at frequent intervals.*

Many items in the military budget tend to be recurrent and relatively fixed, such as military pay scales and long-range research and development contracts. They are not subject to drastic alteration by Congress without interfering with a sustained defense effort. Still, opportunities exist

---

some cases the same senators serve on the Foreign Relations Committee and the Appropriations Committee concurrently—a phenomenon that does not occur in the House.

*Some items in the military budget must be "carried over" from year to year to assure needed continuity. This is true, for example, of long-range defense contracts, research and development costs, and commercial leases.

every year for Congress to change the national defense policy by amending budget requests to reflect the legislative will. These opportunities have been utilized repeatedly throughout the postwar period. Spurred by the recommendations of its Appropriations Committee, the House in 1949 was adamant in support of a 55-group air force—in 1948, it had approved a 70-group force—despite the fact that President Truman had recommended only 48 groups. Even though the Senate was inclined to support the President, in the end it, too, was forced to accede to insistent House demands for increased air power. Here was a forceful legislative attempt to determine an important phase of national security policy—a phase that had profound repercussions for foreign affairs—even over the opposition of the Chief Executive. Again, under President Eisenhower, Congress endeavored to compel the White House to expand the Nike–Zeus missile system. Later, during the Kennedy administration, Congress also tried to compel executive officials to contruct more nuclear aircraft carriers.

In nearly all such cases during the postwar era, in the end Congress has had little success in relying upon its control over appropriations to effect major changes in the composition of the armed forces or in strategic doctrines. President Truman and those who succeeded him in the White House, simply *refused to spend* military appropriations which they did not request for expanding the air force, building additional nuclear ships, or other purposes desired by Congress. Viewing congressional appropriations as essentially permissive, rather than mandatory, expenditures, successive Presidents have in effect "put the money in the bank" instead of spending it for purposes they did not believe were warranted by national defense needs.[18]

In contrast to Congress' treatment of the foreign aid budget, in the vast majority of cases appropriations for national defense (which in recent years has been running $70 billion or more annually) receive cursory legislative scrutiny. More often than not, Congress is inclined to accept the President's budgetary requests, and in some cases even to *increase* them. Since World War II (and memories of the "unpreparedness" that contributed to disaster at Pearl Harbor are still vivid with many legislators), Congress has been as generous with the Department of Defense's budgetary requests as it has normally been parsimonious in its treatment of the foreign aid and State Department budgets.

Despite its constitutional prerogative to "raise and support" the armed forces, in recent history Congress has been reluctant to intrude actively into the determination of military strategy and doctrine. Perhaps even more than most citizens, legislators are aware of the inordinate *complexity* of military–strategic issues; they know too that a

refusal to provide adequately for national defense may risk catastrophe; and they have no desire to face the consequences (political and other) that would almost certainly accompany a major military defeat abroad. Few legislators have the time (and many do not have the inclination) to become real specialists in military strategy or to acquire the kind of expertise enabling them to produce viable alternatives to proposals formulated by the Pentagon. Moreover, few members of Congress really *desire* to be privy to the Pentagon's war plans or other military secrets. Nor is military strategy a subject which generally arouses strong constituency interest or "grass-roots pressures" upon Congress, as do foreign aid programs, trade and tariff bills, some actions of the United Nations, or other developments in foreign affairs. The result is that Congress is generally content to give the Defense Department the funds it asks for and to permit civilian and military leaders in the executive branch to determine military strategy.

One member of the House Armed Services Committee has said candidly: "We mostly reflect what the military people recommend; military policy is made by the Department of Defense." This same legislator added that the House Armed Services Committee was principally "a real estate committee"—that is, it was more interested in such questions as what military bases were going to be closed (or opened), than in more basic issues of military strategy![19] Or, as another commentator has expressed it, in dealing with national defense policy, the tendency of Congress has been to "monitor" executive decisions and to determine "political perimeters of tolerance and expectation" rather than decide upon the substance of national security policy or the precise composition of the armed forces.[20] In contrast to other spheres of foreign policy (and foreign aid is a conspicuous example), in dealing with the Defense Department Congress *encourages* long-range planning; it tends to be generous in allowing defense planners to "obligate" funds for many months ahead (since a new missile can take several years to become operational); and it urges military strategists to engage in innovation, experimentation, and continual change in all aspects of national security policy.[21]

By the late 1960s, however, an obvious restiveness could be discerned in both houses of Congress with regard to national defense. Public discontent over the Vietnam War—coupled with domestic strife in the cities, concern for conditions of poverty, and rising apprehensions about the impact of the military–industrial complex upon American society*—produced significant changes in legislative attitudes toward the national defense budget. Content for many years to

---

*The "Military–Industrial complex" is discussed in Chapter 4.

"go along" with the Pentagon's budgetary requests, Congress now appeared determined to examine defense requirements more carefully and to assert firmer legislative control over military spending. The national controversy which erupted at the end of the 1960s over the ABM (antiballistic missile) system witnessed sharp disagreements between legislators and executive officials over strategic questions; in the same period, the Pentagon was heavily criticized on Capitol Hill for "wasting" billions of dollars on abortive defense projects and for its lack of candor in informing Congress about such projects. Even groups, like the House Armed Services Committee, that in the past had been favorably disposed toward the military establishment pledged that hereafter the military budget would be scrutinized much more thoroughly than had been the case in previous years. For many legislators, the "credibility" of civilian and military officials in the Pentagon had been heavily compromised as a result of disappointments in Vietnam.

One commentator is convinced that congressional restiveness over the activities of the Pentagon had in fact been building up for several years, leading Congress to search for new techniques and procedures for exerting its influence in this vital area of national policy. Three specific forces engendered uneasiness and criticism on Capitol Hill. One was the fact that, more than at any other time in American history, technological progress was rapidly rendering existing weapons systems and strategic doctrines obsolete; under these conditions, all previously "orthodox" principles and doctrines were subject to question. Second, as we noted in Chapter 4, the armed services themselves were often *divided and uncertain* about the strategic implications of new weapons systems (like missiles). Disunity within the military services created new opportunities for legislative initiatives to "settle" intraservice quarrels. Third, a number of experienced legislators (particularly those serving on key committees like Armed Services and Appropriations) could often match executive officials in their experience in dealing with military questions and their level of *expertise* on at least some aspects of national defense. It was not uncommon for senior members of these committees to have twenty-five or more years service in Congress; their involvement in questions affecting national defense extended over the administrations of several Presidents and an even greater number of Secretaries of Defense. When, for the first time in recent history, they discovered growing *public* interest in the problem of national defense, such legislators were not loath to challenge the viewpoints expressed in the Pentagon.[22]

Congressional uneasiness over the defense establishment is but part of a larger phenomenon alluded to earlier in the chapter: a legislative desire to exert greater influence in the foreign policy field. How well equipped is Congress to exercise more effective control over the defense budget? What problems must it overcome in doing so? We may more intelligently examine these questions at a later stage, when we evaluate the obstacles in the path of more forceful legislative leadership in foreign relations.

The Congressional Power to "Declare War"

The internal discontent over America's involvement in the Vietnam conflict during the late 1960s often centered upon another legislative prerogative in foreign affairs: the congressional power to "declare war." The Vietnam conflict, critics alleged, was an "undeclared war" in which the United States was "illegally" involved; in this view, the President lacked constitutional authority to order American troops to Vietnam or other combat zones without a declaration of war by Congress.

The Constitution (Art. I, Sec. 8) gives Congress the power to declare war; the same article gives it the power to raise and support the armed forces of the United States. Yet—as we noted in Chapter 3—Article II, Section 2, designates the President as the Commander-in-Chief of the military forces. As with other grants of authority in the Constitution, power is thus divided between the executive and legislative branches. Even so, it is evident that the Founding Fathers intended that Congress play a leading (perhaps decisive) role in deciding whether the nation would go to war. During the eighteenth century, a "declaration" of war normally was given weeks or months before hostilities erupted between nations; Congress, it was therefore anticipated, would debate and finally decide whether the nation ought to resort to arms. Even in that earlier age, it should be noted, a "declaration" of war normally came from the nation that *initially* took up arms in behalf of its policy goals; nations that were attacked seldom had time to deliberate at leisure how they would respond!

Like other legislative powers in foreign relations, and perhaps more than most, Congress' power to declare war has proved an increasingly weak instrument of legislative control. No longer do nations give notice of their intention of resorting to armed force. Warfare entered a new era, for example, during the 1930s—when Japan attacked Manchuria without warning in 1931 and when Nazi Germany used *Blitzkrieg* tactics in its invasion of Poland in 1939. Today, Communist-supported "wars of national liberation" routinely depend upon stealth and deception for success. During the Cuban missile crisis late in 1962, President Kennedy informed the American people by national television that he had *already ordered* American naval forces to enforce a "quarantine" against Cuba and that he had directed the armed forces "to prepare for any eventualities." He further warned that any nuclear missile launched from Cuba upon any nation in the hemisphere would be regarded "as an attack by the Soviet Union on the United States, requiring a full retaliatory response upon the Soviet Union." It is noteworthy that congressional leaders were informed of Kennedy's message approximately one hour before his broadcast (well after the Strategic Air Command and other military units had been placed on full "alert").[23] The Cuban crisis illustrates well the reasons why Congress' power to declare war has largely become a dead letter in the Constitution. Modern military technology, together with strategic doctrines emphasizing stealth and often "surprise attack," have largely outmoded this constitutional provision. It has been estimated, for example, that if an enemy decided to launch a missile attack against the United States, the President and his military advisers would have from fifteen to thirty minutes' warning before the missiles struck!

Yet we should not draw the contrast between the contemporary era and earlier periods too sharply in this connection. Over a century ago, when he confronted the disruption of the American republic by the secession of the southern states, President Lincoln was also compelled to act promptly and decisively. Without ever asking for, or receiving, a "declaration of war" from Congress, Lincoln took many steps on his own authority designed to save the Union. When the constitutionality of his actions was challenged in the courts, the Supreme Court held that the President is not only authorized but bound to resist force by force. He does not initiate the war, but is "bound to accept the challenge without waiting for any special legislative authority."Citing British precedents, the Court held that ". . . war may exist without declaration on either side." The President, the Court asserted, was required to respond to the crisis "in the shape it presented itself, without waiting for Congress to baptize it with a name; and no name given to it by him or them could change the fact. . . ." After it was convened in extraordinary legislative session in 1861, the Court noted, Congress subsequently approved and legitimitized virtually all of Lincoln's actions.[24]

The fact is that American history has witnessed far more "undeclared" wars than those, like World Wars I and II, which were formally "declared" by Congress.* One student of the

American Constitution has written that the congressional power to declare war "has never prevented war when the President wanted one."[25] Historical evidence abounds to support this contention—from Polk's belligerent position toward Mexico in the 1840s, to Cleveland's militant stand during the Venezuelan boundary dispute with Britain in 1897, to FDR's "shoot on sight" order to the navy in dealing with Nazi U-boats before World War II, to Truman's intervention in the Korean War in 1950, to President Kennedy's military intervention in South Vietnam and his proclamation of a naval blockade against Castro's Cuba in 1962. Presidents have clearly not hesitated to protect national security whenever it was threatened and in whatever manner was required under the circumstances.

Critics of America's involvement in the Vietnam conflict thus were unable to make a persuasive case on the basis of American history. Moreover, in the postwar period a new procedure designed to promote unity between the executive and legislative branches in dealing with international crises—a congressional resolution "authorizing" the President to rely upon armed force to protect the nation's diplomatic interests—has been utilized on several occasions. In the executive view at least, such resolutions constitute a kind of de facto "declaration of war" giving legislative sanction to the President's actions. We shall examine this recent development more fully later in the chapter.

The right of Congress to declare war is less important as a legislative permit to engage in hostilities than in two other particulars. One of these relates to public opinion. Nothing perhaps so dramatically conveys the unified determination of the American people to protect their interests as the spectacle of both houses of Congress overwhelmingly approving the President's resort to armed force in a crisis.* This gesture both unites the home front and serves notice to the enemy that all agencies of the government are wholeheartedly behind the national effort required to

---

*One student of American government has noted that Congress has "declared" war only five times in American history: in the War of 1812; the Mexican War; the Spanish–American War; and World Wars I and II. Even in these instances, Congress declared war only when it was asked to do so by the President. See Louis W. Koening, *The Chief Executive*, rev. ed. (New York: Harcourt Brace Jovanovich, 1968), p. 213. Another study finds

that, beginning with America's "undeclared war" with France in 1798–1800, there have been "at least 125 prior instances in which presidents have ordered our forces into battle or to maintain positions abroad without a congressional declaration of war." See "Vietnam: Vital Issues in the Great Debate" (New York: Foreign Policy Association, 1966), p. 4.

*This aspect of Congress' power to declare war was fully understood by President Eisenhower in dealing with Communist Chinese threats in the Formosa Straits in 1955. Early in that year, the President asked Congress to pass the Formosa Resolution, giving him stand-by authority to use armed force if necessary to repulse a Communist attack on the Nationalist Chinese regime on Formosa. A "suitable congressional resolution" would "clearly and publicly establish the authority of the President" and make clear "the unified and serious intentions" of the United States. Dwight D. Eisenhower, *Mandate for Change: 1953–1956* (Garden City, N.Y.: Doubleday, 1963), pp. 467–468.

safeguard the nation's interests. Second, a congressional declaration of war has important legal consequences. Numerous legislative grants of authority to the President take effect during periods of war and national emergency; these give the Chief Executive vast powers he does not ordinarily have in peacetime.

General Legislative Authority in Foreign Affairs

Along with specific prerogatives bearing upon foreign relations, like the Senate's role in treaty-making or the legislative power over appropriations, Congress has general legislative authority over measures intimately related to foreign policy and domestic programs impinging upon external affairs. Indeed, as the line between "foreign" and "domestic" affairs has become more and more eroded, nearly every important legislative enactment, resolution, or investigation has some impact upon foreign affairs. If Congress raises the level of taxes, it will unquestionably affect America's balance of payments problem. If it refuses to lower tariff duties on commodities sold by the emerging nations, it may influence American relations with the Afro–Asian nations. Legislative enactments dealing with nuclear energy have inhibited America's ability to "share" atomic secrets with the NATO allies. Congressional authority is required to establish new executive agencies like the National Security Council and the U.S. Information Agency, or to undertake major reorganizations of the State Department and the Defense Department. New programs, like the Peace Corps or the "Food for Peace" program, require legislative approval.

While Congress' authority over programs relating directly or indirectly to foreign affairs is thus vast—wider than at any time in American history —the key fact about its role, Robert Dahl has written, is that the legislative branch "rarely provides the initiative. . . . In foreign policy the President proposes, the Congress disposes and in a very large number of highly important decisions . . . the Congress does not even have the opportunity to dispose."[26] In Chapter 3, considerable attention was paid to the President's role as a *legislative* leader. As we have mentioned, the American Congress is the only major legislative body in the world that still has the power to *initiate* legislation. Yet in practice the initiative in legislation has passed increasingly to the White House. Under the Kennedy administration, for example, some forty government officials engaged in "legislative liaison," under the supervision of the President's Special Assistant for congressional affairs. One presidential assistant has quoted President Johnson, who said on one occasion that "no person in his respective department could ever be any more important than the head of the congressional relations activity."[27]

Although congressional initiative in formulating proposals relating to foreign relations is rare, it is by no means unknown. An outstanding example was the Battle Act (officially called the Mutual Defense Assistance Control Act) of 1951, sponsored by Representative Laurie C. Battle (Democrat of Alabama). Passed during the Korean War, this act was comparable to other enactments in the years that followed. It set forth stringent legislative prohibitions regulating the extension of American foreign aid to other countries, particularly those trading with Communist nations or refusing to inform the United States about the scope of their trade with Iron Curtain countries. But it also contained a provision allowing the terms of the act to be disregarded when the President believed the extension of American aid to countries violating it served the national interest.[28]

As a rule, members of Congress are aware of the necessity for presidential leadership and direction in the foreign policy field. They realize that internal disunity and strife within the American government (and we shall treat that problem more fully in Chapter 6) can nullify diplomatic efforts abroad. Even advocates of expanded legislative influence in foreign relations, like Senator J. William Fulbright (Democrat of Arkansas), acknowledge the President's primacy in the foreign policy field, and that Congress should not attempt to usurp the Chief Executive's role, but merely endeavor to redress the balance which they feel has become weighted too heavily in favor of unrestrained executive control.[29]

EXTRACONSTITUTIONAL AND INFORMAL TECHNIQUES

Legislative Investigations

During the year 1961, the Senate alone conducted the following investigations touching national security and foreign policy: the Aeronautical and Space Science Committee investigated the National Aeronautical and Space Administration; the Armed Services Committee carried on three investigations—into problems in the Defense Department, strategic weapons and delivery systems, and secret hearings on the Central Intelligence Agency; the Commerce Committee looked into the problem of foreign competition in textile manufacturing; the Foreign Relations Committee held eight different investigations into various aspects of foreign policy; the Government Operations Committee evaluated national policy machinery; and the Judiciary Committee held seven hearings having ramifications for foreign affairs.[30]

These examples call attention to the extent to which a highly effective instrument for asserting legislative influence in foreign relations is Congress powers of investigation. Legislative investigations had comparatively little influence upon foreign policy before World War II. The only significant exception was the Nye Committee investigation during the 1930s into the influence of the munitions makers on American foreign policy before and during World War I. Its findings were highly instrumental in creating an isolationist climate of opinion within the United States by supporting the view that America had been drawn into the war by the intrigues of profit-hungry industrialists.[31]

During and after World War II, legislative investigations probed virtually every phase of American foreign policy. Conducted by several important committees of Congress, whose members differed widely in knowledge about foreign policy and in attachment to traditional democratic principles of fair procedure, these investigations had decidedly mixed results. Some committees unquestionably injured the prestige of the United States at home and abroad and jeopardized the stability of its foreign relations. Other investigations resulted in needed clarifications of national policy and in improved administration.

One of the most far-reaching clashes in American history between executive and legislative prerogatives over national defense policy occurred when the Committee on the Conduct of the War tried to compel President Lincoln to follow congressional advice during the Civil War. The Committee on the Conduct of the War

was encouraged . . . by the public impatience at the slowness with which military operations against the Confederacy were proceeding. . . . They consistently urged a more vigorous prosecution of the war and less lenience toward the institution of slavery. . . . So far did the committee depart from its legitimate purpose that it became a veritable thorn in the flesh of the President. The members took over partial control of military operations. Their investigating missions to the front undermined army discipline and discouraged the more capable commanders. . . . Interrogating generals as if they were schoolboys and advising the President like military experts, they sought to intimidate Lincoln by threatening to arouse Congress against him.[32]

With certain modifications, this description might also apply to postwar investigations of American foreign policy in the Far East, of the problem of East–West trade, and of the operations of the Voice of America.

Yet legislative investigations have also made important positive contributions to American foreign and closely related domestic policies. A model constructive investigation was that carried

on by the Truman Committee during World War II.* Binkley believes that the "highest development of the congressional investigating committee," and that Senator Truman perhaps contributed more than any other civilian except the President to the winning of the war.[33] The committee grew out of Senator Truman's conviction that Congress ought to carry on investigations while waste could still be eliminated from the war effort and unsound practices could be corrected, instead of waiting until after the war when it could do no more than try to assess the blame for failures. By contrast, after World War I there had been over a hundred congressional investigations, most of them "motivated by partisan desires to fix blame on the opposition"; they had "raked over the coals for more than fifteen years after the war."[34]

The model afforded by the Truman Committee was forgotten by many investigating committees after World War II. The relationship between their activities and traditional legislative purposes was often ill defined, if not completely tenuous.† This was especially true of committees whose primary jurisdictions lay outside the fields of foreign relations and national security and whose members had little first-hand knowledge of these areas. During the 1940s and 1950s, subcommittees of the House Un-American Activities Committee, the Senate Judiciary Committee, or the Senate Committee on Government Operations roamed afield looking for officials who were responsible for the "loss" of China to Communism, for Soviet control over Eastern Europe, or for subversive groups that supposedly led national policy-makers astray at critical junctures throughout recent dip-

*This committee, known as the Special Senate Committee Investigating the National Defense Program, was established in March, 1941, and was named for its chairman, Senator Harry S. Truman (Democrat of Missouri).

†Even under ideal circumstances, it should be noted, since Congress has surrendered much of its traditional power to initiate legislation to the executive branch, the nature of legislative investigations has changed accordingly. Theoretically, such investigations are held to provide information for the guidance on Congress in formulating legislation. In reality, they more often than not serve other purposes in the contemporary era. They afford an opportunity for diverse groups to make their viewpoints known and get their opinions "on record"; they demonstrate the need for legislative action; they highlight problems that will be encountered if a particular bill is passed and serve to allay the fears of the bill's opponents; they sometimes generate support for a particular bill among "wavering" legislators; they allow Congress an opportunity to sense how influential public groups divide on the bill; they give Congress an opportunity to "monitor" administrative performance. Some students of the legislative process believe that the last—the "control of administration"—is perhaps Congress' main function today. See Nelson W. Polsby, *Congress and the Presidency* (Englewood Cliffs, N.J.: Prentice-Hall, 1964), p. 68; and Samuel P. Huntington, "Congressional Response to the Twentieth Century," in David Truman, ed., *The Congress and America's Future* (Englewood Cliffs, N.J.: Prentice-Hall, 1965), p. 25.

lomatic history. If such investigations were noteworthy for their barren results, a fundamental long-range consequence indirectly stemming from them was to inculcate an utterly false—one might say, potentially disastrous—illusion in the public mind, which often compounded the problem of formulating and carrying out effective policies in the recent period. This was a new devil theory of diplomacy, comparable to the one gripping the American mind after World War I. If the foreign policy of the United States during and after World War II sometimes left much to be desired in an area like the Far East, for example, the assumption guiding such investigations was that the nation's diplomatic interests had been "betrayed" by officials in high places. Such assumptions typified the "illusion of American omnipotence," a corollary of which was the widespread belief that events in the outside world could be altered at the will of the United States. When experience sometimes proved otherwise, then betrayal—not pervasive ignorance and indifference about complex developments abroad, not lack of sound diplomatic judgments, not failure to appraise global political currents correctly, not realization that America's great power is *finite* —was advanced as the only possible explanation. If even intensive legislative investigations frequently had difficulty identifying the subversive influences operating upon American policies, in many cases this was because they were such obvious and fundamental, if unspectacular, forces as widespread public apathy about international events, unrealistic public and official expectations, and unwillingness to pay the price that a successful policy exacted—failures often as evident on Capitol Hill as anywhere else in the nation.

Another lasting consequence of certain congressional investigations in the postwar period (particularly those having an evident partisan motivation) was to disrupt morale in agencies like the State Department and the U.S. Information Agency. Harboring a deeply ingrained skepticism and suspicion of the diplomatic service, many legislators took obvious delight in "exposing" State Department failures and deficiencies or in holding Foreign Service officers up to public ridicule and derision.* The result in some periods

(like the 1950s) was a serious decline in State Department morale, difficulty in recruiting well-qualified candidates for the Foreign Service, and over-all impairment of the nation's ability to achieve its external objectives.

Nevertheless, with all their apparent faults—many of which can be, and some of which have been, corrected—congressional investigations can make a useful contribution to American foreign policy. A most valuable investigation in the postwar era was the joint Senate Foreign Relations—Armed Services Committee investigation into President Truman's dismissal of General Douglas MacArthur in 1951. MacArthur was a distinguished national hero. During the Korean War, he seemed to many citizens to stand unflinchingly against certain unwholesome tendencies: appeasement of the Communists, kow-towing to the Allies, and undue surrender of sovereignty to the United Nations. His dismissal precipitated what William S. White has called "the gravest and most emotional Constitutional crisis that the United States has known since the Great Depression."[35] Seldom in American history has the principle of civilian control over the military been in such great jeopardy as when President Truman, after repeated provocations, finally ordered MacArthur home from Korea.

Under the strong leadership of Senator Richard Russell (Democrat of Georgia), the joint committee conducted a prolonged investigation into MacArthur's dismissal, and in the process probed into recent American policies in the Far East. As the facts came to light, the congressional and national furor subsided. Not even Republicans cared to challenge the President's *right* to dismiss the General. Throughout its investigation, the committee sought unity among its members. Its final "Message to the American People," says White "dissolved a national emotionalism the exact like of which had not heretofore been seen. . . ." The committee "protected not only the American tradition of the pre-eminent civil authority; [it] halted what was then an almost runaway movement toward rejection of the United Nations."[36]

During the 1960s, several legislative investigations made a constructive contribution to American foreign policy. Reference was made in Chapter 4 to the lengthy investigations into the machinery of national security policy carried on by the Subcommittee on National Security and International Operations of the Senate Government Operations Committee (the "Jackson Committee"), led by Senator Henry M. Jackson (Democrat of Washington). Studies produced by this committee were of continuing interest to government officials and scholars concerned with foreign policy.

*Congress' innate skepticism about the State Department has deep historical roots, going back to President George Washington's admonition that the United States avoid "foreign entanglements." An experienced Foreign Service officer has written: "The fact is that no other branch of officialdom is so often berated in public, so frequently accused of pursuing the wrong policy, so roundly scolded by the demagogues from the grass roots, so thoroughly misunderstood by the masses in whose behalf it labors" as the State Department. "Badgered by Congress, kicked around by the ill-informed, tackled by the politicians like a dummy at a football practice, the department which bears the chief burden

for our safety in a predatory and tricky world is everybody's whipping boy." Henry S. Villard, *Affairs at State* (New York: Thomas Y. Crowell, 1965), pp. 2–3.

Similarly, investigations by the Senate Foreign Relations Committee on a variety of questions— American relations with Communist China, Congress' powers in foreign affairs, and the Vietnam conflict—produced valuable testimony from well-informed witnesses and generated public interest in important foreign policy issues. As a rule, these investigations were characterized by fair procedures, by a desire to *inform* Congress and the public about national policy questions, and by a relative absence of partisan or personal motivations.

The verdict then on legislative investigations in foreign affairs is clearly mixed. Some have unquestionably impeded the realization of national policy goals and produced deleterious long-range consequences. Others have been beneficial, have undoubtedly served to improve both the conduct of foreign relations and specific national policies, and have played a valuable role in enlightening legislative and public opinion about problems in the outside world. In contrast with the 1950s, the 1960s probably witnessed more investigations in the latter category than in the former.

Congressional Resolutions

Legislative resolutions expressing the opinion of Congress on questions of public policy are not law and have no binding force on the executive. Nevertheless, they can be important techniques by which Congress influences the course of foreign relations. We have already mentioned the Vandenberg Resolution, which initiated negotiations leading to the North Atlantic Treaty in 1949. Similarly, American relations with Red China have been heavily influenced by two legislative resolutions adopted in 1951. At that time, both houses of Congress branded Red China an "aggressor" for intervening in the Korean War late in 1950. The Senate resolution went further by expressing the conviction that Red China should not be admitted to the United Nations. These resolutions unquestionably expressed the dominant sentiment of the American people. Presidents Truman, Eisenhower, Kennedy, Johnson, and Nixon have been unprepared to override legislative and public opinion on this issue.

Neither the White House nor Congress operates in a vacuum. Each is highly sensitive to public opinion and to deep convictions held by officials in the other branch. Whenever possible, the President and Congress prefer to adopt policies that can command wide public support. Congressional resolutions on foreign policy issues are thus important barometers of opinion for the executive. They may reflect deep public concern about contemporary policy issues; they may call attention forcefully to widespread dissatisfaction with existing policies; and they may strengthen the President's hand in dealing with other countries by

conveying the impression abroad of unanimity within the American government.

Two kinds of congressional resolutions in foreign affairs may be distinguished: those initiated by Congress itself, often in the face of presidential opposition; and those formulated by the executive branch (sometimes in concert with selected congressmen), which reflect viewpoints held by both executive and legislative policy-makers. Throughout the postwar period, Congress has from time to time passed resolutions condemning Soviet policy in Eastern Europe, calling upon the President to use American influence to keep Communist China out of the United Nations, or asking for a re-examination of national policies in Southeast Asia.[37] Although such resolutions have no binding force as legislation, a President will of course acknowledge them as an expression of opinion on Capitol Hill; if he desires harmonious relations with Congress, he will take account of such legislative sentiment in formulating national policy.

Much more influential, however, is the other kind of resolution which is drafted in (or with the concurrence of) the executive branch. Its principal purpose is to provide a graphic display of governmental unity in dealing with a foreign crisis. Congress has passed several resolutions of this kind since World War II. Confronted with a threat by Communist China to invade Formosa and adjacent islands in 1955, President Eisenhower asked Congress to authorize the use of force to protect the area. Early in 1955, the Senate completed passage of a resolution granting the President the authority he requested.* A comparable resolution was passed in 1957, several months after the Suez Crisis. This resolution empowered the President to frustrate the expansion of "international Communism" in the Middle East. In 1962, two similar resolutions were approved by Congress. One supported the President's determination to maintain the security of Berlin against Communist encroachments. The other expressed opposition to the Marxist regime in Cuba and reiterated Ameri-

---

*The Formosa Resolution of 1955, and those modeled after it later, involved a troublesome constitutional issue. When the President asked Congress to grant him "authority" to employ armed force in behalf of some foreign policy goal, did this mean that he *lacked* such authority if Congress withheld it? Successive Presidents (along, most probably, with a majority of legislators) would answer in the negative: Both under the Constitution and in the light of ample precedents from American history, any Chief Executive possesses the authority to use armed force for the protection of the nation's vital interests. Thus, President Eisenhower said in connection with the Formosa Resolution: "Authority for some of the actions which might be required would be inherent in the authority of the Commander-in-Chief." Nevertheless, he asked Congress for a "suitable resolution" in order to "clearly and publicly establish the authority of the President" to act and to "make clear the unified and serious intentions" of the American Congress. See Dwight D. Eisenhower, *Mandate for Change* (Garden City, N.Y.: Doubleday, 1963), p. 468.

ca's determination to prevent Communist penetration of Latin America.[38]

The most celebrated and perhaps most controversial resolution of this type was the Tonkin Gulf Resolution of August 10, 1964. Requested by President Johnson, after North Vietnamese naval vessels attacked American ships off the coast of Vietnam, this resolution put Congress on record as approving and supporting "the determination of the President as Commander-in-Chief, to take all necessary measures to repel any armed attack against the forces of the United States and to prevent further aggression." The resolution reiterated an earlier congressional finding that the maintenance of "international peace and security in southeast Asia" was "vital" to America's national interest and to world peace; and it pledged that the United States would "take all necessary steps" to fulfill its treaty obligations and the provisions of the UN Charter to assist any nation "in defense of its freedom." Adopted unanimously in the House of Representatives, and by a vote of 88 to 2 in the Senate, the Tonkin Gulf Resolution figured prominently in subsequent years, both as a basis for national policies in Southeast Asia and as a target for criticism by those who deplored America's involvement in Vietnam. Ironically, this resolution—formulated in the interest of demonstrating maximum national *unity* in foreign affairs—became a primary source of *disunity* among supporters and critics of American policy in Southeast Asia.[39]

The Tonkin Gulf Resolution illustrates some of the advantages and drawbacks of such executive-sponsored resolutions. Ostensibly, a resolution of this kind does reflect a high degree of unanimity between the executive and legislative branches on a particular foreign policy issue, especially at the time it is passed and in the weeks immediately thereafter. Literally any step a President might take could be justified by reference to the wide grant of authority such a resolution confers upon him. Other than a declaration of war (rare as that is), it would be difficult to think of any step which more forcefully symbolizes the existence of a consensus within the American government than a resolution of this type.

Yet time has also revealed that such resolutions may, and not infrequently do, produce tensions, controversies, and intense personal antagonisms among policy-makers in the executive and legislative branches. Nearly always, as in the case of the Tonkin Gulf Resolution, Congress deliberates in an atmosphere of crisis and urgency; little opportunity is afforded for legislative investigation and debate; legislators complain (later, if not at the time) that they were "pressured" into supporting the resolution or that the President and his agents did not reveal "all the facts" when the resolution was being considered. With the passage of time also it is not uncommon for legislators to disagree with the President and the Secretary of State over the extent of the "authority" granted by Congress in the resolution. The resolution becomes, to the minds of some senators and representatives, a "blank check" permitting the President to carry out any policy he desires—presumably with the concurrence of Congress. Especially when national policy fails to achieve its stated goals, whether in Vietnam or in the Middle East, legislators may be expected to complain that the President has exceeded his authority under the resolution or that, in any event, Congress did not anticipate the course of events that would follow under it. Critics of the Vietnam War expressed many of these criticisms about the Gulf of Tonkin Resolution, just as many Democrats voiced complaints about the Middle East Resolution which many of them had voted for under President Eisenhower in 1957.[40]

Experience with the Vietnam conflict suggests that hereafter, Congress may well be hesitant to pass resolutions of this kind, while the President may be no less reluctant to ask for such an expression of legislative opinion.

Speeches and Activities of Individual Legislators

Unlike the British Parliament and most other legislative bodies in democratic governments, the Congress of the United States is characterized by very loose party lines and little or no "party discipline." The absence of party discipline, along with the tradition of legislative freedom of speech, most notably in the Senate, accords legislators wide latitude to comment publicly on outstanding international issues. Moreover, the relative autonomy surrounding the operations of congressional committees (and subcommittees within them) accords wide scope for individual congressmen sometimes to exercise great influence upon foreign relations.

Legislators may express their viewpoints on foreign policy questions by delivering speeches on the floor of Congress; by inserting material into the *Congressional Record;* by holding press conferences; by making speeches over radio and television; by "leaking" information to the press; by traveling abroad, where opportunities exist both for influencing foreign opinion and for familiarizing American diplomatic officials with their views; by interrogating witnesses at legislative hearings; and in a variety of other ways. Expressions of opinion on Capitol Hill are studied carefully by other governments, as well as by agencies like the Office of Congressional Relations in the State Department.

From time to time throughout American history, key legislators have acquired sufficient influence to enable them to become the "spokesmen" for a significant body of opinion in Congress on foreign policy issues. Thus Senator Henry Cabot Lodge emerged as the leading opponent to the League of Nations after World War I. Following World War II, Senator Pat McCarran (Democrat of Nevada) almost single-handedly shaped legislative attitudes on questions of immigration and refugee relief; McCarran was an outspoken opponent of the "liberalized" immigration laws sponsored by the Truman administration. By contrast, Senators Arthur H. Vandenberg (Republican of Michigan) and Tom Connally (Democrat of Texas) became symbols of "bipartisan" cooperation between Republicans and Democrats in formulating key undertakings like planning for the United Nations, extending Marshall Plan aid to Western Europe, and drafting the North Atlantic Treaty. Both held strong opinions about foreign affairs; their voices carried considerable weight in the deliberations of Congress; and both maintained firm control over the proceedings of the Senate Foreign Relations Committee (where they served as chairmen when their respective parties controlled Congress). Under President Eisenhower, Senator Walter George (Democrat of Georgia) similarly worked closely with the White House, often protecting the President's program against attacks from Democratic (and occasionally Republican) dissidents.

During the 1960s, other legislators exercised an influential role in legislative deliberations on foreign police issues. American relations with African nations, for example, were impaired for a time in 1963 following a trip to the African continent by Senator Allen J. Ellender (Democrat of Louisiana). In an 800-page report on conditions there, Senator Ellender accused the State Department of "tiptoe diplomacy" in dealing with African nations governed by "thin skinned politicians." The truth was, in Ellender's view, that there was no "part of Africa where Africans are ready for self-government." To say that Ellender's remarks made him *persona non grata* in newly independent African nations would be to understate the case.[41] In the Senate, an even more influential voice on foreign policy issues was that of Senator Mike Mansfield (Democrat of Montana). Mansfield was a member of the Foreign Relations Committee and the Democratic Majority Leader under Presidents Kennedy, Johnson, and Nixon. Keenly interested in foreign policy problems, and usually very well informed about them, Mansfield took the lead in shaping congressional opinion on questions like the Vietnam War, a consular treaty with the Soviet Union, and the level of American troops stationed in the NATO area. Although he served as Majority Leader, Mansfield did not hesitate to differ with the administration's foreign policy on several major issues. Late in 1966, for example, he sponsored a resolution in the Senate calling for a reduction of American forces in Europe, despite the Johnson administration's known opposition to this move.[42] Several months

later, Mansfield joined a number of other senators in expressing strenuous objection to further American involvement in the Congo, at a time when that country was experiencing an internal political upheaval.[43] Known as a "moderate critic," Mansfield did not, on the other hand, normally associate himself with the "doves" who advocated a unilateral American withdrawal from Vietnam, although he did frequently criticize various aspects of American policy in Southeast Asia (such as over-optimistic predictions of victory in the Vietnam contest).

Individual legislators influential in foreign affairs were not of course confined to the Senate alone. In recent years, two members of the House of Representatives deserve special mention. One is Representative Otto E. Passman, powerful chairman of the House Appropriations Committee's Subcommittee on Foreign Operations. In this capacity, Passman was perhaps the most influential voice on Capitol Hill in determining the fate of the President's foreign aid budget. Known as a determined opponent of foreign aid—"Foreign aid," he once declared, "has been one of the greatest foreign-policy failures in history"—Passman viewed his function as to "contain" foreign aid, to encourage common sense in its policies and operations, and to curb as much as possible its waste and mismanagement." So potent was his influence in determining the magnitude of the annual foreign aid budget that his name became synonymous with opposition to foreign assistance. To "passmanize" the foreign aid budget meant to cut it massively, to criticize the administration of the program, and to attach various provisions to the program greatly inhibiting its flexibility.[44]

In a different sphere of foreign relations—the State Department's budget for domestic and overseas operations—another member of the House of Representatives was no less influential. This was Congressman John J. Rooney (Democrat of New York), chairman of the subcommittee of the House Appropriations Committee which dealt with the State Department's annual budget. One State Department official admitted candidly in 1958: "Let's face it. When Rooney whistles, we've just got to dance."[45] Several years later one commentator wrote an article on "The Foreign Policy of John J. Rooney."[46] An acerbic critic of State Department waste and "mismanagement," Rooney could be counted upon to examine the agency's budget with great care and considerable skepticism.

The following excerpts, taken from hearings on the State Department budget for 1960, illustrate Rooney's attitude. At the outset, the State Department had requested an item involving $2.7 million to cover expanded intelligence activities:

Congressman Rooney: I must be fair and say this: This proposal being presented to us seems to me, for one, to be unwarranted. You are going to have a job justifying this. If you can do so, go right ahead.

After the State Department requested funds to create 47 new diplomatic posts and to expand other posts, this exchange took place:

Congressman Rooney: That means this would be a beef-up of practically 330 positions?
Mr. Henderson: That is right.
Congressman Rooney: Go ahead and see if you can justify it.

Further along, this exchange occurred:

Congressman Rooney: Let me try to summarize it this way . . . is it a fair conclusion to say that there are no real [staff] reductions of any kind?
Mr. Hall: No, sir; because there is a—
Congressman Rooney: Do not elaborate. 'No, sir' is enough.

At a later point, this dialogue occurred:

Mr. Henderson: . . . We are asking for 17 additional people . . . who are to observe carefully all the maneuvers of international communism in its efforts to penetrate economically the various countries of the world, and are to try to devise methods of frustrating these efforts of international communism.
Congressman Rooney: You mean this has not been done for the last 4 or 5 years?
Mr. Henderson: It has not been done in the way it should be done. . . . There has not been . . . a world approach to this problem . . . we should have a global approach. . . .
Congressman Rooney: . . . You have had more Assistant Secretaries in the last few years than you can shake a stick at. What do those people do? Do you mean to say they have been sitting around and not considering this on a global approach basis? . . . Are they not capable, competent, and able?
Mr. Henderson: Some of the people would be if they—
Congressman Rooney: They are not capable, competent, and able to attack this on a worldwide basis?
Mr. Henderson: If they could be freed from their other duties. . . .

After Mr. Henderson had completed his statement, Rooney retorted: "So far we have proceeded two pages, and you have not as yet pointed out anything a youngster in high school in the United States is not familiar with." Pressing this official on the matter of the 17 additional appointments requested, Rooney continued:

Congressman Rooney: Let me explore this. Are you saying you have not been doing anything with respect to combating communism on a global scale up to now?
Mr. Henderson: No, sir.

Congressman Rooney: It would appear so from your statement.
Mr. Henderson: Mr. Chairman, we are not doing as much as we should do.
Congressman Rooney: Every time the Department has come here in the last 14 or 15 years that I have been on this committee, it has gotten additional money because it was fighting global communism.
Mr. Henderson: We are fighting global communism, but we have been fighting it on a continent-by-continent scale, or a country-by-country scale.
Congressman Rooney: You used to do it on a country scale, and then you got into it on a regional scale. What is this? . . . It is now "global." . . . Each year you add more and more people, and the world picture becomes sicker. The picture we listen to today is certainly the worst I have listened to in 15 years.

Further on, Rooney shifted his attention to another budgetary allotment:

Congressman Rooney: What is the representation and liaison activity with public groups. Is that in order to get bigger and better appropriations?
Mr. Henderson: No, sir. . . .
Congressman Rooney: [Speaking of personnel in the Office of Congressional Relations] These are the people you want to get interested in bigger and better appropriations for the State Department; are they not?
Mr. Hall: No, sir. . . .
Congressman Rooney: Would they not primarily be lobbying in behalf of more money for foreign aid?

And another State Department official who confronted Rooney by saying, "Mr. Chairman, we are keeping our shop the same size as last year," was greeted with the retort:

Congressman Rooney: Why could you not cut it in half?
Mr. Macomber: It is a pretty busy operation, Mr. Chairman.[47]

For powerful personalities like Congressman John J. Rooney, there is another side of the coin concerning their role in foreign policy. Once Congressman Rooney has become persuaded of the *need* for certain items included within the State Department's budget, he (in common with nearly all chairmen of subcommittees and committees in Congress) defends the budget vigorously on the floor of the House from those who wish to cut it further. With his considerable prestige and fund of knowledge, Rooney normally experienced little difficulty in having his way both with the State Department and with his fellow legislators.

Congressional Travel and "Representation" at Conferences

During the first six months of 1957, study missions from the House Foreign Affairs Committee visited the following countries:

Austria	Guatemala	Norway
Belgium	Luxembourg	Poland
France	Mexico	Spain
Germany	Netherlands	United Kingdom
Greece	Nicaragua	Yugoslavia

In this period, members of the committee also attended the NATO Parliamentary Conference, the autumn meeting of the 12th session of the United Nations General Assembly, and the inauguration of the President of Nicaragua.[48]

During a four-year period (1962–1965), senators participated as delegates or representatives for the United States at some thirty-five international conferences, whose subject matter ranged from nuclear energy, to international trade agreements, to the Inter-American System.[49]

Congressional travel, a comparatively recent development in American foreign policy, has increased greatly in the postwar period. The first year in which legislators traveled abroad to inspect the operations of an overseas diplomatic mission was 1936. Since then (but especially since the 1950s), foreign travel has become an established procedure with most congressional committees. Nearly two hundred legislators, for example, went abroad in 1947–1948 to study conditions in Europe that necessitated the Marshall Plan. Today it is a rare congressman who cannot find some legitimate reason to take a foreign trip every year or two—perhaps to gain "first-hand knowledge" of conditions in India (or other nations assisted by the United States), or to determine the likelihood of new hostilities in the Middle East, or to "inspect" the readiness of NATO defense forces, or to judge Latin America's economic progress. Such overseas visits have been greatly facilitated by the accumulation of large "counterpart balances" in several countries (like India and Egypt) which are often used to defray the expenses of visits by legislators (whose transportation is often supplied by the armed services).*

Information gained by legislative travel now gives Congress a competence in foreign affairs it did not possess in an earlier period, when it had to depend almost entirely upon the judgments of

---

*"Counterpart funds" are credits accumulated by the United States as countries repay American foreign aid in their own local currencies. Such balances are usually not "convertible" into dollars (since this would imperil the country's foreign exchange balance); but they *may* be expended within the country to defray American embassy expenses, or of operating military bases, or the expenses incurred from visits by congressmen.

executive officials. In certain cases, investigations abroad can have highly significant consequences for foreign policy. Thus the Herter Committee which devoted weeks to collecting data abroad about Europe's economic condition in the 1947–1948 period was extremely influential in generating legislative support for the Marshall Plan.

That foreign travel provides legislators opportunities to develop greater expertise and deeper insight in the realm of foreign affairs can hardly be doubted. The State Department, in fact, has on occasion even suggested to committes that some of their members go abroad to inspect overseas operations, such as administration of the Mutual Security Program. In such cases, and even when the initiative comes from the committee, the State Department works closely with legislative groups to plan itineraries, furnish liaison officers and guides, arrange interviews and entertainment, and make other necessary arrangements.

Travel abroad has come to be relied upon by many congressmen as one method of making themselves less "dependent" upon information supplied them by the executive branch. To the extent that senators and representatives acquire first-hand information about problems and conditions abroad, they are (or *believe* they are) often as qualified as the State Department to formulate effective American responses. An expanding circle of legislators is becoming convinced that its understanding of international relations is good enough to challenge many viewpoints prevailing in the executive branch.

REVITALIZING CONGRESS' ROLE IN FOREIGN POLICY

The "Decline" of Legislative Influence

By the end of the 1960s, a conviction prevailed on Capitol Hill that Congress had lost substantial influence vis-à-vis the executive branch in the foreign policy process and that this tendency ought to be reversed. Such legislative discontent had been evident for many years. Brought to the surface by internal dissension over the war in Vietnam, this sentiment reflected a realization that Congress, as Senator J. William Fulbright expressed it, had been relegated to the periphery of foreign affairs. In most cases, its influence was marginal; and it was virtually impossible in the short run for Congress to compel changes in policies made by the executive branch.

As we have emphasized in this chapter, the Senate's constitutional powers in treaty-making had largely been nullified by the President's use of executive agreements; the right of Congress to "declare war" had been ignored by Presidents who involved the nation in hostilities in Korea and Vietnam, and in various lesser conflicts; even the legislative control over appropriations—theoretically Congress' most potent weapon—had been of little avail in holding down military expenditures at home and abroad or in assuring the nation the kind of foreign aid program many legislators wanted. In brief, a massive feeling of frustration existed in the legislative branch because of an apparent inability to influence events abroad.

This sentiment gave rise to repeated demands that Congress regain its position in the foreign policy process and that it "reassert" its prerogatives in the face of growing executive power. Since 1789, declared Professor Ruhl Bartlett in hearings before the Foreign Relations Committee, there had occurred a "reversal of roles" in relations between Congress and the presidency: Congress had virtually "abdicated" its responsibilities in foreign affairs when it had been confronted with forceful claims of executive leadership advocated with "breakneck speed."[50] Senator Fulbright called upon the Senate to "reclaim" its constitutional prerogatives and responsibilities in foreign relations; since the 1940s, in his view, the Senate had been losing power during an "era of crisis in which urgent decisions have been required . . . of a kind that the Congress is ill-equipped to make with what has been thought to be the requisite speed." Distinguishing between two kinds of power in foreign policy—one relating to long-range direction, purpose, and philosophy, and the other to more immediate, day-by-day decisions—Fulbright contended that at least in the former sphere, congressional initiative could and must be more forcefully asserted.[51] Such opinions have by no means been confined to the Senate alone. Late in 1966, Representative Paul Findley (Republican of Illinois) urged the House of Representatives not to leave legislative initiative in foreign relations solely to the Senate. Observing that in the present era, one out of every five bills coming before Congress had some significant bearing upon foreign relations, Congressman Findley contended that the House furnished a kind of continuing "plebiscite on foreign policy," since its members had to submit to the opinions of the electorate at frequent intervals. The House, he complained, had been consistently underrated as a participant in the foreign policy process.[52]

Such sentiments came to a focus in a resolution introduced in mid-1967 by Senator Fulbright. It was designed to prevent the executive branch from engaging in "national commitments" without legislative approval. If the principal commitment to which Fulbright and his supporters objected was America's involvement in Vietnam, Fulbright envisioned the resolution more broadly, as an effort "to recover in some degree the constitutional role of the Senate in the making of foreign policy. . . ."[53] Citing pledges made by the Secretary of State in a press conference, presidential expressions of support for Israel, and other examples, Fulbright declared that he did not regard such "commitments" as binding upon Congress or the United States.[54] That the President, Secretary of State, and other executive policy-makers opposed Fulbright's resolution was not surprising. Thus far, however, most legislators (including many who agreed with Fulbright's motivations) have found the resolution too sweeping and imprecise to vote for it. Even if a majority did support it, there is no assurance that the White House would regard this resolution itself as anything more than an expression of legislative opinion!

Prospects for Expanded Legislative Influence

What is the likelihood that Congress will be able to recapture at least some of its prerogatives in the foreign policy field and achieve a more nearly equal balance with the executive's influence in foreign relations? Achieving this goal, we must acknowledge at the outset, will not be easy. It will require more than lamentations on Capitol Hill about the "decline" of Congress, recurrent expressions of legislative discontent, or congressional resolutions "demanding" a greater voice in the foreign policy process to reverse the trend of more than a century and a half during which executive power has been greatly augmented.

Several formidable obstacles confront advocates of expanded congressional influence. One of these is the fact that *legislative bodies in all countries* have lost power in recent history to executive officials. The contraction in Congress' influence in the United States is no isolated phenomenon. The British Parliament (whose power, in the English constitutional system, is "supreme") probably has even less influence than the American Congress in determining Britain's relations with the outside world.

There is the further question of whether foreign relations, in an age of recurrent crises on a planet where modern technology has "shrunk" distances to insignificance, is susceptible of being managed effectively on a collegial basis. Take merely one requirement—the need for speed in decision-making in the nuclear-missile era. Whether Congress, even under optimum circumstances, is capable of such rapid decision-making is open to doubt.

Still another hurdle on the path of greater legislative involvement in the foreign policy process stems from the fact that *deficiencies within Congress itself* are in large part responsible for its loss of influence to the executive branch. Even critics like Senator Fulbright have conceded that enhancement of the President's powers in foreign relations has occurred in part because Congress itself has left a vacuum which has been ultimately filled by dynamic executive leadership. The failure of Congress to adapt to the challenge of fast-moving events at home and abroad; its resistance to change (at the very time it demanded "streamlining" of the executive branch); its inability to check centrifugal forces preventing over-all direction in legislative activities; its continued attachment to old modes (like the "seniority system" for assigning committee chairmanships); the great expansion in the congressional workload since World War II—these realities militate heavily against Congress' effectively rivaling the President as the director of foreign policy.

This consideration raises a complex collateral problem—the "reform" of Congress—which is too complex to treat adequately in limited space. We can do little more than indicate the magnitude of the challenge and underscore its importance for a more dynamic congressional role in foreign policy. In the opinion of many governmental officials (not excluding a number of legislators) and political scientists, a sweeping reform of the legislative branch of the American government is long overdue. It seems, in fact, indispensable if Congress is to regain its former eminence. As far back as 1946, George Galloway observed that Congress had "fallen from its once high estate" and that "the streamlined age . . . seemed to have passed it by."[55] The last major reform program undertaken—the Legislative Reorganization Act of 1946—did little, as events proved, to provide lasting solutions or to alter the underlying conditions weakening Congress' influence. To cite but one example: As a result of this act, the number of committees in Congress was cut approximately in half; but in time the number of legislative *subcommittees* grew severalfold! As the wartime euphoria of Soviet-American cooperation for peace evaporated, and as the international environment witnessed one cold war crisis after another, Congress rapidly began to lose ground as an effective mechanism of national policy.

What specific problems within Congress demand attention and correction? Primary attention needs to be given to a cluster of interrelated problems, the net effect of which is to produce a *dispersion and fragmentation of effort* within the legislative system and to frustrate the ability of Congress to react *promptly and decisively* to developments abroad. Given the nature of external affairs in the contemporary world, Congress is probably less well-equipped now than twenty-five years ago to challenge executive leadership. Party discipline within Congress is almost nil (and what little exists derives chiefly from the *President's* role as national party leader). Legislative committees operate with almost total independence—maintaining virtually no liaison either with the corresponding committees in the other chamber or with the House and Senate Appropriations Committees. With the proliferation of subcommittees, the power exercised by key individuals

has grown, while control over the activities of subcommittees has diminished. Committee chairmen (still assigned on the basis of their "seniority") have accumulated vast independent power; and some subcommittee chairmen have only slightly less power. All congressmen have been caught in a continuing dilemma in recent years: As urgent national issues demand solutions and as legislative business increases, the time available for intelligent congressional study and policy formulation has declined. Consequently, legislators find it very difficult to give complicated foreign policy questions (such as the national defense budget) the kind of informed scrutiny they deserve, much less to formulate alternatives for proposals submitted by ths executive branch. Developments like growing specialization within the committees of Congress, expansion of legislative staffs, and more frequent congressional travel have no doubt aided Congress in responding to the challenge of contemporary events. At the same time, the resources available to the President for dealing with external challenges have expanded even more rapidly, leaving Congress in a more inferior position than it was before. Professor James A. Robinson, for example, is convinced that Congress' limited access to information (particularly its inability to *evaluate* information) is crucial in explaining its declining influence.[56]

Professor Clinton Rossiter identified another roadblock which must be surmounted by those favoring a greater legislative voice in national policy. This relates to the *different constituencies* served by the President and Congress. The President (along with the Vice President) is the only official *elected nationally* by the whole electorate. His constituency is therefore *the nation*, the entire American society. By contrast, senators and representatives are elected on a statewide or local basis. Their responsibility is to represent this limited segment of American society. Often, there is tension between the requirement of Congress to "think nationally" and the fact that relatively small constituencies decide the political fate of legislators. This fact goes far toward explaining why a pronounced tendency toward provincialism colors Congress' approach to transcendent issues like the defense budget. Many legislators are really more concerned about whether an air force base in their district will be closed than whether the strategic doctrine of "massive retaliation" is a sound basis for defense policy! As we shall see in Chapter 7, very few constituents express themselves vocally on the latter subject. Referring to the President, Rossiter has said: "His constituency is, in effect, a nation of citizens, that of Congress a nation of interests."[57]

A closely related problem affecting Congress' role is more intangible but nonetheless important. In the light of its reluctance to set its own house in order, Congress has acquired a reputation synonymous with internal deadlock, delay, antiquated procedures, provincialism, and over-all inefficiency. The executive branch, on the other hand (which has been reorganized on a greater or lesser scale several times since World War II) is much more identified with "modernity" and contemporary values. Nearly all postwar Presidents have been concerned (some of course more than others) with problems growing out of urbanization, with minority rights, with social welfare programs, and with an active involvement by the United States in global affairs. Congress has often opposed such presidential programs or refused to grant the funds required for their implementation. Its approach has been stodgy, cautious, and parsimonious, in contrast to the more "progressive" course charted by the White House.[58]

Commenting upon the eclipse of Congress as an effective policy-making institution, Samuel P. Huntington has said that the process really began in the early 1930s, when vigorous leadership was demanded in dealing with the Great Depression and the rising Axis menace abroad. In his view, Congress has unquestionably lost ground to the executive in four key areas: (1) formulating legislative proposals; (2) assigning legislative priorities among the bills and resolutions introduced into Congress during each session; (3) arousing support within Congress and the American society for needed legislation; and (4) determining the final content of legislation ultimately passed by Congress.[59] Congress, in other words, has substantially lost its power *as a law-making institution.* Actually, if not constitutionally, its contributions lie in other spheres.

Another study has identified five positive contributions made by Congress in national policy. First, it *legitimatizes* governmental decisions, making them "acceptable" to the people, thereby converting "power" into "authority." Second, it performs a *representative function:* Congress is responsive to the needs and wishes of the people and communicates their views to executive policy-makers. Some legislators think that this is perhaps Congress' most vital role. Third, Congress *informs public opinion* and "educates" the electorate on complex policy issues (a role it fulfilled repeatedly during the Vietnam contest). Fourth, Congress endeavors to creates *a broad national consensus* in behalf of policies; it generally allows interested groups and individuals a hearing and permits a wide airing of divergent opinions. Nearly all its actions reflect an attempt to satisfy most groups interested in particular legislation. Fifth, Congress *oversees governmental administration.* By relying upon its investigative powers, it supervises executive performance, exposing maladministration and publicizing policy inadequacies. If Congress itself seldom changes existing programs, it can usually compel the executive branch to do so.[60]

Any possible "return" by Congress to its former position of eminence in the national government will be heavily conditioned, as we have suggested, by its ability and willingness to undertake far-reaching changes. In the early 1970s, there was no evidence that required reforms were imminent. As long as this situation obtains, Congress will probably remain in the dilemma which characterized many legislative viewpoints in the midst of the Vietnam War. A significant number of congressmen objected to executive policies in Southeast Asia; some legislators were convinced that successive Presidents had brought the nation to the verge of national disaster. Yet in the main, senators and representatives had minimum success in changing executive policies and still less in formulating viable policy alternatives of their own.

NOTES

1. Clinton Rossiter, "President and Congress in the 1960s," in Cyril Roseman *et. al., Dimensions of Political Analysis* (Englewood Cliffs, N.J.: Prentice-Hall, 1966), p. 34.
2. Bernard Cohen, *Foreign Policy in American Government* (Boston: Little, Brown, 1965), p. 157.
3. John Bibby and Roger Davidson, *On Capitol Hill: Studies in the Legislative Process* (New York: Holt, Rinehart and Winston, 1967), p. 3.
4. Holbert N. Carroll, "The Congress and National Security Policy," in David Truman, ed., *The Congress and America's Future* (Englewood Cliffs, N.J.: Prentice-Hall, 1965), p. 152.
5. Data on the activities of the House Foreign Affairs Committee during 1965 are drawn from the committee's publication, *Survey of House Foreign Affairs Committee.*, 89th Congress, 1st Session, 1965, pp. 1–40.
6. See the findings of George Goodwin, "The Seniority System in Congress," *American Political Science Review* 53 (June, 1959), 433. By two different criteria, this committee led the list of the most coveted committee positions in the Senate.
7. See Senate Foreign Relations Committee, *Background Information on the Committee on Foreign Relations,* 90th Congress, 2nd Session, 1968, pp. 27–31; and *The New York Times* (August 25, 1963).
8. Senate Foreign Relations Committee, *Background Information on the Committee on Foreign Relations, op. cit.,* pp. 8–9, and *The New York Times* (August 25, 1963).
9. The process of drawing up and ratifying the Japanese peace treaty is described in John Foster Dulles, *A Peace Treaty in the Making* (San Francisco: Japanese Peace Conference, September 4–8, 1951).
10. Senate Foreign Relations Committee, *Background Information on the Committee on Foreign Relations, op. cit.,* pp. 31–32.

11. Felix Nigro, "Senate Confirmation and Foreign Policy," *Journal of Politics* **14** (May, 1952), 281–283.
12. *Ibid.*, pp. 290–291.
13. *Ibid.*, pp. 292–293.
14. Senate Appropriations Committee, *The Departments of State, Justice, and Commerce, the Judiciary and Related Agencies Appropriations for Fiscal Year 1968*, 90th Congress, 1st Session, 1967, p. 117.
15. Our discussion of the appropriations process in Congress relies heavily upon Aaron Wildavsky, *The Politics of the Budgetary Process* (Boston: Little, Brown, 1964), pp. 47–61; Nelson W. Polsby, *Congress and the Presidency* (Englewood Cliffs, N.J.: Prentice-Hall, 1964), pp. 91–96; Nicholas A. Masters, "Committee Assignments," in Robert L. Peabody and Nelson W. Polsby, eds., *New Perspectives on the House of Representatives* (Skokie, Ill.: Rand McNally, 1963), pp. 33–59; and Richard F. Fenno, Jr., "The House Appropriations Committee as a Political System," *American Political Science Review* **LVI** (June, 1962), 310–324.
16. Elias Huzar, *The Purse and the Sword* (Ithaca, N.Y.: Cornell University Press, 1950), p. 19. This is a study of congressional control over military appropriations, focusing upon the pre-World War II period.
17. Quoted in *ibid.*, p. 132.
18. For President Eisenhower's views on this issue, see see the first volume of his memoirs, *Mandate for Change* (Garden City, N.Y.: Doubleday, 1963), p. 454.
19. The views of this (unidentified) member of the House Armed Services Committee are cited in Lewis A. Dexter, "Congressmen and the Making of Military Policy," in Peabody and Polsby, *op. cit.*, p. 311.
20. Holbert N. Carroll, "The Congress and National Security," in Truman, *op. cit.*, p. 151.
21. *Ibid.*, p. 166.
22. Raymond H. Dawson, "Innovation and Intervention in Defense Policy," in Peabody and Polsby, *op. cit.*, p. 276.
23. For the text of President Kennedy's message to the American people during the Cuban crisis, see *Documents on American Foreign Relations: 1962* (New York: Harper & Row, 1963), pp. 374–380.
24. *The Prize Cases*, 67 U.S. 635 (1863).
25. Quincy Wright, "International Law in Relation to Constitutional Law," *American Journal of International Law* **17** (April, 1923), 235.
26. Robert A. Dahl, *Congress and Foreign Policy* (New York: Harcourt Brace Jovanovich, 1950), p. 58.
27. See the views of Lawrence O'Brien, as cited in Sidney Warren, ed., *The American President* (Englewood Cliffs, N.J.: Prentice-Hall, 1967), pp. 135–136.
28. For the provisions of the "Battle Act," see 22 U.S. Code 1611.
29. On a number of occasions, Senator Fulbright has denied any intention to invade the execu-tive domain, by calling for a reinvigoration of legislative influence in foreign relations. In 1967, for example, he conceded that many decisions in foreign policy lie outside Congress' jurisdiction and competence; in this instance, he reiterated his idea that Congress could not properly take over the day-by-day management of foreign affairs, despite its desire to be more instrumental in shaping its long-range future and direction. He underscored the idea that the need for *urgent decisions* militated sharply against legislative participation in foreign policy decision-making. See Senator Fulbright's statement before a subcommittee of the Senate Judiciary Committee on July 19, 1967, as reproduced in Martin B. Hickman, *Problems of American Foreign Policy* (Beverly Hills, Calif.: Glencoe Press, 1968), pp. 98–104; and Senator J. William Fulbright, *The Arrogance of Power* (New York: Random House, 1966), pp. 44–67.
30. *Congressional Quarterly Almanac: 1961* **17** 996–998.
31. James A. Perkins, "Congressional Investigations of Matters of International Import," *American Political Science Review* **34** (April, 1940), 285.
32. Wilfred E. Binkley, *President and Congress* (New York: Knopf, 1947), p. 115.
33. *Ibid.*, pp. 268–269.
34. Stephen K. Bailey and Howard D. Samuel, *Congress at Work* (New York: Holt, Rinehart and Winston, 1952), p. 296.
35. William S. White, *Citadel: The Story of the U.S. Senate* (New York: Harper & Row, 1957), p. 242.
36. *Ibid.*, p. 250.
37. For a discussion of a resolution, signed by 52 members of the House, asking for re-examination of American foreign policy in Southeast Asia, see *The New York Times* (September 26, 1967).
38. These resolutions are analyzed in Carroll, *op. cit.*, pp. 155–156.
39. The text of the Gulf of Tonkin Resolution, together with a citation of relevant precedents and testimony by executive officials, is contained in Senate Armed Services and Foreign Relations Committees, *Hearings on Southeast Asia Resolution*, 88th Congress, 2nd Session, 1966.
40. For subsequent criticisms of the Gulf of Tonkin Resolution, see Joseph Kraft, "The Dean Rusk Show," *The New York Times Magazine* (March 24, 1968), pp. 134–140; and Marvin Kalb, "Doves, Hawks and Flutterers in the Foreign Relations Committee," *Ibid.*, (November 19, 1967), pp. 56–82.
41. For Ellender's views, see *The Washington Post* (March 8, 1963).
42. *The New York Times* (September 1, 1966).
43. *The New York Times* (July 11, 1967).
44. For Passman's views on foreign aid, see Otto E. Passman, "Why I Am Opposed to Foreign Aid," *The New York Times Magazine* (July 7, 1963), pp. 16–7. That his views on foreign aid

had not changed in the interim—except to become even more antagonistic toward the program—is indicated by an Associated Press dispatch in mid-1969. Passman called President Nixon's request for a $2.6 billion foreign aid program "shocking," and he expressed his intention of cutting this figure to $1 billion! In his opinion, foreign aid should be "phased out" completely. See the *Morning Advocate* (Baton Rouge, La., June 17, 1969).

45. Quoted in Wildavsky, *op. cit.*, p. 54.
46. William L. Rivers, "The Foreign Policy of John J. Rooney," *The Reporter* **24** (June 22, 1961), 36–38.
47. These excerpts are taken from House Appropriations Committee, *The Departments of State and Justice, the Judiciary and Related Agencies—Appropriations for 1960*, 86th Congress, 1st Session, 1959, pp. 1–20, 24–41, 105–109. This series affords an illuminating source for illustrating legislative attitudes toward the State Department.
48. House Foreign Affairs Committee, *Survey of Activities of the Committee on Foreign Affairs, op. cit.*, p. 6.
49. Senate Foreign Relations Committee, *Background Information on the Committee on Foreign Relations, op. cit.*, pp. 70–71.
50. *The New York Times* (August 17, 1967).
51. See the excerpts from Fulbright's speech in *The New York Times* (July 20, 1967).
52. See the views of Representative Findley, as cited in *The New York Times* (October 6, 1966).
53. The text of Fulbright's resolution, and his defense of it, are reproduced in *The New York Times* (August 1, 1967).
54. A speech by Fulbright giving his views on the President's authority to make "national commitments" without the consent of Congress is included in Hickman, *op. cit.*, pp. 114–115.
55. See Galloway's judgment, as cited in Bibby and Davidson, *op. cit.*, p. 260; and George Goodwin, Jr., "Subcommittees: The Miniature Legislatures of Congress," *American Political Science Review* **56** (September, 1962), 596–601.
56. James A. Robinson, *Congress and Foreign Policy-Making*, rev. ed. (Homewood, Ill.: Dorsey, 1967), p. vii.
57. Rossiter, *op. cit.*, p. 35.
58. Bibby and Davidson, *op. cit.*, p. 262.
59. Samuel P. Huntington, "Congressional Responses to the Twentieth Century," in Truman, *op. cit.*, pp. 5–32.
60. Bibby and Davidson, *op. cit.*, pp. 15–16.

Six

BIPARTISANSHIP: The Problem of Consensus in Foreign Policy

THE RECURRENT CHALLENGE OF DISUNITY

When he retired from the Foreign Service in 1950, one of America's most distinguished diplomats, George F. Kennan, left Washington in a mood of despair about the ability of the United States to conduct its foreign relations intelligently and successfully. Frankly skeptical about whether the government really valued "cool and rational analysis" in the foreign policy process, Kennan lamented: "Altogether, I could find no comfort in what I could observe of the general conduct of foreign policy by our government in that hectic summer." Witnessing the internal reaction to the Korean War, Kennan concluded:

Never before has there been such utter confusion in the public mind with respect to U.S. foreign policy. The President doesn't understand it; Congress doesn't understand it; nor does the public, nor does the press. They all wander around in a labyrinth of ignorance and error and conjecture, in which truth is intermingled with fiction at a hundred points, in which unjustified assumptions have attained the validity of premises, and in which there is no recognized and authoritative theory to hold on to.[1]

George Kennan of course was by no means the first eminent student of government to raise doubts about the capacity of the United States to manage its foreign relations effectively. Early in the history of the republic, in his classic *Democracy in America,* the Frenchman Alexis de Tocqueville observed that a democracy

is unable to regulate the details of an important undertaking [in foreign affairs], to persevere in a design, and to work out its execution in the presence of serious obstacles. It cannot combine its measures with secrecy, and it will not await their consequences with patience.[2]

More recent commentators at home and abroad have called attention to many of these same problems. The late Professor V. O. Key was convinced that policy procedures in the United States inherently promoted delay in making national policy decisions. Professor Stanley Hoffman has deplored America's "immobility" in its relations with Western Europe. The British commentator Alistair Buchan has referred to the "frustration" which Europeans feel with regard to American foreign policy because of the "cumbrous process of internal debate" within the United States. Repeatedly, President Kennedy complained that Congress threatened to deny him the means necessary to protect the national interest.[3] And a former Assistant Secretary of State for Congressional Relations has remarked:

It is often easier to communicate U.S. intentions to a tribal chief in central Africa through a Swahili interpreter, or to Kuala Lumpur [the capitol of Malaysia] across 10,000 miles of cable or radio, or to the U.N. General Assembly with its diverse dialects, than across the two miles from Foggy Bottom [the popular name of the main State Department building in Washington] to the Capitol.[4]

Proof that these concerns remained timely was provided by the experience of the Vietnam War. Perhaps no diplomatic issue in the whole of American history evoked such pervasive and sharp disunity as America's military commitment in Southeast Asia. Public opinion was fragmented and confused;* relations between the President and Congress were acutely tense; during some periods at least, the executive branch was internally divided over problems of military and diplomatic strategy; congressional viewpoints were fractionalized—with "hawks" demanding an American victory in Vietnam and "doves" calling for a liquidation of America's involvement while a majority of legislators basically supported the policies of the Kennedy, Johnson, and Nixon administrations. Meanwhile, North Vietnam and the

*Considerable attention is devoted to public opinion and the Vietnam conflict in Chapter 7.

Viet Cong—mindful that they had won the earlier contest against French colonialism when opinion within France no longer supported the government's policies—unquestionably counted in some degree upon a repetition of this pattern within the United States. According to one report, North Vietnamese Premier Pham Van Dong anticipated that ultimately public opinion in America would compel the President to abandon the nation's commitment in Southeast Asia; Dong was encouraged by President Johnson's inability to "soothe the ever more acute opposition in the United States Congress."[5] President Johnson's decision in 1968 not to seek re-election to the White House —a move dictated primarily by internal opposition to his Asian policies—did little to discredit North Vietnamese predictions. Even after President Nixon took office in 1969, it was far from certain that public and congressional sentiment would provide the support necessary to permit his policies in Vietnam to succeed.

The Necessity for Consensus

These developments indicate that the fundamental problem identified over a century ago by de Tocqueville continues to plague the United States in its foreign relations. Indeed, as we shall see, there is evidence for believing that the problem has become progressively more acute—worse today than in the early postwar period. It would be foolhardy to assume that the oldest and most powerful democratic nation in the history of the world has solved the problem alluded to by these and many other commentators. In its simplest terms, that problem can be posed as follows: Is a democracy intrinsically under certain disadvantages in the conduct of foreign policy, sufficient on some occasions to prevent it from formulating and carrying out national policies which serve and protect its interests?

Since our discussion is confined to American foreign policy, we must note at the outset that we are dealing with a particular (not to say unique) system of democratic government, very different in several respects from either the British or the French "parliamentary systems." To cite but one significant contrast: In these countries, a centralized party system, along with a rigid adherence to "party discipline" within the legislature, goes far toward providing a high level of internal unity on foreign policy issues that is lacking in the United States. American politics, on the other hand, are characterized by a strong local and state orientation, by a relatively weak (sometimes almost nonexistent) *national* party organization, and by the virtual impossibility of disciplining members of Congress who refuse to support the party platform or who defy the wishes of their party leaders.

The most novel—and, insofar as foreign policy is concerned, the most troublesome—feature of the American system of government is, however, the concept of *separation of powers.* As every student is aware, the Founding Fathers divided the powers of the national government among three supposedly co-equal branches. The Supreme Court, as we noted in Chapter 3, plays a marginal role in foreign relations. In that chapter the point was also made that American diplomatic experience and precedent have greatly amplified the powers of the President vis-à-vis Congress in foreign affairs. From a constitutional standpoint, Congress may be an "equal partner" with the executive in this sphere; in reality, it is not—and perhaps never will be.

Even so, the concept of separation of powers continues to afford ample opportunity and incentive for each branch to maximize its power in the foreign policy field, to assert its own viewpoints, and to insist upon respect for its constitutional and historic "prerogatives." With the American Republic approaching its second century as an independent nation, it still could not be assumed that the boundaries of executive and legislative power in foreign relations were fixed or agreed upon by each branch; to the contrary, they remained fluid and subject to determination in the light of events and of the impact of particular personalities in the White House and Congress. The Vietnam contest in the 1960s, for example, indicated convincingly that because many Presidents in the past had committed armed forces abroad without congressional approval did not mean that this right would always be admitted without protest on Capitol Hill. Moreover, the fact that Congress since World War II had habitually approved defense appropriations (sometimes *increasing* them beyond the President's requests) did not prevent legislators by the 1970s from abandoning precedent and scrutinizing the Pentagon's budgetary requests minutely. These and numerous other examples can be cited to prove that Congress is prone to *use* its prerogatives from time to time, despite White House objections.

Such considerations decree that among the perennial problems confronting policy-makers in the United States, few are more compelling and difficult than *creating and maintaining a consensus supporting America's international commitments.* Informed citizens need no reminder that such a consensus is elusive and unstable. Achieving it requires a fortuitous combination of circumstances that is not easy to attain. The natural tendency of the American government—particularly in executive–legislative relations (but to a lesser degree perhaps, in the policy-making process *within* each branch as well)—is toward disunity, fragmentation, and diffusion of effort. A former State Department official, experienced in building such a consensus, has written this.

Whatever the shifting outlook in the rest of the world, one area of chronic tension and even occasional guerrilla warfare is the two-mile gap in Washington between the Hill and Foggy Bottom —between Congress and the State Department.

In the gamut of American government probably no greater antagonism has been generated over the years than that between the legislative branch and the nation's foreign-policy apparatus.

This official also quoted the earlier view of Henry Adams. "The Secretary of State exists only to recognize the existence of a world which Congress would rather ignore."[6]

Internal Dissension in American Diplomatic History

The extent to which disunity within the American democracy has posed an obstacle to the achievement of diplomatic goals may be indicated by a brief examination of historical examples. As a generalization, it may be said that important questions of foreign policy have always engendered some degree of internal controversy within the national government and throughout the nation at large. The only noteworthy exceptions were the two great international conflicts—World Wars I and II—in which the country was engaged; and even in these cases, in time considerable disagreement arose over how and why the United States became involved and over what its participation had achieved. Internal dissension over foreign policy questions can be traced from the earliest days of the republic over such major issues as the Jay Treaty, the Louisiana Purchase, and the War of 1812, on through the course of the nineteenth century over the Texas controversy and Mexican War, the many ramifications of the slavery issue, and Manifest Destiny, down to the mid-twentieth century. As an example of disunity in the modern period, the student of American foreign relations has but to examine closely the fierce partisan and intragovernmental wrangle that characterized the Roosevelt administration's efforts to deal with the rising Axis threat during the 1930s, and especially its efforts to secure repeal of American neutrality legislation.[7]

Of all the examples of such disunity that might be cited, one stands out—both because it precipitated an unusually intense domestic controversy over a diplomatic issue and because its ultimate consequences were of singular importance. This was President Wilson's bitter fight with Senate Republicans over United States membership in the League of Nations. Wilson's opponents, led by Senator Henry Cabot Lodge of Massachusetts, protested vigorously against his failure to consult the Senate in the early stages of planning for the

League of Nations and to include one or more of their number among his official negotiating party in Euope. Wilson had attempted a rudimentary kind of bipartisan collaboration when he took the former diplomat and nominal Republican Henry White with him to Paris to provide liaison with the Republican opposition at home. Republicans, however, had little confidence in White, and he proved completely incapable of providing the expected liaison. Meanwhile, Republicans left no doubt about their intentions regarding the Treaty of Versailles; they proposed to emasculate the League of Nations proposal with crippling amendments and reservations which would be completely unacceptable to Wilson.

For his part, Wilson evinced little awareness of the strength of his Republican foes and of the isolationist bloc in the Senate. Nor did he demonstrate any inclination to reach agreements with it. He adamantly refused to accept even minor modifications of the treaty, and the Senate proved equally unyielding. This deadlock—resulting in America's refusal to join the League of Nations— colored the American approach to international relations for two decades thereafter. While it does not constitute a particularly praiseworthy chapter in American diplomatic experience, it at least taught valuable lessons for future policy-makers. This episode, for example, was the chief impetus in shaping the determination of President Roosevelt and Secretary of State Cordell Hull to avoid a partisan battle during and after World War II, and to work for integrated governmental support for the new international organization growing out of the war.

Post-World War II experience abounds with examples illustrating the difficulties involved in achieving and preserving a consensus on major foreign policy issues. Hardly a presidential or congressional election in the past twenty-five years has been devoid of political controversy over foreign policy questions. Democrats have routinely been required to defend the record of their party against Republican accusations that, under Democratic leadership, China was "lost" to Communism, Eastern Europe was "sold out" to the Soviet Union, or that successive Democratic administrations were "soft on Communism." A contradictory charge was also made that under Democratic Presidents, the nation had become embroiled in one foreign war after another. For their part, Republicans were criticized for bringing the country to the "brink of war" under Secretary of State John Foster Dulles; for alienating the neutralist countries (by following Dulles' theory that neutralism was "immoral"); for relying upon "massive retaliation" with nuclear weapons, thereby neglecting the need for conventional military forces to achieve diplomatic objectives; and for opposing enlightened international measures like an adequate foreign aid program. By the mid-1960s, the Vietnam conflict furnished political ammunition for both sides. Many Democrats attributed the blame for America's involvement in this struggle to decisions made by President Eisenhower in supporting the government of South Vietnam; Republicans were equally certain that America's massive commitment in Southeast Asia began only with the Kennedy and Johnson administrations. Once America became committed in Southeast Asia, the question of how to terminate the war—including decisions about whether to expand or curtail military activities in Vietnam, or whether to accept the concept of a "coalition government" for the country—evoked no less sharp controversy. On a different front, after the mid-1950s, foreign aid programs submitted to Congress by Republican and Democratic Presidents alike encountered almost certain opposition; nearly every year, the President complained that Congress was denying him the funds needed to achieve national objectives overseas. Key agencies—like the State Department and the United States Information Agency (USIA)—continued to face deep-seated legislative skepticism regarding their budget requests, as well as pervasive doubts on Capitol Hill concerning their accomplishments.

Ironically, within a relatively brief span of some fifteen years, the United States had evolved from a period of relatively high "bipartisan" cooperation in foreign affairs to an era of unprecedented acrimony surrounding most significant foreign policy questions. Legislative and public opposition to the war in Vietnam (expressed in nearly all cases by a vocal minority) reached such a pitch under the Johnson administration that the President and Secretary of State Dean Rusk were compelled to cancel or defer public speaking engagements. Perhaps the most graphic indication of internal contention over foreign policy issues was the fact that, for a prolonged period in the late 1960s, Secretary Rusk declined to meet publicly with the Senate Foreign Relations Com-

mittee. By contrast, in the early postwar era, harmonious collaboration between this committee and leading executive officials had epitomized the "bipartisan" approach to foreign relations.

BIPARTISAN TECHNIQUES AND PROCEDURES

Whatever its precise causes, disunity has not become a chronic problem in American foreign policy because policy-makers were indifferent to the need for agreement among all individuals and groups involved in decision-making. To the contrary, at no stage of American history have officials devoted *more* attention to, or perhaps been *more* genuinely concerned about, the desirability of uniting the executive branch, Congress, and public opinion behind major programs and commitments in foreign relations. A superficial verdict on results achieved down to the early 1970s would be that the more policy-makers have endeavored to forge unity in foreign affairs, the more *disunity* they have in fact created! Although such a conclusion must be regarded as a *non sequitur*, it remains true that considerable disagreement has surrounded, and continues to surround, the question of *the procedures and techniques best designed to promote a consensus in the foreign policy field.* The White House and State Department favor certain procedures, in the conviction that these contribute to genuine bipartisanship in foreign relations. Legislative committees often prefer other techniques for assuring bipartisan collaboration. Alternatively, the party controlling Congress (as a rule in recent years, the Democratic party) may believe that the requirements of bipartisanship are satisfied when leading members of the opposition are "briefed" on foreign policy questions. The opposition party (most frequently in the contemporary period, the GOP) may regard bipartisanship as necessitating consultations *before foreign policy decisions are actually made.*

The point is that the techniques associated with achieving a consensus in foreign affairs are themselves debatable and sometimes productive of acute disunity. New procedures are continually evolving and old patterns of consultation being modified or abandoned. Nevertheless, certain procedures have come to be identified with the concept of bipartisanship in foreign relations since World War II. Although the procedures themselves may at times be controversial, they have nonetheless contributed to the achievement of consensus in support of a number of America's postwar overseas programs and commitments.

*The concept of bipartisanship in foreign affairs, it must be frankly conceded, possesses no universally accepted meaning. In a very loose sense, it is synonymous with unity or consensus in behalf of foreign policy undertakings. Yet, as our treatment in this chapter emphasizes, it is a particular kind of unity—one which grows out of attempts to involve spokesmen for both major political parties, and both the executive and legislative branches, in policy formulation. The tacit assumption is that such policies will, in some measure, reflect a basic consensus about goals and programs. In its origins, bipartisanship in the postwar period was an effort to extend the kind of internal unity prevailing during World War II (as suggested by the slogan, "politics is adjourned") to difficult problems arising from America's encounter with expansive Soviet Communism. For a more detailed treatment of the concept of bipartisanship, see Cecil V. Crabb, Jr., *Bipartisan Foreign Policy: Myth or Reality?* (New York: Harper & Row, 1957), pp. 156–184.

Prior Consultations on Foreign Policy Measures

Among the practices associated with bipartisan foreign policy, none is more fundamental than the requirement of prior consultation in the initial stages of policy formulation. Senator Arthur H. Vandenberg (Republican of Michigan), the foremost advocate of bipartisan cooperation in the postwar period, once defined the goal as a "meeting of the minds" toward problems prevailing in the international field.[8] Legislative action on important foreign policy measures since World War II has almost invariably been preceded by a greater or lesser amount of prior consultation between officials in the executive and legislative branches. A notable example was the United Nations Charter. State Department officials worked closely with the Senate Foreign Relations Committee over a period of almost three years to assure Senate acceptance of the nascent United Nations.[9] Similarly, the Marshall Plan was finally approved by Congress in 1948 after what was probably the most intensive collaborative stocktaking in American diplomatic history.[10] Significant bipartisan consultation also preceded the China Aid bill of 1948, the North Atlantic Treaty, the Mutual Defense Assistance Program, and later programs of American economic, technical, and military aid to foreign countries.[11]

The requirement of prior consultation as an essential ingredient in a bipartisan approach to foreign relations is a prime example of a procedure often generating as much disunity as unity among policy-makers. To say that such consultation is requisite to achieving a consensus in foreign policy leaves several basic questions unanswered. What particular bipartisan techniques and procedures are best calculated to generate a consensus? What individuals and groups are to be included in these consultations? What is their proper scope, in terms of the subject matter to be included in the discussions? And at what stage in the policy-making process should such consultations be held?

Formal and Informal Procedures

Bipartisan consultations are of many and diverse types, ranging from *formal and continuing* procedures to *informal and ad hoc* ones. In the former category are the legislative liaison activities regularly carried on by the Office of Congressional Relations in the Department of State, by the White House staff, and by legislative specialists in other executive agencies (like the Department of Defense). Growing out of Secretary of State Cordell Hull's cordial relations with Congress before and during World War II, the Office of Congressional Relations was established in 1949. Its task, as Robert Elder has written, is "to interpret Congress to the Department, and the Department to Congress." Deliberately kept small (Congress is overtly skeptical about legislative liaison or lobbying activities by executive agencies), the office normally serves as a kind of clearinghouse for the exchange of information on foreign policy questions between the two ends of Pennsylvania Avenue.* This office handles inquiries from legislators (who often relay constituency mail to the State Department for a reply); it keeps abreast of legislative opinion as expressed in the *Congressional Record* and other sources and informs policy-makers of sentiment on Capitol Hill; it often assists legislators who plan to travel abroad; it furnishes information to congressional committees on all aspects of external policy. When Congress is in session, the liaison officers from the Office of Congressional Relations spend most of their working day on Capitol Hill; nearly every day, the Assistant Secretary of State for Congressional Relations "calls" on the Senate Foreign Relations and House Foreign Affairs Committees. Within the State Department, legislative specialists regularly advise the Secretary of State and other high officials on congressional attitudes and join in devising strategies for winning Congress' approval for the President's foreign policy programs.

How effective are the efforts of the Office of Congressional Relations? On one level, they have been conspicuously effective. Congressmen themselves acknowledge that the office handles inquiries efficiently and capably (it assigns highest priority to requests for information from Capitol Hill). But by other criteria, it is evident that the State Department's congressional relations leave much to be desired. Criticism of the department has, if anything, increased in recent years; the department still has to fight for its inadequate annual appropriation; in the elusive realm of "confidence" in executive policy-makers, legislative attitudes remain skeptical andd sometimes hostile. Despite the activities of the office, legislators continue to complain about the "wall of secrecy" surrounding American foreign policy and their inability to get information from executive policy-makers. By the standard which perhaps matters most—the degree of national unity underlying the nation's overseas commitments—it is no less

---

*If the Office of Congressional Relations in the Department State might be likened to one "terminal" of the communications link with Capitol Hill, the other is provided by the consultative subcommittees of the Senate Foreign Relations and the House Foreign Affairs Committees. These subcommittees (especially in the Senate) were established primarily to facilitate an exchange of ideas and information with the State Department. As an ever-growing number of congressional committees has become involved in foreign affairs, however, the State Department has been confronted with a proliferation of congressional "terminals."

clear that efforts by the Office of Congressional Relations has failed to achieve a bipartisan consensus on many foreign policy questions. The new global environment of relaxed cold war tensions and a tendency toward miltipolarity in the international system add to the challenge of achieving and maintaining unity in foreign relations. Given the most effective efforts imaginable by the Office of Congressional Relations and other groups seeking to build a foundation of national consensus under American foreign policy, considerable doubt would still exist—more so as the United States was reducing its global commitments in the aftermath of Vietnam War than earlier—regarding the nation's proper role abroad and the policies needed to fulfill it successfully. Executive officials, no less than those on Capitol Hill, seemed increasingly uncertain about how climactic events like the Vietnam War would (or ought to) affect American foreign policy. That national policy was in a state of transition could hardly be doubted. The nature and direction of change, were less apparent. These considerations greatly compounded the problem of achieving bipartisan cooperation in foreign relations.[12]

In one way or another, nearly every unit within the State Department is concerned with congressional relations, from the Secretary of State down. Several years ago, Secretary of State Dean G. Acheson estimated that around one-sixth of his time normally was assigned to cultivating harmonious relations with Congress; in some periods, legislative functions took half his working day. In a typical month in the 1960s, Secretary of State Dean Rusk made 11 trips to Capitol Hill, devoting 22 hours to congressional liaison. Lesser State Department officials, along with those in agencies like the USIA and AID, were also required to spend significant portions of time on "the Hill." During 1967, for example, over 40 meetings were held by such officials with the Senate Foreign Relations Committee alone.[13]

Superimposed on the pattern of formal and continuing consultations are numerous informal and *ad hoc* procedures designed to engender unity in foreign relations. Crises abroad are apt to evoke efforts by the White House and State Department to "brief" legislative leaders on events overseas and on proposed American responses to them. Thus in 1965, President Johnson informed a selected group of congressmen that he had ordered American marines to land in the Dominican Republic; after the landing, the administration endeavored to built a consensus for its Dominican policy by asking well-known political liberals like Arthur Schlesinger, Jr., and John Bartlow Martin to take diplomatic assignments. The latter, for example, went to the Dominican Republic, where he attempted to "open contact" with rebel forces.[14] (These steps, it might be noted, did little

to stem the tide of criticism directed at President Johnson's policies in the Dominican crisis.) Besides White House meetings of this type, earlier in his administration, President Johnson also invited a small group of congressmen to attend meetings of the National Security Council, where they were briefed on foreign policy and defense issues.[15] President Kennedy invited Senator Fulbright to participate in discussions leading up to the disastrous Bay of Pigs episode in 1961. A year later, when the White House had received proof of a Soviet missile buildup in Cuba, a group of legislators were hurriedly called back to Washington (Congress was not in session) to a White House meeting; an hour before President Kennedy announced his strategy publicly, they were informed about the crisis and notified how the President proposed to respond to it.[16]

The Circle of Bipartisan Participants

A wide range of procedures has come to be relied upon to promote a bipartisan foundation for American foreign policy. But what individuals and groups ought to be included in these consultations? The question has elicited controversy throughout the postwar era, and it continues to evoke disagreement. Indeed, by they 1960s it seemed that the question had become more productive of controversy within the government than ever. On the executive side, no particular problems exist. The President, the Secretary of State, and the Secretary of Defense, or their designated agents, act as spokesmen for the foreign policy of the incumbent administration. In Chapter 4, however, it was noted that even within the executive branch an expanding group of departments and agencies are being drawn into the foreign policy process. The Agriculture Department plays a key role in programs designed to sell American farm produce abroad; the Atomic Energy Commission is deeply involved in questions like the nuclear nonproliferation agreement; the Treasury Department remains keenly interested in the nation's balance-of-payments deficit. Nevertheless, all executive activities in foreign affairs are under the ultimate authority of the President and must support policy as decided in the White House.

But with whom shall executive officials consult in their attempt to achieve a foreign policy consensus? During and immediately after World War II, the principal congressional representatives were the chairmen of the Senate Foreign Relations Committee and the House Foreign Affairs Committee; alternating as chairman of the former, Senators Tom Connally (Democrat of Texas) and Arthur H. Vandenberg (Republican of Michigan) became symbols of "bipartisanship" in foreign relations. Under President Eisenhower,

Senator Walter George (Democrat of Georgia) carried on this tradition. As time passed, however, the problem of the individuals and groups participating in bipartisan consultations become vastly more complicated. A growing number of congressional committees in the House and Senate were becoming involved with foreign policy decisions. Sometimes (as in the case of scrutiny by the two Appropriations Committees of the foreign aid program), these committees exercised an even greater influence on foreign policy measures than the Senate Foreign Relations or House Foreign Affairs Committees. In brief, *a steady dispersion of power within Congress* placed the executive branch in a recurrent dilemma. It could continue to follow the early postwar practice of consulting mainly with the Senate and House committees dealing directly with foreign affairs— at the risk of ignoring other committees whose influence was sometimes greater. Or it could attempt to "spread" its activities over a large number of committees on Capitol Hill, of making bipartisan consultation a highly unwieldly and time-consuming process, which on some occasions entailed a considerable risk that a "leak" might jeopardize national security.

As the term "bipartisanship" implies, a dominant goal is to unite the two main *political parties* in support of the nation's overseas commitments. This fact dictates that influential *political leaders,* no less than spokesmen for congressional committees, be included in bipartisan consultations. In some instances, the two groups overlap. Senator Walter George, for example, was both chairman of the Senate Foreign Relations Committee and a recognized leader of the Democratic party on Capitol Hill. By contrast, Senator Vandenberg had great stature as a spokesman of foreign affairs, but he had little influence within party circles (his contemporary, Senator Robert Taft of Ohio, was popularly called "Mr. Republican"). In the more recent period, much the same could be said of Senator J. William Fulbright (Democrat of Arkansas). By virtue of his position as chairman of the Senate Foreign Relations Committee, Fulbright wielded considerable power; during the Vietnam conflict, for example, he used the committee repeatedly to criticize and challenge the Johnson administration's policies in Southeast Asia. But Fulbright was *not* a member of the Democratic "power structure" in Congress. In this sphere, he had much less influence than Senator Mike Mansfield (Democrat of Montana), who was also a member of the Foreign Relations Committee. On some issues, Mansfield did not hesitate publicly to take positions on foreign policy issues without consulting either Fulbright or the committee.

In what must be regarded as a classic model of bipartisan consultation on an important foreign policy issue—wartime planning for the United Nations organization—the Roosevelt administra-

tion made an effort to solicit the widest possible circle of Republican viewpoints. The President and his agents consulted GOP leaders in Congress, Republican governors, presidential candidates (like Governor Thomas E. Dewey and his chief foreign policy adviser, John Foster Dulles), and prominent members of the Republican party from private life. Roosevelt carefully included spokesmen for the GOP among the American delegation to the San Francisco Conference in 1945, at which the UN Charter was drafted.[17] If this case was admittedly exceptional in that it did *not* involve a foreign policy crisis demanding an urgent response from the United States, experience since World War II has indicated that some members of the opposition party—such as the Majority and Minority Leaders in the House and Senate—need to be included in the interests of maximum unity in foreign relations. To assure continuity in foreign policy, it has also become customary for an outgoing administration to include the President-elect and his chief advisers in foreign policy decision-making during the transitional period.

The exact composition of the group included in bipartisan consultations, it must be reiterated, hinges in no small measure upon *personal relationships* existing among key policy-makers. In some periods since World War II, this variable has clearly been crucial in determining the nature of bipartisan consultations—and to no insignificant extent, the nature of American foreign policy itself. Under the Truman administration, for example, Secretary of State Dean Acheson was *persona non grata* with many leading Republicans. For his part, Acheson did little to conceal his irritation and contempt for many of his partisan critics; nor did he disguise his obvious chagrin at congressional efforts to initiate proposals in the foreign policy field. An episode which occurred during the Eisenhower administration also sheds light on the role of personal relationships in the quest for unity. Seeking to elicit maximum legislative support for his foreign aid program, President Eisenhower invited the most outspoken foe of foreign assistance—Representative Otto E. Passman (Democrat of Louisiana)—to a White House discussion.* Passman's demeanor so irritated the President that he was not extended another invitation.[18]

Personal animosities and suspicions among policy-makers, however, set some kind of an all-time "record" during the Johnson administration—so much so that "bipartisanship" all but disappeared from American foreign policy. Ill-will and tension between President Johnson and Secretary of State Rusk, on one side, and their critics, like Senators

---

*Representative Passman's key position on the House Appropriations Committee, which virtually gave him the power of life or death over the foreign aid program, is discussed more fully in Chapter 5.

Wayne Morse (Democrat of Oregon) and J. William Fulbright, on the other side, created such a hostile atmosphere that meaningful communications between them became impossible. The President and the Secretary of State found not only their judgments, but their ethical and moral values, under attack. The President's detractors believed that he was endeavoring to "suppress" legitimate criticism; they resented the implication that critics were giving aid and comfort to the enemy. The result was that normal bipartisan consultations fell into disuse; for a prolonged period in the late 1960s, the Secretary of State did not even consent to meet publicly with the Senate Foreign Relations Committee (although he did offer to meet privately, an offer which the committee rejected). When, early in 1968, Secretary Rusk finally consented to testify before the committee, little was achieved beyond the now-familiar reiteration of the Johnson administration's policies in Vietnam, followed by the no less familiar criticisms of those policies by its opponents.[19]

If any fact is evident about attempts to achieve bipartisan agreement on American foreign policy during the past twenty-five years, it is that the personal dimension—the presence or absence of mutual trust and good will among officials participating in decision-making—has been, and will probably remain, a cardinal element in the success or failure to create and maintain a consensus toward foreign policy issues.

The Scope of Bipartisan Consultations

Efforts to achieve unity in behalf of national policy goals by reliance upon bipartisan procedures also confront another difficult problem. What ought to be the scope of questions included on the agenda of such consultations? The question relates closely to another which we shall analyze below: At what *stage* in the policy-making process should bipartisan consultations be held?

To illustrate the problem of scope, let us refer to the prolonged debate over the Vietnam War. Part (although by no means all) of the difficulty encountered in achieving a unified national policy toward Southeast Asia could be attributed to a profound disagreement between the Johnson administration and its critics over the proper bounds of inquiry regarding America's involvement in Vietnam. President Johnson and his principal advisers were convinced that they had "inherited" a frustrating conflict in Asia from the two previous administrations. Again and again, these officials reiterated the idea that the *constancy* of American foreign policy was on trial before the world; the commitment in Vietnam had to be honored, if for no other reason than that failure to do so would call other commitments (like America's pledge to defend West Germany and Berlin) into doubt. For the Johnson Administration, America's involvement in Vietnam was *a given*, a fact which policy-makers had to acknowledge, a starting point in the discussion of alternative policies in Asia. Accordingly, the main preoccupation of President Johnson and Secretary of State Rusk became what to do *now and in the future*, to conclude the war in Vietnam on terms that achieved (or, at any rate, did not seriously jeopardize) American diplomatic and security interests. Quarrels over "mistakes of the past" or decisions made in the 1950s or whether America really *should* have "gotten involved" were of little value in resolving the overriding problem: how to terminate the war satisfactorily. Officials in the executive branch tended to find the ideas and proposals offered by critics as less than constructive in terms of offering viable alternatives for achieving this goal.

Critics of American policy in Vietnam tended to reason from a different set of premises, making their approach to the basic issue broader and less restrictive. In their view, intelligent policy planning for the present and future had to begin with an objective analysis of the past. Answers had to be found for such vital questions as how the Vietnam conflict began, how America became embroiled in it, and how the goals of the United States in Asia could be reconciled with its global objectives. Responsible critics (and some who attacked existing policy did not fit this category) insisted that discussions of the Vietnam problem had to be carried back to the period of World War II and the Vietnamese struggle against French colonialism. Nor did they think that a unified policy on Vietnam was possible without some consensus on related issues, like the relaxation in Soviet–American tensions, the disintegration of the Marxist monolith (in which the Sino–Soviet dispute was crucial), and the problem of American relations with Communist China. The Johnson administration's critics said, in effect, that a consensus on the issue of Vietnam could not be attained without prior unity on nearly all other major aspects of American foreign policy.

This clash produced a kind of "dialogue of the deaf" between the Johnson administration and its opponents. Seeing very little point in rehashing the history of American policy toward Southeast Asia since the 1950s, or getting involved in prolonged discussions of whether certain commitments should have been made to the Saigon government in the early 1960s, executive policy-makers pressed their critics to offer alternatives for current and future policy. Meanwhile, with very little success, time and again critics called for a sweeping review of American policy in Asia and elsewhere, *before* a new consensus could be arrived at over Vietnam.

Generalizing from American foreign policy in Vietnam is perhaps a hazardous undertaking. Several unique aspects characterize that chapter in recent American diplomacy. Popular feelings about Vietnam, for example, reached a level of intensity that was perhaps unprecedented for a foreign policy question. Moreover, as crises gripped the cities of America and as the nation became deeply concerned with the problem of poverty, Vietnam became associated in the minds of many citizens with wasted money, lack of concern for disadvantaged groups at home, and with a venture maintained by the military–industrial complex. Scarcely a dimension of American life—from the military status of teenagers and the problem of unrest on college campuses, to the level of governmental taxation and America's balance-of-payments deficit—escaped some connection with the Vietnam War.

Yet the internal disagreement over Vietnam may teach certain lessons about the conditions under which bipartisan consultations can succeed. With all its unique features, the Vietnam question was not altogether untypical of other foreign policy issues in the sense that *all* such issues have become more and more "domesticated": That is, they have ramifications for many spheres of domestic life to an extent that did not exist in the early postwar era. Difficult as it might be to prove, the 1960s seemed to have witnessed a tendency toward *wider scope* for discussions of any foreign policy problem. The reasons for this shift are not altogether clear. Perhaps the American people are becoming more personally interested in foreign policy questions (we shall discuss public attitudes more fully in Chapter 7). Or perhaps the nature of America's commitments overseas—in which traditional measures like the use of force to achieve national goals is to some extent being superseded by a variety of other techniques, like involvement in the "national development" programs of Afro–Asian societies—is changing. Or perhaps Congress and the electorate are becoming increasingly frustrated by the failure of the United States to attain many of its long-standing objectives overseas. Whatever the reason, it is obvious that considerable difficulty exists today in keeping the focus of bipartisan discussions on foreign policy issues sufficiently narrow to permit general agreement on the nature of the problem and on the best means available for solving it.

The Timing of Bipartisan Discussions

At what stage in the foreign policy process should bipartisan consultations be held for the sake of maximum unity in foreign relations? This question, more than any other we have posed thus far, comes close to the heart of the matter of achieving a durable consensus among those involved in decision-making. Bipartisan consultations may satisfy all the other criteria identified; yet if they fail to satisfy this one, it is probable that no consensus

will be reached concerning national objectives or methods of attaining them.

Again, the case of wartime planning for the United Nations stands as a model of bipartisan cooperation. As in that instance, the incumbent administration should attempt to elicit the views of key legislators and opposition party members *at an early stage in policy formulation*, in time to permit *a full and frank discussion of alternative proposals before decisions are finally made.* Presumably, the course of action decided upon would, to some extent, reflect the viewpoints of all participants. At a minimum, legislators and members of the opposition party would be given, so to speak, their "day in court"; if their views were not adopted, they would at least be considered. Under these conditions, bipartisanship would become synonymous with a genuine exchange of ideas and a careful weighing of alternatives drawn from a wide variety of sources in an attempt to forge a consensus. This occurred with respect to the UN Charter; and it may be a dominant reason why American membership in the UN thereafter never became an issue eliciting serious partisan discord in the United States.

Very rarely, however, was this model of bipartisanship duplicated after World War II. As often as not, the timing of bipartisan consultations was such as to evoke as much disunity as unity among those taking part in them. Successive Presidents have been accused of "using" bipartisanship (or pseudo-bipartisan techniques) to create a facade of unity which did little to mask underlying disunity; critics have asserted that the Chief Executive was seeking to "silence opposition" by wrapping his foreign policies in a mantle of spurious bipartisanship. Such complaints have been heard off and on ever since World War II, but they became especially pervasive during the 1960s.

On the face of it, critics had ample grounds for dissatisfaction. As far back as 1947, when the Truman administration submitted the epochal Greek–Turkish Aid Program to Congress, the President was accused (in this case, correctly) of having arrived at his decision *before* resorting to bipartisan procedures. In effect, Truman presented Congress and his Republican opposition with a *fait accompli*. They had the choice of either approving his program or repudiating the President before the world during an era of grave international crisis—which was no real choice at all. Not unexpectedly, Congress approved this first great postwar effort to apply the concept of "containment" against Soviet expansionism. According to the Truman administration, containment now had firm bipartisan support.[20]

Presidents after Truman did not hesitate to follow his example. Under Eisenhower, for example, Democrats periodically lamented that the White House was "consulting" them only after decisions had been reached, leaving them no real opportunity to participate in policy formulation. Leading Democrats expressed this criticism after the Suez crisis of 1956, when President Eisenhower asked Congress for authority to use armed force against the expansionism of "international Communism" in the Middle East. On March 9, 1957, Congress granted this authority, but not without evident Democratic discontent over the administration's failure to utilize bipartisan procedures before determining its basic policy in the area.

President Kennedy faced the same criticism. Having reached a decision to sell wheat to the Soviet Union in 1963, he *informed* a bipartisan delegation of his decision two hours before he announced it to a press conference. Critics labeled this another *fait accompli* that failed to meet truly bipartisan standards.[21] Similarly, after a prolonged and highly secretive consideration of policy alternatives for dealing with the Soviet missile buildup in Cuba in 1962, a short time before he was scheduled to announce his decision to the American people, President Kennedy told a bipartisan meeting of legislators about it. It was made clear that the President's policy had already been determined; under the circumstances, it was much too late for significant changes to be made at this "eleventh hour" meeting.[22]

Bipartisanship under President Johnson suffered from this same defect. Time and again, the President's opponents alleged, he utilized bipartisan meetings at the White House and other procedures to "silence his critics" and merely to "brief" members of Congress concerning decisions already taken. Circumstances often did not encourage (nor did the President apparently desire) any real exploration of policy alternatives. With regard to the Dominican crisis early in 1965, for example, Senator Fulbright has commented that the atmosphere of urgency surrounding White House discussions—with executive officials convinced that the lives of Americans and other foreigners in the Dominican Republic were endangered—precluded a calm and full appraisal of American foreign policy. According to Fulbright's account, before bipartisan discussions began the White House had already ordered American marines to land on the island. Several weeks later, after the Senate Foreign Relations Committee had conducted hearings on American policy in the Dominican crisis, Fulbright became convinced that President Johnson and his advisers had deliberately or involuntarily deceived legislators concerning the situation and the nature of the threat to American diplomatic interests. In brief, this kind of bipartisanship fell far short of meeting Fulbright's conception of genuine consensus in policy-making.[23]

Many of these same reservations were expressed by Senator Fulbright and other critics about the Gulf of Tonkin Resolution of the previous year. After American naval vessels were attacked by North Vietnamese PT boats off the coast of Vietnam, in an effort to demonstrate maximum national unity in behalf of American foreign policy, President Johnson on August 5, 1964, asked Congress to grant him authority to use armed force to protect American interests in Southeast Asia. Congress promptly granted this request by passing the resolution. Ultimately, however, the resolution generated intense discord between the Johnson administration and its critics. Despite the fact that he voted for it and defended it on the floor of the Senate, Senator Fulbright called the resolution a "blank check . . . signed by the Congress in an atmosphere of urgency that seemed at the time to preclude debate." This blank check, in Fulbright's view, had subsequently been "waved in our faces" to justify America's growing involvement in Vietnam and to silence those who opposed this course.[24]

This aspect of the problem of bipartisan consultations in foreign affairs, as we emphasized earlier, perhaps qualifies as the essence of the matter of achieving and maintaining a consensus in behalf of diplomatic commitments. Given the utmost good will and sincerity on all sides (and these elements of course have not always been present), the over-all context of policy-making in the United States militates sharply against regularly employing bipartisan techniques like those used in the case of the UN Charter. Postwar experience strongly suggests this model of bipartisan collaboration is, at best, difficult to reproduce—and nearly impossible to follow in dealing with international crises. We shall examine some of the main reasons why in the concluding portion of this chapter.

Legislators as Negotiators

A bipartisan practice rich with tradition is the use of legislators and members of the opposition party

---

*The Gulf of Tonkin Resolution is discussed at greater length in Chapter 5. In this context, it is worth reiterating a point made in our earlier treatment: President Johnson and other Presidents who have used such resolutions did not believe they "needed" the approval of Congress to employ force to protect American interests abroad. Neither then nor afterwards did the White House concede any presumed legislative right to limit the President's power over the armed forces in Vietnam or in other settings. Replying to critics, several months later President Johnson said that "before we go in there to a more advanced state or involve ourselves more substantially, I want the Congress to go in with me." Yet he also admitted: "I did not feel that it was essential that the President have a resolution in order to take the action that was taken. As a matter of fact in the Tonkin Gulf I took the action before the resolution." See the text of the President's news conference, as reproduced in *The New York Times* (February 27, 1966).

as negotiators and observers at international conferences. This custom dates back to the War of 1812, when two legislators participated in negotiating the peace treaty. McKinley followed the same practice at the end of the Spanish–American War; the treaty of peace with Spain might have been rejected by the Senate except for this fact. Henry White's inability to provide liaison between President Wilson and Senate Republicans to assure acceptance of the Treaty of Versailles constituted a lesson which executive officials in later years were careful to observe: Bipartisan support for policy is not likely to emerge unless care is taken to work through the *acknowledged leaders* of the opposition party.

The individual most closely identified with bipartisanship in the modern period was Senator Arthur H. Vandenberg. Vandenberg once wrote of "wearing three hats." He was, first of all, the chairman of the Foreign Relations Committee in the 80th Congress (1947–1948); then he was the acknowledged Republican spokesman in foreign policy questions; finally, he served as President of the Senate and consequently came in close touch with that body's opinions and activities. Because of his great prestige and influence with reference to foreign policy issues, Vandenberg could provide invaluable assistance to the Truman administration in the immediate postwar period, especially in negotiating with the Soviet Union. His presence at the right hand of Secretary of State James Byrnes, during negotiations over the minor Axis peace treaties, for instance, provided a forceful demonstration of American unity.[25]

Much the same purpose was served under the Kennedy administration, when the President asked a bipartisan delegation of legislators to attend the signing ceremonies of the nuclear test-ban agreement in Moscow. Fearing that a delegation consisting solely of the administration's supporters might give the pact a "partisan flavor," President Kennedy counteracted this impression by including spokesmen for the Republican party. For reasons that we shall discuss presently, several GOP leaders were reluctant to serve in this capacity, since they were known to be opposed to the nuclear test-ban and did not wish to be identified with the agreement.[26] As a rule, however, as D. F. Fleming has written:

When powerful Senate leaders act as negotiators of a treaty they acquire a paternal interest in the document and are likely to defend it vigorously. ... Other Senators, too, are likely to look upon the treaty as made by capable, friendly hands and therefore to be attacked with much more restraint.[27]

BARRIERS TO UNITY

Constitutional Obstacles

Formidable barriers to bipartisan collaboration in foreign affairs are inherent in the American constitutional system. Following the concept of separation of powers, the founders deliberately divided control of foreign relations between the President and Congress. Whatever may have been the original intention of the Founding Fathers, American diplomatic experience has clearly elevated the President into a position of leadership in this realm, as we discussed in Chapters 3 and 5. The role of Congress is important, and has become increasingly so in the modern period, but it is nevertheless a *subordinate* role. Congress may modify proposals made by executive officials; and, for short periods at least, it can block at least certain steps contemplated by the White House. Yet the initiative in foreign affairs rests with the President and his chief advisers. Efforts to achieve bipartisan cooperation, therefore, must always be carried on within a framework of executive dominance in foreign relations.

This fact has profound significance for bipartisanship. It means, first, that the President must always remain at the helm of the ship of state. Under the Constitution, it is his responsibility to preserve national security, and he cannot abdicate this responsibility merely because greater unity within the government may be desirable. Obviously, attempts to create unity may contribute to the broad goal of national security. At times, however, as when President Truman decided upon American assistance to Greece in 1947 and intervened with troops in Korea in 1950, a Chief Executive must take steps the demanded by the diplomatic interests of the country, regardless of whether such steps have received widespread initial bipartisan support. This was basically President Johnson's dilemma in the midst of the internal dissension over the conduct of the Vietnam War. After listening to the viewpoints of critics, and after carefully assessing possible alternatives, the President in the end had to decide upon the policies required to achieve American goals in Southeast Asia and promote its diplomatic interests generally. When it came down to a choice between between doing this and conciliating his critics by modifying his policies, President Johnson time and again chose the former course. For, in the final analysis, the President is responsible constitutionally for the management of foreign affairs; more than ever, he is also held accountable by the electorate for the success of failure of national policy in all spheres. Bipartisan cooperation always has to take place with this limitation.

Second, under the American Constitution, Congress bears little or no direct responsibility for certain kinds of activities in the sphere of foreign relations. This is true, for instance, of the recognition of other governments, which is purely an executive function. It is difficult to see how completely satisfactory bipartisan procedures can be worked out within the existing constitutional framework to cover such problems.* For if, on the one hand, the President permits Congress to share in making policies in these instances, then he is allowing the legislature to make decisions for which he is constitutionally responsible. If, on the other hand, he excludes such questions from the area of bipartisan cooperation, then he invites the charge that he has arbitrarily limited the bipartisan process, that he really does not want unity on the issue in question, and that he has freed the opposition party to criticize policy openly. No example from postwar experience better illustrates the complexities of this kind of problem for the bipartisan approach than the Truman administration's diplomacy toward Nationalist China.[28]

In the third place, a constitutional no man's land exists in regard to the control of domestic aspects of foreign relations, notably the use of troops in behalf of diplomatic objectives. After a century and a half of constitutional history, the exact boundaries between legislative and executive prerogatives remain shadowy. This virtually invites the two branches to struggle for supremacy, to maximize their own power, and to resist expansion in the powers of the other branch. Such considerations were undoubtedly behind the so-called Great Debate on American defense policy late in 1950 and early in 1951. Although the ostensible issues involved the commitment of American ground troops to Europe, this debate must be at least partially explained as a recurrence of a constitutional struggle that has erupted many times in American history over the exact scope of legislative and executive prerogatives in the military and defense field. Genuine bipartisan cooperation is predicated upon some kind of understanding as to the jurisdictions of the President and Congress, in order that a profitable division of labor in foreign affairs may result.

Many of the same arguments were heard at the end of the 1960s, when opponents of the Vietnam War introduced a resolution in the Senate designed to prevent the President from assuming

new "national commitments" overseas without the consent of Congress. The resolution was aimed specifically at commitments involving the use of military forces abroad, but it was in effect a resurgence of an old constitutional struggle involving the respective powers of the executive and legislative branches in foreign affairs. To the minds of executive policy-makers, the resolution infringed upon the President's established prerogatives; to many legislators it was a belated attempt to redress the balance in the foreign policy process by restoring to Congress certain powers rightfully belonging to it. Whatever the merits of the argument, it could safely be predicted that Presidents from both political parties would look upon such expressions of legislative sentiment as purely advisory and as marking no real diminution of the President's influence over foreign relations.*

Disunity Within the Executive Branch

The postwar emphasis upon a bipartisan consensus underlying American foreign policy suggests that internal divisions on diplomatic issues have their origins primarily in hostile executive–legislative relations, or in partisan discords, or (as is normally the case) in a combination of the two. These sources of disunity in foreign relations obviously must not be minimized; as our treatment thus far has shown, they exist and they continue to complicate the task of formulating policies having firm bipartisan support.

Yet the postwar period has called attention to another source of internal dissension, which has sometimes rendered bipartisan agreement on foreign policy questions more elusive than ever. This is *disunity within the executive branch.* In Chapters 3 and 4, we emphasized the growing number of executive agencies involved in the foreign policy process. In turn, this fact severely taxes the ability of the White House and State Department to impart central direction to the activities of these agencies. A fundamental prerequisite for bipartisan accords in foreign policy would seem to be that executive officials agree among themselves over basic goals and programs. In the absence of such unanimity, bipartisan understandings (even when they can be reached) can accomplish little. Time has not blunted the force of Senator Vandenberg's complaint about the Truman administration in the early postwar period. Expressing his views at a time when delicate negotiations were under way with the Soviet Union, Secretary of Commerce Henry A. Wallace publicly criticized the administration's increasingly "tough" line with Moscow. Greatly discon-

---

*It is clear that, in some instances, Congress does not *want* to share the responsibility for decisions in foreign affairs, particularly those that might prove domestically unpopular. See Sherman Adams' discussion of legislative unwillingness to "share" in Eisenhower's contemplated use of sanctions against Israel in 1956 or in possible American intervention in Jordan, in *First-Hand Report: The Story of the Eisenhower Administration* (New York: Harper & Row, 1961), pp. 285, 291.

*The "national commitments" resolution is analyzed more fully in Chapter 5.

certed by this evidence of disunity within the administration itself, Vandenberg commented that Republicans wanted to collaborate with Democratic leaders on a bipartisan basis, but that they could only cooperate with one Secretary of State at a time! Realizing that bipartisan understanding was in jeopardy, President Truman promptly called for Wallace's resignation.[29]

The problem by no means disappeared in the months that followed. During the Eisenhower administration, for example, conflicting positions were taken by different executive agencies on the issue of disarmament negotiations with the Soviet Union. In the midst of this confusion, it was not always clear just where President Eisenhower himself stood on the matter.[30] Much the same phenomenon occurred in the early 1960s with respect to American policy in Vietnam. The State Department, the Defense Department, the Central Intelligence Agency, the Agency for International Development, the United States Information Agency—these and other federal agencies had large contingents in Vietnam, and during some periods, it was evident that they were often operating at cross-purposes.[31] Small wonder that confusion existed in the American public's mind about the nation's goals and accomplishments in that country.

Such examples underscore an elementary point: Before there can be a *bipartisan* foreign policy, there has to be a *foreign policy*. Uncoordinated statements and activities by executive officials can destroy bipartisan unity fully as much as acrimony between the President and Congress. For new and established policy undertakings, successful bipartisanship would seem to demand reasonable unity among executive officials in behalf of programs for which a consensus exists.

Disunity Within Congress

Another impediment to bipartisan accord in foreign relations is a problem treated in considerable detail in Chapter 5. This is *growing disunity within the legislative branch* with respect to foreign policy issues. The problem of fragmented and diffuse efforts within Congress has, in some respects, become more critical than ever. The Legislative Reorganization Act of 1946, perspective makes clear, did little to offer permanent solutions. Foreign affairs in the present era have become a matter of great concern to citizens, and as we observed earlier, foreign policy has ramifications for nearly every important realm of domestic policy, with the result that the line separating these two domains has all but disappeared. For Congress, this fact means that it is a rare committee in the House or Senate that is not involved in some way with foreign policy. And given the highly decentralized organization of the national legislature, this extensive involvement tends to be

characterized by a high degree of independence in committee operations; by little or no liaison among them; by a diminution in the once almost exclusive jurisdictions of the House Foreign Affairs and Senate Foreign Relations Committees in dealing with international issues; by a growing level of confidence and expertise on the part of other committees concerning some aspects of American foreign relations; by the tendency of most congressmen to acquire first-hand information (or in some cases, impressions) about conditions overseas from travel abroad; by chronic skepticism in the legislative mind about the "achievements" of the State Department and other executive agencies charged with responsibilities in external affairs; and by a progressively more formidable challenge posed to the White House in trying to achieve a unified approach to foreign policy issues.

The change that has come about in this respect in recent years may be highlighted by contrasting the early postwar period with the late 1960s. When the Truman administration reached bipartisan understandings with key legislators like Senators Tom Connally and Arthur H. Vandenberg, it could do so with confidence that the agreements would "stand up" in Congress as a whole. Once the support of the chairman of the Senate Foreign Relations Committee had been obtained for a program like the Marshall Plan or the North Atlantic Treaty, that is to say, there was every reason to expect Congress itself to enact the legislation required to carry out the policy in question. Even during the 1950s under President Eisenhower, William S. White has written, this same expectation could be held with reasonable assurance. Then, Senator Walter George (Democrat of Georgia) played the role Connally and Vandenberg had played earlier. White has written of Senator George:

He spoke, and speaks, on world affairs for the entire Democratic party in the Senate as few men can have done in history. In effect, he pledged, and indeed committed, the whole power of the Democratic party in this field to the President. And while he was at it he flung about the President the capacious cloak of the immense, incontestably conservative prestige of the Southern Democrats.
. . . Thus, when Mr. George began to make it plain that he saw no reason whatever why the Administration should not negotiate with the Communists, or move a bit away from the China Nationalists, it was impossible even for the most implacable Senate Republican right-wingers to cry out "soft on communism." [32]

Under President Johnson, this requisite for the success of bipartisanship in foreign affairs was almost totally lacking. When it dealt with Congress, the White House faced two highly disconcerting realities: a larger number of legislative committees than ever played a role in dealing with foreign policy issues, and there appeared to be fewer formal or *ad hoc* methods capable of imparting some kind of unified direction to Congress' activities. The problem was exemplified by the fragmentation which occurred within the Senate Foreign Relations Committee itself. Instead of a Vandenberg or a George, the committee was headed by Senator J. William Fulbright, who developed a deep personal dislike for President Johnson, who evinced little confidence in the administration's foreign policies (especially in Vietnam), and who came to regard himself in time as one of its chief critics. Fulbright was not a member of the Senate's "inner circle," nor was he a person of any noteworthy influence within the Democratic party. Presiding over what was often a deeply split committee, Fulbright also witnessed the intrusion of numerous other committees into the domain of foreign relations. Even if the President had been inclined to seek bipartisan agreements with Senator Fulbright (and President Johnson reciprocated Fulbright's distrust), there was little assurance that such understandings would have been accepted either by the Foreign Relations Committee or by Congress as a whole.[33]

Political Hurdles to Unity

Discussing the Republican party's prospects in the presidential election of 1960, Vice President Nixon, the GOP candidate for President, declared: "If you ever let them [the Democrats] campaign only on domestic issues, they'll beat us —our only hope is to keep it on foreign policy." Finding a majority of their political advisers in agreement, Republican strategists settled upon the choice of Henry Cabot Lodge of Massachusetts for vice presidential candidate, since "Lodge was the best man to lift Americans' imagination to the problems of foreign policy...."[34] That Democratic political leaders were not unmindful of the importance of foreign policy issues in the campaign was borne out by such indications as Adlai Stevenson's view that American foreign policy had become "a thing of wonder and mirth" to other countries, and the polls conducted by the Kennedy camp showing that America's declining prestige in international affairs was the dominant issue of the political campaign.[35]

A document prepared by the Republican National Committee explaining the result of the presidential election of 1968 asserts that in that election, the GOP "achieved a monumental success" by winning control of the White House and making gains in Congress and on the state level. In explanation of this result, the study relied upon public opinion polls to show that the voters rated the GOP significantly higher than the Democratic party in its ability to deal with the "top problems" facing the American society. Among these problems, polls showed that the Vietnam War outranked all others in terms of voter concern; the electorate believed that Republican leadership would deal with this issue more effectively than Democratic leadership.[36]

These examples focus attention upon what is perhaps the most durable obstacle to implementation of a bipartisan approach to foreign relations: those inherent in the American political system. At the time of his confirmation as Secretary of State in 1953, John Foster Dulles explained the seeming contradiction between his support for the bipartisan principle and his often sharp attacks upon the policies of Democratic policy-makers, by saying:

. . . under our Constitutional system we have a general election every four years . . . one side presents his case, and the other side presents the other case, as two lawyers do when they go into court. At that stage the two parties are not judges and they are not judicial. In my opinion they should not be . . . but when that time is past, then I believe we should try to work together on a bipartisan basis. . . .[37]

Dulles's statement highlights two contrary and powerful forces that tend to pull any discussion of foreign policy questions in opposite directions: the widely admitted need for maximum unity when important international issues are at stake, and the equally compelling necessity for full and periodic debate on paramount questions of public policy.

Let us consider first an assumption implicit in the process of a bipartisan approach to foreign policy questions: the principle that under this approach both parties share equally in the credit or blame for developments in external affairs. This principle collides head-on with another deeply ingrained precept of the American democratic system. This is that the party in power is held responsible by the electorate for the successful management of domestic and foreign affairs. Postwar experience suggests that it is virtually impossible to reconcile these two principles and that, in practice, leaders and adherents of both political parties are prone (especially during national elections) to abandon the former in favor of the latter. Such a result is almost guaranteed by two other tendencies that have emerged on the basis of experience with the bipartisan principle. One is that the party in power almost invariably claims credit for *successful* policies. The other is that the opposition party no less invariably divorces itself from responsibility for *unsuccessful* policies. Thus, since World War II, Republicans have campaigned repeatedly on issues such as the Roosevelt administration's "appeasement" of the Soviet Union at Yalta and its "loss" of Eastern Europe and China to Communism. Democrats periodically attack the Republican party's traditional "isolationist" record in foreign affairs; they condemn the strategy of "brinksmanship" advocated by President Eisenhower's Secretary of State John Foster Dulles; and they point to the lack of "experience" of many Republicans in the foreign policy field. By the late 1960s, both parties routinely derived political capital out of America's involvement in Vietnam. Without saying precisely how, Republican candidates in 1968 proposed to extricate the nation from this unwanted commitment. Even significant numbers of Democrats divorced themselves from the President's position on the war, attacked his Secretary of State, and advocated policies that had long been rejected by the White House. Since the war was unpopular with almost all segments of the American population, it was a rare candidate who did not in some way attack the policies leading to America's role in it.

In any election year, despite the most diligent attention to bipartisan procedures and the deepest commitment to the cause of unity by policymakers, the political system erects many barriers against a high degree of national unity on foreign policy issues. It remains true, for example, that gains and losses in foreign affairs cannot be shared equally by the two major parties without radical innovations in the American political system and perhaps in the process of democracy itself. If the incumbent party has governed well, it is natural—in a democracy, perhaps desirable and inevitable—that it should seek to be returned to office on the basis of its record. Conversely, an opposition party cannot voluntarily forego opportunities to inject international questions—especially those involving alleged *failures* in American policy—into the political arena without inviting the charge that it "lacks alternatives" of its own or that it can do no better than acquiesce in ineffectual efforts by incumbent officials. In brief, the opposition party cannot accept a theory of bipartisanship that entails a moratorium on criticism. If it did so, it would largely forfeit any claim it may make to being an effective opposition. As we have already observed, in the last analysis the administration in power must decide upon the foreign policies the national interest requires. The opposite side of this coin is that the opposition party must likewise decide when policies have proved unsuccessful and must assume the responsibility of calling these policies to the attention of the electorate.

All of this suggests that bipartisanship in foreign policy may place the opposition party in a peculiarly vulnerable position. Advocates of the bipartisan principle have proclaimed, almost as a matter of ritual, that there must be no moratorium on public debate, but criticism of delicate foreign policy questions ought always to be "construc-

tive." Aside from the difficulty of interpreting this stipulation objectively, this idea means that the opposition party is always in danger of being compromised. Either it attacks policies that, in its judgment, need criticizing—thereby risking the accusation that it has abandoned the concept of bipartisanship and is indifferent to the need for unity in critical times. Or it withholds its criticisms for the sake of unity or the *appearance* of unity—and risks the no less damaging charge that it is no longer an effective opposition party and that it is equally to blame for ineffectual efforts in foreign relations. Either way, it can be penalized. For its leaders know full well that, however much participants in the process of foreign policy may agree that credit and blame ought theoretically to be shared equally, this is the view neither of the electorate as a whole nor of rank-and-file party members, whose principal concern is winning elections.*

It cannot perhaps be too often emphasized that a cardinal distinction between totalitarian and democratic governments lies in the degree to which each believes the creation of unity to be a pre-eminent goal of policy-makers. Democracies operate upon the basis of consent, which inevitably implies a certain amount of dissent and dissension over important public issues. Totalitarian governments eliminate dissent openly and forcibly, but democracies may accomplish the same purpose, consciously or unconsciously, by more indirect and subtle means. Adlai Stevenson has observed that

. . . in many minds "criticism" has today become an ugly word. It has become almost *lèse-majesté*. It conjures up pictures of insidious radicals hacking away at the very foundations of the American way of life. It suggests nonconformity and nonconformity suggests disloyalty and disloyalty suggests treason, and before we know where we are, this process has all but identified the critic with the saboteur and turned political criticism into an un-American activity instead of democracy's greatest safeguard.[38]

*This dilemma was highlighted in 1963 by the interest displayed by the Kennedy administration in permitting American grain dealers to sell wheat to the Soviet Union. Such a move represented a reversal of American policy of many years' standing. The President and his advisers were, therefore, highly desirous of gaining assurance of widespread bipartisan support before undertaking it. Thus one news dispatch pointed out that officials of the administration had been consulting Republican leaders in Congress "in an attempt to gain an advance and public endorsement of the move that would make it impossible for Republican candidates to make a campaign issue out of the sale if it were made—and if United States–Soviet relations then took a turn for the worse." In other words, in the Republican view, the President was seeking GOP concurrence with the move, which would emerge as an "achievement" of the Democratic administration if successful, and GOP silence on the move if it failed! *The New York Times* (October 1, 1963).

Under a bipartisan approach to foreign relations, there is not only the problem of *whether* criticism will emerge, but also the problem of *when* it emerges. Surely one purpose of enlightened criticism is to bring about needed changes in policy while there is yet time to prevent major policy failures. *Ex post facto* criticism whose purpose is merely to identify the individuals responsible for diplomatic ineptitude often serves little constructive purpose. This kind of criticism has been all too common in recent American experience.

One final point requires emphasis. "History," to quote Republican members of the House Foreign Affairs Committee, "is strewn with wreckage of countries that were united but on the wrong course." The paramount goal shared by both branches of the government and by both political parties is *successful foreign policy*. Unquestionably, bipartisan procedures sometimes contribute to reaching that goal. But sometimes too, other techniques and practices—firm executive leadership, clear public delineation of the issues by party spokesmen, replacement of incapable officials by more capable ones—can advance the nation's diplomatic interests better than an uncritical attachment to the bipartisan principle. In the last analysis, one condition above all others is likely to prove the most durable incentive for national unity in foreign affairs: a conviction that the incumbent officials are aware of crucial problems in the international community and that they are working conscientiously to formulate intelligent and realistic policies for dealing with these problems.

NOTES

1. George F. Kennan, *Memoirs* (New York: Bantam, 1969), pp. 526–527.
2. Quoted in William L. Langer, "The Mechanism of American Foreign Policy," *International Affairs* 24 (July, 1948), 321.
3. The views of Key, Hoffman, Buchan, and President Kennedy on the problem of instability in American foreign relations are cited in Kenneth N. Waltz, *Foreign Policy and Democratic Politics: The American and British Experience* (Boston: Little, Brown, 1967), pp. 105–106.
4. Cited in Smith Simpson, *Anatomy of the State Department* (Boston: Houghton Mifflin, 1967), p. 154.
5. See the dispatch in *The New York Times* (May 1, 1966).
6. Frederick G. Dutton, " 'Cold War' Between The Hill and Foggy Bottom," *The New York Times Magazine* (September 15, 1963), p. 36.
7. For more detailed discussion, see Julius W. Pratt, *A History of United States Foreign Policy* (Englewood Cliffs, N.J.: Prentice-Hall,

1965), pp. 77–80, 86–104, 125–140, 201–219, 220–236, 367–394; William L. Langer and S. Everett Gleason, *The Challenge to Isolation* (New York: Harper & Row, 1952), pp. 136–147, 280–291; George H. Haynes, *The Senate of the United States*, Vol. II (Boston: Houghton Mifflin, 1938), p. 700; and Allan Nevins, *Henry White* (New York: Harper & Row, 1930), pp. 397–404.
8. Arthur H. Vandenberg, Jr., ed., *The Private Papers of Senator Vandenberg* (Boston: Houghton Mifflin, 1952), p. 550.
9. *Ibid.*, pp. 90–171.
10. Preliminary studies of the Marshall Plan are described in Senate Foreign Relations Committee–House Foreign Affairs Committee, *The European Recovery Program*, Senate Document No. 111, 80th Congress, 1st Session, 1947.
11. Cecil V. Crabb, Jr., *Bipartisan Foreign Policy: Myth or Reality?* (New York: Harper & Row, 1957), pp. 74–116.
12. Our discussion of the activities of the Office of Congressional Relations in the Department of State is based upon Robert E. Elder, *The Policy Machine* (Syracuse, N.Y.: Syracuse University Press, 1960), pp. 93–111; and James A. Robinson, *Congress and Foreign Policy-Making*, rev. ed. (Homewood, Ill.: Dorsey, 1967), pp. 119–124.
13. See Waltz, *op. cit.*, p. 101; Joseph Kraft, "The Dean Rusk Show," *The New York Times Magazine* (March 24, 1968), p. 130; and Senate Foreign Relations Committee, *Background Information on the Committee on Foreign Relations*, 90th Congress, 2nd Session, 1968, pp. 21–22.
14. Rowland Evans and Robert Novak, *Lyndon B. Johnson: The Exercise of Power* (New York: New American Library, 1968), p. 541.
15. Simpson, *op. cit.*, p. 177.
16. J. William Fulbright, *The Arrogance of Power* (New York: Random House, 1966), p. 48.
17. Bipartisanship with respect to American participation in the United Nations is discussed in detail in Crabb, *op. cit.*, pp. 44–54.
18. This episode is recounted in Nelson W. Polsby, *Congress and Presidency* (Englewood Cliffs, N.J.: Prentice-Hall, 1964), p. 107.
19. See Kraft, *op. cit.*, pp. 35, 130; and *The New York Times* (November 8, 1967, and March 13, 1968).
20. Bipartisanship in connection with the Greek–Turkish Aid Program is analyzed more fully in Crabb, *op. cit.*, pp. 54–60.
21. Evans and Novak, *op. cit.*, pp. 385–386.
22. The Kennedy administration's use of bipartisan procedures in the Cuban missile crisis is discussed in Theodore C. Sorensen, *Kennedy* (New York: Harper & Row, 1965), pp. 702–703.
23. Fulbright, *op. cit.*, p. 49.
24. *Ibid.*, p. 52.
25. For historical precedents involving the use of senators as negotiators, see Haynes, *op. cit.*, pp. 596–598; Vandenberg, *op. cit.*, p. 318;

and *The New York Times* (September 15, 1946).

26. *The New York Times* (July 29, 1963).
27. D. F. Fleming, *The Treaty Veto of the American Senate* (New York: Putnam's, 1930), p. 169.
28. Crabb, *op. cit.*, pp. 93–116.
29. President Truman's controversy with Secretary of Commerce Henry Wallace is treated in Harry S. Truman, *Memoirs*, vol II (Garden City, N.Y.: Doubleday, 1955), pp. 555–559.
30. *The New York Times* (July 2, 1957).
31. *The New York Times* (September 22, 1963).
32. William S. White, "Two Parties and One Foreign Policy," *The New York Times Magazine* (August 7, 1955), p. 34.
33. For a discussion of the problem of disunity within the Senate Foreign Relations Committee, see Marvin Kalb, "Doves, Hawks and Flutterers in the Foreign Relations Committee," *The New York Times Magazine* (November 19, 1967), pp. 56–57, 60–82.
34. William S. White, *Citadel: The Story of the U.S. Senate* (New York: Harper & Row, 1957), pp. 206–207.
35. *Ibid.*, pp. 120, 319–320.
36. See the publication by the Republican National Committee, "The 1968 Elections" (Washington, D.C., 1969), pp. 169–180.
37. Quoted in Joseph C. Harsch, "John Foster Dulles: A Very Complicated Man, *Harper's Magazine* 213 (September, 1956), 29.
38. Adlai E. Stevenson, "Party of the Second Part," *Harper's Magazine* 212 (February, 1956), 33.

Seven
THE PUBLIC CONTEXT OF FOREIGN POLICY

PUBLIC OPINION AND DEMOCRACY

Among the presuppositions underlying the concept of democratic government, none is perhaps more central than the notion that the most intimate and direct connection must exist between the wishes of the people and the policies adopted by their leaders. Few students of democratic government in the modern period would push this relationship to the point carried in the old Roman aphorism: *vox populi, vox dei* ("the voice of the people is the voice of God"). Yet in the writings of nearly every European or American philosopher who has contributed to the American political tradition, the responsiveness of the government to society's needs and demands has been viewed as an essential element in democracy. Classical philosophers like Montesquieu referred to the *esprit général;* the *volonté général* was a prominent theme in Rousseau's writings. The Declaration of Independence stressed the need for government to manifest a "decent respect for the opinions of mankind." The first words of the Constitution of the United States are: "We the People of the United States . . . do ordain and establish this Constitution. . . ." In President Lincoln's well-known characterization of the American system—as government of the people, by the people, and for the people—this relationship is again conspicuous. The phrase "the people" occurs in all three terms; and in the first two, the implication is that the people constitute an *active force*, endowing government with its authority and legitimacy. The folklore and customs of American political life call attention to this idea at every turn. Incumbent leaders are continually at pains to demonstrate that they are heeding the "voice of the people." Their political opponents vow to turn the management of public affairs "back to the people" or to formulate national policies representing the wishes of "all the people." Interest groups making overtures to government invariably cast them in terms of what "the American people demand"; or, if they *oppose* governmental policies, they are likely to insist that "the people will not stand for"

whatever policies they are attacking. Meanwhile, since World War II, policy-makers have routinely condemned Soviet and Chinese Communist conduct on the grounds that it offends international sensibilities and reflects disregard for the opinions of mankind.

Although such developments cannot of course be dated with exactitude, the role of public opinion as a crucial force in foreign policy seems to stem from World War I and the efforts to "democratize" diplomacy led by President Woodrow Wilson. Before that time, long after public opinion had begun to have an impact on domestic policy, foreign affairs were still regarded as largely outside public control or scrutiny. The "secret treaties" among the great powers during and after World War I illustrated this reality. By contrast, the first of Wilson's war aims, as set forth in his famous Fourteen Points (January 8, 1918), was "open covenants, openly arrived at." Not only should agreements among governments be publicized, but what was even more radical, Wilson advocated the idea that *the process of reaching agreements* should also be subject to public scrutiny. Wilson had almost unlimited confidence in both the judgments of the people and his own ability to influence them. During World War I, he frequently differentiated between the views of the German *people* (who presumably desired peace and justice) and their misguided rulers (who had plunged the world into a bloody international conflict). On one occasion, Wilson asserted: "The real people I was speaking to were neither the

*It has not escaped the attention of modern students of diplomacy that even President Wilson, the champion of "open covenants, openly arrived at," found it virtually impossible to adhere to his own doctrine in negotiating the Treaty of Versailles. Commenting on the secrecy surrounding these negotiations, Thomas A. Bailey has written that some 150 American reporters went to Paris, but the "door was barred against these eager reporters; and at the end of the first day a secretary slipped out and read to them a dry five-line summary. The correspondents thereupon made a tremendous outcry." See Thomas A. Bailey, *A Diplomatic History of the American People*, 3rd ed. (New York: Appleton-Century-Crofts, 1947), p. 657.

Senate nor foreign governments, but the people of the countries now at war." And speaking to the Paris Peace Conference, Wilson declared that "we are not representatives of governments, but representatives of people. It will not suffice to satisfy governmental circles anywhere. It is necessary that we should satisfy the opinion of mankind."[1]

Presidents after Wilson were no less concerned with the impact of public opinion upon national policies, foreign and domestic. Usually opposed by a majority of newspapers, President Franklin D. Roosevelt utilized his "fireside chats" with the American people to generate public support for his policies at home and abroad. President Harry Truman once commented: "The biggest problem facing any President is to sell the American people on a policy. They have had to be led forward. . . . That's the biggest challenge every President faces, and one which he cannot escape."[2] Secretary of State George C. Marshall was convinced that "no policy—foreign or domestic—can succeed without public support."[3] And a more recent student of the foreign policy process in the United States has concluded: "The Secretary of State must sell as well as negotiate American foreign policies today. He is a contender in the publicity marts of the world for support."[4] This comment underscores a dimension of the subject we shall deal with at greater length in Chapter 14: the attempts by governments to influence public opinion outside their own borders. Here our interest is confined to *domestic* opinion as it influences the conduct of foreign affairs.

PUBLIC OPINION: ITS COMPONENTS AND PROPERTIES

Since the end of World War II, the investigation of public opinion has forged ahead rapidly and on many fronts. Scholars have probably learned more about the nature and role of public opinion in the past generation than they knew for centuries before that time. If any generalization can be drawn from the innumerable studies made in the postwar era, it is that the concept of public opinion is a fascinatingly complex and variegated phenomenon. Simplistic ideas and assumptions have had to totally discarded or seriously modified. For example, the conception implicit in the views of many classical writers of "public opinion,"—the idea that a homogeneous "public" expressed a unified and unambiguous "opinion" to policy-makers—possesses little or no validity. Even today there remain many unanswered questions about the nature of public opinion, about how it is formed, how it is expressed, and precisely how it enters into the conduct of national policy. At the same time, competent scholars have advanced the frontiers of knowledge significantly with respect

to public opinion. Although they have not been eliminated, areas of uncertainty and supposition have been narrowed, and tools and skills needed for further investigations have been greatly refined.

The Concept of "Public Opinion"

A logical starting point in our discussion is the question, "What exactly *is* public opinion?" What are the necessary components of a satisfactory definition?

Great variation is encountered in the attempts of competent authorities to answer this question. Definitions of public opinion range from succinct (and hence often simplistic) to highly complex (and sometimes unintelligible). Authorities differ concerning the primary ingredients inherent in the concept. Thus, the eminent student of British government A. V. Dicey called public opinion a "body of beliefs, convictions, sentiments, accepted principles, or firmly-rooted prejudicies, which, taken together, make up the public opinion of a particular era. . . ." The sociologist Kimball Young conceived of it as the "beliefs, convictions, or views of individuals on matters or issues of widespread or public interest and concern." Another definition envisions it as the viewpoints held by a group of people on public issues concerning which discussion and controversy occur. Still other commentators regard public opinion as "the distribution of individual opinions about public matters" with respect to "issues that have, or could have, consequences affecting the entire community."[5]

The Components of Public Opinion

These and other definitions of public opinion that might be cited call attention to several ideas implicit in the concept. First, it refers to the viewpoints of a larger or smaller *group of individuals;* it is *collective*, rather than individual, opinion. The size of the group may vary from a few people to many thousands or perhaps millions. Without knowing precisely the line of demarcation, scholars customarily refer to the latter as *mass opinion* (the kind usually tested by public opinion polls), while the former is regarded as *group opinion* (as reflected in the resolutions of a labor or veterans' organization). Mass opinion often includes group opinion, in the sense that individuals comprising the mass also belong to groups within it. Yet it is important at this stage to note that the opinions of the masses of citizens may or may not be identical to those expressed by the largest or most vocal groups in society.

Second, the concept of public opinion logically suggests a fairly high degree of citizen *concern* about public issues; and this in turn requires citizen *awareness* of problems facing policy-makers.

For people to react at all to questions of public policy, they must presumably feel some minimal involvement in them; they must be at least remotely interested in the decisions of their government. For this assumption to be valid, the further ideas must be posited that citizens have access to information concerning important policy issues, and that they avail themselves of this information. To put the matter in its simplest terms: If pollsters found that a majority of the American people had never heard of the Arab–Israeli dispute and exhibited no interest in the conflict, it would be questionable whether "public opinion" on the issue actually existed. Studies of public opinion in the postwar era have in fact demonstrated that for many issues confronting the American people, citizen awareness and interest were substantially lacking.

Third, a group of people must not only be aware of, and concerned about, public issues; they must also hold, and in one way or another express, some kind of judgment or viewpoint about them. Here we encounter one of the most intricate questions associated with the analysis of public opinion. What precisely is an *opinion?* What kinds of reactions from or by the public qualify for inclusion as an "opinion"?* Treatments of public opinion by traditional political theorists (especially those, like the Enlightenment philosophers, who stressed its central role) more often than not envisioned public opinion as a *highly rational force*, reflecting public awareness and *considered judgment* about matters requiring the attention of policy-makers. One of the pillars supporting the case for democratic government in fact is the presupposition that citizens engage in *rational thought and discourse* when they consider major questions of public policy. After hearing the pros and cons of such questions debated in an atmosphere of free speech, they can and will arrive at intelligent judgments about them. In this conception, public opinion becomes synonymous with *reasoned deliberation* followed, at some point, by the formulation of *logical conclusions* by the citizenry.

Now it is apparent that for certain foreign policy issues in the contemporary world, some segments of the American society arrive at their opinions in this way. Substantial numbers of Americans think intelligently about the future of the cold war, or the meaning of the Vietnam conflict, or America's proper role in the Middle East. In a literal sense, it is correct to say that such citizens hold opinions on these and other subjects. What percentage of the American people arrive at their opinions in this way? It is perhaps impossible to generalize about the matter. The percent-

age undoubtedly varies from one issue to another. With some exceptions, however, it is fair to say that this kind of rational and informed judgment is held by *a minority of the mass public*—in some cases, a very small minority.

In the more usual case, the reactions of citizens in the United States (and all other countries, for that matter) cannot properly be termed "opinion" without straining that term beyond its literal meaning. In his study of the New Deal, James M. Burns has portrayed the public opinion context confronting the Roosevelt administration:

Outside Washington were the millions of voters who held the destinies of foreign policy makers in their hands. And here was the most unstable foundation of all on which to build a consistent program of foreign relations. Great numbers of these voters were colossally ignorant of affairs beyond the three-mile limit. . . . The American people, lacking stable attitudes built on long experience in foreign policy making, swung fitfully from one foreign policy mood to another, from isolation to neutralism to participation in world politics.[6]

In countless different ways, citizens *react emotionally* to foreign policy issues. They are "hurt" by anti-Americanism exhibited by General de Gaulle's government in France—the country receiving the largest allocation of postwar foreign assistance. They are "shocked" by Red China's persistent "Hate America" campaign. They are "suspicious" of Soviet Russia and oppose any policies that might be construed as appeasement of Moscow. They are "frustrated" because of America's involvement in the Vietnam War. They are "disillusioned" with the results (or lack of them) achieved with the foreign aid program. They are "skeptical" of the ability (or sometimes even the desire) of the State Department to protect American interests abroad. By the 1970s, they had become "apprehensive" about the influence exercised in American society by the military–industrial complex. Besides such essentially emotional reactions, a significant proportion of Americans had *no opinion at all* on many foreign policy issues. They either were not aware of the problem, or, if they were, had no position with respect to it. In short, as opposed to the kind of rationally held judgments attributed to the public by many political thinkers, the evidence has shown that a variety of emotional responses are included in the term "public opinion." Irrational as they may be, these reactions may, and often do, influence public policy decisively. The fact that public opinion is not based upon careful intellectual analysis does not permit policy-makers to ignore it. Our discussion of American public opinion toward Red China will provide concrete examples.

Fourth, the concept of public opinion necessarily implies that the viewpoints of citizens *are*

*In *Webster's Third New International Dictionary*, the first meaning of "opinion" is: "A view, judgment, or appraisal formed in the mind about a particular matter or particular matters."

expressed and in some way *communicated to policy-makers.* Such communication takes many forms. It may be essentially *passive*, as when the public is asked by pollsters for their reactions to selected aspects of national policy, or when the President deliberately requests newsmen or private citizens to express their views on some aspect of current policy. Expressions of public sentiment may be, and frequently are, *active:* Citizens write letters to newspapers, to the White House, and to Congress; organizations adopt resolutions setting forth their viewpoints on various internal and external problems; lobbyists undertake campaigns designed to impress the executive and legislative branches with the extent and intensity of public sentiment on a given issue; delegations visit the State Department to transmit their viewpoints on some foreign policy matter.

Thus, in contrast with totalitarian environments, a democratic government is seldom left in doubt about the sentiments of its citizens. For democracies, the problem is the reverse: In the midst of what is normally a cacophony emanating from the public, the real challenge consists in obtaining an *accurate* assessment of public attitudes. Filtering out the static and "background noise" (some of which is deliberately created by groups trying to confuse leaders about the strength or direction of public sentiment) often requires the utmost ingenuity on the part of policy-makers.

Finally, the concept of public opinion (at least in its democratic setting) suggests that the viewpoints of citizens are *carefully considered by policy-makers* and that the wishes of the public are ultimately reflected in the activities and programs of the government. Every informed citizen of the United States is aware that "government by the people" does not mean that the mass of citizens actually formulates and carries out public policy. But it does mean that as a generalization (to which it is possible to cite many exceptions), the activities of the government must have the approval of society. At a minimum, these activities must not be consistently *disapproved* by the public or viewed by it as inimical to its interests and welfare.

To what extent does American public opinion actually influence the formulation and execution of American foreign policy? This is a question with many important ramifications. We may more profitably discuss it after we have examined other aspects of public opinion more closely.

The Properties of Public Opinion

As the tools of public opinion analysis have become more refined, scholars have shed new light upon many characteristics of society's viewpoints toward public policy questions. Public sentiment possesses several basic properties relevant to a more intelligent understanding of the foreign policy process.

The most familiar property of public opinion is the *direction* of citizen viewpoints. Is the public "for" or "against" a continuation of foreign aid? Does it "approve" or "disapprove" efforts to resolve cold war tensions? The customary tripartite division of public sentiment in measuring the direction of opinion is: affirmative, negative, and "no opinion" (a category whose importance should not be underestimated). When a specific question is asked—like, "Do you favor efforts by the United States to prevent the spread of nuclear weapons among the nations of the world?"—replies are usually grouped into one of these three categories. A somewhat more refined system for measuring the direction of mass opinion is to present the public with a series of policy alternatives, asking them to express their preferences for A, B, C, D, or E. On that basis, the proportion of public opinion favoring each alternative is tabulated. All measurements of the direction of public opinion, it should be pointed out, are to some degree a function of the questions to which the public is asked to respond. In the latter case, for example, some citizens may identify none of the alternatives listed as actually describing their preferences; nor will the list of choices always include the most attractive course of action recommending itself to policy-makers.

Another fundamental property of public opinion is its *intensity* or firmness. Policy-makers may be just as interested in how strongly the public is attached to its views as in the direction of public sentiment. Some issues evoke public reactions of very low intensity; these are questions about which a majority of the public (in the popular phrase) "couldn't care less." Conversely, other foreign policy questions evoke public responses of extremely high intensity. On these issues the public reacts strongly and vocally; its viewpoints obviously stem from deep conviction and commitment. Postwar studies of public opinion have revealed time and again, for example, that high intensity usually accompanies issues affecting national security and perceived threats to the nation, particularly as these arise from American relations with Communist nations. The anti-Communist sentiments of the American people are clearly "a given" in the over-all context of foreign relations; political leaders ignore such pervasive and intensely held feelings at their peril.

In determining the latitude available to governmental officials for modifying national policies, the intensity of public opinion can be a crucial factor. The *malleability* of public attitudes is another key consideration for policy-makers. Even if the public currently disapproves of some contemplated step in foreign relations (such as new overtures to improve relations with Red China), officials in the White House and State Department are keenly interested in the degree to which these attitudes are susceptible of change. What prospect is there that a series of statements by the President and Secretary of State might gradually alter the climate of opinion on this question? If this technique shows some probability of success, officials might seriously consider launching such a campaign. If not, doing so could have no other result than undermining public confidence in the incumbent administration and turning public sentiment against other foreign policy measures identified with it. The intensity of public opinion also largely determines whether citizens will "accept" certain policy innovations, even if no great public enthusiasm exists for them.

Closely related to this characteristic of public opinion is the property of *saliency*. How deeply "involved" is the public in developments overseas and the government's response to them? To what extent do citizens perceive a direct connection between events abroad and their normal preoccupation with personal and family concerns like health, prosperity, security, and welfare? Is there a significant qualitative difference between the way individuals and groups react to developments like inflation or tax increases at home and the response of their government to a crisis in the Middle East or American efforts to promote economic advancement for Afro–Asian societies?

Throughout the postwar period, public opinion in the United States with respect to foreign policy issues has tended to be characterized by relatively *low saliency*. Citizens normally perceive a difference between internal and external policy; they have been much more involved and interested in the former than the latter. This tendency derives in part from America's prolonged isolationist tradition. Even though most Americans acknowledge that the era of isolationism has ended, this does not mean that they are as personally interested in foreign affairs as internal affairs, nor does it mean that they have fully accepted the implications inherent in America's position as a superpower. After studying the results of the State Department's continuing investigation of public attitudes, Robert E. Elder has written: "Americans deeply interested in foreign policy constitute a dedicated few." Foreign policy issues arouse deep citizen concern only when people's lives or livelihoods are directly affected.[7] In instance after instance, sizable percentages of public opinion sampled have fallen into the "no opinion" category.[8] A study published in 1954 concluded that "the majority of Americans are not interested in foreign affairs as such, as they appear to take an interest only in those problems clearly affecting their own interests."[9]

Considerable evidence exists, however, for believing that the traditional public apathy toward foreign relations is gradually changing. In his study of the national election of 1960, the late Professor V. O. Key cited several public opinion polls to show that foreign policy and national defense concerns ranked ahead of domestic considerations in the minds of the electorate.[10] Another recent study has shown that, among 23 leading concerns of the American people, the first 5 were in the area of foreign affairs and national security. Ranked on a scale from 0 to 300, these dominant concerns were:

Keeping the country out of war	—269
Combating Communism	—257
Keeping military defense posture strong	—250
Controlling nuclear weapons	—248
Maintaining respect for the United States abroad	—244

The nearest internal concern was maintaining law and order, which ranked 240 on the scale.[11]

Still another significant property of public opinion is its *concentration* or distribution among various segments of society. The properties of public opinion, as we have already suggested, tend to interact with one another. One group of people is likely to feel that a particular issue is more important to it than some others; when that situation occurs, we would expect a higher concentration, or greater homogeneity, of opinion within that group than is found throughout the population as a whole. Because their members already share certain common goals and values, group opinion is usually (although by no means always) more concentrated than mass opinion.

Policy-makers are not interested only in what the public thinks and how strongly it feels about a given subject. Sometimes they are even more influenced by the pattern of opinion concentration. For obvious reasons, in formulating policies concerning foreign trade in agricultural commodities, officials are prone to listen more attentively to the viewpoints of farmers than to factory workers. A decisive majority opinion expressed by American scientists on nuclear disarmament is likely to carry more weight than the opinion of lawyers or ethnic minorities. Concentrated opinion among ethnic minorities, on the other hand, can be expected to have an impact upon American foreign policy toward Eastern Europe or toward the Arab–Israeli dispute. Not infrequently, highly concentrated opinion has an influence far out of proportion to its numerical strength.[12] (This is notably true for a group we shall discuss below, "elite opinion.")

Hierarchies and Categories in Public Opinion

Several schemes for classifying public opinion and identifying hierarchies within it, are available. No single system has universal validity, however.

Each system's usefulness and value depend heavily upon the purpose for which the classification is being made.

A former State Department official has written that this agency customarily conceives of three categories of public opinion. Each has its own unique role in the foreign policy process, and each presents a different challenge to officials seeking to understand public attitudes. First, there is the *general public* or what we have previously called mass opinion. Consisting of the views of citizens at large (or, in the popular phrase, "average" citizens), in a democratic system these attitudes form the foundation upon which public officials must erect their major policies at home and abroad. In the long run, such policies cannot succeed unless they are substantially accepted by the society as a whole.

Yet one of the characteristics of mass opinion is that it has little sustained interest in, and is often poorly informed about, its government's activities overseas. Minimally concerned with most foreign policy questions, the general public may periodically become aroused by some crisis abroad, after which a groundswell of popular sentiment may sweep the country. More often than not, this occurrence is essentially an *emotional* reaction, and it seldom lasts more than a few weeks or months (although toward a few issues, like American relations with Communist China, it may last several years). While it exists, however, policy-makers have little latitude in their ability to alter American foreign policy significantly.

Officials engaged in formulating and administering American foreign policy evince a mixed reaction toward mass opinion. On one hand, they seldom derogate its central importance as a force setting the boundaries within which policy-makers must function. They know too that mass opinion often is the source of many *idealistic* elements in American foreign policy like the "Good Neighbor Policy" toward Latin American or the provision of American economic assistance to other countries. The American public has perhaps been more favorably disposed toward foreign aid for many years during the postwar period than has Congress. Yet mass opinion in America also harbors an underlying distrust and skepticism about diplomacy and officials engaged in it. The "public relations" of the State Department are in a chronic state of disrepair in the United States. Somehow, to many Americans, diplomacy seems difficult to reconcile with other ideas deeply entrenched in the national ethos—like the "common man," or freedom of speech and the press, or "straightforward dealings" among people. The image of the diplomat as the "striped-pants cookie pusher" who has lost touch with the "plain people" of America remains a part of national folklore. The State Department has not yet (and may never) overcome many of the antidemocratic qualities associated with the origins of diplomacy in aristocratic societies.

At the other end of the spectrum is *elite opinion*, or what is sometimes referred to as the "informed public." Enormous qualitative differences, as we have already observed, characterize the "opinions" expressed by the public and its components. These range from undisguised prejudice and emotional responses to the most careful and intelligent judgments, based upon a high degree of information about foreign policy issues. Although the State Department and White House cannot ignore mass opinion, policy-makers are often more interested in the reactions of elite opinion to existing or proposed policies. Elite opinion represents the viewpoints of those individuals and groups in American life who are evidently interested in international relations, who keep abreast of important developments abroad, and who endeavor to arrive at thoughtful and reasonably objective conclusions about American relations with other countries. Individuals in this category keep themselves informed by reading *The New York Times* or other good metropolitan newspapers; they belong to organizations like the Foreign Policy Association, the Council on Foreign Relations, the League of Women Voters, and other groups whose main purpose is *understanding* foreign and domestic policy more fully; they read books and periodicals devoting attention to global developments and their implications for the United States; they attend lectures and seminars; they express their views in letters to newspapers, Congress, the White House, and the State Department; they travel abroad; they occasionally attend conferences dealing with international questions. In brief, this segment of public opinion can usually be counted upon to give foreign policy the time and attention it deserves, to acquire the background necessary to develop enlightened viewpoints about it, and to approach external problems with as much detachment as can be found among any groups in American life.

Traditionally, the State Department has leaned heavily upon elite opinion in policy formulation; and until the 1960s, a generally good rapport existed between the agency and this stratum of the public. From the ranks of elite opinion, the State Department often drew "consultants" to advise it on selected aspects of foreign policy. From time to time, the President would appoint a committee of distinguished citizens to investigate some problem in foreign relations and report its findings to him. Not only did this technique apprise the Chief Executive of what intelligent and informed Americans thought about the policies of their government; another result (in some cases, possibly the principal goal) was to eliminate (or at least mute) charges that American policy had become a purely partisan program identified with the incumbent administration. For its part, the elite public has customarily been more prone than any other group to defend the State Department to its critics, to call attention to the complexities of foreign policy that are often poorly understood by ordinary citizens, and to accept the idea that America's policy alternatives in dealing with the outside world are usually much more restricted than most citizens realize.

By the early 1960s, however, much of this traditional rapport between elite opinion and foreign policy officials had begun to evaporate in the heat of dissension over the Vietnam War. Many individuals and groups forming part of the informed public had become "alienated" from the State Department and the White House and were now in the vanguard of the administration's critics. This development could be explained to some degree as arising from personal antipathy toward President Lyndon B. Johnson and (to a lesser extent) his Secretary of State Dean Rusk. Yet in the view of some commentators this explanation was inadequate to account for the alienation of groups like the American intellectuals—who not only objected to President Johnson's leadership at home and abroad, but who also were clearly out of sympathy with many of the fundamentals of American foreign policy, as these had evolved since World War II. Agreeing with many of the criticisms made by spokesmen like Senator J. William Fulbright, a significant number of intellectuals demanded a sweeping re-examination of American foreign policy, to be followed by radical changes in the country's overseas commitments and programs; concurrently, and as a necessary preliminary to improvement in American relations with other countries, the group demanded a kind of national repentence and renunciation of the "arrogance of American power." Elite opinion, Smith Simpson has written, "has expressed more and more frequently the opinion that the Department is lagging far behind the times."[13] In a curious reversal of roles, by the 1970s, the policies of the United States in Southeast Asia and other settings were likely to have greater support in mass opinion than among the well-informed segments of society.[14]

A third classification recognized by policy-makers is *group opinion*. The American "public" consists of an almost infinite number of groups, which are themselves often fragmented and factionalized. Among these, those based upon *occupational status* are perhaps most consistently concerned with foreign affairs, in large part because members of such groups see a connection between their individual and family welfare and the nation's activities abroad. Yet other groups are also active in at least selected aspects of foreign relations. Veterans' organizations, for example, take a keen interest in national defense policy; ethnic minorities are interested in American policies affecting relations with the "old country" or nations like Israel.

The dominant characteristic of group opinion is that it is devoted to a particular point of view, which it seeks to have reflected in national policy. Such groups exist, and often maintain an elaborate public relations organization, to protect and promote the special interests of their members. Thousands of lobbyists representing interest groups are active on Capitol Hill; in recent years, lobbying directed at the executive branch, or aimed at creating a "grass roots" expression of public opinion in the states and localities, has also become routine. All interest groups operate upon a common premise: that their goals and those of the American society as a whole are equivalent. They equate their special interests with the "national interests" of the United States. Groups favoring a higher tariff are convinced that the "prosperity of the nation" depends upon it (while groups advocating lower tariffs believe the same thing). Groups calling for a reduction in defense expenditures are certain that the well-being of the American society requires it (as are groups favoring higher expenditures for national security). If the State Department should, and does, listen to the demands of special interest groups, it is also obliged to keep in mind that the opinions they express are not necessarily identical with American public opinion.[15]

Traits of American Opinion on Foreign Policy

Studies of public opinion have focused upon certain traits or qualities of public sentiment about international relations which are of genuine interest, both to students of American government and to policy-makers. These qualities form part of the normal public opinion background against which policies must be formulated and administered. Admittedly, public opinion is not static or frozen; it is responsive to events, and it can be influenced by officials themselves who seek to create a more receptive opinion environment for their policies and programs. Nevertheless, investigations of the American society's attitudes have uncovered a number of relatively durable and consistent traits characteristic of public sentiment.

As a rule, we have already observed, Americans give foreign relations relatively low priority vis-à-vis domestic policy in terms of their most urgent concerns. If Americans are perhaps becoming more interested in developments abroad, this trend is a recent and gradual one. The society's historic preoccupation with internal pursuits (in the belief that these were more intimately associated with "the good life") continues to be a deeply ingrained tradition.

Another noteworthy characteristic of American opinion on world affairs is its *low level of information and understanding* about problems outside

America's borders. Nearly every commentator on public opinion in the United States has underscored this reality. In poll after poll, a distressingly high percentage of people (routinely running up to 25 percent, but sometimes reaching 50 percent or more) either has "no opinion" about the issue concerned or cannot answer the most elementary questions about external problems. A study published in 1949 cited data showing that, as a generalization, 30 percent of the American people were *totally unaware* of a given international event or issue; 45 percent might be aware of the event, but they could not be regarded as really "informed" about it; and only 25 percent were aware of developments in the external world and possessed reasonably enlightened opinions about them.[16] In the late 1940s, only 14 percent of Americans polled could identify and explain the purpose of the Marshall Plan for aiding European recovery.[17] In the same period, a poll in Cincinnati revealed that only 30 percent of the respondents were able to give an elementary explanation of the purposes for which the United Nations was established; only 1 percent could correctly answer six simple questions about it.[18] This poll was followed by a six-month educational campaign in the city to familiarize citizens with the UN, but a later study found that public understanding of the organization had undergone little significant improvement.[19]

Many commentators are convinced that public enlightenment on foreign policy issues is slowly rising. The steady advancement in educational levels in the United States—along with the nation's continuing involement in global affairs—makes this a natural expectation. The tendency of American public opinion during the Vietnam War, for example, to shun extremism in favor of a more balanced, "middle-of-the-road" position in support of American policy, lends credence to this view. The general public apparently realized (better than some members of the supposedly "well-informed public") that simplistic solutions to this complex struggle offered very little promise of achieving America's goals or protecting its vital interests.[20]

Yet contrary tendencies also exist which may pose serious obstacles to growing public enlightenment. Foreign affairs are, in some aspects at least, becoming *increasingly complex*, often defying intelligent understanding even by members of the "informed public." Recent examples include the national debate over the antiballistic missile (ABM) system—the intricacies of which divided scientists and other experts inside and outside the government; disarmament negotiations (which included a host of complicated questions, like how to establish and operate a viable system of inspection and control); tariff discussions involving the United States and the European Economic Community (EEC) or the industrialized and developing nations; and innumerable issues associated with the concept of "limited war" (like the precise relationship between indigenous nationalist forces and Communist-instigated revolutionary campaigns). It is at least arguable whether the level of public understanding about foreign affairs generally can and will keep pace with, and eventually surpass, the rate at which international issues today are coming to require expert knowledge as a basis for forming intelligent opinions. This tendency toward a growing complexity in the issues has also occurred against a background of mounting and frustrating international crises. The effect may be to "benumb" the American public, causing it to tire of being confronted with one crisis after another, and driving it into a kind of frustrated apathy toward developments in the outside world.

At any rate, recent studies have revealed conclusively that American public opinion on foreign policy issues *remains* qualitatively poor and unsophisticated. In 1964, for example, it was found that 25 percent of the people did not even know that China was governed by a Communist regime; the same percentage, incredible as it appears, were unaware that America was involved in hostilities in Vietnam; a Gallup poll indicated that around two-thirds of the American people admitted they regularly paid little or no attention to events in Vietnam. In the same period, some 25 percent of the population could not identify the North Atlantic Treaty Organization (NATO), and close to 60 percent of the public was ignorant of the fact that the United States belonged to it. On the basis of such findings, Free and Cantril have classified American opinion on Foreign affairs as follows:

Well informed on foreign policy issues	—26%
Moderately well informed	—35%
Uninformed	—39%

(While it may not be conclusive, a comparison of this study with the one cited earlier shows an *increase* in the category of Americans who fall into the "uninformed" class.)[21]

Another interesting trait of contemporary American opinion—one which marks a sharp break with the nation's tradition down to World War II—is the disappearance of significant *sectional* or geographical differences in the people's attitudes. We shall have more to say about this phenomenon at a later stage. Here, it is sufficient merely to note that, with rare exceptions, sectional viewpoints have receded as forces significantly affecting public attitudes on foreign relations.[22]

Public opinion in the United States with respect to foreign affairs is also marked by the presence of *numerous incongruities and inconsistencies* in the attitudes of citizens. The nonideological tendency of the American people is a fact too well known to require documentation. Americans tend to shun elaborate and highly structured philosophical systems; their frame of mind is nearly always eclectic, pragmatic, and attuned to "one problem at a time." Accordingly, their attitudes about international relations tend to be unstructured and fragmented. Taken collectively, their views defy arrangement into a logical system or a consistent philosophy. Americans, for example, have tended to *support* foreign aid programs by their government throughout most of the postwar period. Yet they often *oppose* the conditions (like higher taxes, or fewer restrictions on spending dollars abroad) required to make such programs successful.

A different kind of incongruity is the almost total *absence* of any correlation between the American people's viewpoints toward internal and external policies. Labels like "liberal" and "conservative" or "right-wing" and "left-wing" have little meaning, insofar as attitudes toward a range of global issues are concerned. An "internationalist" (and we shall not attempt to define that elusive term) may be as politically conservative as an "isolationist." Even traditional party labels signify little in defining American sentiments toward other countries. The differences between the Democratic and Republican parties on foreign policy questions have become less and less distinct.[23]

With this general background on American public opinion as it relates to foreign affairs, let us turn now to an examination of a specific case illustrating the key role sometimes played by public opinion in the formulation of national policy. The case will highlight many of the generalizations made about public opinion thus far; it will emphasize also a number of unique features. The case chosen for analysis is American policy toward China in the postwar period.

PUBLIC OPINION AND SINO–AMERICAN RELATIONS

The Over-all Pattern of Postwar Relations

With over 700 million people, China contains around one-fifth of the population of the world. Although that country's designation as a Great Power at the end of World War II (when China was awarded one of the five "permanent" seats in the UN Security Council) was largely honorary and a tribute to its war effort, since 1949 China's Communist leaders have been determined to make this great-power status a reality. China, Mao Tse-tung once declared, "has stood up." When it did so, its bulk cast an ominous shadow over adjacent countries in Asia. By the 1960s, Peking was

contesting with both Washington and Moscow for leadership, not only in Asia itself but in parts of the Arab world and Africa. Policy-makers in the Soviet Union and the United States alike found themselves preoccupied with China's aims and capabilities. Officials in America found that many issues in global affairs involved China. How extensive was the Chinese commitment in the Vietnam War? And how "limited" were North Vietnam and the Viet Cong in settling the war, because of ties with the Chinese mainland? How active was China in fomenting revolutionary movements in nearby countries like Laos, Burma, and Thailand? In formulating national security policy, American officials increasingly took account of China. What were the implications of China's growing nuclear arsenal and its expanding (if still fairly primitive) ballistic missile system? How successful would Peking be in weakening America's long-standing ties with Japan? Would Japan gradually gravitate toward mainland China's orbit? Was an over-all *détente* in Asia—perhaps the most unstable region in the world throughout the postwar period—possible without some kind of reconciliation between Red China and the United States? On their side, Chinese policy-makers seemed no less concerned with the United States. "American imperialism" in their view was the root cause of most of China's problems, from economic setbacks, to China's quarrel with India, to the deterioration in Sino–Soviet relations.

Yet if relations between the United States and China were regarded on both sides as pivotal, the remarkable fact was that for over two decades these relations remained turgid and frozen. Under Mao Tse-tung, the Chinese Communist movement finally defeated the rival Nationalist forces under Chiang Kai-shek in 1949. Ever since, contacts between America and China were characterized by tension, ill-will, and in some instances violence or the threat of violence. Normal diplomatic relations between the two countries were almost totally lacking (although American and Chinese representatives occasionally exchanged viewpoints in Warsaw); cultural and informational exchange between them was virtually nonexistent; trade and commerce had come to a standstill (with the United States still trying to maintain an embargo on trade with China); China's absence from the United Nations meant that some 20 percent of mankind was unrepresented in the world forum. Most crucially, the over-all atmosphere of Sino–American relations was still characterized by mutual suspicion and distrust, ongoing polemical exchanges (especially by Chinese propagandists), and until the early 1970s no evident inclination in either Peking or Washington to change the state of affairs appreciably.

What forces and events had produced a condition which (in the bureaucratic phrase) seemed so "counterproductive" for all concerned? A discussion of the substantive issues engendering Sino–American controversy must be reserved for a later chapter.* Here our interest is confined to the role of public opinion in shaping the policy of the United States toward Communist China in the postwar period. Many variables obviously influenced that policy. Among them, however, few were consistently more important than the force of public opinion in the American society. As always, of course, public opinion and events abroad interacted. Awareness of events among Americans produced certain public sentiments; this opinion played a role (in the case of policy toward China, often a decisive role) in determining national policy; this policy in turn gave rise to new events, which once more affected public attitudes. Although there is nothing unusual about this cycle, with regard to American foreign policy toward China the impact of public opinion was singularly influential. It would be necessary perhaps to go back to the years before World War II —when President Roosevelt sought to evolve a viable American policy for dealing with the rising Axis menace—to find an instance when public sentiment played so decisive a role.†

Why did American foreign policy toward China after 1949 lend itself to unusually massive influence by public opinion? To answer that question, some background on Sino–American relations is needed. Even today, many public attitudes toward China—and, what may be even more important, most of the *intensity* of American feeling toward that country—derives from the prewar period.

American Images of China

More than nearly any other country, China historically has occupied a very special place in the American mind. Ties between the American and Chinese societies go back to colonial times: The American ship *Empress of China* established the first commercial links between the two countries in 1784. From that time on, the "China trade" acted as a powerful magnet attracting Yankee businessmen (as it does for some American business firms today). Many Americans entertained fanciful notions about the profits to be derived from the Chinese market.** One of America's

best-known foreign policy principles before World War II— the "Open Door policy" toward China, proclaimed at the end of the nineteenth century—was designed to guarantee American trading interests equal treatment in the face of British, French, Russian, and other efforts to establish preferential positions on the mainland.

The early nineteenth century also witnessed the beginning of perhaps the most influential movement affecting Sino–American relations for decades thereafter. This was the *American missionary enterprise,* sponsored in time on a massive scale by Protestant and Catholic churches. By the 1930s, American religious organizations had a larger number of missionaries in China than in any other country.[24] The missionary impact upon China was profound, in both its beneficial and deleterious consequences. Throughout China, missionaries built schools and hospitals (often the only ones available to the Chinese masses); they distributed books, translated Western literary works into Chinese, and served as a major "Westernizing" influence; in countless ways (much as China's current leaders would deny it), missionaries manifested deep concern for the Chinese people, by such measures as trying to uplift the status of women and opposing the "binding" of children's feet (which produced deformities). The primary missionary goal—which, on balance, was a failure—was to convert the Chinese to Christianity, inducing them to desert their "heathen" and primitive customs, such as ancestor worship. A significant number of Chinese were in fact converted, but an undisclosed number also fell into the category of "rice Christians"—that is, those who ostensibly embraced Christianity in order to gain access to missionary-operated schools and health centers. As for the mass of Chinese society, it became clear in time that it was largely unmoved by missionary entreaties.

More relevant for our purposes was the impact of missionary viewpoints about China on American public opinion. In time, there was scarcely a church in America that did not wholly or partially support some kind of missionary enterprise on the Chinese mainland. This meant that literally millions of Americans were interested in developments there (even while they were isolationist-minded toward other countries). Letters, articles, and books written by Chinese missionaries flooded the American scene; first-hand reports on conditions in China were delivered by missionaries "on leave" or those who had recently retired from service in China; religious publications were filled with accounts of the achievements and promise of missionary activities in far-off China. These sources flowed together to form a mighty stream of information (or misinformation), impressions, convictions, and mental images which became the basis for much of the American public's thinking about China down to the present

---

*The principal issues in American foreign policy toward China are analyzed more fully in Chapter 13.

†The role of American public opinion in the Roosevelt administration's policies during the late 1930s is discussed in a case study included in the second edition of *American Foreign Policy in the Nuclear Age* (New York: Harper & Row, 1965), pp. 132–137.

**One idea (perhaps apocryphal) which was popular during the hey-day of the Yankee clipper was that the Chinese could be induced to add an *inch* to the length of their shirttails; with millions of Chinese affected, this change would keep the textile firms of New England busy for years to come!

day. Lacking other sources about this distant civilization, the American people depended heavily upon missionaries. What the missionaries reported, in turn, more often than not coincided with what countless Americans *wanted* to believe about this ancient land. By the twentieth century —especially after the Chinese dynasty was overthrown by the Revolution of 1911, led by Sun Yat-sen—the missionary voice was often reenforced by the viewpoints of another group, consisting of American "political advisers" who went to China during the 1920s and 1930s. Assisting Dr. Sen and his successor, Chiang Kai-shek, to reorganize China politically along democratic lines, many of these advisers became convinced that, within a few years, China would emerge as the world's largest democracy—a fact which could be attributed in no small measure to American tutelage.

What were the leading elements in the viewpoints about China inculcated in the American mind from these sources? In general terms, the picture was of a vast country longing for deliverance from primitive religious and political customs; of a society where opportunities were boundless for the application of American ideals, energy, and humanitarian impulses; of a people who—under constant American direction—were making steady progress in the direction of modernity; and, cutting across all these assumptions, of a nation that was eternally grateful to the United States for its concerns and ministrations toward China (which faced only imperialistic designs from other foreigners). If, as events amply proved after World War II, the people of China themselves did not concur in this assessment, this fact seldom served as a deterrent to American optimism about developments there.

After 1900, missionaries comprised one of the largest and most influential elements in the group of "old China hands" upon which the State Department in Washington and American officials in China depended for advice. The humanitarianism often evident in America's approach to China— such as Washington's refusal to accept an indemnity after the Boxer Rebellion in 1900, or President Wilson's opposition to Japan's "Twenty-One Demands" made at the expense of China during World War I—undoubtedly owed much to genuine American concern about China and a pervasive conviction that a "special relationship" bound the American and Chinese societies. Japan's aggressive moves in Manchuria in 1931–1932 elicited a wave of official and public resentment in the United States; a new surge of Japanese expansionism after 1937 intensified the anti-Japanese sentiment in the United States. Overwhelming American sympathy for China produced a hardening in Japanese–American relations and led Japanese officials to their fateful decision to attack Pearl Harbor on December 7, 1941.

The emergence of Chiang Kai-shek in the late 1920s as the leader of the Kuomintang party seemed to Americans to presage a new future for the Chinese society. Chiang (like Sun Yat-sen before him) had accepted Christianity; he was dedicated to modernization, often with the assistance of American advisers; he subscribed to the idea of "democracy" (although later events, along with his own writings, made it clear his conception of it differed fundamentally from Western models). Madam Chiang also did much to cement more cordial Sino–American relations. Educated in the United States, she was perhaps Nationalist China's most effective publicity agent in arousing favorable American opinion. Her visit to America during World War II, for example, contributed greatly to Sino–American amity. In the 1930s also, Americans were becoming more "China-minded" because of the activities of certain novelists. A prominent example was Pearl Buck, whose *The Good Earth* (1931) and other novels depicting life in China sold widely in the United States. Such books supplied a dimension often lacking in the reports of missionaries and political officials: They focused upon the lives of ordinary Chinese.*

The Wartime Experience

After the Japanese attack on Pearl Harbor in 1941, Sino–American relations remained close, if sometimes strained by wartime developments. Throughout the war, American opinion remained highly sympathetic to China; the "heroic" struggle put up by the Chinese against Japanese aggression received wide publicity in the United States. The American government (which early in the war had agreed with its allies to give the European theater priority over the Pacific) sent troops, supplies, and advisers to Chiang's government in Nanking, although the magnitude of this effort seldom satisfied either Chiang or some of his American advisers.

*The student who is interested in studying Ameican attitudes toward China before the Communist victory in 1949 is referred to the illuminating analysis by Harold R. Isaacs, *Scratches on Our Minds: American Images of China and India* (New York: John Day, 1958). Briefer treatments are John K. Fairbank, *The United States and China*, rev. ed. (New York: Viking, 1962), pp. 106–128, 146–161, 246–274; C. P. Fitzgerald, *The Chinese View of Their Place in the World* (New York: Oxford University Press, 1964), pp. 27–36; and Franz Schurman and Orville Schell, *The China Reader: Imperial China* (New York: Random House, 1967), pp. 269–282. A skillful novelist can sometimes portray the kind of American frame of mind we have described toward China better than an essayist. For a fascinating fictional account, written by an author who spent several years in China, see the novel by the late Richard McKenna, *The Sand Pebbles* (New York: Harper & Row, 1962). The impact of Western "advisers" to the government of China for a period of some 350 years has been appraised in a recent study by Jonathan Spence, *To Change China: Western Advisers in China, 1620–1960* (Boston: Little, Brown, 1969).

Yet fissures were beginning to open in the wall of Sino–American solidarity and friendship. Americans knowledgeable in Asian affairs—like General Joseph W. Stilwell (Chiang's American Chief of Staff)—developed a strong aversion to China's President and his Kuomintang movement.[26] Often reenforced by the reports of other Americans in China, Stilwell's conviction was that under Chiang China had lapsed into a morass of corruption and profiteering (often at America's expense); censorship and oppression increasingly marked China's political life; the country's economic system was approaching collapse; inefficiency and personal aggrandizement had become institutionalized. (Other American military officers in China, like General Albert C. Wedemeyer, it ought to be noted, were much more favorably disposed toward Chiang's government.)

Against these disillusioning reports about a society from which Americans expected so much was set another China—one concerning which most Americans were totally ignorant. This was the Chinese Communist movement, led by Mao Tse-tung, which (after the "Long March" of 1934 to escape Kuomintang suppression) was centered in Yenan, in northwest China. Only a small minority of Americans were aware that since the early 1930s China had been engaged in *two conflicts concurrently*. One was the familiar struggle against Japanese imperialism. The other was an internal political contest between Chiang's Kuomintang party and Mao's Communist party. During World War II, the first real American consciousness of this latter conflict began to emerge. A number of American observers visited Communist-ruled China during the war; their articles and books introduced this aspect of China's life to at least better-informed American opinion. One report (still useful for background on China's recent history) was Edgar Snow's *Red Star Over China* (1937).* Snow and other commentators visiting Yenan drew a sharp contrast between the two regimes contesting for leadership. China under Chiang seemed to be gravitating toward rule by a self-seeking political elite, indifferent to the problems of pervasive corruption, economic stagnation, and despotism. In Yenan, however, many observers discovered the kind of disciplined, honest, dedicated, and seemingly efficient political system they felt was lacking in the South. Mao's Communist forces were concurrently resisting the Japanese and carrying out overdue changes in a society long burdened with ancient customs impeding progress. Chinese Marxists gave particular attention to land reform (leading some observers to conclude that they were only or mainly "land reformers"). At this stage, Mao and his followers expressed good will toward the United States and evinced a desire only to participate in (not dominate) China's political life. Yet down to the time of his defeat, Chiang Kai-shek refused to accept American suggestions that he form a coalition government including his Marxist opponents.

The Trauma of Communization

The end of World War II witnessed a renewal of the civil strife that had gripped China since the 1930s. Several efforts by the United States to effect a reconciliation between rival Chinese political forces failed. Even while it tried to promote political stability, Washington supported Chiang Kai-shek's government. After the war, the United States expended more than $2 billion in Chiang's behalf; his troops were transported to North China by American ships and planes, and American military advisers endeavored to assist his commanders in the field. As the months passed, however, the military, economic, and political position of Chiang's regime became more and more hopeless. A detailed discussion of the reasons why the Nationalist government lost the civil war is beyond our scope. It must suffice to say that, despite vast military and other forms of aid from the United States, Nationalist troops proved no match for their Communist adversaries in the field. Inflation destroyed the economic stability of Nationalist-controlled China. Most crucially, perhaps, Chiang's regime proved unable to hold the allegiance of the masses; and as its popularity fell, the government resorted increasingly to terrorism and police-state methods.

By the end of 1949, this chapter in China's history had been closed. Defeated in one engagement after another, Chiang's regime fled to the island of Formosa where (not without a new wave of terror against the native Formosans) it established the Chinese government-in-exile, or what came to be called the Republic of China on Taiwan (the island's Chinese name). Mainland China was now in Communist hands. During this period of aggressive Marxism, the Sino–Soviet axis appeared to confront the United States and its supporters with the most ominous victory by "international Communism" witnessed since the Bolshevik Revolution.

To assert that the communization of China was a traumatic event for the American people would be to understate the matter. It would be difficult to conceive of an episode in the nation's diplomatic history in which popular expectations were so much at variance with reality. On the basis of their information and understanding down to 1949, Americans had anticipated the emergence of a united, progressive, and democratic Chinese government that was prepared to cooperate with the great powers (particularly with the United States) in behalf of a new international order. In-

*Published initially by Random House in New York, Snow's account subsequently became available in paperback edition.

stead, the United States found itself confronted with a totalitarian political system that was cooperating with the Soviet Union to construct a monolithic political structure at home and to export aggressive Marxism abroad. American opinion toward Communism in China was in many respects even more adverse than it was toward Soviet Russia. Russia, after all, had never enjoyed the kind of "special relationship" with the United States that had characterized Sino–American relations. Americans had never entertained the hopes for Russian society that they had held out for the Chinese. Added to this was the fact that Mao Tse-tung's government soon began to rely on a continuing "hate America" campaign which set some kind of record in vilification and exaggeration.

Dominant Themes in Sino–American Relations After 1949

From 1949 down to the 1970s, Sino–American relations were cast in a mold of inflexibility and tiresome reiteration of policy dogmas. For America's part, public opinion (in some cases, official interpretations of public opinion) provided a major explanation. Policy-makers believed, in many instances undoubtedly correctly, that American public opinion toward China was highly adverse to any *détente* between the two countries; whatever their own viewpoints, officials saw themselves as prisoners of public sentiment, which would not sanction overtures by the United States to improve relations with mainland China.

Any reconciliation between China and the United States had to dispose of several specific issues. First, there was the question of formal diplomatic relations, involving the "recognition" of Communist China by the United States. Public opinion polls since the late 1940s have shown what Steele has described as a "generally consistent but variable opposition to diplomatic recognition of the Communist government" in China. A poll taken late in 1949 showed only 25 percent of the public in favor of recognition. Although this percentage more than doubled briefly after the Korean War, by 1964 a new poll showed 36 percent favored recognition, 39 percent opposed it, and 25 percent were undecided.[27] On this issue, as always, events affected public attitudes. It seemed likely, for example, that within a few months after the collapse of Chiang's government, the United States and Red China would move toward normal diplomatic relations. American public opinion (especially if it had been carefully prepared by officials in Washington) might at least have tolerated this move. But for many years to come, this prospect was killed by the Korean War, particularly by Red China's entry into that conflict late in 1950. Now Chinese and American troops fought each other directly. China's incorporation of Tibet in 1951 added to American anxieties. A decade later, Chinese troops attacked the Republic of India, arousing new apprehensions in the West about Peking's intentions. In the years that followed, as the United States became deeply involved in a frustrating war in Vietnam, China was again regarded as a primary threat to American security, more dangerous in some respects than the U.S.S.R.

A second and related issue is Communist China's membership in the United Nations. On this issue too American public opinion has shown a fairly consistent pattern of stability *against* Red China. A poll taken in 1953, for example, revealed that some three-fourths of the respondents opposed China's admission to the UN; a decade later, this percentage had fallen (to some 53 percent) but was still negative. Yet American opinion heavily opposed the idea, advocated by pro-Chiang groups within the country, that the United States should withdraw from the UN if Red China gained admission.[28]

Trade and commerce with China has been a third issue dividing the two countries. The China trade, we need to remember, was the earliest force arousing American interest in the country. Postwar studies of public opinion have yielded some interesting results. The percentages of Americans favoring and opposing trade in *nonstrategic* commodities* have been approximately equal, giving no clear sense of the public's position. Opinion among groups in the United States that opposed such trade has been held with relatively high intensity, whereas those favoring expanded trade have held their views with considerably less intensity.[29] Under these conditions (and considering that the government's position has been against an expansion in trade ties), the views of the former group are perhaps more influential.

Fourth, a sharp change in American opinion toward Chiang Kai-shek's regime on Formosa has occurred over the past two decades. Although there was overwhelming support for Chiang before, during, and right after World War II, American opinion has become less enamored of, and even hostile toward, his government. Chiang's often avowed goal of "returning to the mainland" finds no support in American public thinking, particularly if (as seems certain) Chiang counts on active intervention by the United States to achieve his aim. On one point, however, American opinion has remained fairly stable: In 1964, as on many occasions earlier, a majority (62 percent) of the American people believed that the United States should continue to protect Formosa against incorporation by Communist China.[30] Since one

*Down to the early 1970s, the United States government had embargoed *all* trade by Americans with mainland China; and it had endeavored (with little success) to get its cold war allies to follow the same course.

of the outstanding issues between Washington and Peking remains the disposition of Formosa, Americans countenanced no change in the island's status detrimental to Chiang's interests.

On a fifth issue—re-establishing contacts and communications between the two societies—opinion studies in America have again highlighted some striking ambivalences in the public mind. Although American policy-makers believed themselves to be locked in to their present position on China by public opinion, on this issue at least the general public's attitudes were highly flexible. After examining a series of public opinion polls, Steele has concluded that

. . . if there is any question of China policy on which there is overwhelming agreement in all our public opinion samplings, it is on the desirability of increased communication between the American and Chinese peoples.

Beginning in 1957 (when there existed the possibility that newsmen might be exchanged between China and America), down to the mid-1960s, public sentiment in the United States has overwhelmingly approved expanded contacts between the two societies. Americans have likewise favored negotiations with Chinese representatives on issues dividing them. Even during the Vietnam War, the American people were well disposed toward the idea of Sino–American discussions.[31]

Pervading all these specific sources of tension between China and the United States, however, has been *a general apprehension* in the United States concerning Red China's intentions and capabilities. Steele has concluded: "Communist China has succeeded Soviet Russia in American eyes as our 'most dangerous enemy.' " This shift in American attitudes dates from the mid-1960s; it is apparently shared by the general public and by members of the "elite public." Recent studies have indicated that many of the iniquitous features Americans earlier identified with the Soviet Union (e.g., a tendency toward barbarous behavior, hostility toward the United States, and warlike impulses) are now associated with Communist China.[32] For China, there is another anxiety which (though seldom mentioned publicly or officially) is probably present in the American mind. That is the ancient specter of the "Yellow Peril": China's vast multitudes may someday engulf all of Asia, perhaps Russia, and then the world!

Pressure-Group Activity and China Policy

Thus far, we have concentrated primarily upon the attitudes of the general public toward relations with Communist China. A highly significant aspect of this problem in American foreign policy, however, has been the role of *group opinion*—

particularly by groups opposing any normalization of Sino–American relations. Resistance to change in American foreign policy toward Red China has come from a vocal, active, and sometimes extremely influential organization loosely called the "China Lobby." Actually a collection of organizations and individuals deeply concerned about China (a kind of group of groups, as it were), the China lobby has been active since the late 1940s in influencing official and public opinion in the United States. Consisting of "old China hands," former military officers, admirers of Chiang Kai-shek, militantly anti-Communist groups, certain writers and publishers, members of Congress, ex-missionaries, and other religious groups, this lobby has firmly resisted efforts to arrive at a *détente* with Red China. During some periods, the activities of the China lobby have unquestionably been supported by, and coincided with, public relations campaigns carried out by the Nationalist Chinese Embassy in Washington.* Gradually, as many of its founders died or retired, the China lobby's activities were taken over by a new group whose aims were more or less identical. This was the Committee of One Million (Against the Admission of Communist China to the United Nations)' For over twenty years after 1949, these organizations carried on propaganda operations designed to prevent any fundamental change in American policy toward China. In articles and news reports, films, radio and TV programs, advertisements in major newspapers, public lectures, and other media, the public was presented with propaganda designed to preserve close ties between the United States and Chiang Kai-shek's regime on Formosa. Executive policy-makers were continually reminded of the lobby's opposition to any attempt to improve relations with mainland China. Legislators expressing viewpoints contrary to the lobby's position were promptly made the the the target of its activities (perhaps a "grass-roots" publicity campaign directed against them in their districts or states).[33]

Judged by the results such groups have achieved during the past two decades—chiefly, the absence of any perceptible change in American foreign policy toward Mao Tse-tung's regime —the lobbying activities of these groups have unquestionably been successful. Down to the 1970s, a President could expect that the lobby's operations posed a real obstacle to any substantial modification in national policy toward Red China

---

*Considerable light upon the lobbying and "public relations" campaigns sponsored in the United States by Chiang Kai-shek's regime on Formosa after 1949 was shed by the hearings conducted by the Senate Foreign Relations Committee in 1963. For the evidence presented to the committee, see Senate Foreign Relations Committee, *Activities of Non-Diplomatic Representatives of Foreign Principals in the United States*, Part 7. 88th Congress, 1st Session, 1963.

—or, what may be even worse, to a public re-examination, in an atmosphere of reasonable objectivity, of the pros and cons of existing policy. Yet in acknowledging the role of the China lobby and the Committee of One Million in affecting official and public attitudes, it is also possible to *overemphasize* their influence and to fall into the error of thinking that public policy was in effect *dictated* by special interests. Critics of America's involvement in Vietnam and its policies in Asia generally are especially apt to rely upon a kind of demonological explanation of the stalemate in Sino–American relations, attributing it almost exclusively to pressure-group machinations.

Conceding that the influence of the China lobby upon American foreign policy has been great, it is necessary to recognize certain special circumstances prevailing in this case that have enhanced the group's influence and created a highly favorable environment for its activities. For one thing, other groups not directly concerned with the problem of China—like the American Legion and other veterans' organizations, the CIO–AFL, the American Farm Bureau Federation, the United States Chamber of Commerce, and many others—have basically *supported* the militantly anti-Communist position of the China lobby. That is to say, very few groups in the American society with any real power or resources *favored* a radical change in existing policy toward China. The China lobby and groups allied with it, in short, had little or no effective competition in the marketplace of ideas. This meant that the kind of "equilibrium" among competing pressure groups normally present in American public life was almost totally absent with respect to China policy.

Moreover, an elementary principle of propaganda campaigns is that the most effective propaganda is that which re-enforces the pre-existing opinion tendencies of the group toward which it is directed. This is perhaps the real key to the success achieved by the China lobby and the Committee of One Million. For over twenty years, the predominant sentiment of the American people was opposed to reconciliation with Communist China by recognizing Mao's government, supporting its admission to the UN, or allowing Peking to gain control over Formosa. The traditions and mental images most American brought to bear on the problem of Red China strongly predisposed them in favor of the China lobby's viewpoints and against a policy reformulation. Added to this was the fact that, for most political candidates, little "political capital" could probably be won by public debates over policy toward China. The Americans who were really interested in the question comprised a small minority; and of these, most opposed the kind of policy changes or concessions (such as an agreement with Peking over the future of Formosa) that would almost

certainly be necessary to achieve a rapprochement with Mao Tse-tung's government. In brief, little incentive existed to modify current policy or even to discuss its adequacy publicly.*

The "Leadership" of Public Opinion

Throughout our discussion of public attitudes toward Communist China, the reader has perhaps noticed the relative absence of attention to efforts by the President, the Secretary of State, and other high-ranking policy-makers to "guide" or modify public thinking. The omission was not indeliberate. Efforts by successive administrations to lead public opinion on this issue have indeed been minimal. Steele's informative study of public opinion toward China concludes that there has for many years been "a kind of congressional paralysis," induced by fear of "a hostile public reaction," in regard to discussion of Sino–American relations. Officials in the executive branch have perhaps been even more reluctant to express their views on the subject publicly.[34] In rare cases when national leaders raised the question of China policy publicly, emotionalism was likely to displace calm, objective analysis of the issue.[35] It is interesting to note, for example, that the same kind of forthrightness and "no-holds-barred" criticism voiced in Congress toward America's involvement in Vietnam has seldom been expressed about American foreign policy toward Communist China. Most officials, Steele is convinced, view the question as "a can of worms which they would rather walk around than pry into"![36]

On several occasions since 1949, national leaders have appeared to be on the verge of changing (or at least raising the possibility of changing) American foreign policy toward China. In nearly every case, however, such initiatives proved abortive. A typical example was President Kennedy's known dissatisfaction with the condition of Sino–American relations. A former White House aide has written that Kennedy "considered the state of our relations with Communist China as irrational," and he "did not exclude the possibility of doing something to change them in the course of his administration." But like Presidents before him, Kennedy was also aware of "the uproar it

*One theory of pressure-group activity in the United States holds that: "What may be called public policy is actually the equilibrium reached in the group struggle at any given moment, and it represents a balance which the contending factions or groups constantly strive to weight in their favor. . . ." Congress, in this view, "referees the group struggle"; legislation merely "ratifies the victories of the successful coalitions. . . ." See The views of Earl Latham, as cited in Joseph Monsen, Jr., and Mark W. Cannon, *The Makers of Public Policy: American Power Groups and Their Ideologies* (New York: McGraw-Hill, 1965), p. 2. Whatever validity this theory may have depends upon the existence of groups on both (or all) sides of major policy issues—a condition largely absent in American policy toward China since 1949.

would cause at home" if he allowed America's long-standing opposition to a UN seat for China to be reversed or took other concrete steps to relieve tension between the two countries.[37] Another Kennedy assistant has written that the President was fully mindful of the importance of China; he informed himself in detail about the country's development under a Communist system. But he was deterred from altering American foreign policy significantly by the belief that "any American initiative now toward negotiations, diplomatic recognition or UN admission would be regarded as rewarding aggression," since Red China had recently attacked India's northern provinces. Kennedy nevertheless instructed the State Department to study Sino–American relations anew. Characterizing America's approach to China as one of "rigidity," Kennedy expressed the hope that ultimately some kind of normalization would take place between the two nations. A prerequisite to this development, he believed, was for the President to have "a friendlier Congress and more public understanding."[38] Whether because he felt this prerequisite was lacking, or for some other reason, Kennedy made no noteworthy effort during the early months of his administration to alter American policy.

Several months later, in the weeks just before President Kennedy's tragic death, the administration made a new attempt to reorient American policy toward China. Assistant Secretary of State Roger Hilsman scheduled a carefully prepared speech for delivery in San Francisco late in 1963. The basic theme of this address, in Hilsman's words, was that "the policy of the Kennedy administration was based on a willingness to reach an accommodation with the Chinese Communist regime," provided an important criterion was satisfied. This was that "the Chinese Communist regime was willing to modify its hostility in the same direction."* Abandoning the older Eisen-

hower–Dulles view that Communism in China was a passing phenomenon, Hilsman acknowledged that American policy no longer subscribed to this idea. The United States, Hilsman declared, was prepared to negotiate with any country, including Red China. He reiterated America's historic attachment to the Open Door principle, urging Americans and Chinese alike to adapt to new conditions and seek harmonious relations in a world of diversity. Delivered just after President Kennedy's death, the Hilsman speech was widely praised by those in America and overseas who looked forward to a less rigid American approach to China. Not unexpectedly, it was vigorously condemned by the China lobby and the Committee of One Million, which accused the administration of being "soft on Communism" and urged the American people to repudiate any proposed policy change.[39] The main point about this episode, however, is that as in several earlier instances, the main lines of American policy toward Red China underwent no discernible change.

To a degree perhaps unequalled by any other substantive problem in postwar American foreign policy, Sino–American relations have been devoid of initiatives by high-level policy-makers to educate American opinion or to prepare it for changes in a policy whose essentials remained unaltered for more than twenty years. Many observers believe this fact alone accounts for much of the inflexibility characterizing the American position toward Communist China.[40] What factors explain the passivity of executive policy-makers in this regard? One deterrent was unquestionably the painful recollection of the late 1940s and early 1950s, when the Truman administration was widely castigated for having "lost China" to Marxism and when morale in the State Department (some of whose members were viewed as having abetted Mao Tse-tung's victory) sank to perhaps its lowest point since World War II. Later administrations had no desire to revive this divisive episode, especially when other issues (like the Vietnam War) were engendering great public contention. Moreover, as we have already observed, the "timing" of new American efforts to resolve underlying differences with Red China

---

*At several points in our discussion of American foreign policy toward Red China it is possible that the impression has been that an improvement in Sino–American relations hinged entirely upon decisions made in Washington. This view is of course much too simple. It overlooks, for example, the role of the "hate America" campaign in Red China's own domestic and foreign policy. As Voltaire said about God, if "American imperialism" did not exist, it might have been necessary for Chinese policy-makers to invent it, since the evil designs of American "foreign devils" provided a convenient rationalization for the regime's failures at home and abroad. How ready were the leaders of mainland China to make the kind of concessions required to reach an accord with the United States? On a number of vital issues—China's determination to extend its hegemony over Formosa, its ongoing propaganda vituperations against America, its continued advocacy of revolution in non-Communist countries, its involvement in the Vietnam War—Peking gave no indication of a genuine *desire* to normalize its relations with the United States on a basis acceptable to American policy-makers.

Perhaps the most crucial source of disagreement be-

tween America and Red China in this period and afterward was the issue of Formosa. In this respect, Hilsman's speech marked less of a break in existing policy than might be supposed. For while he sought to promote greater Sino–American understanding, he was also careful to reiterate America's support for Chiang Kai-shek's regime on Formosa—thereby linking American policy again to the concept of "two Chinas." Time and again, however, policy-makers on the mainland had rejected a "two Chinas" formula for resolving the issue of representation in the UN or the matter of recognition by the United States. Judging from its public statements, Peking was determined sooner or later to incorporate Formosa within its Marxist system. See *The United States in World Affairs: 1963* (New York: Harper & Row, 1964), pp. 211–213.

was seldom propitious. Some new crisis—a threatened Chinese strike against Formosa, or the Chinese incursion into India, or an escalation of the conflict in Southeast Asia—intervened to frustrate any improvement in relations between the two countries.

A different kind of deterrent has been the apprehension, grounded in experience since 1949, that even if policy-makers risked the internal storm that might be precipitated by new overtures to Peking, there would be little assurance that their efforts would meet with anything more than ridicule and new polemical condemnations from Mao Tse-tung's government. Where was the evidence, many Americans might legitimately ask, that Red China itself actually *desired a détente* with the United States? There was considerable evidence to support the view that down to the 1970s, hostility toward the United States served a useful purpose for China's leaders.

The passivity of policy-makers in endeavoring to change the intensity and direction of public thinking about China policy undoubtedly stems from another consideration. Unlike President Roosevelt's efforts to educate public opinion about the Axis menace during the late 1930s, thus far executive, and for the most part legislative, opinion in America has not been convinced that a *radical* change of policy towards China is required. Even the Kennedy administration, it must be recalled, was unwilling to change American foreign policy significantly on specific issues like China's admission to the United Nations or America's defense commitments to Formosa. Presidents in recent years have been disinclined to use the resources of their office to modify public attitudes in large part because there was no noteworthy discrepancy between public thinking and their own thinking on the question of China. Faced with the continuing hostility of Red China toward the United States, the President and his subordinates have themselves been uncertain about the direction in which they desired public sentiment to move. Under these circumstances, any dialogue between the citizens and their leaders on the issue of Communist China has remained very limited and, for the most part, unoriginal.

GROUP OPINION AND AMERICAN FOREIGN POLICY

Students of the political process in the modern period have become keenly interested in the role of *groups* in policy formulation. To some social scientists, the public opinion that "counts," that really influences decision-making, is nearly always *group opinion.* Thus a recent study asserts that "today power to affect public policy rests mainly upon an individual's relationship to a major group or organization. Single individuals in this country,

unless affiliated with some power group, seldom influence the course of government."[41] Without necessarily subscribing to the view that *all* governmental activity is ultimately a function of group competition, or that groups are the only forces influencing national policy, it is important to recognize the role of groups in American national life and in the determination of America's relationships abroad.

American society is distinguished by the number of group associations that abound and the decisive part these groups often play in the political life of the nation. That America is a "nation of joiners" is a commonplace fact of unequalled significance for any understanding of American politics. Every American belongs to a number of groups: the family, the neighborhood, religious organizations, business associations and service clubs, labor unions, trade associations, political parties, and fraternal organizations. Besides these, he may be a member of a racial or national minority; his section of the country has distinctive viewpoints on at least some questions of public policy.

A central fact about the American, however, is not so much that he is a joiner, but that he belongs to a number of groups at once and that these create within him what the sociologists call "cross-pressures" in molding his opinions on contemporary issues. Kimball Young has defined a cross-pressure "as the operation of two or more determinants of opinion on the same individual or group."[42] Such cross-pressures are key factors in explaining an important and often bewildering characteristic of public opinion about foreign policy issues. This is the presence of fundamental *incongruities* in public attitudes. Polls have shown repeatedly, for example, that public viewpoints on foreign and related domestic problems are highly inconsistent and often contradictory.* Although there may be a number of significant explanations for this phenomenon, one surely is the fact of multigroup membership in American society. In arriving at his viewpoints about public policy issues, an individual often finds himself torn

---

*Such anomalies show up strikingly, for instance, with reference to public opinion about support for the domestic measures (such as higher governmental spending and increased taxes) needed to expand activities in foreign affairs. Conversely, studies have also shown that a substantial number of Americans would be classified as "isolationist–liberal," in that they believe in a comparatively high level of governmental welfare programs at home and will support them, but concurrently they are opposed to foreign aid programs abroad and other measures identified with an "internationalist" foreign policy. After surveying evidence available from polls, Key believed that an often crucial factor in shaping public viewpoints toward global affairs is the state of the domestic economy at any given time. Such incongruities are discussed at length in V. O. Key, Jr., *Public Opinion and American Democracy* (New York: Knopf, 1961), pp. 155–163.

by forces tending to pull or push his thinking in several different directions and to produce contradictions and anomalies in his attitudes toward a range of important questions.

Economic and Other Interest Groups

The distinguishing feature of American life, writes the sociologist Bradford Smith, is the "enormous proliferation of special-interest associations. . . ."[43] Political scientists have long regarded such groups as providing a useful complement to the nonideological two-party system within the United States. If special economic, regional, racial, religious, professional, and other interests are unable to get the two major parties to take strong and unambiguous positions on policy issues, they are able to express and agitate for their peculiar viewpoints through the thousands of pressure groups active within the nation. The role of interest groups in the American politico-governmental system is a vast and fascinating subject. Here, we shall look briefly at some of the principal interest groups active in foreign affairs, and identify certain problems that have special pertinence for the study of foreign relations.

It would be well-nigh impossible to enumerate or perhaps even to estimate the total number of pressure groups within the United States. Even if we could, highly subjective judgments would have to be made about the extent to which hundreds and perhaps thousands of organizations that might be interested in a narrow range of public issues really qualified as "pressure groups."* We may, however, get some idea of their multiplicity and variety by looking at a sampling of the groups that testified before the House Ways and Means Committee on the Trade Expansion Act of 1962, since trade bills are among those generating intense pressure-group interest and activity. The following represents only a small sampling among the groups represented:

For the Bill (sometimes with amendments)
  Small Business Administration
  International Telephone and Telegraph Company
  American Association of University Women
  United Automobile Workers
  American Veterans Committee
  Committee for a National Trade Policy

*One helpful study admits that "No one knows how many groups there are in America." Yet it cites various calculations that have been made showing the range of groups in American life. Such estimates range from only 60 groups that possess real political *influence*, to an upper limit of well over 50 million "spending units" in the population, as revealed by the census. One study showed that there existed 40,000 to 50,000 local labor groups and some 5000 local and national business groups. For more detailed discussion, see Donald C. Blaisdell, *American Democracy Under Pressure* (New York: Ronald, 1957), pp. 58–60.

  Cooperative League of the USA
  American Bankers Association
  Tobacco Institute of America
  League of Women Voters

Against the Bill (in whole or in part)
  National Machine Tool Builders Association
  Nationwide Committee on Import-Export Policy
  Hatters' Fur Cutters Association
  Fine Hardwoods Association
  Optical Manufacturers Association
  International Brotherhood of Operative Potters
  Synthetic Organic Chemical Manufacturers Association
  National Board of Fur Farm Organizations
  Rolled Zinc Manufacturers Association
  National Piano Tuners Association

SOURCE: *Congressional Quarterly Almanac* 18 (1962), 266–270.

This list, as is apparent, does not include some of the best-known and most influential interest groups in American political life. There are, in the first place, the "big three"—the clusters and coalitions representing agriculture, labor, and business. Three national organizations are active in behalf of farmers: The National Farmers Union, The National Grange, and The American Farm Bureau Federation. The Farmers Union is the smallest of the three (claiming a membership of one-quarter million farm families). Growing out of the Populist movement, the organization has, since its founding in 1902, advocated radical measures to protect farmers, especially those in the lower economic groups. Strongest in the Great Plains area and the Northwest, the Farmers Union takes a strong "internationalist" position toward such issues as American support for the United Nations, the development of world law, and the expansion of foreign aid. Not unexpectedly, in international trade policy it supports steps to safeguard farmers from the adversities of the world market.[44]

Established in 1867, the National Grange began as a social and fraternal movement; in time, it became the second largest group representing the interests of farmers, mainly in New England, New York, the Ohio Valley, and New Jersey. Toward most issues of public policy, the Grange takes a middle-of-the-road position. It has supported foreign aid programs overseas and the lifting of restrictions on international trade.[45]

Perhaps the best-known organization speaking in the farmers' behalf is the American Farm Bureau Federation, the largest, and in many respects most active, of the three groups. Founded in 1903, the Farm Bureau became particularly strong in parts of the South and Midwest. A factor setting it apart from other farm organizations has been its close ties with the Department of Agriculture and the department's "county agents" on the local level. The Farm Bureau is generally more conservative politically than the Farmers Union or the National Grange. Devoted to free enterprise and the competitive principle, the Farm Bureau opposes tariff restrictions on trade (although it has been apprehensive about the impact of the European Common Market upon the American economy); it is skeptical about expanding the activities of the United Nations and about America's reliance upon it; and it favors a high level of American military preparedness.[46]

Historically very great, the influence of the "farm bloc" upon national policy is perhaps declining. From an overwhelmingly rural society, America has now become mainly urban and suburban (farmers now constitute only about 10 percent of the population). Differences among agricultural interest groups often undermine unity within the agricultural community. Yet the agricultural segment still has an influence on the legislative and executive branches disproportionate to its numbers, in part because it has a relatively high degree of "access" to Congress and executive agencies, and because Americans still identify with many of the values and viewpoints associated with rural society.

Among groups representing the viewpoints of workers, the American Federation of Labor–Congress of Industrial Organization (AFL–CIO) is the most prominent and influential. Created by a merger between these two organizations in 1955, the AFL–CIO, it is important to note, is a *federation* of labor unions. Behind the façade of unity, a considerable divergence in attitudes and policies can still be detected. Of the more than 70 million members of the American labor force, some 17 million are affiliated with close to 200 national and international labor unions. However, in the recent period, labor unionism in the United States has suffered from declining membership and an often tarnished public image. An advancing standard of living, public aversion to revelations of corruption in labor's ranks, resentment that unions are often controlled "undemocratically," the accomplishment of many of labor unionism's traditional goals—such factors have often posed obstacles to labor's effectiveness as a pressure group.

The mainstream of the American labor movement has been (vis-à-vis its European counterpart) remarkably nonideological and pragmatic. It has tended to be concerned primarily with immediate goals, like higher pay and better working conditions, related chiefly to *domestic* policy. Yet in recent years, American unions have also become involved in international activities, developing contacts with unions in other countries and taking a lead in international labor organizations. Critics inside and outside the labor movement have accused the AFL–CIO of being too "conservative"

in its international policies (few groups, for example, are more outspokenly anti-Communist) and too closely identified with official American policy. Issues like international trade tend to divide labor organizations internally and generate disagreements among them, with some workers favoring government protection for domestic industry and other workers advocating liberalized trade. As a rule, the AFL–CIO has officially supported efforts to eliminate trade barriers.[47]

Because of the enormous resources available to them, it has long been thought that business groups were perhaps the most influential organizations in American public life. A study in 1962, for example, found that out of the 200 largest American corporations, 130 maintained lobbyists or "public relations" programs in Washington. Even more perhaps than agriculture and labor, the business community is divided and subdivided into literally thousands of large and small organizations and associations on a national, regional, and local basis. At the top are the two giants: the National Association of Manufacturers (NAM) and the Chamber of Commerce; the former has industry as its clientele, while the latter represents some 3400 local and state chambers. Another vocal business organization on the national level is the Committee for Economic Development (CED).

On international questions, business opinion is often distributed over a wide range. It can usually be counted upon of course to support an anti-Communist position on most issues; many business groups are included within the so-called "military–industrial complex" which seeks larger appropriations for national defense and the space program. Yet business opinion even on these issues is seldom monolithic. On other questions—like trade policy—it is even more fragmented, with exporters clashing with importers over tariff rates. Traditionally, business groups have tended to favor commercial expansion overseas. In the contemporary period, business interests on the West coast have urged the government to resume trade relations with Communist China.[48]

Nonoccupational Interest Groups

Within the space available, it is possible to do little more than mention a few of the more active nonoccupational groups influencing opinion about foreign relations. Earlier in this chapter, reference was made to the activities of the China lobby since 1949. This lobby (itself a coalition of disparate groups and individuals whose common bond was concern about America's China policy) was often supported by other interest groups or segments of them. Among these, veterans' organizations—particularly the American Legion—played a prominent role. Toward this issue, as toward many others, the Legion supported a militantly anti-Communist stance by the United States. Actively concerned with arousing public interest in the concept of "Americanism," with more than 3 million members and several thousand local posts, the Legion was often in a strategic position to bring its viewpoints to the attention of policy-makers and insist that governmental policy reflect them.[49]

Certain international issues often forge new interest-group coalitions or activate groups not directly interested in foreign policy questions. This situation occurred when the Zionist lobby—favoring the creation of a separate Jewish state in Palestine—emerged in the United States during and after World War II. Consisting of Jewish citizens and Zionist organizations, Protestants and Catholics who sympathized with Zionist goals, some labor organizations, and certain writers, editors, and publishers, this lobby has been extremely active in its effort to hold American policy on a pro-Israeli course.*

The Vietnam War focused attention upon another opinion stratum which, literally speaking, may not qualify as an "interest group," but whose viewpoints became more clearly identifiable in the 1960s. This is *intellectual opinion* in the United States. Little unanimity exists about the composition of this group; nor, by most criteria, could it really be regarded as a lobby. Still, this population segment reached a new level of "self-consciousness" during the Vietnam contest. From that experience, one commentator has concluded that "the intellectual lays claim . . . to moral authority over the intentions of political leaders"; acting as a kind of self-appointed critic of national policy, intellectuals have assumed much the same role discharged in earlier periods by priests and prophets (many of whom were also of course "intellectuals"). That large numbers of American intellectuals had become alienated from the makers of public policy during the 1960s seemed incontestable. As we observed earlier in the chapter, the State Department had become estranged from this influential element of the elite public, which in the past had tended to defend the department before the public at large.[50]

Ethnic communities have frequently provided intensive interest-group activity in the foreign policy process. As a rule, such groups are peculiarly sensitive to relations between the United States and the "old country." German–Americans, for example, perhaps played a disproportionate role in shaping American attitudes toward

Germany during the 1920s and 1930s.[51] Italian–Americans often derived a sense of pride from Mussolini's accomplishments in Italy before World War II; after the war, they were keenly interested in lenient treatment for Italy and the country's rapid reconstruction.[52] Americans of Eastern European and Russian origin have been at the forefront of anti-Communist movements in the United States and have often insisted that Washington adopt a "hard line" against Soviet expansionism.

Throughout American diplomatic history, few ethnic minorities have surpassed the Irish–Americans in the vigor (and sometimes the violence) of their demands. There were many Irish

> Who think that freedom must consist
> In proving points, with sticks and fists.[53]

Uncompromisingly anti-British and inherently suspicious of "perfidious Albion," Irish–Americans down to World War II could be counted upon to support any American policy directed against British interests and to oppose Anglo-American cooperation in ventures like the League of Nations.[54]

Although, by definition, individual ethnic minorities constitute a small fraction of the nation's total population, their influence upon public attitudes, and sometimes their impact upon national policy, is often enhanced by several factors. One is the *intensity* with which they hold and express their viewpoints. Another is their *strategic location politically.* Outstanding examples are the concentration of Jewish citizens in New York City and its environs and, in an earlier era, the strength of the Irish–American population in the Boston area. Still another factor enhancing the influence of such groups is that on a number of issues arising in American foreign relations (e. g., Soviet treatment of its Ukranian citizens or the provision of military aid to Israel) the bulk of the population neither knows nor cares strongly about the matter—thus ethnic groups that do feel deeply about it are the only "concerned" public.

Sectional Viewpoints and Foreign Policy

One of the most fundamental changes in public opinion in the United States has been *the decline of sectional viewpoints* toward foreign relations. During the nineteenth century, regional disparities in outlook were often pronounced. The Civil War, for example, stemmed in some measure from the clash between eastern and southern attitudes toward the tariff. Traditionally, the Midwest has been the center of isolationism in American opinion. The East coast has always been more concerned about, and interested in, European affairs than the West coast, where attitudes were more oriented toward developments in Asia.

*A great deal of information concerning the extent and nature of Zionist lobbying in the United States was made public by the Senate Foreign Relations Committee's investigation into propaganda and public relations campaigns in behalf of foreign governments and movements. See the committee's hearings, *Activities of Non-Diplomatic Representatives of Foreign Principals in the United States,* Part 12, 88th Congress, 1st Session, 1963.

"The impact of World War II," one student of American public opinion has written, "in large degree erased regional differences in mass opinion on broad foreign-policy problems."[55] Studies of public attitudes in recent years have shown that —in a society as increasingly mobile as the American—geographical location no longer accounts for significant differences in attitudes toward foreign policy issues.* Differences of degree can of course still be detected. The South, for example, may support a strong American defense posture more vocally than the East; or citizens of the West coast may be more interested in an American *détente* with Communist China than the Midwest. In the main, however, public opinion in the United States has become "nationalized" to a degree unknown to earlier periods.[56]

Lobbying by Foreign Interests

By the early 1960s, an increasingly widespread phenomenon involving public opinion and foreign policy was the extensive lobbying activities carried out within the United States by foreign countries or political groups. By 1963, these activities had become so widespread that they prompted a detailed investigation by the Senate Foreign Relations Committee.[57] Its inquiry divulged wholesale evidence of efforts by foreign interests to influence American public opinion and official viewpoints in a manner favorable to the cause advocated by such lobbies.† The problem, as defined by the chairman of the committee, Senator J. William Fulbright (Democrat of Arkansas), is that:

. . . in recent years there have been increasing numbers of incidents involving attempts by agents of foreign principals to influence the conduct of U.S. foreign policy using techniques outside normal diplomatic channels. Various

members of this committee have become disturbed by this trend which has been paralleled by an upsurge in the hiring within this country of public relations men, economic advisers, lawyers, and consultants in miscellaneous areas by foreign governments or groups acting in the interest of foreign governments. The tempo of this non-diplomatic activity has picked up in almost direct proportion to our Government's growing political, military, and economic commitments abroad.

Senator Fulbright, along with many other members of Congress, did not believe that such activities were necessarily wrong or that they were always opposed to the interests of the United States. In some instances (as in hearings before the U.S. Tariff Commission) opportunities were accorded foreign interests to be represented.* Yet, in general, the senator believed that the United States

. . . should have only one foreign policy, and that policy must . . . reflect our own interests. We should, however, be given the facilities necessary to distinguish between those activities which arise from genuine domestic interest in foreign policy and those which are inspired by foreign governments acting through paid U.S. citizens.[58]

Earlier investigations of the same problem had led Congress in 1938 to enact the Foreign Agents Registration Act, according to which paid agents of foreign principals were required to register with the Department of Justice and to disclose information about the nature of their interests and their finances. By 1960, some 500 such agents had registered as required. Even so, congressional and executive officials alike were convinced that many such agents active in prompting the cause of foreign interests had *not* registered; and, among those who did, some disclosed little useful information about the scope and nature of their activities in behalf of their clients.[59] The chief cause of legislative concern about lobbying by foreign principals therefore was that frequently the activities of such groups remained shrouded in secrecy. In company with their counterparts in

---

*Perhaps more than for other determinants of public opinion, or factors correlating with public attitudes, sectionalism interacted closely with other forces—the ethnic distribution of the population, income levels, educational attainment, religious orientations—in shaping the viewpoints of citizens. The "isolationism" of the Midwest, for example, could be partially explained by the larger than average number of German–Americans in that region. The South's well-known pro-British sentiments derived in some degree from the relatively large number of people in that region of British descent. As always, it is extremely difficult to demonstrate that geographical location alone is a decisive factor in shaping opinion toward the outside world.

†The evidence gathered by the Senate Foreign Relations Committee is voluminous. The interested student will find this a rich source of information on the problem, since the committee utilized its power to subpoena records not ordinarily available to other observers. Two secondary accounts are: Douglas Cater and Walter Pincus, "The Foreign Legion of U.S. Public Relations," *The Reporter* 23 (December 22, 1960), 15–22; and "Foreign Lobbyists: The Hidden Pressures To Sway U.S. Policy," *Newsweek* (July 30, 1962), 18–22.

*That the activities of individuals representing foreign interests are by no means always detrimental to the United States was indicated by Under Secretary of State George W. Ball, who told the committee on February 4, 1963, that foreign agents "can often serve as an interpreter of systems and habits of thought—as a medium for bridging the gulf of disparate national experiences, traditions, institutions, and customs." Sometimes, such individuals can be of "great use to the Department of State in explaining its own views" to other governments and foreign groups. Inherently, there is no reason why individuals representing other countries "should present any dangers to the integrity of American foreign policy." Senate Foreign Relations Committee, *Activities of Nondiplomatic Representatives of Foreign Principals in the United States*, 88th Congress, 1st Session, 1963, p. 11.

domestic affairs, pressure groups representing outside interests have cultivated the art of "indirect lobbying" into a highly ingenious, intricate, and surreptitious process. Primary reliance is placed upon "educational campaigns" to influence public opinion and prominent news media, in which the role of the lobbyist is often studiously concealed from the general public and from governmental officials. Occasionally, selected foreign policy issues elicit open and direct lobbying activities by individuals and organizations representing foreign interests. This occured, for example, in 1962, with respect to congressional consideration of a bill proposing to eliminate the premium the United States has traditionally paid on foreign sugar imports. The records of the Stnate Foreign Relations Committee reveal that

. . . foreign governments and foreign sugar interests hired more than 20 lobbyists, to our knowledge, some of them on straight salary, some with contingent fees [i.e., the lobbyist's fee depended upon the success of his efforts in defeating the bill]. The final legislation contained both the global concept [i.e., elements of the Kennedy administration's proposals] and the lobbyists' premium concept.[60]

Citing this as an illustration of the success sometimes achieved by such groups, Senator Fulbright was concerned that foreign governments and interests would come to believe that such lobbying campaigns are "an essential procedure if you are going to succeed in Washington. . . ." Other recent instances in which foreign lobbying has been more than ordinarily successful in creating a public or official atmosphere favorable to foreign clients include the generation of widespread support for interests supporting secessionist Katanga Province during the Congo crisis in the early 1960s, and sympathetic treatment by the American government of the claimants to ownership of alien property confiscated by the American government during World War II.[61]

As with domestic lobbying, it is always difficult, if not almost impossible, to "control" such pressure-group activities, or even to achieve the more limited objective of requiring such groups to disclose their activities so that citizens and officials alike are aware of the efforts by foreign interests to influence American opinion. Constitutional guarantees of free speech and the right of petition preclude stringent regulatory measures; and the line between "lobbying" and "public relations" or "education" remains so indistinct as to make it virtually impossible to discriminate meaningfully and legally between them. It can therefore be safely predicted that such lobbying activities will remain much like an iceberg: Those activities that became visible will constitute only a small proportion of those that remain clandestine and largely unknown to the American people and theiɪ officials.

POLICY AND OPINION: THE INTERACTION

Thus far in our discussion of the role of public opinion in the foreigɪ policy process, we have devoted attention only indirectly to a central question: "What is the impact of public opinion upon the formulation and administration of American foreign policy?" Even today, it has to be admitted, the question is a difficult one. Policy-makers themselves may often be unaware of the degree to which public sentiment affects their approach to other countries. Officials within the American governmeɪt differ concerning the *proper* role of public opinion in decision-making. Moreover, much greateɪ progress has been made in the postwar era in discerning *what* public opinion is on national policy issues than on how it is conveyed to policy-makers or in determining the precise role it plays in, let us say, the Nixon administration's policies toward Southeast Asia. No less difficult to determine is the extent to which officials *do not* propose a certain policy, or refrain from certain activities abroad, because of constraint by public opinicn. In some cases, their *conception* of public opinion also may differ markedly from the reality. Recognizing these and other qualifications, let us move on to examine the relationship between public sentiment and policy-making in foreign relations.

Official Efforts to Assess Public Opinion

Even in a democracy like the United States, the systematic study of public attitudes on external issues is a relatively recent phenomenon, dating from World War II. Officials before that time were not of course totally oblivious to public opinion. President Wilson's views on the subject were cited earlier in the chapter; during the 1930s, President Roosevelt was continually mindful of restrictions placed upon his freedom of action by public attachment to isolationism. Yet prior to World War II, policy-makers usually conceived of public opinion as a force to be led or "educated" to support desired steps (like America's entry into the League of Nations); if national leaders were induced to influence public attitudes, they felt little inclination to study and analyze data informing them of society's viewpoints. The change that has occured since World War II is highlighted by one commentator's remark that today, no government agency is more sensitive to public opinion than the Department of State.[62]

Several factors have played a part in this change. Foreign affairs were perhaps the last realm of governmental activity to become subjected to "democratization" (and many citizens perhaps believe that process has still not be carried far enough). The speed and global extent of modern communications have inevitably accelerated the interaction between the public and its leaders, greatly facilitating the exchange of ideas between them. Recent techniques for measuring and analyzing public opinion make possible the collection of data often unavailable in earlier periods. Above all, the vast change in the nature of America's overseas commitments since World War II dictated a new approach to public thinking about international problems. During the long era of isolationism, as one student has expressed it, American policies tended to be "mainly negative and hortatory."[63] Today, successful American policies require *positive public support,* perhaps over extended periods of time, for their success. Moreover, this support often has to be acquired for certain key *domestic* policies and programs closely related to activities overseas.

Although the State Department created a Division of Information as early as 1909, World War I witnessed the first intensive effort by the department to inform the public about events overseas. Some thirty years elapsed, however, before the department formally conceived of public opinion as a two-way process involving "public relations" campaigns by government and efforts by officials to inform themselves more adequately of public attitudes. In 1943–1944, an Office (now a Bureau) of Public Affairs was created in the department to facilitate an exchange of viewpoints between citizens and policy-makers. This office concerned itself actively with studying public attitudes concerning the nascent United Nations and seeing to it that a broad spectrum of American opinion was brought to the attention of the Roosevelt administration.[64]

Along with other units within the State Department, the Bureau of Public Affairs has been reorganized several times in the postwar period. The bureau concentrates upon *domestic* opinion, leaving the United States Information Agency (USIA) to deal with opinion in other countries.* Containing several internal units, the Bureau has some 150 clerical and staff employees. A news office within the Bureau handles the State Department's relations with the press, radio, TV, and other media. The Historical Office arranges to make the State Department's archives available to scholars and other students of American foreign policy; from time to time, it publishes official compilations, like the series *The Foreign Relations of the United States.*

The Office of Public Services performs a key role in State Department efforts to collect infor-

mation about public opinion and to disseminate it to policy-makers. This office is especially concerned with *group opinion* in the United States. It maintains liaison with some 3000 groups (although its efforts are concentrated on no more than a few hundred). It seeks to inform itself about the attitudes of such groups and, in turn, it presents the State Departments position to them. As many as 1000 speakers annually are sent by this office to address group meetings, conventions, conferences, and the like; the office answers inquiries sent to it (or often to Congress) about American foreign policy, which number as many as 100,000 a year; it publishes pamphlets, booklets, brochures, and the like, for distribution to the public; periodically, it conducts briefings in Washington devoted to explaining America's relations with other countries.[65]

The Public Opinion Studies Staff within the Bureau concentrates upon bringing the attitudes of the American society to the attention of officials in the State Department, the White House, and other agencies involved in the foreign policy process. This office is concerned principally with *mass opinion* as it is expressed in newspapers and magazines, in public opinion polls; in letters written to the department, the White House, and other agencies; and in contacts between governmental officials and the public.[66]

For data bout mass opinion, the office relies heavily upon public opinion polls taken on a national and regional basis. During 1948–1957, the State Department commissioned its own polls dealing with foreign policy issues. This practice was discontinued, however, when it aroused opposition in Congress. Legislators were convinced that public sentiment in the United States opposed programs like foreign aid and accused the State Department of using the results of its polls to support existing or proposed policies. It is true that for many policies and programs, polls have shown public sentiment to be more favorably disposed than legislative opinion or than legislative conceptions of public opinion.[67]

Once it has examined public attitudes, the Bureau of Public Affairs prepares studies of American opinion which are circulated at frequent intervals to policy-makers in the department, the White House, other agencies in Washington, and diplomatic installations overseas. Daily, weekly, and monthly summaries of opinion are sent to interested policy-makers; sometimes special studies of public sentiment are undertaken on a current foreign policy question. Meanwhile, it must be kept in mind, other studies and "soundings" of public opinion are going on concurrently throughout the executive branch. Officials in the White House, for example, keep track of the mail count and prepare studies of public sentiment based upon it; the President and his subordinates are continually meeting with pri-

*The activities of USIA are dealt with at length in Chapter 14.

vate citizens and public groups; the viewpoints expressed in magazines and newspapers are brought to the attention of the President; advisers report to the President and Cabinet officers on public sentiment they have encountered, perhaps on a trip to the West coast. At no stage in American history have policy-makers made such an ongoing effort to keep themselves informed about public attitudes on foreign, and related internal, policy issues.

The Role of Public Opinion in Policy Formulation

A recurrent criticism made of the Johnson administration's policies in Southeast Asia during the 1960s illustrates the fundamental question with which we are concerned at this stage. The criticism (expressed most widely by "doves") was that the President, the Secretary of State, and other key officials involved in decision-making on Vietnam did not listen to their critics. Significant numbers of Americans (and the complaint was pervasive among intellectuals) felt frustrated because, in this view, policy-makers appeared indifferent to public sentiment.

In reality, this complaint entailed two distinct allegations. It might have meant that national leaders *did not care about public opinion*, that they were isolated from it, that criticisms and ideas expressed by the citizenry were not "getting through" to the White House and State Department. Assuming that the procedures described in the preceding section of this chapter were operating normally (and there is no evidence to the contrary) this criticism possessed very little merit. It seems incontestable that the President, the Secretary of State, and other high-ranking officials heard the chorous of dissent over Vietnam. The Secretary of State's reluctance to subject himself and the government to public displays of criticism and dissension seems convincing evidence of this fact. President Johnson's decision in 1968 not to seek re-election was based primarily upon awareness that his Asian policies had generated prolonged public disagreement. However, it must be recognized that such officials could, and unquestionably did, take issue with their critics over the *degree and nature* of popular dissatisfaction or over the kind of policy or approach the American people favored in Southeast Asia.

The second question involved in this complaint was really the crux of the controversy. When critics complained that the administration was not listening to their ideas, what was usually meant was that policy-makers were presumably *taking no account* of the criticisms expressed; as far as they could determine, critics could see no evidence that their viewpoints *had an impact upon national policy*. The administration was ignoring public opinion, in the sense that its policies seemingly remained unchanged in spite of unmistakable evidence of popular disaffection with them. Judged by the relatively high degree of continuity in American policy in Vietnam throughout most of the 1960s, critics could make a plausible case on this point. Little evidence existed that President Johnson was prepared to alter his policies significantly to take account of complaints voiced by either the "doves" or the "hawks." If he was familiar with the positions of such groups, he showed little sign of being guided by their ideas.

The Vietnam conflict was by no means the first time in recent history that such complaints have been voiced. Some students of the foreign policy process in fact are convinced that, in the last analysis, public opinion plays a minimum role in policy formulation. Despite the State Department's systematic efforts to keep abreast of public thinking and to inform policy-makers about public attitudes, much of this activity seems wasted. Even today, according to this view, policy-makers in the field of diplomacy still do not feel an obligation to take account of society's attitudes and wishes. When they do, their conception of public opinion is apt to be highly impressionistic, or they are likely to view public oipnion as a force to be *used* to support the policies and programs they deem necessary. In any case, some commentators have asserted, public opinion does not normally play a central and continuing role in policy-making.[68] That there is considerable validity to this point of view can hardly be doubted. It is expressed by scholars and by commentators who have had long experience in government service.

The pivotal question here becomes the extent to which governmental officials in a democracy *ought to be guided* by public sentiment in formulating their policies at home and abroad. Two polar positions, and a much more complicated intermediate one, are possible. One extreme envisions the concept of democratic government as requiring a direct and essentially simple, almost mechanistic, relationship between the views of citizens and their leaders. Held by many critics during the Vietnam War, this position interprets "government by the people" quite literally: Leaders ought to discover what the people want and then do it! Obviously, this requires policy-makers to keep themselves infomed about society's attitudes; but above all, it obligates them to view public opinion as perhaps the most important input of national policy. Adherence to the principle of democracy thus requires policy-makers to keep closely attuned to public sentiment and to follow it in all phases of policy formulation and execution.

The other polar position—expressed from time to time by retired diplomats, ex-military officers, and even some intellectuals—is that even in a democracy public opinion can and ought to play a minimal role in foreign affairs. In this conception, foreign relations have historically been the province of the ruler and the aristocracy; even in the recent period, they are most successfully managed when left to "professionals" who are trained to understand their complexities. Foreign policy is an extremely complex subject, and getting more so all the time; in most instances, it is beyond both the understanding and interest of ordinary citizens. Those who are deeply concerned about it often belong to groups whose interests may be at variance with the national welfare. At best, advocates of this viewpoint are convinced, public opinion is so amorphous, so variegated, so attached to incongruities and ambiguities, and so variable that policy-makers simply cannot follow it or derive their policies from it. This is an *elitest* conception of public opinion which, it is safe to say, has little mass support among American citizens today.

There is a third point of view with respect to the proper role of public opinion in foreign policy. It is more difficult to state succinctly, since it contains many qualifications and reservations not present in the two positions described earlier. This conception comes closer to being compatible with the idea of the American system of government as *a representative democracy* or a *republican* form of government. A basic premise of this third position is that, in a democracy, public opinion does and must "count" in policy formulation. Unless it does, no policy can succeed over the long run. Public opinion thus has to be regarded as a major policy input. It follows that efforts to assess public attitudes are a legitimate and indispensable governmental activity. National leaders cannot take public sentiment into account unless they know what it is and understand something of its nature and characteristics. Moreover, officials have to be continually receptive to criticisms and ideas emanating from all segments of the American society.

But this conception of the proper role of public opinion in the foreign policy process also rests upon several qualifications, keeping the relationship between public opinion and policy-makers from being mechanistic and automatic. The American system of government, it must not be forgotten, is republican or a *representative democracy*. If it is one thing to assert that national leaders cannot govern successfully without public support; it is a very different thing to assert (or assume) that *public opinion itself governs* in the United States or any other democracy. Constitutionally, the American pattern of government is not (in the current phrase) a "participatory democracy." The Constitution does not require a national referendum before major policies are adopted; nor do national elections in the United States constitute mandates for successful presidential and congressional candidates to carry out a detailed program that has won massive public

endorsement. In a representative democracy, the people decide *who* shall govern; only in rare instances is it possible to say what their choice means in terms of specific policies and programs, especially in meeting problems arising after the election is over. Once they have assumed office, executive and legislative officials accept certain constitutional responsibilities which are assigned *to them*, not to the electorate, nor to public opinion. As we observed in Chapter 3, the President is charged constitutionally with the management of foreign relations. He should, and all Presidents as a matter of course do, receive advice and proposals from numerous sources, not excluding the mass public, groups, and private citizens. Ultimately, however, he bears the responsibility for making necessary decisions.

If the President and his advisers *consider* public sentiment, they normally regard it as only one among several major policy inputs. It has to be acknowledged that in many instances, policy-makers may conclude that public opinion (assuming a clear expression of it to exist) *is wrong* or that it is poorly informed about particular policy questions. They may believe that the public as a whole has very little interest in the issue concerned; or, even if it does, that its attitudes are compounded largely of emotion and prejudice. The evidence presented earlier in the chapter suggests that, for many foreign policy issues confronting the government, such assessments of public sentiment are justified. Presidents are reminded almost daily that, in a society as heterogeneous as that of the United States, there is, literally speaking, no such thing as public opinion *in the singular*. Rather, there is an almost infinite variety of *publics*, expressing or attached to a broad spectrum of *opinions* about matters of national policy. Only in exceptional cases (as, for example, when the American people were united in their response to the Japanese attack against Pearl Harbor late in 1941) can it be said that the "voice of the people" comes through unambiguously and powerfully to the nation's leaders.

Officials involved in making key foreign policy decisions are also conscious of another aspect of the relationship between public sentiment and national policy. The "dialogue" between national leaders and the American society is *a two-way process of communication*. It is a *dialogue*, not a monologue. If leaders obviously must listen to viewpoints expressed by public groups and citizens, a reciprocal obligation exists: The President and his advisers must inform, educate and guide public opinion. They must familiarize citizens with the factual information needed for sound policy decisions (since the President's access to such information, as we emphasized in Chapter 3, is unequaled); they must explain the importance and rationale of existing and proposed policies;

they must set forth the pros and cons of policy alternatives, showing why some courses are preferable to others; they must call the public's attention to changing circumstances at home and abroad that call for policy modifications; they must point out the risks inherent in any policy undertaking, including the most attractive one. In a democracy, such steps are implicit in the idea of "leadership" by those officials bearing the responsibility for governing successfully.

The Leadership of Public Opinion

"A Secretary of State who waited for public opinion of the right kind to develop before taking action," John Foster Dulles once declared, is "derelict in his duty." Yet Dulles also believed that no administration could move too far ahead of public sentiment, and that officials should not neglect to inform the public at frequent intervals and seek to "bring it along" in support of needed policies.[69] Academic commentators have made basically the same point a bit differently. A key fact about public opinion, one study holds, is that it "supports or permits, rather than decides, policy choices."[70] Another study has identified "a wide range of government activity acceptable to the public"; normally, therefore, national leaders select among several possible courses of action within the bounds prescribed by public approval.[71] Or, as Elder has expressed the idea, in analyzing public attitudes, the State Department is interested primarily in determining *the broad limits* within which policy-makers must function; it is less interested in looking to the public for *future* policy alternatives or innovations.[72] The balance which incumbent officials must strike and try to maintain in this matter was alluded to by Secretary of State Cordell Hull. Describing the Roosevelt administration's effort to formulate a response to Axis expansionism in a domestic environment of entrenched isolationist sentiment, Hull declared: "In our policies toward Europe, as in our policy toward Japan we sought to keep reasonably ahead of public opinion, even while seeking to educate public opinion to the importance of our position in the world and to the fatal fallacy of isolating ourselves."[73]

Since World War I, a steady evolution has occured in making the Chief Executive and lesser officials available to the mass media, affording them the opportunity both to listen to the concerns expressed by reporters and to present their viewpoints to the public. From the highly restrictive format imposed upon their press conferences by Presidents Coolidge and Hoover, President Roosevelt moved to "open" the White House to reporters for the press and radio. For the first time, FDR permitted reporters to "attribute" statements directly to the President. More than

any Chief Executive before or since, FDR created a rapport with the American people, renewed from time to time by his "fireside chats" with citizens over radio networks. President Truman largely continued FDR's approach, although he lacked the latter's magnetic radio appeal. Under President Eisenhower, two significant developments occured. The resources available due to the development of nation-wide television facilities were exploited for the President's press conferences and other occasions when Eisenhower desired to communicate directly with the people. American leaders were enabled to convey their appraisal of developments overseas by their appearance, demeanor, gestures, and the like. Eisenhower also introduced what has come to be one of the most influential instruments of presidential leadership: the "official transcript" of the President's news conference. President Kennedy was the first Chief Executive to permit "live" TV coverage of his news conference to be transmitted, without an opportunity for prior White House scrutiny and correction. Presidents Kennedy and Johnson also held numerous private meetings with reporters to explain their policies and to answer their inquiries.

In the summer of 1969, President Nixon undertook a tour around the world, beginning in the Pacific region, passing through the Middle East, and finally to Europe. He was accompanied by a large news contingent, augmented by many more reporters in each country he visited. President Nixon was using one of the most effective techniques available for influencing public attitudes, both within the American society and overseas. In 1959, President Eisenhower had made a "grand tour" covering over 22,000 miles and including 11 countries from India to Italy. In India particularly, Eisenhower's tour was viewed as having been highly successful in cementing friendly relations and exhibiting America's concern for perhaps the most influential nation in the "third world."[75]

In the contemporary period, Presidents are mindful of a dilemma that may easily arise when they attempt to influence and lead public opinion. On the one hand, they may be criticized, as in our case study of American foreign policy toward China, for *failing* to educate public thinking, for neglecting to present the facts to it, or for avoiding needed discussion of policy alternatives. In brief, they may face the charge that they are defaulting upon a central obligation of national leadership. When this occurs, policy-makers permit or acquiesce in the development of a policy vacuum; American policy becomes characterized by a kind of diplomatic hardening of the arteries.

The other prong of the dilemma can be no less painful—as President Johnson (and, to a lesser extent, President Kennedy) discovered. Under

Kennedy and Johnson, newsmen complained vocally about "news management" by the incumbent administration to generate public support for its policies, President Johnson's predicament was well known. Few Presidents made such a concerted effort to cultivate the news media and to maintain a rapport with the public; no White House occupant was apparently more preoccupied with his administration's image. Yet no President suffered from such a "credibility gap." In time, the existence of this gap (or its assumed existence) went far toward undermining public confidence in the President's leadership. The charge was not that the President was failing to communicate with the public or that he and his advisers were "unavailable" to newsmen. It was that the information dispensed was either *inaccurate* or designed primarily to *win public endorsement* for the administration's policies in Vietnam and elsewhere, or both. In spite of some of the most intensive efforts made by any President to influence public opinion, the alleged existence of a credibility gap hampered the administration's activities down to the time President Nixon took office in 1969.

Experience since the Roosevelt period clearly indicates that Presidents must maintain a very delicate equilibrium in their approach to public opinion. Indifference to the public's views and role can of course ultimately prove fatal to the success of any foreign policy. Less crucially, it can perpetuate policy rigidities and re-enforce inertia. Outmoded policies are continued simply because they have "been supported by public opinion" for many years and it is too unsettling to change them!

By contrast, undue preoccupation with America's "image" at home and abroad can lead to a kind of narcissism or policy imbalance in which what people think about the government's activities becomes the all-important factor shaping national behavior. When this situation prevails, there may be a tendency for harsh realities abroad or unpalatable policy choices to be glossed over for fear of an adverse public reaction (or, what may be just as bad, a *confused* public reaction). When policy-makers operate under such restraints, a kind of "credibility gap" becomes almost inevitable. The root cause of this phenomenon in the Johnson administration may well have been a consistent failure to make one sobering reality clear to the American people. Always present to a degree in foreign policy, this fact today seems ubiquitous. It is that nearly *any policy alternative is a calculated risk*, containing both attractive and unattractive features. Under the best circumstances imaginable in a turbulent world, America is likely to achieve *only some of its objectives*, and many of these *partially*. This is the "hard saying" that must lie at the center of any

effort to avert a credibility gap and to promote intelligent citizen understanding of America's foreign relations.

NOTES

1. President Wilson's views are cited in Sidney Warren, ed., *The President as World Leader* (New York: McGraw-Hill, 1967), p. 97; and Louis W. Koenig, *The Chief Executive*, rev. ed. (New York: Harcourt Brace Jovanovich, 1968), p. 184.
2. Quoted in Joseph E. Kallenbach, *The American Chief Executive: The Presidency and the Governorship* (New York: Harper & Row, 1966), p. 370.
3. Quoted in Robert E. Elder, *The Policy Machine* (Syracuse, N.Y.: Syracuse University Press, 1960), p. 137.
4. John S. Dickey, "The Secretary and the American Public," in Don K. Price, ed., *The Secretary of State* (Englewood Cliffs, N.J.: Prentice-Hall, 1960), p. 163.
5. For these and other definitions of public opinion, see Dan Nimmo and Thomas D. Ungs, *American Political Patterns* (Boston: Little, Brown, 1969), pp. 171–173; Daniel Katz *et al.*, eds., *Public Opinion and Propaganda* (New York: Holt, Rinehart and Winston, 1954), pp. 50–51; and Kimball Young, *Social Psychology* (New York: Appleton-Century-Crofts, 1956), pp. 330–332.
6. James M. Burns, *Roosevelt: The Lion and the Fox* (New York: Harcourt Brace Jovanovich, 1956), p. 248.
7. Elder, *op. cit.*, p. 127.
8. Angus Campbell *et. al.*, *The American Voter* (New York: John Wiley, 1960), p. 101.
9. Katz, *op. cit.*, p. 35.
10. V. O. Key, *The Responsible Electorate* (New York: Random House, 1968), pp. 130–131.
11. Lloyd A. Free and Hadley Cantril, *The Political Beliefs of Americans: A Study of Public Opinion* (New York: Simon & Schuster, 1968), p. 52.
12. Our discussion of the properties of American public opinion relies heavily upon Nimmo and Ungs, *op. cit.*, pp. 177–179.
13. Smith Simpson, *Anatomy of the State Department* (Boston: Houghton Mifflin, 1967), p. 194.
14. An illuminating discussion of the process by which intellectual opinion in the United States became "alienated" from American foreign policy during the Johnson administration may be found in Irving Kristol, "American Intellectuals and Foreign Policy," *Foreign Affairs* 45 (July, 1967), 594–610.
15. Our discussion of how the State Department regards various segments of American public opinion is based upon the account in Simpson, *op. cit.*, pp. 190–194.
16. Lester Markel, ed., *Public Opinion and Foreign Policy* (New York: Harper & Row, 1949), p. 51.

17. James L. McCamy, *The Administration of American Foreign Affairs* (New York: Knopf, 1950), p. 313.
18. *Ibid.*, p. 315.
19. Katz, *op. cit.*, p. 38.
20. A detailed analysis of American public opinion toward the Vietnam War—emphasizing the middle-of-the-road position of most citizens—is contained in Sidney Verba *et al.*, "Public Opinion and the War in Vietnam," *American Political Science Review* LXI (June, 1967), 317–334.
21. The results of various public opinion polls illustrating this point are cited in Free and Cantril, *op. cit.*, pp. 60–61.
22. A voluminous study of southern attitudes on international issues—which also presents considerable data on other sectional viewpoints—is Alfred O. Hero, *The Southerner and World Affairs* (Baton Rouge, La.: Louisiana State University Press, 1965).
23. For further discussion of significant traits of American opinion on foreign affairs, see Campbell, *op. cit.*, pp. 113, 281–283; and Free and Cantril, *op. cit.*, p. 61.
24. A. T. Steele, *The American People and China* (New York: McGraw-Hill, 1966), p. 8. Our case study of public opinion toward China in the recent period relies heavily upon Steele's illuminating analysis.
25. America's policy during and after the Boxer Rebellion in China is discussed in Julius W. Turner, *A History of United States Foreign Policy* (Englewood Cliffs, N.J.: Prentice-Hall, 1955), pp. 436–441; Washington's reactions to Japan's "Twenty-One Demands" upon China are treated in *ibid.*, pp. 540–541.
26. General "Vinegar Joe" Stilwell's frustrations in dealing with Chiang Kai-shek's government during World War II are candidly depicted in Theodore H. White, ed., *The Stilwell Papers* (New York: Macfadden Books, 1962).
27. Steele, *op. cit.*, pp. 98–99.
28. *Ibid.*, pp. 101–102.
29. *Ibid.*, pp. 100–101.
30. *Ibid.*, p. 106.
31. *Ibid.*, pp. 97, 99, 104–105.
32. *Ibid.*, pp. 106–109.
33. Accurate information on the nature and activities of the China lobby is not easy to acquire, even today. For a revealing background study, focusing upon the origins of the lobby and its early postwar activities, see the two articles on "The China Lobby," *The Reporter* 6 (April, 1952), 4–24; and (April 29, 1952), 112–118; see also Steele, *op. cit.*, pp. 112–118.
34. Steele, *op. cit.*, p. 205
35. *Ibid.*, p. 208.
36. *Ibid.*, p. 210.
37. Arthur M. Schlesinger, Jr., *A Thousand Days* (Boston: Houghton Mifflin, 1965), p. 479.
38. Theodore C. Sorensen, *Kennedy* (New York: Harper & Row, 1965), pp. 665–666.
39. The background and events surrounding this proposed policy change toward China are discussed in Roger Hilsman, *To Move a Nation* (Garden City, N.Y.: Doubleday, 1967), pp. 350–357.
40. Steele, *op. cit.*, pp. 221–222.
41. R. Joseph Monsen, Jr., and Mark. W. Cannon, *The Makers of Public Policy: American Power Groups and Their Ideologies* (New York: McGraw-Hill, 1965), p. 1.
42. Young, *op. cit.*, p. 340.
43. Bradford Smith, *A Dangerous Freedom* (Philadelphia: Lippincott, 1954), p. 253.
44. Monsen and Cannon, *op. cit.*, pp. 102–108.
45. *Ibid.*, pp. 108–113.
46. *Ibid.*, pp. 114–121.
47. *Ibid.*, pp. 65–95.
48. *Ibid.*, pp. 24–46; Steele, *op. cit.*, pp. 84–86.
49. San Stavisky, "Where Does the Veteran Stand Today?" *Annals of the American Academy of Political and Social Science* 259 (September, 1948), 131; and R. Baker, *The American Legion and Foreign Policy* (New York: Bookman Associates, 1954).
50. See Kristol, *op. cit.*, pp. 594–610.
51. Samuel Lubell, *The Future of American Politics* (New York: Harper & Row, 1952), pp. 132–148; and for a discussion of ethnic minorities in the election of 1960, see Theodore H. White, *The Making of the President. 1960* (New York: Atheneum, 1961), pp. 150–152.
52. R. M. MacIver, ed., *Group Relations and Group Antagonisms* (New York: Harper & Row, 1944), p. 37. See particularly the chapter by Max Ascoli dealing with the viewpoints of Italian–Americans.
53. A worthwhile study of the influential Irish-American minority is Carl Wittke, *The Irish in America* (Baton Rouge, La.: Louisiana State University Press, 1956), p. 105 and *passim.*
54. The viewpoints and activities of Irish–Americans with respect to specific diplomatic issues are treated in Thomas A. Bailey, *Woodrow Wilson and the Great Betrayal* (New York: Macmillan, 1945), pp. 24–27; Wittke, *op. cit.*, pp. 163, 288–291; and Cordell Hull, *The Memoirs of Cordell Hull*, vol. II (New York: Macmillan, 1948), p. 718.
55. V. O. Key., *Public Opinion and American Democracy* (New York: Knopf, 1961), p. 106.
56. The disappearance of significant sectional differences in American opinion on international questions is highlighted in nearly every chapter of Hero's study of southern attitudes, *The Southerner and World Affairs, op. cit., passim.*
57. Senate Foreign Relations Committee, *Activities of Non-Diplomatic Representatives of Foreign Principals in the United States*, 88th Congress, 1st Session, 1963. This series affords a wealth of data about lobbying and "public relations" campaigns undertaken by or in behalf of foreign governments and political movements.
58. *Ibid.*, pp. 2–3.
59. *Ibid.*, pp. 3–4, 10, 55–57.
60. *Ibid.*, p. 17.

61. *Ibid.*, pp. 17, 122.
62. Elder, *op. cit.*, p. 137.
63. Dickey, *op. cit.*, pp. 140–142.
64. *Ibid.*, pp. 142–143, 147.
65. Elder, *op. cit.*, p. 131.
66. Simpson, *op. cit.*, p. 184.
67. Elder, *op. cit.*, p. 146.
68. Simpson is but one among a number of commentators who believe that, despite the State Department's systematic study of public attitudes, in the final analysis policy-makers take little account of public sentiment. See *Anatomy of the State Department, op. cit.*, pp. 184–205.
69. Andrew Berding, *Foreign Affairs and You* (Garden City, N.Y.: Doubleday, 1962), p. 169.
70. Nimmo and Ungs, *op. cit.*, p. 173.
71. William H. Flanigan, *Political Behavior of the American Electorate* (Boston: Allyn & Bacon, 1968), p. 74.
72. Elder, *op. cit.*, p. 150.
73. Hull, *op. cit.*, p. 575.
74. Several studies of the President's relations with, and use of, the major news media have appeared in recent years. See Pierre Salinger, *With Kennedy* (New York: Avon Books, 1966); James Reston, *The Artillery of the Press: Its Influence on American Foreign Policy* (New York: Harper & Row, 1967); and an older, but still useful, study by Douglas Cater, *The Fourth Branch of Government* (New York: Random House, 1965).
75. For a detailed description of President Eisenhower's Asian tour, see Dwight D. Eisenhower, *Waging Peace* (Garden City, N.Y.: Doubleday, 1965), pp. 485–514.

Eight
THE COLD WAR:
Orthodox and Revisionist Interpretations

For a quarter-century after World War II, the omnipresent reality dominating the international environment was Soviet–American hostility. Labeled the "cold war" in the late 1940s, this contest extended into virtually every quarter of the globe and affected almost all other major and minor international issues. The economic recovery and defense of Western Europe; the political development of societies in Eastern Europe; the ability of the Arabs and Israelis to settle their long-standing differences; the economic development of Africa; the provision of American, Soviet, Chinese, and European economic assistance to needy societies; the stability of Asia; the effort to reduce worldwide expenditures for armaments and the diversion of at least some of these funds for peaceful, more constructive purposes; the success of the United Nations—all these and many more significant issues were directly affected by the condition of Soviet-American relations. This is not to suggest of course that serious international problems would not have existed in the absence of the cold war; the decline in Soviet-American tensions during the 1960s (when both countries were confronted with an expansive and nuclear-armed China) indicates that international relations would be far from idyllic even if the cold war had never erupted. By the 1970s, it was also apparent that certain other global issues—like the population explosion, the world food shortage, and the concern of needy societies with national development—were tending to overshadow the Soviet–American rivalry as a source of acute international concern.

Yet the cold war was perhaps *the* principal challenge to international stability and peace for almost a generation after World War II. American policy-makers and defense planners continued to think first and foremost of the Soviet Union's intentions and capabilities. If officials in Moscow were increasingly preoccupied with rising Chinese hostility, they nevertheless continued to give American diplomatic behavior high priority in their own external policy moves. The newly independent nations knew—and deplored the fact—that their own needs and concerns were still viewed in Washington and Moscow largely within a cold war context; most of the funds these societies might have access to for national development continued to be expended for rising armaments stockpiles.

What precisely was this conflict that had come to be known as the cold war? What were the stakes at issue between the two super-powers, the United States and the Soviet Union? How did the contest arise? What were the objectives on each side? How did one side respond to moves by the other? Was the cold war susceptible of negotiation—and if so, on what basis? Has the Soviet-American confrontation changed significantly from the late 1940s to the early 1970s? The dominant global problem of the contemporary era cannot be understood without an effort to answer such questions, however tentative these answers must be. Although authoritative evidence was often unavailable to explain why the Kremlin periodically launched a war of nerves against the Western position in Berlin, or to account fully for America's implication in the campaign against Communist groups in Iran in the late 1940s, relevant materials often remained locked in the archives of the Kremlin or the State Department. The student of international relations was compelled to depend upon official statements, journalist accounts, secondary sources, and the like; his conclusions about Washington's or Moscow's intentions frequently consisted of inferences and suppositions based upon "reading between the lines" of diplomatic communications, logical assumptions, and (perhaps most unsatisfactory) efforts to divine the true motives of policy-makers in both countries. Even that final authority, the "historian of the future," will probably be confronted with some insoluble problems related to the cold war, particularly those involving what might be viewed as the "irrational" nature of Soviet behavior or deciding what President Truman really had in mind when he proclaimed the Truman Doctrine early in 1947. Even when additional source materials become available, the *motives* and *true intentions* of decision-makers are likely to remain a subject of intense controversy.

For convenience, we have divided this chapter on the emergence of the cold war into two parts. The first deals with a subject that too many Americans even now have neglected: Russian diplomatic goals and behavior before the Bolshevik Revolution of 1917. Here the emphasis is upon a fact about the cold war which has received insufficient attention in America. The principal diplomatic antagonist of the United States since World War II has been Communist *Russia*. However, for most Americans, the cold war has arisen and been perpetuated by the behavior of *Communist Russia*, or by the "Communist global conspiracy" aimed at achieving global domination. The main preoccupation is thus with Russia's Marxist political program and platform, particularly with its claim to universal validity and its supposed historical inevitability. It is Communism or Marxism or Marxism-Leninism-Stalinism that is seen to threaten American security and the peace of the world; Russia simply happens to be its bastion and principal advocate. Without in the least denying the antipathy between Marxist ideology and Western conceptions of liberal democracy, the early portion of this chapter suggests that Moscow espouses certain goals, and relies upon certain diplomatic methods, which are identified with *Russia as a state*, irrespective of its system of government or political coloration. It calls attention to the often remarkable continuity between Russian policy under the Czars and under the Commissars.

In the latter part of the chapter, an attempt is made more directly to answer the questions posed above about the cold war in the postwar era. The origins of this conflict are examined. Specific issues generating tensions between America and Soviet Russia are analyzed. Trends in the pattern of cold war animosity are identified. Recognizing that nearly every question that might be raised about recent Soviet–American relations is controversial, the discussion is placed in a context of what might be called "orthodox" and "revisionist" assessments of the origins of the cold war and its development after World War II.

ENDURING GOALS OF RUSSIAN FOREIGN POLICY

The Centrality of Historical Insights

Engraved upon the National Archives building in Washington are the words: "What Is Past Is Prologue." These words serve as an appropriate introduction to the subject of Russia's diplomatic behavior before 1917. Americans venerate their past; they "commemorate" outstanding events from their own history on innumerable occasions. It may be questioned, however, whether they are inclined to view the past "as prologue," at least

insofar as the cold war is concerned. To many citizens, that conflict began no earlier than the closing months of World War II, when the Red Army overran Eastern Europe; for others, perhaps, it really started when Lenin seized control of the Russian government in 1917, imposing a Communist system upon it and launching the U.S.S.R. on the path of world domination. All too willingly (if unintentionally), large numbers of Americans have accepted the Kremlin's view: that Russia under Marxism became a totally new state, whose goals and methods bore no relation to czarist regimes or to other non-Communist systems. Along with all other features of Russian life, they feel, the nation's diplomacy was "revolutionized" in the new Marxist era.

Yet, as we have suggested, history shows a remarkable continuity in Russia's external behavior, irrespective of its system of government or ideology. At this stage, two examples must suffice. (Others will become apparent as our discussion proceeds.)

Is world domination believed to be the cardinal diplomatic goal of the Kremlin? "A strange superstition prevails among the Russians, that they are destined to conquer the world . . . ," said a State Department dispatch in the mid-nineteenth century.[1] And is the Kremlin thought by the West to be utterly unprincipled in its dealings with other countries, so much so that its promises are looked upon as worthless? A Russian historian once described czarist diplomacy as follows:

The diplomatic methods of the Muscovite boyars often threw the foreign envoys into desperation, particularly those who wanted to carry on their business forthrightly and conscientiously. . . . [I]n order not to fall into their nets it was not enough to make certain that they were lying; it was also necessary to decide what the purpose of the lie was; and what was one to do then? If someone caught them lying, they did not blush and they answered all reproaches with a laugh.[2]

At the time of the Russo–Japanese War in 1905, Theodore Roosevelt declared that "Russia is so corrupt, so treacherous and shifty . . . that I am utterly unable to say whether or not it will make peace, or break off negotiations at any moment."[3] Western diplomats in the modern period would probably find these descriptions remarkably apropos in characterizing the difficulty of maintaining harmonious relations with the U.S.S.R.

These examples are cited at the beginning of our study of Russian–American relations to stress the importance of setting contemporary cold war problems within the requisite historical context. Americans are prone to think of the cold war as a conflict between Soviet Communism and Western democracy. Ideological elements are unquestionably present. Yet such an oversimplified approach gives rise to many dangers and misapprehensions. Students of foreign policy must not jump to the conclusion that Russian diplomacy before 1917 is unrelated to present-day Soviet diplomatic behavior. They must be skeptical of the viewpoint—a cardinal article of faith in the communist creed—that Marxist–Leninist–Stalinist ideological compulsions furnish the most useful keys to understanding Russia's activities in the international community since 1917. They must not try to arrive at a guide to Soviet diplomatic conduct merely by piecing together the utterances and writings of high-ranking Communist spokesmen.*

What is basic for understanding Soviet diplomatic goals and methods at any stage is not so much what Lenin or Stalin or lesser Communist luminaries have *said* Soviet Russia was doing or going to do in world affairs, but rather what Russia has in fact *done* in both the czarist and in the Communist periods. The creation of "People's Democracies" by the bayonets of the Red Army in Eastern Europe does not differ from old-style czarist imperialism in the same area merely because Stalin baptized his hegemony with quotations from Marx and Lenin. The Czars could invoke a variety of slogans too, such as "legitimacy" and Pan-Slavism, to justify what was in essence *Machtpolitik.*

Age-old Russian foreign policy goals and methods, blended and overlaid with Communist ideological compulsions, provide the key to the foreign policies of the Kremlin. More and more since 1917, Soviet Russia has given evidence of diplomatic atavism, a characteristic which is not, of course, peculiar with Russia. One of the most fascinating aspects of Soviet diplomacy is the degree to which Stalin and his successors have ingeniously fused the historic diplomatic ambitions of Old Russia with the Communist faith. As much as any other single factor, it is this union that confronts the free world coalition, led by the United States, with a formidable and continuing challenge. Because Americans generally give insufficient attention to the historical elements of Russian foreign policy, we shall devote considerable space here to analyzing them.

*A number of studies of Soviet foreign policy in the recent period implicitly foster such a view. One outstanding example is Nathan Leites's work, *A Study of Bolshevism* (New York: Free Press, 1953). This a thorough and valuable compendium of Communist doctrinal statements on a variety of subjects. Leites attempts, as it were, to provide a kind of "code" to the behavior of the Kremlin in world affairs. Yet, by focusing almost entirely upon ideological influences, this study inherently suggests that motivations arising from historical, geographical, strategic factors—not to mention the Soviet Union's day-by-day response to developments in the outside world—are relatively unimportant in explaining the U.S.S.R.'s diplomacy. As we shall see in this chapter and the next, this seems at best a highly questionable assumption.

Expansionism—The Keynote of Historic Russian Policy

A newspaper reporter during the Crimean War in the mid-1850s wrote of Russia:

The Russian frontier has advanced: towards Berlin, Dresden and Vienna . . . towards Constantinople . . . towards Stockholm . . . towards Teheran. . . . The total acquisitions of Russia during the last 60 years are equal in extent and importance to the whole Empire she had in Europe before that time.

And in another dispatch the same reporter declared that:

And as sure as conquest follows conquest, and annexation follows annexation, so sure would the conquest of Turkey by Russia be only the prelude for the annexation of Hungary, Prussia, Galicia, and for the ultimate realization of the Slavonic Empire. . . . The arrest of the Russian scheme of annexation is a matter of the highest moment.

So wrote a German correspondent—Karl Marx—who was to have no little influence on the future course of Russian history.[4] The word that best characterizes Russian foreign policy throughout history and furnishes the most evident and important link between Russia's past and present policies in the international community is the word *expansionism.* Beginning as an insignificant twelfth-century city in the valley of the Dnieper, by the post-World War II period Moscow was the center of an empire that embraced one-fourth of the human race and 13 million square miles, excluding countries like China and Yugoslavia that are ideologically affiliated with the Kremlin.[5]

The saga of Imperial Russia was a story of almost uninterrupted territorial expansion, initially over the great Eurasian plain that stretches from Poland and European Russian to the borders of Persia, India, and China; and then, after the plain had been occupied and consolidated, of continual pressure against the natural boundaries that surround Russia, such as the Dardanelles, the Himalayas, the deserts of Central Asia, and the river systems of Manchuria.

Patiently, bit by bit, successive Czars pushed back the boundaries of Russia, and in doing so they sometimes created troublesome international problems. Peter the Great finally won the long-coveted "window on the West" when he wrested much of the Baltic region from Sweden; Catherine the Great participated in Poland's three partitions, in 1772, 1793, and 1795, and pushed Russian frontiers steadily southward to encroach upon the Turkish empire. Her successors continued the march southward and eastward by maintaining pressure against the frontiers of Turkey, Persia, Afghanistan, and India—thereby generating one of the most persistent diplomatic problems of the nineteenth century. At Tilsit in 1807, Alexander I and Napoleon attempted to divide most of Europe between them. And after Napoleon's defeat, Alexander annexed Poland, Finland, and Bessarabia, and engaged in intrigues in virtually every country in Europe. Nicholas I and Alexander II sponsored explorations and colonization movements eastward into Central Asia and Siberia, bringing Russia ultimately into conflict with Japanese and, to a lesser extent, British and American diplomatic ambitions in the Orient.

It is instructive to recall czarist territorial ambitions at the beginning of World War I. Had Imperial Russia been victorious, it expected to push its territory westward to incorporate what was the Poland of 1919–1939; annex East Prussia and all of the area west of the Vistula; annex Eastern Galicia; overthrow the defunct Turkish government and realize Russia's ancient ambition to control the Straits; and annex Turkish territories bordering Transcaucasia.[6]

Czarist expansionism derived from several impulses. First of all, Russia pushed inexorably across the Eurasian plain in much the same way as Americans trekked across their continent. Prince Michael Gorchakov wrote of his country's history that Russia, in common with all countries, was "forced to take the road of expansion dictated by necessity rather than by ambitions, a road on which the chief difficulty is to know where to stop."[7] The tendency to expand into territorial vacuums is not a peculiarly Soviet, nor even czarist, trait.

Second, the expansionist tendencies of the czarist state sprang in part from politico-strategic necessities. The vast, frontierless Eurasian plain facilitated Russian internal expansionism, but it also greatly aided foreign incursions into the interior of Russia. Historically, the response of the czarist state was to provide for defense in depth by creating an extensive buffer zone around its vulnerable geographic heartland. Safeguarding the military approaches to the interior has been a cardinal principle of Russian diplomacy since the time of Peter the Great, as it would have to be a diplomatic principle of any great power faced with a comparable threat.

Third, expansionism by the nineteenth century came to have an economic rationale. Russia, along with the other great powers, wanted a stake in foreign markets, to increase both the treasury and Russian prestige. The search for colonies led primarily to Manchuria, where Russian imperialism clashed with the territorial and economic ambitions of Japan, England, and the United States. As was true of American and British imperialism, economic concessions necessitated protection by Russian diplomats and soldiers. From 1904 to 1905, the Manchurian venture drew Russia into

the most humiliating war in its history, when it was humbled by the small island kingdom of Japan.

Fourth, a recurrent motif in Russian expansionism was the "historic mission" of Russia to deliver lesser people from their cultural and spiritual backwardness and to usher in the earthly millennium. Since we shall examine Russian Messianic thought in a later portion of the chapter, we shall merely observe here that the Messianic aspirations of certain secular and religious thinkers within Russia coincided perfectly at several points with the diplomatic ambitions of the czarist state. The foreign policies of Alexander I (1801–1825) illustrate the point. Alexander exhibited a calculating Machiavellianism, combined with a fervent and mystic idealism. He was capable of both the Treaty of Tilsit (1807), whereby he and Napoleon divided Europe between them; and of the high-minded, if totally impractical Holy Alliance (1815), in which Christian principles were to be made the basis of international conduct. Europeans, writes a contemporary British historian, must have wondered whether Alexander was not "just a cunning hypocrite, cultivating liberal sympathies and evangelical piety as a cloak to hide vast plans of aggressive ambitions. . . ." He was apt to "identify his own interest, or whims, with the good of humanity." Professing that all men ought to be free—at the very time he was annexing Poland, Finland, and Bessarabia—Alexander, "desired all men to be free on condition they did what he wanted them to do."[8]

The Search for Warm Water Ports

Closely related to expansionism is Russia's age-old search for warm water ports. Land-locked around most of its borders, Russia has always needed accessible and usable outlets to the sea. The ports of Murmansk, Archangel, and Leningrad are ice-bound a considerable portion of the year. To the south, Russian traffic on the Black Sea has always been at the mercy of Turkey, which controls the Dardanelles, or Turkey's protectors, such as Great Britain and, to a lesser degree, France during the eighteenth and nineteenth centuries. Since 1947, the United States has filled the vacuum created by the decline of British power in the Straits area and throughout the Near and Middle East as a whole.

South and eastward, Russian diplomacy has sought to force a breakthrough to the sea by intermittent pressure upon Persia, Afghanistan, and India. In addition to furnishing rich prizes to incorporate into the Russian empire, acquisition of passageways through these countries would give Russia access to the trade routes of the world. The modern American policy of containment had its origins along the Persian–Russian border and in the bleak hills of the northwest frontier in India during the nineteenth century. A dominant objective of British diplomacy during the age of *Pax Britannica* was to prevent Russian penetration of the Middle East. Throughout British colonial history, Russia was continually probing soft spots in the British defense perimeter and endeavoring to enlist other people, such as the Afghan tribesmen along the Indian frontiers, to further Russia's diplomatic ambitions.

Still further eastward, Russia advanced over Siberia and Central Asia toward the shores of the Pacific. The czars at last acquired outlets to the sea when they obtained or leased ports in Siberia and Manchuria late in the nineteenth century. With the completion of the Trans-Siberian Railroad by 1900, these ports became useful, although they were ice-bound a goodly part of the year, were extremely vulnerable to foreign attack, as the Russo-Japanese War proved, and even though they were some 6000 miles from European Russia. Russia's search for eastern seaports, coupled with the necessity to assure their accessibility over the railroads of north China, inevitably drew it into the maelstrom of great-power imperialistic rivalry in the Far East.[9]

Are Soviet policy-makers today still seeking outlets to the sea? The question hardly requires an answer. Soviet incorporation of the Baltic states, intermittent pressure on Turkey to give the U.S.S.R. a larger voice in safeguarding the Turkish Straits and determining policy toward them; Communist intrigue in the northern provinces of Iran in 1946, support for the Greek rebels in 1946–1947, more recent economic blandishments to Afghanistan, India, and Burma, Communist machinations in Syria, Egypt, and other Middle Eastern countries—all of these indicate that there has been little diminution in the traditional Russian urge to the sea.

The "Iron Curtain Complex"

When Winston Churchill stated in 1946 that an iron curtain had descended over Europe, he was coining a phrase that applied equally well to earlier stages in the history of Russia's relations with Europe. An "iron curtain complex" has been characteristic of the Russian attitude toward the outside world for centuries. When a *cordon sanitaire* or formidable geographical barriers did not effectively seal Russia off from contact with its neighbors, then a spiritual iron curtain has done so during most periods of Russian history. Estrangement and hostility took many forms: rigorous government censorship of ideas and communications from abroad; limited contacts between Russian citizens and foreigners; official coolness, amounting often to outright discrimination, toward foreign diplomats in Russia; belief in the inherent superiority of Russian customs and institutions;

and unwillingness to cultivate sincere and lasting ties of friendship with other countries. With some significant exceptions, almost every period of Russian history has exhibited a deep-seated xenophobia.*

In pre-Soviet history many factors engendered suspicion and hostility toward the outside world. In some periods, like the late nineteenth and early twentieth centuries, Russia was militarily much weaker than other countries suspected. The Russo–Japanese War and World War I showed this. Furthermore, Russia was economically backward. The contrast between its rate of industrialization and standard of living and that of its advanced Western neighbors was a source of constant embarrassment and insecurity. Moreover, under both the Czars and the Communists, Russia has feared the impact of Western political ideals upon a population restive under despotism. Then, too, neither the Czarist nor Communist regime has relished having the whole apparatus of state oppression—the ubiquitous secret police, the massive bureaucracy, the Siberian prison camps, the policies of censorship and suppression of designated minorities—exposed to the gaze and ridicule of the world. Lurid accounts of these aspects of Russian life have always fostered tension between Russia and other countries. To avoid unfavorable reports in foreign countries, Russia has preferred to close the door to foreigners entirely or to permit them to see only a few selected showplaces.

Intense suspicion and fear of the outside world has been engendered also by Russia's historical experiences under both the Czars and the Bolsheviks. The motif of cataclysm, perennial danger from abroad, and impending doom is a recurrent theme in Russian literature and political writing. In large measure it is a product of Russian geography and of history dictated by geographical conditions. The eminent British scholar Sir Bernard Pares has written: "The Great Russian people were hammered out of peaceful, silent pacific elements by constant and cruel blows from enemies on all sides, which implanted into the least intelligent of Russians an instinct of national defense. . . ."[10] And Mazour adds that "The motivating background of Russia's foreign policy is predom-

*While xenophobia has been characteristic of the Russian *government*, there existed a considerable interchange of cultural and political ideas between Russian citizens and the outside world under the czars. Barghoorn in fact maintains that the Russian population as a whole has traditionally been highly receptive to ideas from abroad and that even under the Communists, Soviet citizens have shown keen interest in the viewpoints of foreigners. See Frederick C. Barghoorn, *Soviet Russian Nationalism* (New York: Oxford University Press, 1956), pp. 162–164. For an illuminating treatment of the impact of American political ideas upon the czarist state in the eighteenth and nineteenth centuries, consult Max M. Laserson, *The American Impact on Russia* (New York: Macmillan, 1950).

inantly the need for security. . . ." He continues:

The Napoleonic Wars culminating with the occupation of Moscow, the Crimean War ending with the disaster at Sevastopol, the Russo–Turkish War . . ., World War I ending with Allied intervention, and above all World War II with its appalling devastation—these are experiences which no nation can forgive or forget.

Whether justified or not, he feels that, inevitably, Russia will seek "a *cordon sanitaire* in reverse, with its bayonets turned westward. . . . it is the ABC of national strategy."[11]

Fostered by countless invasions throughout history, the Russian legacy of suspicion and fear of the outside world is exemplified in the attitude of the reactionary Pobedonostsev, adviser to Alexander III (1881–1894). Pobedonostsev was convinced that "it is impossible to rely upon any of our so-called 'friends' and 'allies,' that all of them are ready to hurl themselves upon us at that very minute when our weakness or errors become apparent."[12]

The "Third Rome" Idea and Russian Messianism

The Communist hope of redeeming mankind through the "world revolution" and achieving utopia is a variant of a theme that pervades historic Russian theological and philosophical thought. In a penetrating study of Russian national character, Nicolas Berdyaev states that: "Messianic consciousness is more characteristic of the Russians than of any other people except the Jews. It runs all through Russian history right down to its communist period."[13] Its earliest origins are to be found in the conception of Moscow as the "Third Rome." After the fall of Rome in the fifth century and the collapse of the Byzantine Empire in the fifteenth, the center of Orthodox Christianity shifted to Moscow. To Russian theologians this signified a profound and God-ordained change in the direction of history. Thus the monk Philotheus informed Basil III, Grand Duke of Moscow:

The first Rome collapsed owing to its heresies, the second Rome fell victim to the Turks, but a new third Rome has sprung up in the north, illuminating the whole universe like the sun. . . . The first and second Rome have fallen, but the third will stand till the end of history, for it is the last Rome. Moscow has no successor; a fourth Rome is inconceivable.[14]

"The Mission of Russia," comments Berdyaev, "was to be the vehicle of the true Christianity. . . . There enters into the messianic consciousness the alluring temptation of imperialism."[15]

Strongly reinforcing the theological designation of Moscow as the Third Rome were the viewpoints of the Slavophils and their nineteenth-century successors, the Pan-Slavists. Compounded of Russian nationalism, mystic ties of race, German idealism, and Hegelian philosophy, Slavophilism predicted the inevitable decay of Europe and the redemption of mankind by the Slavs. "Western Europe is on the high road to ruin," Prince Odoevsky wrote. Advancing the theme of *ex Oriente lux* that permeates Russian philosophic and religious thought, he believed that:

We Russians, on the contrary, are young and fresh and have taken no part in the crimes of Europe. We have a great mission to fulfill. Our name is already inscribed on the tablets of victory: the victories of science, art and faith await us on the ruins of tottering Europe.[16]

And the Russian mystic Peter Chaadaev believed that "we have a vocation to solve a great many of the problems of the social order . . . to give an answer to questions of great importance with which mankind is concerned."[17] Describing man's quest for spirituality and holiness, the immortal Dostoevsky stated in 1880: "I speak only of the brotherhood of man, not of triumphs of the sword. . . . For I am convinced that the heart of Russia, more than any other nation, is dedicated to this universal union of all mankind. . . ."[18]

The Pan-Slav movement late in the nineteenth century also contained Messianic elements. According to its leading spokesmen, Russian cultural–historical affinity with the Slavs gave the Russian state a special responsibility as protector and defender of their interests. The Pan-Slavs, writes Florinsky, "were in general agreement that it was the historic mission of Russia to liberate the Slavs from a foreign and religious and political yoke. . . ."[19]

Other influences evident in certain periods of Russian thought also supported Messianism and assigned to Moscow a dominant role in achieving the salvation of mankind. One of these was nihilism. Another was anarchism. Berdyaev summarizes the viewpoint of the most famous Russian anarchist, Michael Bakunin, as follows:

What is needed is to set fire to a world-wide blaze; it is necessary to destroy the old world; upon the ashes of the old world, on its ruins, there will spring up a new and better world of its own accord. . . . Collectivism or communism will not be an affair of organization; it will spring out of the freedom which will arrive after the destruction of the old world.[20]

Also important is the attention given in Russian Orthodox theological thought to the coming of the Kingdom of God. In contrast to Roman Catholic and Protestant thought, Russian Orthodox theology has always emphasized the early apocalyptic message of the Church. The coming of the Kingdom of God will mean the "transfiguration of the world, not only the transfiguration of the individual man." Salvation is conceived of as total and corporate for society.[21]

Russian Messianism, concludes Berdyaev, is perfectly compatible with the mission of Marxism–Leninism–Stalinism to redeem mankind and recreate society anew upon the ruins of the old order. "Russian communism is a distortion of the Russian messianic idea; it proclaims light from the East which is destined to enlighten the bourgeois darkness of the West."[22] Analyzing the Messianic elements in contemporary Soviet policy, Barghoorn observes that the Kremlin "holds out to mankind the vision and prophecy of the earthly paradise, the harmonious society without coercion and inequality. This is the utopian aspect of Soviet Russia's message to the world. . . ."[23] The point is well exemplified by an article in *Izvestia* on February 22, 1948, which discusses Russia's contribution to humanity in World War II:

The Soviet Army . . . stretched out a brotherly, helping hand to the peoples of Europe languishing in Fascist Slavery. The European peoples have to thank the Soviet Army for their liberation. . . . The Soviet Army saved European civilization from the Fascist barbarians, honorably and worthily perfomed its historic liberating mission. . . . As always, the Soviet Army stands on guard to protect the peaceful labor and tranquility of the peoples. Always, it stands on guard for peace throughout the world.[24]

THE SOVIET–AMERICAN CONFRONTATION

The Pattern of Relations Before World War I

One of the keys to understanding the tensions developing between the United States and the Soviet Union after World War II is to be found in the history of relations between the two countries down to the time of Nazi Germany's attack upon Russia on June 22, 1941. Lack of trust and of meaningful communication between the two were conspicuous features of the cold war. The antipathy between Marxism and Western liberal democracy unquestionably fostered animosities. Less widely grasped, however, was the fact that the pattern of Russian–American relations before the contemporary period played a part in setting the stage for cold war hostilities.

In general terms, relations between Russia and America throughout the nineteenth century and for some forty years of the twentieth could be described as *fragmentary, intermittent, and not infrequently hostile*. The absence of sustained contact between the two societies was a noteworthy reality. Insofar as European affairs were concerned, the United States was dedicated to an isolationist mentality which dictated a policy of noninvolvement in the Old World's quarrels and diplomatic rivalries. After 1815 (most Americans did not realize until many years later) the *Pax Britannica* produced conditions of relative stability in Europe, enabling the United States to enjoy its isolationist existence. Czarist Russia did not espouse isolationism. To the contrary, even while czarist governments experienced one internal crisis after another, they pursued an "active" foreign policy abroad, intervening repeatedly in Europe's affairs, trying to extend Russian influence into the Mediterranean and Persian Gulf, threatening Britain's position in Afghanistan and India, and extending their interests to eastern Asia. At the same time, like America, Russia was heavily occupied with domestic affairs. America's westward expansion had its counterpart in Russia's eastward expansion into Asia and Siberia, to the shores of the Pacific. By 1900, czarist Russia had become deeply immersed in diplomatic competition over China. Even before the Spanish–American War at the end of the century, America was also becoming a "Pacific power." Isolationism, we need to remember, applied only to *European* affairs. When the United States championed the principle of the "Open Door" in China early in the twentieth century, Washington was as concerned about an exclusive *Russian* influence over Chinese affairs as by any other threat to its trading and commercial opportunities on the Asian mainland.*

The ideological rivalry characteristic of the cold war in the modern period was foreshadowed by the clash between American democratic ideas and ideals and czarist absolutism before 1917. To the American mind, czarism stood as the epitome of Old World political reaction and despotism. Nor could a starker contrast be found than that between dynamic American capitalism and Russia's stagnant economic system, which was marked by periodic famines. At intervals, as during the suppression of Louis Kossuth's revolt in Hungary against the Austro–Hungarian empire (which received massive support for its anti-revolutionary activities from Moscow), Americans vocally railed against autocracy and predictably supported the revolutionary cause. Kossuth received a hero's welcome when he visited the United States; Secretary of State Daniel Webster delivered a passionate endorsement of Hungarian

---

*America's policy of the "Open Door" in China—one of the nation's best-known foreign policy principles—is discussed in greater detail in Chapter 13. The Russian threat to China's territorial integrity occasioned considerable anxiety in Washington. One diplomatic historian has said that Russian expansionism constituted "the main threat to the open door" in China. See Richard W. Leopold, *The Growth of American Foreign Policy: A History* (New York: Knopf, 1962), pp. 218–219.

independence. Again in 1863, Americans denounced Russian intervention to crush a Polish revolt against czarist autocracy.[25] Ideological estrangement between the two countries was fostered late in the century by the lectures and writings of George Kennan,* who had traveled widely in Russia. To thousands of Americans, Kennan depicted life in the Czar's Siberian prison camps and other evidence of Russian political backwardness.[26]

Successive czarist regimes reciprocated hostility toward the United States. To the Russian nobility, the youthful and "upstart" American republic had embarked upon a democratic experiment that was bound to fail. Meanwhile, however, its very existence encouraged revolts against established and "legitimate" authority in Europe. Americans could always be counted upon to believe the worst about the government of Russia; their continuing support for political revolutionaries alienated the Czar and all other politically conservative groups. Toward America (as, for that matter, toward nearly all other countries), Russian officialdom exhibited rudeness and a lack of consideration which nearly every American resident in Moscow deeply resented. American diplomats deplored the restrictions which nearly always inhibited their movements and contacts in the Czar's domain. Censorship, the activities of the Czar's secret police, and other evidences of "barbarous" Russian behavior alienated Americans. Czarist Russian did not even formally recognize the American republic until 1809; treaty relations between the two governments were not established until 1824.[27]

As is not uncommon in the annals of diplomacy, even in the contemporary era, ideological estrangement did not necessarily preclude harmonious Russian–American relations on other levels. Strategically and diplomatically, Moscow and Washington were sometimes drawn into collaboration against a common enemy: Great Britain. After 1815, London took the lead in checking Russian expansionist tendencies in areas like the Middle East and western Asia. For a century or more after their own revolution, Americans remained intensely suspicious of British power and intentions, despite the fact that enforcement of the Monroe Doctrine depended for many decades upon England's sea power. Occasionally, therefore, Russia and America found themselves in agreement against Great Britain, although these episodes were usually short lived and involved little sustained cooperation.†

*The George Kennan alluded to above was a distant relative of the contemporary American diplomat and historian, George F. Kennan, who is widely (and perhaps erroneously) regarded as the "author" of America's postwar containment policy.

†An outstanding example of Anglophobia as a force producing Russian–American good will was provided in

By 1900, a new common enemy had replaced Great Britain. This was Imperial Japan, which in time posed the severest threat to America's "Open Door" principle in China. In 1904–1905, Japan administered a humiliating defeat to czarist Russia in the Russo–Japanese War. Thanks to the mediation of President Theodore Roosevelt, however, the ensuing settlement in the Treaty of Portsmouth proved more favorable to Moscow than Russia had a right to expect on the basis of its poor military showing. Although Japan had long been regarded as America's protégé (the country had been opened to Western contact by Commodore Matthew Perry in 1853), by the early 1900s its diplomacy engendered growing apprehension in Washington, as well as in London. Seeking to create a more favorable balance of forces in the Far East, President Roosevelt used his position as "honest broker" between Russia and Japan to mitigate Tokyo's harsh demands upon Moscow.[28]

America and the Communist Revolution

The origins of the cold war, some commentators are convinced, must be traced back to World War I, particularly to the months immediately following the seizure of power in Russia on November 7, 1917, by Nikolai Lenin and his Bolshevik followers. As every student of modern history is aware, Lenin's revolution did not topple the ancient and increasingly inept czarist political structure; that had been accomplished in the spring by the revolutionary group (in which Marxists were in a minority) which chose Alexander Kerensky as its leader. Dedicated to democracy and pledged to hold national elections, Kerensky was warmly approved in the West. At last, the hard crust of Russian political backwardness had been penetrated and democracy appeared on the verge of becoming established in the largest nation on the globe.

Lenin's seizure of power from the Kerensky regime appeared a tragedy to many Western minds for several reasons. It aborted what seemed a certain Russian progression toward democratic government and delivered the control of Russia's affairs to a conspiratorial group employing

1863, when a Russian fleet entered New York harbor. Americans interpreted this move as czarist support for the Union during the Civil War; the presence of the fleet apparently signified Moscow's readiness to provide tangible assistance to the Union cause. As historians discovered much later, Britain and Russia were on the verge of hostilities (czarist forces had just crushed the Polish Revolt); Moscow thus used New York harbor as a sanctuary for its inferior fleet, to escape the Royal Navy in the case of hostilities. If war erupted, the Russian fleet might have used this American base to attack British commerce. For a discussion of this episode and citation of available evidence, see Thomas A. Bailey, *A Diplomatic History of the American People*, 8th ed. (New York: Appleton-Century-Crofts, 1969), pp. 364–365.

totalitarian methods. It presaged the emergence of a new and perhaps more dangerous form of despotic rule in Russia, one possibly even more dangerous than czarism. It brought to power a band of revolutionaries who were openly scornful of the Judeo–Christian moral code and other canons of civilized conduct. It raised innumerable questions about Russia's behavior abroad, since a fundamental tenet of the Marxist credo was promotion of "world revolution." But the most immediately pressing problem was the impact of events in Russia on the Allied war effort. Lenin's government was determined to withdraw from the war, even if (as events turned out) it had to make a humiliating peace with Germany to do so. This step placed new and ominous burdens on the other Allies. With the eastern front now pacified, Germany could turn its formidable war machine against the West.

For these reasons, it would be an understatement to say that President Wilson and other Allied leaders greeted the Communist Revolution in Russia with something less than enthusiasm. For a longer period even than its European allies, the United States withheld diplomatic recognition, refused to trade with the Soviet Union, and otherwise pursued a policy of noncooperation with the Communist regime. President Wilson's preference (in Russia and elsewhere) for "orderly reform" of antiquated governmental and political systems was well known. Moreover, Lenin's government showed no disposition to pay czarist war debts or to compensate foreigners for confiscated property. The executions and imprisonments which followed the Communist *coup* alienated Western opinion. Above all, perhaps, the international objectives of Bolshevism—the undisguised Marxist goal of fomenting "proletarian revolutions" in other countries—aroused deep apprehensions outside Russia.[29]

The months that followed Russia's withdrawal from World War I (formalized by the Treaty of Brest-Litovsk with Germany early in 1918) witnessed an intensification of tensions between Lenis's government and the Western Allies. Indeed, some commentators—the "re-examinists," who dispute official and "orthodox" interpretations of the cold war—are convinced that this period was crucial in bringing Soviet–American hostilities to a new peak after World War II. In their view, the Allies tried to apply the strategy enunciated by that militant foe of Communism, Winston Churchill, who advised Western governments to strangle the Bolshevik baby in its cradle! Beginning in 1918, America, Britain, France, and Japan actively intervened in Russia's affairs. For several months thereafter (American troops withdrew early in 1920), Western governments supported the "White Invasions" that sought to overthrow Lenin's regime. Beset on several fronts simultane-

ously, Communist officials in time defeated the counter-revolutionaries—and in the process emerged with greater national strength and a more monolithic political control than they had possessed earlier. Some students of Soviet–American relations are convinced that these foreign incursions into Russia inevitably turned the Communist government in a totalitarian direction and convinced the Marxist elite of the enduring reality of "capitalist encirclement."[30]

Against this "re-examinist" point of view, the official and more orthodox interpretation holds that America's participation in the foreign interventions within Russia was always very limited vis-à-vis the French, British, and Japanese roles. America's *military* goal was to prevent Allied war materials from falling into German hands and to assist a military force known as the Czech Legion to escape from Russia and continue the war on the western front. Far from endeavoring to overthrow Lenin's government by outside force, America's *political* objective was to block and limit Japanese expansionism in Siberia and possibly Tokyo's annexation of Soviet territory in Asia. Admittedly opposed to Communism, President Wilson declared on several occasions that America could not seek to eliminate it by military force.[31] It is noteworthy that the Soviet government itself tacitly acknowledged Wilson's aims in 1933, when the State Department presented documentary evidence that Washington was seeking primarily to restrain Japanese incursions at Russia's expense.[32]

This episode in Soviet–American relations, however, is a classic example of the fact that what is objectively true may be less important than what people (or governments) *believe to be true*. Unquestionably, the Allied interventions in Russia provided evidence to support the pre-existing Marxist conviction that hostility and enmity surrounded the Soviet system on all sides. Believing in the concept of "capitalist encirclement," Lenin and his supporters were quickly confronted with its reality. Nor, as Robert P. Browder has asserted, were Communist policy-makers prepared to draw fine distinctions concerning the reasons why British or French or American troops were on their soil.[33] The "White Invasions" no doubt also reenforced traditional Russian fears about the security of their country and the vulnerability of many of their frontiers. However, it also has to be acknowledged that dedicated Marxists believed in "capitalist encirclement" long before 1918. The hostility of the outside world was a basic Marxist assumption, requiring no foreign intervention for its validity. If the Allied interventions had never occurred, there is no reason to suppose that Lenin, and (after 1924) Stalin, would have abandoned this fundamental Communist tenet.

From the Revolution to the New Deal

For nearly fifteen years after the Bolshevik Revolution, the policy of the United States toward Soviet Russia underwent little significant change. After it became apparent that the Soviet regime was not going to be overthrown, American policy under Wilson and successive Republican Presidents was shaped by three fundamental considerations: extreme ideological hostility between American democracy and Soviet Communism; disagreements between the two countries over Communist repudiation of czarist war debts and confiscation of foreign-owned property; and Communist intrigue in the internal affairs of other countries through the instrumentalities of the Third International and local Communist parties directed from Moscow. As late as 1933, an official State Department memorandum cited these three reasons in support of continuing American refusal to recognize the Soviet government.

By the early 1930s certain influences growing out of internal affairs within the two countries and out of the international community were reshaping relations between them. One of these was the desire of both countries to expand their foreign trade. By the late 1920s Russia had embarked upon the ambitious First Five-Year Plan, by which she hoped substantially to raise agricultural and, to a lesser extent, industrial output. Imports from America would greatly assist in this goal. Meantime, vocal groups throughout the United States were calling for an extension of American markets to Russia, and were bringing pressure to bear upon Congress and the White House to achieve that end.

On the international scene, the imperialistic designs of Japan, Germany, and Italy signaled the end of traditional American–Japanese friendship and drove both the United States and Russia to take steps to promote their own security. Once again, a common enemy was forcing the two nations to collaborate. The first step was the resumption of diplomatic relations. They were renewed between the two nations after the Kremlin pledged noninterference in the internal affairs of the United States through Communist groups directed from Moscow, and agreed to make a satisfactory settlement on repudiated Russian debts and confiscated foreign property.[34] For the first time since the Communist Revolution, the United States and the Soviet Union were prepared to maintain normal and friendly relations.*

---

*Neither of these conditions was fulfilled to the satisfaction of the State Department. Tension characterized relations between the two countries from 1933 to World War II over such questions as the activities of the Comintern and the harassment of State Department officials in Moscow. Department of State, *Foreign Relations of the United States. The Soviet Union: 1933–1939* (Washington, D.C.: U.S. Government Printing Office, 1952), pp.

The Road to War

As the Axis menace began to threaten the security of Europe and the world, events moved in a series of diplomatic crises toward their inexorable climax in World War II. Not until it was attacked by Japan at Pearl Harbor on December 7, 1941, did the United States officially abandon its policy of nonintervention in Europe's diplomatic quarrels, although private and governmental opinion in the United States nearly always was favorable to the victims of Axis aggression. America's policy of "aid short of war" to Great Britain in the months before Pearl Harbor was a crucial element in that country's heroic stand against Germany after the defeat of France. President Roosevelt's detractors also pointed to a hardening of America's attitudes toward expansionist Japan—a posture which some observers at the time and later were certain "drove" Japanese officials to attack the United States. Nevertheless, the United States in the main stood aloof from efforts inside and outside the League of Nations to stem the tide of Axis aggression against countries like China, Ethiopia, Austria, Czechoslovakia, and Poland. Receiving little beside moral support from Washington, policy-makers in London and Paris resorted to a policy of "appeasement" of Axis demands, on the tragically mistaken assumption that reasonableness and conciliation would satisfy Axis territorial ambitions and avert war.

The emergence of the cold war in the late 1940s cannot be understood intelligently without some grasp of the sequence of steps leading to World War II. In the "re-examinist" view, Soviet behavior during and after World War II is explicable only in terms of events during the 1930s. Intense Soviet suspicion of the intentions of Western governments; Moscow's wartime and postwar moves in Germany and Eastern Europe; the U.S.S.R.'s view of, and behavior in, the United Nations after 1945; the inability of the wartime Allies to agree upon postwar settlements for Germany or to preserve Allied unity after the Axis defeat—these and other cold war controversies must be evaluated against a background of mounting diplomatic crisis during the 1930s.

While space is not available to reconstruct this sequence of events in great detail, we must at least take note of the major developments which may have contributed to later cold war animosities. For our purposes, perhaps the central fact was the growing distrust prevailing between the Soviet Union and the West as the world moved toward the abyss of war. The existing pattern of alienation and suspicion that had characterized relations between Soviet Russia and the Western

---

132–134, 224–225, 446–451. The debt question dragged on for years before it was settled, with the State Department convinced that Russia had never intended to resolve the issue fairly.

powers became greatly intensified during the interwar period. As they faced a resurgent Germany under a Nazi dictatorship, an expansionist Italy, and a Japan devoted to aggrandizement in the Pacific, Western policy-makers operated upon the premise that the Communist government of Russia was as untrustworthy and unreliable as ever. In some measure (by discrediting socialist and other non-Marxist political groups in Europe), Marxists had in fact contributed to the rise of Naziism; weakened by economic dislocations and by Stalin's "purges" of some of Russia's best military leaders, Russia was in no position to contribute to League of Nations efforts designed to contain Axis expansionism. Consequently, Western leaders were unimpressed by Soviet delegate Maxim Litvinov's impassioned pleas at Geneva for collective action against the dictators. Such demands were regarded as either insincere propaganda gestures, or efforts by Soviet policy-makers to embroil Western governments in a conflict with Berlin, Rome, and Tokyo, while Russia remained aloof. Confronted with their own internal political and economic problems after the Great Depression, Britain and France ignored Russian entreaties in favor of "appeasement."

From their perspective, Soviet policy-makers might legitimately have concluded that the Western powers were so blinded by their antipathy toward Communism that they were unable to discern their own vital interests, much less Russia's. Soviet officials had read Hitler's *Mein Kampf,* and they had to assume that Western officials were also familiar with Hitler's avowed objectives. Foremost among these was the *Drang nach Osten,* the "drive to the East," in which the major targets were Poland and the Ukraine, Russia's agricultural heartland. In short, Hitler proposed to *dismember Russia.* Besides this, Hitler had another goal that met with widespread approval in certain Western circles: Time and again, he proclaimed his determination to *eliminate Bolshevism* as a political force disturbing international stability. Conditioned by Marxist ideology to be profoundly distrustful of the motives of capitalist states, Russia's Communist elite found their worst fears confirmed by Western behavior in dealing with Axis aggrandizement. Did the evident lack of Western interest in joining with the U.S.S.R. in a common front against the Axis mean that Washington, London, and Paris regarded Communism as a greater threat than Hitlerism? So long as the dictators expanded *eastward,* were Western officials content to let aggression go unchecked? Did conservative groups in the West actually *favor* Hitler's effort to liquidate the Communist threat forever?

Such questions even today are very difficult to answer with assurance. Lacking access to the Kremlin's archives, and even to relevant materials from Western sources, the student of the cold war must often rely upon partial evidence; his conclusions frequently are little better than inferences based upon a "reading between the lines" of available sources, and he must often judge the behavior of nations during the 1930s on the basis of their behavior in earlier periods. Even when such problems do not exist, judging the *real motives* of policy-makers, as distinct from their apparent or declared objectives, is always risky. Yet it seems a safe enough assertion that, during the 1930s, Western diplomatic activities strongly reenforced existing Soviet conceptions of the outside world. Similarly, Western views of Communism were strengthened by Soviet behavior during this fateful era.

Munich and the Nazi–Soviet Pact

Two developments during the late 1930s brought many of the attitudes and suspicions we have described into focus and led to new tensions in Western–Soviet relations. One of these was the Munich crisis (September 29–30, 1938) and its aftermath. Earlier in the spring, Hitler had executed his *Anschluss* with Austria, whereby that country was "reunited" with the German Fatherland and its independence lost. Next on Hitler's timetable was Czechoslovakia, whose Sudentenland was inhabited largely by Germans. Harassed by an escalating German war of nerves, backed ultimately by the threat of an invasion, the government of Czechoslovakia remained prepared to fight for its freedom, provided its military allies—France and Soviet Russia—supported its independence. (Britain had a defense treaty with France, although it had none with Czechoslovakia.) If Czechoslovakia and its allies stood firm, war seemed inevitable, since Hitler gave no indication of retreating from his demands for the dismemberment of the most promising democracy in Eastern Europe. To avert this calamity, Britain's Prime Minister Neville Chamberlain and France's Premier Edouard Daladier met Hitler at his headquarters near Munich in September. The ensuing Munich Agreement—heralded by Chamberlain as achieving "peace in our time"—was a triumph for the Axis. Hitler got the Sudentenland; and when he moved to incorporate the whole of Czechoslovakia into the Third Reich several months later, he acquired one of the most important munitions factories in Europe (the modern Skoda arms works), as well as a strategic gateway for pursuing his *Drang Nach Osten.* If it had any appeal at all by this stage, the concept of "collective security" under the League of Nations had been totally undermined.

What was Moscow's behavior during the Munich crisis? Ostensibly, it was exemplary. Perhaps because it realized Czechoslovakia's strategic importance for Russia's own security, or because it was convinced that the Axis threat was ultimately aimed at Russia, or because it believed that only *collective* action could deter the dictators, for these or some other reasons the Kremlin reiterated its pledge to defend Czechoslovakia—alone, if necessary. Soviet representatives were not invited to the Munich Conference (nor, for that matter, were Czech delegates); Moscow was not consulted about what steps it was ready to take to contain aggression. For reasons we have already noted, London and Paris seriously doubted Moscow's ability to oppose the Axis powers effectively. Collective defense efforts were, therefore, rejected by the West in favor of appeasing Hitler's demands.

Whatever the truth of the matter—and even today, the diplomatic record of the 1930s (particularly of Soviet intentions and behavior) is far from clear—the Munich crisis was unquestionably a watershed in modern history. That it whetted Hitler's appetite for new conquests can hardly be doubted; within a few months he had annexed the whole of Czechoslovakia, and a year after the Munich Conference, he had launched his *Blitzkreig* against Poland. The Munich Conference also greatly widened the "credibility gap" between the West's professions and its behavior. Munich emerged as the acme of unprincipled disregard for the rights of small states and of calloused indifference to ethical precepts in statecraft. Most fundamentally for our purposes, the Munich Conference destroyed any prospect of Western–Soviet cooperation against Axis aggression. While they may have gained time at Munich (as defenders of the agreement frequently argue), Western governments ultimately confronted an infinitely more dangerous Axis—and, as we shall see, they now faced it *alone*.

Within a few brief weeks, Berlin and Moscow arrived at a *détente*, leaving Hitler free to attack the West and giving Stalin a free hand to establish Soviet hegemony in Eastern Europe, and perhaps in time in the Middle East. Frustrated in its efforts to forge an anti-Axis front, after Munich the Kremlin abandoned the effort and arrived at an understanding with Nazi Germany. To the West, the Nazi–Soviet agreement (August 31, 1939) symbolized totalitarian duplicity, proving to many minds that little choice existed between dictatorships of the political right or left. At Munich, the appeasers had sowed the wind. Now—confronted with a far stronger Axis and a neutralized Russia—they were reaping the whirlwind. Stalin was prepared, as he was many times before and after, to lay aside ideological considerations for the sake of Russian strategic and diplomatic objectives. From this treaty, he gained time in which to build up Soviet forces for a possible showdown with Hitler; he acquired territory—the Baltic region and eastern Poland—which served as a military buffer zone and as a new frontier for Communist penetration, and a base from which to exert new pressures against Turkey and Persia.

The Nazi–Soviet Pact was a disaster for the West and a masterpiece of *Realpolitik* for the Kremlin. Proof of Soviet perfidy, to many Western minds, was the fact that Russia was negotiating with both German and Western representatives *concurrently*, when it decided to arrive at an accommodation with Berlin!

No sooner had this accord shocked the world than Hitler moved (on September 1, 1939) to attack Poland. With eastern Poland now under Russian domination, and western Poland quickly overrun by German forces, the independence of the country disappeared. After conquering Poland, having no fear of a "two-front war" with Russia, Hitler launched his attack against the Low Countries and France; the latter surrendered on June 22.

What interpretation can legitimately be placed upon Soviet Russia's conduct during this period? By the Nazi–Soviet Pact, the Kremlin had plainly turned the tables on the advocates of appeasement. The diplomatic historian Thomas A. Bailey has stated the "orthodox" interpretation. In his view, Stalin "cleverly contrived to turn Hitler against the democracies in the expectation that they would bleed one another white, while he emerged supreme."[35] Soviet gains from the understanding with Germany both advanced traditional Russian foreign policy goals and furthered the Marxist objective of world revolution—all at the expense of the West. Re-examinist commentators hold a contrary view. They interpret the Nazi–Soviet Pact as Stalin's "answer" to Western diplomacy at Munich, whose result (if not deliberate intention) was to turn Hitler's ambitions eastward at Russia's expense. If Soviet policy-makers could not persuade the West to collaborate in "collective security" measures to stop Axis expansionism, then they had no alternative but to protect their interests unilaterally, by making a deal with Hitler.[36]

As though Stalin's conduct in dividing Europe with Hitler were not outrageous enough, another Soviet move evoked new Western (especially American) disapprobation. This was Russia's attack upon Finland late in 1939 and into 1940. Not unexpectedly, American opinion was overwhelmingly pro-Finnish in this David-and-Goliath contest. President Roosevelt outspokenly denounced Moscow's "wanton disregard for law" in its absorption of Finland.[37] But to re-examinist commentators then and later, Russia's move against Finland was but part of a Soviet effort to consolidate its defenses against Germany (whose influence in the Baltic region was strong). This was, and remains, a minority viewpoint. Russia's Finnish campaign aroused world wide indignation—so much so that the League of Nations (in a move of dubious legality) *expelled* the Soviet Union from the world organization. To the Kremlin and its apologists, this constituted still further evidence of the outside world's deep aversion to Communism. Japan, Italy, and Germany, for example, had flagrantly disregarded the League's instructions and had openly embarked upon a path of conquest; yet they had tamely been permitted to "withdraw" from the League of Nations, at their own option. Russia alone had been given eviction papers. Small wonder, re-examinists argued in the years ahead, that thereafter the Soviet Union would be loath to entrust its security or its vital diplomatic interests to another international assembly, such as the United Nations.[38]

The "Strange Alliance" During World War II

Modern history has witnessed a number of diplomatic revolutions—none perhaps more epochal than the one that took place less than two years after the Nazi–Soviet Pact. That Hitler had altogether abandoned his cherished goal of attacking Russia was dubious. Having conquered Western Europe, and momentarily expecting Britain's collapse, Berlin began to plan *Operation Barbarossa:* the long-awaited offensive against the U.S.S.R. There was no reason to think—and many Western observers shared the view with the Germans—that Russia could successfully resist the Nazi war machine any better than other victims of Nazi aggression. On June 22, 1941, German troops crossed the Russian frontier. Overnight, official and unofficial opinion in the West reversed itself: Russia was now the underdog, and "Uncle Joe" Stalin quickly took his place with President Roosevelt and Prime Minister Churchill, to form the Big Three directing Allied strategy. Churchill expressed the prevailing sentiment, when he said that if the Devil himself opposed Hitlerism, then Britain would ally itself with the Devil! FDR promptly promised Moscow American assistance; and during the course of the war, American aid to Russia totaled some $11 billion.[39]

Yet even this climactic turn of events in no sense eliminated long-standing sources of discord among the wartime Allies or produced an era of wholehearted cooperation among them. Major and minor frictions characterized their relations throughout the conflict. Repeatedly, Western governments complained about Russia's lack of cooperation (such as Moscow's refusal to make airfields available to Allied planes) and the absence of Soviet "appreciation" for supplies (sent at great hardship on the dangerous "Murmansk run" through the Baltic) furnished during Russia's darkest hour. Americans stationed in Moscow during the war echoed the familiar refrain that they were subjected to numerous restrictions by Soviet authorities and often humiliated.

From the Soviet viewpoint, Western attitudes and behavior during the war often confirmed Communist suspicions. Some segments of Western opinion had long desired a confrontation between Hitlerism and Stalinism; after this mutual exhaustion, Western nations would be arbiters of the world. An advocate of this idea in the United States was Senator (later President) Harry Truman, who urged the Roosevelt administration to assist *both* Germany and Russia in the hope that two obnoxious dictatorships would be eliminated![40] Although President Roosevelt rejected this view, many high-ranking American military leaders (including Chief of Staff General George C. Marshall) were certain that Russian defenses would soon collapse before the Nazi onslaught.[41] As time passed, and as Soviet forces turned (after the decisive Battle of Stalingrad early in 1943) from the defensive to the offensive, Americans widely attributed Russia's survival chiefly to American aid.

If these disputes tended to be minor, military strategy and (as the end of the war approached) political issues fomented real tensions among the Allies. Remembering the Nazi–Soviet Pact, Western officials were apprehensive throughout the war about a new German–Soviet understanding at the expense of the West. Keeping Russia in the war—and doing everything possible to inhibit Moscow from making a separate peace—remained dominant Western objectives. In addition, American military leaders repeatedly urged President Roosevelt and his civilian advisers *to secure Soviet entry into the war against Japan at the earliest possible date.* Through the early months of the war (particularly while the contest with Germany hung in the balance), Moscow held to a position of neutrality toward Japan, while American and other Allied forces bore the brunt of the Pacific campaign. American commanders understandably sought Russian assistance in this theater; it was deemed vital for the final assault on the Japanese home islands, when the Allies expected very high casualties. Finally, at the Yalta Conference early in 1945, Stalin gave his pledge: Soviet forces would enter the war against Japan 90 days after the defeat of Germany (which occurred on May 7, 1945). When Russia did declare war against the Japanese empire (on August 8)—between the dropping of the first and second atomic bombs on Japanese cities—its participation was no longer needed. As it had done many times in the past, orthodox historians and many Americans concluded, the Kremlin had calculatingly timed its moves, not to make an effective contribution to Japan's defeat but merely to share in the spoils of peace-making. The re-examinist contention was that Stalin had kept his word: At America's insistent urging, Soviet troops engaged Japanese forces in Manchuria on virtually the same day Stalin had pledged at Yalta.

In the early phase of the war, Soviet leaders had their own demands—the leading one perhaps being for the West to open a "second front" in Europe to relieve German military pressure or

Russia. In the Soviet view, Churchill and Roosevelt had promised to invade Europe as early as 1942; yet it was not until June 6, 1944, that the D-Day Invasion actually took place. What accounted for this delay? The explanation in Washington and London was that a military operation of this magnitude took time and massive preparation; it simply could not be mounted without the most careful planning and military buildup. As it was, even when Europe was invaded on D-Day, the outcome remained uncertain for several weeks. Meanwhile, Western air assaults were reducing the Axis war capability and destroying morale in occupied Europe. The Western attack against German and Italian forces in North Africa, moreover, ultimately destroyed a powerful Axis army, prepared the way for restoration of Allied control over the Mediterranean, and saved the oil supplies of the Middle East for the Allied war effort.

Soviet leaders, Moscow's protests and inquiries made clear, were unconvinced by such arguments. Was the West *deliberately* delaying the second front, while Russia's existence was in peril? Was Western antipathy toward Communism prolonging the German presence on Russian soil? Did Western policy-makers intentionally seek the "mutual exhaustion" of Germany and Russia, so that London and Washington could dictate a postwar settlement? Western officials rejected such ideas categorically. Re-examinist commentators during the war and afterwards were convinced that Soviet Russia had legitimate grievances and causes for deep concern about Western conduct.[42]

Political Issues in World War II

Many of the political questions that were to become sources of sharp cold war animosity in the late 1940s periodically challenged Allied cohesiveness during World War II. Particularly after the tide of battle had turned against the Axis powers, these issues came more and more to the forefront. Toward most of them, President Roosevelt's approach was uncomplicated: He preferred to *delay decision* until the war had been successfully terminated. Recalling the secret agreements that had compounded the problem of peace-making after World War I and that had aroused great public resentment, FDR repeatedly demanded that major political questions be deferred, lest they impair Allied unity. However, British Prime Minister Churchill, an active opponent of Communism before the war and a keen student of history, consistently urged the American President to keep political and diplomatic considerations in mind in shaping military strategy. Far better than Roosevelt, Churchill recognized the intimate and indissoluble *connection* between military and political decisions; he knew that the shape of the

military frontiers at the end of the war would have a vital bearing upon political settlements made thereafter. Time and again, Churchill advocated military moves dictated wholly or in large part by *political* objectives. An outstanding example was his plan for an invasion of the "soft underbelly" of Europe, carrying Western forces into the Balkans and Eastern Europe, instead of a cross-channel invasion through western France. Churchill's avowed goal was to interpose Western troops between the Soviet Red Army and as much of Europe as possible, leaving Germany and much of Eastern Europe under Anglo–American control. President Roosevelt had little sympathy with this scheme. Even more fundamentally, American military advisers ruled it out as being militarily infeasible, possibly even disastrous: Europe's "soft underbelly" was in reality a formidable military challenge which American commanders did not care to assume. Such an invasion would require Allied troops to fight in some of the most difficult terrain on the continent and would make Allied supply lines (stretched from America and England to the Adriatic and the eastern Mediterranean) extremely vulnerable. American officials thus held out for an invasion of France, a strategic plan which the British in time accepted. With hindsight, in the light of cold war tensions developing after 1945, Churchill's idea still seems attractive to many Americans. If it had been carried out successfully, much of Europe might now be free of Communist control! Leaving aside the question of its military hazards, we need to keep in mind that all through the war, a fear haunted Western policy-makers: the specter of a separate Russian peace with Germany. We can of course do little more than speculate about the possible outcome of Churchill's plan. A few years earlier, however, when Moscow believed its interests were being jeopardized by Britain and France, Stalin's "answer" had been the Nazi–Soviet Pact, which virtually guaranteed Germany a free hand against the West![43]

Not even Roosevelt could successfully defer all important political questions until the war's end. On the eastern front, Soviet forces held back the German attack at Stalingrad; by early 1943, the Red Army had begun a series of offensives that would place Soviet forces in Berlin two years later. As it cleared Russian territory of the Axis invaders, the Red Army liberated Eastern Europe. Decisions about the political future and boundaries of these nations had to be made. By the second half of 1944, Western forces were moving toward the Rhine. Despite some success in its Ardennes counter-offensive at the end of the year, the German army was being defeated (Italy had already surrendered on September 8, 1943). Only in the Pacific (which was always regarded as a secondary theater of war) was the end of the war viewed as perhaps still two years away.

More than any other single issue, the problem of the postwar political order in Eastern Europe ultimately destroyed Allied unity and produced the cold war. As it had many times in history, this region engendered intense diplomatic and political antagonisms. Even today, many commentators are convinced that the problems of Germany and Eastern Europe *remain* the principal obstacles to a Soviet–American *détente*.

Even before the war was over, it became apparent that Western and Soviet conceptions of the future of Eastern Europe and Germany tended to diverge significantly. Western governments (British and French officials, more than American) were aware of traditional *Russian* ambitions in Eastern Europe and of ancient animosities such as that between the Poles and the Russians. The Czars had "partitioned" Poland three times at the end of the eighteenth century; Russian troops had crushed Poland's independence movement in 1863. In the Nazi–Soviet Pact, Stalin had successfully gained Russian dominance over half of Poland. On their part, the Poles were understandably apprehensive about Russian expansionism and often outspokenly anti-Communist. Polish forces had played a prominent role in the "White Invasions" that sought to overthrow Lenin's government. During the 1920s and 1930s, Polish–Russian relations were more often than not hostile. As for the Baltic states and Finland, these had been created out of *Russian* territory by the peace-makers after World War I. The new Communist government of Russia, gripped by pressing internal problems and threatened by foreign invasions, was in no position to resist the Versailles settlement. Yet there was no reason to suppose that Russian policy-makers regarded the map of Europe as it was drawn after World War I to be permanent. Several of the lesser Axis states (specifically, Hungary, Rumania, Bulgaria, and Finland) had joined Germany in attacking Russia, causing billions of dollars' worth of property damage and millions of civilian and military casualties. Western officials thus had ample grounds for concern about Soviet moves in Eastern Europe.

The problem of Poland epitomized the challenge of preserving Allied unity over political issues. After Poland was overrun by Hitler's *Wehrmacht*, a Polish government-in-exile established itself in London. Throughtout the war, it presented Poland's "case" to Washington and London; with much less success, it sought to influence Soviet policy. Relations between this Polish group and the Kremlin were always tense—and after April, 1943, they became openly hostile. For at that time, Nazi propagandists announced that Russian troops had in 1940 committed the "Katyn forest massacre," in which some 8000 Polish officers had been executed while they were prisoners of war in Russia. To many Poles and to their sym-

pathizers in the West, this report at least partially explained the disappearance of many Polish officers whose whereabouts had been unknown since Stalin's troops entered Poland in 1939. In time, Polish groups in the West became convinced that Berlin's charge was true, and many Western commentators also ultimately accepted the fact of Moscow's guilt. Stalin's government of course vehemently denied the accusation, blaming the massacre on Hitler's forces. Several investigations of the Katyn massacre were held (including one later by the American Congress). The evidence even now remains ambiguous, although the dominant view still is that Stalin ordered the executions. A minority view—advocated by the re-examinist school of cold war commentators—maintains that the episode was a skillfully contrived Nazi fabrication, designed to destroy Allied unity.[44] In any case, the Katyn massacres *did* mark the beginning of a deterioration in Allied relations on the Polish question, leading in time to an open break among them on Poland and Eastern Europe generally. The Kremlin broke with the Polish government-in-exile over the matter. As the Red army advanced across Eastern Europe, a Kremlin-supported Committee of National Liberation (popularly called the Lublin government) was recognized by Moscow as the rightful Polish political authority.

A few months later another crisis erupted involving Poland; this one added to Western apprehensions about Soviet designs in Eastern Europe. In August, 1944, after witnessing the steady advance of the Red Army, the Polish underground directed the population of Warsaw to "rise" against the hated Nazi conquerors. Support for the uprising was expected momentarily from Soviet troops. But the support never came—at least not in time to prevent a massive bloodbath, in which superior German forces killed thousands of Poles, before Hitler evacuated Warsaw. During this slaughter, the Red Army remained halted fifteen to twenty miles away from the city for nearly two months. Nor would Stalin permit Western aircraft to supply the beleaguered city. Critics of Soviet behavior then and afterward were certain about Stalin's objective: It was to eliminate any organized opposition (such as the Warsaw underground) to the Marxist regime soon to be imposed upon Poland by the victorious Red Army. Then and later, Soviet leaders denied the charge. The official Soviet explanation—and many re-examinist students of the cold war later believed it was justified—was that military necessity compelled the Red Army to stop its advance, in preparation for a new offensive against strong German forces in Poland. The Polish underground, in the Soviet view, had called for an uprising without any "clearance" from Moscow or any prior assurance of Soviet support. Again, Roosevelt and Churchill were highly disturbed by Russia's conduct (the latter referring to Stalin's "strange and sinister behavior").[45] Anti-Communist groups in the West believed that the Warsaw uprising was an essential step in the communization of Eastern Europe and the imposition of iron-fisted Soviet rule.

By the end of 1944, these and other issues eliciting disagreement among the Allies (like the nature of the proposed United Nations) demanded settlement. They became the main items of the Big Three conference at Yalta in the Crimea on February 3–11, 1945.

Yalta—The Pinnacle of Unity

The military situation existing at the time of the Yalta Conference had a direct bearing upon the results achieved.[46] Russian forces were moving against Vienna, having already liberated most of Poland and East Prussia. By contrast, Anglo-American troops were just beginning to move forward again, after stopping Germany's counter-offensive in the "Battle of the Bulge." In the Pacific, Western leaders looked forward with considerable anxiety to a massive and bloody "island hopping" campaign, climaxed by a fierce struggle against the Japanese home islands. (The Yalta Conference was held, it must be remembered, before the atomic bomb had been successfully tested; it was, one American official said, a "scientific question mark.") In Europe, the Red Army was moving forward, while the Western Allies had yet to cross the Rhine.

The future of Poland—called by Churchill the key issue at the conference—was an urgent and highly contentious matter. FDR and Churchill proposed that Poland's borders as of 1941 (which followed the "Curzon line" drawn after World War I) be recognized. At length, Stalin accepted this idea, with the understanding that, to compensate for the loss of territory in the east, Poland would be given territory in the west at Germany's expense. The formal delineation of Poland's frontiers was deferred until a peace conference; but since none was ever held, this agreement became the de facto determination of postwar Poland's boundaries.

The future political orientation of Poland was also an urgent matter. President Roosevelt had for months been subjected to complaints by Polish-American groups concerning Russian conduct in their homeland; the Polish government-in-exile in London maintained steady pressure upon Churchill and Roosevelt to protect Poland's interests. Meanwhile, the Soviet military occupation of Poland threatened to present outsiders with a *fait accompli*. Refusing to recognize the London Poles, Moscow demanded that the Lublin government be "recognized" as the new Polish government, with the understanding that this regime would be "reorganized on a broader democratic basis" and that it would hold free elections in the near future. All "democratic and anti-Nazi parties" in Poland were to be free to participate—a proviso that engendered no end of controversy between the Anglo-Americans and the Russians as time passed.

Faced with the prospect of unilateral Soviet control over most of Eastern Europe, Churchill and Roosevelt prevailed upon Stalin to accept basically this same formula for other liberated nations. In a "Declaration on Liberated Europe," the Big Three pledged to support "interim governmental authorities broadly representative of all democratic elements in the population"; these regimes were expected to hold free elections "responsive to the will of the people" at an early date.

No less crucial to the future of Anglo-American-Soviet cooperation was the problem of Germany. Hitler's defeat was now imminent. Accordingly, in the Yalta Agreement, the Allies reached a consensus upon the terms of surrender and upon the principle of the "complete disarmament, demilitarization, and dismemberment" of the Third Reich. Each of the major Allies was to have a zone of occupation in Germany, with France being given its zone out of the spheres administered by Britain and the United States. An Allied Control Commission was to serve as a unifying mechanism for occupation policy. And in what was to become another source of intense disagreement within a few months, it was agreed "as a basis for discussion" that Germany would pay $20 billion in reparations, one-half of which would go to the U.S.S.R. Aware that after World War I the United States had to take care of European nations burdened with huge reparations payments, FDR refused to accept massive Soviet reparations claims that would leave Germany impoverished. Since no formal peace treaty with Germany was ever possible, reparations claims were settled on an *ad hoc* basis. Moscow regarded the figure of $10 billion (which was merely a "basis for discussion") as its due and shaped its policies in East Germany accordingly.

As the war in Europe approached the closing phase, American officials were becoming increasingly preoccupied with the struggle in the Pacific. Before the atomic bomb (successfully tested in early summer) had been perfected, it was anticipated that the war against Japan might last another 18 to 24 months.* For Americans, Soviet

---

*In the light of the development of nuclear weapons by the United States in the closing months of World War II, it is perhaps difficult today to understand the apprehensions among American military advisers concerning the prospect of a long and difficult military campaign against Japan after the defeat of the Axis powers in Europe, entailing a series of battles expected to last perhaps a year and a half or more after Germany surrendered. Robert E. Sherwood has written, in connection with the Yalta Conference early in 1945, that American officials counted heavily upon Russia's participation in

participation in the war against Japan was deemed essential; FDR went to Yalta determined to obtain Stalin's pledge on that point. At Yalta, Stalin promised that within 60 to 90 days after the defeat of Germany, Soviet troops would strike Japan. In return, Britain and America agreed to several concessions to Russian interests in Asia: They recognized Outer Mongolia as a Soviet satellite; they agreed that gains made by Japan in the Russo–Japanese War (1904–1905), such as the southern half of Sakhalin Island and the Soviet naval base at Port Arthur would be returned to Russia; they acknowledged Russia's pre-eminent position in the railway system of Manchuria and north China (the system had originally been built largely with Russian funds). Churchill and Roosevelt also persuaded Stalin to conclude a treaty with the Nationalist government of China, thereby providing de facto recognition of Chiang Kai-shek's government as the legitimate ruling authority vis-à-vis the Chinese Communist movement under Mao Tse-tung.

At Yalta the Big Three also made several key decisions affecting the future of the emergent United Nations, scheduled to be established later in the spring. Two major issues resolved were that the United Nations would consist of those countries that had joined in the struggle against the Axis powers, plus a few (like Argentina) that had not. A compromise was reached when Stalin accepted the idea that, in the great-power dominated Security Council, important issues would be "vetoed" by the negative vote of one of the Big Five (France and China were also counted as great powers); but the veto would not extend to procedural issues.*

Yalta is often referred to as the "high tide of Allied unity." All the participants in the conference were ostensibly pleased with its results, even if some issues (like German reparations) had been

left formally unresolved. Western leaders believed at the time—and a goodly number of commentators later agreed with them—that they had obtained several major concessions from Stalin, particularly respecting the "democratization" of European zones which were then (or were rapidly falling) under Russian military control. Moscow also pledged to enter the war against Japan, thereby lessening the prospect of high British and American casualties. Despite earlier indications to the contrary, Allied unity had been preserved; progress had been made in postwar planning; the evidence indicated that the same spirit of wartime cooperation among the Big Three would assure international stability and order after the war was over.*

Cold War: The "Orthodox" View

The euphoria produced by the Yalta Conference lasted only a few weeks. President Roosevelt's death in April, re-examinists are convinced, was a tragedy not only for America, but for international politics as well. FDR, according to this view, was certain that Allied unity would endure into the postwar stage, introducing a new era of global

---

this contest; in the Pacific, General Douglas MacArthur's strategy for defeating Japan was "based on the assumption that the Russians would contain *the great bulk* of Japanese forces on the Asiatic mainland as they had contained the Germans in Eastern Europe." If Moscow did so, this would mean "the saving of countless American lives" and might make the invasion of the Japanese home islands "unnecessary." See Robert E. Sherwood, *Roosevelt and Hopkins*, vol. 2 (New York: Bantam, 1948), p. 512, italics inserted. As events turned out, this strategy was based upon faulty Allied intelligence about Japan's military strength. In reality, the "great bulk" of Japan's forces in Asia did not exist! They had been periodically drained off to supply Japan's island defense bastions, but this fact was unknown to American military strategists, since of course it was carefully concealed by Tokyo. By early 1945, Japan was much closer to military defeat—even in the absence of the atomic bomb, much less Soviet Russia's entry into the war—than the Roosevelt administration realized. See E. M. Zacharias, *Behind Closed Doors: The Secret History of the Cold War* (New York: Putnam's, 1950).

*These and other provisions of the UN Charter, along with Western and Soviet views of the UN, are discussed at greater length in Chapter 15.

*The euphoria that surrounded the Yalta Conference at the time stands in strange contrast to the furor which it generated in the years ahead. By the late 1940s and early 1950s, the Yalta Conference had become synonymous with FDR's "softness" toward Communism and his "appeasement" of Stalin. FDR's poor health (the President died on April 12) is often cited as a primary cause of the wholesale "concessions" allegedly made to the Soviet Union. As we have seen, overt concessions were made, chiefly in the Far East; as events turned out, the atomic bomb obviated the necessity for Soviet participation in the war with Japan. But at Yalta, American policy-makers had no knowledge either that development of the a-bomb was imminent or that it was so powerful. Even without the a-bomb, as navy officials in the Pentagon insisted, Japan was closer to defeat than was generally realized; but this was a minority view among FDR's military advisers at the time. Curiously, the charge of American "appeasement" is usually directed at the Eastern European provisions of the Yalta Agreement. In this area, Americans had nothing to "concede": The entire region within a short time would be under Russian military domination. Apprehensive about Moscow's intentions, Churchill and Roosevelt obtained Stalin's pledge to "democratize" the political regimes established in this region and to hold "free elections" in the future. Events after Yalta made clear that, at worst, Stalin was totally disregarding this pledge or, at best, Western and Soviet interpretations of it were antithetical. Monolithic Marxist political systems soon apppeared in Eastern Europe. Repeatedly, London and Washington protested this development *on the basis of the Yalta understanding*. After the Republicans won the presidency in the United States in 1952, many leading members of the GOP urged President Eisenhower and Secretary of State John Foster Dulles to "repudiated" the unpopular Yalta Agreement. Eisenhower and Dulles in time refused, because they realized that if America did so, its legal basis for objecting to unilateral Soviet activities in the region would be impaired. See Sherman Adams, *First-Hand Report* (New York: Harper & Row 1961), pp. 92–93.

stability and understanding. His death left the management of American foreign affairs in the hands of a new Chief Executive who was both inexperienced and, as events soon revealed, antagonistic toward the Soviet Union. President Truman's advisers were regarded as even more skeptical than he about cooperation with Moscow and prone to adopt a "tough" stance in dealing with the Kremlin.[47]

While FDR's death admittedly created new uncertainties for international politics, it must also be recognized that even before he died Roosevelt had expressed real apprehension about the future course of Soviet–American relations.[48] Had he lived several months longer, FDR would have been faced with problems like reconciling divergent interpretations of the Yalta Agreement; finding a formula that would balance Western and Soviet interests in Eastern Europe; and securing Allied agreement upon a peace treaty with Germany. Undeniably, Roosevelt had a rapport with "Uncle Joe" Stalin which Truman lacked. Yet considerably more than personal compatibility was required to resolve the *substantive issues* fomenting increasingly serious tensions among the wartime Allies.

As in the past, Eastern Europe began to strain Allied unity to the breaking point. At Yalta, the Big Three thought they had reached a *modus vivendi* on Eastern European issues. Yet Western officials watched with rising concern the imposition in this region of monolithic Marxist systems whose authority was supported by the might of the Red army. This was, to say the least, a strange interpretation of Stalin's pledge at Yalta to "democratize" the political base of governments in the area; and while Britain and America had agreed at Yalta that "anti-fascist" elements could be eliminated from political participation, it became clear to London and Washington that Moscow viewed "anti-fascist" as synonymous with "anti-Communist." Significantly, the first day he took office, President Truman was informed by a State Department report that:

Since the Yalta Conference the Soviet Government has taken a firm and uncompromising position on nearly every major question that has arisen in our relations. The more important of these are the Polish question, the application of the Crimea [Yalta] agreement on liberated areas, the agreement on the exchange of liberated prisoners of war and civilians, and the San Francisco Conference [at which the United Nations was established]. In the liberated areas under Soviet control, the Soviet Government is proceeding largely on a unilateral basis and does not agree that the developments which have taken place justify application of the Crimea agreement.

On the specific problem of Poland, the report informed President Truman that the present situation was "highly unsatisfactory," with Soviet authorities refusing to cooperate in efforts to assure *joint* supervision of the Yalta Agreement. The future status of Poland, the State Department believed, "remains one of our most complex and urgent problems both in the international and the domestic field." The same Soviet tendency was identified in the Balkans, where unilateral Soviet decisions in Rumania, Bulgaria, and Hungary amounted to "political interference in the respective countries" involved, in violation of the Yalta Declaration on Liberated Europe. American protests based upon this declaration had been rejected by the Kremlin.[49] Although as Vice President he had been generally familiar with Allied negotiations during the war, President Truman later recorded in his *Memoirs* that very shortly after he succeeded Roosevelt the "full picture" of what was happening in Eastern Europe became clear:

The plain story is this: We and the British wanted to see the establishment in Poland of a government truly representative of all the people. The tragic fact was that, though we were allies of Russia, we had not been permitted to send our observers into Poland. Russia was in full military occupation of the country at the time and had given her full support to the so-called Lublin government—a puppet regime of Russia's own making.

Even by this early date, Truman was convinced, Moscow had shown disregard for the Yalta Agreement. "Properly carried out," this understanding would have satisfied the legitimate interests of the Big Three in Poland and elsewhere in Eastern Europe. But Britain and America now faced "the failure of the Russians to live up to this agreement."[50] A short time later, American Ambassador Averell Harriman in Moscow cabled the President that the West confronted a "barbarian invasion of Europe," growing out of Russia's imposition of totalitarian regimes upon areas under its military control. A "reconsideration" of America's policies toward the Soviet Union was imperative; American policy-makers had to accept the idea that Moscow was unlikely to "act in accordance with the principles to which the rest of the world held in international affairs." Citing Stalin's indicated interest in American aid to rehabilitate Russia, Ambassador Harriman, reflecting the views in no small measure of his top assistant in the Moscow Embassy, George F. Kennan,* urged

*Regarded (not altogether correctly) as the formulator of America's policy of containment early in 1947, George F. Kennan became one of the State Department's leading Kremlinologists. Kennan was fluent in the Russian language and extremely well informed in Russian history, and had spent several years of diplomatic service in Moscow. In a still illuminating essay written in September, 1944, Kennan analyzed Soviet

the Truman administration to adopt a hard line in dealing with the Kremlin and to insist that concessions to Russia be matched by Soviet concessions to American demands.[51] This approach increasingly characterized Truman's attitude toward the Soviet Union.

Re-examinist Appraisals of the Cold War

In time, this official or "orthodox" view of how the cold war began—attributing it primarily to expansionist Soviet moves in Eastern Europe—was vigorously challenged by re-examinist commentators and historians. Rejecting the idea that Russia's wartime and early postwar behavior stemmed from a "Communist global conspiracy," this school of thought held that Stalin's diplomatic moves in Eastern Europe and elsewhere were essentially *defensive*, motivated by Russia's age-old quest for *security* on its vulnerable frontiers, and carried out in response to certain Anglo–American statements and deeds arousing *bona fide* apprehension in the Kremlin. We have already alluded to several themes conspicuous in the re-examinist interpretation: initial Western opposition to the Communist Revolution and America's policy of nonrecognition of the Soviet government thereafter; the attempt by foreign powers to overthrow the Communist regime after 1917; the refusal of Western governments during the 1930s to take Soviet pleas for "collective security" seri-

---

domestic and foreign policy. Several themes are prominent in his essay, such as the basic continuity between czarist and Stalinist goals and behavior. Stalin, Kennan wrote, "had settled firmly back into the throne of Ivan the Terrible and Peter the Great." Differing with other postwar American Kremlinologists, Kennan did *not* view Communist ideology as the driving force behind Soviet behavior at home and abroad; he saw Marxist dogma primarily as *instrumental* to the achievement of Russia's goals and as a rationalization of them. Always mindful of Russia's vulnerable position and its humiliation at the hands of foreign nations since 1917, Stalin's government relied upon its own efforts to alter this state of affairs; it had no real confidence that other nations would protect Russian interests. Even before the war had ended, the Kremlin's objective was "to increase in every way and with all possible speed the relative strength of the Soviet Union in world affairs, and to exploit to the utmost this purpose the rivalries and differences among other powers." As Germany's defeat loomed, Moscow saw an opportunity to complete what it had begun with the Nazi–Soviet Pact of 1939: the establishment of its power in Eastern Europe. Less interested in whether governments in this area were avowedly Marxist, the Kremlin was concerned with whether they were pro-Soviet and amenable to Soviet influence. By the end of 1944, it was clear to Kennan that Moscow was committed to the goal "of becoming the dominant power of Eastern and Central Europe." In another essay written in May, 1945, Kennan analyzed Soviet policy in this region in terms of two objectives: gaining Western "recognition" of Soviet control over the region, and obtaining American aid for Russian rehabilitation and economic progress. See George F. Kennan, *Memoirs* (1925–1950) (New York: Bantam, 1967), pp. 531–582.

ously or to join in an anti-Axis front with Moscow, followed by the attempt of Western appeasers to turn Hitler eastward; Western animosity toward Russia because of the Nazi–Soviet Pact and Stalin's attack against Finland—these, according to re-examinist interpretations, were major causes of Soviet–American hostility after World War II.

Developments late in the war fed this underlying ill-will. Besides Russia's understandable suspicion, engendered by Western delay in opening a second front against Hitler's European fortress, there was the matter of the Soviet Union's role in World War II and its staggering war losses. Western opinion had never recognized the magnitude of either. Legitimate concern was also aroused in Moscow by Anglo–American behavior in dealing with Italy's surrender and arranging its military occupation—a matter in which Stalin's government was accorded no role whatever. The same pattern was repeated after Japan surrendered on September 2, 1945. Russia was excluded from any meaningful participation in the Japanese occupation (which tended to become a kind of personal fiefdom of General Douglas MacArthur).

Indifferent to Russia's enormous war losses,[*] American officials were unmoved by Soviet suggestions that it needed outside assistance for postwar relief and rehabilitation. After the surrender of Germany, the Truman administration abruptly terminated Lend-Lease aid to Russia. In the context of events, Stalin's government could legitimately conclude that America's act was part of the new policy of "toughness" in dealing with Soviet behavior in Eastern Europe. Later Soviet aid requests to the United States either went unanswered or were subject to conditions which were totally unacceptable to Moscow. This same anti-Communist prejudice, re-examinists are persuaded, also governed America's attitude about aiding Russia much later, when the Soviet Union was invited to participate in the Marshall Plan for promoting European reconstruction in the fall of 1947. Since the Truman administration really did not *desire* Soviet participation (since the Marshall Plan was "sold" to Congress primarily as an anti-

---

[*]Among re-examinist commentators, great emphasis is placed upon the U.S.S.R.'s almost incalculable devastation as a result of World War II, which rendered Moscow *incapable* of following expansive impulses after the war and forced the Kremlin to devote its attention chiefly to internal reconstruction. Some 20 million Russians lost their lives during the war; around 25 percent of the nation's fixed capital investment was destroyed; the labor force was reduced by 3 million people; 15 of Russia's largest cities and nearly 70,000 villages were devastated; nearly 6 million buildings were demolished, leaving 25 million Russians homeless; over 30,000 industrial installations and more than 35,000 miles of railroads were ruined. For additional statistical data on Russia's war losses, see D. F. Fleming, *The Cold War and Its Origins*, vol. I (Garden City, N.Y.: Doubleday, 1961), pp. 252–253; and George F. Kennan, *Memoirs* (1925–1950) (New York: Bantam, 1969), pp. 534–535.

Communist program), the conditions America attached to the program again made it totally unacceptable to the Kremlin.[52] In brief, America's response to Russia's wartime suffering and its massive peacetime needs confirmed the conviction of Stalin and his Marxist advisers that capitalist nations bore only enmity toward the U.S.S.R. and really desired Russia's economic collapse!

As for the cockpit of cold war tensions—Eastern Europe—re-examinist and official explanations of how Soviet–American hostility arose also differ fundamentally. Stalin's moves in this region, re-examinists insist, were dictated by a mixture of concern for Russian security, of understandable hostility toward anti-Russian groups in the area, of fears of a German resurgence, of reluctance to entrust Russian security to "collective" efforts, and of apprehensions about the motives of Britain and America as the war drew to a close. The Kremlin was unquestionably familiar with Prime Minister Churchill's desire to cordon Russian influence out of Europe, keeping it as far to the east as possible; but Stalin was determined not to repeat the Paris Peace Conference which followed World War I, in which Russia had no voice in the proceedings and the Allies made several decisions highly inimical to Russian interests.

Yet if Russia were determined to establish itself as the dominant great-power influence in Eastern Europe, Stalin was realistic enough to accord the United States and Britain the same right in their security zones. Russia asked no voice in the application of the Monroe Doctrine or the management of affairs in the Western Hemisphere, nor did it contest the existence of the British empire. All Stalin wanted, re-examinists believe, was a *quid pro quo:* a "spheres-of-influence" agreement delimiting Russian and Western zones in Europe, much like that which Stalin and Hitler had negotiated in 1939. And, in fact, the foundations for such an agreement were laid at the end of 1944, when Churchill visited Moscow. There, the British and Russian leaders arrived at an understanding whereby Russia was given a preponderant voice in the affairs of Rumania, Bulgaria, and Hungary; Britain would have a free hand in its traditional sphere of influence, Greece; and Britain and Russia would share responsibility for events in Yugoslavia.* Adherence to this formula through-

out the months ahead, in the opinion of re-examinist commentators, would have avoided cold war disputes in Eastern Europe and the rupture in Western–Soviet relations globally.[53]

Why did this Anglo–Russian delimitation of spheres of influence collapse? Re-examinists are certain of the answer. It lay in *Western violations* of both its letter and spirit, when Churchill and Truman early in 1945 began protesting Soviet conduct in Eastern Europe. Concurrently (beginning at the end of 1944), British forces intervened actively and decisively in the civil war in Greece, ultimately restoring a rightist and pro-British monarchy to power. In the process, British troops broke the power of ELAS (the Communist-controlled Greek resistance movement against the Nazi occupation authorities). Even then, Stalin lodged no protest with London and Washington over British conduct. The Russian leader thus appeared prepared to accept British primacy in Greece, provided Soviet primacy in Eastern Europe were similarly acknowledged.[54] But such reciprocity was impossible, owing to American and British determination to involve themselves in the affairs of Eastern Europe, a region where they had no legitimate interests and where the urge to economic penetration by Western (especcially American) capitalists naturally elicited deep Soviet misgivings. Only after Britain and America themselves demonstrated an unwillingness to accord Russia a comparable freedom in Eastern Europe did the Kremlin protest Britain's conduct in Greece and America's pre-eminent influence in other areas.[55]

Communist Expansionism and "Containment"

Events after the surrender of Nazi Germany moved steadily in the direction of a deterioration in Anglo–American relations with the Soviet Union. Two interludes offered some hope that Allied unity would survive. The United Nations was finally established by the 46 nations attending the San Francisco Conference, April 25–June 26, 1945. A few weeks later (July 17–August 2) the last of the great wartime conferences was held at Potsdam.[56] Ostensibly successful, the conference clarified principles to be followed in the administration of Germany; it established a Council of Foreign Ministers to draft peace treaties for the smaller Axis powers; it tried once again to arrive at a consensus among the Allies on German repa-

---

*Several points about this Anglo–Soviet understanding (sometimes glossed over by re-examinists) ought to be grasped. The United States was never a party to it. Before it was reached, and even earlier, the Roosevelt administration had steadfastly refused to accept or participate in any "spheres-of-influence" division of Europe or the world. This was the kind of "secret deal" that could be counted upon to offend American sensibilities, based in part upon aversion to the secret agreements made during World War I. Much as they might have an American one in the Western Hemisphere, American officials rejected the idea of "spheres of influence" in principle. Besides this limitation, the Churchill–Stali⌐

understanding *did not include Poland*—viewed by many commentators as the most difficult diplomatic problem in Eastern Europe. Even if America had accepted the Moscow accord, the future of Poland would have remained uncertain. Adherence to the Yalta Agreement made a few weeks later also put Britain and Russia in a highly equivocal position—since that Big Three accord anticipated *joint* Anglo–Russian–American responsibility for the political future of Eastern ⌐urope!

rations and the future of Poland. At the conference, Stalin reiterated the pledge he had made at Yalta: Russia would declare war against Japan within 60 to 90 days after Germany's defeat. President Truman (now knowing that the atomic bomb had been successfully tested, as Stalin's intelligence had probably informed him) seemed indifferent. Cold war clouds were already beginning to overhang Anglo–American–Soviet negotiations. To British and American insistence upon *joint* Allied supervision of political developments in Eastern Europe, Russia's reply (beyond denying any wrongdoing in the area) was to raise the matter of British intervention in Greece. New Soviet demands expressed at Potsdam were for a "trusteeship" over the former Italian colony in Tripolitania (Libya) and for a revision of the international agreement governing administration of the Turkish Straits. These demands suggested that Moscow had expansionist ambitions into the Mediterranean, which was largely a British sphere; Western officials, needless to say, showed no enthusiasm for them.[57]

America dropped the first atomic bomb on Hiroshima on August 6; Soviet troops attacked Japanese forces in Manchuria on August 8; and the second atomic bomb destroyed Nagasaki on August 9. On August 14, the Japanese Emporer ordered a cease-fire. World War II had ended. But the cold war that was to dominate international relations for a generation or more thereafter had already begun. During the remainder of 1945 and 1946, it escalated rapidly. On nearly every issue confronting them, Western and Soviet officials disagreed; mutual suspicion gave way to open expressions of distrust and animosity.

By late 1945, American officials had largely abandoned hope that Moscow would honor its commitments at Yalta and Potsdam respecting Eastern Europe. Repeated Western protests to the Kremlin did little to interrupt the imposition of Soviet-supported Marxist regimes in the area. The aftermath of the war in Western Europe added to Western apprehensions: Communist (or Communist-led) organizations threatened to emerge as the dominant political forces in several European societies. In Asia, Soviet behavior also aroused deep concern in Washington and London. Occupying Korea down to the 38th parallel, Soviet forces lost little time in converting the area under their control into the People's Democracy of North Korea. After Japanese troops surrendered in China, Soviet forces carried out the "rape of Manchuria"—stripping China's industrial heartland of its factories and anything else of value and shipping them to Russia. (At a later stage, even Mao Tse-tung's government condemned Moscow's behavior.) Aside from specific instances of Western–Soviet disagreement, the over-all atmosphere of international relations was also deteriorating. By the end of 1945, Marxist theoreticians had begun to reiterate a familiar (but, during the war, a dormant) Communist theme: the growing economic dislocations that would plunge capitalist nations into crisis and revolution. Early in 1946, Stalin himself referred to the "violent disturbances" that gripped the West and revived the Leninist idea that "two hostile camps" had emerged in global affairs.[58] By 1946, Western officials were certain that they faced the reality of Soviet expansionism. In addition to Soviet policy in Eastern Europe, two other cases offered convincing proof. One was Iran— where Stalin still maintained troops in the country's northern provinces and was evidently intriguing against the Shah's authority. The first case which the fledgling UN Security Council had to consider was Iran's complaint against the Soviet Union. Moscow finally agreed to withdraw its troops and eventually did so. The other instance of Soviet expansionism was China. Despite substantial American aid to Chinag Kai-shek's government at the end of the war, the military and political position of Nationalist China declined rapidly in the civil war against Mao Tse-tung's Communist movement. Although most authorities on China doubted that Mao was dependent upon, or materially aided by, the Kremlin,[59] Western officials tended to assume that the spread of Communism in China was a major victory for "international Communism," with headquarters in Moscow.

These Western concerns were openly expressed by that eloquent and militantly anti-Communist wartime leader, Winston Churchill, in a speech at Fulton, Missouri, on March 5, 1946. From the Baltic to the Adriatic, Churchill declared, an "iron curtain" had descended upon Europe; "police governments" controlled by Moscow ruled east of the line. Acknowledging that the Russians did not want war—they wanted "the fruits of war and the indefinite expansion of their power and doctrine"—Churchill called for a "fraternal association" of the English-speaking peoples to thwart Communist expansionism. Relying upon the atomic might of America, this Anglo–American bloc was needed to preserve world peace against the rising Soviet danger.[60]

From the Soviet perspective, Churchill's views, obviously accepted by his host President Truman, were the most blatant form of "atomic diplomacy." The speech, said *Pravda*, was nothing less than a "call to war with the Soviet Union" and an admission of an Anglo–American desire to "rule over the remaining nations of the world."[61] Re-examinist commentators then and afterward also identified Churchill's speech as the West's "declaration" of cold war against Soviet Russia.[62] The kind of tough line toward Russia epitomized by Churchill's approach ignored the fact that the Soviet Union was too weak and debilitated after World War II to mount any kind of military or political offensive, particularly since it (unlike Britain and other Western allies) received no help from America to meet its postwar needs. The most ominous aspect of Churchill's proposal, critics of a hard line toward Moscow pointed out, was its explicit reference to the American nuclear monopoly (in which Britain also shared). Ever since the Truman administration had used atomic weapons against Japan, Washington had pursued a policy of atomic secrecy aimed chiefly at Soviet Russia. Moreover, several American officials had said openly that America's nuclear arsenal ought to make Moscow "less barbarous" and "more manageable" in the years ahead.[63] Would the United States now use its nuclear advantage to compel Soviet acceptance of demands in Eastern Europe and other key areas? Even worse, did Churchill's speech signal a new era of *Pax Americana,* in which the United States would displace a greatly weakened Britain as the custodian of world order? The Anglo–American–Canadian declaration on the control of atomic energy on November 15, 1945, followed by the Baruch Plan for achieving nuclear disarmament the following June 14,* clearly assumed the continuation of the cold war and the West's determination to "negotiate from strength" in dealing with the U.S.S.R.[64]

Throughout 1946, cold war tensions continued to mount. In the new United Nations, Western and Soviet representatives exchanged recriminations in a series of cases. In every Eastern European state except Czechoslovakia (which was brought under Moscow's control early in 1948), Marxist political orders consolidated their positions, eliminating opposition groups. In China, Mao Tse-tung's Communist forces were defeating Chaing Kai-shek's government. Two developments in the months after V-J Day especially troubled American policy-makers: the decline of British power and the debilitated condition of Western Europe.

Although it was one of the victors in World War II, Great Britain emerged from this conflict with its formerly influential position in world affairs seriously jeopardized. The war shattered London's once leading financial position at the head of the "Sterling bloc"; Britain's industrial complex had suffered extensive war damage, and what was left was depleted and outmoded; the British merchant marine fleet had been severely reduced; the British Empire was torn by anti-colonialist movements; under a Labor government, the British society demanded internal reforms and costly welfare programs. If it was not clear at the time, events in the years ahead made it evident that Great Britain was now a first-rank power in name only; it lacked the resources to maintain its world-

wide international commitments. Without perhaps doing so *consciously* (during the war, for example, FDR and other Americans were often highly critical of British imperialism), the United States ultimately had to assume many of the obligations in international affairs carried for many years by the British.

Conditions in postwar Europe also elicited growing apprehension in Washington. Fought over (in some areas, several times during the war), its industrial complexes bombed and burned, its transportation system in ruins, many of its farms out of cultivation, its population dispirited, Europe faced a grim future. The inability of the wartime Allies to agree upon a peace treaty with Germany added to the region's instability. Europe was a "power vacuum"—a region attracting political extremist groups and perhaps even aggression by predatory powers. Interim aid and relief measures by the United States for two years or so after the war achieved little by way of European rehabilitation and reconstruction.

Many of America's concerns about Europe and Britain's decline came to a focus in the problem of Greece. That country, as we have already noted, was part of Great Britain's Mediterranean sphere of influence. Beginning at the end of 1944, London endeavored to reimpose its control over the country. The right-wing, authoritarian regime supported by British power, however, soon evoked opposition both inside and outside Greece (not least, from critics in the United States). Communist elements in Greece, aided by Marxist governments in the Balkans, fomented insurrection; Greek rebels relied upon "sanctuaries" in Yugoslavia and other Marxist nations to the north to escape British forces and to resupply their own partisans. Compelled to abandon many of its global responsibilities, and gripped by acute internal difficulties, Great Britain found itself overextended in Greece and elsewhere. By early 1947, American officials had become aware that a British retrenchment was likely; and on February 21, London officially notified Washington that British forces would evacuate Greece on April 1.[65]

America's response to this announcement constituted one of the most momentous foreign policy decisions in the nation's diplomatic history. Immediately, the Truman administration undertook a thorough study of the implications of Britain's impending withdrawal. The result of the study, as former President Truman later summarized it, was:

Greece needed aid, and needed it quickly in substantial amounts. The alternative was the loss of Greece and the extension of the iron curtain across the eastern Mediterranean. If Greece was lost, Turkey would become an untenable outpost in a sea of Communism.

*The Baruch Plan—America's first major postwar disarmament proposal—is analyzed in considerable detail in Chapter 15.

... Greece and Turkey were still free countries being challenged by Communist threats both from within and without. These free peoples were now engaged in a valiant struggle to preserve their liberties and their independence.[66]

After consultation with legislative leaders, President Truman on March 12, 1947, recommended the Greek–Turkish Aid Program, calling for an expenditure of $400 million (with $300 million allocated to Greece). In his message to Congress, the President enunciated what came to be called the Truman Doctrine. First describing the crisis in Greece and the threat to Turkey, Truman related these to the wider conflict between freedom and a totalitarian system in which minority rule was "forcibly imposed upon a majority." Accordingly, Truman declared:

I believe that it must be the policy of the United States to support free peoples who are resisting attempted subjugation by armed minorities or by outside pressures.

I believe that we must assist free peoples to work out their own destinies in their own way.

It did not escape notice that President Truman had committed the United States to the support of "free peoples" who opposed externally assisted threats—in Greece, Turkey, or elsewhere in the world. Congress' passage of the Greek–Turkish Aid Act (on May 15) signified legislative acceptance of Truman's strategy and willingness to use American resources to support it.[67] As the culmination of America's increasingly tough stance toward the Soviet Union, the Truman Doctrine marked the beginning of the containment policy followed by the United States for more than two decades thereafter. The concept of containment received its theoretical justification in a widely-quoted article by George F. Kennan a few months later.* From the Greek crisis to America's intervention in Vietnam, the United States followed the strategy of containment in dealing with the Soviet Union, Communist China, and what Wash-

ington viewed as "extensions" of Soviet or Chinese power in smaller countries like North Korea and North Vietnam.

In 1947 and for years thereafter, critics of American foreign policy deplored the Greek–Turkish Aid Program; even more vocally did they denounce the worldwide doctrine of containment which it presaged. Instead of a *détente* to relieve cold war tensions, the Truman administration had now assumed the war's permanence and proposed to wage it on a global scale! Critics asserted that America had discovered a "doctrine" which could easily be reconciled with its own deep anti-Communist impulses, its desire to dominate the world economically (and perhaps even politically), and its opposition to revolutionary political movements. Pursuing the doctrine of containment, the United States would now be allied with dictatorships; it would be identified with economic exploitation in the emerging nations; it would be committed to an indefinite expansion in the level of world armaments; and it would be compelled to neglect overdue welfare programs and reforms at home. By adopting containment, the indictment held, the United States had surrendered the initiative to the Communist bloc, permitting Marxists to become the apostles of progress and change, while America became the guardian of the economic and political status quo. Containment, in this view, was a diplomatic blunder of monumental proportions—from which America and the whole world were to suffer for years to come.[68]

The Debate Continues

Our discussion of the Soviet–American confrontation which dominated the international environment after World War II has been presented within the framework of two conflicting interpretations of the origins and nature of the cold war. The "orthodox" viewpoint—identified with successive administrations in Washington and numerous students of American foreign policy—is that hostility between the United States and Soviet Russia springs almost entirely *from Soviet behavior*, not excluding Moscow's often intemperate propaganda campaign against non-Communist countries. Throughout most of World War II, the Roosevelt administration sought the friendship and good will of Stalin's government; FDR (many detractors argued) accepted most legitimate, and many unreasonable, Soviet demands in order to preserve Allied unity during and after the war. Believing that he had established a durable rapport with "Uncle Joe" Stalin, Roosevelt conscientiously tried to preserve a Western–Russian *détente* upon which to build postwar cooperation and peace. But in the few weeks before his death, even FDR became dubious about whether this accord would endure.

*See his article, written under the pseudonym of "X," on "The Sources of Soviet Conduct," *Foreign Affairs* 25 (July, 1947), 556–583. Although many governmental officials and commentators identified Kennan as the "author" of the containment strategy—since his ideas closely coincided with President Truman's—in later years, Kennan dissociated himself from the "doctrine" which Truman enunciated. Even early in 1947, Kennan did not share the administration's alarm about the crisis in Greece or the security of Turkey. Even more did he reject the *global* implications of Truman's speech. In his later writings, Kennan agreed with many of the trenchant criticisms of containment expressed by Walter Lippmann and other commentators. See his views on containment in George F. Kennan, *Memoirs (1925–1950)* (New York: Bantam, 1967), pp. 330–341. For Lippmann's highly critical analysis of the Truman Doctrine, see his *The Cold War, A Study of U.S. Foreign Policy* (New York: Harper & Row, 1947).

The "blame" for the collapse of wartime unity, in this conception of the cold war, is unambiguous: It rests with the Kremlin. During the war, there was always more "cooperation" from the American, than the Soviet, side. As the military balance shifted against the Axis powers, Stalin took advantage of the Red Army's great military superiority in areas under its control to impose Soviet-dominated Marxist systems upon defenseless peoples, and in some cases (like the Baltic states) he annexed territories directly into the U.S.S.R. Stalin made a choice between friendship with America and unilateral Soviet conduct alienating the West: His preference, it became clear, was to advance Communist objectives at every available opportunity, using whatever methods were most effective. Only after there was no doubt about the direction of Soviet policy did the United States abandon the effort to retain Russia's friendship and adopt containment as its strategy for frustrating Communist expansionism. While it may have imperfections, on balance containment *has worked reasonably well.* Moscow has gained no new satellites since the early postwar era; Western Europe has been preserved from Communist domination; Marxist attempts to take over the whole of Korea and Vietnam have been checked; and since the late 1950s, the Kremlin has concentrated its attention more than ever upon *domestic* problems.

As we have seen, the re-examinist or revisionist position on the origins and nature of the cold war is fundamentally different. It begins with an earlier chain of historical causation, going back to the Bolshevik Revolution of 1917 or earlier. Western societies were always profoundly hostile to Communism—and they remain so today. America's policy of containment is merely a new version of an old strategy, followed when foreign governments tried to overthrow Lenin's government at the end of World War I. Its real goal is the *elimination* of Communist systems in Russia, China, and elsewhere. As such, it is part of a pattern of Western opposition to Marxism, evidenced by Russia's ostracism during the interwar period, by Western refusal to cooperate with Moscow in an effective coalition to halt Axis expansionism, and by the efforts of some Western groups to direct Hitler's aggressive impulses against the U.S.S.R. Western relations with Russia during World War II did little to reassure Stalin's government or convince it that a new era of Western–Soviet cooperation had dawned. Anglo–American procrastination in opening the second front in the West; Western failure to recognize Russia's crucial contributions in the defeat of Hitler; Roosevelt and Churchill's own version of Western unilateralism in dealing with the surrender and occupation of Italy (and later Japan); Washington's indifference to Russia's postwar needs and its refusal to extend assistance—all of these confirmed Marxist policy-makers in their suspicions of Western intentions. At the end of the war, Anglo–American "meddling" in the affairs of Eastern Europe removed all doubt in the Kremlin's mind. Although Britain had its empire, and America enjoyed an exclusive security sphere in the Western Hemisphere, the West would not accord Russia a comparable privilege in the region from which most threats to Russian safety have originated. Even after the Kremlin revealed its willingness to accept Western pre-eminence in Greece, with the accompanying suppression of Greek Communists, Britain and America persisted in intruding into the affairs of Eastern Europe. There, and as time passed elsewhere, America's policy of "atomic monopoly" at the end of the war suggested Anglo–American attempts to *compel* Soviet compliance with Western directives. Finally, by 1946 (and Churchill's Fulton, Missouri, speech was a landmark) anti-Communism became America's new postwar crusade, having all the earmarks of the earlier crusade against the Axis. Every revolution abroad became a "Communist plot" to destroy America and communize the world. Every international problem troubling the American government could be blamed on the "global Communist conspiracy." Better than any other conceivable policy, containment accorded with the desires of conservative circles in the United States, particularly the highly influential military–industrial complex, which defined all problems in military terms and demanded a constantly expanding stockpile of armaments. Deep and underlying hostility toward Soviet Communism, coupled with a failure to understand the legitimate needs of the Russian state, lay at the root of the cold war.

How is the student of American foreign policy to reconcile these obviously divergent interpretations of the dominant problem in international relations since World War II? How is it possible for equally qualified and well-informed scholars to be found in both the orthodox and revisionist schools? It must be frankly acknowledged that even today the answers to such questions are not simple. A point made earlier in the chapter needs to be reiterated: Much of the evidence (particularly concerning Soviet goals and intentions) required for a thorough and objective study of the cold war remains inaccessible. What did Stalin's government *really* propose to do when the Red Army overran Eastern Europe at the end of the war? Was Stalin himself at this stage still capable of rational thought and long-range decision-making? On these and many related issues, competent scholars can often do little more than deduce and surmise; too frequently, their conclusions boil down to guesswork based upon a careful analysis of *Pravda* or an attempt to apply Communist ideology to some Soviet decision in Poland. Even when most of the evidence *is* available (as, for example, on Soviet diplomacy in the 1920s and 1930s), it must be borne in mind that disagreement among qualified commentators is not an uncommon phenomenon—as witness the continuing debate among historians on the causes of the American Civil War or the degree of German "war guilt" in World War I. The *significance* of evidence is always controversial.

Differing assessments of the cold war are also produced by divergent judgments on a host of collateral issues. Nearly all cold war commentators *start* from an initial state of mind about such issues as the role of ideology in shaping Marxist attitudes toward the outside world, the political influence exerted by America's so-called "ruling class" (or political elite), or the nature of the international community itself. On the matter of Communist ideology, revisionist commentators tend to attribute a relatively *low* priority to it as a determinant of Soviet policy; orthodox interpreters generally give it greater weight in explaining Russian behavior. A related question is how "rational" are Soviet moves to Western observers, or vice versa. Orthodox commentators believe that the Communist mentality possesses a rationality all its own, rendering it incomprehensible o someone not steeped in Marxist dogma. Concepts like "democracy" or "peaceful coexistence" mean the opposite for an avowed Communist of what they mean for an advocate of Western liberal democracy. The re-examinist also calls attention to "irrational" elements present in the cold war, but they are of a different kind. They feel that the Western approach to the Soviet Union since 1917 has exhibited irrationality at every stage—as, for example, in rejecting some concept (like peaceful coexistence) merely because it emanates from the Kremlin, or opposing revolutions as *automatically* advancing Soviet interests, or failing to recognize the Russian people's genuine concern with the problem of security.

At issue also between the orthodox and revisionist interpretations of the cold war is a deep difference of opinion about the nature of international relationships. Revisionist thought, it seems safe to say, is rooted in the Englightenment era and the idealism of Woodrow Wilson. It tends to be essentially optimistic about the possibility of achieving world peace and a stable international order. It has great confidence in the peaceful instincts of the "plain people" of America, Russia, and other countries, whose impulses (especially in America) are frustrated by political leaders. It places considerable confidence in the United Nations (which it believes would be an even better instrument if America would use it more). It identifies with change in the international system, which it feels in most instances is *beneficial*, being equivalent to progress. Accordingly, it views the status quo in all countries, and in global affairs generally with skepticism. Above all, perhaps, it tends to attribute cold war tensions to a lack of true "understanding" (more by Americans than by Russians) of the legitimate aspirations and feelings of other societies. The most fundamental reason that American and Russia quarreled is that there has been an absence of needed understanding, sympathy, and good will, notably on the part of the United States. Given this, a cold war *détente* would quickly emerge. There is, in brief, no necessary or unalterable reason why conflict should characterize Russian–American relations.

The orthodox viewpoint is founded upon a more *pessimistic* evaluation of international relations, and perhaps of the human condition itself. Its operating premise is the idea that the international environment resembles the jungle: *It contains predatory and expansionist nations.* This was a reality which America learned at the end of World War II, at some peril to itself and to the security of its friends. After a fair trial, American officials concluded that, lamentable as the fact was, the behavior of Stalin's government placed Soviet Russia in this category. No amount of talk about Russia's historic concern for "security" or the lack of "mutual understanding" between the two countries could erase the fact that on two recent occasions—in the Nazi–Soviet Pact of 1939, and at the end of World War II—the U.S.S.R. used its power to expand its hegemony significantly over weaker nations. Soviet suppression of Czechoslovakia's freedom in the late 1960s is seen to afford recent evidence that this threat was neither a delusion in the minds of President Truman and his advisers nor a bogey invented by the so-called military–industrial complex.

As for Russia's desire for "security," orthodox commentators make two points. First, *every nation is entitled to security*, not merely Soviet Russia. Unfortunately, Moscow has not demonstrated a similar interest in the security of Poland, the Baltic states—or, for that matter, the United States. Virtually every diplomatic or military move the Kremlin has made since 1917 has been justified as, in one way or another, enhancing Soviet security. But one nation's fixation with security may, and does, promote feelings of massive *insecurity* among its neighbors. Second, if Russia has legitimate security interests, it follows that America, Western Europe, and other nations have them as well. If it is granted that Russia is entitled to accord security a high priority in policy formulation, American officials are free to do the same. No more in Washington than in Moscow are officials prepared to allow the *other side* to define national security objectives or specify how they shall be achieved. In the absence of some supranational authority powerful enough to mediate between the cold war giants and impose a *modus vivendi* upon them, America must safeguard its own interests as American officials define them.

Clearly, both the revisionist and orthodox interpretations have their strengths and weaknesses. At every turn re-examinists emphasize the need for citizens and policy-makers in the United States to "understand" the Soviet point of view; to recognize that events in recent history often take on a different perspective and meaning for other countries; to acknowledge that, like every nation, Soviet Russia has certain long-standing security and diplomatic interests which are as vital for it as American objectives are for Washington; and to be cautious in imputing evil or aggressive intentions to diplomatic adversaries. Revisionist interpretations of the cold war afford a useful and often necessary antidote for cant, hyprocisy, and self-deception in American foreign policy. This group of commentators also properly insists upon the necessity for ongoing re-examination of hallowed policy dogmas which often tend to become deeply embedded in American consciousness through sheer repetition.

Revisionism also of course has its defects. One of these is a fact which ought to be faced squarely: For a variety of reasons (more so today perhaps than ever) revisionist interpretations of the cold war *are likely to be intellectually fashionable.* In the first place, they are *different,* offering an explanation of how and why the cold war emerged that is novel and stimulating, affording an appealing contrast to the stale account many students became familiar with in high school. The revisionist viewpoint also challenges the official "power structure" and its explanation of why tensions appeared in Soviet–American relations; for many Americans today, the official rationale of national policy at home and abroad is automatically suspect. Revisionism is appealing for another reason: Its explanations of the cold war tap a recurrent American tendency to engage in self-criticism, "honest confession," and a kind of psychological self-laceration. Many citizens of the United States enjoy nothing more than reading about the "ugly American" and his failures throughout the world; more than in any society in the world, confessions of *mea culpa* have become a kind of national pastime. Perhaps the tendency stems from America's "guilt feelings" because of its vast wealth. But whatever the reason, the masochistic tendencies of numerous Americans in dealing with the cold war, or relations with Latin America, or the contest in Vietnam, are too evident to be denied. The appeal of revisionism is assured in part because it tells Americans something many of them find psychologically rewarding: that the United States is responsible for the cold war.

Re-examinist commentators have another tendency which often raises real questions about the objectivity and validity of their findings. They are apt to reverse the procedure followed by official and orthodox commentators. In dealing with many contentious issues in Soviet–American relations since 1917, for example, revisionists tend to

be extremely charitable towards the Soviet Union's external behavior, while being highly critical of American behavior. Soviet Russia's words and deeds can be "accepted" at face value; their sincerity is seldom questioned. The same is almost never true, however, of American deeds and words. It is a curious phenomenon that toward a totalitarian society—where intrigue, duplicity, disingenuousness, and deceit are commonplace— the behavior of the government is credited with a greater degree of sincerity and genuine concern for the welfare of mankind than is true of one of the oldest democracies known to history. Revisionists are highly reluctant to accept any kind of conspiratorial or Machiavellian explanation of Soviet diplomatic conduct, while readily accepting such an explanation of American behavior (dictated presumably by the machinations of the military–industrial complex, which supposedly determines cold war policy). Soviet fears about the nation's "security" are held to be legitimate; comparable American apprehensions about the security of the United States and its allies, however, are deemed to be nothing more than aberrations growing out of Western dread of Communism. Nor are revisionists normally troubled about the *means* which the Kremlin has employed to achieve its goals. One finds little attention paid in their accounts to Stalin's ruthlessness (still less, to his psychological degeneration), the record of Soviet economic and political exploition in the satellite zone, or Marxist contempt for the "bourgeois morality" of the West. Apparently, once the U.S.S.R.'s quest for security is granted, then *any method* may be legitimately utilized for achieving it. (No such readiness, it might be noted, is shown in justifying American foreign policy in Latin America, Vietnam, or other settings. The argument that American "security interests" dictated involvement in Indochina or the Dominican Republic is anathema to revisionist commentators!)

The "orthodox" or official explanation of the origins and nature of the cold war similarly possesses strong and weak points. Among the former, one of its major contributions is recognition that gratitude, good will, and personal affinities among policy-makers can seldom serve as a lasting basis for diplomatic relationships. The Soviet Union's diplomatic and security intersts during World War II were intrinsically independent of the rapport between Stalin and Roosevelt or Russia's "gratitude" for American wartime assistance. The orthodox viewpoint also rests upon a realization, belated as it may have been, that *the United States is one of the world's super-powers*, with all this status implies about *a permanent and extensive involvement in world affairs.* The orthodox commentator is not intimidated by the charge that, in pursuing containment, the United States sought to be the "policeman of the world." To this criticism, he replies: What other country was in a position to play the role? Would it have been better to leave that assignment to the Soviet Union alone? Or, if it is asserted that the world needs no "policeman," the reply is that this has not been the lesson of experience in international relations since World War I. In both great global conflicts, eventually the United States was *required* to bring its vast power to bear in behalf of peace and stability—in World War II, under conditions that were initially *militarily disadvantageous*. In the atomic age, there is no assurance that another opportunity would exist for the United States to recover from a disaster like Pearl Harbor and once more tilt the balance of military power favorably. Should the "policeman," in effect, sit quietly in the stationhouse until the community has been engulfed in an epidemic of law-breaking, which even he at that point might be incapable of handling? Or are *preventive measures* not essential to avert crises?

The orthodox point of view also exhibits understanding of a fact that seldom emerges in revisionist attitudes. Far from being motivated by imperialist impulses or a desire to dominate the world, even today most Americans are probably still strongly devoted to *isolationism*, much as they may realize its impracticality in the contemporary era. Their involvement in global affairs, as in the isolationist period, remains reluctant, distasteful, and much less psychologically satisfying than their own private domestic pursuits. Failing to achieve quick results abroad, Americans become highly impatient and frustrated; it is very difficult for them to sustain a program like foreign aid or a strategy like containment over a period of many years, especially when results are often unimpressive. If official explanations of the cold war sometimes tend to exaggerate the "Communist danger," one reason is that policy-makers know that the American people require some evidence of a threat to their security to overcome their isolationist tendencies.

Orthodox treatments of the cold war also highlight another fact which receives very little attention from revisionists. From whatever source (whether Russian history and traditions, Communist ideology, or a combination of both), Moscow is devoted to the achievement of certain goals, many of which can be traced back to the czarist era. It simply will not suffice to "explain" the Nazi–Soviet Pact of 1939 solely as a Soviet reaction to Western neglect or indifference to Russia's security needs. There have been too many more or less comparable treaties and agreements throughout Russian history, in which the Kremlin acquired new territory or expanded its hegemony over weak neighbors when opportune occasions arose. Great Britain encountered such Russian moves repeatedly during the era of *Pax Britannica*. There is no evidence that Communist policy-makers since 1917 have abandoned this tendency, much as they might rationalize it differently or justify their actions by reference to "capitalist encirclement." Now, as in the past, some kind of superior force is needed to frustrate Russia's designs at the expense of other countries. After World War II, only America was in a position to supply that force.

Orthodox commentators acknowledge that "mutual understanding" is a useful and desirable element in statecraft today, as always. But they also insist that there are some problems in international relations that no amount of "mutual understanding" and recognition of the other side's point of view can resolve harmoniously. Washington may comprehend fully *why* the Soviet Union dominates Eastern Germany and wishes to displace Western power from Berlin and the rest of Germany. Given the premises of Soviet policy, this may be a completely rational, not to say necessary, Soviet position. This realization, however, does not alter the fact that achievement of Russia's goal would be highly prejudicial to Western security interests and perhaps fatal to morale in the NATO area. Being aware of the reasons for Soviet moves is one thing; it is quite another to accept these moves as compatible with American security and world peace. The same is obviously true for Soviet policy-makers, when they assess American diplomatic moves. Conceivably, to their minds, American conduct is dictated by compulsions arising out of capitalist economic forces. Even though the Communist elite "understands" this fact, this does not make the Kremlin any more willing to accept American hegemony in Vietnam.

Certain defects are present also in the orthodox approach to the cold war. Most fundamentally, perhaps, this approach tends nearly always, in one way or another, to be *egocentric*. Its starting point is *American* national interest and security; it serves as a rationale for the policy of the United States government. Too often, orthodox observers assume the inherent superiority of the American viewpoint and the essential rectitude of the American position. Nearly always too, American moves are presented as "defensive," undertaken as a "reaction" to Soviet aggressiveness. Legitimate Soviet concern for American, or more broadly Western, diplomatic behavior is almost never conceded. In their way, some orthodox interpreters of the cold war become as polemical and as dogmatic as Marxists, repeating clichés, reiterating dogmas from the late 1940s, and engaging in propaganda duels with their Communist adversaries. A constant tendency among official and orthodox interpreters is for American attitudes to become frozen, for a kind of diplomatic hardening of the arteries to displace imaginative policy-making.

This approach to the cold war also tends to

suffer from a tendency which has unquestionably impaired the effectiveness of 'American foreign policy on innumerable occasions since the late 1940s: For many orthodox interpreters, the cold war becomes a kind of *theological and metaphysical encounter*, a kind of morality play in which Righteousness confronts (and ultimately overcomes) Evil. On the premise that Soviet diplomatic moves stem from an irresistible Communist urge toward "world domination"—that they are part of a "Communist global conspiracy"—official and orthodox commentators are often dubious about *any* prospect of negotiated settlements between the United States and the Soviet Union. Police departments, after all, do not "negotiate" with conspirators! For some students of the cold war, the lessons of the Munich era have perhaps been learned too well—so well that any proposed Soviet–American settlement is in danger of being equated with appeasement, entailing a "sell-out" of American vital interests. What might be called the "Munich mentality" is conspicuous in the approach of many orthodox commentators; they have forgotten that it was not so much the *attempt* to resolve diplomatic issues at Munich, as it was the *terms* of the Munich Agreement, that became odious.

When this mentality exists, it tends to create a massive contradiction at the center of America's containment policy in dealing with the Communist world. Very few advocates of containment believe that the dominant (or an attainable) goal is the *overthrow* of Communist systems in Russia, China, or elsewhere. The objectives are more limited: to teach the Kremlin that "aggression does not pay" and perhaps induce some "mellowing" within the Communist system. Yet, if it is assumed that Communist officials are permanently committed to global domination or engaged in an immutable international conspiracy, then they are apparently incapable of learning the lessons taught by successful containment or modifying their behavior in a manner acceptable to Americans. When Soviet imperviousness to Western influence, or the unalterability of Communist goals, is postulated, then containment is inherently doomed to failure.

The two conflicting interpretations of the cold war which have provided the framework for this chapter thus derive from antithetical premises and assumptions concerning such still controversial issues as the "real" motives of Soviet and American policy-makers, the forces actuating the diplomatic moves of Washington and Moscow, and the nature of international politics. In dealing with an ongoing controversy of this kind—where interpretations of key events and trends are often so divergent—it is tempting to say that both the orthodox and the revisionist viewpoints offer useful insights into the pivotal issue. Inconclusive as it appears, there is considerable merit in this con-

tention. As we have seen, both points of view have certain attractions and defects; neither can be accepted without qualifications. Moreover, as with all traumatic experiences in the nation's history (such as the American Revolution, the Civil War, and World War I), it is perhaps inevitable that sooner or later, revisionist interpretations challenge conventional wisdom. The re-examinist school of thought was telling the American society, in effect, that its own leaders and citizens bore no small share of the responsibility for the disruption of wartime unity and the era of Soviet–American hostility. This group of commentators sought to do something which is always difficult and psychologically unpalatable: to apply the same critical standards to their own country's behavior which were normally used in judging the conduct of other countries. Evaluating American diplomacy by this criterion, revisionists were convinced, yielded conclusions about it which were often sharply at variance with accepted interpretations. (The same basic result was obtained by those commentators who believed that prolonged animosity between America and China could be attributed chiefly to failures by the United States over the past half-century or so to understand important developments on the Chinese mainland.) The principle that any society, especially a democratic one, ought periodically to examine its own behavior objectively and critically seems incontestable. The *very process of re-examination itself* keeps a society from lapsing into sterile orthodoxy and diplomatic ossification. Mankind learns from history only to the extent that he is prepared to review its record dispassionately and with a genuine desire to profit from past mistakes. And one lesson of history which supporters of orthodox and "establishment" doctrines need to remember continuously is that there is always a tendency for a widely accepted point of view to become sacrosanct; too many times, the test of patriotism has been the extent to which members of society were willing uncritically to subscribe to the majority's opinion. The history of natural science, for example, abounds with examples too numerous to list of initially heretical (not to say, incredible) ideas which in time became established doctrine. Similarly, there is always the chance that some novel, even shocking, interpretation of America's relations with the Soviet Union, with Asia, with Latin America, or with other regions will become as widely accepted as Newton's laws of motion or Pasteur's ideas about the causes of disease. Indeed, such continual re-evaluation of national behavior goes on routinely and constantly. To cite but a single example: Diplomatic historians today are more inclined than in the 1930s to accept many revisionist contentions about the nature and purpose of America's "Open Door" policy toward China after 1900.

After conceding the necessity for periodic re-examination of national policy, we must be no less cognizant of *the dangers inherent in romanticizing the concept of historical revisionism.* Given the climate of American society in the contemporary period, students are perhaps naturally and unconsciously prone to give the benefit of the doubt to any *new* interpretation of American experience—particularly those which challenge prevailing explanations. The "Muckraking" tradition is firmly established in the American ethos. In foreign affairs, in minority–majority groups relations, in the field of economic history—in these and other key areas of American life, revisionist commentators can often count on receiving a sympathetic hearing, especially among well-educated youth. As we have noted, foreigners have repeatedly observed that Americans have a singular penchant for *self-criticism;* they derive a certain satisfaction from being told how much their performance falls short of their professions. For some revisionist commentators, as for many contemporary novelists, "shock value" has become a stock-in-trade. Evidence which tends to disprove their contentions is ignored or explained away. While the professions of Soviet or Chinese officials can be taken at face value, those of American officials cannot be accepted; Soviet policy is really motivated by identifiable and legitimate goals (like the desire for security), while American policy (always more Machiavellian than it appears) is dictated by the intrigues of the military–industrial complex; Soviet behavior in Eastern Europe or Chinese suspicion toward the outside world can be justifiably explained by reference to the wrongs done to these societies in recent history, but American policy which is similarly based in part upon the impact of crucial historical episodes (like the Munich Conference or the conflict with Japan during World War II) is unacceptable; in regions like Southeast Asia, the massive involvement of the United States can be explained by reference to the "arrogance of American power," although comparable Soviet or Chinese involvements in regions outside their own borders (such as a growing Soviet presence in Egypt) are merely *defensive responses* to American provocations. With respect to the cold war, as in revisionist interpretations of World War I, the existence of a double standard of this kind sometimes raises a serious question about the validity of the re-examinists' conclusions. America's conduct tends to measured by an *ideal* standard, while that of its opponents is judged by a *relativist* standard, according to which nearly *any* Soviet or Chinese move becomes both fully explicable and ethically acceptable.

Many revisionists appear to operate upon the premise that orthodox viewpoints are inherently suspect *because they are widely believed.* The very fact that a majority of America's leaders and citizens attribute the origins of the cold war

primarily to Soviet behavior in world affairs—the fact that this point of view has become the doctrine of "the establishment"—calls its validity into serious question. Every revisionist perhaps sees himself as a new Galileo, Newton, or Pasteur, whose ideas revolutionize the age in which he lives. (Yet a fascinating book could be written about the history of natural science focusing upon the hundreds or thousands of "heretical" ideas which in time came to be viewed as erroneous, unsubstantiated, and in some instances utterly nonsensical! Indeed, investigation would probably reveal that this was the outcome for *most* ideas seeking to challenge established scientific thought.) For scientific heretics like Pasteur, the key point which needs to be remembered is this: In the final analysis, his views prevailed within the scientific community not merely because he "confronted" existed scientific wisdom, nor because his views were "different" from orthodox ideas, nor because they were psychologically satisfying, but instead because they *successfully stood the test of experimental and other evidence.* After it was clear that they had done so, in time they came to be incorporated into the corpus of scientific knowledge. This remains the only real test for the validity of "heretical" ideas today. The fact that they appeal to us because they are "different," that they satisfy the psychological yearnings of many Americans who enjoy being told how culpable their own government was for initiating the cold war and other diplomatic crises in the postwar period,* that they provide an *exposé* of the intrigues supposedly carried on by the military–industrial complex or some other influential group against the true interests of the American people —all such considerations are fundamentally extraneous and misleading. The only standard by which revisionism ought to be judged is the one which has been applied throughout the history of scientific thought: How well does the explanation offered *accord with the available evidence?*

When that standard is applied to the origins and nature of the cold war, three conceivable responses are possible: (1) For some important questions related to that conflict (e.g., whether the Kremlin really had any intention of permitting Anglo–American influence in postwar Eastern Europe, or what Stalin's precise role was in precipitating the Korean War), we must concede frankly that to date the evidence remains highly fragmentary and inconclusive, permitting few authoritative conclusions; (2) for other aspects of the cold war, the evidence available tends to support

*For a recent and provocative discussion of the tendency of many Americans toward self-flagellation and emotional satisfaction derived from what one writer terms their sense of America's "supreme criminality and unpopularity," see Robert Conquest, "The American Psychodrama Called 'Everyone Hates Us,'" *The New York Times Magazine* (May 10, 1970), pp. 28–29, 92–96.

orthodox interpretations; and (3) for still other aspects (as, for example, the once-prevalent notion of a monolithic "international Communism" controlled from Moscow), the evidence indicates that a reappraisal of many pervasive ideas and interpretations is indeed required. On the basis of evidence available at the present time, however, the chances are that the first and second responses are more nearly justified than the third.

NOTES

1. Thomas A. Bailey, *America Faces Russia* (Ithaca, N.Y.: Cornell University Press, 1950), p. 62. A history of Russian–American relations, focusing on the role of public opinion.
2. Frederick C. Barghoorn, *Soviet Russian Nationalism* (New York: Oxford University Press, 1956), p. 163. An analysis of nationalism and Soviet Communism since 1917.
3. Quoted in Bailey, *op. cit.*, p. 198.
4. Marx's views were paralleled by those of his colleague, Friedrich Engels. See the essay by Engels, from his *The Russian Menace to Europe*, included in Robert A. Goldwin *et al.*, eds., *Readings in Russian Foreign Policy* (New York: Oxford University Press, 1959), pp. 74–92.
5. George B. Huszar *et al.*, *Soviet Power and Policy* (New York: Thomas Y. Crowell, 1955), pp. 22–23. A helpful symposium, covering various aspects of historic and more recent Soviet policy.
6. E. Carman Day, *Soviet Imperialism* (Washington, D.C.: Public Affairs Press, 1950), p. 11.
7. Michael T. Florinsky, *Russia: A History and an Interpretation*, vol. II (New York: Macmillan, 1953), p. 982. A thorough and scholarly account that is rich in detail and short on interpretation.
8. K. W. B. Middleton, *Britain and Russia*, vol. II (London: Hutchinson, n.d.), pp. 33–34.
9. Florinsky, *op. cit.*, pp. 1262, 1270–1271.
10. Anatole G. Mazour, *Russia: Past and Present* (New York: Van Nostrand, 1951), p. 114. A succinct and readable textbook on Russian history, with many illuminating insights.
11. *Ibid.*, p. 116.
12. Melvin C. Wren, "Pobedonostsev and Russian Influence in the Balkans, 1881–1888," *Journal of Modern History* 19 (June, 1947), 132.
13. Nicolas Berdyaev, *The Russian Idea* (New York: Macmillan, 1948), pp. 8–9. A highly original, provocative study of Russian character and viewpoints.
14. Quoted in Mazour, *op. cit.*, pp. 51–52.
15. Berdyaev, *op. cit.*, pp. 8–9.
16. Quoted in Mazour, *op. cit.*, p. 31.
17. Quoted in Berdyaev, *op. cit.*, p. 37.
18. Quoted in Mazour, *op. cit.*, p. 19.
19. Florinsky, *op. cit.*, vol. 2, p. 987.
20. Quoted in Berdyaev, *op. cit.*, p. 148.
21. *Ibid.*, p. 195.
22. *Ibid.*, pp. 249–250.
23. Ernest J. Simmons, ed., *Continuity and Change in Russian and Soviet Thought* (Cambridge, Mass.: Harvard University Press, 1955), p. 531. A symposium containing several thought-provoking essays on Russian policy.
24. Quoted in Department of State, *Communist Perspective* (Washington, D.C.: Division of Research for USSR and Eastern Europe, Office of Intelligence Research, 1955), p. 512.
25. Harold E. Blinn, "Seward and the Polish Rebellion of 1863," *American Historical Review* 45 (July, 1940), 828–833.
26. See, for example, the reissue of George Kennan's *Siberia and the Exile System* (Chicago: University of Chicago Press, 1958).
27. American aversions to czarism are discussed in "Russian–American Relations, 1917–1933: An Interpretation," *American Political Science Review* 28 (June, 1934), 388. The author contends that American estrangement from Russia stems from attitudes formed in the czarist period.
28. Winston B. Thorson, "American Public Opinion and the Portsmouth Peace Conference," *American Historical Review* 53 (April, 1948), 439–464.
29. For official and unofficial American opinions on the Bolshevik Revolution, see George F. Kennan, *Russia Leaves the War* (Princeton, N.J.: Princeton University Press, 1956); Jules Davids, *America and the World of Our Times* (New York: Random House, 1960), pp. 115–117; Bernard S. Morris, *International Communism and American Policy* (New York: Atherton Press, 1966), pp. 125, 130; William A. Williams, *American–Russian Relations: 1781–1947* (New York: Holt, Rinehart and Winston, 1952), pp. 105–131.
30. This viewpoint has perhaps been most forcefully presented by D. F. Fleming, *The Cold War and Its Origins*, Vol. I (Garden City, N.Y.: Doubleday, 1961, two vols.), pp. 31–32; see also Williams, *op. cit.*, pp. 131–157.
31. See Bailey, *op. cit.*, pp. 636–637; Davids, *op. cit.*, pp. 115–117. Monographic studies of this still controversial episode in American diplomatic history are L. I. Strakhovsky, *The Origins of American Intervention in North Russia, 1918* (Princeton, N.J.: Princeton University Press, 1937); the same author's *Intervention at Archangel* (Princeton, N.J.: Princeton University Press, 1944); and Betty M. Unterberger, *America's Siberian Expedition, 1918–1920* (Durham, N.C.: Duke University Press, 1956).
32. See *The Memoirs of Cordell Hull*, vol. I (New York: Macmillan, 1948), p. 299.
33. Robert P. Browder, *The Origins of Soviet–American Diplomacy* (Princeton, N.J.: Princeton University Press, 1953), p. 9.
34. Department of State, *Foreign Relations of the United States, The Soviet Union: 1933–1939* (Washington, D.C.: U.S. Government Printing Office, 1952), pp. 6–9; Williams, *American–Russian Relations, op. cit.*, pp. 236–237.
35 Bailey, *op. cit.*, p. 709.

36. Our treatment of Soviet–Western relations during the 1930s draws from a large number of sources. One of the most scholarly and dispassionate is Max Beloff, *The Foreign Policy of Soviet Russia, 1929–1941* (New York: Oxford University Press, 1949, two vols.). In general, Beloff takes a very limited view of both Russia's capabilities and its desire to cooperate with the West to halt Axis expansionism during the 1930s. A more recent analysis is by the distinguished Russian scholar, George F. Kennan, *Russia and the West Under Lenin and Stalin* (Boston: Little, Brown and Co., 1960). A detailed treatment of the Munich crisis is John Wheeler-Bennett, *Munich: Prologue to Tragedy* (New York: Duell, Sloan and Pearce, 1948). Interpretations emphasizing the essentially defensive nature of Soviet diplomatic behavior during this period are Peter G. Filene, ed., *American Views of Soviet Russia* (Homewood, Ill.: Dorsey, 1968); William A. Williams, *The Tragedy of American Diplomacy* (Cleveland: World Publishing, 1959), pp. 135–143; and the same author's *Russian–American Relations, op. cit.*, pp. 234–253. Perhaps the most capable assertion of the "re-examinist viewpoint" on the interwar period is Fleming, *op. cit.*, vol. I, pp. 53–97. The official American view of the Nazi–Soviet Pact, highly critical of Moscow's diplomacy, is the State Department's publication, *Nazi–Soviet Relations, 1939–1941* (Washington, D.C.: U.S. Government Printing Office, 1948).
37. Bailey, *op. cit.*, p. 713.
38. For the re-examinist explanation of Soviet Russia's attack against Finland, see Fleming, *op. cit.*, vol. I, pp. 101–104; and Williams, *American–Russian Relations, op. cit.*, pp. 254–255. Even American opinion normally favorable to Moscow, however, was shocked by the Finnish War; see Filene, *op. cit.*, pp. 137–141.
39. Bailey, *op. cit.*, pp. 726–727.
40. The views of Truman and others in this vein are cited in Fleming, *op. cit.*, vol. I, pp. 135–137.
41. See the views of General Marshall in George C. Marshall, *Ordeal and Hope* (New York: Viking, 1965), pp. 72, 240.
42. See Williams, *American–Russian Relations, op. cit.*, p. 265; and Walter LaFeber, *America, Russia, and the Cold War, 1945–1966* (New York: Wiley, 1968), pp. 5–6.
43. Churchill's politico-military strategy, involving an Allied invasion through the "soft underbelly" of Europe, is discussed in Fleming, *op. cit.*, vol. I, pp. 154, 159–160, 164–167; and Gaddis Smith, *American Diplomacy During the Second World War: 1941–1945* (New York: Wiley, 1966), pp. 46–47.
44. For discussions of the Katyn massacres, presenting evidence pro and con regarding Russia's involvement, see Smith, *op. cit.*, pp. 70–71; Fleming, *op. cit.*, vol. I, pp. 228–230. Alexander Werth, *Russia at War, 1941–1945* (New York: Avon Books, 1964), pp. 606–612,

presents a balanced analysis of this and other wartime issues involving the Soviet Union. Werth makes the significant point that at the Nuremberg war crimes trials, the evidence of German complicity in the Katyn massacres was regarded as too slender to indict Nazi officials for the crime.
45. Evidence on the controversial "Warsaw uprising" is still mixed and incomplete, particularly as regards Soviet intentions. Indictments of Moscow's behavior are Stanislaw Mikolajczyk, *Rape of Poland* (New York: Whittlesey House, 1948); and Arthur B. Lane, *I Saw Poland Betrayed* (Indianapolis: Bobbs-Merrill, 1948). Less polemical, but favorable to the Soviet view, is Fleming, *op. cit.*, vol. I, pp. 233–237. Werth's account in *Russia at War, op. cit.*, pp. 786–801, is thorough, presenting many of the military difficulties confronting Soviet commanders as they approached Warsaw.
46. For the text of the Yalta Agreement, see the useful compendium prepared for the Senate Foreign Relations Committee, *A Decade of American Foreign Policy: Basic Documents, 1941–1949*, 81st Congress, 1st Session 1950, pp. 27–34. Useful commentaries are Werth, *Russia at War, op. cit.*, pp. 876–886; Smith, *American Diplomacy During the Second World War, op. cit.*, pp. 129–136; Fleming, *op. cit.*, vol. I, pp. 191–218. Primary sources on the Yalta Conference are James F. Byrnes, *Speaking Frankly* (New York: Harper & Row, 1947), pp. 21–45; and Edward R. Stettinius, *Roosevelt and the Russians: The Yalta Conference* (Garden City, N.Y.: Doubleday, 1949).
47. See the views of Fleming, *op. cit.*, vol. I, pp. 214–215, 266; and Williams, *The Tragedy of American Diplomacy, op. cit.*, pp. 163–169.
48. See Byrnes, *op. cit.*, pp. 54–55; 57–59.
49. This report is reproduced in Harry S. Truman, *Memoirs*, vol. I, (Garden City, N.Y.: Doubleday, 1955, two vols.), pp. 14–17.
50. *Ibid.*, pp. 23, 25.
51. *Ibid.*, p. 71. See also the views of George F. Kennan, whose interpretations of Soviet behavior were proving increasingly influential within the Truman administration during this period, in his *Memoirs (1925–1950)* (New York: Bantam, 1967), pp. 227–284.
52. For re-examinist treatments of the question of aid to Russia during and after World War II, see John Lukacs, *A History of the Cold War* (Garden City, N.Y.: Doubleday, 1962), pp. 35–36; LaFeber, *op. cit.*, pp. 22–23, 48–49; and Fleming, *op. cit.*, vol. I, pp. 140–141, 481. For a detailed and objective appraisal of the problem of American aid to Russia during World War II, see Raymond H. Dawson, *The Decision to Aid Russia, 1941: Foreign Policy and Domestic Politics* (Chapel Hill, N.C.: University of North Carolina Press, 1959).
53. For discussions of the Anglo–Russian "spheres-of-influence" agreement in Eastern Europe, see LaFeber, *op. cit.*, pp. 10–11, 18;

Williams, *Tragedy of American Diplomacy*, *op. cit.*, pp. 160, 163, 273; and Filene, *American Views of Soviet Russia*, *op. cit.*, pp. 152–156.

54. LaFeber, *op. cit.*, p. 18; Williams, *Tragedy of American Diplomacy*, *op. cit.*, p. 160; Fleming, *op. cit.*, vol. I, pp. 174–187.

55. Fleming, *op. cit.*, vol. I, pp. 249–251, 254–255; Williams, *Tragedy of American Diplomacy*, *op. cit.*, p. 163; and see the speech by Vice President Henry Wallace, highly critical of the Truman administration's increasingly tough stance toward Moscow, as reproduced in Filene, *op. cit.*, pp. 167–170.

56. For the text of the Potsdam Agreement, see Senate Foreign Relations Committee, *A Decade of American Foreign Policy*, *op. cit.*, pp. 34–49.

57. A primary source on the Potsdam meeting is Byrnes, *op. cit.*, pp. 67–87. An excellent secondary account is Herbert Feis, *Between War and Peace: The Potsdam Conference* (Princeton, N.J.: Princeton University Press, 1960).

58. LaFeber, *op. cit.*, pp. 13–14, 30.

59. For a discussion of the extent of Soviet aid to Chinese Communism during and immediately after World War II, see Robert C. North, *Chinese Communism* (New York: McGraw-Hill, 1966), pp. 144–145; 176–177; recurrent *conflict* between Stalin's government and the Chinese Communist movement under Mao Tse-tung is a basic theme of Kennan's discussion in *Russia and the West Under Lenin and Stalin*, *op. cit.*, especially pp. 260–278.

60. For the text of Churchill's speech, see *The New York Times* (March 6, 1946); and for commentary, see LaFeber, *op. cit.*, pp. 30–31.

61. Quoted in LaFeber, *op. cit.*, p. 31.

62. See Fleming, *op. cit.*, vol. I, p. 350.

63. See the views cited in LaFeber, *op. cit.*, p. 21; and in Williams, *The Tragedy of American Diplomacy*, *op. cit.*, pp. 169–170.

64. The texts of the Anglo–American–Canadian declaration on nuclear disarmament, and the subsequent Baruch Plan for disarmament, are contained in Senate Foreign Relations Committee, *A Decade of American Foreign Policy*, *op. cit.*, pp. 1076–1087.

65. Truman, *Memoirs*, *op. cit.*, vol. II, pp. 99–100.

66. *Ibid.*, pp. 100–101.

67. For a discussion of the Greek–Turkish Aid Program, see Cecil V. Crabb, Jr., *Bipartisan Foreign Policy: Myth or Reality?* (New York: Harper & Row, 1957), pp. 54–61.

68. For criticisms in this vein, see Fleming, *op. cit.*, vol. I, pp. 433–476; Williams, *American–Russian Relations*, *op. cit.*, pp. 258–283; and *The Tragedy of American Diplomacy*, *op. cit.*, pp. 184–212; and for a recent indictment of the American postwar diplomatic record—in which the dominant theme is America's hostility toward revolutionary movements—see Richard J. Barnet, *Intervention and Revolution: America's Confrontation with Insurgent Movements Around the World* (New York: World Publishing, 1968), *passim;* the Greek crisis is treated on pp. 97–132.

Nine
THE COLD WAR AFTER STALIN:
Peaceful and Competitive "Coexistence"

In an era of nuclear stalemate, Soviet-American relations remain in most respects the most influential force affecting the future of the international system and the prospect for global peace and stability. Since the death of the Soviet dictator Joseph Stalin in 1953, the cold war has undergone significant changes. The recovery and revitalization of Western Europe; the emergence of Communist China and the deterioration in Sino-Soviet relations to the point of armed conflict between the two countries; the "liberalization" of many features of the Soviet system under Stalin's successors; the defection of Yugoslavia from the Communist satellite zone of Eastern Europe and growing "polycentric" tendencies behind the Iron Curtain; the corresponding desire of several Western nations (France being a conspicuous example) to pursue a more independent course in foreign affairs; the achievement of independence by new nations in the Afro-Asian world and their adoption of a nonaligned position in the East-West conflict; perhaps above all, the condition of nuclear "parity" whereby the two super-powers achieved a rough equilibrium in weapons of mass destruction—these developments affected the cold war fundamentally. But they did not eliminate it. Although both Washington and Moscow encountered many more limitations upon their ability to control international events than in the period immediately after World War II, it remained true that Soviet-American relations would probably continue to have a decisive impact upon such diverse phenomena as the likelihood of global war, the future of the United Nations, the prospect for stability in the Middle East, and the ability of the emerging nations to achieve many of their developmental goals.

These and other cold war issues will be discussed in detail in future chapters. Here our purpose is to provide an over-all frame of reference within which to evaluate specific questions affecting Soviet-American relations, by focusing upon two broad aspects of the cold war in the contemporary era: ideological disputes and the military-strategic confrontation between the two nuclear giants.[*]

THE IDEOLOGICAL FRONT

Save perhaps for a profession that Communist and Western democratic ideologies seek to achieve the best interests of humanity and strive to bring about a more just political–economic–social order, the two philosophies are antithetical on almost every concrete issue that confronts society. Their disagreement over most goals and, more crucially, over the means for reaching them, is so deep and all-pervasive that common agreement on seeking the welfare of society affords very little real affinity between the two ideologies. Their differences necessarily color relations between Communist and non-Communist nations in international affairs. Our interest here centers on the limited topic of the relationship between Communism as an ideology and Russian behavior in the sphere of foreign relations.[†] We shall explore that question

[*]A third important arena of the cold war—economic competition between the U.S. and Soviet Russia—was discussed in Chapter 1.

[†]The literature on Communist ideology is voluminous. Among the many helpful summaries and critical commentaries are: Sidney Hook, *Marx and the Marxists* (Princeton, N.J.: Van Nostrand Reinhold 1955); R. N. Carew Hunt, *A Guide to Communist Jargon* (New York: Macmillan, 1957), and *The Theory and Practice of Communism* (London: Geoffrey, Bles, 1957); Barrington Moore, Jr., *Soviet Politics—The Dilemma of Power* (Cambridge, Mass.: Harvard University Press, 1950); George F. Kennan, "The Sources of Soviet Conduct," *Foreign Affairs* 25 (July, 1947), 566–583, and *Russia and the West Under Lenin and Stalin* (Boston: Little, Brown, 1960); Ernest J. Simmons, ed., *Continuity and Change in Russian and Soviet Thought* (Cambridge, Mass.: Harvard University Press, 1955); Alvin Z. Rubinstein, *The Foreign Policy of the Soviet Union* (New York: Random House, 1960); Philip E. Mosely, ed., *The Soviet Union: 1922–1962* (New York: Praeger, 1963), and *The Kremlin in World Politics* (New York: Vintage Books, 1960); Abraham Brumberg, ed., *Russia Under Khrushchev* (New York: Praeger, 1962); Robert V. Daniels, *A Documentary History of Communism* (New York: Random House, 1960); Richard C. Gripp, *Patterns of Soviet Poli-*

first by examining the main tenets of Communist thought and then relating this credo to the diplomatic behavior of the Soviet Union.*

Communist Ideology—An Overview

Communism is a materialistic creed. This means not so much that it is concerned with material advancement—which of course it is—as that it rejects supernatural phenomena, and confines what is known and can be known about human nature and behavior solely to historical experience. This fact at once places it outside the Judeo–Christian tradition. Rejecting such ideas as that man is a creation of the Almighty, that he is constantly tainted with sin, and that consequently no perfect social order can be established on earth, Communism claims to "be able, through science and social action, to create an ideal order in which the needs and desires of mankind will be fully satisfied. . . ."[1]

Through the insights afforded by the processes of "dialectical materialism,"† Communism purports to have found the key to social organization

---

tics (Homewood, Ill.: Dorsey, 1963); Alexander Dallin and Thomas B. Larson, eds., *Soviet Politics Since Khrushchev* (Englewood Cliffs, N.J.: Prentice-Hall, 1968); Robert C. Tucker, *The Marxian Revolutionary Idea* (New York: Norton, 1969); Samuel Hendel and Randolph L. Braham, eds., *The U.S.S.R. After Fifty Years: Promise and Reality* (New York: Knopf, 1967); Alfred G. Meyer, *Communism* (New York: Random House, 1967).

*More than ever before, it is essential for the student to recognize at the outset that the term "Communism" is subject to widely differing interpretations. To some extent, the dispute between Soviet Russia and Red China revolves around the issue of what Communism *means* in theory and practice. In recent years, the problem has been compounded by the distinctive brand of Communism practiced by Yugoslavia and by advocacy of the concept of "national Communism" by several Eastern European states. There are of course various *non-Marxist* versions of Communism, such as that practiced by the early Christian Church and the "Brook Farm" experiment early in American history. Even before the Bolshevik Revolution in Russia, it must be recalled, the Marxist movement was itself split into two major factions—the Mensheviks and the Bolsheviks, with the former advocating peaceful and evolutionary methods, while the latter (which ultimately recognized Lenin as its leader) urged reliance upon violence and revolution.

As used in this chapter, the term "Communism" is meant to describe the ideology identified with Soviet Russia. This philosophy can perhaps most accurately be called Marxism-Leninism-Stalinism or Bolshevism, to differentiate it from other movements (ranging from Titoism to Maosim) purportedly derived from the teachings of Karl Marx.

†Marxist thought took from Hegel the idea of the "dialectic"—that is, arriving at truth by the synthesis of opposites. One stage of human history (the thesis) gives rise to tendencies (the antithesis) that ultimately bring in a new stage (synthesis), which is formed by a combination of the old and new. Thus, in Marxist thought, feudalism engendered antifeudal forces. The synthesis of these two stages ushered in the new stage, capitalism.

in the "mode of production." At any stage in history, whether in the feudal, capitalist, socialist, or Communist era, the prevailing mode of production determines the nature of a society's laws, institutions, ethical and moral codes, class relationships, political systems—in short, every aspect of the societal order. But there is one feature common to all societies, until the Communist utopia has been reached. This is the class conflict. In every pre-Communist society a struggle takes place between the owners of the means of production—under capitalism, the bourgeoisie—and the workers, or proletariat. The latter are denied their rightful share of the fruits of industry by the entrenched bourgeoisie. Until the prevailing system of production is overturned by revolution, this situation continues. Nothing short of a revolution can usher in a new socialist* order, since the entrenched owners will never relinquish control voluntarily. Ostensible improvements in the standard of living of the working class, through such techniques as higher wages and better working conditions, extensions of governmental regulation over economic enterprise, or democratic political reforms, merely constitute efforts on the part of the bourgeoisie to consolidate its power by beguiling the proletariat into believing that its condition is improving, when in fact the exploiting class remains firmly in control. Hence, Bolsheviks reserve some of their sharpest invective for labor union movements, socialist parties, the British Labour party, and other groups—collectively condemned for the sin of "bourgeois reformism"—that divert the masses from a revolutionary course. Down to the 1960s, it remained a fixed canon of Communist belief that "the ruling classes do not yield power of their own free will." Although, under Khrushchev, Communist ideology emphasized "peaceful coexistence" and proclaimed that violent revolution was not *re-*

---

*Despite a widespread misconception in the United States, from the point of view of strict ideological correctness, it must be emphasized that the U.S.S.R. is *not* now, and has never regarded itself as, a *Communist* state, even by its own version of Marxist criteria. Down to 1961, the Soviet Union, its theoreticians said, was engaged in creating a *socialist* order—the stage prior to Communism. In that year, Soviet ideologists announced that the socialist stage had been completed and the stage of "Communist construction" had begun. But after Premier Khrushchev's ouster in 1964 this line was modified and with it the timetable announced for the achievement of Communism. Once more officials in the Kremlin announced that the U.S.S.R. was in the process of constructing *socialism;* when that process was finished (and it was not clear when it could be expected), there would occur a "gradual transition" to Communism. Internal economic problems in the Soviet Union, for example, evidently compelled a cutback in the goals projected under Khrushchev. See Wolfgang Leonhard, "Politics and Ideology in the Post-Khrushchev Era," in Alexander Dallin and Thomas B. Larson, *Soviet Politics Since Khrushchev* (Englewood Cliffs, N.J.: Prentice-Hall, 1968), p. 57.

quired for the overthrow of capitalism, the equivocal qualification was added that the necessity for violence would depend upon "the strength of the reactionary groups' resistance" to the demands of the proletariat.[2] At a later stage in the chapter, we shall examine the Kremlin's concept of "peaceful coexistence" and its major implications more fully.

"World Revolution" and Conflict with Capitalism

Perhaps no aspect of Marxist thought has engendered such disquiet and apprehension among non-Communist states as the movement's *international ambitions and goals.* A clear (if not always consistent) theme in Marxist ideology for many decades has been the idea that Communism will eventually embrace the world; one after another, capitalist and non-Communist societies will be gripped by "proletarian revolutions" that will destroy existing orders, paving the way for a Communist utopia. Even more alarming to non-Bolsheviks is the idea that this worldwide revolutionary struggle is likely to be *violent,* involving internal insurrections and external wars. A celebrated doctrinal pronouncement from Lenin in 1919 asserted:

. . . We are living not merely in a state but in a system of states and the existence of the Soviet Republic side by side with imperialist states for a long time is unthinkable. One or the other must triumph in the end. And before that end supervenes, a series of frightful collisions between the Soviet Republic and the bourgeois states will be inevitable.[3]

The following year, Lenin wrote that: ". . . As long as capitalism and socialism exist, we can not live in peace; in the end, one or the other will triumph —a funeral dirge will be sung over the Soviet Republic or over world capitalism."[4]

Such prophecies of doom for capitalism were echoed even by the advocate of "peaceful coexistence," Nikita Khrushchev, in 1963, when the Central Committee of the Communist party affirmed that:

We are wholeheartedly for the destruction of imperialism and capitalism. We not only believe in the inevitable downfall of capitalism, but we do everything to ensure this will be achieved by means of the class struggle and as quickly as possible.[5]

In mid-1968, the world discovered that this Leninist idea had not disappeared from the minds of Soviet officials; indeed, it was readily available when needed to rationalize Russian policy moves —in this instance, the ruthless suppression of Czechoslovakia's internal freedom. After the

armed forces of the Soviet Union and the Warsaw Pact countries invaded Czechoslovakia on August 20, the Kremlin announced the so-called Brezhnev Doctrine justifying reliance upon force. In essence (and we shall discuss it more fully below), this doctrine provided that Communist reliance upon military might was permissible whenever, in Moscow's judgment, a threat was posed to "the interests of world socialism and the world revolutionary movement."[*]

Admittedly, in common with many other aspects of Communist ideology, Soviet officials have been ambivalent in their pronouncements concerning the degree and nature of violence expected to characterize relations between Marxist and non-Marxist societies. Are Communists committed to the use of *military* means to achieve their objectives? Does the hostility which Lenin and other Marxists identified as inherent in the international class struggle decree an escalation in the level of violence, possibly precipitating a new global war fought with nuclear weapons? Lenin (as Marxists themselves have recognized) lived in the prenuclear age; he could not have anticipated the nuclear stalemate between the Soviet Union and the United States that has made both nations extremely cautious about triggering a nuclear confrontation. It is also significant that, in their ideological quarrel with the Chinese Communists, Soviet officials condemned Peking for its "adventurism" and its apparent indifference to the prospect of global nuclear war.

Marxist ideology has also been reasonably consistent for many years in emphasizing the point that the danger of war arises from the "general crisis" of capitalism: As capitalist nations are increasingly gripped by revolutionary forces, they will be tempted—in their death throes, so to speak —to lash out at the source of their tribulations, the Soviet Union. In the Marxist lexicon, "imperialism" and "war" are synonymous; by its very nature, capitalism cannot rid itself of reliance upon "militarism" and violence to perpetuate exploitation and to defend itself against its ultimate downfall. A perennial theme (as a Soviet source expressed it in 1961) is that modern-day capitalism "stimulates militarism"; the party faithful

---

[*]See the article in *Pravda* (September 25, 1968), as cited in Senate Committee on Government Operations, *Czechoslovakia and the Brezhnev Doctrine,* 91st Congress, 1st Session, 1969, pp. 1–3. As officially formulated and announced by Soviet party leader Leonid Brezhnev, this new doctrine justified use of force by Communist states to prevent a "deviation from socialism," to avert the "restoration of the capitalist order" in states having a Marxist regime or to counter "a threat to the security of the socialist community as a whole." See *ibid.,* p. 4. In later justifications for Soviet intervention in Czechoslovakia, Soviet journals referred to the "two antithetical social systems—capitalism and socialism. . . ." The "socialist community," said Politburo member Mazurov, is "always ready to defend its revolutionary gains. . . ." See *ibid.,* pp. 15 and 21.

were warned that a "new war was being hatched by the imperialists" which threatened mankind "with unprecendented human losses and destruction."[6] For many years also, as we shall see in later pages, the Soviet Union's armed forces have been designed primarily for defensive warfare. From an analysis of its military strength, there is no evidence that Moscow has designed a military machine capable of mounting a major global or regional offensive in behalf of an ideological goal like world revolution.

The post-Stalinist emphasis upon "peaceful coexistence" in Communist thought, however, implied no lessening in *ideological hostility* between Marxist and non-Marxist societies. Premier Khrushchev's widely celebrated challenge to capitalism —"We will bury you"—was explained to mean not "the physical burial of any people, but the question of historical force of development"; Communism would supercede capitalism "and capitalism thereby would, so to speak, be buried." Or, as one commentator has expressed the idea, the Kremlin does not envision that the cold war will be ended by a process of mutual accomodation with capitalism; at no time has "peaceful coexistence" anticipated that result. The cold war—arising primarily out of capitalist hostility toward the U.S.S.R.—will end after the Communist "revolutionary struggle" has achieved victory. Ideological "coexistence," Premier Khrushchev once declared, was possible only "under Communism." If reliance upon military force were ruled out, peaceful coexistence did not anticipate "reconciliation of Socialist thought and bourgeois ideology." According to a declaration made by Moscow in 1960, it meant "intensification of the struggle of the working class . . . for the triumph of Socialist ideas."[7] As the United States, the center of global capitalism, was gripped by progressively more acute crises, it became compelled to become a "world gendarme" and to rely increasingly upon militarism—proof, to Marxist analysts, that capitalism was in its last stages and was "digging its own grave."[8] Stalin's successors were prepared to assist the forces of history in relegating capitalism to oblivion.

Communist "Morality" and Law

The moral–humanitarian basis of Communist ideology has always formed a conspicuous element in the movement's rationale and programs. If Communism rejects "the class morality of the exploiters," it affirms "Communist morality," identified as encompassing "the fundamental norms of human morality which the masses . . . evolved in the course of millenniums. . . ." Among the specific items enumerated in the Communist moral code are the obligation to assume an "uncompromising attitude to the enemies of Communism, peace and the freedom of nations" and

devotion to the "fraternal solidarity with the working people of all countries, and with all peoples."[9] In practice, as Westerners are painfully aware, it is usually almost impossible to distinguish this code of "Communist morality" from outright expediency and opportunism in advancing the interests of the Soviet Union in world affairs. Communist "morality," said an official Soviet publication in 1941, is "that which facilitates the destruction of the old world, and which strengthens the new, Communist regime." Invoking an unidentified quotation from Lenin, the article continued that: " 'At the foundation of Communist morality lies the struggle for the strengthening and perfecting of Communism.' "[10]

The outside world was provided with a dramatic example of the unique nature of Communist ethical and legal principles late in 1968, when the Soviet Union and five of its Warsaw Pact allies invaded Czechoslovakia, crushing that nation's efforts to liberalize its internal regime. Catching many Western observers by surprise, this intervention was in direct violation of numerous treaty commitments between Czechoslovakia and its Communist neighbors.* After the suppression of Czech freedom, the Kremlin (responding perhaps to the censure which greeted its behavior, even by Marxist groups outside Eastern Europe) justified its conduct on the basis of the distinction between "bourgeois law" and "socialist law." The former, as Marx taught, was identified with, and subservient to, the interests of capitalism; the latter was a new and more progressive system of law, stemming from the Bolshevik Revolution in Russia and binding upon all Marxist states. Over against the bourgeois idea of "national sovereignty," for example, the Kremlin posited "the interests of world socialism and the world revolutionary movement" to which sovereignty always had to yield. Asserting that Czechoslovakia's exercise of self-determination would "run counter to Czechoslovakia's fundamental interests and would harm the other socialist countries," *Pravda* rejected any charge that intervention in the country's affairs was "illegal." Anyone invoking "legalistic considerations" to condemn Russia's behavior overlooked the basic Marxist tenet that "laws and the norms of law are subordinated to the laws of the class struggle and the laws of social development." The "yardstick of bourgeois law" was thus totally inapplicable. Intervention in Czechoslovakia, said another *Pravda* article, was not merely legal; it was imperative for the Krem-

---

*For relevent treaty provisions, see Senate Government Operations Committee, *Czechoslovakia and the Brezhnev Doctrine,* 91st Congress, 1st Session, 1969, pp. 27–35. To cite but one example, in 1964, Soviet Premier Kosygin said concerning the Czech-Soviet Treaty of Friendship that it "guaranteed the restoration of independence, sovereignty and freedom to the Czechoslovak Republic. . . ." (Cited on p. 3.)

lin and its supporters to discharge "our internationist duty to them and to the international Communist workers' and national-liberation movement. For us this duty is the highest of all." The Communist conception of law and morality served as a foundation for the new Brezhnev Doctrine (announced November 12, 1968), which provided an ideological support for intervention in Czechoslovakia. This doctrine cited the existence of "common laws governing socialist construction"; foremost among these was the principle that whenever a threat to any one socialist country arises, this "is no longer only a problem of the people of that country but also a common problem, concern for all socialist states." Several months later, another Soviet theoretician declared that "Socialism and sovereignty are indivisible"; dedication to the principle of "proletarian internationalism" required "the unconditional fulfillment of its revolutionary duty."[11]

The case of Czechoslovakia merely affords a recent example to illustrate an idea obvious since 1917. Any policy, any move or maneuver that advances the aims of Communism, as determined by the Kremlin, is ipso facto moral and legal. Conversely, immorality and illegal conduct are those acts which hinder or impair the achievement of Communist objectives. Accordingly, the methods by which Marxists pursue their goals are exceedingly flexible and opportunistic.* Said Stalin in 1923: "The strategy of the Party is not something

*Some recent writers on Communist thought have differentiated rather sharply between strategy and tactics, (the former being the long-range plan of action, the latter the short-run techniques utilized for carrying out that plan). It is by no means certain, however, that Communist spokesmen themselves make such a clear delineation. It is true that Stalin declared: "Strategy deals with the main forces of the revolution" and that it "remains essentially unchanged throughout a given stage. . . ." Yet he also said that: "The strategy of the Party is not something permanent, fixed once and for all. It changes to meet historical turns and shifts. These changes are expressed in the fact that for each separate historical turn there is worked out a separate strategic plan appropriate to it and operating for the whole period. . . . For every historical turn there is a strategic plan which corresponds to its needs and is adapted to its tasks."

This problem highlights the underlying ambiguity of Marxist thought and the impact of exigencies at home and abroad upon the viewpoints advocated by the Kremlin in any period. Whether or not the Kremlin does differentiate between strategy and tactics may be of interest chiefly as a matter of philosophic speculation. For our purposes, a more significant point may be the keynote that has recurred frequently in Communist ideology. As expressed by Lenin in 1900, the theme urged loyal Communists to utilize "all methods of political struggle, as long as they correspond to the forces at the disposal of the Party and facilitate the achievement of the greatest results possible under the given conditions!" For addition quotations on this subject, see Department of State, *Communist Perspectives* (Washington, D.C.: Division of Research for USSR and Eastern Europe, Office of Intelligence Research, 1955), pp. 440–455.

permanent, fixed once and for all. It changes to meet historical shifts. . . ."[12] Or, as Lenin had phrased it earlier in 1920: ". . . the strictest loyalty to the ideas of Communism must be combined with the ability to make all the necessary practical compromises, to 'tack' to make agreements, zigzags, retreats and so on."[13]

The extreme flexibility of Communist methods has significant implications for Russia's relations with the outside world. It means that there is no predetermined timetable for ushering in the world revolution. As George Kennan has put it: the Kremlin "is under no ideological compulsion to accomplish its purposes in a hurry." Realization of the ultimate goals of world Communism is made contingent upon the development of favorable circumstances in the external environment. Time and again after 1917, Lenin and Stalin cautioned the party faithful against rashness and precipitate action that could only bring injury to the Communist cause. They warned, in effect, that "enemies aim at the annihilation of the Party. . . . An all-out attack may come at any time. . . . Until final victory, the very survival of the Party is always uncertain; when the enemy is already severely wounded, he lashes out with unprecedented reckless ferocity."[14] If the final victory of Communism depends upon propitious developments in the non-Communist world, then the "inevitable victory" of Communism may be postponed indefinitely.

Failure to heed these admonitions—accompanied by pursuit of a "reckless" and "adventurist" foreign policy—was one of the chief indictments which Soviet Russia brought against the Chinese Communist government, after these two former allies became increasingly antagonistic. To the Kremlin, the Communist rulers of China were engaging in "anti-Marxism" and "Trotskyism." Apparently indifferent to the prospect of global nuclear devastation and obsessed with the notion that the United States was a "paper tiger," Peking was failing to adapt its ideological pronouncements to the "objective conditions" prevailing in the outside world. Its failure placed the entire Marxist movement and the security of all Communist countries, not least Russia's, in jeopardy! Similarly, its ill-advised summons to revolution in most nations throughout the Afro-Asian zone was premature and doomed to failure. The only possible result would be to discredit Communism in societies where revolutionary prospects were *nil;* to strengthen the position of indigenous governments vis-à-vis Marxist groups; and perhaps to make it more difficult than ever to achieve Marxist objectives in the future.[15]

From this ideological verbiage, several principles of Marxism, as identified with the Kremlin, can be extracted. Moscow believed that "world revolution" proceeded on many fronts and had to be pursued by a variety of techniques adapted to the circumstances existing at any given time. The successful pursuit of world revolution did *not* require global war, although it might (and probably would) entail more limited forms of violence (like "wars of national liberation") or armed intervention in a country (like Czechoslovakia) to protect revolutionary gains. Since no timetable existed for the victory of world revolution, the Communist world had to accomodate itself to numerous setbacks (Lenin's publication, "Two Steps Forward, One Step Backward" served as an appropriate guideline); more might be lost than gained if Marxists pressed the revolutionary struggle under adverse circumstances—more so during a period of nuclear stalemate than in any other era since 1917. Implicit in Communism as identified with the Soviet Union is an idea that has increasingly produced contention among Marxist nations in recent years and lies at the heart of the Sino-Soviet dispute. This is the notion that the Kremlin, in the last analysis, is the *authoritative interpreter* of the Communist credo; and that the Soviet "model" of Communism has been, and remains, the only one having universal validity and legitimacy.

The U.S.S.R.—Bastion of World Communism

In the previous chapter we remarked upon the threat posed by the merger of traditional Russian foreign policy goals with the imperatives of Communist and ideology. At this point, let us examine this identity more closely.

Time and again since 1917, Communist leaders have called upon all who accepted the Marxist–Lenist–Stalinist faith to work unceasingly for the support of the diplomatic ambitions of the Soviet Union in world affairs. Following the diplomatic line laid down by the Kremlin is tantamount to advancing the interests of world Communism. True believers in Communism, said Stalin in 1925, will "support Soviet power and foil the interventionist machinations of the imperialists against the Soviet Union . . . mainstay of the revolutionary movement in all countries."[16] And a Communist journal stated in 1948 that

. . . the only determining criterion of revolutionary proletarian internationalism is: are you for or against the USSR, the motherland of the world proletariat? . . . A real internationalist is one who brings his sympathy and recognition up to the point of practical and maximal help to the USSR in support and defense . . . by every means and in every possible form. . . . The defense of the USSR . . . is the holy duty of every honest man everywhere. . . .[17]

Again, in the new Communist manifesto announced in 1961, it was affirmed that: "The existence of the Soviet Union greatly facilitates and accelerates the building of Socialism in the peoples' democracies," that "isolation from the Social-

ist camp" impedes the development of countries not already under Communism, and that true devotion to the Communist cause requires "love of the Socialist motherland. . . ."[18] Equation of the national interests of the Soviet Union with the professed ideological goals of the world Communist movement had become, by the 1960s, both a highly controversial and prominent element in Communist ideology. It constituted a crucial point of disagreement between Moscow and Peking, since Mao Tse-tung's regime increasingly challenged the Soviet Union's traditional "leadership" of the world Communist movement. However much they might reject other Chinese doctrinal assertions or criticize Peking's behavior at home and abroad, Marxist groups outside the U.S.S.R. often *approved* of this aspect of China's ideological heresy. If the Communist states of Eastern Europe, for example, often did not possess enough power to contest the Kremlin's claim to ideological leadership, events by the 1960s left no doubt that support for the idea of "national Communism" was strong in this zone. Yugoslavia's defection from the Cominform in 1948 had led the way; for over twenty years, Tito's government had successfully defied the Kremlin's authority. Gradually, other Communist states in Eastern Europe (by the late 1960s, Rumania had become an outstanding example) came to subscribe to the concept of "national Communism," or (as it was defined by the Italian Communist party) the concept of "polycentricity," involving several centers of Communist orthodoxy and authority. By the late 1960s, polycentric tendencies had destroyed the monolithic character of Communism in Eastern Europe. To a greater or lesser degree, all Marxist states in this region (with the possible exception of East Germany) endorsed the idea of polycentricity, thereby indirectly joining Red China in its defiance of Moscow's leadership. A logical corollary of national Communism was the idea that greater "democracy" ought to prevail in decision-making by representatives of the international Communist movement. For the first time, the Kremlin encountered effective resistance to the idea that gatherings of Marxist leaders in Moscow or elsewhere should routinely approve proposals advanced by the U.S.S.R. Soviet policy-makers were forced to win support among Marxists outside Russia by persuasion and compromise; sometimes even these methods failed to give Moscow the kind of unified support it sought at Marxist conferences.

Although the Soviet Union's once-uncontested position at the head of the international Communist movement had been sharply challenged by the 1960s, the identification of Russia's needs and policies as a state with the interests of global Marxism remains a *tour de force* that has proved extremely valuable to the Kremlin. Communist groups everywhere in the world have been at least potential agents of Moscow; they have been required to take any steps—treason and espionage not excepted—to carry out the interests of the international Communist movement, as the Kremlin defined them. Moreover, the process of identification assigned to the Soviet Union the prerogative of interpreting both the *meaning* of contemporary Marxist doctrine and the *methods* required to carry it out, thereby giving the U.S.S.R. a preferential position over all other claimants in the Communist community. Third, it baptized the goals of Russian foreign policy—expansionism, Messianism, the search for warm water ports, the fixation with national security, and the rest—with a mystique and an ideological rationalization that made them appealing to dedicated Communists, fellow-travelers, and even certain non-Communists throughout the world. For, once the Kremlin's claim was conceded, advancement of Soviet Russia's goals in world affairs was made equivalent to the uplift and progress of humanity at large! Fourth, it eliminated any contradiction that might arise between the ideological aims of Communism and the diplomatic ambitions of the Soviet Union and its supporters, by declaring: (1) that those were identical to begin with, and (2) that the Soviet Union was the final and authoritative interpreter of both, leaving the Kremlin free to adjust its ideological concepts to its diplomatic interests, or vice versa, while equating its goals with the purpose of humanity at large. That non-Communists regard such pretensions with incredulity does not prevent the U.S.S.R. from realizing considerable diplomatic and propaganda advantage from them.

Recent Ideological Modifications

Communist ideology, we have already emphasized, is an evolving philosophical system; "creative Marxism" is one of its central tenets. Experience since 1917 has simply demonstrated that the Kremlin can and does adapt its doctrinal position to the exigencies facing it at home and abroad. Indeed, this effort to bring ideological pronouncements into harmony with Soviet policy requirements is one of the more striking features of Communist policy-making. Insofar as precedent serves as a reliable guide for the future, we may expect this ideological adaptation to continue. For a variety of reasons to be noted at a later stage, it may in fact become even more pronounced in the future than in the past.

The period of "de-Stalinization" under Premier Khrushchev witnessed a number of significant ideological modifications in the Soviet Union. Although the concept of "peaceful coexistence" was not an innovation, it received unprecedented emphasis during the Khrushchev era. Rapid economic progress within the U.S.S.R., coupled with the demonstration of its economic "superiority" globally, were regarded as the principal instru

ments of Communist advancement. Soviet officials viewed the eruption of nuclear war as a calamitous prospect—not only for other societies, but for the U.S.S.R. as well. With a few exceptions (Khrushchev's effort to emplant Soviet missiles in Cuba was an example), Russian officials concentrated upon internal economic progress, upon trying to maintain maximum unity within the Communist zone of Europe, and upon preserving a *détente* with the West.

These goals were by no means entirely abandoned by Khrushchev's successors. "Peaceful coexistence" remained the Kremlin's cardinal principle in relations with the United States. The consequences of nuclear war were regarded by Soviet policy-makers as still ominous. Even more than under Khrushchev, Moscow was obviously troubled by Chinese "adventurism" and the growing might of Peking's nuclear arsenal. A nuclear exchange between the United States and the Soviet Union, Russian officials commented on more than one occasion, would reduce both nations to the "level" of China! Soviet policy-makers after Khrushchev also continued to take a sober and realistic view of American society. The Vietnam conflict aside, America's international behavior was judged "reasonable" and restrained. Understanding of the magnitude of America's vast power permeated Moscow's ideological pronouncements. Nor did the Kremlin anticipate a repetition of the Great Depression in the United States.[19]

Nevertheless, after Khrushchev some "hardening" in the Kremlin's world view could be detected. Ideological conflict between Communist and non-Communist nations remained as intractable as ever. While nuclear war would be ruinous in its effect, Marxist ideologists by the late 1960s were more confident than a few years earlier that Communist societies could survive it, if capitalist nations could not. Militarily, the post-Khrushchev era witnessed a moderate expansion in Soviet expenditures for the armed services; Russian strategists were less prone than earlier to accept nuclear "parity" with America as a satisfactory defense posture. In a major doctrinal pronouncement in 1967, commemorating the fiftieth anniversary of the Bolshevik Revolution, the Kremlin called upon its supporters to employ both "peaceful and nonpeaceful" methods to achieve Marxist objectives, as circumstances dictated. Although the risks of nuclear war were not minimized, both theoretically and actually Soviet officials called attention to the importance of military force as a necessary instrument of Communist diplomacy.[20]

Armed Conflict in Communist Ideology

By the 1970s, Communist ideology recognized three categories of armed conflict that were legitimate, even in the nuclear age. One of these was "just wars." Although no precise definition of such conflicts has ever been offered by Marxist theoreticians, in practice a just war is an encounter in which the Soviet Union or any other Communist nation finds it expedient to engage in armed conflict to defend its interests. From the Communist perspective, resistance to American "aggression" in Vietnam was an example of a just war, as was support for the Communist cause in the Korean conflict several years earlier. Ideologically (if not of course always actually), in "just wars" Communist states are victims of armed attack by other nations.[21]

A second category of armed encounter in which Communist nations or forces might legitimately participate is "wars of national liberation." In general, these are struggles against colonial domination (such as guerrilla warfare against Portugal's rule in Angola), efforts by blacks or other oppressed minorities to break the dominant position of whites (as in Southern Rhodesia or South Africa), or possibly attempts by Arab societies to resist encroachments by "outposts of Western imperialism" such as Israel. The 1960s witnessed no decline in the Kremlin's ideological endorsement of wars of national liberation. Indeed, on some occasions (particularly when it was accused by Peking of abandoning its support for revolutionary causes), Moscow renewed its devotion to such conflicts.*

A third category of armed struggle in which it has been legitimate for Communist states to participate was highlighted by the Soviet and Warsaw Pact invasion of Czechoslovakia in 1968. According to the Brezhnev Doctrine announced later in the year to justify this reliance upon force, the Soviet Union and other Communist nations

might legitimately employ armed force against "counter-revolutionary" activities and to maintain the security of the "socialist commonwealth" against internal and external threats. As a principle of action, as distinct from a mere doctrinal pronouncement, the Brezhnev Doctrine was perhaps the most ominous ideological innovation made in Marxist thought during the 1960s.

Ideological Conflicts and International Tensions

What conclusions can we draw about the effects of ideological conflicts on Russian–American relationships in the contemporary era?

In the first place, the evident antithesis between Western and Communist political ideals affects the very language employed in diplomacy. A good illustration is the long-standing controversy between Russia and the United States over interpretation of the Yalta and Potsdam Agreements pertaining to Soviet occupation of former Axis territory in Eastern Europe. When the West and Russia talked in terms of establishing "democratic governments" and holding "free elections" in the Axis satellite territories overrun by the Red Army, they were talking a different language. The West obviously thought this agreement demanded free elections by secret ballot, as practiced in America, Britain, or France. It soon discovered that "free elections" according to the Kremlin's interpretation meant elections preceded by the elimination of all "fascist elements" and disfranchisement of "enemies of the people"—or in effect disfranchisement of all groups that could not be faithfully counted on to follow the line dictated by Moscow. The point here is not whether Moscow really intended to abide by the letter and spirit of the Yalta and Potsdam Agreements; the point is that these agreements were couched in language bound to foment misunderstanding and ill will in later interpretations. So fundamental is the divergence between Western political ideology and Marxism–Leninism–Stalinism that ordinary terms which formerly had a widely accepted meaning in diplomatic parlance no longer possess a clearly defined content. Ideological conflicts means, in other words, that the two most powerful nations on earth sometimes *cannot even communicate* with assurance that their positions are being completely understood by the other side.

In the second place, injection of ideological conflict into international affairs on a scale seldom experienced in recent history has intensified existing sources of disagreement and made problems, which were already inordinately difficult, wellnigh insoluble. Select any problem that has engaged the attention of foreign policy-makers throughout recent history—maintaining the balance of power, establishing a system of collective security and international law, seeking disarmament agreements, trying to achieve solutions of

---

*On this, as on several other major tenets of Marxist ideology, it is necessary to keep in mind the difference between what might be called the Kremlin's *declaratory* policies and its *operational* policies. Not infrequently, a wide gulf separates these two policy realms—for the U.S.S.R. as for other countries, not excluding the United States. With regard to "wars of national liberation," this dichotomy is especially marked. Ideologically, the Kremlin's support of them remains undiminished. In practice, there has been a noteworthy *reduction* in Russia's tangible support for, and participation in, such conflicts. Several commentators have called attention to the fact that, as judged by its *behavior,* Moscow apparently has little interest now in fermenting revolutionary situations abroad, in part perhaps because its recent experience in a number of countries (like Algeria, Ghana, Guinea, Iraq, and Indonesia) has not been overtly successful. Soviet involvement in the Vietnam War, for example, has been quite limited. The U.S.S.R. has been cautious about committing its own armed forces to support wars of national liberation. In brief, this is the kind of ideological tenet that appears to have minimum relevance to the Soviet Union's conduct in international affairs. See William Zimmerman, "Soviet Perspectives of the United States," in Alexander Dallin and Thomas B. Larson, eds., *Soviet Politics Since Khrushchev* (Englewood Cliffs, N.J.: Prentice-Hall, 1968), pp. 174–176; Robert C. Tucker, *The Marxian Revolutionary Idea* (New York: Norton, 1969), pp. 143–145; George Lichtheim, "What Is Left of Communism?" *Foreign Affairs* 46 (October, 1967), 78–95.

colonial conflicts. All of these and more have served as focal points for intense ideological discord. It is difficult enough under optimum conditions to make a system of collective security operate, without having the United Nations perverted into a propaganda forum which resounds with Soviet vituperations against "capitalist warmongers" and "Wall Street imperialists" *ad nauseam*, and in which the West in turn and largely in self-defense excoriates Moscow's record in internal and external affairs. Over the course of time, in such bodies as the United Nations, both sides have given evidence of being more interested in proving the soundness of their ideological positions than in negotiating settlements of existing cold war tensions. With respect to issues before the UN and other international questions, the era of "peaceful coexistence" has not basically altered the fact that Marxist societies envision non-Marxist states *as adversaries*. Whatever its precise form, and irrespective of the methods employed, the relationship between Communist and non-Communist states is regarded as essentially *hostile* and characterized by recurrent tensions.

Third, many students of Communist philosophy believe that the ideological conflict foredooms any genuine or lasting settlement between the United States and the U.S.S.R. or between the Communist bloc and the free world. Pointing to doctrinal assertions by Lenin and Stalin, they argue that conflict between the two worlds is inescapable as long as "world revolution" remains the Kremlin's announced goal. According to this view, Communist advocacy of "peaceful coexistence" is merely a siren song calculated to lull the West into complacency, to paralyze its defense efforts, and in the end to yield the world by default to Communism. The only realistic course for the United States, therefore, is to accept Communist pronouncements about the coming world revolution at face value and to prepare for continuing conflict, perhaps ultimately a third world war.

Fourth, Marxist–Leninist–Stalinist philosophy gives the Kremlin a powerful advantage over its diplomatic opponents: belief in the inevitable victory of its ideological cause. Besides inculcating in Communist groups a fanaticism and earnestness seldom seen outside religious groups in non-Communist countries, conviction that Communism is the "wave of the future," that it is being swept forward by the irresistible tides of history, serves as a powerful tonic to sustain the Kremlin and its supporters during lean years. It gives them a vision that, regardless of day-to-day adversities, remains undimmed; and it evokes loyalties to a cause worthy of their best and untiring efforts. In some degree this advantage partially accounts for the fact that the United States—in spite of its economic advancement, idealism, and remarkable lack of imperialistic motives—sometimes experiences great difficulties in countering Communist propaganda and diplomatic maneuvers.

Ideology and Soviet Foreign Policy

. . . There will develop two centers on a world scale: the socialist center drawing together to itself the countries gravitating toward socialism, and the capitalist center drawing together to itself the countries gravitating toward capitalism. The struggle between these two camps will determine the fate of capitalism and socialism throughout the world.

Statements such as this, made by Stalin in 1927, focus attention upon a crucial question for the present age. The answer to it is likely to determine the course of international affairs for generations to come. To what extent generally can the Communist credo as declared and interpreted by the Kremlin be taken as a reliable guide to the foreign policy of the Soviet Union? More specifically, does the Communist world's professed belief in the inevitability of "world revolution" foreclose any possibility of averting a new global holocaust? Does the presence of deeply ingrained and irreconcilable ideological disagreements rule out the possibility of an over-all "settlement" of diplomatic issues between East and West, or even limited and specific settlements of outstanding problems such as Berlin or Soviet domination over Eastern Europe?

Such questions are as difficult as they are fundamental. The basic inquiry involved in them is, "What is the precise role of ideology in Soviet policy-making?" More concretely, is Russia's internal and external behavior primarily a result of rigid adherence to the requirements of Marxism–Leninism–Stalinism? Alternatively, does its ideological system serve chiefly as a *rationalizer and legitimizer* of Soviet conduct, which is dictated mainly by nonideological considerations? Over a half-century after the Bolshevik Revolution, competent authorities on the Soviet Union are divided on this issue—perhaps more so than they were a decade or two earlier. At one stage in the postwar period, some Soviet scholars evinced a high degree of confidence in their ability to "predict" the Kremlin's behavior at home and abroad. The basic premise followed by this school of thought was that Soviet authorities adhered to an "operational code" derived from the principles of Marxism–Leninism–Stalinism; the main elements in this code could be identified from a careful examination of Communist thought. Therefore, Soviet responses to internal and external problems, being more or less automatic, could be anticipated with reasonable assurance.* By the late

*This approach is epitomized in the writings of Nathan Leites, *A Study of Bolshevism* (New York: Free Press, 1953), and *The Operational Code of the Politburo* (New York: McGraw-Hill, 1951).

1960s, it is fair to say, most scholars had considerably less confidence in their ability to predict Soviet (or other Communist) conduct with a high degree of accuracy; the limitations inherent in an analysis of the Kremlin's "operational code" (assuming that it even existed) had been dramatically revealed. Developments like the adoption of certain neo-capitalistic processes by Soviet economists; the Kremlin's toleration for many years of "polycentric" tendencies among Marxist nations in Eastern Europe; the unexpected and massive Soviet invasion of Czechoslovakia in 1968; Moscow's "gamble" when it tried to establish an offensive missile base in Cuba in the early 1960s; the Kremlin's restraint during the Vietnam War; the rising level of Sino–Soviet hostilities—these were but a few of the more widely publicized Soviet moves that took many Western observers by surprise.

To evaluate the role of ideology in Soviet foreign relations, one can think in terms of two polar positions. One of these conceives of ideology *as the most influential force* affecting the Soviet decision-making process. In this view, philosophical compulsions outweigh geographic factors, historical traditions, Russia's long-standing concern for security, expansionist impulses and other drives (discussed at length in Chapter 8), expediency and pragmatic considerations, and all other influences that might conceivably determine Soviet conduct. For those who hold this position, the fact that Soviet Russia is a *Communist* state is the dominant reality from which all appraisals of its behavior proceed.

The opposite position is that, among all the forces or variables affecting Soviet foreign policy, ideology is among the *least influential.* Some authorities (George F. Kennan is a leading example) are convinced that, from 1917 onward, Marxism–Leninism–Stalinism has *never* played the decisive role in shaping Moscow's international relationships which the Kremlin claims or which many Western observers have supposed. Other commentators (some of of whom are convinced that ideology may once have been a major factor actuating Soviet foreign policy) believe that the role of ideology has declined perceptibly *in recent years;* for neither domestic nor foreign affairs does it currently serve as a primary policy determinant.

While it is possible to postulate these two extreme positions with respect to the relationship between ideology and Soviet foreign policy, it must be recognized at the outset that this dichotomy probably does not accord with reality. This kind of either–or choice between ideology on the one hand, and Russian national interest (or security, or expediency, or some other force) on the other, as the dominant element in Soviet foreign policy is probably artificial and misleading.[22] In common with policy-making in all other nations, Soviet domestic and foreign policy almost invariably stems from some *combination* of forces, among which is ideology. Aside from the fact that Soviet officials make the claim, there is no good reason to suppose that ideology alone (or any other single causative factor) functions as the source of official decision-making. Like all other states, the Soviet policy-making apparatus is subjected to a multitude of diverse pressures and influences propelling it in one direction or another. The formulation of national policy thus resembles the process of vector analysis in physics: The ultimate direction in which an object or a policy will move involves the *resolution of all forces* acting on it at any given time. Ideology is of course one of these forces; in Russia's case, it may even be more influential than it is in other countries. But ideology must also compete with history and tradition, geographic factors, considerations of national security, the impact of key personalities upon the policy process, expediency and pragmatism, the often crucial impact of science and technology, and sheer bureaucratic inertia. Officials in the Kremlin have to "resolve" these forces before deciding upon a given course of action in foreign affairs. (In this connection, it is worth recalling a comment which Secretary of State Dean Rusk once made in discussing de facto principles of policy-making: The natural tendency of a governmental bureaucracy, when confronted with a new challenge or problem is *to do nothing.* In many cases, for Russia as much as for America, *bureaucratic inertia* may in reality be the strongest force operating upon the policy process!) Numerous and varied forces thus are brought to bear upon decision-making in the U.S.S.R. Almost never is Soviet behavior a function of ideology alone.

This statement leaves unanswered the question of the *relative importance* of Marxism–Leninism–Stalinism as an influence shaping Soviet foreign policy. If it is granted that Communist philosophy is one among several forces determining Moscow's foreign relations, is it a major or a minor force? Or, precisely *how* does ideology affect the U.S.S.R.'s relations with other countries? It may be helpful to conceive of two levels on which ideology operates in the Soviet decision-making process. It may function *subconsciously,* affecting how Russian officials understand, interpret, and react to events abroad; their immersion in the principles of Marxism–Leninism–Stalinism may prehaps color (and often distort) their images of the outside world to an extent of which not even they themselves are aware. On this level, it is perhaps impossible for a non-Communist observer to determine satisfactorily how ideology influences Moscow's relations with East Germany, its diplomacy in the Middle East, or its latest proposal on nuclear disarmament. In countless ways, Communist ideology (like, of course, other ideology) may produce a "world view" on the part of its adherents that is an integral part of their being and mental processes, affecting their behavior in ways that are impossible to detect, much less measure. It is logical to assume that ideology is a potent *subconscious* force among Soviet decision-makers, although even on this level it is but one influence shaping their world view.

Insofar as Soviet officials are *consciously* aware of Marxist objectives when they shape national policies, the role of ideology may be quite different. Difficulties abound in trying to arrive at satisfactory answers to the influence of ideology even at the level of conscious and deliberate policy-making. A key fact that must be borne in mind in this connection, for example, is that—as the leader of at least most of the Communist world—it is incumbent upon the Soviet Union to *appear* to be consistently dedicated to achieving Marxist goals. Any obvious discrepancy between its avowed Communist principles and its diplomatic behavior may tend to undermine its leadership position. Soviet officials, therefore, are continually obliged to demonstrate that no such dichotomy in fact exists.

Three characteristics of Communist ideology are relevant to the point under discussion. One of these is Communism's *pervasive ambiguity*. This feature may in fact constitute one of its greatest virtues for Soviet policy-makers, for it means that they are never at a loss for a suitable quotation from Marx, Lenin, or some other apostle of the Communist faith with which to legitimatize their conduct, no matter how often they shift their diplomatic stance. Expediency aside, an effort made in good faith by Soviet officials to be guided chiefly by ideological requirements would present formidable problems. For policy-makers in the Kremlin, the challenge is in determining *which* Marxian concepts (and there are many differences between the "early Marx" and the "late Marx") currently apply to Soviet relations with Afro-Asian societies; or deciding *which* passages from Lenin's writings are applicable to the competition in missile technology with the United States; or agreeing upon *which* of Stalin's deeds (especially after many of them have been repudiated by the Soviet hierarchy itself) are worthy of emulation by his successors; or *which* among the ousted Khrushchev's doctrinal statements are to be ranked among his lasting contributions to Communist thought. Significantly, more than a half-century after Lenin seized power in Russia, the Kremlin had still not permitted an authorized "codification" of the Marxist credo to provide an official and unambiguous (or at any rate less ambiguous) compilation of Communist doctrine.[23] This failure suggests two possibilities: Either Moscow believes that such a codification would be too difficult (and perhaps ideologically divisive among Marxist groups) or the Kremlin *prefers* to leave its ideology conveniently ambiguous and flexible.

Second, the post-Stalin era has called attention to the fact that Communism is a *continually* *evolving* philosophical system. Time and again during the past two decades, the Kremlin has invoked the concept of "creative Marxism" to make ideological innovations dictated by realities at home and abroad.[24] There is no reason to suppose that Moscow has discarded its attachment to "creative Marxism"—and, as we shall see, there are many compelling reasons for believing the contrary.

Third, we must reiterate a point made earlier in the chapter. For the Kremlin, pursuit of ideological objectives and promotion of the welfare and interests of the Soviet Union in global affairs are identical and inseparable goals. Moscow recognizes no distinction between them. To the extent that the world moves closer to the Marxist utopia, the Soviet Union is strengthened, and vice versa. The emergence of polycentric tendencies in Eastern Europe and traumatic developments like the Sino–Soviet dispute have not fundamentally changed this identification. Indeed, as a result of their progressively more hostile disagreement with Red China, it is quite possible that officials in Moscow are more convinced than in the past that this identity must be retained. Differentiating a nation's military–diplomatic objectives from its ideological goals is permissible, in the Kremlin's view, only for the purpose of analyzing the behavior of *non-Communist states*.

With these qualifications in mind, let us return to the question posed earlier. Of what importance is Communist ideology as a force *consciously* actuating Soviet foreign policy? The evidence since 1917 strongly suggests that its role as *a major causal influence* in Soviet diplomacy is more often than not *minimal and expendable*. There is no convincing reason that Moscow's contention that its ideological and military–security interests are identical needs to be accepted at face value. Indeed, at many critical junctures in Russian diplomatic history during the past fifty years, it has seemed evident to qualified observers that the Kremlin has been compelled to "sacrifice" ideological consistency or doctrinal purity for the sake of national security, the acquisition of territory, or the extension of Russian power into other countries and regions. Space is not available to deal with these instances in detail, but many of them were discussed in Chapter 8. A leading example occurred in the late 1920s, when Stalin abandoned, or at least drastically modified, the concept of "world revolution" in favor of "socialism in one country." After experience during the post-World War I era made it clear that revolutions were *not* undermining capitalist orders in countries like Hungary, Germany, Great Britain, and America, Soviet theoreticians accommodated themselves to this fact. "Socialism in one country" meant that a Marxist order *could* be created successfully in Russia alone and that Moscow did not "need" revolutions elsewhere to build a Communist regime within its own borders. Another significant implication of this new doctrinal concept was that the U.S.S.R. was *not* prepared to engage in questionable (perhaps even dangerous) revolutionary ventures abroad when these jeopardized its security or diplomatic interests. Much the same mentality governed the response of Soviet officials to Red China's revolutionary zeal during the 1960s. Moscow was obviously concerned about the extent to which Communist Chinese "adventurism" threatened the delicate nuclear balance with the West and increased the prospect for a new global war, in which Communist gains within Russia would be imperiled.

A more recent example of the extent to which doctrinal innovations have been made to take account of realities which the Kremlin could not ignore involves the concept of "peaceful coexistence." From the time of Stalin's death onward, this doctrine was at the forefront of Moscow's ideological pronouncements and programs, especially in Russia's relations with the United States. Peaceful coexistence became a watchword of Premier Khrushchev's regime; and while his successors toughened some aspects of Soviet foreign policy, they did not depart fundamentally from this principle in dealing with the West. Endlessly, Moscow's theoreticians pointed out (particularly to advocates of violent revolution in Communist China) that failure to be guided by the concept of peaceful coexistence in international relations could jeopardize the future of civilization, not excluding Communist civilization.[25] Once more, most western commentators were convinced, the U.S.S.R. had accommodated itself to existing realities—in this case, the grave risks inherent in armed conflict between nuclear super-powers.

As in other doctrinal modifications, the Kremlin was able to cite Lenin, Stalin, and other authoritative sources on *both sides* of the issue of "peaceful coexistence." Earlier in this chapter quotations were cited from Lenin in which he envisioned a series of "frightful collisions" between capitalist and noncapitalist societies which would occur before Marxist goals were achieved. (It has never been clear, however, and perhaps was not clear even to Lenin, precisely what *form* these clashes would take. Lenin, as Soviet authorities are no doubt well aware, lived in the pre-atomic age and had no way of anticipating the extent to which nuclear weapons have revolutionized warfare and compounded the consequences of armed conflict.) But Lenin also made other statements indicating his confidence that peaceful coexistence between Marxist and non-Marxist states was possible. Under Khrushchev and his successors, these statements were featured in Communist doctrinal pronouncements, while Lenin's more militant predictions were totally ignored (except by Com-

munist officials in Peking, who now claimed to be the only genuine heirs of Leninism). Small wonder that Western observers often had difficulty deciding what the doctrine of peaceful coexistence meant or agreeing upon its implications for nations outside the Communist zone. Was this example of "creative Marxism" a genuine and reasonably *permanent* doctrinal change? Or was it merely an expedient tactic, designed to lull the United States and other nations in the free world into a sense of false security, while Communism pursued its "unchanging goal of world revolution" by new and perhaps more effective methods? For that matter, was the Kremlin itself clear about the meaning and implications of the concept? It was difficult to give totally satisfactory answers.* Perhaps the most significant fact, however, was that by espousing peaceful coexistence, policy-makers in the Kremlin had demonstrated, as in the past, that they *were* capable of comprehending external realities and of tailoring their ideological program to them, especially when the security of the U.S.S.R. itself was at stake. The danger posed by the nuclear age, it was safe to predict, would be a part of the international environment for many years, perhaps decades, to come. On that basis, it was reasonable to suppose that peaceful coexistence would remain a central Communist tenet as long as the circumstances giving rise to it remained basically unchanged.

In these and other cases in which realities at home and abroad compelled revisions in Communist ideology, Soviet officials in no sense formally abandoned their commitment to Marxism–Leninism–Stalinism; instead, they were usually at pains to demonstrate how some sudden shift in the Soviet diplomatic line (like the Nazi–Soviet Pact of 1939) was in fact compatible with ideological requirements. As we have noted, the ambiguity of Communist doctrine facilitated such transitions and supplied convenient quotations to "prove" that ideological purity was being preserved. Periodic reinterpretations of the Communist faith and reliance upon "creative Marxism" enabled the Kremlin to retain some semblance of compatibility between its deeds and its ideological professions. But in the process, Communist ideology was converted into a philosophical credo

*The degree to which peaceful coexistence was emphasized in the new Communist program, announced in Moscow in 1961, is highlighted in the text of the program, together with commentary upon it, given in Harrison E. Salisbury, *Khrushchev's "Mein Kampf"* (New York: Belmont Books, 1961), especially pp. 87–93. For appraisals of the meaning and implications of the doctrine, see Philip E. Mosely, "The Meaning of Coexistence," *Foreign Affairs* **41** (October, 1962), 36–46; several essays by various authorities reproduced in Abraham Brumberg, ed., *Russia Under Khrushchev* (New York: Praeger, 1962), pp. 46–69, 114–153, and 531–657; and Louis J. Halle, "The Struggle Called Coexistence," *The New York Times Magazine* (November 15, 1959), pp. 14, 110–118.

that would, in many vital respects, be unrecognizable to Marx or even to Stalin.

Earlier it was asserted that Communist ideology does not appear to be a direct *casual factor* shaping the Soviet Union's relations with other countries, in the sense that Russian policy-makers are motivated mainly by ideological compulsions. Especially during periods of external crisis, ideology has been sacrificed to security or diplomatic gain. This is not to say, however, that ideology plays *no* role in Soviet policy-making or has *no* value for Soviet officialdom. If it is not a central causal influence, it has other uses for the Kremlin. One of these is underscored by Louis J. Halle's remark that, ironically, Communist doctrine itself "has tended to become the 'opium of the people.' " It has come to serve the same purpose that Communists have traditionally associated with religion in non-Communist societies. It legitimatizes, sanctions, rationalizes, and endeavors to make morally and ethically acceptable whatever policies are adopted by the Soviet hierarchy. It identifies the Soviet Union and, more broadly, the Communist zone, with progress, the forces of history, change, revolution, attacks against the "power structure," justice, and other ideas and ideals having great appeal for citizens throughout the world. It transforms what, for other nations, might be interpreted as Machiavellian diplomacy, imperialism, extensions of national power, or diplomatic moves dictated by *Realpolitik* into crusades for uplifting oppressed humanity, achieving justice for the masses, or some other cause generating wide public support. Since these are, by the decree of Communist theoreticians, Moscow's true goals, they are immediately surrounded with a mantle of ethical–moral purity and removed from the realm of objective criticism. And, as we have mentioned, attachment to the Communist faith by citizens inside and outside the U.S.S.R. has benefited the Kremlin in another respect: Belief that the future "belongs" to Marxists unquestionably serves as a potent tonic for the Soviet Union's supporters, giving them a vision and a fervor strengthening the Communist movement during periods of adversity and generating confidence that sooner or later the "class struggle" will be carried to a victorious conclusion. Obstacles to Communist gains are thus regarded merely as temporary setbacks, requiring detours on the road to victory, not permanent barriers to ultimate success.

The "Erosion" of Ideology

Our discussion of the role of Marxist ideology in Soviet foreign policy has made no reference to what is surely one of the most noteworthy and interesting tendencies in the contemporary world. This is the "erosion" or decline of *all ideologies* and the eclipse of ideological discords as forces engendering international tensions. Beginning in the 1960s, ideologies tended to lose their appeal to masses throughout the world. The "de-ideologization" of the political process in Western Europe, for example, was especially marked; Marxist and other political movements seemed concerned predominantly with immediate issues, rather than philosophical goals and abstractions. In international relations, the emergence of the neutralist nations (by some counts, nearly half of the membership of the UN General Assembly) signified that much of mankind had little interest in old cold war discords and ideological contentions.

Many forces contributed to the de-emphasis of ideology. History has witnessed many instances in which ideological conflicts eventually waned after many years, perhaps generations, of intense hostility. The clash between Islam and Christianity, which led to numerous armed encounters during the Crusades, in time diminished (if it has not entirely disappeared, even today). Religious conflicts within Europe produced the Thirty Years' War (1618–1648); but as time passed Catholics, Protestants, and other religious groups in that region learned to coexist in reasonable harmony. With all ideological discords, ultimately the contestants become subject to a certain war weariness and psychological enervation; other issues and problems come to the forefront, demanding the attention of leaders and masses. Oncoming generations find the "battles of the past" no longer relevant to their concerns and capable of eliciting their devotions.

Ideological erosion is likely to occur also for another reason emphasized in our earlier discussion of Marxism. Philosophical dogmas and systems *change in response to new circumstances*. Even proponents of the Marxist creed have abandoned or drastically modified many of its tenets, making it more relevant to current problems and conditions. Such change has been especially notable with respect to Communism's *millennial aspects*. Just as Christianity witnessed a declining sense of the imminence of the coming of the Kingdom of God, Marxism has lost much of its Messianic character. The coming of the Marxist kingdom through "world revolution" is still an avowed Communist goal; but, as in Christianity, it is a goal that has been deferred to *an unspecified future time*, when circumstances favor its realization. Unlike Bolshevik leaders during the 1920s, Soviet policy-makers do not expect to achieve it next year, or in the next decade, and perhaps not for many generations. Indeed, so long as achievement of the goal remains contingent upon favorable circumstances, it may be *indefinitely postponed*. In any case, it seems clear that the millennial aspects of Marxist thought have very little relationship to day-by-day Soviet policy-making. There is no evidence that Moscow's adherence to the objective of "world revolution" plays any significant role in shaping the Kremlin's position in the Vietnam War or in the formulation of its defense budget.

Interest in ideological disputes has also waned because, with the passage of time, masses of citizens have become increasingly preoccupied with immediate, often urgent, problems related to their standard of living, the education of their children, the elimination of poverty, and other concerns to which their leaders are forced to respond. The new Afro–Asian societies, for example, regard national development as perhaps their most pressing requirement. Ideological disputes between East and West are irrelevant to that goal; moreover, to the extent that Moscow and Washington prolong their ideological controversy, they divert funds which might be used to elevate living standards in the emerging nations into armaments, propaganda, and other nonproductive activities. The developed nations (and Afro–Asian spokesmen place the Soviet Union in this category) have failed to respond to the requirements of needy societies largely because ideological ill will provides an impetus for ever-expanding defense budgets. Even within Marxist societies, citizens today are reluctant to make sacrifices for future results. Promises of a glorious Communist utopia no longer suffice (except possibly in Communist China) to generate mass enthusiasm for Marxist programs. Citizens within the U.S.S.R. and Eastern European societies increasingly demand *tangible gains for their own generation*, not merely formulas for assuring the well-being of their grandchildren. The masses within Marxist societies are perhaps engaging in behavior that is commonplace in revolutionary movements: Public discontent with the government, the political elite, and the official ideology are often likely *to increase directly as progress is made*. Mass discontent is associated with a condition not of pervasive poverty but of *rising standards of living* and *expanding public expectations*.

Another phenomenon identified with many ideological movements throughout history is relevant to the current era. Nearly all ideologies are challenged to maintain their "credibility" over time. Sooner or later a gap develops between the promises made by the movement's leaders and popular expectations, on the one hand, and the ability of the rulers to "deliver" upon their pledges and to satisfy public demands, on the other. For a time (and the Soviet society waited from 1917 until Stalin's death in 1953), the construction of the new socialist order was given top priority, according heavy industry preference over consumer production. The benefits promised by Communist leaders also had to await the reconstruction of Soviet society after World War II. Eventually, however, the gap must be narrowed between what the regime promises and what it delivers. By the mid-1950s, many Soviet citizens demanded that their leaders give increasing attention to the latter, even if it meant scaling down programs (like Soviet aid to Red China) designed to achieve some global Communist objective.

Philosophical heresies and schisms on both sides of the Iron Curtain in recent years have also weakened the appeal of ideological claims and perhaps induced a widespread feeling of psychological enervation with respect to ideological discord. Concepts applicable to the cold war in an earlier era—that it was a contest between freedom and tyranny or between Marxism and capitalism—had become subject to many qualifications by the 1970s. The supposedly monolithic nature of the "Communist global conspiracy" (whose internal cohesion was never as great as many Western observers believed) has been severely undermined in recent years. Beginning with the defection of Yugoslavia from the Soviet satellite system in 1948,* followed in the early 1950s by the program of "de-Stalinization" that was undertaken within the U.S.S.R. and Eastern Europe, the Kremlin's claim to be the judge and expositor of Marxist orthodoxy came under increasing attack. By the late 1950s, Communist China had begun to question Moscow's leadership; and by the early 1960s, Peking accused the Kremlin of nothing less than apostasy from the true Marxist course. For the emerging nations at least, "Maoism" was offered as the proper Communist model. Several versions or models of Communism were thus available: the Soviet Union's brand; Yugoslavia's unique version (which had wide appeal for a number of Afro–Asian societies); several species of "national Communism" in Eastern Europe (which by no means disappeared, in spite of the Soviet intervention in Czechoslovakia in 1968); Red China's distinctive systhesis of Marxism–Leninism–Maoism; and in Western Europe (where there had been a notable trend away from ideological programs and discords), the concept of "parliamentary Communism." This ideological fragmentation was bound to weaken philosophical campaigns and loyalties generally, to confuse masses being subjected to appeals by rival Marxist groups, and to raise serious questions about *which variety* of Communism represented the "wave of the future." One observer has described the Kremlin's dilemma, under these conditions, as follows:

Caught between a Western environment which imperceptibly transforms communists into social-democrats, and an Eastern [Chinese] heresy which eliminates the last surviving remnants of classical Marxism, the Soviet regime has come to

*As a matter of historical record, it ought to be remembered that technically Yugoslavia was *expelled* from the Soviet-dominated Cominform on June 28, 1948. Moscow would not permit an ideologically deviate government to remain in the organization.

wear a defensive look. No longer a lodestar for revolutionaries in Africa or Asia, and not yet acceptable to the democratic labor movements of the West, it is in danger of appearing irrelevant to both.

Having lost its ideological primacy, Moscow was now reduced largely to the role of "mediator" between the United States and Red China![26]

Less acute schismatic tendencies were also evident in what formerly had been a cohesive "Western bloc" led by the United States. From its inception, of course, the West was more pluralistic than the Communist bloc. While America was devoted to capitalism, European societies often espoused non-Marxist socialist economic principles. After Europe recovered its economic vitality following World War II, Washington experienced growing reluctance among its allies to support its involvement in Vietnam, to participate in its economic blockade against Red China, or otherwise to follow its diplomatic lead automatically. From 1958 until 1969, under President Charles de Gaulle, France epitomized Europe's new independence from America; under de Gaulle's successors, there was no indication that Paris would abandon its independent stance. Outside Europe, America discovered much the same inclination on the part of countries like Pakistan, the Philippines, and Japan. Pakistan all but defected outright from the SEATO alliance and arrived at a *détente* with Red China; the Philippines and Japan also asserted their diplomatic freedom and endeavored to reduce their "dependence" upon the United States. Latin America was another area in which Washington encountered political and diplomatic restiveness. The United States and the Latin American republics, for example, differed fundamentally over the nature and future of the Organization of American States (Washington's attempt to organize an OAS "peace force" won very little approval south of the border); the Alliance for Progress to raise living standards in Latin America met with only limited success; and no evident consensus existed between Washington and other capitals in the hemisphere over the meaning of "democracy" or the proper course for the United States to follow in dealing with Latin American revolutionary movements.

Ideological unity within the non-Communist world was also impaired by another problem which the United States encountered throughout the world: formulating a successful policy toward *nondemocratic governments*. This designation of course embraced a wide variety of regimes, ranging from undisguised personal dictatorships (as in Haiti), to a large number of countries (especially in Africa and Latin America) ruled by military juntas, to monarchies (like those of Saudi Arabia and Iran), to "one-party systems" (as in Tanzania or Egypt), to regimes which appeared to be kept in power largely by American aid (like that of South Vietnam), to Communist systems (as in Poland and Rumania) which possessed considerable internal and external freedom. Whatever its justification in any given instance (and it seems clear that often all policy alternatives were unattractive), the close identification of the United States with such governments diluted its claim to leadership of a coalition of states devoted to "democracy" versus totalitarianism.

The process of ideological erosion which had become marked by the late 1960s did not mean that the cold war had ended or that tensions had disappeared in Soviet–American relations. From the beginning, as we emphasized in Chapter 8 and as we shall observe further in this chapter, the cold war was never concerned with ideology alone; in some respects, ideology may have been its *least serious* dimension and the realm *most subject* to de facto (if not necessarily formal) settlement. Among the nonideological sources of cold war antagonisms, none perhaps remains more fundamental than the strategic and geopolitical causes of Soviet–American hostility.[27]

THE STRATEGIC–GEOPOLITICAL FRONT

Speaking to the National Press Club in 1950, Secretary of State Dean Acheson discussed the problem of East–West relations, saying:

. . . I hear almost every day someone say that the real interest of the United States is to stop the spread of communism. Nothing seems to me to put the cart before the horse more completely than that. Of course we are interested in stopping the spread of communism. . . . Communism is the most subtle instrument of Soviet foreign policy that has ever been devised, and it is really the spearhead of Russian imperialism which would, if it could, take from these people [of Asia] what they have won, what we want them to keep and develop, which is their own national independence, their own individual independence, their own development of their own resources for their own good and not as mere tributary states to this great Soviet Union.[23]

Acheson was calling attention to a facet of the cold war that is often neglected by Americans. The United States obviously dislikes Communism and all other totalitarian ideologies wherever they are found. Yet, abstract fear of "world revolution" causes no great perturbation in Washington, London, and Paris. What does occasion grave concern is the fear of Soviet or Chinese expansionism and the consequent imposition of alien, totalitarian political orders, directed from Moscow or Peking. Communism has confronted the West at least as far back as the publication of the *Communist*

Manifesto in 1848. The novel element in international affairs is not, therefore, that Russia is communistic, or even that the Communist movement has gained adherents in other countries; it is rather that, since World War II, Russia, and more recently Red China, has gained a new geopolitical base from which to expand and to infiltrate other countries. So formidable is the threat created by this fact that the cold war might have ensued, in many respects unchanged, even if the Communist Revolution of 1917 had never occurred. By the same logic, modifications in the internal character or the ideology of the Soviet or Chinese systems might do little to diminish the strategic threat posed to free world security.

The origins of the cold war late in World War II and in the immediate postwar period can be traced to the strategic–geopolitical conflict. When the military tide turned in the east after the Battle of Stalingrad (1943), the Red Army began to drive the Germans out of Russia, across the Eurasian plain to the north and toward Czechoslovakia in the south, and finally to the very gates of Berlin. In the process, Russia overran and occupied the belt of small countries separating Germany from the U.S.S.R. Rounding out occupation of these countries with the Czechoslovak coup in 1948, Russia has remained in direct or indirect control of this territory to the present day.

Why did Soviet annexation and control over the Eastern European satellite belt precipitate the cold war? There are many reasons. In the first place, Russia's action constituted eloquent testimony to Western policy-makers of Soviet duplicity and of the Kremlin's apparently insatiable appetite for territory. Secondly, the communization of Eastern Europe was at variance with many wartime pledges, such as those given at Yalta, and in opposition to almost every principle of the United Nations Charter. Furthermore, by annexing these territories, Russia was engaging in undisguised imperialism, after the fashion of Japan in Manchuria or Germany in Austria before World War II.

The Postwar Geopolitical Revolution

Yet beyond these reasons there was another which by itself would have necessarily foreordained the cold war. This was that World War II ushered in a geopolitical revolution which profoundly altered the world balance of power. Militarily, as one observer has put it, Communist-dominated Eastern Europe was

a deployment area of great strategic importance, by building up the satellite armies to over one million men . . . to the point where Soviet and satellite forces together cast their shadow over all of Europe and stand as a threat to the security of the free nations beyond their borders. Nothing

brings home to free Europeans the reality of the Soviet threat more than to see the Russians encamped on the Elbe and the Danube, and to hear the ancient European capitals of Prague and Budapest speaking with the voice of Moscow.[29]

This was written in the mid-1950s. Although the Communist nations of Eastern Europe may be less prone today to speak "with the voice of Moscow" ideologically and politically, the strategic threat posed by Soviet military control of the region remains basically unchanged.* The occupation of Czechoslovakia by the U.S.S.R and its Warsaw Pact allies in 1968 in many respects increased the danger to the military security of the NATO area and had several other far-reaching consequences for Western defense. We shall examine some of these implications at a later stage.

From a strategic point of view, Soviet occupation of east-central Europe came close to what one observer described as the "fulfillment of the Western geopoliticians' bad dreams."[30] For Soviet hegemony over this zone gave the Kremlin substantial control over an area that the famous geographer Sir Halford Mackinder described as the "world island," from which he feared that any would-be conqueror would be in a well-nigh impregnable position to control the destiny of the world.† It is not necessary to accept Mackinder's

*Down to the late 1950s, the Soviet "satellite zone" in Eastern Europe included: Latvia, Lithuania, and Estonia, along with parts of Poland, Eastern Germany, Rumania, Czechoslovakia, and Finland, which had actually been incorporated into the U.S.S.R. Communist nations in Eastern Europe closely linked with the Soviet Union were Poland, Rumania, Bulgaria, Hungary, Czechoslovakia, and East Germany. Albania had cast its lot ideologically and diplomatically with Red China, while Communist Yugoslavia was diplomatically "nonaligned."

†Mackinder's ideas were developed during World War I and reiterated, in modified form, during World War II. His most famous dictum was: "Who rules East Europe commands the Heartland; Who rules the Heartland commands the World Island; Who rules the World Island commands the World." East Europe was the area between the Volga and the Elbe rivers. The Heartland, never precisely defined, was the great Eurasian hinterland, roughly conterminous with the U.S.S.R. The World Island was the land mass of the European–Asian–African continents. Thus Mackinder, in opposition to advocates of sea power like Captain Alfred Mahan, believed that ultimate victory belonged to a firmly entrenched, militarily impregnable land mass. For commentary on Mackinder's views, see George B. Huszar, *et al.*, *Soviet Power and Policy* (New York: Crowell, 1955), pp. 567–586; T. Hammer, "The Geopolitical Basis of Modern War," *Military Review* 35 (October, 1956), 75–82; and General Paul M. Robinett, "Survey of the Land Routes into the Soviet Union," *Military Review* 35 (August, 1955), 6–12.

Although many of Mackinder's ideas have to be drastically modified in the age of jet airplanes and missiles, the effect of which has been to "erase distances" on the globe, modern technology has not totally eliminated the strategic concepts and premises upon which his thinking was based. For example, the presence of Soviet jet fighters along the western border of Czechoslovakia

views literally to recognize that Soviet military dominance over the greater part of the Eurasian land mass presents the United States and its free world allies with a strategic problem of unparalleled magnitude. This fact per se is sufficient to generate continuing apprehension about the security of Western Europe and about the gravity of the Soviet threat to countries along the periphery of its Eurasian empire.

American Policy and the Strategic Imbalance in Europe

The ability of the Red Army to overrun Western Europe in the event of a new war prompted the United States initially to formulate the Marshall Plan for rehabilitating Western Europe's war-devastated economies and, after that, to create the NATO defense system as the sheet anchor of the free world's military efforts. The threat or likelihood of a Soviet-instigated military invasion of Western Europe diminished sharply after the late 1940s. By the early 1970s, Western policy-makers were much less concerned with this prospect than about the escalation of hostilities in the Midde East or Red China's reliance upon its nuclear arsenal to support an expansionist policy toward neighboring Asian states. Moreover, Soviet officials gave no indication that they contemplated aggression in Europe or even supporting Marxist insurrectionary activities in the NATO area. These facts did not, however, completely dispose of the strategic danger posed to Western security by the military imbalance in Europe. For if the *intentions* of Soviet policy-makers in this region were no cause for serious concern, Soviet and Warsaw Pact *military capabilities* vis-à-vis NATO forces still produced anxieties among Western defense planners. One lesson gained from the experience of the Korean War was that defense estimates based upon an enemy's apparent intentions, rather than on his capabilities, may be highly deceptive, sometimes disastrously so. By the 1970s, by that criterion, the strategic imbalance in the heart of Europe remained detrimental to Western security interests. Even with its massive nuclear arsenal, it remained highly doubtful whether the United States, in conjunction with its NATO allies, could really *defend* Western Europe against a Communist attack. In the event of a *non-nuclear* attack by Communist forces, for example, the United States would face an excruciating dilemma: It could rain nuclear devastation upon the Soviet Union, with the certain knowledge that much of America itself would quickly be reduced to radioactive rubble; or it could refrain from us-

ing nuclear armaments, thereby conceding the Soviet Red Army and other Communist forces a substantial advantage on the level of "subnuclear" warfare. At an intermediate level of warfare—in which only "tactical" nuclear weapons"* and conventional armaments were employed—the West could well find itself at a marked military disadvantage. By the late 1960s, the Soviet Union possessed an ample supply of tactical nuclear weapons (one of Russia's strongest military arms historically has been artillery). Since they had never actually been employed in warfare, it was not possible to be dogmatic about their most effective use or their limitations. Nevertheless, it seemed possible (if not probable) that they might be most militarily advantageous when employed against *fixed defensive positions*, such as airfields or military bases in the NATO area. In any of these situations, the NATO nations confronted very difficult choices and sometimes highly unpalatable military alternatives.

Soviet evacuation of that part of Europe overrun by the Red Army toward the end of World War II has remained a fixed goal of American foreign policy ever since 1945. Few diplomatic objectives in the postwar era have met with so little success. At the same time, the problem of Soviet control over Eastern Europe remains a root cause of conflict between the Communist and non-Communist worlds.

Settlement of issues growing out of Soviet military occupation of Eastern Europe was a major item on the agenda of the Yalta Conference (February, 1945). At Yalta, the United States and Britain thought they had secured Soviet agreement to proposals guaranteeing the establishment of freely elected, democratic political regimes in Eastern Europe, even while the West conceded that such regimes must remain "friendly" to Russia. Stalin, for example, had agreed to a four-part memorandum on Allied policy toward occupied countries in Eastern Europe, the key phrase of which was that the Big Three *jointly* would assist these countries to "form interim governmental authorities broadly representative of all democratic elements in the population and pledged to the earliest possible establishment through free elections of governments responsive to the will of the people."

Agreements reached at the Yalta Conference thus bound the U.S.S.R.: (1) to establish democratic political orders in the liberated and oc-

---

gives NATO defense forces considerably less time to prepare for and resist a military incursion into Western Europe than they would have if these planes were based upon Soviet territory.

*No totally satisfactory definition of "tactical nuclear weapons" is available. But (like "tactical aircraft") they embrace nuclear armaments designed to be used primarily to support troops and armored forces *on the battlefield*. Such weapons consist mainly of nuclear projectiles fired from artillery and short-range nuclear rockets. "Strategic" weapons, on the other hand, are nuclear bombs and missiles designed for use chiefly against industrial centers, cities, and the like, as distinct from battlefield troop concentrations.

cupied countries of Eastern Europe, and (2) to carry out such steps in concert with the other major Allied powers. Since 1945, the United States and its Western allies have protested in vain against the Kremlin's domination over the nations of Eastern Europe.*

For its part, the U.S.S.R. has held steadfastly to the position it assumed in the closing months of World War II: Developments in Eastern Europe are no concern of the United States. The Kremlin refuses to acknowledge any legitimate American interest in the area or to permit even the United Nations to become officially involved in the affairs of Hungary, Czechoslovakia, or any other Communist nation in the region. Although several Eastern European nations were exhibiting much greater internal and external independence by the late 1960s than they had during the Stalinist era, the military occupation of Czechoslovakia in 1968 underscored the idea that the Kremlin's basic position in Eastern Europe had undergone little significant change. The Brezhnev Doctrine gave ideological and legal sanction to Moscow's interference in the affairs of other Communist nations. Once again, the outside world was reminded that the Soviet Union viewed Eastern Europe as its own vital security zone. If Soviet power had unquestionably receded in the area, the intervention in Czechoslovakia signified that it had by no means disappeared; the Communist elite in Russia followed developments in this region closely and were prepared, in key instances, to assert Soviet power. No more than in the 1940s was the Kremlin prepared to relax its grip when it believed that Russia's security and diplomatic interests would be adversely affected.†

Prospects for a Strategic Realignment

Memories of invasion from the west—by Napoleon, by Germany and the Allies during World War I, by Hitler during World War II—are too deeply woven into the fabric of Russian national consciousness to be removed by mere promises from the West that Russia has no reason to fear for the security of its borders or by assurances that its security is safeguarded by the United Nations. For basically the same arguments were heard before

World War II, when Russian security was presumably guaranteed by the French system of alliances in Eastern Europe and by the League of Nations. Both of these supports ultimately collapsed, permitting Hitler's war machine to penetrate to the gates of Moscow and, in the process, to inflict millions of casualties and billions of dollars' worth of property damage on the U.S.S.R.

In whatever degree Western observers may believe Soviet fears about the security of Russia's western frontiers to be irrational, it cannot be denied that they are *real* and that they enter heavily into Soviet diplomatic calculations. Events since World War II—particularly the Soviet suppression of revolts and lesser indications of restiveness in East Germany, Poland, Hungary, and Czechoslovakia—indicate conclusively that de facto Russian control over the military and political destiny of Eastern Europe is a fixed principle of the Kremlin's foreign policy. The legitimacy of the principle appears no more debatable than whether the Western Hemisphere ought to be included within the American security zone. Russian willingness to countenance no Western "interference" in the Hungarian Revolt of 1956 or the Czech crisis of 1968, in fact, had its counterpart in the American unwillingness early in the 1960s to permit the U.S.S.R. to establish missile sites in Cuba. In both instances, each side regarded its vital interest as at stake and would not tolerate the prospect of hostile control over a zone deemed vital to its security.

These considerations suggest that the prospects for an *unconditional* Soviet withdrawal from Eastern Europe, as demanded unceasingly by the United States since 1945, remain as remote as ever. At a minimum, two conditions would almost certainly have to be fulfilled before such a withdrawal would become a reality, or even a subject of serious East–West negotiation. The first is that there would almost assuredly have to be some kind of equivalent American concessions, entailing reductions in American military strength in Western Europe. Under no conceivable circumstances is the Kremlin likely to be induced to relinquish its military–strategic position in this area unilaterally. The second condition is that there would also probably have to be some genuine relaxation in international tensions, perhaps due to the successful implementation of a disarmament agreement or some other mutually acceptable endeavor, that would have the effect of dispelling Soviet apprehensions about security, assuming that these can be affected by logic and by events. Postwar experience has indicated that verbal assurances to the Soviet Union do little or nothing to mitigate these fears. An extended period of relatively harmonious "coexistence" with the West, on the other hand, might gradually allay them sufficiently to induce the Soviet Union to test the good intentions of the West by a settlement. This prospect, in turn, might be enhanced

---

*Developments in Eastern Europe during World War II and in the early postwar period are discussed in Chapter 8.

†However, the Czech crisis of 1968 did *not* mean that the Stalinist era of monolithic Soviet domination of Eastern Europe had returned. The Brezhnev Doctrine aside, Communist regimes, in Rumania and Poland particularly, still exercised a considerable degree of freedom from the U.S.S.R. Czechoslovakia's location, bordering the NATO area, may account in part for Moscow's extreme sensitivity about developments in that country. Soviet military strategists were also no doubt mindful of the country's key role in Hitler's expansionist plans against the U.S.S.R.

by the extent to which modern military technology de-emphasizes the importance of military bases and territorial defense in depth.

For the United States the problem of Soviet hegemony over Eastern Europe remains as baffling as it is crucial. Despite the widespread political slogans in the United States about "liberation" of the Iron Curtain countries and a rollback of Soviet power, that were conspicuous during the Eisenhower administration, the simple truth was and remains that the future of Eastern Europe lies in Soviet, not American hands. As the Hungarian Revolt of 1956 and the Czech crisis of 1968 drove home to Americans, there is no way short of an all-out nuclear war to compel Soviet evacuation from this zone. This reality has confronted American policy-makers since World War II. And this fact—rather than any imagined "sell-out" of Eastern Europe by officals of the Roosevelt administration—explains the strategic revolution in Europe ushered in by World War II. The verdict of one commentator in the mid-1950s has lost none of its cogency for the 1970s:

Soviet successes . . . have been our failures, or rather our losses, in terms of the world balance. These are losses that were perhaps inevitable, given the postwar situation with which the United States found itself. We may regret instances of our lack of foresight, of misplaced hope and confidence, or of less than realistic negotiation. But the United States is not the arbiter of the world, least of all in areas which the Red Army overran in our common war against Hitler.[31]

Cold War Strategic Postures

The Soviet occupation of Eastern Europe was, as we have emphasized, a crucial phenomenon affecting the strategic balance between the Communist and non-Communist worlds. Yet this fact *alone* might not have engendered serious anxieties about Western security. It was the Soviet Union's acquisition of a new strategic base, greatly augmented when China joined the Communist camp, *coupled with its vast military power and potential* that created deep apprehensions among Western policy-makers. In our earlier discussion of Marxist ideology, the point was made that Communism, as Soviet interpreters have expounded it, does not "need" war to achieve its goals. However, even this idea, it must be remembered, is far from consistently held by expositors of Marxism; and in the recent period the Kremlin has not hesitated to endorse "just wars" and "wars of national liberation." It remains true that general or global war is not an ideological compulsion.

Even so, Western students of Marxism are conscious of a paramount historical reality: Communism established itself within the Soviet Union in large part because of World War I; and as a result of World War II, the Communist zone was extended from Eastern Europe to China and Korea. Whatever the precise ideological relationship between Marxist ideology and war, the fact is that the two world wars provided a powerful impetus to Communist expansionism! At a minimum, the Kremlin had demonstrated great skill in exploiting the chaotic conditions accompanying such conflicts to advance its own interests. And in some instances (Moscow's forcible incorporation of Czechoslovakia into the Soviet satellite empire in 1948 furnished a dramatic example), it was clear that the U.S.S.R. was not averse to relying upon armed force to achieve its goals. The apparent reluctance of the Soviet Union to scale down its armed forces drastically at the end of the Second World War—at a time when American forces were being demobilized at a rapid rate—added to existing concerns about Western security. America's nuclear monopoly, which lasted only until 1949, did not offset the Communist bloc's superiority in ground forces on the European continent and in Asia.

Comparisons of military strength can never be more than crude approximations. This is true for several reasons. One is that nations are always at pains to *conceal* their true military power and potential, especially as regards the development of new weapons. This limitation is perhaps less significant today than ever; it is very difficult, for example, to "hide" military bases, airfields, missile sites, industrial centers, and the like from orbiting space satellites equipped with high-resolution cameras. Another reason is that, as much now as in earlier eras of history, *intangible elements of national power* still weigh heavily in the military balance. Perhaps as much as any other factor, the American people's morale affected the outcome of the Vietnam War; the Soviet society's demand for increased consumer-goods production sets limits to Russian military power; both America and the U.S.S.R. are in some degree inhibited in their behavior by the reaction of global public opinion. Many weapons and strategic doctrines today are also *relatively new;* some have never been tested under combat conditions; others (like nuclear bombs) have been used rarely or under conditions which have little application to cold war encounters. The American military historian Samuel L. A. Marshall has cautioned that:

War, and the risks of war, are never a matter of counting the chips on both sides of the table, and then coming forth with a plus or minus answer. The wisest man . . . could not forecast the true capability of the United States for a war with limits yet undefined, fought with weapons the effects of which remain unmeasured, engaging peoples whose moral strength in the face of unfathomed danger is unknown and unknowable.[32]

From the Western perspective, the Communist nations possess certain real strategic–military advantages. A leading one is *territory*. The Soviet Union is the largest nation on earth, encompassing one-sixth of the land surface of the globe. Counting Red China and the Marxist nations of Eastern Europe, the Communist zone covers one-fourth of the world's land area. Although mere numbers are not necessarily elements of national strength, it remains true that a large manpower pool is required both economically and militarily by any nation or coalition aspiring to global influence. The Communist zone includes over 1 billion people (including over 700 million Chinese), or approximately one-third of the world's population. Save for its historically vulnerable western frontier, the Soviet Union is relatively well protected by geographical barriers, like the mountains and deserts of Asia and the ice fields of the Arctic region. Traditionally, the Soviet Union's defense strategy, invoked for coping with the German attack during World War II, has been to "trade space for time." From Napoleon to Hitler, foreign armies have found that the combination of Russia's vast territorial expanse, the dispersion of its population centers, and the severity of its winter climate in time posed an insurmountable military challenge. The military problem of maintaining secure supply lines over great distances (often against attacks by guerrilla forces) has proved insoluble. Sometimes, however, as in building and maintaining an adequate internal transportation system or defending Russia's 5000-mile frontier with Communist China, Soviet policy-makers have discovered that vast distances could also work to their disadvantage.

The United States possesses different strategic assets. Historically, its security has always been greatly enhanced by a fortuitous combination of *geographical remoteness* from Europe and Asia and the presence of militarily impotent neighbors along its northern and southern frontiers. Down to the postwar period, the polar ice cap served as an effective deterrent to attack from the north, while formidable geographical barriers, along with the chronic instability and economic weakness of Latin American governments, militated against threats from the south. On the east and west, thousands of miles of oceans served as a "moat" to protect North America. Throughout the nineteenth century, an inarticulate premise of American policy (evident, for example, in the Monroe Doctrine) was that the superior naval power of Great Britain could be counted upon to keep potential enemies at bay. By World War I, America was on the way to surpassing Britain as monarch of the seas—a position which went largely unthreatened in the postwar era until the mid-1960s, when the U.S.S.R. embarked upon an ambitious naval contruction program. Even then, as we shall see, American naval strength would not be seriously challanged for many years, certainly not in the waters of the Western Hemi-

sphere. With abundant raw materials, a large and vigorous population (which was still attached to the Puritan ethic of devotion to hard work), a salubrious climate, and abundant space, the American society had created the most productive economic system known to history. America's power base was sufficently strong to enable it to construct and maintain the most powerful navy and air force on the globe and to staff some 2500 major and minor military bases around the world. Joined with the United States and Canada in the NATO alliance were some twelve allies in Western Europe—by many criteria, the most economically dynamic region on the globe. The European industrial complex, when added to the American, created a power nexus which no combination of Communist nations or other potential enemies could hope to equal for an indefinite period in the future. Against this advantage, on the other hand, was Europe's relative *vulnerability* to a possible attack from the east; the urbanized nature of much of its population; and the limited space available to NATO forces in which to conduct mobile defense operations (especially in case of *nuclear* attack).

Ground Forces and "Conventional" Warfare

For both cold war power blocs, the particular components of armed strength have undergone continuous change and "modernization," especially in the light of technological and scientific developments. For many centuries, Soviet military strategy emphasized powerful land forces. As recently as World War II, the Red Army often crushed German forces by a combination of sheer bulk, overwhelming firepower, and in some instances brilliant tactics. Russian artillery and tank strength, for example, were exceptionally effective elements in accounting for the Red Army's victories. With over 3 million men in its armed forces, in the 1960s the U.S.S.R. continued to give priority to infantry, armored, and other ground units, concentrating two-thirds of its total military manpower in land forces. Relying upon conscription, the Soviet Union drew about 1 million recruits annually into its armed forces. Although, as we shall see, the U.S.S.R. has begun to challenge the United States in some aspects of seapower, the Red Army remains what is sometimes called the "the soul" of modern Soviet military power.[33] Consisting of just under 150 peacetime divisions (some at less than full strength),* the Red Army must be spread from the German border to Siberia. By the 1970s, recurrent hostilities and "border incidents" on the long Sino–Soviet frontier required Moscow to build up its ground (and air) forces in Asia, in part by shifting troops from the

---

*A Russian division customarily numbers some 10,000 troops, versus 16,000 men in NATO's divisions.

west. Supported by powerful modern tanks, self-propelled artillery, and excellent rapid-fire infantry weapons, the Red Army was unquestionably in many ways the strongest ground force in the contemporary world.

Augmenting the Soviet Union's own ground troops were the forces supplied by the members of the Warsaw Pact, Russia's Eastern European security alliance system.* Including Soviet troops, in the late 1960s the Warsaw Pact had some 4.5 million forces at its disposal, with close to 3 million men in its ground components. It maintained 40 combat divisions and many more could of course be raised after general mobilization. During the Stalinist era and for several years thereafter, a substantial question existed about the political reliability of the Soviet Union's Eastern European military allies. In a crisis, would these troops remain loyal to their Communist leaders or obey the Kremlin's orders? (Many Western commentators recalled that even some Soviet forces defected after Germany attacked Russia during World War II.) Even now, the reliability of some of the Warsaw Pact contingents remains in some doubt; much would depend upon the circumstances under which the forces were committed and the particular European nations concerned. Yet one result of the Czech crisis of 1968—when Czechoslovakia was invaded by fourteen Soviet divisions, along with six from East Germany, Poland, Hungary, and Bulgaria—was to suggest that Moscow had no hesitation in using troops supplied by its allies and held no strong doubts about their reliability, at least in dealing with a political crisis within the Communist zone.[34]

By some standards, ground forces are perhaps the *weakest* component in the Western defense network. America has had a long-standing constitutional and cultural tradition against the existence of a "standing army." Except for periods of general mobilization like World War II, the United States has given naval, and in more recent years air, power priority over land forces. Beginning around 1900, the United States gradually surpassed Great Britain as the world's leading sea power. During World War II America built the greatest air armada in the history of warfare; and in the postwar era, this superiority was maintained. A rapid demobilization of its land forces followed the end of World War II (when American

troops fell to a dangerously low level), and America did not build up its strength in this sphere until the Korean War. This struggle demonstrated that (especially when nuclear weapons were not used), the infantry remained "the queen of battle" and strength in conventional weapons had lost none of its importance. In the years that followed, the United States continued to emphasize the need for maintaining a moderate level of modern mobile ground units. By the late 1960s, over 500,000 American combat troops were committed in Southeast Asia. Five combat divisions, with supporting armored cavalry regiments, were stationed in West Germany. In addition, American forces manned over 400 large military installations overseas, (together with nearly 3000 smaller ones) located in some 30 foreign countries.[35]

Insofar as the cold war between the United States and Soviet Russia was concerned, the American military commitment to NATO was crucial. If it was not large, the American military "presence" on the European continent was both symbolically and strategically significant; it not only served as a token of Washington's determination to defend Europe against aggression, but also provided a powerful nucleus for NATO's defensive shield. European apprehensions about America's massive involvement in Vietnam stemmed in no small measure from fear that the United States might sooner or later find it necessary to withdraw a major portion of its troop commitment from the European continent. Temporarily at least, by the end of the 1960s the deescalation of hostilities in Southeast Asia, along with Western apprehensions generated by the Czech crisis of 1968, made the danger of a substantial American troop reduction in Europe remote. Total ground forces available to the United States and its military allies were over 4.5 million troops, of which the NATO partners furnished around 3 million. NATO forces were equipped with modern weapons, possessed numerous mechanized units, had a large stockpile of tactical nuclear weapons (plus long-range artillery and rockets to deliver them), were maintained in a high degree of readiness, and were "backstopped" by both tactical and strategic airpower, armed with nuclear weapons.* Whatever its shortcomings, NATO presented a potential aggressor with a defensive military array that could not be dismissed lightly.

Are NATO forces capable of defending the West in case of aggression? Or is the Soviet Red Army, supported by troops from the other Warsaw Pact nations, superior on the European continent? Fortunately, the world has been spared the

---

*The Warsaw Pact was created in 1947–1948 as Moscow's "answer" to the NATO defense system. The ostensible purpose of the pact was to protect Communist countries from the danger of a resurgent Germany. Members of the Warsaw Pact are: Albania, Bulgaria, Czechoslovakia, East Germnay, Hungary, Poland, Rumania, and the Soviet Union. Albania was excluded from its meetings in 1962. From its inception, it has been controlled by the Kremlin; its headquarters are in Moscow; and its military commander is a Soviet general. See Lt. Col. Paul R. Shirk, "Warsaw Treaty Organization," *Military Review* XLIX (May, 1969), 28–38.

*Our discussion here is not intended to suggest that NATO was without problems as regarded strategic doctrine, political differences among its members, or other issues. These are discussed more fully in Chapter 10.

only conclusive test: a clash of arms between the contending forces. For a number of years after World War II, the Communist side appeared to have an overwhelming advantage in ground forces. Fears existed in Washington and other Western capitals that the Soviet Red Army could penetrate Western defenses and push to the English Channel in (at most) a few weeks. By the early 1960s, these military estimates were revised in NATO's favor. Western strategists believed that NATO and Warsaw Pact forces were very close to being equally matched in manpower and armaments. Considering that any attacking force must enjoy a substantial advantage (perhaps from three- to fivefold over defending units), this reassessment indicated that Europe was relatively secure, all the more so since Soviet *intentions* by this period appeared less belligerent. The risk of war in Europe seemed—and still seems—minimal.

The late 1960s, however, witnessed another reappraisal of the military balance in Europe. Again, the Czech crisis of 1968 was a crucial development, since it afforded Western defense planners an opportunity to study how Warsaw Pact forces were actually *used* in a military operation. The new assessment was not altogether reassuring for the West. Militarily (if not politically), the invasion of Czechoslovakia was an outstanding success. Once the Kremlin decided to reassert its control over the country, the Warsaw Pact executed a rapid and highly efficient military operation, which within a few hours rendered the Czech government impotent. Moscow's *coup de main* impressed several facts upon Western commanders and military analysts. Some 650,000 Soviet, Polish, Hungarian, Bulgarian, and East German troops were moved into Czechoslovakia —a force some 20 percent larger than the United States maintained in Vietnam. The heart of this military operation was the successful "airlifting" of Soviet troops into Prague; Moscow showed its ability to perform such an operation rapidly and effectively. Staff planning for the Czech invasion, Western commentators believed, must have gone on for some six months or so before the event; it had obviously been highly secretive, thorough, and efficient. Within four hours after receiving their orders, Warsaw Pact troops had entered the country; the invasion revealed that the Communist logistical and communications systems were well enough developed for a maneuver of this magnitude; troops from the Warsaw Pact nations were armed with modern weapons, could be dispersed quickly throughout the country, evinced a high degree of morale and discipline, and were armed with tactical nuclear weapons. Two aspects of the episode were particularly disturbing to NATO strategists. One was the fact that Western intelligence agencies had *not* anticipated the invasion of Czechoslovakia, despite the months of preparation it required. This failure naturally raised the question of whether a larger attack by Communist forces, perhaps into the NATO area itself, would be similarly undetected. The other disturbing aspect was the fact that a large Communist military contingent was brought much closer to NATO's eastern defense line. Before the Czech crisis, the bulk of NATO defense forces were stationed in northern and central Germany (deemed the most vulnerable salient); now Communist armed forces occupied territory adjacent to the Czech–German frontier opposite Bavaria, NATO's *weakest* defense zone.[37]

Airpower, Missile Strength, and Deterrence

Down to the early 1960s, a fundamental premise of American defense policy was that any military conflict between the United States and the Soviet Union was likely to be a "total" war in two senses: It would be (or quickly would become) *worldwide* in scope, and it would be conducted with *nuclear weapons*. This was the conviction that underlay the Eisenhower–Dulles policy of "massive retaliation" during the 1950s. Any Communist penetration of the free world (and in this period, it was assumed that Russia and China were militarily and ideologically allied) would provoke a devastating nuclear response by the West, carried out by American bombers and missiles. As a strategic doctrine, massive retaliation had its imperfections. The Korean War, and after that the Vietnam conflict, showed that it had little application to "limited" engagements, "wars of national liberation," civil wars, or other conflicts in which the great powers were reluctant to use their nuclear arsenals. In these and other cases, the stakes were not worth nuclear devastation—for America, as much as for Russia. In reality, therefore, both Moscow and Washington exercised great caution in preventing violence from reaching the nuclear threshold. By the 1960s, America had modified the concept of massive retaliation to the point of admitting that "limited" (or "conventional") warfare could and probably would erupt, requiring the United States to possess a capacity for waging it successfully.

Yet if the principal cold war antagonists were obviously aware of the dangers of the atomic age, it could not be assumed that nuclear weapons would never be used or that either side was indifferent to the nuclear strength of the other. It is worth recalling that during the Cuban missile crisis of 1962, President John F. Kennedy asserted that the United States would regard any missiles launched from Cuba against the American continent as coming from Russia itself.[38] Washington, that is to say, would *not* treat a missile attack from Cuba as a "limited war." A recent study of the military capabilities of the NATO area asserts this.

The Soviet Government cannot suppose that a large-scale attack on Western Europe could be even briefly restricted to conventional forces, and therefore, if a massive attack is to be made, it will surely begin with a nuclear strike against Western Europe and North America, not a march of great armies across NATO's eastern boundaries.[39]

One of the most striking tendencies in the past two decades has been the extent to which the Soviet Union has achieved a position of "nuclear parity" with the United States, both in terms of the size of its nuclear arsenal and in terms of means of delivery—planes and missiles. The U.S.S.R. broke the American nuclear monopoly in 1949; it exploded a hydrogen bomb in 1953. In the years that followed, Moscow proceeded to construct a bomber fleet and missiles capable of delivering nuclear warheads to distant targets. According to one standard—the total "megatonnage" of its nuclear arsenal*—the Soviet Union had perhaps acquired the most powerful nuclear arsenal in the world. By the opening of the 1970s, Moscow had a fleet of around 1000 intercontinental missiles (ICBM's) with nuclear warheads capable of reaching targets some 6000 miles away. Moscow also had some 50 missile-firing submarines, with a range of up to 1500 miles, along with a family of short-range (700–900-miles) missiles. Most Soviet ICBM's used liquid fuel, making them less defensible than comparable American missiles using solid propellants. But the Kremlin appeared to be modernizing its missile fleet at a steady pace in order to overcome any qualitative superiority held by the United States. On the basis of recent experience, there was no reason to expect that Soviet policy-makers would fail to close (or at least greatly narrow) this gap.

Since World War II, the emphasis in Soviet airpower has been chiefly upon *tactical aircraft*, whose primary mission is to support the Red Army in the field. Tactical airpower continues to be one of the Soviet Union's great sources of military strength. By the end of the 1960s, Moscow had over 3000 aircraft in this category; from bases in Eastern Europe, many of them could of course reach cities and military targets in the NATO area. Qualitatively, the Soviet Union's fighter planes and light bombers compared favorably with those of the West. In contrast to its determination to rival America in missile strength, the Kremlin has never seriously contested American superiority in "strategic airpower" employing long-range bombers. The U.S.S.R. has a relatively small fleet of strategic bombers (around 150–200 planes); it has many more (700–1200) medium-range bombers. The great preponderance of airpower and missiles available to the

Warsaw Pact is supplied by the Soviet Union.[40]

By other criteria, America and its NATO allies have retained their superiority in nuclear weapons and delivery systems. The Soviet nuclear arsenal was greater in its total destructiveness. And, by 1970, the Kremlin was catching up with the United States in terms of numbers of missiles, producing around 150 annually. But America and its NATO partners still had several important advantages. The American missile arsenal was *numerically larger* than the Soviet arsenal. America (which had forged substantially ahead in "miniaturization") had a greater quantity of missiles with smaller warheads; the total number of ICBM's available to the West was three to four times the number available to Soviet Russia. Moreover, the United States had around 1000 solid-fuel Minuteman missiles protected in "hardened sites" (Russia had a much lower number of protected missile sites), making them relatively difficult to destroy; it also had some 50 older Titan missiles in "semi-hardened sites." Perhaps the most commanding lead the United States held was in missile technology was in missile-firing submarines. The American navy had over 40 Polaris-type submarines, each carrying 16 nuclear-armed missiles. These submarines could stay submerged for long periods and fire their weapons from the depths of the sea. By the 1970s, the United States was manufacturing a new generation of missiles: Minuteman III and IV were designed as Multiple Independently Targeted Reentry Vehicles (MIRV's), meaning that each rocket booster would propel a *cluster* of missiles, each of which could be aimed at a separate target. One version of the MIRV was the new Poseidon missile, replacing the Polaris (and possessing greater firepower) in the American submarine fleet. Relying upon MIRV's, it was anticipated that, by the early 1970s, the United States would probably widen the gap between itself and the Soviet Union in terms of the number of missiles which could be trained upon an enemy and its missile sites. Since it consisted of a larger number of missiles and missile sites, the American nuclear arsenal would be more difficult to knock out in a "first-strike" blow and would have a substantially higher "second-strike" capability.

In the missile age, long-range bombers seemed to many commentators outmoded and destined to be rapidly "phased out." For a time during the early 1960s this was a fashionable and pervasive viewpoint. Still, the planes in the American Strategic Air Command (SAC), numbering more than 650, remain a vital element in Western defense. America and its NATO partners have nearly three times as many B-52's, B-58's, and other heavy bombing planes as the Communist nations. As we have observed, however, in medium bombers the Communist zone has approximately a fivefold advantage. Although many

---

*A "megaton" is a unit for measuring the destructive power of nuclear weapons. One megaton is equal to the explosive force of 1 million tons of TNT.

strategic bombers have indeed been phased out in recent years, modern technology may have given such planes a new lease on life. For example, the new SRAM (short-range attack missile) was designed to be carried aloft by bombers, from which it would be fired toward its target. This method both frees the missile from a fixed site and greatly increases its effective range. A new Walleye "guided bomb" combined features of the bomber and the missile; it employed a miniature television camera to locate its target. Another new device was SCAD (subsonic cruise armed decoy). Launched from bombers, SCAD was designed to serve as a decoy to "confuse" enemy antiaircraft and antimissile defenses, causing them to expend their fire against harmless targets. A few SCAD's in each salvo, however, might carry nuclear warheads, preventing the enemy from "ignoring" the attack.[41]

The ABM and International Stability

By the end of the 1960s, strategic positions in the cold war were being significantly affected by the emergence of the ABM (antiballistic missile) defense system. Unlike certain other developments in offensive and defensive weapons, the ABM system threatened to become a highly "destabilizing" influence, triggering a new arms race and jeopardizing global disarmament negotiations.* Moreover, the ABM introduced greater unpredictability in defense planning by Western and Communist policy-makers.

The ABM issue must be placed in the context of over-all progress in nuclear missile technology in the recent period. During the late 1950s, many Americans became convinced that a "missile gap" had developed; in Congress and elsewhere, fears were expressed widely that the United States had fallen behind the Soviet Union in missile strength. President Eisenhower and his advisers contended at the time (and ultimately the evidence showed that they were substantially correct) that the so-called "missile gap" was illusory.† At any rate, by giving high priority to new missile construction, by the early 1960s the United States had largely closed this gap, achieving a condition of approximate "nuclear parity" with the Soviet Union. As we have observed in this chapter, the nature and variety of their military arsenals differed, in some respects fundamentally. Yet they were regarded as more or less equal in the sense that each had the capacity to devastate the other—with a substantial degree of "overkill" capability, as well.

Under conditions of nuclear parity, a highly complex and sophisticated set of assumptions and theories evolved which supposedly governed strategic planning on both sides of the Iron Curtain. Western policy-makers assumed (and it was never more than an assumption) that the Kremlin accepted the "ground rules" imposed by the ability of each side to destroy the other, in which the principal goal was to "deter" an attack by the other; deterrence was feasible because Washington and Moscow alike realized that if deterrence failed, its own society would be devastated by the nuclear arsenal of the enemy. Paradoxically, then, the fact that America and the Soviet Union each possessed sufficient military power to destroy the other many times over was, according to the calculus of nuclear parity, a *stabilizing factor* in international relations, reducing the likelihood of war and promoting caution by officials in nuclear-armed countries.

For true stability to exist, each side was required to have two kinds of nuclear missile forces. It needed a "first-strike" capacity: Russia would use such a force if it contemplated aggression against the West, while America would use it in case of a massive attack against the NATO area. It also required a "second-strike" capability, such as Minuteman missiles in "hardened" sites, which was able to survive an initial attack and rain destruction upon an enemy. Existing strategic doctrine held that neither side could possibly eliminate the "second-strike" capability of the other; if one side unleashed aggression, therefore, it would do so only at the risk of bringing catastrophe upon itself. Realizing this, the nuclear giants would want to maintain this delicate military equilibrium to assure their own survival. In this situation, of course, each cold war belligerent operated upon a premise that every great power in history has accepted: Its own (usually expanding and ever more modern) weapons stockpile was "defensive," while its enemy's arsenal (similarly being improved continually) was "offensive" in character.

Delicate at best, the military equilibrium tended to be upset by two tendencies in the early and mid-1960s. One of these was Communist China's acquisition of nuclear weapons. (Its first nuclear-armed missile was tested in 1966.) Since nuclear weapons were useless without a delivery system, American defense planners believed that Communist China could and would develop an arsenal of ICBM's equipped with nuclear warheads. It was predicted that by the early 1970s, Red China would be a formidable nuclear power, capable of inflicting massive damage upon either the United States or the Soviet Union. Neither with respect to the "ground rules" for preserving

---

*Postwar disarmament negotiations are discussed at greater length in Chapter 15.

†Answers to whether a "missile gap" really existed depended in large part upon whether *total megatonnage* (in which the Soviet Union excelled) or *number of missiles* (in which America led) was viewed as the most militarily significant indicator. The question cannot be answered abstractly; much depends upon the kind of war and the circumstances in which missiles are used.

nuclear stability nor in any other realm did Red China indicate a willingness to accept agreements worked out between Washington and Moscow.*

The second development tending to destroy the cold war military balance was Soviet Russia's decision to contruct an ABM system to safeguard Moscow, Leningrad, and other urban centers in case of global war. To the Russian military mind —which has traditionally emphasized *defensive* weapons and strategies to protect the country's great land mass—the ABM system posed no threat to American security; it was Russia's "answer" to the new generation of American missiles like Minuteman and the improved Polaris. But to the Pentagon, the Soviet ABM appeared in a very different light. It threatened to destroy nuclear parity altogether and to disregard the ground rules that had evolved for keeping Soviet–American military competition in check. For the Soviet ABM network loomed as a serious challenge to an indispensable condition for peace—America's "second-strike" missile capability for deterring a Soviet "first-strike" attack against the West. If that capability were impaired, American strategists reasoned, then Moscow might have no fear about undertaking aggression, since its ABM system could be relied upon to destroy American missiles launched in retaliation. Furthermore, as long as the United States lacked its own ABM complex to destroy Soviet missiles, Moscow might be tempted to take advantage of its superiority, knowing that within a few years it would no longer exist. Such reasoning, to be sure, was highly suppositional; it was based upon countless hypotheses and speculations, many of which could easily be erroneous. The same could be said perhaps for theories of nuclear deterrence existing before the ABM controversy arose. More than is ordinarily the case in policy-making, intelligence and planning projections have been essentially "guesstimates" often grounded upon dubious premises. Despite its "scientific" guise and its reliance upon the computer, strategy in the nuclear age, as in the past, has depended upon trying to anticipate the enemy's intentions or reconstructing his point of view or calculating when and where hostilities would erupt in the future—none of which lends itself to precise prediction or a high degree of certainty. The only justification for such calculation is that, if they are to plan defense strategy at all, military and civilian policy-makers have to operate upon *some* set of assumptions and expectations and plan their strategies accordingly.

*Communist China's foreign policy and military capabilities are analyzed more fully in Chapter 13. Meanwhile, it may not be amiss to point out that there has been a tendency in the West (particularly in America) to exaggerate Red China's capabilities. Some experts doubted that China could ever seriously rival America or the U.S.S.R. as a missile power. See *The New York Times* (January 27 and November 8, 1967).

Defense estimates that are only partially correct are better than none at all.

The question of how the United States ought to respond to the Soviet ABM generated intense controversy within the American society. The debate was closely related to a phenomenon we examined in Chapter 4: growing criticism of the military–industrial complex and reaction against steadily rising military expenditures. After thorough study, both the Johnson and Nixon administrations decided that the United States had to construct an ABM complex of its own. Really "adequate" ABM defenses were estimated to cost upwards of $40 billion! This unpopular prospect, plus public opposition to building new missile sites near large urban centers, compelled officials to settle for a considerably less expensive "thin" ABM network which, it was hoped, would afford adequate protection against Chinese missiles and offer a measure of security against Soviet ones. Officials in both the Johnson and Nixon administrations pointed out, however, that neither this nor a "thick" ABM network was impenetrable; if general war erupted, some enemy missiles would be bound to find their targets, resulting in millions of American casualties. Critics wondered why, in view of this reality, *any* ABM system, costing several billion dollars, was warranted. Defenders of the proposed ABM complex replied, in effect: Was it not worth the price to save millions of American lives, even if many millions more would be killed in a nuclear exchange? Besides, since the earliest days of warfare, the defense had always "answered" the offense; there was no known way of stopping the advance of military technology. It was Russia, after all, which had embarked upon ABM construction initially, not the United States. Even if America chose to "freeze" the nuclear arms race by not building the ABM, what grounds existed for believing that the U.S.S.R. would bind itself not to produce some new weapon giving Moscow a substantial military advantage? If the arms race were to be halted (and all parties agreed in principle that it should be), it could only be ended by *international agreement* in disarmament discussions.[43]

The Challenge of Soviet Seapower

By the close of the 1960s, another tendency affected the cold war balance of forces, in some ways even more fundamentally than competition in missile technology. Throughout modern history, as we have already noted, Russian military strength has been heavily concentrated in ground forces; in the postwar era, Moscow built up aircraft and missile power to a level which, by some standards, equalled that of the West. Beginning in the late 1950s, the Kremlin began to expand what had customarily been the weakest arm of Russian military might: seapower. The growth in Russian naval power was instigated by Premier Nikita Khrushchev; after his ouster in 1964, the expansion of the Soviet fleet continued apace. By the 1970s, the Russian navy was the second largest in the world (after the American navy). No longer regarded by the Kremlin as a mere "adjunct" of Soviet land power, the fleet was now viewed as what one commentator has called "an instrument for *global* support of Soviet interests."[44] As a report for the House Armed Services Committee described it: "For the first time in history, the Soviet Union is developing an *offensive* maritime strategy and is seeking *supremacy* at sea."[45] Although the analogy is not perfect, the student of history is reminded of Germany's challenge to British naval supremacy at the end of the nineteenth century. From a relatively small naval force, designed chiefly for coastal defense and short-range operations in the Baltic or Black Sea, the U.S.S.R. moved rapidly to the construction of a large, modern, well-equipped navy capable of sustained operations in international waters. Within some fifteen years, Moscow has built (and is still building) an "ocean-going navy" able to extend Russian power into the Atlantic, the Mediterranean, the Indian Ocean, and other distant waters.

Both qualitatively and quantitatively, Soviet seapower was impressive—and becoming more so every year. By the 1970s, Soviet Russia had four large fleets stationed in the Pacific, in the Arctic region, in the Baltic Sea, and in the Black Sea (with units of the last operating routinely in the Mediterranean). Consisting of modern vessels carrying sophisticated equipment, the Soviet navy was increasingly making its presence felt throughout the world. For many years, the strongest unit in the Soviet navy was the submarine force. Moscow had over 350 submarines, some 55 of which were nuclear powered; many of the latter were armed with missiles carrying nuclear warheads. Ten new submarines a year were being added to the Soviet fleet. Supported by modern Soviet tankers and other auxiliary vessels, Soviet submarines could cruise any waters on the globe; in case of war, they could fire missiles having a range of some 1500 miles.

The expansion in the Soviet merchant marine in the contemporary period has been little short of spectacular. While the American merchant marine was in a state of stagnation and neglect, the U.S.S.R. forged ahead rapidly. Although the total tonnage was less than that of the American merchant marine, Russia's cargo fleet was newer and on many counts superior. As every American citizen was probably aware, Russia's "fishing trawlers" had become ubiquitous off America's coasts and regularly harrassed NATO naval maneuvers. The announced "target" of Moscow's naval construction program called for doubling the size of the Soviet merchant fleet by 1980s. If the goal were achieved (and, like other Soviet "targets," it could be abandoned or revised), the Kremlin would possess the largest total tonnage of cargo shipping in the world.

In other categories of seapower, Soviet strength was also noteworthy. The Kremlin had close to 600 torpedo and small missile ships to protect Russia's long coastline and ports; America had no ships in this category. Soviet and American strength in amphibious landing craft was approximately equal (around 100 each). This meant that the U.S.S.R. had given high priority to creating an "amphibious force" which could be transported and supported by the Soviet navy. In destroyers, frigates, and smaller escort vessels, the U.S.S.R. had some 170 ships (versus well over 300 for the United States). Soviet inferiority in this category of vessels meant that Moscow's large merchant marine remained highly vulnerable to attack from enemy submarines and surface ships.

Although it had made considerable progress in the recent period, the Soviet navy was still relatively weak in such "capital ships" as heavy and light cruisers, battleships, and aircraft carriers. The Soviet Union had more cruisers and battleships (19) than America (14). But in small and large aircraft carriers—considered the nucleus of a modern naval task force—Moscow lagged significantly. Russia, for example, had only 2 helicopter and "support" carriers (while America had 17); and the Soviet navy had *no* large "attack" aircraft carriers (the American navy had 15).

Another notable feature of the Soviet navy was that nearly all of its surface combat ships were armed with modern missiles; its "helicopter carriers" were an innovation which gave Moscow's ocean-going infantry (comparable to the American marine corps) great mobility for short distances. In recent years, the Kremlin has had no hesitation about "showing the flag" to promote some diplomatic objective. Perhaps the greatest weakness of the Soviet navy as a combat force is *its relative lack of naval airpower.* The Soviet fleet remains vulnerable to Western superiority in aircraft carriers and overseas naval bases. Even Soviet spokesmen have admitted that Moscow's strength in missiles does not completely offset this weakness of the Russian fleet. Offensively, the absence of a strong naval air arm also detracts from the Russian navy's capabilities (although in this sphere, its missile strength on the sea may come closer to serving as a substitute for the lack of naval aircraft).

For a number of reasons, Soviet Russia's newly acquired seapower has had unique implications for the Mediterranean area. This was the region in which the cold war had compelled the United States to abandon its isolationist position; the Greek crisis of 1947, together with a lesser threat to Turkey, prompted the United States to adopt the Truman Doctrine of containment. Under

Czars and Commissars alike, Moscow sought access to warm water ports and spheres of influence in the Mediterranean area. The postwar era witnessed no diminution in the Kremlin's interest in the Mediterranean. The prolonged Arab–Israeli conflict kept the region in a state of active or incipient violence. By the 1950s, the U.S.S.R. had emerged as an active champion of Arab rights against Israel, which continued to rely heavily upon the United States. Civil strife on the island of Cyprus kept relations between Greece and Turkey inflamed, impairing the unity of NATO. Internally, Greece continued to experience political unrest and instability. Britain and Spain had been engaged for many years in an increasingly bitter controversy over the future of Gibraltar. Suffering from a chronic balance-of-payments problem, and aware that the era of colonialism had ended, Britain was scaling down its international commitments. After giving up its great naval base in the Suez Canal, London cut back on other political and military obligations "east of Suez"; by the end of the 1960s, for example, the traditional British position in the Persian Gulf area had been substantially liquidated.

Utilizing elements of its Black Sea fleet, by the mid-1960s, Moscow had embarked upon a substantial expansion of its naval forces in the Mediterrean and adjacent waters. Within a few years, the U.S.S.R. maintained as many ships (close to 50) in the Mediterrean as the United States (although the combined American–NATO naval force was much larger). Soviet Russia's naval presence, in what for many years had been an "American lake," was dramatic and pervasive. Russian ships routinely shadowed American warships in the area. To support its fleet, and to call attention to its growing might on the sea, Moscow had acquired the use of port facilities in Egypt, Syria, and North Africa. As one of the world's greatest sea powers, the U.S.S.R. had also become a principal user of the Suez Canal. Its closing in 1968 posed an obstacle to the Kremlin's shipment of supplies and military equipment to North Vietnam, as well as impeding its political and diplomatic activities in the Persian Gulf area, where British power had been dominant throughout modern history. Relying upon a two-pronged thrust based upon seapower—by building up its naval strength in the Baltic to the north and in the Mediterrean to the south—Moscow had gone far toward "outflanking" NATO's land defense nexus. In the event of general war, Soviet submarines firing nuclear warheads could devastate Europe from the Mediterrean or the eastern Atlantic; Moscow's submarine fleet (far larger than Germany's at the beginning of World War II) could attack trade and communication routes connecting Europe and the United States.

Since the prospect of general war seemed remote, the expansion in Soviet seapower in the Mediterranean seemed more relevant to the problem of "limited war" and the extension of Russian power southward. In these respects, there seemed little doubt that the existence of a modern Soviet fleet in the Mediterranean gave Moscow additional military options and greater diplomatic leverage. The consequences of this fact were not always fully predictable, although it seemed a safe assumption that Western interests in the area were *not* automatically impaired. The presence of Soviet ships in Arab ports, for example, might have a deterrent effect upon Israel's military plans; fearing a confrontation with the Soviet Union, the Israeli government might become more cautious about employing military force to achieve its goals. Insofar as Israel relied upon a tacit American pledge or the likelihood of U.S. protection against the Arabs, this premise could be called into question by the growth in Soviet military influence throughout the area. With respect to Soviet relations with Arab governments, other consequences might be expected. Conceivably, the Soviet Union's strength in the Mediterranean might make the Arabs more reckless in their conflict with Israel, in the expectation that in a crisis Moscow would use force to prevent another massive Arab defeat. In fact, however, events during the late 1960s did *not* support the idea that Moscow was prepared to be "dragged into war" by recalcitrant Arab governments. The presence of the Soviet navy—coupled with Moscow's extensive arms-aid program to countries like Egypt and Syria—might also serve to de-escalate the level of crisis in the Middle East, in two ways. Israel, as we have noted, would be less prone to pursue its objectives by military means; and the Arab states—more than ever dependent upon Moscow for arms-aid and military advice— might be more amenable to Soviet viewpoints concerning the dangers of a general war in the region.

At the same time, the expansion of Soviet power in the Mediterranean–Middle East region clearly set new limits on Western (especially American) policy alternatives. Western policy-makers could no longer assume that they enjoyed a position of preponderant military strength in any cold war encounter in the area. We may illustrate the manner in which the military balance had shifted within the decade by noting that American marines, supported by overwhelming naval power, landed in Lebanon in 1957 to avert what Washington believed was a threat to the security of that government. Although the move was vocally condemned by the Soviet Union and most Arab governments, the United States encountered little or no effective opposition. A decade later, Soviet Russia's strong naval presence in the area rendered a repetition of this kind of *tour de force* dubious, possibly even hazardous for world peace. Conceivably, a Soviet naval squadron could interpose itself between the U.S. Sixth Fleet and some Arab country to frustrate the application of Western power in behalf of a political objective. Some Western observers, not to mention those in the Communist or Arab zones, might regard this as a beneficial turn of events.* Whatever its precise consequences, however, the main point is that the emergence of the Soviet Union as a sea power, in this region and elsewhere, unquestionably *changed* the configuration of cold war forces, requiring corresponding modifications in Western military and diplomatic behavior.

NOTES

1. R. N. Carew Hunt, *The Theory and Practice of Communism* (London: Geoffrey, Bless, 1957), p. 264.
2. Harrison E. Salisbury, *Khrushchev's "Mein Kampf"* (New York: Belmont Books, 1961), p. 69.
3. Department of State, *Communist Perspective* (Washington, D.C.: Division of Research for USSR and Eastern Europe, Office of Intelligence Research, 1955), pp. 383–384.
4. *Ibid.*, p. 384.
5. Quoted in Jerry A. Hough, "The Stalin–Trotsky Split: A Lesson for Kremlinologists," *The Reporter* 29 (December 5, 1963), 39.
6. See Department of State, *op. cit.*, p. 18; Salisbury, *op. cit.*, pp. 52 and 56.
7. See *The New York Herald Tribune* (February 5, 1962); and Sir William Hayter, "The Cold War and the Future," in Evan Luard, ed., *The Cold War: A Re-Appraisal* (New York: Praeger, 1964), pp. 307–328.
8. Salisbury, *op. cit.*, pp. 52–62.
9. Salisbury, *op. cit.*, pp. 155–156.
10. Department of State, *op. cit.*, p. 238.
11. Senate Government Operations Committee, *Czechoslovakia and the Brezhnev Doctrine*, 91st Congress, 1st Session, 1969, pp. 3–4, 14, 22–24.
12. Department of State, *op. cit.*, p. 442.
13. *Ibid.*, p. 443.
14. Quoted in Nathan Leites, *A Study of Bolshevism* (New York: Free Press, 1953), p. 416.
15. Red China's "cultural revolution," for example, was repeatedly denounced by the Kremlin because it endangered Communist international gains and often engendered anti-Communist sentiments abroad. See the text of the Soviet statement in *The New York Times* (September 1, 1966).
16. Department of State, *op. cit.*, p. 177.
17. *Ibid.*, p. 273.
18. Salisbury, *op. cit.*, pp. 45–49, 156.
19. See William Zimmerman, "Soviet Perception of the United States," in Alexander Dallin and Thomas B. Larson, eds., *Soviet Politics Since Khrushchev* (Englewood Cliffs, N.J.: Prentice-Hall, 1968), pp. 168–170.
20. See Richard Lowenthal, "The Soviet Union in the Post-Revolutionary Era," in Dallin and Larson, *op. cit.*, p. 14; and Robert Conquest, "The Limits of Detente," *Foreign Affairs* 46 (July, 1968), 734, 737–738.
21. Perhaps the key point about the doctrine of the "just war" is that it is one in which the Soviet Union is the victim, leaving it no choice but to fight. Always, the instigator is the "capitalist" world. See Alfred G. Meyer, *Communism*, 3rd ed. (New York: Random House, 1967), pp. 180–182; Robert V. Daniels, *The Nature of Communism* (New York: Random House, 1962), pp. 172–176.
22. For a recent study analyzing the forces operating upon Soviet foreign policy—and stressing the multiplicity of factors present—see Jan F. Triska and David D. Finaly, *Soviet Foreign Policy* (New York: Macmillan, 1968). In the introduction, pp. xiii–xix, the authors deal succinctly with various theories advanced about the basic influences motivating Soviet behavior in foreign relations.
23. Quoted in Leites, *op. cit.*, p. 17.
24. *Ibid.*, p. 245.
25. For an authoritative exposition of the Communist interpretation of this concept, see Nikita S. Khrushchev, "On Peaceful Coexistence," *Foreign Affairs* 38 (October, 1959), 1–18.
26. George Lichtheim, "What Is Left of Communism?" *Foreign Affairs* 46 (October, 1967), 79.
27. The "erosion" of ideology—a conspicuous theme in recent commentaries on Marxism—is treated more fully in Lichtheim, *op. cit.*, pp. 78–95; Wolfgang Leonhard, "Politics and Ideology in the Post-Khrushchev Era," in Dallin and Larson, *op. cit.*, pp. 41–71; Vernon V. Aspaturian, "Foreign Policy Perspectives in the Sixties," in *ibid.*, pp. 129–133; and George F. Kennan, "The Russian Revolution—Fifty Years After: Its Nature and Consequences," *Foreign Affairs* 46 (October, 1967), 1–22.
28. *Documents on American Foreign Relations: 1950* (Boston: World Peace Foundation, 1951), p. 429.
29. C. Grove Haines, ed., *The Threat of Soviet Imperialism* (Baltimore: Johns Hopkins, 1954), p. 209.
30. T. Hammer, "The Geopolitical Basis of Modern War," *Military Review* 35 (October, 1956), 77.
31. Haines, *op. cit.*, p. 217.
32. Quoted in *ibid.*, p. 200.
33. Hanson W. Baldwin in *The New York Times* (October 30, 1967).
34. See R. Rockingham Gill, "Europe's Military Balance After Czechoslovakia," *Military Review* XLIX (January, 1969), 49.
35. See the excerpts from a report to the Pentagon on American overseas bases and installations in *The New York Times* (April 9, 1969).

*As we shall see more fully in Chapter 11, the American landing in Lebanon did little to enhance Western–Arab relations or, in the long run, to bolster the Western position in this area.

36. For data on NATO's military forces vis-à-vis those of the Warsaw Pact, consult Senate Foreign Relations Committee, *Thirteenth Meeting of the North Atlantic Assembly*, 90th Congress, 1st Session, 1968, pp. 22–30.

37. The Czech crisis of 1968 had many far-reaching implications for NATO's defense strategy and planning. For further discussion of them, see Wilhelm Meyer-Detring, "Red Army at the Bavarian Border," *Military Review* **XLIX** (May, 1969), 77–85; Stanley L. Harrison, "NATO's Role After Czechoslovakia," *ibid.* **XLIX** (July, 1969), 12–24; and the dispatch by Tad Szulc in *The New York Times* (September 10, 1968).

38. In his broadcast to the American people informing them of the presence of Soviet missiles in Cuba (October 22, 1962), President Kennedy stated: "It shall be the policy of this nation to regard any nuclear missile launched from Cuba against any nation in the Western Hemisphere as an attack by the Soviet Union on the United States. . . ." *See Documents on American Foreign Relations: 1962* (New York: Harper & Row, 1963), p. 378.

39. Senate Government Operations Committee, *The Atlantic Alliance: Unfinished Business*, 90th Congress, 1st Session, 1967, p. 6.

40. Data on the Soviet Union's strength in nuclear weapons, missiles, and aircraft are drawn from Major Edgar O'Ballance, "Megatonnage and Missile Gaps," *Military Review* **XLIX** (March, 1969), 65–71; R. Rockingham Gill, "Europe's Military Balance After Czechoslovakia," *ibid.* **XLIX** (January, 1969), 50–51; Senate Foreign Relations Committee, *op. cit.*, pp. 22–25.

41. For comparisons of Western and Communist military strength in missiles and aircraft, see O'Ballance, *op. cit.*, pp. 65–71; Senate Foreign Relations Committee, *op. cit.*, pp. 25–31;

The New York Times (September 13, and November 8, 1968; and February 5 and 13, 1969).

42. Studies of "deterrence" and other strategic theories may be found in Raymond Aron, *The Great Debate* (Garden City, N.Y.: Doubleday, 1965); André Beaufré, *Deterrence and Strategy* (New York: Praeger, 1966); T.C. Schelling, *The Strategy of Conflict* (Cambridge, Mass.: Harvard University Press, 1960); Morton H. Halperin, *Limited War in the Nuclear Age* (New York: Wiley, 1963).

43. Our discussion of the ABM controversy is based on data supplied in *The New York Times* (January 27, September 24, and November 8, 1967; February 10, 13, and 16, 1969); Herman Kahn, "Why We Should Go Ahead With an ABM," *Fortune Magazine* **79** (June, 1969), 119–121, 212–216; "What's the Answer to ABM and the War?" *U.S. News and World Report* **LXVI** (April, 7, 1969), 30–36.

44. Thomas W. Wolfe, "Projection of Soviet Power," *Military Review* **XLIX** (February, 1969), 67. Italics inserted.

45. *The New York Times* (December 8, 1968). Italics inserted.

46. The nature and implications of Soviet Russia's new emphasis upon seapower are dealt with at length in Wolfe, *op. cit.*, pp. 63–72; Curt Gasteyger, "Moscow and the Mediterranean," *Foreign Affairs* **46** (July, 1968), 676–688; "The Soviet Navy," *Military Review* **XLIX** (April, 1969), 10–18; "How Adventurous Are the Soviets?" *Atlas* **16** (December, 1968), 18–21; "Growing Threat of Soviet Sea Power," *U.S. News and World Report* **LXVI** (January 20, 1969), 49–54; and *The New York Times* (June 2 and October 23, 1967; January 15 and 24, April 17, September 25, October 9, November 20, 24, 28, and December 8, 1968).

Ten

WESTERN EUROPE: Pivot of American Foreign Policy

The postwar transition in American foreign policy toward Western Europe serves as a symbol of the revolution in American policy toward the outside world as a whole. As we have noted in earlier chapters, the cold war originated in Europe; the wartime alliance gradually disintegrated over Soviet–American hostility with respect to events in Eastern Europe. The Greek crisis in the immediate postwar era elicited the Greek–Turkish Aid Program and the enunciation of the doctrine of containment by President Truman early in 1947. When it signed the North Atlantic Treaty early in 1949, the United States formally abandoned its historic policy of isolationism with respect to European affairs;* by joining NATO—and from the beginning American power was, and remains, the organization's sheet anchor—the United States acknowledged that its security was inextricably connected with developments on the European continent.

During the 1950s and early 1960s, as the United States assumed a variety of international commitments, America's vital link with Europe sometimes tended to become eclipsed. Embroiled in armed conflicts in Asia—first in Korea, and then in Southeast Asia—America, many Europeans believed, tended more and more to "neglect" the area to which they were most closely tied. Much of the opposition to the Vietnam War in the United States and on the European continent stemmed from a feeling that, because of its massive military involvement in Southeast Asia, Washington had weakened its ability to defend the Atlantic community; the longer the conflict dragged on unresolved, the greater the risk of disunity, conflicting purposes, and over-all weakness within the NATO area. Whatever its other implications, the readjustment in American foreign policy which grew out of public dissatisfaction with the Vietnam War would most likely

*The traditional American policy of isolationism, we need to recall, applied only to American relations *with Europe;* as we shall see in future chapters, it did not govern the relations of the United States with Latin America or Asia.

involve a new emphasis upon the relations of the United States with its NATO allies. As in the early postwar era, many segments of public and official opinion in the United States viewed Western Europe as the real pivot of American foreign policy. Retrenchment might be indicated in American relations with Asia or the Middle East; in these and other regions, America's "involvement" might require curtailment. The opposite was true, however, of American–European relations. In that sphere the Atlantic alliance needed to be "revitalized," and the ultimate goal of Atlantic community needed to be pursued with new vigor.[1] The twentieth anniversary of NATO in 1969, for example, served as the occasion for officials on both sides of the Atlantic to reaffirm their common destiny and to pledge themselves afresh to the creation of new forms of economic and political collaboration.

A Century of the Monroe Doctrine

From the earliest days of the republic, the United States has conceived of itself as a new and unique nation whose appointed mission required it to stand aloof from the quarrels and vicissitudes of the Old World. Geography separated the two worlds by thousands of miles of ocean; the American Revolution signified a spiritual–ideological breach. For well over a century thereafter, Americans were concerned primarily with domestic problems and challenges, especially expansion across the continent. George Washington had sounded the keynote of the American outlook in his Farewell Address in 1796, when he declared that "Europe has a set of primary interests, which to us have none or a very remote relation." This view was also supported by Thomas Jefferson, who stated in 1813 that: "The European nations constitute a separate division of the globe; their localities make them a part of a distinct system; they have a set of interests of their own in which it is our business never to engage ourselves." America, on the other hand, "has a hemisphere to itself. It must have its separate system of interests;

which must not be subordinated to those of Europe. . . ."[2]

Thus, when President Monroe delivered his classic message to Congress in 1823, he was adding very little to the position already taken by the United States in regard to European affairs since independence. The key thought expressed by the Monroe Doctrine with respect to Europe,* was that: "In the wars of European powers in matters relating to themselves we have never taken any part, nor does it comport with our policy so to do. It is only when our rights are invaded or seriously menaced that we resent injuries or make preparation for our defense." Warning the Holy Alliance to stay out of American affairs, Monroe stated "that we should consider any attempt on their part to extend their system to any portion of this hemisphere as dangerous to our peace and safety. With the existing colonies or dependencies of any European power we have not interfered and shall not interfere."[3]

At the time neither the United States nor Europe was conscious that Monroe was enunciating a principle of American foreign policy that would apply for over a hundred years thereafter. The influences that prompted Monroe's speech were twofold: threatened intervention by the Holy Alliance to return the newly independent states of Latin America to Spain, and machinations of czarist Russia in the Northwest, climaxed by the imperial ukase of 1821 which virtually proclaimed the Pacific Northwest a Russian sphere of influence.[4] The Monroe Doctrine had been America's response to these two threats. Over the course of time it became the most famous principle of American foreign policy.

However, the self-abnegation pledge that the United States would not interfere in European affairs was not nearly so sweeping as is sometimes supposed. Monroe pledged only noninterference in "the wars of the European powers in matters relating to themselves. . . ." Thus, the Monroe Doctrine from its inception applied only (1) to Europe's *wars* and (2) to those wars that *were exclusively of European concern.*

Although President Monroe was not conscious of laying down a precept that would bind American foreign policy-makers through successive decades, the Monroe Doctrine's stipulations relating to America's relationships with Europe became the guiding principles of American foreign policy until the Truman Doctrine was proclaimed

---

*The Monroe Doctrine had two aspects, one governing America's relations with Europe, the other, Europe's relations with the Western Hemisphere. While the first aspect remained relatively unchanged for over a century, except of course for World War I, the other was subject to numerous amendments and modifications in the years that followed 1823. The Western hemispheric applications of the Monroe Doctrine are discussed in Chapter 12.

in 1947. There were, of course, a number of exceptions to noninterference in Europe, notably America's participation in World Wars I and II. But even these examples can be deemed compatible with the Monroe Doctrine, since in both cases American vital interests were very much involved. German submarines forced the United States into World War I. The Japanese attack on Pearl Harbor, followed by the German declaration of war against the United States, compelled our entry into World War II. It is significant that all through World War II the United States believed that the greatest threat to its own security emanated *from Europe;* hence American policy-makers consistently gave a higher priority to the European theater of war than they did to the Pacific theater.

For nearly a hundred years after 1823, American involvement in the politics of Europe was episodic and transitory. Woodrow Wilson's ill-fated attempt to reorient American foreign policy around the principle of "collective security" is too well known to require elaboration here. Senate rejection of the League of Nations graphically reaffirmed American isolationist attitudes toward Europe. America did not officially participate in the League's activities, although it sent unofficial "observers" to attend League deliberations, and cooperated on a limited scale with a number of the League's social and humanitarian activities.[5] Prolonged vacillation by the Senate in considering American membership in the World Court constituted further evidence of isolationist tendencies, with the World Court proposal being finally rejected by the Senate in 1935.[6] Then during the 1930s, isolationism made the population insensitive to the most elementary facts concerning the nation's security and the security of the North Atlantic region with which America's destiny was increasingly linked. "Aid short of war" was the most that the American people would support—and sometimes there was very little public support even for this—prior to the Japanese attack of Pearl Harbor in 1941.

Prerequisites of an Isolationist Policy

For almost a hundred years, isolationism accorded both with the desires of the American people and with existing geographic–diplomatic realities, although by the turn of the century many of these realities were beginning to change. At first, few Americans were aware of these changes, preferring as late as the 1930s to cling to old ways long after conditions had passed that had made traditional habits of thought and policies possible. Isolationism was finally abandoned as the policy of the United States, not willfully, but as an inescapable reaction to the facts of international life in the postwar nuclear age, and more specifically a reaction to the inescapable challenge posed by the Soviet threat. Yet, even in the postwar period, many Americans fail to understand why isolationism has been possible historically and why it is an untenable policy today.

Three conditions made possible America's historic withdrawal from the political affairs of the Old World. These conditions have either disappeared altogether today or else they have so changed as to make an isolationist course by the United States nothing short of suicidal.

1. America was geographically isolated from the world. This fact, as much as any other, explains America's ability for over a hundred years to stay out of great-power conflicts in Europe and to a lesser degree in Asia. America could follow isolationism as a policy because the United States was separated from the storm centers of diplomatic controversy by formidable geographical barriers. Thousands of miles of ocean cut America off from Europe and Asia; the polar icecap and northern Canadian wastelands posed an impenetrable obstacle to the north; no threat could come from the weak, unstable governments that existed in Latin America. In the modern period, annihilation of distance by the fast ocean liner, the submarine, radio and telephone, and finally the jet airplane and supersonic missile has eliminated the geographical fact of isolation from the outside world. Within minutes, destruction could be rained on American cities by a potential aggressor; and, conversely, American retaliatory power could be launched speedily against an enemy. Isolationism will not suffice as a policy, therefore, because isolation is no longer a reality.

2. Europe's diplomatic troubles were America's well-being. The United States was also fortunate that suspicion and rivalry among the great powers of Europe prevented them from uniting behind an anti-American policy. As a rule, the United States had only one thing to fear from the Old World: a new grand coalition that might arise to despoil the young nation and to jeopardize its continued independence. Occasionally this danger appeared imminent, as illustrated by the Holy Alliance's threatened intervention in Latin America in the early 1820s. In the main, however, European countries could never subordinate their differences sufficiently to collaborate against the United States. Repeated diplomatic conflicts on the Continent during the nineteenth century—occasioned by Russia's several attempts to penetrate the Near East, France's efforts to re-establish its former position of greatness, countless nationalistic rebellions against entrenched autocracies, Bismarck's determination to make Germany a great power—kept the great powers in an almost constant state of diplomatic ferment and intensified existing hostilities. Europe's infrequent incursions into Western hemispheric affairs—such

as French intervention in Mexico during the Civil War—produced controversies among the European states themselves, out of fear that one country would increase its power over the others. Meantime, on the Continent age-old jealousies and antagonisms made European countries reluctant to embark upon expansionist policies in the Western Hemisphere, so long as the fear existed that the first danger to their security lay in Europe.

Continuance of this state of affairs in turn depended on several factors: the existence of a number of European states, roughly equal in power; determination by these states to fight wars for limited ends, in contrast to the doctrine of "total wars," followed by the principle of "unconditional surrender" that has been one factor making a balance of power inoperative in more recent years; recognition by the states of Europe that preservation of the balance-of-power system was in the best interests of all concerned. These conditions do not obtain in the contemporary age. They were destroyed by a combination of World War I, the imperialistic ambitions of Hitler and Mussolini, World War II, the wartime and post-World War II policies of the U.S.S.R., independence movements in former colonial areas, the injection of ideological considerations into world politics on a far greater scale than in the nineteenth century—all contributing to the decline of Britain, Germany, France, and Italy as great powers on the European scene and militating against reinstitution of a balance-of-power system comparable to that prevailing earlier.

3. American security was protected by the Pax Britannica and the subsequent Anglo–American entente. The nineteenth century was the age of *Pax Britannica*—unquestionably one of the most stable and benign eras known to the history of international relations. Britain ruled the seas. Utilizing strategic bases in its scattered colonies, it intervened repeatedly to put down threats to international peace and order, whether they came from the diplomatic intrigues of Russia in the Near East, or Germany in Persia, or the Holy Alliance in Latin America. For more than a century after independence, the American people were suspicious of Great Britain, believing firmly that Downing Street harbored territorial ambitions on the American continent and, in more general terms, that it sought to frustrate American diplomatic goals. This frame of mind persisted until around 1900.

Actually, in spite of this prevailing antagonism toward Britain, a fundamental identity of interest lay beneath the surface of Anglo–American relations throughout most of the nineteenth century. Historians are agreed that British acceptance of the principles of the Monroe Doctrine—at least those parts relating to European activities in the

Western Hemisphere—largely explains whatever success the doctrine achieved for several decades after 1823 in realizing American diplomatic objectives. Britain was perhaps even more concerned than America about the possibility of other great powers' establishing a strong position in Latin America, thereby enhancing their capacity to jeopardize British sea communications and trade routes. Britain could accept the idea, therefore, that this hemisphere was a special preserve of the United States—a country that possessed no navy worth mentioning and that harbored no expansive tendencies at British expense.

Until about 1900, Americans rarely perceived the relationship between their own security and British power. After that date, however, both countries began openly to acknowledge their mutual interests. Britain feared the growing naval might and imperialist ambitions of Germany and Japan. The age-old imperialistic objectives of czarist Russia threatened more than ever to infringe upon British colonial and trade interests in the Far East. America, although beginning to expand its navy, had few imperialistic designs that clashed with those of Great Britain. As maritime and trading countries, both nations shared a desire to preserve freedom of the seas and unimpeded access to world markets. Ideological affinity provided another link in the chain of Anglo–American cooperation. British support of the Open Door policy in China at the turn of the century and negotiation of the Hay–Pauncefote Treaty in 1901, preparing the way for American construction of the Panama Canal, signified the new official harmony that characterized Anglo–American relations.

Nevertheless, it could not be said that American citizens as a whole understood the crucial role of this entente in preserving their security. Periodically, vocal citizens' groups "twisted the lion's tail" and railed against the alleged evils of the British Empire. Anglophobia abated during World War I, but in the era of "normalcy" and isolation that followed the war, a majority of Americans appeared to be ignorant of the part played by Anglo–American cooperation in defending the vital interests of the United States. The "inarticulate major premise" of American foreign policy after 1900 has been the assumption that Great Britain and the United States are friends and that in an overwhelming majority of cases their diplomatic objectives are complementary, rather than antagonistic. Britain's dramatic decline as a great power after World War II, a process that actually began with World War I, drove home to Americans as never before how vital for international peace and stability had been Britain's former role as protector of the balance of power in Western Europe and chief defender against Russian expansion across the frontiers of Europe, the Middle East, and Asia. Moreover, as

America discovered painfully in the turbulent postwar period, in its colonial affairs Britain had contributed to international stability through its policies of preparing dependent peoples for orderly and enlightened self-government.

For nearly a century the United States enjoyed the benefits of *Pax Britannica*. In the postwar years the roles became reversed. Now it was Great Britain that was protected by a *Pax Americana* whose aims differed in few material respects from Britain's efforts to enforce the peace during the nineteenth century.

CONTAINMENT, RECOVERY, AND REARMAMENT

The Origins of Containment

By 1947 the Monroe Doctrine had been superseded by the Truman Doctrine's principle of containment as the guiding rule of America's relationship to Europe. Reduced to its essentials, the new policy anticipated firm and sustained American resistance to Soviet expansionist tendencies. Containment received its most persuasive justification at the hands of George F. Kennan, a high-ranking State Department official and recognized authority on Soviet Russia. In a widely circulated article on "The Sources of Soviet Conduct,"[7] Kennan enunciated the containment idea as America's response to the challenge of Soviet expansionism and hostility toward non-Communist countries. The immediate postwar period had witnessed Soviet hegemony over Eastern Europe, Communist intrigue in such countries as Iran, Turkey, Greece, Indochina, and China, as well as Soviet intransigence on such questions as disarmament and control of nuclear weapons. By 1947 it had become apparent on all sides that the wartime policy of great-power collaboration had collapsed.

It was Kennan's belief, sharply challenged by other leading students of international politics,[8] that successful implementation of the containment idea would not only prevent further Soviet incursions into the non-Communist world but would also in time bring about a "mellowing" in the Kremlin's attitudes and policies toward the outside world, possibly aiding the emergence of a less despotic, less xenophobic political order within the U.S.S.R.

Containment received its first application in the Greek–Turkish Aid Program of 1947. After that came the Marshall Plan, the North Atlantic Pact, the Mutual Defense Assistance Program, and the Mutual Security Program. Hand in hand with these developments went efforts by the United States to encourage greater economic, military, and political integration on the continent of Europe. All of these were manifestations of the containment idea, because a major impetus in each case was the threat to the security of the North Atlantic community posed by the expansionist policies and impressive military power of the Communist bloc. Whatever specific forms America's relations with Western Europe in the postwar period might take, one goal remained uppermost: to make the North Atlantic area as impregnable as possible against threats to its security emanating from behind the Iron Curtain, irrespective of whether they came from a threatened Soviet military attack or Communist intrigue in the political affairs of Western Europe.

European officials in the main shared Washington's assessment of the Communist threat; but to their minds there were perhaps even more compelling reasons for cooperating with the United States to rebuild Europe's devastated economies, strengthen its defenses, and initiate movements aimed at transcending deeply entrenched nationalistic tendencies on the Continent. One was to impart a feeling of greater security among Europe's citizens. Another was to lessen dependence upon the United States, a dependence which, in Europe's weakened position, was both inevitable and widely resented. Still another was ultimately to recreate Western Europe as a more powerful independent force in world affairs. Throughout the postwar era the viewpoint has gained adherence among leaders on the Continent that the countries of Europe must forsake ancient nationalistic bickerings and pool their energies and resources, if Western Europe is ever again to play the decisive role in international politics witnessed in earlier eras of modern history.

In examining these developments, our study will focus on four dominant problems in postwar American foreign policy toward Europe. These are: European economic recovery and rearmament; economic unification movements; defense and military collaboration within the North Atlantic region; and movements directed at the political unification of the North Atlantic area.

The Greek–Turkish Aid Program

In an historic foreign policy address on March 12, 1947, President Truman declared that "it must be the policy of the United States to support free people who are resisting subjection by armed minorities or outside pressures."[9] Truman's address was prompted by the crisis in Greece, where Communist-led rebels were seeking to overthrow the existing government. For almost two years, British troops had supported the Greek government's effort to restore stability. But Britain was near bankruptcy. Some liquidation of British overseas commitments therefore became imperative, leaving the United States the alternative of either assuming many of these commitments or accepting further Communist intrusions into

the free world. The situation in Greece took on added urgency because, at long last, Russia appeared on the verge of achieving its age-old desire to break through into the Mediterranean area.

President Truman consequently asked Congress for an appropriation of $400 million to resist Communist expansionism in Greece and to bolster the defenses of nearby Turkey, which had also experienced intermittent Soviet pressures during and since World War II. After prolonged study, Congress granted this request in May, thereby establishing the pattern of economic–military aid to countries confronted with Communist aggression. Such aid was to become a permanent feature of American foreign policy in the contemporary period. Along with Yugoslavia's later defection from the Soviet bloc, American economic and military aid proved to be of crucial importance in preserving the political independence of Greece and assuring its continued adherence to the free world alliance.*

The European Recovery Program

Even before Congress had approved the Greek–Turkish Aid Bill, the Truman administration had begun studies of Western Europe's progressively critical economic plight. Wartime and early postwar relief programs like the United Nations Relief and Rehabilitation Administration (UNRRA) had done little or nothing to eliminate the underlying causes of economic instability in Europe. By mid-1947, widespread economic distress, contributing

---

*American intervention in Greece in 1947, along with Yugoslavia's defection from the Soviet satellite system a few months later, proved decisive in averting a threatened Communist seizure of power in that country. For some twenty years thereafter, Greece appeared to have a reasonably stable government and was firmly committed to the Western alliance system. Two developments during the 1960s, however, raised fundamental questions about its future role. One was the dispute on the island of Cyprus, which pitted Greece against Turkey, as each sought to offer effective "protection" to its clients on that strife-torn island. Although a UN "presence" kept the Cypriot dispute from flaring into open warfare, the underlying issues engendering conflict between the island's Greek and Turkish communities remained unresolved. Then on April 20–21, 1967, Greece itself experienced a military-led *coup d'état*. The officers who seized power were identified with a conservative and ultra-nationalistic point of view; not unexpectedly, the regime was fiercely anti-Communist. Both inside and outside Greece, the junta was sharply criticized for its repressive internal policies, such as the dissolution of parliament and severe censorship. Some critics of American foreign policy said, in effect, that the new regime in Greece was the culmination of twenty years of "containment" and but another instance in which Washington supported *any government* which opposed Communism. For a forceful statement of this view, see Richard J. Barnet, *Intervention and Revolution: America's Confrontation with Insurgent Movements Around the World* (New York: World Publishing, 1968), pp. 97–132.

to political turbulence, existed in Europe. In a major foreign policy address on June 5, 1947, Secretary of State George C. Marshall took note of Europe's crisis and suggested that America would be prepared to extend long-range assistance for reconstruction, provided Europe itself took the lead in presenting a carefully worked-out plan for utilizing American resources to promote lasting regional recovery. Europe was quick to respond. Even Soviet Russia and its satellites expressed an interest in participating in the Marshall Plan. By midsummer, however, Communist propaganda organs had begun to denounce the Marshall Plan as an instrument of American imperialism. Neither Russia nor its satellites participated in the discussions that finally resulted in the presentation of a concrete program to the State Department. Lacking access to the Kremlin's archives, no Westerner can be certain of the reason behind Moscow's refusal to participate in the Marshall Plan. No bars originally existed against Russia's association with the plan, although as time passed, the program came more and more to be presented to Congress and the American public as an anti-Communist measure. Several hypotheses may be suggested. Russia was apparently unwilling to accept any "conditions" for the use of American aid, particularly any that would involve extensive American "supervision" of its administration. Moreover, in the light of an increasingly anti-Soviet attitude within the United States and especially in Congress, Russia may have actually feared an expansion in American influence in the sensitive Eastern European satellite zone. Several countries in this area had expressed keen interest in participating in the Marshall Plan. Czechoslovakia, for instance, appeared highly enthusiastic about the prospect of American assistance. If extensive American aid to Eastern European countries led to significant progress in rehabilitating them, American prestige would be greatly enhanced to the detriment of Soviet influence. Ideological considerations may also have colored Russia's decision. The Kremlin may have thought that long-awaited revolutionary forces could work more successfully in economically debilitated countries.

Whatever the reasons for the Kremlin's obduracy, it is apparent that Soviet refusal to join in the plan was a major blunder in Russia's postwar foreign policy. Perhaps more than any other factor, the Marshall Plan was responsible for the decline of Communist influence in Western Europe after 1948. Initially there had appeared considerable opposition within the United States to so costly a measure. This opposition was largely overcome by presenting the plan to Congress as part of the "containment" strategy, a maneuver that would hardly have been possible had Soviet Russia been a participating country. Soviet participation, therefore, probably would have killed the Marshall Plan outright, or, at a minimum, sharply reduced its scope.

In accordance with American demands, the nations of Western Europe formed a regional association, ultimately called the Organization for European Economic Cooperation (OEEC), to make exhaustive studies of the region's long-term needs and to draw up plans for using American assistance in the most effective way.* By mid-August, the OEEC had submitted a proposal calling for nearly $30 billion in American funds, an estimate that was eventually scaled down to $17 billion over a four-year period. By the end of the program, $12.5 billion had actually been appropriated by Congress for European recovery.[10]

The Marshall Plan officially came to an end in 1951. At the time of its expiration, there was no question but that it had largely achieved its basic purpose of rehabilitating the economic systems of the OEEC countries. By 1951, European production had either reached or exceeded prewar levels. Using American assistance as a kind of catalyst, the Europeans recovered their economic vitality and began to stabilize their internal political conditions. In the years that followed, as we shall see, Western Europe became in some respects the most economically dynamic region on the globe, challenging economic growth rates attained by both the United States and the Soviet Union.

The Shift to Military Aid

The change to military aid, for reasons to be discussed later, began in 1950 with the Mutual Defense Assistance Program. In 1952, economic, military, and technical assistance for underdeveloped countries were combined into a single program, known as the Mutual Security Program. Military aid extended under the MSP resulted in a vast increase in Western Europe's defense efforts. By 1957, Europe was spending $13 billion on its own defense.[11]

By the late 1950s and early 1960s, it had become apparent that Europe's military defense position was infinitely stronger than it had been ten years earlier. This did not mean that no problems beset NATO's efforts to strengthen Western security; we shall examine many of these later in the chapter. Western Europe, nevertheless, was no longer considered one of the most inviting areas for Communist expansionism. This realization underlay the reduction in American military assistance to Europe. In submitting his foreign aid

---

*The OEEC remained in existence until 1961, when it was superseded by the Organization for Economic Cooperation and Development (OECD). While OEEC had been concerned primarily with fostering regional economic cooperation to achieve the goals of the Marshall Plan, as we shall see, OECD was responsible chiefly for coordinating economic policies among its European members and for integrating their foreign aid activities.

budget for 1965, President Johnson could report to Congress that: "The Western European nations in the North Atlantic Treaty Organization now supply almost all the financial support for their own military forces and also provide military assistance to others."[12] From this point on, American military assistance to Europe consisted chiefly of the five infantry divisions, plus supporting ground and air forces, which the United States maintained on the European continent. These not only afforded a visible symbol of America's deep involvement in European security; they also served as an integral part of the NATO "shield" designed to safeguard Europe from attack.

EUROPEAN ECONOMIC INTEGRATION

The American Objective

As early as 1942, John Foster Dulles expressed the thoughts of many leading Americans when he stated that:

Continental Europe has been the world's greatest fire hazard. This has long been recognized, but it has seemed impractical to do anything about it. Now the whole structure is consumed in flames. We condemn those who started and spread the fire. But this does not mean that, when the time comes to rebuild, we should reproduce a demonstrated firetrap.[13]

When the Senate was considering interim aid to Europe in 1947, Dulles told the Senate Foreign Relations Committee that the "basic idea should be, not the rebuilding of the pre-war Europe, but the building of a new Europe which, more unified, will be a better Europe.[14]

Consistently throughout the postwar period the United States has encouraged the movements looking toward European unity or European integration. Congress in particular has been keenly interested in the progress of European integration and has not hesitated to express its viewpoints in legislation providing American assistance to Western Europe. Thus the Mutual Security Act of 1954 contained the following expression of congressional sentiment:

The Congress welcomes the recent progress in European cooperation and re-affirms the belief in the necessity of further efforts toward political federation, military integration, and economic unification as a means of building strength, establishing security, and preserving peace in the North Atlantic area. . . . the Congress believes it essential that this Act should be so administered as to support concrete measures to promote greater political federation, military integration, and economic unification in Europe.[15]

Throughout the postwar period, America's support for the *idea* of European economic integration has remained more consistent than its conception of the precise forms such integration was expected to take and of the relationships that were to prevail among economic unification movements on the Continent.* Over the two decades that followed the inauguration of the Marshall Plan, it became evident that a great variety of alternatives existed for promoting economic cooperation in the North Atlantic region. These ranged from limited forms of economic collaboration, as in the Benelux customs union; to "sector" collaboration involving a single commodity or enterprise, as in the European Coal and Steel Community; to extensive supranational cooperation among several European nations, as in the European Common Market (EEC); to proposed schemes for extending the EEC to most of Western Europe; to projected plans for "Atlantic partnership" involving close economic (and eventually political) ties between Europe, on the one side, and the United States and Canada, on the other.

---

*The term European "unification" or "integration" possesses no very clear definition. Even the more specific term "economic unification" is sometimes also imprecise and ambiguous. Robert Marjolin conceives it to envision "free circulation of goods, persons, and capital between the European countries," in turn requiring a "single tariff" for its members, a "single currency with a single bank of issue, and a common budget. In a word, it would mean practically the creation of a single state." The more limited concept of *economic integration* is "any process which brings about a greater degree of unity." Quoted in Michael T. Florinsky, *Integrated Europe?* (New York: Macmillan, 1955), p. 28.

Walter Hallstein, a European advocate of regional cooperation, has defined the goal of economic unification by saying more simply that "it may be regarded as a means of establishing throughout the territory of its member states as much as possible of the uniformity of economic conditions that normally obtains within a single country." Walter Hallstein, *United Europe: Challenge and Opportunity* (Cambridge, Mass.: Harvard University Press, 1962), p. 40.

The literature on integration and unification movements in postwar Europe is voluminous. The following provide detailed and illuminating coverage: Michael T. Florinsky, *Integrated Europe?* (New York: Macmillan, 1955); H. A. Schmitt, *The Path to European Union* (Baton Rouge, La.: Louisiana University Press, 1962); Isaiah Frank, *The European Common Market* (New York: Praeger, 1961); Ernest B. Haas, *The Uniting of Europe* (Stanford, Calif.: Stanford University Press, 1958); Emil Benoit, *Europe at Sixes and Sevens: The Common Market, the Free Trade Association and the United States* (New York: Columbia University Press, 1961); George Lichtheim, *The New Europe* (New York: Praeger, 1963); Walter Hallstein, *United Europe: Challenge and Opportunity* (Cambridge, Mass.: Harvard University Press, 1962); Kurt Birrenbach, *The Future of the Atlantic Community* (New York: Praeger, 1963); Richard Mayne, *The Community of Europe: Past, Present, and Future* (New York: Norton, 1962); Michael Curtis, *Western European Integration* (New York: Harper & Row, 1965); David P. Calleo, *Europe's Future: The Grand Alternatives* (New York: Norton, 1967); and George E. G. Catlin, *The Atlantic Commonwealth* (Baltimore: Penguin, 1969).

Support for the *goal* of European economic co-operation has been strong on both sides of the Atlantic since World War II. Despite French opposition to the idea under the presidency of General Charles de Gaulle (1958–1969), it is an objective to which all governments concerned continue to subscribe. The progress made by the European Common Market during the past decade testifies to the fact that the goal is something more than a vague ideal. Yet neither now, nor in the early postwar period, has a consensus existed among the United States and its European partners concerning the *form* such economic collaboration ought to take. Even more fundamentally, the precise *stages* by which the goal was to be reached have remained unspecified. Behind these issues has existed a reality which—in spite of Europe's phenomenal postwar recovery—has not, in many vital respects, basically changed: the vast economic power of the United States, particularly in activities like space and computer technology, in which America has maintained superiority over Western Europe. This "technology gap" (which is, in some respects, widening in favor of the United States) posed a major problem to agreement on the most desirable form of economic cooperation and the sequence of steps by which it might be achieved. American opinion on the issue was ambivalent and often divided for another reason. Much as they subscribed to the principle of greater economic collaboration among nations in the North Atlantic region, American officials appeared indifferent to a question asked increasingly by Europeans: What concessions was the United States prepared to make, in order to translate the ideal of Western economic cooperation or unification into reality? In the European view, America's insistence that its partners transcend "narrow nationalism" was not matched by a corresponding willingness in Washington to relinquish American sovereignty in behalf of the common goal.

Nevertheless, progress in various kinds of supranational economic collaboration in the North Atlantic area since World War II has been considerable. If gains have fallen short of expectations, they have perhaps exceeded what might have been predicted by anyone familiar with the nationalistic rivalries of European nations throughout modern history.

Early Forms of Economic Integration

Throughout modern history, Europe has been plagued by the existence of excessive customs duties and numerous national trade barriers impeding the movement of goods and services across frontiers. In the midst of World War II, the Netherlands, Luxembourg, and Belgium took the first steps to overcome this traditional problem when they established a customs union. For several years, this union accomplished very little. As it became apparent in the early postwar era that only limited steps toward economic cooperation among the nations of Europe had any chance of success, the Benelux countries revived their wartime customs union. A comparable agreement was reached between France and Italy in 1949. Many of the goals implicit in the idea of these customs unions were incorporated into the much more ambitious and successful European Common Market, which came into existence in 1959.

When the Marshall Plan to promote European economic recovery was launched in 1948, its stated objective was to facilitate "the recovery of Western Europe in the form of an integrated unity, which, it was hoped, would be capable of maintaining itself economically, politically, and militarily."[16] Throughout the life of the Marshall Plan, the theory (if not always the practice) in the administration of the program was to foster *regional* economic collaboration among the European recipients, in order to transcend long-standing economic rivalries and to make the best possible use of Europe's collective resources. Consequently, the Organization for European Economic Cooperation (OEEC), established by the recipients to plan effective use of Marshall Plan aid, continually emphasized the necessity for mutual planning to achieve the program's goals. Yet, OEEC possessed very little actual power to compel adherence to this ideal. In spite of these limitations, OEEC succeeded in overcoming some obstacles facing European economic collaboration.[17]

That OEEC proved its worth as an instrument of regional cooperation on the European continent was indicated by the fact that it remained in existence until 1961, long after the Marshall Plan was terminated. Gradually, its compass was broadened to deal with economic problems and tendencies throughout the North Atlantic area. In 1961, as a result of American initiative, the organization was transformed into the Organization for Economic Cooperation and Development (OECD); its membership was broadened to include the United States and Canada. By the mid-1960s, Japan (which had cooperated with OECD's activities from the beginning) had applied for membership, and was ultimately accepted.*

More than its predecessor (OEEC), the new OECD is concerned with *global* economic problems, particularly as these affect the economic re-

---

*In 1960, the older OEEC was reorganized and became the OECD. It consisted of the 18 nations originally belonging to OEEC, plus the United States and Canada; Japan joined in 1964; Yugoslavia and Finland were granted an associated status. Governed by a council on which all members are represented, the OECD requires unanimity for decisions, but no member which abstains from voting is bound by its decisions. Between sessions of the council, an executive committee makes necessary decisions.

lations and welfare of its members. OECD has a threefold objective: encouragement of economic growth and expansion; enhancement of multilateral trade and removal of discriminatory trade barriers; and promotion of the economic expansion of the developing countries through extension of financial and technical assistance to needy societies. The last objective has been the subject of intense OECD activity in recent years. Close to forty of the new nations achieving independence in the postwar era were once colonies of OECD members. More than any other region, Africa has been recognized on both sides of the Atlantic as an appropriate sphere for OECD activities; the United States has been content to let Europe provide the great bulk of economic and technical assistance given to Africa by the free world. This task has fallen to the Development Assistance Committee of OECD, which often works in close concert with agencies like the International Bank for Reconstruction and Development (IBRD) and the International Monetary Fund (IMF). Lacking funds of its own, the Development Assistance Committee serves as a planning and coordinating mechanism for the foreign aid activities of its members and as facility for undertaking periodic "reviews" of past and present programs. Besides its interest in economic growth in the developing areas, OECD is also active in spheres like encouragement of integrated transportation systems within its orbit, promotion of scientific education, manpower training and utilization, support for scientific research, and the collection of statistics and other information useful to its members.[18]

Meanwhile, economic integration and unification in Western Europe was also being achieved by various "sector" schemes designed to accomplish this result within a specific, and often quite limited, sphere of economic enterprise. A leading example of this approach was the European Coal and Steel Community (ECSC), an outgrowth of the Schuman Plan, set up by the Benelux countries, France, Germany, and Italy on April 18, 1951. As a prominent advocate of European economic integration, Walter Hallstein, has described ECSC: "Its essential characteristics were that it was 'supranational,' that it was practical, and that it was partial [in its scope]."[19] Unlike OEEC or OECD, the Coal and Steel Community possessed supranational authority to formulate regulations and directives binding upon its members in coal and steel production. Moreover, as Hallstein has emphasized, a singular characteristic of ECSC was its *evolutionary* character. From the beginning, its instigators conceived of ECSC as an undertaking that would gradually, and on the basis of experience, chart a course toward expanded supranational collaboration in other phases of European economic life.[20] As an ultimate goal (whose realization would take years and would encounter many obstacles), ECSC envi-

sioned creating what Robert Schuman had called "the European federation which is indispensable to the maintenance of peace."[21]

ECSC was a significant step down the path of European economic unity, therefore, not alone because it represented a successful venture in supranational collaboration in one industrial segment. It was perhaps even more significant for what it foreshadowed. This was the far more ambitious European Common Market, whose goals, organizational pattern, and implications for America we shall examine below.

Another sector approach to economic collaboration among European nations was Euratom, which began operating in 1958. Its members were the Benelux nations, France, Germany, and Italy. Unlike ECSC, which it resembled in many respects, Euratom dealt with an area—the peaceful application of atomic energy—in which there was no backlog of competing national traditions to be overcome. The organization was intended to deal with one of Europe's most pressing shortages—fuel; short on coal reserves, Europe had become increasingly dependent upon importations of oil, especially from the Middle East. The Suez crisis of 1956—when oil supplies from the Arab world to Europe were cut off for several months—underscored the region's economic and military vulnerability when the flow of oil from the outside world was impeded. For this reason, perhaps more than any other, the generation of nuclear power for civilian uses has received a higher priority in Western Europe than in any other area.

Intended to function as a common market in all aspects of peacetime nuclear technology, Euratom exercises control over the production of raw materials, trade, production, and other important aspects of nuclear technology. Theoretically, it controls the allocation of fissionable materials within its orbit, inspects the operation of nuclear installations, enforces safety regulations, fosters nuclear research, and prevents its members from using nuclear technology and fissionable materials for military purposes. In practice, Euratom's performance has not fulfilled initial expectations. The principal barrier to accomplishment of its goals was French President Charles de Gaulle's insistence upon acquisition of a nuclear striking force, the *force de frappe*, giving France membership in the "nuclear club" and presumably enhancing its global influence. Development of the *force de frappe* inevitably dictated French refusal to cooperate in many spheres of Euratom's activities, especially if these diminished French sovereignty; nor was France willing (before or after de Gaulle) to accept a nuclear nonproliferation treaty barring the country from access to nuclear weapons. Under these conditions, the over-all unity of Euratom was lessened. As in other European unity schemes, progress in one sphere of cooperation (or lack of it) was likely to affect fundamentally the prospects for cooperation in other spheres.[22]

The European Economic Community

The European Economic Community (EEC), popularly known as the Common Market,* is the culmination of the movement toward European economic union, and the most promising step toward political union in the postwar era. EEC is far more comprehensive than Benelux, ECSC, and its other predecessors on the European scene. It visualizes the substantial economic merger of the participating countries. What is more, the ultimate goal of EEC is *political* unification. So far as the United States is concerned, few developments in postwar Europe have posed as many far-reaching implications for American foreign policy as the emergence of the European Common Market. EEC came into existence on January 1, 1958, as the result of a 378-page treaty among its signatories: France, the Federal Republic of Germany, Italy, and the Benelux nations (widely referred to as "the six"). It began operations a year later. The appearance of EEC marked the emergence of a new "trading area," in which internal tariffs and other barriers to trade were to be removed. Concurrently, EEC would move toward the goal of a common tariff toward the outside world, based upon an average of the tariff rates applied earlier by its members.

The emergence of the European Economic Community has to be reckoned one of the most crucial developments of the postwar era—if not of modern history. The EEC served as both a cause and a symbol of the "new era" in Europe's relations with the outside world. If the European allies, for example, were exhibiting a greater degree of independence from America than ever, a major explanation was that Europe had a new base of economic growth and vitality upon which to build new political and diplomatic postures. By the late 1960s, the nations belonging to EEC collectively represented an area of some 700,000 square miles and a population not far from 200 million people.† For several years after its formation, the EEC

achieved one of the fastest economic growth rates in the world. By the mid- and late 1960s, some of this momentum had been lost. (The 18 European members of OECD and Japan, for example, were expanding their economic activity slightly faster than EEC.) Faced with problems like a contraction in its labor force and a slowdown in population growth, EEC was likely to experience more moderate economic expansion in the years ahead. Yet many of these problems were "normal" for an industrially advanced region. In spite of them, the EEC gave every sign of moving ahead economically at a healthy and sustained rate.[23]

The projected aims of EEC are sweeping; as the institution's popular name implies, its ultimate goal is creation of a "common market" among its members, entailing the removal of trade barriers, currency restrictions, and obstacles to the movement of capital, goods, and labor across national frontiers within the EEC area. Progressive steps toward economic integration will in time produce a single industrial and agricultural market for "the six," while a uniform tariff will prevail toward nations outside the EEC area. Such changes, needless to say, cannot be achieved quickly. When the Treaty of Rome was signed in 1958, it was anticipated that progress toward creation of a common market would be made in three stages, extending over a period of 12 to 15 years. In the main, "the six" have harmonized their economic decisions on schedule, and in some instances ahead of schedule. Progress has not always been easy; and some setbacks have occurred. As we shall see, disagreements within EEC over procedures for reaching decisions, over the difficult problem of a common market in agriculture, and over the still pending question of Great Britain's admission to the organization have engendered tensions and occasionally called the very future of EEC into question. Nevertheless, undeniable gains have been made toward the achievement of EEC's goals. Trade within the EEC area itself has been largely freed of tariff and other restrictions; labor moves without hindrance from Italy to Germany to Belgium; significant progress has been made in facilitating the exchange of industrial goods among EEC countries; many currency restrictions have been lifted and common policies have been arrived at dealing with monetary problems (French devaluation in 1969, for example, caused no noteworthy repercussions throughout the EEC area); steps have been taken in the direction of a common system of taxation, with the ultimate objective of making taxes uniform throughout the EEC region; and several hurdles have been overcome in resolving one of the most

---

*As time passed, semantic confusion was fostered by the evolution of EEC. Popularly called the European Common Market, in fact after 1967, the EEC was widened to include three organizations which had hitherto been separate: the European Common Market, the European Coal and Steel Community, and Euratom. Thus the Common Market is only one of the EEC's three main agencies. All three are administered by common institutions of EEC, although each retains its own executive organ.

†The main "rival" to EEC in Europe was EFTA, the European Free Trade Area. We shall discuss EFTA at a later stage. Here, however, it is worthwhile noting that if and when Great Britain and its other EFTA partners join EEC, a giant trading and industrial nexus will come into existence that will, in many ways, overshadow both America and Russia economically. Combined, EEC and EFTA would encompass 1.6 million square miles of territory and well over 300 million people. Total exports by both organizations in the late 1960s were more than $75 billion in goods and services, some ten times Russia's exports and over three times America's.

difficult issues confronting movement toward a common market: disparities in agricultural productivity, levels of government subsidies, and food prices among the participating nations, notably France and West Germany. In brief, by the close of the 1960s, EEC had eliminated all internal tariffs among its members and had adopted a common tariff toward non-EEC nations. No matter how much it applauded Europe's movement toward economic unification, these events presented Washington with difficult choices. To mention only one specific problem—American agricultural exports to the European continent—the United States was encountering considerable difficulty in getting the kind of tariff concessions from the members of EEC that would allow the level of exchange in agricultural commodities to remain normal, much less to expand. For their part, members of the EEC assumed a "tough" stance about American trade restrictions, such as provisions favoring American chemical manufactures over European.[24] Not the least of its accomplishments since 1958 has been the building of a body of tradition and experience in reaching and administering economic decisions involving six nations. The "Eurocrats" who serve the institution have demonstrated that the dream of economic unification is not unattainable, notwithstanding the opposition and obstruction (chiefly from France under General de Gaulle) that sometimes hindered their activities.

The organizational structure of EEC was adapted from the oldest of its three communities, the ECSC. The highest decision-making body is the Council of Ministers. Consisting of one delegate from each of the six countries, the council normally meets two or three times a year. Its decisions are binding and final (unless challenged on legal grounds in the court of EEC). On most major issues, it is required to reach decisions on the basis of unanimity. Consensus within EEC is obviously promoted by doing so. Yet from the beginning, a qualified or extraordinary majority could make certain decisions; and as the years passed it was anticipated that the trend would be away from the unanimity requirement. Between meetings of the council, the permanent representatives (with the rank of ambassador to EEC) meet, usually several times weekly, to prepare for council sessions and undertake necessary background studies before decisions are reached.

The EEC Commission is the main executive agency. Its nine members serve four-year terms; both theoretically and actually, they are "Eurocrats" who cannot be "instructed" by their own governments but are expected to put the interests of EEC as a whole ahead of national interests. The presidency of the commission symbolizes the idea of European unification, particularly when it is held by forceful personalities like Walter Hallstein. With a staff of close to 3000, the commission

is concerned with a variety of subjects, such as agricultural and financial affairs, and transport questions throughout the EEC area. Permitted to arrive at its decisions by majority vote, in practice (especially while General de Gaulle led the government of France), the commission seeks unanimity in behalf of major decisions. Besides serving as an over-all "watchdog" for all the EEC's activities, the commission formulates proposals for consideration by the Council of Ministers.

The court of EEC is the institution's highest legal tribunal. Its seven judges (serving six-year terms and eligible for reappointment) are appointed by "the six." The court's function is to hear contentious cases arising under the Treaty of Rome and other legal instruments. Although decisions of the court do not automatically override decisions by the national courts of nations belonging to EEC, national courts are expected to take account of the rulings of the EEC's tribunal. The court of EEC has had a full docket of cases, arising chiefly from the activities of the European Coal and Steel Community.

The stated goal of EEC, as we have already observed, is to achieve eventual *political unification* among its members. Of parliamentary institutions concerned directly or indirectly with European unification before 1958, there was no lack. In part, this goal stems from the realization that economic and political decision-making are closely intertwined; progress on one level required corresponding progress on the other if genuine unity is to be achieved and, once achieved, maintained.*

The fourth major organ of EEC is the European Assembly (popularly called the European Parliament). Choosing members from their own national parliaments, "the six" send 142 delegates to the assembly; the political configuration of EEC's parliament thus corresponds more or less closely with that prevailing in the parliaments from which members were selected. Required to meet at least annually, in practice the assembly convenes for brief sessions several times a year. It serves mainly as a consultative body, receiving reports from EEC's supervisory and administrative organs; not infrequently, the latter consult the assembly *before* making important decisions. In the most vital sense, the assembly is *not* a true parliament: It lacks the power to enact legislation. Depending primarily upon moral suasion and its not inconsiderable influence over European opinion, the assembly provides a mechanism for fur-

---

*One of the oldest and best known was the Council of Europe, created in 1949, meeting in Strasbourg. In the years thereafter, other parliamentary bodies—like the assembly of ECSC and the assembly of the Western European Union (WEU)—had been created. When EEC was formed in 1958, the ECSC assembly was transformed into its parliamentary organ.

nishing policy guidelines for the EEC's administrators and for focusing public attention upon problems confronting "the six" in their attempt to arrive at common policies.[25]

Although it has made impressive progress in achieving many of its proclaimed goals, the European Economic Community faces several challenges affecting its development in the years ahead. Three major problems may be identified, two of which are concerned mainly with relations among the European nations, while the last has to do with the relations of the EEC with the United States.

EEC and Gaullism

The first problem might be designated: the European Economic Community in the post-Gaullist era. For over a decade (from mid-1958 until mid-1969), a pall hung over the future of EEC, as well as other supranational ideas and movements on the European continent. Military collaboration among the nations of the West, as we shall see, was momentously influenced by this challenge. Even before he became the first President of the Fifth French Republic, General Charles de Gaulle made it clear that he had little confidence in true supranationalism, whether in the European region or in the United Nations. Dedicated to restoring *la grandeur* for France, to the assertion of French "independence" from both Washington and Moscow, and to the elevation of France to a position of acknowledged leadership in Western Europe, de Gaulle viewed EEC with strong misgivings, as an actual and a potential infringement upon French sovereignty.[26] Against the idea of European economic, and future political, unification de Gaulle advanced his own idea of a *Europe des patries* ("Europe of the fatherlands"), in which the nation would remain with its sovereignty largely intact as the organic unit in creating a new Europe. De Gaulle's conception of the desired European realignment—a "Europe from the Atlantic to the Urals"—anticipated the disappearance of the Iron Curtain; the recognition by the Soviet Union of its essentially European orientation (de Gaulle expected that in time Moscow would lose some of its eastern territories to China); and the appearance of a revitalized Europe as a counterpoise to the "Anglo–Saxons." France, having gained membership in the "nuclear club," would of course play a leading role in this new scheme of things; perhaps a Franco–Soviet *entente* would confront both the Anglo–Saxons and the West Germans with superior strength!

Although he did not totally reject the idea of regional cooperation among the increasingly prosperous European nations, De Gaulle did not conceal his antipathy to ECC's announced goal of economic, and ultimate political, unification

among "the six."* At a minimum, he insisted that efforts by the members of the EEC to harmonize their economic policies be carried out within carefully specified parameters and by use of procedures acceptable to the participating nations. This insistence led de Gaulle to attack many of the principles and procedures whereby (in his view) EEC's "Eurocrats" made decisions, sometimes to the detriment of France. The French President adamantly opposed any departure from the unanimity rule in EEC decision-making. Limited supranational cooperation by the sovereign members of EEC was one thing; de Gaulle seldom attacked that conception directly. But government by "Eurocrats," who were in turn supported by a mere majority of "the six" against the interests of France, presented an unacceptable situation; de Gaulle repeatedly denounced it as incompatible with French sovereignty. Realizing that the other members not only approved of EEC as it had evolved since 1958, but in many respects desired to hasten its progress in the future, de Gaulle did not withdraw France from the organization. Instead, for a period of several years, he carried on a kind of cold war against "Eurocrats" and other advocates of regional unification; alluded to innumerable times to the "problems" inhibiting EEC from making further advances; vetoed Great Britain's application for membership in the organization in 1963; and opposed its reapplication thereafter. Dramatically following the policy of "the empty chair," under de Gaulle French representatives absented themselves

*General de Gaulle's views on the future of European unification, as on a number of other issues, were sometimes contradictory—on some occasions, deliberately so. Disguising his true feelings and surrounding them with an air of mystery was a calculated tactic of the French leader. When he became President of the Fifth Republic in 1958, de Gaulle accepted the European Economic Community; on numerous occasions thereafter, he asserted belief in the ultimate goal of European unity. On September 5, 1960, for example, he declared: "To build Europe . . . to unite it, is evidently something essential." Again on May 15, 1962, he asserted that ". . . Western Europe must form itself politically." Yet such evidences of de Gaulle's support for European integration were always qualified by insistence that the time was not ripe for supranational ventures; that the towering "reality" in Europe was the existence of national sovereignty—leading him to favor a "Europe of states" vis-à-vis the approach of the "Eurocrats"; that Great Britain should not be admitted to the EEC; and that the ultimate goal must be a "European Europe," taking an independent position between the "two hegemonies" of America and the Soviet Union. Robert Aron is convinced that de Gaulle's views on this question were always subordinated to his determination to assure French dominance on the European continent. "He would probably accept a united Europe if it were under French hegemony"; he opposed it when it seemed almost certain that a united Europe would be under American domination. See Robert Aron, *An Explanation of de Gaulle* (New York: Harper & Row, 1966), pp. 190–191; and Roy C. Macridis, ed., *De Gaulle: Implacable Ally* (New York: Harper & Row, 1966), pp. 155–167.

from many EEC meetings and activities. Mindful that French secession from the organization would probably signal its disintegration, the other EEC members hesitated to press their demands upon a reluctant French government.[27]

After his defeat in the French national elections in the spring of 1969, General de Gaulle retired from active political life. Would his departure eliminate the difficulties from "Gaullism" confronting EEC? Critics of the French President in Europe and America were prone to assume so—perhaps prematurely. Although he was the center of the movement, however, General de Gaulle and Gaullism were in many ways distinct phenomena. Many aspects of Gaullism had existed before 1958; the movement might well persist after the retirement of its leader. For the President of France had often expressed—at times brutally and irritatingly—what millions of Frenchmen and other Europeans sincerely believed. Frustrated as they might become with his unique political style, Europeans not infrequently shared many of de Gaulle's anxieties and agreed with his assessment of regional and global developments. It was de Gaulle's predecessors in the Fourth Republic, we need to remember, who took the first steps towards the acquisition of the French *force de frappe*. This move indicated deep attachment to the Gaullist goal of defending and expanding French independence; it implied dissatisfaction in Paris with Anglo–Saxon dominance of the Western alliance; and it reflected a pervasive feeling on the European continent—the widespread fear of West Germany's growing economic and political power. Few Europeans outside France relished the prospect of a Gaullist-led EEC; but they were even less ecstatic about a German-controlled regional organization (which would perhaps mean, in practice, a German–American axis dominating European affairs). Master practitioner of *Realpolitik* that he was, de Gaulle realized a truth about the evolution of Europe whose implications had never been faced squarely by his detractors. The locus of power in an evolving EEC had to rest *somewhere*, and the choices were very limited. Would it be in America or possibly a German–American axis? Would West Germany emerge as the leader of a united Europe west of the Iron Curtain? Would France, as de Gaulle anticipated, become the pivot of the new Europe? Or would a resurgent Europe build upon a foundation of Franco–German rapport? This fundamental dilemma lay at the heart of economic and political unification movements in Europe, although advocates of supranationalism seldom faced it candidly. The rejection of French dominance in Western Europe would almost inevitably mean German (or German–American) dominance—and most Europeans really wanted neither. The power disparities within the EEC area were such as to rule out other alternatives, as

long as Great Britain remained outside the organization. In his way, de Gaulle attempted to force Europeans to face these realities. His opposition to the principle of "majority rule" within EEC was in part an effort to drive home the point that the creation of true community required that these problems be confronted honestly and that efforts be made to resolve them before EEC entered its next stage.

Observers on both sides of the Atlantic counted upon the retirement of General de Gaulle to resolve many of the difficulties besetting the drive toward European economic unity. The new French government, however, initially made no major innovations in the nation's foreign policy, although the tone of its relations with other countries changed significantly. Late in 1969, Paris announced the first important modification in France's diplomatic stance as a result of de Gaulle's departure: Although it still foresaw a number of difficult problems associated with the move, Paris would no longer block Great Britain's bid for membership in the European Economic Community. This announcement cleared the way for European economic unification to forge ahead into the next stage.

Great Britain, EFTA, and EEC

In the years during which "the six" were preparing the groundwork for the European Economic Community, Great Britain was invited to join these discussions and to become a charter member of the organization. For a variety of reasons, London refused—primarily because Britain's heritage of "splendid isolation" from continental affairs had traditionally dictated attachment to the policy of the "free hand" in dealing with Europe. Throughout modern history, Britain had avoided *permanent* association or alliance with any particular group of European states. Its decision to decline membership in EEC, it soon became apparent (and as was evident at the time to many Britons and Europeans) was probably a cardinal error. Its most likely consequences would be to isolate Britain from one of the most economically dynamic regions on the globe, to compound London's economic and financial problems, and to guarantee even greater British dependence upon the United States. With its Commonwealth ties undergoing drastic change, often to its disadvantage, Britain's economic and diplomatic prospects did not look promising.

In 1956, after deciding against participation in preliminary EEC discussions, London took the lead in creating its own counterpart to the nascent organization. Called the European Free Trade Area (EFTA), it consisted of European states that had customarily been linked closely with Britain in economic and financial affairs: Sweden, Denmark, Norway, Austria, Portugal, and Switzerland. EFTA (popularly referred to as "the seven") created an impressive economic bloc. By the end of the 1960s, it encompassed a total area of close to 1 million square miles and contained a population of some 100 million people. Its total trade (counting both imports and exports) ran some $68 billion annually.[28]

From the beginning, however, a number of fundamental differences existed between EEC and EFTA. First, the members of EFTA were scattered around the periphery of Europe; they lacked EEC's geographic cohesion. Second, EFTA possessed little cultural unity or political homogeneity. Third, it was strictly an *economic* organization; and even in this sphere, its goals were more limited than those of EEC. EFTA, for example, did not contemplate the creation of a "common market"; still less did it envision the ultimate political unification of its members. Fourth, EFTA was always visualized (at least implicitly) as an *interim measure:* Sooner or later, it was expected that Britain and its smaller partners would join, or otherwise associate themselves with, EEC. EFTA as a whole might even someday merge with its rival. Meanwhile, the existence of EFTA afforded its members some leverage with which to gain more favorable terms when a decision was made to join EEC. Fifth, EFTA gave priority to facilitating trade among its members in *industrial* goods; little progress was made in lifting barriers to agricultural trade. Seventh, a not inconsiderable difference was that EEC plainly enjoyed the support of the United States, which regarded it as the nucleus of a united Europe.

Despite these limitations, EFTA made some real progress. In a series of steps, it eliminated nearly all tariffs on the exchange of industrial goods among its members; its exports expanded appreciably (although they fell to the EEC area); the trade balances of several of its members improved; it contributed in some measure to Britain's progress in overcoming many of its chronic trade and financial problems; and it facilitated preliminary work on a proposed "Nordic Economic Union," consisting of Denmark, Finland, Norway, and Sweden. Not the least of its achievements was in affording an avenue whereby Finland might expand its contacts with Western Europe without arousing Moscow's apprehensions.[29]

A few months after the EEC began operations, a high British official conceded that London had made a mistake in refusing membership in the organization. Early in 1961, the British government formally expressed its desire to join EEC—a move enthusiastically endorsed by all the organization's members except de Gaulle's France. Then on January 14, 1963, in an unusually harsh and undiplomatic speech, General de Gaulle "vetoed" Britain's application for admission to EEC.[30] The French President referred to a number of difficulties, but the main impediment was the "special relationship" which Great Britain had with the United States. Resistance to the "Anglo–Saxons," and fear that the United States would indirectly dominate EEC, prompted de Gaulle's opposition to British membership—a position he held consistently until his retirement in 1969. In 1967, when London renewed its application for admission to EEC, de Gaulle reiterated his opposition.[31]

Yet neither Great Britain nor the other members of EEC were prepared to accept French adamancy as irrevocable. West Germany, finding itself at odds with many aspects of de Gaulle's foreign policy, supported British membership; the smaller EEC nations—desiring maximum protection from both German and French dominance on the Continent—remained firm advocates of British admission. Across the Atlantic, the United States also urged London not to abandon the quest; American officials continued to believe that EEC was destined to evolve into a broader European partnership, bringing the goal of an Atlantic community one step closer. Curiously enough, during the mid-1960s, some segments of British opinion began to lose their enthusiasm for membership in EEC. If they were admitted to the organization, the British would undoubtedly face a substantial increase in food prices, along with other economic and financial readjustments that might eclipse the benefits of membership. Yet the passage of time did not weaken what had perhaps always been the strongest argument in favor of the move: As long as it remained outside EEC, and while its position in Asia, the Middle East, and other areas was declining, Great Britain faced a highly uncertain future in terms of its regional and global influence.

By the early 1970s, the prospect that EEC would be expanded to include Great Britain, along with several of its EFTA partners, had improved markedly. General de Gaulle's departure from the French political scene in 1969 provided fresh impetus for London to renew its bid. Then in June, 1970, the British people elected a Conservative government; almost immediately, British negotiators opened discussions with representatives of the EEC on the question of British membership. Negotiations were likely to be hard and prolonged (lasting, some commentators expected, perhaps until 1972). Great Britain obviously desired belated entry into EEC, and most members of the organization approved its entry in principle. Yet neither side was prepared to make wholesale concessions to achieve the goal. London demanded that the terms of its membership in EEC be fair and reasonable; the members of EEC did not wish to lose the momentum their organization had generated since its creation or to assume onerous burdens (like underwriting the stability of the British pound). British consumers were sensitive about the possibility of higher food prices; nor could Britain's traditional ties with the Commonwealth nations be abruptly terminated. Yet, with negotiators on both sides desiring agreement, it seemed likely that in time agreement would be reached, significantly expanding the size and scope of EEC. If so, it would be another landmark in Europe's resurgence.[32]

The United States and EEC: Partnership or Rivalry?

Officials in the United States enthusiastically welcomed the emergence of the European Economic Community. Among all the schemes for promoting supranationalism within the North Atlantic area since World War II, EEC seemed by all odds the most promising. A successful EEC, said an American policy-maker in the early 1960s, would be followed by a "trade partnership" between the United States and a united Europe; this new union would then take the initiative in establishing "a free world economic community." Several years later, another former State Department official identified many ways in which de facto economic and commercial unity existed among the nations of the West. Atlantic cooperation was "a living reality" and was rapidly producing "a relatively integrated Atlantic economy."*

Advocates of greater American–European economic cooperation could point to a number of

*A perceptive study of American viewpoints toward European unification since World War II is Max Beloff, *The United States and the Unity of Europe* (New York: Random House, 1963); see esp. pp. 144–168. A more recent study is Harold van B. Cleveland, *The Atlantic Idea and Its European Rivals* (New York: McGraw-Hill, 1966); the above quotation is on p. 161. Both studies focus attention upon a common theme: the basic *ambivalence* of America's response to European, and broader North Atlantic, integration. Officially, Washington has endorsed both European unification and concepts like "the Atlantic community"; nearly any statement by the President or Secretary of State on intra-Western relations supports these ideas warmly. Yet both studies doubt America's real commitment to these goals (especially the latter) when they involve *some diminution of American sovereignty*, not only in crucial areas like nuclear strategy, but in lesser areas like economic decision-making. Beloff draws an analogy between American views on this subject and American attitudes toward the United Nations. As long as the latter proved useful in the containment of Communism, it received enthusiastic American approval; when (by the late 1950s), it had begun to come largely under the influence of the Afro–Asian nations, which had little interest in participating in cold war contests, Washington began to make major decisions outside the UN. Beloff has observed that "the obsolescence of national sovereignty that was the key to the process going on in Europe was something with which the American people had still to be confronted." Consequently, he anticipated that in the near future there would not be "any important institutional innovations" in the sphere of Atlantic unity. Beloff, *op. cit.*, p. 167. In the early 1970s, the evidence afforded no compelling reasons for modifying Beloff's judgment.

favorable developments during the 1960s. In monetary problems, for example, considerable harmonization of policies went on continuously throughout the West to maintain stable currencies, mitigate balance-of-payments deficits, and cushion the economic shocks involved in British or French devaluation. The growing economic dynamism of EEC was perhaps the principal reason why President John F. Kennedy recommended, and Congress passed, the Trade Expansion Act of 1962, the first thorough revision of American tariff legislation in many years. Desiring to avert an "inward-looking" EEC, whose common tariff might discriminate against American and other foreign imports, Washington sought new trade agreements with Europe that would expand commerce across the Atlantic. Accordingly, in 1964 the "Kennedy round" of tariff negotiations opened; these talks proved to be one of the most complex and prolonged series of trade discussions in modern history. The United States had three primary goals: the reduction of tariffs on industrial goods; the promotion of agricultural and commodity exchange; and the elimination (or at least curtailment) of tariff restrictions in the West against imports from the developing nations.

The first goal was substantially achieved: Industrial tariffs between the United States and the EEC nations were lowered from 50 to 30 percent. On the second and third goals, however, considerably less progress was made. Agriculture—in which America sought easier "access" to European markets for its farm products—proved a highly contentious realm. Fearful of the impact of massive American farm imports, and unable to agree even among themselves on a Common Agricultural Policy (CAP) for EEC, "the six" were prepared to make few concessions to accommodate American demands. Although some limited steps were taken to liberalize agricultural exchange, the United States did not get the "assured outlet" to the European market which its negotiators sought. Even less progress was made in giving the emerging nations access to markets in the West. As many Afro–Asian governments complained in succeeding months, the terms of trade available to them were becoming more and more unfavorable.*

*For more comprehensive discussions of the results of the "Kennedy round" of tariff discussions, see *The United States in World Affairs: 1967* (New York: Harper & Row, 1968), pp. 190–193; and Werner Feld, *The European Common Market and the World* (Englewood Cliffs, N.J.: Prentice-Hall, 1967), pp. 89–112. One explanation of why efforts to lower barriers to agricultural trade among the nations of the West met with little success was that "the six" were themselves sharply divided on the matter of EEC agricultural policy. This was a major obstacle to Britain's membership in the EEC; it also fomented discord between France and West Germany. For appraisals of the problem, see Jon McLin,

American officials may have been surprised to discover during the "Kennedy round" how tough European negotiators were in dealing with American demands. The day of European economic subordination to the United States had plainly ended. Efforts to achieve a consensus on trade policy underscored an idea which had become evident in other ways as well: There were few grounds for thinking that a consensus within the Western community would necessarily grow apace with Europe's economic revival. On the question of whether EEC would become an inward-looking organization, the results of the "Kennedy round" were clearly mixed. In 1969, for example, American officials became vocally concerned about European efforts to impose new restrictions on agricultural imports, particularly from the United States. Nor did the European allies show any sign of lowering their tariffs on imports from the Afro–Asian states. For their part, Europeans feared a revival of "protectionist" sentiment in the United States. Even more fundamentally, they were apprehensive about the growing American economic penetration of the European continent. A large number of American corporations had "jumped" the EEC fence by establishing European branches. Within a few years, American industries largely dominated the European market in products like computers, communications and space technology, and nuclear energy. Some Europeans viewed this as a form of "technological imperialism" which threatened Europe's economic and political independence. Others, like the French commentator Jean-Jacques Servan-Schreiber, regarded it as an unparalleled opportunity for European enterprise to modernize itself and become truly competitive with American industry. In any case, America's economic penetration of Europe—a phenomenon having a number of significant *political* implications—added a new source of controversy on the agenda of issues facing proponents of Western economic cooperation.

NATO: SOVIET CHALLENGE AND WESTERN RESPONSE

Origins of NATO

A significant landmark in American postwar foreign policy toward Europe was the creation of the NATO defense community.* Just as economic as-

sistance to Greece and Turkey in 1947 had led to the much more comprehensive and prolonged European Recovery Program, so too was sustained economic assistance to Europe followed by efforts to bolster the military strength of the free world. Initially, these efforts took the form of a military alliance among the nations of Western Europe, which became the nucleus of the North Atlantic Treaty. Within a short time this was supplemented by substantial American military assistance to NATO and to other regional defense organizations.

Several developments in the 1947–1949 period spurred efforts within both the United States and Europe to establish a unified defense system for the North Atlantic area. European Communist parties had agitated militantly against the Marshall Plan. During the late 1940s Communist groups in such countries as France and Italy appeared to be gaining in strength. Moscow's propaganda organs meanwhile were carrying on a virulent anti-American campaign. In China, the Nationalist government was collapsing before the Communist rebel forces. Then in the spring of 1948 came the Soviet-engineered *coup* in Czechoslovakia, an event that hastened favorable congressional action on the Marshall Plan. There followed the Berlin blockade of 1948–1949. Here an avowed objective of Soviet foreign policy was to drive the West—and above all, the United States—out of Germany. Had the Kremlin succeeded in this goal, Western Europe would have been left in a highly precarious military–economic position.

Increasingly, Europe's leaders were aware of the need for closer military cooperation among members of the North Atlantic area. With the active encouragement of the United States, five of them on March 17, 1948, signed the Brussels Treaty.* This pact formed a "collective defense arrangement within the framework of the United Nations Charter. . . ." Concurrently, the Senate Foreign Relations Committee, working in close conjunction with the State Department, was attempting to draft a legislative resolution paving the way for American association with a European security system. This resolution, known as the Vandenberg Resolution for its instigator, Senator Arthur H. Vandenberg, was approved by the Senate on June 11, 1948, by a vote of 64–6. It called for "association of the United States, by constitutional process, with such regional and other col-

---

"Rethinking Common Agricultural Policy," and "Agriculture 1980: The Mansholt Plan," *American University Field Service Reports* IV (June, 1969).

*The text of the North Atlantic Treaty is reproduced in Department of State, *American Foreign Policy: 1950–1955* I, 812–815. Original signatories of the treaty were the United States, Canada, the United Kingdom, Belgium, Luxembourg, Norway, Iceland, the Netherlands,

Denmark, France, Italy, and Portugal. Countries that later joined NATO were: Greece and Turkey (1952) and the Federal Republic of Germany (1955).

*The text of the treaty is reprinted in Department of State, *American Foreign Policy: 1950–1955* I pp. 968–971. Original signatories were Belgium, France, Luxembourg, the Netherlands, and the United Kingdom. Italy and the Federal Republic of Germany joined the Brussels defense system in 1954

lective arrangements as are based on continuous and effective self-help and mutual aid, and as affect its national security."[33] The Senate, in other words, was overwhelmingly in favor of a closer military union between the United States and Western Europe. Europe had created the embryo of such a union under the Brussels Pact; it remained for the United States to join in this effort and for the pact to be extended to other countries. This was done under the North Atlantic Treaty, which the United States ratified on July 21, 1949.

The American Military Commitment Under NATO

By making explicit what had been implicit in the Greek–Turkish Aid Program, the Marshall Plan, and in the firm resistance to Soviet pressure during the Berlin blockade earlier, the North Atlantic Treaty signified that the United States had accepted the principle that its own security was inextricably linked with the well-being of its North Atlantic neighbors. The North Atlantic Treaty is a short document, containing only 14 articles. The key article, expressive of the philosophy behind this military union, is Article 5 by which: "The parties agree that an armed attack against one or more of them in Europe or North America shall be considered an attack against them all. . . ." In the event of an attack, each signatory will exercise the "right of individual or collective self-defense" and will "individually and in concert with the other Parties" take "such actions as it deems necessary, including the use of armed force, to restore and maintain international peace and security."

Several points about the obligations assumed by the United States under the North Atlantic Treaty require emphasis. An obvious, although sometimes overlooked, fact about the treaty is that it created essentially *a military alliance*, designed to protect its members from what was envisioned as the gravest threat to Western security: a Soviet military thrust westward into a highly vulnerable Europe. Western Germany—with its largest city isolated and surrounded by Communist forces—was considered the most likely target of a hostile Soviet move. As we noted in Chapter 9, the preponderance of Soviet ground forces over those available to Western governments placed Europe in a position of serious military jeopardy.

To say that NATO was, and remains, essentially a military alliance is not to overlook its expanding circle of activities in various nonmilitary spheres, like political consultation, cultural affairs, and education. Article 3 of the North Atlantic Treaty, for example, commits the members to engage in "continuous and effective self-help and mutual aid," which will "maintain and develop their indi-

vidual and collective capacity to resist armed attack." Such ancillary activities since 1949 have no doubt proved beneficial and have enhanced the over-all goal of greater Western security. Nor does emphasis upon NATO's intrinsically military character ignore a theme conspicuous in the statements of American officials about the alliance. The idea was reiterated by President Nixon, in connection with NATO's twentieth anniversary in 1969, when he characterized the alliance as a "new means of partnership, and an invigorated forum for new ideas and new techniques"; Nixon anticipated that NATO would develop its capabilities as a means of political consultation and progress. A successful NATO, in the President's view, was an essential step toward "an independent Europe increasingly united."[34] NATO, in other words, not only satisfied an urgent need to strengthen Western security; it was regarded as an "acorn" (one of several) from which the "oak" of Western political and economic unity would someday grow. Such expectations, especially strong in Washington, could, and not infrequently did, obscure the fact that NATO was fundamentally a form of *military* collaboration, designed to meet a *military* danger. As such, experience after 1949 amply demonstrated, NATO was to suffer many of the vicissitudes of military alliances throughout history. Its fortunes, and its degree of internal cohesion, were above all *a function of the perceived danger facing its members*.

The geographic compass of NATO, as specified in the treaty, also is noteworthy. NATO's orbit is Europe and North America, a fact that has been productive of misunderstandings on both sides of the Atlantic.* From the beginning, attempts to "internationalize" NATO by extending its activities beyond the North Atlantic area have been uniformly unsuccessful. During the 1960s, for example, the United States repeatedly failed to gain NATO support for its involvement in Vietnam. Far from viewing the Vietnam conflict as an issue requiring their participation, most of America's Western allies regarded the struggle in Southeast Asia not only as peripheral to their interests but as a threat to the unity and security of the North Atlantic area.

America's obligations under NATO, in the event of an attack against one or more signatories, also require brief elaboration. In reality, the responsibility assumed by the United States under this treaty is unique; the contrast with the terms

---

*Article 6 of the treaty refers to an "armed attack against the parties in Europe or North America" and includes the "Algerian departments of France." Yet even though France's position in Algeria was specifically included in the alliance, during the 1950s Paris had no success in winning the support of its NATO allies for its effort to defeat the Algerian rebels—a fact which undoubtedly prejudiced General de Gaulle against the alliance.

of the SEATO treaty in Asia, for example, is striking. Article 5 of NATO provides that "if such an armed attack occurs, each of them . . . *will* assist the Party or Parties so attacked by taking forthwith, individually and in concert with the other Parties, such action as it deems necessary including the use of armed force, to restore and maintain the security of the North Atlantic area." The language of the treaty thus *requires* the United States to respond to an enemy attack against the NATO area, while leaving the mode of response discretionary. In reality, America's response to aggression against the West has not been in real doubt since World War II. The nature of modern warfare, coupled with the lessons taught by America's involvement in two global conflicts during the twentieth century, have created a de facto obligation upon which the NATO security system is built. Secretary of State Dean Acheson made this clear to the Senate in 1949;[35] Secretary of State John Foster Dulles admitted publicly in 1957 that, if the NATO area were attacked, American forces would almost certainly engage in battle without waiting for a declaration of war by Congress;[36] the same idea was implicit in the "warning" delivered by NATO to the Soviet Union after the crisis in Czechoslovakia in 1968.[37]

In summary then, NATO entailed a profound change in American foreign policy by making clear the determination of the United States to fight beyond its own shores to protect the security of the Atlantic system. And it signified a de facto, if not de jure, alteration in the American constitutional system by notifying potential aggressors that the United States would retaliate instantly, without waiting for a declaration of war, if an attack occurred against its friends in the North Atlantic sphere.

Structure and Organization

NATO's organizational structure reflects the fact that it is a military alliance of independent states, not a supranational body possessing power to coerce its members. The highest decision-making organ is the Council, consisting of civilian representatives (foreign ministers or other ministers of cabinet rank) from the member nations. As the supreme authority, the council decides all major administrative, financial, and general strategy questions coming before the organization. Reflecting the principle of the sovereignty of its

members, the council reaches its decisions on the basis of unanimity.* Normally, the NATO Council meets two or three times annually (although it can of course be summoned into emergency session). Between its meetings, decisions are made at a lower level by the Permanent Representatives (with the rank of ambassador) from the NATO countries. The permanent representatives meet at least once weekly, and sometimes more frequently. As with all parliamentary bodies, the real work of the council is usually performed by its committees (those for Political Affairs, Nuclear Defense Affairs, Economic Affairs, and several others), which study issues in considerable detail, preparing reports and recommendations for the council as a whole.

The chief administrative officer is the Secretary-General, who heads a large staff; he is accountable to the council. The staff in turn consists of several divisions—for Political Affairs, Cultural Affairs, Defense Planning and Policy, Defense Support, and the like—which administer NATO's manifold activities, undertake studies for submission to the council and other organs, and generally seek to achieve the alliance's goals.

The principle of civilian supremacy in NATO decision-making is preserved by making the military command structure accountable to the council. On the military side, the highest organ is the Military Committee, consisting of a high-ranking military officer from each NATO country (usually a member of its national military staff), except France, which withdrew its representation to NATO in 1966–1967. The Military Committee usually holds two meetings each year, although it may meet more frequently. Between its sessions, each nation designates a permanent military representative; these representatives collectively deal with less important military issues and prepare the groundwork for meetings of the Military Committee. The Military Committee has its own integrated staff, headed by a director, which is comparable to the supreme military

---

*The comparable article in the Southeast Asia Treaty (1954) provides simply that an attack against the signatories requires each to "meet the common danger in accordance with its constitutional processes." For the text of this treaty, see Marvin E. Gettleman, *Viet Nam: History, Documents, and Opinions on a Major World Crisis* (New York: Fawcett Publications, 1965) pp. 92–96.

*Throughout his administration (1958–1969), French President Charles de Gaulle expressed his opposition to NATO's *organizational structure*, in contrast to the alliance itself, which France supported and continues to support. Accordingly, de Gaulle "disengaged" France from the varied activities carried out by NATO organs, such as defense planning, economic collaboration among its members, and other forms of cooperation. French ground, sea, and naval forces were "withdrawn" from the NATO command (although, de Gaulle said on several occasions, they would cooperate with NATO in case of an attack against Europe). French representatives were absent from meetings of the NATO Council and other bodies. When de Gaulle ordered NATO installations to be removed from French territory by 1967, NATO headquarters moved to new and more modern quarters in Mons, Belgium. France continued, however, to maintain some links with NATO, by participating in the radar air defense system and stationing a French military "liaison group" at the new headquarters in Mons. See *The New York Times* (January 24, 1969).

staff maintained by most NATO members.

At the operational level, NATO has three "commands" plus a Regional Planning Group. NATO's major ground forces are of course maintained in Europe, as part of the European Command (ACE), under the authority of the Supreme Allied Commander, Europe (SACEUR). After 1967, SACEUR's headquarters were located at Mons, Belgium (Supreme Headquarters Allied Powers, Europe, or SHAPE). The first SACEUR was General Dwight D. Eisenhower, who served until 1952; thereafter, an American general has always been designated SACEUR. Some 1 million troops, together with 4000 aircraft and over 300 naval combat vessels, are available to SACEUR to meet a threat to the security of Europe. The Atlantic Ocean Command (SACLANT), with headquarters in Norfolk, Virginia, is responsible for defending the waters extending from the eastern shores of the United States to the western coast of Europe and Africa. Although it has no naval forces of its own, SACLANT utilizes national forces designated for assignment to NATO for training purposes and in time of war. A smaller Channel Command protects the English Channel and the North Sea, cooperating with SACEUR in air defense. A planning group is concerned with the problem of strengthening the defense of North America, collaborating with the national efforts of the United States and Canada.[38]

Problems and Prospects in the Western Alliance

The year 1969 marked the twentieth anniversary of the North Atlantic Treaty. By many criteria, NATO had made a creditable record during the two decades that had elapsed since its creation. Ironically, what was sometimes referred to as "the NATO crisis" (and, as we shall see more fully below, the crisis in fact involved *several* problems) was in some measure an outgrowth of NATO's very success. The dominant goal of the alliance—preserving the security of the West against Communist aggression—had unquestionably been achieved. The danger of a military thrust by the Warsaw Pact into the NATO area seemed altogether remote. Even the Warsaw Pact's intervention in Czechoslovakia in 1968 did not change that prospect fundamentally. Many of NATO's difficulties after 1949 in fact stemmed from a pervasive feeling on the European continent that NATO was no longer really "needed." After Stalin's death in 1953, Moscow became much more preoccupied with the Middle East, Africa, and other regions outside Europe; the Kremlin showed no disposition to press its demands against Germany to the point of precipitating a military showdown; it accorded its Eastern European satellites a much greater degree of internal freedom; and it revealed a growing apprehension about differences with Red China which led in the

1960s to warfare on the Sino–Soviet border. NATO thus seemed designed to protect against perhaps the *least likely* danger to Western security: a Soviet-instigated attack against Western Europe. NATO's existence over the past twenty years was, however, one reason that the threat to European security had substantially diminished.

Other NATO accomplishments include: creation of a unified defense system for the NATO area; contributions to mutual cooperation in raising living standards; limited progress in promoting political collaborating among the NATO partners (a matter to which we shall return in due course); the significant mitigation of tensions arising among the nations of Western Europe, especially concerning the restoration of Western Germany to a position of influence and acceptance among its European neighbors; and progress in fostering greater regional cooperation by the members of NATO in a variety of nonmilitary activities. The experience gained over two decades by NATO provides many useful lessons for those seeking broader political and economic cooperation among nations in the North Atlantic region.[39]

To acknowledge NATO's achievements, however, is not to disguise the fact that throughout its history the organization has faced—and continues to face—a number of problems. As we have suggested, some of these arise from NATO's success in reducing the military danger to the West. Others are perhaps inherent in any military alliance. Still others grow out of certain realities which have confronted the alliance since its inception—principally, the great disparity between the power of the United States and that of the other NATO allies. During the early and mid-1960s, NATO was referred to widely as a "troubled partnership" and as an alliance whose very future was threatened by "disarray."[40] Until 1969, there was perhaps a tendency (particularly in America) to attribute the NATO crisis to a single source: French President Charles de Gaulle's well-known antipathy toward regional military and other forms of collaboration and his obstructionist tactics within the Western alliance. Under de Gaulle France admittedly did little to strengthen NATO. Yet it would be a mistake to ascribe disunity within the alliance to Gaullist opposition alone. Toward this issue, as toward others, Gaullist behavior was frequently as much a symptom as it was a cause of underlying contentions and unresolved issues. It was noteworthy that many of NATO's problems continued to exist after de Gaulle's retirement from political life.

Since some selectivity is imperative, within limited space let us focus upon three basic problems influencing NATO's effectiveness and internal cohesion since 1949. As we do so, it is necessary to keep in mind the *interdependence* of many of these questions. Progress in securing agreement upon a common NATO defense strategy, for example, will undoubtedly facilitate achieving a consensus upon consultation within NATO on political issues. Similarly, lack of agreement on one fundamental issue will (and has) made the resolution of other issues more difficult.

1. *The Problem of NATO Defense Strategy.* From its inception, NATO has sought to evolve an acceptable set of strategic guidelines capable of meeting a twofold test: They must provide maximum *deterrence* against a military threat to the West; and, if deterrence fails, they must assure the most effective *defense* possible to the NATO members. For obvious reasons, it is infinitely better to *prevent* an attack against the NATO area than to defend against it once aggression has occurred. Throughout the postwar era, the people of Europe have been mindful of a painful reality associated with World War II: The "liberation" of Europe from Axis domination was, in some ways, a more destructive process than initial Axis conquest. Judged by the results since 1949, NATO has been eminently successful in achieving the goal of deterrence. As a NATO publication has expressed it: "Not one square inch of free territory in Europe has fallen under Soviet domination since the signature of the Treaty."[41] Whether because of NATO's efforts or other factors (and developments like de-Stalinization behind the Iron Curtain unquestionably diminished the threat to Europe), concern with Europe's security has diminished considerably during the past two decades.

Nevertheless, one element in the "NATO crisis" during the 1960s was a widespread conviction, particularly in Europe, that Western defense strategy was faulty and was, in many respects, ill adapted to conditions in the contemporary world. Circumstances prevailing at the time of NATO's creation had changed—in some respects drastically; NATO's strategic doctrines had not been correspondingly altered. For example, NATO was founded on the premise that the United States enjoyed a monopoly of nuclear weapons, a condition that was expected to last for several years. Even after the Soviet Union acquired such weapons (beginning in 1949), the United States continued to hold an impressive lead in nuclear armaments. By contrast, Communist forces were superior on the ground; NATO's infantry, armor, and other land contingents (never in fact up to their proposed strength) were no match for the Soviet Red Army, supplemented by forces supplied by the Warsaw Pact.

In the light of these conditions, during the 1950s NATO adopted a military strategy of "the sword and the shield." NATO ground forces supplied the shield. They served the dual purpose of blunting an enemy's initial attack and (sometimes referred to as the "trip wire") alerting Western governments to the threat. Then the NATO "sword"—overwhelming nuclear air and missile power—was to strike against both the source of aggression and hostile armies in the field. The doctrine of the sword and the shield was thus fully compatible with the strategic concept that had guided American military thinking since World War II—massive retaliation against any nation or group of nations undertaking aggression against the free world.

To be effective, the concept of the sword and the shield depended upon several presuppositions. First, it assumed that the United States possessed, and would continue to possess, a commanding superiority in nuclear weapons and methods of delivery. Second, it postulated the idea that massive retaliation against an aggressor was a "credible" response: not only must America be capable of undertaking it, but an enemy must in fact *be convinced that America's nuclear arsenal would be used.* Third, the doctrine of the sword and the shield assumed that aggression against NATO would present itself in a recognizable and unambiguous form, such as the crossing of an international frontier by the armed forces of an enemy state or a coalition bent upon conquest (the crossing of the 38th parallel by Communist forces in Korea in 1950 provided a recent instance of such aggression). Fourth, the concept rested upon the presupposition that invoking it would inflict maximum damage upon the enemy, while incurring minimum damage for the United States and its allies.

By the late 1950s, it had become evident that many of these assumptions were wholly or partially erroneous. After 1949, the Soviet Union forged rapidly ahead in the military aspects of nuclear technology; its first hydrogen bomb was detonated in 1953. Although never attempting to rival the United States in strategic bombers, after launching its Sputnik I in 1957 Moscow took an initial lead in space competition and missile technology. By the end of the decade, many Americans were convinced that a significant "missile gap" had developed in favor of the Soviet Union. The Soviet Union, that is to say, had achieved a level of approximate nuclear parity with the United States; and in some aspects of missile development, it was ahead of America.

These new conditions raised serious questions about the credibility of America's nuclear arsenal —the "sword" of NATO's defense forces. Retaliation against an enemy which lacked nuclear weapons was one prospect; retaliation against a nuclear-armed adversary, was a very different matter. For a nuclear first strike by the United States would almost certainly be answered by a nuclear second strike by the Soviet Union, in which much of America itself would be devastated. When President Charles de Gaulle expressed doubt about the willingness of American officials to "trade" New York City for Paris or Berlin, he was alluding to a dilemma that lay at the heart of the nuclear stalemate between the cold war giants. In a crisis, would the United States use its nuclear power to defend Europe, if the price were the destruction of many American cities and millions of American casualties? At the very least, de Gaulle and other Europeans contended, some threats to the security of Europe might be deemed sufficiently limited or ambiguous to dissuade American officials from pulling the nuclear trigger. Moreover, even if Washington were determined to direct its nuclear-armed missiles and bombers against the Communist world, Moscow might well retaliate with its "second-strike" force *against Western Europe.* Either way, Europe stood to suffer grievously. If America unleashed nuclear war, much of America and Europe would almost inevitably be destroyed; if it did not, then NATO forces would have to defend Europe with conventional weapons against superior ground forces. Neither alternative constituted the kind of defense that was reassuring to Europeans.

If an attack occurred on the NATO area, many Europeans reasoned, the probability was that the United States would *not* use nuclear force against an aggressor. Assurances in Washington to the contrary, critics of the doctrine of massive retaliation pointed to three forces acting as restraints upon American behavior. In the first place, nuclear retaliation by the United States might well mean the destruction of American civilization itself. In the second place, in the two wars in which the United States had been actively involved in the recent period—the Korean and Vietnam conflicts—Washington had carefully refrained from employing nuclear weapons (including even so-called "tactical nuclear weapons"). In Vietnam, it had even been willing to incur a defeat (or what was widely interpreted as a defeat) rather than risk nuclear escalation. In the third place, sentiment in the international community was running heavily against the testing or use of nuclear armaments. America was already the only nation that had actually employed such weapons against an enemy, at the end of World War II. Out of "respect for the decent opinions of mankind," America might hesitate to offend global opinion (especially in the Afro–Asian states) by using its even more destructive nuclear armaments. Convincing or not, such reasoning was widespread in Europe. It was one consideration prompting the government of France (even before de Gaulle became President in 1958) to develop its own nuclear *force de frappe.* In the French view, this admittedly limited force was better than an unreliable American nuclear guarantee of European security.[42]

Awareness of the many limitations inherent in the concept of massive retaliation; Moscow's growing and varied missile capability; the thaw in Russia's relations with the West after Stalin's death; the loosening of the Kremlin's grip upon Eastern Europe; the shift in cold war rivalries from Europe to the developing nations; America's expanding involvement in Southeast Asia; the growth of Soviet seapower, notably in the Mediterranean—these factors coalesced in the early 1960s to produce a fundamental change in NATO defense policies. Instead of massive retaliation, the new slogan became "flexible" or "graduated response" to threats against European security. Initiated by President John F. Kennedy and his Secretary of Defense Robert McNamara, the principle of flexible response was officially adopted by NATO as a whole in 1967. As a NATO publication explains it:

The basis of this concept, which retains the principle of forward defence, is that credible deterrence of military actions of all kinds is necessary, and that this can be secured with a well-balanced mixture of conventional and tactical and strategic nuclear weapons. The purpose of this balance of forces is to permit a flexible range of responses combining two main principles. The first principle is to meet any aggression with direct defence at approximately the same level and the second is to deter through the possibility of escalation. If an attack cannot be contained our response must at least be sufficient to convince the enemy of NATO's determination to resist and to force a pause during which the risks of escalation must be considered.[43]

The doctrine of "graduated response" thus emphasizes several key ideas. NATO is committed to a "forward strategy"—that is, its forces will defend Western Europe as far to the east as possible, in an attempt to limit enemy penetration of the NATO area. Effective implementation of this strategy demands maintenance of large NATO contingents, kept in a high state of military readiness, in a position to defend the alliance's eastern frontiers. In this connection, America's contribution of five combat divisions stationed in Germany (a total of some 225,000 American forces in Europe altogether) is viewed by officials in Washington and other NATO capitals as essential.*

*By the 1970s, the American military commitment to NATO, as in other areas of the world, had come under sharp attack, especially in the Senate. Led by Senator Mike Mansfield (Democrat of Montana), a number of legislators called for a reduction in the American forces stationed in Europe, maintained at an annual cost of approximately $14 billion. Although there was no indication that they would in fact do so, Mansfield and his supporters believed that the NATO countries were able to make a substantially larger commitment to their own defense. Concurrently (with France still playing a limited role in the affairs of NATO), both Britain and Canada were also cutting back their troop commitments on the European continent. The Johnson and Nixon admin-

The doctrine of "graduated response" is also designed to cope with "military actions of all kinds"—ranging from a full-scale nuclear attack against the West to a limited and perhaps non-recurring probe of a NATO defense salient. NATO therefore depends upon a diversified arsenal consisting of conventional (nonnuclear) armaments and tactical and strategic forces. Relying upon a more flexible military capacity, NATO is prepared "to meet any aggression with direct defence at the same level [as the attack itself]"—which means that an attack by conventional forces would be answered by conventional NATO forces; while an enemy employing tactical nuclear weapons could expect to confront NATO defense forces using the same weapons. Theoretically, "the possibility of escalation" would serve as a force tending to hold down the level of violence. Below the nuclear threshold, NATO forces would be strong enough to "force a pause" on the part of an advancing enemy, compelling it to confront the issue squarely: Halt its advance or risk the threat of nuclear devastation against its troops in the field, as well as its homeland. Flexible response thus recognizes that, in the end, aggression against Europe *might* lead to global nuclear war; but it permits several options before that calamity ensues; and it does *not automatically* assume instant nuclear retaliation against an enemy attacking the NATO area.

Several points about this new defense doctrine require comment. It is unquestionably an improvement over the earlier concept of "massive retaliation." It reduces the risk, for example, that the world would be quickly plunged into a nuclear conflict by accident or inadvertence; it affords political leaders (who can communicate on the "hot line" facilities connecting Washington and other NATO capitals with Moscow) time in which to pull back from the nuclear abyss; it opens the possibility that even in Europe, as in Asia, wars may remain limited geographically and in terms of the weapons employed; it goes far toward placing the onus upon the enemy for resorting to nuclear weapons; and it contributes toward relieving

fears in Europe that the Continent would almost certainly be devastated if hostilities erupted in the area.

Yet the concept of flexible response does not dispose of all dilemmas associated with "massive retaliation," and it raises some new controversies of its own. By providing a range of graduated responses to an attack against the NATO area, the new policy permits the United States to postpone a decision to retaliate massively against an aggressor. Ultimately, however, that decision still may have to be faced; and when it is, the old question of whether Washington would be willing to unleash nuclear war will still arise. Would the United States be willing to risk destruction of its own territory, for example, to defend West Germany? And if not, can Western Europe be successfully defended against Communist ground forces?

Another imponderable in the concept of graduated response is the role of tactical nuclear weapons. NATO and Warsaw Pact forces alike are now equipped with artillery, short-range rockets, and other weapons designed to fire nuclear explosives against battlefield targets. Let us suppose that, in accordance with the doctrine of flexible response, NATO faces an attack launched by enemy forces using these new armaments. Since tactical nuclear weapons have never actually been used in warfare, experience furnishes no guidelines about the results to be expected or the general military implications. Nevertheless, several outcomes might reasonably be anticipated. Relying upon the element of surprise, an aggressor might use these weapons with telling effect against NATO forces and installations, blasting a "hole" in Western defenses which its mobile forces would quickly exploit. (Since the Czech crisis of 1968, NATO strategists have concluded that they have much less "warning time" for such a possible attack than they previously supposed.) In the main, damage done by tactical nuclear weapons *would be confined to the NATO area*, since the aggressor would choose the time and place of attack—presumably those most advantageous to itself. The more the enemy penetrated across the NATO defense perimeter, the more Western Europe would be damaged by conflict confined to conventional and tactical weapons; Eastern Europe, the Soviet Union, and the United States would escape devastation. If the enemy advance continued, at some point the President of the United States would have to choose between maintaining the scale of combat at the existing level or escalating it to the level of global nuclear war. In either case, Europe would incur widespread damage; but in the former case, America might escape it. Under graduated response, *at what point* would America decide to use its strategic nuclear power against an enemy? In some ways even more crucially, how would the Kremlin know the conditions under which its behavior might trigger

istrations alike opposed any significant reduction in America's contribution to NATO. High-ranking White House and State Department officials contended that, logistically, such a move would weaken Western defenses (they simply did not agree that adequate American forces could be "airlifted" to Europe in a brief period of time); politically and psychologically, curtailing America's European presence would "destabilize" the situation in Western Europe by suggesting a waning of American interest in the region; and militarily, this step might *compel* Western military planners to use nuclear weapons *immediately* if hostilities erupted on the European continent, thereby returning to the concept of "massive retaliation" as the basic Western defense strategy. Yet, some reduction (largely symbolic, perhaps) in American forces in Europe seemed likely in the near future. See *The New York Times* (January 25, and March 8, 17, and 22, 1970).

global nuclear war?[44] This uncertainty raised the question in the minds of many Europeans of whether graduated response signified that Washington was more reluctant than ever to expose America to destruction for the sake of European security.*

2. *The Problem of "Nuclear Sharing."* Closely related to the matter of NATO defense strategy is a second issue: the problem of "nuclear sharing" among the members of the alliance. Since 1945, the United States had been committed to a rather rigid policy of nuclear secrecy, especially as regards the military applications of nuclear technology. Congressionally imposed restrictions prevented executive policy-makers from giving nuclear weapons to other countries; in Europe and elsewhere, such weapons were kept under the strict control of American officials. Whether to use them was a decision which only the President of the United States could make.

With one exception, the NATO alliance was therefore an inherently unequal partnership. That exception was Great Britain, which had participated with the United States in the development of the atomic bomb during World War II and had shared in many (if not all) aspects of nuclear technology ever since. This situation in large part formed the basis of the "special relationship" between the Anglo-Saxons which General de Gaulle found so objectionable. When the United States declined de Gaulle's request in 1960 for a reorganization of NATO—whereby an Anglo–French–American "directorate" would manage the alliance's affairs—the Fifth Republic became more determined than ever to develop its own nuclear *force de frappe.* Nor would the French government under de Gaulle support efforts by the United States and the Soviet Union to secure an international agreement designed to prevent the proliferation of nuclear weapons to countries not currently possessing them.

Recognizing the existence of discontent within NATO over its nuclear monopoly, the United States took two steps to give its allies a greater voice in decision-making involving nuclear weapons. One was the "two keys" proposal, under which an American officer and an officer from a NATO country in which nuclear installations existed, each held a key required to set in motion the steps required to fire nuclear weapons. Neither official could activate such weapons without the concurrence of the other (in practice, the concurrence of his government). Thus, the nonnuclear NATO partners could exercise a "veto" over their use. The "two keys" scheme, however, did little to change the reality of the power disparities characterizing the alliance. The bulk of America's nuclear arsenal, as its allies were well aware, remained in the United States, under Washington's exclusive control.

A second approach to the problem of nuclear sharing was an outgrowth of the first. Since the two keys idea did not eliminate dissatisfactions within NATO or hinder France from developing its own nuclear deterrent, in 1960 Washington proposed the creation of a "multilateral force" (MLF). This force would consist initially of five American Polaris submarines carrying nuclear warheads (the plan was later enlarged to include surface ships as well), to be manned by "mixed fleets" representing all the NATO members. The ultimate decision to fire nuclear missiles, however, would remain where it had always rested—with the President of the United States. Assuming that Europe moved forward along the path of political and economic unity, in time the MLF could evolve into a "NATO force," comprising a powerful nuclear arsenal, and with decision-making democratized to include all the NATO allies.

The MLF was enthusiastically supported by only one government besides the United States— West Germany. Bonn viewed it as a first step toward achieving nuclear parity with Britain and France and overcoming the limitations on German rearmament. France rejected the MLF outright, while Britain was lukewarm. In addition, the plan encountered opposition from many

---

*In a perceptive study of nuclear strategy, particularly as the problem of nuclear parity in the cold war appeared to the Europeans, Raymond Aron conceded that "graduated response" had several advantages over the older doctrine of "massive retaliation." Yet, for Europeans, the new strategic concept re-enforced certain European anxieties and created new ones. The idea of flexible response "left Europeans more troubled than convinced." Now "the disparity between European and American risks stood out with new clarity." The new strategic doctrine, Aron has pointed out, "does not necessarily coincide with the national interest of Frenchmen and Germans because the primary purpose of the policy is to minimize the risk of a big war that might involve the continental United States at the price of putting up with little wars (little, that is, when viewed from across the ocean), in which only Europeans would be killed." If "graduated response," as Aron argues, left many Europeans dissatisfied with alliance strategy, the basic reason perhaps was that *geography had made America's and Europe's strategic situations basically different.* Europe and the U.S.S.R. occupied an adjacent land mass, from which America was isolated. In this sense, the idea that America and its European allies "were in the same boat" strategically was totally misleading. See Aron's analysis of nuclear strategy in *The Great Debate: Theories of Nuclear Strategy* (Garden City, N.Y.: Doubleday, 1965), pp. 66–99. The concept of graduated response was coupled with another strategic reassessment in the early 1960s, when military planners in America concluded that NATO ground forces *could* successfully counter a Communist attack on land, without resort to nuclear weapons. One study says of this idea: ". . . it seemed to the Europeans that Washington was looking for a way out of its suicide pact with Europe." See Richard J. Barnet and Marcus G. Raskin, *After 20 Years: The Decline of NATO and the Search for a New Policy in Europe* (New York: Random House, 1966), p. 49.

members of the U.S. Congress. Even President Kennedy gradually became skeptical about its advantages. Devising a scheme which provided something other than "a different facade" to disguise the reality of America's nuclear monopoly, Kennedy admitted, "will require a good deal of negotiation and imagination."[45] As the months passed, the MLF was quietly shelved.

Something more than negotiating skill and imagination was needed to solve the problem of nuclear sharing within NATO. A solution required the kind of talents necessary to square the circle! It would be difficult to think of a current problem in American foreign policy containing more contradictory and irreconcilable elements. Washington obviously desired greater cohesion and improved morale within NATO. Yet it also wished to *limit* access to nuclear weapons by states not already possessing them by the end of 1969, even the Soviet Union had subscribed to that objective. And if American officials sought broader consultation within the alliance, they showed no disposition (nor could they under existing legislation) to relinquish America's unilateral control over its nuclear stockpile. True, MLF assumed that *someday* a genuinely integrated NATO force might evolve. But this goal encountered two difficulties tending to counteract its appeal. The appearance of such a force was tied to Europe's progress toward political and economic unification. Moreover, even if a NATO force were ultimately created, it was not clear that all, or even a major portion, of America's nuclear stockpile would pass under its control. If it did not, then America's pre-eminent position within the alliance would remain substantially unaltered.

The problem of "nuclear sharing" was intimately related to another recurrent source of controversy within NATO after 1949: the matter of political consultation and cooperation among the members of the Western alliance.

3. *The Problem of Political Consultation.* In 1966, a group of American citizens concerned about the future of the Atlantic alliance declared that NATO had to be modernized to facilitate greater political and economic unity among its members. Among the steps needed to revitalize the alliance was "joint formulation of policies before they are crystallized and before they reach crisis proportions."[46] Discussing the future of the Atlantic alliance as it entered its third decade, President Nixon declared early in 1969: "The United States fully intends to undertake deep and genuine consultation with its allies, both before and during any negotiations directly affecting their interests."[47]

These statements are only two examples of the concern among members of NATO about the lack of progress achieved by consultation among the allies, particularly in realms outside the problem of Western military security. If NATO was in a state of actual or potential disarray, a major reason was that during the first twenty years of its existence its members had shown little disposition to concert their policies toward a variety of international issues. By this standard, NATO seemed in many respects less cohesive in 1970 than it was in 1950.

Evidence of such disunity was not lacking. France under General de Gaulle was dedicated to achieving greater independence in French policy-making. The cultivation of closer ties with Eastern Europe, General de Gaulle's repeated overtures to the "third world," Paris' attempt to improve relations with the Arab world during and after the Middle East crisis of 1967—such steps reminded the other NATO partners of the disunity in the West on major political questions. For many years, Britain and Spain had been engaged in an acrimonious dispute over the future of Gibralter. Greece and Turkey remained in disagreement—sometimes approaching violent conflict—over Cyprus. As the most powerful member of the alliance, the United States had bypassed or neglected NATO in its approach to several global issues. As early as the Korean War in 1950, President Truman ordered a unilateral American military commitment to defend South Korea; NATO's contribution to Korean defense in the months that followed was marginal. In perhaps the most dangerous Soviet–American confrontation in the postwar period—the Cuban missile crisis of 1962 —the NATO partners were informed *only after the decision had been reached.*[48] From the early 1960s onward, officials in Washington expanded the American commitment in Southeast Asia. Insofar as the NATO allies were consulted at all about these moves, American policy-makers endeavored (with very little success) to convince them to recognize the Vietnam conflict as "their war" and to expand their contribution to the defense of freedom in Southeast Asia.[49]

A Gaullist criticism of NATO, shared widely throughout Europe, was that after 1949 the alliance faced conditions basically different from those prevailing two decades earlier. On this basis, France derogated NATO's importance and withdrew from its formal organizational structure, a move having little appeal for the other European members of the alliance. Rather than abandon NATO, the other members desired to revitalize it and to make it more responsive to contemporary conditions. Accordingly, during the late 1960s the members of the alliance undertook a detailed self-study, with a view toward making NATO a more viable instrument of Western collaboration. The result was the Harmel Report (named for the Belgian Foreign Minister Pierre Harmel). After detailed consideration, this report was adopted by all 15 members of the alliance (including France) at the end of 1967.

The Harmel Report endeavored to steer a middle course between two extremes: the ideas of those who called for greatly increased cooperation on political questions, leading perhaps to a "NATO decision" toward them; and those (like France) who believed that the lessened danger to Western Europe reduced NATO's importance and left greater scope for more independent diplomatic and political initiatives. As it approached its twentieth anniversary, the Harmel Report declared, NATO had a twofold objective: "military strength and political solidarity." The report underscored the latter as a particularly urgent requirement. A number of outstanding political questions—from the standpoint of European stability, the paramount one being the future of Germany—continued to foment discord within the alliance and weaken its military efforts. Success in resolving these political issues was contingent upon a cold war *détente* between the United States and the Soviet Union; hence NATO should use its influence to bring about more amicable Soviet–American relations and to create an environment within which issues like the German problem could finally be resolved. Acknowledging that NATO still consisted of independent nations, the Harmel Report proposed no supranational mechanism for harmonizing political decisions among its members; nor did it specifically provide new mechanisms whereby the goal of greater political cooperation could be achieved. Yet (accepting a long-standing American position) it emphasized the idea that problems within NATO did not exist in geographic isolation; crises arising in Asia, the Middle East, or other areas could and did affect NATO's future. The alliance's cohesion could be strengthened by "frank and timely consultations" among its members before their national governments reached decisions on major policy questions. In an obvious effort to conciliate France, the report did not propose the formulation of common "NATO policies" toward political issues likely to engender controversy among the partners.

Although considerable time would be required before the effects of the Harmel Report could be fairly judged, early indications were that it had done little to change the nature of the alliance fundamentally. French attitudes toward NATO in the post-Gaullist era, for example, had not perceptibly altered. American policy-makers showed no particular inclination to consult NATO before making important decisions in Southeast Asia. Perhaps the case for greater consultation within NATO rested upon a premise that was at least questionable: that more frequent and better discussions among the fifteen nations belonging to NATO would produce a *consensus* among them on outstanding political questions. In some cases, at least, the lack of consultation was symptomatic of the fact that basic policy differences existed among the Western governments which no amount of formal or informal discussion among them was likely to disguise.[50]

POLITICAL UNIFICATION IN THE NORTH ATLANTIC AREA

In 1948, a committee of the Hague Congress on European unity observed that:

Judged from any standpoint—political, economic or cultural—it is only by uniting herself that Europe can overcome her immediate difficulties and go forward to fulfill her mission for the future. . . . It is impossible to keep problems of economic collaboration and defense separate from those of general political policy.

Successful implementation of joint economic or military policies, the committee was convinced, required sooner or later "the renunciation or, to be more accurate, the joint exercise of certain sovereign powers."[51]

The dream of a politically unified Europe is as old as history. The list of illustrious personages advocating this ideal—Dante, Pope Leo X, Erasmus, Grotius, Thomas More, Sully, Fichte, Kant, Mazzini, Churchill, to list but a few—testifies to the importance and durability of the idea. Yet down to World War II, the idea of European political unification was a dream espoused chiefly by intellectuals. The same historical forces that engendered extensive economic and military collaboration among nations in the North Atlantic community—Soviet hegemony over the heartland of Eurasia; the decline of England, France, and Germany as great powers; Europe's early postwar economic debilitation and military vulnerability; the continuing challenge posed by expansive Communism—convinced Western policy-makers that political unification must at least be postulated as an ultimate goal, if indeed in some spheres it was not an urgent necessity.

Such convictions have spawned a profusion of often highly varied plans, institutions, and approaches whose professed goal is political unification. More often than not, several movements and organizations simultaneously embraced this goal; frequently, there was little coordination among their efforts. The results were that, paradoxically, proponents of European "unity" were in danger of jointly creating highly disunified and competing efforts, that in some ways vastly complicated the task of finding common ground among advocates of the same goal. In the space available, we may focus only upon the more important tendencies and developments in the recent period.

The Council of Europe

In March, 1948, the French National Assembly called for the creation of a European constituent assembly to lay the basis for a European federation. Accordingly, on May 5, 1949, the Council of Europe came into existence, with its headquarters at Strasbourg. From ten original members, the council ultimately expanded to seventeen, making it the largest body on the Continent concerned with political and economic integration (except for the OECD). Unlike NATO, the Council of Europe contained several "neutrals" (e.g., Austria and Ireland), which took no formal part in Western defense activities.

From the beginning, the Council of Europe has mirrored, more than it has overcome, disunity on the European continent. It has been torn between those seeking an "organic" unification of Europe in which national sovereignty would be significantly reduced, and the "functionalists" who desire cooperation among the European nations in limited areas of activity. It has been weakened by the division between the EEC and EFTA and by the internal disagreements within NATO over regional defense policies. Created as an organ to promote the political integration of Europe, the council has drifted away from this objective toward more attainable and immediately useful goals. If it has not been successful in achieving its original purpose, it has nonetheless made several useful contributions. Its most constructive service perhaps has been as a convenient and prestigious platform from which to "keep alive" the ideal of European unity. It has sometimes played a valuable role in coordinating the activities of regional organizations within Europe; it has performed useful functions in social, cultural, and legal spheres. And—in what is surely one of the landmarks of contemporary international law—it established the European Court and the Commission of Human Rights.[*][52]

The Rise and Fall of EDC

The urgency of the Communist threat, and the implementation of the American "containment" policy to counter it in the late 1940s, induced American policy-makers to modify early postwar policy toward defeated Germany. NATO, American defense planners became convinced, could never defend Europe from Communist aggression without substantial contributions from West Germany; and this contribution could only be made if the Allied occupation of Germany were terminated. Yet, American officials were keenly aware of the existence of deep-seated apprehensions among the European allies to this step. The minimum necessity was a new agreement on Germany rendering it impossible for a revived, rearmed Germany to embark upon the path of *revanche*. The lessons of history and geographical proximity understandably made France more apprehensive about the dangers involved than was generally true of other European societies. Many Frenchmen, in fact, feared a rearmed Germany infinitely more than an expansive Communist bloc.[53]

Efforts to reconcile American insistence upon German rearmament with European misgivings about the move led to the signing on May 27, 1952, of an agreement to establish a European Defense Community (EDC). Although its immediate goal was to terminate the Allied occupation of Germany and to provide for German participation in NATO, EDC was widely regarded as the forerunner of an emergent European political union.

Except in one sense, EDC is now of historic interest only. As, one by one, its signatories ratified the agreement, with the strong encouragement of the United States, its fate finally rested with the French National Assembly. Ironically, it had been to mollify French misgivings that EDC had sought to restrict West Germany's future military power and to assure that it could never again threaten the peace of Europe or the world. Yet after a long and acrimonious debate—in the course of which Secretary of State Dulles was led to threaten Europe with an "agonizing reappraisal" of American relations with Europe if EDC failed—on August 30, 1954, the French Assembly rejected the agreement. This act brought American–European relations to perhaps their lowest point in the postwar era.[54] The defeat of EDC, it had become apparent by the 1960s, did however highlight certain fundamental divergencies among the Western allies concerning the scope and nature of any agreement contemplating the ultimate surrender of national sovereignty to a supranational political institution. As we shall see, many of the issues that explained the demise of EDC reappeared several years later when the United States and its European partners debated other approaches designed to impart greater political unity to the North Atlantic community.

The Western European Union

French rejection of EDC did not deter the United States from its objective of lifting most of the war-

*Under the auspices of the Council of Europe, the nations of Western Europe agreed to a European Convention for the Protection of Human Rights and Fundamental Freedoms; the Convention was signed in Rome in 1950. To implement the Convention, three organs— a Committee of Ministers, the European Commission of Human Rights, and the European Court of Human Rights—play a role. For more detailed discussion, see Michael Curtis, *Western European Integration* (New York: Harper & Row, 1965), pp. 41–45; and Philip E. Jacob and Alexine L. Atherton, *The Dynamics of International Organization* (Homewood, Ill.: Dorsey Press, 1965), pp. 593–602.

time restrictions imposed upon Germany and of gaining its participation in Western defense efforts. Accordingly, on October 23, 1954, the Western occupation of Germany was terminated. Concurrently, the signatories of the Brussels Treaty of 1948 (France, Belgium, Luxembourg, the Netherlands, and the United Kingdom), invited Italy and Germany to join this defense agreement, to which were appended protocols specifying limitations upon German rearmament. These prohibited Bonn from manufacturing chemical, biological, or nuclear weapons, long-range bombers and missiles, or large naval vessels. A separate body—the Agency for the Control of Armaments—was set up to supervise compliance with this new treaty.[55] This agreement, creating the Western European Union, was made possible by an offer that might have allayed earlier French misgivings about EDC: a British commitment to station its military forces *permanently* on the European continent, marking a radical departure from Britain's historic policy of "splendid isolation."

The Political Future of EEC

From the beginning, the European Economic Community anticipated the ultimate political merger of its members, at least respecting those matters affecting the economic well-being of the Common Market area. As one commentator has observed: "What lifts the Community far above the importance of a common economic effort— great as that is—is the basic political aim of many influential statesmen of the constituent nations." EEC thus must be viewed as "the first stage in the building of a genuine United States of Europe."[56]

After witnessing the progress made by EEC in creating supranational cooperation among its members, one commentator observed: "Today, Europe is no longer only an idea, but an institution—a *political community* which not only disposes of formidable and ever-growing power, but which already possesses the basic structure necessary to form the government of a new European federal state." This is, at any rate, the judgment of those who favor European political unification and believe that EEC offers the most promising avenue to date for achieving it.[57]

Such confidence is far from unwarranted. As our earlier treatment of the economic progress made by EEC emphasized, gains by the organization since its establishment have been impressive. Its accomplishments in the economic sphere aside, it has also gone far toward translating the goal of political cooperation among "the six" into reality. In instance after instance, the members of EEC have avoided pitfalls capable of destroying the whole experiment and perhaps of triggering a new wave of nationalist competition among the nations of Europe. Even during the crisis of the mid-1960s (when France under General de Gaulle all but seceded from the organization), EEC managed to arrive at a consensus which enabled necessary decisions to be made. Blending both national and supranational elements, the three "communities" forming EEC, as David P. Calleo has observed, have "posed an ideal that has appealed to many powerful interests, and permanently affected the drive to unite Europe."[58] Thus far, experience with EEC gives encouragement to those who believe that effective supranational cooperation in one important sphere—in this case, the economic—will "spill over" into other spheres, providing an irresistible momentum for expanded *political* cooperation among the European nations. In this view a threefold sequence can be envisioned: EEC as presently constituted will prove the feasibility of greater political integration among "the six"; in time, the European Free Trade Area will disappear and its members (possibly with other European countries) will join a greatly enlarged EEC, further extending the scope of supranational political collaboration; finally, an "Atlantic community" will be created when the United States and Canada join with the nations of Europe in a new regional organization dedicated to political, economic, and other forms of supranational cooperation among its members.

Without derogating EEC's accomplishments, it is not amiss to suggest certain inadequacies in the "spillover" theory of European (and eventually Atlantic) political unification. As with all theories of automatic progress, this one tends to assume an inevitability about developments that takes little account of future contingencies and that reduces the nations concerned to passive objects having little control over their political destinies. The theory often tends to confuse the European commitment to political unification *as an abstract ideal*, to which nearly all groups on the Continent (not excluding Gaullists) subscribe, and as *an operating principle of national policy-making*. There is considerably less evidence, for example, that the success of EEC has resulted in any appreciable "spillover" into the latter realm. Calleo has cautioned: "It can be argued persuasively that the Common Market, by strengthening the economies of the members, has increased their means of political independence."[59] Another recent study of EEC, focusing upon the organization's relations with the outside world, concludes that thus far "the six" have "had serious difficulties in finding agreement on the extent and substance of common external policies." In the crucial area of foreign affairs, experience has shown "the persistent inclination of individual member states to pursue independently their own foreign policy goals rather than to submit to common procedures and common objectives under Community auspices."[60] It was perhaps more than coincidence that, at a time when EEC was achieving noteworthy economic gains, NATO was in a state of "disarray," leading some groups in Europe and America to question its future. During the latter part of the 1960s, Franco–German relations had deteriorated markedly although those two countries signed a treaty of friendship early in 1963. After that date, Bonn and Paris disagreed fundamentally on cooperation with the United States in NATO, on the prospects for German reunification, on Britain's admission to EEC, and on a host of other questions.[61] Fashionable as it was (especially in America) to attribute these disagreements to the personality and inimitable style of General de Gaulle, the French President may merely have identified *publicly* certain sources of disagreement among the nations of Europe which advocates of political unification chose to ignore or to assume somehow would be dissolved by the solvent of universal commitment to an ideal. De Gaulle's plan for a *Union des Patries* (a union of fatherlands) evoked very little support either in Europe or in America. To many commentators, it seemed indistinguishable from the kind of nationalism which EEC and other forms of regional integration were designed to surmount. Yet two points need to be made about de Gaulle's idea. First, the French President repeatedly expressed his support for the *ultimate goal* of European regional cooperation; in his view, a *Union des Patries* was an attempt to reach it by accepting the existence of strong national loyalties as a starting point. As even some of de Gaulle's detractors recognized, his scheme had the virtue of honestly facing the fact that very little political consensus actually existed among the nations of the West. Second, de Gaulle's plan accepted the reality that the key to European political cooperation was *concurrence of the national governments involved.* At every step, the nations of Europe would have to be convinced that their interests were served by supranational cooperation; they had to believe that their interests would be promoted, not jeopardized, by relinquishing national sovereignty. To the extent that they were so convinced, a true and lasting "community" might evolve. It was likely to be neither genuine nor durable, however, as long as the fact of national loyalties, and of conflicting national goals, was evaded.

The United States and "Atlantic Partnership"

Early in 1964, Secretary of State Dean Rusk observed that: "Until Western Europe attains a substantial degree of political unity, it is unlikely to make a contribution to world leadership commensurate with its resources." Rusk went on to add that, thus far, policy coordination is much further advanced in the spheres of economics and defense than in that of political action; he urged "all of the Atlantic nations—including the United States" to "improve their performance in seeking common lines of policy and action." Otherwise, the Western partners would "frustrate one another's efforts all over the world"[62]

Another former American diplomatic official, ex-Under Secretary of State George W. Ball, has written that a dominant theme of modern history is the European "civil war," of which the two great world wars of the twentieth century were but a part. For some four centuries, this "dramatic cycle of rivalry" destroyed one European empire after another and contributed to the emergence of both the Soviet and Chinese threats to Western civilization. Only European unity could avert a new disaster. In Ball's view, "the logic of European unity was inescapable" and "sooner or later Europe will unite."[63] From the time that advocates of European unification seriously proposed supranational cooperation after World War II, Ball has written, American officials "were firmly convinced that a united Europe would be stronger and less dangerously unstable and no longer a seedbed of war."[64]

By the 1960s, official thinking in the United States had extended the idea of European unity to the broader concept of "Atlantic partnership," presumably embracing the European and North American continents. Thus, one high State Department official stated in 1962: "We have regarded a united Europe as a condition to the development of an effective Atlantic partnership." In mid-1962, President Kennedy observed that the United States visualized a united Europe as "a partner with whom we could deal on a basis of full equality in all the great and burdensome tasks of building and defending a community of free nations." He added: "The first order of business is for our European friends to go forward in forming the more perfect union which will some day make this partnership possible." At some future time, Kennedy pledged, the United States would be ready for a "Declaration of Interdependence," that would afford the basis for discussion of "ways and means of forming a concrete Atlantic partnership . . . between the new union now emerging in Europe and the old American Union. . . . Let the world know it is our goal."[65]

American foreign policy toward postwar Europe has thus been consistent in its endorsement of European—and, in recent years, Atlantic—cooperation, leading in time to substantial political and economic unity. It has been much less clear and consistent on either the reasons why this goal was beneficial or the means best designed to achieve it. As the material in this chapter has emphasized, the impulse toward regional collaboration in Europe has taken a variety of forms since World War II; the very proliferation of regional bodies on the European scene has itself posed something of an obstacle to effective supranational cooperation.

One explanation of this phenomenon was that fundamental disagreement existed among advocates of the goal concerning the precise course regional integration ought to take. Did European, and eventually Atlantic, unification envision *organic unity,* with common political institutions having power to make binding decisions upon member nations? If so, this dream was likely to go unfulfilled for many decades to come; its advocacy would seem to be mere utopianism. Or, did European (and later, Atlantic) unity contemplate a much looser *federation* (or confederation), in which substantial power, except perhaps in economic and defense matters, would be reserved to the member states? The prospect of achieving this more limited goal also seemed remote for the immediate future.

Less important than the precise form of future supranational cooperation perhaps was the issue of the distribution of power within the proposed "Atlantic community." The official American view was simple: A true Atlantic community could only come into being after the non-Communist states of Europe had formed a political union. After that—according to what was sometimes referred to as the "dumbbell scheme"—an Atlantic partnership could be created as a "community of equals," by a merger between the United States and Canada on one side, and a united Europe on the other. The new political entity would, so to speak, consist of two senior partners, instead of one senior partner and several, much less influential, junior partners. Thus, without a previously united Europe, the idea of Atlantic community was likely to prove abortive and unappealing.[66]

To many Europeans, however, such logic was less than totally convincing. As long as the United States retained its commanding lead in nuclear weapons, leaving it the strongest power in the Western alliance, it could be wondered whether the two ends of the "dumbbell" could ever be truly equal, or even approximately so. For equality to exist, America might have to encourage a united Europe to develop its own nuclear force— a kind of European *force de frappe.* However, this move would conflict with the American and Soviet goal of preventing the "proliferation" of nuclear weapons and their interest in an international agreement toward that end. Alternatively, the United States would have to give Europeans an effective share of control over American nuclear armaments; this course would violate statutory prohibitions and encounter outspoken opposition in the American Congress. To date, there has been little tendency among American officials to follow either course—or even to acknowledge that the dilemma exists at the heart of the problem of "Atlantic community."

Europeans have also pointed out that, by insisting upon European unification as a prerequisite for Atlantic partnership, the United States puts the onus for the lack of progress upon its Allies. In effect, the American position seems to be: To achieve an Atlantic community, *the Europeans must act boldly and imaginatively.* Europe must eschew narrow nationalism and must forego its historic rivalries for the sake of the common goal. Meanwhile, Europeans ask, what sacrifices are Americans prepared to make to achieve what would unquestionably become the most promising step toward supranational cooperation in modern history? The kind of "boldness" demanded of Europeans does not always have its counterpart in American behavior. Demands in Congress that America *reduce* its military commitment to NATO; American unilateralism in going to the brink of war in Cuba in 1962; the periodic reassertion of "protectionist" sentiment within the United States on tariff and trade issues; the unwillingness of Washington, during both the Korean and Vietnam conflicts, to admit the Allies to military decision-making—such moves did not impress Europeans with a sense of America's willingness to transcend nationalism or relinquish its own sovereignty.

Moreover, a tacit premise of American policy toward the issue of Atlantic partnership has been that the movement toward greater political and economic unification would result in *greater unanimity* among the nations of the West on major international issues. Instead of "NATO in disarray," a unified Atlantic community would arrive at *common positions* toward a variety of global issues. In one sense, of course, this correlation was reasonable enough. It could be logically contended that if the nations of the West can successfully resolve the multitudinous problems associated with political unification, then they ought to be able to arrive at a consensus toward many lesser issues tending to elicit controversy. The argument is, however, more plausible than convincing. It assumes that the most difficult problem— the reallocation of political power, involving inevitable diminution of national sovereignty— can and will be disposed of before less fundamental questions, like "nuclear sharing" within NATO or common positions toward the security of Southeast Asia. In the improbable event that this occurs, it still does not follow that consensus will appear within an Atlantic community. As Henry A. Kissinger has pointed out in connection with disunity within NATO: "The American historical experience causes our policy-makers to be reluctant to admit that the process of consultation may have objective limits." Down to the 1960s, at any rate, the experience of the American society encouraged the view that "all problems are soluble through goodwill and a willingness to compromise"; Americans are prone to believe that "agreement is sure to emerge if the interested parties gather around a table."[67] Certain other American habits of mind, discussed at length in

Chapter 2—like faith in legal documents and institutional procedures as means for producing agreement among the nations of the world—are also worth recalling in our discussion of the matter of Atlantic community.

As the postwar record of the United Nations amply suggests, legal documents, procedures for maximizing consultations among nations, and established machinery *may or may not* produce a consensus on major policy issues and a sense of *true community*. It is at least an open question whether there is a greater consensus among the members of the UN today than in 1950. Admittedly, the analogy has its imperfections. The degree of heterogeneity prevailing among the members of the UN greatly exceeds that existing among the nations of the West. Difficult as it might be to define precisely, "Western culture" clearly has a number of unifying elements, like the Judeo–Christian tradition, which are lacking in an international organization. The example of the UN is cited merely to underscore the idea that true community and unanimity of opinion are not *automatically* engendered by documents like the UN Charter or by new institutional patterns. Indeed, as political philosophers since antiquity have been aware, the successful operation of political institutions and processes at all levels of society may well depend upon *the prior existence* of a sense of community and shared values. Such institutions are likely to receive public support to the extent that they contribute to the well-being, and promote the interests of, the groups and societies concerned.

A final problem regarding the goal of Atlantic unity requires brief attention. The case for greater political and economic cooperation among the nations of the West rests upon another implicit premise that needs to be be made explicit and examined critically. In the "dumbbell scheme," North America would someday join with a united Europe to form an Atlantic partnership. The Europe involved in this process of course consists of those nations outside the Communist zone. The "dumbbell scheme," that is to say, *presupposes the permanent division of the European continent.* In this connection, it is worth remembering that when the United States proposed the European Recovery Program in 1947–1948, Soviet Russia and the smaller Communist nations were invited to participate; the invitation was refused. One reason Washington made the offer, however, was that the United States did not want to bear the responsibility for dividing Europe permanently.[68] In the years that followed, American officials repeatedly condemned the division of Europe by the Iron Curtain as unnatural and temporary. The partition of the German nation epitomized the problem. [Time and again, the United States and West Germany insisted that the reunification of Germany

was a key to lasting stability in Europe and perhaps the leading requirement for a true cold war *détente.* Proposals for Atlantic partnership thus collide with this long-standing goal. In the absence of German reunification—and, more broadly, a "normalization" in the relationships among all the European nations—the concept of Atlantic community might prolong the division of Europe indefinitely and make a resolution of cold war differences infinitely more difficult.[

NOTES

1. This is the theme of the new book by former Under Secretary of State George W. Ball, *The Discipline of Power* (Boston: Atlantic–Little, Brown, 1968). See esp. pp. 29–169.
2. Quoted in Julius W. Pratt, *A History of United States Foreign Policy* (Englewood Cliffs, N.J.: Prentice-Hall, 1955), p. 168.
3. *Ibid.,* p. 169.
4. *Ibid.,* pp. 169–173.
5. *Ibid.,* pp. 527–528.
6. D. F. Fleming, *The United States and the World Court* (Garden City, N.Y.: Doubleday, 1945).
7. George F. Kennan, "The Sources of Soviet Conduct," *Foreign Affairs* 25 (July, 1947), 556–583. Although widely regarded as the "author" of the containment policy, Kennan later denied its authorship, indicating several respects in which he did not subscribe to the doctrine, particularly as it became a *global military* response to the Communist challenge. See his *Memoirs* (New York: Bantam, 1969), pp. 373–388.
8. For a penetrating analysis of the deficiencies of the doctrine of containment, many of which were clearly illustrated in time, see Walter Lippmann, *The Cold War* (New York: Harper & Row, 1957).
9. *Congressional Record,* Vol. 93, 1980–1981.
10. See William A. Brown and Redvers Opie, *American Foreign Assistance* (Washington, D.C.: Brookings Institution, 1953), p. 175.
11. House Foreign Affairs Committee, *Hearings on the Mutual Security Act of 1957,* 88th Congress, 1st Session, 1957, p. 24.
12. Text of the President's budget message in *The New York Times* (January 22, 1964).
13. U.S. Department of State, *American Foreign Policy, 1950–1955,* General Foreign Policy Series, No. 117, vol. I, p. 1442. This publication and the volumes issued periodically in the series provide an invaluable collection of materials on American foreign policy.
14. *Idem.*
15. Senate Foreign Relations Committee, *Legislation on Foreign Relations,* 85th Congress, 1st Session, 1957, p. 5.
16. *United States in World Affairs: 1951* (New York: Harper & Row, 1952), p. 215.
17. *United States in World Affairs: 1955* (New York: Harper & Row, 1956), p. 79.
18. For a more detailed discussion of the OECD,

see Michael Curtis, *Western European Integration* (New York: Harper & Row, 1965), pp. 57–70.

19. Walter Hallstein, *United Europe* (Cambridge, Mass.: Harvard University Press, 1963), p. 12.
20. *Ibid.*, p. 13.
21. Quoted in *ibid.*, p. 17.
22. Émile Benoit, *Europe at Sixes and Sevens: The Common Market, the Free Trade Association, and the United States* (New York: Columbia University Press, 1961), pp. 17–19; and Curtis, *op. cit.*, pp. 224–237. See also *The New York Times* (June 12, 1965; October 25 and November 20, 1966; and January 15, 1967).
23. See *The New York Times* (January 15, 1968). Current data on developments and economic progress within the EEC and other regional organizations in Europe are provided conveniently in the annual volumes of *The Europa Year Book* (London: Europa Publications).
24. *The New York Times* (March 10, 1967; January 13, 15, and 19, 1969).
25. For further discussion of the institutions and internal procedures of the EEC, see Curtis, *op. cit.*, pp. 155–174; and Werner Feld, *The European Common Market and The World* (Englewood Cliffs, N.J.: Prentice-Hall, 1967), pp. 23–31. A lengthy analysis of decision-making within the EEC is Hartley Clark, *The Politics of the Common Market* (Englewood Cliffs, N.J.: Prentice-Hall, 1967), pp. 1–130.
26. General de Gaulle's somewhat enigmatic views on supranationalism within Europe are dealt with in Roy C. Macridis, *De Gaulle: Implacable Ally* (New York: Harper & Row, 1966), pp. 155–168. This is a useful compendium of excerpts from de Gaulle's writings and speeches. See also Alexander Werth, *De Gaulle* (New York: Simon and Schuster, 1966), pp. 305–354.
27. Gaullist opposition to the EEC during the early and mid-1960s led to a "crisis" within the organization and an evident slowdown in its forward momentum. See *The New York Times* (January 2, 21 and 26, 1966; December 11, 1968).
28. *The Europa Year Book: 1969* pp. 210–216. Current data on progress within EFTA and developments affecting its future are provided in this series.
29. An informative brief analysis of EFTA is Jon McLin, "EFTA: Condemned to Live," in *American Universities Field Staff Report*, vol. IV (January, 1969), pp. 1–9. See also *The New York Times* (January 21, May 14, and December 31, 1966; October 27, 1967; and January 15, 1969.
30. For General de Gaulle's speech vetoing Great Britain's request for membership in the EEC, see "Major Addresses, Statements and Press Conferences of General Charles de Gaulle: May 19, 1958–January 31, 1964," (New York: Press and Information Division, Embassy of France, 1964), pp. 208–223.
31. See the discussion of General de Gaulle's press conference in *The New York Times* (November 28, 1967).
32. British views on the EEC during the 1960s are discussed in *The New York Times* (January 22 and 24, March 2, March 9, March 17, and October 25, 1967; January 15, 1968; and January 13, 1969). A more detailed analysis of the issues posed by Britain's bid for membership, expressing many reservations about the advantages of the move, is George E. G. Catlin, *The Atlantic Commonwealth* (Baltimore: Penguin, 1969).
33. U.S. Department of State, *American Foreign Policy, 1950–1955, op. cit.*, vol. I, pp. 819–820.
34. See the viewpoints of President Nixon as set forth in the speech by Secretary of State William Rogers, "U.S. Foreign Policy: Some Major Issues," *Department of State Bulletin* **LX** (April 14, 1969), 309.
35. Department of State, *American Foreign Policy, 1950–1955, op. cit.*, vol. I, pp. 822, 835.
36. Hugh Sidey, *John F. Kennedy: President* (New York: Atheneum, 1963), p. 184.
37. Following the Warsaw Pact invasion of Czechoslovakia, NATO issued "a warning" to the Communist countries concerning threats to the security of Europe. Secretary of State Dean Rusk declared that the future security of Yugoslavia and Austria (which were not members of NATO) were of direct concern to the Western alliance. See *The New York Times* (November 16 and 17, 1968).
38. See *NATO Handbook* (Brussels, Belgium: NATO Information Service, 1968), pp. 7–19.
39. For a more detailed discussion of NATO accomplishments, see the symposium in *Atlantic Community* 7 (Spring, 1969), particularly the article by Richard J. Wallace, "This Is the Twentieth Anniversary Year," pp. 11–17.
40. Detailed examinations of problems within NATO during this period may be found in Henry A. Kissinger, *The Troubled Partnership* (Garden City, N.Y.: Doubleday, 1966); and Alastair Buchan, *NATO in the 1960s: The Implications of Interdependence*, rev. ed. (New York: Praeger, 1963).
41. See *The NATO Handbook* (Paris, France: NATO Information Service, 1965), p. 19.
42. Critical appraisals of the doctrine of massive retaliation, focusing upon its limitations, are contained in Henry A. Kissinger, *Nuclear Weapons and Foreign Policy*, rev. ed. (New York: Norton, 1969), *passim;* and Morton W. Halperin, *Contemporary Military Strategy* (Boston: Little, Brown, 1967), pp. 48–50, 102–104.
43. *Aspects of NATO: Defense Policy* (Brussels, Belgium: NATO Information Service, 1969), p. 10.
44. The concept of "flexible response" and its implications are dealt with in Buchan, *op. cit.*, pp. 27–42; and Halperin, *op. cit.*, pp. 14–32.
45. The origins of, and reactions to, the MLF proposal are discussed in Theodore C. Sorensen, *Kennedy* (New York: Harper & Row, 1965),

pp. 567–569; see also Ball, *op. cit.*, pp. 198–220.

46. *The New York Times* (July 19, 1966).

47. See "Address by President Nixon," *Department of State Bulletin* **LX** (April 28, 1969), 353.

48. Although they received no advance warning of President Kennedy's decision to go to the brink of war over the installation of Soviet missiles in Cuba, Theodore Sorensen has written, the NATO allies "did not flinch or complain." See his *Kennedy, op. cit.*, p. 705. Yet many Europeans believed that the absence of consultation within NATO underscored Europe's "dependence" on America and the fact that, in a crisis, Europe could be devastated because of a decision made in Washington. See Raymond Aron, *The Great Debate: Theories of Nuclear Strategy* (Garden City, N.Y.: Doubleday, 1965), pp. 160–164.

49. See, for example, Secretary of State Dean Rusk's speech to NATO at the end of 1965, in *The New York Times* (December 13 and 15, 1965); and *Documents on American Foreign Relations: 1965* (New York: Harper & Row, 1966), pp. 85–86.

50. For a detailed discussion of this point, see Henry A. Kissinger, "What Kind of Atlantic Partnership," *Atlantic Community* 7 (Spring, 1969), 18–38. The Harmel Report is discussed in "The Future Tasks of the Alliance," Mons, Belgium: North Atlantic Treaty Organization, 1968).

51. Quoted in F. C. S. Northrop, *European Union and United States Foreign Policy* (New York: Macmillan, 1954), pp. 6–7.

52. For further information on the Council of Europe, see Curtis, *op. cit.*, pp. 29–47.

53. Northrop, *op. cit.*, p. 163.

54. The viewpoints of the Eisenhower adminis-

tration on the EDC are presented in Dwight D. Eisenhower, *Mandate for Change: 1953–1956* (Garden City, N.Y.: Doubleday, 1963), pp. 395–409.

55. Department of State, *American Foreign Policy, 1950–1955, op. cit.*, pp. 978–984.

56. Robert Heilbroner, *Forging a United Europe: The Story of the European Economic Community,* Public Affairs Pamphlet no. 308 (New York: Public Affairs Press, 1961), pp. 3–5.

57. David P. Calleo, *Europe's Future: The Grand Alternatives* (New York: Norton, 1967), p. 45. Italics inserted.

58. *Ibid.*, p. 46.

59. *Ibid.*, p. 64.

60. Werner Feld, *The European Common Market and the World* (Englewood Cliffs, N.J.: Prentice-Hall, 1967), p. 161.

61. This disagreement is analyzed in detail in F. Roy Willis, *France, Germany and the New Europe: 1945–1967*, rev. ed. (London: Oxford University Press, 1968), pp. 312–365.

62. Text of Secretary Rusk's speech in *The New York Times* (February 1, 1964).

63. Ball, *op. cit.*, pp. 34, 44–45.

64. *Ibid.*, p. 48.

65. See *Documents on American Foreign Relations: 1962* (New York: Harper & Row, 1963), pp. 215–216, 226.

66. This conception is presented and discussed in detail in Ball, *op. cit.*, pp. 57–68.

67. Henry A. Kissinger, *The Troubled Partnership: A Re-appraisal of the Atlantic Alliance* (Garden City, N.Y.: Doubleday, 1966), p. 224. Kissinger's analysis of the question, "What kind of Atlantic partnership?" on pp. 221–249, is well worth careful study.

68. See Dean Acheson, *Present at the Creation* (New York: Norton, 1969), p. 232.

Eleven
THE MIDDLE EAST AND AFRICA:
America Confronts Emerging Societies

Among the far-reaching changes in the international community brought about by World War II, few surpass in importance the emergence of the Middle East as a maelstrom of great-power conflict. In recent years, the Middle East has exhibited many of the characteristics associated with the Balkans of the pre-War I era.* Turmoil and ferment, engendering manifold controversies and antagonisms among great and small powers, appear endemic to the region. While the United States at an early stage in its history developed a fairly well-understood body of principles that governed American diplomatic behavior toward Europe and Asia, it had no foreign policy at all for the Middle East before World War II. This fact furnishes one key to American diplomatic efforts in the Middle East in the postwar period. Foreign policy officials in the United States have been required to formulate and carry out policies and programs toward an area with which they have had little or no historical experience and for which lessons from their domestic history afforded minimum guidance—and to do this at a time when turbulence within the area necessitated quick and difficult judgments.

How has the United States responded to the challenge of events in the contemporary Middle East? We may conveniently seek the answers to this question by centering attention upon three basic problems in the region: the Arab–Israeli dispute; strategic–military issues in the Middle East; and the Western response to Arab nationalism and neutralism.

THE ARAB–ISRAELI CONFLICT

The United States had no foreign policy toward the Middle East prior to World War II, because it thought it had no vital interests in this far-away and backward region. Until the 1930s, American activities in the region were limited chiefly to those carried on by educators, missionaries, and philanthropic groups. These groups won the friendship of the Arab populations, which lasted until it was dissipated by the partition of Palestine in 1947–1948. During the 1930s, American oil companies began to acquire a stake in Middle East fields. By the postwar period, American oil concessions surpassed those of any other country.[1]

During World War II, the United States became conscious as never before of the strategic–military role of the Middle East. Iran provided an indispensable base from which to send war matériel into Russia. Middle East oil was essential to the Allied war machine.

Nevertheless, during World War II, the United States was content to play a subordinate role in Middle Eastern diplomatic and political affairs. Still, it was not beyond giving gratuitous advice to Britain and France concerning their colonial interests in the Middle East.[2] Immediately after the war, the Middle East became a focal point of international discord. During 1946, for example, the nascent United Nations was compelled to deal with a succession of crises involving the Middle East, including Soviet intrigues in northern Iran, complaints by Syria and Lebanon against France, and Soviet efforts to gain control of nearby Greece. In these crises, especially those involving liquidation of colonial empires, the United States often gained the good will of Arab societies, as a country that opposed colonialism.[3]

*Contemporary usage varies widely concerning the territory formerly called the Near East and now usually designated the Middle East. Definitions tend to be arbitrary and to be shaped by the criteria employed to explain the cohesiveness of the region. A recent study uses the phrase Middle East to include Turkey, Iran, Egypt, Libya, Saudi Arabia, Iraq, Syria, Lebanon, Jordan, and Israel. See Robert C. Kingsbury and Norman J. G. Pounds, *An Atlas of Middle Eastern Affairs* (New York: Praeger, 1963), p. 2. A noted geographer prefers the term Southwest Asia to include the area from Turkey to the Arabian peninsula and from Egypt through Afghanistan. George B. Cressey, *Crossroads: Land and Life in Southwest Asia* (New York: Lippincott, 1960), pp. 8–9. In our discussion, the principal focus will be upon Egypt, the Arabian peninsula, Lebanon, Jordan, Israel, Syria, and Iraq.

The Partition of Palestine

Whatever good will existed toward the United States throughout the Arab world was soon dissipated by the inflamed passions accompanying the dispute between Arabs and Jews (or more correctly, Zionists)* over the partition of Palestine in 1947, followed by creation of the State of Israel. Partition was the culminution of a long and progressively more bitter controversy between Zionist and Arab groups, each of which had its partisans among great and small powers on the world scene. The long sequence of events leading to the partition of Palestine is too complex to be traced out here.† Our purpose is served by taking note of one transcendent fact which, perhaps more than any other in the postwar era, colored American relations with Arab states. This was that after World War II, the United States came to be identified by Arabs as the chief backer and defender of Israel. Conversely, Arabs came to look upon America as a country that was insensitive to their demands and interests in the dispute with Israel and was prepared, in nearly every case, to give Israel the benefit of the doubt in the continuing controversy. The result was an alienation of American and Arab opinion that has continued to the present day and has, in turn, affected almost every other significant aspect of Arab–American relations.

This alienation grew out of the fact that, during World War II, influential Zionist organizations in the United States and their supporters carried on an intensive and often highly successful campaign to generate American support for their goal of a separate Jewish state in Palestine. Millions of dollars were raised in the United States to support the Zionist cause; state legislatures passed resolutions calling upon officials in Washington to ac-

cede to Zionist demands; politicians in both major political parties widely endorsed Zionist goals; pressure groups in Washington and throughout the country at large conducted a highly organized drive to win supporters for the Zionist program. As a result, the United States supplanted Great Britain as the center of Zionist agitation and, at least so far as this issue was concerned, largely displaced Britain and France as an object of Arab enmity and suspicion.[4]

Arab apprehensions about the course of American policies became evident immediately after World War II, when Washington began to exert pressure upon Great Britain (as the League of Nations mandate power in Palestine) to relax barriers against massive Jewish immigration into Palestine, a move which, both in this period and earlier, London steadfastly opposed.[5] Chiefly upon American instigation, an Anglo–American Committee of Inquiry visited Palestine early in 1946. It endorsed increased Jewish immigration to the country; but it also emphasized that any solution to the Palestine problem must protect both Arab and Jewish rights in the country. Within a few months, the United States and Britain formulated a plan for a federal government in Palestine, upon which the later UN partition plan was largely based.[6] As time passed, however, Great Britain made known its coolness toward partition, and its unwillingness to support the plan in the face of rising Arab hostility. For this reason, and because Britain was liquidating many of its overseas commitments, London notified the nascent United Nations that it was relinquishing its mandate authority in Palestine. From April to November, 1947, the UN General Assembly debated the future of the country. It finally voted to accept the partition scheme, although Arab spokesmen expressed their unanimous opposition to the idea and voiced their determination to resist it by force if necessary. The United States played a central role in these events. It emerged as Israel's foremost advocate in the UN and used its influence to rally global support for Israel's cause among disinterested states, such as those in Latin America.

Three dominant influences shaped American policy. One was humanitarianism. Many Americans supported Presidents Roosevelt and Truman in believing that Hitler's barbarous policies toward the Jews created an obligation for Western societies to alleviate somehow the still desperate plight of European Jewry, in part by permitting those who so desired to emigrate to Palestine.[8] A second influence shaping American policy was historical ignorance of the Arab world and, as an important contributory factor, ingrained suspicion of British colonial policies. In brief, many Americans were disposed to believe that the British were emotionally and blindly pro-Arab, an attitude engendered by Britain's own interests in

---

*While Zionism has roots in the Hebrew religious faith, it is predominantly a *political* movement. Its objective has been the creation of a "national home" for the Jews in Palestine. Many Jews are Zionists, others are not; some are in fact vigorously anti-Zionist. Similarly, many non-Jewish groups and individuals support the Zionist cause. The writer has heard spokesmen for the Arab countries make the distinction between being anti-Semitic and being anti-Zionist. To Arab minds, the key fact about Zionism is that it is a Western-sponsored political movement, detrimental to their interests.

†For the pre-World War II background on events leading to the partition of Palestine in 1947, the student is referred to the following sources: J. C. Hurewitz, *Diplomacy in the Near and Middle East* (New York: Van Nostrand Reinhold, 1956), vol. II of which deals with developments after World War I; L. Larry Leonard, "The United Nations and Palestine," *International Conciliation* 454 (October, 1949), an objective and illuminating discussion of the issue; and Charles D. Cremeans, *The Arabs and the World* (New York: Praeger, 1963), pp. 180–213, a perceptive analysis of problems in the Arab world. The best recent study is Fred J. Khouri, *The Arab–Israeli Dilemma* (Syracuse, N.Y.: Syracuse University Press, 1968), which provides a thorough and balanced account.

the Middle East. Only in the State Department and among military officials did awareness exist of the long-range repercussions of trying to implement the partition scheme in the face of adamant Arab opposition. The White House not only disregarded State Department warnings, but it also ignored President Roosevelt's earlier wartime pledges that nothing would be done in Palestine inimical to Arab rights. Similarly, the Truman administration chose to disregard FDR's earlier admonition that partition could be carried out in Palestine only by military force.[9]

Third, and perhaps most galling to Arabs, there was no question that American foreign policy toward the Arab–Israeli dispute was substantially shaped by domestic political considerations. In Chapter 7, we examined the influence of pressure groups on American foreign policy, of which the activities of Zionist groups in this period afford an outstanding example. Moreover, in political contests during the 1940s, politicians in both the Democratic and Republican parties widely supported the Zionist position. In local elections (particularly in states like New York, New Jersey, Pennsylvania, and Illinois), the Zionist viewpoint received widespread endorsement by candidates.[10]

It would be difficult to cite an example from the record of postwar American diplomacy in which national policy-makers were more insensitive to the long-range diplomatic interests of the nation, and less prepared to evaluate policy alternatives in the light of their implications for American objectives in a vital region such as the Middle East, than in the Palestine controversy.

Conflict After 1947

Hardly had the United Nations adopted the partition plan before open warfare erupted in the Middle East between Jewish and Arab forces. Displaying resourcefulness and a brilliant command of military tactics, and materially aided by internal divisions prevailing among their Arab enemies, Jewish forces successfully defeated or held at bay three Arab armies. On February 24, 1949, both sides finally accepted a UN-sponsored armistice. Meanwhile, on May 14, 1948, the Jewish National Council in Tel Aviv had proclaimed the existence of the state of Israel. Within minutes after the event, the Truman administration extended American recognition to the new Jewish state. Contrasting this haste with the reluctance displayed by the United States in recognizing Communist states like Soviet Russia and Red China, or even new political regimes in Arab countries, Arab spokesmen interpreted Truman's act as another indication of Washington's pro-Israeli bias.

The truce negotiated in 1949, it was expected, would bring an end to military hostilities between the antagonists and open the way for a durable peace between them. In reality, it did nothing of the kind. For over twenty years thereafter, the hostility between Israel and its Arab neighbors kept the Middle East in a state of active tension and sometimes open warfare. Border incursions into Israel by Arab commando groups like Al Fatah who were dedicated to the "liberation" of Palestine; retaliatory attacks by Israeli forces into Egypt, Jordan, and Syria; continuing propaganda vilification by one side against the other; a persistent refusal by the governments of the area to cooperate in the development of water resources and other regional projects; Arab determination to maintain an economic boycott of Israel and to deny its use of the Suez Canal; Israel's insistence that its existence be "recognized" by Arab governments and that the latter agree to negotiate outstanding issues in good faith; a failure by all parties to the Arab–Israeli controversy to resolve the tragic refugee issue, leaving several hundred thousand refugees as wards of the United Nations —after 1949, these became permanent features of the Middle Eastern political environment, keeping the region in a state of ongoing instability and violence.

On two occasions after 1949, warfare erupted between Israel and the Arab states. The "second round" in the Arab–Israeli conflict opened a few weeks after President Nasser of Egypt nationalized the Suez Canal on July 26, 1956. On October 29, Israel's armed forces invaded the Sinai Peninsula; and on November 5–6, British and French military units landed in the Suez area, ostensibly to "protect" the canal from Israeli forces, but actually to overthrow Nasser's outspokenly anti-Western regime. Militarily, the "Suez crisis" of 1956 was a disaster for the Arab world, particularly for Nasser's Egypt. Egyptian troops proved no match for the military might of Britain, France, and Israel. Politically, however, the Suez crisis was in many respects a victory for President Nasser and his Arab supporters. Responding to initiatives by the United States, the United Nations condemned the Israeli–British–French invasion of Egyptian territory and demanded the prompt withdrawal of foreign forces. Acceding to world opinion, London and Paris evacuated their troops; Israel was much more reluctant to do so, but it finally yielded, after receiving assurances from the United States that its security would not be left unprotected. A UN Emergency Force was created and stationed in Egyptian (although not in Israeli) territory to maintain peace between Israel and the Arab states. As for President Nasser, his position as a hero to Arab masses inside and outside Egypt was strengthened as a result of his skill in surviving a crushing military defeat and in successfully defying the "foreign imperialists." Moscow's offer to send Soviet "volunteers" to assist Egypt (declined by officials in Cairo), along with the Kremlin's support of the Arab cause in UN debates, went far toward cementing friendly relations between the Arab and Communist zones, at a time when Western–Arab relations had become extremely tense.[11]

The years that followed the Suez crisis of 1956 witnessed no diminution in Arab–Israeli animosities. On both sides, positions tended to harden; Arabs and Israelis reiterated their demands with monotonous regularity; neither UN officials nor governments outside the area experienced any noteworthy success in discovering a basis for agreement between the belligerents. Meanwhile, with the underlying causes of tension unresolved, the Middle East reverted to the familiar pattern of Arab raids across the Israeli frontier, followed by "retaliatory strikes" by Israeli forces against Arab territories; each side increased its propaganda activities and endeavored to enlist allies in the international community; and while Israel sought new armaments in the West, the Arab governments increasingly turned to the Communist bloc to rebuild their military forces for the expected "third round."

The "Six-Day War"

It came in the spring of 1967, when Egypt demanded the withdrawal of the UN Emergency Force from its territory.* Once UNEF was removed, Egyptian troops moved in to occupy the strategic heights of Sharm el-Sheikh, controlling the southern entrance to the Gulf of Aqaba, Israel's only sea route to the south and east. With its shipping blocked from the Suez Canal, Israel regarded this outlet as economically and militarily vital (most of its oil imports, for example, came through the Gulf of Aqaba); the route also served as Israel's principal channel of contact with Asia and Africa. Predictably, authorities in Tel Aviv viewed Egypt's action as a *casus belli.* Rejecting efforts by the United Nations, the United States, and other nations to resolve the crisis without war, on June 5 Israel launched a surprise air attack against Egypt, followed by air strikes against Jordan and Syria. As a result, Arab air power (includ-

*UN Secretary-General U Thant's withdrawal of UNEF elicited considerable criticism, particularly in the West. Yet it must be recalled that UNEF had initially been stationed inside Egypt's borders with Cairo's concurrence (Israel had refused to concur). Since the UN was not a supranational government, it lacked authority to "impose" its forces upon an unwilling member. Moreover, the nations contributing forces to UNEF (particularly India) were unwilling to do so after Cairo demanded its withdrawal, if for no other reason than that UNEF might find itself in a crossfire between Israeli and Arab troops. For a discussion of the legal and political complexities involved in Egypt's request for the withdrawal of UNEF, see the account by the former Indian diplomat, Arthur Lall, *The UN and the Middle East Crisis, 1967* (New York: Columbia University Press, 1968), pp. 11–21.

ing many Soviet-supplied planes) was largely wiped out. Lacking air cover, Egyptian troops in the Gaza and Sinai regions were left defenseless against superior Israeli power. In the "Six-Day War," Egyptian infantry, armor, and support forces east of the Suez Canal were decimated; Jordanian forces were defeated in a series of encounters; and Syrian troops along Israel's northern frontier were similarly overcome. In brief, Israel won a spectacular victory, demonstrating its unquestioned military superiority over its more numerous Arab enemies. As in the past, divisiveness among Arab governments prevented effective military collaboration among them; one of the strongest military establishments in the Middle East, for example—the armed forces of Saudi Arabia—took no part in the conflict.

Peace Talks and Hostile Acts

The net effect of the "third round" in the Arab–Israeli hostilities was to exacerbate underlying antagonisms and render an early resolution of outstanding differences more remote than ever. By virtue of its victory, Israel had greatly enlarged its frontiers—which now encompassed the entire Sinai region, up to the Suez Canal; the "West Bank" of the Jordan River, Jordan's most productive area; certain strategic points along the Israeli–Syrian border (such as the Golan Heights); and the entire city of Jerusalem. Altogether, Israel had extended its authority over some 32,000 additional square miles of Arab territory, encompassing 1 million people (mostly, of course, Arabs).[12]

In marked contrast to events in 1956, Tel Aviv showed no inclination to be deprived of its victory. Israel steadfastly refused to relinquish occupied territories until the Arab states were prepared to enter into serious negotiations designed to resolve the issues which kept the Middle East inflamed. For some twenty years, Israel's most fundamental demand had remained unchanged. It was that Arab governments recognize its existence, enter into normal relationships with it, and negotiate disagreements (like the troublesome refugee issue and the matter of Israel's boundaries) engendering regional tensions. Whatever the theoretical pros and cons of the Palestine question, on three different occasions Israel had successfully asserted its claims on the battlefield. Having survived Arab harassment and intimidation for over twenty years, Israel was not prepared to abandon its demands now; and it was perhaps even less inclined than earlier to propose compromises for the sake of agreement. Exploiting to the utmost its position of strength vis-à-vis its Arab enemies, Israel gave Arab governments three choices. They could finally decide to negotiate with Tel Aviv by agreeing initially to accept Israel's legitimacy. They could accept the *fait accompli* of Israel's occupation of Sinai, Gaza,

Jerusalem, and other former Arab territories. Or, they could prepare for the "fourth round"—a contest which might (and, in the Israeli view, surely would) prove even more injurious to their interests than the 1967 crisis. Tel Aviv was equally opposed to efforts by the United States, the Soviet Union, the United Nations, or other outside powers to "impose" a settlement of the Arab–Israeli dispute. Lasting peace, in the Israeli view, could come only as a result of direct negotiations between the parties concerned.[13]

Arab attitudes after the crisis of 1967 were no less intransigent. Defeated in three military encounters against Israel, with each defeat more humiliating than the last, Arab leaders and masses showed less disposition than ever to "accept" Israel or enter into negotiations with it. One of the most neglected aspects of the Palestine question perhaps was the extent to which it had produced *profound psychological shocks* within Arab societies, strengthening emotional and irrational political forces and hardening popular attitudes. Few people on the globe were as preoccupied with their pride and their "dignity" as the Arabs; and few had experienced such repeated blows to their ego in modern history. Arabs were mindful that during an earlier era, the Islamic empire had ruled much of the civilized world and that it had excelled in many aspects of science, learning, and culture. European medicine, for example, benefited enormously as a result of contact with the Arab world during and after the Crusades, For the Arabs, the creation of Israel and its subsequent military victories appeared as but another stage in a long train of events in which, for several centuries, Arabs had been oppressed and humiliated by outsiders, like the Mongols, the Turks, the European colonialists, and (in a new version of Western control) Israel. Established in the Middle East during a period of Arab weakness and colonial subordination, Israel (like the Kingdom of Jerusalem set up by the Crusaders) was a remnant of Western power which had to be, and someday would be, eliminated. More galling than any other fact for the Arabs was the reality that revolutionary Arab governments (which gained power widely after the Egyptian Revolution in 1952 overthrew the monarchy) had been even less successful in containing Zionist expansionism than Western-controlled governments throughout the Arab world.

As Arab frustrations mounted, so did Arab extremism, emotionalism, and over-all unwillingness to compromise with Zionism. Over the years, Israel had unquestionably become a symbol of Arab resentments and discontents. Even if they so desired, moderate Arab leaders (like King Hussein of Jordan) dared not alienate domestic opinion by seriously proposing negotiations with Israel.* Is-

rael stood as a visible reminder of Western colonialist impulses. Nearly all colonial enclaves in the Middle East had been (or were being) liquated—except in Palestine. Correctly or not, Arabs were convinced that Israel owed its existence and its survival—not to speak of its military prowess—to ongoing Western (principally American) support. To the Arab mind, Israel was also to blame for another pervasive phenomenon: the gap (which was often widening in some Arab societies) between popular expectations and the achievements of native Arab governments. Why was the monarchy in Jordan increasingly hard-pressed to maintain economic and political viability? Why did Syria experience continuing political unrest? Why was the government in Egypt severely challenged to solve the country's economic problems or check the ever more critical population crisis? Why had it proved impossible for Arab unity to be achieved? For millions of Arabs, the answer in

---

given key consideration in discussing the internal and external policies of those Arab states (Egypt, Jordan, Syria, and increasingly Lebanon) at the forefront of the conflict against Israel. This is the degree to which the real decision-makers within these countries have come to be various commando and guerrilla organizations dedicated to the "liberation" of Palestine. In the spring of 1970, for example, King Hussein's government in Jordan was thrown into an acute crisis, threatening both the monarch's life and his authority within the country. Precipitated by an organization called the Popular Front for the Liberation of Palestine, among the most militant guerrilla groups, the crisis was resolved only after Hussein made substantial concessions to the demands of the insurgents. By 1966, Jordan contained some 2 million people, of whom a majority were Palestinians; many of the latter bore deep grievances against both King Hussein and his grandfather Abdullah (the latter had been assassinated by a political extremist earlier). That the Jordanian monarchy faced an uncertain future was a considerable understatement; the real miracle perhaps was that it had survived as long as it had. Meanwhile, guerrilla organizations in the Middle East were extending their influence into a country which had hitherto taken a minor part in the Arab confrontation with Israel—Lebanon. During 1969 and 1970, Lebanon experienced several governmental crises and, like Jordan, was compelled to grant guerrilla forces considerable de facto autonomy. Any attempt by Beirut to enforce the government's authority against these groups could well precipitate civil war, spearheaded by the 300,000 Palestine refugees living within Lebanon's borders. Guerrilla and commando organizations within the Middle East confronted a problem which had long plagued the Arab world: rivalry and lack of cooperation among a number of separate groups, all of which were pledged to regain Palestine but often by different methods and strategies. In June, 1970, a 27-man central committee was formed to coordinate these guerrilla activities; its chairman was Yasir Arafat, head of the Palestine Liberation Organization and leader of the largest guerrilla group—Al Fatah. According to one report, this organization regarded itself as "a Palestinian legislature in exile." Whether this step would succeed in unifying guerrilla operations in the region was of course uncertain. For more detailed discussion, see "A Guerrilla Leader's Reply: To Turn Israel into Another Vietnam," *Atlas* 19 (April, 1970), 47–48; *The New York Times* (June 2, June 13, and July 5, 1970); and *Time Magazine* 95 (June 22, 1970), 22–34.

---

*Within recent years, Jordan has presented merely the most extreme case of a phenomenon that must be

each case tended to be clear and simple: Israel's existence and its successful expansionism fomented economic dislocations for Arab societies, aggravated political tensions in the area, and encouraged intra-Arab conflicts. Tel Aviv *deliberately* sought to keep the Arab world divided and weak; but even if it did not, Zionist expansionism required that Arab governments divert large sums for armaments and neglect critical internal problems. Israel's ambitions also required the Arabs to develop a high degree of "dependence" upon outside nations like the Soviet Union, to counteract Western influence channeled through Israel.

Logically defensible or not, such Arab attitudes were extensive throughout the Middle East. Like many psyhchological issues, the *reality* of Arab animosity toward Israel could not be questioned, and the intensity of this animosity was perhaps higher than at any time since the late 1940s. Far from "accepting" Israel or reaching agreements with it, responding to pressures exerted by extremist groups like Al Fatah and other guerrilla organizations, Arab governments were adamant in their refusal to negotiate with Tel Aviv. Instead, Arab spokesmen increasingly spoke of the coming "fourth round" of hostilities; Arab governments maintained their policies of economic boycott and blockade; and anti-Israeli forces throughout the Arab world dedicated themselves to the "liberation of Palestine." Relying largely upon Soviet assistance, Egypt, Syria, Iraq, and other Arab states rebuilt their armed forces in preparation for what appeared to be an inexorable tendency toward a new outbreak of violence in the Middle East.[14]

The United States and the Palestine Question

Two dominant conclusions emerge as a result of American involvement in the Arab–Israeli dispute since World War II. The first is that the controversy *has affected virtually every major issue with which the United States has been concerned in the Middle East in the past twenty-five years.* It is not possible to understand the obstacles facing the United States in its attempt to inhibit Soviet influence in the area without reference to American policy toward the Arab–Israeli controversy. Or take another American goal in the Middle East: encouragement of regional economic advancement. Incipient and actual warfare between the Arab states and Israel poses a major obstacle to realization of this objective. Nor is it likely that *political stability* will emerge, especially in Arab states adjacent to Israel, as long as the conflict exists. No problem, it is safe to say, stands as a more formidable barrier to Arab–American understanding and cooperation than does the involvement of the United States in the Arab–Israeli controversy.

The second conclusion is *the declining ability of the United States to influence the course of events in the Middle East,* particularly in the direction of an Arab–Israeli *détente.* For the past quarter-century, the tendency has been for the United States to be consigned more and more to the role of spectator in the Middle East drama. Despite its position as a great power, by some criteria the greatest power in world history, America's ability to shape developments in this vital region appears to have steadily deteriorated.

During World War II and the early postwar era, as we have already observed, the United States replaced Great Britain as the principal base of Zionist activities in behalf of a Jewish state in Palestine. Time and again, Washington used its influence with London in efforts to achieve Zionist goals, like more rapid and expanded Jewish immigration to Palestine. Great Britain (where, Americans assumed, "pro-Arab" influences controlled Middle Eastern policy) was reluctant to accept American viewpoints; but with the rapid decline in British power, London could often do little more than delay American proposals. Then, after Britain decided to relinquish its mandatory authority in Palestine, more than any other nation the United States took the initiative at the United Nations for "partitioning" Palestine and creating the state of Israel. In this process, the affirmative votes of the Latin American republics were crucial to the outcome.[15] Yet when it became quickly apparent that partition faced implacable Arab opposition (a fact of which the British had been aware since the 1920s), the Truman administration reverted to the idea of a UN "trusteeship" for Palestine. With Israel already in existence, and with first round in the Arab-Israeli conflict underway, the American plan offered no prospect for stability, and it was soon abandoned.[16]

Thereafter, the United States gradually moved to an official position of "neutrality" in the conflict between Israel and the Arab states. Their major interest, officials in Washington declared, was in a just and durable settlement of outstanding differences and in the restoration of stability to one of the most strategically vital regions on the globe. America's effort to assume a posture of impartiality was illustrated, for example, in the Tripartite Declaration (issued with Britain and France) of May 25, 1950, which committed the Western powers to opposing "the use of force" by either side and pledged them to refrain from supplying arms (except for "self-defense") to either Israel or the Arab nations.[17] Variations on this policy were expressed by American officials many times in the years ahead, as when UN Ambassador Arthur Goldberg declared late in 1966 that "violence breeds violence and . . . it must be opposed in the Middle East, regardless of the direction from which it comes."[18] By the 1960s, American officials sometimes adopted the nomenclature of the Afro-Asian "third world" in describing their position. [Toward the Arab-Israeli quarrel, the United States regarded itself as "nonaligned"—a position it also assumed toward other quarrels disturbing the peace and security of the Middle East.] Or, as the officials of the Nixon administration declared, the United States proposed to be more "even-handed" in its treatment of the Arab-Israeli controversy, avoiding favoritism for one side over the other. Israeli sources treated this development (probably correctly) as signaling a more pro-Arab orientation in American policy; Arab sources (many of whom doubted that the United States was really capable of changing its former pro-Israeli position) theoretically approved this new direction in American foreign policy.[19] But, as time passed, Arab spokesmen were dubious about American impartiality in the Middle East, especially as regards supplying military equipment to Israel.

Yet from the beginning, the attempt by the United States to assume a neutral or impartial position toward the Arab-Israeli conflict was subject to a "credibility gap" of such major proportions as to render its attainment extremely difficult. Arab governments rejected America's claim as both factually inaccurate and morally indefensible. Israel owed its birth to American diplomatic efforts; after 1948, its continued existence had been contingent upon massive economic and military aid from the United States, the effect of which was to "keep Israel in business."* In whatever degree

*The effect of each new crisis in the Middle East, it appeared, was to strengthen Arab opinion in the conviction that the United States was allied with Israel to the detriment of Arab interests. This was a conclusion which seemed to have little or no connection with objective reality—since official American policy toward the Arab-Israeli dispute during the 1960s appeared to be *less* openly pro-Israeli than had been in the late 1940s and 1950s. Yet after visiting twelve Arab states during 1968, one reporter found majority sentiment in the area convinced that America was "a greedy imperialist, pledged to support Israel, the Arab's enemies, under any conditions." An Egyptian official declared that once the United States opposed colonialism; but in recent years "you have planted your own colony, Israel, in our midst." This reporter concluded that "most Arabs seem to believe that the United States has been thoroughly pro-Israel. The charge is repeated ceaselessly by their rulers, their newspapers and their broadcasters"—an accusation which, needless to say, had been re-enforced by Communist propaganda activities. This belief was *not*, however, confined merely to chronically anti-Western circles in Cairo or Damascus; one striking fact in the recent period was the extent to which it had been expressed by pro-Western Arab leaders like King Hussein of Jordan and King Faisal of Saudi Arabia. The latter, for example, asserted that America's "neglect" of Arab viewpoints, and its intimate identification with Israel, had greatly facilitated Soviet penetration of the Middle East. Not unexpectedly, spokesmen for revolutionary Arab regimes were even more vehement. Thus a close adviser of President Nasser in Egypt declared that because of their association with Israel, "the Americans

Arabs were prepared to forget the Soviet Union's earlier role in championing Zionist claims to Palestine, their recollection of America's part in the establishment of Israel was indelible. A major reason was that, in contrast to the U.S.S.R., America's identification with, and support for, Israel had remained strong since the late 1940s. To cite but two examples, at a time when the United States professed "neutrality" in the Arab-Israeli dispute, during the mid-1960s it authorized West Germany to supply modern tanks to Israel out of NATO military stockpiles.[20] Again in the early 1970s, nearly every day Egyptian and Syrian military forces faced attacks by Israeli-manned American Skyhawks, Phantoms, and other jet aircraft obtained in the United States or Western Europe. As the Soviet Union expanded its military assistance to Arab states, the United States came under extreme pressure—from Israel and from its friends in Congress and the American public—to maintain Israel's military superiority, by selling Tel Aviv Phantom aircraft and other modern military equipment. Arab nations regarded Washington's commitment to the preservation of a "military balance" in the Middle East as doubly objectionable: In their view, this was tantamount to acquiescing in Israel's demonstrated military superiority; and, Arabs asked, how could Israel's strength really be "balanced" against that of 80 to 100 million Arabs? Arabs were certain that America's commitment to Israel meant in effect that the United States was a party to—and at some point might intervene directly in—the Palestine controversy.[21]

From the Arab point of view, America's affinity for Israel in no way produced *restraints upon Israeli policies or behavior* inimical to Arab interests. It had long been apparent that policy-makers in Israel were not deterred by adverse reactions in the United States or by world public opinion. The United States, Arabs were convinced, was not prepared to *do anything concrete* to restrain Israeli behavior. Symbolic gestures—like official American condemnation of Israel's annexation of the Old City of Jerusalem or military raids against Beirut and other Lebanese cities and villages—did nothing fundamentally to change Arab convictions that America had become Zionism's fore-

have no real friends left in the Arab world." See *The New York Times* (May 23 and July 17, 1968), dispatch by Drew Middleton. That Arab resentment toward the United States for supporting Israel had not diminished was indicated by the remarks of Egypt's President Nasser in 1970. Speaking on March 5, Nasser declared that Israel intended to occupy more Arab lands and that it was directly supported in this goal by the United States. A few weeks later, Nasser accused the United States of enabling Israel to defeat Arab forces in 1967 and maintain military operations against them ever since. See *The New York Times* (March 6, 1970), dispatch by Raymond H. Anderson; and the interview with President Nasser in *U.S. News and World Report* **LXVIII** (May 18, 1970), 60–63.

most advocate and protector. Referring to the American role "as a principal creator of Israel" and to "two decades of strident pro-Israel statements by political leaders" in the United States, one of America's most experienced commentators on the Middle East concluded that Arabs believed "any American impartiality [in the Middle East] must stop short of the borders of Israel."[22]

For altogether different reasons, the American claim to neutrality proved no less ineffectual in dealing with Israel. The dominant reason perhaps was that the masses and leaders in Israel simply did not believe the assertion. As early as World War II, Americans had "identified" closely with Israel. The idea of a Jewish "national home" in Palestine appealed widely to Americans for several reasons. One of these was the close affinity between Judaism and Christianity. Then too the emigration of thousands of Jews to Palestine would go far toward solving the troublesome refugee problem in postwar Europe; after Hitler's barbarities against the Jews, the latter were "entitled" to achieve their goals in Palestine. This consideration strongly influenced President Truman's position toward the Palestine question.[23] Besides, Israel's history bore many resemblances to America's own. The "pioneers" who were settling Israel faced many of the same challenges overcome by America's pioneer settlers. Jewish citizens were "making the desert bloom" in the Negev and elsewhere. Anyone who visited Israel after 1948 (and Americans did so by the thousands) could see that the dedication, hard work, and ingenuity of Israeli citizens were transforming what had formerly been an arid country; they were perhaps making it into a model which Arab, African, and other governments might properly emulate. In contrast to other areas, private and public aid extended by the United States to Israel was *being used effectively;* results were evident and rapid. Most crucially to many American minds, Israel was *a democracy*—nearly the only one in a region characterized by growing resentment against Western democracy, by revolutionary Arab regimes espousing authoritarian programs and systems of government, and by an increasing Soviet (and in some instances, Chinese) presence. As the traditional champion of the underdog, the American society also visualized the Arab-Israeli dispute as a David and Goliath contest. Against overwhelming odds (the Arab states had 30 to 40 times the population of Israel, with Egypt alone being more than 10 times larger), Israel had successfully defended itself and vindicated its right to exist in the military arena. Mention must also be made of another factor that was sometimes extremely influential in shaping American attitudes: Israel's intensive, and at times extraordinarily successful, public relations campaign designed to keep American opinion favorable and to counteract Arab propaganda in the United States.*

*From the time of America's earliest involvement in the Palestine question, during World War II, the efforts of Zionist and Arab groups to influence public and official opinion in the United States have been what one reporter terms "an uneven match," with the outcome nearly always favoring the former. There was little doubt that "friends of Israel have won the hearts of the American people, the votes of Congress, and usually, but not always, the mind of the President, no matter who he is." As we have observed, several factors (America's sympathy with Europe's Jewish refugees, Israel's existence as a democracy, and other considerations) predisposed Americans to favor the Zionist point of view. Other factors—the backwardness and political turmoil characteristic of the Arab world, Arab rejection of the concept of Western democracy, intimate relations between several Arab states and the Soviet Union—have perhaps conditioned the American mind against Arab viewpoints on the Palestine issue. Two other considerations have greatly facilitated Israel's attempt to influence American attitudes. First, nearly 6 million Jewish citizens live in the United States. They tend to be concentrated in four of the nation's most important states: New York (New York City has a larger Jewish population than Israel itself), Pennsylvania, Illinois, and California. In addition, throughout the American society, Jewish citizens tend to be articulate, politically active, and at the forefront of citizen concern with public issues. In many states, Jewish voters contribute funds to political campaigns on a scale greatly disproportionate to their numbers, particularly for candidates of the Democratic party (with which some three-fourths of the "Jewish vote" is traditionally affiliated). Second, few organizations in recent history have surpassed the efforts of the Israeli Embassy in Washington, working in concert with groups like the America-Israel Public Affairs Committee, to disseminate its viewpoints and to win converts for them within the United States. Even Arab spokesmen have praised the effectiveness of Zionist lobbying and informational activities.

By contrast, for most of the postwar era, pro-Arab informational activities in America have been much more limited and considerably less influential. Although American oil companies have investments in the Middle East totaling some $1.6 billion, this fact has not somehow been convertible into pro-Arab sentiment within America. A few organizations (like the American Friends of the Middle East and Arab student groups on American campuses) have presented the Arab side of the Palestine controversy. Within the American government, the Arab point of view has most consistently been expressed by officials in the State Department, many of whom have served tours of duty in Arab societies. As we shall see, by the late 1960s this imbalance between Zionist and Arab groups in their influence on American opinion was perhaps shifting somewhat in favor of the latter. After winning three military victories within twenty years, Israel was no longer viewed as the "underdog"; many Americans also perhaps feared that Israel would sooner or later "involve" the United States in a military conflict in the Middle East. See *The New York Times* (April 6, 1970), dispatch by Robert H. Phelps; Fred J. Khouri, *The Arab-Israeli Dilemma* (Syracuse, N.Y.: Syracuse University Press, 1968), pp. 25–36 and *passim;* and John S. Badeau, *The American Approach to the Arab World* (New York: Harper & Row, 1968), pp. 27–28. For evidence of recent changes in American attitudes toward the Arab-Israeli dispute, see *the New York Times* (February 4 and 10, 1969); and the dispatch by the Associated Press in the *Morning Advocate* (Baton Rouge, La., February 6, 1969). At the end of 1969, Israeli Prime

Yet these affinities between America and Israel did not mean that Tel Aviv was necessarily receptive to suggestions from Washington, particularly those that might act as *restraints* upon Israel's behavior or bring about some modification of its more rigid demands. Arabs might be convinced that Israel was a mere creature of the United States or an "extension of American power" in the Middle East. But the Israelis obviously did not believe this, nor were they prone to formulate their policies on this assumption. After each military victory, Israeli diplomatic independence increased—until by the early 1970s it appeared that the United States had as little influence with Tel Aviv as it did with Cairo or Damascus. On the ideological, cultural, and economic levels, Israeli-American relations remained close. The American society still was, for example, the major center for Zionist fund-raising activities; American candidates for office continued to side with Israel much more frequently than they championed the Arab cause. Officials within Israel could assume a high degree of American support (or, at a minimum, tacit acquiescence) for whatever policies they adopted, since they had no real fear of efforts by the United States to compel Israeli compliance with UN directives or to compromise some of their more militant demands on the Arab states. During the late 1960s, Tel Aviv had no hesitation in vocally opposing joint American-Soviet efforts to achieve stability in the Middle East. In the Israeli view, this was an unacceptable effort by outside powers to "impose" peace terms upon nations in the area.[24] Although Arab governments repeatedly rejected the idea, Tel Aviv continued to insist upon direct negotiations between the parties to the controversy.

[Having alienated Arab opinion by its support of Israel, and being unable to translate that support into influence upon Tel Aviv, the United States found its role in the Arab-Israeli controversy sharply curtailed. Its professions of neutrality in the dispute were really believed by neither side.] In no area of the world (with the possible exception of sub-Saharan Africa) did American power appear to have such a marginal impact in shaping the course of events.

American-Sponsored Peace Initiatives

By the early 1970s, the Nixon administration had become genuinely apprehensive about the ongoing crisis in the Middle East; with every passing month, the danger of a new war—entailing the risk of a direct Soviet-American encounter in the area—became more acute. White House spokesmen announced, for example, that Washington was more disturbed about developments in the Middle East than in Southeast Asia, where American forces were being reduced. Accordingly, American officials undertook diplomatic initiatives designed to produce a military cease-fire in the Middle East and, in time, an over-all settlement of the Arab-Israeli controversy. Despite its support of the Arab position, the Soviet Union had apparently concluded that a new round of military hostilities involved serious risks. Even if a great-power collision could be avoided, the Kremlin did not look forward to rescuing its Arab clients from a new military disaster; yet if hostilities broke out anew, Soviet failure to provide tangible support to the Arab side could significantly lessen Russian prestige and influence among the Arabs. Consequently, Moscow was willing to join with Washington in proposing a cease-fire agreement and in urging both Israel and the Arab states to accept its terms. Assured of Soviet support, on June 19, 1970, Secretary of State William Rogers announced the proposal which he hoped would bring stability to the Middle East.*

To the surprise of many observers, Egypt's President Nasser soon signified his willingness to accept the American plan; Jordan quickly followed suit; the Syrian reaction was ambivalent (although not totally hostile). That Soviet influence weighed heavily in Cairo's decision seemed evident. Nasser's acceptance of the plan put the onus for blocking the path to peace squarely upon Israel. Israeli authorities did not conceal their distaste for many features of the American proposal; they doubted Soviet and Arab sincerity in accept-

*The American-initiated cease-fire agreement called for a 90-day military standstill on the Israeli-Egyptian front (technically, cease-fire accords had existed since 1967 on the Jordanian, Syrian, and Lebanese frontiers, and these had never been formally abandoned), effective on August 7, 1970. Concurrently, diplomatic negotiations under United Nations auspices were to be resumed in an effort to resolve the underlying sources of conflict on the Palestine question. Israel and Egypt would monitor each other's compliance with the truce terms, with assistance provided by some 100 UN observers in the area (American aircraft also provided photographic evidence of military movements along the cease-fire line). The Nixon administration claimed it had received a "categorical commitment" from the Soviet Union to cooperate in enforcing the accord; on this basis Washington assured Israel that its security would not be impaired by accepting the scheme. One significant feature of this proposal was that, for the first time, Egypt (soon followed by Jordan) agreed to seek a "just and lasting peace" with Israel; for its part, Israel accepted the idea of withdrawing its forces from Arab lands captured in 1967, except for the Old City of Jerusalem, the Golan Heights, portions of the Sinai region and other areas which Israel deemed "vital" to its security. To Arab minds, Israeli annexation of Jerusalem removed one of the most controversial issues from the negotiating table, thereby presenting Arabs with a *fait accompli*. For the text of official statements announcing acceptance of the cease-fire agreement, see *The New York Times* (August 8, 1970), and the commentary provided in *Newsweek* LXXVI (August 10, 1970), 15–16.

Minister Golda Meir publicly expressed concern about the decline in American sympathy toward the Israeli position. See *The New York Times* (October 7, 1969).

ing it; and they were highly dubious about the prospect of any permanent settlement of the Palestine question consistent with Israel's security requirements. The Gahal party (representing "Hawkish" sentiment within Israel) rejected the proposal outright, thereby precipitating a new political crisis within the country. Eventually, however, one dominant reality dictated Israel's reluctant agreement to a cease-fire: awareness that failure to do so would leave Israel diplomatically (and perhaps militarily) isolated, with neither the United States nor any other outside power prepared to support its policy. On August 7, therefore, Washington, Cairo, and Jerusalem jointly announced the beginning of a 90-day cease-fire along the Arab-Israeli frontier. Concurrently, UN Ambassador Gunnar Jarring and other diplomatic officials undertook new efforts to discover the basis for a permanent peace in the Middle East. Limited (and, as events showed, brief) as it was, this agreement was a significant diplomatic accomplishment for the United States.

Yet from its inception, the American peace initiative in the Middle East faced numerous and serious obstacles. The intense suspicions existing between Israel and the Arab states made each side doubt the good faith of the other. Israeli officials questioned whether their Arab opponents really desired peace; Arabs doubted whether Israel was prepared to make any meaningful concessions for the sake of Arab good will. Not without reason, Israel was extremely suspicious of Soviet motives in the area, while many Arab nations were similarly dubious about America's intentions. After more than two decades of acute hostility, neither side was inclined to accept compromise solutions or make conciliatory gestures. Beyond these deleterious environmental factors, three specific problems beset this new effort to stablize the Middle East.

One source of ongoing controversy involved the question, "How is the military cease-fire to be effectively policed to assure compliance on all sides?" In the main, the American plan contemplated that the belligerents themselves would assume the main responsibility for monitoring compliance with the truce provisions. Almost immediately, the cease-fire agreement was imperiled by charges and countercharges concerning violations of the truce terms.

A second obstacle to a durable accord between Israel and the Arab states was the requirement that Israel relinquish *all* former Arab territories occupied or annexed after the 1967 war. Arabs viewed this stipulation as fundamental to any lasting settlement. Yet Israeli officials had already stated publicly that they would never relinquish control over the City of Jerusalem, nor were they prepared (in the absence of iron-clad security guarantees) to give up their hold on the Golan Heights in Syria or Jordan's West Bank. As long as Israel persisted in this attitude, Arabs were convinced, peace talks would prove fruitless.

A third deterrent to an Arab-Israeli accord became painfully obvious to the international community during the early fall of 1970, when several commercial airliners were "hijacked" by Palestinian guerrilla organizations. This episode underlined the implacable opposition of the guerillas to a cease-fire agreement, not to speak of a political settlement recognizing the existence of Israel. As we have already observed, after 1967 several Palestinian groups became key political forces in the Arab states adjoining Israel; their influence was especially strong in Jordan and Syria and, most recently, in Lebanon—so much so as to make them collectively a kind of state within a state. Even the government of Egypt was obliged to recognize the popular appeal exercised by guerrilla organizations, whose overt opposition to Israel was often more evident than that exhibited by some Arab armies. Yet the guerrillas were themselves far from being a monolithic political force. They were divided into several rival organizations, epousing diverse programs and strategies. Opposition to Israel tended to be their only unifying link; and as the Arab governments themselves had discovered long ago, this was not enough to create real cohesion among them. More than any other Arab state, Jordan had a large and militant refugee population; its presence in the country posed a continuing challenge to the authority of King Hussein's government and sharply limited his ability to arrive at a *détente* with Israel. Yet, after a series of internal political clashes, by the early 1970s, the government of Jordan had successfully reasserted its authority and had significantly reduced the influence of Arab guerrilla organizations. Although Arab political leaders certainly could not disregard refugee opinion, they were perhaps less influenced by it now than in the immediate past.

For these reasons, the prospects for peace in the Middle East looked far from encouraging. American influence over established Arab governments remained extremely limited; it was nonexistent with the guerrilla organizations. For all its visible "presence" in the area, Soviet Russia clearly could not (or would not) dictate peace terms to the Arab nations; nor did Moscow have any overt rapport with the guerrilla forces. The more responsible leaders of the Arab world might realize that a new regional, or possibly global, war would be a disaster for all countries involved, not least the Arab countries. Yet they were sometimes equally hard-pressed to control extremist elements within their own country. Meanwhile, Israel had growing doubts about Arab and Soviet good faith, and its supporters in the United States demanded substantial American help to prevent a deterioration in Israel's military position. There was no real evidence that the *sine qua non* of genuine peace—a willingness to make mutual concessions in the interests of a reasonable settlement—had finally appeared. Until it did, the Middle East would probably remain characterized by strife and continuing hostility.

In the fall of 1970, what appeared to be still another obstacle to a possible Arab-Israeli settlement was added: the death of Egypt's highly influential President Gamel Abdel Nasser. Much as they might disagree with many of his policies, Israeli leaders recognized that, among Arab leaders, Nasser often espoused a relatively *moderate* position on the Palestine question. Yet to the surprise of many observers (including perhaps many Egyptians), Nasser's successor, Anwar Sadat, was even more conciliatory, so much so that he frequently succeeded in placing the onus upon Israel for refusing to engage in peace negotiations. If Sadat lacked Nasser's charisma, he also had fewer public commitments, enabling him to approach the Palestine crisis more flexibly. For several months after Nasser's death, Sadat appeared to be supported by a united Egyptian nation. Then in late spring, 1971, the internal political crisis which many commentators expected earlier gripped Egypt. High-level governmental and political leaders were arrested; a purge was conducted in the leadership of the Arab Socialist Union; Sadat accused many of his associates of plotting to bring about his overthrow. Left-wing critics of Sadat's regime were singled out for severe treatment by the government. Although the precise combination of forces producing this political turbulence in Egypt was not altogether clear to outsiders, it seemed evident that the dissession stemmed in part from public (and perhaps military) disaffection with Sadat's policies toward Israel. In that sense, Nasser's more rigid position may have been a more accurate reflection of Arab public opinion than Satat's flexible stance. At any rate, Israeli sources did not believe a power struggle in Egypt enhanced the prospects for stability in the Middle East.*

The Search Continues

Despite the manifold difficulties besetting the path to peace in the Middle East—and America's own apparent inability to influence either side decisively—American officials believed that the effort to discover a basis for agreement must continue. While Soviet and American goals in the Middle East might differ in many respects, both great powers desired to avoid a new conflagration,

risking nuclear war. Accordingly, the Nixon administration renewed its efforts to resolve the Arab-Israeli controversy. In May, 1971, Secretary of State William Rogers undertook a tour of the region, the first by an American Secretary of State in eighteen years. Rogers' reception in most Arab countries visited was cordial (and this fact alone was perhaps significant in cultivating more amicable Arab-American relations). Not unexpectedly, Rogers found that Arab resentments and suspicion of Israel remained intense; Arab leaders were not disposed to make substantial concessions (like recognizing Israeli territorial annexations) for the sake of peace. In Cairo, some progress was made toward a normalization of Egyptian-American relations, although there was no sign of an *early* restoration of regular diplomatic relations between the two countries.

By this period, it was no secret that relations between the United States and Israel had become somewhat strained. Officials of the Nixon administration made it clear that, as much as any other factor, Israeli intractability blocked the restoration of stability in the Middle East. Israel's refusal even to discuss the annexation of Arab territories, in Washington's view, was an unreasonable attitude, leaving the Arabs little choice except to resort to force. Jerusalem's persistence in this rigid posture, Washington was convinced, would leave Israel diplomatically isolated and in a more militarily precarious position than before. For a change, Senator J. William Fulbright (Democrat of Arkansas) agreed with many officials of the Nixon administration. Fulbright accused Israel of "Communist-baiting humbuggery" and of seeking to "manipulate" American foreign policy in the Middle East for Zionist ends. Fulbright feared that (like South Vietnam) Israel was exploiting America's phobia about Communist expansionism in a crucial area. In brief, many American officials believed that Israeli attitudes had become highly "negative," rigid, and difficult for the United States to defend.

Predictably, Secretary of State Rogers' visit to the Middle East produced no spectacular "breakthrough" in the Arab-Israeli impasse. Indeed, events like political upheaval in Egypt during this period—along with the announcement of a new federation among Egypt, Libya, and Syria—may have made the search for a peace formula more elusive than ever. Considering that hostility between the Arabs and the Zionists erupted in the aftermath of the First World War, experience suggested that a deescalation of that dispute would be a more difficult process than settlement of the Vietnam War.*

---

*For discussions of political conditions in Egypt after Nasser's death, see *The New York Times*, October 21, 1970; May 14, 1971; and *Newsweek*, Vol. LXXVII (April 5, 1971), 40–41.

*Our discussion of Secretary of State Rogers' visit to the Middle East relies upon *The New York Times*, December 28, 1970; January 13, February 21, March 8, March 14, March 21, April 5, April 11, and May 9, 1971.

THE MIDDLE EAST AND WESTERN SECURITY

The Strategic Role of the Middle East

The strategic significance of the Middle East makes it one of the central arenas of international politics and an area of continuing concern to the United States. This strategic importance arises chiefly from three factors. First, the Middle East is a "crossroads" or bridge connecting the continents of Europe, Asia, and Africa. Land, sea, and air routes criss-cross the region, giving it a crucial role in world trade and commerce and, during time of war, making it an area of prime military importance. According to some commentators, for example, the North African campaign of World War II constituted a major turning point in that conflict.

Second, the Middle East is peculiarly vital to the West in its cold war strategy of containment of expansive Soviet Communism. The doctrine of containment was announced by the United States in 1947 in connection with the political crisis in Greece and the threat to nearby Turkey. The Middle East safeguards the southern flank of NATO and is a vital security zone for protecting the sea and air approaches across the South Atlantic to the Western Hemisphere. Today, even more than when Hitler's forces invaded North Africa during World War II, enemy control of the Middle East might prove disastrous for the security of the West. In this connection, it is worth reiterating a point discussed in Chapter 9: The rapid buildup in Soviet naval forces in recent years—with the Mediterranean serving as the major region in which Moscow has expanded its seapower—enhances the strategic significance of the Middle East for the United States and its Western allies. Some Western military analysts have interpreted the Kremlin's program of naval construction as an effort to "turn" NATO's southern flank, providing it with new opportunities to establish a strong position in North Africa and involve itself actively in political conflicts throughout the area.

The West and Middle East Oil

The vast oil resources of the Middle East rank as a third reason why the region is strategically vital.[25] The area contains between two-thirds and three-fourths of the known oil reserves of the world, the bulk of it being concentrated around the Persian Gulf. On the basis of recent discoveries and explorations, there is reason to believe that the oil reserves of the Middle East are even larger than previously supposed. Tiny Kuwait alone (smaller than the state of New Jersey) has a 30–40-billion barrel supply of oil—perhaps exceeding the oil deposits of the United States (including

Alaska). Saudi Arabia has even more extensive reserves; Iran has some 35 billion barrels; while other oil-producing states (like Iraq, Libya, the Arabian sheikdoms, and most recently, Egypt and Syria) also have petroleum deposits. Natural gas (once considered a waste product by the petroleum industries of the Middle East) has also come to be regarded as an extremely valuable resource, especially as supplies decrease in the West, while demand increases. In recent years, the Middle East has produced one-fourth of the world's entire petroleum output; one-third of all the oil available to the non-Communist world comes from this source. And present indications are that such proportions are likely to *increase*, as American domestic oil supplies are depleted, as demand for oil products continues to rise in regions like Western Europe, and as even Soviet Russia (traditionally an oil *exporter*) begins to purchase oil products from the Arab world.

The United States has an undeniable interest in access to the oil resources of the Middle East.[26] Beginning in the 1920s, American firms acquired oil concessions in Iran; oil was discovered on the Arabian Peninsula in 1933. After that period, American companies became actively involved in oil exploration and rapidly expanded their concessions in the area. World War II underscored Allied dependence upon the oil reserves of the Middle East; during and after the war, the demand for petroleum products climbed steadily in America and Western Europe; and as Japan embarked upon a path of rapid economic expansion, it became one of the largest consumers of oil from this area.

As time passed, and as a result of a series of negotiations and renegotiations, nearly all the major oil concessions of the Middle East came to be held by consortia formed by agreement among American, British, French, Dutch, and other large oil corporations. Five giants of the American oil industry—Standard Oil of New Jersey, Standard Oil of California, Gulf Oil, Mobile, and Texaco—controlled concessions encompassing some two-thirds of the known petroleum reserves of the Middle East. Two of the best-known corporations active in the Middle East were the Iraqi Petroleum Corporation (IPC) and the Arabian-American Oil Company (Aramco). Most recently, American companies have been at the forefront of oil exploration efforts in Egypt and Libya; Algeria has also signed agreements with American corporations to export oil and natural gas products.

Despite the fact that the oil-producing states of the Middle East had insisted upon, and in nearly all cases won, a larger share of the proceeds from oil production and marketing, it was still true that foreign-owned oil concessions in the region were highly profitable. Income from Middle East oil operations benefited American firms, workers, and stockholders; it provided a significant plus item in the nation's balance of payments (which had been chronically adverse for many years). The United States itself was not dependent upon foreign oil. With its own large reserves (including the new discovery on Alaska's north slope), along with limited imports from Venezuela, America remained more or less self-sufficient in meeting its oil and gas needs. American firms engaged in Middle East production sold most of their output abroad, chiefly in Western Europe. Yet few Americans seemed aware that, at present and anticipated future consumption levels, the nation's self-sufficiency in oil production was rapidly changing; even the new discoveries in Alaska did not fundamentally alter the fact that within a decade or two, the United States would almost certainly become a primary oil importer, turning to the Middle East to supply a large part of its oil and natural gas needs.[27]

Western Europe's current dependence upon the oil supplies of the Middle East was another matter. Europe has traditionally lacked petroleum reserves; and although oil and gas have been recently discovered in the North Sea and in various offshore sites, its dependence upon oil products from the Persian Gulf and North Africa remains heavy. At the time of the Suez crisis of 1956, Europe obtained some 80 percent of its oil requirements from the Middle East, most of this being transported through the Suez Canal. Although short-lived, that crisis caused considerable hardship in the NATO area. For a brief period, Middle East oil supplies were cut off; a prolonged interruption would have brought European industry to a standstill and would have seriously impaired North Atlantic security. If, for example, the burden of supplying oil to Western Europe had fallen upon the United States and Caribbean countries like Venezuela, reserves in the Western Hemisphere would have been rapidly depleted. From a military perspective—with Soviet Russia possessing the world's largest submarine fleet—Western military strategists would face a grave challenge. Lacking significant oil reserves of its own, Japan would also suffer extreme economic dislocations and military jeopardy if it no longer had access to the oil of the Middle East.

In the light of their massive dependence upon the petroleum products of the Middle East, since the mid-1950s the nations of Western Europe have taken several steps to reduce their economic and military vulnerability. As we noted in Chapter 10, Europe has forged ahead in the application of peacetime nuclear energy; extensive explorations have been carried out in the North Sea and other areas; with the Suez Canal closed since 1967, European oil has increasingly been transported in "supertankers," which can carry cargo economically around the horn of Africa; North and West African sources, closely accessible to

Western Europe, now supply almost as large a proportion of the Continent's oil needs as nations adjacent to the Persian Gulf; most recently, countries like Austria, West Germany, and Italy have begun purchasing oil and natural gas from the Soviet Union and other Communist nations. Yet, counting North Africa, Western Europe still acquires some three-fourths of its oil requirements from the Arab world. With consumption levels in Europe continuing to increase, the region *remains* heavily dependent on the petroleum products of the Middle East.

Any reference to the interest of the United States and its European allies in the oil reserves of the Middle East is likely to conjure up visions of the most Machiavellian kind of "oil diplomacy" by Western nations. Some critics of American foreign policy in the Middle East are convinced that the diplomatic moves of the United States in this region are "dictated by American oil companies"—a charge which has been a standard item of Communist propaganda for years. America's well-known identification with politically conservative regimes—like King Faisal's in Saudi Arabia or the monarchy in Iran—is often accounted for on this basis. Conversely, America's supposed opposition to concepts like "Arab socialism" is attributed to apprehension about the future of its oil interests in the Middle East. There is no point in denying that the United States and its European allies *are* deeply concerned about the continued accessibility of Middle Eastern oil fields; any prolonged interruption in oil supplies from this area could have momentous consequences for the West's security and economic well-being. The Western stake in the oil reserves of the Middle East is direct and important. Protecting this interest unquestionably ranks as a prime American objective in the area.

Having acknowledged this, it must also be emphasized that *the oil-producing nations of the Middle East also enjoy many benefits growing out of Western oil operations in the area;* in some respects, they are even *more* dependent upon the continued production and sale of oil in Western markets than America and its allies. For many nations in the area, oil reserves are the only significant natural resource that exists in any appreciable quantity, and which can be developed economically. The production and sale of petroleum and natural gas offer the only (or the main) hope for industrialization and national development; even agricultural development programs depend heavily upon income derived from oil royalties and taxes levied upon foreign oil companies; nearly all the oil-producing countries have increased both the proportionate share and the total income they derive from oil operations. By general consent, companies like the Iraqi Petroleum Corporation and Aramco have set an example sharply at variance with the activities of other foreign concerns (in regions, for example, like Latin America). In the main, these corporations have reinvested heavily within the host countries; they have been willing periodically to renegotiate existing oil concessions; they have applied the royalty rate to a broad range of activities besides the mere production of oil; they have deliberately sought to employ and train thousands of Arabs or Iranians at all levels of the oil industry; they have paid fair wages and provided liberal fringe benefits to their employees; they have built schools and provided educational scholarships for foreign study; they have endeavored to protect oil-rich states in the Middle East against the fluctuations in the world oil market (which has suffered acutely since the 1960s from the problem of oversupply). That this behavior stems, in the final analysis, from the desire of foreign oil corporations (supported in some cases by their governments) to *preserve* their concessions in one of the most turbulent regions on the globe is perhaps self-evident. But the point we are emphasizing here is that the relationship between foreign oil corporations and the nations of the Middle East has proved to be *mutually profitable and beneficial.* (There is no reason to assume that the relationship is necessarily a "zero-sum game.")* The lesson of the Iranian oil crisis of 1951 was not lost on governments within the area: When oil production and sales stop, they are perhaps the principal losers! In the short run at least, they would suffer the most acute economic dislocations; and in the long run, their hopes for modernization and economic growth would be unrealized. It is significant that the Six-Day War of 1967 witnessed no lasting stoppage of Middle East oil shipments; efforts by extremist political groups, some nonoil-producing states, and Communist organizations inside and outside the area since 1967 to deny the West access to the Middle East oil have all failed. Ironically, some of the most outspokenly anti-Western governments in the Middle East, like Nasser's Egypt, were dependent upon keeping the flow of oil unimpeded: Since 1967, with the Suez Canal blocked, Cairo has received a "subsidy" from Kuwait, Saudi Arabia, and Libya, without which Egypt's financial position would probably be untenable. It is also noteworthy that —in spite of periodic denunciations of America's "oil imperialism" by certain Arab groups—Egypt requested that American oil corporations carry on exploration and development of its petroleum resources! Even Syria (perhaps the most vehemently and consistently anti-Western Arab

government) has been reluctant to cut the oil pipelines crossing its frontiers or to permit guerrilla organizations to carry out this threat.

Yet it must be frankly conceded that by the 1970s, Western oil interests in the strife-torn Middle East faced an uncertain future.* While recent events had not brought about any radical change in the relationship between Western oil companies and producing states of the Middle East, this was of course no guarantee that such changes had been ruled out for the future. Arab resentment against the United States (and to a lesser degree Western Europe) because of its support for Israel showed no sign of diminishing. The overthrow of the Libyan monarchy late in 1969 protended a further decline in Western influence: Another pro-Western regime had been ousted, and within a few months the revolutionary government issued nationalization decrees affecting Western oil concessions. Earlier, Iraq had compelled the Iraqi Petroleum Corporation to accept new agreements greatly limiting its concessions; the Soviet Union won new exploratory rights for expanding Iraq's oil output. Moscow also arrived at an agreement to purchase natural gas and other petroleum products from Iran; Syria was similarly relying upon Soviet assistance to prospect for and develop its oil resources.

These developments suggested that—after a period of many years in which Moscow did little to challenge the position of Western business concerns in the Middle East oil industry—the Soviet Union had decided to displace America and Europe. The oil fields of the Middle East, some commentators were convinced, was the paramount prize to be awarded the winner of Soviet–American rivalry in this zone. Apparently, Moscow was determined to capitalize upon its rapport with Arab governments, and even the desire of other pro-Western states (like Jordan and

---

*A "zero-sum game" is illustrated by a football game or a chess match (which does not end in a tie or "draw"): If one side wins, then the other side loses. By contrast, a "nonzero-sum game" is one (like a tariff agreement or labor-management bargain) in which both sides may win (or lose); a gain by one side is not necessarily a setback for the other.

*Western dependence upon Middle East oil was underscored by the results of negotiations between the major oil-producing states of the region and some 23 oil corporations over new royalty agreements, early in 1971. For the first time, the oil-rich states of the Middle East presented a united front through the Organization of Petroleum Exporting Countries (OPEC). Not unexpectedly, OPEC demanded higher royalties and other benefits from Western oil companies. Negotiations were prolonged and often acrimonious. In the end, the members of OPEC largely won their demands: over the next five years, for example, the oil companies agreed to pay to the six principal oil-exporting states of the Persian Gulf region some $10 billion in additional oil royalties and benefits. The new agreement would almost certainly raise the price of petroleum products in Western Europe and, eventually perhaps, in the United States. Even more significantly, the agreement marked what might prove to be a turning point in economic relations between the industrialized and the developing nations. The Shah of Iran, for instance, called on other nations exporting commodities needed in the West to form organizations capable of gaining them better terms of trade. See *The New York Times,* February 7 and 21, 1971.

Iran) to reduce their dependence upon the West, in pursuit of a twofold objective: to break the almost exclusive grip which Western companies had on Middle East oil concessions, and to establish itself as the dominant foreign power in the area. Successful pursuit of this strategy would both deal a grave blow to Western security and consolidate Soviet Russia's hold over key Middle Eastern states. In brief, Russia would emerge from this process as the new master of the Middle East.[28]

The evidence left no doubt that Moscow's involvement in the Middle East oil industry had expanded significantly since the 1960s; nor was there any reason to suppose that its role would diminish in the years ahead. As we have mentioned, Soviet Russia was itself becoming a petroleum importer: The combination of its own internal needs, which were increasing, plus the needs of Eastern Europe, plus its sales (for "hard currencies") in Western Europe meant that Moscow needed oil from the Middle East and was willing to pay attractively for it. Both politically and economically, the oil-rich states of the area were finding it desirable to accept Soviet terms. Russia's emergence on the Middle East oil scene improved the market for oil sales and provided Western companies with what many governments in the area believed beneficial "competition." Politically, some governments did not of course object to the fact that America and Western Europe were apprehensive: The situation might compel greater Western sympathy for Arab grievances toward Israel!

Meanwhile, the oil-producing states of the Middle East were not likely to forget three key considerations tending to confine the Soviet Union's new "oil offensive" within narrow limits. The first was that the West afforded by all odds the *largest* market for the oil products of the Middle East, while Japan's purchases were not inconsiderable. This fact was not likely to change in the near future. The second was that Soviet domination of the oil reserves of the Middle East could prove even more inimical to the interests of the producing states than the dominant role traditionally played by Western business concerns. Much as they might welcome Soviet assistance against Israel, or look upon Moscow's competition as a healthy antidote to Western dominance in the oil industry, governments within the region were aware that Soviet trade and commercial policy nearly always had *political objectives*. The Kremlin's oil offensive was but one prong of its over-all efforts to penetrate, and perhaps dominate, the Middle East. A third reality was that throughout the postwar period, Soviet Russia had been *a major competitor* with Middle East oil producers in the petroleum markets of the world. On several occasions, Moscow has "dumped" oil on the world market at cut-rate prices, impairing an already fragile price structure and reducing the royalties

to Middle Eastern nations; Russia's effort to win new customers in Europe had been in part at the expense of Persian Gulf and North African producers. Whatever their political and ideological differences, governments as dissimilar as Iraq and Iran, or Saudi Arabia and Libya, were cognizant that Moscow's interest in the oil reserves of the region did not stem basically from a concern for the welfare of the countries involved. They knew that a displacement of Western involvement, followed by a Soviet monopoly over Middle Eastern oil fields, served only the interests of the Kremlin.

The Baghdad Pact and CENTO

Awareness of the strategic importance of the Middle East led officials in Washington to accord its defense high priority in the cold war conflict. In the first important case coming before the United Nations, the United States supported Iran's complaint against Soviet intrigue in its northern provinces. Less than a year later, the United States had extended some $400 million in assistance to Greece and Turkey. As British and French power steadily declined in the Middle East and North Africa, American officials became convinced that further steps were needed to promote the security of the Middle East. Using NATO as a model, in the early 1950s Washington proposed a "Middle East Command"—a plan which quickly aroused the opposition of Arab governments, chiefly Egypt, and was soon abandoned.[29] Rebuffed in its efforts to establish a broad regional security system, the Eisenhower administration narrowed its objective to the creation of a defense network for the "northern tier" countries of Greece, Turkey, Iraq, Iran, and Pakistan. Situated along the Soviet border, these nations were perhaps most vulnerable to Communist pressures; a tight security fence through them would, it was hoped, serve to bar Soviet penetration southward. Using Britain's historic links with several of these nations as a nucleus, Washington strongly encouraged a new defense treaty—the Baghdad Pact (actually a series of pacts), signed in 1955.

From the start, the Baghdad Pact probably did as much to *weaken* the security of the Middle East, and to *reduce* its ability to withstand Communism, as it did to strengthen the region. Arab opposition to it remained implacable; the pact became a rallying cry for opponents of "Western imperialism." Only one Arab nation, Iraq, belonged to it; in 1959, following the overthrow of the Iraqi monarchy, Iraq withdrew from the pact. Israel was apprehensive about the treaty, especially after American arms-aid began to flow to its signatories. Having sponsored the pact, the United States decided not to join it (perhaps out of fear of Israeli and Arab reaction), although Washington did participate "informally" in its deliberations. To Arab nationalists, the Baghdad

Pact symbolized Western opposition to their policy of "neutralism" or "nonalignment," a key element of which was their desire to avoid military alliances with either major cold war bloc.[30] Following Iraq's withdrawal from the Baghdad Pact, the alliance was reorganized and renamed the Central Treaty Organization (CENTO).

In the years that followed, CENTO seemed less and less relevant to the most urgent problems of the Middle East. Finding Arab resentment against the pact still intense, the United States continued to participate only as an "observer" in CENTO's deliberations. Turkey—involved in the continuing dispute with Greece over Cyprus—found the alliance of minimum assistance in achieving its goals. Nor did Pakistan receive any noteworthy benefit from CENTO in its ongoing quarrel with India. The government of Iran—considered in the 1950s one of the staunchest opponents of Communism in the Middle East—in time improved its relations with the Soviet Union; by the late 1960s, Tehran had accepted a limited program of Soviet military and economic assistance. The most urgent foreign policy issue facing the Iranian government perhaps was mounting tensions with certain Arab states over their respective influence in the Persian Gulf (or what Cairo preferred to call "the Arab Gulf") after Britain's traditional power in the area was withdrawn. The possibility of an overt Soviet attack against the Middle East seemed altogether remote. Yet CENTO appeared to afford little protection against what had become an evident reality: a growing Soviet "presence" in the Middle East, stemming from the rapid expansion in Russian naval power in the Mediterranean; Moscow's ongoing programs of economic and technical assistance to selected Middle Eastern nations (including, by the late 1960s) "traditional" as well as "revolutionary" states; and the Kremlin's vast program of arms-aid to Arab nations, especially those (like Egypt, Syria, and Iraq) which suffered massive losses in the "third round" conflict with Israel in 1967.*

*Many of the regional and international implications of the buildup in Soviet naval strength in the Mediterranean and adjacent waters were discussed in Chapter 9. Voluminous data on varied Soviet military activities in the Middle East in recent years are provided in J. C. Hurewitz, *Middle East Politics: The Military Dimension* (New York: Praeger, 1969); see especially his account of arms-aid to Egypt, pp. 123–145, and to Syria–Iraq, pp. 145–163, and his more general discussion of the continuing arms race in the Middle East, pp. 438–489. Other recent evidence of the growth of Soviet influence in the area is cited in *The New York Times* (January 15, July 16, October 13, October 22, and December 25, 1968; January 26, February 9, and June 15, 1969). Unquestioned evidence of an expanded Soviet "presence" in the Middle East, does not of course prove Russian *control* over, or domination of, nations in the area. A number of the above sources allude to complaints by Soviet officials, for example, about the lack of "gratitude" by Egyptians or other societies for Russian aid; neither in 1967 nor afterwards were Arab officials prone to accept Moscow's "ad-

The "Eisenhower Doctrine"

The next stage in America's efforts to bolster Middle Eastern defenses occurred as a response to growing Communist influence in the area. Egypt and Syria were receiving large stockpiles of arms from behind the Iron Curtain. During the Suez crisis of 1956–1957, when British–French–Israeli troops attacked Egypt, there arose the possibility that "Soviet volunteers" might enter the Middle East, ostensibly to rescue Egypt from British–French–Israeli domination. These threats prompted the Eisenhower administration to ask Congress to approve what came to be designated the "Eisenhower Doctrine," making more explicit Washington's concern with Middle Eastern security. Congress gave the President substantially the authority he requested. A joint resolution passed on March 9, 1957, declared that "preservation of the independence and integrity of the nations of the Middle East" was vital to the American national interest. The key phrase in the resolution granted the President authority "to use armed forces to assist any such nation or group of such nations requesting assistance against armed aggression from any country controlled by international communism."[31]

As the months passed, the Eisenhower Doctrine was broadened in scope, particularly by giving an elastic definition to the concept of "armed aggression." Washington began to invoke the doctrine to deal with cases of "indirect aggression," citing a UN General Assembly resolution of 1949 calling on all states "to refrain from any threats or acts, direct or indirect, aimed at impairing the freedom, independence, or integrity of any state."[32] On July 1, 1958, Secretary of State Dulles stated that "we do not think that the words 'armed attack' preclude treating as such an armed revolution which is fomented abroad, aided and assisted from abroad."

The immediate occasion for this expanded interpretation of the Eisenhower Doctrine was the threat of internal subversion in pro-Western Lebanon. In Washington's view, rebellion against the regime of President Chamoun was being morally and materially aided by pro-Communist Syria and Egypt, then joined as the United Arab Republic. American officials also feared that a revolution in nearby Iraq had greatly enhanced Communist influence in that country and had given anti-Western elements a new base of operations from which to threaten Lebanon. King Hussein in neighbor-

vice" in dealing with Israel. As former American Ambassador to Egypt John S. Badeau has emphasized, it is very difficult for America and Soviet Russia alike to "translate" their programs of economic and military assistance to other countries into any significant degree of policy control (or even the lesser goal of *policy restraint*) over such countries. See his perceptive study, *The American Approach to the Arab World* (New York: Harper & Row, 1968), pp. 58–62, 67–75, 84–90.

ing Jordan was able to maintain his authority only with the help of British troops. As the crisis mounted in Lebanon, local authorities requested the United States to render assistance. Accordingly, on July 15, 1958, President Eisenhower ordered American marines to enter Lebanon to preserve order in that internally divided country. For the time being, Lebanon was successfully held in the Western camp.

In the long run, however, it could be questioned whether the American landing in Lebanon enhanced the position of the West in the Middle East. Predictably, it became a symbol of Western "interventionism" in the area and supplied ammunition for fanatical anti-Western groups. It compromised Lebanon's attempt to remain neutral in intra-Arab controversies. Above all, perhaps, it tended to polarize political opinion within Lebanon itself. No country in the world endeavored to maintain such a delicate political equilibrium—between the dominant Maronite (Christian and pro-Western) element and the Moslem (pro-Arab) element. When the United States intervened on behalf of the former, it invited counter-intervention by President Nasser of Egypt and other Arab leaders on behalf of the latter. Lebanon's political crisis in 1969 could be traced in part to resentments against the West created by American intervention in 1958.[33]

THE WEST AND ARAB NATIONALISM

Sources and Nature of Nationalist Ferment

Since the end of World War II, Arab nationalism has become a mighty stream fed by numerous tributaries. It has threatened to sweep away Western influence throughout the Middle East and to inundate that area in wave after wave of fanaticism and xenophobia, spawning numerous intraregional tensions and inviting great-power antagonisms.

Nationalism has infused virtually every issue troubling the Middle East in the contemporary era. The complaints in 1946 of Syria and Lebanon to the United Nations against French colonialism were anchored in nationalism. Part of the Arab states' opposition to the creation of Israel lay in their historical resentment of Western dictation. Nationalism was a key factor in the Iranian oil dispute which began in 1951 and was not settled until 1953, when Iran successfully nationalized the holdings of the Anglo-Iranian oil company.[34]

Not since the time of the Crusades have the Arab states been politically united.* Their in-

ternal weaknesses have greatly facilitated the imposition of colonial domination over them. Pan-Arabism is a natural reaction against former colonial subjection and, in the minds of many Arab leaders, the necessary preliminary to restoration of the greatness that once belonged to Islam. Pan-Arabism is sustained by many forces, of which three have been of lasting historical significance: a common language—Arabic; a common religion—Islam; and common racial ties—Semitic. Since World War I, other forces have fostered Arab unity. Most of the Arab states received their independence after that war from either Britain or France, their colonial masters. Economic backwardness and widespread poverty have given the Arab masses a sense of unity and feeling of separateness from the more advanced Western countries. To a greater or lesser degree, all the Arab states resent involvement in the cold war and desire to retain their independence of action from both the Communist bloc and the Western alliance. Finally, since 1947, there has been a powerful new bond of Arab unity: intense hostility to Israel.

Middle Eastern nationalism differs from other nationalist movements with which the student of history is familiar, such as those in nineteenth-century Europe or in India under the leadership of Gandhi and Nehru. In Europe, nationalism meant predominantly "self-determination," a goal that grew out of the philosophy of the French Revolution. But the Middle East "received nationalism in isolation, without liberalism, democracy, and the humanitarian aims. . . ."[35] That is why nationalism in the Middle East has so often "taken . . . the form of chauvinism, of emotional aggression, and of opposition to everything foreign rather than of genuine patriotism." In its over-all manifestations, Middle Eastern nationalism is

. . . distinguished by the over-estimation of one's own nation and the denigration of others, the lack of the spirit of self-criticism and responsibility, an ambivalent appraisal of the destiny of one's nation based on a feeling of inferiority, and a general tendency to attribute anything wrong with one's nation to the evil-doing of others.[36]

A perceptive student of the Islamic religion has made much the same point about Arab nationalism.

---

*Once again it is necessary to remind the reader that the term "Middle East" and "Arab world" are not coterminous; the former is much broader than the latter. In

earlier portions of the chapter, we have construed it to include countries like Turkey and Iran which, by most interpretations, are geographically a part of the Middle East. Yet these countries are not usually regarded (certainly not by *Arabs*) as part of the "Arab world." Many criteria might be used to define this concept, but the most common perhaps is use of the Arabic language. By this definition, the Arab world extends from Morocco through Iraq and from Syria through Egypt and the Arabian peninsula. Admittedly, even by this criterion, borderline cases (like northern Sudan and much of the eastern "horn" of Africa) remain.

To resist aliens, to work against their domination, even to hate or despise them, is one thing. To respect all members of one's own nation, to envisage its welfare, to evolve an effective loyalty to that welfare, and to work constructively so as to bring it about, is quite another. It is easier to see what one is or should be fighting against, than to imagine what one is or should be fighting for. . . . [I]t is sometimes not appreciated how negative until now have been the nationalisms of the Islamic world.[37]

Another conspicuous theme in Arab nationalism has been its defensiveness and its massive sense of insecurity. "The modern Arab," Wilfred C. Smith has observed, "is first and foremost a person defending himself and his society against onslaught." Contemporary Arabs believe themselves to be "still under attack, still reacting to an insecurity almost greater than they can bear."[38] This aspect of Arab nationalism has many sources, too numerous and complex to discuss here.[39] Suffice to say that it imparts to the Arab nationalist movement an emotional fervor, a hypersensitivity, and deeply ingrained suspicion toward the outside world, that is distinctive. Arabs are quick to discern affronts to their honor and dignity or plots against their newly gained freedoms by foreigners, especially by Western societies. Arab leaders caution the masses continually against the alleged attempts of "imperialists" (meaning principally Western imperialists) to reimpose colonial control over their affairs or to dominate their policies by economic and military means.

In the contemporary period, another source of frustration—often producing emotionalism, irrational behavior, and fanaticism—has often pervaded the Arab world. This is the hiatus between what the Arabs have achieved in the past, and what they hope to achieve under "revolutionary" regimes today, on the one hand; and what they have in fact accomplished, on the other hand. For a number of Arab societies, this gap has *widened* in recent years; in other cases, progress has been minimal. The "glories" of the Arab empire—in territorial extent, one of the largest in world history—remain vivid in the Arab mind. Beginning with the revolution in Egypt in 1952, ultimately led by President Nasser, several Arab societies had great hopes that, under their own political leadership devoted to programs of radical change, the Arabs would once more be restored to a position of influence and respect abroad and rapid progress at home. In Egypt, in Syria, in Iraq, in Algeria, and most recently in Libya, revolutionary Arab governments committed themselves to these goals and promised quick results. In nearly all these cases, of course, some progress was unquestionably made—such as land reform in Egypt and Iraq, expanding educational opportunities in nearly all countries, the gradual "emancipation" of women, and other gains. Yet it was also true that, by the 1960s, many of the internal problems of Egypt were becoming more critical than ever; Syria and Iraq had not succeeded in achieving real political stability; Algeria continued to confront major economic problems. The gap between expectations and realities was especially marked in foreign relations. At a time when much of the Arab world was governed by revolutionary governments, Israel had made its largest incursions against Arab territory! The concept of "Arab unity" seemed perhaps more incapable of realization than ever. Until Nasser's death in 1970, Egypt's government remained dependent upon a subsidy provided by *monarchies* in Kuwait and Saudi Arabia, fact which seemed to underscore the hiatus we have identified. Unable to resolve the Arab–Israeli dispute by their own efforts, Arab governments could do little more than acquiesce in efforts by the United States and the Soviet Union to do so. In brief, the gulf between promises and performance seemed to have *expanded* in the period when Arabs were becoming masters of their own political destinies. This fact was bound to exacerbate frustrations throughout the Middle East and to serve as a continual source of political ferment, xenophobia, and over-all instability. In such situations (and an analogy might be Red China's "Hate America" campaign) it was perhaps an irresistible temptation for Arabs to blame "foreign imperialists" (meaning chiefly *Western* imperialists), Zionists, or other external forces for their tribulations.

Goals of Contemporary Arab Nationalism

The foregoing discussion is not intended to suggest that modern Arab nationalism was devoid of *positive* goals. Admittedly, the things that contemporary Arab nationalists *oppose* have sometimes been more evident to the outside world than what they are seeking to achieve. The revolutionary regimes which have come into power in the Middle East since the 1950s have often required a period of several years to produce a detailed program of positive objectives; and even when they have done so (Egypt under Nasser, 1952–1970, furnishes a notable example) goals are sometimes left vague and inexplicit. In a word, contemporary Arab nationalism seeks, above all else, "modernization" of some of the most primitive social, economic, and political structures on the globe. The concept of modernization of course has many facets; its precise requirements naturally vary from one society to another. The nations of the Middle East also differ widely in terms of their resources for achieving modernization. Countries like Jordan and Lebanon face extraordinarily difficult problems, while the oil-producing states—principally Iran, Iraq, Saudi

Arabia, and Kuwait—possess the means to finance ambitious development programs.

Many of the positive goals of contemporary Arab nationalism are epitomized in the concept of "Arab socialism" identified with President Nasser's regime in Egypt. Arab socialism is an extremely pragmatic and flexible concept, incorporating a range of diverse elements—from the historic Islamic emphasis upon the welfare of the community and the subordination of individual rights to it, to the American New Deal and Fair Deal programs, to the humanitarian goals espoused by European Socialist and Communist parties. Nasser's goal of creating a "democratic, socialist, cooperative society" and his conviction that democracy "must be social as well as political," has translated itself into a variety of programs designed to promote the welfare of the Arab masses and to establish a political order that has solid mass support. Specific goals of socialism —and in this respect his program enjoys widespread support from Morocco to Iraq—are land reform, industrialization and enhanced agricultural production, the promotion of cooperative societies, expanding educational opportunities, improved sanitation and health facilities, a rising standard of living for the Egyptian masses, creation of new areas of arable land, the emancipation of women, and other steps designed to modernize one of the most primitive and economically backward societies found anywhere on the globe.* The stated goals of Nasser's regime, in the Egyptian President's own words, were

. . . to end the exploitation of people, to realize national aspirations and to develop the mature political consciousness that is an indispensable preliminary for a sound democracy. . . . Our ultimate aim is to provide Egypt with a truly democratic and representative government, not the type of parliamentary dictatorship which the Palace and a corrupt "Pasha" class imposed on the people.[40]

Westerners, particularly critics of "Arab socialism," are apt to find such objectives extremely vague and mystical. To some minds, they are in fact little more than attempts to rationalize, and make publicly acceptable, the exercise of authoritarian political power in Egypt and other revolutionary Arab states and perhaps to anesthetize the masses in an effort to disguise the relative lack of progress under indigenous leaders. Such judgments, however, seem much too simple and are in some ways highly deceptive. There is not the slightest doubt, for example, that the Egyptian government, the Ba'ath party in Syria and Iraq, and the revolutionary regimes in Algeria and Libya are *genuinely committed* to the improvement of their societies; if nothing else, the sheer political survival of the regime dictates this course. Even the remaining monarchies of the Middle East, like Kuwait, Jordan, Saudi Arabia, and Iran, have adopted ambitious development schemes. It is no less true, however, that groups espousing national development programs face monumental problems and difficult choices. Among these are creating a national consensus on the *order of priorities* to be adopted by the government. Should limited resources, for example, be used initially to promote education or to attack age-old health problems? Should industrialization take precedence over expanded agricultural production? Or take another pervasive dilemma: Without losing popular support, how can indigenous governments generate internally the funds needed to raise development capital? Will the masses tolerate the level of taxation, the limitation of consumption and imports, needed to make this possible? Again, how can land reform programs be carried out without *reducing* farm output? Such questions confront every Arab government devoted to modernization; they are unusually difficult for those countries in the Middle East which lack oil reserves or other resources with which to finance ambitious development projects. Small wonder that the specific objectives of contemporary Arab nationalism often appear imprecise and vague. Even now, Arab leaders themselves are perhaps still at a loss to know how the goals are to be achieved with the resources available or the approach to national development that promises the most effective results.

The "Confrontation" Between Revolution and Evolution

If all governments in the Middle East (with the possible exception of the Arabian sheikhdoms) subscribe to the goal of "modernization," two broad paths have been open for achieving it. We have already identified one of these: a "revolutionary" movement whose initial goal is to seize power and then to undertake the radical transformation of political, economic, and social life. The military junta which deposed the Egyptian monarchy in 1952, and until 1970 was led by Gamal Abdel Nasser, set the pattern of revolutionary activity in the contemporary Middle East. After 1952, Nasser's movement generated wide support among the Arab masses; his Arab Socialist Union (a movement which underwent several changes

*More detailed treatment of the positive ingredients in modern Arab nationalism, particularly in its Egyptian setting, may be found in: J. S. F. Parker, "The United Arab Republic," *International Affairs* 38 (January, 1962), 15–29; Gamal Abdel Nasser, "The Egyptian Revolution," *Foreign Affairs* 33 (January, 1955), 199–212; P. J. Vatikiotis, *Egypt Since the Revolution* (New York: Praeger, 1968), pp. 19–143; Tom Little, *Modern Egypt* (New York: Prager, 1967), pp. 177–256; J. H. Thompson and R. D. Reischauer, eds., *Modernization of the Arab World* (New York: Van Nostrand Reinhold, 1966), pp. 178–212.

of name after 1952) tended to be regarded as the prototype of revolutionary Arab nationalism. Despite two major military defeats by Israel, and the existence of massive problems within Egypt itself, until his death Nasser's prestige remained high and his appeal for many Arab groups stronger than ever!

But Nasser's model of Arab socialism was not without rivals in the Middle East. The leading one was perhaps the Ba'ath party, founded in Syria and having branches in several other Arab countries, particularly Iraq. Devoted to Arab unity and Arab socialism, the Ba'ath espoused objectives similar in many respects to those of Nasser's regime. Yet there were also a number of major differences (the Ba'ath, for example, emphasized *democratic* decision-making within the party). In some areas, especially in the Levant, the Ba'ath and Nasser's movement were competitors for the political loyalties of the Arab masses.[41]

The other path to modernization in the Middle East has been taken by those societies that have thus far avoided revolution, preferring an *evolutionary* approach to modernization. In the main, these societies are still governed by monarchs, such as the Hashemites in Jordan, the Saudi family in Saudi Arabia, the sheiks in Kuwait, and the royal dynasty in Iran. For many years Libya was numbered in this group, until its military officers seized power, ousting King Idris, in 1969. Conscious of the "winds of change" which threaten antiquated institutions and practices throughout the Afro–Asian world, the monarchies of the Middle East have committed themselves to programs of national development. Possessing vast oil resources, several of them are in a position to achieve rapid progress. Kuwait, for example, has emerged as the "welfare state" *par excellance*. Its per capita income is the highest in the region; health services and education are free; economic diversification is proceeding apace; it has established a record for progress in many spheres that is the envy of its neighbors.[42] In recent years, the government of Saudi Arabia has also forged rapidly ahead along the path of modernization. Admittedly, the Saudi dynasty was late in adopting this objective; but the "palace revolution" in 1964 —which designated Crown Prince Faisal as Viceroy (and later King)—might be said to mark the country's entry into the modern world. King Faisal was dedicated to the reform of one of the most primitive societies on the globe. Under his leadership, changes were being made rapidly and, in some instances, drastically.[43]

Another example of the evolutionary approach was Shah Reza Pahlavi's "White Revolution" in Iran, which was not a "revolution" in the usual sense, but a sweeping program of reform and modernization carried out by the monarchy. The Shah's efforts encountered hostility from two groups: the aristocratic elite (who were the proto-

type of "absentee landlords") and revolutionary forces favoring elimination of the monarchy and other radical transformations. Promulgating land reform by royal decree, expanding educational opportunities, attacking the country's age-old health and sanitation problems—by such steps, the Shah's regime hoped to usher Iran into the twentieth century. By 1970, Iran had achieved one of the most outstanding records of economic progress made by any "developing" nation. As in the other monarchies of the Middle East, least progress had been made in democratizing *political* decision-making.[44]

Dilemmas for American Policy

The conflict between the forces of evolution and revolution in the Middle East presented American policy-makers with a number of difficult choices and dilemmas. With some critics of American policy, it had become commonplace to assert that the United States "opposes revolution" in the Middle East and elsewhere. To some minds, the close ties between America and nations like Saudi Arabia and Iran offered presumptive evidence that Washington was too intimately identified with political reaction and authoritarianism. By contrast, American relations with countries like Syria, Iraq, and Egypt—where revolutionary regimes dominated—were characterized by misunderstandings, tensions, and in some periods hostility. Monarchies in the Middle East could count upon generous American economic assistance and arms-aid; revolutionary governments received far less, or none at all.

Choosing the American response to the confrontation between revolutionary and evolutionary methods of national development in the Middle East was far from a simplistic or clear-cut matter. However the United States responded, it was likely to be criticized and to discover obstacles to the achievement of American goals in the area. A case could be made, of course, for the idea that revolutionary Arab nationalism constituted the "wave of the future" in an area long weighted down by the forces of traditionalism and backwardness. The coup in Libya in 1969 strengthened the idea that the trend of history (in the Middle East, as elsewhere) was perhaps against monarchies, which seemed more and more out of place in the modern world. Advocates of revolution inside and outside the Middle East contended that the most urgent necessity was *political modernization;* without it meaningful social, economic, educational, and other transformations were not possible. Because of their past associations with the colonial powers and their modern ties with Britain and America, the monarchies of the Middle East appeared tainted. Jordan, for example, depended upon British and American assistance for its survival; without Western aid, the monarchy might have collapsed long ago. Nor was it coincidence, critics asserted, that throughout the postwar period American military bases in the Middle East (another object of resentment among revolutionary groups in the area) were located almost entirely in countries still ruled by monarchies. Followers of Nasser and the Ba'ath party regarded such bases as incompatible with the Arab desire to remain nonaligned in the cold war. That officials in Washington since the early 1950s have preferred the evolutionary to the revolutionary approach to modernization in the Middle East seems incontestable. Since 1952, for example, America's relations with Egypt have been strained; formal relations between the two governments were broken during the "Six-Day War" in 1967, and they have not yet been restored. Syrian–American relations have perhaps been characterized by even greater tensions. American officials would unquestionably identify Cairo, Damascus, and Baghdad as the leading centers of anti-Western, anti-American (not to mention anti-Zionist) agitation in the Middle East. Conversely, the governments of Jordan, Saudi Arabia, and Iran have obviously desired cordial relations with America and other Western countries. These governments have not been in the forefront of those seeking to "drive Israel into the sea"; in general, they have not sought to interfere in the internal affairs of their neighbors; nor have they intervened in conflicts outside their area (such as the Congo crisis of the early 1960s); like the West, these states have a stake in maintaining uninterrupted oil production and access to Western markets. For evident reasons also, the monarchies of the Middle East abhor Communism; they have not hesitated to take steps, either with other countries or unilaterally, to curtail Marxist influence within the area. By the mid-1960s, Washington had discovered another reason for preferring evolutionary to revolutionary methods. Judged by the *results achieved,* the evidence suggested that Saudi Arabia, Kuwait, and Iran (Jordan excepted) had in fact made *substantially greater internal progress* than countries in which modernization was more of a slogan than a reality. The contrast between conditions in Iraq and Iran—both oil-rich nations—was especially marked. The former had gravitated from one political and economic crisis to another; Baghdad's development schemes had seldom been translated into positive gains. As we have observed, Iran had established an enviable record of gains in the direction of modernization. Politically, both governments were authoritarian, the former being ruled by the Ba'ath party (with military support), while the latter remained under control of the Shah (who also relied upon the army).

American policy toward the problem of evolution versus revolution in the Middle East also had to take account of another factor: In some societies there, little or no evidence existed that the masses themselves actually preferred a movement like the Arab Socialist Union to the existing monarchy. Monarchial institutions in Saudi Arabia and Iran (less so perhaps in Jordan) had deep roots in tradition, where they were viewed as compatible with (if not required by) the Islamic religious heritage. In areas like the rural portions of Jordan and Iran, for example, the masses themselves supported existing political institutions—which was perhaps a key fact in the monarchy's survival.

One thing seemed clear: In the light of the great diversity existing among the governments of the Middle East, no single or totally consistent American policy toward the area was possible. Any policy had to be grounded initially upon recognition that America's power to affect the political future of the Middle East *was very limited.* Unilaterally, the United States could neither overthrow a revolutionary regime in Egypt nor maintain it in power; it could neither "maintain" the Iranian monarchy in the face of popular disaffection nor depose it against the wishes of the Iranian people. The only defensible principle upon which American policy could be based was the idea that the future political development of societies in the Middle East rested with the peoples in the area themselves; only they could determine what kind of government they wanted and which approach to national development they preferred. The United States had no choice other than to accept their decisions. This did not mean that America had to *agree with the policies* of all governments in the region, irrespective of whether they were adopted by evolutionary or revolutionary regimes. Friction between the United States and Egypt, for example, could arise (and in the past had arisen) fully as much over differing approaches to the Arab–Israeli dispute as over disagreements concerning the character of the Egyptian government; the United States could not be expected to support an Iranian threat against Iraq, or vice versa. For the United States to sponsor, or otherwise support, revolutionary activities in the Middle East would be the most blatant form of interventionism; it would be no less interventionism for America to align itself unalterably with the status quo. The governing principle had to be the idea that America supported the right of the *peoples themselves to determine their own political future.* After they had done so, America would seek to maintain constructive relations with the existing government, whatever its complexion or its avowed ideology.

ARAB NEUTRALISM AND NONALIGNMENT

A central tenet of Arab nationalist ideology has been the acceptance and advocacy of a foreign policy of "neutralism" or "nonalignment" by the overwhelming majority of Arab countries from Morocco to Iraq. Nonalignment in foreign affairs is regarded by Arab leaders and masses as both a visible symbol, and a necessary consequence, of the gaining and maintenance of Arab independence, as indicated by Nasser's remark in an interview with American newsmen: "We want, above all and everything, to feel that we are free."[45] The connection between the goal of Arab independence and a neutralist position in foreign affairs was further suggested by a speech by Nasser on March 5, 1958, upon the establishment of the United Arab Republic (the union between Syria and Egypt, which was dissolved in 1961). After recounting the Arab effort to achieve independence, Nasser noted:

You won as a result of a long and bitter struggle. You won in the battle of freedom. You won in the battle of independence. You won in the battle of alignments and alliance. . . . You won when you decided to have an independent policy for yourselves emanating from your own country, land, and conscience. . . . Today, brethren, we must fight and be on the alert in order to preserve this independent policy.[46]

In whatever terms it is expressed by individual Arab leaders—and in whatever degree it had to be recognized that a foreign policy of "neutralism" or "nonalignment" often encompassed highly diverse national policies toward regional and global issues*—the Arab states were agreed on certain essentials of their neutralist credo. One common denominator, as Nasser expressed the idea, was that the voice of Arab states "in international forums is not counted as an automatic one attached to a particular bloc . . . which can be added to or discounted in accordance with the position of a certain great power . . ."[47] This in turn implied Arab unwillingness to join in foreign-sponsored military pacts or to become *permanently* identified with either cold war power bloc. Nonalignment also implied diplomatic freedom of action. Arab states, along with other neutralist countries in Africa and Asia, were free to evolve

policies according to the merits of diplomatic issues confronting them, in accordance with their own interests as their governments perceived them. A neutralist policy, on the other hand, did not preclude *temporary* diplomatic, economic, or military association with either the East or West, or with both concurrently. Yet toward some issues (the dispute with Israel is an example) it meant formulating distinctively Arab policies, which not even other neutralist states outside the Arab zone necessarily accepted or supported.

Another element in a neutralist or nonaligned policy commanded widespread support throughout the Arab world. This was that such a policy in no way implied traditional "neutrality" toward global controversies, noninvolvement in international political discussions and negotiations, or a lack of deep concern about global problems and tendencies. Nor did it signify an absence of moral or ethical standards in approaching cold war developments, particularly in evaluating issues involving the risk of a global nuclear conflagration.*

Still another idea deemed incompatible with the Arab conception of a neutralist or nonaligned foreign policy was the theory invoked to justify Western efforts to establish a Middle Eastern defense organization during the 1950s. With the emergence of the cold war, coupled with the withdrawal of French and British military power from the Middle East, American officials become convinced that a "power vacuum" existed in the Arab world that would invite Communist expansionism.[48] The "power vacuum" conception deeply offended Arab sensibilities and violated their neutralist credo. "We have no need for the protection of either the Eastern or the Western blocs," Nasser said in 1958. "We have no need for instructions to us by either the East or the West."[49] Arabs thus agreed with an Indian observer that, in the Western view, "any rich area without some Western power or other occupying it, or dominating the spot, is a vacuum."[50] In whatever degree Americans believed such Arab viewpoints to be exaggerated or naïve, events revealed that such statements correctly described prevailing Arab attitudes.

The United States and Arab Nonalignment

During the 1950s, American officials scarcely concealed their skepticism about, and opposition to,

---

*Even Arab commentators acknowledged that "neutralist" policies in the Arab world often yielded diverse results. Thus, one Arab writer has identified four classifications of Arab neutralist policies, utilizing the extent to which identification with the policies of India (assumed to be the symbol of a truly "nonaligned" nation) could be detected: (1) Iraq and the United Arab Republic (at that time, Syria and Egypt) evinced a high correlation in policies with India; (2) Saudi Arabia, Morocco, and Yemen revealed a fair correlation—but were sometimes more outspokenly anti-Communist; (3) Lebanon and Libya gravitated between a "neutralist" and a pro-Western position; and (4) Tunisia and Jordan were usually pro-Western, but sometimes sided with neutralist states. This appraisal is based upon an analysis of voting patterns in the 13th session of the UN General Assembly. See Khalid I. Babaa, "Arab Positive Neutralism" (New York: Arab Information Center, mimeo., no date), p. 43.

*The Arab mentality on this point—widely misunderstood in the West—is illustrated by the viewpoint of an Egyptian publication: "Neutralism does not imply retirement within one's self. Such an attitude would constitute a negative and niggardly stand towards world society and a betrayal of the human ideal. . . . Nonaligned states are in reality committed in the sense that they must exert their efforts for the preservation of peace and the defense of the intangible principles without which the world would be ruled by the law of the jungle." "A Decisive Action for Peace," *The Scribe* 2 (Cairo, May-June, 1961), 11.

the Arab determination to remain diplomatically nonaligned. As long as cold war antagonisms remained intense (and this was before Moscow adopted "peaceful coexistence" as its watchword in relations with the West), American policy-makers were deeply concerned about Communist expansionism—especially into the kind of "power vacuum" afforded by the Middle East. One goal of the American containment strategy, therefore, was strengthening the security of the free world by the creation of a network of regional defense systems like NATO, SEATO, and the Baghdad Pact. The adverse Arab reaction to the last, as we have already noted, significantly hampered American containment efforts in the Middle East; among these regional security systems, the one created by the Baghdad Pact (CENTO) has been the least effective. In the 1950s also, Secretary of State John Foster Dulles labeled diplomatic neutralism "immoral"—a judgment widely resented by Arabs, as well as other groups throughout the Afro–Asian world subscribing to the concept.[51] Arabs believed (with considerable justification) that Secretary Dulles and other American officials really did not *understand* the concept of nonalignment, the reasons why Arabs almost universally supported it, or its major implications for international relations.

As much as any other specific development, Syria's growing ties with the Soviet Union prompted Dulles' harsh verdict.[52] The American opposition to Arab nonalignment, however, was most sharply revealed in one of the most momentous episodes in the postwar Middle East: the controversy over Egypt's Aswan High Dam. In turn, this issue led directly to the Suez crisis of 1956. Construction of a high dam on the upper reaches of the Nile had been a long-standing goal of Egyptian officials (the British had earlier constructed a "low dam" at Aswan). After Gamal Abdel Nasser became President of Egypt in 1954, Cairo endeavored to gain foreign support for this project —in some respects, perhaps the most complex and costly engineering project in history. It was anticipated that the total cost would run to $1.5 billion; 10–15 years would be required for the dam's construction. After numerous studies, the United States and Britain, along with the World Bank, agreed to extend a substantial loan to Nasser's government to build the Aswan High Dam. It was hoped that this agreement would usher in a new era of Arab–Western friendship, following what had been a period of often acute Arab anticolonial agitation.[53]

To the growing dismay of officials in Washington, however, Nasser's regime was also cultivating more intimate ties with the Communist bloc, by purchasing arms from behind the Iron Curtain, by recognizing Communist China, and by providing substantial assistance to rebel groups in Algeria (who were also aided by Moscow and Red China). Egypt was at the forefront of the Arab countries opposing the Baghdad Pact; and Nasser had emerged as the symbol of Arab opposition to Israel. Unquestionably, American disenchantment with Nasser and his followers was rising. Congressional opinion, for example, had become outspokenly critical. On July 19, 1956, therefore, the State Department canceled its offer to assist in financing the Aswan High Dam; Britain and the World Bank quickly followed suit. Secretary of State Dulles cited a number of reasons for this decision, such as various engineering difficulties and the lack of agreement between Egypt and the Sudan over the allocation of Nile waters. But Arabs believed (and probably correctly) that the most persuasive reason for the change was Dulles' opposition to Egypt's policy of nonalignment. Dulles referred to Cairo's "ever-closer relations with the Soviet bloc countries." He admitted that Nasser's behavior posed the issue for America: "Do nations which play both sides get better treatment than nations which are stalwart and work with us? . . ."[54] Nasser's retort was to nationalize the Suez Canal on July 26—thereby plunging the Middle East into the most serious crisis it had experienced since World War II. Although Arabs credited the United States with a decisive role in bringing about British, French, and Israeli evacuation of Egyptian territory in the months which followed, the net result of the Suez crisis of 1956 was an over-all *reduction* in Western influence in the Arab world, the emergence of the Soviet Union as a self-appointed protector of "Arab rights," and further exacerbation of the Arab–Israeli dispute.

By the late 1950s, a combination of factors induced American officials to reappraise the neutralist movement, not only in the Arab world but in Asia and Africa as well. One impetus for this new approach came from the retirement and death of Secretary of State Dulles, whose celebrated strictures against a position of diplomatic nonalignment were well known. Another came from the growing realization among State Department officials that forceful and undisguised opposition to neutralism, however it might be urged by American public opinion, seldom paid diplomatic dividends. Still another influence was the growing American insight into the origins, ideology, and implications of neutralism—leading to an over-all realization that prevailing popular judgments (e.g., that "neutralism is the next thing to Communism" or that "the neutralists are playing the Communist game") were often unwarranted and detrimental to American diplomatic interests.

Finally, throughout the months that followed the Suez crisis, the activities and policies of neutralist nations in the Arab world and elsewhere made abundantly clear that the overwhelming majority of countries holding to a nonaligned diplomatic position were determined to preserve their freedom from *Communist,* as well as from Western, domination and control. As Senator Frank Church (Democrat of Idaho), a member of the Senate Foreign Relations Committee, observed in 1961:

We have for a long time been terribly concerned about the United Arab Republic being a satellite of the Communist bloc by virtue of this arms supply, which is bigger than any [Communist] arms supply elsewhere in Africa. We are beginning to wake up to the fact that the United Arab Republic may not be a satellite at all, despite the extent of Soviet involvement there. It is one African country where all the Communists are in jail.[55]

Or, as a State Department official stated the following year, although the U.S.S.R. had maintained "unrelenting pressure" on the Arab countries for many years, it had not achieved "any noticeable new gains" in this region. He continued:

The fact that the Sino–Soviet bloc has been held at bay may be attributed mainly to the resolute determination of the countries in the area to maintain their independence. . . .[56]

The fact that, by the early 1960s, American policy-makers no longer seriously contested the right of Afro–Asian governments to remain diplomatically nonaligned did *not* of course mean the absence of tensions or misunderstandings in their relations. It must be borne in mind that, strictly speaking, *nonalignment is not a foreign policy.* It is an *approach* to foreign policy; it provides guidelines for determining how foreign policy shall (or shall not) be decided. Thus, knowing that Egypt or Syria or Iraq or some other nation in the Middle East is nonaligned *tells us little or nothing about its specific policies toward major regional or global issues.* Under the rubric of nonalignment, such nations may (and frequently do) maintain highly diverse relations with each other, with Western nations, and with Marxist nations. America may have cordial relations with some nonaligned countries; and it may have tense relations with others. Or, as has come to be a prevailing pattern, it may agree with a nation like Egypt on some questions, while disagreeing no less sharply with it on others.

Put differently, by the 1960s, executive officials in the United States had come to understand the fact that *several levels of alignment or nonalignment existed.** Insofar as *military pacts* were con-

cerned, nearly all nations of the Middle East subscribed to nonalignment: They were determined to remain outside the alliance systems sponsored by the great powers. With regard to *military aid,* the general pattern was that nonaligned nations would accept it on the best terms available from the outside world. Once they had achieved their independence, most Arab nations (including those like Egypt and Syria which later became identified with anti-Western sentiments) initially requested arms-aid *from the West.* As a rule these countries turned to the Communist bloc only when their requests were refused in the West or when the terms of Western military assistance were deemed unfavorable. Some nations (e.g., Jordan, Saudi Arabia, and Iran) still depend chiefly upon arms-aid from the West; others (e.g., Egypt, Syria, Iraq, Algeria) have tended to lean more heavily upon Russia and other nations in the Marxist zone.

Much the same pattern prevailed with respect to *economic and technical assistance:* During the 1950s, requests for such aid were made initially to Western governments. When these requests were refused, or aid was provided in insufficient quantities or extended on unfavorable terms, economic assistance was requested from Moscow, from Eastern Europe, and in more limited quantities from Peking. By the mid-1960s, it was not uncommon for some governments in the area (like Egypt, Algeria, and Iran) to receive such assistance from both Western and Communist sources.

In the 1950s, Secretary of State Dulles had reacted most adversely to the tendency of neutralist nations to "shop both sides of the street" in their quest for arms-aid or economic assistance. As time passed, however, several considerations induced American officials to re-examine Dulles' position: (1) The needs of the developing nations as a whole were nearly always greater than the volume of outside assistance available; and these needs were *increasing steadily.* (2) By contrast, most industrialized nations (including, for this purpose, Red China) were *reducing* their foreign aid programs; the "competition" for available assistance for developing societies was thus constantly rising. (3) As America itself had discovered in several settings (India and South Vietnam were but two examples), economic or military aid to a country were not necessarily tantamount *to control over that country.* Sometimes, just the opposite appeared to be true! Foreign military and economic assistance programs, under some conditions, could introduce *new tensions* in relations

---

*The attitudes we are describing here, it must be emphasized, were evinced much more frequently by State Department officials than by legislators. As in many foreign policy problems, legislative opinion tended to "lag" behind opinion in the executive branch, particularly the attitudes displayed by rank-and-file legislators not on the Senate Foreign Relations or House Foreign Affairs Committees. Executive policy-makers may largely have

"come to terms" with nonalignment; this did not necessarily mean that Congress had done so. Judged by legislative attitudes on foreign aid, military assistance, and the Arab–Israeli dispute, it seemed clear that a strong residue of Dullesian opposition to neutralism remained on Capitol Hill—and perhaps in the American society at large.

between the donor and host nation. There was, for example, the perennial problem of America's (or Russia's) desire that aid be utilized "efficiently" versus the recipient's resistance to any form of outside control or interference in its domestic affairs. With respect to military aid, once a country had acquired weapons from abroad, there was virtually no way that the donor could prevent their being used for purposes detrimental to its own interests. Arab governments had turned Communist-supplied weapons against Marxist groups. Israel and Jordan both used American-supplied armaments against each other. (4) There was another troublesome dimension to foreign aid in the Middle East and other regions: Assistance to a country inescapably implied *some degree of responsibility for the country's welfare and progress.* Foreign aid enhanced America's or Russia's image to the extent that it produced visible results in terms of evident progress within the host society. When it did not, such aid might in fact *impair the image* of the nation providing it. With many of Egypt's critical economic problems worsening, for example, it could at least be debated whether in the long run the Soviet Union would receive more blame than praise for its programs of economic assistance. The benefits provided by the Aswan High Dam, it was estimated, might improve Egyptian living standards for no more than twenty-five years, unless the country's population growth were drastically curtailed.

The last level of nonalignment was in many respects the most crucial. Although the process required several years, in time American officials realized that, to the countries of the Middle East, nonalignment *was synonymous with freedom.* The concept signified the determination of the governments subscribing to it to resist *all outside efforts to subordinate them politically*—Communist efforts no less than Western. Thus, nonalignment coincided fully with America's own ideological professions, as well as with its avowed cold war objectives. No persuasive evidence existed that the nonaligned nations of the Middle East had abandoned, or become indifferent to, this aspect of nonalignment. By the late 1960s, Soviet spokesmen complained about Arab intransigence as frequently as American officials. Even in the revolutionary regimes of the Middle East, Moscow appeared to be having no more success than Washington in imposing its control over native governments or gettings its "advice" accepted. In nearly all states in the area (Israel was an exception) Communism was illegal; native governments imposed rigorous bans against Marxist political activity. With respect to the most inflammatory issue affecting the region—the Arab-Israeli dispute, for which both America and Russia sought a solution—the striking fact in recent years was the *declining ability of both Russia and America* to control events.

Soviet–American Rivalry in the Middle East

Although official American attitudes toward Arab nonalignment had changed fundamentally since the 1950s, this fact did not mean that Washington had become less apprehensive about the foreign policies pursued by several Arab governments. After the "Six-Day War" in 1967, Egypt, Syria, Iraq, and a number of other Arab states developed closer ties than ever with the Soviet Union. Throughout the region as a whole, the evidence of a growing Soviet presence seemed incontrovertible. Moscow, for example, replaced Egypt's aircraft, tank, and other equipment losses after its defeat at Israel's hands; by the early 1970s, Egyptian defenses were armed with modern Soviet missiles (like the SAM-3); and Soviet pilots (according to Israeli reports) were actually flying defensive missions within Egyptian territory. Several thousand Soviet advisers and technicians were present inside Egypt. With massive Russian assistance, Cairo had completed contruction of the Aswan High Dam.

To the north, after a period of hostile relations between Moscow and the dominant Ba'ath party in Damascus, following the "Six-Day War" Syria also moved closer to the Soviet Union. After breaking relations with West Germany (which had originally proposed to finance the project), Syria accepted a Soviet offer to assist with the construction of an ambitious Euphrates dam project—a decision almost certain to lead to new tensions between Syria and pro-Western Turkey. Moscow provided Damascus with aid to renovate Syrian railroads and to expand the country's limited oil production. Eastward, the U.S.S.R. endeavored to cultivate more cordial relations with Iraq and Iran. To conciliate the government in Baghdad, the Kremlin soft-pedaled its long-standing demands for Kurdish autonomy, substantially reduced its support of the Iraqi Communist party, and extended limited economic and military aid to the Iraqi government. Nor did Soviet officials permit ideological differences to interfere with an effort to win the friendship of the Shah's government in Iran, hitherto one of the staunchest Western allies in the Middle East. Offering aid and attractive terms of trade, Moscow brought about a marked improvement in Soviet–Iranian relations. The Red Sea area was another zone of Soviet political and diplomatic activity. Having supported rebels groups in Yemen (with no very marked success) during the mid-1960s, Moscow turned next to the People's Republic of South Yemen (formerly British-ruled Aden and the Aden Protectorate), which emerged as an independent nation in 1967. As one of the world's leading naval powers—and perhaps the nation which was most dependent upon the Suez Canal—Soviet Russia sought to displace traditional British power in this strategic region. Jordan—before 1967, possibly the most pro-Western Arab government in the Middle East—received offers of Soviet cultural and military aid; fearing the almost certain end of Western support, Hussein's government accepted the former but declined the latter. Almost alone among Arab nations, Saudi Arabia experienced no improvement in relations with the Communist zone.

Behind these separate Soviet moves, there was the reality to which we have already referred in Chapter 9 and again in this chapter: the growing Soviet naval presence in the Mediterranean. Within a relatively few years, Moscow had constructed a formidable Mediterranean fleet. Its ships were new and equipped with modern armaments (like surface-to-surface missiles); its crews were obviously well trained and efficient; and (as long as the Dardanelles remained open), the eastern Mediterranean was readily accessible to Soviet naval power. As we noted in Chapter 9, the American Sixth Fleet, together with the naval forces of the NATO allies, provided the West with over-all military superiority in the area, although in some categories (such as submarine strength) Russia already possessed an advantage. To date, perhaps the principal gain accruing to Moscow from its enhanced naval presence lay in the *psychological realm.* The Mediterranean was no longer a "Western lake" in which the United States and its allies enjoyed a military monopoly. If the Kremlin desired (and thus far, there was no evidence that it did), Russia possessed a greater capability than ever for challenging Western military strength in the Mediterranean area. Justifiably or not, the more militant Arab opponents of Israel no doubt viewed the rapid growth in Soviet naval power as a force held, so to speak, "in reserve" to protect them against further Israeli encroachments (and possibly even their own military foolhardiness).

That Moscow's involvement in the affairs of the Middle East had grown steadily within the past few years was a fact too evident to be seriously contested. Conversely, Western influence continued to decline: By the 1970s, American and British (if not necessarily French) power to affect events in the region was minimal. To many students of international politics, this situation had all the earmarks of a "zero-sum game," in which the *expansion* of Soviet influence meant a corresponding *contraction* in Western influence.* It

would be difficult to think of an area of the world in which Moscow had enjoyed greater success in hurdling the containment fence which Western governments had tried to erect against it.

Yet recognition of these realities did not necessarily justify the kind of alarmist conclusions which some commentators (especially those closely identified with Israel's position) drew concerning Russia's new role in the Middle East. The eastern Mediterranean had *not* been converted into a "Soviet lake"; the American Sixth Fleet, augmented by the naval forces of the NATO allies, gave the West a position of continued superiority on the sea. Short of an outright Soviet military invasion of the area, which seemed altogether unlikely, the strategic balance continued to favor the West. This advantage was admittedly offset to some extent by the fact that Soviet equipment and personnel were in countries like Egypt *by invitation of the government,* while few Arab regimes dared become so closely identified with America or other Western countries. Israeli propaganda to the contrary, Egypt, Syria, Iraq, Libya, and other countries governed by revolutionary regimes have *not* become "Russian satellites" whose policies were dictated by the Kremlin. The vital oil reserves of the Middle East have *not* passed under Soviet control. There was no credible evidence that Soviet policy-makers sought a new military crisis in the region, risking an American military involvement on the side of Israel. Indeed, judging by the Soviet Union's behavior and statements after the 1967 conflict, it might be easier to stabilize the Middle East if radical Arab governments *were* more amenable to Soviet suggestions (assuming of course that Israel were similarly receptive to American influence)!

Soviet Russia's growing activities and commitments in the Middle East provided an object lesson in one of the major defects in the concept of national power, viewed by many political scientists as the central idea in the study of international politics. As we noted in Chapter 1, no concept is perhaps more fundamental for an understanding of global political relationships. Yet, as the case of increased Soviet involvement in the Middle East amply illustrates, the doctrine of national power is both highly imprecise and subject to innumerable qualifications, so much so that it may actually convey a *misleading* impression of the true interaction between the Soviet Union and the smaller Arab states. It is manifestly clear that <u>Soviet</u> military, economic, and diplomatic *activity* in the Middle East has <u>expanded</u> percepti-

---

*In Soviet–American rivalry in the Middle East, it must be recognized that, although this contest had many characteristics of a zero-sum game, appearances could be (and probably were) highly deceptive. An expanding Soviet presence in the Middle East might well have been more a *result* than a cause of the decline in Western influence within the region; the latter could well have been a precondition for the former! Alternatively, it was no less possible that the situation was a nonzero-sum game: All things considered, both Russia and America had perhaps suffered setbacks because of devel-

opments in the Middle East during the 1960s and early 1970s. The de facto political control exercised by guerrilla organizations in several Arab governments, for example, was a reality which neither Washington nor Moscow desired; nor did either of the great powers approve of the intractability demonstrated by all parties to the Arab–Israeli dispute.

bly since the mid-1960s. It is, however, open to serious question whether this change is tantamount to a corresponding growth in Soviet *power* to determine the course of events in this highly unstable environment. Although the two situations are in some respects very dissimilar, an analogy might usefully be drawn with the growth of American commitments in Southeast Asia during the 1960s. According to many of the usual criteria relied upon to measure national power, we would be justified in concluding that America's control over the destiny of Southeast Asia had risen sharply, in at least rough proportion to the magnitude of its military, economic, and political involvement in the region. As every citizen knows, however, such a verdict would be totally erroneous. Existing theories of national power do not afford satisfactory explanations of a fact which, in the era of nuclear stalemate, has become rather commonplace in the international environment: Nuclear giants like the United States and the Soviet Union can reach a point of diminishing returns, beyond which their power to alter the course of events declines sharply. It may always have been true in international relations, but restraints growing out of the nuclear balance of terror re-enforce the idea, that a nation's "involvement" or "activity" in a region may be something very different from its "power" over that region. Considerable evidence exists for believing that this is Moscow's predicament in the Arab world.

Another limitation upon Soviet power in the Middle East is the demonstrated imperviousness of Arab societies to Marxist ideology and the lack of success achieved by local Communist organizations. Much as they might applaud Arab acceptance of the concept of nonalignment, as signifying a weakening of Western influence throughout the region, Moscow and Peking alike have discovered that this credo is aimed fully as much at preventing Communist control as it is against a revival of Western domination in the Middle East. In several respects, the Arab version of nonalignment is uniquely resistant to Marxist influence. In Moslem countries, religious faith and values are deeply embedded; nearly all Arab governments recognize Islam as the official state religion; Moslems tend to be repulsed by Marxism's explicit antireligious bias. Except in Israel, Communist party activity is banned by nearly all governments in the area. On innumerable occasions in recent years, incumbent Arab governments have suppressed Marxist political activities. The concepts of Arab nationalism and Arab unity, evoking the loyalties of millions of people from Morocco to Iraq, stand as formidable obstacles to Communist influence within the Middle East. Arabs are cognizant of a fact which many Americans have forgotten (if they ever really knew it): Penetration of the Middle East has been a goal of

the Russian state *for several centuries,* going back at least to the era of Peter the Great. And while experience does not of course provide an infallible guide to future events, thus far Russian efforts to dominate or subordinate the region have been successfully thwarted. Arab nationalism is directed against efforts by *any alien power* to impose its will upon the region. The idea of Arab unity (admittedly, thus far little more than a political slogan) collides with the Marxist doctrine of "proletarian internationalism," which means in practice that Moscow determines the diplomatic line to be followed by its supporters.

The particular nature of Soviet–Arab relations in the recent period also set limits to what Russia will probably accomplish in the Middle East. A number of countries (prominent examples are Egypt, Syria, Iraq, Yemen, and South Arabia) are indebted to Moscow for economic and military assistance; both financially and psychologically, Egypt is heavily "mortgaged" to the Kremlin for Soviet aid since 1967. Yet experience in the Middle East and other regions has shown that the creditor–debtor relationship in international politics is often much more complex than is often supposed; in several fundamental ways, it differs from the relationship between an American home owner and the bank holding his mortgage. A massive Soviet commitment to Egypt, for example, may mean in reality that Moscow is as "dependent" upon Cairo as the reverse. Following the Arab defeat in 1967, the Kremlin was almost compelled to replace equipment lost by Egypt; failure to do so would have been tantamount to Russia's acquiescence to Israel's permanent military superiority and acceptance of a sharp decline in Soviet prestige among the Arab nations. Regarding economic assistance, with its internal economic situation in many ways deteriorating, Egypt has followed the path of other third-world countries in asking that its debts be "rescheduled"—and, concurrently, that *new* assistance be extended. Having already invested huge sums in Egypt's future, Soviet Russia has little choice but to accede to Cairo's wishes. Successful completion of projects like the Aswan Dam almost inevitably generated new pressures upon Egypt's creditors to furnish additional assistance, so that the project's benefits may be realized and shared by the Egyptian masses. Meanwhile, by the 1970s, the evidence indicated that Cairo was making little real progress in overcoming Egypt's deep-seated economic dislocations, much less in achieving the regime's proclaimed goal of rapid economic advancement for the masses. Neither in Egypt nor in any other Arab society was there any convincing evidence that incumbent governments had become subordinate to Soviet influence. (If any political force tended to rival established governments, increasingly it was the guerrilla and commando organizations, over which neither established Arab leaders nor Moscow and Peking had any discernible control. Several times in recent years (Algeria, Syria, and Iraq provided examples), Soviet-supplies arms had been used against Marxist groups within Arab societies; Moscow evidently had been no more successful than America in preventing the "misuse" of its assistance to other countries. The presence of several thousand Soviet technicians and advisers in Egypt not infrequently produced frictions with the local population; much as they might concede its necessity, Egyptians and other Arabs basically resented their dependence upon a great power as a source of their economic and military needs. As in earlier periods of history, there was no evidence that a smaller country's gratitude for the assistance furnished by a great power would directly affect its internal and external policies; in this kind of ostensibly dependent relationship, Arab leaders might well in fact be compelled to demonstrate that the government had *not* lost its independent decision-making power. Short of occupying the country militarily, there was very little Moscow could do to "foreclose" the mortgage it held on Egypt, Syria, Iraq, or other countries receiving massive Russian aid. For their part, Arab leaders did not bother to conceal their attitude (just as America and Soviet Russia cooperated as allies in World War II, without either accepting the politico–economic system of the other) that Soviet assistance *was instrumental to their purposes*, that they asked for such aid because they had no other choice, and that they would control its use.

To many American observers, Arab attitudes seemed naïve and oblivious to the dangers inherent in becoming overly dependent upon Moscow's largess. Their professions of independence aside, the real question, many Western commentators were convinced, was whether the Arab nations would be able to prevent encroachments upon their sovereignty, leading ultimately to a complete loss of independence. According to many traditional conceptions of the connection between economic or military power and political power, this prospect could not be dismissed lightly. Yet, as we have seen, a number of forces in the Arab world made the prospect largely a *potential* danger, which thus far had not become an actual one; nor did there appear to be any imminent prospect of its realization. On the basis of results thus far, Soviet policy-makers might well ask themselves the same question which American officials had asked on innumerable occasions since World War II: "What has our aid *actually achieved* in terms of promoting some major national interest or tangible gain?" Over against a few concrete benefits Moscow may have derived from its new role in the Middle East, there were several fundamental liabilities—such as the kind of apparently endless commitment Moscow faced in Egypt; the Arab nations' persistence in the be-

lief that Soviet power was "available" to safeguard them from Israeli military might; the unwillingness of Arab governments to be guided by the Kremlin's diplomatic advice; the loss by several Arab states of American and other Western sources of aid (thereby throwing a greater burden than ever upon the Soviet Union); a political *milieu* which continued to be inhospitable to Marxist ideas; the substantial power exercised by guerrilla organizations which acknowledged no outside control over their decisions; ongoing political ferment and upheaval in countries like Yemen, South Arabia, Syria, and Iraq (it is questionable whether Communism, any more than Western democracy, can thrive in conditions of actual or incipient anarchy); and undeniable evidence of considerable economic progress in countries like Morocco, Tunisia, Saudi Arabia, Kuwait, and Iran —societies where Soviet influence was minimal or nonexistent. In brief, Soviet policy-makers might well discover, as Americans had in time concluded about their involvement in Southeast Asia, that the expenditure of several billions of dollars returned them chiefly constantly growing obligations and a multitude of unwanted (and in some cases at least, insoluble) problems!*

THE AWAKENING OF AFRICA

Africa's Entry upon the World Stage

By the year 1969, the continent of Africa contained 38 independent states—close to one-third of the total membership of the United Nations and well over half of that group of nations considering themselves "nonaligned" in global affairs. This number was bound to increase (if much less rapidly than in the past), as the few remaining colonial dependencies in Africa, like Portuguese Angola, achieved their independence.

Encompassing an area four times that of the United States, the continent of Africa contains more than 11 million square miles, most of which is in the tropics. Africa is a region of infinite variety and contrasts. The northern portion of the continent is divided from east to west by the greatest desert on the globe, the Sahara; that portion lying athwart the equator includes a dense, at some points an almost impenetrable, tropical rain

*More extended discussions of Soviet–American rivalry in the Middle East—focusing upon the nature and implications of growing Soviet influence in the area— are provided in: J. C. Hurewitz, *Middle East Politics: The Military Dimension* (New York: Praeger, 1969)— primarily a country-by-country analysis; the same author's *Soviet–American Rivalry in the Middle East* (New York: Praeger, 1969)—a symposium on the topic; and Walter Laqueur, *The Struggle for the Middle East: The Soviet Union in the Mediterranean, 1958–1968* (New York: Macmillan, 1969)—a perceptive and balanced account.

forest. Elsewhere there is "small bush" country, isolated barren wastes, grasslands, and mountain ranges. Most of the interior of Africa is a great plateau. Africa has the shortest coastline, proportionate to its area, of any continent; with few exceptions, the coastline is unsuitable for the construction of harbors. Climate and geography have conspired to make transportation and communication arduous among African countries and between them and the outside world. Today, the only dependable method of transportation for much of Africa is the airplane.

In Africa's inhospitable environment, there dwell approximately 330 million people, of whom some 5 million are of European stock, with half the latter group living in the Republic of South Africa. Over 700 languages and dialects are spoken throughout Africa. The largest (and most rapidly growing) religious faith on the African scene is Islam, with over 80 million adherents; around one-fourth of Africa embraces Christianity; the remainder of the Africans are pagans or adherents of various animistic religious faiths.[57] Illiteracy has been estimated to run between 80 and 90 percent of the *total* African population, although several newly independent African nations have begun to make progress in raising literacy and educational levels. The vast majority of Africa's population lives at a "subsistence level"— the highest proportion (when South Africa is excluded from the calculation) of any continent. By the late 1960s, the per capita income for all of Africa (again excluding South Africa) was $125 annually; Africa as a whole produced a gross national product which was only 3 percent of the world's total, or only half as much as Latin America contributed. By this period also, the evidence indicated that, for many African societies, productive levels and standards of living *were declining;* food production in a number of African nations was barely keeping pace with the population growth, expanding at a rate of 2.4 percent each year, which (as contrasted with rates pushing 3 percent in Asia and Latin America) was relatively low for societies outside the West.[58]

Yet Africa's economic and strategic importance, and its potential for development, are in some respects outstanding. The African continent is the source of many minerals, a number of which are vital in Western defense programs. Africa is a major supplier of uranium ore to the non-Communist world. Nearly all of the world's industrial diamonds come from Africa. As we observed earlier in the chapter, Western Europe is beginning to seek alternative petroleum supplies in Africa, thereby lessening its dependence upon Middle Eastern oil. Other raw materials—like columbite, cobalt, beryllium, manganese, chrome, and gold —are found in significant quantities on the African continent. Africa's economic potential is, therefore, unquestionably impressive. One of the noteworthy facts about the continent, a recent study points out, is that: "Less than 10 per cent of the entire African continent has been geologically surveyed."[59] Even under colonial administrations, Africa's mineral wealth was inefficiently exploited. There is every prospect that, as mineral surveys and other studies proceed, Africa's capacity for development will become greater than ever. Not only are raw materials present in large quantities; Africa also possesses a largely unrealized potential for hydroelectric power generation —perhaps the greatest potential of any region in the world.[60]

Barriers to African Development

A recognition of Africa's potential for development, however, must be coupled with the realization that difficult and often deeply embedded obstacles impede the continent's present and future progress. African development lies in the future—and it may be *a very distant future.* Perhaps no region on the globe affords such a stark contrast between present conditions and potentialities. In the contemporary period, as measured by its mineral *output,* Africa ranks at the bottom of the list for all the continents. Africa lacks fuels needed to support industrialization. Much of its vast forest reserves are inaccessible—and this is one illustration of a problem impeding nearly every aspect of African economic development: the inadequacy of its transportation system. All-weather roads are almost nonexistent. Harbors and port facilities are inferior. Africa's vast river system has thus far been minimally useful in opening up the interior or serving as arteries of trade; rapids and other hazards interfere with navigation. The railroad network—the principal method of transportation before the air age—is antiquated and often in disrepair; constructed during the colonial era, the rail system in one independent African nation is often "incompatible" with the system of an adjacent nation (a condition sometimes *deliberately* created by the colonial powers for strategic and defense reasons). The most convenient mode of transportation for most of Africa today remains the airplane.

Besides these difficulties, African states lack capital for national or regional development. For the Afro–Asian world as a whole, capital requirements have been rising, while capital generated either internally or from outside sources has been *declining.* Both the United States and the Soviet Union, for example, have *reduced* their foreign assistance programs since the mid-1960s. Low levels of literacy and education impede economic progress throughout Africa; some African nations are hard pressed to keep these levels from *declining* as populations continue to rise. Although progress is continually being made by the African governments, in concert with the United Nations and foreign countries, in eradicating age-old scourges—like locusts, the tsetse fly, typhoid fever, malaria, Bilharzia, and other parasitical diseases—health and sanitary conditions throughout Africa remain depressingly poor and serve as major obstacles to development, especially in the rural areas. African nations face another impediment to advancement, shared with several Latin American states. Economic prosperity is heavily dependent upon *exports of primary raw materials,* chiefly agricultural goods and minerals. This fact makes Africa peculiarly vulnerable to the uncertainties of the world market for its principal exports. Unfortunately from the African viewpoint, the price levels of what Africa sells abroad have *declined,* while the price levels of what African nations normally import (mainly industrial and other finished goods from the West) have *risen.* Like other developing societies, the African states have thus faced a *widening gap* between the prices they pay and those they receive in the world market. The over-all effect has been to impose additional strains upon already overburdened, and often fragile, African economic systems.[61] The adverse trade balance encountered by most African nations accounts in no small measure for widespread apprehensions on the continent about regional organizations like the European Economic Community.* A number of African countries (primarily those once belonging to the French colonial system) are "associated" with the EEC; this association confers numerous benefits, such as preferential terms of trade, which African nations not affiliated with the EEC do not enjoy. For the latter, the EEC—especially if and when Britain and other members of the European Free Trade Area join it—is visualized as a threat whose very success may compound Africa's problems.

In company with many other newly independent nations, the African states have belatedly been confronted with another reality that is likely to serve as a brake upon rapid economic advancement. Throughout the Afro–Asian world, there was a tendency for masses and leaders to regard "industrialization" as the panacea that would usher in an unprecedented era of prosperity and plenty, once the age of colonialism came to an end. Agriculture—the economic sector in which the vast majority of the population tended to engage—was largely ignored. Yet if it was not evident during the period of anticolonialist agitation,

within a few years after independence was achieved it became obvious that *agriculture was likely to remain the most crucial sector of economic activity, perhaps for decades to come.* Intelligent Africans in time comprehended a key fact about America's own economic development: The agricultural revolution had preceded the industrial revolution, and the former was in large measure responsible for the success of the latter. And if the realization was often overlooked earlier, by the 1960s it seemed convincingly clear that societies in which "subsistence agriculture" was the traditional way of life were *not* likely to achieve rapid industrialization. Indeed, successful industrialization itself is largely contingent upon maintaining a steadily rising agricultural output. In almost all African nations, a majority of the population still depends upon agriculture for its existence. As urbanization has occurred, Africa's growing cities are perhaps even more dependent than ever upon rising farm outputs; agricultural commodities, as we have noted, are among Africa's main exports. Yet traditionally, agriculture as practiced in Africa has, in the main, been inefficient, uncertain, and unproductive as compared with that in other regions of the world. Contrary to popular impressions in the West, the tropical and semitropical soils of Africa are *not* fertile; they tend in fact (particularly when cultivated intensively) to be highly *infertile,* subject to erosion and other debilitating conditions. African farmers have to contend with a wide variety of plant diseases; chemical fertilizers are usually lacking; modern scientific agricultural techniques are still unknown throughout much of Africa; many African countries suffer from acute drought conditions, while others suffer from floods and the "waterlogging" of soils; the absence of satisfactory transportation systems impedes the marketing of crops. Even when the African farmer overcomes these problems, he confronts world market conditions that are often highly detrimental to his interests. Political leaders in Africa find themselves caught between the demands of the poverty-stricken masses—whose first impulse is to *consume* increases in food production—and the requirements of national development—which often dictate restrictions upon consumption, in order to generate additional development capital.[62]

Among the barriers to rapid African economic progress, we must take note of two which are pervasive and fundamental. One of these is the *political instability* that has been characteristic of post-colonial Africa. Thus far, the evidence indicates that this problem is *chronic* and may be becoming *more serious with each passing year.* Scarcely an African state has escaped some form of civil war, insurrection, separatist movement, *coup d'état,* or ongoing revolutionary activity. Bloody civil war in Nigeria and the Sudan; the

*Africa's relations with the European Economic Community, a subject outside the scope of our study, is dealt with more fully in: Vernon McKay, *Africa in World Politics* (New York: Harper & Row, 1963), pp. 134–169; Arnold Rivkin, *Africa and the European Common Market* (Denver, Colo.: Univeristy of Denver, 1966); Werner Feld, *The European Common Market and the World* (Englewood Cliffs, N.J.: Prentice-Hall, 1967), pp. 113–148.

overthrow of civilian governments by military juntas in Ghana and several other African states; a rising crescendo of political unrest in Kenya and Tanzania; the failure of Africans to translate the ideal of Pan-Africanism into a functioning and forceful regional organization—such developments are both the signs of deep frustrations within African societies and the reasons for widespread failure to achieve the goals of national development. Under optimum conditions—even when they are successful in preserving national cohesion and political stability—native African governments will be sorely challenged to satisfy mass aspirations for social betterment. It will be almost impossible to do so as long as governments are gripped by political tensions, growing distrust among rival political factions, and the threat of civil war.

Any discussion of the problems besetting contemporary Africa must also call attention to one of the continent's most ancient and ubiquitous forces: *tribalism and other forms of separatism.* Writing in 1969, one observer who visited 32 African nations declared: "Africa's central problem is separatism—regional, tribal and religious—and it is getting worse. . . . Separatist tensions underlie most African violence, and African political leaders have been unable to dampen them." The Nigerian civil war afforded perhaps the most dramatic example of a fragile political structure— considered in the early post-colonial era as the most "promising" example of democracy in Africa —destroyed by separatist tendencies growing out of ancient tribal animosities. In a number of other African nations as well—Zambia, Ghana, Kenya, Tanzania, Ethiopia, the Sudan, Chad—separatist tendencies arising from tribal and religious differences pose perhaps the most critical challenge to political stability and economic advancement. Some 2000 different tribal units (a number of them very small) inhabit the African continent. Jealousies and conflicts among them, often perpetuated by educational and economic disparities, antedate the period of European colonial domination; after independence, these animosities have asserted themselves forcefully, threatening both to undermine the internal political cohesion of the state and to inject new sources of discord into intra-African relations. In the late 1960s, the government of Kenya—led by the venerable nationalist Jomo Kenyatta—provided merely the most recent example of an African nation in which tribal jealousies generated mounting political unrest. Once regarded as the "showplace of East Africa," Kenya was experiencing a series of political crises growing out of distrust between the dominant Kikuyu tribe (embracing some 20 percent of the population) and the other 40 or so tribal units into which the majority of the population was divided. Another prominent African nationalist, President Kenneth D. Kaunda of Zambia, asserted that at least several decades would be required before the problem of tribally instigated separatist movements in Africa would be successfully overcome.*

The American "Discovery" of Africa

Even more than in the case of the Arab world, American officials were often ill prepared to deal successfully with events in Africa. American contact with Africa down to World War II had been fragmentary. Very early, Yankee traders had participated in the lucrative slave trade. In its infancy, the American republic had continuing quarrels with the rulers of the Barbary Coast. The United States was instrumental in establishing Liberia as an independent country in 1822. Moreover, American delegates participated in the Berlin Conference of 1884–1885, from which the European colonial "scramble" for Africa is dated. The boundaries of many African countries were agreed upon at this conference. During World War II, American military planners became acutely conscious of the strategic significance of Africa and the adjacent Arab world. One of the most decisive battles of this conflict was fought along the desert strip of North Africa. For many decades, American missionaries and educators have also been active on the African continent.[63] Beyond these developments, American contact with Africa has been minimal, leaving the United States little experience upon which to draw in dealing with contemporary African societies.

"As Africa was the last continent to be opened to the world at large," writes Rupert Emerson, "so it was the last to be discovered by the United States. . . ."[64] Africa perhaps remained "the dark continent" more for Americans than for any other group in Western society. Indicative of America's lack of interest in, and knowledge about, Africa is the fact that as late as 1958 the United States had more Foreign Service officials in West Germany alone than in the whole of Africa. If official recognition of the importance of Africa has been slow, within recent years it has been almost frenziedly rapid. For many years, African affairs tended to be dealt with by officials whose primary concern was Western Europe or the Middle East. Finally, in 1958, the State Department set up a Bureau of African Affairs. Besides this new agency, other State Department and governmental agencies became heavily involved with African affairs—like the Bureau of International Organization Affairs

*For recent reports on the nature and extent of tribalism in Africa, see *The New York Times* (October 1 and November 23, 1969), dispatches by R. W. Apple, Jr. Background on particular tribal conflicts in Africa is provided in Lawrence Fellows, "The Duka-Wallas Are Outcasts in Africa," *The New York Times Magazine* (June 25, 1967), pp. 20–29; Lloyd Garrison, "The Ibos Go It Alone," *ibid.* (June 11, 1967), pp. 31–36.

in the State Department, which was keenly aware of the greatly enhanced role of African states in the United Nations.[65] In addition, educational exchange programs with Africa have expanded significantly. In 1953, there was only one officer in the United States Information Agency assigned exclusively to Africa! By 1962, USIA planned to operate 43 information centers in Africa, with 133 officers and almost 500 local employees. The Peace Corps, from its inception in 1961, has been strongly oriented toward Africa. Out of almost 4400 members, nearly a third served in Africa in 1963.[66]

America "Adjusts" to African Independence

If America was relatively late in "discovering" Africa, a number of years were required before the United States developed a reasonably clear conception of its interests on the African continent and evolved an approach calculated to promote them. By the late 1950s, American officials acknowledged (Africans often said belatedly) that the era of Western colonialism was over—a realization underscored by Washington's opposition to the attempt by Britain and France to invade Egypt in 1956. By the late 1950s, official American representation on the African continent expanded rapidly. The civil rights movement in the United States also supplied an impetus to closer Afro–American relations. Rupert Emerson has written: "The ferment of Africa and the ferment of the Negro American could not possibly be kept separate from each other in watertight compartments."[67]

By the early 1960s, American foreign policy toward Africa was being pulled in two somewhat contrary directions. President John F. Kennedy was keenly interested in Africa; earlier, as a senator, he had espoused the cause of independence for Algeria and other nations. In an effort to create more cordial relations with the newly independent nations of Africa, he appointed ex-Governor G. Mennan Williams—an outspoken advocate of civil rights—as Assistant Secretary of State for African Affairs; Williams devoted himself actively to the cause of Afro–American understanding. Yet the Kennedy administration was seldom able to generate significant interest in Africa on Capitol Hill or to convince Congress that American assistance to Africa ought to be substantially expanded.[68]

Although the Kennedy administration was making an evident effort to "identify" with the aspirations of the African people, new sources of misunderstanding and tension were provided by the role of the United States in the Congo crisis which began in the summer of 1960 and continued, in one form or another, for almost four years. The events encompassed by this political explosion are too complex and detailed to discuss

here; it must suffice to make a few brief points. Justly or not, the United States was widely criticized by African nationalist groups for insisting upon the political integrity of the newly independent Democratic Republic of Congo (formerly, the Belgian Congo) and opposing the "secession" of the mineral-rich Katanga Province. Inside and outside the United Nations, Washington took the lead in supporting the central government against separatist groups, like the secessionist movement led by the left-wing nationalist Patrice Lumumba. When Lumumba was assassinated, the United States was blamed for his death. UN forces in the Congo—regarded by many Africans as instruments of Western political domination—were financed largely by the United States, since countries like France and the Soviet Union refused to contribute to their support. After the UN forces were finally withdrawn, the Congolese government under Premier Moise Tshombe—vocally denounced in many Afro–Asian circles as a lackey of the West—employed "white mercenaries" in an attempt to suppress insurrectionary activities. At the end of 1964, American aircraft were utilized to send Belgian paratroopers into the Congo to rescue white hostages endangered by rebel forces. This intervention also aroused widespread resentment against America throughout Africa. It seemed to suggest that America's interest in African affairs was limited to the welfare of *white groups;* and many Africans interpreted the incident as signifying America's willingness to rely upon armed force to protect its interests against Africans!*⌊For Africans, as well as for Americans, the Congo crisis left a residue of distrust, resentment, and bitterness.⌋

Diplomatic Retrenchment in Africa

By the mid-1960s, a combination of forces and considerations produced a reassessment in Washington of America's diplomatic role in sub-Saharan Africa. As we have observed, necessary as it might have been, the UN intervention in the Congo alienated many Africans; in the United States, Congress was obviously concerned about the disproportionate burden borne by America in this affair and about what had apparently become a permanent UN "financial crisis" because of such peace-keeping operations. The Congo crisis also seemed to many Westerners to presage the erup-

*The literature on the Congo crisis of the early 1960s and America's role in it is voluminous. See, for example, Smith Hempstone, *Rebels, Mercenaries, and Dividends: The Katanga Story* (New York: Praeger, 1962); Rupert Emerson, "American Policy in Africa," *Foreign Affairs* 40 (January, 1962), 303–315; Colin Legum, *Congo Disaster* (Baltimore: Penguin, 1961); Clark D. Moore and Ann Dunbar, eds., *Africa: Yesterday and Today* (New York: Bantam, 1968), pp. 258–276; Richard N. Gardner, *In Pursuit of World Order* (New York: Praeger, 1964), pp. 75–83

tion of new political upheavals on the African continent; earlier hopes that African societies would evolve from colonial status to stable democracies seemed doomed to disappointment. Eruption of the Nigerian civil war early in 1966 was a grave disappointment to many admirers of African nationalism, since it shattered widespread hopes that Nigeria could serve as a model of a politically stable democracy in a multiracial African society. At the same time, developments in post-colonial Africa also underscored the fact that the African political environment was no more congenial for the establishment and expansion of Marxism.* During the late 1950s and early 1960s, considerable apprehension existed in Washington that Africa constituted a fertile field for Communist political intrigue—and perhaps eventual domination. Such African nations as Guinea, Ghana, and Mali in West Africa—closely identified with radical political orders in Algeria and Egypt—had developed intimate relations with Soviet Russia; by the early 1960s, Communist China had also embarked upon a campaign to win footholds in Africa, in an effort to compete with both American and Soviet influence there and in other regions.

Events soon revealed, however, that Western apprehensions were largely unfounded. For many years, African nationalists had asserted that Marxism—along with Western-style democracy—was an alien ideology and system of government unsuited to Africa's needs and desires. Guinea's abrupt expulsion of Soviet officials and advisers in 1961 for interference in the country's political affairs indicated that "African socialism" was not synonymous with Soviet or Chinese Marxism.[69]

The outside world was reminded again of Africa's dedication to independence in 1966, when a military junta overthrew the government of President Kwame Nkrumah in Ghana; Ghanian opinion, developments made clear, was overwhelmingly against Communist efforts to subvert the government or establish a bridgehead in West Africa. Nkrumah's ouster was a significant diplomatic defeat for the Kremlin (and a lesser one perhaps for Communist China); within a few months, the new government of Ghana had moved to normalize its relations with the West.[70] A few months earlier, a Communist-instigated attempt to seize control of Zanzibar was similarly frustrated by the union between Tanganyika and Zanzibar, to form Tanzania.[71] Perhaps even more than in West Africa, East African political leaders had no desire to become subservient to Moscow or Peking. Throughout Africa as a whole, Marxist organizations were making little headway in their competition with African nationalism. Africans appeared to be fully alert to the dangers of Communist penetration and capable—without massive assistance by the West—of dealing with such threats.

America's role in Africa was being reappraised for another reason. By the mid-1960s, the United States had become heavily committed to the defense of South Vietnam. As this commitment expanded, frustrations in America mounted.* One result of the American involvement in Vietnam was to raise questions about whether the United States was not "overextended" in its global responsibilities; the climate of public and legislative opinion in the United States was clearly against the assumption of any *new* international obligations in distant regions. Among all the regions of the world, Africa seemed in many respects most remote from American interests and responsibilities. African political leaders were almost unanimous in wanting the great powers to stay out of their affairs—a goal which seemed more and more compatible with America's own desire to reduce its foreign commitments.[72]

A related consideration fostering a retrenchment in America's involvement in African affairs was the fact that the United States (followed soon thereafter by Soviet Russia and Communist China) was *curtailing its economic and military aid programs to other countries.* Foreign aid had never been overly popular on Capitol Hill or with some segments of American public opinion; every year, legislative skepticism about it became more widespread. American military aid programs, critics asserted, often served to bolster reactionary political regimes in power and to identify the United States as an opponent of revolutionary political movements. Such aid always carried the risk

---

*By the early 1970s, a decade or so after most African nations had received their independence, three-fourths of the continent's population lived under some form of "one-party" political system or were governed by a military junta; one-tenth of the population lived in South Africa, Southern Rhodesia, Mozambique, and other countries where black Africans had no voice in political affairs. Since 1960, Africa had experienced some 30 *coups d'état* or other violent changes in government; two countries (Dahomey and Burundi) had witnessed eight coups within a decade! In the main, the African nations which had achieved apparent stability (and the appearance could of course be deceptive), were governed by authoritarian leaders like Col. Joseph Mobutu in the Congo, President Felix Houphouët-Boigny in the Ivory Coast, and President Tubman in Liberia (who had ruled since 1944, and whose True Whig Party had been in power for 90 years). Throughout independent Africa, pervasive disillusionment existed, growing out of the discrepancy between what the masses expected independence to achieve and what it in fact accomplished. Unemployment, for example, remained widespread—and in many African countries was growing; the gap between rich and poor appeared in many societies to be widening. A projection by the British Institute for Strategic Studies anticipated that new military-led coups would erupt in Africa in the years ahead; the military role in African political life could be expected to increase. See the reports in *The New York Times* (June 14, 1970).

*America's role in the Vietnam conflict is discussed more fully in Chapter 13.

—as events in South Vietnam abundantly illustrated—that America would somehow become "responsible" for the security of the governments receiving it and would be compelled steadily to increase its military support of such governments. Different criticisms tended to be leveled at American economic aid: Outside Western Europe, the results achieved with American assistance often seemed minimal; for example, the gap between economic conditions in the developed nations and the developing nations *was widening;* innumerable instances of waste, mismanagement, and maladministration in the foreign aid program could be documented; America appeared to have earned little gratitude from recipients for the assistance extended thus far—and in some cases, American aid seemed to generate nothing but ill will for the United States; recipients resented American efforts to supervise or control the administration of aid programs; many Americans were disillusioned because they believed (not altogether correctly) that the European allies were not carrying their share of the burden for providing assistance to Africa and other economically backward regions. In brief, Americans saw little connection between the extension of economic assistance abroad and the immediate realization of their major foreign policy goals. More than any other principal region, Africa seemed an appropriate area in which to reduce American economic and military commitments.

American ties with Africa had always been tenuous and episodic. In contrast to Europe or Asia, America had no formal defense agreements with African states; its few bases on African soil (such as air bases in Morocco and Libya) were being closed, since the development of guided missiles and a large *Polaris* submarine fleet had made them largely superfluous. As long as there existed no real danger of Communist penetration of Africa—and on the basis of recent experience, that danger appeared remote—American officials were content to respect the African desire to escape involvement in the cold war. Ongoing political turbulence on the African continent did not create an attractive environment for rapid economic progress; with some 38 independent African nations seeking American assistance, aid necessarily had to be fragmented, often to such an extent that its value was at best questionable; for some African nations, five (or even ten) times as much aid as the country currently received from the outside offered little promise of overcoming economic backwardness. Concurrently, Americans had finally become deeply concerned about conditions in Latin America, a region with which the United States had long-standing and numerous ties. Cooperating with the Latin American states in the Alliance for Progress, the United States was pledged to make a massive contribution to improving economic conditions within the Western Hemisphere.*

The net result of this policy reassessment by the United States was Washington's adoption of what might be called a "low posture" in African affairs. By 1964, the State Department was endeavoring to *reduce* its commitments and responsibilities on the African continent. Or, as an authoritative study expressed the idea: Africa was an "area of residual interest" for the United States. Africa received the smallest percentage of American foreign aid (10 percent of the total) allocated to any major region; and, in more general terms, African problems tended to receive "the least attention from American policy makers."[73] Preoccupied with the Vietnam conflict, President Lyndon Johnson devoted little attention to African problems; the "waning threat of Communist takeovers" on the African continent contributed to a curtailment of American responsibilities in the area.[74] As we shall see, the African response to this policy readjustment in the United States was ambivalent. Insofar is it signified American willingness to allow Africans to manage their own affairs, or testified to American acceptance of African nonalignment in the cold war, it was widely applauded. To the extent, however, that it suggested American indifference toward Africa's needs, or that it was evidence of American unwillingness to increase its assistance to African societies, it tended to be widely criticized.

We may gain greater insight into the implications of America's "low posture" in dealing with African issues by focusing upon three concrete problems in Afro–American relations: racial and colonial conflicts on the African scene, American foreign aid to African societies, and the African concept of nonalignment.

Colonial and Racial Conflicts in Africa

Addressing the United Nations in 1959, President Sékou Touré of Guinea enunciated the fundamental principle that would determine African attitudes toward East and West. In Touré's view, the test could be stated simply: "Yes or No—are you for the liberation of Africa."[75] Or, as another spokesman expressed the same basic idea:

. . . the Western powers must realize that in most of Africa "colonialism," with its connotation of a ruling European group and subordinate African masses, is widely held to be *the* worst enemy. Communism is a secondary peril, and *apartheid* [the policy of racial separateness followed by the Republic of South Africa] is to most Africans a greater danger than the dictatorship of the proletariat.[76]

*The Alliance for Progress is dealt with at greater length in Chapter 12.

By beginning our discussion of specific issues in Afro–American relations with colonial and racial problems we start with what is, to the African mind, the matter of highest diplomatic priority: ridding the African continent of remaining colonial enclaves and eliminating racial discrimination in all African societies. Writing in 1969, an African nationalist from Southern Rhodesia noted that 38 African nations had acquired their independence, making some 88 percent of the African population free from colonial domination. This left some 30 million Africans (or about 12 percent of the population) still to be emancipated; this group inhabited about one-sixth of Africa's total territory. Among the larger African territories still to be freed from alien control, this spokesman listed Angola, Mozambique, Southern Rhodesia, South Africa, South-West Africa, and Spanish Sahara.* The inclusion of states like Southern Rhodesia and South Africa on this list underscored the *organic relationship between "colonial" and "racial" conflicts in African society*. However much Western observers might regard them as distinct, the African tended to view them as inherently related and inseparable. Racial discrimination against Africans in Southern Rhodesia, for example, was a product of the colonial experience; British colonial policy gave preferential treatment to white groups over black, in part, African nationalists charged, to guarantee the *permanent* supremacy of the former over the latter. Much the same explanation is offered by African nationalists for the dominant position of the whites in South Africa; South Africa constitutes perhaps the most serious "colonial problem" remaining on the African continent. The case of Portugal's African empire was even clearer. After Great Britain, France, and Belgium had relinquished their colonial rights in Africa, Portugal continued to hold large territories like Angola and Mozambique; thus far, Lisbon has showed no disposition to be influenced by the "winds of change" that have swept away colonial structures in Africa and other regions.[77] Regardless of whether the issue were Portugal's remaining colonial possessions in Africa, or racial discrimination in "independent" nations like Southern Rhodesia, black Africans were convinced that colonialism and racism were inseparable phenomena, representing the most serious threat to African independence.

Almost all African leaders are mindful of the

---

*By the end of the 1960s, five countries—France, Portugal, Spain, Great Britain, and South Africa—still had (or claimed) colonial possessions in Africa. Among the largest of these were Angola and Mozambique, owned by Portugal; the Spanish Sahara; South-West Africa, over which South Africa exercized de facto control; and Southern Rhodesia, still recognized as a British colony by nearly all countries except Southern Rhodesia itself.

traditional American opposition to colonialism, as symbolized by Presidents Wilson and Franklin D. Roosevelt. The United States has no "colonial record" in Africa; African governments also know that Washington has often encouraged the prompt liquidation of the British, French, and other empires on the African continent. Yet such facts do not prevent African governments, like the revolutionary regime that gained control of Zanzibar in 1964, from labeling the United States as the "leader of world imperialism and colonialism."[78] Frequently, Americans have succumbed to the temptation to dismiss such judgments as untypical of prevalent African opinion or as merely another tiresome instance of Communist-inspired propaganda. Admittedly, the American position on colonialism is seldom condemned so harshly by most responsible African governments. Yet, when even Emperor Haile Selassie in Ethiopia has called for the use of force to remove colonialism from the African scene, we may be sure that African opposition to colonialism is endemic and that America's policies on this issue are subjected to very close scrutiny by *all* African countries.[79] An American official has called attention to a widespread tendency in Africa and elsewhere to believe that the Americans "are lined up with the Western European powers" and that the United States will "always support . . . any European country when it has a colonial problem."[80] Whether such a conclusion is fully warranted is not our concern. But that Africans widely *believe* it is a justified conclusion can hardly be contested.

To the African mind, America's identification with, if not active support of, colonialism is confirmed by a number of facts. Members of NATO, like France and Portugal, have unquestionably used American-supplied arms against anticolonial movements on the African continent. Africans explain Washington's failure to restrain Lisbon by alluding to the fact that Portugal's anti-Communist sentiments are evident and that the United States desires continued access to Portuguese bases, like the Azores. African spokesmen believe that, despite its historic identification with anticolonial causes, American "leadership" in behalf of African independence has been feeble, massively qualified, and devoid of real conviction. Down to the early 1960s, American officials in the United Nations, for example, cautioned Africans against the dangers of "premature independence" and emphasized the need for an "orderly" transition from colonialism to national independence—ideas evoking little enthusiasm from impatient nationalist groups on the African scene.[81] For the first time, in 1961 American officials at the UN unequivocally denounced Portuguese colonialism in Angola.[82] Thereafter, although Washington was seldom prepared to support African nationalist demands in full, the United States moved closer to the African position in resolutions dealing with colonial issues.*

In the long run, however, it seemed doubtful that this change in American policy fundamentally altered African attitudes concerning America's apathy about the struggle against the remaining colonial regimes on the continent. It was evident that the "liberation" of Africa was *not* high on the list of American diplomatic priorities. Even more distrubing to African nationalists was the obvious fact that the United States was unprepared to assume any commitment to, or to materially assist, anticolonialist movements in Africa. By contrast, vocal and tangible support for the "liberation" of Africa was extended by Moscow and Peking. Throughout the postwar period, the strongest bond between African governments and nations in the Communist bloc was supplied by their common opposition to colonialism. Routinely, the Soviet Union sided with the African nations in voting for anticolonial resolutions in the United Nations. Within Africa itself, groups like the Angolan Popular Liberation Movement—supplied with weapons by Moscow and Peking, and utilizing bases in countries like Guinea and the two Congos—conducted an increasingly active guerrilla campaign against Portugal's West African empire. Across the continent, the Mozambique Liberation Front, also aided by Communist governments and by African countries like Tanzania and Zambia, led the struggle against Portuguese rule in East Africa. Meanwhile, Portugal was relying more upon cooperation with South Africa in order to maintain its African empire.[83]

Racial conflicts on the African continent posed many of the same problems for Afro–American relations. As we have noted, Africans tended to regard the problem of racial discrimination as an offshoot of the larger colonial question: It stemmed from the subordination of Africans by alien white groups, chiefly Europeans, during the colonial period.* This problem was embodied in two specific issues which, by the 1960s, were matters of urgent concern to Africans: the cases of Southern Rhodesia and South Africa.

The Case of Southern Rhodesia

Claimed late in the nineteenth century for Great Britain by the African explorer Cecil Rhodes, Southern Rhodesia became a "self-governing colony" in 1923. Its abundant raw materials, rich lands, and salutary climate attracted white settlement, although whites never comprised more than 5 percent of the total population of the country. In time, however, the white element became economically and politically dominant. The white philosophy of "parallel development" for the blacks—or, as Prime Minister Ian Smith recently described it, a policy of "meritocracy"—was clearly designed to perpetuate white rule, until such a time as the black majority was "fit" for political participation, development which lay many decades, perhaps generations, in the future. As anticolonialist agitation swept postwar Africa, white attitudes in Southern Rhodesia hardened. Defying efforts by British officials, African nationalists, and the United Nations to improve the condition of Rhodesia's black majority, on November 11, 1965, the government of Southern Rhodesia proclaimed its "independence." This act—held to be illegal by Great Britain, the United States, and African governments alike—precipitated a continuing conflict between Rhodesia and the outside world. Finding that racial discrimination in Rhodesia constituted a threat to international peace, the UN Security Council on December 16, 1966, voted to impose economic sanctions against the country; this embargo was tightened by subsequent Security Council resolutions.

American diplomacy in the Rhodesian crisis paralleled Washington's position toward African colonial disputes. Time and again, American officials at the UN and outside it denounced discriminatory racial policies adopted by governments like those of Southern Rhodesia and South Africa. Beginning with the Kennedy administration in 1962, official American criticism became sharper than ever. Washington also joined London and the majority of nations at the UN in holding that Southern Rhodesia's declaration of independence was contrary to international law and in refusing to recognize the act as valid. After it became evident that the govern-

---

*Early in 1970, the Nixon administration issued a new policy statement on Africa, advertised as a "restatement" of the American position on several African questions. Regarding colonial issues, the statement held: "We shall continue to believe that their [i.e., dependent] peoples should have the right of self-determination." Yet the statement also stated that "resort to force and violence" to terminate colonialism "is in no one's interest." With regard to racial oppression in South Africa and Southern Rhodesia, President Nixon committed his administration to support "the side of . . . fundamental human rights in southern Africa as we do at home and elsewhere." Yet the United States would continue its relations with South Africa, while making clear "that our limited Governmental activities in South Africa do not represent any acceptance or condoning of its discriminatory system." By contrast, Washington would not recognize the white-ruled government of Southern Rhodesia and would support UN-imposed sanctions against it. Pledging the American government to "work to bring about change in parts of Africa where racial oppression and residual colonialism still prevail," the new statement emphasized that "we are linked [to Africa] by the cultural fact that one out of every ten Americans has his origin in Africa." See the summary of this new policy declaration in *The New York Times* (March 29, 1970).

*Africans tended to give considerably less urgency to other forms of racial conflict on the continent, such as the tensions between Africans and Asians (mainly Indians) in East Africa. Justifiably or not, the latter often interpreted the program of "Africanization" adopted by East African governments as a form of ethnic discrimination against them.

ment of Southern Rhodesia was taking little account of global opinion in its internal policies, early in 1970 the Nixon administration moved to deny formal recognition to it by closing the American consulate in Salisbury. A few days later, Washington sharply condemned racial discrimination in Africa and pledged to bring about its elimination.[84] Little enthusiasm could be found among American officials, however, for the stronger measures (such as military intervention) often advocated by militant African groups. The idea of a new, black-ruled Rhodesia (called "Zimbabwe") received little encouragement from Washington. Besides its own reluctance to accept new obligations in Africa, the United States was dubious about more stringent measures against Southern Rhodesia for another reason. In the cases of both Southern Rhodesia and South Africa, American officials disagreed with African governments on three specific points: (1) Washington doubted that racial discrimination in Africa or elsewhere constituted a "threat to the peace," enabling the United Nations to take jurisdiction; (2) it had genuine doubts about the *effectiveness* of boycotts, embargoes, and the like; and (3) it was skeptical that, even if they were successful, such sanctions could ultimately benefit *black* citizens in these countries. By the 1970s, experience appeared to confirm many of these American reservations. Even African governments—like Zambia, Malawi, and Botswana—found it all but impossible to sever their economic ties with Southern Rhodesia and South Africa; Portugal and South Africa, needless to say, took no part in the boycott of Southern Rhodesia and, in fact, seemed determined to make it fail (Southern Rhodesia, for example, continued to import oil through ports in Mozambique); beset with continuing financial problems, Great Britain had all but abandoned its earlier efforts to compel a change of policy in Salisbury. Most crucially, perhaps, the white-dominated government of Southern Rhodesia showed no sign of collapse or even of a willingness to modify its policies toward the country's black majority. One reporter found a "remarkable resilience to world pressure" and a "will to resist" throughout white society that would last a long time.[85] With most of Rhodesia's black African nationalists in prison, resistance to white rule remained weak and disorganized. Pressured by adverse world opinion, and facing growing discontent among white groups that desired greater cooperation with South Africa, the government of Southern Rhodesia gave no indication of altering its position fundamentally.[86]

Apartheid in South Africa

For American foreign policy officials, the case of racial discrimination in the Republic of South Africa posed even more agonizing policy choices. The South African government's policy of *apart-*

heid (racial "separateness" or segregation) was in most essential respects even more discriminatory against blacks and other nonwhite groups than the policies of Southern Rhodesia. It is neither possible, nor necessary for our purpose, to discuss the theory and practice of *apartheid* in detail. It must suffice to note briefly that the objective of the policy is to safeguard the racial "identities" of South Africa's major ethnic groups by legally enforcing racial separation. The ultimate goal—sometimes called "grand (or big) *apartheid*"—insofar as the black majority is concerned, is the creation of "Bantustans" or separate and self-governing political units for blacks within South Africa. Meanwhile, in virtually every sphere of South African life—education, religion, housing, employment, social and cultural affairs—rigidly-enforced *apartheid* laws preserve racial segregation.* Writing in the mid-1960s, one commentator believed that *"apartheid* has been getting sharper and sharper." Several years later, another commentator said that "white South Africans who oppose apartheid have little influence and less power." Blacks and other nonwhites who opposed the policy were, in most cases, in jail, in exile, or perhaps striving clandestinely to change it.* To Afro–Asian groups, *apartheid* served as perhaps the most exploitive form of racial discrimination encountered on the planet. Critics frequently referred to the South African "Reich" and likened the government's policies to Hitler's program designed to assure "Aryan supremacy."[87] A Zulu chief from South Africa, for example, has characterized the white-dominated government as a "museum piece in our time, a hangover from the dark past of mankind, a relic of an age which everywhere else is dead or dy-

---

*By 1969, South Africa's population stood at 19.6 million people, divided as follows: African (Bantu, or black), 13.3 million; white, 3.7 million; colored (or people of "mixed blood," e.g., white and black, or black and Asian, almost 2 million; and Asian (e.g., Indian or Malay), almost 600,000. During 1960–1970, the white population had the fastest rate of increase, growing by some 700,000 over 1960. See *The Star* (Johannesburg, December 13, 1969).

*See Philip Mason, "South Africa and the World: Some Maxims and Axioms," *Foreign Affairs*, Vol. 43 (October, 1964), 154; and *The New York Times*, September 6, 1969, dispatch by Tertius Myburgh. Legally, the application of the *apatheid* in South Africa had, in many respects, become more severe with the passage of time. Yet, as South Africa continued to make rapid economic progress and to experience unrivalled prosperity, this fact made it more difficult than ever for the ultimate goal of *apartheid*—creation of separate black-ruled Bantustans—to be reached. Blacks workers, for example, continued to move into the larger cities; this accelerated the breakup of the black family structure and tended to relegate less productive blacks to the rural areas. Even more than in the past, it seemed clear that a *rigid* enforcement of South Africa's segregation policies would prove highly disruptive to the country's economy, which depended massively upon the availability of black labor in the mines and cities. See *The New York Times*, May 27, 1969, dispatch by Tertius Myburgh.

ing." In his view, "the golden age of Africa's independence is also the dark age of South Africa's decline and retrogression"; white power in the country "rests on the most heavily armed and equipped military machine in Africa."[88] A white South African has written of his native country: "Apartheid is a horror which can no longer be hidden or denied. The whole world condemns and execrates it."[89]

As early as the first session of the UN General Assembly, racial discrimination in South Africa has been on the agenda. By the late 1950s, as the deliberations of the United Nations became increasingly responsive to the views of the Afro–Asian states, resolutions dealing with South Africa became more uncompromising. Seeing little evidence that South Africa's white elite was responsive to the force of world opinion, by the early 1960s critics of *apartheid* succeeded in forging a majority in the UN General Assembly in support of sanctions against the country; in 1963, the Security Council called for an embargo of arms shipments from the outside world to South Africa; efforts were made (usually unsuccessfully) to exclude South African delegates from auxiliary bodies like the UN Conference on Trade and Development. Afro–Asian campaigns to enforce a *general* economic and diplomatic boycott against South Africa, however, have thus far been unsuccessful. As the years passed opinion on both sides hardened. Condemnations of South Africa grew more frequent and more militant, while South Africa's overt defiance of its critics in the international community also became more outspoken and self-confident.[90] That the racial situation in southern Africa was becoming more inflamed could hardly be doubted, if for no other reason than that African nationalists were more determined than ever to "liberate" South Africa, while the white-controlled government was equally resolved to resist external pressures and to assist other countries, like Portugal and Southern Rhodesia, to preserve the political status quo against violent change.*

*Eloquent evidence of South Africa's determination to defy world opinion was provided in the mid-1960s by the controversy over the future of South-West Africa—a territory some two-thirds as large as South Africa itself and rich in resources. The country had been a German colony prior to World War I; after the war, it was assigned to South Africa as a "mandate" by the League of Nations. Under the United Nations, South Africa refused to recognize any UN right to supervise its administration of the country, nor did it acknowledge that the UN was the successor organization to the League of Nations in administering League mandates. Finally, following many months of prolonged diplomatic and legal wrangling over the future of South-West Africa, the matter was submitted to the World Court for adjudication. This body ruled on a technicality that the UN had no jurisdiction over the territory—a decision which was almost universally condemned by black Africans and naturally applauded by South Africa and its supporters. The effect of the decision was to leave South Africa in control of the

To assert that American diplomatic behavior with respect to the problem of South Africa commanded little enthusiasm among independent African nations would be to understate the matter. On innumerable occasions, American officials have expressed their opposition to *apartheid*. Among all possible forms of racial discrimination, this variety—stemming from *governmentally sponsored* programs of racial separation—seemed an especially objectionable violation of human rights. Moreover, on many occasions Washington has communicated its viewpoints to Pretoria, urging officials in South Africa to modify their intractable position and to recognize the force of world opinion in behalf of racial justice.[91] At the same time, however, the United States has refrained from taking a leadership position at the United Nations to ostracize, boycott, or otherwise coerce South Africa; for example, it has *not* favored efforts to enforce a trade embargo (except for arms shipments); even less was it prepared to join in or support military intervention against South Africa.

America's hesitancy to take an active part in the campaign against *apartheid* in South Africa stems from several considerations. Officials in Washington have always been skeptical about the *legality* of UN sanctions against the country; they did not accept the Afro–Asian view that such action was legal under the Charter merely because a majority of nations at the UN found *apartheid* abhorrent or felt strongly about racial discrimination. Grave doubts also existed among American officials concerning the *effectiveness* of boycotts or other sanctions against South Africa. Events had made it abundantly clear that a number of countries in the international community would refuse to recognize or participate in such sanctions, *including some African countries*. Some of South Africa's most outspoken critics—not excluding a number of Marxist nations—carried on trade with South Africa (in some instances, disguised in the form of "third country" trade). A few nations in black Africa also continued to exchange goods with South Africa; for some of the smaller African nations (like Lesotho, Botswana, and Swaziland) the cessation of such trade could have the most serious economic implications. Indeed, several African nations close to South Africa had even begun to evince some interest in the creation of a "Common Market" for this region of the continent, with South Africa inevitably the dominant

country. It cannot be said, however, that the opinion of the World Court in any significant way diminished outside opposition to South Africa's unilateral rule there or dampened the determination of black African nationalists to "liberate" South-West Africa from what they viewed as alien domination. See *The New York Times* (July 17, August 7, 10, and 12, October 29, 1966; June 14, 1967). A excellent background study of the problem is Ruth First, *South West Africa* (Baltimore: Penguin, 1963).

member—a prospect which had the attraction not only of expanding trade among the members but also of considerably augmenting the sources of foreign assistance available to black African states.[92]

But even if sanctions could be successfully applied against South Africa, would they produce the results—progress toward a true "multiracial society" within the country—which its proponents sought? American officials had strong reservations. It was certainly conceivable that the opposite could as easily occur: The more the white elite of South Africa became isolated, fearful, and motivated by a "seige mentality," the greater the chances that they would move even further in the direction of a more totalitarian, monolithic political order dedicated to defying adverse opinion at home and abroad. Growing economic dislocations in South Africa would almost certainly *strengthen* the authority of the white-dominated government, aggravate existing apprehensions and psychoses, and produce an over-all movement *away from political liberalization and democracy*. As long as the prospect seemed remote that South Africa's critics actually possessed the *power* to alter policies in the country—and South Africa's armed forces were probably stronger than all other African armies combined—a head-on attack against *apartheid* appeared doomed to failure.

American policy toward South Africa, as African nationalists often pointed out, also unquestionably reflected cold war considerations. As part of its campaign to inhibit Communist penetration of Africa, the United States sought to minimize political upheavals and violent conflicts on the African continent. Washington was aware too of the extent of American financial holdings in South Africa. By the late 1960s, over 250 American business firms had combined assets of over three-quarters of a billion dollars in the country. South African–American trade (with the balance favoring the United States) was not insignificant.[93] South Africa's dominant position in the international gold market was also a fact well known in the West. More crucial than America's economic involvement in the country, however, was Great Britain's massive investment in South Africa—totalling some $3 billion. Impairment of this trade would surely trigger a new and acute financial crisis in Britain, conceivably leading to financial dislocations throughout the West as a whole. A fundamental disagreement thus existed between the United States and the nations of black Africa over both the legitimacy of a UN-sponsored "confrontation" with South Africa and the consequences to be expected from undertaking it.*

*The most vigorous defense of recent American policy toward South Africa is perhaps given by former Under Secretary of State George W. Ball. Besides the considerations already noted as motivating American policy-makers, Ball cites a number of other factors as

American Foreign Assistance to Africa

The general principle of assuming a "low posture" in African affairs was also reflected in the foreign assistance extended from the United States to African nations. From 1946 through 1966, the United States provided a total of some $4.6 billion in economic aid to some 33 African states, or an average of over $200 million annually for a period of two decades. As political leaders on the African continent are mindful, this fact alone makes it apparent that Africa has never ranked high on the scale of American diplomatic priorities. The total of American aid to Africa is less than half of what the United States provided for European reconstruction after World War II, and it is about half of the commitment America made during the 1960s to the Alliance for Progress. Moreover, during this period, American aid to African nations tended to be heavily *concentrated*, with the bulk of it going to a few countries (e.g., South Africa, Algeria, the Congo Republic, Morocco, Liberia, and Nigeria).[74] Military assistance from the United States to Africa has always been very limited, running around $25 million annually in recent years. American arms-aid to Africa has totaled less than .05 percent of Washington's global military assistance programs.[95]

Beginning in the mid-1960s, American economic assistance to African states was reappraised and, in time, reduced, following a study conducted by Edward M. Korry, former ambassador to Ethiopia. American assistance to all countries was declining. In an effort to achieve maximum gains with more limited funds, the Johnson administration decided to restrict American aid to

significant in the problem. He notes, for example, that the white population of South Africa, having arrived in the country *before* the Bantu majority, is no more "alien" to it than most blacks living within its borders. He is convinced that, for an indefinite period ahead, the government of South Africa is strong enough to defy both international revolutionary movements and external pressures. Attempts to compel changes in *apartheid* are likely to have only one result: to work severe hardships upon the country's black majority and to lessen its chances for greater political participation. A policy of "confrontation" with South Africa is thus "self-defeating," producing little more than "enforced solidarity" within South Africa "against a hostile world." Ball likens this problem to the issue posed by American relations with Communist countries earlier; and he urges a similar approach in dealing with South Africa. Insofar as the outside world has *any* influence on racial questions within South Africa, it is likely to be achieved by *maximizing the country's contact with the West;* by letting the "winds of change" blow through the country and giving it the widest possible exposure to foreign opinion; by endeavoring to *reduce* the fears and psychoses of the white elite, not aggravating them; and by encouraging the closest diplomatic, economic, religious, cultural, and other ties between South Africa and the outside world. Even then, foreigners must reconcile themselves to the fact their influence upon the problem is likely to be marginal. See George W. Ball, *The Discipline of Power* (Boston: Little, Brown, 1968), pp. 245–259.

fewer African nations; an attempt to impart an "over-all direction" to American aid activities was made by allocating most of such assistance to regional and multilateral programs (like the African Development Bank) instead of to individual countries. American officials agreed with many private commentators that Africa was afflicted with "Balkanization": Many of its new nations were simply too small and economically unpromising to utilize outside assistance constructively. This reduction in the volume of American economic aid (together with comparable reductions in Soviet and Chinese aid programs after the mid-1960s) meant that the gap between Africa's need for development capital and the supply of funds available to Africa's detriment.[96] African leaders known for their pro-Western orientation —like President Tubman of Liberia—complained openly about America's "neglect" of African needs; he and other officials in Africa proposed a moratorium, for example, on the space race, with funds to be rechanneled into expanded assistance for needy societies.[97] Writing late in 1969, one observer noted that Africa, which obtained its independence later than any major region, "had the singular misfortune to arrive at this stage of development at a time when foreign economic aid is drying up." A report by the World Bank in the same period found that prospects for a considerable expansion in outside assistance for Africa were far from encouraging. The nations of Western Europe—Africa's principal source of foreign aid in recent years*—were similarly tapering off

their aid programs on the African continent. Britain was cutting down its aid and subsidies to several African governments; in the post-Gaullist era, France was also reducing its assistance to Francophile African states. For their part, neither Soviet Russia nor Communist China gave any indication of desiring to assume the responsibility for promoting the economic development of the African continent or even a major part of it.[98] Although the World Bank planned to increase its lending activities in Africa, this favorable development was largely offset by two factors: Adverse conditions in the world market continued to impair Africa's ability to generate its own capital from exports; and the needs of most African nations for outside assistance of all kinds continued to increase at a rapid rate.[99] One sobering index of Africa's requirements, for example, was provided by the viewpoint of a UN official who said that if it were possible (and of course, it was most unlikely) to allocate *solely to Africa* the foreign assistance available from the United States and the United Nations for all countries in the world, this substantial increase would still fall short of meeting Africa's needs![100]

From the perspective of the United States, the problem of Africa's foreign aid requirements was but part of the larger question of assistance from the industrialized nations to the developing world as a whole. For nearly all nations south of the equator, the demand for developmental assistance outstripped both the supply available and, in many cases, the country's capacity to absorb outside aid constructively. For reasons that we shall examine more fully in Chapter 14, the American people and their leaders had become disenchanted with foreign aid—an attitude reflected most graphically in the unwillingness of Congress to approve increases in the foreign aid budget. Under President Nixon, for example, the foreign aid allocation was the smallest in recent history. As the area of lowest American diplomatic and military involvement, Africa suffered uniquely from the over-all reduction in foreign assistance by the United States. Moreover, Africa's record of civil wars, insurrectionary activities, and ongoing political turmoil, and its inability to translate the ideal of Pan-Africanism into a functioning regional organization created an adverse "investment climate" for suppliers of private and governmental capital alike. Africa's need for foreign assistance was unquestionably great; but its capacity to utilize outside aid often appeared small.

For African nations, the problem of access to external assistance, particularly from the United States, was in some measure an outgrowth of their very success in insulating the African continent

---

*As was pointed out in our discussion of the European Economic Community in Chapter 10, the members of this organization have taken the lead in extending foreign assistance to developing societies in Africa, especially to their former colonial possessions. Among the 38 independent African nations, 18 (the largest group being former French colonies in West Africa) have "associate membership" in the EEC; two other groups of African states—the Maghreb (Algeria, Morocco, and Tunisia) and the 12 African members of the British-led Commonwealth of Nations—have expressed keen interest in EEC membership. During the first seven years of the 1960s, the African states associated with the EEC received some $1.5 billion in assistance from the organization's members; in addition, France (for several years during the 1960s, the largest single provider of foreign aid to Africa) maintained a number of "bilateral" aid programs to African nations maintaining their membership in the French Community; Belgium extended comparable assistance to its former colony, the Democratic Republic of the Congo. See George W. Ball, *The Discipline of Power* (Boston: Little, Brown, 1968), p. 238. Americans who sometimes have complained about the reluctance of the European allies to assume their "share" of the burden of foreign aid tend to be unaware of the extensive assistance extended by the European nations to African societies. Even by the late 1950s, for example, France contributed a larger percentage of its national income (1.5 percent) to foreign aid than did the United States (0.5 percent). By the late 1960s, French aid, concentrated primarily in Africa, totaled some $1.5 billion annually vis-à-vis the total American foreign aid budget for fiscal year 1970 of some $2 billion. See

---

"French Aid to Developing Countries," (French Information Service, New York) no. 1310 (November, 1969).

from the cold war. As we shall see, by the 1960s, the United States had largely accepted the desire of African nations to remain diplomatically nonaligned. Ostensibly at least, so did Soviet Russia. In contrast to Korea or South Vietnam—or even "northern tier" countries like Turkey and Iran—the African states faced no overt danger of aggression or even of successful Communist-led internal subversion. In the main, the African continent was not a crisis area in which threatened Communist expansionism had to be countered by an American program of containment. On balance, this fact conferred many benefits upon African nations—no one of which desired to become "another Vietnam." Justifiably or not, a price that had to be paid for this situation was the relatively low level of official American interest in African problems and—while American policy-makers were under pressure to reduce the nation's global commitments—an unwillingness in the United States to expand its responsibilities for African welfare.

African "Positive Neutralism" and Nonalignment

Like the newly independent Arab states, African countries that have recently won their freedom tend to regard a foreign policy of noninvolvement with cold war blocs, variously defined as a position of "neutralism," "positive neutralism," or "nonalignment"—as an integral feature of true national sovereignty. Expressing a viewpoint pervasive throughout Africa, one observer has said of Guinea:

Guinea desires to be friends with East and West, to seek help from anyone who will give it, and to avoid embroilment in a worldwide ideological conflict while at the same time creating a revolutionary one-party socialist state.

Guinea's animating impulse in foreign affairs, President Touré has explained, can be expressed simply: "We want to be ourselves—not drawn to either bloc."[101] President Keita in nearby Mali echoed this idea when he declared that Mali refused to become "a pawn of this or that bloc" in diplomatic affairs; citizens of his country "realize that to make our country a satellite is against our traditions of honour and dignity."[102] Lest it be imagined that such ideas are dominant only in regimes that are conspicuous for their anti-Westernism, it must be emphasized that openly pro-Western African governments espouse a basically identical foreign policy credo. Emperor Haile Selassie of Ethiopia, for example, has repeatedly voiced his "independence" of either the West or the Communist bloc; he has underscored this determination by accepting aid from both camps.[103] The African concept of positive neutralism or nonalignment is basically similar to the policy widely embraced by other newly independent Arab and Asian states. African spokesmen insist that such a policy is *not* tantamount to a position of "neutrality" or "isolationism" or "fence straddling" or other postures often erroneously equated with it by outsiders. Nor is it synonymous with a position of diplomatic "equidistance" or *equilibrisme:* African nations feel no obligation to assume a "midway" position between the United States and the Soviet Union on a given international issue, to balance criticism of one of these countries with denunciations of the other, or to "walk a tightrope" between the cold war giants. Nonalignment intrinsically has nothing to do with these things. Rather, its essential meaning is *diplomatic independence* or freedom to agree, and to disagree, with one great-power bloc or the other, as the interests of African states dictate. Nonalignment is thus viewed by African nations as an extension of, and a major guarantor of, national sovereignty; for the first time in many years, native governments possess the freedom to formulate their own diplomatic positions without external dictation and without having decisions "made" for them in a foreign capital. Nonalignment has two specific requirements. It prohibits African states from joining cold war military alliance systems, like NATO or the Warsaw Pact; and it means that African nations do not regard themselves as *automatically or permanently* identified with the Western or Communist blocs in the United Nations or outside it.[104]

As in other regions, the theory and practice of nonalignment is affected by environmental factors. The African conception of nonalignment, therefore, possesses certain characteristics not necessarily found (at least not in the same degree) in the Middle East or Asia. Africa was the last major colonial area to receive its independence. Its memories of Western colonial exploitation remain vivid, and its suspicions of Western colonial and "neo-colonial" impulses are still strong. Anti-Western sentiment thus sometimes reaches an intensity in Africa that is rarely found today in Asia. While it is close to Europe, the African continent is remote from the Soviet Union—and even more distant from Communist China. In contrast to some countries in the Middle East, African nations have experienced no historical, and face no current, threats from Russian expanionism. Communist China's capacity to penetrate Africa is almost nil. It is perhaps impossible for most Africans to envision any real danger from Communism, a movement which has had minimum success on the African continent. On the other hand, Africans tend to identify the gravest threat to their independence and welfare—existing colonial regimes and racial discrimination against black Africans—as deriving from the behavior of Europeans inside and outside Africa. These considerations often impart an anti-Western coloration to

African nonalignment, leading Western observers to complain about the "double standard" which Africans are prone to apply in judging American and European vis-à-vis Soviet or Chinese behavior.[105]

Yet, if African nonalignment often has an evident anti-Western bias, it is also true that *African ties with the West have remained close*—closer, in some respects, than those of any other region in the Afro–Asian world. The West provides the largest market for African exports; inadequate as it might be in terms of African needs, aid from America and Western Europe provides Africa with its largest quantum of foreign assistance; Western private investments in Africa are extensive and, in many African nations, continue to grow; English or French is the *lingua franca* throughout much of Africa; in several African societies, the number of Westerners living in the country has *increased* since independence; Western culture, philosophies, and political ideologies have permeated Africa; in the most vital sector of African economic enterprise—agriculture—native governments look to the West (along with countries like Israel and Taiwan) for expertise and scientific know-how in order to raise agricultural output (a sphere in which neither Soviet Russia nor Communist China has much to offer Africa).[106]

Imprecise as they often are, concepts like African socialism and African democracy owe a great deal to Western antecedents and models.[107] Much as they might denounce the idea of American-style capitalism as a synonym for exploitation, African leaders are aware that *private entrepreneurship is deeply embedded in the African tradition*. Even the most radical versions of African socialism accept the fact that native private enterprise—along with private investment from abroad—must play a key role in Africa's economic future.

Another important tie linking Africa and the West—in the sphere of political relations, among the most crucial—is the basic agreement between native African and Western governments that the "African revolution" has already occurred, that it is entitled to acceptance, and that the new political regimes on the African scene are, for the most part, those which represent the desires of the African peoples themselves. This of course does not mean that American policy-makers have *no preferences* among the highly variegated political systems existing among almost 40 independent African states. As in the Middle East, officials in Washington have openly expressed their interest in promoting "moderate" political movements in Africa and in maximizing political stability in an environment in which instability seems the rule.[108] Thus policy-makers in the United States did not conceal their approval when the regime of President Kwame Nkrumah in Ghana—at the

time, the epitome of anti-American sentiment and ongoing revolutionary agitation among African nations—was overthrown by a military junta in 1966; as the United States hoped, Ghanian–American relations improved significantly in the years that followed.[109] In the allocation of foreign assistance, an American preference for political moderation in Africa has also sometimes weighed heavily.

Yet the fact remains that, in spite of such undisguised preferences by American policy-makers, the United States: (1) has maintained reasonably cordial relations with a broad spectrum of political regimes throughout Africa; (2) has provided assistance even to some of the more radical African governments (such as those of Guinea, Ghana, and Algeria); and (3) has, in the overwhelming majority of instances, left the Africans to work out their own political destinies without outside dictation. Irrespective of whether the African choice is a "one-party" authoritarian system (as in Guinea and several other African nations), a military junta (as in Ghana, Algeria, the Sudan, and a number of other African countries), an "African democracy" (as in Tanzania and Kenya), or a reform-minded monarchy (as in Ethiopia), the United States has accommodated itself to the existence of political heterogeneity on the African continent.* On this issue, America's position coincides with Africa's: The choice of political system and ideology should be made by the Africans themselves.

Overtly, Soviet Russia and Communist China also subscribe to this view. Even before the United States reappraised its position with respect to African nonalignment, Moscow and Peking had endorsed the concept and welcomed neutralist states into the "peace zone." After a period during the early 1960s—when a number of Soviet or Chinese-instigated intrigues and insurrections accomplished little more than alienating African leaders and masses—Moscow and Peking dampened their support for revolutionary movements in this area. Communist machinations against native governments did not, however, completely

---

*The great political diversity represented among the African recipients of American assistance is illustrated by examining the foreign aid allocations for fiscal year 1969. Some 18 African nations benefitted from economic and technical assistance from the United States; in addition, American aid went to 6 regional and multilateral organizations, such as self-help projects involving several African states and regional schemes in East Africa and in southern Africa. Among the larger recipients of foreign aid from the United States were: Cameroon ($10 million); Ethiopia ($2.3 million); Guinea ($15 million); Ivory Coast ($26 million); Malagasy Republic ($2 million); Nigeria ($7.5 million); Tunisia ($1.3 million). Among the group receiving a smaller quantity of American aid, a comparable diversity of political regimes and of attitudes toward the West, was represented. See Agency for International Development, *Operations Report as of December 31, 1968* (Washington, D.C.: U.S. Government Printing Office, 1969), pp. 9–10.

come to an end; during the late 1960s, for example, officials in East Africa openly complained about Communist-supported intrigues against established governments.[110] Yet in general Communist policy-makers have apparently concluded that Africa is *not* (in the words of Chinese Foreign Minister Chou En-lai) "ripe for revolution"; ongoing revolutionary agitation against native governments, even Peking's recent conduct seems to admit, wins few converts for Communism on the African scene. Attempts to identify with and support anticolonial movements; the extension of economic, technical, and military assistance to African governments; programs of educational and cultural exchange; extensive propaganda activities directed at African societies—these are the techniques used by both Soviet Russia and Communist China to influence Africans and to win adherents to Marxism.

A formidable barrier hindering such efforts, however, is the fact that Moscow and Peking do *not* accept the "African revolution" in the form of native African governments as permanent or legitimate. African political elites are fully aware that in Soviet Marxist jargon, they constitute the "national bourgeoisie"—that is, they are neither capitalists nor true Marxists, but an intermediate group whose basic purpose in the Communist scheme of things is to prepare the way for the ultimate African revolution under Marxist auspices. In the Marxist conception, native African governments are thus regarded as *instrumental and expendable*. African political leaders are cognizant of the long-standing ideological antipathy between nationalism and Communism; they know that in the Marxist conception of "Communist (or proletarian) internationalism" only Soviet (or Chinese) nationalism is recognized as legitimate. African political elites are also fully mindful that Soviet or Chinese economic and military aid programs, assistance to anticolonial movements, cultural programs, and the like are techniques employed ultimately *to weaken and destroy African nationalism.* Experience thus far indicates rather convincingly that African political leaders not only recognize this fact; when necessary, they are prepared to take steps to protect their independence.[111]

Although issues like colonialism, foreign aid, the problem of South Africa, and other specific questions continue to foment misunderstandings and disagreements between Americans and Africans, Africa's ties with the West nevertheless remain strong. With rare exceptions, Western policy-makers acknowledge that independent African nations belong to that group known as the "free world." African nonalignment is directed against *all* foreign intervention in African affairs. Few Western governments desire to dominate Africa politically; nearly all acknowledge that the era of Western colonialism has ended. In fact, most Western nations have *reduced* their involvement in African affairs. Although the "Communist timetable" for establishing Merxist orders on the African continent appears also to have been slowed down significantly, ideologically at least both Soviet Russia and Red China still refer to African political elites as the "national bourgeoisie." Thus far, there is no reliable evidence that Communist policy-makers have abandoned their underlying hostility toward African nationalism or that they have come to terms with Africa's desire to determine its own political future.

NOTES

1. America's limited role in the Middle East prior to World War II is discussed in William R. Polk, *The United States and the Arab World* (Cambridge, Mass.: Harvard University Press, 1965), pp. 261–263.
2. Cordell Hull, *The Memoirs of Cordell Hull*, vol. 2 (New York: Macmillan, 1948), pp. 1540–1547.
3. Harry N. Howard, "The Arab–Asian States in the United Nations," *Middle East Journal* 7 (Summer, 1953), 279–922.
4. For extensive evidence of lobbying activities by Zionist organizations in the United States, see the data included in Senate Foreign Relations Committee, *Activities of Nondiplomatic Representatives of Foreign Principals in the United States*, 88th Congress, 1st Session, 1963, pp. 1695–1775.
5. Harry S. Truman, *Memoirs*, vol. 2 (Garden City, N.Y.: Doubleday, 1955), pp. 136–150.
6. See *ibid.*, pp. 145–146, 151.
7. Edward B. Glick, "Latin America and the Establishment of Israel," *Middle Eastern Affairs* 9 (January, 1958), 11–16.
8. Truman, *op. cit.*, pp. 132–138.
9. American diplomacy with respect to the partition of Palestine is discussed at length in Truman, *op. cit.*, pp. 132–169; and Dean Acheson, *Present at the Creation* (New York: Norton, 1969), pp. 169–183.
10. Truman, *op. cit.*, p. 154; *The New York Times* (October 5 and 7, 1946).
11. The Suez crisis of 1956 is dealt with more fully in Peter Calvocoressi, ed. *Suez: Ten Years After* (New York: Random House, 1967); Anthony Eden, *The Suez Crisis of 1956* (Boston: Beacon Press, 1960); and Dwight D. Eisenhower, *Waging Peace* (Garden City, N.Y.: Doubleday, 1965), pp. 20–58, 177–205.
12. For more detailed analysis of the origins and consequences of the Middle East crisis of 1967, see the symposium on the subject in *Foreign Affairs* 46 (January, 1968), 304–347, especially the articles by Charles W. Yost, "How It Began," pp. 304–321, and Bernard Lewis, "The Consequences of Defeat," pp. 321–336. A more recent account is Nadav Safran, *From War to War: The Arab–Israeli*

Confrontation, 1948–1967 (New York: Pegasus Press, 1969).

13. Israel's position after its victory over the Arabs in 1967 is discussed more fully in Fred J. Khouri, *The Arab–Israeli Dilemma* (Syracuse, N.Y.: Syracuse University Press, 1968), pp. 326–338; and in Frank Gervasi, *The Case for Israel* (New York: Viking, 1967), pp. 170–181; and Amnon Rubinstein, "'Damn Everybody' Sums Up the Angry Mood of Israel," *The New York Times Magazine* (February 9, 1969), pp. 24–27, 93–99.

14. For Arab viewpoints after their defeat in 1967, see Khouri, *op. cit.,* pp. 319–326; "An Interview with Nasser," *Time Magazine* 93 (May 16, 1969), 31; *Newsweek* LXXIV (October 6, 1969), 89; and *The New York Times* (July 24, 1969).

15. America's role in the establishment of Israel is highlighted in Truman, *op. cit.,* pp. 132–169; and Khouri, *op. cit.,* pp. 55–56.

16. See Khouri, *op. cit.,* pp. 60–61.

17. For discussions of the Tripartitite Declaration of 1950, see Khouri, *op. cit.,* pp. 295–296; and John C. Campbell, *Defense of the Middle East* (New York: Praeger, 1960), pp. 85–87.

18. For official expressions of American "neutrality" or "impartiality" in the Arab–Israeli conflict, see the speech by Ambassador Arthur Goldberg to the UN Security Council on November 16, 1966, in *Documents on American Foreign Relations: 1966* (New York: Harper & Row, 1967), pp. 175–181; and the views of Assistant Secretary of State Joseph J. Sisco, "The United States and the Arab–Israeli Dispute," *Annals of the American Academy of Political and Social Science* 384 (July, 1969), 66–73.

19. See John S. Badeau, *The American Approach to the Arab World* (New York: Harper & Row, 1968), p. 90; and *The New York Times* (December 10, 1968).

20. For details of this transaction see J. C. Hurewitz, *Middle East Politics: The Military Dimension* (New York: Praeger, 1969), p. 469.

21. See *ibid.,* pp. 484–488. For discussions of the role of the United States in trying to preserve an arms balance in the Middle East during the 1970s, see *The New York Times* (January 25, March 24, and July 12, 1970).

22. Badeau, *op. cit.,* p. 91. For earlier statements by Arab spokesmen in this same vein, see *The New York Times* (January 23 and 24, 1964). See also H. P. Castleberry, "Arab's View of Postwar American Foreign Policy," *Western Political Quarterly* 12 (March, 1959), 9–36.

23. For President Truman's views, see his *Memoirs, op. cit.,* pp. 132, 140.

24. Our discussion of the Middle East cease-fire agreement relies upon *The New York Times* (July 3, 18, 24, 25 and 30 and August 8, 9, 20, 27, 29, and 30, 1970). See also *Newsweek* **LXXVI** (August 10, 1970), 15–16; and *Time Magazine* **96** (August 10, 1970), 14–23.

25. See Charles E. Cremeans, *The Arabs and the World* (New York: Praeger, 1963), pp. 234–238, 310; and Badeau, *op. cit.,* p. 21

26. Badeau, *op. cit.,* p. 22.

27. The nature and extent of American involvement in the oil industries of the Middle East are discussed at greater length in Robert Engler, *The Politics of Oil: Private Power and Democratic Directions* (Chicago: University of Chicago Press, 1967), pp. 65–79; Badeau, *op. cit.,* pp. 20–26; and Stephen H. Longrigg, "The Economics and Politics of Oil in the Middle East," in J. H. Thompson and R. D. Reischauer, *Modernization of the Arab World* (New York Van Nostrand Reinhold, 1966), pp. 102–115.

28. Soviet Russia's efforts to gain a foothold in the Middle East oil industry began in the early 1960s. See Leon M. Herman, "The Soviet Oil Offensive," *The Reporter* 26 (June 21, 1962), 26–28; for more recent data, see the detailed discussion in Walter Laqueur, *The Struggle for the Middle East: the Soviet Union in the Mediterranean, 1958–1968* (New York: Macmillan, 1969), pp. 118–137; and *The New York Times* (June 21 and July 12, 1970).

29. An evaluation of this proposal in provided in Campbell, *op. cit.,* pp. 39–48.

30. The negotiations leading to the Baghdad Pact and a discussion of its history are included in Campbell, *op. cit.,* pp. 39–161. For more recent developments, see the reports on the activities of CENTO in *The New York Times* (April 24, 1966; February 11, 1967; and May 27, 1969).

31. See Department of State, *United States Policy in the Middle East,* no. 6505, Near and Middle Eastern Series, vol. 25 (1957), p. 45.

32. *Documents on American Foreign Relations: 1957* (New York: Harper & Row, 1958), p. 237; and *Documents on American Foreign Relations: 1958* (New York: Harper & Row, 1959), 300.

33. America's intervention in Lebanon in 1958 is discussed in greater detail in Eisenhower, *op. cit.,* pp. 262–291. For commentatary on some of the long-range implications of this intervention, see J. C. Hurewitz, "Lebanese Democracy in Its International Setting," in Leonard Binder, ed., *Politics in Lebanon* (New York: John Wiley, 1966), pp. 213–239; and Richard J. Barnet, *Intervention and Revolution: America's Confrontation with Insurgent Movements Around the World* (New York: World Publishing, 1968), pp. 132–153.

34. Department of State, *The Development of United States Policy in the Near East, South Asia, and Africa, 1951–52,* no. 4851, Near and Middle Eastern Series, vol. 9 (1953), pp. 892–895.

35. Walter Z. Laqueur, *Communism and Nationalism in the Middle East* (New York: Praeger, 1956), p. 7.

36. *Ibid.,* p. 8.

37. Wilfred C. Smith, *Islam in Modern History* (New York: Mentor Books, 1957), p. 82.

38. *Ibid.*, pp. 117, 164–165.

39. See *ibid.*, pp. 97–165.

40. Gamal Abdel Nasser, "The Egyptian Revolution," *Foreign Affairs* 33 (January, 1955), 208.

41. For the ideology and program of the Ba'ath party, see Kamel S. Abu Jaber, *The Arab Ba'ath Socialist Party: History, Ideology, and Organization* (Syracuse, N.Y.: Syracuse University Press, 1966), pp. 1–23.

42. See Fakhri Shehab, "Kuwait: Super-Affluent Society," in Thompson and Reischauer, *op. cit.*, pp. 126–141.

43. Discussions of Saudi Arabia's attempts to modernize may be found in George Rentz, "Saudi Arabia: The Islamic Island," in Thompson and Reischauer, *op. cit.*, pp. 115–126; George Lenczowski, "Tradition and Reform in Saudi Arabia," *Current History* 52 (February, 1967), 98–105; and Dana Adams Schmidt, "Faisal Modernizes but with Caution," *New York Times Magazine* (November 1, 1964), pp. 38, 78–86.

44. For a detailed and informed discussion of the "White Revolution" in Iran, focusing upon progress and prospects for further modernization, see William G. Miller, "Political Organization in Iran: From Dowreh to Political Party," *The Middle East Journal* 23 (Spring, 1969), 159–168, and 24 (Summer, 1969), 343–351.

45. "Nasser Replies to Questions of U.S. Editors," *Egypt News* 5 (February 12, 1958), 1.

46. *Documents on International Affairs: 1958* (London: Oxford University Press, 1962), p. 245.

47. "Abdel-Nasser Says 'Russia Took Our Hand,'" *Mideast Mirror* 12 (July, 1960), 2.

48. Dwight D. Eisenhower, *Mandate for Change* (Garden City, N.Y.: Doubleday, 1963), p. 154.

49. See the *Egyptian Mail* (Cairo, November 18, 1961).

50. Quoted in "Syria and the United States," *The Arab World* 3 (November, 1957), 4.

51. The views of Secretary of State John Foster Dulles toward neutralism in the Arab world and elsewhere are analyzed in greater detail in Cecil V. Crabb, Jr., *The Elephants and the Grass: A Study of Nonalignment* (New York: Praeger, 1965), pp. 168–177.

52. See Eisenhower, *Waging Peace, op. cit.*, pp. 21, 145–146, 196–204.

53. The Aswan Dam episode is treated more extensively in *ibid.*, pp. 30–34, and 663; see also Sherman Adams, *First-Hand Report* (New York: Harper & Row, 1961), pp. 245–251. Several years after Dulles revoked the American offer to assist in financing the dam, Vice President Nixon conceded that this step had been a mistake by the United States. For his views, see *Arab News and Views* IX (July 1, 1963), 1.

54. See *Documents on International Affairs: 1957* (London: Oxford University Press, 1960), p. 216.

55. Senate Foreign Relations Committee, *International Development and Security*, 87th Congress, 1st Session, 1961, p. 761.

56. House Foreign Affairs Committee, *Foreign Assistance Act of 1962*, 87th Congress, 1st Session, 1962, pp. 564, 566.

57. For more detailed discussion of the Islamic tradition in Africa, providing an important link between many African and Arab countries, see Abdul A. Said, *The African Phenomenon* (Boston: Allyn and Bacon, 1968), pp. 31–35; and for a more detailed historical account of the impact of Islam upon Africa, consult J. Spencer Trimingham, *The Influence of Islam upon Africa* (New York: Praeger, 1968), esp. pp. 103–126. An illuminating account of the Christian impact upon African society is contained in Ndabaningi Sithole, *African Nationalism*, 2nd. ed. (New York: Oxford University Press, 1969), pp. 84–95.

58. The most authoritative study of the economic, geographic, and other major characteristics of the African continent is perhaps George T. Kimble, *Tropical Africa* (Garden City, N.Y.: Doubleday, 1962, two vols.). For current data on the economic development of Africa, see the Agency for International Development, *AID Economic Data Book—Africa* (Washington, D.C.: U.S. Government Printing Office, 1968); this series is published annually.

59. See Agency for International Development, *op. cit.*, p. 6 and *passim* for data on individual African countries; see also Reginald H. Green and Ann Seidman, *Unity or Poverty? The Economics of Pan-Africanism* (Baltimore: Penguin, 1968), p. 53.

60. See Chester Bowles, *Africa's Challenge to America* (Berkeley, Calif.: University of California Press, 1956), p. 2; and Walter Goldschmidt, ed., *The United States and Africa* (New York: Praeger, 1963), p. 162.

61. Current data on trade by African nations may be found in Agency for International Development, *op. cit., passim*. For an analysis of the problems confronted by African nations in world trade, see Green and Seidman, *op. cit.*, pp. 31–200; and for a discussion of the larger problem of economic growth by the Afro-Asian nations generally, see Branislav Gosovic, "UNCTAD: North-South Encounter," *International Conciliation*, no. 568 (May, 1968).

62. Kimble, *op. cit.*, vol. 1, pp. 120–121; Clark D. Moore and Ann Dunbar, eds., *Africa: Yesterday and Today* (New York: Bantam, 1968), pp. 334–337.

63. Goldschmidt, *op. cit.*, p. 4.

64. Rupert Emerson, "The Character of American Interests in Africa," in *ibid.*, p. 3.

65. For the evolution of official American concern with Africa, see Vernon McKay, "The African Operations of United States Government Agencies," in *ibid.*, pp. 273–296.

66. Cited in Goldschmidt, *op. cit.*, pp. 31, 285–286, 288; see also Thomas A. Sorensen, *The World War: The Story of American Propa-*

ganda (New York: Harper & Row, 1968), pp. 165–170, for a discussion of American propaganda activities in Africa.

67. Rupert Emerson, *Africa and United States Policy* (Englewood Cliffs, N.J.: Prentice-Hall, 1967), p. 26.

68. See Arthur Schlesinger, Jr., *A Thousand Days* (Boston: Houghton Mifflin, 1965), pp. 552–557.

69. Guinea's experience with Soviet aid, leading to a sharp reaction against Russian political intervention in the country, is discussed more fully in David Hapgood, "Guinea's First Five Years," *Current History* **45** (December, 1963), 355–361. For a broader analysis of Soviet aid activities in Africa down to the early 1960s, see David Morison, *The U.S.S.R. and Africa: 1945–1963* (New York: Oxford University Press, 1964).

70. Events in Ghana leading to the overthrow of President Kwame Nkrumah are discussed in *The New York Times* (February 26, March 6 and 13, 1966); and in Lloyd Garrison, "Exit Nkrumah, an Old Dreamer; Enter Ankrah, a New Realist," *New York Times Magazine* (April 3, 1966), pp. 32–33, 117–120. For developments in the months which followed, see *The New York Times* (September 7, 1969).

71. Political developments leading to the Communist-led insurrection in Zanzibar, followed by the union between that country and Tanganyika, are discussed in A. J. Hughes, *East Africa: The Search for Unity* (Baltimore: Penguin, 1963), pp. 194–213; *The New York Times* (February 20, March 25 and 28, and April 24, 1964); and Norman N. Miller, "East Africa—1969," *American Universities Field Staff Reports* **VIII** (September, 1969), 1–8.

72. See *The United States in World Affairs: 1964* (New York: Harper & Row, 1965), p. 276.

73. *The United States in World Affairs: 1965* (New York: Harper & Row, 1966), p. 192.

74. *The United States in World Affairs: 1966* (New York: Harper & Row, 1967), pp. 239–240.

75. "Sékou Touré in America," *Africa Special Report* **4** (November, 1959), 9.

76. Emmet V. Mittlebeeler, "Africa and the Defense of America," *World Affairs* **121** (Fall, 1958), 82. Italics in original.

77. For discussions of Portugal's colonial possessions in Africa, see James Duffy, *Portugal in Africa* (Baltimore: Penguin, 1959), *passim;* and *The New York Times* (August 6 and October 7, 1969).

78. *The New York Times* (February 20, 1964).

79. *The New York Times* (October 7, 1963).

80. See, for example, the statement of George V. Allen, then director of the USIA, in Senate Foreign Relations Committee, *Review of Foreign Policy,* 85th Congress, 2nd Session, 1958, p. 218.

81. *Ibid.,* p. 736.

82. The change in American foreign policy toward colonialism in Africa, with specific reference to Portugal's empire, is discussed in Schlesinger, *op. cit.,* pp. 509–512.

83. See *The New York Times* (August 6, 1969), dispatch by Richard Eder; and (October 7, 1969), dispatch by R. W. Apple, Jr.

84. Discussions of recent American foreign policy toward Southern Rhodesia may be found in John A. Davis and James K. Baker, *Southern Africa in Transition* (New York: Praeger, 1966), pp. 101–157, and *The New York Times* (March 10 and 29, 1970).

85. See *The New York Times* (January 24, 1969), dispatch by Ronald Legge.

86. See John Worrall, " 'Our Independence is Real,' Says Ian Smith," *New York Times Magazine* (October 27, 1968), pp. 40–66.

87. An "indictment" of South African *apartheid,* comparing the white-ruled government to Nazi Germany, is Brian Bunting, *The Rise of the South African Reich* (Baltimore: Penguin, 1964); a more recent, and less polemical, study is Douglas Brown, *Against the World: Attitudes of White South Africa* (Garden City, N.Y.: Doubleday, 1969).

88. Chief Luthuli's views are presented in Moore and Dunbar, *op. cit.,* p. 293.

89. See Bunting, *op. cit.,* p. 322.

90. "Issues Before the 24th General Assembly," *International Conciliation,* no. 574 (September, 1969), 108. Issues in this series, published annually, provide an up-to-date account of UN actions regarding South Africa. For a summary of UN-sponsored activities toward South Africa down to the end of the 1960s, see *ibid.,* pp. 107–110.

91. *The United States in World Affairs: 1966, op. cit.,* pp. 253–255; for more recent data, see later volumes in this series.

92. See *The New York Times* (May 28, 1967; and September 6, 1969).

93. Recent data on the nature and scope of American investments in, and trade with, South Africa is contained in House Foreign Affairs Committee, *Report of Special Study Mission to Southern Africa,* 91st Congress, 1st Session, 1969, pp. 4–5, 98–101.

94. For current data on American foreign aid activities in Africa, see the publication by the Agency for International Development, *Operations Report* (Washington, D.C.: U.S. Government Printing Office); this series is published semiannually. An appraisal of recent American foreign aid programs to Africa is contained in Emerson, *Africa and United States Policy, op. cit.,* pp. 35–42; and see *The New York Times* (January 27, 1967).

95. *The New York Times* (January 20, 1964; and July 5, 1966).

96. The findings of the Korry Report on American aid to Africa, and the changes made in the program as a result, are included in Agency for International Development, *Proposed Foreign Aid Program: Fiscal Year 1968* (Washington, D.C.: U.S. Government Printing Office, 1967), pp. 201–203. Com-

mentaries on the report and its implications are Anthony Astrachan, "AID Reslices the Pie," *Africa Report* **12** (June, 1967), 8–15; and Dean Rusk, "The Foreign Assistance Program," *Department of State Bulletin* **57** (August 14, 1967), 212.

97. President Tubman's views may be found in the *African Recorder* **6** (January 15–28, 1967), 1541.

98. Africa's access to foreign aid in the years ahead is evaluated in *The New York Times* (November 24, 1969), dispatch by R. W. Apple, Jr.

99. Foreign aid programs by Soviet Russia, Communist China, and other Marxist nations on the African continent are analyzed in Zbigniew Brzezinski, *Africa and the Communist World* (Stanford, Calif.: Stanford University Press, 1963), pp. 49–84, 142–204; and in Green and Seidman, *op. cit.*, pp. 191–199. In several African countries, the "ugly American" has had its counterpart resentments directed toward Russian and Chinese aid activities. Although its tone is rather stridently anti-Communist, this is the theme of the study by Victor Lasky, *The Ugly Russian* (New York: Pocket Books, 1966); Lasky cites innumerable examples of the negative impression created by the "ugly Russian" in Africa.

100. Cited in "A Progress Report on Economic Development," in Moore and Dunbar, *op. cit.*, p. 346.

101. *The New York Times* (October 25, 1959).

102. Quoted in the *Iraq Times* (Baghdad, September 25, 1961).

103. *The African Recorder* **1** (January 1–14, 1962), 56.

104. The concept of Afro–Asian "positive neutralism" or "nonalignment" is dealt with in Crabb, *op. cit.*, *passim*.

105. African conceptions of nonalignment are identified and evaluated in Thomas P. Melady, "Nonalignment in Africa," *Annals of the American Academy of Political and Social Science* **362** (November, 1965), 52–62; Said, *op. cit.*, pp. 128–161; Vernon McKay, *African Diplomacy: Studies in the Determinants of Foreign Policy* (New York: Praeger, 1966), pp. 12–23, 69–91, 119–176; Ali Mazrui, *Towards a Pax Africana* (Chicago: University of Chicago Press, 1967), pp. 147–212.

106. Africa's underlying ties with the West are identified and evaluated in Arnold Rivkin, *Africa and the West: Elements of a Free World Policy* (New York: Praeger, 1962), pp. 21–60; Vernon McKay, *Africa in World Politics* (New York: Harper & Row, 1963), pp. 134–169, 245–397; and Goldschmidt, *op. cit.*, pp. 3–39.

107. Two informative studies of the concept, including the related idea of "African democracy," are William H. Friedland and Carl G. Rosberg, Jr., eds., *African Socialism* (Stanford, Calif.: Stanford University Press, 1964); and Léopold Sédar Senghor, *On African Socialism* (New York: Praeger, 1964).

108. See, for example, official references to countries like Ghana, Liberia, Tunisia, Morocco, and several other African states, in Agency for International Development, *Proposed Foreign Aid Program for Fiscal Year 1968*, *op. cit.*, pp. 213–227.

109. For reactions to President Kwame Nkrumah's ouster by a military *coup d'état*, see *The United States in World Affairs: 1966*, *op. cit.*, pp. 236–237.

110. During the second half of the 1960s, numerous complaints were expressed throughout East Africa about Communist intrigue in countries like Kenya and Tanzania. See, for example, *The United States in World Affairs: 1965*, *op. cit.*, pp. 198–201; and *The New York Times* (March 12 and 17, May 20, 1966; February 26, 1967).

111. For discussions of the Marxist ideological conception of African and other Afro–Asian nationalist movements and goals, see Leonard Schapiro, ed., *The U.S.S.R. and the Future* (New York: Praeger, 1963), pp. 69–86; Robert Tucker, *The Marxian Revolutionary Idea* (New York: Norton, 1969), pp. 92–130; and Lazar Pistrak, "Soviet Views on Africa," *Problems of Communism* **11** (March–April, 1962), 24–31.

Twelve
THE WESTERN HEMISPHERE:
Vicissitudes of the Good Neighbor Policy

LATIN AMERICA IN WASHINGTON'S GLOBAL POLICIES

President John F. Kennedy once described Latin America as "the most critical area in the world." President Lyndon B. Johnson said that, next to the maintenance of world peace, "no work is more important for our generation of Americans than our work in this hemisphere." And a recent commentator has referred to Latin America as "a volcano on the verge of violent eruption." After witnessing a series of political crises in the Caribbean, this observer described it as "the Middle East" of the Western Hemisphere.[1]

From the end of World War II down to the early 1960s, Latin America occupied a subordinate place in the foreign relations of the United States. Preoccupied with the cold war—and compelled to give primary attention to Western Europe, Asia, and other arenas of Soviet–American rivalry —policy-makers in Washington appeared to be indifferent to hemispheric problems and developments. Latin America, after all, had escaped the devastation of the Second World War; and it was geographically isolated from the main centers of cold war conflict in the recent period. Its governments faced no overt threat of external aggression; nor (until Fidél Castro gained control of Cuba in 1959) did there appear to be any significant threat of internal subversion in most Latin American societies. Accordingly, before the 1960s the preponderance of American economic, technical, and military assistance went to Europe, Asia, and other regions where the danger of Communist expansionism was greater and where the strategic interests of the non-Communist world were more directly threatened.

Justifiable as it might have seemed to policymakers in Washington, this "neglect" of Latin America gradually aroused deep resentments against the United States south of the border. Although they had been independent almost as long as the United States itself, the Latin American countries were beginning to be influenced by many of the same forces that were shaping contemporary nationalist movements in the Afro-Asian world. If colonialism was no longer a dominant force on the Latin American scene, societies in this region were being buffeted by the winds of change; the "revolution of rising expectations" affected political movements from Argentina to Mexico. Hierarchical political and social structures, feudal conditions in the rural areas, poverty in the countryside and in the urban slums, undemocratic political systems designed to enrich the *caudillo* and his coterie, unfair price discrimination against Latin American exports, "exploitation" by foreign (mainly American) corporations, a rate of population growth that was often the highest in the world—these were among the main targets against which revolutionary forces throughout Latin America were directed. In nearly every Latin American nation, modernization had become the watchword. Societies that had long lived in economic backwardness were determined to advance rapidly into the twentieth century. For many groups throughout Latin America, violent revolution was preferable to a perpetuation of the status quo, which they regarded as debilitating and exploitive.

By the 1960s, it had become apparent that a new era had opened in relations between the United States and its neighbors in the Western Hemisphere. Latin Americans widely viewed the "North American colossus" as both a major cause of their economic backwardness and perhaps the key to their future advancement. Washington's neglect of hemispheric problems was in large part responsible for keeping Latin America backward and depressed; only if officials and masses in the United States became aware of the "time bomb" that was ticking in the other American republics, and responded generously to Latin American needs, could a major crisis within the hemisphere be averted. Even after the Kennedy administration inaugurated the Alliance for Progress in 1961 to promote Latin American development, tensions between the United States and its hemispheric neighbors continued to mount. As we shall see at a later stage, the Alliance for Progress fell short of Latin American demands; and within a fairly brief time, it became apparent that few of its goals would be achieved. Thus, in mid-1969, Foreign Minister Gabriel Valdés of Chile, speaking in behalf of 21 Latin American nations, informed President Richard M. Nixon of the existence of a "deep crisis" in hemispheric relations. He referred to "growing and harmful resentment" toward the United States throughout the hemisphere. On behalf of this group of states, Foreign Minister Valdés demanded sweeping changes in the economic relations between the United States and its neighbors, such as more favorable terms of trade, increased public and private assistance, and the repeal of certain laws discriminating against Latin American products. Even officials in Washington, for example, admitted that in recent years private corporations in the United States were receiving more profits *from* Latin America than they were investing *in* the region; in this sense, private investment from the United States was actually *impeding* the process of capital formation in the other American republics.[2]

Late in 1969, the Nixon administration released a report on conditions throughout Latin America written by a special study committee headed by Governor Nelson Rockefeller. The Rockefeller Report painted a grim picture of life in most of the 26 American republics studied. Almost without exception, over-all conditions were worsening; political extremism and instability appeared to be increasing; and anti-United States sentiment was becoming more vocal than ever. By the end of the 1960s, Latin America contained some 250 million people; with some of the highest rates of population growth found anywhere in the world, it was expected to have close to 650 million by the end of the century! Meanwhile, little progress was being made in most Latin American countries to raise per capita incomes, provide schools and housing for the masses, expand health facilities, or significantly narrow the gap between "advantaged" and "disadvantaged" groups within society. The demand for government services in nearly all countries south of the United States was growing more rapidly than the ability of governments to provide them. Increasingly, disaffected political groups were relying upon violence to achieve their goals; terrorism in the urban centers had become a common phenomenon; while Castroism and other Marxist political movements had thus far made only limited gains, the political and economic environments in many Latin American states were attractive for Marxist or other totalitarian solutions. Resentment against the United States was also rising. "The United States," the Rockefeller Report concluded, "has allowed the special relationship it has historically maintained with the other nations of the Western Hemisphere to deteriorate badly." Without a new approach to Latin America, Governor Rockefeller informed Congress, the United States could anticipate "utter chaos" within the Western Hemisphere.[3]

The latest crisis in inter-American relations was but the most recent chapter in the history of diplomatic relationships among the nations of the Western Hemisphere—a saga frequently characterized by conflicting national interests, misunderstandings, and ill will. Current resentment against the United States in Latin America stemmed fully as much from recollections of the era of "dollar diplomacy" and the "big stick" as they did from more contemporary relationships. For its part, the United States had sought for many years—with no very notable success—to find a formula or principle that would assure hemispheric solidarity. Some understanding of at least the highlights of relations between the United States and Latin America before World War II is essential if more contemporary developments are to be intelligently appraised.

HEMISPHERIC SECURITY AND SOLIDARITY

The Monroe Doctrine

For over a century the Monroe Doctrine defined the diplomatic behavior of the United States toward the Western Hemisphere. Two developments in the third decade of the nineteenth century induced President Monroe to enunciate what came to be the most famous principle of our foreign policy. There were, first of all, Russian colonial activities in the west. Especially significant was the czarist imperial ukase of 1821. It virtually declared the Pacific waters around these Russian colonial outposts a closed sea, a pronouncement that seemed to the United States to presage renewed Russian colonizing efforts in North America. A second danger arose from the threatened intervention of the Holy Alliance in the affairs of the former Spanish colonies in Latin America. The United States feared that the Holy Alliance would invoke the principle of "legitimacy" in an attempt to reimpose Spanish hegemony over newly independent American possessions; or failing this, that another European country might supplant Spain as a colonial power in the Western Hemisphere.

The key portion of Monroe's message of December 2, 1823, was that:

The political system of the allied powers is essentially different . . . from that of America. . . . We owe it, therefore, to candor, and to the amicable relations existing between the United States and those powers, to declare that we should consider any attempt on their part to extend their system to any portion of this hemisphere as dangerous to our peace and safety. With the existing colonies or dependencies of any European power we have not interfered and shall not interfere. But with the governments who have declared their independence and maintained it . . . we could not view any interposition for the purpose of oppressing them, or controlling in any other manner their destiny, by any European power, in any other light than as the manifestation of an unfriendly disposition toward the United States.[4]

Several points about Monroe's pronouncement require emphasis.* The first is that this was a *unilateral* declaration by the United States. The noncolonization principle, to be sure, was also supported by the British Foreign Office and, what was much more crucial for the continued independence of the Latin American states, enforced on several significant occasions by the Royal Navy. Yet other powerful nations were not inclined to regard the doctrine as a fixed canon of international law, much less as a precept to which they had freely given consent. Second, as originally expressed, the noncolonization principle of the Monroe Doctrine prohibited *future* colonization by European countries. It did nothing to interfere with *existing* colonies; nor did it proscribe European diplomatic or economic influence throughout the New World. Later amplifications and corollaries of the Monroe Doctrine, which we shall treat below, broadened the scope of the noncolonization principle and introduced new prohibitions against European diplomatic activity in the Americas. But no such sweeping prohibitions were included in the original message.

Third, in the years following Monroe's proclamation the United States was unprepared on a number of occasions to back up the Monroe Doctrine with military and diplomatic force. This became evident almost immediately after 1823, when Latin American diplomats asked Washington for treaties of alliance that would commit the United States to support their continued freedom from Spanish colonial rule. These requests met with an unenthusiastic reception on the part of the State Department. Moreover, when the nations of Latin America sought to cement closer hemispheric relations at the Panama Congress of 1826, the United States held aloof from the meet-

ing. The viewpoint of the new President John Quincy Adams—"There is no community of interest or of principle between North and South America"—was in strange contrast with the community of interest which had seemingly been postulated by Monroe's message of 1823.[5]

From the time of its inception, and even after its scope had been broadened in the light of experience, the Monroe Doctrine remained essentially a unilateral response by the United States to conditions believed to threaten its security. In substance, wrote Robert Lansing in 1914, it reflected the view that "the United States considers an extension of political control by a European power over any territory in this hemisphere, not already occupied by it, to be a menace to the national safety of the United States." Compliance with the doctrine in the last analysis rested upon the "superior power of the United States to compel submission to its will. . . ."[6] That the Monroe Doctrine has been proclaimed unilaterally by the United States meant, in the words of Secretary of State Charles Evans Hughes in 1923, that

the government of the United States reserves to itself its definition, interpretation, and application. . . . Great powers have signified their acquiescence in it. But the United States has not been disposed to enter into engagements which would have the effect of submitting to any other power or to any concert of powers the determination either of the occasions upon which the principles of the Monroe Doctrine shall be invoked or of the measures that shall be taken in giving it effect.[7]

Schooled as they are in the idea that Monroe's classic foreign policy principle was ideally suited to their country's historic desires and needs, North Americans find it difficult to understand that the doctrine could arouse apprehension in their neighbors south of the border. Over the course of time, however, Latin American nations often viewed "Yankee imperialism" as a more imminent threat than reimposition of European colonial domination. Occasionally, Latin American countries were inclined to regard the doctrine as nothing more than a thinly veiled scheme whereby the United States invoked hemispheric security as a pretext to exercise a de facto protectorate over weaker American states and, under the guise of protecting them from European intervention, practiced intervention itself in the affairs of nations to the south. In recent years, therefore, one recurring task of United States foreign policy-makers has been to try to convince the countries of Latin America that the Monroe Doctrine has not been directed against them but against powerful nations in Europe. Later portions of the chapter will illustrate how the United States has sought to translate the unilateral guarantees contained in the Monroe Doctrine into guarantees supported and enforced by all the

*Here our concern is with the Western Hemispheric aspects of the Monroe Doctrine. The European aspects, by which the United States pledged itself not to interfere in wars on the continent of Europe, are discussed in Chapter 10.

The historic meaning and evolution of the Monroe Doctrine are ably treated in the studies by Dexter Perkins: *The Monroe Doctrine, 1823–26* (Cambridge, Mass.: Harvard University Press, 1927); *The Monroe Doctrine, 1826–67* (Baltimore: Johns Hopkins, 1937). James W. Gantenbein, *The Evolution of Our Latin-American Policy* (New York; Columbia University Press, 1950), pp. 301–425, provides documentary materials on the Monroe Doctrine.

countries belonging to the Inter-American System.

Corollaries of the Monroe Doctrine

Today, when the student of American foreign policy studies the Monroe Doctrine, in reality he is studying an aggregate of diplomatic pronouncements and actions based upon President Monroe's message to Congress in 1823. Collectively, these have vastly expanded and modified the original meaning of the Monroe Doctrine in order to cover specific diplomatic situations that have arisen in the Western Hemisphere. Let us look briefly at some of the more important highlights in the evolution of this cardinal principle of American foreign policy.

The first important amplification of the Monroe Doctrine was the *Polk Corollary* in 1845–1848. President Polk declared that the noncolonization principle of the Monroe Doctrine "will apply with greatly increased force, should any European power attempt to establish *any new colony* in North America. . . ."[8] A half-century later, in the midst of the Venezuelan boundary dispute with Great Britain, Secretary of State Richard Olney informed the British that the noncolonization principle of the Monroe Doctrine has been "universally conceded" and that it had been the "controlling factor" in the "emancipation of South America" from Spanish rule. Olney, more gifted in the role of prosecuting attorney than historian or diplomat, went on to inform the British Foreign Office categorically that:

Today the United States is practically sovereign on this continent, and its fiat is law upon the subjects to which it confines its interposition. Why? . . . It is because . . . its infinite resources combined with its isolated position render it master of the situation and practically invulnerable as against any or all other powers.[9]

The Olney letter translated the Monroe Doctrine into a pronouncement that in effect designated the Western Hemisphere as a Yankee sphere of influence, a claim which the nations of Europe and of Latin America were reluctant to accept.

Coincident with the age of "dollar diplomacy" toward Latin American and Asian affairs in the early 1900s was the *Roosevelt Corollary* to the Monroe Doctrine. Certain Latin American nations, chiefly in the Caribbean region, were notoriously lax in the management of their governmental and fiscal affairs. Outside intervention in their affairs for the purpose of collecting legitimate debts was consequently a perennial risk. President Theodore Roosevelt concluded that the United States could not prohibit foreign intervention to enforce payment of debts unless it were willing to assume responsibilities itself for preventing gross fiscal mismanagement by its southern neighbors. In 1901, Roosevelt stated that the Monroe Doctrine did not protect any Latin American country "against punishment if it misconducts itself. . . ." A year later he warned that it behooved each country in Latin America to "maintain order within its borders and to discharge its just obligations to foreigners." This line of reasoning ultimately led him to the conclusion in 1904 that any nation that "knows how to act with reasonable efficiency and decency" need not fear intervention. But:

Chronic wrongdoing, or an impotence which results in a general loosening of the ties of civilized society, may in America, as elsewhere, ultimately require intervention by some civilized nation, and in the Western Hemisphere the adherence of the United States to the Monroe Doctrine may force the United States, however reluctantly . . . to the exercise of an international police power.[10]

This then was the first Roosevelt's characteristically forthright response to the threat of intervention in Latin America affairs by European countries. Either the southern neighbors of the United States would keep their own affairs in order, thereby minimizing the risk of such intervention, or else the United States would be compelled under the Monroe Doctrine to undertake necessary housecleaning duties in such countries. This was no idle boast. On repeated occasions after 1904, the United States invoked the Roosevelt Corollary to justify intervention in Latin American affairs. This fact inevitably conveyed the impression to the other American republics that the Monroe Doctrine might protect them from the diplomatic ambitions of countries outside the Western Hemisphere, but that it could also be invoked to rationalize control over them by the United States, and to their minds this was often a distinction without a difference. Not until the administration of the second Roosevelt were all the military contingents of the United States finally withdrawn from Latin America.

The scope of the noncolonization principle contained in the Monroe Doctrine was also broadened by the *Lodge Corollary*, expressed in a Senate resolution of August 2, 1912. Prompted by threatened Japanese acquisition of ports in Lower California, this corollary held that the United States could not permit occupation of harbors within the Western Hemisphere "for naval or military purposes" by a foreign power, if such occupation would "threaten the communications or safety of the United States. . . ."[11]

The Good Neighbor Policy

The impact of Wilsonian idealism, along with the evident deterioration in relations between the United States and its hemispheric neighbors as a result of the Roosevelt Corollary from 1904 onward, demanded corrective measures on the part of the State Department. Recurrent outcries from the south against "Yankee imperialism" could no longer be ignored in Washington. A significant change in the foreign policy of the United States was therefore presaged by the "Clark Memorandum" of 1928, the gist of which was that the Roosevelt Corollary had been a perversion of the original intention of the Monroe Doctrine. Then with the election of Franklin D. Roosevelt came the "Good Neighbor" policy, enunciated in FDR's First Inaugural Address and reiterated in a series of messages thereafter by Roosevelt and Secretary of State Cordell Hull. The first step in establishing good neighborly relations was to reassure the Latin American countries that the Monroe Doctrine was not a pretext to conceal Yankee imperialistic ambitions toward them. Secretary Hull stated in 1933 that the people of the United States believed that the so-called right of conquest "must be banished from this hemisphere and, most of all, they shun and reject that so-called right for themselves." In the same year, FDR repeated Wilson's earlier pledge that the United States would never again seek additional territory by conquest. Paving the way for an effective inter-American system of defense and solidarity, Roosevelt observed that political turbulence and threats to hemispheric security were no longer of special concern to the United States alone, but that they were "the joint concern of a whole continent in which we are all neighbors."[12] As it related to the Monroe Doctrine, the new Good Neighbor policy came down to this: The traditional interest of the United States in Western hemispheric security must be translated into a policy shared by all the American countries. All must support it and all must act in concert to deal with conditions threatening the peace and stability of the hemisphere. This was in substance the purpose of the Inter-American System.

The Pan-American Movement

No sooner had the countries of Latin America won their independence in the early 1800s than their leaders began to think in terms of a Pan-American movement to preserve their freedom, not alone from Europe but from their northern neighbor, the United States, as well. The great South American leader Simon Bolivar early took the lead in laying the basis for the Pan-American movement. The United States, largely for reasons of domestic politics and the desire to preserve an attitude of nonentanglement with other countries, did not participate in the first Panama Congress of 1826. As was often characteristic of such conferences in the years that followed, the delegates were quick to pass resolutions proclaiming their mutual attachment to idealistic goals, such as political nonintervention and economic coopera-

tion. But in this and later instances, such resolutions frequently received little or no tangible support afterwards from the governments concerned. The first attempt to establish a Pan-American system therefore was a failure. For a half-century thereafter, the dream of Pan-Americanism languished, despite the fact that considerable support for it existed in Latin America and within the United States.

Fifty years later the movement received new impetus under Secretary of State James G. Blaine, who proposed a meeting of all the American republics in Washington in 1881 for the purpose of preventing war in the Western Hemisphere and of promoting closer economic collaboration among the nations of the region. A change in political administrations within the United States delayed these plans for eight years. But finally, in 1889, the conference was held. This conference was also devoid of tangible results, except for one: establishment of the Bureau of American Republics, later renamed the Pan-American Union, which in time evolved into one of the principal organs of the Inter-American system.[13]

The pace by which the Pan-American movement grew from little more than expressions of affinity among the American republics, accompanied by occasional conferences at which actual gains were usually negligible, was leisurely between the late 1800s and the New Deal. Interventions carried out by the United States under the Roosevelt Corollary understandably made the other American republics highly suspicious of Uncle Sam's intentions. Uppermost in the minds of Latin American statesmen was the ubiquitous specter of Yankee domination; they looked askance at frequent endorsements of the ideal of Pan-Americanism by the United States because they feared domination of Latin American affairs by an international body controlled from Washington. Repudiation of the Roosevelt Corollary and the inauguration of the Good Neighbor policy were therefore necessary before significant progress could be expected toward establishing more intimate relations among countries in the Western Hemisphere.

Once the diplomatic atmosphere had cleared after 1932, Pan-American cooperation gradually became a reality. The threat of Axis aggression provided another stimulus, by binding the nations of the Western Hemisphere together against a common enemy and by emphasizing their economic interdependence. Beginning with the conference at Montevideo in 1933, the Inter-American system began to take shape. The United States accepted a resolution directed principally at itself, pledging all American republics to a policy of nonintervention in the affairs of their neighbors. In return, the United States received widespread support from the Latin American governments for the New Deal principle of reciprocal trade, whereby national tariffs were lowered on the basis of mutual concessions. Three years later, at the Inter-American Conference in Buenos Aires, the American republics accepted the principle of joint consultation among all the American countries in the event of a threat to the security of the hemisphere. Additional conferences were held in 1938, 1939, 1940, and 1942. An important milestone was the conference at Mexico City in 1945, at which the Act of Chapultepec was adopted, formally declaring the determination of the American republics to pursue a common policy in meeting any threat to their security from abroad.[14]

Building on these foundations, the Rio Conference of 1947 resulted in the Treaty of Reciprocal Assistance, signed on September 2. This regional defense agreement, like NATO and similar agreements, was drawn up under Article 51 of the United Nations Charter, providing for the right of individual and regional self-defense. Pending action by the Security Council of the UN, threats to the peace within the Americas were to be dealt with by the Inter-American system.[15] Then at the Ninth Inter-American Conference at Bogotá in the spring of 1948, the formal machinery necessary to make these goals a reality—the Organization of American States (OAS)—was established. Finally, the Pan-American movement had come to fruition. After nearly a century and a quarter, the American republics had moved from highly generalized and usually ineffectual declarations of mutual affinity to the creation of a regional defense system, containing permanent machinery for dealing with threats to the security and stability of the Western Hemisphere that might arise from such diverse sources as the activities of international Communism, conflicts among individual American states, or widespread hemispheric economic dislocations.

OAS—Procedures and Principles

The Inter-American system rests upon three basic "charter documents" defining its scope and procedures. First, there is the Rio Treaty of mutual assistance, safeguarding the defense of the Americas from an attack originating outside or inside the hemisphere; second, there is a document specifying the scope, organs, and duties of OAS; and third, there is a document setting forth procedures to be followed for bringing about the pacific settlement of disputes among members of the system. Similarly, the Inter-American system has three principal organs: international conferences, the Pan-American Union, and specialized agencies. The high-level policy-making body is the international conference. General conferences are supposed to be held at five-year intervals. Within shorter periods, lower-level conferences dealing with limited, sometimes highly

technical, subjects are held. In the event of a threat to the security of the Americas, Meetings of Consultation are summoned immediately to deal with the threat. The foreign ministers of the member states attend these meetings, whose purpose, in the words of a State Department document, is "to bring together on short notice the top spokesmen on foreign affairs in the executive branches of the 21 governments for rapid discussion and resolution of emergency issues."

The Pan-American Union is the permanent organ of the Inter-American system. PAU maintains its headquarters in Washington. Its governing board consists of representatives chosen by each member state. Frequently, the state's highest diplomatic representative in the United States is selected. To assure that the PAU does not become the diplomatic organ of one country alone, and is not too strongly influenced by one country, such as the United States, the chairman of PAU's governing board is not eligible for re-election. The Director General and his assistant, the highest administrative officials, serve for ten years, and they, too, are ineligible for re-election, nor can their successors be of the same nationality as the incumbents.

PAU was established in 1910 primarily as an information-gathering and information-disseminating body, and its functions were confined largely to this task until after World War II. Much of its activity today is still devoted to the collection and spread of information of common interest to the American states in the economic, social, technical, scientific, cultural, and legal fields. In addition, it has become the secretariat of OAS. It arranges for inter-American conferences, provides the required staff, and does the paper work that invariably accompanies such meetings. Moreover, many of the scientific and technical bodies associated with OAS operate under the supervision of the Pan-American Union. After the Rio Treaty of 1947, for the first time PAU acquired important *political* duties. Now it is empowered to act in response to a threat to the Inter-American system until a Meeting of Consultation can be convened.[16]

The guarantees of hemispheric security contained in the Monroe Doctrine and its corollaries have been assumed by the Inter-American system. Certain precepts have emerged to guide OAS in dealing with threats to the peace. As far back as the end of the nineteenth century, the states in the Western Hemisphere agreed to abstain from using force unilaterally in settling disputes among themselves. This principle was translated into a series of treaties during the 1920s and 1930s, providing that each state would rely upon the "good offices" of other countries, mediation, conciliation, and the like, in settling conflicts within the Inter-American system. Then, during World War II the principle of "all for one, one for all" was incorporated into the Inter-American system. Any attack or threat against any part of the hemisphere would be regarded as an attack against all the American republics. Under the Rio Treaty of 1947, therefore, OAS is empowered to deal with any threat to the hemisphere, irrespective of whether the threat arises from within or outside the American system. Decisions taken by the Meetings of Consultation are binding on all members, regardless of whether they vote for them or not, provided the decision is taken by a two-thirds vote and with the further qualification that no state can be required to use armed forces without its consent.

The five most salient features of the Inter-American system as it has evolved throughout a long, and sometimes discouragingly slow, historical process are: Each member of the system is obligated to cooperate in resisting an actual or threatened attack against any American country; a two-thirds vote of a Meeting of Consultation is binding on all members; no distinction is made between threats to the peace arising from outside or inside the hemisphere; the Pan-American Union now exercises political responsibilities, along with those it has in the cultural, social, economic, and related fields; and finally, the Inter-American system is firmly integrated with the United Nations.

OAS—Problems and Prospects

On the basis of postwar experience, what kind of verdict can be rendered on the Organization of American States? In general terms, it might be said that OAS has both disappointed its supporters and surprised its critics. It has failed to realize its full potentialities, but it also has some significant accomplishments to its credit.

In the sphere of promoting hemispheric peace and security, one commentator has observed, OAS "deserves a fairly high rating. By and large, its greatest achievement during the postwar period has been in the realm of maintaining peace and security among its members." The performance of the OAS "has fully justified the idea of establishing a regional organization for the purpose of settling regional problems in a manner satisfactory to its members."[18] Within a few months after its creation in 1947, OAS was called upon to deal with a dispute between Costa Rica and Nicaragua. The first of the organization's "investigating committees" was quickly dispatched to Central America; in due course, the OAS brought about a cessation of hostilities (although the long-smouldering dispute between the two countries erupted again five years later).

In the years which followed, OAS dealt with other conflicts and quarrels within the hemisphere, such as the charge of aggression against the Dominican Republic, brought by Haiti in

1949–1950; a second invasion of Costa Rica by Nicaragua in 1955; a boundary conflict between Honduras and Nicaragua in 1957; and hostilities between the Dominican Republic and Venezuela in 1960.[19]

In 1964, OAS was confronted with a different kind of conflict—one which had far-reaching implications for Western hemispheric solidarity and regional cooperation. This was a quarrel between the United States and Panama, which threatened to erupt into armed conflict; as the dispute became more intense, Panama ultimately severed diplomatic relations with the United States. The underlying source of disagreement was the Panama Canal Treaty of 1903. Panamanians had become increasingly convinced that this agreement was discriminatory and inimical to their sovereignty—a conclusion shared by many groups throughout Latin America. While officials in Washington stated their readiness to "discuss" possible revisions of the treaty, they were not willing to commit themeselves to renegotiating it or to accepting a host of Panamanian "demands" concerning it. As tension mounted—and as Panama threatened to charge the United States with "aggression'" before the United Nations— OAS was asked to appoint a five-nation Peace Committee to mediate the controversy. Rather than have the dispute taken to the UN, OAS in time voted 16 to 1 to consider Panama's charges against the United States. At length a 17-nation OAS committee was established to bring about agreement between the two countries. Owing to these mediatory activities, the crisis subsided, although events made it clear in time that many of the basic sources of contention between the two countries had been left unresolved.* This case was important, however, for one paramount reason: For the first time, OAS was utilized to deal with a complaint brought *against* the United States. Hitherto, there had been a tendency in Washington to regard the OAS primarily as a mechanism for achieving its own hemispheric goals, such as imposing sanctions against Castro's Cuba. The case of Panama illustrated a long-standing idea held by the nations of Latin America about Western hemispheric solidarity: A central purpose of

---

*In the months that followed, negotiators from Panama and the United States reached agreement on three accords, removing most of the recent causes of tension between the two countries. These dealt with joint administration of the existing Panama Canal, with the possible construction of a new canal in Panama, and with the defense of the Panama Canal Zone. These agreements were to replace the old 1903 treaty which Panamanians contended had been "imposed" upon it by Washington, shortly after the country became independent from Colombia. The seizure of power late in 1968 by a group of young military officers in Panama, however, introduced new strains into United States–Panamanian relations and suspended deliberations within each country on the new agreements covering the Panama Canal. See *The New York Times* (July 2 and September 8, 1967; December 8, 1968).

an organization like OAS was to *protect them* against their more powerful North American neighbor.[20]

Other examples of reasonably successful efforts by OAS to deal with crises within the hemisphere may be mentioned briefly. After considerable initial reluctance, most members agreed that Cuba's conversion to Communism, and Castro's sponsorship of subversive activities in other American republics, were incompatible with continued membership in the Inter-American system. In the months which followed the Cuban missile crisis of 1962, nearly all members of OAS were ready to join the United States in imposing sanctions against Castro's regime. Then in 1965, OAS played a significant role in the Dominican crisis, precipitated when armed forces from the United States intervened on that troubled island. Encountering widespread criticism inside and outside the hemisphere for its intervention in the Dominican Republic, the Johnson administration willingly accepted the idea that OAS ought to bring the crisis to an end. Gradually, a newly created OAS Inter-American Peace Force assumed responsibility for preserving order in the country until new national elections could be held; in time, Washington even placed its own troops under OAS authority. For nearly a year, the Inter-American Peace Force remained in the Dominican Republic, until the country chose a new government.[21]

Another challenge to OAS was presented in the summer of 1969. Alleging that Honduras was committing "genocide" against Salvadorians resident in the country, El Salvador invaded Honduras, after which the former charged the latter with aggression. Within hours, the Organization of American States responded to this outbreak of violence by sending a peace commission to Central America. As the conflict continued, on July 23 the Council of OAS renewed its demand for a cease-fire between the belligerents and threatened to impose sanctions unless armed conflict came to an end. Confronted with the possibility of an economic boycott by the other American republics, El Salvador evacuated its troops from Honduran territory. Enmity and suspicion between the two countries of course remained; it would not be unprecedented for new violence to erupt between the two countries in the future. Yet OAS had performed efficiently and creditably in this case to put a stop to armed conflict. A noteworthy aspect of this episode was the degree to which the United States was *not* required to assert leadership in behalf of OAS peace-making activities. In contrast to other instances in which OAS has sought to preserve peace within the hemisphere, in this case Washington largely left the initiative to the other members and to OAS Secretary-General Galo Plaza to draft, and to enforce, a cease-fire agreement in Central America.[22]

Despite its achievements, the Organization of American States possesses certain defects as a regional body. One authority, for example, refers to the "ever-increasing state of crisis" surrounding its existence. In common with the United Nations, OAS has experienced a "crisis of confidence" regarding its effectiveness and its future.[23] The organization functions within an over-all environment of inter-American relations; inevitably, its activities and future are momentously affected by trends within that environment. Two such forces seem especially important: relationships between the United States and the other American republics in political and diplomatic affairs; and the increasingly acute economic and social problems prevailing in most societies in the Caribbean, Central America, and South America. With regard to the first of these forces, for many decades Latin American nations have been fearful that OAS would in time become merely an instrument by which the United States imposed its will upon weaker neighbors. No evidence existed that, by the 1970s, this apprehnesion had significantly diminished. Indeed, for many groups throughout Latin America, such anxieties had been *confirmed* by Washington's tendency to gain OAS support for its anti-Communist policies and by its belated search for OAS "cooperation" in its unilateral intervention in the Dominican Republic in 1965. Latin America's increasing preoccupation with social and economic progress has been reflected in the recurrent desire of the countries involved to give OAS a larger role in promoting hemispheric economic development, under such programs as the Alliance for Progress. However officials in the United States have scarcely concealed their reluctance to accept a greatly enhanced role for OAS in regional development. Aside from Congress' refusal to surrender its own authority over appropriations (and the question of whether this is even constitutionally permissible), policy-makers in the United States have been deterred by the tendency of meetings of the OAS to become confrontations in which the other American republics indict the "North American colossus" for neglecting their needs. Nor have officials in Washington disguised their dislike of "sloganizing," sterile debate, and the tendency for the enthusiastic adoption of idealistic principles by the members of OAS to outstrip *performance* in carrying out those principles.

Disagreement among the members of OAS over political questions has also impeded the organization's effectiveness. From the late 1940s onward—particularly after a Communist regime gained control of Cuba—the United States has regarded the containment of Communist expansionism and influence in the hemisphere as a matter of urgent priority for OAS. Occasionally, as during the Cuban missile crisis of 1962, the United States found widespread agreement with this objective among the other American republics. But such agreement has tended to be exceptional. As a rule, Washington's efforts to gain OAS support for sanctions against Cuba have collided with Latin America's insistence upon adherence to the "nonintervention" principle. In Latin American eyes, John C. Drier has written, the anti-Communist goals of the United States have conflicted with one of the basic purposes of OAS: "the protection of the small Latin American countries against the intervention of the United States."[24] The lament of Secretary of State John Foster Dulles during the late 1950s—that most Latin American states preferred to "leave themselves exposed to international communism rather than run the risk that the doctrine of collective security might be turned . . . into a doctrine of collective intervention"—had lost none of its validity by the 1970s.[25]

Still another issue dividing the members of OAS —the promotion of democracy and respect for human rights throughout the Western Hemisphere—is a problem we shall discuss more fully at a later stage. Here, it must suffice to observe merely that little unanimity exists within the Inter-American system on a host of questions and dilemmas relating to these broad issues. The United States, for example, has sought to encourage "political stability" throughout the hemisphere. By contrast, many groups in Latin America—including non-Communist (sometimes, anti-Communist) groups—advocate revolutionary political change. A related problem, which had lost none of its urgency or complexity by the 1970s, asks the perennial questions: "How should the United States and the other American republics respond to a military-led *coup d'état* against civilian authority in one of the Latin American societies?" and "What action should the OAS take against a government which consistently violated the human rights of its own citizens?" Postwar experience gave no indication that the members of the Inter-American system were close to agreement upon the principles that ought to be followed in such cases.

Widely criticized for its unilateral intervention in the Dominican Republic in 1965, the Johnson administration endeavored to strengthen OAS by the creation of a hemispheric "police force" which would presumably obviate the necessity for such intervention in the future. This idea was supported by several Latin American nations, chiefly Brazil and Argentina. Yet a number of other American republics—notably Mexico, Panama, Colombia, and Ecuador—vigorously opposed it. The smaller Latin American nations were no more enthusiastic about intervention in their affairs carried out by their larger neighbors than they were about that perpetrated by the "North American colossus." After several months of discussion within OAS, early in 1967 the organization voted to *reject* a proposal aimed at strengthening its peace-keeping powers.[26] In Washington's view, this development highlighted the dilemma which had faced the OAS for many years. The nations of Latin America had made known their opposition to "Yankee interventionism" on innumerable occasions; yet they were unwilling to provide an effective alternative—a revitalized OAS—which could make such unilateral behavior by the United States unnecessary.

THE CHALLENGE TO DEMOCRACY IN THE HEMISPHERE

Few problems have tested the resourcefulness and ingenuity of policy-makers in the United States more than the issue with which we are concerned here—the challenge of formulating a satisfactory response to nondemocratic political movements throughout Latin America. It would also be difficult to think of an issue which has been more productive of dissension and fundamental disagreement within the Inter-American system than this problem. At the risk of oversimplifying what is in reality an extremely complex political pattern in many Latin American societies, for the purpose of analysis we may think of this challenge as embracing two reasonably distinct political tendencies: Communist expansionism and influence in the Western Hemisphere; and the active, sometimes decisive, role of military elites in Latin American political life.

Latin America as a Cold War Arena

The importance of Latin America as an arena of cold war hostilities may be gauged by recalling briefly the Nazi menace to the Western Hemisphere during World War II. Nazi agents were active in a number of Latin American states, particularly Argentina. There was perhaps never a time when the Axis powers were in danger of gaining control over Latin America—nor could the threat to the security of the United States existing in that quarter compare with the danger from Europe or Asia—but the United States was nonetheless compelled to divert over 100,000 troops for protection of that vital region. In the postwar period, according to a high Defense Department spokesman, "In enemy hands the Latin American countries could provide bases for attack which would be dangerously close to the United States"—a fact that was brought home with the utmost gravity to citizens of the United States, when aerial photographs showed Soviet guided missiles being installed by Castro's regime in Cuba. These weapons were capable of bringing the great industrial northeastern heartland of the United States within their field of fire. Similarly, a potential aggressor would find that the "bulge" of

Brazil afforded a tempting foothold for any enemy seeking to penetrate the Western Hemisphere across the South Atlantic, especially if the Middle East and northern and western portions of Africa were in hostile hands. Conversely, Brazil and its neighbors offer needed bases for air power and for radar defense units to safeguard the Americas and the South Atlantic sea lanes. Latin America also supplies the United States with a number of strategic imports. One of the most important now is thorium from Brazil, used for thermonuclear technology. The states along the northern periphery of the South American continent and in Central America are in close proximity to the Panama Canal, while those along the continent's western fringe can protect vital sea and air approaches to the hemisphere.

Latin American Communism—An Overview

Although the United States did not become aware of the "Communist danger" in the Western Hemisphere until the postwar period, Communist political organizations were established in the area soon after the Bolshevik Revolution in Russia in 1917. By the early postwar era, one or more Marxist parties existed in every Latin American country, despite the fact that in nearly all of them Communist movements were illegal. Legal strictures against the Communist party have often compelled it to assume another name (like "Popular Socialist" or "Labor" party) under which to carry on its activities. Moreover, the prevalent tendency of Marxist groups in Latin America to collaborate with other political organizations, or to reach an accord with the government in power, sometimes makes it difficult to gauge the true size and influence of Communism within a country. Note must also be taken of the fact that right-wing political forces within Latin America routinely denounce political opposition groups as "Communists"—a tactic designed in part to strengthen the government's chances of receiving military and economic aid from the United States! Despite what are perhaps unavoidable differences in estimates of Communist strength and influence throughout Latin America, most informed commentators agree that avowed Marxists comprise a relatively small, and often politically uninfluential, minority in nearly all Latin American societies. Writing in the mid-1960s, one commentator estimated the maximum number of Communists in the region at one-tenth of 1 percent (.001) of the total population. Countries like Argentina (with upwards of 80,000 Communists) and Brazil (with some 50,000) naturally had larger Communist organizations than the smaller countries like Colombia (with some 5000 Communists) and Ecuador (which had only 1000).[27] Later studies have shown limited gains by Communist groups in countries like Colombia, Ecuador, Honduras,

Mexico, and Uruguay. A State Department estimate in 1970 placed the total number of Communist party members in Latin America at approximately 300,000. On the whole, the number of avowed Marxists throughout Latin America remains small; and in many countries Communists constitute a negligible political minority.[28]

Yet two qualifications must immediately be made about such estimates of Communist strength south of the Rio Grande. The first is that the revolutionary group under Lenin which seized power in Russia was also a small minority of the population; similarly, the followers of Mao Tse-tung in China represented nothing more than an insignificant fraction of the people until the 1940s. In Marxist ideology, as expounded by Lenin and his successors, the Communist party has always been envisioned as a political minority, a small band of dedicated and well-trained revolutionary forces. For more than fifty years, the U.S.S.R. has retained this elitest conception of the Communist party. The second point that must be kept in mind is that Latin American Communism received a new impetus from the successful communization of Cuba under Fidel Castro after 1959. After that date Marxism possessed a revolutionary base from which to foment insurrection within the Western Hemisphere. Despite severe economic dislocations, the evident hostility of the United States, Washington's more or less effective application of economic sanctions against Castro's regime, and even the hostility of several Latin American governments, the Marxist government in Cuba has survived and continues to offer itself as a model for other Latin American societies. Although it is entrenched in one of the smaller and more geographically isolated countries in the hemisphere, Castroism exercises an influence outside its own borders which cannot be ignored.

As in other settings, Communist movements in Latin America combine familiar and unique features. Marxist goals are orthodox and unexceptional: the seizure of power through a successful "proletarian revolution," followed by the imposition of a Communist order upon the society. Down to the 1960s, for nearly all Marxist groups in Latin America Soviet Russia provided the correct revolutionary model. As Marxist international unity was destroyed by the Sino–Soviet dispute, upheavals in Eastern Europe, and other polycentric tendencies, however, the unity of Marxist movements in Latin America was inevitably impaired. In time, Brazil and Bolivia had three Communist parties; in Mexico and several other Latin American nations an open split developed between pro-Soviet and pro-Chinese factions; Castroism provided still another alternative, which was more appealing for some individuals and groups than either Soviet or Chinese Communism. Schismatic tendencies in nearly all Latin American Communist movements have weakened Marxism's appeal and resulted in prolonged internal disagreements.

Traditionally, Latin American Communist movements have directed their appeals to two major elements within society: industrial workers and intellectuals. With neither group have such appeals been conspicuously successful. In the recent period a third group—the peasants and rural elements in Latin American society—has become a prominent target of Communist political activities. Perhaps the most neglected of all groups in Latin American society, these workers have age-old grievances which Marxists have sought to exploit. According to Robert J. Alexander, three specific issues have often enhanced Marxism's appeal throughout Latin America: (1) Communists have sought to gain acceptance for the idea that they are "the most efficient and faithful purveyors of revolutionary change," in a region where the idea of revolution enjoys wide support; (2) Communist groups have disseminated the idea that the Soviet Union provides an applicable model for rapid industrialization and national development for Latin America; and (3) Marxists have enjoyed considerable success in depicting the United States as the embodiment of imperialism and in exploiting pervasive grievances against the "North American colossus"—a theme which has from time to time been given credibility by the behavior of the United States in the Western Hemisphere.

Many of the general observations made about Communism in Latin America were illustrated by events in Chile at the end of 1970. Chile has a population of some 10 million people; its population growth is 1.9 per cent annually (relatively low, by Latin American standards); its per capita annual income is some $600—less than one-sixth that of the United States, but some fifty percent greater than the average for Latin America as a whole. Chile, in other words, ranks ahead of most Latin America nations in its standard of living. The majority of the Chilean population is Spanish-Indian descent, with two-thirds classified as urban. In common with most other Latin American countries, Chilean trade is dominated by a single commodity—copper exports—which accounts for some seventy-five percent of its foreign sales. Although business corporations from the United States have traditionally controlled Chilean copper mining and processing, some ninety percent of Chile's copper exports are sold to Western Europe and Japan.

On October 24, 1970, at the end of a prolonged and heated political campaign, Dr. Salvador Allende was elected President of Chile. Dr. Allende was an avowed Marxist; he had repeatedly emphasized that he was an "independent Marxist," who owed no allegiance to Moscow or Peking. He was the candidate of the Socialist party of Chile, whose strategies were often more extreme than those advocated by the Chilean Communist Party (which follows Moscow's preferred strategy of relying mainly on the electoral process to gain power). In Chile, only some 1.3 percent of the electorate (or 45,000 voters) were registered Communists. It was evident, therefore, that Dr. Allende's victory had been possible only because of the support of many non-Marxist groups in Chile. Although he had gained the presidency, Dr. Allende's regime still had to reckon with a non-Marxist majority in the Congress. In contrast with most other Latin American states, the Chilean army traditionally has played little role in the political process. Yet, as his government formulated new policies for the country, the Allende regime could not count on the fact that the Chilean military would remain politically neutral, particularly if the danger arose that Chile's sovereignty were being infringed upon by other Marxist nations.

The Nixon Administration, needless to say, did not greet this turn of events in Chile with unbounded enthusiasm. For reasons we have already discussed, Allende's victory did not necessarily mean that the Chilean people had been converted to Marxism; still less did it signify that Moscow or Peking had gained a new "bridgehead" in Latin America, enabling them to sponsor subversive activities throughout the region. Yet Allende's election unquestionably did indicate the presence of widespread disaffection in Chile, and perhaps throughout Latin America as a whole, with the policies of the United States; it did reveal the existence of deep-seated resentments toward the traditional conduct of United States business corporations in the region; it did afford persuasive evidence that the Alliance for Progress (which we shall discuss at greater length presently) had not made the impact in Latin America which officials in Washington desired; and (because Chile was at the forefront of Washington's critics in the organization), it undoubtedly portended greater disunity within the Organization of American States. In short, the United States could discern little cause for rejoicing over political developments in Chile.

Yet the Nixon Administration reacted mildly—more mildly than many of its critics expected—to the Marxist victory in Chile. By this stage, it was perhaps not too much to expect policy-makers in Washington to understand that the era of overt "interventionism" in Latin America's political affairs had ended—if for no other reason than such behavior *aggravated* Latin American resentment toward the United States, thereby perhaps guaranteeing the success of political extremist movements. Besides, the Nixon Administration had very little leverage in Chile. Short of a military invasion of the country (which no official seriously suggested), there was little Washington could do to change the outcome in Chile. Chile received an insignificant amount of economic assistance from the United States; the United States had, several years earlier, begun to reduce its arms-aid to Latin American nations, the result being that these countries were now beginning to acquire modern armaments from Western Europe. At the end of 1969, President Nixon publicly declared that in dealing with non-democratic governments of both rightist and leftist coloration in Latin America the United States must adhere to a policy of nonintervention in the region's political life. Officials of Washington were also aware of a crucial difference between the case of Cuba and Chile: unlike Castro's regime, Dr. Allende's government showed no sign of trying to "export" its Marxist program to neighboring countries by sponsoring revolutionary activities in them. By the 1970s, another consideration induced policy-makers in Washington to react cautiously to events in Chile. That Marxism had scored a victory in an important Latin American nation was undeniable. Yet, based upon experience in other developing nations, it remained to be seen whether in the long run the election of Dr. Allende benefited the cause of Communism in Latin America. If this regime *failed* to bring abut significant improvement in Chile, the chances were perhaps just as great that this fact would discredit Marxism as a model for other Latin American nations.[29]

Crisis in Guatemala

The first serious encounter between the United States and Latin American Communism occurred in Guatemala in 1954. Revolutionary ferment had long marked the political scene in Guatemala, as elsewhere in Latin America, in large part because non-Communist groups had been unable to effectuate lasting socioeconomic reforms. Like its counterparts in Asia, the Middle East, and other Latin American nations, the Guatemalan Communist party was able to pose as the champion of nationalist aspirations while promising progress in solving bedrock economic problems.[30]

The year 1944 witnessed the beginning of a new revolutionary regime under Juan José Arévalo, who overthrew the government of the military dictator Jorge Ubico. The new government received substantial support from the lower middle classes and from the intellectuals, with many of the latter believing that a Marxist approach offered the best hope of progress for Guatemala. As is customary following revolutions in Latin America, a number of prominent and less prominent political exiles returned to Guatemala. Among these were influential individuals who espoused Communism; some of these had received revolutionary training in Moscow. Until the early 1950s, however, Guatemalan Communists tended to operate clandestinely and to work through popular movements to advance their goals.

As time passed, Communists infiltrated the Guatemalan labor movement and other organizations commanding wide popular support. Through such groups Communists carried on intensive propaganda campaigns closely paralleling the diplomatic line of the Kremlin. The equivocal policies of President Arévalo, who encouraged "participation of Communists as individuals" in the government and labor movement while "discouraging the formation of an open organized Stalinist party," enabled Communist groups to gain more and more control over Guatemalan affairs.[31] As the time for the national elections of 1951 drew near, the tempo of Communist agitation and propaganda greatly increased. Election of the Communist-sponsored candidate, Colonel Jacobo Arbenz, as President was soon followed by the open establishment of the Guatemalan Communist party *(Partido Communista de Guatemala,* PCG). At home Arbenz, supported by the PCG, embarked upon a long overdue program of land reform. As the largest landholder in the country, the United Fruit Company—with headquarters in Boston—became the principal target of Arbenz's reform measures. Guatemalan nationalism was also directed against the alleged power of the *Empresa Eléctrica,* owned by investors within the United States, that generated four-fifths of the country's electric power.[32]

In external affairs, the Arbenz government was making little effort to conceal its growing hostility toward the United States. Moreover, as the months passed, policy-makers in the United States were convinced they detected the hand of Guatemalan Communists in fomenting political unrest in such countries as British Guiana and British Honduras. Guatemala provided a base for Communist-inspired intrigue throughout all the neighboring Central American states. In international affairs Guatemala's position coincided with the Kremlin's with remarkable frequency.[33] On June 30, 1954, Secretary of State Dulles publicly called attention to the "evil purpose of the Kremlin to destroy the inter-American system. . . ." He noted that "For several years international communism has been probing . . . for nesting places in the Americas. It finally chose Guatemala. . . ."[34] As early as April 7, 1951, the foreign ministers of the American republics, largely at the instigation of the United States, had issued the "Declaration of Washington," calling for "prompt action . . . against the aggressive activities of international communism. . . ."[35] But as it watched the steady accretion in the influence of Guatemalan Communism, the Eisenhower administration was persuaded that stronger measures were demanded. Hence Secretary of State Dulles personally attended an OAS meeting in Venezuela on March 28, 1954, where he was successful in getting the "Caracas Declaration" approved by an overwhelming vote. This sharply worded resolution declared that

the domination or control of the political institutions of any American States by the international communist movement . . . would constitute a threat to the sovereignty and political independence of the American States, endangering the peace of America, and would call for a Meeting of Consultation to consider the adoption of appropriate action in accordance with existing treaties.[36]

The Caracas Declaration was widely hailed in the West, especially in militantly anti-Communist circles, as an outstanding diplomatic victory for the United States on the cold war front. Now the weight of the entire Inter-American system could be thrown against the "Communist beachhead" in the Western Hemisphere. Discriminating observers, however, pointed to a number of signs indicating significant differences of opinion among the American republics about the proper attitude toward Guatemalan Communism. It was clear that Latin America was much less concerned about the threat of Communism in Guatemala, and much more alarmed about State Department interference in hemispheric affairs, than the United States.*

Events moved toward a climax in the spring and summer of 1954, when Guatemalan Communists supported a strike in Honduras and when a shipload of arms from behind the Iron Curtain arrived in Guatemala. Denouncing Guatemala as already the "heaviest armed state" in Central America, the State Department moved immediately to increase the flow of armaments to other countries in that area.[37] In the ensuing diplomatic tug of war, Guatemala, supported by the Communist bloc, sought to have the United Nations consider alleged United States intervention in

Guatemala's affairs; Washington, on the other hand, was insistent that the United Nations did not have initial jurisdiction in the matter and demanded that it first be considered by the Organization of American States. Meanwhile, tension was growing in Central America. On June 18 an anti-Communist force under Colonel Castillo Armas crossed into Guatemala from Honduras. Within a short time the pro-Communist Arbenz government collapsed. "Each one of the American States has cause for profound gratitude," said Secretary of State Dulles. The "impressive solidarity" of the Inter-American system, he continued, "undoubtedly shook the Guatemalan Government." All Americans could rejoice that the citizens of that country "had the courage and the will to eliminate the traitorous tools of foreign despots."[38]

From one perspective—that of a dramatic victory of the free world against Communism—the United States had scored an impressive diplomatic coup in the Guatemalan affair. Whatever else Armas was, and we shall examine this question more fully below, he was certainly anti-Communist. Temporarily at least, the "Communist beachhead" in Guatemala had been eliminated.

But many Latin American countries, joined by some of the United States' Western allies, were less given to unqualified rejoicing than were supporters of Secretary Dulles. Skepticism, in the first place, was directed against State Department complicity in the counter-revolution that had ousted the Arbenz government. The exact nature and scope of United States involvement in the movement that overthrew the Arbenz regime may never be known, although there seems little question that the Central Intelligence Agency was highly active in the affair and that it perhaps supplied the increment of power needed by the anti-Communist forces under Colonel Castillo Armas to achieve victory.*

---

*At this meeting of the OAS, Latin American delegates voiced a theme that was recurrent in their attitudes about the Communist problem in the Americas. Although the Caracas Declaration had been approved by a vote of 17 to 1 (with Guatemala predictably voting no, and Mexico and Argentina abstaining), many Latin American spokesmen expressed strong reservations about Washington's preoccupation with the issue of Communism. Justifiably or not, then and throughout the years that followed, Latin American states believed that the interest of the United States in their problems tended to vary directly according to the intensity of the Communist threat to the hemisphere. Put differently, they often gained the impression that Latin America was "useful" to the United States only in the degree to which it played a role in "containing" Communism. Thus a Bolivian delegate to the conference demanded "something more than a new way of fighting communism . . . something appropriate to improve welfare and progress" in the Americas. A delegate from Uruguay confessed that he supported the Caracas Declaration "without enthusiasm, without optimism, without joy and without feeling that we were contributing to the adoption of a constructive measure." See William Benton, *The Voice of Latin America* (New York: Harper & Row, 1961), p. 73.

*In his memoirs, former President Eisenhower did not conceal the fact that CIA Director Allen Dulles played a key role in the White House deliberations on this issue. Upon his recommendation, Eisenhower agreed to supply the anti-Communist forces with aircraft and to replace those that had previously been lost. Eisenhower was convinced that: "The major factor in the successful outcome" of the struggle in Guatemala was "the disaffection of the Guatemalan armed forces and the population as a whole with the tyrannical regime of Arbenz." His judgment upon the new President Armas was that he proved "a farseeing and able statesman, who enjoyed the devotion of his people." Dwight D. Eisenhower, *Mandate for Change* (Garden City, N.Y.: Doubleday, 1963), pp. 424–426. The judgment of more disinterested observers is rather different. One authority, for example, noted that it was easy for Armas "to crush the Communist and the radical left" in Guatelmala; it was a different matter for him to implement the principles of the country's revolution of 1944, in the face of the entrenched oligarchy's opposition. Indeed, Armas's seizure of power "was a gen-

In the second place, there was the unmistakable determination of the United States to prevent the United Nations from considering the Guatemalan issue. The State Department's view was that the UN could not properly take jurisdiction in the affair until the OAS had disposed of it—which was, to say the least, a novel interpretation of the power of the international organ charged with preserving global peace and security.[39]

Finally, there was the strong belief, shared by critics of Washington's policy inside and outside the hemisphere, that the victory against Communism in Guatemala might prove short-lived and self-deceiving. In Guatemala, as elsewhere in Latin America, the only lasting anti-Communist measures would be those that were directed against the conditions within which Communism and other extremist movements thrive.

Aftermath of the 1954 Crisis

That the American-supported overthrow of the Arbenz government in Guatemala did little to bring true political stability was indicated by recurrent crises in that country throughout the years which followed. Writing in the mid-1960s, one observer found that in Guatemala, there had been "virtually no political, economic or social progress" since the 1954 crisis. In this view, Guatemala had experienced nothing but "stagnant dictatorship" for more than a decade.[40] As a nation in which poverty and malnutrition were ubiquitous, in which three-quarters of the population were illiterate, in which housing and health facilities were inadequate, in which the tax system was grossly inequitable, and in which corruption pervaded the government, Guatemala offered a fertile field for Communist and other revolutionary activities. Leftist guerrilla campaigns and terrorism—increasingly supported by Castro's government in Havana—in turn produced "counter-revolutionary" movements by Guatemalan military elements, supported by powerful business and landowning interests. Political authorities tended to depend more upon force than upon internal reform programs for counteracting political unrest. A report early in 1968 depicted Guatemala as "one of the battlegrounds of Latin America," in which Washington's efforts to produce evolutionary political change were pitted against revolutionary political forces. Exploiting deep resentments against "Yankee imperialism" in Central America, Communists and other terrorist groups called for the "liberation" of Guatemala from domination by the United States.[41]

In 1966, a civilian government finally came to power in Guatemala, pledged to a "middle-of-the-road" approach to the country's manifold problems. Yet, as in many other Latin American contexts, the government's commitment to reform often appeared more nominal than real; its commitment to change was seldom translated into programs which really altered old social and economic patterns.[42] Thus far, prospects for true political equilibrium in the country—not to mention the achievement of Western-style democracy —were not encouraging. Political developments in Guatemala were likely to be heavily conditioned by two tendencies we shall discuss more fully later in the chapter: revolutionary activities carried on by Marxist groups, especially those identified with Castro's Cuba; and, even more fundamentally, progress throughout Latin America in achieving economic, social, educational, and other forms of national development.

The Communization of Cuba

The gravest challenge to democracy by leftist political forces in the Western Hemisphere has come from the regime of Premier Fidél Castro in Cuba. Castro and his followers not only succeeded in imposing a Marxist order upon Cuban society; after doing so, they offered *Fidelismo* as the only "correct" revolutionary path for neighboring Latin American countries and actively sponsored insurrectionary activities in Central and South America.

From 1933 to 1944, the island of Cuba was the personal enclave of a *caudillo,* former army sergeant Fulgencio Batista. Like most Latin American dictators of his ilk, Batista depended heavily upon military support; under his administration, the Cuban army was pampered with pay increases, lucrative appointments, and access to graft. Surprisingly, in 1944, Batista accepted the defeat at the polls of his own hand-picked candidate for President; shortly thereafter, the *caudillo* announced his "retirement" from the army and subsequently moved to Florida, leaving Cuba for the next eight years to be governed by civilian leaders. By a coup carried out in 1952, Batista took back the reins of power. Thereafter, opposition to his regime—now widely hailed by conservative circles in the United States because of its "stability" and its anti-Communist complexion—steadily mounted. Student disturbances broke out in 1955, followed by signs of discontent among the military, attempted assassinations, and invasions by rebel groups led by a man who was soon to dominate the center of the Cuban stage—Fidél Castro.

As the pressure in the Cuban political boiler rose, Batista reacted in traditional *caudillo* fashion by clamping a ruthless despotism upon the Cuban people. But the end was not far away. Relying chiefly upon rural support, Castro's rebellion in the eastern section of the island slowly gained

uine counterrevolution." Edwin Lieuwen, *Arms and Politics in Latin America* (New York: Praeger, 1963), p. 94.

momentum. As one element of Cuban society after another defected from Batista's camp, Castro advanced upon Havana. On January 1, 1959, the dictator left Havana and went into exile. On January 7, the United States recognized Castro's regime, under President Manuel Urrutia, as the government of Cuba.* Although the Eisenhower administration had not suspended arms shipments from the United States to Batista until March 14, 1958, it extended cordial greetings to Cuba's new revolutionary government and gave every indication of seeking to cooperate with Castro's regime to achieve many of its stated goals.

Within a few weeks, however, relations between the United States and Cuba began to sour. By the end of 1959, Castro's government had executed over 600 Cubans for counter-revolutionary and pro-Batista activities. Very soon after taking office, Castro began a program of expropriation and nationalization of foreign properties on the island. Throughout this period, State Department officials repeatedly emphasized that the United States supported many of the goals of Castro's regime, such as land reform; nor did it contest Castro's right to expropriate private property in Cuba, provided just compensation were paid for properties seized, as international law required.

In whatever degree such quarrels alienated the United States and Cuba, the most serious issue became Castro's perceptible gravitation toward the Communist bloc. Tensions mounted between Havana and Washington, as Castro accused the United States of supporting counter-revolutionary activities against him and as the Eisenhower administration watched with deep concern Castro's evident determination to alienate the United States completely. A trade agreement between Red China and Cuba at the end of 1959 did not improve the atmosphere of Cuban–American relations. Castro received a visit from Soviet First Deputy Premier Anastas Mikoyan on February 13, 1960, after which the first of a series of Soviet–Cuban trade agreements was announced. On March 20, "Che" Guevara, one of Castro's principal subordinates, stated openly that: "Our war . . . is against the great power of the North." This announcement was followed by the statement of another Cuban official in June that Cuba was "the Soviet Union's greatest and most loyal friend." Congress responded to these provocations by giving the President authority to reduce Cuba's sugar quota in the United States, a power first

invoked by President Eisenhower on July 6. The Kremlin's answer to this gambit was to inform the world that the U.S.S.R. was "raising its voice and extending a helpful hand to the people of Cuba." Ominously, Khrushchev added that "Soviet artillerymen can support the Cuban people with rocket fire."

By August 1, the United States had become sufficiently disturbed by these evidences of Cuban-Soviet collaboration to submit a lengthy document concerning Communist infiltration of the Western Hemisphere to the Inter-American Peace Committee of the OAS. By the end of the month at a meeting in San José, Costa Rica, the foreign ministers of the American republics condemned extrahemispheric intervention in American affairs. Castro's reply was to castigate the United States anew for its "intervention" in Cuban affairs and to reaffirm Havana's close ties with the Communist world.

The early months of 1961 might well be taken as marking the turning point that led to a complete rupture between the United States and Cuba. Two developments, occurring more or less simultaneously, led to the final break. One was the disastrous Bay of Pigs episode, in which a small group of anti-Castro forces, morally and materially assisted by agencies of the United States government, endeavored to invade Cuba and topple Castro's regime. After months of preparation (in which nearly all their plans became known to the public, and to Havana as well), early in the morning of April 17 this group landed in Cuba at the Bay of Pigs. From the beginning, the invasion force had no chance. Counting on air cover by the United States, which was never supplied, within a few days this pathetic group was expeditiously liquidated by Castro's army. In the process, the United States was administered a humiliating diplomatic defeat. That the Kennedy administration would even permit and sanction such an invasion from Florida, much less give it nominal but totally inadequate support, indicated both the implacable opposition of the United Sates to Castro's regime and its apparent unwillingness to take firm measures to oppose it.[43]

In the same period, unmistakable evidence appeared of Castro's continued gravitation toward the Communist bloc. The first in a series of Soviet arms shipments arrived in Cuba on November 18, 1960. Throughout the weeks that followed, Cuban officials openly proclaimed their allegiance to the Communist cause. On January 3, 1961, the United States broke relations altogether with Castro's regime. Finally, on December 2, Castro openly admitted that: "I believe absolutely in Marxism. . . . I am a Marxist–Leninist and will be a Marxist–Leninist until the last day of my life." He confessed that this had been his "true" political ideology ever since he embarked upon his revolutionary course. Early in 1962, the Inter-American

---

*For the background to Castro's successful revolution in Cuba, see Edwin Lieuwen, *Arms and Politics in Latin America* (New York: Praeger, 1963), pp. 97–100.

Our discussion of communization of Cuba relies heavily upon studies prepared for the Senate Foreign Relations Committee, particularly: *Events in United States–Cuban relations: A Chronology*, 88th Congress, 1st Session, 1963.

Peace Committee found Castro's ties with the Communist bloc incompatible with its obligations under the Inter-American system; this judgment was formally confirmed when the foreign ministers of the American republics, meeting at Punta del Este on January 31, expelled Cuba from the Inter-American system. On February 3, the United States proclaimed a total embargo on trade with Cuba.

Throughout the weeks that followed, Havana received new shipments of arms from the Communist world, together with "technical advisers" from behind the Iron Curtain. On September 4, President Kennedy finally warned Castro's government that the United States was determined to take whatever steps were necessary to prevent the installation of offensive weapons on Cuban soil.

The Cuban Missile Crisis of 1962

Then, on October 22, came the long-deferred showdown: In a dramatic coast-to-coast television appearance, President Kennedy announced that Communist missiles had been installed in Cuba and that these were capable of launching nuclear weapons at the United States and other American nations. Kennedy outlined seven steps the United States was taking to deal with this threat to hemispheric peace and security. These included a naval blockade against the shipment of offensive weapons to the island; re-enforcement of American strength at the Guantánamo Bay naval base; a request for an immediate meeting of the OAS; and a similar request for an emergency session of the UN Security Council. To Soviet Premier Khrushchev, President Kennedy issued a warning that the United States would retaliate against the U.S.S.R. itself if any Soviet missiles were launched from Cuba; and he urged the Kremlin to eliminate this dangerous threat to global peace.

The controversy between Washington and Havana had now become openly transformed into a major cold war confrontation between the United States and the Soviet Union. This "secret, swift, and extraordinary build-up of Communist missiles" in Cuba, President Kennedy told the American people, "in an area well known to have special and historical relationship to the United States . . . is a deliberately provocative and unjustified change in the status quo which cannot be accepted by this country. . . ." The United States "will not prematurely or unnecessarily risk the costs of worldwide nuclear war . . . but neither will we shrink from that risk at any time it must be faced.[44]

At no time in the postwar period had the United States gone so perilously to "the brink of war." As tense White House and State Department officials awaited the next moves by Havana and Moscow, they feared that an outright military invasion of Cuba might soon be required.[45] Meanwhile, the UN Security Council was summoned into extraordinary session, where the United States presented incontestable proof of Soviet missile sites inside Cuba. Contemporaneously with these developments, the OAS demanded the immediate and total dismantling of Communist missiles in Cuba and called upon its members to resist, by force if necessary, any further Cuban importation of Communist arms. At the same time, Soviet ships bearing new arms shipments from behind the Iron Curtain held their course for Havana; heavily armed naval forces of the United States waited to intercept them.

The first break in the crisis came when these Havana-bound ships finally altered course and turned back with their lethal cargoes. Then, in a succession of swiftly moving events, the crisis receded: The State Department received an unusually conciliatory message from the Kremlin, indicating its desire to avoid provocations against the United States; both the United States and the U.S.S.R. (if not Cuba) indicated their readiness to have UN Secretary General U Thant mediate the crisis; nonaligned countries in the UN called on the parties to the conflict to avoid provocative actions and used their influence in behalf of peaceful settlement; Khrushchev pledged that no further arms from behind the Iron Curtain would be sent to Cuba, and this assurance was followed on October 27 by a new pledge that all offensive weapons would be removed from the island; with this assurance, and upon the understanding that the removal of such weapons would be clearly verified, the United States agreed to lift its naval blockade. By November 20, President Kennedy announced that all Communist missiles had been dismantled and that Premier Khrushchev had pledged to have remaining IL-28 bombers removed speedily. With that announcement, the White House also declared that it had ordered the termination of Cuba's naval quarantine. On December 12, the White House stated that the evidence indicated that all offensive missiles and aircraft had been dismantled in Cuba; thereafter, as in the preceding weeks, American high-level reconnaissance aircraft kept up a constant inspection of the island to assure that there was no clandestine violation of the *détente* that had led to a resolution of the crisis.

The Kennedy administration's handling of the Cuban missile crisis must surely be ranked as one of the most spectacular cold war diplomatic victories the United States has scored in recent years. Nearly every American goal was achieved, as Soviet machinations were dealt one of their most severe setbacks since World War II. For once, a major diplomatic undertaking by the United States won approval by the overwhelming majority of countries in the OAS and in the United Nations; even many of the neutralist countries of

Africa and Asia, formerly sympathetic to Castro in his David-and-Goliath drama with the United States, were remarkably uncritical of the United States and notably passive in championing Cuba's cause before the bar of world opinion. Among other results, the Soviet-American confrontation over Cuba exploded many myths, such as the bogey of Soviet missile invincibility, the hollowness of Khrushchev's pledges to defend Castro's regime with rockets, and the stereotype of the United States as a wavering democracy unable to take a firm stand when its vital interests are at stake.

Without discounting the gains resulting from Washington's skillful diplomacy, however, it is necessary also to call attention to what the removal of Soviet missiles from Cuba did *not* achieve. It did not bring about the downfall of Castro's Marxist regime. It did not disrupt the Cuban-Soviet axis. It did not put a stop to Communist or other revolutionary activities in the Western Hemisphere. It did not prevent many Latin Americans from championing *Fidelismo* as an ideology or program uniquely suited to their conditions. It did not assure the victory of democracy over totalitarianism in any Latin American country. It did not transform the Organization of American States, infusing it with new power and authority. It did not eliminate anti-United States sentiment south of the border. It did not promote regional economic progress. In brief, most of the basic problems in Inter-American relations remained unresolved; and many of them became more critical in the years which followed.

The Dominican Crisis of 1965

Officials in Washington soon became aware that the removal of Soviet missiles from the Caribbean did not dispose of the Communist threat to the Western Hemisphere. Fidél Castro and his followers openly sponsored insurrections in neighboring countries; by the mid-1960s also, Communist China's distinctive brand of Marxism—in which the necessity for ongoing "revolutionary struggle" was continually emphasized—had won a limited number of converts in Latin America. Correctly or not, the Johnson administration became convinced that the Dominican Republic was next on the Marxist revolutionary timetable.*

Occupying two-thirds of the Caribbean island of Hispaniola, the Dominican Republic has had a

*The Dominican crisis of 1965 is included in our discussion of the Communist threat to hemispheric security only because the danger of a Marxist takeover in that country was cited by the Johnson administration as a major reason for intervention by United States military forces. The author agrees with several studies of this crisis that the Communist danger, while undoubtedly present in some degree, was in the main remote and considerably exaggerated by policy-makers in Washington.

long history of violence and political upheaval. The dictator Rafael L. Trujillo, who ruled the country from 1930 until his assassination in 1961, epitomized the Latin American *caudillo*, whose main interest was personal (or family) gain and aggrandizement at the expense of his countrymen. After Trujillo's death, a subordinate—Joaquin Balaguer—led the government briefly. At the end of 1962, the first national election in years brought Juan Bosch to the presidency. Bosch was an enigmatic and controversial figure; his regime lasted only until September, 1963, when it was overturned by a military *coup d'état*. Supporters of Juan Bosch, Communists, and other radical political elements precipitated an insurrection against the government at the end of April, 1965.

From that point on, for a period of several weeks, political developments within the Dominican Republic became clouded by uncertainty, rumor, and confusion. Even now, it is not always possible to recount events accurately or dispassionately, and interpretations of the Dominican crisis continue to differ widely concerning key developments and personalities. Was the opposition to military rule a "Communist conspiracy," possibly directed from Havana, Moscow, or Peking? Were Juan Bosch and his followers dedicated Marxists? And if so, was it possible to distinguish between their belief in "national Communism" and subservience to a foreign power? By contrast, was the ruling military junta engaging in a familiar political gambit by labeling its critics "Communists" in order to discredit them and to assure larger quantities of aid from the United States? Were the American ambassador in Santo Domingo, W. Tapley Bennett, Jr., and former Ambassador John Bartlow Martin (who visited the country in this period), along with other officials in the embassy, accurately informed about political developments? Or did they panic in advising Washington that a Marxist seizure of power was imminent? These and other relevant questions remain highly controversial.

Whatever the true facts, on April 28, 1965, President Johnson responded to increasingly insistent pleas from embassy officials by ordering U.S. marines to land in the Dominican Republic. In time, some 25,000 American troops were sent to the country or adjacent waters; after May 6, most of these forces were placed under the authority of a newly formed OAS Inter-American Peace Force, which assumed responsibility for maintaining order for more than a year thereafter. President Johnson justified this intervention in the affairs of another American republic by reference to the fact that the lives of several thousand citizens from the United States and other foreign countries were endangered.[46] Other observers and critics were certain, however, that the intervention could actually be explained by reference to two other interrelated factors: They felt that embassy officials in Santo Domingo had totally misread the Dominican political situation in mistaking opposition groups for a "Communist conspiracy" (a misapprehension fostered by the military junta itself). They also believed that, as in several other Latin American nations, policy-makers in the United States *preferred* right-wing military regimes to left-wing movements embracing Marxists and other dissident elements. In brief, Washington's response to the Dominican political crisis stemmed from ignorance, from an ingrained antipathy toward Communism, or from a combination of both tendencies.[47]

The consequences of United States military intervention in the Dominican Republic would doubtless be felt for a long time to come. It did not escape the attention of the other American republics that Washington ignored the OAS until the marines had landed; then the Johnson administration sought OAS approval and support for the undertaking—despite the fact that unilateral intervention of this kind was expressly prohibited by Article 15 of the organization's Charter. With few exceptions, the members of OAS were not impressed with the administration's claim that some Latin American governments had been consulted before the event or that insufficient time existed in which to call for a meeting of the OAS to consider the crisis. To Latin American minds, such reasoning merely underscored how little value the United States really put on the OAS and how reluctant it was to allow its own conduct to be inhibited by the opinions of its neighbors. Belatedly, the members of the OAS were willing to create an *ad hoc* police force, as a substitute for the unilateral power exercised by the United States in the Dominican Republic. But as we have already noted, the other American republics were not willing to convert this force into a *permanent* military organization.

Except for other right-wing governments and oligarchies in the area, Latin American opinion of Washington's conduct in the Dominican affair was almost uniformly hostile. Outspoken opposition by Marxist groups could of course be anticipated; much more disturbing was the criticism expressed by individuals and groups normally friendly toward the United States. The Dominican intervention seemed to symbolize what was wrong with American foreign policy—its undue fixation with "Communist conspiracies," its lack of sophistication and understanding about political movements in other countries, its readiness to rely upon military force, its ill-concealed preference for right-wing military dictatorships, its reluctance to accept restraints upon its own freedom of action, its indifference to the opinions of the international community. At no point in the postwar period, it would be safe to say, had the United States alienated Latin American sentiment so widely.[48]

More disturbing than the temporary occupation of the Dominican Republic by United States armed forces was the principle enunciated by President Johnson on May 2. Referred to in time as the "Johnson Doctrine," the statement affirmed that: "The American nations cannot, must not, and will not permit the establishment of another communist government in the Western Hemisphere." Although the President claimed that this was "the unanimous view of all the American nations," many Latin Americans wondered whether the doctrine would be invoked again in the future to justify intervention whenever officials in Washington detected signs of a Communist conspiracy in another American republic.[49]

As in the case of Guatemala, it was difficult to show that direct intervention by the United States in the affairs of the Dominican Republic contributed to lasting political stability or enhancement of democracy in the country. In the national elections, held under OAS supervision in June, 1966, Joaquin Balaguer defeated Juan Bosch for the presidency; the former strengthened his position by victories in municipal elections in 1968. Balaguer's government embarked upon a 15-year program of national development and promised other overdue reforms, financed in large part by economic and technical assistance from the United States. On the surface, reasonable political calm had been restored to the turbulent country. Yet many commentators were convinced that this equilibrium was deceptive: Ancient political rivalries—re-enforced by animosities and resentments growing out of the crisis of 1965—remained unresolved. The Dominican Revolutionary party, Juan Bosch's old movement, still militantly opposed the government and called for an insurrection against it. As in the past, opposition groups claimed that the government suppressed dissent and that a free election in the country was impossible. Officials of the United States within the country, one observer wrote, sought to "maintain a publicly neutral position" on political struggles within the nation, "while working privately to keep lines open to all non-Communist political groups."[50]

Prospects for Communism in Latin America

According to the chief ideologist of Castro's revolutionary movement in Cuba, Ernesto "Che" Guevara, "New uprisings will take place in Our America, and they will continue to grow in the midst of all the hardships inherent to this dangerous profession of being modern revolutionaries."[51] That Guevara's prophetic gifts were less than outstanding was demonstrated when he and other Marxist revolutionaries, who sought to overthrow the government of Bolivia, were hunted down and summarily executed. Before he died,

Guevara proclaimed his Bolivian revolutionary movement a "fiasco."[52]

As a rule, this judgment could also be passed upon Cuban-instigated revolutionary activities in Guatemala, Venezuela, and Colombia during the late 1960s. In none of these countries did Marxist insurrections succeed.[53] Nor was there any very convincing evidence that Communist attempts to seize power elsewhere in Latin America were close to achieving their objectives. By contrast, gains had sometimes been made by "old line," Soviet-oriented Communist parties which eschewed insurrections and terrorism. A conspicuous example was the Communist party of Chile, identified with the Soviet Union and vocally anti-Castro. This party had become one of the most influential groups in Chilean political life. For years, it had cooperated with the socialists and other left-wing groups to form a large bloc in the Chilean Congress; its prospects for gaining strength in the future were perhaps better than at any previous time. Not untypically for Marxist groups oriented toward Moscow, the Communist party of Chile was regarded as relatively *conservative* (vis-à-vis other radical forces within Chile), opportunistic, and devoid of revolutionary fervor. Its lack of revolutionary zeal, for example, made it *passé* for much of Chile's youth, not to speak of proponents of *Fidelismo* and Mao Tse-tung's revolutionary approach.[54]

These examples suggest several general conclusions about future Communist gains in Latin America. Marxist organizations oriented toward Cuba or Communist China thus far have experienced very little success in "liberating" Latin America by reliance upon insurrection and terrorism against established governments. Isolated revolutionary acts have occurred and can be expected to recur. By the late 1960s, the growth in *urban terrorism* was marked in several Latin American nations. But little evidence exists that Marxist revolutionary movements have gained widespread popular support. Even the leaders of such insurrections have complained that the masses (especially in the rural areas) are apathetic —and sometimes overtly hostile. Moreover, problems of supplying and maintaining effective revolutionary campaigns in the Andean mountains, the jungles, and other adverse settings have thus far proved insurmountable. Cuban-sponsored revolutionary activities in Central and South America also generate resentments because they represent foreign attempts to determine the political destinies of Latin American societies. Nor does the recent experience of the two leading advocates of Communist revolution in Latin America—Castro's Cuba and Mao Tse-tung's China—offer an attractive model for Latin American societies. Whatever mode or pattern of economic development is adopted by these societies (and considerable diversity is likely to prevail in this respect), the dominant objective is likely to be real economic and social *progress*. The Marxist systems of Cuba and China win little support by this criterion. Another obstacle to successful Communist revolution in the hemisphere is a problem alluded to earlier: ongoing factionalism and infighting among competing Marxist groups. Disputes over doctrines and tactics among Communist organizations in Latin America, as in other regions, have destroyed the unity of Marxism and vitiated much of its public appeal. Communist revolutionary activities in Latin America also confront a reality which, in the recent period and for the foreseeable future, serves as a pervasive obstacle to successful insurrections. This is the fact that the most influential political force in many Latin American societies is *the military elite*. As we shall see, military elements in Latin America today often espouse the cause of reform and national development; in contrast to earlier periods, rule by military *junta* is not necessarily tantamount to political reaction or preservation of the status quo. Nevertheless, military officers in Latin America have not abandoned their traditional antipathy toward Communism or their determination to suppress Marxist-led revolutions. Thus far, in the vast majority of Latin American states, the odds continue to favor military elites over their Marxist rivals in the struggle for political supremacy.

In assessing the prospects for Communist revolutions throughout Latin America, however, one key distinction must be borne in mind at all times. The evidence indicates that successful *Marxist-led* insurrections are a remote danger. Yet this is *not* to imply that Latin America will escape revolutionary or radical political change—spearheaded, more often than not, by *indigenous* (non-Marxist) political forces in the Caribbean, Central America, and South America. More so today than ever, perhaps, the *non-Communist political left* has wide popular appeal. Unless economic and social conditions throughout the region rapidly improve, this force may be expected to become even stronger; in some Latin American societies it may emerge as the dominant instrument of radical political change.*

*The non-Marxist political parties referred to here are what Robert J. Alexander calls the "national revolutionary" parties of Latin America which have "grown out of the changing circumstances and recent history of their respective countries." Although some differences from country to country can be discerned, these parties have certain similarities. In contrast to Marxist parties (which theoretically, if seldom actually, represent the working-class elements), these parties have broad constituencies —urban workers, peasants, middle-class groups, and other segments of the population. Traditionally, these parties have sought to break the political hold of the landowners and commercial aristocracy; in several Latin American societies (like Peru and Bolivia), they have endeavored to enhance the political role of the Indians; they have advocated the redistribution of

THE PROBLEM OF MILITARY ELITES IN LATIN AMERICA

Military Dictatorships and American Foreign Policy

In May, 1911, the long-awaited revolution in Mexico erupted against the thirty-year rule of the dictator Porfirio Diaz. Advocates of democracy inside and outside Mexico had high hopes that the end of authoritarian government in the country (popularly called "Diazpotism") would usher in a new era of expanding political freedom and needed reforms. After a brief interval, however, the new leader (Francisco Madero, a known advocate of democracy) was deposed, and later executed, by General Victoriano Huerta. Huerta imposed an even more despotic regime upon Mexican society; and his seizure of power opened one of the most frustrating and tragic chapters in the history of inter-American relations.

Huerta's *coup d'état* quickly elicited a denunciation from President Woodrow Wilson who (in contrast to his predecessor, President William H. Taft) took few pains to conceal his desire for democratic political systems in the Americas. Perhaps no President in the history of the United States was a more fervent believer in the democratic ideal—for Latin America and for all other regions. His goal for Mexico, Wilson declared, was "an orderly and righteous government"; his avowed sympathies were with "the submerged eighty-five percent of the people of that Republic who are now struggling toward liberty." Characterizing the new regime as "a government of butchers," led by the "unspeakable Huerta," President Wilson refused to extend diplomatic recognition to it and announced his unequivocal opposition to it. "I am going to teach the South American republics to elect good men!" the President declared. Within the United States, one group of Wilson's critics urged him to follow Great Britain's example by recognizing the Huerta regime in the interests of political stability in Mexico and regard for American investments in the country. Other critics urged the White House to take a firm line toward dictatorship south of the border, by using armed force if necessary to restore democracy.

For some three years, Mexican–American relations went from bad to worse. President Wilson insisted upon Huerta's resignation and encouraged the arming of anti-Huerta groups within Mexico—steps which aroused resentment not only within Mexico itself but throughout Latin America as a whole. The climax came in April, 1914, when the armed forces of the United States seized the Mexican port city of Vera Cruz, a move which was of course tantamount to an act of war against Mexico. President Wilson left little doubt that his ultimate objective was to overthrow Huerta's government. Even outspoken enemies of General Huerta in Mexico joined the government in condemning this invasion of their territory by the "North American colossus"; Latin American reaction to the occupation of Vera Cruz was similarly hostile. Open war between the United States and Mexico was averted only because Argentina, Brazil, and Chile offered to mediate the dispute—a proposal readily accepted by President Wilson. Within a few weeks after the Vera Cruz crisis, General Huerta fled to Spain. He was succeeded by General Venustiano Carranza, a vocal critic of the United States. Carranza's attacks upon the Roman Catholic Church—along with his support for General Pancho Villa, who terrorized American citizens close to the Mexican border—evoked new denunciations from proponents of democracy inside and outside the country. Except for his avoidance of outright war with Mexico, President Wilson's effort to teach Latin Americans "to elect good men" had achieved little, other than to leave a lasting residue of resentment and bitterness against the United States.[55]

Every occupant of the White House who followed Woodrow Wilson has confronted the problem of despotic government in Latin America, more often than not imposed by military elites. In the second half of the twentieth century, it was remarkable how little the scenario had changed. With due regard for different circumstances and personalities, the basic elements in the plot—the seizure of power by a military junta in some Latin American nation; the outcry against this threat to democracy by its opponents inside and outside the country; denunciations of the regime by officials in the United States; Washington's resort to nonrecognition and other measures to express its displeasure; growing resentment against the United States (even by groups opposing the military junta) for its "intervention" in Latin America's political affairs; the eventual deposition of the incumbent dictatorship, followed by the imposition of a new one in the society concerned—have

---

wealth, agrarian reform, and greater state control over the economic system. While they urge massive restrictions against the influence of foreign corporations, these parties are *not* as a rule xenophobic; under proper state supervision, foreign business investments are encouraged. These parties have also opposed the intrusion of the Church in the political sphere. Several significant differences between these parties and Marxist organizations exist. "National revolutionary" parties, for example, are *not* generally anti-Western in their outlook on foreign affairs; they envision an important role for private industry in national development; and they operate democratically in their internal affairs. Examples of non-Marxist revolutionary parties include the *Aprista* party of Peru; the *Accion Democratica* of Venezuela; the *Movimiento Nacionalista Revolucionario* of Bolivia; the *Partido Revolucionario Dominicano* of the Dominican Republic and possibly the *Partido Revolucionario Institucional* of Mexico. See Robert J. Alexander, *Latin-American Politics and Government* (New York: Harper & Row, 1965), pp. 62–74.

recurred with distressing regularity. Perhaps no problem in inter-American relations has been more productive of ill will and misunderstanding among the American republics than the issue of military rule in Latin American societies.*

For policy-makers in the United States, the problem abounds with complexities. A half-century after Wilson's time, little evidence existed that officials in Washington had resolved them successfully. Indeed, in some respects the effort to evolve a frame of reference for guiding American foreign policy in dealing with the problem was more difficult than ever. Inevitably, the approach of the United States to Latin American nations governed by military elites tended to be schizophrenic and productive of dissension. As in Wilson's era, two basically contrary forces pulled policy in opposite directions. Responding to these forces, policy-makers often tended to adopt a "compromise" approach which satisfied no one completely and which invited the accusation that the foreign policy of the United States was "devoid of principle."

One powerful force was America's traditional identification with the ideal of democratic government. As the oldest successful democracy in the world, the United States properly championed the ideal of political freedom. The Constitution of the United States has served as a model for many new governments; the Bill of Rights—along

*In what might be regarded as almost a "textbook case" of a military seizure of power in Latin America, on October 11, 1968, a military junta ousted the civilian government in Panama, led by Dr. Arnulfo Arias. Two national guard officers—Col. Omar Torrijos and Col. Boris Martinez, both relatively young men—emerged as the dominant personalities within the junta. The coup was bloodless and encountered no active opposition; Dr. Arias took refuge in the embassy of the United States, where he spearheaded opposition to the new regime. Both the ruling military elite and groups opposing it accused each other of being under Communist influence. Asserting that the Arias government was infused with corruption and had failed to solve the country's problems, the new regime pledged itself to "restore" democracy, to eliminate waste and mismanagement, to promote economic advancement and generally to lay the foundation for durable civilian rule. Concurrently, the junta imprisoned large numbers of political dissenters, imposed censorship, and placed government agencies under military control. Proclaiming that Panama needed a "rebirth of democracy," the junta promised new election laws and elimination of abuses which had long impaired efficient governmental operations; as always, the public was assured that military domination of the government was merely "temporary," or what one observer called "a parenthesis in the history of Panama." The junta was closely identified with the United States, since most officers in the National Guard had received extensive training in the U.S. The new government sought to reach agreement with Washington concerning the future of the Panama Canal. Yet, like other members of the "new" military in Latin America, the government also expressed its desire to adopt a more "independent" foreign policy and reduce its "dependence" upon Uncle Sam. See *The New York Times,* (October 16 and December 8, 1968; February 8, 1969).

with the writings and speeches of American leaders like Thomas Jefferson, Abraham Lincoln, Woodrow Wilson, and Franklin D. Roosevelt—have had a potent influence upon democratic movements in Latin America and other regions. In the postwar era, officials in the United States have interpreted the cold war as a clash between democracy and totalitarianism. For these and other reasons, successive Presidents have reaffirmed America's attachment to democracy and its preference for it in other countries. When President Wilson condemned Huerta's despotic rule in Mexico; or when President Truman denounced the dictatorship of Juan Perón in Argentina; or when President Johnson deplored Brazil's acceptance of military rule; or when President Nixon confronted an outspokenly anti-Yankee government ruled by military elements in Peru— in these and countless other cases, officials in the United States have expressed their strong preference for democracy and their opposition to military or other antidemocratic regimes throughout Latin America. Proponents of democracy in the Western Hemisphere had high hopes that the Alliance for Progress would provide a new impetus for expanded political freedom throughout the Americas. Among the several announced goals of this program, the one listed first was the improvement and strengthening of democratic political institutions in the countries participating in it.[56]

During the late 1960s, another inducement was added to the argument that the United States ought to champion the principle of democracy in the Western Hemisphere. Much of the domestic criticism directed at the Johnson administration's management of foreign affairs focused upon America's "consorting with dictators" in recent years. In Southeast Asia, in Latin America, and other settings, critics charged, the image of the United States had been tarnished because of Washington's apparent preference for right-wing dictatorships in other countries, especially those which were conspicuously "anti-Communist." Among other results, this stance tended to align the United States with the political status quo and to leave the initiative for promoting radical political change to Moscow or Peking. Most crucially, perhaps, it made it impossible for the United States to characterize the cold war as a contest between "freedom and tyranny."

If the case for encouraging democratic movements overseas was clear and compelling, the difficulty for policy-makers in the United States was that the case *against* doing so had equally forceful arguments. In no region of the world was the dilemma more complex than in Latin America. In the first place, there was the concept which Latin Americans viewed as the keystone of the Inter-American system: nonintervention by one American republic in the internal affairs of another. In practice, Latin Americans interpreted this to mean chiefly nonintervention *by the United States* in the affairs of its neighbors. For well over fifty years—from Wilson's difficulties with Mexico to President Johnson's interference in the political life of the Dominican Republic—Latin Americans have complained about efforts by the United States to determine their political destinies. It was no coincidence that—at Latin American insistence—President Franklin D. Roosevelt's attempt to win hemispheric support for the "Good Neighbor policy" during the 1930s was coupled with Washington's acceptance of the nonintervention principle.[57]

In the second place, the history of inter-American relations since 1900 affords little or no evidence to support the assumption that efforts by the United States to eradicate despotism and implant democracy in Latin America (or any other region) are likely to succeed. On the basis of experience, the principal result is likely to be an escalation in popular resentment against the United States for seeking to "dictate" to other societies! Even opponents of the Huerta regime in Mexico, it needs to be recalled, resented efforts by President Wilson to overthrow the Mexican dictator. In the two leading cases in the postwar period—Washington's interventions in Guatemala and the Dominican Republic—the prospects for genuine democracy remain, at best, remote and uncertain. A case can be made for the contention that such intervention may have actually *impeded* the emergence of democracy in these societies. Antidemocratic groups of both the left and right were able to exploit popular resentment against Washington's interventionist behavior; indigenous governments could cite the danger of a foreign threat as justification for even more repressive measures; and even groups genuinely devoted to the ideal of democratic government were to some extent discredited because of their identification with a foreign power. After reviewing the record of efforts by the United States to instill democracy throughout Latin America, the diplomatic historian Dexter Perkins concluded several years ago: ". . . it is extremely doubtful whether the United States strengthens democracy in fact by active participation in the affairs of other states. Appeals from the outside by a government over the head of constituted authority in another country seem in general to have been unsuccessful in the past, and are likely to be unsuccessful in the future."[58] Experience in recent years has not invalidated Perkins' conclusion. President Kennedy, for example, arrived at much the same verdict. A firm believer in the democratic principle, Kennedy deplored "military takeovers" in the Western Hemisphere. Yet he was no less convinced that relying upon U.S. marines to prevent or remove them "is not the way for democracy to flourish." President Kennedy

tried various approaches to the problem; but one of his aides concluded that "his policy was neither consistently applied nor consistently successful. Both economic and diplomatic relations were cut off, restored or not cut off without any discernible pattern in a situation which itself had little discernible pattern."[59]

Presidents Johnson and Nixon were no more successful in reversing the trend toward military juntas in Latin America. Despite the clear emphasis in the Alliance for Progress on the promotion of democracy within the hemisphere, it soon became clear that little immediate progress was being made in reaching that goal—in part perhaps because the *Alianza* itself was only partially successful. Early in the 1970s, one report found that over half of Latin America's total population lived under governments controlled directly or indirectly by military elites.[60] Adopting a recommendation made by Governor Nelson Rockefeller, as a result of his intensive study of Latin America's problems, President Nixon declared that under his administration the United States would "deal realistically with governments in the Inter-American system as they are." In effect, this meant that the <u>Nixon</u> administration would no longer refuse to extend formal recognition to military-controlled governments, deny foreign aid to them, or otherwise attempt directly to change nondemocratic political systems south of the border.[61] This reorientation in American foreign policy was dictated in part by a realization among officials in Washington that fundamental changes were affecting the character of military elites throughout Latin America.

The Military Tradition in Latin America

From the early nineteenth century—when Latin American countries acquired their independence —the armed forces have often played a dominant role in the political life of that region. This phenomenon has manifold origins, which we cannot discuss in detail here. It is enough to observe that, under Spanish rule, the colonial tradition in Latin America often exalted military leadership; Spanish culture had nothing corresponding to the principle of civilian supremacy over military elements which is central to the constitutional system of the United States. The wars of Latin American independence were prolonged and destructive, leaving chaos and social disorganization in their wake. The new civilian governments often lacked both the legitimacy to give them popular support, and the capacity to deal with national problems successfully. By contrast, military leaders—like José de San Martín and Simón Bolívar, along with many lesser-known figures—emerged with great prestige and mass appeal. For well over a century, Latin American political life involved the interplay of three potent forces: the wealthy landowners, the Roman Catholic Church, and the armed forces. More often than not, the army (frequently allied with one or both of the other groups) served as the real locus of political power. Based perhaps on the army's decisive role in achieving independence, Latin American military elites asserted a claim which was to be heard many times in the years ahead. This was the idea that the armed forces were the true repository of national power and welfare; they were the real "custodians" of the society's well-being; and governmental officials were ultimately accountable to them for the welfare of the nation.[62] The logical corollary of this doctrine of course was that military elites could, and not infrequently did, depose incumbent governments; sometimes they selected a new civilian regime, and sometimes a military junta ruled directly. Even disgruntled civilians often turned to the military for assistance in overturning the government in power. Military-led coups thus became a recurrent feature of Latin American political life. Or, as a recent student of political behavior in the area has expressed the idea: "The *normal* business of the military in these countries is politics."[63]

The pattern of government by the *caudillo* system thus became ubiquitous throughout Latin America.* While due allowance of course had to be made for differences among Latin American societies, and among different personalities within a single country, the *caudillo* system had certain common characteristics./*Caudillo* rule tended to be extremely *personal:* The acquisition and retention of political power per se—rather than concern with ideological principles or specific programs—became the dominating impulse of the system./The *caudillo* demanded unquestioning loyalty and obedience from his followers. The leader's orders had to be obeyed, and orders issued by his subordinates in his name were similarly authoritative. Absolutism and *caudillo* rule thus tended to become synonymous terms. Constitutional restraints upon arbitrary governmental power, laws, elections, and other safeguards (with which the constitutions of Latin America often

abounded) were customarily disregarded or circumvented by the *caudillo* and his coterie. Ultimately, the extent of his own power or ambitions served as the only effective limitation upon his behavior. In return for virtually uninhibited political power, the *caudillo* had certain obligations— foremost among which perhaps was to enrich and enhance the welfare of the coterie which installed and maintained him in office. Functioning in a region where loyalty to family and friends often ranked ahead of concern for society as a whole, the *caudillo* system customarily produced fortunes for the leader and his clique, while despoiling society at large. Ruling groups thus enriched themselves, their families, and supporters (often with the active connivance of foreign corporations seeking concessions from the government), while the masses sank deeper into economic and social backwardness.

Latin American political life acquired a kind of predictable rhythm. Inevitably opposition would appear to the rule of the incumbent *caudillo*. Sooner or later, a revolt would oust the existing government; a new regime—frequently professing its devotion to national welfare and its intention to "restore democracy"—would seize power. In due course, disaffection would arise against the new *caudillo* and his coterie; detecting plots against its rule, the government would adopt increasingly repressive measures to maintain its authority. But in time the *caudillo* would be either assassinated or exiled (the latter being customary under the distinctive ground rules of Latin American political life). After that, the familiar cycle would begin anew.

Despite the fact that the term "revolution" was loosely applied to the frequent changes of regime throughout Latin America, in reality the replacement of one *caudillo* government by another was not *revolutionary* at all. With one notable exception—the gradual diminution in the political power of the Church in most Latin American societies—nothing really changed when a new government took office. To the contrary, most *caudillos* had (or soon developed) a powerful vested interest in the status quo, including the system of landed estates and peasant peonage, the influential role of foreign corporations in economic and political affairs, and the poverty-stricken condition of the masses. Insofar as fundamental changes occurred at all, these were usually in the direction of greater economic and social *inequality* among the various strata of society and the general deterioration in conditions throughout Latin America vis-à-vis those in Europe, the United States, or other "developed" regions./*Caudillo* rule thus became synonymous with despotism, the personal enrichment of political elites at the expense of society, widening social and economic disparities, and economic decline./

---

*In the period immediately following Latin American independence, Edwin Lieuwen has written, the new republics quickly came under the control of *caudillos*, who were "ambitious local chieftains," usually military officers. These "army-officer politicians" normally "ruled by the sword, perverted justice, and pillaged the treasury"; the *caudillo* and his followers tended to live "as parasites upon the society they were supposed to protect." Down to the recent period, the "plethora of ambitious, opportunistic military men made politics in nearly every country little more than an endless process of dissension, intrigue, and revolutionary turmoil." Opponents of the *caudillo* (often individuals and groups "left out" in the distribution of spoils) would eventually form a new conspiratorial group and, if successful, install a new *caudillo* in office. See Edwin Lieuwen, *Arms and Politics in Latin America*, rev. ed. (New York: Praeger, 1961), pp. 18, 20.

The "New" Military Elites of Latin America

Even in the second half of the twentieth century, vestiges of the traditional *caudillo* system survived in the Western Hemisphere, particularly in the Caribbean area and Central America. Throughout Latin America as a whole, military elites remained the most influential political force; in nearly every country, a military junta ruled directly or "installed" civilian leaders in power who were dependent upon the support of the armed forces. Nor was there any real prospect that the crucial political role of military groups would be diminished in the near future. Yet students of Latin American affairs could discern significant changes in the *nature and goals* of military regimes in Latin America.[64]

In general terms, we may characterize these developments by saying that military elites in the Western Hemisphere were employing the levers of political power to become the main agents of political change and modernization within their societies. The Rockefeller Report late in 1969 referred to a "new type of military man" in Latin America, who was "coming to the fore and often becoming a major force for constructive social change in the American Republics." Latin American military officials were motivated by "impatience with corruption, inefficiency, and a stagnant political order"; they were prepared to adapt authoritarian political traditions "to the goals of social and economic progress."[65] In several Latin American societies, military officers were referred to as "revolutionaries in uniform." One commentator detected a "new mentality" among the military leaders of Peru, Bolivia, Brazil, and other Latin American states. In these countries, the armed forces had "dropped the traditional defense of the social order"; they had "adopted, in the name of national pride, a theory of economic development through radical social reform." Military elites were interested perhaps above all in *industrialization*. In addition, they often favored encouragement of foreign investments, an expansion of the state's role in economic management and decision-making, greater regional economic cooperation, and measures to alleviate poverty. Although the military junta currently governing Peru had recently carried out a program of land reform (and the junta in Brazil had formulated a similar program), in general rural problems received less attention from military leaders. More than at any time in history, military regimes in Latin America were mindful of the need to broaden their base of popular support. In Peru, for example, "The Government . . . [sought] support with well-publicized reform measures, propaganda, and an appeal to nationalism."[66]

What factors accounted for the change in the outlook and goals of military leaders in many of the American republics? Mention may be made briefly of several influential forces. As early as the nineteenth century, military service offered one of the few avenues of social mobility and advancement for individuals who otherwise found such avenues closed. In the postwar period, Latin American military establishments have been broadened by the inclusion of a larger number of lower- and middle-class elements. Moreover, in the larger Latin American states, military groups have given an impetus to "nationalist" sentiments vis-à-vis the provincial viewpoints endemic in the regions and localities. Increasingly, a spirit of professionalism and *esprit de corps* has infused the Latin American armed forces. The acquisition of modern weapons; the creation of a strong and stable national base upon which to build an up-to-date military machine; a desire for greater military self-sufficiency; the realization that a modern military establishment demands improved training and education; prolonged residence and study abroad, enabling military officials from Latin America to contrast conditions in their own countries with those existing in others; rising confidence among military elites that they are best qualified to "lead" in national development; a new determination to solve long-standing problems which thus far have defied solution by civilian governments; the conviction that military-initiated reform is the only alternative to Marxist and other insurrectionary movements— these considerations have combined to alter military attitudes in many Latin American societies.[67]

Care must be taken of course not to romanticize or distort the nature of the "new" Latin American military elites. There has been no indication, for example, that military officers have become widely converted to Western-style democracy or have abandoned their traditional belief that they are the ultimate repository of national power and sovereignty. Much of the impetus for reform carried out by military groups, it also must be recognized, stemmed from a desire to make *the armed forces* more modern and efficient; to some extent, concern for the welfare of the nation as a whole is a by-product of that objective. Nor is there any convincing evidence that most military regimes have succeeded in acquiring a foundation of mass popular support. As in the past, the gap between promise and performance by military-controlled governments continues to be great; the failure of such regimes to solve increasingly difficult social and economic problems could easily lead to growing public disillusionment and new outbreaks of political instability. Rivalries *within* Latin American military establishments—with the air force and navy becoming increasingly resentful of army dominance—often have made a unified approach to national problems difficult. By the late 1960s, it was apparent that more intense anti-United States sentiment was also characteristic of military rule in a number of Latin American societies. Military-controlled governments objected to the significant decline in U.S. arms-aid to Latin America; in some instances, the nationalization of assets of Yankee corporations created tensions between Washington and other American capitals. Military regimes often favored a more "independent" foreign policy for their countries, due to their resentment of Latin America's subordination to the cold war strategy of the United States. There was, therefore, no assurance whatever that changes in the nature of goals of military elites in Latin America would guarantee the emergence of democracy in the Western Hemisphere or automatically foster more harmonious inter-American relations.[68]

Admittedly, President Nixon's decision to adopt a new approach to the problem of military regimes in the Americas was a calculated policy risk. In common with earlier approaches to this vexatious problem, it offered no inevitable success in achieving the goals of the United States in the Western Hemisphere. Nixon's approach invited the charge that the United States was "indifferent" to democracy and that it was "consorting with dictators." The strongest argument to be made in favor of the policy, perhaps, was that it offered as good a prospect as any alternative approach to achieving the nation's objectives.

HEMISPHERIC ECONOMIC DEVELOPMENT

Social and Economic Backwardness in the Americas

By the 1960s, it had become belatedly evident to policy-makers in the United States that many of the hemispheric problems we have identified—the accusation that Washington had "neglected" its neighbors, threats to the security of the American republics, challenges to democracy by right-wing and left-wing groups—had their origins in Latin American social and economic backwardness. In contrast to Africa, the Middle East, and Asia, most of the states throughout Latin America have been independent for some 150 years. Except for societies in the Caribbean area, before World War II the American republics had a higher standard of living than prevailed in the Afro–Asian world. For several years prior to the war, Latin America achieved a reasonably impressive record of economic growth; the expansion in manufacturing was especially marked; farm output increased less rapidly, in some countries barely exceeding population growth. Through the early 1950s, Latin American exports generated high earnings, although the region's share of total world exports began to decline (falling by almost 50 percent from 1948 to 1968). In many Latin American nations, however, larger export earnings were more than offset by even more rapidly rising *imports*. This imbalance contributed to inflation, proved economically unstabilizing, and impeded Latin America's ability to accumulate savings for national development.[69]

A root cause of Latin America's deteriorating social and economic condition was the accelerating rate of population increase. Although it did not have the largest population *base* (Asia held that distinction), Latin America epitomized the "population explosion": Population growth rates tended to be higher than in any other region of the world. From an annual growth rate of 1.9 percent in 1920 and 1930, Latin America's population increase grew to 2.3 percent annually by the 1940s; it climbed to 2.8 percent annually in the 1950s; and it reached 2.9 percent annually in the 1960s. The rate for the 1960s was almost 50 percent greater than the *highest* anticipated population growth rate for the world (2.1 percent) by the year 2000![70]

Few individuals living in the United States or Western Europe are in a position to comprehend the momentous, not to say disastrous, implications of the kind of population growth rates prevalent in Latin America today. A population expanding at the modest rate of 1.5 percent annually will double in size within approximately a half-century; if the yearly growth rate is 2.0 percent, it will double within 35 years; a 2.5 percent rate means that the population will double within 28 years; and an increase of 3.0 percent each year—close to the rate for Latin America as a whole, but *less* than the rate for several countries in the region—will reproduce the population in only 23 years.[71] A few Latin American societies in recent years—Costa Rica, Brazil, and Haiti are examples—have expanded their populations by 3.5 to 4.0 annually; at such rates, these countries will double their populations in less than two decades![72]

With the population of most Latin American countries growing at approximately 2.9 percent annually, the region will have some 378 million people by the year 1980; and by the year 2000, projections of Latin America's total population range from 532 million to 686 million, depending upon the kind of assumptions made concerning developments in the area during the next generation. Projections based upon "high" assumptions indicate that, by the year 2000, Latin America will have more than 9 percent of the world's people, versus some 6.5 percent in 1965.*

*The student should bear in mind that population projections are, at best, approximations. They are calculations which are normally based upon *present* population growth rates applied to a given demographic base. Normally, such projections are based upon several sets of differing assumptions. For example, one projection may envision some slowdown in population increase; it will make "low assumptions" of future population increase. At the other end of the scale, the application of "high assumptions" will of course yield a significantly higher

Nearly every aspect of life in Latin American societies is adversely affected by unchecked population growth. Educational facilities throughout the region are in general already overcrowded and inadequate. In 1961, only half of Latin America's youth attended school at all; and of this proportion, only one-fifth completed over two years of elementary school. By 1975, most Latin American nations will face a substantial increase (30 to 60 percent over 1960) in their school-age populations. Governments will be required to expand educational facilities merely to *avert a decline* in per capita educational resources and to preserve what are often low literacy rates.[73] Health and sanitary services throughout the region face the same challenge. Bolivia has six times the number of inhabitants per doctor, Guatemala eight times, and Haiti twelve times, as does the United States. Life expectancy in Argentina is some 51 years, in Brazil it is 36 years, in Mexico 34 years, in Haiti 29 years—versus 66 years for the average citizen in the United States.[74] In order to prevent a deterioration in already minimal (and in some areas clearly inadequate) health facilities, Latin American governments will need to double their expenditures (at constant prices) over the next generation. Improving such services on a per capita basis could easily entail a threefold, fourfold, or greater increase in expenditures.

High unemployment, rapid urbanization (with the accompanying problem of slum conditions in nearly every Latin American city), chronic housing shortages, a widening gulf between the "have" and "have-not" segments of society, deepening backwardness in the rural areas—these are to some extent all functions of the population explosion in the Western Hemisphere. Among the Malthusian implications of runaway population growth, however, none is more urgent than the elemental challenge of providing food for Latin America's people, many of whom are already undernourished. By the early 1960s, Western agricultural experts had become deeply concerned about a "world food crisis."[75] Except for North America, Western Europe, and a small number of nations outside these zones, societies (including Soviet Russia) were proving incapable of satisfying their food needs. While scientific agriculture and modern technology promised to alleviate this growing food shortage (several Asian

countries, for example, had raised agricultural output significantly with new strains of "miracle rice"), the probability still existed that food scarcities would become worse, perhaps producing famine conditions in some countries. For the less developed regions of the world as a whole, per capita food output slightly exceeded population growth during the 1960s. Yet in this group of societies—embracing two-thirds of mankind—the average person consumed half the over-all caloric intake and one-fifth the vital protein intake of his counterpart in the developed world. Merely to *hold* food consumption at this minimal level, by the year 2000 Latin America must expand its grain supplies by over 200 percent. To make a real breakthrough in raising dietary standards (particularly in protein intake), a 400 percent increase would be required![76] Yet by the late 1960s, in several Latin American nations per capita food production was already lagging behind population growth. For the region as a whole, from 1962 to 1965 per capita agricultural output grew by only one-tenth of 1 percent; food imports into the region were rising steadily, creating balance-of-payments problems and curtailing the ability of societies to amass development capital. Despite great agricultural potential, Latin America lagged behind the world average in grain and certain other major agricultural yields.[77] In 1969, the UN Economic Commission for Latin America found that, while the American republics had made some noteworthy economic advances during the 1960s, progress in raising farm output, in promoting land reform, and in taking other steps necessary to raise agricultural levels had been minimal.[78] In common with other developing regions, Latin American governments were likely to discover that rural problems were at once the most *intractable*, and in many ways the most *urgent*, of all those impeding national development.

The Alliance for Progress

By the late 1950s, officials in the United States had become deeply concerned about conditions in the other American republics. An ominous portent of impending political explosions was provided by Vice President Nixon's "good-will tour" of Latin America in 1958. The trip was marked by a number of violent incidents; instead of good will, he encountered widespread disaffection because of Washington's neglect of the region's economic and social needs.[79] A few months later, the report submitted by a fact-finding mission directed by Dr. Milton Eisenhower confirmed the existence of a worsening crisis in inter-American relations; a report submitted to the Senate Foreign Relations Committee in the same period also underscored the region's economic problems and the likelihood of growing political upheavals.[80] The communization of Cuba under Fidél Castro in this

total population for the future; reliance upon "medium" assumptions will yield a projected future population somewhere in between these extremes. While there is nothing deterministic or inevitable about the population explosion in Latin America or other areas, by 1970 with some exceptions few societies in the "third world" had successfully curtailed population growth; there was no reason to expect *early* progress in reducing such rates of population expansion. For various projections of the future populations of the major regions of the world, see Philip M. Hauser, ed., *Overcoming World Hunger* (Englewood Cliffs, N.J.: Prentice-Hall, 1963), pp. 16–17.

period supplied additional evidence of Latin America's political instability and vulne ability. Latin American leaders themselves warned Washington that—in the absence of some new and constructive approach to the region's problems—violence and revolutionary unrest would become inevitable.[81]

With these realities in mind, the Kennedy administration concluded that the time was overdue for a fundamental reorientation concerning the problem of Latin America by the United States. North Americans, the President confessed, had "not always grasped the significance" of the needs of their southern neighbors, just as the latter had "not always understood the urgency of the need to lift people from poverty and ignorance and despair." Accordingly, on March 13, 1961, Kennedy proposed what he labeled "a vast new 10-year plan for the Americas, to transform the 1960s into a historic decade of democratic progress." If successful, at the end of the decade the plan would witness "the beginning of a new era in the American experience. . . . [E]very American republic will be the master of its own revolution and its own hope and progress." Kennedy's proposal was soon known as the Alliance for Progress. Like the Marshall Plan that had revitalized Western Europe in the early postwar period, the Alliance for Progress emphasized *mutual collaboration* among the participants and accorded a key role to maximum self-help by the recipients of American economic aid. Among the ten points cited by the President as fundamental to the plan, key ones were: regional planning by the Inter-American Economic and Social Council; an initial allocation by the United States of $500 million to launch the Alliance for Progress; increased economic integration and cooperation among nations in the Western Hemisphere; and an attempt to stabilize the commodity market for Latin American exports.

The most far-reaching change contemplated by the Alliance for Progress, however, was its implicit demand for nothing less than a social and economic revolution throughout Latin America. It demanded "vital social change" in this region; its funds would be used to "improve productivity and use of . . . land," to "attack archaic tax and land-tenure structures," and to assure "abundance to all" throughout the region. In short, successful fulfillment of the projected goals demanded a radical reconstruction of traditional Latin American society, in which oligarchies based upon vast land holdings and ancient privilege would be eliminated, personal fortunes that had traditionally been used for luxuries or had been invested overseas would be directed into national development, and sweeping transformations in all levels of society would usher in an age of equal opportunities for all. To carry out this ambitious ten-year scheme, President Kennedy pledged the United States to supply $10 billion in governmental funds, to be supplemented by an additional $10 billion from other public and private sources for Latin American economic development. Thus from the beginning, the role of *private investment capital* was recognized as indispensable in promoting economic progress in the southern zone of the hemisphere. The charter formally establishing the Alliance for Progress was signed by all the American republics (except Cuba) at Punta del Este on August 17, 1961. Latin American countries themselves were expected to furnish some 80 percent of the resources needed to achieve the program's goals.[82]

Only a few months were required before the Alliance for Progress began to suffer from a "credibility gap" which became steadily more pronounced. If officials in the Western Hemisphere had not realized it in the beginning, it soon was obvious that the "modernization" of Latin America was a very different matter from the postwar "reconstruction" of Western Europe—a region where, prior to World War II, the level of industrialization had been high, scientific and technological ability was impressive, social mobility existed, and (with some exceptions) reasonable political stability prevailed. A crucial difference between the Alliance for Progress and the European Recovery Program was that the governments and peoples of Europe were deeply committed to the goal of reconstruction; with assistance from the United States, they had provided the great preponderance of resources, energy, and administrative skill required to make the ERP an outstanding success. By contrast, experience with the Alliance for Progress soon highlighted the fact that many governments in the Western Hemisphere either would not or (because of the opposition of conservative oligarchies, the vested interests of the regimes themselves, ongoing political upheaval, or other reasons) could not undertake the kind of "controlled revolution" which the Alliance for Progress envisioned. Admittedly, the challenge confronting the Latin American nations was *infinitely more difficult* than was true of Western Europe in the early postwar period. Most Latin American societies lacked adequate administrative systems; for centuries, governments in the area had been plagued with corruption, favoritism, and maladministration. Ongoing political turbulence destroyed the continuity of programs and perhaps inescapably compelled incumbent governments to be cautious and to shun major innovations. Economic and social conditions throughout much of Latin America approximated those prevailing in Europe during the Middle Ages. By the 1960s, conditions in the world market had become highly adverse to Latin America and other less developed areas; within a number of Latin American societies, inflation threatened to "get out of control," precipitating new economic strains and political instability. The allocation of development funds sometimes exacerbated rural–urban tensions (with masses in the rural areas increasingly resentful of the central government's indifference toward their poverty and backwardness). Foreign corporations and other private investors often found Latin America's investment climate unprofitable and unappealing—particularly after a rash of nationalization decrees by Latin American governments jeopardized foreign assets in the late 1960s. Unfortunately for the other American republics, the Alliance for Progress was also launched at a time when the United States Congress and segments of United States opinion were becoming disenchanted with foreign aid programs generally, in large part because the results achieved with them (outside Western Europe) often seemed minimal; growing involvement in the Vietnam War perhaps inevitably decreed a new period of "neglect" of hemispheric problems by the United States. Above all, perhaps, the Alliance for Progress never acquired the kind of *mystique* engendered by the Marshall Plan in Europe. The program lacked popular support throughout Latin America; powerfully entrenched interests in Latin American society (like the landowners and some business groups) remained opposed to it; Marxist and other revolutionary political forces denounced it; the United States itself sometimes discouraged public support for it by such moves as the intervention in the Dominican Republic. In brief, the alliance lacked the kind of *public consensus* upon which the success of the European Recovery Program had been based.

Despite these limitations, during the 1960s the Alliance for Progress unquestionably made some gains in achieving its objectives. By the midway point in the program, the *over-all* economic growth rate for Latin American countries had surpassed the annual rate of 2.5 percent projected for the alliance, although several nations in the area failed to attain this rate of economic advancement.[83] And by 1969, the average yearly growth in the gross national products for the American republics (excluding the United States) collectively was almost 5 percent—higher than the rates currently existing in the United States, Western Europe, and Africa. Significant progress could also be detected in the purification of water supplies, in the eradication of malaria and other health hazards, and the extension of medical services throughout the hemisphere. In nearly every country participating in the alliance, expenditures for education were rising rapidly—in some instances reaching twice the level achieved before 1961. Expansion in "infrastructure"—new electric power facilities, improved transportation networks, better communications systems—had also been commendable. In several Latin American nations industrial growth was also impressive,

although in others it was moving only slowly ahead.[84] National and local governments throughout the region were gaining experience and expertise in mobilizing and utilizing resources for development. Several countries (Brazil and Chile were prominent examples) were progressing in the campaign against ruinous inflation. A number of American republics had attracted significant quantities of private investment capital, although in a few Latin American nations (Peru and Bolivia could be cited) governmental policies inhibited private investments from abroad. An official of the United States who had been deeply involved with the Latin American area for many years said in 1968 that more progress had been made there since the Alliance for Progress was launched—in spheres like land reform, the reorganization of tax systems, the improvement of government administration, and the extension of health and educational services—than had been made during the preceding quarter-century.[85] In most of the American republics, domestic savings had climbed impressively. By 1969, the Latin American nations themselves had contributed a total of some $115 billion (or 90 percent of *all* funds available for national and regional development) to various development programs; this was well in excess of the $80 billion originally envisioned by the Alliance for Progress.[86] The end of the 1960s found most over-all economic indicators moving upward; Latin American exports were expanding and earning higher sales prices abroad. In the political realm, externally promoted revolutionary activities throughout Latin America had thus far achieved little or no success.

Regional Integration in the Western Hemisphere

The 1960s also witnessed impressive activity—and some noteworthy gains—in another sphere: regional economic cooperation and integration. In reality, Latin America mirrored the experience of postwar Europe by initially creating several schemes for regional economic collaboration. The first was the Central American Common Market (CACM), proposed early in the 1950s and finally established in 1959. The CACM gradually broadened its activities to fiscal and economic cooperation among its members, while pursuing its original goal of removing obstacles to free trade in the Central American area.* A Central American Bank for Economic Integration operates under CACM auspices. A novel feature of the CACM is its goal of creating "integrated industries"; traditionally dependent upon "one-crop" agricultural enterprises, the countries involved were gener-

---

*Members of the CACM are Guatemala, El Salvador, Nicaragua, Honduras, Costa Rica; Panama does not belong to the organization.

ally unable to establish and operate industries efficiently on a purely national basis. As time passed, the CACM achieved a significant expansion in trade among its members, although political rivalries and conflicts in the area tended to overshadow economic gains by the organization.[87]

With the strong encouragement of the United States, the nations of South America also sought to promote economic collaboration on a regional basis. Early in 1960, in the Treaty of Montevideo, they set up the Latin American Free Trade Association (LAFTA).* LAFTA's members produced four-fifths of Latin America's total goods and services. This organization sought to remove tariff and other trade restrictions and to encourage expanded trade among the members.[88] Developments soon made it apparent that LAFTA faced a difficult challenge likely to last for several years, possibly decades. Trade obstacles were prevalent, and often deeply embedded, throughout Latin America. Euthusiasm for removing them varied widely among LAFTA's members. Thus a Mexican economist asked candidly: "Can development be undertaken better, or sooner, by creating conditions for freer trade among the Latin American countries or by leaving each country to its own devices?"[89] The example of the European Common Market provided persuasive evidence that *regional* economic integration had many advantages; this organization served both as a *model* for Latin American efforts and as a *threat* to the well-being of regions which failed to overcome purely national approaches to economic problems. Despite the example of regional integration in Europe, however, it was clear that national sovereignty remained deeply rooted in Latin America and that some governments were unable to participate in LAFTA on anything more than a token basis.

Besides the CACM and LAFTA, smaller regional organizations had evolved in Latin America or were being discussed. A very old ideal came to fruition when the Andean group—consisting of Venezuela, Colombia, Ecudor. Peru, Bolivia, and Chile—was created in 1969 to facilitate economic collaboration among its members. The River Plate countries—Brazil, Argentina, Uruguay, Paraguay, and Bolivia—were also exploring the possibility of creating a comparable organization.[90] The Caribbean area witnessed another subregional group designed to promote free trade among its members.[91]

What have these steps in the direction of regional economic integration and collaboration in the Americas actually accomplished? The Alliance for Progress anticipated that a Latin American common market would begin operations by 1985. Several regional and subregional schemes for reaching that objective have been agreed upon by the Latin American nations; organizational frameworks have been established; and some limited progress has been made by the CACM and (to a lesser extent) by LAFTA. Beyond these results, progress in implementing the idea of regional economic cooperation has been minimal. During the first half of the 1960s, the CACM made impressive strides in facilitating trade among its members. But by the end of the decade, the unity and future of the organization had been called into question because of the war between El Salvador and Honduras; momentum in achieving other goals—like improving the members' balance-of-payments positions and establishing viable "integrated industries"—had been slowed down. Nor had proposed cooperation between the CACM and LAFTA been carried further than the discussion stage. As for LAFTA itself, the organization had been increasingly confronted with an inescapable and troublesome reality plaguing efforts to concert hemispheric economic activities: *The growing disparity in the economic performances and capabilities of the American republics.* The giants of Latin America, like Brazil and Argentina, favored the rapid elimination of trade barriers; these countries were sufficiently large and economically diversified to run the risks involved and to benefit from such steps. Countries like Bolivia and Ecuador, however, were much more reluctant and fearful; governments in the smaller Latin American nations were concerned that the elimination of tariffs and other restraints upon trade would jeopardize already vulnerable domestic industries and would result in accelerating expenditures for imports. As in other regions, economic growth among the nations of Latin America has been *highly uneven;* assuming that this trend will continue, as seems likely, disparities among the southern neighbors of the United States will probably become even sharper with the passage of time. Moreover, trade by the Latin American nations has encountered two major obstacles: growing competition from the products sold abroad by Afro–Asian countries; and massive restrictions against exports from Latin America (except for raw materials and agricultural commodities) in the United States and Western Europe. By the end of the 1960s, Latin America's share of total world exports had declined markedly, from 11 percent in 1959 to 5.1 percent by 1969.[92] Such distrubing trends prompted the Rockefeller study group in 1969 to urge that the

---

*The original signatories of the Montevideo Treaty creating LAFTA were Agentina, Brazil, Chile, Paraguay, Peru, Uruguay, and Mexico; in the months which followed, Colombia, Ecuador, Venezuela, and Bolivia joined the organization. For a discussion of the problems which have beset the organization, see Miguel Teubal, "The Failure of Latin America's Economic Integration," in James Petras and Maurice Zeitlin, eds., *Latin America: Reform or Revolution?* (New York: Fawcett World Library, 1968), pp. 120–144. See also John M. Hunter, "Latin American Integration and the Alliance," *Current History* 53 (November, 1967), pp. 257–263.

Nixon administration grant the other American republics substantial trade concessions, without which hemispheric integration schemes would probably achieve little. While the White House supported such recommendations, the congressional reaction to them, along with other pleas for a lowering of trade barriers by the United States, was likely to be at best cautious and skeptical.

Hemispheric Progress: The Road Ahead

What were the prospects for Latin America and inter-American relations during the 1970s and beyond? In over-all terms, the Rockefeller study mission painted a grim picture of developments in the Western Hemisphere in the future, unless the bulk of some 83 recommendations included in its final report were adopted by the President and Congress. These recommendations covered a broad spectrum of substantive issues in inter-American relations—from the reorganization of foreign policy machinery in Washington concerned with Latin American affairs; to encouragement of regional economic collaboration within the hemisphere; to revitalization of the Organization of American States; to greater commitment by the President and his subordinates to providing "moral leadership as a force for freedom and justice in the Americas"; to the elimination of tariffs, quotas, and other restrictions impeding greater trade between the United States and the other American republics.[93] Failure by executive and legislative policy-makers in the United States to adopt these proposals, and to implement them effectively, Governor Rockefeller testified in 1969, would result in "utter chaos" throughout the Americas.[94]

That this prediction was not exaggerated was confirmed by persuasive evidence that conditions in Latin America had, on balance, *deteriorated seriously* since the early 1960s. The Alliance for Progress, we have already pointed out, had some gains to its credit. But it was equally apparent that these had done nothing to change fundamental conditions in most Latin American societies. A number of the American republics were doing little more than holding their own against the population explosion and its social and economic consequences; some countries were not doing even this well. If there existed a key problem impairing Latin American development (and in reality, there were of course *many* basic problems) it was unchecked population growth. As we have mentioned, collectively, the Latin American nations continued to lead all other regions in the *rate* of population expansion. From 1960–1970, the region's population grew by some 35 percent; this same percentage increase was anticipated for 1970–1980. Consequently, the demands upon Latin American governments for health, educational, and other services continued to mount; the

percentage of young people in Latin American societies—where dissatisfaction with existing conditions and determination to change them were often most deeply felt—became larger with each passing year; unemployment levels (reaching from 25 to 40 percent of the labor force in some Latin American societies) remained alarmingly high; urban centers—whose rate of population increase was often two or three times the national rate—fell further behind in meeting the demands for jobs, housing, and other necessities. Throughout Latin America, reliance upon violence to express mass discontent and demands for change was on the increase, particularly in the cities. Revolutionary agitation by Marxist and non-Marxist groups showed no sign of diminishing. Latin American suspicion and hostility toward the United States and Yankee business corporations remained ubiquitous; in some countries (as in Peru and Bolivia) they reached the point of acute tension and possible diplomatic rupture. In many Latin American nations, the payment of interest and repayment of principal owed on government and private assistance already received produced a *net outflow* of capital.

For several years to come, therefore, it seems relatively certain that Latin America will remain in ferment. South of the United States, political upheavals can be expected to continue—perhaps even *increase*, as mass expectations outpace the ability of governments in the area to solve social and economic problems. Thus far, efforts to curb runaway population growth have had little or no impact; and even if the required steps are energetically fostered by governments and private groups concerned about the "Malthusian trap," several years will be needed before such measures really begin to reverse the upward curve of population expansion.

Inter-American relations are also likely to remain characterized by misunderstandings, controversies, and sometimes acute tensions. Justifiably or not, governments and masses throughout the Western Hemisphere hold the United States in large part "responsible" for Latin America's social and economic backwardness, its recurrent political instability, and its other manifold problems. Both historically and in the postwar era, some of these grievances are unquestionably warranted. From the era of "big stick" diplomacy during the early 1900s to Washington's intervention in the Dominican Republic in 1965, the response of the United States to Latin American problems has perhaps properly induced an attitude of resentment, fear, and distrust among its neighbors. As a great power with *global* commitments, the United States has inevitably neglected its friends in the Western Hemisphere and failed to satisfy *their* expectations with regard to a proper scale of diplomatic and economic priorities. If considerations of cold war strategy have sometimes influenced Washington's economic and military aid programs unduly, it is no less true (as some Latin Americans have difficulty understanding) that cold war threats to the security of the non-Communist world *do* exist and that they have to be met by a massive and sustained response by the United States. Nevertheless, as the Rockefeller mission emphasized, by the 1970s the United States could take a series of steps calculated to improve the atmosphere of inter-American relations and to facilitate Latin America's quest for modernization and democracy.

At the same time, relations among the American republics are unlikely to become harmonious and constructive until societies south of the United States accept a reality which emerged after many years of frustrating conflict in Vietnam: The power of the United States is *finite* and often heavily *circumscribed* in what it can achieve outside its own borders. Policy-makers in Washington are not the only ones who need to be disabused of "the illusion of American omnipotence." Governments, political elites, and masses overseas are sometimes no less prone to exaggerate the scope and effectiveness of the power of the United States—to the point of believing on occasion that it is the crucial element in successful modernization or the key ingredient in achieving political stability. Undoubtedly, the United States can *assist* Latin America and other less developed regions to accomplish their objectives. Decisions made in Washington will sometimes incontestably either encourage or hamper efforts by governments in the Western Hemisphere to move into (or toward) the twentieth century.

Yet the United States cannot make Latin American governments more efficient or less plagued by corruption; it cannot revise and enforce tax laws for the other American republics; it cannot make economic elites in the area more prone to place the welfare of society ahead of private gain; it cannot curb unrealistic mass aspirations concerning what governments ought to achieve over a short interval of time; it cannot prevent disaffected political groups from soliciting the aid of military elites to gain control of the government; it cannot *compel* its neighbors to forego long-standing rivalries and jealousies in order to achieve regional economic integration; it cannot formulate and carry out land reform programs for Latin American societies; it cannot inhibit the tendency for many groups in Latin America to use Yankee-phobia as a scapegoat for their own lack of discipline or constructive solutions to problems. In short, the United States cannot unilaterally "save" or modernize the societies of Latin America. Whether the goals of societies throughout this region are achieved will be determined, in the last analysis, largely by decisions made by the governments and peoples in Latin America themselves.

NOTES

1. Peter Nehemkis, *Latin America: Myth or Reality* (New York: New American Library, 1966), p. 18. The views of Presidents Kennedy and Johnson are cited on p. 15.
2. *The New York Times* (June 12, 1969).
3. The findings and recommendations of the Rockefeller study mission on Latin America are included in: *The New York Times, The Rockefeller Report on the Americas* (Chicago: Quandrangle, 1969), *passim;* excerpts from the mission's report are available in *The New York Times* (November 10 and 16, 1969).
4. James W. Gantenbein, *The Evolution of Our Latin-American Policy* (New York: Columbia University Press, 1950), p. 324. A helpful compendium of official sources on historic U.S. policy in Latin America.
5. Julius W. Pratt, *A History of United States Foreign Policy* (Englewood Cliffs, N.J.: Prentice-Hall, 1955), pp. 180–181.
6. Gantenbein, *op. cit.*, pp. 371–372.
7. *Ibid.*, pp. 387–388.
8. *Ibid.*, p. 330. Italics added.
9. *Ibid.*, pp. 344–348.
10. *Ibid.*, pp. 360–364.
11. *Ibid.*, p. 208.
12. *Ibid.*, pp. 401–407, 165–166.
13. Pratt, *op. cit.*, pp. 181–183, 346.
14. *Ibid.*, pp. 610–611, 765; Gantenbein, *op. cit.*, p. 285.
15. Pratt, *op. cit.*, pp. 767–768.
16. Department of State, *Sovereignty and Interdependence in the New World*, no. 3054, Inter-American Series, vol. 35, (1948), pp. 157–163. This document traces out the evolution and operation of the Inter-American system.
17. *Ibid.*, pp. 165–168.
18. John C. Drier, *The Organization of American States: The Hemispheric Crisis* (New York: Harper & Row, 1962), p. 58.
19. For these and other examples of cases handled by the OAS dealing with hemispheric peace and security, see *ibid.*, pp. 58–68.
20. For discussions of the dispute between the United States and Panama, see *The New York Times* (January 19, 26, and 28; February 3, 7, 9, and 27; March 14, 15, and 16, 1964).
21. For analyses of the challenge presented to the OAS by the Dominican crisis, see G. Connell-Smith, "OAS and the Dominican Crisis," *World Today* 21 (June, 1965), 229–236; and J. Slater, "The United States, the Organization of American States, and the Dominican Republic, 1961–1963," *International Organization* 18 (Spring, 1964), 268–291.
22. For discussions of the activities of the OAS in dealing with the conflict between El Salvador and Honduras, see *The New York Times* (July 16, 24, 30, and August 3, 1969).
23. O. C. Stoetzer, *The Organization of American States* (New York: Praeger, 1965), pp. 76–77.
24. Drier, *op. cit.*, p. 91.
25. Dulles' judgment is quoted in *ibid.*, p. 92.

26. See *The New York Times* (November 24, 1965; March 13, 1966; and February 23, 1967).

27. John Gerassi, *The Great Fear in Latin America* (New York: Macmillan, 1965), pp. 306–307.

28. For an enlightening appraisal of Communism in Latin America, including recent data on the strength of Marxist parties in the area, see Federico G. Gil, "Communism in Latin America," in Dan N. Jacobs, ed., *The New Communisms* (New York: Harper & Row, 1969), pp. 184–210.

29. Our discussion of the Communist victory in Chile is based upon the treatment in *The New York Times*, September 23, October 3, and November 26, 1970; April 11, 1971. For a more comprehensive discussion, see Claudio Véliz, "The Chilean Experiment," *Foreign Affairs*, **49** (April, 1971), 442–454.

30. For the Eisenhower administration's assessment of developments in Guatemala, see Dwight D. Eisenhower, *Mandate for Change* (Garden City, N.Y.: Doubleday, 1963), pp. 420–427.

31. Department of State, *Intervention of International Communism in Guatemala*, no. 5556, Inter-American Series, vol. 48 (1954). p. 49. This document presents the State Department's "case" against the Arbenz regime in Guatemala.

32. *Survey of International Affairs:1954*, (New York: Oxford University Press, 1956), pp. 376–378.

33. *United States in World Affairs:1954* (New York: Harper & Row, 1955), p. 372.

34. Dept. of State, *Intervention of International Communism in Guatemala, op. cit.*, p. 30.

35. Department of State, *American Foreign Policy:* 1950–55, no. 6446, General Foreign Policy Series, vol. 117 (1957), p. 1292

36. *Ibid.*, p. 1301.

37. *Ibid.*, p. 1308.

38. *Ibid.*, p. 1315.

39. Frederick B. Pike, "Guatemala, the United States, and Communism in the Americas," *Review of Politics* 17 (April, 1955), 258–259. An illuminating analysis of many aspects of the Guatemalan crisis.

40. See the views of Dan Kurzman, as cited in Eduardo Galeano, "With the Guerrillas in Guatemala," in James Petras and Maurice Zeitlin, *Latin America: Reform or Revolution?* (New York: Fawcett Publications, 1968), pp. 374–375; see also Mario Rodriguez, "Guatemala in Perspective," *Current History* **51** (December, 1966), pp. 338–344.

41. See *The New York Times* (November 4, 13, and 14, 1966).

42. *The New York Times* (January 21 and September 8, 1968).

43. The Bay of Pigs episode is described more fully in Hugh Sidey, *John F. Kennedy: President* (New York: Atheneum, 1963), pp. 124–144.

44. See the text of President Kennedy's broadcast to the American people on October 22, 1962, in David L. Larson, ed., *The "Cuban Crisis" of 1962* (Boston: Houghton Mifflin, 1963), pp. 41–46.

45. Sidey, *op. cit.*, p. 346.

46. See President Johnson's message on May 2, 1965, explaining the intervention in the Dominican Republic, in *Documents on American Foreign Relations: 1965* (New York: Harper & Row, 1966), pp. 241–247.

47. For a comprehensive and sympathetic treatment of events leading up to America's intervention in the Dominican crisis, written by a former diplomatic official, see John Bartlow Martin, *Overtaken by Events* (Garden City, N.Y.: Doubleday, 1966), esp. pp. 705–743. A highly critical account of the intervention is Richard J. Barnet, *Intervention and Revolution: America's Confrontation with Insurgent Movements Around the World* (New York: World Publishing, 1968), pp. 153–181. Another indictment—the basic theme of which is that in the future, as in the past, the United States wished to dominate Dominican affairs —is Fred Goff and Michael Locker, "The Violence of Domination: U.S. Power and the Dominican Republic," in Irving L. Horowitz *et al.*, eds., *Latin American Radicalism* (New York: Random House, 1969), pp. 249–291.

48. *United States in World Affairs: 1965* (New York: Harper & Row, 1966), pp. 82–83.

49. The Johnson Doctrine was stated as a paragraph in the President's speech, included in *Documents on American Foreign Relations: 1965* (New York: Harper & Row, 1966), p. 245.

50. *The New York Times* (November 5, 1969), dispatch by Juan de Onis.

51. Quoted in *The New York Times* (July 7, 1968), dispatch by Paul L. Montgomery.

52. *The New York Times* (October 15, 1967).

53. *The New York Times* (July 7, 1968).

54. *The New York Times* (September 2, 1968), dispatch by Malcolm W. Browne.

55. For Wilson's views on the Huerta regime in Mexico, and his commentary on the crisis in Mexican–American relations, see Thomas A. Bailey, *A Diplomatic History of the American People*, 8th ed. (New York: Appleton-Century-Crofts, 1969), pp. 554–560; and Pratt, *op. cit.*, pp. 426–431.

56. J. Warren Nystrom and Nathan A. Haverstock, eds., *The Alliance for Progress* (Princeton, N.J.: Van Nostrand Reinhold, 1966), p. 23.

57. See Gantenbein, *op. cit.*, pp. 165–166, 401–407.

58. Dexter Perkins, *The United States and the Caribbean* (Cambridge, Mass.: Harvard University Press, 1947), p. 165.

59. Theodore Sorensen, *Kennedy* (New York: Harper & Row, 1965), pp. 535–536.

60. See *Newsweek* LXXV (January 5, 1970), 26.

61. *The New York Times* (November 2, 1969), dispatch by Malcolm W. Browne.

62. Alexander, *op. cit.*, pp. 168–169.

63. Nehemkis, *op. cit.*, p. 58. Italics in original.

64. Our treatment of the *caudillo* system depends heavily upon Alexander, *op. cit.*, pp. 168–171; and Frank Tannenbaum, *Ten Keys to Latin America* (New York Random House, 1966), pp. 112–172.

65. See the excerpt from the findings of the Rockefeller study mission, in *The New York Times* (November 10, 1969).

66. *The New York Times* (December 31, 1969), dispatch by Joseph Novitski.

67. See *idem;* and Alexander, *op. cit.*, pp. 171–177.

68. For an able exposition of the dangers inherent in militarism in the Western Hemisphere, and a critical interpretation of the "new military" in Latin America, see Irving L. Horowitz, "The Military Elites," in Seymour M. Lipset and Aldo Solari, eds , *Elites in Latin America* (New York: Oxford University Press, 1967), pp. 146–190.

69. See the data on economic and social conditions in Latin America prior to World War II, in Report of the Commission on International Development, *Partners in Development* (New York: Praeger, 1969), pp. 237–260.

70. *Ibid.*, p. 239; and Clifford M. Hardin, ed., *Overcoming World Hunger* (Englewood Cliffs, N.J.: Prentice-Hall, 1969), p. 15.

71. Garrett Hardin, ed., *Population, Evolution, and Birth Control* (San Francisco: W. H. Freeman, n.d.), p. 21.

72. Gerassi, *op. cit.*, p. 36.

73. Philip M. Hauser, ed., *The Population Dilemma* (Englewood Cliffs, N.J.: Prentice-Hall, 1963), p. 40.

74. Gerassi, *op. cit.*, pp. 36–37.

75. The growing global food shortage is the basic theme of Hardin, *Overcoming World Hunger, op. cit., passim.*

76. See *ibid.*, p. 59.

77. See *U.S. News and World Report* LXII (April 17, 1967), 36.

78. *The New York Times* (April 20, 1969).

79. Vice President Nixon's "good will tour" of Latin America in 1958 is discussed in Dwight D. Eisenhower, *Waging Peace* (Garden City, N.Y.: Doubleday, 1965), pp. 519–520.

80. Dr. Milton Eisenhower's study mission to Latin America is treated in *ibid.*, pp. 514–539; for other warnings about conditions south of the border in this period, see Senate Foreign Relations Committee, *Latin America: Venezuela, Brazil, Peru, Bolivia, and Panama*, 86th Congress, 2nd Session, 1960, *passim.*

81. Quoted in William Benton, *The Voice of Latin America* (New York: Harper & Row, 1961), p. 147.

82. See the text of President Kennedy's message outlining the nature and goals of the Alliance for Progress in *Documents on American Foreign Relations: 1961* (New York: Harper & Row, 1962), pp. 395–408; see also Department of State, *Report to the Congress on the Foreign Assistance Program for Fiscal Year 1962* (Washington, D.C.: U.S. Government Printing Office, 1963), pp. 7–8.

83. Lincoln Gordon, "Inter-American Cooperation: the Road Ahead," *Department of State Bulletin* LV (December 26, 1966), 946–952; and *The Rockefeller Report on the Americas, op. cit.*, pp. 67–68.

84. Lincoln Gordon, "Alliance for Progress: Next Steps for Effective Action," *Department of State Bulletin* LIV (May 9, 1966), 740.

85. See the views of Sol M. Linowitz, in *The New York Times* (February 28, 1968).

86. *The New York Times* (January 20, 1969), dispatch by Robert J. Cole.

87. *The New York Times* (February 4, 1969).

88. For discussions of the Central American Common Market, see *The Rockefeller Report on the Americas*, p. 51; and *The New York Times* (January 20 and November 11, 1969).

89. See the views of Victor Urquidi in *The New York Times* (April 10, 1967).

90. *The New York Times* (April 16, 1969).

91. *Idem;* and *The Rockefeller Report on the Americas, op. cit.*, p. 51.

92. See *The New York Times* (April 20, 1969).

93. For the mission's detailed recommendations to the White House concerning needed changes in the policy of the United States toward Latin America, see *The Rockefeller Report on the Americas, op. cit.*, pp. 57–140.

94. *The New York Times* (November 16, 1969).

Thirteen
ASIA: New Nations and Ancient Problems

ASIA IN PREWAR AMERICAN FOREIGN POLICY

In the turbulent postwar period no region has presented the United States with so many diplomatic challenges as has that far-flung arc of territories extending from Afghanistan to Japan and southward to Indonesia and the Philippines. As in the Middle East, the United States has been compelled to formulate viable policies toward countries and problems in this area when swiftly unfolding events often left very little time for working out intelligent decisions.

Guidelines from earlier diplomatic experience toward Asia unfortunately offered minimum help to American policy-makers in today's world. Some authorities doubt whether, prior to World War II, the United States ever possessed what can meaningfully be called a "foreign policy" toward Asia in the sense of a realistic conception of its diplomatic interests there, together with reasonably effective methods for advancing them. Broad segments of American public opinion and even influential political and government leaders tend to seek guidance for contemporary policy in America's historic relations with Asia. Their attachment to images and conceptions derived from this experience goes far toward explaining many of the nation's policy inadequacies in that vital region during recent years. Let us look briefly at the highlights of America's relations with Asia in the past.

Three episodes were of singular importance: Commodore Perry's opening of Japan to Western influence; proclamation of the Open Door policy toward China; and America's acquisition of the Philippines and other strategic bases in the Pacific. The visit of an American naval expedition under Commodore Perry to Japan in the mid-1850s climaxed a period of westward continental expansion at home. By 1848 the United States had acquired a 1200-mile Pacific coastline, thereby whetting its interest in the affairs of Asia. Perry's visits in 1853–1854 at last forced the hermitlike kingdom of Japan to open its doors to Western influence and, more specifically, to trade with the outside world.[1] In the years following Perry's visit, Japan became America's protégé in the Orient.

The second historic landmark in American policy toward Asia was proclamation of the Open Door policy toward China at the end of the nineteenth century. Preservation of the Open Door remained a professed goal of American foreign policy until World War II. Even after the victory of Communism in China in 1949–1950, part of America's resentment toward the Communist government derived from the fact that Soviet Russia enjoyed a preferential position in Chinese affairs. Peking had abandoned the Open Door policy. Just what was this policy? What were its implications for later American–Asian relations?

Strict accuracy should make us hesitate to call the Open Door a policy at all. In a brilliant diplomatic coup, on March 20, 1900, Secretary of State John Hay announced that he had been able to secure British, German, Japanese, and American concurrence to a pledge which, in the words of a British diplomat, assured that these countries would "maintain free and equal commercial relations for all time in the Orient."[2] More concretely, Hay professed he had secured agreement to the general principle that future economic concessions granted to one of these governments by China must be granted on the same basis to the other governments. The gist of the three-fold pledge was that: Each party agreed not to interfere with commercial spheres of influence currently maintained by other powers in China; Chinese tariffs would apply equally to the goods imported from these countries; and harbor dues, railroad charges, and the like, within any power's sphere of influence would be the same for other powers using these facilities.

Actually, Hay had not secured the agreement of the powers to these terms, but after his public announcement the countries involved hesitated to deny their acceptance of what appeared to be a fair, almost idealistic, agreement respecting diplomatic rivalry in China.

Historical scholarship has shown convincingly that the Open Door policy grew out of competing diplomatic ambitions in China, not the least of which were ambitions entertained by the United States. The policy was aimed specifically at czarist Russia, whose advances in the Orient caused widespread alarm among other imperialistic countries, not so much out of abstract concern for the territorial integrity of China as out of fear that Russia's seemingly insatiable diplomatic appetite might eventually close China, Manchuria, and Korea to Western influence.[3] The United States was insisting upon equality of treatment chiefly because recent concessions wrested from China by other countries threatened to imperil America's position in the current economic rivalry and, most especially, to jeopardize American access to the lucrative Chinese trade. The Open Door was Washington's way of trying to safeguard its own political and economic interests in China at a time when an all-out diplomatic struggle for control of that country—in which America had neither the inclination nor the means to compete vigorously —would almost certainly result in the disappearance of American influence. Says Werner Levi of the Open Door: ". . . every nation sought its own advantage in the policy, not the least its official originator. . . ."[4] In the light of these facts, it may seem strange that over the course of time the Open Door policy came to be widely regarded by the American people as the quintessence of a moral, unselfish foreign policy whose dominant purpose was preservation of Chinese territorial integrity against powerful imperialist forces.

Yet the Open Door policy did nothing whatever to interfere with *existing* foreign concessions in China; nor did it prevent future ones, so long as the countries enumerated above were treated *equally* by China. A four-way monopoly of Chinese trade was by no means prohibited under the Open Door policy—if indeed this was not what its framers ultimately anticipated. The Open Door policy said nothing about the *political* inviolability of China. The principle of equal concessions applied to commercial matters only, and it did not apply to all of them. For instance, future industrial or railroad concessions were excluded. Whatever influence the Open Door may have had in protecting Chinese sovereignty was therefore largely incidental. The objective was to assure equality of treatment for the United States in the midst of an impending imperialist struggle on the Chinese mainland. That China itself greeted the Open Door with something less than unrestrained enthusiasm was indicated by the fact that it did not formally adhere to the principle until it signed the Nine-Power Treaty in 1921.[6]

More basic still in evaluating the implications of the Open Door policy in shaping the future American outlook toward Asia is the fact that neither at the time nor later was the United States prepared to take steps to enforce compliance with its provisions. As the years passed after 1900, American foreign policy in the Far East sometimes appeared deliberately designed to undermine the Open Door, perhaps not so much by commission as by omission. The United States was either unwilling or unable to halt progressive Japanese encroachments against the Open Door principle; and willfully or through ignorance, American policies sometimes actually facilitated Japanese expansionism at the expense of the Open Door.[7]

Nevertheless, the Open Door policy was one of the most profound influences which shaped popular attitudes toward China and, more broadly, toward Asia as a whole. Its most lasting consequence was to inculcate the view that in China's relations with the outside world, the United States occupied a preferential position. This idea had a number of important corollaries: that China was a kind of "ward" of the United States and that it looked to Washington for guidance in its internal and external affairs; that China's leaders were highly amenable to American suggestions and leadership in all fields; that China was pro-American in its attitudes and could be counted on to remain America's firm ally in Asia; that China was moving slowly but perceptibly down the path of political democracy and economic stability; that China owed a great "debt of gratitude" to the United States for moral and material help extended to it after 1900, and that this debt would weigh heavily in shaping China's attitudes toward domestic and foreign issues.

Since World War II, Americans have often been psychologically unable to accept the fact—and this has been a key element in explaining the ineffectuality of their policies—that events inside and outside China have long since overtaken the Open Door policy. That policy was postulated upon the existence of a weak, internally divided China which was an easy prey to foreign influence. In general these conditions persisted until the end of World War II. Even during the war and in the immediate postwar period, however, Chiang Kai-shek had demonstrated time and again that *China's interests* were uppermost in his mind and that in critical areas of policy the United States and other foreign countries could be expected to exert minimal influence over Chinese affairs. This fact was made even plainer after Communism's victory under Mao Tse-tung. The American people have been unable to adjust their thinking and their policies to the existence of a politically unified, ambitious, self-confident China.

The third landmark in American Far Eastern policy before World War II was acquisition of the Philippines in 1899. This development climaxed the acquisition of other Pacific islands such as Midway and Hawaii, obtained in 1867 and

1898, respectively. Its new strategic island bases for the first time made the United States a "Pacific power" in the military sense.[8] This fact drew America deeper and deeper into the vortex of great-power rivalry there, ordaining that sooner or later conflict would arise between the United States and the rising Japanese empire, whose diplomatic ambitions led it eventually to challenge the United States and Great Britain for mastery over the eastern Pacific area.

With other territories in Asia—India, Burma, Southeast Asia, Indonesia—the United States had no significant and direct relations at all before World War II. Washington recognized British primacy in India and Burma, French in Indochina, and Dutch in Indonesia. At intervals the United States did not hesitate to offer gratuitous advice to European countries about the management of their colonial affairs. But it was not until former dependencies emerged as independent nations after World War II that the United States established formal and direct diplomatic relations with them.

The principal elements of American foreign policy toward the Far East in the prewar period afforded very poor preparation for the new role of responsible American leadership of the West's policies toward Asian affairs throughout the postwar period. Novel and complex problems, often totally alien to American experience and arising under conditions of urgency, required a fundamental change and reorientation in American policies. We may conveniently discuss postwar American relations with Asia by examining three categories of issues confronting policy-makers in the United States: Sino–American relations since the Communist victory on the Chinese mainland; Asian neutralism, as symbolized by the problem of American–Indian relations; and rival cold war strategies in Asia, as illustrated by the Korean War and the conflict in Southeast Asia.

THE UNITED STATES AND COMMUNIST CHINA

In the light of the historic background of Sino–American relations described in Chapter 7, it is not surprising that with the Communist victory in China at the end of 1949, the United States suffered one of the most far-reaching diplomatic reverses in its history. Morally, economically, and militarily, the United States had supported the regime of Chiang Kai-shek in its struggle against Mao Tse-tung's Communist forces. With Chiang's defeat, and his subsequent retreat into exile on Formosa (Taiwan), a breach appeared in Sino–American relations that has proved unbridgeable down to the present day.

Space is not available here to discuss the course of the Chinese civil war, or even to analyze in detail why Communist forces ultimately won this contest. Basically, Mao Tse-tung's movement emerged victorious because, in spite of massive quantities of American aid to Chiang's regime, the Nationalist government was unable to hold the allegiance of the Chinese masses, unwilling to eliminate corruption from its own ranks, and incapable of offering a constructive program to the people of China as an alternative to Mao's forward-looking, if ruthlessly authoritarian, platform.*

The Deadlock in Sino–American Relations

Following the Communist victory in China, relations between Peking and Washington entered a stage of intense animosity, suspicion, and recrimination that has endured until 1971. The thaw that became conspicuous in Soviet–American relations during the era of "peaceful coexistence" after 1955 had little effect upon the Sino–American deadlock. Mao Tse-tung's regime regarded the United States as the embodiment of a "capitalist warmonger"; Washington, in Peking's view, manifested a degree of enmity toward Red China that it did not exhibit even toward Soviet Russia. Nearly every week after 1949 witnessed vitriolic outbursts of intemperate Chinese propaganda against the United States.†

Toward a Sino–American Détente

It was ironic that a "thaw" in Sino–American relations began under Republican President Richard M. Nixon, whose political party had for so many

*Political developments in China during and after World War II, and America's relations with China during this period, are discussed in the following sources: Department of State, *United States Relations with China*, Far Eastern Series, no. 30 (1949). This is the Truman administration's "white paper" on China, tracing the course of Sino–American relations since the era of the Open Door. Werner Levi's *Modern China's Foreign Policy* (Minneapolis: University of Minnesota Press, 1953) appraises China's foreign relations from around 1900 to the early postwar period. Herbert Feis, *The China Tangle* (Princeton: Princeton University Press, 1953) is an authoritative and dispassionate discussion of the Chinese civil war and America's role in it. John K. Fairbank, *The United States and China*, rev. ed. (New York: Viking, 1962), provides a succinct and illuminating treatment by one of America's foremost authorities on China. Foster Rhea Dulles, *China and America* (Princeton: Princeton University Press, 1946) is an historical account, focusing on the prewar period. More recent studies, emphasizing the period of active American involvement in the Vietnam War are: Edwin O. Reischauer, *Beyond Vietnam: The United States and Asia* (New York: Random House, 1967); Bernard K. Gordon, *Toward Disengagement in Asia* (Englewood Cliffs, N.J.: Prentice-Hall, 1969); Fred Greene, *U.S. Policy and the Security of Asia* (New York: McGraw-Hill, 1968); and Robert C. North, *The Foreign Relations of China* (Belmont, Calif.: Dickenson, 1969), pp. 72–101.

†The stage of acute tensions in Sino–American relations is dealt with at greater length in Chapter 7.

years condemned earlier Democratic administrations for allegedly being "soft" on Communist China. Yet by the end of the 1960s, President Nixon was prepared to take limited steps designed to restore normal relations between the two nations. In July, 1969, the administration relaxed certain long-standing travel and trade restrictions applicable to Red China; Peking was invited to make some reciprocal gesture of good will. Reporting to Congress early in 1971, President Nixon declared that during the 1970s, "there will be no more important challenge than that of drawing the People's Republic of China into a constructive relationship with the world community, and particularly with the rest of Asia." (Nixon's statement was noteworthy for several reasons, but one was that for the first time an American President officially referred to Communist China by its official title.) Committed to reducing the American military presence in Asia, Nixon sought a new Sino–Soviet–American equilibrium to produce and maintain stability in Asia. For reasons not fully apparent to outsiders (the still acute condition of Sino–Soviet relations and Peking's desire to engender greater stability after the disruptive Cultural Revolution were leading ones), at this stage Red China was prepared to play its part in a reconciliation with the United States.

In mid-April, 1971, the first graphic evidence of a thaw came from an unexpected quarter: an American ping-pong team, accompanied by American newsmen, crossed the frontier of Communist China from Hong Kong. It became quickly evident that Communist China was endeavoring to treat its American guests graciously. Premier Chou En-lai granted the group an audience; he informed the Americans that their visit had "opened a new page in the relations of the Chinese and American people." Hereafter, Chou declared, American newsmen would be "welcome" in China. With the full knowledge and concurrence no doubt of the Nixon Administration, the Americans invited a Chinese ping-pong team to tour the United States, and the Chinese announced their acceptance of this invitation. During this period, the White House announced a further liberalization of trade regulations affecting Communist China. Concurrently, a prestigious presidential commission, headed by former Ambassador Henry Cabot Lodge, Jr., proposed that Communist China ought to be admitted to the United Nations. (This recommendation, it should be noted, did not necessarily reflect the viewpoints of the Nixon administration.) Secretary of State William Rogers also alluded to the possibility of educational exchange programs between the two nations. After more than twenty years of animosity and ill-will, the course of Sino–American relations, it now seemed, was being reversed.

The impact of these developments was indeed significant. Lasting peace and stability in Asia, for example, was clearly impossible without some kind of *détente* between the United States and Communist China. President Nixon regarded this change in Sino–American relations as one of the most outstanding accomplishments of his administration. As we indicated in our earlier discussion of American attitudes toward Red China (in Chapter 7), public and legislative opinion on this matter was perhaps more flexible, and more inclined to favor reconciliation between the two countries, than successive presidents had assumed. Attitudes in Congress, for example, were in the main heavily *in favor* of a reduction of Sino–American tensions. On its side, Red China had perhaps also concluded that a stance of revolutionary militancy and intractable opposition to the United States, as well as to other non-Marxist nations, paid very few dividends; throughout the world, Peking was seeking to counteract the impression that China encouraged violence, political upheaval, and ideological militancy in pursuit of its goals. American policy-makers were heartened by another implication of change in China's diplomatic posture: its evident desire to improve relations with the United States signified that (in spite of recent American and South Vietnamese incursions into Laos and Cambodia), the Chinese government apparently accepted the idea that the United States was actually reducing its military presence in Asia.

In the midst of the euphoria surrounding these events, it was possible to lose sight of the fact that they marked only the *beginning of a thaw* in relations between the United States and Red China. Difficult substantive issues continued to divide the two nations—chief among which was the future of Taiwan (Formosa) and other offshore islands. Communist China continued to reiterate its claims to these islands; and the United States still maintained close ties (including a security treaty) with Nationalist China. As in the past, American and Chinese viewpoints on this issue appeared to be irreconcilable. The future of Nationalist China was also crucial to another issue: admission of Communist China to the United Nations. Technically, this was really not a dispute over whether to "admit" China to the UN; China already belonged to the organization, and it held one of the five permanent Security Council seats. The controversy revolved around which government was entitled to represent China in the UN. While most nations of the world unquestionably believed that Communist China ought to take its place in the UN, they were equally reluctant to expel Nationalist China (which had engendered considerable good will for itself among the Afro–Asian states in recent years).

Expanded trade relations between the United States and Communist China also appeared to be a likely prospect. Yet obstacles existed in this sphere as well. As we observed in Chapter 7, Americans had engaged in the "China trade" since the Colonial period; for generations, Yankee traders had visions of the potentialities of the "China market," and this vision apparently remained undimmed. Business groups within the United States called for a restoration of Sino–American trade links, in the expectation that sales on the Chinese mainland would boom. Except for goods which directly strengthened Red China's military power, the Nixon Administration was willing to relax most trade restrictions. There were, however, at least two major hindrances to a significant expansion in Sino–American trade during the 1970s. With one of the lowest standards of living in the world, Red China would be hard pressed to buy heavily in the American market (many finished goods, for example, could be obtained from Japan or perhaps Western Europe more cheaply). Even more crucially, what could the Chinese *sell* Americans, which the latter really wanted? Mainland China's principal exports were items like agricultural and food products, textiles, hog bristles, peanuts, and feathers —goods which competed with American products or for which the American market was very limited. At a time when American labor and business groups were more than ever concerned about "unfair foreign competition" it seemed rather unlikely that Sino–American trade would expand appreciably. Fashionable as it often was to think otherwise, experience offered few grounds for believing that expanded trade per se automatically improved *political* relations between the countries involved.*

Insofar as the future stability of Asia, and perhaps the question of world peace, was concerned there remained another major problem in Sino–American relations. What were the implications of Peking's determination to acquire a nuclear arsenal and a modern delivery system? In their arguments justifying construction of an American antiballistic missile (ABM) system, both Presidents Johnson and Nixon alluded to the threat of a nuclear-armed China.† For many years, American

officials also believed that Chinese intractability (much more than Soviet opposition) accounted in no small measure for Hanoi's reluctance to negotiate an end to the Vietnam War. In the light of these tensions, a radical change in the relations between the two countries did not seem likely in the near future.[9]

The Sino–Soviet Axis

After 1949, American apprehensions about China's intentions were re-enforced by the Sino–Soviet alliance. China's accession to the Communist camp raised the number of people within the Communist orbit to around 1 billion; territorially, the Communist empire now extended from the Pacific and the China Sea to the Adriatic, the gates of Berlin, and the Baltic Sea. Not since the time of Genghis Khan has such an empire appeared in history.

Down to the late 1950s, the official American view was that the Sino–Soviet axis was durable and that its policies were highly unified. The American tendency to refer to the machinations of "international Communism" in Europe or the Middle East or Asia indicated a belief in the United States that the Communist conspiracy against the free world was monolithic. A State Department memorandum of 1958 held that "the two partners in the Sino–Soviet alliance clearly realize their mutual dependence and attach great

---

*Our discussion of the thaw in Sino–American relations is based upon coverage provided in *The New York Times* for April 14, 15, 16, 17, 18, 19, 21, 27, 28, and 29; and May 2, 5, and 6, 1971.

†The nature and magnitude, but above all the implications, of the Chinese nuclear arsenal were difficult to judge with certainty. Against which countries specifically was it directed? What would be the impact upon China's influence over India, Southeast Asia, or Japan? The answers to such questions were far from clear, even by the 1970s. A number of informed commentators, like former American ambassador to Japan Edwin O. Reischauer, were convinced that the West had always been prone to exaggerate China's military power. In reality, economic weakness and internal political upheaval made China the "paper tiger"; it would not be able to rival the military might of the United States or Soviet

Russia until the 1980s. For this viewpoint see *The New York Times* (February 1 and October 22, 1967; and August 7, 1969). Other commentators noted that China had acquired nuclear weapons faster than had been predicted (its first atomic explosion took place in 1964). Soon thereafter, China embarked upon a program of missile construction; Peking was expected to have a limited arsenal of long-range missiles by the early 1970s and a larger stock of medium-range (1000-mile) missiles prior to that time. A study by the British Institute of Strategic Studies, released late in 1969, estimated that Red China could manufacture about 100 nuclear weapons (or a smaller number of hydrogen bombs) annually; yet its missile-construction program was found to be behind schedule. A British observer who toured China and visited its nuclear installations at the end of the 1960s found that Peking was concentrating on the production of *hydrogen* bombs; the testing of a 6000-mile Chinese missile was expected soon; and, incredible as it appeared, Chinese officials were devoting 15 to 20 percent of the country's entire national product to building a nuclear missile arsenal! According to this view, China's compulsion to acquire a nuclear striking force was related most closely to its increasingly grave dispute with Soviet Russia. See the report by Oxonian James for the *London Sunday Times*, reproduced as "China's Nuclear Zone—First on the Inside," in *Atlas* 18 (August, 1969), 19–23; and *The New York Times* (January 12, June 18, and June 25, 1967). An American student of Asian affairs had concluded that, on balance, China's accession to the ranks of the nuclear powers will have an effect "not pleasant to contemplate." It will mean for Asia, "the continual eruption of low-level acts of violence that could entangle the major powers in nuclear confrontations." See Fred Greene, *U.S. Policy and the Security of Asia* (New York: McGraw-Hill, 1968), p. 273.

importance to bloc unity vis-à-vis the free world." The memorandum detected "no evidence" for believing "it would be possible to exert leverage on the Peiping regime which might ultimately be successful in weakening or even breaking the bond with Moscow."[10]

Ostensibly, the Kremlin's policies toward its increasingly powerful Asian ally were designed to take account of Chinese viewpoints and to maintain intimate relations between the two power giants of the Communist movement. In ideological affairs, the doctrine of "different paths to socialism" was designed to accommodate the fact that Chinese Communism—based upon the peasantry, instead of the urban proletariat—was a legitimate, if different, manifestation of Marxism. This meant, in the words of an announcement from Peking in 1951, that: "The classic type of revolution in the imperialist countries is the October revolution" in Russia. But the "classic type of revolution in the colonial and semi-colonial countries is the Chinese revolution, the experience of which is invaluable for the peoples of these countries."[11]

Similarly, in economic affairs, during the early and mid-1950s the U.S.S.R. provided massive economic aid to Peking and negotiated generous trade agreements, assisting Peking with its "great leap forward." Diplomatically, the Kremlin was at the forefront of countries calling for the admission of Red China to the United Nations and denouncing American "imperialistic" intervention in Chinese affairs, as exemplified by Washington's determination to prevent Formosa from passing under Red China's hegemony.

The Split Between Moscow and Peking

Such outward signs of Sino–Soviet solidarity did not, however, conceal a growing rift between the two giants of the Communist world. In retrospect, it is clear now (if it was not apparent at the time) that the death of Stalin in 1953 marked a watershed in Sino–Soviet relations. The process of de-Stalinization and the reforms introduced by the new Soviet Premier Nikita Khrushchev had a profound impact upon relations between Russia and its Chinese ally. In reality, the period of the mid-1950s served to bring to the surface a number of underlying differences between the two nations which, over the course of time, shattered the cohesiveness of the international Communist movement and led to fears in both capitals that war between them was at least a possibility.

What forces were responsible for the disruption of the Sino–Soviet axis? While a detailed discussion of Sino–Soviet relations in recent history is beyond our scope, we may briefly allude to a number of long-range and short-range influences which produced a growing divergence in outlook between Moscow and Peking.* In the first place, Western observers had perhaps always been prone to attribute greater cohesiveness to the Sino–Soviet alliance than the facts warranted. As far back as the 1920s, and continuing through the 1930s and World War II, fundamental differences existed between the Soviet and Chinese Communist parties. On numerous occasions, Moscow sacrificed the interests of the Chinese Communists to achieve goals deemed important by the Kremlin. Not only did Mao Tse-tung finally win in China with minimum assistance from Stalin; he did so in the face of attempts by the Kremlin to impede Mao's campaign and to encourage his principal enemy, the Kuomintang movement headed by Chiang Kai-shek. Having successfully established his movement as the dominant political force on the Chinese mainland, Mao Tse-tung showed no inclination after his victory to become subservient to the Kremlin. Moreover, after Stalin's death, Mao became the "senior member" of the Communist partnership. In whatever degree he might have been inclined to acknowledge Stalin's preeminent position in the international Communist movement, there was no reason whatever why he should accept Khrushchev's claim to that position, especially in view of the latter's inconspicuous role in leading the Communist revolution within the U.S.S.R.[12]

Ideological issues also furnished ammunition for continuing philosophical discord between the U.S.S.R. and Red China. Although the Kremlin accepted the theory of "different paths to socialism," it was obviously unwilling to accept a Chinese corollary to this idea, assiduously advanced by Mao's regime. This was the idea that Red China had succeeded—where the Soviet Union had earlier failed—in finding the path that permitted a prompt and direct transition to the Communist utopia. This was the "commune" system for agriculture, progressively abandoned by the Kremlin. Mao Tse-tung offered the commune system as the long-missing key that would open the door to the Communist utopia of material plenty and the "classless society." In effect, as Harry Schwartz

---

*The origins of the Sino–Soviet split in the recent period are related to political and diplomatic developments in China before World War II, in George F. Kennan's perceptive treatment, *Russia and the West Under Lenin and Stalin* (Boston: Little, Brown, 1961), pp. 241–278. See also: Louis Fisher, *Russia, America, and the World* (New York: Harper & Row, 1961), pp. 52–79; G. F. Hudson, "Russia and China: The Dilemmas of Powers," in Philip E. Mosely, ed., *The Soviet Union: 1922–1962* (New York: Praeger, 1963), pp. 417–428; Vidya P. Dutt, *China and the World: An Analysis of Communist China's Foreign Policy* (New York: Praeger, 1966), pp. 58–147; Conrad Brandt, *Stalin's Failure in China* (New York: Norton, 1966); Dennis J. Doolin, "China vs. Russia," in Dan N. Jacobs, ed., *The New Communisms* (New York: Harper & Row, 1969), pp. 47–74; and James R. Townsend, "Chinese Communism" in *ibid.*, pp. 131–159.

has observed, this amounted to claiming "ideological leadership of world communism, since it implied that Peking had found a magic formula for doing in a few years what Moscow has not been able to do in more than four decades."[13] Khrushchev joined Western observers in predicting openly that Mao's commune system would ultimately fail.

Another source of doctrinal discord, more directly relevant for East–West relations, lay in differing Soviet and Chinese assessments of the prospect and implications of nuclear war between the non-Communist and Communist worlds. In 1963, the Kremlin released a statement attributed to Mao Tse-tung at an earlier conference in Moscow, in which the Chinese leader deprecated the dangers of a nuclear holocaust, particularly for the future of global Communism. The leader of China purportedly acknowledged that in a full-fledged nuclear contest between East and West, "a half of humanity, and perhaps even more than a half, will perish." Yet he contended that "if a half of humanity were destroyed, the other half would still remain, but imperialism would be destroyed entirely and there would be only Socialism in all the world and within a half of a century or a whole century the population would again increase even by more than a half."[14] Moscow heatedly denounced China's "erroneous and adventuristic platform on questions of war and peace, which was emphatically rejected by the peace-loving peoples." Severely criticizing Peking's manifest desire to "acquire their own atomic bomb at any cost," the Kremlin reiterated its conception that "in modern conditions the forces of peace, of which the mighty community of Socialist states is the main bulwark, can, by their joint efforts, avert a new world war." Peking's tendency to believe that "the atomic bomb is a paper tiger" was held to be "in crying contradiction with the ideas of Marxism–Leninism."[15] As in the conflict over agricultural communes, Moscow's insistence upon "peaceful coexistence" versus Peking's insistence upon continuing the "revolutionary struggle," even at the risk of nuclear war, amounted to a contest over whether the Soviet or the Chinese version of Marxism–Leninism would become the authoritative interpretation of Communist principles for the conduct of international relations in the nuclear age.

Behind such ideological disputations there was increasingly emerging what one commentator called "the respective dynamism of the two great Communist states."[16] By the 1960s, an ancient theme had come prominently to the fore in Asia: the rivalry between the Russian and Chinese empires, each of which sought to expand its influence, sometimes at the expense of the other. It was largely to prevent *Russian* hegemony over China, for example, that the United States proclaimed, and the powers of Europe supported, the Open Door policy at the turn of the century. Throughout history, Russian and Chinese interests have conflicted over important territories such as Manchuria, Outer and Inner Mongolia, Sinkiang, and Tibet. Nathaniel Peffer has pointed to the congruence of ideological and national goals in Soviet policy in Asia by saying: ". . . the strategy for world revolution coincided point for point with the historic strategy of old Russia. It worked to the interest of world revolution to strike at Great Britain in Asia; but it had also worked to the interest of tsarist expansion to strike at Great Britain in Asia." Thus, imperialist-minded Russian Czars "might gleefully have burned Lenin at the stake, but they would also have applauded his foreign policy." Referring to certain concessions exacted at China's expense, as Moscow's price for entering World War II against the Japanese, Peffer notes that Russia "got back all of its classical imperialist tokens. In this respect in the Far East Russia has never acted out of its traditional character since the Bolshevik revolution."[17]

As for China's goals in Asia, one authoritative study has concluded that its dominant ambition is:

the establishment of China as a recognized world power with a position of primacy in East Asia. This is not a uniquely Communist aim; it is one which has deep roots in traditional Chinese thinking. . . . Traditional Chinese attitudes have led many Chinese to believe that their country naturally deserves leadership in Asia and hegemony over surrounding areas. Chinese do not forget that if one views the last two millennia rather than the past century, China has been the strongest country in Asia over long periods, and many Asian countries have at some time been tributary to China.[18]

Werner Levi points out that since 1949, Red China has presented itself as "the savior of all Asia, leading its peoples to a glorious future." Especially significant to an understanding of present-day Chinese policy is the fact that "the area of major interest, Southeast Asia, is also the area in which imperial China had or claimed a paramount position. . . ."[19] Traditionally conceiving of itself as the "Middle Kingdom," throughout history Imperial China sought to create and to maintain a system of political dependencies—known in earlier diplomatic parlance as "client states"—around the periphery of the Chinese heartland. At various stages in history, Chinese dominion has extended over what are now the states of North and South Korea, North and South Vietnam, Laos, Cambodia, Thailand, Burma, Tibet, Nepal, and parts of Malaya and Indonesia. Relating this fact to contemporary Chinese diplomatic behavior, an authoritative British study group summarized Chinese ambitions in Asia by concluding that "the Central People's Government will aim at the formation around China of a ring of satellites under

Chinese influence, following in many respects the Chinese political way of life, insulating China's borders from undesirable contacts."[20]

Events following Mao Tse-tung's victory in China have tended to corroborate this prediction. North Korea has become a de facto Communist Chinese satellite; North Vietnam is not perhaps, strictly speaking, a "satellite," but it has maintained intimate ties with Peking and has in many instances accepted its interpretations of the Marxist creed over competing Soviet interpretations. As we shall see, Western observers were persuaded that it was Communist China, rather than Russia, that sought to undermine a great-power agreement calling for "neutralization" of Laos. Chinese power also actively supported a campaign of subversion against the government of South Vietnam. In the face of evident Soviet embarrassment, late in 1962 Peking launched an attack against India's Himalayan frontier, thereby risking a cold war confrontation in the Himalayas, at the very time that the United States and the U.S.S.R. were embroiled in the Cuban missile crisis.

By the 1960s, conflicting territorial claims along the 4500-mile border between Russia and China created extremely tense relations on the frontier of Sinkiang and in the disputed Amur River district of Manchuria.* Now it was the Kremlin's turn to be subjected to Chinese "map diplomacy." Peking vocally complained about old and "unequal" treaties, supposedly alienating Chinese territories at a time when China was too weak and too internally divided to protect its territorial integrity. Thus, an Indian source took note of a report that the Chinese were studying history in order to revive claims to territory in Eastern Siberia, notably areas originally colonized by Chinese during the seventeenth century! This Indian observer detected ample realization among Chinese officials that their "biggest territorial loss in the latter half of the last century was in the north at the hands of tsarist Russia." An initial surrender of 93,000 square miles of Chinese territory to Moscow was followed by other cessions that proved highly deleterious to China's interests.[21]

China's growing inclination to "discover" some ancient and allegedly authoritative map, substantiating its border claims to Russian or Indian or Burmese territory, was but one response that Mao's regime was making to a problem that could

be expected more and more to color China's relations with the outside world. This was the fact that by the mid-1960s, China had a population of more than 700 million—close to one-fourth of the human race! United Nations studies indicated that by 1975, Red China would probably have a population of 900 million people; by the end of the century it might well reach 1.5 billion people. As China's mushrooming population pressed against the country's limited food supplies—and as Peking encountered severe difficulties in its efforts to expand productivity significantly—internal population pressures might well-nigh dictate expansionist policies abroad. With India and most of Southeast Asia already severely overcrowded, Russian provinces in East Asia offered the most inviting sites for untold millions of Chinese settlers.[22]

The Future of Sino–American Relations

For a number of years—long after the evidence had become convincingly clear that the quarrel between Soviet Russian and Red China was genuine—policy-makers in Washington were inclined to discount the prospects for a rupture in the Sino–Soviet alliance. Even if controversies existed between the two nations, some American officials asserted, they neither concerned the United States directly nor contributed to the achievement of American foreign policy goals.[23] The concept of "international Communism" had become so deeply ingrained in the American public and official consciousness that it was difficult to accept the reality of a Marxist world rent by ideological discords and clashing nationalist ambitions. It was perhaps simpler and more publicly acceptable for the United States to have a policy directed against the "Communist global conspiracy" than to have *several* policies—for Soviet Russia, for Communist Eastern Europe, for Red China, for North Vietnam, for North Korea, and possibly for other Marxist or semi-Marxist systems. As was emphasized in Chapter 7, both public and official opinion in the United States concerning affairs in China exhibited distortions, stereotypes, and illusions which posed many obstacles to a basic reformulation of American policy toward the Communist regime on the mainland.

On its side, the Communist government of China showed no sign of *desiring* more amiable relations with the United States. To the contrary, the "hate America" campaign that had been a conspicuous theme of official Chinese propaganda for many years continued to be pushed energetically by Chinese policy-makers. Confronted as they were with grave and recurrent domestic problems, and encountering definite limits to their ability to achieve regional and global objectives, Chinese officials perhaps still *needed* the "American imperialists" to serve as a convenient

---

*By the early 1970s, China's westernmost province, Sinkiang, had become an active center of conflict along the 4500-mile Sino–Soviet border. This province contained some 10 million people and was rich in natural resources. Moscow was supporting separatist movements among the Turkestan minorities in this area, seeking to detach the province from Chinese control. In this period also, Chinese officials condemned the Soviet Union for "social imperialism"—that is, imperialism carried out under the guise of socialism. See *The New York Times* (December 1, 1969; March 2, 1970).

scapegoat for the nation's inability to accomplish many of its internal and external goals. As in other respects, the Communist tendency to blame "foreign devils" for the ills afflicting society accorded with Chinese traditions and exhibited a behavior pattern which was endemic in Chinese history. [The new campaign against the "Wall Street warmongers" diverted the society's attention from domestic problems and tended to create internal unity in the face of a foreign threat. From this perspective, the Communist regime in China perhaps had little incentive to abandon its "hate America" propaganda line and to seek a resolution of Sino–American differences.]

The long-standing enmity between Red China and the United States was also of course grounded in fundamental disagreements over substantive diplomatic issues. [Peking's announced revolutionary strategy collided, needless to say, with America's global objectives, as well as with Moscow's proclaimed policy of "peaceful coexistence."] Despite Communist Chinese setbacks in one country after another during the 1960s, there was no evidence that Peking had abandoned its avowed intention to support the "revolutionary struggle" of Africans, Arabs, Asians and (in some countries) Latin Americans against established governments.* In 1962, Communist Chinese troops had attacked India, occupying that country's northern provinces and threatening its security; in the years which followed, Sino–Indian relations remained hostile. One significant victory for Chinese diplomacy during the 1960s was the encouragement of a more independent, and in some respects avowedly anti-American, stance by Pakistan—an Asian nation which, during the 1950s

*A highly significant statement of Communist Chinese strategy in foreign affairs was the article by Marshal Lin Piao, entitled "Long Live the Victory of People's War," published in the *People's Daily* (September 3, 1965). Breaking sharply with the Soviet conception of "peaceful coexistence" toward the capitalist zone, this statement endeavored to apply Mao Tse-tung's strategy against Japan during World War II to the continuing struggle against "imperialism" outside China's borders. Lin Piao's theory of "protracted war" sought to demonstrate how a poor rural country like China was able to defeat an industrialized nation like Japan; by relying upon a "people's war," China proposed to establish rural "base areas" and to "encircle the cities and finally capture them. . . ." Extending this strategy to the international arena, Lin Piao contended that this approach promised success in the "revolutionary struggles" of the Afro–Asian and Latin American peoples against American domination. For the text of this statement, see Senate Committee on Government Operations, *Peking's Approach to Negotiation*, 91st Congress, 1st Session, 1969, pp. 84–92. In the years that followed, the Chinese government's attitude on revolutionary struggle abroad tended to be somewhat muted. Yet, on November 30, 1969, Premier Chou En-lai called upon the people of the world to resort to revolutionary warfare against both the United States and the Soviet Union, since each of these countries was guilty of aggression. See his statement as reported in *The New York Times* (December 1, 1969).

and early 1960s, had been regarded as a firm member of the CENTO and SEATO alliance systems. Owing primarily to Pakistan's continuing antagonism toward India, and the still-unresolved Kashmir dispute between the two countries, the government of Pakistan arrived at a *détente* with Communist China; as a result, Chinese economic and military aid, commercial agreements, and diplomatic support tended to displace Western (chiefly American) influence in Pakistan.[24] Chinese diplomacy in Southeast Asia also disturbed officials in Washington and other Western capitals. Although the magnitude and nature of its aid to North Vietnam was perhaps not fully known, Red China unquestionably supplied vital military equipment, economic assistance, diplomatic support, and other forms of aid to Hanoi in the Vietnam conflict. [Hanoi's reluctance to engage in serious negotiations to settle the war could also perhaps be attributed in some measure to Communist China's "hard-line" position and its commitment to ongoing "revolutionary struggle" against American, as well as other forms of, "imperialism." Similarly, Peking had openly called for the overthrow of the pro-American government in Thailand and had unquestionably sponsored insurrectionary activities against the "lackeys of American imperialism" in Bangkok.][25] The government of Burma—which during the 1950s and early 1960s had maintained friendly relations with Red China—complained about Chinese-supported revolutionary activities within its borders. As in the earlier case of India, Sino–Burmese agreement upon the principles of "peaceful coexistence" did little in the long run to prevent frictions between the two countries.[26] The Communist-led insurrection which sought to gain control of Indonesia in 1965 was unquestionably aided and abetted by Red China. The Communist party of Indonesia (PKI) was oriented toward mainland China, rather than Soviet Russia; the PKI had been one of the largest recipients of Chinese funds and arms. The attempted coup against the Indonesian military was crushed by the armed forces; in the months which followed untold thousands of Indonesian Communists and suspected Communists were massacred; and the PKI disappeared as an organized political force in Indonesian political life. The new government of Indonesia under General Suharto adopted a militantly anti-Communist stance and sought to normalize its relations with the United States.[27]

Throughout Asia, Red China's pursuit of a revolutionary strategy alarmed both Moscow and Washington. By the early 1970s, Peking had reestablished friendly relations with the government of North Korea; its ties with North Vietnam and Viet Cong forces in South Vietnam were closer than ever; it assisted the *Pathet Lao* and other insurgent movements in Laos and Cambodia (serving as a base for the deposed Prince

Sihanouk of Cambodia, who established a government-in-exile after his overthrow in 1970); and with Chinese assistance, insurgent movements were active against Thailand, Burma, and Malaysia. In brief, every radical revolutionary group in east Asia was aligned with Chinese (rather than Soviet) power. Even Moscow was disturbed by this trend; Soviet officials, for example, publicly warned North Vietnam in 1970 that undue dependence upon Red China courted "defeat and destruction."[28]

Among the sources of Sino–American animosity, none outranked the issue which had existed since the late 1940s: the future of Formosa, site of the Republic of China ruled by Chiang Kai-shek and his followers. Ever since their victory on the mainland, Red China's leaders had proclaimed their determination to "liberate" Formosa, along with certain smaller offshore islands. These territories were viewed as forming an integral part of China; they remained alienated only because American power preserved the security of Chiang's regime. Although its pronouncements were uncompromising, Peking had in fact been careful to avoid a direct clash with the United States in the Formosa Straits (one indication that Red China's foreign policy was actually less "reckless" than it was often depicted to be). Yet there was no reason to suppose that Peking had abandoned its ultimate objective of bringing Formosa under Communist rule and of trying members of Chiang's government as war criminals.[29]

In his attempt to improve the climate of Sino–Soviet relations, President Nixon would be required to reassess America's long attachment to Nationalist China. That the United States had invested its prestige heavily in Chiang Kai-shek's regime was undeniable; it would no doubt prove difficult for any American administration to "abandon" Nationalist China, particularly if Communist Chinese sovereignty resulted in a bloodbath on the island. Meanwhile, neither Nationalist nor Communist China was prepared to accept a "two Chinas" formula which might serve as a compromise of this intractable issue.[31] Even groups in the United States favoring more amicable Sino–American relations acknowledged that the Formosa question posed the most serious cause of contention between the two nations.[32]

The United States and the Sino–Soviet Dispute

How does the continuing controversy between the two giants of the Marxist world—Soviet Russia and mainland China—affect the United States? What are the implications of the Sino–Soviet dispute for American foreign policy? Some of the consequences of this schism within the Communist system are obvious; others are less easy to identify with assurance. It is evident, for example, that the Sino–Soviet controversy underscores the fact that "international Communism" (if it ever really existed) is no longer the primary threat to Western security. It is no less clear that the quarrel between Moscow and Peking is real and very deep-seated; it involves something much more fundamental than mere semantic or ideological quibbling over how best to "bury" the United States. It is also apparent that the controversy is *far-reaching* in its implications, affecting such diverse issues as defense spending by Russia and China, the strategy each pursues toward the "third world," and the effort by Marxist nations to agree upon doctrinal questions. Increasingly, the area of *disagreement* between Moscow and Peking appears to have widened; each capital seems to have become more preoccupied than ever with the threat of overt hostilities. As for the United States, the disruption of the Sino–Soviet alliance would logically dictate a different approach to these leading Marxist countries from that which was followed when the Moscow–Peking axis was (or appeared) cohesive.

Yet on the level of concrete policies, the implications of the Sino–Soviet dispute for America are complex and ambiguous. As in every foreign policy decision, alternative proposals have their attractions and limitations; almost never are policy proposals entirely free of the latter. On the one hand, the Sino–Soviet dispute reduces the dangers posed to the United States and its allies by a Marxist monolith; the strife between Moscow and Peking unquestionably weakens the appeal and effectiveness of Communism throughout the free world. As they have become progressively concerned with the threat of war along their common frontiers, policy-makers in Moscow and Peking have become distracted from challenging American influence in Western Europe, Latin America, or Asia. Indeed, as the danger of open violence becomes more acute, there is perhaps a tendency for both mainland China and Soviet Russia to temper their anti-American activities and to "protect their rear" by avoiding conflict with the United States.

On the other hand, policy-makers and the United States cannot remain oblivious to the consequences for their own nation and the world at large of unlimited escalation in Sino–Soviet hostility. As the tension between Russia and China rises, so does the risk of regional—perhaps global —war. Some "accident" along the Russian–Chinese border might trigger a nuclear conflagration. More so for China perhaps than for Russia, the dispute keeps the government in a state of anxiety and war readiness—hardly a frame of mind designed to instill greater *rationality and moderation* into its policy-making. Arms competition between the two nations well-nigh guarantees higher defense budgets—and this fact in turn alarms officials in the United States! As long as it confronts a nuclear-armed Russia, Red China is unwilling to forego nuclear weapons or to join in agreements seeking to prevent the proliferation of nuclear arsenals.

Four basic alternatives are open to policy-makers in the United States in responding to the Sino–Soviet controversy. First, America can *unequivocally support the Soviet Union against China.* This strategy would make even more explicit the mutual American and Soviet interest in "peaceful coexistence." It would underscore the fact that, in most vital respects, the two countries have much more in common with one another than either has with China. It could lead to a new axis between the world's super-powers, thereby making Peking reluctant to attack either—and certainly not both combined. It would mark America's formal abandonment of the idea that international Communism represented the main threat to global stability and would make more explicit the principle that any *aggressive nation,* irrespective of its ideology, endangers the well-being of the international community.

Yet a Soviet–American common front against Red China also possesses some serious policy defects. It would be an extremely difficult policy to pursue from the viewpoint of *domestic political considerations.* Segments of Congress and public opinion would probably have real difficulty comprehending how or why the United States is friendly toward a Communist regime in Russia and hostile to a Communist regime in China. Nor is there any persuasive evidence that Soviet Russia really desires to conclude a formal or de facto alliance with the United States directed against its erstwhile ally, Red China; Soviet officials themselves might have considerable trouble rationalizing such a policy. Most fundamentally, perhaps, it must be seriously questioned how "credible" a Soviet–American axis against mainland China would actually be in a crisis. Would the United States *really* be prepared to engage in war with Red China if the latter found itself at war with Soviet Russia? And would Peking take such a threat of American involvement (particularly after the traumatic experience of the Vietnam conflict) *seriously?* The same question of course applies to the credibility of Moscow's commitment. Would policy-makers in the Kremlin seriously consider going to war against China because of a Sino–American conflict over Formosa? At best, the prospect seems doubtful.

A second conceivable policy alternative for the United States is to arrive at a *détente* with Communist China directed against the Soviet Union. Strategically, this step would confront Soviet defense planners with the prospect they dread the most—the possibility of a "two-front war" against powerful enemies. It would mean abandonment of America's long-standing policy of hostility toward, and nonrecognition of, Communist China, followed almost necessarily by an attempt to re-

solve the major issues fomenting tension between the two countries. Such a Sino–American *détente* might contribute positively to the future political security of Asia, especially vulnerable Southeast Asia.

Yet a Sino–American axis against the U.S.S.R. would also have many of the defects discussed in connection with the first alternative. The political difficulties facing such a policy within the United States would be even more serious than those confronting a Soviet–American alliance; adoption of the policy would require nothing less than a *revolutionary change* in public and official American attitudes toward the Communist regime in China. It might be even more difficult to induce Red China to abandon its "hate America" campaign, and impossible to do so as long as the United States remained closely identified with Taiwan. The question would have to be faced also of what a Sino–American axis would do to the Western alliance system in Asia. How would it affect Japanese attitudes toward the United States and Red China? The credibility of such an alliance also appears to be exceedingly dubious. In a crisis, would the United States risk devastation by Soviet missiles for the sake of Chinese border claims? Even if America did so, it appears certain that its European allies would be totally unprepared to run such a risk. For both of the policy alternatives we have analyzed thus far, there is a further risk: No evidence exists that either the U.S.S.R. or Red China is prepared to be *used* for the achievement of policy objectives defined *in Washington.*

A third alternative—widely proposed by some groups in American society—is for the United States to take any step necessary *to encourage the Sino–Soviet dispute,* possibly inflaming it to the point of open war. This proposal rests on the premise that *any quarrel* between Marxist nations promotes America's diplomatic interests. If the earlier Sino–Soviet alliance posed a grave *threat* to international security, then it might be natural to assume that a military conflict between Russia and China would *enhance* the security of the West and other countries outside the Communist zone. Plausible as this argument might seem, it verges on being a *reductio ad absurdum.* Among all the policy alternatives available to the United States, this one seems the most potentially dangerous, and possesses the fewest compensating advantages. This course of action resembles the strategy widely advocated in the West in the early stages of World War II: encouraging a conflict between Hitler's Germany and Stalin's Russia, in the hope that the two tyrannies would "exhaust each other." In the case of the Sino–Soviet dispute, the overriding risk, of course, is that an escalation in the quarrel could lead to open warfare, embracing much of Asia and possibly the entire world. There is no assurance that a war between Russia and China would remain limited to conventional (nonnuclear) weapons; and with both antagonists possessing a nuclear arsenal, the chances are great that such weapons would be used. In that event, neighboring Asian societies would almost certainly suffer massively from nuclear fallout; and in time Europe and North America could themselves be contaminated, making much of the planet uninhabitable. If it is meaningful any longer to refer to a winner and a loser in a nuclear contest (and there are persuasive reasons why such terms are misleading), the final outcome would be inimical to the diplomatic interests of the United States. A Soviet victory over China, for example, would give Moscow a greatly expanded power base from which to pursue its global objectives; it would remove any threat of a two-front war for Soviet strategists; and it would go far toward healing the breach in the international Communist movement. A Chinese victory would, from the American viewpoint, be even more calamitous. In such an event, Chinese power would be extended to Eastern Europe and the Mediterranean. Peking would acquire vast new resources and territory from which to launch revolutionary campaigns against established governments. Asian states proximate to China could scarcely resist being drawn into its orbit (not perhaps excluding Japan and the Philippines) Meanwhile, the devastation caused by a nuclear conflict between Russia and China (even if the West itself escaped direct damage) would create worldwide havoc, probably dooming Afro–Asian societies to *permanent* poverty and misery, with attendant political instability and chaos. As the only remaining powerful nation (with the possible exception of Western Europe) capable of extending vast sums for postwar reconstruction, the United States would then have the choice of providing billions of dollars for relief and rehabilitation programs, or of witnessing the descent of most societies outside the West into the abyss of famine and misery7

A fourth alternative for the United States in responding to the Sino–Soviet dispute resembles the position of nonalignment followed by many nations toward the cold war. There are of course many degrees and gradations of nonalignment; no two advocates of the doctrine define it identically. The basic ingredients of the policy for the Sino–Soviet conflict would consist of: avoiding any active "involvement" in the quarrel, on the ground that America had no direct stake in it; eschewing permanent identification with either the Soviet or Chinese positions; refraining from any temptation to "use" either country—least of all, to incite a war between them; seeking to preserve (in China's case, to establish) channels of communication with the antagonists, in the interests of maintaining an impartial stance; endeavoring by direct and indirect means to impress upon both Moscow and Peking the need for restraint; and calling attention to the grave consequences for humanity at large of a nuclear holocaust.

That this policy has certain disadvantages cannot of course be denied. It may fail to prevent war between the two giants of the Communist world. Neither Soviet Russia nor Red China may be receptive to American persuasion and influence. This approach might also be criticized as too passive: It leaves the initiative to Moscow and Peking, with America simply "reacting" to their moves. Admittedly, the credibility of a nonaligned stance by the United States might well be in doubt. Moscow might be convinced that Washington was *really* supporting Peking, and it would perhaps be even more difficult for Peking to believe in Washington's *bona fides*.

On balance, however, the fourth alternative seems the most promising (or the least damaging) course available to the United States. Any other response to the Sino–Soviet dispute appears to entail greater risks. This last alternative reflects recognition of a reality about the quarrel which most other courses obscure: In the final analysis, the influence of the United States *is likely to be marginal* in determining the outcome of the controversy. Efforts to make it decisive could well produce consequences diametrically opposed to American diplomatic interests and possibly to the security of the world.73

THE CHALLENGE OF ASIAN NATIONALISM AND NEUTRALISM

Over 1 billion people in Asia have been involved in nationalist movements since World War II. Out of the fires of Asian nationalism, 13 newly independent nations have been forged: Pakistan, India, Burma, Ceylon, Laos, Cambodia, North and South Vietnam, Malaysia, Indonesia, the Philippines, and North and South Korea. In addition, profound social, economic, and political transformations have taken place as a result of the Communist victory in China and changes carried out in Japan by the American occupation authorities and by successive Japanese governments. No nation in the Orient has escaped nationalist ferment.

As far as the domestic programs and policies espoused by nationalist regimes in Asia are concerned, the dominant interest of the United States might be said to consist of two closely related goals: to encourage, and assist with, the maintenance of *stable* political regimes throughout Asia, capable of enforcing central governmental authority over what is, in nearly every case, a sharply divided and fragmented society; and to create the conditions under which Asian governments may progress in the achievement of a "democratic" political order, accompanied by rising standards of living, a goal to which every Asian nation from Pakistan to the Philippines is ostensibly committed. A major technique of American foreign policy in pursuing these goals, to which we shall refer in more detail presently, has been the extension of economic and technical assistance to Asian governments to enable them to overcome formidable social and economic problems impeding their quest for modernization.

As in the Arab, or African, or Latin American contexts, great diversity has characterized the political orders appearing on the Asian scene. Military dictatorships, exercising greater or lesser authoritarian powers, govern such countries as Pakistan, Burma, Thailand, Indonesia, South Vietnam, and South Korea. The government of Cambodia was a constitutional monarchy. Only in India, Malaysia, the Philippines, and Japan did regimes adhere to constitutional and political precepts long viewed by the West as integral features of democratic systems. Even so, widespread agreement existed among newly independent states of Asia upon two propositions. One was that "democracy" had to be defined fully as much in social and economic systems as it was in political terms. Asian nationalists tended to believe that democratization of the social and economic systems prevailing in their countries was perhaps an indispensable *prerequisite* for the achivement of political democracy. This led to the second dominant idea: *Ultimately* Asian states hoped to achieve a substantial measure of political democracy. Progress toward that goal remained a fixed objective of all governments on the Asian scene.

Our concern with Asian nationalism, however, is more with its diplomatic than its internal aspects. In this respect, a dominant fact about contemporary Asia was widespread attachment to a neutralist or nonaligned position in world affairs. Pakistan, Thailand, South Vietnam, South Korea, Japan, and the Philippines had formal defense ties with the United States. North Vietnam and North Korea were members of the Communist bloc. The largest and most influential non-Communist countries of Asia—India and Indonesia—along with Burma, Ceylon, Laos, Cambodia, and Malaysia, adhered to the principle of nonalignment with rival cold war power blocs. Moreover, by the mid-1960s, in certain other countries that were formally "aligned" with the West, neutralist currents were strong. After the Sino–Indian Himalayan crisis of 1962–1963, the government of Pakistan assumed a de facto position of diplomatic nonalignment by signing a border agreement with Red China and by reaching other accords with Peking, in the face of evident American opposition. The evidence therefore indicated that, as in regions like Africa and Latin America, nonalignment was gaining converts in Asia and that the United States would probably be confronted with new manifestations of this diplomatic ideology in the Asian context.[34]

What were the leading ingredients in the concept of neutralism or nonalignment in Asia? What were some of its more important regional variations? How did it compare with Arab or African manifestations of the idea? What were the principal implications of the trend toward nonalignment for the United States? These questions may be most meaningfully evaluated as we focus upon the one Asian country that, throughout the postwar period, epitomized the concept of nonalignment and provided guidance in its expression and application to many other newly independent countries—the Republic of India.[35]

The Indian Conception of Nonalignment

An editorial appearing in the Ceylon *Daily News,* commemorating Indian Prime Minister Nehru's seventy-fourth birthday on November 14, 1963, referred to Nehru as "one of the dominating figures of the age." Among his achievements was listed "the influence he has exerted in international affairs as initiator of [the] neutralist policy so favored by newly independent countries." This tribute (written after the Chinese attack late in 1962) commended Nehru because he "constantly adhered to the policy of neutralism."[36] Several years earlier, Woodrow Wyatt, a member of the British Parliament, observed that India

has set the pattern by which states that are numerically strong but weak as yet in physical resources can "live with all" and find the means of developing themselves economically while retaining independence of judgment and maintaining democracy.[37]

And a former American ambassador to India, Chester Bowles, has said that Nehru of India expressed "not only his own convictions but also the yearnings and the attitudes of the vast majority in free Asia and in Africa. . . . I am convinced that what Nehru says, most free Asians think."[38] In no sphere are such comments more relevant than in the area of foreign relations. Nehru emerged as the architect of the policy of nonalignment that has gained a growing circle of converts throughout the Afro–Asian world.

The great variety of viewpoints and practices associated with neutralist or nonaligned foreign policies in Asia, and in other regions in the contemporary world, lends considerable credence to the judgment expressed by an Indian observer in 1961: "There is no measuring tape for determining nonalignment."[39] Asian versions of the concept—ranging from the "nonalignment" professed by India, to the "neutralization" imposed upon Laos, to the "positive neutralism" espoused by Indonesia until 1965—reveal numerous differences, both in principle and in practice. At the same time, there is a substantial consensus among states in Asia and elsewhere devoted to nonalignment about its central ingredients. As in the Arab world and Africa, the core of the doctrine is the idea that genuine national independence both makes possible and demands nonalignment in foreign affairs. One student of Asian affairs has thus linked the emergence of the neutralist credo with the nationalist ferment that swept Asia during and after World War II:

The policy of nonalignment with power blocs was an offshoot of the strong sentiments of nationalism in these countries. The pursuit of an "independent" foreign policy provided a tremendous satisfaction to their national pride and sense of independence. . . . [S]uch a policy makes a tremendous mass appeal in all these countries. . . . Nonalignment . . . was seen to be the best possible guarantee by these states to preserve . . . their national integrity and independence.[40]

In the same vein, the editor of the *Times of India* declared in 1961 that for India a policy of nonalignment "in world politics . . . is an insurance against being treated lightly or with calculated disrespect."[41]

The crux of the doctrine of nonalignment was identified by Nehru in 1957, when he declared that such a policy "seems to me as the natural consequence of an independent nation functioning according to its own lights. After all, alignment means being regimented to do something you do not like and thereby giving up a certain measure of your own independent judgment and thinking."[42] On another occasion Nehru asked:

Are we copies of Europeans, Americans or Russians? We are Asians or Africans and none else. For anyone to tell us that we have to be campfollowers of Russia or America or any country in Europe is not very creditable to our new dignity, our new independence, our new freedom, our new spirit.

To Nehru's mind—and in this, he was unquestionably voicing the dominant sentiment prevailing in Asia—*permanent* diplomatic or military identification with either cold war power bloc would be "most degrading and humiliating to any self-respecting people or nation. It is an intolerable thought to me that the great countries of Asia and Africa should come out of bondage only to degrade themselves in this way."[43] As early as 1946, therefore, Nehru declared that in foreign affairs India proposed to "keep away from power politics of groups aligned against one another" in the world community. Several years later, Nehru reiterated that military or diplomatic "alignment" with a great power would reduce India to the status of a "camp-follower"; Indian policies would then become shaped by its more powerful allies. Fervently, Nehru told the Indian Parlia-

ment, "I would rather India sank and died than she should be a camp-follower of other nations."[44]

Implicit in this conception of foreign affairs is the idea of diplomatic *freedom of choice* as the hallmark of a nonaligned foreign policy. *Permanent* identification with the East or West (or, as each bloc has tended to lose its monolithic character, with powerful countries within them) is prohibited by a policy of nonalignment. *Temporary* cooperation or association with great powers in military, economic, diplomatic, or other affairs is permissible without departing from a "nonaligned" diplomatic status. Thus, for India and other states espousing this principle, four alternatives are available: (1) to formulate policies of their own toward major global issues; (2) to agree on some issues with the West; (3) to agree with the Communist bloc on other issues; and (4) to agree in part with the West and in part with the East on some issues, such as disarmament.

Indian officials, along with those in almost all other nonaligned states, have repeatedly rejected what they deem to be a deep-seated Western misconception about the concept of nonalignment. This is the expectation (to use a phrase conspicuous in Yugoslav formulations of the doctrine) that nonaligned countries must assume a position of "equidistance" between the diplomatic positions of the great powers. Adherence to nonalignment does not demand a "middle-of-the road" diplomatic course between cold war contestants, nor do states professing this doctrine actually follow such a course, since each nonaligned country "takes a different attitude on a number of questions, in keeping with its geographical position, its special interests, concepts, traditional ties" and other factors.[45]

Indian voices have been conspicuous in making another distinction deemed essential by nonaligned states throughout the Afro–Asian world. This is the difference between "neutralism" (or nonalignment) and "neutrality." For two reasons, advocates of nonalignment reject the use of the label "neutral" to describe their position. First, under international law "neutrality" has a fairly precise meaning; it describes the position of a country toward *belligerents in a war*. Hence it is inapplicable to East–West relations in the contemporary era. Second, neutrality implies a kind of ethical-moral indifference or relativism, a lack of concern about major global issues, that nonaligned states believe is in fact directly contrary to the objectives they actually pursue. For this reason, New Delhi and many other capitals throughout the Afro–Asian world prefer "nonalignment" to describe their foreign policy orientation. The Indian ambassador to the United States declared in 1959:

It is a grave error to accuse India of neutralism. Neutralism means knowing the difference between right and wrong and refusing to side with either. It is an obnoxious expression which can only be true of cowardly people without a backbone.

Nehru once said categorically: "One cannot be neutral to right or wrong." And he emphasized that "neutralism . . . means a person who sits on the fence and who cannot decide between right and wrong. India is certainly not neutral, and her policy of nonalignment is anything but a neutral policy."[46]

A corollary of this idea is that nonalignment does not entail isolationism, noninvolvement in global affairs, or passivity toward major international developments. Suggestions (prevalent in the West) that nonalignment implies an isolationist or passive stance, the leader of Indonesia once declared, "is wrong and altogether beside the point." Asian countries dedicated to nonalignment "are not neutral; we are not passive spectators of the events happening in the world; we are not without principles, we are not without a standpoint. We do not conduct the independent policy just for the sake of 'washing our hands clean' " in the face of thorny international issues.[47] Instead, a major goal of nonaligned states, an Indian spokesman has said, is to restrict the area of the cold war and to work in behalf of international peace and stability "by persuading other countries also to remain unaligned." India was "actively and vividly interested in improving the climate of the world by bringing about more tolerance and understanding" among powerful nations professing different ideologies.[48] A desire to call attention to such goals has induced some nonaligned countries to designate their foreign policy as "positive neutralism," to distinguish it from "neutrality" or mere passivity in global affairs.

If these are the leading elements in nonalignment, as defined by one of its outstanding exponents, the Republic of India, brief mention must be made of some of the more distinctly *Asian* characteristics of the doctrine. In the spectrum of viewpoints and policies embraced under the concept of nonalignment, India and Asian states generally have gained the reputation for being among the "moderate" neutralist countries. As time passed, officials in India were much less inclined than "radical" neutralist countries (like the former "Casablanca group" on the African scene, led by Ghana, Guinea, and Egypt), to engage in intemperate denunciations of Western colonialism, while giving minimum attention to Communist oppression behind the Iron Curtain. While Nehru always insisted that, literally speaking, it was incorrect to call Communist domination of European countries "colonialism," he nonetheless endorsed the principle of self-determination for Communist satellites and stated that Communist rule was "even worse from the human point of view" than Western-style colonialism. Nehru denounced Moscow's suppression of Hungarian freedom in 1956 as a "terrible thing" and condemned the U.S.S.R. for behaving "in a brutal manner in Hungary." Moreover, Nehru often repeatedly criticized the agitational tendencies of some of India's neutralist partners, leading to fiery "resolutions" on subjects like colonialism that did little more than alienate the countries they were endeavoring to influence. To his neutralist compatriots, Nehru cautioned:

It is rather difficult to deal with these matters in this way. There are what might be called a diplomatic approach to these problems, and an agitational approach and various other approaches. Now as a nation grows in maturity, it adopts a mature approach to these problems. It may be occasionally satisfying to a country to utter condemnations of other countries, but if it wants to achieve results that is hardly the shortest way. Sometimes silence is a little bit louder than noise.[49]

However, India's version of nonalignment—widely praised throughout the West as a moderating and conservative influence at gatherings like the neutralist Belgrade Conference in 1961—increasingly came to be widely criticized by some neutralist countries for its lack of dynamism and "commitment" to causes high on the list of neutralist priorities.

At the same time, the nonalignment avowed and practiced by Nehru's government differed fundamentally from the "pro-Western neutralism" of such countries as the former French states of West Africa, Tunisia, and Malaysia. New Dehli's resort to military force to liquidate the Portuguese enclave in Goa illustrated, even to the satisfaction of Indonesians, that Nehru believed: "There can be no compromise with colonialism" and that "when it becomes evident that the colonial Power in question does not intend to give way, all means must be used to resolve the situation." To the Indian mind, once Portugal joined NATO, the existence of Goa as a colonial enclave on Indian soil not only signified the perpetuation of Portuguese colonial rule; it also meant that the dispute over Goa might sooner or later involve the intervention of NATO powers.[50]

India's middle-of-the-road conception of nonalignment enabled New Delhi to serve a valuable role in mediating and ameliorating cold war tensions. Being neither overtly pro-Western nor pro-Communist in its practice of nonalignment, New Delhi was acceptable to all belligerents in the Korean War. Nehru's government made a valuable contribution in bringing about talks that finally broke the deadlock in the truce negotiations. Similarly, in the years that followed, India played a leading role in efforts by the United Nations to preserve peace in the Middle East and in other peace-keeping activities, to which the major cold war belligerents and their supporters were unable to contribute.

America and India: An "Uneasy Dialogue"

Considerable attention has been devoted to India's *conception* of nonalignment. Theoretical formulations of this foreign policy principle undoubtedly owe much to Indian influence. Yet, like any formal set of foreign policy guidelines, these principles may be less important as a true index of what motivates a nation in international affairs than the nation's *actual behavior* in dealing with concrete issues and problems arising in foreign relations. Sometimes, a nation's professions and its behavior are not completely harmonious. Or, even if there is no overt disparity between them, the precise meaning of guiding principles is often supplied as they are *applied* to specific situations confronting the nation abroad. The United States and other nations may be more interested in what nonalignment means in terms of *actual Indian behavior patterns* than in abstract formulations of the doctrine.

The record of Indian–American relations throughout the postwar period affords many examples illustrating this general point. American officials undeniably had certain qualms about the concept of diplomatic nonalignment during the 1950s. Yet even during this period, Secretary of State John Foster Dulles pointedly exempted India from his harsh dictum that neutralism was "immoral."[51] As early as the Truman administration, India had begun to receive American economic and technical assistance; it continued to be one of the largest beneficiaries of American foreign aid down to the 1970s.* One key considera-

*In the period 1946–1968, the government of India received approximately $7 billion in military and economic assistance from the United States, after allowing for the fact that India had repaid close to $1 billion in American aid; the vast bulk of this assistance was *economic* aid designed to advance India's national development programs, feed its people, promote industrialization, and otherwise contribute to the country's economic advancement. Next to South Korea, India was the largest recipient of American assistance outside Western Europe. See the data presented in the Congressional Quarterly Service's publication, *Global Defense: U.S. Military Commitments Abroad* (Washington, D.C., 1969), p. 39. As he was planning what proved to be an extremely successful tour of Asia toward the end of his administration, President Dwight D. Eisenhower explained the purpose of his visit by saying: "My . . . purpose was not tourism. It was an obvious fact that the Free World should do everything possible to make certain that India—an announced neutral in the polarized power struggle—should never be allowed, with its 400 million people, to fall within the Communist orbit." See Dwight D. Eisenhower, *Waging Peace* (Garden City, N.Y.: Doubleday, 1965), p. 487. One of President John F. Kennedy's principal advisers wrote: "Of all the neutral countries, Kennedy was most interested in India, which he had long regarded as 'the key area' in Asia. . . . The

tion shaping American policy toward India was the fact that the Republic of India was *a democracy*—in terms of population, the largest one in the world. In contrast with certain newly independent Arab nations, for example, it had not rejected Western liberal democracy as a system imposed by the colonial powers and alien to the society's traditions. American officials also tended to regard India as a kind of testing ground or "showcase," demonstrating the successful operation of democratic political institutions and the effective modernization of an ancient society by evolutionary and nontotalitarian methods. Two facts dictated India's pivotal role in this respect. One was India's enormous influence throughout the third world, owing to the country's size, its long campaign of leadership against colonial domination, and the great prestige of its leaders like Mohandas K. Gandhi and Jawaharlal Nehru. The other was India's size, its location, and its long-standing ties with the West, which made it perhaps the principal alternative to Communist China's model of national development for the emerging nations. A successful democratic solution by India to age-old problems like poverty, inequality, the population explosion, and the need to raise living standards would go far toward undermining Peking's contention that the Maoist system was the "wave of the future" for Afro–Asian societies. Officials in the United States thus tended to regard India as in many respects *the key* to whether systems patterned after Western or Communist (particularly Chinese Communist) models would ultimately prevail in the zone of less developed societies.[52] This consideration overrode official and public doubts about India's policy of nonalignment, its quarrel with Pakistan, its readiness to accept Soviet aid, and its disagreements with the United States on specific international issues. More than was the case for any other single country outside the members of its alliance system, the United States acquired a massive stake in India's success as a nation; Washington's relations with New Delhi were in some ways closer than its relations with several of its formal allies.

On its side, the government of India had been, and remained, heavily dependent upon American economic and technical assistance, along with loans and private investment by business firms from the United States, to achieve its development goals. Although they might not do so as frequently as Americans deisired, Indian officials periodically expressed their gratitude for assist-

struggle between India and China 'for the economic and political leadership of the East, for the respect of all Asia,' he said in 1959, would determine the Asian future." On another occasion, Kennedy had stated that "'If China succeeds and India fails, the economic-development balance of power will shift against us.'" Arthur M. Schlesinger, Jr., *A Thousand Days* (Boston: Houghton Mifflin, 1965), p. 522.

ance supplied by the United States and acknowledged its vital role in promoting the progress of their country. In contrast to certain Arab, African, and (more recently) Latin American nations, the "investment climate" for foreign business concerns in India has not been unfavorable. New Delhi has made a real effort (again in marked contrast to a number of Afro–Asian states) to hold down military spending; thus far, India has refused to embark upon the production of nuclear armaments, although it has the capability of manufacturing them; by the standards of the Afro–Asian world, its use of American and other forms of outside assistance has been reasonably efficient and productive. By the 1970s, several leading indicators of Indian progress and modernization—like industrial production, agricultural output, the extension of educational and other services, the eradication of disease, and the nation's balance of payments—showed a marked improvement over the late 1950s and early 1960s. If it would be premature to assert that India has solved its multitudinous internal problems, it is not amiss to say that its accomplishments thus far are impressive and that its record compares very favorably with that of most other Afro–Asian societies.[53] Moreover, despite a number of external and internal crises, India *remains a democracy;* Indian political elites have rejected totalitarian solutions to the nation's problems; and mass support for democratic ideology is still pervasive. India has thus far escaped the kind of internal political convulsion that impaired Communist China's modernization efforts during the 1960s; and it has not joined other countries in Asia in relying upon the military establishment to provide discipline and direction for the society.*

In spite of these achievements, several specific issues have caused frictions and misunderstandings in Indo–American relations. One of these is

---

*The national elections in the Spring of 1971 (the fifth since the country's independence) provided a crucial test of India's political stability. Some 275 million voters participated in the electoral process. Despite considerable evidence of citizen disenchantment with the ruling Congress Party—and growing factionalism within the party's ranks—to the surprise of many outside observers, Mrs. Indira Gandhi's wing of the party (called the New Congress party) received the overwhelming endorsement of the Indian electorate. Although it advocated socialism, Mrs. Gandhi's political supporters rejected both right-wing and left-wing extremism, in preference to a moderately left-wing pragmatism. With political upheavals taking place in several parts of India (for many years, for example, Kerala had been in turmoil), Mrs. Gandhi favored the use of strong central authority to counteract such centrifugal forces. Given the magnitude of India's problems (many Indians, for example, had a poorer diet in 1970 than in 1960, and virtually no progress had been made in checking the country's population growth), it was perhaps something of a miracle that democratic government remained viable in the largest nation in the third world. See *The New York Times,* March 11, 1971.

India's continuing quarrel with Pakistan. The animosity between these two countries has its origins in the "communal strife" between Moslems and Hindus which antedates the "partition" of the Indian subcontinent by Great Britain (announced by London early in 1947), which created India and Pakistan as independent nations. A related source of antagonism between the two nations—the problem of Kashmir—also stems from this period. Kashmir's Hindu rulers "invited" India to assume jurisdiction over the country; supporting the demands of Kashmir's Moslem majority, the government of Pakistan has refused to accept Kashmir's accession to India and demands that the wishes of the country's inhabitants be respected. For more than twenty years, the Kashmir dispute has inflamed Indo–Pakistani relations; it shows no signs in the 1970s of being peaceably resolved.[54]

Until 1962 (when it was attacked by Communist China) India refused to participate in American-sponsored Asian security systems or to accept arms-aid from the United States. By contrast, Pakistan was a member of both the Baghdad Pact (CENTO) and SEATO alliance systems; it became a major beneficiary of American arms-aid programs, as well as being a recipient of economic assistance from the United States. Military aid to Pakistan, as for other countries deemed vulnerable to Communist expansionism, was designed to be used against aggression, specifically *Communist* aggression. The aid agreements signed between the United States and Pakistan spelled out this requirement. American military assistance provided to India in 1962 was similarly intended to bolster the security of that country primarily against *Chinese* encroachment. Yet when the dispute between India and Pakistan over Kashmir erupted into open warfare in the summer of 1965, both nations used American-supplied weapons. As a result, Washington suspended arms shipments to both countries; and it found itself accused by each belligerent of making possible (if not encouraging) aggression by the other. This embarrassing episode highlighted the fact that, in a crisis, provisions in arms-aid agreements governing the use to which weapons and other military supplies can be put by the recipient are of dubious value. The United States can neither *prevent* the misuse of such military equipment, nor *stop* wars fought with American weapons once they have erupted. In this crisis, it was the Soviet Union which (in the Tashkent Agreement, early in 1966) served as a mediator and secured Indo–Pakistani consent to a cease-fire accord. America's influence fell with both countries—more so perhaps in Pakistan than in India. Thereafter, Pakistani–American relations became extremely cool, not to say tense. Although it formally remained in the CENTO and SEATO alliances, Pakistan took little

part in their deliberations; its officials sharply criticized American policy in Southeast Asia; and after
the mid-1960s, Pakistan's relations with Communist China became cooperative, while its relations
with India remained hostile.[55] Although Indo–
American relations in time were restored to a reasonably cordial basis, New Delhi also began to
cultivate more harmonious relationships with
Moscow.[56]

By the early 1960s, the problem of Indian
security had also begun to concern American policy-makers. The country's vulnerability was graphically displayed when Communist China attacked
its Himalayan provinces late in 1962. Chinese
troops easily overran Indian defenses and threatened to invade the subcontinent itself. For reasons that are not yet altogether clear, however,
Peking unilaterally halted its military advance,
and the immediate crisis passed. To assert that the
military encounter with Red China was a traumatic experience for India would be to understate
the matter. It destroyed, forever perhaps, India's
trust in *Panch Sheela* (the five principles of "coexistence" agreed upon with Communist China in
1954) as a guarantor of national security; after the
crisis, Sino–Indian relations remained tense and
suspicious.* In India's hour of danger, the United
States and Great Britain promptly supplied
needed military aid; Soviet military assistance
(especially modern aircraft) was also instrumental
in bolstering Indian defenses. As a result of this
confrontation, India largely abandoned hope that
relations with Red China could be peaceful and
cooperative; at the same time, New Delhi became
more careful than ever to maintain harmonious
relations with the U.S.S.R., the United States, and
other Western nations.[57]

The Himalayan conflict with China naturally
raised the issue of the adequacy of India's defense
program. The crisis revealed the fact that India's
armed forces were inadequate to maintain national security; its military establishment was too
small, too poorly trained, and lacking in modern
equipment (particularly for mountain warfare).
By the late 1960s, the government of India had
taken a number of steps to strengthen its armed
forces. Did the continuing threat of Chinese expansionism require New Delhi to abandon its
long-standing opposition to nuclear weapons?
India undoubtedly had the capacity to manufacture nuclear armaments; and some segments of
Indian opinion advocated this course, as a counterpoise to China's great strength in ground
forces. For several reasons, however, the Indian

government rejected such suggestions. Asian
opinion remained highly adverse to the proliferation of nuclear weapons, and it was even more
opposed to the prospect of nuclear war in the
area.* Nuclear weapons were extremely *costly* to
manufacture; and a modern delivery system of
aircraft and missiles could be even more expensive. The diversion of funds for this purpose would
unquestionably impede (if it did not entirely crip-
ple) India's international development programs.
Moreover, certain realities—like the remoteness
of China's principal cities and population centers
—influenced strategic thinking in New Delhi.
After 1962, India confronted two imminent dangers, neither of which lent itself to elimination by
reliance on nuclear weapons. One was a new Chinese encroachment against India's northern territories; based upon recent experience, this was
likely to be a relatively small and limited military
encounter. Neither in 1962 nor afterward had Peking revealed any strong urge to conquer India or
engage in a prolonged war with it. The other
threat to Indian security grew out of the nation's
internal problems. Age-old "communal strife"
among religious groups; ancient rivalries among
numerous tribal and ethnic minorities; Communist intrigues in Kerala and other Indian states;
the impatience of the population with the pace of
progress and improvements in the standard of living; by the late 1960s, a growing popular disaffection with the ruling Congress party, viewed by
many segments of Indian opinion (particularly
youth) as a conservative, self-serving "power
structure" that was unresponsive to the society's
needs; above all perhaps, India's population explosion, which remained largely unchecked and
which created new slums and other problems
faster than they could be ameliorated—these
forces gave rise to "fissiparous tendencies," serious internal stresses tending to shatter national
unity and to fragment Indian society into a multitude of small, hostile, atomistic units. The government's decision to manufacture nuclear weapons
could well exacerbate these internal conflicts,
which threatened to destroy national integrity.[58]

In company with several other middle-rank
powers, the government of India supported international efforts to reduce armaments stockpiles
and to decrease the risk of nuclear devastation.
Yet it also believed that a key step in this process
was willingness by the nuclear powers to arrive at
a disarmament accord. There is no evidence that

*Five principles of "peaceful coexistence" were enun-
ciated in a treaty of mutual friendship between Communist China and India, signed in 1954; these principles
were reiterated many times thereafter—in China's relations both with India and with other neutralist nations.
See Beatrice Pitney Lamb, *India: A World in Transition*
(New York: Praeger, 1963), pp. 311–312.

*More so than in any other region, opinion in Asia has
always been extremely sensitive about nuclear testing or
warfare. Thus far, Asians have been the only victims of
atomic warfare, when the United States used two atomic
bombs against Japan at the end of World War II. Asians
are also uniquely vulnerable to nuclear "fallout," both
because atomic weapons have been widely tested in the
Pacific and because strontium-90 tends to replace calcium in food supplies; the latter element is a major constituent in rice, the basic diet of millions of Asians.

India itself has acquired nuclear weapons.* Yet—with a nuclear-armed China on its borders—this decision might well be changed in the future.[59]

Despite its reservations about India's policy of nonalignment, the American government showed no real interest in negotiating a defense treaty with India, requiring the United States to assume a major responsibility for defending the subcontinent. America's frustrations in Vietnam would probably be insignificant vis-à-vis the challenge of maintaining the integrity of India's northern provinces against Chinese encroachment! Nor did the United States show any overt desire to assume the main burden for promoting the welfare of the Indian society. In the early 1970s, as in the 1960s, *domestic problems* constituted the most crucial challenge facing the government of India. Whether the Republic of India would survive as a nation—or whether its democratic political system would continue to operate successfully, after those in other Asian countries had collapsed —would probably be decided primarily by the record of progress in raising urban and rural living standards, in building schools, in expanding food output, and most crucially in curbing population growth. The United States could not accept primary responsibility for the modernization of India. (Incidentally, this was not an obligation which Soviet Russia showed any marked willingness to assume.) Relying upon the Indian government's own efforts and its commitment to national development, the United States was prepared to join with other countries (not excluding the U.S.S.R.) in extending economic assistance and, when needed, military aid. Beyond that, India's future rested with its own leaders and citizens.†

---

*As we shall see in our discussion of the Nixon Doctrine at a later stage in this chapter, one major provision of the doctrine extended the American nuclear shield to nonaligned nations, in part to induce countries like India to refrain from producing or acquiring a nuclear arsenal.

†Although India's progress toward economic advancement and modernization has in some respects been impressive in recent years, by the 1970s the evidence indicated that the country still confronted a number of serious problems, some of which were becoming *more acute* with the passage of time. Over-all agricultural production, for example, has risen impressively; but agrarian unrest is prevalent throughout India. The widely heralded "Green Revolution," using new "miracle" strains of seed grains, fertilizers, and other methods for increasing farm output, has thus far affected only a small fraction (around 10 percent) of India's 400 million farmers; land reform either has not been carried out at all or has not really altered the traditional pattern of land ownership; Indian peasants remain heavily in debt to money-lenders, whose rates of interest are usurious; rural diets are still nutritionally deficient. Above all, little progress has been made to date in checking India's population growth: With more than 500 million people in 1970, if the present rate continues, India will have *1-billion people* by the year 2000! New Delhi aspires to make the country "self-sufficient" in food production within a few years; but even if this goal is achieved, it contemplates no over-all *improvement* in Indian dietary levels, which often tend to be near the subsistence level.

America and the Smaller Asian Neutralists

Relations between the United States and the smaller neutralist states of Asia have ranged from decidedly cool to reasonably cordial. Several of the Asian neutralists are small nations, incapable of influencing the course of global (or even regional) events decisively. Ceylon, for example, has only some 12 million people (about the same as Pennsylvania); Burma has a population of around 27 million (about equal to Pennsylvania and New York State combined); tiny Cambodia has only 7 million people (less than the population of Michigan).

After the civilian government of U Nu was overthrown by a military coup (March 2, 1962), Burma's policy of nonalignment took the form of an inward-looking, isolationist position. Advocating "Burmese socialism," the regime of General Ne Win deliberately shunned ties with the outside world; although the country's internal needs were great, the government decided not to seek massive assistance from abroad. Tribally instigated rebellions against the central government, abetted during the 1960s by Chinese and possibly North Vietnamese aid, kept Burma in a state of chronic instability. Under Ne Win, internal economic progress during the 1960s was minimal; and in some sectors (like rice production and inflation) the country clearly *retrogressed*. By the 1970s, some evidence existed that Burma was beginning to broaden its contacts with other countries and to solicit at least limited assistance from abroad in meeting its needs.[60]

The problems plaguing small and economically backward Cambodia were of a different kind. From the time it became independent in 1953 until early 1970, Cambodia was governed by a constitutional monarchy, with power exercised by the voluble and mercurial Prince Norodum Sihanouk. Fiercely devoted to his country's independence, Sihanouk espoused a policy of "neutrality" in the hope that Cambodia would be saved from two imminent dangers. One of these was the threat of Communist encroachment, aided by North Vietnam and Red China. By the 1960s, Cambodia had been drawn into the Vietnam conflict; the main supply artery used by Communist forces (the Ho Chi Minh Trail) passed through Cambodia's northern provinces, and the port of Sihanoukville was an important point of entry for

---

If India succeeds in attaining the goals projected in its new five-year plan, launched in 1969, the effect would be to raise the per capita income for the lowest stratum of the population from $35 to $42 dollars annually. Thus far, India has managed to keep its food production somewhat ahead of population expansion; without some curtailment of the latter (and that prospect does not seem imminent), it may be sorely challenged to do so in the years ahead. See several reports on India's economic record and future in *The New York Times* (January 19, 1970).

Communist supplies. Possessing a small and poorly trained army, Cambodia appeared unable to prevent such Communist inroads.

The other danger to the country's independence arose from threats by two heavily armed American allies in Southeast Asia—Thailand and South Vietnam. Historically, both countries had claimed Cambodian territories; and Sihanouk was convinced that these claims had never been relinquished. Relations between both governments and Sihanouk's regime became increasingly strained.

Caught between these conflicting forces, Sihanouk pursued an erratic course in foreign affairs, alternately blaming both Communism and "American imperialism" for Cambodia's insecurity. In a typically inscrutable utterance, Sihanouk declared in 1969 that only the presence of "American imperialism" in Southeast Asia allowed Cambodia to exist as a free country! Early in 1970, while Prince Sihanouk was on a tour of the Communist zone, Cambodia followed in the wake of several other Afro–Asian nations in recent years. The Cambodian military elite seized power, and Sihanouk promptly declared himself head of the Cambodian government-in-exile, which would return to power after Cambodia's "liberation." Led by Lieutenant General Lon Nol, the new regime committed itself to a policy of "independence, sovereignty, peace, strict neutrality and territorial integrity"—goals which differed little in principle from Sihanouk's objectives, but which in practice dictated Cambodia's gravitation toward the West. The growing Communist threat to Cambodian security had perhaps been the main concern leading military elements to carry out their coup. Within a few weeks, Cambodian officials had cast their lot irretrievably with America and its allies, when they cooperated with Washington's decision to launch an offensive into Cambodian territory. Tactically, this military strike was highly successful. Yet, after its completion, two-thirds of Cambodia was more or less controlled by Communist forces, while the capital city of Phnom Penh remained highly vulnerable.

Cambodia's destiny had been linked with developments in Indochina, Thailand, and Laos since 1953, and the change of regime in Phnom Penh did not radically alter that reality. It was evident that General Lon Nol's government faced the same dilemma which Sihanouk had been unable to resolve; Would Cambodia lose its independence to Communism, or would it become a de facto dependency of South Vietnam and Thailand (and indirectly of the United States)? If all neutralist or nonaligned nations did not face the same hard choice, Cambodia's unique circumstances made preservation of its neutralist position highly problematical.[61]

Next to India, Indonesia is the largest and most influential neutralist state in Asia. Almost twice the size of Texas, Indonesia contains a population of some 113 million people (over half as many as the United States). In contrast with some developing nations, Indonesia possesses vast raw materials and rich land; yet down to the 1970s, its potential for economic development had barely been tapped.

Throughout the postwar period, America's relations with Indonesia have varied from cordial to extremely tense. Following a long and bitter struggle, Indonesia finally achieved its independence from the Netherlands on December 27, 1949. Because of its pressure upon the Dutch government, the United States could properly claim some credit for the victory of Indonesian nationalism, led by Dr. Achmed Sukarno. Sukarno's regime governed the country until 1966, when he was ousted by the armed forces in the aftermath of an abortive Communist effort to seize power. Under Sukarno's leadership, internal affairs deteriorated to the point of economic collapse; Indonesia embarked upon an unsuccessful campaign to "crush Malaysia" (a new federation having close ties with the West); and Sukarno emerged as one of the most outspoken critics of "Western imperialism" in the world. By the 1960s, Indonesia had developed intimate ties with Soviet Russia and Communist China; many Western commentators were convinced that Indonesia had become a de facto Chinese satellite. During the 1950s, American assistance to Indonesia had been generous; yet few countries in the world could rival Indonesia in the extent to which such aid had been mismanaged and wasted on dubious projects appealing to Sukarno's ego. American officials, therefore, had ample grounds for becoming disenchanted with Indonesia's leader; from Sukarno's point of view, America's involvement in secessionist movements in the archipelago merely confirmed his suspicion that Washington sought his downfall.[62]

An abortive Marxist coup in 1965 transformed Indonesia's internal and external policies. Blaming the Communist party of Indonesia (PKI) and its Chinese sponsor for precipitating a rebellion, the Indonesian armed forces launched (or acquiesced in) a campaign of repression against Marxist and suspected pro-Marxist groups; untold thousands were killed or imprisoned in the ensuing political upheaval. The PKI disappeared as an organized political force, and Sino–Indonesian relations entered a new phase of acute animosity. The new regime under General Suharto sought to improve Indonesia's relations with the West. The "crush Malaysia" campaign was abandoned; Indonesia resumed its place in the United Nations; American, Soviet, and other external sources of aid were solicited in an effort to rehabilitate Indonesia economically. For the first time since independence, the government of Indonesia seemed prepared to attack the country's problems in a reasonably disciplined and methodical manner.

America's approach to Indonesia since 1966 resembles its recent policy toward a number of new African nations. Washington's posture in Indonesia might best be described as one of "low profile" or "low visibility." American officials scarcely concealed their pleasure at Sukarno's political downfall. Efforts by the new Indonesian government to create more cordial relations with the West were reciprocated in Washington, although American officials were cognizant that General Suharto's regime was pledged to continue Indonesia's policy of nonalignment toward the super-powers. Moreover, Indonesia was governed by a military junta; from all appearances, the army was likely to exercise effective power until well into the 1970s. By Western standards, Indonesia hardly qualified as a democracy; yet some liberties (like freedom of the press) had been restored; and the regime was clearly dedicated to economic advancement and modernization.

Indonesia served as a prototype for many (though by no means all) of the countries in the zone of "developing" nations. Its potential for national development was vast—but so were its problems. Sukarno's administration had left the country bankrupt and economically disorganized. By 1970, the average Indonesian worker's standard of living was lower than in 1950; up to 15 percent of the labor force was unemployed; with great agricultural potential, Indonesia was required to import food to feed its burgeoning population—which was growing at a rate of 3 percent annually (and at that rate, the population would double in less than twenty-five years); the country was heavily in debt to foreign creditors (with a quarter of its foreign exchange earnings devoted to debt repayments); private investment from abroad had largely ceased; and corruption remained pervasive in the bureaucracy, the military, and other groups. Turbulent political forces —growing out of ancient religious, tribal, and regional animosities—added to uncertainty about the future.

General Suharto's government endeavored to attack such problems head on. Indonesia's non-Communist creditors (chiefly, the United States and Japan, leading a 10-nation consortium) agreed to "reschedule" the country's debts and to extend new loans (thus far, Moscow has not shown a similar willingness); the government successfully induced some 200 private business corporations to invest in Indonesia; inflation control measures were successfully introduced; and a five-year development plan was inaugurated to lift the country out of its traditional poverty (per capita income in Indonesia averaged less than $100 annually). General Suharto's visit to Washington in the spring of 1970 signified Indonesia's desire for cooperative relations with the United States and Washington's recognition of the country's importance and potential. Insofar as America succeeded in persuading Asian nations to assume greater responsibility for the security of their region after it withdrew from Southeast Asia, Indonesia (along with India and Japan) would have to play a major role. Yet American policy-makers were also conscious that a "low profile" by the United States in Indonesian affairs was dictated by the strained history of relations between the two countries in the recent past and by Indonesia's desire to remain diplomatically nonaligned. Indonesia was also endeavoring to restore normal relations with the Soviet Union and perhaps eventually to bring about a restoration of Soviet aid. As in India, American officials saw in this policy no inherent threat to the sovereignty of the country, whose determination to resist subordination to Communism had been graphically demonstrated.[63]

DEFENSE AND SECURITY IN THE PACIFIC

The strategic importance of Asia arises from a number of factors. India and Southeast Asia, along with Indonesia, lie athwart the main sea and air routes connecting Europe and the Middle East with the Far East. Japan, Formosa, Okinawa, the Philippines, and many lesser Pacific islands, form links in the defense chain safeguarding the military approaches to the Western Hemisphere and to two stalwart Western allies, Australia and New Zealand. Southeast Asia offers sources of food and raw materials needed both within and outside Asia. This region, for instance, supplies 90 percent of the world's natural rubber and 55 percent of its tin.

Three additional considerations enhance Asia's importance in the contemporary era and combine to make it perhaps the most volatile region in world affairs. First, it is the only major region in which Soviet, Chinese, and American power tend to intersect and to collide directly. All three nations have historically been "Asian powers"; each has vital interests to protect and diplomatic objectives to promote in the region. The kind of de facto delineation of spheres of influence which has kept Europe relatively stable and secure in recent years has not yet been achieved in Asia. The fact that agreement requires the concurrence of *three* powerful nations—whose mutual antagonisms remain acute—renders the achievement of Asian equilibrium unusually difficult. Second, the size of Asia and the magnitude of its problems perhaps inevitably make it a cockpit of international conflict and tension. Asia already contains more people than the rest of the world combined; by the year 2000, if present rates of population growth continue, it will have some two-thirds of the world's total population. Postwar Afro–Asian nationalism first emerged as a potent force in Asia, where nationalist movements successfully undermined British, French, Dutch (and, during the Vietnam War, some critics would say American) colonial hegemony. Much of the turmoil witnessed in contemporary Asia stems from a long tradition of anticolonial agitation, coupled with a widespread determination to eliminate pervasive poverty. Yet many Asian governments have been sorely challenged to prevent a *deterioration* in standards of living, much less to raise them appreciably. Third, and possibly the most fundamental source of Asia's lack of equilibrium, there are certain deep-seated conflicts which seem endemic to the region and which coalesce to make it in many respects the most unstable regional subsystem on the globe. The existence of many different ethnic and linguistic groups, which are often antagonistic toward their neighbors; marked geographic differences, both between and within Asian countries, making national cohesion extremely difficult; the lack of adequate transportation facilities, especially land routes; sharp (and growing) dichotomies in many Asian societies between the "Westernized" elite, whose standard of living has risen perceptibly in recent years, and the majority of the population, whose way of life has changed little for centuries and whose existence today may be closer than ever to poverty and hopelessness; the presence within Asia of several unassimilated communities (like the "overseas Chinese" and the "overseas Indians"), who are often resented by the people in whose society they live and who are suspected of being "agents" for foreign powers— these are among the major forces producing instability throughout Asia and serving to attract interventionist policies by outside powers.[64]

The United States has a unique and long-standing involvement in Asian affairs. Many Americans are perhaps unaware that contacts between their country and Asia are in many respects older than those with Europe or even Latin America. The "Yankee Clippers" carried on trade with Asia in the infancy of the American republic; the United States played a leading role in exposing Japan to contact with the outside world (thereby beginning possibly the most successful example of "modernization" by a non-Western society in recent history); acquisition of the Philippines by the United States as a result of the Spanish–American War made America "a Pacific power," at a time when its policy toward Europe remained isolationist; and despite its policy of "aid short of war" to Great Britain, the United States did not actually enter World War II until its military installations *in Asia* were attacked by Japan. During and after the war, American influence was important (and in some instances, decisive) in the decisions of Britain, France, and the Netherlands to grant independence to their colonial empires in Asia. In the postwar era, the United States has been in-

volved in two violent conflicts in Asia—the Korean War and the contest in Vietnam. By the 1970s, America was rapidly liquidating its own military involvement in the Vietnam conflict. Even then, there was no assurance that lasting stability would be achieved in Asia. Other threats to the region's security (in Thailand, in Laos, and in Korea) might well compel the United States to defend its interests and support its military allies against new dangers. In the concluding portion of this chapter, we shall examine efforts by the United States to preserve Asian security since World War II and evaluate the problem of instability in Asia for the 1970s.

The Asian Revolutionary Environment

Americans are well aware that the security of Asia has been threatened by Communist revolutionary activities and other sources of instability in the postwar period. Asia has enjoyed high priority among Communist policy-makers since the earliest days of the Bolshevik Revolution. A statement widely attributed to Lenin—"the road to Paris lies through Calcutta and Bombay"—may be apocryphal; but it accurately describes Marxist strategy toward Asia since 1917.[65] Lenin and later Soviet leaders were convinced (more than ever, after revolutionary movements failed to succeed in the West) that the capitalist nations were most vulnerable *in their colonial empires.* World War I precipitated nationalist upheavals throughout Asia and other areas where colonial systems flourished. Lenin advocated Marxist support for Afro–Asian nationalist movements, on the grounds that the collapse of European colonial structures would gravely weaken capitalist nations in Europe, thereby accelerating the process of worldwide revolution. Accordingly, as early as 1920, the Soviet-controlled Comintern Congress called for a "close alliance of all national and colonial liberation movements with Soviet Russia" and instructed Marxists to support liberation movements in Afro–Asian societies.[66] The 1920s and 1930s thus witnessed the establishment of Communist political organizations in Asia and revolutionary agitation against European rule.

Yet it was not until World War II that Asian Marxist movements gained wide popular support or were able actually to control governments in the area. As in other regions, World War II provided a potent stimulus for Communist political activity. One by one, the European colonial powers were defeated by Japan; the myth of European invincibility was forever shattered; and one of the major arguments in favor of colonialism—that it afforded "protection" to weaker societies against outside threats—was undermined. During the war, Communist groups throughout Asia gained great prestige for their role in leading resistance movements against Japanese rule; wartime experience acquired in these guerrilla operations proved invaluable to Marxist groups in later revolutionary campaigns. Asia suffered grievously from the devastation and chaos caused by the war. With the end of hostilities, Marxist organizations often emerged as the only political groups sufficiently well organized and disciplined to exercise governmental powers in an environment where political and economic disintegration were pervasive.[67]

Several other wartime and early postwar developments in Asia favored an increase in Communist gains. The victory of Mao Tse-tung's Communist movement on the Chinese mainland enhanced the prestige of Marxists and gave them a new power base to extend their activities into neighboring countries. Korea emerged from the war with a Communist regime north of the 38th parallel; with Soviet and Chinese support, North Korea maintained its existence as a "People's Republic" and threatened the security of South Korea. Southeast Asia became a major center of Communist political activity. During the war, the Vietminh (the anti-Japanese resistance movement led by Ho Chi Minh) led the struggle against Tokyo's authority; after the war, the Vietminh was at the forefront of the campaign against French colonialism. Next to Mao Tse-tung, Ho Chi Minh was perhaps the most influential Marxist leader in Asia and easily the most respected political figure in Indochina.[68] In some Asian societies, political in-fighting and rivalries among non-Communist groups weakened their ability to compete against disciplined Marxist organizations. Ancient tribal, linguistic, and ethnic antagonisms impaired the authority of postwar governments in a number of Asian countries. Efforts by European nations to reimpose colonial administrations fomented political strife and generated anti-Western sentiments (Indochina and Indonesia were conspicuous examples); Marxists were skillful in exploiting these discontents for their own advantage.

The process of decolonization in several Asian countries was prolonged, bitter, violent, and left a residue of hostility toward the West. As always, Communist groups identified with Asian anticolonialism; organizational ability and skill in guerrilla warfare made them effective instruments of anticolonial agitation; Soviet Russia's own colonial record was too historically and geographically remote to concern Asian nationalists, while China's record of dominance over many smaller Asian nations engendered even less apprehension among groups struggling against *European* colonial control. At length, as Lenin had predicted, European colonial systems were undermined, despite the efforts of some former colonial powers to maintain their hegemonies.

Nor did opportunities for Communist gains disappear once independence from Europe had been achieved. In contrast to what many Asians anticipated, the achievement of political freedom did not usher in the Age of Plenty, transforming primitive societies into modern nations. Decolonization in fact often involved *economic disruptions*, as trade links were broken and as private business investments were withdrawn. With the disappearance of alien political control, in nearly every Asian society centrifugal forces—conflicts between different religious, tribal, and ethnic groups; rivalries between the government (the "center") and the provinces; and rural–urban conflicts—threatened to destroy national cohesiveness. In Asia, as in other regions experiencing successful revolts against European colonialism, native governments found themselves sorely pressed to satisfy popular demands (or even a portion of them), often with limited resources. Irrational as they might be, public expectations concerning what the government *should* accomplish usually were far ahead of what the government *could* reasonably manage. Understandably, Asians were not attracted to Western political and economic models or ideologies; for many Asians capitalism was an epithet—a system inherently exploitive and oppressive. Soviet Russian and Chinese experience seemed more relevant to their problems than Western traditions. Under such conditions, Communist appeals were often attractive. Marxists contended that only they could really lead the Asian revolution to its successful consummation and asserted that the complete transformation of Asian society required adoption of the Communist program.

In recognizing that Asia provided a favorable environment for Communist gains after World War II, we must be wary of *overemphasizing* the extent to which the instability of the region was *caused* by Moscow, Peking, or Communist groups within other Asian countries. For it was Western influence that initially ignited the fuse of Asian nationalism and held out a new vision of material progress and political self-determination. In a literal sense, no force was more "subversive" of established political and economic orders in Asia than American idealism. President Woodrow Wilson's Fourteen Points, for example, fed nationalist aspirations during and after World War I. One historian has written that: "It may not be an exaggeration to say that in modern times only the *Communist Manifesto* of Karl Marx was more subversive. Indeed, in the relations of empires and colonies Marx was probably less subversive than Wilson."[69] Asians also identified many of their political and economic aspirations with President Franklin D. Roosevelt. Wartime pronouncements like the "Four Freedoms" (1941), along with FDR's widely circulated criticisms of British, French, Dutch, and other colonial regimes, encouraged Asian nationalists. Presidents Roosevelt and Harry S. Truman did not conceal their opposition to attempts by France and the

Netherlands to re-establish their colonial administrations in Asia after the war; and in some cases (Indonesia was one), the United States sided openly with the anticolonial movement. America's granting of independence to the Philippines after the war also heartened millions of Asians. Neither Moscow nor Peking, then, created the widespread unrest and instability throughout Asia. Conditions in Asia would not necessarily be more favorable to Western influence if the Communist Revolution in Russia had never occurred or if Mao Tse-tung's movement in China had been defeated. Moreover, as a number of commentators have pointed out, Asian political traditions and precedents can be more easily reconciled with Marxist than with Western patterns. One of America's leading students of Asian affairs, Edwin O. Reischauer, believes that Communism

forms in some respects an almost perfect continuity of tradition with the supposedly benign autocracies of Asia's past. . . . There is no part of Asia in which democratic methods of organization and control do not represent a far greater and more difficult break with past political practices than does Communist dictatorship.[70]

The Korean War and Its Implications

The Korean peninsula has served as a center of cold war conflict since the end of World War II. Like Germany and Indochina, Korea emerged from the war as a divided country; each of its separate governments remained closely linked with one of the cold war power blocs.* In all three cases, the division of the country was expected to be "temporary"; ultimately, Korea was supposed to be reunited under a government chosen by national elections. Cold war tensions made international agreements designed to achieve Korean unity impossible. In May, 1948, the American-supported Republic of Korea (South Korea) officially came into existence; in the same month, the People's Democratic Republic of Korea (North

Korea) was created under Communist auspices.

Recurrent tensions between these two states erupted into open warfare on June 25, 1950, when North Korean troops crossed the frontier of South Korea. Within hours, the United States committed its forces in behalf of South Korean defense. For the next three years, the Korean peninsula was an arena of prolonged and bloody fighting between South Korea, the United States, and several smaller free world allies versus North Korea, Communist China, and other Marxist nations supplying various kinds of support. As a result of the armistice (signed on July 27, 1953), a formal cease-fire among the belligerents was proclaimed; yet throughout the years that followed, the frontier between North and South Korea witnessed innumerable military clashes, indicating that genuine peace in the area was still remote.

Space is not available to discuss the history of the Korean War, nor is such a discussion necessary for our purpose. Our interest must be confined to the major long-term implications of the conflict for American foreign policy. Omitting the Greek crisis in the late 1940s, the Korean encounter was the first "limited war" between the American-led coalition and the Communist bloc. As such, the war in Korea opened a new era in American foreign policy; and some of the consequences of that contest were clearly felt in later conflicts, like the struggle in Vietnam. Perhaps the most fundamental characteristic of the Korean War was that it remained a *limited* military engagement. Although the decision precipitated an acute internal political crisis within the United States—which reached its peak after President Truman relieved the theater commander, General Douglas MacArthur, on April 11, 1951—the Truman administration was determined that conflict in Korea would expand neither *territorially* (by American attacks against the Chinese mainland) nor *militarily* (by using nuclear weapons against Communist ground forces and installations).[71] To American officials, acceptance of an inconclusive result on the Korean battlefield seemed infinitely preferable to running the risk of starting World War III. Yet this was not a decision congenial to many American citizens. General MacArthur's maxim— "In war, there is no substitute for victory"—commanded wide support in public and legislative opinion; it unquestionably described the traditional American mentality, growing out of the nation's experiences in past wars. Americans had not been accustomed to having their military efforts limited to "fighting with one hand tied behind their backs"; the doctrine enunciated during World War II (when the "unconditional surrender" of the Axis powers was the goal) accorded much more closely with American experience and expectations. Supporters of General MacArthur at the time and later tended to believe that the strategy followed in Korea was a mistake—if

---

*Korea became part of the Japanese empire in 1910; until the end of World War II, it served mainly as a source of raw materials for Japan and a market for its manufactured goods. Yet Japan did undertake significant industrialization in Korea, especially in the north; the south remained largely agricultural. After Japan's defeat in 1945, American military authorities drew up a hastily devised plan whereby American forces would accept the surrender of Japanese troops south of the 38th parallel, while Soviet forces would accept the Japanese surrender north of this line. Designed merely as a military demarcation line, the 38th parallel in time proved the de facto frontier between North and South Korea. Yet this boundary, one study contends, "cut across the grain of the land like a knife and had none of those characteristics, natural or social, which give real meaning to a boundary line." Shannon McKune, "The United States and Korea," in Willard L. Thorpe, ed., *The United States and the Far East* (New York: Columbia University Press, 1956), p. 81.

not a disaster. As a result of the Korean conflict, for example, a number of air force officers, supported in their viewpoints by certain legislators, formed a group called the "Never Again Club": Never again would the United States wage a war under the kind of restrictions imposed upon the armed forces in Korea. In the mid-1960s, this group vocally advocated massive American bombing of North Vietnam.[72]

Advocates of a "hard line" military strategy were not the only groups who felt frustrated and dissatisfied by the Korean War. Even many Americans who basically supported the Truman administration's policies there found the concept of limited war strange, novel, psychologically unpalatable, and difficult to adapt to America's traditional reliance upon *sea and air power* to maintain the security of the nation and its allies. For significant numbers of Americans, the results achieved in Korea—where some 34,000 American troops were killed in battle, and almost 158,000 were wounded—seemed incommensurate with the military commitment and expenditure of resources involved. What had this massive American military involvement really accomplished? In terms of positive gains, America's commitment *had* preserved the independence of South Korea; in the years ahead, this small nation would emerge as one of the more politically stable and economically dynamic states in Asia. The decision of the Truman administration to place the defense of South Korea under the auspices of the United Nations also revitalized that organization, possibly saving it from the fate of the League of Nations in dealing with international crises. Moreover, America's determination to defend South Korea did perhaps contribute in some measure to encouraging restraint by North Korea, Communist China, Soviet Russia, and perhaps other Marxist nations throughout the years ahead. Other Communist-instigated threats to the security of the free world of course occurred after 1953. Nevertheless, Communist nations were careful thereafter to avoid the kind of flagrant violation of an international frontier that had occurred in Korea; Communist China's evident reluctance to clash openly with the United States over Formosa undoubtedly had some connection with the earlier contest in Korea.

Yet the positive results attained in Korea fell considerably short of what many Americans regarded as normal (much less ideal) when the United States involved itself heavily in crises overseas. True, South Korea still existed as an independent nation. But it remained a *divided* nation and a vortex of continuing regional tension. Until 1960, Korea had an authoritarian regime under President Syngman Rhee; some Americans detected little difference between North and South Korea in terms of the lack of democratic political procedures. Popular resentment against Rhee's regime brought the President's ouster in 1960. A year later, a military coup brought General Chung Hee Park to power. His regime was also authoritarian; General Park maintained close ties with the United States (South Korea sent some 40,000 troops to Vietnam); and under his leadership Korea achieved an impressive level of economic growth. Yet America's intervention in the Korean War and its support of South Korea thereafter had not converted the country into a democracy; it had not prevented rule by a military elite; and, as events during the late 1960s made clear, it had not removed the Communist threat to the security of South Korea. America's intimate identification with the Park regime, along with South Korea's substantial involvement in the Vietnam conflict, constituted evidence to critics of national policy that the United States "preferred" right-wing military governments, especially those prepared to support its anti-Communist campaigns abroad. By such idealistic criteria, America's cooperative relationship with South Korea appeared to have achieved very little.*

Korea as a Source of Asian Insecurity

A new crisis involving North Korea on one side, versus the United States and South Korea on the other, erupted on January 23, 1968, when North Korean air and naval forces attacked and seized the American vessel *Pueblo* off the coast of the peninsula. All parties to the dispute were agreed that the *Pueblo* was engaged in intelligence-gathering operations. American officials insisted, however, that the ship was in international waters and that its seizure was a patent violation of international law. Authorities in Pyongyang claimed that the *Pueblo* had intruded into the coastal waters of North Korea, thereby infringing on the country's sovereignty. Prolonged investigation by executive

---

*By the 1970s, South Korea had achieved one of the most impressive rates of economic growth among the Afro–Asian nations. South Korea had been of course a major recipient of American economic and military assistance (totaling some $7.4 billion from 1946 through 1968). In contrast to other countries which had also received substantial aid allocations, South Korea had used this assistance effectively. In 1969, for example, South Korea experienced an overall expansion of 16 percent in its Gross National Product; this rate fell to a still impressive 10 percent in 1970. Manufacturing and export expansion grew at an even faster rate. Politically, gains have been considerably more limited. General Park was reelected President in the spring of 1971, amidst charges that his support continued to rest upon control of the army and the secret police. Many Koreans indicated that they had voted for Park without real enthusiasm and out of fear that, without his reelection, political chaos would erupt in South Korea. See the voluminous data provided on South Korea in the publication by the Agency for International Development, *Economic Data Book—East Asia* (Washington, D.C., 1971), pp. 1–12; and *The New York Times,* January 18 and May 2, 1971.

officials, legislative committees, and other groups left considerable doubt about the facts of the case. The officers and men of the *Pueblo* were captured and held prisoner in North Korea for more than a year, during which time they were mistreated by their captors. The United States finally negotiated their release. With American military forces deeply involved in Vietnam during this period, both the Johnson and Nixon administrations avoided escalating the crisis with North Korea, although President Nixon issued a stern warning to Pyongyang and re-enforced American air and naval power in the area.[73]

The *Pueblo* crisis was perhaps as much a symptom as a cause of instability in the Korean peninsula. The Korean War cease-fire agreement in 1953 had done little to remove underlying sources of tension; as in other instances of cold war conflict, no peace treaty had been agreed upon by the belligerents. The military front between North and South Korea was porous and witnessed almost daily "incidents" involving armed clashes.[74] Nor had time brought any notable diminution in hostilities between the two Korean governments. The Communist regime in Pyongyang, headed by the veteran Premier Kim Il Sung, periodically announced its intention of unifying Korea under a Communist system; General Park's government in the South was militantly anti-Communist and advocated a hard line in dealing with Communist-sponsored insurrections and other threats to its security. Ideologically, North Korea was closely identified with Communist China's revolutionary strategy abroad. That its dedication to the "liberation" of South Korea was something more than a doctrinal pronouncement was indicated early in 1968, when North Korea dispatched a team of commandos (who were killed or captured) to assassinate President Park. Both before and after that episode, North Korea supported insurrections and endeavored to foment revolt against the government of South Korea.[75]

Several other factors kept Korea in a state of greater or lesser tension. Internal pressures in North Korea were one of these. Marshal Kim, who assumed power in 1948, has sometimes been referred to as "the last of the Stalinists." His regime was an absolute dictatorship; purges eliminated opposition to his rule; North Korea had fewer contacts with the outside world in some respects than Communist China; and Kim had created a "personality cult" rivaling Stalin's and Mao Tse-tung's. Yet North Korea suffered from economic stagnation and retrogression; the disparity between the progress in North and South Korea was widening steadily, to the former's detriment.[76] North Korea's position in the international Communist system also perhaps induced erratic and unpredictable behavior by Pyongyang. North Korea adjoined both mainland China and Soviet Russia. Consequently, it was directly in

the cross-fire of the Sino–Soviet dispute. Marshal Kim clearly sought to preserve the independence of his small nation from both Marxist giants. To achieve this goal, he followed an erratic course in external affairs—accepting Moscow's line in some matters, Peking's in others, and trying to elicit economic, military, and other forms of assistance from both. North Korea agreed with Red China that Communist nations must be free to formulate their own policies at home and abroad; yet Pyongyang also sought to preserve friendly ties with the U.S.S.R. and to resist becoming a Chinese satellite. At the same time, neither Moscow nor Peking revealed any marked willingness to help Kim's government reunite Korea under Marxist control or to encourage provocative moves against the United States.[77]

The instability of Korea was plainly related also to the continuing crisis in Southeast Asia. Pyongyang's seizure of the *Pueblo* quite possibly was designed both to induce a withdrawal of South Korean forces from Vietnam and to reveal the United States as a "paper tiger" which was incapable of protecting its military allies. There is no evidence that Kim's government accomplished either objective. Yet, as the conflict in Southeast Asia moved closer to a de facto settlement, it was obvious that the Korean peninsula would remain a center of cold war animosity and Asian instability for many years to come.*

Origins of an Asian Security System

Two developments in the early 1950s combined to create great anxiety in Washington about the vulnerability of Asia: the Communist attack against South Korea and the collapse of French power in Southeast Asia. The growth of neutralist sentiment among Asian nations was also interpreted by some American officials in this period as signifying weakness in the region's defenses. Accordingly, the Eisenhower administration began to lay the basis for an organized Asian security

---

*At a later stage, we shall discuss President Nixon's new doctrine for Asia, the key principle of which was that, in the post-Vietnam War era, the United States intended to put primary responsibility for the region's defense upon the nations within the area. Among all the Asian countries affected by this redefinition of American policy, South Korea was perhaps most apprehensive about its implications. Authorities in Seoul were convinced that North Korea posed a grave and continuing threat to the security of South Korea and that, despite American aid, Communist forces possessed new and better armaments. They regarded the presence of over 60,000 American troops within their country as essential; without them, South Korea might become converted into "another Vietnam." Yet on July 9, 1970, Secretary of Defense Melvin R. Laird announced that, as part of a program to reduce its global military commitments, the United States would gradually curtail its troop strength in South Korea (with total reductions to run from 15,000 to 20,000 men in the months ahead). See *The New York Times* (June 24 and July 10, 1970).

system, more or less modeled after NATO in the West. The first step in this process was terminating the American military occupation of Japan and restoring that influential Asian power to the family of nations. Following prolonged study, the United States sponsored a conference at San Francisco which, despite Soviet opposition, agreed upon a Japanese peace treaty and restored sovereignty to the Japanese people on April 28, 1952. In the same period, a new Japanese–American defense agreement gave the United States the right to "dispose . . . land, air and sea forces in and about Japan."* As time passed, America's continued military presence in Japan proved a contentious issue, particularly among Japanese critics of the Vietnam War.[78] A new security treaty between the two countries was negotiated in 1960. This agreement, subject to revocation after one year's notice by either party, stipulated that the United States could deploy its armed forces only after "prior consultations" with the Japanese government; in effect, Tokyo now had a veto over the use of American military forces on its soil.† Another source of friction between the two nations for many years had been the future of the Ryukyu Islands, a former Japanese possession occupied by the United States since World War II. The largest island, Okinawa, had served as a major American Pacific base since World War II; it had played a key role in the bombing of North Vietnam and other parts of Southeast Asia. Late in 1969, Japanese Premier Eisaku Sato and President Richard Nixon agreed upon the return of Okinawa to Japan by 1972. To compensate the United States for the loss of this important base, Tokyo agreed that American military forces stationed within Japan might be used for purposes other than the defense of Japan itself, provided the Japanese government concurred.

The end of the occupation in Japan raised the issue of safeguarding Far Eastern countries from a renewal of Japanese aggression, a matter causing apprehensions particularly in Australia and New Zealand. Accordingly, a security treaty among Australia, New Zealand, and the United States—popularly called ANZUS—entered into force on April 29, 1952. Under Article 5, each party recognized that "an armed attack in the Pacific Area on any of the Parties would be dangerous to its own peace and safety and declares that it would act to meet the common danger in accordance with its constitutional processes." Then on August 27, 1952, a United States–Philippine treaty of defense became operative. Article 4 of this treaty duplicated Article 5 of the ANZUS treaty. On November 17, 1954, following the armistice in the Korean War, a mutual defense treaty between the United States and the Republic of South Korea entered into force. Article 3 of this treaty contained the same key stipulation as found in the ANZUS and Philippine treaties. Then on March 3, 1955, a new defense treaty was signed between the United States and the Republic of China on Formosa. Article 5 of this treaty was similar to the articles contained in the treaties cited above.

SEATO—Organization and Principles

During this period, sentiment was growing both within the United States and within allied countries in the Pacific in favor of a regional security system modeled after the earlier NATO pattern. Consequently, after extended consultations, the South East Asia Collective Defense Treaty was signed at Manila on September 8, 1954, by the governments of the United States, the United Kingdom, France, Australia, New Zealand, the Philippines, Pakistan, and Thailand. The South East Asia Treaty Organization (SEATO) began operating on February 19, 1955. To allay apprehensions among neutralist countries that SEATO threatened their freedom, there was attached a "Pacific Charter," which put the signatories on record as favoring the principle of self-determination and pledging to assist Asian states in maintaining it.

While SEATO bears a superficial resemblance to NATO, there are several fundamental points of contrast. The heart of SEATO is Article 4, providing that in case aggression occurs each party will "act to meet the common danger in accordance with its constitutional processes." The same article declares that threats of internal subversion or other threats to the peace, shall oblige the signatories to "consult immediately in order to agree on the measures which should be taken for the common defense." The treaty area is defined as the general area of Southeast Asia up to 21 degrees 30 minutes north latitude. A separate protocol to the treaty, however, designates the states of Cambodia, Laos, and South Vietnam as lying within the treaty area. In still another protocol the United States expresses its understanding that references in the treaty to aggression and armed attack apply only to *Communist-instigated* attacks. If aggression arises from any other quarters, the

---

*Quotations from the texts of treaties between the United States and Asian countries here and in the remainder of the chapter are taken from House Foreign Affairs Committee, *Treaty Provisions Relating to the Use of United States Forces for Mutual Defense*, 84th Congress, 2nd Session, 1956. This document provides a valuable comparative study of all defense treaties to which the United States is a party, pointing out significant differences in the obligations assumed under them.

†After 1960, the Japanese–American security treaty became a highly controversial issue in Japanese internal politics, leading to repeated political demonstrations against it by opponents of the agreement. Much to the surprise of many commentators, on June 22, 1970, Tokyo announced that the treaty had been renewed for another ten years; reaction to the announcement within Japan was unpredictably restrained. See *The New York Times* (June 23, 1970).

United States will consult with the SEATO powers concerning appropriate steps to be taken.

SEATO in the Balance

Has the existence of SEATO enhanced the security of Asia or weakened it? Is SEATO a source of strength for American foreign policy in Asia or a hindrance to it? From the beginning, the SEATO defense system has been criticized by substantial numbers of Americans and foreigners, who view it as epitomizing the kind of "pacto-mania" guiding the foreign policy of the United States during the Dulles–Eisenhower period.

SEATO has unquestionably suffered from several conspicuous weaknesses. Insofar as it attempted to create a replica of NATO in Asia, it was perhaps always doomed to failure, chiefly because the nations of Asia lacked Western Europe's resources, political stability, and other qualities required to promote a common defense effort. After a cease-fire had been proclaimed in Korea, the danger of direct Communist aggression against independent Asian nations seemed minimal. Yet another ominous danger—revolutionary upheaval, civil strife, and insurrectionary movements, aided by Communist nations—presented the most serious challenge to Asian security. In countering such threats, the usefulness and value of SEATO was at best questionable. Neutralist sentiment in Asia and other regions was often outspokenly opposed to Western-sponsored defense systems. Not only did states like India, Indonesia, Ceylon, and Burma refuse to join SEATO; their officials expressed the view that SEATO was a detriment to a more influential American role in Asia.

Among the nations initially joining SEATO, two in time virtually abandoned the organization. Pakistan, for example, became alienated from the United States because of Washington's refusal to support it in the conflict with India; Pakistani officials believed that Washington in fact *favored* India over Pakistan. After arriving at a *détente* with Communist China, Pakistan played little part in SEATO deliberations.* Under President

Charles de Gaulle, France similarly de-emphasized the importance of SEATO and virtually seceded from the organization. France vocally opposed America's involvement in the Vietnam War; and Paris regarded itself as a competitor with Washington for influence in Southeast Asia. While Great Britain remained a member of SEATO, it was unwilling to assume responsibilities for the defense of South Vietnam. As part of the process of liquidating its military commitments "east of Suez," London was relinquishing its historic position in the area of Singapore. Meanwhile, by the early 1970s, insurgencies (aided to a greater or lesser degree by Hanoi, Peking, and Moscow) posed threats to the security of such nations as Thailand, Laos, Cambodia, Burma, and Malaysia. By the 1970s, the contrast between the security of the NATO and SEATO areas was indeed striking. With some critics, perhaps the most serious indictment of SEATO was that the treaty was cited as a major justification for America's involvement in the Vietnam War.[79]

In the view of other commentators, however, many of the criticisms directed at SEATO missed the mark. Some critics had a distorted understanding of what the alliance was originally *intended* to accomplish. Despite superficial resemblances to NATO, in reality SEATO was never designed as "an Asian NATO"; Secretary of State Dulles realized full well that the NATO system was not applicable to Asian affairs; nor did he actually desire the kind of American commitment in that region that had been made for safeguarding European security.[80] SEATO was designed to call attention to the fact that, after the collapse of French power in Southeast Asia in the mid-1950s, the United States "intended to play a continuing and potentially larger role in the defense and security of Southeast Asia."[81] American officials were under no illusions that SEATO could replace *bilateral* defense guarantees between the United States and key Asian nations; and they were aware that, in the final analysis, *American power* was perhaps the crucial ingredient in promoting the

---

*Early in 1971, Pakistan's role in Asian affairs—perhaps its future as a nation—was called into question by a civil war erupting when East Pakistan sought to form a separate state (called *Bangla Desh*). Separated by 1200 miles of Indian territory, East and West Pakistan comprise very different cultural, linguistic, and economic regions. Since the country's creation in 1947, tensions and ill-will have characterized relations between East and West Pakistan. One of the poorest regions on the globe (with an annual per capita income below $50), East Pakistan has long resented its subordinate position in the political and economic affairs of the nation, despite the fact that it has a population of some 75 million versus 55 million in West Pakistan. The Bengali population of East Pakistan has little in common with the Punjab culture prevailing in the West; but the Bengals of East Pakistan are linked to the Bengali provinces of

northeast India. For over two decades, East Pakistanis have been convinced that they have been denied their rightful share of political power; nor has the central government treated the region equitably in economic and financial affairs. Long-standing recriminations between the two regions reached a climax early in 1971, when revolt against the central government swept East Pakistan. The rebellion was quickly and ruthlessly suppressed by the government's armed forces (in many cases, using American-supplied arms). Although the Bengali secession movement appeared to have been crushed, two conclusions seemed warranted. Few of the underlying causes of political upheaval in Pakistan had been removed; and new outbreaks of violence within the country appeared to be inevitable. For an informative and objective discussion of Pakistan's internal problems, see Peggy Durdin, "The Political Tidal Wave That Struck East Pakistan," *The New York Times Magazine*, May 2, 1971, pp. 24–25, 88–94; and see *Newsweek*, LXXVII (March 22, 1971), 35–36.

security of Asia. As for the objection that certain Asian countries opposed America's role in regional defense, it was noteworthy that some Asian neutralists (Cambodia was an example) actually *sought* a defense agreement with the United States, while others (a prominent case was India, after the attack by Red China in 1962) implicitly relied upon America's readiness to support its defense efforts. Indeed, India and several other Asian countries perhaps depended upon the existence of an American "nuclear umbrella" to protect them from a Soviet or (what was more likely) a Chinese attack. Whether expressed formally in the existence of SEATO or not, intimate American involvement in the security of Asia has been, and remains, a reality and a factor momentously affecting the region's future.[82] SEATO has also served another function. According to American officials, it has provided a principal justification under domestic and international law for the commitment by the United States to the defense of South Vietnam and other Southeast Asian nations. Since the treaty was ratified by the Senate, by a vote of 82 to 1, executive officials maintained that America's involvement in Vietnam had the approval of the Senate and that it conformed with the requirements of international law.[83] This interpretation was, needless to say, sharply contested by critics of the Vietnam War.[84]

On balance, SEATO perhaps *added* little to the security of Asia. The language of the SEATO treaty did not *require* the United States to assume a massive defense commitment for South Vietnam, although the treaty certainly *permitted* this development and gave it legal sanction. The terms of the treaty did not obligate America to do anything it could not (or probably would not) have done in the absence of a treaty. As we shall see, the Nixon Doctrine, enunciated in 1969, underscored the fact that the United States still had a responsibility for the defense of Asia and that it would continue to accept this obligation.

THE AGONY OF VIETNAM

The Vietnam Debate in Perspective

For almost a generation—from World War II to the 1970s—the United States has been directly or indirectly involved in the affairs of Southeast Asia. Beginning with the first half of the 1960s, America became engaged in what was, by many standards, the most agonizing and frustrating military conflict in its entire history. Controversy had surrounded the Korean War, but the contest in Vietnam presented even greater complexities for American policy-makers and proved infinitely more divisive for public opinion in the United States. While these two conflicts had some points in common, the differences between them were

striking. The Korean War had occurred because of a clear-cut case of "aggression" by Communist forces across an international frontier. The Vietnam War really embraced *several* kinds of hostility and violent upheaval: To some extent, it was a continuation of the anticolonial campaign against French, and later American, influence in Southeast Asia; in part, it was an effort by North Vietnam, supported by Red China and Soviet Russia, to unify Indochina under Communist rule; it was also an attempt by South Vietnam, relying heavily upon the United States, to preserve its existence as a separate nation under a government opposed to Marxist rule; in South Vietnam, it entailed a clash between the rural provinces and the central government in Saigon, as well as political competition among rival groups and movements for control of the government; it also involved conflict in adjacent Asian states (like Cambodia, Laos, and Thailand) between groups oriented toward North Vietnam and Red China, on the one hand, and those supporting the incumbent government and the United States, on the other hand.

Another key difference between the earlier Korean conflict and the Vietnam War was that in the latter case, *virtually every significant fact and decision relating to America's involvement in Southeast Asia after the mid-1950s was controversial*, even among informed students of Asian affairs.* How did the Vietnam conflict "begin"?

*The literature on the Vietnam conflict is voluminous and highly varied; some of it is polemical and ought to be used judiciously. Among the more worthwhile studies and collections of materials bearing on the contest are: Douglas Pike, *Viet Cong* (Cambridge, Mass.: M.I.T. Press, 1966), perhaps the most illuminating study of this movement available; George M. Kahin and John W. Lewis, *The United States in Vietnam*, rev. ed. (New York: Delta, 1967), a critical but scholarly treatment of America's role in Vietnam; Marcus G. Raskin and Bernard B. Fall, eds., *The Viet-Nam Reader* (New York: Random House, 1965); Marvin E. Gettleman, ed., *Viet Nam* (Greenwich, Conn.: Fawcett, 1965); Edwin O. Reischauer, *Beyond Vietnam: The United States and Asia* (New York: Random House, 1967); Chester A. Bain, *Vietnam: The Roots of Conflict* (Englewood Cliffs, N.J.: Prentice-Hall, 1967); Denis Warner, *The Last Confucian* (New York: Macmillan, 1963); Donald S. Zagoria, *Vietnam Triangle: Moscow, Peking, Hanoi* (New York: Pegasus, 1967); Bernard Newman, *Background to Viet-Nam* (New York: New American Library, 1966); Roger Hilsman, *People's War—People's Army* (New York: Bantam, 1968), a presentation of the guerrilla warfare theories of General Vo Nguyen Giap; Ernst Benz, *Buddhism or Communism: Which Holds the Future of Asia?* (Garden City, N.Y.: Doubleday, 1965); P. J. Honey, *Communism in North Vietnam* (Cambridge, Mass.: M.I.T. Press, 1963); Jean Lacouture, *Vietnam: Between Two Truces* (New York: Random House, 1966). One of the most scholarly and balanced students of Vietnam and Southeast Asia was the late Bernard B. Fall, author of several books and many articles, including *The Two Vietnams: A Political and Military Analysis*, rev. ed. (New York: Praeger, 1964), *The Viet Minh Regime* (Ithaca, N.Y.: Cornell University Press, 1954), *Ho Chi Minh on Revolution: Selected Writings, 1920–1966* (New York: Praeger, 1966), *Last Reflections on a War* (Garden City, N.Y.:

When and how did the United States become inextricably involved in it? What were the strategic and diplomatic interests of the United States in Southeast Asia? By what process did the American commitment in Vietnam steadily expand—reaching more than 500,000 troops and an expenditure of more than $24 billion annually by the late 1960s? What factors accounted for the inability of the United States to accomplish its major objectives in Southeast Asia? Why was public opinion in America confused and disunified concerning the conflict in Vietnam? These and a number of other basic inquiries engendered sharp disagreement among government officials and citizens in the United States. Even when facts about the Vietnam War were not in dispute (it could hardly be denied, for example, that the United States was the instigator of the SEATO defense treaty and its most powerful member), the *meaning* of these facts in terms of their implications for American foreign policy remained highly debatable. Far more than was the case in the Korean conflict, viewpoints about the struggle in Vietnam, even among academicians, tended to be expressed fervently, often polemically. Like the Arab–Israeli dispute, the Vietnam issue was a question on which commentators found it difficult to preserve detachment and objectivity; any discussion of the problem was apt to be colored by implicit and explicit value judgments.

Vietnam in the Early Postwar Period

During World War II, President Roosevelt endeavored to persuade the French to make concessions to Indochinese nationalist demands, most militantly expressed by the Vietminh led by Moscow-trained Ho Chi Minh. Despite mild American opposition, in 1946 Paris asserted its authority over the country once more, although France admitted Indochina into the newly formed 'French Union.' Such concessions (leaving the exact status of Indochina highly ambiguous) did not satisfy nationalist demands; at the end of 1946, the Vietminh spearheaded a revolt against French rule that lasted until 1954, when the French were finally defeated in a decisive military contest at Dienbienphu.[85] At the ensuing Geneva Conference of 1954, Indochina was partitioned at the 17th parallel, into the State of Vietnam (South Vietnam) and the Democratic Republic of Viet-

nam (North Vietnam). Other articles in the Geneva accord called for the independence and "neutralization" of neighboring Laos and Cambodia.*

As the first independent leader of South Vietnam, President Ngo Dinh Diem, a Western-trained and Western-educated figure, endeavored to unify the country, to eliminate pervasive corruption, and to impose a modern system of administration. Meanwhile, approximately a million refugees from Communist North Vietnam poured across the border into South Vietnam. This group both imposed enormous economic and social strains upon Diem's new regime and introduced Communist infiltration into the country, who later served as a nucleus for Communist-led Viet Cong forces. Under Diem, Vietnam undoubtedly made some progress in economic modernization and in laying the basis for a stable political order. Such gains were imperiled, however, by the growing estrangement between Diem's regime and the masses. From the beginning, Diem was suspect because of his ties with, and active encouragement by, the West. Moreover, nepotism became rife under his administration, as the government of South Vietnam became a personal enclave of Diem and his relatives. Nor was Diem receptive to suggestions involving the liberalization and reform of his government made by officials in Washington. In whatever degree Diem was prepared to accept vast quantities of American aid, he was disinclined to introduce measures curtailing his own extensive authority or in any way satisfying the growing complaints of diverse groups within the country.[86]

By 1959, Communist-led Viet Cong forces— materially and morally aided by North Vietnam

---

*An international conference called at Geneva assembled on April 26 and lasted until July 21, 1954, in an effort to arrive at a permanent agreement upon the future of Southeast Asia following the defeat of French forces by the Vietminh and other anticolonial groups in Indochina. Officially, the United States was not a party to this conference; Secretary of State Dulles attended it only briefly; and the United States did not sign the Geneva accord. Under the agreements arrived at, Indochina was divided at the 17th parallel; French forces were to carry out military evacuations south of this line and Communist forces led by Ho Chi Minh were to withdraw north of it. Within two years (by July 20, 1956) national elections were supposed to be conducted throughout the country under United Nations supervision. In nearby Laos, all Vietminh forces were to withdraw into two northeastern provinces. Thus the Geneva Conference created four separate states—South and North Vietnam, Laos, and Cambodia—which were expected to be free of foreign military influence. Although America did not sign the Geneva agreements, it pledged to abide by them; but its representative also warned that the United States would view any renewal of aggression in the area with grave concern and as a threat to global peace. For the agreements and commentary on them, see Marvin E. Gettleman, *Viet Nam: History, Documents, and Opinions on a Major World Crisis* (Greenwich, Conn.: Fawcett, 1965), pp. 118–178.

Doubleday, 1967). See also J. William Fulbright, *The Vietnam Hearings* (New York: Random House, 1966); Henry A. Kissinger, "The Viet Nam Negotiations," *Foreign Affairs* 42 (January, 1969), 211–234; John T. McAlister, Jr., *Viet Nam: The Origins of Revolution* (New York: Knopf, 1969); Richard M. Pfeffer, ed., *No More Vietnams: The War and the Future of American Foreign Policy* (New York: Harper & Row, 1968); Senate Foreign Relations Committee, *Background Information Relating to Southeast Asia and Vietnam.* 5th rev. ed. (Washington, D.C.: U.S. Government Printing Office, 1969)

and by Red China—opened a drive to subvert Diem's government. As the months passed, in spite of growing assistance to Saigon by the United States, the Viet Cong steadily consolidated its position. The government in Saigon was losing the loyalty of the masses. As the Viet Cong's activities mounted, the United States in turn became openly insistent that radical changes be made by Diem's administration while there was still time to defeat the insurgents. The Diem regime was unresponsive to such pleas. Finally, at the end of 1963, a military-led *coup d'état* overthrew the Diem government. South Vietnam was governed by military juntas until 1966, when a constituent assembly was elected. The new constitution, adopted in 1967, provided for a new government, led by a strong President and a two-house legislature. As a result of elections held late in that year, General Nguyen Van Thieu was chosen President, with Marshal Nguyen Cao Ky as Vice President. Supporters of American policy in Vietnam regarded these developments as marking at least some progress toward the democratization of the South Vietnamese government; critics of the Vietnam War tended to view them as meaningless changes, doing little to alter the authoritarian character of the Saigon regime.

The Growing American Commitment in Vietnam

Meanwhile, the American commitment to the defense of South Vietnam grew steadily. As early as October, 1954, President Eisenhower offered economic assistance to the government in Saigon; a few months later, the United States agreed to train South Vietnamese military forces, while in the same period the SEATO treaty was extended to protect the security of Vietnam.[87] By the late 1950s, America had a large Military Advisory Group (MAG) in South Vietnam; in mid-1959, the first American soldier was killed in the Vietnam conflict. At the end of 1960, North Vietnam announced the creation of the National Liberation Front (NLF), deemed by the Viet Cong and Hanoi the only "legitimate" government of South Vietnam. In the months which followed, North Vietnamese–Viet Cong efforts to communize Vietnam increased steadily, as did the magnitude of America's commitment to the security of South Vietnam.

Yet by the end of 1962, only some 4000 American forces were stationed in Vietnam. After he entered the White House early in 1961, President John F. Kennedy had ordered a thorough study by executive agencies of the problem of Vietnam. From the beginning, Kennedy was convinced that the challenge of Vietnam was not essentially a *military* one; the crisis was more of a political, economic, and diplomatic conflict which had to be resolved chiefly by reliance upon nonmilitary

methods. Kennedy endeavored, with no very conspicuous success, to build up the capacity of the United States for waging counter-insurgency warfare successfully. He urged the Diem regime in Saigon (again with little apparent result) to make concessions to popular demands and to strengthen village security against Viet Cong terrorism.* In a statement, later quoted widely by critics of America's involvement in Vietnam, President Kennedy asserted: "In the final analysis, it is their war. They are the ones who have to win it or lose it. We can help them, we can give them equipment, we can send our men out there as advisers, but they have to win it, the people of Vietnam."[88] President Kennedy was no less persuaded, however, that the United States had to honor the commitments made to the government of South Vietnam, extending back to 1954; he blamed the Communists for rejecting peaceful solutions to the problem (like the "neutralization" of Southeast Asia); he was convinced that Communist China sought to dominate Southeast Asia and to eject American influence from the region; he was certain that many of the insurgents in South Vietnam were agents of North Vietnam and were being supported by that government; he believed that the crisis in South Vietnam was closely related to the security of other Southeast Asian nations; and he did not think the United States could "abandon" South Vietnam without the gravest consequences for regional and global security.[89] Just before his tragic death, President Kennedy declared: "What helps to win the war, we support; what interferes with the war effort, we oppose. . . . We want the war to be won, the Communists to be contained, and the Americans to go home. That is our policy. . . . We are not there to see a war lost. . . ."[90]

By the end of 1963, the United States had committed 15,000 of its own troops to the defense of Vietnam. Thereafter, the conflict became rapidly "Americanized," with the United States bearing an ever-larger share of the military and financial burden for safeguarding the security of South Vietnam. A significant episode in this process occurred in mid-1964, when (on August 2 and 4), North Vietnamese vessels attacked American ships off the coast of Vietnam. On August 7, Con-

---

*For a detailed discussion of the frustrations encountered, both in America and in South Vietnam, in the efforts to evolve an effective counter-insurgency strategy, see Roger Hilsman, *To Move a Nation* (Garden City, N.Y.: Doubleday, 1967), pp. 413–440. Despite Kennedy's efforts, it must be observed that even he had certain doubts about America's ability to wage guerrilla (or antiguerrilla) campaigns successfully. Reflecting on the Bay of Pigs crisis in 1962, when anti-Communist forces tried to overthrow Castro's government, Kennedy said: "We cannot, as a free nation, compete with our adversaries in tactics of terror, assassination, false promises, counterfeit mobs and crises." See Theodore C. Sorensen, *Kennedy* (New York: Harper & Row, 1965), p. 631.

gress approved the <u>Tonkin</u> <u>Gulf</u> <u>Resolution</u> authorizing the President to "take all necessary measures to repel any armed attack against the forces of the United States and to prevent further aggression."* President Lyndon Johnson and his advisers repeatedly invoked the authority of this resolution as one (but only one) of the sources providing a <u>legal</u> <u>basis</u> for America's involvement in the Vietnam conflict. Critics of the war later contended that Congress had not been given the true facts when it passed the resolution and that, in any case, President Johnson had exceeded the authority conferred upon him by Congress when America intervened heavily in Vietnam.[91]

American involvement in Vietnam accelerated rapidly during the Johnson administration. Continuous bombing of North Vietnam began early in 1965; every few months, additional military units from the United States were sent to Southeast Asia, until the total exceeded 500,000 by 1968; by the late 1960s, the war was costing the United States around $2 billion monthly to wage; and by early 1969, American combat deaths in the conflict had reached the level of the Korean War (almost 34,000 fatalities). Officials in Washington and military commanders in Vietnam periodically issued optimistic reports that this extensive commitment of American men and resources was reversing the tide of battle; that the enemy was "hurting badly" as a result of the American–South Vietnamese military effort; that South Vietnam was becoming more politically stable and widening its base of popular support; and that the war was becoming too costly for the enemy to maintain. Late in 1968, South Vietnamese President Thieu asserted that Communist forces had lost the war on the battlefield.[92]

Yet as the pace and magnitude of America's commitment in Vietnam expanded, so did dissatisfaction with the war within the United States. Although dissent had surrounded every war in which the United States had engaged, the Vietnam conflict established some kind of record for internal dissension, public acrimony, lack of confidence in presidential leadership, legislative discontent, and general dissatisfaction with the course of events in Southeast Asia. As time passed, the Johnson administration suffered from a real or imagined "credibility gap": Among many segments of American opinion, official statements about the progress of the war were often sharply

at variance with facts brought to light by news media or with the interpretation of events by informed students of Asian affairs. A case in point was the "Tet offensive" early in 1968, in which Communist guerrillas inflicted widespread destruction in Saigon, Hué, and other cities of South Vietnam. Critics of the American role in Vietnam interpreted this enemy attack as proof that the war could not be won militarily; supporters of the Johnson administration replied that the Viet Cong and Hanoi failed to win their objectives in this campaign and suffered irretrievable military losses in the process, making the Communist side more receptive than ever to a negotiated settlement of the conflict. This was merely one instance among many in which domestic opinion in the United States was sharply fragmented. "Doves" and other critics of America's involvement became more insistent than ever that the United States liquidate its military commitment in Southeast Asia. Although they were never more than a minority of the American people, such critics asserted their viewpoints loudly and incessantly, often relying upon "peace marches," the disruption of public meetings, and other dramatic tactics to communicate their ideas forcefully. The ordinary American, studies of public opinion and of voting behavior indicated, also was frustrated and dissatisfied with the course of events in Southeast Asia. Yet the average citizen rather consistently identified himself with neither the "hawks" nor the "doves." His support for the basic policies of the Johnson and Nixon administrations remained fairly high. Most Americans desired neither to expand the war further nor to "abandon" South Vietnam; while they shared many of the criticisms expressed by the "doves," they *rejected* the idea that the United States should withdraw its forces from Southeast Asia unilaterally or that it could be indifferent to the consequences of a Communist victory in Vietnam.*

---

*The Tonkin Gulf Resolution is discussed at greater length in Chapter 6. For the text of the resolution, see *Documents on American Foreign Relations: 1964* (New York: Harper & Row, 1965), pp. 216–217. As a result of continuing controversy between legislative and executive policy-makers over their prerogatives in foreign affairs, on June 24, 1970, the Senate repealed this resolution by a vote of 81 to 10. President Nixon promptly announced, however, that this action would not affect his authority over the armed forces in Southeast Asia. See *The New York Times* (June 25, 1970).

*In no military conflict in American history perhaps did public opinion play so significant a role as the Vietnam conflict. Yet, as was emphasized in Chapter 7, public opinion is an extremely complex phenomenon; its precise impact upon policy-making is even now far from clear. As in many other foreign policy issues, public opinion toward the Vietnam War exhibited a number of anomalies and inconsistencies; the course of events in Southeast Asia sometimes influenced it heavily. For example, from mid-1965 to mid-1969, the percentage of Americans who said it had been a mistake for the United States to send troops to Vietnam ranged from over 25 percent (in 1965) to 58 percent (in 1969). Yet, the proportion of citizens who favored an immediate American withdrawal from Vietnam remained reasonably stable, at approximately 20 percent, from the beginning of the war. Under the Nixon administration, 6 out of 10 Americans were disillusioned with American involvement in the war; yet late in 1969, over half the people approved the President's handling of the conflict. By early 1970, after peace talks in Paris had gone on for several months, almost three-fourths of the citizens polled declared that the Paris discussions were *not* making headway. Asked

By 1967–1968, the controversy over the conduct of the war in Vietnam had reached a new level of intensity and acrimony. President Johnson and his advisers reiterated endlessly that: (1) The United States would fulfill its long-standing commitments to South Vietnam; (2) the willingness of the United States to honor all its treaty commitments was at stake in the Vietnam issue; (3) the crux of the conflict in Vietnam was the independence of South Vietnam, which the United States intended to preserve; (4) since Vietnam was a test case in the Communist strategy of "wars of national liberation," failure to block Marxist expansionism in that area would encourage Communist intrusions elsewhere; (5) the United States had always been, and remained, willing to negotiate a cease-fire in Vietnam, but Hanoi (supported by Communist China) had shown no readiness to negotiate a cease-fire. Critics of the Vietnam War of course rejected these contentions. In their view, the United States was intruding into a "civil war" in Indochina; the American military presence itself was a destabilizing influence and generated support for the Communist cause; the Johnson administration's reasons for prolonging the war rested upon ideas (like the supposed aggressiveness of "international Communism" and the discredited "domino theory" of Asian vulnerability) having little relevance for contemporary international relations; the American effort in Vietnam was widely resented—especially by Afro–Asian societies; Washington's identification with the military clique governing South Vietnam reflected a deep malaise—the American government's preference for right-wing political regimes whose claim to American aid was their posture of anti-Communism; and the longer the conflict in Vietnam was prolonged, the more urgent domestic problems

what the United States ought to do to extricate itself from Vietnam, over 20 percent had "no opinion"; 26 percent favored a unilateral American withdrawal; while 32 percent thought the war ought to be escalated to a decisive conclusion. A detailed study of public opinion and the Vietnam conflict found several interesting conclusions: Public opinion was *not* in the main a major constraint upon executive policy-makers; throughout the period studied, American opinion was fairly constant in showing both a willingness to negotiate with the enemy and an opposition to abandonment of South Vietnam; the vast majority of Americans could be classified as neither "hawks" nor "doves," but basically supported the policies of Presidents Johnson and Nixon; the opinions of the "informed" (or elite) public and the mass of citizens were remarkably parallel on the Vietnam issue. See Sidney Verba *et al.*, "Public Opinion and the War in Vietnam," *American Political Science Review* **LXI** (June, 1967), 317–334; *The New York Times* (October 5 and 19, and November 27, 1969); and the Gallup Poll early in 1970, as reprinted in the *Baton Rouge Morning Advocate* (March 23, 1970). For a study emphasizing the degree to which "elite opinion" did compel the Johnson administration to change its policies, see Townsend Hoopes, *The Limits of Intervention* (New York: McKay, 1969).

within the American society were neglected. Supporters and critics of American policy in Vietnam based their assessments on fundamentally different premises and value judgments. More and more, the clash between these differing interpretations resembled a "dialogue of the deaf," as meaningful communications between them became impossible.

Finally, on March 31, 1968, President Johnson announced that the United States would unilaterally undertake a de-escalation of the war by ceasing the bombing north of the 20th parallel in Indochina. He invited Communist spokesmen to join in cease-fire negotiations. At the same time, President Johnson announced he would not seek renomination for the presidency—a decision dictated primarily by the evident public dissension over his Asian policies. After several weeks of diplomatic sparring, discussions were opened in Paris on May 13. As was not entirely unpredictable on the basis of the experience in the Korean War, the Paris talks were almost immediately deadlocked —where they remained for many months.

"Vietnamization" and the Cambodian Invasion

Richard M. Nixon's election to the presidency in 1968 (coupled with the defeat of several vocal critics of American policy in Vietnam) was widely interpreted as a mandate for a middle-of-the-road strategy toward the conflict in Southeast Asia. Clearly, the American people desired no widening of the war, as "hawks" demanded. Yet they were equally opposed to a rapid American military evacuation from Southeast Asia, amounting to a graphic defeat for the United States or the "abandonment" of South Vietnam and adjacent Asian countries to Communist control.

After a thorough review of policy alternatives, President Nixon announced his acceptance of the program of "Vietnamization": Gradually, as American forces were withdrawn from the country, the government of South Vietnam would assume the military burden involved in national defense; economic and military aid from the United States would no doubt have to be extended to Saigon for many months in the future. The Nixon administration realized perhaps better than its critics that the strategy of "Vietnamization" was a calculated risk. It offered no guarantees of success; and the future of South Vietnam (along with Cambodia and Laos) clearly hung in the balance. But perhaps better than any suggested alternative, it steered a middle course between the two extremes of immediate American evacuation of Southeast Asia, and an indefinite prolongation of the conflict, which both the new administration and the majority of the American people rejected.[93]

Having announced his policy of "Vietnamization" and made public his plans for the scheduled withdrawal of American forces from Vietnam, President Nixon electrified the world (including some of his own advisers) by informing the country on April 30, 1970, that American troops had invaded Cambodia. Coordinating their attack with the American offensive, South Vietnamese forces also crossed the Cambodian frontier. Although he perhaps underestimated the degree of opposition, President Nixon was cognizant that his decision would cause "deep divisions" within the American society; he also knew that for a time, the peace discussions in Paris (which had remained deadlocked for many months) would be adversely affected. Accordingly, President Nixon set stringent limits on the Cambodian operation: American troops were not to advance more than 21 miles across the border, and they were to be withdrawn within 60 days (or by July 1).

What gains did the While House expect to realize from this highly controversial undertaking? The Cambodian offensive had several major and minor objectives. It was designed to eliminate the enemy "sanctuaries" in eastern Cambodia, which for many years had supported Communist operations against South Vietnam. It was hoped that the enemy's main headquarters (the Central Office for South Vietnam or COSVN) would be captured. The American–South Vietnamese thrust into Cambodia would relieve increasingly ominous Communist pressure against that country and strengthen the defenses of nearby Laos. It would give South Vietnamese (ARVIN) forces needed combat experience—an essential element in the success of "Vietnamization." And above all, with the monsoon season approaching, it would *gain time* (six months or more) in which Saigon could prepare itself for the evacuation of American forces. It was also hoped (although perhaps not seriously expected) that the success of the Cambodian operation would induce Hanoi to negotiate an end to the Vietnam conflict. The Cambodian offensive also had a larger goal. In recent months, as we emphasized in Chapter 11, the Soviet Union had expanded its presence significantly in the Middle East (principally in Egypt); American officials were clearly concerned about this growth in Communist influence. For Moscow and Peking, the meaning of Cambodia was that the United States would use force when necessary to preserve its vital interests.

To the surprise of many "doves," American forces were withdrawn from Cambodia on schedule, although Saigon kept troops within the country. As a result of the operation, the Nixon administration claimed that over 11,000 Communists had been killed and some 2000 captured; a stockpile of some 25,000 enemy weapons—along with 15 million rounds of ammunition and over 60 tons of food and medicine—had been seized. The action in Cambodia had given South Vietnamese forces valuable combat experience, and Saigon's troops had on several occasions performed credit-

ably. Viewing the Cambodian expedition as "visible proof of the success of Vietnamization," President Nixon announced an acceleration in the timetable of American withdrawal from Southeast Asia. By most criteria, the campaign was a military success, giving Saigon a period of several months of preparation for America's withdrawal.

Yet several items had to be entered on the liability side of the Cambodian ledger. Domestic opposition to America's involvement in Southeast Asia was revived, leading to new outbreaks of campus unrest. Antiwar sentiment in Congress, particularly in the Senate, reached a new level of intensity; and the Cambodian invasion gave fresh impetus to those legislators seeking to curtail the President's power to commit American troops abroad without congressional approval.* Predictably, the Paris peace negotiations remained deadlocked. Conflict between the people of South Vietnam and Cambodia, which had its origins in centuries-old strife and suspicion, flared anew. Cambodia's new government, led by General Lon Nol, remained weak and militarily vulnerable; after several weeks of widespread fighting, Cambodia's economic problems had perhaps been magnified. As time passed, there was no sign of a *permanent dimunition* of Communist strength in Cambodia or in Laos to the north. Even if America disclaimed any responsibility for Cambodia's future (and the invasion inevitably strengthened the ties between the two countries), all pretense of "neutrality" or nonalignment had been dropped by Lon Nol's new regime; its destiny was now linked directly with that of South Vietnam. For its part, Saigon was likely to discover that even limited military operations in Cambodia (undertaken, for example, periodically to clean out Communist sanctuaries) were a heavy drain upon its own military capabilities. Although Communist forces suffered a tactical defeat in the Cambodian offensive, there was no evidence either that it curtailed their long-range military capabili-

*Executive and legislative prerogatives in the foreign policy field are discussed in detail in Chapters 3 and 5. America's growing commitment in Southeast Asia spurred efforts in the Senate to curtail the President's authority to use the armed forces overseas without legislative authorization. Thus, as we have noted, following several weeks of prolonged and often acrimonious debate, on June 24, 1970, the Senate voted to repeal the Tonkin Gulf Resolution authorizing the President to use force in support of American objectives in Southeast Asia. Then on July 1, in what most commentators viewed as a largely symbolic gesture, the Senate adopted the "Cooper–Church amendment" to a foreign military sales bill, stipulating various restrictions upon *future* American involvement in Cambodia. These steps were, however, counterbalanced by two forces: the House of Representatives did not share many of the Senate's reservations; and President Nixon (like his predecessors) repeatedly stated that he did not "need" congressional approval in exercising his powers as Commander-in-Chief of the armed services. See *The New York Times* (May 16, June 14, June 25, July 1, and July 10, 1970).

ties in Southeast Asia or that it had induced them to seek a negotiated peace. Strategically, it was difficult to discern any major respect in which the Cambodian operation had changed the nature of the conflict in Southeast Asia?

Whether the expedition into Cambodia had been "worth the price" would depend perhaps mainly upon the outcome of one development: How well did the governments of South Vietnam and Cambodia *use* the time which had been gained by this tactical success? To date—with the military future of Cambodia still uncertain and the success of "Vietnamization" far from assured —the evidence offered only limited encouragement.*

Despite the uncertain prospects of "Vietnamization," the Nixon Administration moved ahead with its announced program of American military retrenchment in Vietnam, and throughout Asia as a whole. At the peak of American military involvement in the Vietnam conflict in mid-1968, the United States had committed approximately 550,000 troops; after that time, phased withdrawals reduced the number of American forces to some 284,000 by early 1971; this number was expected to decline to 180,000 by the end of 1971; and some estimates held that by the end of 1972 around 100,000 American troops would be left in Vietnam.

How far would the process of American military retrenchment in Vietnam and other Southeast Asian nations be carried? What precisely was meant by President Nixon's pledge to bring about a "total American withdrawal" from this vulnerable area? By the early 1970s, it was clear that antiwar sentiment in the United States was strong and that it was becoming more vocal with each passing month. At the same time, the Nixon Administration steadfastly resisted the demands of some groups that the White House publicly announce a "deadline," after which *all* American forces would be evacuated from Vietnam. Three considerations dictated the administration's caution in this matter. First, on the assumption that Hanoi and the Viet Cong ranked an American withdrawal from Vietnam among its foremost objectives, what incentive would the Communist side have to negotiate an acceptable settlement if the United States conceded this objective unilaterally? A second consideration was closely related: the fate of American prisoners of war still in Com-

munist hands. The Nixon Administration was determined to secure their release, using the continued presence of American forces in South Vietnam as a bargaining point toward that end.

Third, there was the question of America's "residual forces" in Vietnam and elsewhere in Southeast Asia. As we shall see, under the Nixon Doctrine the United States planned to assign the primary responsibility for providing ground forces needed for Asian defense to the countries most immediately threatened. Insofar as America's continued involvement in Vietnam is concerned, two points about this provision of the Nixon Doctrine require emphasis. The Asian nations themselves were expected to bear the *primary* responsibility for furnishing ground forces; this did not necessarily mean that *no* American ground forces would remain in the area. Under the Nixon Doctrine, the United States could (and doubtless would) retain "support forces," air and naval units, military advisers and comparable military units throughout Asia. As long as they remained in Vietnam and other vulnerable areas (like Thailand), these forces might have to be "protected" in the event of a new military threat. Hopefully, as the program of "Vietnamization" succeeded, the government of South Vietnam could provide the ground forces needed for that purpose. But, as we have observed, the success of Vietnamization was far from assured; as long as *any* kind of American military contingents were present in Southeast Asia or other combat zones, the risk clearly existed that the United States would need to protect them, perhaps by reintroducing ground troops.

Under these conditions, the only promising avenue for a total American military evacuation of Vietnam and other Southeast Asia countries appeared to be a *political settlement*, laying the basis for Asian security. As long as the Paris peace negotiations remained stalled—and by late 1971 they had entered their fourth year of seemingly fruitless discussions—the probability seemed great that the United States would retain a military commitment in Vietnam for several years in the future.*

The "Nixon Doctrine"

A significant development in American foreign policy toward Asia, and for other areas of the world as well, for the 1970s was the announcement of the Nixon Doctrine in the summer of 1969. Sometimes popularly called the Asian (or

---

*Our account of the American–South Vietnamese invasion of Cambodia relies heavily upon *The New York Times* (May 1, May 3, May 10, June 21, June 29, June 30, and July 12, 1970). For an illuminating analysis of how President Nixon arrived at the decision to undertake the Cambodian campaign (highlighting the extent to which the President makes the foreign policies of the United States, often ignoring his principal advisers), see the analysis by Hedrick Smith in *ibid.*, (June 30, 1970). And for an evaluation of the pros and cons of the operation after American troops were withdrawn, see *Newsweek* LXXVI (July 13, 1970), 16–29.

*For a discussion of America's future military involvement in Southeast Asia and other parts of the region, see President Nixon's report to Congress on American foreign policy, "U.S. Foreign Policy for the 1970s: Building for Peace," (Washington, D.C.: the While House, February 25, 1971), pp. 9–23; 91–114; and *The New York Times*, February 28, March 8, and April 11, 1971.

Guam) Doctrine, this restatement of American foreign policy was perhaps designed most basically to reflect the lessons of the nation's prolonged and frustrating involvement in the Vietnam War. As the conflict in Southeast Asia was being reduced, the Nixon Administration sought to clarify America's future role in Asian affairs and to reaffirm certain fundamental goals of the United States in foreign relations which had often become obscured by the controversy over the conflict in Vietnam.

Before identifying the main elements in the Nixon Doctrine, several qualifications about this reassessment of American foreign policy need to be made. As with previous "doctrines" of this kind (and the Truman Doctrine is a leading example), the new statement represented the *Nixon administration's* conception of America's proper role in Asian and global affairs; there was no guarantee of course that President Nixon's successor would necessarily accept this conception as his own. In contrast with the Truman Doctrine, President Nixon's statement did *not* immediately require congressional approval; it did not call for a large appropriation of funds or a legislative resolution giving if official or de facto congressional sanction. There is no evidence that influential legislators were consulted in the formative stage of the Nixon Doctrine. After its issuance, the legislative reaction to it was mixed some features of the doctrine (such as the administration's determination to reduce American military strength in Asia) were applauded; other features (such as the doctrine's implicit conception that the United States was and *remained* an "Asian power") were greeted with less enthusiasm. On the basis of experience with earlier diplomatic doctrines (and the Monroe Doctrine offers perhaps the best case in point), we may also be certain that considerable time will be required before the full meaning and implications of the Nixon Doctrine will be apparent. How the doctrine is *applied* to specific problems confronting the United States in Asia and other regions will be crucial in determining its importance and in judging the degree to which it results in major foreign policy changes for the United States. We may be no less certain that, as the process of applying the Nixon Doctrine to particular cases goes on and as official "clarifications" of it are issued from time to time, the doctrine's meaning may be *less clear* than when it was initially proclaimed. The Nixon Doctrine typified the kind of "masterful ambiguity" in which the history of diplomacy abounds: its provisions were probably left deliberately flexible, allowing ample scope for interpretation in the light of developments overseas.

The Nixon Doctrine contained three key provisions. First, President Nixon affirmed that "the United States will keep all of its treaty commitments." The results of the Vietnam War, the Nixon Administration declared in effect, should not be interpreted as implying any lessening in America's determination to defend its military allies from new outbreaks of aggression or other threats. This reassurance was no doubt intended to relieve anxieties in West Germany, South Korea, Thailand, and other vulnerable countries. Neither the Vietnam experience nor the retrenchment in American military power overseas indicated any weakening of the determination of the United States to protect its allies.

In the second major provision of the Nixon Doctrine, President Nixon declared that the United States "shall provide a shield if a nuclear power threatens the freedom of a nation allied with us or of a nation whose survival we consider vital to our security." A number of points about this provision require brief emphasis. This section of the doctrine is addressed to the problem of large-scale or nuclear war (although, it should be noted, the doctrine does *not* specifically refer to nuclear war, but to a threat by "a nuclear power"). The obvious reference in this provision is to aggressive behavior by Soviet Russia or Communist China, in the post-Vietnam War era. If either (or both) of these nations threatens the security of another nation, the United States will provide "a shield" to protect the endangered country. The Nixon Doctrine recognizes two categories of such countries: military allies of the United States; and nations "whose survival we consider vital to our security," irrespective of whether they are formally allied with the United States or not. A conspicuous example of a nation in the latter category is India. To the Republic of India, the Nixon Doctrine seems to say that, although India remains militarily nonaligned, the United States *may* conclude that its survival is vital, thereby bringing India under the protection of the American nuclear shield. It should be noted, however, that this determination rests with *American officials: if* the survival of India or some other nonaligned nation is deemed vital to American security, then a nuclear shield will be extended to that country. Recognizing the contingent nature of this commitment, we may still conclude that conceivably the Nixon Doctrine *could* extend the defense obligations of the United States to nations not belonging to American-sponsored alliance systems.

The third important provision of the Nixon Doctrine related to new outbreaks of limited or nonnuclear war, such as "indirect aggression," wars of national liberation, attempts to subvert established governments, and the like. For this category of threats, the Nixon Doctrine declared that the United States "shall furnish military and economic assistance when requested in accordance with our treaty commitments. But we shall look to the nation directly threatened to assume the primary responsibility of providing the manpower for its defense." This section of the Nixon

Doctrine clearly reflected many of the "lessons of Vietnam." In general terms, it signified an effort by the United States to shift the burden for defense in limited hostilities to the country most directly affected. In effect, it was an effort to apply the concept of "Vietnamization" to Asia as a whole and (since the Nixon Doctrine nowhere mentioned Asia alone) to other regions.

Insofar as the Nixon Doctrine contemplated a retrenchment in American overseas commitments, three limitations present in this provision are noteworthy. First, the United States intended to furnish military and economic assistance to other countries *in accordance with its treaty commitments:* according to the Nixon Doctrine, America's aid to countries threatened by nonnuclear conflicts was limited to *allies* of the United States. (In contrast to the second provision of the Nixon Doctrine, here the United States undertook no commitment to defend India from limited military threats.) Second, the allies had to *request* such aid when they faced a threat to their security. And third, the American response would be confined primarily to providing "military and economic assistance"; the allies themselves would supply their principal manpower requirements.

Yet it is essential to understand this provision of the Nixon Doctrine correctly. It did *not* state that the United States would never again become involved in a land war in Asia. It did *not* say that American ground forces were henceforth excluded from participating in the defense of Asia or any other region. It did *not* anticipate that America's strategic role in Asia would be limited to sole reliance upon sea- and airpower. Despite what many critics of America's involvement in Southeast Asia might have hoped, the Nixon Doctrine declared that the United States would place "primary responsibility" for supplying military manpower needs upon its allies; this idea suggested that America had what might be termed a "secondary responsibility" in this matter, and in some cases that could conceivably involve a *substantial* manpower commitment. Note should be taken also of the fact that, under the Nixon Doctrine, the United States *is* committed to furnishing military and economic assistance to its allies. As officials of the Nixon Administration made clear after mid-1969, this commitment (particularly for military assistance) could and no doubt would *increase*, as the level of American combat forces in Asia declined.

Summarizing the main provisions of the Nixon Doctrine, we may say that the emphasis in all three of them was upon America's *obligations and responsibilities* in Asia and other regions. The end of the Vietnam conflict would witness no significant reduction in America's overseas commitments. Indeed, as we have observed, the second provision of the doctrine explicitly recognized that the United States had defense obligations to nonaligned nations. In effect, the Nixon Doctrine endeavored to provide a new and more effective approach for achievement of the nation's overseas goals.*[94]

The Prospects for Asian Stability

Earlier in the chapter, the inherent instability of postwar Asia was emphasized. In the early 1970s, there was no reason to change that judgment. The evidence indicated rather convincingly that Asia (in company perhaps with the Middle East) would *continue* to witness political turmoil, produced by some combination of two basic forces: internal political rivalries and revolutionary movements; and conflicts among nations in (or having interests in) Asia. Grounds existed for believing that *international* rivalries within the region might possibly *decline,* once the Vietnam War was formally or informally settled. If the war had been a trauma for the United States, it may have been a no less agonizing experience for nations on the Communist side. Yet the resolution of the conflict in Vietnam would not automatically dispose of difficult questions which had confronted American policymakers in Asia since the mid-1950s. Was the principal source of the region's chronic instability to be found in Asian nationalism and anticolonialism? And if so, was Asian nationalism always a force that could be reconciled with the diplomatic interests of the United States? Alternatively, did *domestic* political rivalries among competing groups furnish the key to understanding the region's ferment? And could the United States remain totally indifferent to how these political contests were resolved? Or, were the conflicts prevailing in the region mainly a clash between the forces of "traditionalism" and "modernization," with the latter process perhaps being intrinsically disruptive and revolutionary? Because of its geographic location and its record of ongoing political strife, did Asia inescapably attract outside powers, which often became the "sponsors" of contending political groups? If the earlier dichotomy between "Communist tyranny" and "the free world" seemed much too simple for the contemporary world, it was nonetheless true that Asia remained an arena of Soviet versus American, or Soviet versus Chinese, or Chinese versus American, rivalry. In that sense, the tendency toward "polycentricism" on both sides of the Iron

*A detailed elaboration of the meaning and some of the major implications of the Nixon Doctrine may be found in the White House document, "U.S. Foreign Policy for the 1970's—Building for Peace" (February 25, 1971), pp. 9–23 and *passim.* Under the Nixon Administration, the White House established the practice of issuing an annual report on American foreign relations. The student of American foreign affairs will find these reports an informative and useful summary, providing up-to-date treatment of American foreign relations from the official point of view.

Curtain had done little to reduce international competition within Asia. In fact, it might be more difficult to *control* such competition among the stronger powers today than when the United States and Soviet Russia dominated a "bipolar" international order.

The little kingdom of Laos, for example (smaller than the state of Nevada) still experienced political and military strife, pitting the "neutralist" government under Premier Souvanna Phouma against the Communist-led *Pathet Lao* rebels. The internal politics of Laos in recent years were as tangled as the jungles covering much of the country. France granted independence to Laos in 1950. Shortly thereafter, a *Pathet Lao* movement was organized in North Vietnam and Red China to bring Laos under Communist control. International agreements at Geneva in 1954 and 1955 sought to "neutralize" Laos, insulating it from cold war animosities. An agreement in 1962 endeavored to create a durable coalition government. These accords, however, achieved little. Revolutionary activities by the *Pathet Lao* continued. At the end of the 1950s, and again in 1964, right-wing and militantly anti-Communist elements tried to defeat the *Pathet Lao*. These campaigns (the former undertaken with American encouragement) failed, as Communist forces extended the area under their control.

As the conflict in Vietnam escalated, Laos was inescapably drawn into the vortex. American officials tended to regard the struggle in Laos as merely an extension of the Vietnam War, illustrating the validity of the "domino theory" advanced by the Eisenhower administration in the 1950s to explain America's concern for the security of Southeast Asia.[95] For Hanoi and the Viet Cong, Laos was a vital flank protecting the Ho Chi Minh Trail and the main center of revolutionary activity to the east. Anticipating that ultimately the Vietnam conflict would be settled by negotiations, the *Pathet Lao* sought to bring as much of the country as possible under its hegemony prior to a new Asian peace conference.

Since the mid-1950s, American economic and military aid to Laos has been extensive; American military advisers sought to strengthen the government's defense efforts; and once the United States became massively committed to the conflict in Vietnam, American bombers carried out repeated sorties against Communist targets in Laos. Yet a *Pathet Lao* offensive early in 1970 resulted in Communist control of the strategic Plain of Jars, making the Marxists dominant in over three-fourths of the country.

Early in 1971, it was revealed that American helicopters were engaged in supporting Laotian ground forces against the *Pathet Lao* and its followers, particularly along the Ho Chi Minh Trail. A few days later, the Nixon Administration announced that American-supported South Viet-namese forces had invaded Laos; the participation of the United States in this campaign was designed (according to White House spokesmen) to protect "the security and safety of American forces in South Vietnam." Disclaiming any intention of enlarging the conflict in Southeast Asia, the Nixon administration insisted that the Laotian operation in fact shortened the war. It provided South Vietnamese (ARVIN) forces needed combat experience; and the disruption of enemy supply lines and depots was essential for the success of "Vietnamization." Critics of America's involvement in Vietnam were not reassured. Intended or not, to their minds the Laotian invasion did in fact jeopardize the prospects for peaceful settlement; and at least tacitly, it suggested that the United States was somehow involved in the security and political future of Laos.[96] As for the invasion's impact upon the Paris peace negotiations, officials of the Nixon Administration replied that the discussions had already been deadlocked for many months; the Laotian incursion did not basically change that situation.

The South Vietnamese invasion of Laos lasted only a few weeks. In common with the military incursion into Cambodia earlier, the results of the Laotian operation were clearly mixed. Communist supply lines and depots in Laos were disrupted; the Ho Chi Minh Trail was cut; ARVIN forces acquired combat experience; an undetermined period of time was gained in which to make "Vietnamization" successful. On the other side of the ledger, the Laotian invasion revived anti-war sentiment within the United States. It perhaps made North Vietnam, the Viet Cong, and Communist China more suspicious of America's intentions than ever. In the closing phase of the Laotian operation, ARVIN forces suffered a series of military reverses, thereby perhaps publicly underscoring South Vietnam's vulnerability, at a time when the United States was carrying through with its proposed military retrenchment in Southeast Asia.

One thing seemed certain: whatever its specific consequences, the Laotian invasion had done little or nothing to solve the problem of the country's political future. As the months passed, there was no discernible letup in Communist military activity in Laos. Even if it succeeded in South Vietnam, the program of "Vietnamization" might well face its most severe test in Laos and Cambodia. With American air support, ARVIN forces had been sorely challenged to achieve their objectives in Laos; with little or no American support, these forces would be totally unable to guarantee the security of Laos. Yet failure to do so could well undermine the security of South Vietnam itself. In the long run, the future of Laos and other Southeast Asian nations depended upon the ability of the Soviet Union, Communist China, and the United States to reach a settlement laying the foundations for Asian stability. Early in 1971, Secretary of State Rogers indicated America's willingness to participate in a new great power conference toward that end; and by late spring, the beginning of a thaw in long-frozen Sino–American relations provided new impetus for a more stable equilibrium in Asia. Even if it could be achieved, however, many of the sources of conflict in Southeast Asia (like age-old ethnic and national rivalries) would remain.[97]

Another cause for American concern about the future stability of Asia was the situation in Thailand—a signatory of the SEATO treaty and one of the closest military allies of the United States. Thailand has an area of almost 200,000 square miles (slightly smaller than the state of Texas) and a population of some 34 million people; the country has one of the highest rates of population growth of any nation in the world. An Anglo–French agreement recognized the independence of Thailand (formerly Siam) in 1896; since that time, the country has preserved its sovereignty successfully. As in World War II— when Thailand offered no resistance to Japanese expansionism— Bangkok has generally identified itself with the strongest power in the area. In 1932, Thailand adopted a representative form of government, although the monarchy was retained. In reality, however, it has been governed by the armed forces, whose rule might be called a kind of benign dictatorship. A new constitution was promulgated in 1968, but it did not fundamentally change the dominant position of military elites.

By the second half of the 1960s, a number of commentators on Asian affairs had begun to express fears that Thailand was becoming "another Vietnam." Two interrelated factors explained the growing political instability within the country. One was the expanding American military presence in Thailand: By 1970, some 50,000 American forces were stationed on Thai territory. Outside of South Vietnam, Thailand had become the principal base area for American military operations in Southeast Asia. And as elsewhere, the American impact upon traditional ways of life was disruptive and perhaps inherently revolutionary. In large part because of its role in the Vietnam War, Thailand had become a major beneficiary of American economic and military aid (although the total of around $1 billion the United States had granted Thailand since 1946 was approximately one-seventh of what had been granted to India or South Korea). The government of Thailand also sent its own troops to fight in South Vietnam. Periodically, American officials reiterated the determination of the United States to defend Thailand. In 1962, Secretary of State Dean Rusk pledged that the United States would protect the security of Thailand, even if no other SEATO allies contributed to its defense.[98] In the years ahead, American and Thai officials reached agreement on various "contingency plans," providing for collaboration between the two countries to maintain Thailand's independence.

The other cause for apprehension about Thailand's security stemmed from insurrectionary activities in its northeastern and southeastern provinces. Each of these areas presented somewhat distinctive problems. Rebellions and terrorism erupted in the northeast during the early 1960s. In 1965, officials in Communist China called for the overthrow of the government in Bangkok and announced their support for various "liberation movements" (like the United Patriotic Front of Thailand). Insurgencies in this area were clearly related to, and assisted by, the *Pathet Lao*, Hanoi, and Peking. The peoples of the northeast were ethnically related to the Laotians, rather than to the dominant Thais. Sometimes referred to as "Thailand's Appalachia," the northeast had long been neglected by the Thai government; the standard of living was considerably below that of the country as a whole.

Insurrections and separatist tendencies also existed in the Kra Peninsula, where the "Malay Moslems" were the largest group in four southern provinces. Here, the dominant ethnic group was Malay; it was related closely to the people across the border in Malaysia. Moreover, the prevalent religion was Islam, whose adherents were distrustful of the Buddhists (who comprised over 90 percent of Thailand's population). In this region, many of the Communist rebels (mainly Chinese) who had earlier led the rebellion in Malaya had taken refuge after that revolution was crushed. As time passed they actively exploited the grievances of the Malay Moslems and inflamed them against the Thai government.[99]

Conditions in Thailand of course were in many respects very different from those prevailing in Vietnam. Thailand had been independent for many years; unlike Vietnam, it was not a divided country; it had experienced no prolonged anticolonial campaign; since most of Thailand's peasants already owned their land, Communist groups could not use "land reform" as an attractive slogan; although the Thai government was undeniably authoritarian, there was no evidence of widespread popular disaffection with it; nor was there any credible evidence of significant resentment against the United States (Thailand itself, for example, *owned* the military installations used by the United States); the government had an enviable record of economic growth (reaching 8 percent annually by the end of the 1960s); the Thai society was not sharply fragmented along religious lines, except in a few small provinces. Most crucially, perhaps, the authorities in Bangkok were finally using the country's resources, along with American assistance, to respond to the needs of the provinces for economic development and essential services.

Yet it could not be assumed that Thailand would necessarily escape becoming "another Vietnam." Referring to Thailand, one commentator wrote that "the general Maoist model for revolutionary warfare was being applied throughout the former French Indo-Chinese empire with significant results."[100] Both Hanoi and Peking had vowed to overthrow the "puppets of American imperialism" in Bangkok. The problem of Thailand presented difficult choices for American policymakers. By the 1970s, it was clear that opinion in the United States favored some curtailment of American power in Asia, and perhaps globally; this desire was reflected in the Nixon Doctrine. Yet, outside the NATO area, no nation perhaps had received so many assurances of American protection as Thailand. In the same period that President Nixon announced his new doctrine for Asia, for example, he also stated publicly in Bangkok that "the United States will stand proudly with Thailand against those who might threaten it from abroad *or from within.*"[101] Bangkok and other Asian capitals were reassured that the United States proposed to honor its treaty commitments by defending its allies. President Nixon did not speculate publicly about what the United States would do *if* Bangkok (with American assistance) proved unable to deal with foreign-aided insurgencies and *if* Communist forces sharply escalated their activities within the country. These were of course suppositions which might not materialize. Whether they did or did not would depend upon many factors: the results of the military contest in South Vietnam and in Laos; the terms of a cease-fire agreement which might be negotiated for Southeast Asia; the eruption of new revolutionary activities in countries like Malaysia and Cambodia; Thailand's record of economic progress in the future; the capability of Communist China and North Vietnam to support a massive "war of national liberation" in Thailand; the readiness of officials in Bangkok to at least *begin* to democratize the political system. If the earlier "domino theory" now tended to be discredited, there were grounds for being equally skeptical about the opposite viewpoint: that Thailand could retain its independence without massive American involvement in its affairs *irrespective* of what happened in countries adjacent to it. The risk clearly existed that Thailand could become the next center of international crisis in Asia; and this was one reason why the Nixon Doctrine did *not* explicitly rule out the commitment of American military forces in another Asian country.

In an unprecedented report to Congress entitled "United States Foreign Policy for the 1970's: A New Strategy for Peace," early in 1970, President Nixon amplified his new doctrine for Asian affairs. A key concept in the American approach

to Asia in the future, Nixon declared, would be the idea of "partnership," in which *regional cooperation* among the states of the area would be a central concern. Nixon reiterated the idea that "Asian hands must shape the Asian future." Achieving greater regional collaboration required several prerequisites. As in the Marshall Plan era to promote Europe's postwar recovery, Asian nations had to approach problems like reconstruction after the Vietnam War and development of the resources of the Mekong River on a *multilateral* basis. Such collaboration also demanded disciplined and intensive efforts by Asian societies to solve their internal problems—a greater effort than most of them had made in the past. It necessitated new attempts by Asian states to terminate long-standing regional conflicts, like the hostility between India and Pakistan. President Nixon also strongly emphasized another requirement for the 1970s: a considerable expansion in *Japan's responsibilities* for promoting Asian welfare and security. Japan, said Nixon, has a "unique and essential role to play in the development of the new Asia." Inferentially at least, the same point could be made about two other major Asian nations, India and Indonesia. These countries too would be required to assume new obligations outside their own borders.[102]

The obstacles facing effective Asian regionalism had to be faced squarely.[103] For reasons we have already identified, they were numerous and difficult—more critical for Asia (and possibly the Middle East) than for any other region. The prospects for the *early* emergence of Asian regional collaboration seemed most remote, as did the likelihood that there would be an immediate and dramatic change in Japan's role in Asian affairs. Many of the factors contributing to Asia's vulnerability and instability also militated against effective regional cooperation among the states of the area.* One

---

*The difficulties attending the U.S. attempt to encourage greater initiative by Asians for the region's security and well-being can hardly be exaggerated. Efforts to achieve regional economic cooperation in Asia, for example, have thus far proved largely abortive. Although several organizations—an Association of Southeast Asian Nations (ASAN), an Asia—Pacific Council (ASPAC), and an Asian Development Bank—have been established, real progress toward regional integration has been minimal. True, with Asia in a state of actual or incipient military conflict, the idea of regional collaboration has not received a fair trial. But there is no sign that these conflicts, or the internal instability besetting most Asian states, will disappear in the near future. Perhaps one of the principal elements for success—the *desire* of Asian states to collaborate regionally and to reduce their dependence upon the United States—is still lacking in this region. For discussions of the problem, see Bernard K. Gordon, "Economic Impediments to Regionalism in Southeast Asia," in George P. Jan, ed., *International Politics of Asia: Readings* (Belmont, Calif.: Wadsworth, 1969), pp. 362–371; and William C. Johnstone, "The United States as a Pacific Power," *Current History* **58** (April, 1970), 194–195, 243.

thing seemed certain: The ingenuity of American policy-makers would be challenged for many years in the future to translate President Nixon's proposals into reality.

NOTES

1. Julius W. Pratt, *A History of United States Foreign Policy* (Englewood Cliffs, N.J.: Prentice-Hall, 1955), pp. 270–278.
2. Foster R. Dulles, *China and America* (Princeton, N.J.: Princeton University Press, 1946), p. 107.
3. *Ibid.*, p. 107.
4. Werner Levi, *Modern China's Foreign Policy* (Minneapolis: University of Minnesota Press, 1953), p. 52.
5. Dulles, *op. cit.*, pp. 110–111.
6. Levi, *op. cit.*, p. 55.
7. *Ibid.*, pp. 287–297.
8. Pratt, *op. cit.*, 387–392.
9. See the frequent references to the United States in A. Doak Barnett, ed., *Quotations from Chairman Mao Tse-tung* (New York: Bantam, 1967). For efforts by President Nixon to bring about a relexation in Sino–American tensions, and Peking's response, see *The New York Times* (March 13, May 1, July 22, August 1, September 6, October 6, October 9, November 12, and December 1, 1969; March 2, 1970).
10. *The New York Times* (August 10, 1958).
11. Howard L. Boorman *et al.*, *Moscow–Peking Axis* (New York: Harper & Row, 1957), pp. 42–43.
12. An illuminating study of relations between the Communist movements in the U.S.S.R. and China down to the late 1940s is George F. Kennan, *Russia and the West Under Lenin and Stalin* (Boston: Atlantic–Little, Brown, 1961), pp. 260–278. Other helpful studies are Conrad Brandt, *Stalin's Failure in China* (New York: Norton, 1966); and David Floyd, *Mao Against Khrushchev* (New York: Praeger, 1963).
13. *The New York Times* (February 19, 1959).
14. See the text of the Kremlin's record of this statement in *The New York Times* (September 23, 1963).
15. *The New York Times* (July 15, 1963).
16. *Christian Science Monitor* (February 5, 1959).
17. Nathaniel Peffer, *The Far East* (Ann Arbor, Mich.: University of Michigan Press, 1958), p. 421.
18. American Assembly, *The United States and the Far East* (New York: Columbia University Press, 1956), p. 147.
19. Levi, *op. cit.*, p. 329.
20. Royal Institute of International Affairs, *Collective Defense in South East Asia* (London: Oxford University Press, 1956), pp. 58–59.
21. For an informative analysis of territorial and border disputes between Russia and China, containing a map of contested border areas, see Harrison E. Salisbury, *War Between Russia and China* (New York: Bantam, 1970), esp. pp. 1–49. As the title implies, Salisbury is pessimistic about the prospects that these two Marxist nations will be able to avoid open conflict. By the 1970s, each side was building up its military forces close to the frontier; efforts to resolve border controversies by negotiations between Moscow and Peking had been unavailing. See *The New York Times* (July 22, 1970).
22. For discussions of Communist China's population explosion and its implications, see John C. Scott, *China: The Hungry Dragon* (New York: Avon Books, 1967), pp. 99–108; and Ruth Adams, *Contemporary China* (New York: Random House, 1966), pp. 235–253.
23. See, for example, *The New York Times* (December 22, 1963).
24. For discussions of major developments affecting Pakistan's foreign policy in recent years, see J. C. Hurewitz; *Middle East Politics: The Military Dimension* (New York: Praeger, 1969), pp. 179–231; Hafeez Malik, "The Muslims of India and Pakistan," *Current History* 56 (March, 1969), 151–156; and George L. Montagno, "Peaceful Coexistence: Pakistan and Red China," *Western Political Quarterly* 18 (June, 1965), 309–317.
25. For background discussions on threats to Thailand from North Vietnam and Red China, see Richard Butwell, "Thailand After Vietnam" *Current History* 57 (December, 1969), 339–343; and Bernard K. Gordon, "Thailand: Its Meaning for the U.S.," *ibid.* 52 (January, 1967), 19–21.
26. The deterioration in Burma's relations with Red China is analyzed in Robert K. McCabe, "When China Spits, We Swim," *The New York Times Magazine* (February 27, 1966), pp. 27, 44–54; "Mao's Men in Burma," *Atlas* 14 (October, 1967), 31–32; and *The New York Times* (January 30, March 20, July 6, and November 1, 1968).
27. For background on political events leading up to the attempted Marxist coup in Indonesia, see Bruce Grant, *Indonesia* (Baltimore: Penguin, 1964), pp. 43–105; and for discussions of the nature and meaning of the military seizure of power in the country, see Frederick Bunnell, "Indonesia's Quasi-Military Regime," *Current History* 52 (January, 1967), 22–29; and Seth S. King, "The Great Purge in Indonesia," *The New York Times Magazine* (May 8, 1966), pp. 25, 89–92.
28. See *The New York Times* (May 11 and June 6, 1970).
29. See, for example, the recent study of Chinese foreign policy goals in Robert C. North, *The Foreign Relations of China* (Belmont, Calif.: Dickenson, 1969), pp. 83–90; and the reply of the Chinese government to President Nixon's overtures for a resolution of tensions, in *The New York Times* (March 2, 1970).

30. For the text of this resolution, and discussions of it, see Department of State, *American Foreign Policy, 1950–1955*, No. 6446, General Foreign Policy Series, vol. II (1957), pp. 2487, 2370–2371, 2373–2376.

31. Nationalist China's successful effort to cultivate good will among the Afro–Asian nations is described in Leon M. S. Slawecki, "The Two Chinas in Africa," *Foreign Affairs* 41 (January, 1963), 398–409; and for more recent evidence, see the references to foreign aid extended by the Taiwan government in President Nixon's statement, as reprinted in *The New York Times* (February 19, 1970).

32. See *The New York Times*, May 1 and December 28, 1969; January 18, 1970.

33. The literature on the Sino–Soviet dispute is voluminous. In addition to the studies by Kennan, Brandt, and Floyd cited earlier, see also: Edward Crankshaw, *The New Cold War: Moscow v. Peking* (Baltimore: Penguin, 1963); Klaus Mehnert, *Peking and Moscow* (New York: New American Library, 1963); C. P. Fitzgerald, "Tension on the Sino–Soviet Border," *Foreign Affairs*, 45 (July, 1967), 683–694; and Rodger Swearingen, ed., *Soviet and Chinese Power in the World Today* (New York: Basic Books, 1966).

34. The emergence and growth of the concept of diplomatic nonalignment is evaluated in Khalid I. Babaa and Cecil V. Crabb, Jr., "Nonalignment as a Diplomatic and Ideological Credo," *Annals of the American Academy of Political and Social Science* 362 (November, 1965), 6–18.

35. For the origins of the neutralist mentality, focusing upon India's role as an initiator of the outlook, see Cecil V. Crabb, Jr., *The Elephants and the Grass: A Study of Nonalignment* (New York: Praeger, 1965), pp. 3–77. For various points of view about the Indian theory and practice of nonalignment, see Paul E. Power, *India's Nonalignment Policy: Strengths and Weaknesses* (Boston: Raytheon/Heath, 1967); and Robert L. Rothstein, "Alignment, Nonalignment, and Small Powers: 1945–1965," *International Organization* 20 (Summer, 1966), 397 –418. A highly critical evaluation of India's nonalignment policy is Werner Levi, *The Challenge of World Politics in South and Southeast Asia* (Englewood Cliffs, N.J.: Prentice-Hall, 1968), esp. pp. 75–123.

36. Text in *India News* 2 (Washington, D.C.: Embassy of India, November 22, 1963), 2.

37. Cited in *The Times of Indonesia* (March 10, 1960).

38. Chester Bowles, *Ambassador's Report* (New York: Harper & Row, 1954), p. 111.

39. *Hindustan Times* (overseas edition, June 22, 1961).

40. N. P. Nayar, "Non-Alignment in World Affairs," *India Quarterly* 18 (January–March, 1962), 30, 32. An excellent appraisal of the evolution of the neutralist mentality.

41. *Times of India* (November 7, 1961), dispatch by Prem Bhatia.

42. *Asian Recorder* 3 (July 6–12, 1957), 1531.

43. See Nehru's remarks to the Bandung Conference in 1955, as reported in *Hindustan Times* (overseas edition, April 28, 1955).

44. See Nehru's speech to the Lok Sabba on May 14, 1962, as reported in *India News* 1 (May 28, 1962), 1.

45. Dr. Alec Bebler, "Role of the Non-Bloc Countries," *Review of International Affairs* 9 (Belgrade, Yugoslavia, January 1, 1958), 1–2.

46. See *India News* 4 (March 1, 1959), 1; and 6 (January 1, 1961), 1; *Egyptian Gazette* (November 17, 1961).

47. *Times of Indonesia* (August 19, 1960).

48. *India News* 4 (January 26, 1959), 1; and 5 (February 15, 1960), 2.

49. *Hindustan Times* (overseas edition, August 16, 1956).

50. See the reaction of an Indonesian official in the *Asian Recorder* 8 (January 15–21, 1962); and 8 (February 5–11, 1962), 4404–4405.

51. The evolution of American foreign policy toward the concept of nonalignment is analyzed in Cecil V. Crabb, Jr. "The United States and the Neutralists," *Annals of the American Academy of Political and Social Science* 362 (November, 1965), 92–102; and the discussion in Crabb, *The Elephants and the Grass, op. cit.*, pp. 168–198.

52. For official American references to India in this vein, see Cecil V. Crabb, Jr., "The Testing of Nonalignment," *Western Political Quarterly* XVII (September, 1964), 524–525.

53. Recent data on India's progress toward modernization and economic development are provided in the report of the Commission on International Development, *Partners in Development* (New York: Praeger, 1969), pp. 282–302; "Self-Reliant Growth Will Be Attained in 10 Years," *India News* 5 (August 19, 1966); 1; "India—An Agricultural Transformation," *ibid.* 7 (April 26, 1968), 4. For more recent data, see the latest issues of this publication; S. Chandrasekhar, "How India Is Tackling Her Population Problem," *Foreign Affairs* 47 (October, 1968), 138–151; Max F. Millikan, "India in Transition—Economic Development: Performance and Prospects," *Foreign Affairs* 46 (April, 1968), 531–548. For a sobering assessment of India's problems, see Khrishan Bhatia, "India Adrift," *Foreign Affairs* 45 (July, 1967), 652–662.

54. Background on the Kashmir dispute and other sources of tension between India and Pakistan is provided in Selig S. Harrison, "Troubled India and Her Neighbors," *Foreign Affairs* 43 (January, 1965), 312–330; Nicholas Mansergh, "The Partition of India in Retrospect," *International Journal* 21 (Winter, 1965–1966), 1–19; Ronald Segal, *The Anguish of India* (New York: New American Library, 1965), pp. 241–245.

55. Pakistan's growing disaffection with American policy in Asia and its *détente* with Communist China are discussed in *The New York*

Times (March 14 and August 30, 1965; February 23, March 6, and March 28, 1966; February 26 and March 3, 1968; and April 3, 1969).

56. See "A Decade of Indo–Soviet Cooperation," *Indian and Foreign Review* 2 (February 15, 1965), 17–18; Richard L. Siegel, "Evaluating the Results of Foreign Policy: Soviet and American Efforts in India," Monograph no. 4 (Denver, Col.: University of Denver, Social Science Foundation and Graduate School, 1968–1969).

57. For the implications of the Himalayan crisis for Indian foreign policy, see Crabb, "The Testing of Nonalignment," *op. cit.*, pp. 517–542; and Power, *op. cit.*, pp. 33–46, 85–109. More detailed study of the origins and aftermath of the Himalayan crisis is P. C. Chakravarti, *India's China Policy* (Bloomington, Ind.: University of Indiana Press, 1962); and John Rowland, *A History of Sino–Indian Relations and Hostile Coexistence* (New York: Van Nostrand Reinhold, 1967).

58. India's Himalayan encounter with Red China precipitated a continuing debate over the strategic assumptions underlying the former's defense policy—particularly over India's acquisition of nuclear weapons. For appraisals of the issues involved, see Power, *op. cit.*, pp. 47–58; Lorne J. Kavic, *India's Quest for Security: 1947–1965* (Berkeley, Calif.: University of California Press, 1967), pp. 169–219; A. B. Shah, ed., *India's Defense and Foreign Policies* (Bombay: Manaktalas, 1966), pp. 124–165.

59. Indian perspectives on the problem of nuclear "proliferation" are presented in V. C. Trevedi, "Vertical Versus Horizontal Proliferation: An Indian View," in James E. Dougherty and J. F. Lehman, Jr., eds., *Arms Control for the Late 1960s* (New York: Van Nostrand Reinhold, 1967), pp. 195–203.

60. For studies of Burma's foreign policy in the recent period, see John H. Badley, "Burma: The Nexus of Socialism and Two Political Traditions," *Asian Survey* 3 (February, 1963), 89–95; William C. Johnstone, *Burma's Foreign Policy: A Study of Neutralism* (Cambridge, Mass.: Harvard University Press, 1963); Louis J. Walinsky, "The Rise and Fall of U Nu," *Pacific Affairs* 38 (Fall–Winter, 1965–1966), 269–282; Joseph Silverstein, "Military Rule in Burma," *Current History* 52 (January, 1967), 41–47; and Joseph Lelyveld, "Mandalay Must Not Become Indianapolis," *New York Times Magazine* (January 5, 1969), pp. 30–31, 76–79.

61. For discussions of Cambodia's unique conception of neutralism and the major forces influencing its foreign policy, see Michael Leifer, *Cambodia: The Search for Security* (New York: Praeger, 1967); Seth S. King, "Sihanouk—Prince Under Pressure," *New York Times Magazine* (September 13, 1964), pp. 42, 84–88; David Chandler, "Cambodia's Search for Survival," *Current History* 57 (December, 1969), 344–349. And for developments within Cambodia after the overthrow of Sihanouk's government early in 1970, see *The New York Times* (March 19 and 20, and June 29, 1970); and *Newsweek* LXXVI (July 13, 1970), 16–29.

62. Sources of tension in Indonesian–American relations during Sukarno's regime are identified and evaluated in Frank N. Trager, "The U.S. and Indonesia—A Tragedy in Diplomacy," *New York Times Magazine* (August 29, 1965), pp. 26, 70–76; Guy J. Pauker, "The Soviet Challenge in Indonesia," *Foreign Affairs* 40 (July, 1962), 612–626; and Roger Hilsman, *To Move a Nation*, (Garden City, N.Y.: Doubleday, 1967), pp. 361–397.

63. Indonesian policies in the post-Sukarno period are treated in Benedict R. Anderson, "Indonesia's Uncertain Future," *Current History* 57 (December, 1969), 355–361; Guy T. Parker, "Toward a New Order in Indonesia," *Foreign Affairs* 45 (April, 1967), 503–520; and *The New York Times* (March 31 and October 29, 1968; February 13, 1969; May 29 and 31, 1970); and Adam Malik, "Promise in Indonesia," *Foreign Affairs* 46 (January, 1968), 292–304.

64. An illuminating analysis of the inherent instability of the region may be found in Michael Brecher, *The New States of Asia* (New York: Oxford University Press, 1966), pp. 47–110.

65. See Alvin Z. Rubinstein, ed., *The Foreign Policy of the Soviet Union* (New York: Random House, 1960), p. 341.

66. George F. Kennan, *Soviet Foreign Policy, 1917–1941* (New York: Van Nostrand Reinhold, 1960), pp. 65, 151–152.

67. For Communist activities in Asia during and immediately after World War II, see Hugh Seton-Watson, *From Lenin to Khrushchev: The History of World Communism* (New York: Praeger, 1960), pp. 225–227; and for discussion of Marxist activities in individual Asian societies, see A. Doak Barnett, ed., *Communist Strategies in Asia* (New York: Praeger, 1963).

68. Dwight D. Eisenhower, *Mandate for Change* (Garden City, N.Y.: Doubleday, 1963), p. 372.

69. Peffer, *op. cit.*, pp. 272–273.

70. Edwin O. Reischauer, *Wanted: An Asian Policy* (New York: Knopf, 1955), p. 165.

71. The most comprehensive treatment of this dispute is John W. Spanier, *The Truman–MacArthur Controversy and the Korean War* (Cambridge, Mass.: Belknap Press of Harvard University, 1959). Another informative discussion of the Truman–MacArthur dispute is Matthew B. Ridgway, *The Korean War* (New York: Popular Library, 1967), pp. 144–185.

72. The attitudes of the so-called "Never Again Club" toward the crisis of Southeast Asia are discussed in Hilsman, *op. cit.*, pp. 128–129.

73. For discussions of the *Pueblo* crisis, see Joseph C. Kun, "Behind North Korea's New

Belligerence," *The Reporter* 38 (February 22, 1968), 19–21; Flora Lewis, "Seoul Feels a Cold Wind from the North," *New York Times Magazine* (February 18, 1968), pp. 30–31, 104–112; and Joungwon A. Kim, "North Korea's New Offensive," *Foreign Affairs* 48 (October, 1969), 166–180.

74. Erik Amfithaetrof, "The Forgotten Front at the 38th Parallel," *The Reporter* 38 (April 18, 1968), 22–23.

75. For recent developments in relations between the two Koreas, see *The New York Times* (January 28, 1968; April 27, 1969).

76. *The New York Times* (September 14, 1968; April 27, 1969); Joungwon A. Kim, "The Long March of North Korea's Kim," *New York Times Magazine* (February 25, 1968), pp. 32–33, 107–111; and Emerson Chapin, "Success Story in South Korea," *Foreign Affairs* 47 (April, 1969), 560–575.

77. Background on North Korea's position in the international Communist movement is provided in Glenn D. Paige, "North Korea and the Emulation of Russian and Chinese Behavior," in A. Doak Barnett, ed., *Communist Strategies in Asia* (New York: Praeger, 1963), pp. 228–262; see also Kim, *op. cit.*, pp. 107–111.

78. Sources of tension in recent Japanese–American relations are analyzed in Edwin O. Reischauer, *Beyond Vietnam: The United States and Asia* (New York: Random House, 1967), pp. 105–140; and in various articles in the symposium edited by Herbert Passin, *The United States and Japan* (Englewood Cliffs, N.J.: Prentice-Hall, 1966), *passim*. For an analysis of the debate within Japan about its new role in Asia, see Kiichi Aichi, "Japan's Legacy and Destiny of Change," *Foreign Affairs* 48 (October, 1969), 21–39; and Kei Wakaizumi, "Japan Beyond 1970," *ibid.* 47 (April, 1969), 509–521.

79. For criticisms of SEATO, focusing upon the organization's inadequacies, see George M. Kahin and John W. Lewis, *The United States in Vietnam*, rev. ed. (New York: Dell Publishing, 1969), pp. 60–64; Don R. and Arthur Larson, "What is Our 'Commitment' in Vietnam?" in Marcus G. Raskin and Bernard B. Fall, eds., *The Viet-Nam Reader* (New York: Random House, 1965), pp. 99–104; and *The New York Times* (February 19, 1966; September 11, 1968; September 8, 1969).

80. A much more favorable evaluation of the SEATO system is persuasively argued in Bernard K. Gordon, *Toward Disengagement in Asia: A Strategy for American Foreign Policy* (Englewood Cliffs, N.J.: Prentice-Hall, 1969), pp. 133–136.

81. *Ibid.*, pp. 134–135.

82. *Ibid.*, p. 137.

83. See, for example, Secretary of State Dean Rusk's statement to the Senate Foreign Relations Committee, as reported in *The New York Times* (February 19, 1966).

84. See for example, Kahin and Lewis, *op. cit.*, pp. 300–302.

85. France's effort to preserve its colonial rule in Indochina, leading to the defeat of French forces at the battle of Dienbienphu, is appraised in Donald Lancaster, *The Emancipation of French Indochina* (London: Oxford University Press, 1961); and Ellen J. Hammer, *The Struggle for Indochina* (Stanford, Calif.: Stanford University Press, 1954).

86. The achievements and failures of the Diem government in South Vietnam are treated in Hilsman, *op. cit.*, pp. 417–482; Denis Warner, *The Last Confucian: Vietnam, Southeast Asia, and the West* (Baltimore: Penguin, 1963), pp. 220–241; and Robert Scigliano, *South Vietnam: Nation Under Stress* (Boston: Houghton Mifflin, 1963), *passim*, but esp. pp. 26–49. Various viewpoints are presented in Marvin E. Gettleman, ed., *Viet Nam: History, Documents, and Opinions on a Major World Crisis* (Greenwich, Conn.: Fawcett Publications, 1965), pp. 191–282.

87. America's involvement in Vietnam down to 1960 is discussed in Dean Acheson, *Present at the Creation: My Years in the State Department* (New York: Norton, 1969), pp. 671–679; Eisenhower, *op. cit.*, pp. 166–170, 332–376; and the various interpretations in Gettleman, *op. cit.*, pp. 115–191. For the official justification for America's involvement in Vietnam thereafter, see Department of State, *Aggression from the North: The Record of North Viet-Nam's Campaign to Conquer South Viet-Nam* (Washington, D.C.: U.S. Government Printing Office, 1965).

88. Quoted in Theodore C. Sorensen, *Kennedy* (New York: Harper & Row, 1965), pp. 658–659.

89. *Ibid.*, pp. 648–652.

90. Quoted in Hilsman, *op. cit.*, pp. 505–506.

91. For congressional apprehensions at the time and later over the implications of the Tonkin Gulf Resolution, see numerous citations of legislative attitudes in the study by the Congressional Quarterly Service, *National Diplomacy: 1965–1970* (Washington, D.C.: 1970), pp. 65–85; and J. William Fulbright, *The Arrogance of Power* (New York: Random House, 1966), pp. 50–52.

92. See, for example, the views of Secretary of State Rusk as reported in *The New York Times* (July 20, 1967).

93. President Nixon's program of "Vietnamization" is discussed in detail in his lengthy statement on American foreign policy during the 1970s as reprinted in *The New York Times* (February 19, 1970).

94. For statements of the Nixon Doctrine and commentaries on this concept, see *The New York Times* (July 27, August 3, August 10, and December 21, 1969).

95. The "domino theory" is explained in Dwight D. Eisenhower, *Waging Peace* (Garden City, N.Y.: Doubleday, 1965), pp. 607–608. Interestingly enough, this idea was advanced initially with reference to Laos.

96. Prime Minister Phouma's comment is quoted in Elizabeth Urrows, "Recurring Problems in Laos," *Current History* **57** (December, 1969), 367.

97. For discussions of conflict in Laos since the mid-1950s, see *ibid.*, pp. 361–363, 367; Guy Wint, "Southeast Asia in the Twentieth Century," in Guy S. Métraux and François Crouzet, eds., *The New Asia* (New York: New American Library, 1965), pp. 300–324; and the lengthy discussion of recurrent crises in Laos in *The New York Times* (March 1, 1970). Early in March, 1970, President Nixon and Secretary of State Rogers made lengthy statements concerning America's involvement in Laos, as reported in *ibid.* (March 5 and 7, 1970). Our discussion of the invasion of Laos in 1971 relies upon *The New York Times*, January 20, February 6, 9, 10, and 11, 1971.

98. See Richard Butwell, "Thailand After Vietnam," *op. cit.*, p. 339. This article (pp. 339–343, 368–369) is an informative discussion of the security problem of Thailand. A more detailed assessment is Daniel Wit, *Thailand: Another Vietnam?* (New York: Scribner's, 1968), *passim*. A highly critical (in parts polemical) account of America's involvement in Thailand is Louis E. Lomax, *Thailand: The War That Is, The War That Will Be* (New York: Random House, 1967). See also J. L. S. Girling, "Northeast Thailand: Tomorrow's Viet Nam?" *Foreign Affairs* **46** (January, 1968), 388–398.

99. For discussions of the extent and nature of insurgent movements in Thailand, see *The New York Times* (July 12, 1966; October 20, 1967; February 4 and October 2, 1968); and Peter Traestrup, "How the Guerrillas Came to Koh Noi," *New York Times Magazine* (December 10, 1967), pp. 30–31, 49–74.

100. See Wit, *op. cit.*, p. 5.

101. See the text of the President's statement as reproduced in *The New York Times* (July 29, 1969). Italics inserted.

102. The full text of this comprehensive and important message by President Nixon on American foreign policy during the 1970s may be found in *The New York Times* (February 19, 1970).

103. For recent discussions of the problem of creating regional cooperation among Asian nations, see David E. Lillenthal, "Postwar Development in Viet Nam," *Foreign Affairs* **47** (January, 1969), 321–334; Bruce Grant, "Toward a New Balance in Asia: An Australian View," *ibid.* (July, 1969), 711–721; George Thomson, "The New World of Asia," *ibid.* (October, 1969), 123–139; Gordon, *op. cit.*, pp. 131–166; and *The New York Times* (March 2, 1970).

Fourteen
INFORMATIONAL AND ECONOMIC POLICY IMPLEMENTS

In this chapter, we shall focus upon two tools of American foreign policy which came to be utilized heavily and consistently after World War II. These are informational or propaganda activities as an instrument of foreign relations and reliance upon military and economic aid programs to achieve the nation's foreign policy goals.

Late in 1960, a committee appointed by President Eisenhower to investigate the operation of American overseas information programs reported that: "The eventual outcome of the struggle, assuming that general war can be avoided, and that Communist subversion can be countered, will depend in considerable degree on the extent we are able to influence the attitudes of people."[1]

One major consequence of the revolution in techniques of communication witnessed in recent years is that increasingly governments endeavor to influence the attitudes of *masses and leaders* in other countries. No longer are international relations confined to contacts among *governments;* all nations, especially the great powers, endeavor to affect the viewpoints of people outside their own borders, often in order to influence the policies adopted by other governments. A former head of America's overseas information program asserted several years ago that: "Every major foreign office in the world is doing things today which it would have considered startling, if not improper, ten years ago."[2] This official had reference primarily (although not exclusively) to the impact of the "information explosion" upon the conduct of international relations and the organized efforts by nearly all nations of the world to create a favorable climate of opinion in other countries for the realization of their foreign policy aims. One student of American propaganda operations has observed that, by the late 1960s, for the first time in history over half of mankind was literate. "In these new circumstances, public opinion among the masses, as distinct from attitudes of governments, has become a preoccupation of world lead-

ers. . . ." The rapid technological progress of the modern era has had a profound impact upon propaganda activities. Consider merely the proliferation in radio and television sets in recent years. Today, there are over 300 million radio receivers outside the United States and Canada. Programs of "international broadcasting" by all countries total more than 25,000 hours weekly! Within the past two decades, the number of TV sets overseas has grown to over 150 million.[3] In the modern era, the most remote African village or Arab Bedouin tribe is "connected" with the outside world; even illiterate masses are now promptly informed of important events at home and abroad.

For hundreds of years, military commanders have been aware that the morale of their soldiers, and of the civilians behind the lines, can be the decisive element in the outcome of wars. Not infrequently (as in the American Revolution), such intangible aspects of national power can outweigh superiority in economic strength, numbers of troops, and other components of military might. In the contemporary world, morale on the home front and the attitudes of people in societies abroad can be no less crucial in deciding whether the United States achieves its foreign policy goals. How cohesive is the NATO alliance? What degree of support (or lack of it) are other nations prepared to give the United States in maintaining the security of Southeast Asia? What influence will American officials have in efforts to resolve the Arab–Israeli conflict? What will be the future of the Organization of American States and the attempt to achieve Western hemispheric solidarity? These and countless other concrete issues confronting the United States in foreign relations are, to a greater or lesser degree, affected by America's "image" overseas, the degree of confidence which other nations place in its leadership, and the extent to which the United States is able to convince other societies that it "identifies" with their needs and aspirations.

PSYCHOLOGICAL WARFARE: ITS NATURE AND USES

Psychological warfare is as old as history.* When the Greeks failed to capture Troy by force of arms, they resorted to skillful deception—the Trojan Horse—to bring them victory. In early American history, one purpose of the Declaration of Independence was to gain widespread support in England and Europe for the colonial cause by identifying it with the political aspirations of Western society as a whole. During World War I, tons of propaganda in the form of press releases, leaflets, posters, booklets, pictures, and the like, emanated from the Allied side. These were acknowledged by German military leaders as having been singularly effective in undermining the military and civilian morale of the Central Powers and in turning neutral opinion against their cause. One of the most brilliant Allied propaganda victories in the period was won through the proclamation of President Wilson's "Fourteen Points," which were of inestimable value in shortening the war by weakening the will to resist among populations in the enemy camp.[4]

Some Basic Concepts

No universally accepted definition of psychological warfare exists; and, indeed, it may be more difficult than ever in the contemporary period to formulate a satisfactory one. The earlier distinction which many Americans believed existed between peace and war (and it seems clear that the dichotomy was *always* drawn too sharply) is largely untenable today. Concepts like "cold war" or "protracted struggle" or "wars of national liberation," which may be applied to various categories of international crisis, suggest a close conjunction between traditionally peaceful and

violent instruments of foreign policy. Even though it has moderated significantly since the 1950s, the cold war between the United States and the Soviet Union still involves *a synthesis* of diplomatic techniques, ranging from preservation of a "credible" military establishment on each side, to efforts by Washington and Moscow to win the good will of Afro–Asian societies by foreign aid programs and other undertakings, to propaganda competition between Radio Moscow and the Voice of America, to attempts by each side to win favorable majorities in the UN General Assembly, to genuine concern on the part of each great power with its "public image" in activities like disarmament negotiations. There is, in fact, no single major aspect of the cold war which lacks a psychological dimension. In most acute crises, the psychological aspects of foreign policy are even more apparent and perhaps crucial. At every turn during the Vietnam War, the United States confronted the central importance of psychological warfare and successful informational activities; the same of course was true of the Viet Cong, North Vietnam, and Red China. As much as any other factor, America's failure to achieve its objectives in Vietnam could be attributed to lack of success in the psychological realm. Instilling public confidence in the government of South Vietnam; implementing a successful rural "pacification program" in the South; convincing Hanoi that the American society was not "tired of the war" and was willing to support the government's policies indefinitely; persuading the Communists that they would gain more by negotiating than by prolonging the conflict—these were but a few of the specific issues related to the Vietnam War in which the psychological and informational aspects of foreign policy were important, if not crucial.

Although they may often be difficult to differentiate in practice, two broad categories of psychological and informational activities in foreign relations may be identified. One of these is *psychological warfare*. As the term implies, it is a form of *conflict* among nations. It may be used either in *conjunction with* military force or as a *substitute for* it. Nearly all armed conflicts in the modern era have involved intensive propaganda campaigns against the enemy, as well as propaganda programs directed at the home front. Nations utilize psychological instruments during warfare to undermine the enemy's will to fight and to hasten his capitulation, to win victories as cheaply as possible, to convince the enemy that his defeat is certain, and generally to enhance the achievement of victory. Psychological techniques also sometimes can replace the need to apply force; a successful propaganda campaign, for example, can achieve certain goals (like the surrender of an enemy force, or the collapse of an unfriendly government, or the change in a gov-

*In common with many other general concepts, definitions of such terms as psychological warfare and propaganda often vary considerably; any definition offered is likely to reflect the emphases that the user thinks most basic or relevant to his discussion. Numerous definitions are thus available. Psychological warfare may be thought of as "the use of propaganda against an enemy, together with such other operational measures of a military, economic or political nature as may be required to supplement propaganda." Propaganda is a narrower concept, normally comprising only one element in psychological warfare. Propaganda may be conceived to be "planned use of any form of public or mass-communication designed to affect the minds and emotions of a given group for a specific public purpose, whether military, economic, or political." Propaganda is concerned with *the written or spoken word* as an instrument or statecraft. These and other definitions are cited in Urban G. Whitaker, Jr., *Propaganda and International Relations* (San Francisco: Chandler, 1962), pp. 4–5; see also the views presented in Terence H. Qualter, *Propaganda and Psychological Warfare* (New York: Random House, 1962), pp. 15, 27.

ernment's policies) which might otherwise have to be effected by armed force.

The other category of psychological activity in foreign affairs might be designated *normal informational and propaganda programs conducted in an over-all atmosphere of relatively peaceful relationships*. One school of thought in the study of international relations tends to view all contacts among nations (or at least, the most important ones) as involving "conflict resolution"; in this approach, conflict is an omnipresent and inescapable element in relationships among all nations, great and small, in the international community. In brief, international politics *is* "conflict resolution."[5] Provided the idea of "conflict" is defined broadly enough, this is perhaps a legitimate approach to global political phenomena. Yet a major drawback is that it tends to obscure *the broad range of "conflicts" present in international relations*. Cold war animosities between the United States and the Soviet Union, or the tensions characteristic of Sino–American relations, or America's continuing quarrel with Cuba, could be cited as obvious examples involving the resolution of international conflicts. The concept of conflict resolution would seem to have much less applicability, however, to Anglo–American relations, or to U.S.-Japanese relations, or to Washington's efforts to achieve a consensus on military strategy among the NATO partners. The point may be generalized by saying that there are at least two broad categories of international "conflict": those, such as the cold war between the United States and the Soviet Union, in which there is a fundamental clash of values, ideologies, and national interests—possibly leading to an ultimate military collision; and those, such as relations between the United States and its friends (including many "neutralist" nations) in which there is an attempt to arrive at common policies, to eliminate existing sources of tensions, and to conduct normal, amicable relations, to the mutual benefit of the societies involved.

Even in this latter category, however, psychological instruments of foreign policy are routinely employed to achieve the nation's objectives. Thus, the United States has endeavored to create and preserve cohesion among the members of NATO; it has endeavored to eliminate sources of misunderstanding in American–Canadian relations; it has tried to promote a greater sense of common purpose and shared concerns among the nations of the Western Hemisphere; it has sought to convince the free nations of Africa that it respects their independence and will assist them in attaining their development goals. Another important goal of American policy toward this group of nations is *counteracting Communist propaganda* directed at Western Europe and the Afro–Asian societies. Failure to do so would leave an informa-

tion vacuum which could prove highly detrimental to American foreign policy.

In reality, America's relations with particular foreign countries, not excluding its cold war adversaries, are likely to embody elements associated with both psychological warfare and more peaceful propaganda techniques. Thus, Soviet–American relations in the 1970s combine ongoing ideological discord and rivalry, polemical exchanges, and continuing efforts by Washington and Moscow alike to prove the "superiority" of their respective political and economic systems to societies in the zone of emerging nations. Concurrently, however, the United States and the Soviet Union express belief in the principle of "peaceful coexistence" among nations; they carry on active programs of cultural and scientific exchange across the Iron Curtain; in recent years, they have relaxed many barriers to travel and circulation of news media; and their mutual relations are conducted on a reasonably "rational" and harmonious basis.

Propaganda and Diplomacy

In this chapter we shall concentrate upon propaganda as a major technique of psychological warfare, defining it as the effort of one group or nation to influence the actions of another group or nation *by primary reliance upon methods of systematic persuasion, including methods of verbal coercion and inducement*. Propaganda is to be distinguished from other forms of psychological warfare by its utilization of the written and spoken word. Successful utilization of methods of persuasion depends in no small degree upon the effectiveness of other weapons in the arsenal of national power, such as economic strength and military force. Threats, unsupported by the requisite military power, are usually ineffectual; promises and inducements, without the willingness and capacity to make good on them, are equally worthless as diplomatic tools.

The successful propagandist is required to have a well-stocked and versatile arsenal and to be skilled in the use of these weapons. Among the variety of weapons available are radio broadcasts, television programs, speeches, films, public rallies and demonstrations, various symbols like armbands, flags, slogans, or buttons, posters, cartoons, comic books, newspapers, timely "leaks" of official information, libraries, lectures, seminars, clandestine radios, articles in magazines, news conferences, and a host of other techniques.[6] In successfully employing any or all of these techniques, the propagandist is continually conscious of a fact that is at the center of his operations. This is that propaganda is merely a *single instrument* of foreign policy; as such, it is intimately related to, and its success ultimately depends upon, the effective use and skillful coordination of other instruments to achieve diplomatic goals, such as foreign aid, reliance upon (or the threat to rely upon) military force, negotiating skill, and, perhaps above all, a clear sense of what the nation is seeking to achieve in its relations with other countries.

A former Director of the United States Information Agency (USIA) once stated that "Ninety percent of the impression which the United States makes abroad depends on our policies and not more than 10 percent . . . on how we explain [them]."[7] Or, as President Kennedy once expressed the idea: "It is a dangerous illusion to believe that the policies of the United States . . . can be encompassed in one slogan or adjective, hard or soft or otherwise." And referring to propaganda on another occasion, he asserted: "If we are strong, our strength will speak for itself. If we are weak, words will be of no help."[8] After recognizing that propaganda is always an *auxiliary instrument*, whose effectiveness is a function of the nation's over-all foreign policy, it must be added that it can sometimes be a crucial policy component. Utilized in conjunction with instruments like military force, diplomatic techniques, and foreign aid, successful propaganda can facilitate the achievement of national goals; by contrast, an ineffectual propaganda campaign can seriously impede their attainment.

Several further points about propaganda require emphasis. A popular misconception is that propaganda is inherently false. This misconception explains in some measure why Americans have often been loath to support the propaganda activities of their government. Knowing that certain information is "propaganda" tells us nothing about the veracity or falsity of that information. The etymology of the word *propaganda* enables us to keep this point clearly in mind. Its root is the Latin verb *propagare*, meaning to propagate, to spread, to disseminate, to extend, to transmit. The term first came into historical currency after the establishment of the College of Propaganda by Pope Urban VIII (1623–1644), to promote the missionary activities of the Roman Catholic Church. Throughout the greater part of history, propaganda possessed none of the insidious connotations later associated with it in the Nazi or Communist periods. It meant merely the process of trying to gain converts to a particular cause, initially the Christian gospel as expounded by the Vatican. The process of propaganda then is the act of disseminating a belief; or propaganda may describe the belief so disseminated.[9]

Confusion can enter into any discussion of propaganda, however, when we inquire: "What is good and bad propaganda?" In a *tactical* sense, good propaganda is that which attains its intended result—gaining converts for the belief in question —and bad propaganda is that which fails to attain this result. In an *ethical* sense, according to the Judaeo–Christian tradition prevalent in the West,

good propaganda is that which accords as nearly as possible with objective truth, and bad propaganda is that which relies heavily upon various forms of deception, falsehood, and chicanery. Whatever the ethical standards by which propaganda is judged, however, *any* propaganda, including of course American, is to be distinguished from an objective search for truth. Irrespective of whether it is the lobbyist trying to influence the legislator, the advertising agency trying to influence the consumer, or the Voice of America trying to influence public opinion in Indonesia, the object of all propaganda is to utilize *carefully selected* data to induce the hearer to accept a predetermined point of view. The propagandist may *use* the truth—in fact, successful propaganda nearly always necessitates its use—but he is not *seeking* it objectively, nor is he prepared to follow where a dispassionate search for truth may lead * This is the cardinal distinction between propaganda and education.

Propaganda, as we have suggested, often arouses a feeling of revulsion among individuals steeped in the Western liberal or Judaeo–Christian traditions, particularly if it is equated with outright falsehood. These feelings are re-enforced by widespread antipathy to the methods of Nazi or Communist propagandists in recent history, whose conduct frequently has violated standards of behavior deemed acceptable among civilized societies. Yet, from another perspective, propaganda can properly be regarded as an alternative to military force in the conduct of international affairs. Organizations like the United Nations and the World Court exist to confine disputes among nations to the arena of persuasion and argumentation—which is the arena of propaganda. Conversely, wars occur when argumentation and negotiation *fail* to safeguard the vital interests of nations, leaving them no alternative but recourse to armaments. The ultimate objective of the United States therefore is not the elimination of propaganda per se as a permissible technique of international relations; rather, it is the substitution of words for bullets, so that propaganda and other nonviolent techniques may accomplish in the future what machine guns, howitzers, and, in

*The relationship between truthfulness and propaganda may be highlighted by recalling the legal distinction between "the truth" and "the whole truth"; a fact or statement may of course be the former without necessarily being the latter. Effective propaganda must be grounded upon truth, if for no other reason than that falsehoods, when exposed, undermine the propagandist's credibility. Thus a study of American propaganda efforts by a House Foreign Affairs subcommittee in 1967 called for a new approach "based on telling the truth"; but it also demanded greater "selectivity" among the facts and ideas presented. USIA's goal ought to be "attempt at persuasion . . . based on intelligent selection and emphasis"; fact should be used "with an objective in mind." Quoted in John W. Henderson, *The United States Information Agency* (New York: Praeger, 1969), p. 212.

the contemporary era, nuclear weapons accomplish in safeguarding the nation's interests and promoting its diplomatic objectives.

Western political leaders and informed citizens particularly have been disturbed for many years by the kind of psychological "total war" waged by Moscow and Peking, the hallmarks of which have been duplicity, blatant distortions of the truth, repeated imputations of bad faith, and other techniques poisoning the atmosphere of international relations and sometimes rendering any settlement of outstanding global issues all but impossible. Responsible leaders and observers have long recognized the need for agreement upon the kind of propaganda that is permissible in international affairs. Nevertheless, it remains true that words, however false and malicious, are always preferable to bombs, and that the more conflicts among nations can be confined to propaganda exchanges, the less likely that the future of civilization itself will be imperiled by global and regional animosities.

Americans particularly are prone to derogate "mere talk," to believe that "talk is cheap" and to call for "action instead of words." Historically, Americans have been doers, not philosophers; they have admired the man who "gets things done" more than the man who looks for the meaning in action or who seeks to change the thought patterns upon which past or future action takes place. Americans are, therefore, suspicious of diplomats who "do nothing but talk," often about highly technical, dull subjects, frequently beyond the comprehension of a majority of citizens. For reasons that we shall examine at a later stage, agencies of the American government engaging in propaganda in the postwar era have enjoyed very little popular support or understanding. USIA's relations with Congress, for example, are perpetually poor; legislators remain skeptical about the agency's activities and are almost always disposed to limit its budget sharply. Although this frame of mind has diverse origins, one of them is clearly the traditional American distaste for propaganda and the feeling that it is somehow incompatible with democracy or the American society's ethical values.

POSTWAR AMERICAN PROPAGANDA ACTIVITIES

Wartime and Early Postwar Programs

The United States was a comparative late-comer in recognizing the centrality of psychological warfare as an instrument of foreign policy. During World War I, the Creel Committee carried on an intensive campaign of propaganda which made a significant contribution to the Allied war effort. But from 1919 until the late 1930s, the United States conducted no noteworthy psychological warfare activities as a part of its foreign relations. Then in the late 1930s, several agencies within the government, particularly the Division of Cultural Relations in the State Department, began to undertake propaganda operations directed toward Latin America, where the threat of Axis penetration had become imminent.

A host of civilian and military agencies with responsibilities in the propaganda field emerged during World War II. Among the more important of these were the Office of Strategic Services, the Office of War Information, branches of army and navy intelligence, and the Coordinator of Inter-American Affairs, who took the place of the Division of Cultural Relations mentioned above. All of these carried on psychological warfare activities designed to shorten the war and to assure ultimate victory by the Allies. In the process, many valuable insights into the nature of such warfare were obtained, and for the first time the United States began to acquire a backlog of experience and personnel trained in the propaganda field. These were to pay enormous dividends when cold war compulsions finally forced the United States to initiate its first peacetime campaign of systematic propaganda operations.

After the war, many of the functions of these agencies were either eliminated altogether or transferred helter-skelter to the Department of State. Yet neither in the government nor in public opinion during this period was there any noteworthy support for continuance of psychological warfare activities. During the late 1940s and early 1950s, White House efforts to expand propaganda operations encountered extreme budgetary difficulties on Capitol Hill, as well as undisguised legislative hostility toward certain officials engaged in such activities. Events during the period of the Greek–Turkish Aid Program and the Marshall Plan nevertheless made it painfully clear that a greatly augmented informational and propaganda program was a diplomatic necessity, if the free world was to counter the expansive tendencies of the Communist bloc.

Propaganda aspects of foreign policy, however, remained secondary until the Korean War, when President Truman committed the nation to a "Campaign of Truth" abroad. Disturbed by enhanced Soviet prestige in exploding a nuclear bomb, and by initial Communist victories in Korea, Truman launched a propaganda campaign whose stated goals were:

. . . to present the truth to the millions of people who are uniformed or misinformed or unconvinced . . . to reach them in their daily lives, as they work and learn . . . to show them that freedom is the way to economic and social advancement, the way to political independence, the way to strength, happiness, and peace . . . [to] make ourselves known as we really are—not as Communist propaganda pictures us.[10]

The United States Information Agency

Yet these efforts by the Truman administration to strengthen American propaganda efforts proved only partially successful. After President Eisenhower took office in 1952, evidence mounted that the United States was lagging behind its ideological opponents in presenting its point of view to the outside world. Administratively, as one study has concluded, the American propaganda campaign in this period consisted chiefly of a "patchwork of pieces." Organizational responsibility for conducting programs remained scattered, and the programs themselves were inadequate to meet the challenge.[11] Consequently, upon the recommendation of President Eisenhower, the United States Information Agency (USIA), headed by a director appointed by the President, was established on August 1, 1953.* The State Department was divested of operating responsibility for propaganda and informational programs, although USIA remained under the supervision of the State Department for over-all policy guidance.

When it began operations in 1953, USIA had 255 overseas installations in 85 countries; it had some 12,900 employees, three-fourths of which (including 8500 foreign nationals) served overseas. Its first annual budget totaled just over $84 million.[12] By the 1970s, USIA had a total work force of approximately 10,500, substantially less than the number of personnel with which it began its activities. And as it entered the 1970s, USIA was compelled by Congress to reduce its existing staff by an additional 4 percent. By 1970, the agency operated 1380 overseas posts; the Nixon administration, however, had ordered a 10 percent reduction in these installations and a curtailment of American and foreign employees by USIA.[13] From the time of its establishment to the early 1970s, USIA's yearly budget ranged between a low of $82 million and a high of $185 million. Under the Nixon administration, it would probably fall into the $170–180 million range. After allowing for inflation since the early 1950s, that is to say, funds allocated to USIA had been increased insignificantly—and some of the agency's operations had been sharply curtailed.[14]

Since 1953, several statements of USIA's goals have been issued by the agency itself and by study groups appointed to examine its performance. New Directors of the USIA (and the agency has experienced considerable turnover among its high-level executives) customarily redefine and

"clarify" its objectives; and there is no reason to suppose that this process has come to an end. However simple or elaborate such statements of purpose may be, two basic objectives for American propaganda activities are almost always emphasized. First, the USIA exists to *influence opinion among leaders and masses in other countries in a manner favorable to the attainment of American diplomatic aims.* It exists to create an advantageous climate of opinion overseas which will enable the United States to accomplish its purposes in international relations. In countless ways—by convincing Communist policy-makers of the credibility of America's nuclear deterrent, or counteracting divisive tendencies within the NATO alliance, or persuading Africans that the United States opposes colonialism, or inducing North Vietnam and the Viet Cong to negotiate an end to the conflict in Southeast Asia, or stimulating the Japanese to assume greater responsibilities for Asian security—USIA endeavors to enhance foreign receptivity to American diplomatic objectives and behavior.

Second, a major responsibility of USIA is *to advise the President, the State Department, the overseas embassies, the National Security Council, and all other agencies playing a role in foreign relations regarding "the implications of foreign opinion for present and contemplated U.S. policies, programs, and official states."*[15] Thus, USIA serves as a conduit for channeling foreign reactions (and anticipated reactions) to American diplomatic behavior to key policy-makers. This responsibility may in turn be thought of as involving two separate functions: advising American officials concerning foreign attitudes toward the United States *in the present and recent past;* and *predicting* the impact of some new or proposed development in American foreign relations upon opinion overseas, so that decision-makers may take these attitudes into account in policy formulation.

The former goal—influencing opinion abroad—is a very old objective of propaganda campaigns. The latter—trying to anticipate foreign attitudes and informing decision-makers *before* policy has been decided upon—is a relatively recent responsibility of agencies engaged in propaganda activities. Although officials involved in propaganda have long advocated the expansion of USIA's role in policy formulation, this idea has encountered both passive and active opposition among other agencies of government. Some Secretaries of State, for example, have deprecated USIA's contribution or openly disparaged the importance of foreign opinion as an influence upon American foreign policy.* Yet slowly, USIA has gained

---

*The overseas installations of USIA continued to bear the name they had been known by since World War II —the United States Information Service (USIS).

*During the Truman administration, for example, Secretary of State Dean G. Acheson believed that propaganda activities played a marginal role in the outcome

greater influence in the policy-making process. The agency's director has often participated in meetings of the National Security Council; by invitation of the President, he sometimes attends meetings of the Cabinet; and USIA officials are regularly assigned to lower-level interdepartmental committees (like the Senior Inter-Department Group, or SIG under the Johnson administration). In 1966, USIA established a Media Reaction Unit, whose purpose was to keep the President and his principal advisers informed of foreign reactions to American policy rapidly and systematically.[16]

To accomplish its purposes, USIA utilizes a wide variety of techniques and programs. The attempt to influence foreign news media, particularly newspapers overseas, is a significant area of USIA activity. The agency's Press and Publications Service prepares news releases, photographs, interpretive articles, pamphlets, comic strips, and other materials for use by foreign news media. Within individual countries, USIS posts prepare and distribute such materials specifically for a given audience. USIS installations around the world report to embassy officials and to Washington the reaction of the foreign press to American conduct at home and abroad.

The production and distribution of films is another principal USIA activity. Films are especially effective in rural areas and among foreign populations where literacy is low. In the urban centers, films prepared by USIA are supplied to local TV stations and shown at USIS posts. In the main, these films are documentaries and news reels designed to explain and elicit support for American foreign policy objectives.

The "binational centers" (or "information centers") operated by USIS in most of the nations of the world have been called by one USIA director "the single most important activity" of the agency.[17] Under the supervision of a cultural affairs officer, each center serves as a complex where cultural, educational, and informational activities are conducted. The heart of the center is the USIS library—often the largest single collection of "Americana" within the country. The larger libraries contain thousands of fiction and nonfiction books, reference volumes, technical manuals, a representative assortment of Ameri-

can magazines and periodicals, perhaps a record collection, and other resources dealing with the American society. Trained librarians assist foreigners seeking to use these materials; not infrequently, the concept that books may be "borrowed" from a valuable library collection is a novel idea in other countries. Along with a library, the information center normally has an auditorium and other facilities for lectures, talks, concerts, and seminar meetings. Space is available for art exhibits and poster displays. One of the most popular and heavily utilized of USIA's services is its program of English language instruction (an activity in which the wives of American officials overseas often play a leading role). Countless thousands of foreigners have attained a fairly high degree of proficiency in English because of this program. Studies by USIA indicate that upwards of 25 million foreigners annually use the facilities available in its overseas centers.[18]

As every reader of the daily newspaper is aware, the USIS centers abroad constitute a highly visible symbol of America's "presence" in the country and perhaps of its international role. Since they are usually located in the center of the capital or another large city, these posts are conspicuous and highly vulnerable to groups desiring to express anti-American sentiments. Hardly a month passes without some American library overseas being damaged, and occasionally destroyed, by crowds expressing hostility toward the United States. To some minds, the very existence of these installations is provocative, perhaps inherently encouraging inflammatory conduct by groups opposed to the United States. Understandably, damage to American libraries overseas is not calculated to enhance USIA's image with Congress or the taxpayer. Yet, as we shall see presently, there may be another side to this coin. It is conceivable at least that attacks against USIS installations abroad may stem in part from resentment and apprehension that they *are* winning friends for the United States in other societies.

USIA is also assigned responsibility for supervising a number of educational (student and faculty) exchange programs between the United States and other countries. The agency arranges for American artists, musicians, and writers to visit foreign countries and for cultural groups from abroad to tour the United States. American participation in foreign trade fairs and exhibitions is another USIA activity, as is arranging American representation in international scientific and educational conferences abroad.

America's best-known propaganda activity perhaps is the radio arm of USIA—the "Voice of America" (VOA), created during World War II. Transmitting in some 36 different languages, and broadcasting over 800 program hours weekly, VOA relies upon a network of powerful transmitters (some of which are "floating" transmitters) in

---

of American diplomacy. On one occasion he said that "world opinion simply does not exist on matters that concern us." His successor, Secretary of State John Foster Dulles, was equally dubious about the role of informational and propaganda activities in achieving American foreign policy goals. Dulles once stated that "If I so much as took into account what people in other countries are thinking or feeling, I would be derelict in my duty." He was also skeptical about America's acting "behind the backs" of foreign governments by seeking to influence public opinion in other countries. The views of both officials are cited in Thomas C. Sorensen, *The Word War: The Story of American Propaganda* (New York: Harper & Row, 1968), pp. 29, 82.

America and abroad. The power output of VOA's broadcasting facilities exceeds that of all the medium-wave (AM) radio stations in the United States! Using both medium-wave and short-wave frequencies, the VOA's programs literally encompass the globe. USIA officials estimate that VOA signals can be received by some 70 percent of the human race; planned construction of more powerful transmitters will raise that proportion to 90 percent (including people in the interior of China and Siberia). Although audience size naturally varies (depending upon the day of the week, weather conditions, and other factors), studies by the VOA indicate that normally from 42 to 43 million foreigners listen to its programs during an ordinary week. The highest "audience potential" is reached in Eastern Europe (with 23 percent of the potential audience listening to VOA broadcasts); while the lowest figure (only 3 percent) is achieved in Communist China. Impressive as they are, however, USIA's worldwide broadcasting facilities are eclipsed by those of both the Soviet Union and Red China.*

USIA in Action: Two Cases

Greater insight into the complexity of USIA's activities may be gained by examining its propaganda efforts with regard to specific issues having a high propaganda content. Let us examine briefly two such cases—one intrinsically favorable to America's image overseas, and the other unfavorable. The former category is illustrated by the Apollo XI moon mission in 1969. To derive maximum propaganda impact from this historic event, USIA spent months planning how best to exploit it to America's advantage. Every modern propaganda technique—Voice of America broadcasts, TV programs, films, press releases, and a great variety of publications, displays, exhibits, speeches, and interviews, all at a total cost of several million dollars—was utilized to publicize the first moon landing throughout the world. Reports to USIA indicated that some 750 million people listened to VOA transmissions dealing with the Apollo XI flight, the largest radio audience ever reached by the agency. Some 650,000 requests were received by USIA posts for photographs,

booklets, commemorative stamps, and other memorabilia of this space probe. USIA distributed several million pamphlets and brochures calling attention to America's achievement in the "space race." All USIS installations abroad presented exhibits and displays related to the feat; thousands of books, space buttons, and the like were distributed in other countries. USIA worked with foreign television stations to provide "live" coverage of the launch and the "moon walk" by American astronauts; agency officials appeared on many of these programs to explain the events. After the Apollo XI mission had been successfully completed, USIA continued with a massive follow-up campaign, calling attention to the technological and scientific skill required to carry out the exploit and accenting its scientific importance for the entire world. Foreign interest in this historic space accomplishment was extraordinarily high; some USIA installations overseas had to be closed because crowds overwhelmed their facilities. Some 3600 foreign radio stations and 888 foreign TV outlets used materials supplied by USIA. A high official of the agency has termed this propaganda effort "the most complicated and exhaustive they have ever undertaken."[19]

What precisely did this massive expenditure of time, energy, and funds by USIA achieve? That it called attention graphically to America's technological and scientific prowess can hardly be doubted. For an indeterminate period of time, it unquestionably raised foreign admiration for the United States. Beyond that, its impact is difficult to calculate. As we shall see at a later point, the measurement of the results of propaganda is an extremely difficult and often highly subjective undertaking.

A different kind of challenge of course is presented to American propagandists by other subjects—racial conflicts, student unrest, the existence of slum and poverty conditions in the U.S., or the growth in violence within the American society. Many of these subjects are "difficult" propaganda themes; they tarnish America's image in the eyes of foreigners, since they are often viewed (and actively exploited by Communist propagandists) as failures of the American society. How does USIA seek to treat such topics in order, at a minimum, to mitigate their adverse effects upon foreign attitudes? In general terms, USIA endeavors "to analyze the facts and meet the distortions with positive, persuasive documentation."[20]

Take the matter of racial strife in American society. In its propaganda activities, USIA endeavors to place the problem in perspective, to highlight the gains made by minority groups within the United States, to point out that violent episodes are rare and often less intense than widely imagined, to feature positive efforts made by all levels of government and by private organi-

---

*Writing in 1968, an experienced American propagandist stated that, with VOA broadcasting in 38 languages for a total 850 hours per week, America's radio broadcasting arm ranked *fourth* among government-sponsored propaganda programs. The Soviet Union ranked first—with over 1500 hours weekly in 67 languages; Communist China was second—with some 1130 hours of weekly transmissions; while the United Arab Republic (Egypt) transmitted 910 hours of propaganda weekly. Britain ranked below America; West Germany, whose propaganda activities were expanding rapidly, was listed sixth on the list. See Thomas C. Sorensen, *The Word War: The Story of American Propaganda* (New York: Harper & Row, 1968), pp. 226–227.

zations to remove the underlying causes of racial discord, and to reiterate the idea that the policies of the national government are *in favor* of eliminating barriers to equal opportunities for all ethnic groups. As an example, a VOA broadcast dealing with racial crises in 1968 declared:

... in the past two years two million Negroes rose above the government-designated poverty level of $3,000 annual income for a family of four, and ... over the past decade the number of Negro families with annual incomes in excess of $8,000 tripled.

Other USIA efforts to explain the racial situation in America to foreigners underscore the fact that several large and medium-size cities have black mayors; that the number of blacks in Congress has been rising; that some 80 percent of all registered black voters (somewhat over 7 million) voted in 1968. Foreign newsmen and authors writing about race problems in the United States are assisted by USIA in arranging interviews and gaining access to data. Successful efforts by the national government, and often by states and localities, to break down racial barriers in all spheres of life are widely publicized. Statements by the President and lesser officials endorsing the goal of civil rights are given worldwide circulation. Peaceful efforts aimed at improving the status of blacks and other minorities (such as the "March on Washington" on August 28, 1963) are given full publicity, with emphasis upon their nonviolent and positive aspects. Movements seeking to promote "dialogues" between whites and blacks are given conspicuous treatment in USIA media. By arranging foreign tours, performances, and lectures overseas by outstanding blacks and black groups, the USIA tries to provide evidence of the progress made by blacks in the United States.

The facts concerning racial upheavals within the American society *are reported* by USIA to the outside world. They are presented, however, within a framework emphasizing the steps being taken to put an end to violence and to punish law-breakers in the short run, along with measures designed to remove the long-range causes of racial turmoil. In approaching subjects of this kind, USIA officials are aware of a cardinal maxim of effective propaganda: *the need for candor and truthfulness* in the information disseminated abroad. Although this approach is often criticized vocally on Capitol Hill and by private groups in America, Thomas C. Sorensen has echoed the conviction of many other students of the art of propaganda by saying that "a basic law of propaganda was involved: foreigners, hearing the bad news from others if not from us, would be unlikely to believe USIA's good news if unpleasant developments were ignored or shrugged off."[21] Without

attempting to deny the existence of racial tensions within America, USIA sought to underscore the idea that some of this strife was an outgrowth of rising concern for equality in the United States; to emphasize the degree to which black citizens were becoming full participants in a pluralistic American society; and to call attention to the official and private steps being taken continuously to alleviate the causes of racial disharmony.

USIA officials were under no illusions that these steps totally counteracted the adverse effects of American racial strife upon foreign opinion. We might liken the process of propaganda in such cases to that of "retouching" a photograph: Within limits, individuals engaged in both activities can do much to improve the image with which they are concerned, but the results are also fundamentally determined by the nature of the original picture. To reiterate a point made earlier in the chapter: Propaganda is *only one policy instrument* or force influencing the nation's diplomatic effectiveness, and sometimes it is a relatively uninfluential factor. For race problems, along with many other issues affecting America's relations with the outside world, the real "Voice of America"—the voice which is heard most clearly by foreigners and which is most crucial in affecting their attitudes about the United States—is American *behavior* at home and abroad. Carl Rowan, a former director of USIA, once said that "we in USIA are the purveyors of the American image abroad, but not its manufacturers. The image of the United States cannot be concocted in some propaganda factory."[22] Ideally, of course, American conduct and official propaganda statements ought to be harmonious and mutually supportive. When they are not, deeds are likely to be more eloquent testimony than words in expressing America's principles, moral values, ethical codes, and goals to societies overseas. After recognizing these realities, it remains true that skillful propaganda efforts can and do contribute to a clearer understanding by foreigners of racial and other problems troubling the American society. Informed opinion abroad, for example, recognizes a vital distinction between racial tensions within the United States and those within countries like South Africa and Southern Rhodesia; and it is cognizant that—despite instances of racial violence or misunderstanding—minority groups have, by most criteria, made more progress within the United States than in any other society on the globe.*

---

*The fundamental difference between racial strife in the United States and in these African states is of course that in the latter *apartheid* is *the official policy of the government;* the authority of the law, and often force, are used by government officials to *enforce racial segregation;* moreover, in these nations, there is a greater degree of separateness now than one or two decades ago. By contrast, violent episodes often erupt within the

In assessing the impact upon foreign attitudes of the more unpalatable aspects of American society like racial disharmony, violence, and poverty, a point made by a study of the ideological aspects of international relations in 1968 is pertinent. *The impression Americans have of America* is unquestionably a crucial factor is determining what outsiders think of the United States. This study concluded:

. . . foreign opinion about the United States is to a surprisingly large extent the product of our national mood and of what we say and write about ourselves. For example, vocal division over U.S. policy in Vietnam finds an immediate reflection in public attitudes abroad. So do American opinions on most other issues.

According to an expert witness, foreign correspondents derive some 80 percent of their information and impressions about the United States from what American reporters write in our papers and say on our television networks.[23]

Continuing Problems and Dilemmas

A report by a legislative subcommittee in 1967 on American propaganda activities overseas complained about the "frequently undistinguished response to the challenge and the opportunities presented by modern communications technology."[24] When the new USIA Director Frank J. Shakespeare, Jr., took office late in 1969, he expressed his intention to reorganize the agency, making it into a more influential instrument of American foreign policy. This intention reflected recognition of widespread skepticism about USIA's effectiveness and about America's overseas image generally.[25] In the same period, the Nixon administration announced that USIA's staff was being reduced by some 4 percent, while its foreign posts were being cut back by 10 percent.[26]

These developments constituted evidence of a long-standing and continuing reality: Postwar American propaganda operations and programs have been plagued by a number of obstacles. In the space remaining, let us examine four of them.

1. *The Problem of Agency Morale and Support.* By many standards, understanding and support of USIA's activities by officials in other executive agencies, by Congress, and by the public at large has been, and remains, at a relatively low level. Among all the agencies involved in the foreign policy process (with the possible exception of the

CIA), USIA has perhaps the poorest "image" and the least impressive degree of support on Capitol Hill and in public opinion. Evidence of USIA's low prestige abounds. The largest annual expenditure for its operations since World War II was just over $185 million (in fiscal year 1966). This was less than *one two-hundredth* of the Defense Department's budget for that same year; and it was below 10 percent of the amount the United States expended to wage the Vietnam War *for a single month* in the late 1960s. Moreover, USIA has undergone innumerable investigations and assessments of its performance since the early 1950s; it is probably the most thoroughly "examined" federal agency in Washington. Some of these studies have no doubt been valuable and have improved American propaganda programs. Others (especially those undertaken in the late 1940s and early 1950s) sharply impaired morale within the agency and disrupted its operations. The sheer frequency with which USIA's operations have been examined and re-examined, after which its mission has been "redefined," has detracted in some degree from its effective operation.

USIA's relations with Congress have consistently been poor. Legislative attitudes toward the agency normally range from hostile to skeptical. Congress has been indifferent to USIA's pleas for more funds and expanded programs—at the very time that sentiment among legislators was critical of USIA's "failures" to improve the image of the United States in foreign countries. One student of public opinion informed the House Foreign Affairs Committee bluntly in 1968 that it was often Congress' own action (or inaction) which produced a poor image of America abroad or limited USIA's ability to alter that image.[27]

Another indication of difficulties impeding USIA's contribution to American foreign policy has been the high rate of turnover among its top executives. Directors of the agency usually remain in office only a few months; and it is a common pattern for them to resign under controversial circumstances. Not infrequently, they leave USIA disillusioned because of lack of rapport between it and the State Department, the White House, and Congress; and they are usually convinced that USIA does not yet play the role in policy formulation which is essential to achieve America's diplomatic goals.

An important step designed to improve morale within USIA and to impart greater permanence to positions within it was finally taken late in 1968, when Congress passed Public Law 90–494, giving permanent career status to most of USIA's "temporary" employees. Passage of this law (first proposed as early as 1955) was the culmination of the movement seeking to create a career foreign service for USIA comparable to the Foreign Service arm of the State Department. By this act, the United States took a long stride forward in creat-

United States because of efforts by the national government to *abolish* racial segregation and to create greater equality of opportunity for all citizens. In this case, national officials are using their authority to *break down* racial barriers, sometimes against strong state and local opposition, and in nearly all cases of legally imposed (if not de facto) segregation, the power of the national government has eventually prevailed.

ing a corps of propaganda specialists and in according public recognition to the role of propaganda in the foreign policies of modern states.[28]

To some extent, the problem of USIA's low prestige and support derives from a still pervasive *aversion to propaganda* throughout the American society. To many Americans, as we have mentioned, propaganda is incompatible with democracy and the Judeo-Christian tradition. Like the State Department, USIA has no strong and vocal domestic constituency, similar to the Agriculture Department's traditionally close ties with American farmers. When Congress cuts USIA's budget, few local or state citizen organizations object. The low prestige of the agency can be accounted for also by another factor whose importance will be examined in greater detail presently: the problem of devising objective methods for *measuring the results* of propaganda efforts abroad. Thus far, such measurements yield highly uncertain results.

2. *The Problem of Truth vs. Persuasion.* As we have already noted, successful propaganda must be grounded in truth; falsifications and grossly distorted news reports by the Voice of America, for example, would probably in the end damage America's reputation and alienate opinion in other countries. Although nearly all propagandists subscribe to this principle, there is still room for considerable flexibility in interpreting USIA's mission and in formulating the propaganda strategies which ought to guide its operations. Ever since its creation, USIA has experienced internal tensions growing out of the conflict between two more or less distinctive conceptions of its mission.

One approach was symbolized by the viewpoints of former USIA Director George V. Allen, who declared that its task was, above all, to be *truthful and accurate* in its propaganda emanations. Allen asserted that when USIA's functions were "properly conceived and executed," it would be no different from "the Associated Press or the Rockefeller Foundation." Referring to America's diplomatic tensions with Cuba, Allen believed that "nothing could have helped Castro more" than an intensive and strident anti-Communist campaign directed against his regime.[29] This approach maintains that dissemination of truthful information per se is the "best propaganda" the United States can undertake abroad. Conversely, the USIA ought to avoid extolling American democracy and capitalism; it ought to shun any kind of "hard sell" approach to other societies; it should eschew denunciations of Soviet or Chinese Communism; it should refrain from implying any inherent superiority in the American way of life or in the policies of the American government. Its guiding maxim should be the idea that in all its activities—from cultural exchange programs with other countries, to programs broadcast by VOA, to discussions of American racial strife in news releases—emphasis upon truthfulness and artistic creativity will, in the final analysis, promote America's diplomatic interests better than any other operating strategy. This approach reflects the need to maintain maximum "credibility" for propaganda programs and to enhance the receptivity of foreigners to USIA's propaganda efforts.

The opposite conception of USIA's proper mission emphasizes the agency's goal of *persuading foreign opinion* to support American overseas objectives. In this view, USIA has one overriding objective: to promote a greater willingness by outsiders to respond favorably to the policies of the United States. A former USIA official has thus recalled a conversation he had with President Kennedy:

I told Kennedy that I thought USIA's purpose should be to persuade, not merely to inform; that the Agency should be charged with furthering the achievement of U.S. foreign policy objectives by "promoting climates of opinion abroad that will enhance the prospects of achieving these objectives through diplomatic means." . . .[30]

Or, as USIA Director Edward R. Murrow (quoting from an earlier study of USIA's performance) expressed the idea, " ' any program established by government funds can only be justified to the extent that it assists in the achievement of national objectives,' I agree—and that *is* the purpose, the sole purpose of USIA today."[31]

The conflict between these two basic propaganda strategies may be more apparent than real. Both recognize the necessity for adhering to an essentially truthful presentation of information about internal and external American policies; both acknowledge that successful propaganda must be "credible;" both are prepared to inform foreigners about the attractive and the more unsavory aspects of American conduct; both also believe that a continuing informational program by the United States government is essential to the achievement of its diplomatic goals.

Yet differences in emphasis and tone do characterize these two approaches. Take a USIA-sponsored activity like "cultural exchange" between the United States and the Soviet Union. The former approach believes that such exchange is inherently beneficial to the United States; these and other attempts to promote "international understanding" reduce the likelihood of war and lesser forms of international tension. The latter approach evaluates such programs rather differently. It does *not* concede that the diplomatic interests of America are automatically furthered when the New York Philharmonic Orchestra tours the Soviet Union or when the Bolshoi Ballet gives programs in the United States. (Such examples of cultural exchange may simply have no fundamental impact upon political relations between the United States and the Soviet Union.) Similarly, the exchange of students and scholars across national frontiers may, or it may not, enhance opportunities abroad for the United States to realize its foreign policy aims. Sometimes such programs unquestionably are valuable for the United States; at other times, they may not be. It ought to be noted, advocates of this approach point out, that some of the most vocal critics of the West in Africa and other emerging societies were often *educated in the United States and Western Europe.* Moreover, studies have shown that the "exposure" of foreigners to American society by no means automatically results in more favorable attitudes toward the United States; in some instances, the resulting attitudes may in fact be more unfavorable than before. The only applicable yardstick for measuring the value of cultural exchange and other programs operated by USIA is: In what way does the program contribute to a more favorable environment for accomplishing American foreign policy goals?[32] This is unquestionably the criterion applied by Congress in evaluating USIA's performance and by most of the agency's directors for the past two decades.

3. *The Measurement of Propaganda Impact.* Here we examine one of the most difficult, but also one of the most crucial, problems affecting USIA's role in the foreign policy process. How can the results of propaganda activities be accurately assessed? If Congress appropriates around $175 million in a given year for the agency's operations, how can it be certain that this allocation of tax revenues is really achieving a worthwhile purpose vis-à-vis, let us say, expanding the Defense Department's budget or spending an equivalent sum on the State Department? Or, how can one form of propaganda by the United States (for example, cultural exchange programs) be compared with another (such as radio broadcasts by VOA) in terms of their effectiveness?

Over the years, officials of USIA have employed several more or less accurate indicators to measure the impact of their propaganda activities on foreign opinion. The agency has utilized public opinion polls, for example, to determine the attitudes of foreigners toward the United States. Polls by private organizations, together with those specifically commissioned by USIA, have been relied upon for this purpose; results are made available to officials engaged in propaganda, to the State Department, to the White House, and to other agencies involved in foreign policy. The use of such polls, particularly those commissioned by USIA itself, has been heavily curtailed in recent years, however, because of the fact that poll results were injected into the presidential election of 1960. Candidate Richard M. Nixon claimed that America's image abroad was very good; his oppo-

nent, John F. Kennedy, claimed the contrary and relied upon USIA polls of opinion overseas to confirm his contention. USIA was widely criticized for becoming involved in this domestic political contest.[33]

Another category of measuring devices includes several methods for assessing foreign audience response to USIA activities. Making projections of audience potential from analyses of "fan mail" received from those who have heard VOA broadcasts; tabulating the number of requests received from foreign listeners for newsletters and other publications by USIA; in some countries, estimating the membership of "clubs" (e.g., the "Friends of Music USA") formed among those regularly listening to VOA transmissions; estimating total audience size from the percentage of listeners who enter contests sponsored by VOA —by these and comparable means, the Voice of America tries to gauge the size of its audience in individual countries and major regions. The number of foreigners who visit exhibits in USIS installations abroad, the number of readers using the facilities provided by American libraries overseas, the total number of books circulated within a given year by these libraries, and the size of audiences watching USIA-produced films afford data concerning the size and nature of foreign groups exposed to American propaganda activities.*

A different kind of standard for measuring propaganda impact encompasses various types of foreign reactions to the United States. Here, we will limit our attention to two examples. One is *editorial opinion* in newspapers and journals overseas. USIA regularly conducts studies of such opinion abroad and circulates its findings both within the agency and to other departments involved in American foreign policy. Major shifts in foreign editorial reactions are especially important. Referring to the way other countries reacted to racial strife in the United States, for example, one USIA study concluded that *before* Washington began to enforce school integration, foreign editorials "condemned brutality and condemned the United States for permitting it"; *after* federal authority was placed behind efforts to achieve racial equality (and presumably after USIA's propaganda activities began to affect foreign attitudes), editorial opinion abroad, though it still con-

---

*It is evident that nearly all criteria used for measuring the effectiveness of USIA's activities have their imperfections, in some cases perhaps major ones. USIA officials are aware of many of these limitations. Thus former director Edward R. Murrow was skeptical about utilizing figures showing visitors to USIS libraries or total book circulation in a given year as evidence of the impact made by American propaganda efforts overseas. One of his subordinates observed that heavy patronage of USIS posts in other countries, for example, might be accounted for by the fact that "a USIS Library was the only air-conditioned spot in town open to the public without charge"! See Sorensen, *op. cit.*, p. 186.

demned racial inequality in America, was much less critical of government policies toward this issue.[34]

A second category of foreign reaction is *disclosure by other governments* of USIA's effectiveness. This kind of evidence relates especially to broadcasts by VOA. For many years, USIA officials have relied upon Soviet statements and conduct to provide insight into how well American propaganda activities are penetrating the Iron Curtain and the degree to which they influence opinion in the Communist zone. Moscow's words and deeds provide a surprising amount of evidence on this score! From time to time, the Kremlin's own propaganda apparatus warns citizens behind the Iron Curtain about the insidious character of Voice of America broadcasts; occasionally, Communist officials themselves admit (at least tacitly) that VOA transmissions are appealing and that they have gained a growing audience in Communist-ruled societies; in some periods, massive Soviet "jamming" activities indicate that the Kremlin is concerned about the dissemination of news and messages by USIA throughout the Marxist sphere.[35] USIA officials assume that the frequency and intensity with which American propaganda operations are denounced by Communist officials furnishes at least a crude index of their impact. A not untypical comment by the Soviet labor publication *Trud* in 1963—labeling USIA "a perfect example of an instrument for poisoning the minds of the people with deceitful propaganda"—illustrates this kind of Marxist tribute to the agency's performance.[36] Now and again, Moscow publicly concedes that USIA's programs are in danger of surpassing Radio Moscow and other Communist propaganda activities in terms of their audience appeal.[37] In recent years, another index of USIA's impact behind the Iron Curtain has been the extent to which Marxist propaganda and news organs have changed their strategy, in part at least because of fear that Radio Moscow may be "scooped" by the Voice of America in announcing important developments in the international community. Soviet censorship has been relaxed, for example, in some measure owing to the realization in the Kremlin that even events like Russian suppression of Hungary's bid for freedom in 1956, or the invasion of Czechoslovakia in 1968, will quickly be publicized by the Voice of America, the British Broadcasting Company and other Western outlets. Consequently, Soviet officials have stated publicly that attempts to suppress information by Communist media merely enhance the appeal of Western propaganda operations and embarrass the U.S.S.R.[38]

A still different measure of USIA performance is the frequency with which foreign agitators (often with the connivance of, and certainly with the knowledge of, foreign governments) attack USIS posts in other countries. During some periods, violence against American libraries overseas reaches epidemic proportions. The destruction of these installations of course normally indicates a considerable reservoir of anti-American sentiment within the foreign societies concerned; the more frequently these posts are attacked, American congressmen are likely to reason, the more *ineffectively* USIA is conducting its programs. Yet USIA officials are often prone to draw opposite conclusions from these assaults. They indicate, one former official has stated, that "extremists . . . [are] afraid of knowledge, truth, and America"; accordingly, political extremists strike "at the most accessible and most visible symbol of knowledge, truth, and America at hand: the USIS library." In short, American libraries overseas are attacked because they *are* influential propaganda instruments, a fact which even anti-American groups acknowledge.[39]

From this brief examination of techniques relied upon to evaluate the results of propaganda activities, it is apparent that such measurement remains a primitive, subjective, and often unsatisfactory undertaking. Determining what is accomplished with propaganda is a very difficult process, one perhaps that is not, by nature, susceptible to very precise findings. Each of the criteria mentioned above has its limitations as an indicator of USIA's effectiveness, and some must be used with numerous qualifications. The process of propaganda itself is normally so intertwined with other "variables" affecting foreign attitudes toward the United States—such as the policies of the American government at home and abroad, the history of America's relations with particular countries and regions, the incidence and intensity of international crises, and many other factors—that the impact of propaganda alone in shaping America's image overseas is all but impossible to calculate. As we emphasized earlier in the chapter, propaganda nearly always serves as *an auxiliary instrument* of foreign policy. Its success or failure is heavily conditioned by other considerations, ranging from the nation's military posture, to its negotiation skill, to its success in solving domestic problems.

Furthermore, propagandists are often called upon to undertake an assignment for which they receive little credit and for which (even when their efforts are carried out skillfully) the benefits accruing to the United States may often appear minimal. Not infrequently, officials in USIA must try to prevent foreign opinion from becoming *more adverse* to America than it already is, to keep the national image from becoming *more tarnished*, and to make foreigners somewhat *less critical* of American policies than they would be without USIA's programs. Achieving these essentially negative goals does little to impress Congress with USIA's skills or its level of performance. Yet the question can be legitimately asked: "What would foreign attitudes toward the United States be *without* USIA's efforts to influence opinion overseas favorably?"

After recognizing the difficulties involved in documenting results obtained by American propaganda efforts, the USIA will probably continue to engage in a variety of psychological activities for one compelling reason. Confronted with massive propaganda campaigns waged against it by Moscow, Peking and several of the smaller Marxist nations, the United States cannot risk being "left out" of this global psychological contest.

4. *USIA's Role in Policy Formulation.* Finally, it is necessary to refer once more to a problem identified earlier: USIA's participation in national policy formulation. The over-all record since the early 1950s indicates that progress—in some periods, outstanding progress—has been made in integrating the agency into policy planning and formulation. At intervals, the director of the USIA has served on the National Security Council; liaison between USIA and the State Department is unquestionably closer today than ten years ago. John W. Henderson, for example, has concluded that "the tendency in recent years has been for USIA to take increasing initiative in the development of policy guidance" provided by the Department of State.[40]

Yet complaints continue to be expressed by USIA officials that this process has not been carried far enough, that there is sometimes resistance within the State Department and the White House to consulting specialists in opinion overseas *before* diplomatic decisions are made, and that the personalities of leading policy-makers often are crucial factors determining USIA's role in prior policy formulation. USIA, for example, was left out of the Kennedy administration's early deliberations at the time of the Cuban missile crisis of 1962; and when it did learn of the government's proposed response to this threat—in which the persuasive communication of America's intentions to other countries was a key element— the agency was informed *accidentally*.[41] Several months earlier, USIA's views concerning likely foreign reaction were not solicited in connection with the abortive Bay of Pigs invasion of Cuba.[42] Although USIA was brought increasingly into the mainstream of policy, Thomas C. Sorensen has said that "there was little more comprehension of USIA's role in the departments and agencies than there had been under Eisenhower or Truman."[43] Henderson concludes his study of USIA by saying that "greater acceptance by the State Department of the Agency's function as a participant in the policy-making process" is still required.[44] And under the Nixon administration, one report found that, as in the past, the agency's mission, its role in policy-making, and its value as an instrument of American foreign policy remained in question.

Despite recent recommendations by an advisory commission on national psychological programs that USIA's participation in policy formulation be expanded, indications were that under President Nixon it would probably be curtailed.[45]

THE UNITED STATES FOREIGN AID PROGRAM

The remainder of this chapter will be devoted to an analysis of another important instrument of postwar American foreign policy: foreign aid Between world War II and the early 1970s, the United States dispensed approximately $135 billion in various categories of foreign aid to other countries. Out of this total, approximately $95 billion was devoted to loans and grants classified as "economic assistance" to societies overseas; the remainder (close to $39 billion) was allocated to "military assistance," designed to strengthen the security of nations threatened with Communist expansionism or other dangers to their independence.* Earlier chapters focused attention upon American foreign aid programs as they related to specific regions like Western Europe, Asia, and Latin America. Here, our interest centers upon such questions as: What patterns and trends are discernible in American foreign assistance during the past quarter-century? What have been the goals of foreign aid programs administered by the United States, and how have these goals changed throughout the postwar period? What have American foreign assistance activities achieved? In what respects have they facilitated the attainment of American diplomatic goals? Conversely, what have been the chief failures and inadequacies in postwar foreign aid programs and why? And, in the 1970s, what was the future of foreign assistance as an instrument of American

*Considerable variation is likely to be encountered among studies showing the overall scope of American postwar foreign assistance. These differences can largely be accounted for because of: (1) rounding of totals; (2) inclusion or exclusion of aid which has been "allocated" but not yet granted to foreign countries; (3) inclusion or exclusion of loans and other forms of assistance made available by *private* sources in the United States, such as investments by American business firms in less developed societies abroad; and (4) the extent to which such figures take account of past (or scheduled) repayments to the United States by aid recipients. The total of $135 billion cited above refers to assistance extended by the United States government (including loans made available by the Import-Export Bank); it does not include aid made available by private concerns (like the Rockefeller or Ford Foundations or private business firms). The above total represents "gross" American aid, since it does not include repayment of principal and interest or loans extended by the United States to foreign countries. See the data supplied by the Agency for International Development, as cited in *Global Defense: U.S. Military Commitments Abroad* (Washington, D.C.: Congressional Quarterly Service, 1969), pp. 37–44.

foreign policy? We begin our inquiry by briefly examining the scope and nature of American aid programs since World War II.

Scope and Nature of U.S. Aid

Extensive foreign assistance is no new phenomenon in American history. In the post-World War I period the United States advanced nearly $10 billion in loans to some 20 countries. Most of these loans were never repaid. Negotiated agreements between America and its debtors, coupled with the Hoover debt moratorium during the Great Depression, turned most of these loans into outright grants.

Huge sums were advanced by the United States to its Allies during World War II and to deal with severe crises in the immediate postwar period. The Greek-Turkish Aid Program and the Marshall Plan inaugurated continuing programs of economic and military assistance. These programs differed somewhat from later foreign aid ventures, however, in that they were designed to deal with a specific, relatively short-lived crisis. Continuing *military* assistance to other governments began with the Mutual Defense Assistance Program to bolster the defense of Western Europe, following ratification of the North Atlantic Treaty in 1949. Global *economic and technical* assistance programs evolved out of President Truman's "Point Four" program of aid to underdeveloped countries in 1949.* Then, under the Kennedy ad-

*American postwar foreign aid activities have been subjected to a continuing cycle of change and "reorganization," making it difficult for the student of American foreign policy to keep abreast of prevailing administrative patterns. During World War II, the Lend-Lease Administration supervised American assistance to Allied governments; toward the end of the conflict, the United States relied upon the United Nations Relief and Rehabilitation Administration (UNRRA) to supervise assistance to societies suffering from the war. The State Department administered the Greek-Turkish Aid Program of 1947; but at congressional insistence, a separate agency—the European Cooperation Administration, headed by a prominent businessman—was set up to oversee Marshall Plan aid to Europe. Then in 1950, the Technical Cooperation Administration was established to handle President Truman's new Point Four Program of aid to the emerging nations. After the Korean War, in 1951 economic and military aid programs were combined and administered by a new Mutual Security Agency. But this pattern was changed again in 1955, when the International Cooperation Administration (ICA) was set up within the State Department to supervise *economic* aid to other countries, while *military* assistance programs were assigned to the Department of Defense. Another agency—the Development Loan Fund—was created in 1957 to extend loans (sometimes called "soft loans") to needy countries on liberal terms. When President Kennedy entered the White House in 1961, he reorganized the foreign aid machinery again. A new Agency for International Development (AID) was created as a semiautonomous agency, taking its basic policy directives from the State Department (a responsibility carried out directly by the Under Secretary for Economic Affairs); the State Department had

ministration during the early 1960s, the United States became the principal sponsor of the Alliance for Progress, designed to stimulate economic growth and modernization throughout Latin America. Initially envisioned as a ten-year development scheme for the America's involving a commitment of $10 billion in aid by the United States, the Alliance for Progress was subsequently revised. A single decade, it became evident to all governments concerned, was insufficient time in which to achieve the program's objectives. Accordingly, as we observed in Chapter 12, Presidents Johnson and Nixon pledged that the United States would continue to support the Alliance during the 1970s.

Several significant trends and shifts in emphasis in postwar American foreign aid programs may be identified. Down to early 1947, American foreign aid activities were intended chiefly to deal with emergencies and short-term needs—like food shortages in war-devastated Europe and Great Britain's acute financial problems at the end of World War II. With the Truman administration's adoption of a "containment" strategy for countering Communist expansionism, American foreign aid programs became, to a greater or lesser degree, directed at strengthening the free world against Communist intrusions. Two measures in the late 1940s—the China Aid Program and the Greek-Turkish Aid Program—sought to apply the containment principle to countries threatened by Marxist movements. The United States government expended a total of over $2 billion in a futile effort to prevent a Communist victory in China.[46] Then, early in 1947, President Truman recommended, and Congress quickly approved, the Greek-Turkish Aid Program. This measure (involving some $400 million in American funds) was prompted by the effort of Communist-led rebels in Greece to seize power after the evacuation of British forces from that country; secondarily, the program sought to bolster the defenses of nearby Turkey, which was experiencing a renewal of Soviet pressures aimed at gaining control of the

the over-all obligation to prepare the total foreign aid program for presentation to Congress. Within these guidelines, AID actually supervised economic assistance programs abroad; the Office of International Security Affairs (ISA) in the Defense Department was assigned responsibility for formulating and administering *military* aid activities overseas. Other forms of American aid, however, were also being extended by the Development Loan Fund; the Export-Import Bank (which, as a bank, made straight commercial loans to other governments); and the Department of Agriculture, which was coming to play a key role in providing *food aid* under Public Law 480 to needy societies. As a result of several studies of foreign aid in the late 1960s and 1970s, other administrative changes could undoubtedly be expected. For the administrative history of foreign aid, see Burton M. Sapin, *The Making of United States Foreign Policy* (Washington, D.C.: Brookings Institution, 1966), pp. 188–202.

Dardanelles and securing access to the Mediterranean Sea. In the sense that both Greece and Turkey were successfully preserved against internal and external Communist threats, the Greek-Turkish Aid Program achieved its major objective.*

In this same period, it became evident to American policy-makers that emergency and "interim" aid would not suffice to restore stability to countries devastated by World War II or, in the years which followed, to achieve the kind of economic breakthrough required to raise productive levels throughout the Afro–Asian world. Accordingly, within a few weeks after Congress had passed the Greek-Turkish Aid Program, officials within the executive branch began to formulate the European Recovery Program (or "Marshall Plan") to promote the recovery of Western Europe and reduce its vulnerability to Communist penetration. After months of study and investigation, Congress approved the Marshall Plan, entailing some $13 billion in American aid to the European recipients over a four-year period. These funds—in conjunction with several times this total raised by the Europeans themselves—provided the stimulus needed to launch Western Europe upon the path of economic reconstruction and modernization. As we noted in Chapter 10, European recovery was nothing short of phenomenal; by the early 1960s, economic growth rates in the region often surpassed those achieved by both the United States and the Soviet Union. After the termination of the Marshall Plan in the early 1950s, American economic assistance fell off sharply, although limited military aid continued to be extended to the NATO allies. But by the 1960s, Western Europe itself had become a major source of foreign aid, especially to independent Africa; and, in Washington's view, the European nations were now in a position to assume an ever larger share of the assistance provided to developing societies.

Recent Trends and Emphases

The shift in the nature of American foreign aid activities after the early 1950s has been noteworthy. During the Korean War (from mid-1950 to mid-1953), the emphasis in foreign assistance provided by the United States shifted heavily to military aid, designed to bolster the security of the non-Communist world. The war in Korea was fol-

lowed by the collapse of French power in Southeast Asia, raising fears in Washington that this region would succumb to Communist expansionism; in that event, the security of countries like India, Indonesia, the Philippines, and Japan might be seriously endangered. Revolutionary movements in the Arab world (like the junta which overthrew the Egyptian monarchy in 1952), along with the ongoing Arab-Israeli dispute, kept the Middle East in ferment. After the Suez crisis of 1956, Soviet influence in the Middle East became pronounced. Such developments in the mid-1950s dictated substantial military assistance by the United States to its military allies.[47] From this period to around 1960, military aid tended to be the largest category of American foreign assistance. Under the Kennedy administration, a rough equilibrium came to be established between economic assistance to other governments and military aid programs (with the notable difference that the former increasingly involved repayable *loans*, while the latter were usually *grants* requiring no repayment by the recipient). Then by the late 1960s, economic assistance began to eclipse military assistance (for fiscal year 1970, for example, some $1.5 billion was allotted to the former, while $350 million was earmarked for the latter).[48] Congressional and public disaffection over the Vietnam War, coupled with a growing skepticism about programs advocated by the "military-industrial complex," perhaps foreordained a substantial reduction in American military commitments overseas—including military assistance and training programs sponsored by the United States government.

Once the economic recovery of Europe had been assured in the early 1950s, the economic direction of American assistance began to shift to the Afro-Asian and Latin American nations. In these regions, foreign aid provided by the United States had a twofold objective: to strengthen the security of nations (like Turkey, Iran, Pakistan, Thailand, South Vietnam, and South Korea) viewed by policy-makers in Washington as unusually vulnerable to Communist threats; and to contribute to the modernization and development schemes to which nearly all governments in this zone were committed. Military aid to its allies had remained a consistent feature of America's foreign assistance programs since the early 1950s although, as we have noted, by the 1970s the magnitude of such aid had declined sharply. For most nations outside the West, however, the principal goal of the American foreign aid program has been to promote economic development. India, for example, has been a primary beneficiary of American economic and technical assistance; it ranks below Great Britain and France as the third largest beneficiary of American aid since World War II, and almost all American assistance extended to India has been earmarked for either

*For discussions of the origins and purposes of the Greek-Turkish Aid Program, see Harry S. Truman, *Memoirs: Years of Trial and Hope* (Garden City, N. Y.: Doubleday, 1956), pp. 93–109; and Dean Acheson, *Present at the Creation* (New York: Norton, 1969), pp. 220–226. For a recent highly critical account of the Greek aid program, see Richard J. Barnet, *Intervention and Revolution: America's Confrontation with Insurgent Movements Around the World* (New York: World Publishing, 1968), pp. 97–132.

economic development or "emergency aid" to alleviate food shortages. As we noted in Chapter 11, American aid programs to Africa (never large visà-vis assistance furnished to Europe or Asia) has also been allocated almost entirely to economic progress and modernization programs. Since the inauguration of the Alliance for Progress in the early 1960s, the bulk of Washington's assistance to the Americas has been devoted to economic assistance programs. Sentiment in Congress (particularly in the Senate) has become increasingly critical of military assistance to Latin America; it was feared (and often with justification) that armsaid from the United States would be used by indigenous governments to suppress political opposition movements.

In terms of the magnitude of the assistance provided by the United States since World War II, Western Europe, Asia, and Latin America have ranked among the main beneficiaries. Among the twenty-six leading recipients of postwar American foreign assistance, nine countries have been located in Western Europe, eight in Asia, four in the Middle East, four in Latin America, and one in Eastern Europe. Among the European beneficiaries, Great Britain, France, Italy, and Western Germany head the list; in Asia, major recipients have been India, South Korea, South Vietnam, the Republic of China (Taiwan), and Japan; in the Middle East, Turkey, Iran, Israel, and the United Arab Republic (Egypt) have received the largest American aid allocations; in Latin America, significant assistance has gone to Brazil, Chile, Mexico, and Colombia; while Yugoslavia is the only Eastern European nation appearing on the list of major aid recipients. Among the "top ten" nations benefiting from aid from the United States, four were in Europe, five were in Asia, and one (Turkey) was in the Middle East. It was noteworthy that among these twenty-six nations, not a single country from black Africa was represented; except for Egypt (ranked twenty-sixth on the list), no Arab state was included among the major aid recipients.[49]

Still another discernible trend in the postwar American foreign aid program has been the shift toward greater *selectivity* in dispensing military and economic aid from the United States. During the 1950s, for example, American aid tended to be extended broadly and somewhat indiscriminately among a large number of recipients; in the nature of the case, this meant that many grants or loans to individual countries were often quite small— too small, in fact, to provide anything other than a kind of token of American interest in the society involved and to avoid (or at least mitigate) criticisms that country X was being neglected in the foreign aid activities of the United States. In many instances, American foreign assistance had more of a psychological than an economic or military objective.

In time, it became evident to American policymakers and to groups studying the foreign aid program, that the United States was diffusing its funds and efforts much too widely throughout the world. By the late 1950s, popular novels like *The Ugly American* focused public attention upon the waste, "mismanagement," and projects of dubious merit characteristic of the foreign assistance program; while unquestionably present in American efforts to aid other societies, such *lacunae* tended to obscure the *achievements* realized with foreign aid and to cast doubt upon the foreign assistance program as a whole. Yet greater selectivity in extending American loans and grants to other countries was plainly indicated. Thus, in the early 1960s, the Clay Committee which investigated the foreign aid program urged the President to exercise greater discrimination in dispensing foreign aid funds to assure greater effectiveness in their use. New criteria for administering the foreign aid program—emphasizing soundly conceived, long-range development projects, greater "self-help" by host countries, and preference for loans over grants to nations seeking American help—were adopted by the White House. By 1963, some 80 percent of the over-all American foreign aid budget was allocated to only 20 foreign countries.[50] The decline in the foreign aid budget during the 1960s made greater concentration of available assistance funds indispensable. In time, American aid was terminated altogether to several nations (such as Israel and Iran), which had attained an impressive level of economic advancement; only a handful of independent African nations received economic assistance from the United States; by the 1960s, aid to Europe was limited chiefly to military assistance (largely supplied through NATO); and a few nations in Asia (India, South Vietnam, South Korea, Thailand, and the Philippines) obtained the bulk of American assistance to that region; in Latin America (as in Africa), Washington increasingly sought to channel its aid activities toward regional development programs rather than individual nations. In the foreign aid budget enacted for fiscal year 1971, only ten countries were scheduled to benefit significantly from the $1.5 billion in economic assistance made available to other countries by the United States.[51]

Beginning in the mid-1960s, an important development affecting the foreign aid program was the marked decline in congressional and public support for the provision of American aid to other countries. This phenomenon had many and diverse origins, some of which we shall identify at a later stage. Since Americans had been engaged in providing assistance to societies overseas for some twenty years, they had perhaps become psychologically enervated by the burden they had assumed, particularly when the "results" of such assistance frequently seemed minimal. Little correlation seemed to exist between the extension of aid to other societies and an increase in international stability, the expansion of democracy, and other goals cherished by Americans. Rising legislative and popular discontent centering upon the Vietnam War also created an atmosphere hostile to the foreign aid program (especially military assistance). Correctly or not (and we are not concerned with the validity of the contention here), many critics of the conflict in Vietnam believed that American military aid to Saigon was the "first step" leading to the massive military and economic commitment to that country. During the mid-1960s, groups which had long opposed foreign aid were joined by a number of influential legislators (like members of the Senate Foreign Relations Committee) who had earlier supported the program, but who now demanded its elimination or, at the very least, its radical reorganization.

In the months before his tragic death, President John. F. Kennedy proposed a foreign aid budget (for fiscal year 1964) of some $5 billion; his successor, President Lyndon B. Johnson, was compelled to settle for a legislative appropriation of some $3 billion for foreign aid—and even this total was widely construed as a White House victory in the face of mounting congressional skepticism concerning the program. The extent to which the foreign assistance program had contracted within a few years was highlighted by President Richard M. Nixon's foreign aid budget request for fiscal year 1971. The Nixon administration's budget allocation was some $2.4 billion, the smallest total proposed by the White House for foreign aid since the late 1940s. As always, however, Congress was convinced that the President's request could be pared without jeopardy to the program; eventually, President Nixon received approximately $1.8 billion in economic and military aid appropriations, with programs designed to benefit Asia and Africa sustaining the largest reductions.* By the

early 1970s, therefore, the American foreign aid program totaled less than half the amount (averaging around $4 billion annually) made available to other countries by the United States during the early 1960s.[52]

By other standards also, America's commitment to foreign aid had declined sharply. One of the goals of the first Decade of Development (1960–1970) sponsored by the United Nations called for the wealthier nations to contribute 1 percent of their annual gross national products to assist the economic progress of needy societies. By that standard the United States, with an annual GNP exceeding $1 trillion, should make $10 billion a year available for meeting the needs of the developing nations. In reality, by the 1970s the American government's foreign aid efforts (ignoring private American capital made available overseas) were equal to only about one-fifth of the suggested UN standard. Even the less ambitious yardstick proposed for the 1970s by an international commission headed by Canada's Prime Minister Lester Pearson—calling for the wealthier nations to spend .7 of 1 percent of their annual GNP's—was more than double the amount the United States was actually devoting to foreign aid in the early 1970s. Moreover, after allowances had been made for the fiscal implications of tax reduction and of providing for urgent domestic needs, it appeared unlikely that the United States government would expand its foreign aid activities appreciably in the years ahead.[53]

Another recent development affecting the American foreign aid program was the growing preference among executive policy-makers for reliance upon *multilateral agencies and institutions* in making assistance available to needy societies. Executive officials urged a substantial diversion of funds to the World Bank, various United Nations agencies, and regional bodies (like the Inter-American Development Bank and the Asian Development Bank) as the proper channels for distributing American assistance abroad. It was premature perhaps to speak of this develop-

*Throughout this chapter, our attention has been concentrated upon foreign assistance provided by the United States *government* to needy societies overseas. Even then, it ought to be recognized, the so-called "foreign aid program"—economic and military assistance administered by the Agency for International Development and the Defense Department—encompasses *less than half* of the official aid America extends abroad. Thus, the President's foreign aid budget for fiscal 1971 was some $1.8 billion; but the *total* of all foreign aid made available to other countries was some $4.4 billion, the latter including the Food for Peace Program, the cost of operating the Peace Corps, and some $750 million contributed by the United States to international agencies (like the International Bank for Reconstruction and Development). See the testimony of AID Director Dr. John A. Hannah in *The New York Times* (March 20, 1970).

Omitted from our discussion also has been one of the most important forms of American assistance to societies seeking to develop: *private American investment overseas.* From 1956 to 1968, direct investments by Americans in other countries ranged between $566 million (in

1962) and $1.5 billion (in 1968) annually. The Pearson Commission found that the flow of private development capital overseas was a vital ingredient in the modernization of needy societies; by the late 1960s, the magnitude of this aid was rising rapidly. Yet this study also noted several inhibiting factors, preventing private investment from replacing official programs of grants and loans. Private capital is attracted heavily to "extractive" enterprises (like oil fields in the Arab world and Latin America); some regions are much better able to attract such capital than others (Latin America has three times as much private investment as Africa); many developing nations are in no position to attract outside business or bank capital—and they must have grants and loans from other governments for that very reason. For an assessment of the role of private investment overseas, see the report of the Commission on International Development, *Partners in Development* (New York: Praeger, 1969), pp. 99–123.

ment as a "trend"; the vast preponderance of American aid was still extended bilaterally from the United States government directly to other governments. Furthermore (since this proposal was not a new idea), for many years sentiment in Congress had been decisively *against* turning over a major portion of the American foreign aid budget to multilateral agencies. The United States, many legislators evidently feared, would lose control over foreign aid spending; its funds might be utilized for purposes highly inimical to American foreign policy objectives. (What would happen, critics of this idea asked periodically, if a UN agency decided to use American funds for an aid project benefiting Castro's Cuba?) The proposal to "multilateralize" the American foreign assistance program, it had to be recognized, threatened to infringe upon one of Congress' most cherished prerogatives—the "power of the purse" or control over governmental appropriations. That foreign aid funds might conceivably be used more *effectively* by a multilateral agency did not alter legislative skepticism about the proposal.

Yet several forces combined to create a new impetus for this idea. Most governments in the zone of developing nations favored the proposal; it appeared to have many advantages, such as avoiding the implication (often conveyed by bilateral assistance programs) that aid recipients were in a politically dependent relationship to the donor. It was expected that UN supervision of aid would be less detrimental to national sovereignty than "controls" imposed by the United States. Although little evidence existed to support their hopes, the less developed societies undoubtedly also believed that a tendency toward multilateralism would result in a significant *expansion* in the funds made available for economic development and modernization programs. Greater American reliance upon international and regional organizations in dispensing aid was also urged by Robert S. McNamara, the President of the World Bank.[54] Even some legislators, like Senator J. William Fulbright (Democrat of Arkansas), who had become outspokenly critical of bilateral American aid measures, favored an expansion in American assistance channeled to multilateral agencies. This was, in fact, the *only* kind of foreign aid programs Fulbright was prepared to support in the future.[55] In announcing the foreign policy objectives of his administration early in 1970, President Nixon called for a "new American purpose and attitude" in assisting other countries, "if our economic assistance is to contribute to development in the new environment of the 1970s." Among the changes required was realization that

Multilateral institutions must play an increasing role in the provision of aid. We must enlist the expertise of other countries and of international agencies, thereby minimizing the political and

ideological complications with can distort the assistance relationship.[56]

In actuality, the United States had been relying upon multilateral agencies on a limited basis for a number of years in providing assistance to foreign countries. American aid to Africa, for example, was already allocated largely to the African Development Bank and other regional organizations on the African scene. Similarly, multilateral agencies had taken increasing responsibility for administering the Alliance for Progress in the Western Hemisphere. In its report on the economic progress of the Americas in 1969, the Rockefeller study mission recommended that Washington make even greater use of regional organizations in the hemisphere.* Yet the transition from bilateral to multilateral aid programs, it could be predicted, would be far from smooth. There was no sign that congressional opposition to this idea had substantially lessened; nor was there any indication that one of the gains hoped for by advocates of this proposal—a major *expansion* in foreign aid allocations by the industrialized nations—was imminent.

The Goals of Foreign Aid—Illusory and Realistic

What has the provision of some $135 billion in postwar economic and military assistance by the United States to other countries achieved since World War II? How has this expenditure contributed to the realization of American diplomatic objectives? Has foreign aid been, and does it remain, a worthwhile "investment" for the United States? Or is it instead, as many critics have charged since the era of the Marshall Plan, a waste of money, a "global boondoggle," a futile effort by the United States to "buy friends" abroad, and in general a dubious use of American resources which might better be utilized to solve domestic problems?

How the student of American foreign policy answers such questions depends heavily upon his conception of the *proper goals* of the foreign aid program. What precisely is the United States endeavoring to achieve by aiding the economic development of India, by promoting regional economic collaboration in Africa, or by supplying modern military equipment to South Korea? One problem that has beset the American foreign aid effort since its inception has been the evident gap between what members of Congress and segments of American public opinion have expected external assistance to accomplish and what it has *in fact achieved*. Almost never (the Marshall Plan

*See *The New York Times* edition of *The Rockefeller Report on the Americas* (Chicago: Quadrangle, 1969), p. 52. This report is discussed more fully in Chapter 12.

for European reconstruction was perhaps an exception) have anticipated achievement and actual results coincided. Much of the legislative and public disillusionment with foreign aid which had become apparent by the late 1960s could be attributed to this hiatus. For experience with foreign assistance programs since the late 1940s made it clear that they did not—and probably could not—achieve many of the objectives often assigned to them by legislators and public groups. It is doubtful that these goals could have been attained even if the magnitude of American foreign assistance programs had been several times greater.

Since any assessment of the value of foreign aid as a diplomatic instrument must derive from a prior determination of projected aims, clarity regarding such aims is highly desirable. As our discussion has already suggested, for many years the American foreign assistance program undoubtedly suffered because certain *spurious and illusory goals* have been associated with it. In some cases, these pseudo-goals were not only beyond the competence of foreign aid to accomplish, they probably defied attainment by *any* program (or combination of programs) adopted by the United States government. Ever since the late 1940s (if not earlier, during World War II), Americans have expected foreign aid to win the friendship, good will, gratitude, and sympathy of societies benefiting from the generosity of the United States. Reasonable or not, this is a human and natural expectation by one group of people providing assistance to another. One motivation of American aid (and of course there are several) has unquestionably been genuine humanitarian concern among the people of the United States for less fortunate societies. From time to time, governments receiving American assistance *have* expressed their gratitude for American help; and foreign aid has probably contributed in some measure to creating greater good will among foreigners for the United States.

But in the sense in which this objective of foreign aid is usually meant—gratitude by foreign countries expressing itself in a close identification with American foreign policy goals and a greater willingness to "support" these goals enthusiastically—it is evident that foreign aid has failed. Even the most casual reader of the daily headlines is aware that the internal and external policies of the United States have been criticized vocally by foreign countries, sometimes most outspokenly by major recipients of American foreign assistance. France, for example, has been among the chief recipients of economic and military aid from the United States since World War II. Yet during the 1960s, Franco-American relations were more often than not marked by tensions and misunderstandings; this situation (at least in terms of major changes in French foreign policies) did not alter materially after 1969, when Georges Pompidou succeeded General Charles de Gaulle as the leader of France.

This was no isolated phenomenon. It could be essentially duplicated in American relations with India, with South Vietnam, with the Philippines, with Ghana, with Tanzania, with Israel, with several Latin American nations—in fact, at some period of time, in relations between the United States and nearly all recipients of its aid throughout the postwar era. A conspicuous example is afforded by Egyptian-American relations during the 1960s. For several years, the American Food for Peace program (under which the United States sent its agricultural surpluses to needy societies) provided massive and urgently needed food supplies to President Nasser's government. It would be no exaggeration to say that this assistance played an indispensable role in averting famine and malnutrition among Egypt's burgeoning population. Yet ever since the late 1950s, Egyptian-American relations have been strained, and in some periods hostile; they are perhaps even more tension-ridden in the 1970s than in the past. No evidence exists that America's aid program to Egypt significantly improved the climate of relations between Cairo and Washington; and there are even fewer grounds for believing that, as a result of American aid, Egypt has become more prone to support the policies of the United States in the Middle East or elsewhere. Indeed, as former Ambassador to Egypt John S. Badeau has emphasized, the existence of the aid program may have furnished *new sources* of Egyptian-American misunderstanding and contention.[57]

Such experiences suggest that the goals associated by many American with foreign aid are inherently unattainable. Foreign countries do not, of course, formulate their external policies on the basis of a feeling of "gratitude" toward the United States.

Another goal often attributed to the foreign aid program by members of Congress and public groups in the United States is promotion of certain economic and political principles identified with American society—like the concept of democratic government, capitalistic economic principles, and in more general terms, "the American way of life." Again, any expectations that the extension of American foreign assistance to other countries would achieve these aims have largely been disappointing. Among most of the new nations throughout the Afro-Asian world, for example, support for Western-style (not to speak of American-style) democracy is undeniably less widespread in the 1970s than in the 1950s. Democracy, it is true, is the professed objective of nearly all governments throughout this zone, however much they may deviate from it in practice; it is a rare government today (Marxist and other totalitarian systems included) which *denies* belief in the democratic principle, since this is an emotive concept possessing great public appeal. Yet if political leaders in the new Afro-Asian states routinely subscribe to the democratic principle, their definitions of the concept often contrast sharply with Western traditions; they tend to be united in the conviction that true independence requires them to *redefine* democracy in terms consonant with their own traditions and needs. With a few exceptions (India might be cited as a case in point), the European or American models of democracy have *not* been widely embraced by the new Afro-Asian states; when these models were adopted in the early post-independence period, in most cases they were soon abandoned.

Nor has encouragement of democracy proved an easier goal to achieve in an area in which states have been independent since the early 1800s and where support for the democratic principle has been widespread—Latin America. When the American republics adopted the Alliance for Progress in 1961, an avowed purpose of this program was encouragement of democratic political systems throughout the Western Hemisphere. President John F. Kennedy justified the new program to Congress by emphasizing that the "people of Latin America are the inheritors of a deep belief in political democracy and the freedom of man"; in announcing hemispheric agreement on the principles guiding this program, the nations participating in the Alliance for Progress declared that one of its aims was "To improve and strengthen democratic institutions through application of self-determination by the people."[58]

Yet, as our analysis of political trends and prospects throughout Latin America in Chapter 12 underscored, the hope that truly democratic political systems would finally displace the old *caudillo* regimes, military juntas, or other authoritarian-totalitarian systems in the region has thus far remained unfulfilled. The dominant political system in Latin America (and of course there are many different forms and variations of it) is the military junta. Our earlier discussion called attention to the fact that the "new military" in most of these states differs in many fundamental respects from the traditional *caudillo* pattern. Contemporary military elites in Latin America may well be more attracted to the concept of democracy—particularly in its social and economic dimensions—than the regimes that governed before the mid-twentieth century. Indeed, in some Latin American societies, military elites may be more pro-democratic than any rival force capable of governing the country (which may prove only how *undemocratic* most Latin American political movements really are). Yet insofar as the point under discussion here is concerned, there is no reliable evidence that the Alliance for Progress has actually contributed to strengthening democratic traditions and practices south of the border or in any discernible way reversed the widespread Latin American tendency toward government by military elites.

Summarizing the point, we may say generally that from Latin America to Asia the tendency since the late 1950s has been *away from* democratic political systems and concepts, as these have customarily been understood in the West. American foreign assistance programs have in no evident way averted or mitigated this tendency. Thus far, the evidence raises a substantial question about whether foreign aid by the United States (or any other country) has *any detectable impact* in determining the political systems and ideologies of other nations.

The role of foreign aid in promoting worldwide support for the concept of American capitalism may be treated much more briefly. Outside the United States and Western Europe, "capitalism" tends to be a psychologically unpalatable term—often an epithet. In the light of their history and experience with Western colonialism, it is perhaps not surprising that Afro-Asian and Latin American peoples frequently equate capitalism with exploitation by absentee landlords and moneylenders, with privileges exercised by foreign corporations, and with imperialism. In many of these societies, capitalism is synonymous with pervasive poverty, with entrenched economic elites, and with the status quo.* Much as they have endeavored to exploit Afro-Asian and Latin American resentments against capitalism, policy-makers in Moscow and Peking did not *create* that sentiment; nor would capitalism necessarily be a more appealing economic system to leaders and masses in these regions if the cold war did not exist.

Even less than is the case with encouragement of democracy, American foreign aid programs (despite deliberate efforts from time to time by Congress to achieve this goal) have done nothing of consequence to make aid recipients more receptive to capitalistic principles or to increase their admiration for capitalism.

Another goal often identified in the American mind with the foreign aid program is the promotion of political stability and "moderation" in other countries. Aid provided by the United

---

*The student should be aware that, although the *concept* of "capitalism" arouses little enthusiasm outside the West, *in practice* attachment to it—even in societies in which anti-American sentiment is strong—is often deeply rooted in tradition and remains widespread. A leading example of this phenomenon is Syria. Under the leadership of the Ba'ath party, Syria, espouses "Arab socialism" and has been at the forefront of countries denouncing American exploitation of weaker societies. Yet "free enterprise" is a centuries-old tradition in Syria and is still deeply entrenched there. Syrian merchants zealously protect their historic "independence" and resist government regulation of business. In reality, Syria (and counterparts can be found in many other Afro-Asian societies) is perhaps more attached to *laissez-faire* economic principles than is the United States!

States, it is sometimes reasoned, gives recipients an "alternative" to revolutionary programs, perhaps entailing authoritarian (if not Marxist or other totalitarian) rule. Phrases sometimes used to describe the Alliance for Progress in Latin America—"a controlled revolution" or a "revolution in freedom"—suggest this objective. Foreign nations receiving aid from the United States, it is hoped, do not need radical and possibly revolutionary programs to accomplish their aim of national development.

This goal of the American foreign aid program may not be totally unrealistic. It is not an unreasonable assumption that violent political turmoil abroad is in some way connected to mass dissatisfaction and frustration over poverty, malnutrition, entrenched privilege, and the status quo. Lacking any viable prospect of orderly change—and in some societies, *visible and rapid change*—the masses in less developed nations have in the past been, and may in the future be, tempted to embrace revolutionary solutions. Or to put the matter differently: The minimum condition of survival for moderate political regimes in emerging societies is convincing the public that the government *is* responsive to their needs and demonstrating that progress *is* being made in modernization. This in turn necessitates a continuing flow of funds to finance development schemes from the United States, from Western Europe, from the Soviet Union, from agencies of the United Nations, and from other external sources. To the extent that such assistance is available, moderate governments at least have a chance of competing successfully against revolutionary political movements and of retaining their base of popular support. From the American point of view,* a number of Afro-Asian and Latin American nations exemplify this goal: democratic India; the monarchies of Iran, Saudi Arabia, Jordan, Morocco, and Ethiopia; middle-of-the-road governments in the Arab world like Lebanon and Tunisia; in Africa, the governments of Ghana, the Ivory Coast (a widely cited example of political

---

*The term politically "moderate" is highly inexact and subjective. It does not, and perhaps cannot describe a *genus* of government, a particular ideological system, or even a definite orientation in foreign policy. In defining the term, the political context of *individual countries* is crucial: Nasser's regime in Egypt, for example, may have been authoritarian and often anti-American, but it might also qualify as "moderate" *in terms of the alternatives* to it within Egypt, which was one reason American Food for Peace aid was extended to Cairo for several years. In most cases, "moderate" means a regime which seeks to achieve its goals by *evolutionary* methods; which is not *chronically* anti-American (although it may be so occasionally); which, if it is not democratic, is relatively benign in its more authoritarian features; and which is committed to the goal of modernization. By this conception, most Marxist regimes would be eliminated, as would extreme right-wing and "personalistic" governments.

moderation and "responsibility"), Tanzania and Kenya; and several recent regimes in Latin America, such as the governments of Mexico, Venezuela, and (in some periods) Brazil.

While there is undoubtedly some connection between the progress of national development in the emerging nations (including Latin America) and avoidance of political extremism in this zone, several qualifications must be kept in mind about this relationship. The very fact, for example, that Washington identifies an incumbent political regime abroad as "moderate"—and extends foreign aid to it on that basis—can serve to discredit the government in question and undermine popular support for it. Uncongenial as the fact may be to many Americans, the label "moderate" is often an epithet in foreign countries. Conversely, popular sympathies tend to be aroused for any political cause or movement labeling itself "revolutionary." Societies burdened with antiquated social, economic, and political systems may be prone to equate revolution with progress and "the good society," whereas moderate political programs may be identified with the status quo and possibly with subservience to an outside power. Although the *results* achieved by revolutionary movements in recent history, whether Marxist or non-Marxist, may not really justify the idea that revolution is a synonym for progress, Americans must recognize that this identification is widespread outside the West. America's seeming opposition to revolutions abroad undeniably affects its overseas image adversely.

The use of foreign aid to engender political moderation abroad is likely to have only partial success for another reason. Americans (not excluding some government officials) have perhaps always exaggerated the degree of "leverage" which the United States possesses among the recipients of its foreign assistance. Even among the nations benefiting most from American aid, this leverage has never been as great as is often depicted. France, we need to recall again, has been among the leading recipients of postwar American aid—a fact that would be difficult to discern from Franco–American relations in the recent period! The same point might be made about the government of India. For the preponderance of Afro–Asian and Latin American nations, American aid has never been substantial; and since the early 1960s, as we have seen, it has been *declining* and becoming *more selective*. In the vast majority of instances, American aid is too small to be reckoned a crucial factor in determining the future political orientation of governments receiving it.

Criteria for Foreign Aid—The Problem Examined

Having examined certain false or illusory criteria for measuring the accomplishments of foreign aid, we now inquire: What performance goals may be regarded as *realistic and reasonable?* What can the American people legitimately expect foreign assistance to achieve? Several defensible objectives of foreign aid may be cited.

First, as far back as the period following World War I, America extended assistance to foreign countries because it was genuinely concerned about conditions of want and need in other societies. Philanthropy is deeply rooted in the American tradition—more so perhaps than in any other society. "Generous" is an adjective which innumerable foreigners have used to describe the American people. This impulse has undoubtedly been present in various postwar foreign aid programs. Beginning with the extension of relief funds for Europe at the end of World War II, and extending through the Marshall Plan, the Point Four Program, and various grants of "emergency assistance" to societies suffering from famine or natural disasters, Americans have customarily responded to evident need overseas. A related propensity of Americans—magnanimity exhibited toward former enemies, like Germany and Japan—has supported Washington's efforts to assist in the economic reconstruction of defeated nations and attempts to restore them to the family of nations.

To identify concern for less fortunate societies as an important impulse motivating American foreign aid programs is not of course to deny the existence of other considerations underlying such programs. Nearly every foreign aid program undertaken by the United States since World War II has sought to promote some American diplomatic objective. The Marshall Plan, for example, was unquestionably part of America's containment strategy against expansive Communism; Washington viewed European reconstruction as a prerequisite to Western security. More recent aid programs (like large-scale American assistance to India or military aid supplied to countries like South Korea and Thailand) have also been related to the containment of Communism and the achievement of other diplomatic objectives (such as, in India's case, enabling a democratic government to solve its internal problems). Recognition of these facts does not preclude awareness that humanitarianism has been an element in postwar American assistance programs.[59]

A closely related goal of U.S. foreign aid has been creation of a reasonably stable, prosperous, and peaceful international community, in which conflicts among nations are minimized and governments are making progress in solving their domestic problems. More than any other nation in the history of the world, perhaps, America has a clear stake in achieving this result. As the wealthiest nation on the planet, the United States has a direct interest in elevating living standards throughout the world and in assisting other soci

eties in the process of modernization. On idealistic grounds, wealthy individuals, groups, and nations have some obligation to use a portion of their wealth for the welfare of humanity; the doctrine of "stewardship" is a prominent theme of the Christian tradition, just as the Judaic tradition requires tithing and generosity toward the less fortunate. Viewed from the standpoint of sheer self-interest, the United States has the same obligation: Modern history teaches rather convincingly that the wealthy cannot be secure in their position when they are consistently indifferent to deepening conditions of poverty and need around them. Today, masses at the bottom of the economic scale are less content than ever to be told: "Let them eat cake." In an age when democracy, equality of opportunity, and "the winds of change" enjoy well-nigh global support, the minimum demand of the disadvantaged is likely to be that entrenched privilege be abolished, if necessary by violence. Whether this change in reality would improve the lot of the impoverished masses is not the main point. The mentality undoubtedly exists more widely than ever before in history; it influences attitudes toward the United States (along of course with Western Europe and the Soviet Union); it is a reality which American policy-makers dare not ignore. To do so would be to guarantee the increasing isolation of the United States, Western Europe, and the Soviet Union in an enveloping sea of worldwide poverty and degradation.[60]

Assistance to needy countries by the United States also makes some contribution toward identifying America with the forces of change and modernization in the international community. Foreign aid provides tangible evidence that—despite accusations by critics of American foreign policy—the United States does not seek to perpetuate the status quo throughout the Afro–Asian world and Latin America. Admittedly, incumbent governments have sometimes utilized American *military* aid to suppress internal political dissent or to support expansive foreign policies abroad. American economic aid programs have not escaped maladministration, waste, extravagance, and poor judgment by both American officials and those within the recipient countries. Postwar experience indicates that *all* foreign aid activities may suffer from such disabilities, in much the same way that waste and mismanagement are perhaps inherent in warfare.*

*These conditions have also plagued the Soviet foreign aid program, perhaps to an even greater degree than the American program. It would be difficult to prove that Moscow has won many friends or supporters in the international community because of its foreign aid activities; in some instances, its program has in the end created ill will between the U.S.S.R. and the recipient. In several cases, Russian-supplied military equipment has been used by governments receiving it against Communist and pro-Communist groups. For details, see Jo-

Given the often primitive levels of governmental administration existing in many less developed societies, the magnitude of the problems confronting these governments, the inexperience of both the nations extending aid and those receiving it in successfully managing national development schemes, the impatience of the masses with the slow pace of change—in the light of these and other inhibiting factors, the real miracle perhaps is that there has not been a *greater degree* of waste and mismanagement in the American foreign aid program in recent years. Aware that Western Europe utilized Marshall Plan aid rapidly and efficiently to promote its recovery, Americans have tended to expect equivalent results throughout the area from the Philippines to Ghana. As a generalization, to which there are a number of exceptions, such results have not in the main been realized.

For the purposes of deciding what American aid to countries outside the West has accomplished, we may classify the Afro–Asian and Latin American societies into three groups: those in which progress toward economic development and modernization has been impressive, in a few cases outstanding; those in which the over-all record has been more favorable than unfavorable, but in which major impediments to national development remain to be overcome; and those in which progress in national development to date has been minimal or economic retrogression has in fact occurred.

The first category—developing countries making outstanding progress toward economic growth and modernization—encompasses relatively few nations, and some of these can be explained by certain special circumstances, making them untypical cases.* The largest group of emerging nations falls into the second category: Those in which demonstrable progress has been made in raising productive levels and improving social conditions, and in which an impressive "start" has been made in national development, but where major problems remain to be overcome. As measured in *absolute terms*, most countries in this category have made real gains in recent years. For the group as a whole, their gross national products have risen impressively (often at a faster rate than those of America, Western Europe, or the Soviet Union). Approximately 100 nations can be classified as "developing" or ("less developed") countries. Out of this group, 70 attained the 5 percent annual increase in gross national product proposed by the first UN Decade of Development launched in 1960; and 20 developing nations significantly surpassed this target goal in raising their productive levels. According to another criterion —ability to amass development capital internally —this group has also performed creditably: Some 85 percent of the total funds allocated to national development has been raised *within* these societies (a record comparing very favorably with Europe's efforts during the Marshall Plan period). Thus far, in other words, most of the developing societies *have* been able to prevent rising consumption levels from impairing the accumulation of development capital. Considering the pressures upon indigenous governments to raise living standards rapidly and visibly, this must be ranked as an outstanding accomplishment.

Down to the late 1960s, commentators in the West widely referred to an accelerating "world food crisis"; outside of the United States, Canada, and Western Europe, very few nations throughout the world were able to feed themselves; and this crisis, many observers were convinced, was rapidly becoming more acute. Some societies (chiefly in the Afro–Asian region) were faced with imminent famine and chaos.[61] While these dire predictions are not entirely unjustified in the 1970s, the developing nations as a whole have made striking gains in recent years in expanding agricultural output and reversing the Malthusian

---

seph S. Berliner, *Soviet Economic Aid: A New Policy of Aid and Trade in Underdeveloped Countries* (New York: Praeger, 1958); A. Nove, "The Soviet Model and Under-Developed Countries," *International Affairs* 37 (January, 1961), 29–39; Marshall I. Goldman, "A Balance Sheet of Soviet Foreign Aid," *Foreign Affairs* 43 (January, 1965), 352–359. For an illuminating discussion of one region, see David Morison, *The U.S.S.R. and Africa: 1945–1963* (New York: Oxford University Press, 1964).

*Various criteria may of course be employed for measuring concrete results achieved with American and other forms of external assistance by the developing nations. In the past, *economic* indexes have been widely utilized. A list compiled by the UN Conference on Trade and Development in 1969, for example, shows that ten developing nations doubled their gross national products from the late 1950s to the late 1960s. Seven countries on this list were located in Europe; the three nations outside the West were Japan, Sierra Leone, and Taiwan. In the latter category of non-Western nations, the study pointed out, several unique factors were present (e.g., Japan's long commitment to industrialization and its successful birth control program or Taiwan's unusually large influx of skilled labor from the Chinese mainland and its disproportionate share of American economic aid) which largely accounted for the results obtained. A different standard is to cite the number of

countries which have "graduated" from the American foreign aid program; by the end of the 1960s some twenty-seven nations formerly receiving American assistance no longer did so. Again, the nations of Western Europe dominated this list; outside Europe, Israel, Taiwan, Japan, and Iran were leading examples. Some of these former aid recipients (such as Taiwan, Japan, and Israel) were themselves extending various forms of economic and technical aid to needy societies. Nationalist China, for example, had won considerable good will among the other less developed societies (at a time when admiration for Communist China was declining) because of its willingness to assist them with development projects. See Charles F. Gallagher, "Rich and Poor Countries," American Universities Field Staff, *Reports* IV (1969), 10–12; and Lloyd D. Black, *The Strategy of Foreign Aid* (New York: Van Nostrand Reinhold, 1968), pp. 138–140.

cycle which threatened many of them. After an initial period—in which *industrial development* tended to receive priority from the governments in the emerging nations—most of these countries have accepted the reality that, for many years to come, their most important economic segment is likely to be *agriculture*. There are several reasons for this, two of which are that industrial progress in most cases depends upon rising agricultural output, and that agriculture is, and will probably remain, the dominant economic pursuit in most developing societies. For the group as a whole, since the late 1960s the record of growth in farm production has been commendable. Owing in large measure to the "Green Revolution" (whose impact has been felt largely in Asia), new strains of foodstuffs (like rice), improved agricultural techniques, mechanization, growing use of fertilizers, greater readiness among peasants and farmers to accept new agricultural techniques, improved government facilities for distributing and marketing agricultural products—such developments have modified the earlier ominous predictions about an inevitable worldwide food shortage and offered hope that even greater progress can be made in the future in increasing agricultural yields.

According to other key indicators, most of the 100-odd developing nations have made gains in their quest for modernization. During the 1960s, the rate of industrial expansion for this group surpassed the rate for the world as a whole. Progress toward industrialization was especially noteworthy in Asia and Latin America (less impressive in Africa). In another vital sector—transportation, power generation, road construction, communications systems (often referred to as "infrastructure" facilities)—it has not been unusual for the developing nations to surpass growth rates in the West three-, four-, or fivefold since the end of World War II; the same growth rates have existed for the production of key commodities like steel. Progress in elevating health and nutritional levels throughout the Afro–Asian zone and Latin America has also been notable. Ancient killers (like plague, cholera, and smallpox) have been wiped out or brought under tight control; medical services have slowly been extended to masses who were totally devoid of them earlier. Similarly, educational facilities have been expanded. Annual growth rates in primary and secondary school facilities for the developing societies since 1950 are often several times the rates achieved in this same period by the industrialized nations. By another yardstick—export expansion and growth in trade volume—the record of most of these nations is more favorable than unfavorable. Total exports and export earnings have climbed steadily since the 1950s—a gain which has often been offset, however, by *declining prices* for agricultural commodities, raw materials, and other goods nor-

mally exported by countries in this zone. Not infrequently, an even greater rise in *import levels* canceled out foreign sales and tended to aggravate the balance-of-payments problems experienced by a number of these countries.

Other evidence of accomplishments by the developing nations might be cited, but the above data are sufficient to make the point under discussion. In absolute terms, the vast majority of the developing nations *have* made significant progress in their efforts to promote national development since the 1950s. Most governments in these societies are committed to the goal of modernization; nearly all of them have adopted and implemented plans for utilizing resources toward that end; and results thus far offer considerable encouragement that national development *is* proceeding apace and that it will continue in the future. As we have observed, one of the most meaningful indicators—the very high percentage of development funds which these nations have accumulated *internally*—shows that the leaders of these nations are, in the main, seriously committed to modernization and are prepared to use their own domestic resources to attain it.[62]

At the same time, two factors detract from this record of accomplishment and raise genuine questions about whether many of the developing nations will "win" their race to overcome economic and social backwardness. One of these is a problem to which we have already alluded: the requirement for outside sources of development funds is *rising*, while the supply of such funds from the industrialized nations is *declining*. Nearly all Afro–Asian and Latin American states will require outside assistance for an indefinite period in the future, if the momentum toward national development is not to be lost. Some of these countries, several of which began their development programs relatively late, will undoubtedly need greater infusions of foreign capital in the future. While the determination of their capital "needs" may always be somewhat subjective (and influenced in some cases by prestige or other extraneous considerations), it remains true that their capital requirements, from private and public sources, are increasing; the gap between their need for funds and their access to them has widened appreciably in recent years; and there is no significant evidence that it will be bridged by a major increase in American, Western European, or Soviet foreign assistance programs. Nor is there any realistic prospect that another major source of development capital—*private investment* from American or European business corporations—will replace government-supplied funds. Even more in the 1970s than in the 1950s and 1960s, the dilemma plaguing the emerging nations is that countries most in need of private investment capital are often those *least likely to attract it;* and in some instances, such as several of the military-dominated governments of Latin America, government policies are consciously or unconsciously designed to *repel* foreign business corporations. With respect to another possible source of development funds—larger earnings generated by exports—the prospect for the emerging nations remains highly uncertain, and in some cases unpromising. As exporters of agricultural commodities and raw materials, these nations have for years suffered from the adversities of the world market; the disparity between the prices they receive and those they pay, or between the prices their exports earn and those the industrialized nations earn, continues to widen to their detriment. Despite efforts by organizations like the UN Conference on Trade and Development (UNCTAD), and limited trade concessions by the United States and the nations of the European Common Market in dealing with the developing nations, thus far this imbalance remains basically unaltered.[63]

A second factor, however, is perhaps even more crucial in determining whether the absolute gains made by the emerging nations can be maintained and whether progress can be translated into tangible benefits for millions of citizens. This is *the continuing population explosion* in Africa, the Arab world, Asia, and Latin America. When the absolute gains recorded by most countries in these regions are converted into *per capita terms*, the record of achievement made by the developing nations in recent years must be interpreted very differently. By per capita standards, gains have often been minimal; and in several key sectors of development, retrogression has occurred. Unchecked population growth—often at explosive rates of 3 percent annually or higher—continues to characterize the vast majority of developing societies. Very few of them (Japan is a noteworthy, but probably most untypical exception) have succeeded in curbing their population expansion appreciably; and in some cases, a sharp decline in the death rate threatens to give the society an even *higher rate* of population growth than it had in past. Gains in industrialization, in agricultural output, in medical and health services, and in many other areas are threatened by the inexorable expansion of the population. The result is that, for many of these countries, problems are being created more rapidly than they are being solved; despite intensive efforts, schools cannot be built and staffed as rapidly as the school-age population expands; rural and urban unemployment is rising in many developing countries; gains made in raising agricultural output are largely canceled out (or will be within a few years) by the fact that there are now more "mouths to feed" than ever before; rural masses migrate to already overcrowded cities, creating new slum conditions. Politically, runaway population expansion has momentous consequences for the governments of the emerging nations. On a per capita basis, it is often difficult for individual Africans, Arabs, Asians, or Latin Americans to discern any significant progress over the years; citizens and families see little improvement in their standard of living —and in some countries they may have experienced a *decline* in food intake, in educational and employment opportunities, and other activities concerning them directly.* Pressures continue to be built up in favor of *consuming* economic gains made, rather than diverting these gains into development funds. An over-all atmosphere of frustration, impatience, disappointment, and bitterness at the slow pace of progress surrounds political contests, creating an environment in which extremist political groups win new converts. More than ever before, evolutionary and moderate programs advocated by governments are under attack, while radical and revolutionary measures gain popular support. The hope which leaders and masses in the emerging nations originally associated with foreign aid turns to disillusionment and resentment—often directed at the country (or countries) which have supplied foreign assistance; somehow America becomes "responsible" for the fact that societies receiving

*The difference between over-all or absolute progress in the less developed nations and progress measured on a per capita basis is highlighted by examining the problem of food production outside the West. For the decade 1956–1965, for example, over-all food output in the less developed nations improved markedly, from an index of 100 in the mid-1950s to 130 ten years later. In per capita terms, however, results were much less impressive: The index rose from 100 to 105 during this decade, while the index of population growth rose from just under 100 to 125 in the same period. Although the so-called "Green Revolution" in agricultural production began, by the late 1960s, to improve food production dramatically, its effects had been felt (and for many years perhaps would be felt) primarily in Asia. Studies by the American Department of Agriculture in the early 1970s, for example, indicated that South and East Asia had raised their agricultural yields impressively; per capita food output was growing at twice the world average. Other regions, however, showed much less progress—and some showed none at all. Per capita agricultural yields for Latin America had improved insignificantly throughout the 1960s; the same was true of the Near East; Africa had *less* food on a per capita basis in 1969 than it had in 1960; the index (with food production in 1957–1959 = 100) for the less developed nations as a whole stood at 102 in 1960 and at 106 in 1969. Aside from the problem of food scarcities created by this lack of progress, this phenomenon meant that most of the developing nations now had to spend more of the money generated by exports *on food imports;* and this fact in turn greatly aggravated their balance-of-payments difficulties. For more detailed data, see "Food: Better in Asia; Spotty Elsewhere," in Agency for International Development, *War on Hunger,* 4 (March, 1970), 18–20; "A Year of Action," in *ibid.,* 3 (February, 1969), 3–6; Irwin R. Hedges, "A Look at Agricultural Development Strategy," in *ibid.,* 3 (August, 1969), 4–5, 16–17; "Is Famine Inevitable?" in *ibid.,* 4 (January, 1970), 7–9. The publications in this series provide the student of American foreign policy with excellent up-to-date material on the problems confronting the foreign aid program.

its aid in the past have made minimal progress according to per capita criteria.

This leads us to discuss the third category of countries receiving American aid, along of course with assistance from other sources. These are the nations that have made *little or no progress* toward the goal of national development and have, in some cases, actually *fallen behind economically* vis-à-vis their positions one or two decades ago. As we have observed, by per capita standards, many of the emerging nations included in the second category really belong in this group: In sectors like food production, educational and health facilities, and adequate housing output has not kept pace with population growth. Even by absolute standards, some Afro–Asian societies, along with a few in Latin America, have made no noteworthy progress in overcoming poverty and economic backwardness. Within this third group, that is to say, the record is discouraging, even if population expansion is ignored for the purpose of measuring economic gains. Such foreign aid as these countries have received from the United States and other sources, it would appear, has achieved little, except perhaps to slow down economic deterioration. Prospects for an early improvement in many of these countries seems remote. To the contrary (assuming no significant increase in outside sources of aid), a realistic prognosis is that several of them will be subjected more than ever to the Malthusian cycle of poverty and degradation.

Now this is, admittedly, not the kind of report on the record of foreign aid that is congenial to Americans or that arouses support for it on Capitol Hill. As we shall see more fully in Chapter 16, a belief in inevitable progress, in the infinite capacity of human society for self-improvement and in the power of the "American example" to uplift less fortunate societies are deeply embedded in the American ethos. Yet if experience with foreign aid throughout the postwar period furnishes a reliable guide, the idea that economically primitive societies are "underdeveloped" or that they belong to the "developing nations" is an illusion. Some of them may in fact already be "overdeveloped," in the sense that it is a struggle for the present population to *maintain* its existing standard of living! Euphemistically, we refer to all *poor* nations as *developing* nations, as though they have a significant potential for improving their productive levels substantially; the further implication often is that they are apt to *realize* this potential for economic growth rapidly. Undeniably, many of the 100-odd nations belonging to the less developed world may properly be classified as "developing" states; some have enormous potential for growth in the years ahead. Others, however, do not—at least within the limits of present-day scientific know-how and of the assistance they may reasonably anticipate from the outside world.

Writing in the early 1960s, Robert Heilbroner presented a sobering analysis of the challenge of national development in the emerging societies. His study subjected prevalent American expectations about foreign aid to rigorous examination, finding that most of them were utopian. Successful national development, for example, was likely to require a *revolutionary*, as distinct from an evolutionary, approach within most societies concerned; and this revolution would have to be far more sweeping than merely changing political regimes and doctrines. Instead of fostering greater "social contentment" among the masses of Africa, the Arab world, Asia, and Latin America, progress toward modernization was in fact apt to be accompanied by "a growing gap between expectations and achievements"; mass demands were likely to grow even faster than tangible gains by governments, thereby accelerating political ferment. Development, Heilbroner wrote, was likely to prove "a time of awakening hostilities, of newly felt frustrations, of growing impatience and dissatisfaction."[64]

But the point most relevant to our discussion here is Heilbroner's appraisal of the optimistic American assumption "that economic development cannot fail." In reality, the contrary is more likely to occur: In Heilbroner's view, "the likelihood is very great that for the majority of nations now attempting the long climb the outcome in our time will be defeat." For much of tropical Africa, the Near East and North Africa, Central America, portions of South America, and even India and Indonesia, the outcome is, at best, problemmatical and, at worst, foredoomed to failure.[65] Many Americans will regard Heilbroner's assessment as unduly gloomy—almost cynical in its despair. Yet as measured by *per capita* indexes during the 1960s and early 1970s, the records of most of the emerging nations do not negate Heilbroner's predictions. Even with early and effective measures aimed at checking population growth outside the West, a majority of needy countries will require many decades (perhaps generations) before the ideal of national development is translated into significant improvements in living standards for ordinary citizens.

The Prospects for Foreign Aid

If there is one prediction that may be safely made about the American foreign aid program, it is that it will be characterized by change. From the early postwar period to the 1970s, as we have seen, the program has undergone major alterations and shifts in emphasis; that process will undoubtedly continue in the future.

By the early 1970s, several indications, to which we shall refer below, pointed to the fact that sweeping modifications could be expected in the theory and practice of foreign aid in the years ahead. The principal reason perhaps was that

American policy-makers and many citizens still had doubts about the results achieved with foreign assistance thus far; the minimum condition for the program's renewal was likely to be demands by Congress and study groups that the underlying premises of the program be re-examined and its administrative procedures be overhauled.

With the possible exception of the international propaganda activities of the United States government, the American foreign aid program has been the most thoroughly investigated and studied aspect of postwar foreign policy. Innumerable legislative investigations of the program have been carried out since World War II, and these will doubtless continue in the years ahead. In addition, the White House has initiated several studies of foreign assistance by executive agencies and by private study groups. The late 1960s and early 1970s witnessed an unusually large number of such investigations, designed to provide the Nixon administration with new guidelines and administrative improvements.[66]

While the recommendations made as a result of these studies often varied widely (testifying to the fact that even now the purposes and desirable administrative principles associated with foreign aid remain far from clear), certain common themes pervaded them. Tacitly or explicitly, all these studies recognized that the United States had entertained a number of illusory goals with respect to foreign aid in the past. Too often, Washington had misguidedly sought some short-range diplomatic or political advantage from its aid. In earlier programs, the *speed* with which American assistance could be expected to make a major impact abroad had been overestimated. Conversely, the difficulties in the path of successful modernization by needy societies had been consistently underestimated. These studies conceded that sometimes mistakes in judgment and poor administrative practices had detracted from foreign aid programs in the past (although never on the scale which critics often charged). Not infrequently, narrow economic criteria—such as the annual percentage growth in a country's gross national product or its industrial output—had been used to determine the results achieved with foreign aid. Yet American foreign assistance abroad ought to be concerned fully as much with the "quality" of life in the less developed nations; improvements in educational facilities and health services might ultimately prove more crucial in the quest for modernization than industrial growth or expanded farm yields.

A dominant theme in these recent studies of foreign aid was the overdue need for the United States, and the international community generally, *to encourage restrictions upon population growth outside the West*. Many variables of course would determine whether less developed societies would transcend their economic backwardness; but none perhaps surpassed the population

problem as a crucial influence. Thus one authority on foreign aid declared in the late 1960s that external assistance to other governments could not succeed in the long run *without stringent population control* in the Afro–Asian and Latin American nations. "To the extent that foreign aid permits the survival of millions of people without actually raising their levels of living, we are engaged in an essentially ineffective, inhuman and uneconomic enterprise."[67]

Accordingly, by the 1970s one of the leading objectives of the American foreign aid program was support of effective population control. The United Nations expressed its strong interest in that objective beginning in 1962; thereafter, several UN agencies became active in sponsoring birth control measures. In 1965, President Lyndon B. Johnson identified a successful attack upon the population explosion as a major aim of his administration, thereby reversing the earlier reluctance of American officials to deal with the problem directly. In the months which followed, the Agency for International Development furnished assistance to societies seeking to curb population growth. Thus far, however (in spite of some demands by legislators that it do so), the United States has *not* made extension of its aid contingent upon the willingness of recipients to undertake birth control programs or other steps designed to halt population gains.

By the 1970s, many demographers and other students of the population problem viewed such developments as *totally inadequate* to prevent a Malthusian disaster, from which the United States could not fully escape. One group of scientists, for example, labeled "voluntary" family planning as "insanity"; thus far, this approach had done little or nothing to check the population tide which threatened to engulf the planet. One estimate (employing "high projections" of population increase) calculated that there might be close to *8 billion people* on the earth by the year 2000! Even if there were 1 or 2 billion less, within two decades or so, a "perfectly dreadful catastrophe" impended for many societies on the globe; pervasive famine and disease might kill up to 100 million people each year; at best, the "Green Revolution" in agricultural yields *provided time* in which to redress the balance between food output and the world's population. Some demographers called upon the United States to reduce its own population growth rate to zero within a few years (by instituting a "reproductive pause"), to provide an example to the rest of the world. Other commentators believed that *compulsory* birth control measures would soon become essential.*

---

*See the views expressed by a scientific meeting at Aspen, Colorado, as reported by *The New York Times* (September 22, 1969); and see the text of President Nixon's message to Congress on the global population problem, in *The New York Times* (July 19, 1969). Still another

Discussions of the role of foreign aid in American foreign policy will probably revolve around three fundamental questions in the years ahead. The first of these is *the nature and magnitude of America's aid output.* As we have already observed, the foreign aid budget of the United States has contracted steadily in the recent period; under the Nixon administration, it fell to the lowest level ($1.8 billion appropriated by Congress for fiscal year 1971) reached in many years. This tendency occasioned deep concern among governments dependent upon outside assistance and among officials of agencies (like the United Nations and the World Bank) actively involved in promoting national and regional development schemes abroad. From many sources, the United States heard laments that the over-all volume of American aid was "inadequate" for the requirements of needy countries and that Washington was increasingly "neglecting" the welfare of societies outside the West. By the early 1970s, the United States allocated some .35 percent of its annual gross national product to foreign aid—the lowest percentage of its resources throughout the postwar period.

Certain conclusions about the American foreign aid program in the future seem warranted. First, the need for it *remained undiminished.* The capital requirements of the developing nations continued to grow at a rate which surpassed the external assistance these nations received from all sources. Despite contrary predictions in the 1940s and 1950s, it could *not* be anticipated that the need for foreign assistance from the advanced nations would come to an end in the near future. Second, the United States still had a major role to play as a supplier of foreign aid to the less developed countries. Although several Western European nations had become important sources of foreign assistance (particularly for African nations) during the 1960s, and although Japan's efforts to assist other nations had also expanded, there was no substitute for American aid programs. And as other studies earlier had done, most of these groups recommended a *significant expansion* in the magnitude of aid by the United States to needy societies.[68] Robert S. McNamara, President of the World Bank, observed early in

1970 that the United States was the only industrialized nation that was *not increasing* its foreign aid allocation. Predicting that the American economy would expand by around 50 percent during the 1970s, McNamara believed that the United States could easily "afford" to adopt the target suggested earlier by the Pearson Commission: national allocations of .7 of 1 percent of annual GNP for foreign assistance. In America's case (assuming an annual GNP of over $1 trillion), this would necessitate a *fourfold increase* in the current foreign aid budget. By other standards, among sixteen major donors of foreign aid at the end of the 1960s, the United States ranked thirteenth, when is foreign aid program was judged in terms of the nation's capacity to assist other countries; the American program ranked eighth in terms of total aid actually made available to needy societies. Britain and France (both plagued with financial and balance-of-payments problems), along with West Germany, had *increased* their foreign assistance allocation in the recent past.[69]

What were the prospects that the magnitude of American aid would be substantially expanded in the near future? All things considered, they did not seem overly favorable. The United States faced a number of urgent domestic problems, some of which require large governmental expenditures for many years to come. Popular disaffection stemming from the Vietnam War demanded a retrenchment in nearly all international commitments, especially those likely to entail growing American responsibility for the destiny of other countries. Willard L. Thorpe has characterized foreign aid as a "political orphan"; no powerful lobby demands its continuation (much less its expansion); when it must reduce federal spending, Congress is perhaps inevitably attracted to the idea of cutting the foreign aid budget; on Capitol Hill and throughout the public at large, widespread skepticism exists about what earlier foreign aid programs have accomplished. Congressional and public opposition aside, there was no indication that the White House contemplated a sizable expansion in the volume of assistance from the United States. Early in 1970s, for example, President Nixon made a number of proposals to improve the foreign aid program; but Nixon did *not* call for any noteworthy increase in the over-all foreign aid budget. That step, the evidence suggested, would probably have to await both progress in alleviating several internal problems with which Americans were concerned and the disappearance of public dissatisfactions with involvement overseas growing out of the Vietnam War.

Another question central to the future of the foreign aid program is an issue alluded to earlier: *the use of multilateral agencies in dispensing American assistance to other countries.* Both recipient government and study groups investigat-

---

grim warning about the implications of unchecked population growth came from the National Research Council at the end of 1969. Its study found that many natural resources were rapidly being exhausted and that the rate of consumption was climbing steadily. Some important raw materials (e.g., mercury, tin, tungsten, and helium) were already in short supply; global reserves of petroleum and natural gas, the study predicted, could be exhausted within 50 to 60 years; world coal deposits might last only another two centuries or so. This projection admittedly did not consider how this situation could change if the ocean floors were successfully mined. See "Toward a Have-Not World," *Chemical and Engineering News* 47 (November 17, 1969), 13.

ing the program have urged greater reliance upon the United Nations and regional institutions in extending American aid abroad. This proposal arises from several motivations: Most countries receiving American aid desire it because it avoids any appearance of "dependency" upon the United States and largely escapes frictions over such issues as American supervision of loans and grants; such a step might give greater impetus to effective regional cooperation among major aid recipients; many Afro–Asian states no doubt feel that, in UN-administered aid programs, they could exercise a larger voice in the allocation of funds. In his comprehensive statement of foreign policy principles early in 1970s, President Nixon declared that "Multilateral institutions must play an increasing role in the provision of aid." This change, Nixon was convinced, would contribute to "minimizing the political and ideological complications which can distort the assistance relationship."[70] The Rockefeller mission made basically the same recommendation, following its study of hemispheric aid programs.[71] Other study groups in the late 1960s and early 1970s also endorsed this move as needed to improve the administration of American aid programs.[72]

Although such proposals have been put forward with new intensity in the contemporary period, the basic idea common to them is not new. As early as the Greek–Turkish Aid Program of 1947, some critics urged the Truman administration to channel American assistance through the nascent United Nations. In the years which followed, the idea that American assistance ought to be administered by international or regional agencies was advocated from time to time. As we have already observed, *congressional opposition* has always been the principal obstacle to this proposal. One difference between the situation in the 1970s and in earlier periods, however, was that now several legislators (like the chairman of the Senate Foreign Relations Committee, Senator J. William Fulbright) favored a continuation of the foreign aid program *only* if it were administered largely by multilateral agencies. Such viewpoints, it had to be recognized, were still perhaps in the minority in Congress. Indeed, as we shall see in Chapter 15, legislators were perhaps more troubled than ever about recent tendencies within the United Nations and less inclined than ever to rely upon that body to achieve American foreign policy aims. Except for the European Economic Community, nearly all regional organizations (especially in Latin America and Asia) are in their infancy and their ability to administer American aid funds remains largely untested. With the magnitude of the foreign aid budget declining, Congress may be more loath than ever to entrust its administration to institutions over which American policy-makers have little control. In any case, congressional assent to this move can assuredly not be taken for granted.

A third issue around which discussion of the foreign aid program in the years ahead is likely to revolve concerns *the administrative reorganization of the foreign aid machinery.* Omitting legislative investigations, the foreign assistance program has been investigated by some *fifteen* study groups and commissions since the late 1940s. The frequency of these investigations per se may well have proved a hindrance to consistent and effective aid administration. In nearly every case, these studies proposed administrative modifications, with the result that the "reorganization" of the foreign aid program has almost become a national pastime! Earlier in the chapter, the main stages in the administrative history of foreign aid were identified. In 1961, President Kennedy (again accepting the demand for "reform" in the foreign aid structure) created the Agency for International Development (AID). AID was established as a "semiautonomous agency," within the executive branch: It took its basic policy directives from the State Department, but it functioned autonomously in administering American aid funds overseas. As time passed, the Department of Defense largely assumed the responsibility for formulating and administering *military assistance* to foreign countries.

As in the past, the investigations of foreign aid carried out by the Nixon administration called for further reorganization of administrative structures and procedures. Considerably less unanimity surrounded the specific recommendations made by these groups concerning an ideal model for foreign aid administration. Some groups proposed the outright abolition of AID (a suggestion also endorsed by several legislators); others advocated less drastic steps, involving perhaps little more than symbolic changes. All groups, however, agreed upon two principles. Some of AID's responsibilities ought to be transferred to multilateral agencies. And greater imagination and creativity were needed in the formulation of American assistance programs than had sometimes been displayed in the past, perhaps by trying to recruit new personnel who were not identified with earlier guidelines governing the foreign aid program. The same general observation can be made about these periodic demands for the "reorganization" of the foreign aid program that was made in our discussion of the Department of State in Chapter 3. In the case of the State Department—or more specialized agencies like AID and the United States Information Agency—beneficial changes can doubtless be made in its operations; and many such improvements have in fact been made since World War II. Yet the continuing demand for organizational change in the principal agencies involved in

American foreign policy is perhaps as much *symptomatic of public dissatisfaction with the over-all course of foreign policy* as it is dictated by evidence of maladministration. Demands have been expressed for the "reorganization" of the State Department, AID, USIA, and other agencies playing a central role in foreign affairs, in much the same way that business corporations are subjected to reorganization when profit levels began to fall. The crucial difference with government agencies perhaps is that it is infinitely more difficult to determine whether their operations are diplomatically "profitable"; and for foreign aid, even the standards for determining profit and loss remain far from clear.

The Peace Corps

We conclude this chapter with a brief examination of a program which combines both propaganda and foreign aid techniques of American foreign policy: the Peace Corps. The Peace Corps was established by executive order of President Kennedy in 1961. Beginning with 120 volunteers assigned to 3 foreign countries, the organization expanded its size and activities rapidly. By the end of the 1960s, some 15,000 Peace Corps volunteers (PCVs) were serving in 46 foreign countries throughout the Afro–Asian world and Latin America.

One student of American foreign policy has likened the Peace Corps to a "missionary technical assistance" program, since PCVs usually have more in common with "the missionary in terms of techniques and approaches" than they do with State Department officials or foreign aid technicians.[73] Administratively separate from the Department of State and AID, the Peace Corps possesses considerable operational independence. It seeks to *complement* the activities of the State Department, USIA, AID, and other government agencies, by sending idealistic American youth (along with many older PCVs) into societies requesting their services. Peace Corps representatives often succeed in avoiding many of the frictions sometimes associated with foreign aid. After careful training (including intensive foreign-language instruction), PCVs carry on their activities at the grass-roots level, where they endeavor to counteract foreign stereotypes of *The Ugly American;* their presence in a village classroom or as a member of a team seeking to carry out a community project, provides a visible symbol of American humanitarianism and interest in the welfare of other societies.

By almost any standard, the Peace Corps has proved a worthwhile investment of American funds for the purpose of winning good will for the United States abroad. At relatively low cost vis-à-vis other foreign aid programs, several thousand PCVs serve abroad; the demand for their services has nearly always outpaced the organization's ability to supply the need. Some sixteen other industrialized nations have copied the Peace Corps model; the government of Iran has instituted a similar program to attack poverty and illiteracy within its own borders. Communist propaganda organs have experienced minimum success in discrediting the Peace Corps abroad—in part because the organization studiously avoids identification with the Central Intelligence Agency or even with the State Department and other agencies in the diplomatic "establishment." In the main the Peace Corps has been successful in preserving its image as an organization devoted chiefly to helping societies desiring its assistance and willing to contribute a minimum degree of self-help in the venture.[74]

The Peace Corps has also experienced problems in carrying out its activities, along with occasional failures. Some countries (like Zambia) have refused outright to accept PCVs; others (like Tanzania) have become highly critical of the Peace Corps' operations within its borders. Tanzanian disaffection centered upon what is admittedly a built-in anomaly in the program: Peace Corps workers were sometimes (as in the case of the Vietnam War) outspokenly *critical* of the very government they were representing overseas. Tanzania and other societies might well wonder, under these conditions, whether the State Department or the Peace Corps most accurately represented the viewpoint of the American people; and foreign observers were perhaps inevitably puzzled by the behavior of a government which officially sponsored one position through the American embassy and another as expressed by PCVs serving within the country.[75] According to one interpretation, this situation furnished other societies a case study in the successful functioning of American "pluralism." By another interpretation, however, it might also suggest to foreigners that the American government really did not know its own mind! In some countries, too, evident differences have existed *within* the Peace Corps, between PCVs and the organization's older (and perhaps more conservative) staff members. The kind of "confrontations" existing on a number of American campuses have also erupted inside the Peace Corps, with volunteers seeking a larger role in formulating the organization's policies.[76]

Early in 1970, studies made among several hundred Peace Corps workers revealed a number of interesting facts and attitudes. The overwhelming majority of PCVs surveyed found the Peace Corps experience valuable. Surprisingly, however, a majority of present and former PCVs believed the experience had been *more valuable to them* than to the country to which they had been assigned. As the organization approached its first decade of service, a substantial sentiment among PCVs existed that the program should be reorganized and revitalized, to restore some of the initial idealism and creative spirit which was being lost as the organization became more "conservative." By this period, the Peace Corps was also experiencing a decline in legislative support for its activities; Congress had cut its budget; and applications for the Peace Corps were declining.[77] As a novel experiment in providing assistance to other countries, the Peace Corps has been on balance, however, a conspicuous success. From the beginning, it has been and will undoubtedly remain *an adjunct* of American foreign policy. The views of some PCVs to the contrary, it can never replace the State Department; Peace Corps efforts alone cannot revolutionize America's relations with other countries; and, as many PCVs have learned, the obstacles to economic advancement in many nations outside the West are more formidable than many idealistic Americans imagine. For many countries in which the Peace Corps has carried on activities, the PCVs may well be correct: In the last analysis, the main beneficiary of the program *may well be the United States itself.* Experience in the Peace Corps can provide thousands of American citizens with an unexcelled education in the problems confronting the United States in its foreign relations.

NOTES

1. See the text of the Sprague Committee's report in Urban G. Whitaker, Jr., *Propaganda and International Relations* (San Francisco: Chandler, 1962), pp. 38–61.
2. See the views of George V. Allen, as quoted in John Henderson, *The United States Information Agency* (New York: Praeger, 1969), p. 4.
3. *Ibid.*, pp. 6–7; and Thomas C. Sorensen, *The Word War: The Story of American Propaganda* (New York: Harper & Row, 1968), pp. 229–230.
4. See Daniel Lerner, ed., *Propaganda in War and Crisis* (New York: Stewart, 1951), pp. 72–73, 84–85, 276.
5. The idea that international relations is concerned chiefly with problems of "conflict resolution" is pervasive among contemporary students of the subject. For fuller treatment of the point, see the discussion and citations in Cecil V. Crabb, Jr., *Nations in a Multipolar World* (New York: Harper & Row, 1968), pp. 7–8.
6. For more detailed listings of the weapons employed in psychological warfare, see Terence H. Qualter, *Propaganda and Psychological Warfare* (New York: Random House, 1962), p. 74.
7. See the views of George V. Allen, as quoted in Sorensen, *op. cit.*, p. 105.
8. President Kennedy's viewpoints are cited in *ibid.*, pp. 127–128.
9. See Qualter, *op. cit.*, p. 3.
10. American propaganda activities from World War II to the early 1950s are discussed in Henderson, *op. cit.*, pp. 3–62; Sorensen, *op. cit.*, pp. 1–31; and Robert E. Elder, *The United States Information Agency and American Foreign Policy* (Syracuse, N.Y.: Syracuse University Press, 1968), pp. 25–51.
11. Charles A. Thomson and Walter H. C. Laves, *Cultural Relations and U.S. Foreign Policy* (Bloomington: University of Indiana Press, 1963), pp. 97, 119.
12. Henderson, *op. cit.*, pp. 54, 308.
13. See *The New York Times* (December 21, 1969), dispatch by Tad Szulc.
14. See *idem* and Henderson, *op. cit.*, p. 308.
15. Our statement of the goals of USIA relies upon the formulation of objectives by the agency's director, Leonard H. Marks, as presented in the agency's *30th Report to Congress: January–June, 1968* (Washington, D.C.: U.S. Government Printing Office, 1968), p. 17.
16. *Ibid.*, pp. 17–18.
17. See the views of Leonard H. Marks, as cited in Henderson, *op. cit.*, p. 155.
18. *Ibid.*, p. 75.
19. Our treatment summarizes data included in USIA's *32nd Report to Congress: January–June, 1969* (Washington, D.C.: U.S. Government Printing Office, 1969), pp. 6–13.
20. Our summary of USIA's handling of controversial issues draws from the agency's *31st Report to Congress: July–December, 1968* (Washington, D.C.: U.S. Government Printing Office, 1969), pp. 14–19; and Sorensen, *op. cit.*, pp. 100–101, 171–179, 296–298.
21. See Sorensen, *op. cit.*, p. 173.
22. Quoted in *ibid.*, p. 255.
23. House Foreign Affairs Committee, *The Future of United States Public Diplomacy— Winning the Cold War: The U.S. Ideological Offensive*, 90th Congress, 2nd Session, 1968, p. 4R.
24. See the excerpt from the report by the House Foreign Affairs Committee, as cited in Henderson, *op. cit.*, p. 196.
25. The *New York Times* (December 7, 1969), dispatch by Tad Szulc.
26. *The New York Times* (December 21, 1969).
27. See the testimony of Lloyd A. Free in House Foreign Affairs Committee, *op. cit.*, p. 20.
28. See USIA, *31st Report to Congress, op. cit.*, p. 23.
29. Quoted in Sorensen, *op. cit.*, p. 208.
30. Quoted in *ibid.*, p. 122.
31. Quoted in *ibid.*, p. 144. Italics in original.
32. The assumption that international good will and cooperation are engendered to the extent that people "understand each other better" tends to be an unchallenged premise of informational and cultural programs. At best, the assumption can be accepted with reservations. Conceivably, as with the belated American "understanding" of Soviet Russia's foreign policy ambitions after World War II,

clearer understanding of one nation by another can sometimes *increase* international tensions and ill will. As Americans have discovered concerning African and Arab students who have studied in the United States, pro-American sentiments are *not* necessarily fostered by such experiences. Some of the most outspokenly anti-Western figures in postwar Africa, for example, were educated in Europe or America. For evidence on this point, see such studies as William Buchanan, "How Others See Us," *Annals of the American Academy of Political and Social Science* 295 (September, 1954), 1–11; Jacques Freymond, "Americans in European Eyes," *ibid.*, pp. 33–41; Herbert Passin and John W. Bernett, "The American-Educated Japanese," *ibid.*, pp. 83–96; and Sorensen, *op. cit.*, pp. 70–71.

33. Sorensen, *op. cit.*, pp. 114–115, 163.
34. See the study cited in *ibid.*, p. 252.
35. For specific instances, see Henderson, *op. cit.*, p. 169; and Sorensen, *op. cit.*, p. 156.
36. Cited in Henderson, *op. cit.*, p. 289.
37. See, for example, the report from Moscow in *The New York Times* (September 2, 1963), dispatch by Theodore Shabad.
38. See *The New York Times* (July 12, 1965), dispatch by Theodore Shabad.
39. Sorensen, *op. cit.*, p. 268–269.
40. Henderson, *op. cit.*, p. 197.
41. Sorensen, *op. cit.*, pp. 198–200.
42. *Ibid.*, p. 128.
43. *Ibid.*, p. 130.
44. Henderson, *op. cit.*, p. 270.
45. *The New York Times* (December 7, 1969), dispatch by Tad Szulc.
46. American assistance to Nationalist China at the end of World War II and in the early postwar period is discussed at length in the Truman administration's "white paper," entitled *United States Relations with China* (Washington, D.C.: Department of State Publication no. 3573, 1949).
47. See *Global Defense: U.S. Military Commitments Abroad* (Washington, D.C.: Congressional Quarterly Service, 1969), p. 39.
48. *The New York Times* (March 1, 1970).
49. See the list supplied by the Agency for International Development, as cited in *Global Defense, op. cit.*, p. 39.
50. Agency for International Development, *Report to the Congress on the Foreign Assistance Program for Fiscal Year 1962* (Washington, D.C., 1963), p. 4; and Agency for International Development, *The Foreign Aid Program Today: Answers to Four Basic Questions* (Washington, D.C., 1963), p. 9.
51. *The New York Times* (February 21, 1970).
52. See the discussion of President Nixon's foreign aid budget requests in *The New York Times* (January 27, 1970), dispatch by Felix Belair, Jr.
53. *The New York Times* (February 21, 1970).
54. *Idem.*
55. See Senator J. William Fulbright's letter, in *The New York Times* (February 15, 1970).
56. See the text of President Nixon's message on American foreign policy, as reprinted in *The New York Times* (February 19, 1970).
57. For an illuminating case study of American aid to a country with which relations have often been strained, see the discussion of U.S. assistance to Egypt in John S. Badeau, *The American Approach to the Arab World* (New York: Harper & Row, 1968), pp. 67–75.
58. See the text of President Kennedy's message to Congress on March 14, 1961, and the "Declaration to the Peoples of America" on August 17, 1961, as reproduced in *Documents on American Foreign Relations: 1961* (New York: Harper & Row, 1962), pp. 402 and 433.
59. The humanitarian considerations justifying American aid to other countries are evaluated in Lloyd D. Black, *The Strategy of Foreign Aid* (New York: Van Nostrand Reinhold,, 1968), p. 20; and for a more recent statement, see the views of AID Director John S. Hannah, in *The New York Times* (March 20, 1970).
60. See AID Director Hannah's statement in *The New York Times* (March 20, 1970).
61. For analyses of the impending world food crisis, risking the danger of widespread famine in certain areas, see Black, *op. cit.*, pp. 48–52; S. N. Afriat, "People and Population," *World Politics* 17 (April, 1965), 431–440; Richard W. Reuter, "The World's Food and Population Problems," *Department of State Bulletin* 55 (December 5, 1966), 862–866; and "The World Food and Population Crisis," *ibid.*, **55** (August 8, 1966), 199–210. And for a more detailed study of the problem, see I. W. Moomaw, *The Challenge of Hunger* (New York: Praeger, 1966).
62. For evidence of gains—in many cases, outstanding gains—in agricultural output by the developing nations, see the data cited in the report of the Commission on International Development, *Partners in Development* (New York: Praeger, 1969), pp. 32–36; and in Black, *op. cit.*, pp. 48–52.
63. For more detailed treatment of the trade and commercial obstacles confronting the developing nations, see Black, *op. cit.*, pp. 56–59, 61–63; *Partners in Development, op. cit.*, pp. 45–48; and *The Rockefeller Report on the Americas* (Chicago: Quadrangle Books, 1969), pp. 70–80, 87–88, 124–125.
64. Robert L. Heilbroner, *The Great Ascent: The Struggle for Development in Our Time* (New York: Harper & Row, 1963), pp. 17–19.
65. *Ibid.*, pp. 19–20. Although somewhat dated now, Heilbroner's analysis deals realistically and objectively with many problems facing national development; very few of his basic conclusions need to be changed in the light of the events of the late 1960s and early 1970s.
66. These studies and reports on the problems and future of American foreign aid are summarized and appraised in Willard L. Thorp, "Foreign Aid: A Report on the Reports," *Foreign Affairs* 48 (April, 1970), 561–574.
67. Quoted in Black, *op. cit.*, p. 153.
68. See *The New York Times* (March 15, 1970).
69. See Thorpe, *op. cit.*, p. 572.

70. See the text of President Nixon's statement on American foreign policy in *The New York Times* (February 19, 1970).
71. See *The Rockefeller Report on the Americas*, *op. cit.*, pp. 52–54.
72. Several such proposals are cited in Thorpe, *op. cit.*, pp. 565–566.
73. John D. Montgomery, *Foreign Aid in International Politics* (Englewood Cliffs, N.J.: Prentice-Hall, 1967), pp. 10–11.
74. Our discussion of the Peace Corps relies heavily upon Black, *op. cit.*, pp. 83–85; and upon *The New York Times* (March 31, 1966; February 2 and 3, 1969).
75. See *The New York Times* (February 3, 1969).
76. See the account of the Peace Corps' activities in Liberia, as reported in *The New York Times* (April 22, 1969).
77. Recent studies and surveys of the Peace Corps are summarized in *The New York Times* (April 4, 1970), dispatch by Robert M. Smith.

Fifteen
INTERNATIONAL ORGANIZATION AND ARMS CONTROL

Over two millennia separate the mutual defense leagues established by the ancient Greeks from the United Nations organization set up at the end of World War II. Yet statesmen dedicated to the goal of world peace and security in the modern period follow a path through the jungle of international anarchy which has been blazed by countless predecessors. Oftentimes the trail has grown dim; frequently it has veered off into the tangled thickets of wars and the quagmires of competing national interests. The ultimate destination has sometimes been obscured by clouds of suspicion, hate, ignorance.

But the vision has persisted and, in spite of obstacles and digressions in the unfolding of historical events, the quest has gone on. Gradually, mankind has acquired renewed faith in its ability to reach the final goal: greater skill in the use of techniques and institutional devices to cultivate harmonious intercourse among nations, and heightened awareness that the abolition of war as an instrument of national policies may well be a prerequisite for survival of civilization on the planet. Every age has added its legacy to the reservoir of insights and tools available to contemporary statesmen. We must confine our attention to those most directly relevant to American foreign relations.*

*Limitations of space prevent us from dealing extensively with pre-United Nations efforts to achieve workable international organization and respect for world law. Students are strongly urged, however, to familiarize themselves with these earlier movements by reading some of the worthwhile studies available, such as: American Association for the United Nations, *An Eleven Year Review of the League of Nations* (New York: League of Nations Association, 1931); Edgar E. Davis, *Pioneers of World Order* (New York: Columbia University Press, 1944); D. F. Fleming, *The United States and the League of Nations, 1918–1920* (New York: Putnam, 1932); the same author's *The United States and World Organization* (Garden City, N.Y.: Doubleday, 1945); Institute on World Organization, *World Organization: A Balance Sheet of the First Great Experiment* (Washington, D.C.: American Council on Public Affairs, 1942); Gerald J. Mangone, *A Short History of International Organization* (New York: McGraw-Hill, 1954); Gilbert Murray, *From the League to the U.N.* (New York: Harper & Row, 1951).

THE EVOLUTION OF THE UNITED NATIONS

Nineteenth-Century Antecedents

Conditions in the nineteenth century were peculiarly conducive to impressive strides toward reaching the goal of effective international organization and toward inculcating acceptance of world law. After 1815, techniques for "consultation" among powerful European countries emerged within the Concert of Europe. The Holy Alliance sought, admittedly with limited success, to inject Christian principles into the conduct of international affairs. Significant progress came about in socioeconomic–administrative aspects of interstate relations due to agreements establishing such bodies as the Rhine River Commission (1868), the International Telegraphic Convention (1865), the Universal Postal Union (1874), and many others.[1]

Meantime, international law was being strengthened. Noteworthy developments included international agreements on the abolition of the slave trade; various conventions dealing with fisheries and marginal territorial waters; agreements aimed at mitigating the barbarities of naval and land warfare; and the Hague Conferences late in the nineteenth century, which established machinery for arbitrating disputes among nations and for reducing armaments.[2]

By 1900, the United States had assumed an active role in these activities. It supported the Permanent Court of Arbitration at the Hague by submitting cases to it. An attempt was made by President Taft to broaden the area of disputes which the United States would submit to arbitration; but it encountered formidable resistance in the Senate, where so many exceptions were demanded that Taft finally abandoned the effort. President Wilson's idealistic and pacifistically inclined Secretary of State, William Jennings Bryan, resumed the crusade. Eventually, 30 "cooling-off treaties" were negotiated between the United States and other countries, of which 21 were ratified by the Senate and proclaimed. These provided for arbitration of disputes by impartial bodies. The signatories were not required to accept recommendations made, but they pledged not to begin hostilities until after the arbitration commission had submitted its report.[3]

The League of Nations

The League of Nations was the culmination of an evolutionary movement often proceeding on many fronts at once, directed at gaining adherence to principles of international law and at securing formal and informal agreements for the peaceful settlement of disputes among nations. What looked like the total collapse of efforts to avert war in the period 1914–1918 was in reality but a temporary though crucial deviation from the charted course in the history of international organization. World War I witnessed physical destruction, bloodletting, and social disorganization on a scale seldom equaled in human society to that time. It furnished a powerful stimulus to an often complacent Victorian world for eliminating war and creating machinery for nonviolent adjustment of disagreements in the world community. Out of the "war to end wars" and to "make the world safe for democracy" came intensive and widespread study of methods for setting up a viable international organization. From numerous sources, both official and private, suggestions and proposals were made which finally coalesced in the Covenant of the League of Nations, the first international organization in history providing a continuously functioning body to study and deal with issues affecting peace and security for all nations.

In many respects, the structure and operating principles of the League of Nations foreshadowed those of its successor, the United Nations. Three major organs were created. The *Council,* a revised version of the Concert of Europe, consisted of Britain, France, Italy and Japan, plus four smaller nations elected by the Assembly. The *Assembly* embraced the total membership of the League, initially 42 countries; it was roughly analogous to national legislatures. The *Secretariat* was the permanent administrative body, whose head, the Secretary-General, was nominated by the Council and approved by the Assembly. The World Court was the League's legal tribunal. In addition, there grew up a host of lesser agencies in the economic–social field.

An imprecise boundary separated the functions of the two major policy-making agencies, the Council and the Assembly. The Covenant gave both certain independent functions; yet both were also empowered to deal with any question affecting world peace and security. Theoretically, the Council was expected to address itself to issues *directly* affecting peace and security, such as disarmament and the threat of war, while the Assembly was to consider more indirect contributory causes of international instability. The founders of the League, like the founders of the UN, envisioned that the smaller Council, where the great powers had a preponderant voice, would provide leadership and guidance to the larger Assembly in arriving at decisions on major causes of international tension.[4] And in time the Council indeed came to speak for the League, as corroborated by the fact that it held 106 meetings throughout the League's existence, whereas the Assembly met only once a year from 1920 to 1940.[5]

Uppermost among the League's objectives was the maintenance of peace. The Covenant required members to submit disputes to judicial organs or to the League Council and to observe a 90-day "cooling-off" period before resorting to hostilities over a dispute. The League's fatal weakness showed up when it had to grapple with aggression by ambitious dictators after Japan's invasion of Manchuria in 1931. The League possessed no independent power to *compel* acceptance of its decisions by recalcitrant members and nonmembers. Recommendations by the Council, reports by fact-finding commissions, impassioned appeals to protect the "sovereign rights" of weaker countries, aroused public opinion, moral suasion, conferences among the great powers—all of these were used to no avail by the League to dissuade aggressive countries. Dictators in Germany, Italy, and Japan continued to defy the League with impunity, because the great powers hesitated to use collective force to stop them. With each successful aggression the League was rendered more and more impotent.

In some fields, however, the League of Nations accomplished lasting good. Its subsidiary organs vigorously and often successfully attacked problems like widespread disease, narcotics traffic, government barriers to communications, substandard conditions of labor, and the slave trade. Many of the League's less publicized activities made an undeniably valuable contribution in eliminating the underlying causes of war and human misery. Moreover, the League's contribution was of inestimable importance in another respect: Experience gained in establishing and successfully operating the first permanent international organization in history provided a rich backlog of precedents and insights which was drawn upon in innumerable instances by the founders of the United Nations.

The United States did not join the League of Nations, in spite of the fact that one of its greatest Presidents had secured Allied acceptance of it at the Paris Peace Conference. The overwhelming election of Republican President Warren Harding in 1920 was widely—and probably incorrectly—interpreted as a resounding public rejection of the League. The Senate refused to ratify the Treaty of Versailles as submitted by President Wilson, and Wilson refused to accept modifications which would make it palatable to the Senate. The impasse was never resolved, dooming the United States to remain outside the League.

Nevertheless, as time went on, the United States sent "unofficial observers" to Geneva. Working without fanfare, the observers cooperated with certain League activities, particularly in fields such as the suppression of narcotics rings and white-slave traffic. They were able to communicate the American government's position on prevailing international issues to statesmen at Geneva. In 1934, the United States finally joined the International Labor Organization, which was loosely affiliated with the League, and in the same year it agreed to register its treaties at League headquarters.[6] That isolationism still was the dominating impulse in American foreign affairs, however, was indicated in 1935, when not even the politically adroit President Roosevelt could prevail upon two-thirds of the Senate to approve American membership in the World Court.

The United States held officially aloof from the proceedings of the League of Nations dealing with global political developments after 1920. American initiative in sponsoring the Washington Naval Armaments Confeence (1921) and the Kellogg–Briand Pact (1928) denouncing war as an instrument of national policy, however, was indicative of America's willingness to work for peace. In the critical decade of the 1930s, the United States as a rule applauded efforts by the League to deal with aggression in Europe and Asia; and occasionally, Roosevelt and Secretary of State Hull took the initiative in trying to prod the League to even greater efforts. From time to time, vigorous condemnations of German expansionism and of Japanese perfidy emanated from Washington. But American officials were always restricted by two prohibitions: They dared not commit the country to a policy which demanded action, and particularly military action, to halt aggression, nor could they risk the accusation that American policy was being "dictated" by the rejected and still unpopular League of Nations.[7] These limitations, coupled with prolonged indecision in Washington regarding the long-run implications of Japan's expansionism in the Orient, meant that the United States was unprepared to render any tangible assistance to the League of Nations in a showdown and that its own unilateral response to repeated international crises was seldom an improvement over the growing paralysis displayed by the League of Nations. Considering the profound isolationist propensities of the American people, it was perhaps of no crucial significance that the United States failed to join the League of Nations

There is no evidence that, had the United States been a member, it was prepared to go beyond the feeble efforts exerted by England, France, and Russia in meeting the challenge of aggression head-on, with military force if necessary. Anything less could scarcely have averted the League's eventual demise.

The United Nations

Hitler's attack against Poland in the fall of 1939 ignited World War II. Soon every major power of the world was drawn into the vortex of that struggle. After the United States entered the war, following the Japanese attack against Pearl Harbor on December 7, 1941, American officials moved rapidly to integrate Allied war efforts and, more importantly for our subject, to lay the basis for a durable peace in the postwar era. By 1942, the State Department had initiated intensive preliminary studies of problems that would be encountered in assuring international stability after the Axis defeat. Executive and legislative officials collaborated intimately to generate support within the government and throughout the country at large for an international organization to facilitate maintenance of world peace. Careful attention was paid to the experience of the League of Nations.

In a series of conferences dating from early 1942, step by step the contours of the nascent United Nations emerged, as agreements were secured among the Allies concerning its purposes and guiding principles. At Moscow in the autumn of 1943, at Tehran in December, and finally at Dumbarton Oaks in the autumn of 1944 the "Big Five" (Great Britain, France, China, Soviet Russia, and the United States) negotiated agreements laying the foundations for the United Nations. The Dumbarton Oaks agreements indicated that the UN was to be much like its predecessor. The two major policy-making bodies were to be the Security Council and the General Assembly. The former, possessing primary responsibility for dealing with questions of international peace and security, was to reflect the preponderant influence of the Big Five in world affairs. These states were to be the "permanent" members, and six smaller countries were to be rotating "nonpermanent" members elected for two years by the General Assembly. The Assembly's function theoretically was confined to discussing all other matters within the jurisdiction of the UN and, more broadly, to promoting human welfare. The League's Permanent Court of International Justice, renamed the International Court of Justice, was retained as the judicial organ of the new international organization.

Finally, the Dumbarton Oaks proposals included a Secretariat to be headed by a Secretary-General who, according to Article 97 of the UN

Charter, designated "chief administrative officer of the Organization." The Secretariat was to be the UN's continuing executive office, charged with facilitating the carrying out of policies and taking an active part in their formulation. As we shall see, one of the most profound changes in the UN after 1945 was the emergence of the Secretary-General as an active force in negotiations seeking to eliminate causes of international tension.

After Dumbarton Oaks there remained the crucial question of voting within the Security Council —a question involving the guiding philosophy upon which the United Nations was to be constructed and operated thereafter. The great powers had been primarily responsible for the impending Axis defeat. Moreover, they had taken the initiative in planning for the UN, virtually presenting the smaller powers with a *fait accompli*. Two extreme alternatives were possible: The emergent UN, following in the footsteps of the Concert of Europe after the Congress of Vienna, might become merely a mechanism whereby the great powers imposed their will upon the international community. Or else the UN could accept the principle of "one state, one vote," carrying the concept of the equality of nations to the point of giving all states, regardless of size and power, an equal opportunity to shape decisions. The first course led back to the wastelands of a world dominated by the great powers, in which global decisions were made by a handful of governments representing a small minority of the earth's population. The second path led to the swamp of futility, with the new international organization rapidly becoming impotent because decisions were made by a preponderance of weak states which possessed neither the power nor inclination to carry them out in the face of great-power opposition. In short, a formula had to be found which in some way would blend the realities of the existing international power structure with the broad principles of equality, responsibility, and respect for the rights of weaker countries.

Such a formula was agreed upon at the Yalta Conference in February, 1945. Here it was decided that Security Council decisions involving *procedural* (i.e., presumably minor) questions could be made by a majority of any six members of the Council. But on *substantive* matters (i.e., highly important questions affecting peace and security) decisions could be reached only by the *unanimous* vote of the great powers, plus the affirmative votes of at least two of the nonpermanent members. Parties to a dispute before the Council, however, were prohibited from voting. Each permanent member in effect possessed a "veto"—a term not mentioned in the Charter. If the Security Council could not act in matters affecting peace and security with the concurrence of *all* the great powers, then it could not act at all.

The UN Charter was drawn up and signed at the 50-nation San Francisco Conference held April 25-June 26, 1945. The smaller states objected vigorously to the preponderant voice given to the Big Five in the Security Council. While the great powers remained adamant on retention of the veto, other concessions were made to accommodate the viewpoints of smaller countries. As an example, the draft Charter was amended to make more forceful the UN's concern for "fundamental human rights," "social progress," and "better standards of life"—matters of the highest concern to newly independent and dependent countries throughout Asia and Africa. A vastly strengthened Economic and Social Council was elevated into a major organ of the UN.* A completely new body, the Trusteeship Council, was also added and given responsibilities for supervising governments of dependent people and of advancing their welfare.

The UN—Basic Assumptions and Underlying Concepts

For a proper understanding of the United Nations and of America's relationship to it, it is essential to grasp certain assumptions and underlying concepts upon which the UN was founded. First, the United Nations was designed to be, and it remains, *a league of sovereign states, not a world government*. This distinction has sometimes been blurred by both advocates and critics of international organization. The UN was established to

---

*The Charter provision permitting the Economic and Social Council to negotiate working relationships with specialized agencies active in the economic–social field proved especially important. In some cases, these agencies already existed; after 1945, their efforts were coordinated as closely as possible with the UN. In other cases, the UN created certain specialized agencies. Agencies already in the field, and later brought under the jurisdiction of the UN, include the Universal Postal Union (UPU), the International Labor Organization (ILO), the Food and Agriculture Organization (FAO), the International Monetary Fund (IMF), and the International Bank for Reconstruction and Development (IBRD). Agencies which were in the formative stage or were created after 1945 include the International Civil Aviation Organization (ICAO), the UN Educational, Scientific and Cultural Organization (UNESCO), the World Health Organization (WHO), the International Refugee Organization (IRO), and the International Trade Organization (ITO).

A total of 11 "specialized agencies" of the UN exist. While they possess a certain degree of autonomy, they are also loosely under the jurisdiction of the General Assembly and the Economic and Social Council. For a fuller treatment of their precise relationship to the UN, see Leland M. Goodrich and Edward Hambro, *Charter of the United Nations* (Boston: World Peace Foundation, 1949), pp. 73–78. Informative treatments of the activities of these agencies are contained in Graham Beckel, *Workshops for the World: The Specialized Agencies of the UN* (New York: Abelard-Schuman, 1954); and Marian Maury, *The Good War: The UN's Worldwide Fight Against Poverty, Disease and Ignorance* (New York: MacFadden-Bartell, 1965).

facilitate harmonious relationships among *sovereign* countries to achieve ends specified in the UN Charter. While the Preamble to the Charter speaks of "the *peoples* of the United Nations," it goes on to observe that "our respective *Governments* . . . have agreed to the present Charter . . ." (italics added).

The UN possesses virtually none of the attributes associated with sovereign political entities: the power to tax, to pass laws, to impose its will directly upon citizens, and to punish *individuals* who violate its laws. Exceptions exist in one sphere only: enforcement of Charter provisions against violators of international peace and security. Article 2 of the Charter expressly prohibits the UN from intervening "in matters which are essentially within the domestic jurisdiction of any state," leaving it to the states concerned to decide what these matters are.[8] The founders were establishing an institution which accepted national sovereignty as supreme except in the case of threats to the peace. They sought to create an international environment in which sovereignty could be exercised more beneficially for the welfare of mankind.[9]

In the second place, the United Nations was envisioned by its originators as predominantly an instrumentality to *preserve and maintain peace and security.* The implications of this fact for the later development of the UN, and for its subsequent influence upon world affairs, can hardly be exaggerated. For in many crucial respects, the United Nations presupposed the existence or the early establishment of the peace it was expected to preserve; it was not designed to bring that peace into existence.

In at least three important respects, however, the peace which the UN was expected to preserve was not achieved after 1945 and has not been altogether achieved today. The most obvious instance was in relations among the great powers themselves. "Great-power unanimity," the keystone of the arch of collective security, began to disintegrate after 1945 in the face of cold war antagonisms between two rival diplomatic blocs. Having postulated its existence and future effectiveness upon a continuation of wartime unity among the great powers, the UN possessed very few methods for creating an essential condition which its founders had taken for granted. The United Nations was set up to deal with *future* threats to the peace which met a twofold definition: (1) situations which the great powers *unanimously* recognized as endangering international tranquility; and (2) those with which the great powers were prepared to deal on a basis of *collective action.* Quite obviously, disputes among the great powers themselves do not meet this test— a fact which as much as any other explains why the UN's influence in settling cold war disputes since 1945 has often been peripheral.

Another sphere in which the UN presupposed an established peace was in restoring defeated Axis countries to the family of nations. The founders deliberately divorced the UN Charter from the peace treaties for all defeated Axis powers, in order to escape the stigma attached to the League of Nations because of its intimate identification with what proved in some countries a highly unpopular peace settlement. The UN has taken no role in negotiating Axis peace treaties since World War II. One of the problems which lies at the heart of continued cold war tensions—the territorial division of Germany—remains an issue toward which the UN has made, and can make, little positive contribution, so long as the great powers remain divided.

Still another sphere in which the peace the UN was supposed to safeguard did not materialize was in relations between colonial countries and their possessions. Here again, the founders of the UN either did not anticipate postwar tensions over colonial questions, or else they counted on "great-power unanimity" to resolve problems which might arise. In any event, the UN was given no formal jurisdiction over the vast majority of pre-existing colonial relationships. Charter provisions pertaining to dependent areas, in the words of one commentary, applied only to a limited number of "territories administered under League mandates or for which at a later time trusteeship agreements might be negotiated."[10]

Immediately after the war, the UN did experience some success in dealing with colonial disputes, as in Indonesia, Syria, and Lebanon. But in many other critical instances, involving French colonialism in Indochina and North Africa, British colonialism in Kenya and Cyprus, and what can be correctly designated as Russian colonialism in Eastern Europe, the UN has been conspicuously unsuccessful in preserving the peace. Largely because peace did not exist in many of these areas at the time of the UN's establishment and throughout the years that followed, the UN possessed very few facilities for resolving these tensions.

Admittedly, the UN's record in dealing with colonial disputes, or with the consequences of colonial discords, has by no means been totally negative. By the late 1950s, two tendencies combined to inject the UN more than ever into colonial controversies: the increasing influence of the Afro–Asian world in the General Assembly, and the emergence of that organ as, in most important respects, the dominant agency of the United Nations. Newly independent states of Africa, the Middle East, and Asia have tended to take a "dynamic" view of the United Nations, leading them to favor greater reliance upon the UN, and to encourage a more liberal interpretation of the scope of its powers under the Charter, than the great powers often are willing to accept. Hence, such states have often converted the UN into a forum for denouncing Portuguese or French colonialism, for demanding a speedup in the "timetable" of independence for dependent societies, and for calling for outright UN intervention in disputes such as the Congo crisis of the early 1960s.

THE UN AND THE POSTWAR WORLD

Since our task is confined to describing and assessing problems of international organization as they bear upon the foreign policy of the United States, we cannot undertake a comprehensive treatment of the evolution and major activities of the United Nations after 1945.* Nevertheless, some familiarity with the UN's development and its efforts to cope with leading international issues is indispensable for our purpose.

The Security Council and Peacekeeping

Critics of the UN often overlook the solid record of accomplishment which it has amassed throughout the postwar period. Notable achievements have been the withdrawal of Soviet troops from Iran's northern provinces in 1946; termination of colonial rule over Syria and Lebanon in the same year; resolution of the conflict between Indonesia and the Netherlands in 1947–1949; successful adjudication of a dispute between Great Britain and Albania in 1947; assistance in preserving the sovereignty of Greece in 1946–1948; prevention of war between India and Pakistan over Kashmir from 1948 down to 1965; partial responsibility for ending the Berlin blockade in 1949; resistance to armed Communist attack against South Korea from 1950 to 1953, and supervision of the Korean truce; conclusion and subsequent supervision of

*Bibliography on the United Nations is copious. Aside from the *Official Records* of the UN's principal organs, described in the *United Nations Documents Index* issued monthly, a number of valuable summaries and commentaries exist. Official publications include the *Yearbook of the United Nations*, summarizing annual activities; the *United Nations Bulletin*, issued by-weekly; and the *Annual Report of the Secretary-General on the Work of the Organization*. These also cite relevant documentary materials for further reading in selected cases. Also valuable is the State Department's publication entitled *U.S. Participation in the United Nations*, issued annually, summarizing the UN's activities with emphasis upon America's role.

Helpful secondary studies include the summaries and articles appearing in the journal *International Organization*, which contains resumés of UN activities in its quarterly issues; publications in the Carnegie Foundation's series *International Conciliation*, which contains a number of illuminating studies on selected cases involving the UN; studies in the State Department's International Organization and Conference Series; and the summaries and essays in New York University's series *Annual Review of United Nations Affairs*.

an armistice between Israel and the Arab states in 1950, a major contribution in terminating the Suez crisis of 1956, and ongoing UN efforts after the Middle East crisis of 1967 to promote an Arab-Israeli truce; the prevention of anarchy and chaos —followed by the restoration of governmental authority—in the Congo, beginning in 1960; and following an upheaval in Cyprus in 1964, continuing efforts to prevent further conflicts between Greek and Turkish elements on that island. These are merely some of the better-known instances of more or less successful UN activities devoted to the maintenance of global peace and security. Less publicized activities have included sponsorship of disarmament negotiations among the major powers; efforts by the Secretary-General and other UN officials to reduce international tensions, especially among the cold war belligerents (the UN contribution in the resolution of the Cuban missile crisis of 1962, for example, was not inconsiderable); an expanding UN campaign (sometimes referred to as "the good war") to eliminate disease, malnutrition, poverty, illiteracy, and other conditions hindering human progress; and the UN's contributions in the promotion and protection of human rights. The United Nations of course also has experienced failures and innumerable cases in which it has not lived up to the expectations of its founders. We shall refer to its inadequacies in more detail at a later stage. At this point, our interest is confined to underscoring the fact that this international organization has a longer list of *successes* in achieving its principal goals than many commentators recognize.

While this list of accomplishments is not inconsiderable, it is also true that with regard to the most crucial international controversies affecting global peace and stability—conflicts involving the United States, the Soviet Union, and Communist China—the United Nations has experienced very little success since 1945. With a few notable exceptions (such as the UN's role in resolving the Berlin controversy in the late 1940s and producing a settlement of the Cuban missile crisis in 1962), the United Nations' contribution to reducing tensions between Washington and Moscow has been minimal. Indeed, the very effectiveness of the UN itself has been heavily dependent upon Soviet–American efforts (largely outside the United Nations) to resolve cold war discords and make "peaceful coexistence" a reality. Developments like de-Stalinization behind the Iron Curtain; recognition by America and Russia alike of the dangers inherent in a nuclear conflagration; anxiety by both countries concerning the behavior and intentions of Communist China; growing concern in the American and Soviet societies with urgent internal problems—these have done more to lower the temperature of the cold war than debates within the UN Security Council or resolutions passed by the General Assembly. If UN deliberations seldom found the United States and the Soviet Union fully in agreement, on a number of issues the lack of forceful opposition by Washington or Moscow permitted the Security Council to adopt and pursue a course of action.

Communist China of course does not belong to the United Nations. Ever since the late 1940s down to the early 1970s, the United States has successfully opposed Red China's admission to the organization.* Considering the fact that the United Nations (again responding to American initiative) branded Communist China an "aggressor" in the Korean War, Peking's admiration for the organization has not been high. The Communist government of China has demonstrated little active interest in joining the United Nations and has rejected the idea outright as long as Nationalist China is represented in it.[11]

As long as cold war antagonisms remained intense, the UN Security Council was largely immobilized as an instrument for maintaining international peace. Time and again, Soviet vetos prevented Council action in major global disputes; a steady barrage of Russian nyet's rendered this UN organ increasingly impotent. The United States did not formally exercise a veto in the Security Council until 1970 (when it voted against proposed UN sanctions against Southern Rhodesia). Yet there was always the reality of what was often called America's "hidden veto." The known opposition of the United States to a proposal before the Security Council was frequently influential enough to prevent its adoption (or sometimes even its discussion) by the members. The hidden veto derived from several sources. Members of the UN were usually realistic enough to know that Washington's opposition was likely to sway other nations who sought to maintain the good will of the United States; in the light of the fact that the United States customarily contributed up to 40 percent of the budget for many UN operations, measures adopted by the organization in the absence of American support would have little chance of being implemented; the Congo crisis of the early 1960s made it clear that other industrialized nations were seldom prepared to supply the funds and resources required

to make the application of UN measures effective. In brief, whether the United States exercised its veto or not, America's position toward proposals before the Security Council was often crucial in determining the outcome.[12]

Two developments during the 1960s tended to revitalize somewhat the influence of the Security Council and to save the organ from what had earlier seemed certain oblivion. One of these was the reorganization of the council, which became effective on August 31, 1965. In response to the demands of the new Afro–Asian members of the United Nations, the General Assembly approved a revision of the UN Charter, expanding the membership on the Security Council from eleven to fifteen states; the four new representatives served as nonpermanent members on a rotating basis, according to a formula designed to give the Afro–Asian nations a greater voice in Security Council deliberations.*

The second (and probably much more influential) development was the relaxation of Soviet–American tensions that had become evident by the 1960s. A number of forces—most crucially, perhaps, an evident desire in Washington and Moscow alike to avoid the hazards of nuclear war—produced a de-escalation in the cold war. Cold war animosities of course had not entirely disappeared; global armaments were still being stockpiled and very little progress had been achieved (as we shall see later in the chapter) in stopping the armaments spiral; nor had ideological discords between the two leading cold war adversaries come to an end. The Soviet Union's ruthless suppression of freedom in Czechslovakia in 1968 revived anxieties in the West concerning the security of the free world. Yet cold war recriminations had unquestionably been reduced. America and Russia found themselves increasingly the target of Chinese hostility. The Nuclear Test Ban Treaty of 1963 (which Red China vocally denounced), for example, underscored the common interests of Russia and America in reducing the risks of global war. Even during the Vietnam War, Soviet–American relations (as the Chinese government frequently pointed out) were not unduly strained. In some areas (Africa was a prime example), Washington was largely content to keep its

---

*Technically, it should be noted, the question of Red China's membership in the UN is not one of "admission": China already belongs to the UN and is recognized as one of the "permanent members" on the Security Council. The issue is, therefore, more accurately one of "representation." Which government—Peking or Nationalist China on Formosa (Taiwan)—is entitled to China's place? Neither government has been willing to accept a so-called "two Chinas" formula, whereby both countries would be represented in the UN. In fact, Peking has repeatedly rejected this proposal. By the early 1970s, Sino–American relations were improving; American officials were less adamant about Red China's participation in the UN. Yet, the question of what to "do" with Nationalist China remained unresolved.

*Down to 1965, a "gentlemen's agreement" among the members of the UN had distributed the nonpermanent seats on the Council as follows: two seats for Latin America; one each for a member of the British Commonwealth, for the Middle East, for Western Europe, and for Eastern Europe. Under the new formula, the scheme was: five seats for Afro–Asian nations; two for Latin America; one for Eastern Europe; and two for Western Europe and other areas. No change, it should be noted, was made in the *voting privileges* of the members; the permanent members still exercised the power of veto in the Security Council. See William L. Tung, *International Organization Under the United Nations System* (New York: Thomas Y. Crowell, 1969), pp. 61–62.

own involvement to a minimum, provided that Moscow did the same; Soviet policy-makers showed no desire to change this understanding. The existence of at least a limited cold war *détente* held out the possibility that the Security Council could once more become an influential UN organ. Althouth its efforts to date appear to have achieved little, the UN Security Council (along with the General Assembly) involved itself actively in the attempt to restore stability to the Middle East, following the eruption of new violence in that region in 1967.* Conversely, throughout the Vietnam War, despite efforts by the United States to place the matter before the Security Council, the United Nations was able to play virtually no role in resolving the conflict in Southeast Asia.[13]

Based on the *results* it has been able to obtain in reducing international conflicts, the revival of the Security Council may thus be more apparent than real. This may of course be a misleading standard by which to judge the organ's effectiveness. The Security Council now *functions;* it has not been totally abandoned as an instrument of futility; criticisms of the council by the Afro–Asian nations (who often charged that it was an instrument of great-power domination over smaller states) have declined, as these nations have been given a larger voice in its proceedings; the fact that both Russia and America are willing to exert their influence *through* the United Nations (as well of course as outside it) in an effort to stabilize the Middle East greatly enhances the prestige and perhaps the long-run effectiveness of the United Nations. Certainly the United Nations would seem to have an unpromising future *without* the Security Council or a comparable organ. That a revived Security Council has not been able to resolve intractable global disputes like the Vietnam War or the crisis in the Middle East may simply underscore the fact that, at this stage in history, the concept of international organization per se still faces a number of formidable obstacles. At best, the ability of the UN Security Council to eliminate threats to international peace is likely to be a very arduous and discouragingly slow quest.

*Summarizing prolonged UN efforts to find a formula for peace in the strife-torn Middle East, one commentator describes the climax of Security Council deliberations as follows: "The President of the Council called for a vote on the British draft. A tense moment of silence followed. Then all fifteen representatives at the Council raised their hands to signify approval. The British text had been adopted unanimously. Thus ended the long, precarious, and hitherto uncertain search for a widely based consensus on the Middle East crisis." For an informative treatment of UN activity in this crisis, see Arthur Lall, *The UN and the Middle East Crisis, 1967* (New York: Columbia University Press, 1968); the above quotation is from p. 263; the text of this important Security Council resolution may be found in Appendix 23, pp. 309–310.

A New Role for the General Assembly

Contemporaneous with the decline of the Security Council during the 1950s and early 1960s was the transformation of the General Assembly. For several years, the General Assembly was—and for certain purposes it remains—the most influential organ of the United Nations. Our discussion has already called attention to attempts in the Charter to distinguish rather sharply between the functions of the Council and the Assembly, assigning primary responsibility to the former for dealing with issues affecting international peace and security. The Assembly, on the other hand, as specified in Article 10 of the Charter, may discuss any questions or any matters within the scope of the present Charter or relating to the powers and functions of any organs provided for in the present Charter, and, except as provided in Article 12 [prohibiting the Assembly from making recommendations on issues pending before the Security Council], may make recommendations to the Members of the United Nations or to the Security Council or to both on any such questions or matters.

Save for questions directly pertaining to peace and security, therefore, the founders intended that the General Assembly should possess very broad powers and that it should deal with sundry "indirect" and long-range causes of international instability. However, the Assembly is limited to "making recommendations" on matters within its jurisdiction.

Founded upon the principle of the equality of all members, the General Assembly was to be a great international forum in which countries large and small would have an opportunity to discuss any subject within the purview of the Charter. Military behemoths and pygmies alike were given an equal voice and an equal vote. At San Francisco, the United States had joined with the small states in demanding broad powers and equality of voting in the Assembly. One of the crises at the Conference had come when Soviet Russia refused to accept such a conception, only to give way in time to avert a total impasse.[14] A significant advance was made over the Assembly of the League of Nations, where unanimity was required for decisions, by the Charter provision that the Assembly could make decisions on an "important matter" by a two-thirds majority and on less important questions by a simple majority (Article 18). Apprehensive lest some of the smaller states lead the Assembly to discuss questions not properly within the competence of the United Nations, the American delegation at San Francisco took the initiative in inserting the Charter provision already cited (Article 2, Section 7) prohibiting *all* organs of the UN from intervening in matters which were "essentially within the domestic jurisdiction of any state."[15]

As cold war antagonisms increasingly paralyzed the Security Council, the General Assembly began to emerge as the authoritative voice of the United Nations. A critical period was 1947–1948, when the General Assembly voted to partition the strife-torn land of Palestine into separate Jewish and Arab states and was called upon to deal with the violence which this act precipitated. After the Communist attempt to gain control over Greece in 1946–1948, the United States took the initiative in converting the Assembly into the UN's primary organ for dealing with political tensions and possible causes of war.

An important evolutionary step was the American-sponsored "interim assembly" plan introduced in 1947, whereby an interim committee could deal with inflammable international issues between sessions of the Assembly.[16] This was merely the forerunner of a much more sweeping transformation of the Assembly's powers. That step was the American-initiated "Uniting for Peace" resolution, presented in the fall of 1950 and passed by the General Assembly on November 3. Carefully taking note of the Security Council's inability to discharge its primary obligations under the Charter, the resolution observed that this did not "relieve Member States of their obligations or the United Nations of its responsibility under the Charter to maintain international peace and security." The resolution therefore provided that when the Security Council was deadlocked or failed to act "where there appears to be a threat to the peace," then the General Assembly

shall consider the matter immediately with a view to making appropriate recommendations to Members for collective measures, including in the case of a breach of the peace or act of aggression the use of armed force when necessary, to maintain or restore international peace and security.

If the Assembly were not in session when a threat to the peace occurred, it could meet in emergency special session within 24 hours.[17]

When the Assembly had to deal with successive crises in Egypt and Hungary in 1956, the "Uniting For Peace" resolution was put into effect for the first time. It was of no avail in attempting to terminate Soviet oppression of the Hungarian revolutionary movement. This proved once again that the Assembly, where there is no veto, was no more successful than the Security Council in dealing with issues on which one of the world's two power giants refused to accept UN directives.[18] The Assembly debates on the Suez dispute in the same period left no doubt that public opinion the world over was opposed to the Anglo–French and Israeli invasions of Egypt. As a result of negotiations which took place both inside and outside the UN, these countries agreed to withdraw their troops. For the first time in history, a "United

Nations Emergency Force," consisting of military contingents from ten member states, was created. Its task was to patrol the always tense Israeli–Egyptian frontier and to prevent further hostilities from erupting between these countries. UNEF was withdrawn at the request of the Egyptian government in 1967. Whatever other results the Suez crisis of 1956 may have had, one of them was to enhance the prestige of the United Nations and to revivify its sometimes waning fortunes. By turning to the General Assembly in this crisis, it was the United States as much as any other country which took the lead in giving the UN responsibility for restoring stability to the Middle East.[19]

Yet, perhaps somewhat to the surprise of many students of international organization, the Congo crisis that erupted in 1960 and continued for many months thereafter, demonstrated that the UN Security Council was not totally moribund. For it was under Security Council auspices that the UN operations in the Congo (ONUC) were carried out. After the crisis had continued for several months, the General Assembly also took cognizance of the question and passed resolutions seeking to clarify the UN's role in the country. Debate on the floor of the Assembly over the activities of ONUC became heated and intense. Still, technically, it was the Security Council that supervised UN activities in this controversy.*

Although the 1960s witnessed a resurgence in the role of the UN Security Council, and a corresponding decline in the influence of the Assembly on matters related to global peace and security, the latter continued to play a forceful part in the attempt to make the United Nations a dynamic organization. Except for questions directly affecting world peace, the General Assembly remained perhaps the UN's most influential forum. It was the General Assembly, for example, which initiated United Nations concern about the problem of *apartheid* in South Africa and which increasingly called for a "confrontation" with the white-dominated government of that country—a cause which the Security Council began to support in the 1960s. Again, pressure came mainly from the General Assembly upon Spain and Portugal to liquidate their colonial empires, chiefly in Africa. The General Assembly also took the lead (and in time it was joined by the Security Council) in expressing opposition to the declaration of independence by the white-controlled government of Southern Rhodesia on November 11, 1965; thereafter, it was principally the General Assembly which demanded the application of sanctions to

*For a detailed treatment of UN handling of the Congo crisis, see Stanley Hoffman, "In Search of a Thread: The U.N. in the Congo Labyrinth," in Norman J. Padelford and Rupert Emerson, eds., *Africa and World Order* (New York: Praeger, 1963), pp. 63–94; and Colin Legum, *Congo Disaster* (Baltimore: Penguin, 1961).

compel Rhodesia to change its racist policies. In the Middle East, aid to Palestinian refugees has been carried out under the authority of the General Assembly. Debates within the General Assembly were to a major degree responsible for efforts (like the Nuclear Test-Ban Treaty of 1963 and the Treaty on the Nonproliferation of Nuclear Weapons in 1968) to reduce the threat of nuclear destruction. The General Assembly's Committee on the Peaceful Uses of Outer Space has endeavored to confine the "space race" to nonmilitary competition among America, Russia, and other advanced nations. By the late 1960s, the General Assembly had assumed the initiative in undertaking studies of environmental problems throughout the world and alerting mankind to the dangers threatening its environment. The First UN "Decade of Development," launched in 1960, as well as the Second Decade of Development, initiated in 1970, were undertaken under the auspices of the General Assembly. These activities are suggestive of the great importance and wide range of responsibilities falling within the General Assembly's jurisdiction.[20]

From the perspective of American diplomatic interests, these changes in the role of the General Assembly posed a number of policy dilemmas, some of which by the 1960s had induced a "crisis of confidence" in the United Nations among the American people and their leaders. Ever since 1945, the United States had been in the main an enthusiastic supporter of the United Nations. Without substantial financial contributions from the United States, for example, many UN operations would have been impossible; and the future of the organization itself might be in great (or greater) jeopardy. American initiative was in large part responsible for enhancing the powers of the General Assembly, a process which, as we have noted, began with the Uniting for Peace Resolution of 1950. Without that de facto Charter revision, the UN might rapidly have been relegated to the sidelines of history.

It was no less true that, as time passed, official and public opinion in the United States began to exhibit deep apprehension about tendencies in the United Nations, especially within the General Assembly. During the 1960s, for example, several representatives and senators were outspokenly critical of America's "reliance" upon the United Nations to achieve American foreign policy goals. For by the mid-1960s, the UN General Assembly (where the principle of "one nation, one vote" is followed) was theoretically controlled by nations *outside the West*. Between them, the Afro–Asian and Latin American states held the preponderance of political power. In voting strength (if in few other respects), America's vote "counted" for no more than Zambia's or Kuwait's. From 13 members when the UN was founded in 1945, the Afro–Asian nations had expanded their represen-

tation in the United Nations to 68 by the beginning of the 1970s. This total meant that the UN General Assembly was now theoretically controlled by an Afro–Asian majority which (when many of the 24 Latin American states, and 10 Marxist nations joined with it) gave the countries outside the West a preponderance of voting strength in this world forum. The age of colonialism had of course largely come to an end; but as several remaining colonial dependencies (such as Portugal's African colonies) acquired their independence, Afro–Asian strength in the UN would be augmented further.

America and the UN's "Swirling Majorities"

Insofar as it affected American diplomatic interests and behavior, this highly significant change in the composition of the United Nations could be interpreted on two levels: as primarily *a theoretical and potential problem* and as *an actual and immediate problem* inimical to American interests. On the surface, there was no question but that the United States and the Western community generally had found their positions *weakened* by the influx of Afro–Asian members to the United Nations. If countries like Canada, Australia, New Zealand, and Japan were included, the "Western bloc" comprised less than one-fifth of total UN membership. Although they did not comprise the smallest voting group within the UN (with 10 members, the Marxist group had that distinction), the Western nations numbered less than half as many as the Afro–Asian group and less than one-third of the combined Afro–Asian and Latin American membership. Several years ago, Secretary of State Dean Rusk calculated that "Theoretically, a two-thirds majority of the General Assembly would now be formed by nations with only 10 percent of the world's population, or who contribute, altogether, 5 percent of the assessed budget" of the international organization.[21] This prospect gave rise to growing anxiety in the West about the "swirling majorities" which now dominated UN proceedings, rendering that organization increasingly irresponsible and oblivious to American interest. It was easy to demonstrate mathematically that the United States and its cold war allies had lost control of the United Nations to a group of nations which were, at best, indifferent to American viewpoints or, at worst, directly and indirectly supporting the goals of Moscow and Peking. The United States still possessed its power of veto in the UN Security Council; but as we have already observed, that body was being eclipsed by the General Assembly as the real "voice" of the United Nations. Undeniably, the earlier period—when Washington could count fairly regularly upon an automatic majority to support its proposals in the UN—had ended; it was doubtful that it would ever be restored.

What were the *actual* implications of this change in the nature of the United Nations? Did this transformation signify that the UN General Assembly had become an instrument of anti-Americanism and anti-Westernism? Ought it to be supposed that the UN's swirling majorities were congenitally in conflict with American diplomatic purposes? Was the Soviet Union automatically the beneficiary of these changes? Would the United States now be compelled (as in efforts to terminate the Vietnam War) to work *outside* the United Nations to achieve its objectives? The general answer to these questions was negative: With some exceptions (and we shall take note of them below), the UN had *not* in fact been converted into an instrument which routinely disregarded American viewpoints, and in which an "irresponsible" Afro–Asian majority continually put the United States on the defensive (often with the connivance of the Communist bloc). At the same time that he depicted how a possible UN majority could be formed contrary to America's interests, Secretary of State Rusk also pointed out: "In practice, of course, this does not happen; and I do not share the dread expressed by some that the General Assembly will be taken over by its 'swirling majorities.' "[22] Even earlier, America's ambassador to the UN, Adlai E. Stevenson, commented at length on the power exercised by the newly independent nations within the United Nations:

There is an illusion in some quarters that the so-called "Afro–Asian bloc" always votes with the Soviet Union against the so-called "Western bloc." This is three mistakes in one, since, in the first place, neither the Afro–Asians nor, in the second place, the Western nations vote mechanically as blocs in the United Nations—and as long as each member is free to think for itself they never will.

Furthermore, the record abundantly proves that the members from Africa and Asia have not been afraid to find themselves voting on the same side as the United States; indeed, on great issues they have been doing so very often.

The Soviets do the best they can to pit Africa and Asia against the West, and to side with the Africans and Asians. And one of the great untold stories of the United Nations—a story which I hope will one day be told in full—is the failure of this divisive strategy.[23]

With regard to the vast majority of issues arising before the United Nations, these earlier judgments by American officials have *not* been outmoded by events. Thus far, the Afro–Asian and Latin American majority in the UN has not been converted into a kind of anti-Western steamroller; much less has it become an instrument for achieving Moscow's diplomatic aims. For a number of fundamental reasons, the *potential* majority formed by the emerging nations has seldom materialized into an *actual* majority adverse to America's interests. A major reason why this has not happened is that, for most voting purposes, the Afro–Asian states *do not comprise a monolithic voting bloc;* the bloc is even less unified when the Latin American nations are included within it. Numerous studies of voting behavior in the UN General Assembly underscore the *heterogeneity* prevailing among the members of this potential UN majority. Some Afro–Asian states are large, and others are very small; some have a good prospect of making rapid economic progress, and some have little or none; some subscribe to democratic principles of government (almost always, as *they* define these principles), while others are governed by military elites, monarchial institutions, or other nondemocratic systems; some have very close ties with the West, others with members of the Communist bloc, while still others endeavor to maintain links with both camps; some Afro–Asian nations are involved in border controversies or other quarrels with each other; some advocate various forms of regional cooperation, while others do not. Many other differences might be cited, but these are sufficient to make the point that the so-called Afro–Asian "bloc" is as internally fragmented (on some issues, more so) than any other group within the United Nations.[24] Moreover, with the passage of time, the differences among these nations will probably *become more pronounced.*

Other factors have also prevented the UN's non-Western majority from becoming a force congenitally inimical to American diplomatic interests. One of these is the fact that, on a number of important issues arising before the UN, the United States has basically supported many proposals advocated by the Afro–Asian and Latin American nations, such as efforts to reduce the dangers of nuclear war and to curb unchecked population growth. On major political issues, such as efforts to stabilize the Middle East, Washington has favored a dynamic role for the United Nations. It cannot be assumed, in other words, that America and the newly independent nations are always on opposite sides of important issues with which the United Nations is concerned. Another inhibiting factor restraining formation of an "irresponsible" UN majority is awareness by most governments throughout the Afro–Asian world *that effective action by the UN demands the support and concurrence of the industrialized nations.* Whether the issue is a proposed peace-keeping operation in a crisis area, or attempts to reduce the level of global armaments, or programs to meet the economic needs of the developing nations, the leaders of the Afro–Asian governments are cognizant that successful implementation of their proposals is dependent upon the cooperation of the wealthier nations of the world. The United Nations is not a world government; it possesses no power to tax its members; in all spheres of its operations, it requires the *voluntary compliance* of its members. As a group, the newly independent nations are very "UN oriented." They seek to *maximize* the UN's influence in global affairs and to broaden its jurisdiction; they are mindful that—far more than most nations in the West and the Communist zone—they "need" the UN and are the primary beneficiaries of its programs. Their officials at the UN and at home are, in most cases, reluctant to precipitate a crisis of confidence in America, Western Europe, or elsewhere, the net result of which might well be to *weaken* the UN's influence and raise substantial questions about its future.

There are, however, a few areas of UN activity in which, from the American point of view, the danger of irresponsible UN action is real, rather than merely potential. Admittedly, America has found itself at odds with the Afro–Asian members in recent years, particularly in regard to three issues. Two of them, although basically distinct, are closely related: the problem of existing colonial empires and the problem of officially sponsored programs of racial discrimination. Africa is the principal locale for both of these issues. Portugal maintains the largest colonial enclave remaining on the globe; since Southern Rhodesia's declaration of independence from Great Britain is not "recognized" by black Africa, its status might also be regarded as a colonial question; similarly, the position of Southwest Africa (formally annexed by the former mandate power, South Africa) is also viewed as involving colonialism. All three of these countries are looked upon by black African nations as societies which sponsor or condone racial discrimination against their black majorities. The third problem involving conflict between the United States and the Afro–Asian (joined by Latin American) nations in the UN is related to efforts by the developing nations to secure trade concessions, economic assistance, and other forms of aid from the industrialized countries.

To a greater degree than any other international issue concerning the United Nations in recent years, the interrelated questions of colonialism and racism on the African continent epitomize the changes occurring within the UN since 1945. The African nations—the largest regional group represented in the UN, with over half of the total Afro–Asian membership in 1970—are understandably most directly concerned with colonial and racial issues. Indeed, one African leader after another has stated that these issues *outrank all other global problems* in terms of their urgent concern for Africans. If Africans regard themselves as "nonaligned" in the cold war, they are very much "aligned" on the side of anticolonialism and in opposition to racial discrimination; these issues serve as yardsticks whereby Africans measure the concern of America or other nations

outside the continent with Africa's welfare. For Africans, to the extent that the United States supports anticolonial and antiracial causes, it confirms its belief in ideals like freedom, independence, and self-determination; to the extent that it fails to join with Africans against colonial and racial oppression, America contradicts its professed belief in democracy and undermines its claim as leader of the "free world" against political oppression.[25] On these questions, there *is* a high degree of unity among the Afro–Asian members of the United Nations—so much so as to give the term "Afro–Asian bloc" a substantial degree of validity.[26] In each annual session, the UN General Assembly can now be counted upon to pass measures directed against colonial administrations and against governments practising racial discrimination. Invariably, the 10 votes cast by the Soviet Union and the smaller Marxist nations re-enforce the Afro–Asian majority on such questions. Since the mid-1950s, the Kremlin has made a concerted effort to win the good will of nations throughout the third world; one of its most effective tactics has been to take a leading role inside and outside the UN in assaults against existing colonial structures and racist regimes. Although many Africans have become increasingly aware that racial discrimination in reality exists behind the Iron Curtain, Moscow's consistent identification with African aspirations has undeniably enhanced its image and influence outside the West.

The dual problems of colonialism and racial injustice have posed real dilemmas for American policy-makers. Several aspects of the matter have been especially troublesome; and it cannot be claimed that even now American policy has escaped these difficulties. One dimension of the problem is the *constitutional issue* arising under the UN Charter from the attempt of Afro–Asian nations to conduct a progressively more militant campaign of confrontation against Portugal, Southern Rhodesia, and South Africa. The policies of these governments, a majority of UN members are convinced, pose a "threat to the peace," within the meaning of Article I, Section 1 of the Charter; this fact confers jurisdiction upon the United Nations. Indeed, once it is determined that the existence of Portugal's colonial system is a "threat to the peace" (and Afro–Asian spokesmen regard colonialism as a form of aggression against subject peoples), the United Nations *must* endeavor to deal with the matter. By contrast, the United States—joined by several of its allies in Western Europe and, needless to say Portugal, Southern Rhodesia, and South Africa—has taken the position that colonialism and racial discrimination are not per se "threats to the peace," as understood by Charter definitions of that term. The fact that black Africans, along with many Americans, find colonial and racial oppression abhorrent does not, in Washington's view, necessarily confer legal jurisdiction upon the United Nations to deal with colonial and racial disputes. In one instance after another, American officials have cited the Charter provision (Article II, Section 7) prohibiting the UN from intervening "in matters which are essentially within the domestic jurisdiction of any state. . . ." In view of the level of racial strife within the American society itself, spokesmen for the United States were not unmindful that the problem of racial violence within their own country might in the future be put on the agenda of the UN General Assembly! Aside from that concern, legitimate differences of opinion could of course exist concerning the scope of the UN's proper authority and the precise meaning of Charter provisions. On this issue, Washington has opposed the kind of maximalist conception of the UN favored by the Afro–Asian majority.

In addition to the constitutional questions involved, American policy-makers have been confronted with the question of *what kind* of action by the United Nations best contributes to the resolution of racial tensions in South Africa, Southern Rhodesia, and other countries. Down to the early 1960s, American officials at the UN usually limited themselves to criticisms of racial and colonial injustice and to expressions of hope that the governments of Portugal, Southern Rhodesia, and South Africa would moderate their policies in response to rising criticism by the world community. In the Afro–Asian view, American leadership on colonial and racial issues was half-hearted and ineffectual, reflecting little genuine appreciation of the gravity of these problems. Then in 1960, a historic reversal of American policy occurred under President John F. Kennedy, who made intensive efforts to improve the American image in Africa. For the first time, America's UN delegation voted *for* a General Assembly resolution condemning Portuguese colonial policies and calling upon Lisbon to comply with earlier resolutions demanding the liquidation of colonial empires; in fact, in concert with African delegates, American officials participated in drafting this resolution (designed in part to head off a more polemical Soviet resolution on the subject).[27] This shift in American policy was widely acclaimed by nations outside the West: Finally, the United States was prepared to support the cause of anticolonialism, even if it meant voting against a military ally.[28]

Much of the good will which accrued to the United States from this policy shift was largely dissipated in the years ahead, as the Afro–Asian confrontation with governments practicing colonialism and racism became increasingly militant and uncompromising. The tone of the General Assembly resolutions become progressively sharper, as the Afro–Asian minority demanded sanctions (and some called for the application of military force) against these governments. The UN Security Council first invoked sanctions against Southern Rhodesia in 1965; each year, the Afro–Asian nations called for a tightening of these measures and urged Great Britain to use military force against its erstwhile colony, whose declaration of independence was confirmed by a referendum of Rhodesia's white citizens on June 20, 1969. The United States cast its first veto in the UN Security Council early in 1970, in opposing further coercive steps against Rhodesia.[29]

Afro–Asian indignation, however, has reached its apex against South Africa—the epitome of white racism against a black majority. The question of racial discrimination in South Africa was one of the first questions placed on the agenda of the UN General Assembly. Intense UN concern with the question dates from around 1960, after most black African nations had received their independence. By 1964, the UN Security Council had called for an arms embargo against the country; before and after this date, the General Assembly demanded coercive measures (such as economic and diplomatic boycotts) against South Africa by the entire international community.

The American position on the South African question has won few friends for the United States throughout the Afro–Asian world.* Inside and outside the United Nations, American officials have made clear their opposition to *apartheid*, South Africa's policy of racial separation. In 1966, President Johnson declared that "the United States cannot, therefore, condone the perpetuation of racial or political injustice anywhere in the world."[30] Early in his administration, President Richard M. Nixon reiterated America's view on racial injustice. Regarding racial tensions in southern Africa, Nixon declared that "there is no question of the United States condoning, or acquiescing in, the racial policies of the white-ruled regimes. For moral as well as historical reasons, the United States stands firmly for the principles of racial equality and self-determination."[31]

Yet the United States has been *unwilling* to join the Afro–Asian members of the UN in applying sanctions against South Africa or leading a confrontation against it. American officials were fully aware, for example, that the armed forces of South Africa were superior to those of all the black African nations *combined*. After its experience in Vietnam, the United States had no inclination to assume a military commitment for the liberation of South Africa from white rule. American spokesmen, as we have noted, also expressed genuine doubt about the legality of sanctions against South Africa under the UN Charter; offensive as it might be to outsiders, the country's *apartheid* policy was a "threat to the peace" only because other coun-

---

*The problem of *apartheid* in South Africa was discussed at length in Chapter 11, where the American government's views toward the issue, and its assessment of various approaches to it, were analyzed.

tries threatened to use violent measures against the South African government. Based upon the evidence thus far, American officials had little confidence that efforts to apply forceful measures against South Africa could be implemented *effectively*. Many of the black African nations (joined by several in the Marxist zone) continued to trade with South Africa, in defiance of UN resolutions; and some African countries had *expanded* their economic and commercial ties with South Africa in recent years.[32]

American spokesmen have also expressed grave doubts (on the dubious assumption that sanctions could be effectively applied) whether this was the most promising method of bringing about a liberalization of South Africa's internal policies. On the contrary, to the extent that South Africa was converted into a kind of "white fortress," whose white elite was more and more motivated by a seige mentality, it was a reasonable likelihood that the regime would become *more oppressive* than ever; as economic sanctions began to pinch the South African economy, in time millions of blacks would suffer deprivations. Likening the problem of South Africa to that presented earlier by Stalinist Russia, one former American official has asserted that the only course offering hope for a fundamental change in the government's policies was to do *exactly the opposite* of what the UN's Afro–Asian majority proposed. This was to preserve rapport with the white-ruled government of South Africa and to keep open channels of communication with it; to *maximize* South Africa's contacts with the outside world, permitting the "winds of change" to bring new ideas into the country; to *reduce* apprehensions which obviously motivated the country's white community; to use every conceivable occasion for trying to *persuade* South Africa to modify its policies; and to hope that, over the course of time, the white minority would gradually be induced to give the nonwhite majority a greater share in political and economic decision-making. Groups advocating the use of force against South Africa, one former American diplomatic official is convinced, are "pursuing a self-defeating strategy" which (if it has any impact upon white attitudes in South Africa at all) is likely to render a solution of the problem more remote than ever.[33] Shortly after he entered the White House, President Nixon (under massive public pressure to reduce America's global commitments) declared that America did not believe "that progressive change in southern Africa is furthered by force"; instead, violence and counterviolence will "only make more difficult the task of those on both sides working for progress on the racial question."[34]

Two points can be made with reasonable certainty about America's position with regard to UN action on colonial and racial issues. America's stand will probably continue to be unacceptable to the Afro–Asian nations and will serve as a contentious question in America's relations with the third world. And, in the light of America's prolonged involvement in Southeast Asia, there seems very little prospect that the United States will be willing to play the kind of leading role in removing colonial and racial injustices which a majority of the members of the United Nations desire.

Economic and Social Activities

Sometimes overshadowed by the activities of the United Nations in peace and security matters are the myriad operations carried on by the UN in economic and social affairs touching hundreds of millions of people. An earlier portion of the chapter called attention to the fact that, to conciliate the small states, provisions for a strengthened Economic and Social Council were added to the Charter at San Francisco. The Economic and Social Council consists of 27 members elected by the General Assembly, each member serving for three years. As defined in Article 62, its province is sweeping, permitting it to "make or initiate studies and reports" relating to "international economic, social, cultural, educational, health, and related matters"; to "make recommendations . . . to the General Assembly, to the Members of the United Nations, and to the specialized agencies"; and to "make recommendations for the purpose of promoting respect for, and observance of, human rights and fundamental freedoms for all."

Under the Economic and Social Council are eight functional commissions and three regional bureaus. In addition, it has several "operating bodies" like the UN International Children's Emergency Fund (UNICEF), the UN Relief and Works Agency for Palestine Refugees, and the UN Korean Reconstruction Agency. There are also 11 semiautonomous "specialized agencies," which were enumerated earlier in this chapter. Measured by the volume and quality of studies and publications turned out, the subsidiary organs of the Economic and Social Council have done a staggering and immensely valuable job. Frequent publications include a *World Economic Report, Review of International Commodity Problems, Statistical Yearbook, Demographic Yearbook, and Yearbook of International Trade*, to list merely a few titles from among the hundreds of comprehensive and specialized studies released so far.

The activities of ECOSOC are among the least publicized, but in terms of promoting human welfare the most worthwhile, of all UN operations. Functioning under the over-all supervision of the General Assembly, ECOSOC is engaged in what has been described as "the good war" on many fronts throughout the world. The great preponderance of the UN's total staff in fact is engaged in social, economic, and administrative (rather

than political) operations.[35] Whether it is expanding the frontiers of scientific knowledge; or discovering new sources of energy for the world's
population; or expanding the world's supply of
fresh water and making it available to societies
where water is scarce; or promoting regional
development schemes like the Mekong River
project in Southeast Asia; or, through the efforts of
the World Health Organization and other agencies, engaging in programs to eliminate diseases
like tuberculosis, smallpox, and leprosy; or seeking
to provide adequate housing for slum dwellers—
in these and countless other ways, the United Nations carries on a worldwide campaign for human
betterment.[36] Most of these programs are doubtless estimable and beneficial. Yet, as one student
of international organization has observed: ". . .
[I]t is extremely difficult to prove that the economic and social activities . . . of the United Nations' system have contributed, in a tangible
fashion, to an atmosphere of co-operation in the
world." In terms of what is often regarded as the
primary purpose of these activities—eliminating
the long-range and "indirect" causes of war and
misunderstanding among nations—this dimension of the UN's operations "represents only a
small beginning toward a goal of universal contact
and understanding among all peoples."[37]

The UN and the Struggle for Modernization

By the 1960s, the United Nations had become actively involved in the quest which was at the forefront of concern for nearly all societies outside the
West: the process of national economic development and modernization. This goal of course embraced many diverse activities and programs, by
the United Nations, by the industrialized nations,
and by the less developed nations, themselves.
Economic development actually began to receive
the attention of the United Nations as early as
1949, when the Expanded Program of Technical
Assistance (EPTA) was created, as an outgrowth of
President Harry Truman's Point Four program
of assistance to needy societies. EPTA supplied
primarily *technical aid and advice* (as distinct
from grants or loans) to societies requesting its
services.[38] As the United Nations began more and
more to reflect the concerns of its growing Afro–
Asian membership, the demand for greatly expanded UN devlopment programs mounted in
intensity; EPTA's modest efforts, it became apparent, fell considerably short of satisfying it.

Accordingly, in 1959 the Special Fund for Economic Development (SUNFED) was established.
Its purpose was to facilitate the investment of outside capital in developing societies—a goal which
was again less ambitious than those many of its
Afro–Asian sponsors favored. In the face of evident reluctance by the United States, along with
several other industrialized nations, the poorer
members of the UN sought to make SUNFED
a new source of expanded foreign aid from
the wealthier countries. In the Afro–Asian view,
SUNFED was also a mechanism whereby foreign
aid recipients could exercise greater control over
the disposition of aid funds.[39]

EPTA and SUNFED are noteworthy for two
reasons. The latter particularly served as a catalyst, speeding up the process by which the UN
became heavily involved in the process of modernization outside the West. And in these two
early programs, the conflict which became
sharper with each passing year—between the
United States and other industrialized nations (including the Soviet Union) and the Afro–Asian
and Latin American majority in the UN—had already become noticeable. One former American
UN official has stated categorically that the
United States opposed SUNFED and comparable
schemes "precisely because large amounts of capital aid would be disbursed under circumstances
that would not assure the promotion of U.S. foreign-policy objectives."[40]

In response to the speech to the UN General
Assembly by President John F. Kennedy late in
1961, the 16th General Assembly launched the
first UN Decade of Development. Under this program, the proclaimed target was a 5 percent annual increase in the gross national products of the
less developed nations by 1970. The UN Decade
of Development did not (in contrast to what many
Afro–Asian members desired) serve as a substitute
for existing private and governmental foreign aid
programs; still less did it provide a substantial increase in available funds to finance development
schemes in needy societies. Rather it was intended mainly as a stimulus for expanding existing
aid programs, as a coordinating mechanism for
diverse efforts seeking to foster modernization,
and as a central source for issuing information and
reports on how well nations were achieving their
development aims.[41]

A detailed evaluation of the results attained by
the first UN Decade of Development is beyond
the scope of our inquiry. Chapter 14 called attention to the obstacles in the path of successful development for most societies outside the West;
evidence cited there indicated that the record
made by most of these societies during the 1960s
was mixed. A handful of countries made outstanding progress; the vast majority experienced successes as well as failures. For the less developed
societies as a whole, it had become apparent by
the mid-1960s (although most experts were aware
of it much earlier) that *several decades*—for a
number of countries, *several generations*—would
be required to bring about the kind of modernization and level of economic development most of
these societies sought. By some criteria (such as
per capita food production), many countries
throughout the Afro–Asian and Latin American

regions were either barely holding their own or retrogressing by the end of the decade.

Planning began, therefore, well before 1970 for the second UN Decade of Development. The basic objective—accelerating the economic growth and modernization of needy societies—was the same: On the premise that the population of the Afro–Asian and Latin American world would grow by an average of 2.5 percent annually, the program hoped to raise over-all economic output by 6 to 7 percent a year (or 3.5 to 4.5 percent a year on a per capita basis); this would permit the less developed societies to expand their savings by an average of 15–20 percent annually, to raise their export earnings by 7 to 8 percent a year, and to increase their industrial production by 8 to 9 percent annually. But under the second Decade of Development, considerable emphasis would also be given to improving the "quality of life" for populations living in economically primitive societies. To a greater extent than formerly, *social aspects* of development would receive priority, in an effort to avoid some of the adverse consequences of overly rapid industrial growth and urbanization. By the 1970s, for example, the problem of rapdily expanding *urban slums* had become a matter of deep concern for many governments from the Caribbean to the Philippines. The second development decade also emphasized the necessity for redistributing incomes within developing nations and creating new career and employment opportunities for youth (the group which, in many countries was experiencing rapid population growth and constituted one of the largest segments of the society).[42]

Debate within the preparatory committees planning the second UN Decade of Development indicated that, as in the past, major disagreements existed between the United States and other industrialized nations, on the one side, and the less developed countries, on the other side, concerning the desired scope of the program and the obligations which each category of nations was expected to assume for its implementation. As we observed in Chapter 14, by this period the United States was *reducing* its over-all foreign assistance to other governments. President Nixon's foreign aid budget request was the lowest which had come from the White House in many years. Although several industrialized nations (notably Australia, Canada, West Germany, and the Scandinavian countries) were willing to expand their contributions to UN development programs, there was no indication that the United States was prepared to do so. Nor did President Nixon's endorsement of greater reliance by the United States upon multilateral agencies for dispensing foreign aid envision any substantial increase in America's contribution to the needs of less developed societies.[43]

UNCTAD: North–South Confrontation

In some respects, the sharpest conflicts between the industrialized and the developing nations in recent years have occurred in the deliberations of the United Nations Conference on Trade and Development (UNCTAD). UNCTAD grew out of the largest international conference ever assembled, when more than 2000 delegates gathered at Geneva in 1964 to discuss problem of world trade.* Urged by the nations of the West to depend more heavily for their capital needs upon "trade, not aid," the developing nations sought ways to eliminate (or at least reduce) tariff and other barriers impeding their sales in foreign markets. To facilitate their rapid national development, many of these nations urged the West to grant *trade preferences* and other concessions which, for a period of several years, would allow the needy countries to compete successfully against established industries in the advanced countries.

The UNCTAD meeting at Geneva marked a watershed in modern international politics. There, for the first time, the familiar East–West or cold war encounter was overshadowed by a new conflict: the North–South confrontation between the industrialized nations (located for the most part in the Northern Hemisphere) and the developing nations (whose members were in the main situated in the Southern Hemisphere). The latter group included approximately two-thirds of the human race. At Geneva and later meetings of UNCTAD, a very old theme in international relations—the conflict between the "have" and the "have-not" nations—dominated the proceedings. In their attempt to gain major tariff and trade concessions from the advanced countries, the Afro–Asian and Latin American representatives agreed at Geneva to pursue a common strategy; in time, spokesmen for these nations formed what was called the Group of 77 to concert their policies. It is interesting to observe that (despite efforts by the Kremlin to convince nations belonging to this group otherwise), the Soviet Union and the smaller Marxist states of Europe were included among the advanced nations whose policies were believed to be inimical to societies in the Southern Hemisphere. One observer at the first UNCTAD meeting described Soviet Russia's anomalous position as being "rich in the eyes of

---

*The impetus for this conference came largely from the General Agreement on Tariffs and Trade (GATT), initially an organization to promote trade among the nations of the West. Established in 1948, GATT grew from 20 members to around 90 by the late 1960s. Although its deliberations had come more and more to be influenced by the developing nations, the new members still viewed GATT as an organization oriented toward (if not dominated by) the industrialized nations and responsive to their trade policies. See Philip E. Jacob and Alexine L. Atherton, *The Dynamics of International Organization* (Homewood, Ill.: Dorsey, 1965), pp. 456–458.

the poor, but not rich enough to have been interesting."[44] The Group of 77 was aware, in other words, that success in attaining their goals depended chiefly upon the positions of the United States and Western Europe.

Beginning with the Geneva assembly in 1964, the United States found itself continually on the defensive, as it faced the demands of the Group of 77 for a radical transformation of existing international trade policies. Ever since the 1930s, the United States had been committed to the principle of "reciprocal trade," the aim of which was to lower national tariffs and other trade barriers *on the basis of mutual concessions among the nations involved.* By definition, the reciprocal trade policy was at variance with the idea of preferential concessions to a single country or group of countries. This doctrine had been reaffirmed in the Trade Expansion Act of 1962, by which the President's authority to reduce tariffs (provided other countries did the same) was broadened. The developing nations complained, and with some measure of justification, that this act was intended primarily to expand trade between the United States and the members of the European Economic Community; other nations received minimum benefit from this liberalization of American trade policy; indeed, in the tariff negotiations which followed passage of this act, American and European negotiators devoted little attention to the impact of agreements reached upon the trading positions of countries outside the West. Some countries in this group now found it more difficult than ever to penetrate either the EEC or the American market. At the very time that American officials were calling upon governments south of the equator to rely upon "trade, not aid" to generate development capital, the terms of international trade were becoming more adverse than ever for needy societies! Throughout the world, this was unquestionably one major source of anti-American sentiment. To cite but one example, the Rockefeller Study Mission found that this was a major grievance against the United States in Latin America. The mission reported that "Trade policy is the central economic issue facing all Western Hemisphere nations." Its report to President Nixon in 1969 contained a number of recommendations designed to give the Latin American nations greater access to markets in the United States. Along with most Afro–Asian societies, the Latin American republics were exporters of primary products (food commodities, fibers, and industrial raw materials). Existing trade barriers discriminated against these products in the world market, and prices received for their export sales were *declining*, while the prices paid for imports from the advanced nations were *rising*. Under these conditions, even a significant expansion in exports would not necessarily produce an increase in *export earnings* from sales abroad. In fact, a number of these countries were experiencing progressively more acute balance-of-payments problems. Western insistence upon "trade, not aid," therefore, seemed unresponsive to the needs of the emerging nations and, failing a radical transformation of world trade policies, seemed to condemn them to a position of permanent economic inferiority.[45]

Failing to receive the kind of trade concessions they expected at the Geneva trade conference, the developing nations demanded new machinery and procedures under the jurisdiction of the United Nations to promote their objectives in international trade. At Geneva, and in the years which followed, the United States and many Western European nations resisted this demand; Washington preferred to work through GATT and other established machinery to liberalize existing trade restrictions. Moreover, the question of voting procedures in UNCTAD proved a highly contentious matter. Not unexpectedly, the Group of 77 favored the principle of "one nation, one vote" prevailing in the UN General Assembly. Yet in time most members of this group accepted a reality which applied to UNCTAD, as to all UN agencies: Effective decision-making in an international organization required *consensus*, particularly since the wealthier nations were not prepared to have their trade policies dictated by the Group of 77 or any other majority of nations within UNCTAD.[46] As in the General Assembly itself, on most issues arising within UNCTAD the nations outside the West realized the futility of trying to change international trade policies without the cooperation of those nations which had the power to make such changes effective. Even so, the very existence of UNCTAD meant that, for the first time, problems of global trade would be studied, debated, and (as the poorer countries undoubtedly expected) resolved by an *international agency* and perhaps ultimately by the UN General Assembly itself.[47]

That the deliberations of UNCTAD would be characterized by fundamental disagreements and factionalism was perhaps ordained from the beginning. The unity of the Group of 77 was severely tested on many occasions after 1964. United as they were in demanding trade concessions from the Western nations, the members of this group by no means constituted a monolithic entity. Disparities among them (reflecting conflicts between large and small states, or those that had close economic ties with the West and those that did not) became increasingly evident. Yet in most instances, the group remained cohesive and was able to preserve its common front in dealing with the industrialized nations.

Among the other members of UNCTAD, two principal groups emerged. The Western nations became known as the B Group; it tended to rely upon existing machinery (like GATT) to formulate unified policies within UNCTAD. Within the B Group, differences of opinion have sometimes been pronounced; in the end, however, the attitudes of the United States and of the larger nations of Western Europe have usually prevailed.[48] Soviet Russia and the smaller Marxist nations became known as the D Group. The basic strategy followed by this group was to win and preserve the good will of the emerging nations by supporting their demands for sweeping changes (mainly by Western nations) in prevailing trade policies. A noteworthy trend in UNCTAD's deliberations, however, has been the extent to which the Group of 77 has criticized the trade policies of the Marxist zone; in the main, Moscow has failed to convince this group that the trading positions of the B Group and the D Group are fundamentally different.[49]

What has UNCTAD actually accomplished since 1964? From the point of view of the Group of 77, its achievements have fallen far short of expectations. UNCTAD has thus far failed to transform world trade or the take anything more than preliminary steps toward that ultimate goal. The dichotomy which existed at Geneva—the "maximum demands" of the Group of 77 versus the "minimum offer" of the B Group—continues to exist within UNCTAD and to render any prospect of rapid progress in overhauling global trade policies remote. Indeed, by the 1970s, the bargaining position of most members of the Group of 77 may well have *worsened,* as sellers faced growing competition within the world market, as the Soviet–American conflict became muted, and as domestic problems gripped several of the nations belonging to this group.

American participation in UNCTAD was always reluctant; more than any other member perhaps, the United States found itself on the defensive because of its strong commitment to the principle of reciprocal trade concessions. To the minds of officials in most Afro–Asian and Latin American nations, this stance reflected American indifference to their special problems and an unwillingness by the wealthiest nation on earth to make the concessions required to accelerate their economic progress. By the late 1960s, American officials were prepared to make limited concessions by granting preferential terms of trade to nations outside the West and implementing measures calculated to give these nations more favorable prices for their export sales. Even then, however, the American position fell short of meeting the demands expressed by most of UNCTAD's members. With "protectionist" sentiment in the American Congress rising, and with the United States making little progress in recent years in resolving its chronic balance-of-payments problems, there seemed little likelihood that Washington was prepared to go much further in the near future in modifying its long-standing commitment to reciprocal trade concessions.[50]

America and International Human Rights

As the influence of the Afro–Asian nations has risen within the United Nations, so has direct UN concern for a group of related issues encompassed by the concept of international human rights. Never in history has there been such concern for the promotion of human rights as a *global* problem—a phenomenon stemming in part from the growing *national* preoccupation with the question. Earlier, in discussing Portugal's African colonies, Southern Rhodesia, and South Africa, the intense interest of the Afro–Asian nations in these areas was emphasized; each of these cases was important to the United Nations largely because it involved the violation of human rights. Among the major purposes of the United Nations (as defined in Article 1, Section 3 of the Charter) is "promoting and encouraging respect for human rights and for fundamental freedoms for all without distinction as to race, sex, language, or religion. . . ." As one study of the UN observes, this obligation entails two closely related responsibilities: *defining* those human rights entitled to the protection of the UN and *securing* the rights so defined.[51] It has not been easy for the United Nations to do either of these things, but it has had considerably greater success in carrying out the former responsibility than the latter.

The definition and elaboration of international human rights has concerned the United States since its establishment. The General Assembly adopted a Universal Declaration on Human Rights in 1948;* since that time, some 15 addi-

---

*This declaration encompasses a long list of "inalienable rights," including such diverse freedoms as the rights to life, liberty, security, and nationality; to property; to freedom of conscience, of movement, and peaceful assembly. The declaration merely sets forth *recommendations* to governments; it has no binding force under international law. After adoption of the declaration, the UN Commission on Human Rights proceeded to draft *covenants* which, when ratified by the members of the UN, would constitute legally enforceable instruments for promoting human rights. After several years of study and discussion, on December 16, 1966, the UN General Assembly finally adopted two such covenants—one encompassing civil and political rights and the other economic, social, and cultural rights: after a nation ratified these covenants, the rights specified would become legally enforceable in the courts. Even then, however, enforcement was left almost entirely to *national action;* the UN possessed no method of imposing sanctions against individuals or nations violating the rights enumerated. A noteworthy exception was the European Convention for the Protection of Human Rights and Fundamental Freedoms, adopted by the nations belonging to the Council of Europe on November 4, 1950. This document made enforcement of the rights enumerated a *regional* responsibility and established two organs—a European Commission on Human Rights and a European Court of Human Rights—to promote compliance

tional instruments and declarations modeled after this document have been approved, such as the International Covenants on Civil and Political Rights and on Economic, Social and Cultural Rights. A noteworthy document was the International Convention on the Elimination of All Forms of Racial Discrimination, adopted in 1965. In contrast to all other instruments in the human rights field, this one received the requisite number of ratifications by the members of the UN, enabling it to come into legal force in 1969.[52] A long list of agreements covering other subjects— the problem of religious intolerance, the status of women, capital punishment, and freedom of information, to cite only some leading examples— have been debated extensively, and some of them have been passed by the members of the United Nations.[53]

What have UN activities devoted to the promotion of human rights accomplished since 1945? In limited space, it is possible only to identify significant trends briefly.* First, questions of human rights have moved to the forefront of global concern; the Afro–Asian nations may well regard UN activities in this sphere (particularly as they relate to cases on the African continent) as one of the

organization's principal functions. These countries usually concede, for example, that the UN can make only a marginal contribution to the settlement of the cold war—or even perhaps to the resolution of lesser conflicts like the quarrel between India and Pakistan or the Arab–Israeli dispute. Yet they recognize few limitations upon the UN's ability to resolve successfully problems in the field of international human rights. Second, a discernible "credibility gap" has existed for years between the UN's professed concern for human rights and its apparent inability to implement its resolutions, declarations, and the like dealing with the subject. UN efforts in the specification and elaboration of international human rights has no doubt been useful; perhaps the major contribution in this regard has been the *global publicity* accorded to the problem, making all governments more conscious of human rights issues. Beyond this, progress in implementing the rights identified as a result of UN efforts has been imperceptible. Few nations have rejected such instruments as the Covenant on Civil and Political Rights directly; the general tendency has been for them simply to delay ratification indefinitely or to vitiate such instruments with reservations and provisos depriving the documents of any real significance. Not untypically, few concrete results attended the International Human Rights Year in 1968. In the main, effective action in the realm of human rights continues to rest with the *national governments* of the world, although some progress has been made in recent years (notably in Western Europe) in promoting respect for human rights on a *regional* basis.[54]

Our earlier discussion of colonial and racial disputes in Africa underscored the fact that the United States has *not* been in the vanguard of nations seeking to expand the authority of the United Nations in the field of human rights. As reflected in their cautious position in these cases, American officials have doubted the constitutional basis of many proposed measures dealing with human rights questions. Moreover, given the strong attachment to national sovereignty (not least, by some countries leading the campaign to expand the UN's jurisdiction in this sphere) throughout the world, spokesmen for the United States have questioned the value of UN declarations on human rights which had little prospect of becoming more than verbal commitments having no legal effect. In this connection, they have sometimes observed a real dichotomy between Afro–Asian concern for racial discrimination (which in nearly all cases was attributed to the behavior of *white* groups) and the treatment accorded to racial and tribal minorities or the status of women within many societies outside the West. As in all aspects of UN operations, deliberations on human rights questions have been heavily influenced by *political considerations*. Routinely, American

---

with its terms. See William L. Tung, *International Organization Under the United Nations System* (New York: Thomas Y. Crowell, 1969), pp. 147–158.

*One commentator has aptly said of UN activities in the field of human rights that they are "great on production but poor in distribution"; the result of continuing UN efforts in this area has been "a cornucopia of papers proclaiming principles and goals which almost no state dares contradict publicly, but which few observe conscientiously, and which fewer still embrace to the point of allowing their practices to be inspected." The conference at Tehran, marking 1968 as the International Year for Human Rights, became an "exercise in acrimony," in which Arab grievances against Israel and the problem of South Africa were the leading themes. This observer feels that a basic question exists about whether the people of the world actually *share* "common goals and values in the sphere of human rights, or a common concern for the human rights of others." The "wide disparity" between professed common aims and fundamental differences in the practices of nations is perhaps the most basic explanation for the UN's lack of progress in this field. Almost invariably, this commentator emphasizes, governments approach the problem of international human rights in terms of their *political interests:* Black Africans identify *white racism* as the most acute threat to human rights; they are much less concerned about discrimination against the Chinese in Southeast Asia or religious discrimination on the Indian subcontinent, not to mention discrimination by black Africans against Indians. Since the UN manifestly cannot deal with *all* kinds of human rights violations, one of the major problems besetting its efforts in this field is determining *what categories* of human rights questions to consider and *why* certain categories ought to be chosen over others. See Morris B. Abram, "The U.N. and Human Rights," *Foreign Affairs* 47 (January, 1969), 363–375; and for a recent symposium dealing with selected aspects of the problem, see Christopher R. Hill, ed., *Rights and Wrongs: Some Essays on Human Rights* (Baltimore: Penguin, 1969), particularly the two essays by Hilary Cartwright and Christopher R. Hill.

delegates have tried to focus UN attention upon problems like "genocide" or anti-Semitism behind the Iron Curtain; Marxist spokesmen have of course denied that violations of human rights occur within Communist societies and have tried to confine UN attention to cases involving chiefly American or European violations; as we have noted, Afro–Asian governments have been strangely indifferent to violations of human rights (like the still-depressed condition of the "untouchables" in India or discrimination by black governments against racial minorities in East Africa) occurring within their own territories. American officials have stated time and again that the United States was not of course opposed to the concept of human rights per se; its own Declaration of Independence and Bill of Rights attested to the American society's deep attachment to these ideals. But Washington was dubious about the extent to which human rights could really be protected by *international action.*[55]

By the early 1960s, American policy-makers—aware that their position on human rights questions had won little admiration with most UN members—began to take a more energetic role in dealing with this issue. Even before this time, Washington had favored UN activities relating to reporting, research, and advisory services in the sphere of human rights. During the 1950s, the United States had led the way in concentrating UN attention on the problem of "genocide," especially within Soviet Russia and other Marxist societies. But in general, it was not until the Kennedy administration that executive officials publicly endorsed UN human rights declarations and, when necessary, requested the Senate to approve conventions on subjects such as slavery, forced labor, and the rights of women.[56] More than any other postwar Chief Executive, President Kennedy was uniquely sensitive to the importance of international human rights issues and to the desirability of improving America's image in approaching these issues, both within the UN and within its own borders.[57] Under Kennedy, American delegates at the UN were especially active in seeking to gain international awareness of a subject of special concern to many Americans: discrimination against Jewish groups living behind the Iron Curtain.[58]

Yet experience during the remainder of the 1960s and the early 1970s indicated that the change in American policy on international human rights questions may have been more apparent than real. One observer stated that during the 1960s, "the establishment of international norms for human rights met with tepid enthusiasm in the United States."[59] Many of the reservations American officials had entertained about UN activity in this field were still present—and (with mounting racial disorders within the United States) some of them loomed larger than ever. Congressional atti-

tudes about UN human rights proposals had been negative for many years; almost invariably, critics of the UN within the American society cited examples from the sphere of human rights activities to illustrate the danger to "'national sovereignty" of steadily expanding UN power. Executive and legislative officials alike were unquestionably aware that, at some stage in the future, the question of violations of human rights in the United States might be inscribed on the agenda of the UN General Assembly. They were also aware that the records of those UN members (whether Afro–Asian or Marxist) who might raise this issue were hardly exemplary, in serving as models for observing human freedoms. Some proposals advocated by proponents of UN human rights declarations (such as prohibiting groups from advocating racial intolerance) patently conflicted with provisions of the American Constitution, such as the guarantee of free speech. Suggested enforcement proceedings—whereby an international tribunal like the International Court of Justice would adjudicate cases involving the violation of human rights—conflicted with the terms of America's adherence to the ICJ. But even if no such conflict existed, there remained a grave doubt whether the United States or any other nation was willing to accept rulings by the ICJ *as binding* without its prior consent.* It was significant, for example, that India had showed no interest in submitting the case of Portuguese colonialism in Goa to the ICJ before New Delhi resorted to force to liquidate that colony; nor were African states prepared to accept a ruling by the ICJ in 1966 the effect of which was to leave South-West Africa under the de facto control of South Africa. American public opinion on the matter of UN concern for human rights was also fragmented. Some groups (religious organizations were often at the forefront) called upon Washington to exert greater initiative in dealing with such questions. Other groups (which often opposed the United Nations generally) denounced efforts to expand the UN jurisdiction over such issues.

As in the past, policy-makers in the United States continued to believe that real progress in safeguarding human rights depended primarily upon two conditions: encouraging *voluntary compliance* by governments with standards and ideals

---

*When the United States accepted the jurisdiction of the International Court of Justice, the Senate attached an amendment to the agreement (known as the "Connally Amendment"), specifying that the Court's jurisdiction did not extend to several categories of issues. The key reservation was that the ICJ was prohibited from deciding "disputes with regard to matters which are essentially within the domestic jurisdiction of the United States as determined by the United States. . . ." See the text of this agreement, in Senate Foreign Relations Committee, *A Decade of American Foreign Policy: Basic Documents, 1941–49*, 81st Congress, 1st Session, 1950, pp. 155–156.

defining human rights; and creating *favorable political and economic conditions* within the international community conducive to the respect for, and meaningful enjoyment of, human rights.[60]

The U.S. and the UN: A Balance Sheet

It is admittedly difficult to summarize briefly the relationship between the United States and the United Nations for close to a generation. Even a discussion of major trends evident within that relationship risks oversimplification and omission of several important aspects. The United States has been heavily involved in almost all UN activities since 1945, from major peace-keeping operations to attempts to eradicate disease and poverty. By nearly any criterion, the UN owes its creation and its continued existence to American support. At a number of critical junctures during the postwar period, American initiative was largely responsible for the ability of the UN to *adapt itself* to new challenges and crises; if one of the outstanding characteristics of the UN's experience is the organization's *flexibility and ingenuity in meeting unprecedented problems*, the United States may properly claim major credit for ths accomplishment. To cite but one leading example: The Uniting for Peace Resolution of 1950, which enabled the General Assembly to discuss international crises when the Security Council was deadlocked, resulted mainly from American initiative. American financial support of the UN has been, and remains, essential to the organization's operation.

For the first decade and a half of the UN's existence, there was considerable validity to the Communist accusation that it was an instrument of American foreign policy. During that period, the United States could usually count on an "automatic majority" of UN members to support its policies or (as in the case of the admission of Communist China to the world assembly) to block measures at variance with American diplomatic objectives. With the emergence of the Afro–Asian majority, this era came to an end. Toward several issues of international concern, the United States was now as much on the defensive in the United Nations as the Communist bloc had been during the 1940s and 1950s. And while it seldom happened in practice, the theoretical danger existed that the United States could be outvoted by a hostile UN majority in the General Assembly. The fact that this happened with *relative infrequency* indicated that the United States had not "lost control" of the United Nations to a group of nations congenitally opposed to its interests.

In spite of the changes that have occurred within the United Nations since 1945, official and public American support for the organization has remained high. In 1970, President Richard Nixon joined his predecessors in the White House when he called the UN "both a symbol of the worldwide hope for peace and a reflection of the tensions and conflicts that have frustrated these hopes." He commended the UN's "25 years of accomplishments" and he called upon the members to "match idealism in purpose with realism in expectation." Nixon added the admonition, however, that "the UN cannot by itself solve fundamental international disputes, especially among the superpowers." Unrealistic expectations concerning the UN and failure to recognize its limitations could "undermine the UN" as easily as unwillingness to use it at all. In a pointed reference to the inclination of some UN members to pass resolutions irrespective of the prospects for their implementation, Nixon asserted that "good words are not a substitute for hard deeds and noble rhetoric is no guarantee of noble results." On the occasion of the organization's twenty-fifth anniversary, Nixon called upon all members to acknowledge the UN's "realistic possibilities and to devise ways to expand them." America was committed to helping the UN make "steady progress" toward fulfillment of the pruposes for which it was established.[61]

President Nixon's remarks call attention to several ideas basic to the role of the United Nations in American foreign policy. America's dedication to the United Nations was reaffirmed, as was the desire of the United States to transform the UN into a more effective instrument for international peace and security. Nixon's request to Congress for funds to enlarge UN headquarters in New York provided tangible evidence of continued American support. As in the past, Washington sought to protect the UN from two forces detrimental to its future: those groups within the United States that sought to restrict the powers of the UN, perhaps to the point of securing America's nonparticipation in it; and those groups (joined by many members of the UN) who endeavored to give the UN responsibilities (like settlement of the Vietnam War) it was ill-equipped to bear, or even perhaps to discuss seriously, without considerable risk to its own future effectiveness. Despite temporary disenchantment with the United Nations, American public opinion remained basically favorable to the organization; suggestions that the United States curtail its participation in the UN found very little public support in the United States.[62] The greater danger then, as the Nixon administration saw it, was that the UN might be weakened, and popular support for it in America and elsewhere undermined, by failure to admit candidly the UN's limitations and to take these into account in carrying out American foreign policy.

No one was better aware than officials in Washington that the international environment had changed, in some ways radically, since 1945. If the necessary policy modifications had sometimes come slowly (and in some instances had lagged considerably behind events), American policymakers were cognizant that the bipolar order of the early cold war period had been superceded by a multipolar distribution of global power; that "international Communism" no longer existed as a monolithic entity; and that the nuclear balance of terror compelled at least a minimum degree of Soviet–American agreement upon the necessity to avoid violent confrontations. American officials knew too that the emerging nations had little interest in the cold war and that their main preoccupation within the United Nations was with problems directly related to their own interests, like racial discrimination against black peoples or the challenge of economic development. Despite these evident changes, it remained true that many of the assumptions upon which the United Nations was founded were at variance with the facts of international life. Acceptance of the concept of peaceful coexistence by Washington and Moscow alike did not mean, for example, that the kind of "great-power unanimity" envisioned in the UN Charter existed. The existence of the nuclear balance of terror did not signify that controversial issues like the future of Germany, or the Arab–Israeli conflict, or the Vietnam War could be resolved on the basis of Soviet–American unanimity within the United Nations.

Indeed, the decline of bipolarity may in some respects have made the task of converting the UN into an effective instrument for ensuring peace and security even more difficult. As concepts like "international Communism" and the "Western bloc" became more and more *passé*, the ability of both the United States and the Soviet Union (assuming that they agreed upon a course of action) to impose solutions upon other countries was clearly impaired. A number of countries (including several black African states) had made it clear that they had no intention of abiding by UN-imposed sanctions against South Africa or Southern Rhodesia; under both General Charles de Gaulle and his successor President Georges Pompidou, the Fifth French Republic similarly defied UN resolutions dealing with South Africa and pursued its own independent policies in the Middle East, even though doing so greatly complicated the UN's search for peace in the latter area; as the most influential nonmember of the United Nations, Communist China showed no inclination to be influenced by UN resolutions which, in Peking's view, stemmed from "Soviet–American collaborationism" at China's expense; smaller states (like Israel and the Arab nations) defied the UN's authority with impunity, invoking it only in efforts to restrain the conduct of their antagonists. In all countries, not excluding the two super-powers, societies had become heavily preoccupied *with domestic problems;* in varying degrees, all great and second-rank powers were *reducing* their international commitments and responsibilities. If Americans had become disenchanted with the

idea that the United States was the "policeman of the world," the U.S.S.R. likewise revealed little interest in instigating worldwide revolutionary movements or (with the exception of the Middle East) in assuming major responsibilities outside the European Communist zone. For all of its revolutionary polemicizing, Communist China showed no disposition to support revolutionary activities on any major scale beyond its own frontiers.

The weaknesses of the United Nations, to which President Nixon alluded, were not of course entirely the fault of other countries or of changes in the global environment. America's own behavior sometimes has failed to match its official statements of devotion to the UN or to strengthen the organization's authority in dealing with international crises. During the Korean War, for example, the United States clearly viewed the UN chiefly as an instrument for ratifying decisions made in Washington or in some cases by the theater commander in the Pacific, General Douglas MacArthur. American policy-makers showed considerably less readiness to consult the UN *before* important decisions were made or to regard opinion in the UN as a major *constraint* upon American behavior. In a number of key instances in the years which followed—the American landing in Lebanon in 1957, the intervention in the Dominican Republic in 1965, the steady buildup of American involvement in Vietnam during the 1960s, the Nixon administration's decision to send American troops into Cambodia in 1970—the UN played a minor (in some cases, a totally insignificant) role in the foreign policy calculations of the United States. In some cases, as during the Vietnam War, American reluctance to involve the United Nations was, on balance, perhaps warranted. The existence of marked divergencies in the positions of the United States, the Soviet Union, and Communist China (not to mention North and South Vietnam) on this issue clearly precluded effective UN action. Even Secretary-General U Thant acknowledged on several occasions that the UN could make little contribution to the resolution of tensions in Southeast Asia. Nor was there any evident sentiment in favor of involving the UN in the Vietnam conflict among the Afro–Asian nations.* Nevertheless, the impression was

---

*With regard to the role of the UN in the Vietnam War, its contribution can be conceived of on two levels. Officially, neither the UN Security Council nor the General Assembly has adopted proposals dealing with the war, although the Vietnam question has been discussed at intervals in the UN. Opposition to discussion of Vietnam by the Security Council came primarily from the Soviet Union and other Marxist nations. By contrast, UN Secretary-General U Thant sought on innumerable occasions during the 1960s to bring about a cease-fire in Southeast Asia, often at the invitation of the United States. His efforts met with little success. U Thant stated several times that the UN could not "settle" the Viet-

created by such cases that the Unted States fa-vored vigorous UN action in crisis situations only under one of two circumstances: when (as in Korea) the UN was prepared to *support* American foreign policy goals; or (as in cases like the Congo, Kashmir, and Cyprus) when the United States had no vital diplomatic interests at stake and was un-likely to become deeply involved in the crisis. Few members of the UN were convinced by American reasoning during the Dominican crisis that because the Organization of American States was prepared to assume jurisdiction over the case, the United Nations was *precluded* from doing so. Washington was not prepared to accept this same contention from Moscow when the Warsaw Pact countries invaded Czechoslovakia in 1968. Nor, as we have observed, has the United States been pre-pared to work through the UN to any appreciable extent in providing assistance to less developed countries.

In the 1970s, the United Nations continues to face a number of challenges and serious obstacles. There is very little immediate prospect, for exam-ple, that it will become a major peace-keeping force; more than in the 1960s, its capacity to pre-vent or contain violence is extremely limited. The inability of the members of the UN to re-establish the United Nations Emergency Force (UNEF) in the Middle East following its withdrawal in 1967, does not bode well for UN peace-keeping opera-tions in future crises. For, as in that case, even the nonaligned nations are reluctant to assume the responsibility for preventing violence, when they cannot secure the concurrence of the gov-ernments most directly involved. As differences among the nonaligned nations become more pro-nounced (and this tendency seems certain), it may be more difficult than ever to discover that op-timum combination of circumstances which will enable UN peace-keeping ventures to function successfully.

In two key areas—the Middle East and South-east Asia—it has become obvious that the United Nations has only a *limited role* to play in restoring peace and security. In both regions, agreements among the United States, Soviet Russia, Red China, and perhaps some of the less powerful na-tions of the world, are indispensable. Officials like UN Secretary-General U Thant can admittedly contribute to reaching such agreements; the de-gree to which resolutions by the UN Security Council or the General Assembly contribute to global peace, however, is likely to be conditioned in the future, as in the past, by the existence of a

prior readiness among the more powerful nations of the world to concert their policies. There is, consequently, no reason to suppose that the United Nations can become a substitute for unilat-eral defense programs; that it obviates the need for Soviet–American (and Sino–American) efforts to resolve major sources of tension; or that it re-places any of the normal channels of diplomacy.

The disappearance of America's "automatic majority" within the UN is undoubtedly of crucial significance. It has changed both the nature of the United Nations and America's relationship with the organization. Yet it must be reiterated that to date this change has *not* in most instances proved highly injurious to American diplomatic interests. The factors which have contributed to America's success in the UN for many years—the large num-ber of countries supporting the United States be-cause of ties with it or because of basic agreement with its policies; America's continued financial support of the organization, giving it great "bar-gaining power"; and the skill displayed by Ameri-can negotiators in lobbying and other forms of parliamentary maneuvering—continue to oper-ate. To this list should be added a fourth factor which may be an even more decisive restraint upon the Afro–Asian majority: a desire *to preserve and strengthen* the United Nations—a goal not likely to be achieved, as most Afro–Asian govern-ments are fully aware, if the strongest nation in the history of the world becomes alienated from the UN and relegates it to the sidelines of history.

Insofar as American foreign policy is con-cerned, the era of the "automatic majority" has been superceded by what might be called the "convinced majority." Now, the United States must *persuade* the members of the UN of the cor-rectness of its policies; now, as never before, American officials are required to "legitimize" their government's behavior before world opin-ion. The risk, of course, it cannot be denied, is that some American policies will be viewed as illegiti-mate. In some instances, Washington may feel compelled to disregard the views of an adverse UN majority. But as a rule, this process of legitimi-zation may prove very beneficial for American foreign policy and may in the end gain for it the widest possible degree of global support.

DISARMAMENT: THE ELUSIVE QUEST

Arms Control in Historical Perspective

From the time of the League of Nations forward, the concept of international organization has al-ways been closely linked with another idea to which we devote the remainder of this chapter. This is *disarmament*—or, more accurately per-

---

nam conflict; its resolution lay "in the hands of those who have the power and the responsibility to decide," he asserted in 1966. See William L. Tung, *International Organization Under the United Nations System* (New York: Thomas Y. Crowell, 1969), pp. 206–209; and *The New York Times* (May 25 and December 20, 1966; Janu-ary 1, 1967).

haps, *arms control*—as an essential step in the creation and maintenance of global peace and security. One study of the League of Nations held that when this organization was established

no one anywhere doubted that the race in armaments had been largely responsible for the first World War. Therefore, "disarmament" was the largest single item in the peace movement of that time, and there was universal agreement that the first and greatest test of the League of Nations would be its ability to carry out a "reduction and limitation of armaments," which was the more cautious expression for the popular term, disarmament.[63]

That the disarmament question had lost none of its urgency in the intervening years was indicated by President John F. Kennedy's speech to the United Nations on September 25, 1961, when he declared:

Today, every inhabitant of the planet must contemplate the day when this planet may not longer be habitable. Every man, woman and child lives under a nuclear sword of Damocles, hanging by the slenderest of threads, capable of being cut at any moment by accident, or miscalculation or by madness. The weapons of war must be abolished before they abolish us.[64]

The challenge of arms control had become no less imperative by the 1970s. With progress in military technology rapidly accelerating, the weapons balance was continually changing. The only "constant" perhaps was the danger to mankind of an unchecked armaments spiral. President Nixon declared in 1970 that "There is no area in which we and the Soviet Union—as well as others—have a greater common interest than in reaching agreement with regard to arms control."[65]

Arms limitation is one of the oldest and most intractable issues in the history of modern international relations. The world's statesmen became actively concerned about the problem late in the nineteenth century; the First Hague Conference in 1899 was convened for the purpose of ending what many leaders were convinced had become a "runaway" arms race that was certain to end in disaster for the nations engaged in it. Again in 1907, the powers met at the Hague to renew the quest for agreement on arms control. Beyond a consensus on measures to "humanize" war, these early efforts met with virtually no success. The unprecedented destruction accompanying World War I gave new impetus to the quest for international negotiations to limit armaments. In his celebrated Fourteen Points (January 8, 1918), President Woodrow Wilson included among the Allied war aims assuring "adequate guarantees that armaments would be reduced to the lowest point consistent with domestic safety." Article 8 of the

League of Nations Covenant echoed Wilson's idea.

Intensive efforts to scale down the world's armaments were carried on during the 1920s and 1930s. Certain categories of naval armaments were actually reduced (and the manufacture of designated naval weapons "frozen" for the future) at the Washington Conference in the early 1920s. While it was not, literally speaking, a disarmament agreement, the Kellogg–Briand Pact or "Pact of Paris" (signed on August 27, 1928) bound the signatories to renounce war as "an instrument of national policy." Other than serving as one of the legal instruments under which Axis war criminals were tried at the end of World War II, this agreement had little discernible value. Throughout the 1930s, the production of armaments (especially by nations dedicated to expansionism) proceeded apace. World War II of course greatly surpassed World War I as a destructive chapter in the history of armed conflict. For this conflagration (unlike the earlier war) was truly a *world war*, involving most societies on the globe; and the devastation inflicted upon human society sometimes reached levels which were impossible to visualize. In this global encounter, man's ingenuity in "the art of war" reached new heights. Not only did conventional (nonnuclear) weapons attain unprecedented levels of destructiveness; but World War II witnessed a major qualitiative change in the threat posed by modern armaments because of the perfection of nuclear weapons, whose very testing in the years ahead imperiled the survival of at least a portion of human society. The danger of radioactive fallout from the use or testing of these weapons placed the future of the human race itself in the balance, since the genetic changes it could cause endangered future generations. Since the radioactive element strontium-90 tends to replace calcium in the human body, Asian societies (which rely upon calcium-rich rice diets) were, as we have noted, uniquely vulnerable to this danger.[66]

In view of the intensity of destruction caused by World War II, and the injection of the nuclear threat into the always difficult disarmament problem, it is a curious fact that the UN Charter gave less overt emphasis to arms limitation than did the League Covenant. The Charter did express the intention of the founders to "save succeeding generations from the scourge of war" and to guarantee that "armed force shall not be used save in the common interest" of the international community. Admittedly, if the concept of "collective security" contemplated by the UN Charter could be made to operate, large national armed forces would no longer be necessary. Using armed forces supplied by the members of the UN, the Security Council would assume the responsibility for maintaining global peace and security. Yet, as though they conceded that this transition would be extremely difficult, the founders of the UN recognized (in Article 51) "the inherent right of individual and collective self-defense if an armed attack occurs against a member of the United Nations, until the Security Council has taken the measures necessary to maintain international peace and security." As our earlier discussion of the UN emphasized, thus far the Security Council has failed to perform its anticipated peace-keeping function, particularly when the more powerful nations of the world are involved. The result has been that efforts to assure their "individual and collective self-defense" have led the nations of the world to expand their military arsenals at an uninterrupted rate, to establish a network of alliance systems, and as in earlier eras of history to be guided by the old Roman maxim: *si vis pacem, para bellum* (if you want peace, prepare for war).

The Postwar Armaments Spiral

That armaments budgets continue to rise—and that new weapons are being developed continuously—are commonplace facts to anyone who reads a daily newspaper. The tempo of the "action–reaction" pattern characteristic of arms races throughout history appears to increase steadily. Soviet military strategists concentrate upon a new Fractional Orbiting Bombardment System (FOBS); this Soviet move is "answered" by progress in equipping American missiles with multiple warheads, greatly augmenting their firepower. While Moscow pioneers in the production of an "antisatellite satellite," Washington forges ahead with the installation of an Antiballistic Missile System (ABM). Each side of course views progress by the other side as "destabilizing" and as a threat to the condition of nuclear parity which has prevailed between the United States and the Soviet Union for several years. Meanwhile, the destructive level of conventional (nonnuclear) weapons has also escalated sharply in the postwar period. To cite but one example: Combat infantry forces are routinely equipped with automatic weapons enabling them to lay down a deadly "spray" of fire against an enemy force on a scale that was unknown in World War II or the Korean War.

Less well known is the fact that *expenditures on armaments by the emerging nations have climbed steadily throughout the postwar period.* One study in 1969, for example, referred to "the poor man's arms race" which was "gathering speed" throughout Latin America, Asia, and Africa. Arms budgets for most countries in this zone were "rising faster than their gross national products," which meant that a high proportion of funds generated by national development schemes was being diverted to the manufacture or purchase of war matériel. All around the world, this report observed, the arms race was "out of control"; the

sale of military hardware constituted "one of the world's most lucrative markets." A Pentagon study estimated that, unless effective arms-control measures were adopted by the nations of the world, the arms market for the non-Communist countries alone during the ten-year period 1965–1974 would approximate $100 billion! Of this total, some $3 billion annually would be spent on arms *imports;* the United States planned to supply approximately half (or $1.5 billion a year) of these sales to other countries. By the beginning of the 1970s, America was devoting around one-tenth of its national resources to defense expenditures; but, with their armaments expenditures rising rapidly, many nations in the third world came close to reaching this same level. Total annual expenditures on weapons by all the nations of the world were equal to the *total yearly incomes* of 1 billion people living in the less developed countries; worldwide expenditures for education were only two-thirds as large as the world's outlay for armaments; and expenditures for public health were only one-third the military expenditures of all nations.[67] As the United States and the Soviet Union entered into the Strategic Arms Limitations Talks (SALT) at Helsinki, Finland, the armed forces of the world totaled some 20 million men and women, while 30 million additional people were employed in armaments manufacturing and related industries.[68] In the light of the steady upward movement of the arms spiral, it is interesting to speculate on what the level of global armaments would be *without* the efforts to reduce national military arsenals that have been going on inside and outside the United Nations since 1945! We shall examine postwar progress in arms control at a later stage. Meanwhile, let us briefly analyze some of the principal elements in the problem of arms reduction.

Elements in the Disarmament Problem

Based upon the lack of concrete results achieved in reducing the world's supply of weapons since the First Hague Conference, the student of international relations might be amply justified in viewing disarmament as the most difficult and complex problem of the international community. At every turn, the issue of arms reduction presents anomalies and dilemmas. The ramifications of the problem extend into nearly every sphere of human experience. Disarmament is not a single problem but a *cluster of problems,* some of which relate to the most fundamental questions about human existence and motivation. Even today, officials and citizens concerned with disarmament are basically ignorant or only incompletely informed about many important dimensions of the issue.

Why does evidence from the earliest Stone Age cultures show that man has always sought to acquire and perfect weapons? Is aggressiveness and a propensity to engage in violent conflict an innate human trait? Is violent behavior mainly a moral–ethical problem, reflecting man's failure to abide by the precepts of the world's leading religious and moral codes? Are international relations inherently and inescapably concerned with "power politics," entailing armed clashes from time to time among the members of human society? Even if power politics can be shown to be a common denominator of international relations throughout modern history, does it follow that conflicts among nations are unavoidable in the future? Do arms races ultimately generate a certain momentum and inner compulsion of their own, rendering them impervious to control by the will of man? Or does the impulse for new and more destructive weapons arise from the machinations of a military–industrial complex which, in America and other countries, has developed a powerful vested interest in pushing the level of military spending to new heights? Are the main obstacles to success in disarmament discussions to be found in *irrational forces* (such as the desire of every government to maintain its prestige or its ingrained suspicion of its neighbors), making the quest for arms reduction impossible? After more than three-quarters of a century of more or less serious disarmament negotiations, has the scenario become stale, unimaginative, and ritualistic, fostering an atmosphere of futility and boredom among the participants? It may as well be conceded frankly that thus far students of international relations have few satisfactory answers to such questions. Given the best of intentions on all sides among officials involved in disarmament proceedings, this fact alone casts a pall over their discussions.

Although manifold uncertainties continue to surround the disarmament problem, the basic assumption upon which arms-limitation talks are conducted is that an agreed-upon reduction of national military arsenals is on balance beneficial, not only for the nations involved in the agreement but for mankind as a whole. The benefits to be derived from effective arms limitation have been stated and reiterated endlessly since 1899. The reduction of global armaments would serve to lift the "cloud of war" that perpetually hangs over human society. In the era of total war fought with nuclear weapons, successful disarmament would go a long way toward guaranteeing the future of civilization. An arms-limitation accord ought to serve as a kind of catalyst, accelerating agreements among the nations of the world on many other controversial issues. If a breakthrough occured in disarmament proceedings, this fact would raise the level of international confidence and good will sufficiently to make possible the resolution of less intractable questions fomenting international tensions. Once global armaments

have been scaled down, perhaps the earlier goal of the Kellogg–Briand Pact—the elimination of war itself as an instrument of national policy—can be realized.

Another motivation of disarmament negotiations throughout modern history has been awareness of the economic and financial dimensions of an arms race. Today, more than in any other era of history, this argument is pertinent and extremely influential. At one stage, America's military expenditures in the Vietnam War alone approximated $2 billion per month or $24 billion annually. If only half (or even one-quarter) of this total could be recovered and rechanneled to constructive purposes like education or public health or antipoverty programs, within a few years many of the domestic problems besetting the American society might be largely solved. On an international scale, imagine the results if one-half or an even smaller fraction of the world's "armaments bill" of $100 billion during 1965–1974 were devoted to meeting the needs of the developing nations. If no more than one-quarter of this sum could be used for this purpose (assuming of course these funds were used *effectively*), many societies throughout Asia, Africa, and Latin America would be propelled rapidly along the path of modernization. Even a more modest gain—persuading the less developed nations themselves to rechannel funds devoted to armaments into national development programs—would go far toward assuring their economic and social progress. Government officials and concerned citizens alike have deplored the "waste" of huge sums on munitions and have called for the diversion of these funds to more worthwhile programs.*

*Economic motivations have always been among the most powerful forces providing an impetus to disarmament negotiations in modern history. Governments in every age since 1900 have sought to recover the money spent on armaments to finance more "constructive" programs. Yet, by the 1970s, the economic gains from successful arms control had become more evident than ever, especially as the United States, the Soviet Union, and nearly all other countries faced difficult domestic problems—like inadequate housing, education, and health facilities, and other needs requiring massive expenditures of funds. With regard to the United States alone, one study found that a 35 percent increase in Social Security benefits would require a $13 billion expenditure (or approximately what it cost to wage the Vietnam War in the late 1960s for six months). A substantially improved, federally financed welfare program, it was estimated, would cost an additional $20 billion annually. Many critics of America's involvement in the Vietnam War based their objections mainly on the financial waste involved and the consequent "neglect" of urgent internal needs. Upwards of $20 billion annually, many critics asserted, could be saved once the United States liquidated its involvement in Southeast Asia. Yet, it was perhaps an eloquent commentary upon the kind of inherent momentum an arms race generates that the savings involved in America's withdrawal from Southeast Asia would largely prove illusory; at any rate, they would be much smaller than often imagined. Studies by budgetary experts in the American government

The reasons advanced in favor of reducing the level of the world's armaments are as familiar and as logically convincing today as they were at the end of the nineteenth century. Very few governments in the modern world (Hitler's Germany being a possible exception) have denied the theoretical desirability of arms limitation or have questioned the benefits to be derived from its achievement. Irrespective of its form of government or ideological system, almost every nation subscribes to the concept of disarmament "in principle."

Why then are disarmament negotiations usually so unproductive? Why has it proved extraordinarily difficult to convert this universal agreement in principle to the necessity for disarmament into tangible programs and procedures making it a reality? One explanation is that humans always find it difficult to adhere to their idealistic professions. The dichotomy between what governments *say* and what they *do* is present here, as in all other political relationships. But explaining the lack of progress toward genuine disarmament on this basis risks being a form of circular reasoning. Why are governments content with this dichotomy? Why have they apparently been so unresponsive to the appeals of individual citizens and groups and to the logical force of the case in favor of disarmament? Converting an agreement "in principle" into a detailed blueprint for actually reducing armaments, it must be recognized, encounters a number of fundamental obstacles. Indeed, the question of *how to disarm* may be a more difficult one to solve than the issue of *whether to disarm*.

In the first place, the very term *disarmament* is a misnomer. No nation seriously proposes the *total abolition* of weapons, including those belonging to domestic police forces and internal defense forces. The aim is considerably more modest. To

cite Wilson's Fourteen Points, the goal is to reduce armaments "to the lowest point consistent with domestic safety." What precisely is this point? How is it determined? Does it perhaps vary from one country to another? Or might it (as in the case of the United States for the year 1950 vis-à-vis 1970) vary over time for an individual nation? Whatever the concept of "domestic safety" means precisely, is it related to the kinds of *problems and responsibilities* a given nation faces? The qualification that disarmament must not jeopardize domestic safety explains why the concepts of arms control and effective international peace and security are customarily linked. If nations no longer depend upon their own military might, then they must depend upon *something* (such as a functioning United Nations peace-keeping system) to protect their security. The concept of arms reduction rests upon the assumption that military arsenals can and will be reduced *without jeopardy to the internal and external security interests of the nations involved.*

A second obstacle which disarmament agreements "in principle" must surmount is an outgrowth of the first. Disarmament negotiations are carried on upon the premise that the reduction of military stockpiles will produce *no significant change in the existing distribution of world power*, to the detriment of one nation (or group of nations) vis-à-vis another nation (or group of nations). From the First Hague Conference onward, officials engaged in disarmament proceedings have sought to arrive at agreements which met this requirement; in most instances, they have failed. At the SALT disarmament sessions in the early 1970s, for example, any understanding reached to curtail the manufacture of nuclear-armed missiles must not, in the American view, undermine the "deterrent" strategy of the United States by rendering America militarily inferior to the Soviet Union. From their perspective, Soviet negotiators were concerned about any disarmament plan that might leave the U.S.S.R. in a vulnerable position as regards the United States or Communist China, especially since the latter was not bound by any understandings reached. A basic purpose of arms reduction after all is to *enhance global security;* some disarmament schemes (of which America's unilateral reduction of its defense establishment after World War II was a leading example) might in the end foster *greater insecurity*—leading in turn to a new and more ominous armaments spiral.

This consideration leads to a third major problem which disarmament negotiators must overcome. What precisely are *armaments*, and how can the weapons in one nation's arsenal be compared with those in another nation's? How many nuclear-armed missiles would American negotiators have to "trade" for 20 Soviet armored divisions? Or even for comparable weapons, how

showed that these savings would be largely wiped out by: the rising cost of all weaponry, military pay increases already approved, spending on new weapons systems already scheduled, the necessity to "modernize" units of the navy and perhaps the air force which had become obsolete, and perhaps some form of tax relief. Even after the Vietnam conflict, officials of the American government might be sorely challenged to prevent *an increase* in military spending! To cite but one example: During the Korean War, F-86 fighter planes cost $300,000 each; by the 1970s, the navy wanted to adopt the F-14 fighter, which cost $14 million *per plane*. See Jonathan B. Bingham, "Can Military Spending Be Controlled?" *Foreign Affairs* 48 (October, 1969), 52–54. Lest it be thought that the United States had a unique problem in this regard, it should be noted that in 1969, mankind spent some $174 billion collectively on armaments. The nations of the third world expended some $12 billion on weaponry—an amount that was approximately double the funds they received for development aid. All countries of the world, not excluding the Soviet Union and smaller nations like Sweden and Switzerland, were actively engaged in supplying weapons in this lucrative arms trade. See "The Arms Pushers of the World," *Atlas* 18 (December, 1969), 22–25.

many modern American Minuteman missiles in "hardened" sites are the equivalent of larger modern Soviet missiles in "soft" (or unprotected) emplacements? What weapons in its arsenal might the Soviet Union be willing to sacrifice if the United States would abandon its proposed Antiballistic Missile system? To say that such judgments are highly subjective and not susceptible of mathematical determination would be to understate the matter. Traditionally, in disarmament negotiations officials of one country have offered to trade obsolete or marginal weapons for a possible enemy's most important weapons. Or, desiring to protect their "domestic safety," nations routinely identify their principal weapons as "defensive," to be used only if the country is attacked, while their enemy's principal weapons are "offensive," posing a threat to global peace. American officials had no doubt that their planned ABM system was defensive; Soviet officials viewed it as a step greatly enhancing America's offensive capability, which would in time have to be answered by some addition to the Kremlin's arsenal.

This familiar action–reaction cycle in the history of military technology underscores a fourth troublesome aspect of the disarmament conundrum. The attempt to curtail armaments involves two basically distinct, if closely related, stages. One of these is concerned with the question, "How can *existing weapons stockpiles be reduced,* permitting some degree of actual disarmament or *arms reduction?*" The second stage is concerned with limiting the *future production of armaments* (arms control or arms limitation), in an attempt to prevent a renewal of arms competition. The reduction of current military arsenals may or may not entail efforts to prevent the production of new and better weapons in the future (although the former would seem rather pointless without the latter). Or, negotiators may be unable to agree upon the elimination of weapons already in existence, although they may reach an accord prohibiting the production of new weapons (the Nuclear Test-Ban Treaty of 1963 fell into this category). In some disarmament schemes, a "freeze" on existing armaments levels, coupled with a prohibition against the manufacture of new armaments, is proposed to stop the momentum of the arms race. Such an agreement may provide a "cooling off" period among heavily armed nations; it may be a symbol of good will and mutual trust; and it may serve as a preliminary step in the reduction of military stockpiles.

For both the reduction of existing armaments and the prevention of future arms production, the idea of *arms control* suggests an aspect of the problem which has loomed large in postwar negotiations. As we shall see, it has been a pivotal consideration in the American approach to the disarmament question. Arms control implies some mechanism or procedure for *supervis-*

ing national compliance with the terms of the agreements reached. Such control entails determination and verification of facts about national compliance (or noncompliance), along with the application of sanctions against nations violating the agreement. But how is such control to be exercised? How will the international community discover whether infractions of the disarmament agreement occur? And, perhaps most crucially, if noncompliance is discovered, what steps can be taken to enforce the terms of the disarmament accord upon recalcitrant nations? As much as any other problem, failure to solve this dilemma has been responsible for the deadlock in postwar disarmament proceedings.

Postwar Disarmament Efforts—An Overview

Writing in 1956, one student of disarmament cautioned:

It is important to avoid confusing long hours of international debate, vast piles of printed documents, and elaborate charts of institutional structure with meaningful accomplishment. Aside from certain limited and ephemeral successes which were achieved outside the League structure in the interwar period, the movement for arms reduction and limitation has been as unproductive of results as it has been productive of words. The tremendous display of military fireworks from 1939 to 1945 was only the final and most tragic bit of evidence that the League's efforts had been an abject failure, and the equally complete sterility of the work thus far undertaken by the United Nations in this field is one of the most glaring facts of international life.[69]

By the 1970s, it was evident that the characterization of disarmament proceedings as demonstrating "complete sterility" was too harsh a judgment. That progress in reducing global armaments had fallen considerably short of the world's expectations was undeniable. Whatever progress had been made on this front had been insufficient to *reverse* the escalation of military budgets or to permit any noteworthy diversion of funds spent on munitions to more worthwhile purposes. Yet the record of disarmament discussions was not entirely devoid of results. Perhaps the most encouraging sign was that the more powerful nations had *not* given up the quest for arms control; in some respects, the chances for achieving it seemed somewhat more favorable in the 1970s than in the 1950s.

The postwar period began auspiciously enough. Germany, Japan, and the other Axis powers were disarmed by the Allies. The United States and its allies rapidly reduced their military establishments—to the point (as the Korean War in 1950 revealed) of endangering the security of the free world. Among the great nations, only Soviet

Russia continued to maintain a large military establishment.

Even before the end of World War II, American officials were aware that weapons technology had been revolutionized by the development of the atomic bomb; perfection of what was sometimes called "the absolute weapon" gave unprecedented urgency to the search for a disarmament accord. America, therefore, joined with Great Britain and Canada in issuing a declaration (on November 15, 1945) identifying the atomic bomb as a "means of destruction hitherto unknown, against which there can be no adequate military defense. . . ." According to this Anglo–Canadian–American statement, the "prevention of war" was the only certain means of escaping nuclear devastation.[70]

Within a few months, the United States introduced a disarmament plan in the United Nations which contained many of the elements characteristic of the American position on arms control throughout the postwar period. This was the "Baruch Plan," introduced on June 14, 1946. The plan called for the establishment of a new international agency (an International Development Authority) possessing broad powers to own and control all nuclear energy facilities which might endanger world peace. The agency would control, inspect, and license all nuclear activities, would foster beneficial uses of nuclear technology, and would sponsor research and development basic to scientific progress. After these steps had been taken, there would be cessation of production of all nuclear weapons, disposal of all existing stockpiles of such weapons, and transmission to the Authority of complete information concerning nuclear technology. The proposal envisioned rigid enforcement of the provisions of any disarmament proposal adopted, with "immediate, swift, and sure punishments," on the order of the Nuremberg war crimes trials, to be meted out to violators. The Security Council would have no veto of the Authority's findings and operations.[71]

On June 19, Soviet Russia offered a counterproposal to the Baruch Plan. Cardinal features were: an immediate international agreement pledging nations "not to use atomic weapons in any circumstances whatsoever," and requiring them to terminate current production of nuclear weapons and to dispose of existing stockpiles of nuclear weapons within three months after the agreement was reached; a pledge that signatories would regard violation of the agreement as a crime against humanity; and a further pledge that within six months the signatories would "pass legislation providing severe penalties" for violations of the provisions of the agreement.[72]

These two proposals were of lasting significance in shaping the course of disarmament negotiations over the next several years. The proposals defined the positions of the two rival power blocs whose relations colored most global political issues. Each plan reflected certain underlying assumptions indicative of each side's approach to disarmament and closely related questions in international affairs. Although there were some modifications on each side in the years ahead, the deadlock on disarmament which ensued over these two conflicting proposals remained essentially unchanged thereafter.

The cardinal ingredients in the American plan were establishment of foolproof international inspection and control over all phases of nuclear technology, cessation of nuclear weapons production, disposal of accumulated atomic weapons stockpiles, and surrender of full information concerning nuclear technology to the Authority—in that order. The fundamental elements in the Soviet plan were immediate and unconditional prohibition of the use and manufacture of atomic weapons, destruction of existing stockpiles, and establishment of a nationally operated inspection and control system—in that order.

Behind each of these proposals were certain hard realities. The United States possessed the atomic bomb; the U.S.S.R. did not. Therefore, America was unwilling to relinquish its advantage until international control over nuclear processes had been guaranteed. Lacking the atomic bomb, but possessing formidable ground and air forces, the U.S.S.R. was following the ancient stratagem of seeking to deprive its opponent of its strongest weapon, thereby leaving the Communist bloc an overwhelmingly advantageous position in nonnuclear weapons. Meantime, pending negotiation of an acceptable disarmament scheme, Russia would press on rapidly to expand its own scientific–technological knowledge in the field of nuclear energy.

The American-sponsored Baruch Plan was widely hailed as a generous and statesmanlike gesture designed to bring the military applications of nuclear energy under tight international supervision. The United States was the only country currently possessing nuclear weapons; it offered to place this formidable arsenal under international control. It is at least an interesting speculation whether Soviet Russia or Communist China or one of the newly independent African nations would have made such an offer under comparable circumstances. Yet, from the Soviet perspective, the Baruch Plan contained two major defects which perhaps foreordained its rejection by the Kremlin. At this stage, and on many occasions thereafter in disarmament proceedings, the United States insisted upon "ironclad" inspection before it relinquished its nuclear monopoly. The efficacy of an international control system had to be demonstrated *before* America handed over its nuclear arsenal to an international agency. Given the Russian society's traditional suspicion toward the outside world, along with its ideological militancy during the Stalinist period, it was doubtful whether Moscow would accept any plan calling for the inspection of industrial and military installations inside Russia's borders. The "staging" aspect of the Baruch Plan also proved unacceptable to Soviet policy-makers. The Baruch Plan envisioned that, through a process of successfully implemented stages, international control of nuclear energy would be established. America would keep its nuclear arsenal *until the final stage;* it would judge the extent to which the requirements of each stage had been met; and only if Washington were satisfied concerning Soviet behavior and intentions would it relinquish control over its nuclear stockpile to an international authority. This sequence of stages might of course extend over several years, during which time the United States would retain its nuclear superiority, perhaps even increasing its lead over the Soviet Union; and in the end, if the Baruch Plan did *not* produce nuclear disarmament, the United States would retain its nuclear arsenal and perhaps hold a commanding position in nuclear technology which no other country could match. That the Soviet Union would not accept this plan was perhaps predictable. Even a country less antagonistic to the United States (such as the Fifth French Republic under President Charles de Gaulle) would probably have been unwilling to concede such advantages.

As for the Soviet counterplan, its weaknesses were even more glaring and unrealistic. At a time when the United States had reduced its military strength to a small fraction of its wartime level—leaving American nuclear power as the only counterweight to the superiority of the Red Army on the European continent—the Kremlin asked Washington to give up its nuclear monopoly in exchange for vague promises of future compliance with an international disarmament agreement and assurances that at some undisclosed date in the future an effective system of inspection and control would be established. During a period when American officials were deeply concerned about Soviet violations of the promises made at the Yalta and Potsdam Conferences in 1945, concerning Allied cooperation in determining the political future of Eastern Europe, Washington could hardly be blamed for its reluctance to accept Soviet statements of good intentions at face value. Soviet behavior in dealing with weaker nations hardly inspired confidence that its professions could be relied upon to preserve international security.

Recurring Issues in Disarmament Negotiations

The positions taken by the two super-powers and their allies and satellites, during the UN debate on the Baruch Plan were, in most particulars, identical with positions held throughout the disarmament negotiations in the years thereafter. Proposals, counterproposals, and attempts to create syntheses between them, resulted in negotiations that were as prolonged and intricate as they were usually fruitless in halting the steady accretions in national armaments and the destructive power of modern weapons. In the absence of a workable disarmament agreement, both sides pressed forward rapidly in the field of nuclear technology. Soviet Russia broke America's monopoly of the uranium bomb in 1949. The United States, meanwhile, was developing the thermonuclear (hydrogen) bomb, which it perfected in 1952. Less than a year later, the U.S.S.R. had succeeded in making a "hydrogen device," thereby re-establishing approximate nuclear weapons parity with the United States. The Korean War prompted a considerable increase in the level of "conventional" weapons* throughout the non-Communist world. Furthermore, East and West alike pressed forward with the development of a category of weapons fitting neatly into neither classification: "tactical" nuclear weapons, designed for use on the battlefield or against enemy submarines or (potentially, if not by the mid-1960s, actually) as "antimissile" missiles for defense. The result was that the destructive power of *all* categories of weapons reached a new high. One thermonuclear bomb dropped on New York or Moscow, for example, would exceed the total destructive power of all the bombs used in World War II.

In 1964, Communist China joined the ranks of the nuclear powers; three years later, Peking exploded its first hydrogen bomb. And by the early 1970s, the government of Red China had begun to develop a missile capability; although it would require many years before China could seriously rival America or Soviet Russia in missile strength, in time the Chinese would undoubtedly be able to bring much of Asia at least within the range of their nuclear arsenal. Several other countries had the capacity to join the "nuclear club"; faced with

---

*The term "conventional" weapons does not have a universally accepted definition. In Martin's words, it means "all armaments and armed forces except atomic, radioactive, lethal-chemical and biological weapons, and all future weapons having comparable destructive characteristics." Andrew Martin, *Collective Security* (Paris: UNESCO, 1952), p. 81. The principal point of ambiguity arises, however, about tactical nuclear weapons intended chiefly for use against troop concentrations on the battlefield. If these are looked upon as simply highly destructive "conventional" weapons, ironically the destructive force of *several* of these could easily exceed that of a single nuclear bomb used against enemy cities!

For that matter, the definition of "armaments" themselves is extremely difficult to draw precisely and meaningfully. Is the steel-making potential of a nation part of its "armaments"? Normally, it would not be so regarded. Yet in any future military conflict, the side that possesses the greatest economic potential—the greatest ability, that is to say, to "bounce back" from a nuclear attack—could be expected to win the conflict in the end.

continuing Chinese antagonism, the government of India had not ruled out the possibility that it might develop nuclear weapons; Israel could easily become a nuclear power (and, in fact, might have secretly produced a nuclear arsenal).

The postwar period had witnessed two outstanding developments with regard to modern weapons. The *cost* of armaments for all nations had escalated rapidly; sophisticated modern military hardware was extremely expensive, and there was no indication that this trend would be reversed. The destructiveness of nuclear and nonnuclear weapons alike had also risen spectacularly. The widespread use of automatic weapons, napalm, rockets, and other "conventional" methods of devastation meant that even limited wars like the Vietnam conflict reached new heights of destructiveness.

The governments of the world have not been insensitive to these trends or to the urgent necessity for stopping the arms race. Their failure to do so cannot be attributed to lack of studies or of negotiations devoted to all conceivable aspects of the disarmament problem. As in other eras of history, disarmament discussions of course were heavily conditioned by the state of *political* relations among the great and medium powers; during some periods of the cold war, Soviet–American tensions precluded any meaningful negotiations aimed at reducing military arsenals. But the process of de-Stalinization in Soviet Russia, along with the expanding role of the Afro–Asian nations in global affairs, supplied a new impetus to the search for an arms-limitation accord. Except possibly for the Chinese Communists, all nations acknowledged the desirability of curtailing the production of armaments, and all conceded the danger to humanity at large if the arms race went unchecked.

Throughout the months and years of prolonged and often sterile negotiations devoted to arms control since World War II, certain key issues have persisted. Disarmament proposals have often differed fundamentally in their details; but in their essentials, most have been concerned with a number of recurrent questions which might be viewed as "keys" to any successful disarmament accord. Insight into the intricacies of the disarmament debate since World War II can more profitably be gained by focusing our attention upon these key questions instead of tracing out chronologically the pattern of disarmament negotiations since 1946.*

*The following provide detailed, more chronologically oriented, discussions of postwar disarmament negotiations: Louis Henkin, ed., *Arms Control* (Englewood Cliffs, N.J.: Prentice-Hall, 1961); B G. Bechhoefer, *Postwar Negotiations for Arms Control* (Washington, D.C.: Brookings Institution, 1961); J. W. Spanier and J. L. Nogee, *The Politics of Disarmament* (New York: Praeger, 1962); Lincoln P. Bloomfield, "Arms Control

The Scope of Disarmament Proposals

A central issue in disarmament discussions is *the scope* of the arms-control agreement to be adopted. Two alternative positions have been proposed from time to time. One is *general and complete disarmament.* By one decisive step, as it were, the powers would dispose of their military arsenals, perhaps by having a "bomber bonfire" or taking such comparable steps as a wholesale "dumping" of weapons into the ocean depths. General and complete disarmament (sometimes called GCD) has been a prominent theme in Soviet arms-control measures for many years. During the 1930s, Soviet Foreign Minister Maxim Litvinov asserted that "the only way to disarm is to disarm." Some thirty years later, Soviet Premier Nikita Khrushchev urged the UN General Assembly to adopt his proposal for achieving GCD within four years. All nations participating in disarmament discussions endorse GCD *as an ultimate goal* (subject of course to the retention of sufficient arms to equip domestic police forces and perhaps provide for "self-defense").

It may legitimately be questioned, however, whether general and complete disarmament has ever been proposed seriously, other than as a psychological or propaganda gesture. Soviet spokesmen undoubtedly realized that their endorsement of the goal had little prospect of being accepted; by making it, they could reap propaganda capital with virtually no risk that the Red Army would soon be demobilized. Appealing as it may be for idealistic, moral, or other reasons, the case for GCD breaks against the rock of national unwillingness to move, by a single step, from massive reliance upon armaments to no reliance upon

and World Government," *World Politics* 14 (1962), 633–645; Hedley Bull, *Control of the Arms Race* (London: Weidenfeld and Nicolson, 1961); Alexander Dallin *et al., The Soviet Union and Disarmament* (New York: Praeger, 1964); Arthur Dean, *Test Ban and Disarmament* (New York: Harper & Row, 1966); Lawrence Finkelstein, "Arms Inspection," *International Conciliation* 540 (November, 1962); Robert A. Levine, *The Arms Debate* (Cambridge, Mass.: Harvard University Press, 1963); Martin C. McGuire, *Secrecy and the Arms Race* (Cambridge, Mass.: Harvard University Press, 1965); James E. Dougherty, and John F. Lehman, Jr., eds., *The Prospects for Arms Control* (New York: MacFadden-Bartell, 1965); James E. Dougherty and John F. Lehman, Jr., *Arms Control for the Late 1960s* (New York: Van Nostrand Reinhold, 1967); William B. Bader, *The United States and the Spread of Nuclear Weapons* (New York: Pegasus, 1968); Alastair Buchan, ed. *A World of Nuclear Powers?* (Englewood Cliffs, N.J.: Prentice-Hall, 1966); Walter C. Clemens, Jr., "Military Technology in the 1970s," in Abdul A. Said, ed., *America's World Role in the 70s* (Englewood Cliffs, N.J.: Prentice-Hall, 1970); J. I. Coffey, "The Anti-Ballistic Missile Debate," *Foreign Affairs* 45 (April, 1967), 403–414; William C. Foster, "New Directions in Arms Control and Disarmament," *Foreign Affairs* 43 (July, 1965), 587–601; Kenneth Younger, "The Spectre of Nuclear Proliferation," *International Affairs* 42 (January, 1966), 14–23.

them to protect national security or to achieve other goals.

For two reasons, disarmament proceedings have, therefore, been devoted to discussing measures for achieving *partial and limited arms reduction.* If GCD is possible at all, it is likely to be attained only by an evolutionary process, whereby the feasibility of disarmament on a very limited scale is demonstrated. A limited "first step" could conceivably generate the kind of confidence and good will among nations required for ultimately reaching the goal of general disarmament. The other virtue of partial disarmament is that it is the only kind which has any remote chance of being accepted. If arms-control discussions are to be anything more than propaganda exchanges, experience has made it clear that agreement is likely only within rather narrow limits (such as the demilitarization of Antarctica or the ban on nuclear weapons testing), involving perhaps *marginal* military activities not jeopardizing the security of the nation. Yet a demonstration of the feasibility of arms reduction in an area of this kind could, as President Kennedy characterized the nuclear test-ban accord in 1963, "be a step toward reduced world tensions and broader areas of agreement."[73] As President Kennedy stated on another occasion when he called on America and Soviet Russia to engage in a "peace race," both countries should "advance together step-by-step, stage-by-stage, until general and complete disarmament has been achieved."[74] Although the prospect seemed remote, America's commitment to the goal of GCD at least kept the Soviet Union from enjoying monopolistic use of this idea in its efforts to win the good will of other countries.

Political Issues and Arms Control

In a comprehensive review of the foreign policy objectives of his administration in 1970, President Nixon devoted considerable attention to the need for arms reduction. The United States and the Soviet Union were currently engaged in what some observers regarded as among the most important discussions in the postwar period—the SALT talks at Helsinki. Referring to these negotiations, President Nixon underscored the intimate relationship between progress in arms reduction and in resolving the outstanding *political issues* fomenting international tensions:

We continue to be prepared to discuss the issues that divide us from the Communist countries. Whether in addressing the cruel division of Europe or the future security of Asia we shall try to deepen the dialogue with the Communist powers.

In seeking a disarmament accord with Moscow, President Nixon asserted, Washington desired to "build a lasting peace without sacrificing the interests of our allies and friends."[75] President John F. Kennedy expressed the same idea succinctly in 1961, when he said that genuine peace "is not solely a matter of military or technical problems, it is primarily a problem of politics and people." Again in 1963, after the great powers had agreed upon the Nuclear Test-Ban Treaty, Kennedy reminded Americans that this agreement would "not resolve all conflicts, or cause the Communists to forego their ambitions, or eliminate the dangers of war."[76]

To highlight the connection between arms reduction and the settlement of major political disputes, we need to ask: "Why do nations *acquire* armaments and continue to *build up* their military arsenals?" Many reasons (including some essentially irrational ones, like the fact that an arms race creates it own momentum) might be cited. But one fundamental reason is that nations depend upon armed force to safeguard or achieve their most vital *political* interests, most basically their national security. Why, for example, did the United States begin to rearm in the early 1950s? The immediate objective was to ensure the security of South Korea against absorption into the Communist bloc. More generally, it was to strengthen the American position in Asia and the free world as a whole; during this period, for example, the freedom of Berlin and West Germany were being directly threatened by Communist pressures. In brief, American policy-makers concluded that without an expansion in the national defense base, the United States would be unable to protect or achieve certain political goals deemed vital to itself and its allies. Failure to safeguard these political interests could in turn lead ultimately to a major threat to the security of the free world. The Soviet decision to maintain a large military establishment after World War II was undoubtedly dictated by basically the same rationale: The Kremlin's political objectives demanded reliance upon superior military force.

The relationship between the existence of political tensions among nations and a high level of national armaments is unquestionably a mutually interacting one. Soviet–American contention over the future of Berlin, for example, no doubt disposes each side to maintain the kind of armed forces needed to pursue its objectives in Germany; the fact that each side possesses a formidable military machine—and is adding to its armaments stockpile continuously—may serve to "harden" attitudes on both sides, rendering a solution of the political controversy more difficult than ever. America's military involvement in Southeast Asia—in which there appeared to be a kind of built-in compulsion to *expand* military commitments, thereby posing new obstacles to a political settlement—may only be an extreme case of the kind of cycle that has characterized political disputes among nations throughout modern history.

Postwar disarmament negotiations have, therefore, recognized the intimate connection between arms reduction and the resolution of major international controversies, particularly those between the United States and the Soviet Union, likely to engender violence among nations. If they had formally settled very few of the long-standing questions dividing them, by the 1970s the United States and the Soviet Union had at least arrived at de facto and tacit understandings concerning a number of issues (like the removal of Africa from the realm of active cold war strife and the preservation of the status quo in Germany) which improved the prospects for meaningful progress in arms limitation.

The Problem of "Staging" or Phasing

A staff study written for the Senate Foreign Relations Committee in the mid-1950s asserted that: "At the present time, some of the issues of disarmament revolve less around what is to be done than when it is done."[77] And in the same period, Secretary of Defense Charles E. Wilson declared that:

Any agreement for reductions under the terms of a comprehensive disarmament program must be carried out by stages. These stages must be clearly defined and should be progressive, beginning with areas of least sensitivity. Each of the succeeding stages should only be initiated after the preceding stage has been satisfactorily completed.[78]

These assertions call attention to another basic problem in any disarmament negotiations: What will be the exact sequence of steps (or "stages") by which nations move from an existing high level of armaments to a condition of massive arms reduction? The Baruch Plan, it will be recalled, specified several stages in the process whereby the United States would ultimately relinquish control over its nuclear arsenal to an international authority. Soviet disarmament proposals have also enumerated a different sequence of steps by which a disarmed world could become a reality. Fundamental differences—growing out of dissimilar ideological systems, diverse strategic positions, and varying kinds of international responsibilities and commitments—have characterized Soviet and American viewpoints on staging.

Although the details of the American position on this issue have been modified from time to time, Washington's conception of the problem of staging has been reasonably consistent and clear-

cut. The basic idea is that progress toward a major reduction in global armaments would be made by means of a series of steps; progression from one stage to another would occur after—and *only* after—*verified* compliance with the requirements of the earlier stage had been achieved; as the nations of the world successfully demonstrated both the willingness and the ability to fulfill the requirements of each phase, a new stage would be entered, calling for additional reduction of military arsenals on a verified basis; ultimately, as the Baruch Plan emphasized, nuclear arsenals would be curtailed—and the world would be close to the goal of general and complete disarmament. The problem of staging, it is evident, is closely related to another issue we shall discuss below: the problem of inspection and control in disarmament proceedings. American officials have consistently held the position that national compliance with the requirements of any stage must be *verified;* and accurate verification has in turn demanded the existence and successful operation of an inspection-control system, presumably administered by an international authority.

The Soviet position on staging has differed from the American in many respects. The *order* of desired stages in Moscow's disarmament schemes, for example, has contrasted sharply with American proposals. Although the Kremlin has been less explicit about the precise nature of the stages it favors, in general terms, its disarmament plans have called for the total prohibition of the manufacture of nuclear weapons and the use of existing ones in the first stage; the next stage would be the reduction of stockpiles of both conventional and nuclear armaments, along with cuts in military manpower; and the last stage would entail establishment and operation of a system of international inspection and control. Thus, in the Soviet view, an effective international inspection-control system would come *after* disarmament had been achieved, while in the American view such a system would be set up, and its viability demonstrated, *before* nations reduced their weapons stockpiles.

The question of the circumstances under which progress would be made from one stage to the next has also fomented deadlock between the United States and the Soviet Union. Washington has consistently demanded *full and verified compliance* with the requirements of each stage before the next stage is entered. Moscow has favored the idea of *automatic transition* from one stage to another, on the basis of each nation's willingness to certify that it has complied with the conditions of the preceding stage. In the American view, good faith and mutual trust must be clearly demonstrated before a new round of arms reduction is carried out. In the Soviet view, the act of reducing armaments will in time provide the requisite atmosphere of international trust and good will needed for an effective system of inspection and control to be implemented successfully.

Inspection and Control—Key to Disarmament

Throughout the postwar period, perhaps the root cause of deadlock between the United States and the Soviet Union has been *the problem of inspection and control.* From the Baruch Plan forward, the necessity for an adequate (sometimes called "foolproof") inspection-control system has been a central ingredient in American disarmament proposals. Soviet willingness to permit the operation of such a system has been, in the American view, both a token of Moscow's good faith and the key to any really effective disarmament accord. When American policy-makers called upon the Kremlin to demonstrate its belief in disarmament by "deeds, not words," they maintained that the most convincing evidence Moscow could offer would be to accept independent verification of its compliance with any arms-control agreement reached.

As we have noted, Soviet officials have tended to take a very different position on this cardinal issue. In the first place, the Kremlin's disarmament position has relegated an inspection—control system to the final stage, to come about only after substantial disarmament has been achieved. Soviet Premier Nikita Khruschev stated in 1959: "We are in favor of strict control over the implementation of a disarmament agreement when it is reached. . . . We are in favor of general disarmament under control, but we are against control without disarmament."[79] In the second place, Moscow has consistently rejected the concept of international inspection as merely a form of ill-concealed "espionage," whereby non-Communist nations desired to gain secret information about Soviet Russia's military defenses and its industrial complex. In view of the Russian society's traditional suspicion of the outside world, it is perhaps inevitable that any plan contemplating wholesale inspection of military and industrial installations within Russia's borders would be denounced by Soviet policy-makers; and if such inspection were carried out by an agency of the United Nations (where America has traditionally enjoyed majority support for its policies), then the proposal would be doubly objectionable. Moscow's opposition to this idea reflected a reality which sometimes tended to be obscured in American proposals: An effective system of inspection and control *would* entail the most sweeping kind of surveillance within the borders of at least the stronger nations of the world, and a functioning "control" system would (at least within the orbit of its operations) require a substantial relinquish-

ing of national sovereignty.* Beyond limited disarmament measures relying upon various forms of "self-enforcement" (and we shall take note of these below), the Soviet Union has consistently opposed the kind of elaborate inspection-control system which American officials believe is essential to any successful disarmament accord.[80]

By the 1960s, the ongoing progress of science and technology had opened the possibility that certain forms of arms reduction might be successfully carried out on the basis of self-enforcement or voluntary national compliance, without undue danger to the security of the nations participating in the agreement. Gains in space technology were especially crucial in this regard. Orbiting space satellites, launched by the United States, Soviet Russia, and perhaps other countries, were capable of monitoring such military activities as the construction of missile (or antiballistic missile) sites; highly sophisticated radar and other scientific equipment allowed one government to detect launchings by other governments; other detection devices permitted scientists in one country to discover when another government had exploded nuclear or thermonuclear weapons (although such detection was not infallible, particularly for small nuclear devices). The more heavily armed nations also confronted intense pressure from the international community to curtail the testing of nuclear weapons in order to avoid continued contamination of the atmosphere. The strongest inducement to voluntary compliance with at least limited arms-control measures, however, was perhaps the realization among the great and small powers alike that failure to slow the momentum of the arms race endangered *all nations* and perhaps jeopardized the future of civilization itself. The most outstanding example of a self-regulating or voluntary disarmament accord was the Nuclear Test-Ban Treaty of 1963. Literally speaking, this agreement was not a "disarmament" measure: It did not actually reduce weapons stockpiles. At best, it made it

---

*The concepts of inspection and control are usually coupled, although in fact they are separate ideas. *Inspection* refers to verification of national compliance with a disarmament agreement and the disclosure of violations of its provisions. Such inspection would presumably be carried out by an international agency, whose officials would operate without hindrance by national governments; this agency would presumably have the right to inspect any military or industrial installation for evidence of noncompliance with the requirements of the disarmament accord. *Control* refers to procedures to be followed in dealing with nations found to be in violation of an arms-limitation agreement. Once noncompliance had been discovered and verified, steps would have to be taken by the international community to *compel* compliance by the nation concerned and possibly to "discipline" the nation found to be in violation of the terms of the accord. For both functions, of course, a crucial question is: "What nations could be trusted to staff an inspection-control agency and to exercise the powers assigned to it?"

more difficult (although certainly not impossible) for great and medium powers to acquire new nuclear weapons. By this agreement, the signatories pledged not to engage in above-ground or underwater nuclear testing that would produce massive radioactive fallout (some forms of tests, such as those deep underground, were permissible). Compliance with the understanding was voluntary and the degree of adherence by all nations was monitored by national scientific agencies throughout the world. Except for countries like Communist China (which did not sign the agreement), it appeared that the principal nuclear powers were complying with the accord in good faith.[81]

Other forms of arms control depending upon self-enforcement have also been achieved in recent years. At the end of 1959, the United States, the Soviet Union, France, Great Britain, Japan, and several smaller nations signed an agreement prohibiting the creation of military installations in Antarctica; this accord provided for mutual inspection of that continent to assure compliance with the terms of the agreement. On December 19, 1966, the UN General Assembly unanimously adopted a treaty providing for the demilitarization of outer space. This accord was designed to prevent military competition in space exploration by the great powers and to guarantee such exploration on an equal basis for all nations. The Nuclear Test-Ban Treaty of 1963 provided impetus to a movement supported by Africans and Latin Americans to have their regions recognized as "nuclear-free zones," in which the great powers would neither introduce nor use nuclear weapons. Although no formal international agreement has been reached respecting Africa, a kind of de facto understanding has prevailed, the general effect of which has been to inhibit Washington and Moscow from converting Africa into an active arena of cold war competition. The Latin American nations, however, have been more successful in getting their desire incorporated into an international agreement. On February 14, 1967, a Treaty for Prohibition of Nuclear Weapons in Latin America was signed at Mexico City; this accord prohibited the testing, deployment, or use of nuclear weapons throughout the region. Then, after prolonged discussions and negotiations on the problem, on June 12, 1968, the UN General Assembly adopted a draft resolution prohibiting the "proliferation" of nuclear weapons; the nuclear "have" nations were enjoined by the agreement from making nuclear weapons available to the nuclear "have-not" nations. Not unexpectedly, some nations aspiring to become leading nuclear powers (notably France and Communist China) were unenthusiastic about the agreement. French officials indicated their reluctant acceptance of its provisions; Communist Chinese officials denounced it as a form of Soviet-American

collaborationism at China's expense. Even countries like West Germany and India expressed reservations about the understanding. In the absence of a general cold war *détente* and settlement of issues like the Sino-Indian border controversy, the nonproliferation agreement tended to leave vulnerable countries in a position of military inferiority and to deny them the diplomatic influence exercised by members of the "nuclear club."[82] The concept of nuclear nonproliferation unquestionably had the support of a majority of the nations of the world; in time, most of them formally adhered to the treaty. Yet it also had to be observed that this accord did not prevent a nation like Israel or India or Brazil from *developing its own nuclear weapons;* Israel quite possibly had already done so; and countries like India and Brazil were capable of doing so.* At best, this step merely slowed down the momentum toward indefinite expansion of the nuclear club and perhaps imposed certain obstacles which would impede a "have-not" nation from becoming a nuclear power.

Other self-regulating disarmament measures were also possible and would undoubtedly be taken in the future. During its first year in office, for example, the Nixon administration announced that the United States henceforth would refrain from the use of chemical and biological weapons of mass destruction; American development of such weapons was drastically curtailed. In the early 1970s also, the United States, the Soviet Union, and other maritime nations were discussing methods of demilitarizing the ocean floors in order to reserve this vast area solely for peaceful uses. Successful demilitarization of the sea beds would probably depend upon some combination of voluntary national compliance and at least limited international supervision and control.

Encouraging as they were, steps like the nuclear test-ban agreement or the nuclear nonproliferation accord actually did little to slow the momentum of the global arms race. By the 1970s, the level of national armaments was at an all-time high; as we observed earlier, the developing nations were expending large portions of their national budgets for modern weapons. Thus far, the progress made in unilateral and self-regulating forms of arms control had *not* resulted in a real breakthrough in disarmament discussions affecting either nuclear or conventional military arsenals. Stopping the armaments spiral, it seemed clear, depended upon something more than unilateral arms limitation or schemes involving voluntary compliance.

*A key provision of the Nixon Doctrine, discussed in Chapter 13, was that nations like India would be protected by the American "nuclear shield" if they faced a threat by nations armed with nuclear weapons. A major reason for this pledge was to induce India and other countries *not* to produce their own nuclear arsenals.

SALT Negotiations

By the late 1960s, several forces converged to give the search for a disarmament formula renewed impetus. A number of limited accords (although they did not actually reduce the level of global armaments) offered hope that a more sweeping agreement on disarmament could be reached. By the mid-1960s, cold war animosities between the United States and the Soviet Union had lessened significantly; not even the Vietnam conflict rekindled the earlier cold war tensions; the danger of an armed clash between the United States and Soviet Russia in Europe seemed altogether remote; Washington and Moscow jointly supported efforts by the United Nations to arrive at a settlement in the turbulent Middle East. Growing internal problems also shaped American and Soviet attitudes toward national defense. The cost of modern weaponry continued to rise—straining the ability of even the wealthier nations to develop ever more powerful implements of war, particularly when the ones they already possessed had a substantial "overkill" capacity. The Communist hierarchy in Russia was under considerable pressure to devote its resources to a number of more or less critical domestic problems. After several years of extremely high military expenditures in connection with the war in Southeast Asia, the United States was also faced with public dissatisfaction over domestic issues, the size of the defense budget, and the accelerating cost of modern weapons.

Two interrelated conditions pertaining to American and Soviet military strength also contributed to a conviction in Washington and Moscow that the time was propitious for a possible breakthrough in the long deadlocked disarmament discussions. By the late 1960s, a rough equilibrium existed between Soviet and American military strength. In Chapter 1, the point was emphasized that comparisons of national power are always crude and approximate; the power of a nation consists of intangible, as well as tangible, elements, and the former are virtually impossible to quantify. As the United States discovered after prolonged involvement in Southeast Asia, for example, civilian morale can be a crucial factor in determining the degree or kind of power available to policy-makers for the achievement of foreign policy goals. Even in the narrow realm of military power alone, judgments concerning American vis-à-vis Soviet sgrength are always highly subjective. The *conditions* under which the armed forces of each side might be employed, for example, could play a crucial role in determining whether Washington or Moscow were more successful in achieving its diplomatic goals. Yet in the view of many qualified observers, by the late 1960s the United States and the Soviet Union were more or less evenly matched militarily. Each

had a massive "overkill" capability; each possessed a formidable "deterrent" capacity to prevent attack, along with a "second-strike" capacity to devastate an enemy after an initial attack; and each continued to spend a high percentage of its national budget for defense.*

Closely related to the existence of this military equilibrium was the fact that the two super-powers were at the threshold of a new round of competition in weapons development. As in earlier stages of history, the approximate military balance between the more powerful nations of the world was *highly precarious* and would probably prove temporary. Progress in space technology, electronics, and other spheres of scientific technology well-nigh guaranteed that one side would acquire a military advantage, which would quickly be "answered" by new weapons developed by the other side—setting in motion the familiar armaments spiral characteristic of modern history. As always, American and Soviet policy-makers alike regarded their latest weapons as "defensive" and as additions to their national arsenals needed to counterbalance superior force on the other side. Thus, according to American officials,

---

*Various phrases have been used to describe the condition of greater or lesser arms equality between the two super-powers. For a number of years, the condition was referred to as a "nuclear balance of terror"; President Nixon and his advisers referred to a condition of "arms sufficiency" on each side. The basic idea was that both America and Soviet Russia possessed "first-strike" nuclear capabilities, along with a substantial "second-strike" force—meaning that, if one side attacked the other, the aggressor could not itself escape ultimate destruction, producing a condition of "mutual deterrence." But for mutual deterrence to continue to exist the first-strike and second-strike capacities of both sides had to remain reasonably secure. American officials feared, for example, that a steady buildup in offensive Soviet missile strength was "aimed at" impairing the first-strike capacity of the United States—thereby in time "inviting" a Soviet attack on America, during a period when the arms balance had been tipped in Russia's favor.

The arms parity between the two super-powers did not of course mean that they were equally matched in all aspects of armed strength. The United States, for example, was ahead in submarine-based missiles and intercontinental bombers; it was also converting both its land-based and its submarine-based missiles to multiple warheads, thereby greatly expanding their destructive power. By contrast, the Soviet Union had more (and newer) land-based missiles; it was also converting this force to multiple warheads. The U.S.S.R. also possessed a functioning, if limited, antiballistic missile system, while America was just beginning to install such a system. Soviet land-based missiles were larger than American; they could, therefore, accommodate a greater number of independent warheads than those of the United States. Yet America had a headstart in converting its Polaris submarine fleet to the new multiple-warhead Poseidon missiles. See *The New York Times* (November 18 and 23, 1969; February 21, 1970). See also several essays dealing with Soviet and American military strength in Mortan A. Kaplan, ed., *Great Issues of International Politics* (Chicago: Aldine, 1970), pp. 323–431.

a new antiballistic missile system was required as a counterweight to the U.S.S.R.'s ABM system and its newly gained offensive missile strength. By contrast, Moscow regarded the American ABM system as a deliberate threat to the existing military balance and (because it was directed against Russia's offensive missile force) as a move designed to strengthen America's offensive capability. The most serious challenge to the delicate military equilibrium between the two cold war antagonists, however, was the development Multiple Independently Targetable Re-Entry Vehicles (MIRV's)—the next stage in the evolution of long-and middle-range guided missiles equipped with nuclear warheads. MIRV's were "clusters" of warheads attached to a single ICBM; in its most advanced form, a single missile could fire several nuclear warheads (along with "dummies" to deceive enemy defenses). The wholesale conversion of single missiles to MIRV's would obviously raise the striking power of America's or Soviet Russia's military arsenal severalfold, perhaps (depending upon which country made this conversion more rapidly) giving one a decisive military advantage over the other. The United States appeared to be ahead in this process, although the Soviet Union was unquestionably making progress toward development of its own MIRV system. By contrast, the U.S.S.R. led the United States in producing a Fractional Oribital Bombardment System (FOBS). FOBS missiles were fired on an orbital trajectory, giving them the versatility to utilize a flight path capable of eluding enemy defenses. More specifically, Soivet FOBS missiles could be fired on a trajectory enabling them to orbit the earth and to re-enter the atmosphere over South America, thereby possibly evading America's radar defense network in Canada and the Arctic region. Although the Nixon administration committed the United States initially to developing a "thin" ABM system, the threat presented by Soviet FOBS missiles could compel Washington to expand its ABM defenses.

Such ongoing progress in military technology had a destabilizing impact upon the Soviet-American arms balance; less obviously, it also greatly complicated the task of disarmament negotiators. To cite but one example, orbiting space satellites might be able to detect major missile installations in the United States and the Soviet Union; they could *not*, however, detect whether such missiles were equipped with single or multiple nuclear warheads. As long as either country had MIRV's, it might reduce the *number* of its missile sites, while *increasing* the over-all firepower of its remaining missile sytem. No matter how accurately it was conducted, a "missile census" would convey little information about the actual military strength of the super-powers and it would be more difficult than ever to determine if and when a condition of rough military parity existed between them. It was equally true of course that sophisticated military hardware of this kind had become extraordinarily expensive, even for America. Both countries thus had an incentive to halt the arms race. But as in earlier periods of history, arms limitation had to be carried out in a way that did not give one country a military advantage over the other or (what could be no less crucial) create even the *impression* of favoritism for one side vis-à-vis the other. It was against this background that a new effort to resolve the disarmament deadlock was launched by President Johnson in 1966–1967; but it was not until the end of 1969 that Soviet and American negotiators began a series of meetings at Helsinki, Finland, to search for a formula that would avert another, perhaps deadly, round of arms competition. The Strategic Arms Limitation Talks (SALT) might well prove to be the most influential disarmament discussions in modern history.[83]

Several considerations favored the success of SALT negotiations. Officials in Washington and Moscow—joined by nearly all governments throughout the world—repeatedly emphasized the overdue necessity for disarming and enumerated the benefits for all mankind that would accrue from doing so. "There is no area in which we and the Soviet Union—as well as all others—have a greater common interest than in reaching agreement with regard to arms control," President Nixon declared early in 1970. In preparation for SALT discussions, American officials carried out a thorough reappraisal of the government's past position on disarmament questions, in an effort to produce fresh proposals capable of avoiding familiar stalemates (like American insistence on inspections and control versus Soviet rejection of this idea) that had blocked disarmament proceedings previously. The United States, President Nixon asserted, wanted to avoid turning SALT conversations into "the kind of propaganda battle characteristic of some previous disarmament conferences."[84] The fact that SALT negotiations were being held at all, after many months of futile efforts to break the disarmament impasse, was itself an encouraging sign that the super-powers acknowledged the urgency of ending the arms race. A few months before the Helsinki meetings, a high Soviet official reiterated his government's desire for a *general* disarmament accord, greatly exceeding in scope the limited agreements (like the nuclear nonproliferation treaty) reached in the recent past.[85] No nation of course opposed disarmament in principle. Moreover, in the light of Russia's internal economic problems and the steadily rising cost of modern weaponry, there seemed little doubt that Moscow genuinely desired to arrive at an acceptable arms-control program with the United States.

Yet if there is any lesson to be learned from disarmament proceedings since the First Hague

Conference in 1899, it is that good intentions and the realization of the grave consequences of *not* curtailing arms expenditures do not suffice to avert a new arms race. The need for reducing the level of global armaments is exceeded only by the difficulties in the path of doing so. As SALT discussions opened, the participants sought to achieve a consensus on a two-step disarmament scheme: First would come a *"freeze"* on the construction of new missile systems and other forms of modern weapons to avoid upsetting the delicate arms balance; once arms stability had been assured, Soviet and American negotiators would then try to devise a formula for actually *reducing* weapons stockpiles. At SALT discussions, no less than in past disarmament negotiations, participants were apprehensive lest agreement to eliminate one category of weapons (like ABM systems) tilt the military balance decisively in favor of a possible enemy. It was equally true of course that failure to include other categories of weapons (like MIRV missiles) might just as easily destroy the military equilibrium.

The outcome of SALT talks also hinged to no insignificant degree upon *psychological factors* and the differing interpretations which each side gave to recent developments in military technology. Soviet policy-makers, for example, were expanding the *size* of their ballistic missiles. What did this move indicate about Soviet "'intentions" toward the United States? Were these larger missiles possibly designed to knock out America's hardened missile sites, which hitherto were relatively safe from attack? Conversely, even before SALT discussions began, the United States was pushing ahead with its "thin" ABM system, ostensibly intended as a defense against *Chinese missiles*. Was Washington endeavoring to have ABM's installed *before* a disarmament accord was reached in Helsinki, thereby strengthening its position at the bargaining table? Or did America's program of ABM construction signify grave doubt in Washington that SALT negotiations would be productive? Inevitably, Soviet and American assessments of such developments differed fundamentally.

SALT discussions were also complicated by another problem which, if not new, had perhaps reached a higher stage of intensity by the 1970s. Both the American and Soviet governments were *internally divided* over the wisdom and possibility of reaching an acceptable disarmament accord. In the United States, a number of military leaders openly expressed their reluctance to support disarmament without the traditional safeguards (like on-site inspection and control) which America had insisted upon throughout the postwar period. With regard to MIRV missiles, for example, Pentagon spokesmen were convinced that it would be relatively easy for the Kremlin to produce and test such missiles clandestinely, to the

great jeopardy of American security. The Soviet Union also had its "military-industrial complex." By the 1970s, in fact, military influence upon Soviet decision-making appeared to be growing. At a time when Soviet society suffered (in some respects acutely) from economic shortages and failures, the Russian military establishment continued to demand new and better weapons. Technologically, the Soviet Union was falling behind the other industrialized nations of the world—except in technology directly applicable to warfare. Meanwhile, the Soviet military machine (and, as we observed in Chapter 9, the Soviet navy was an outstanding example) was being equipped with the latest weapons, enabling it to challenge the West and Communist China and to build up a strong military position in regions like the Middle East. The Soviet Union's annual expenditure of some $70 billion for national defense was about equal to America's military budget, although Russia's gross national product was only two-thirds of the American output. Would Russia's military elite accept a substantial reduction in military strength, in the absence of a *détente* with Communist China? In common with military elites in all countries, do Soviet commanders believe that Soviet defenses are inadequate to the challenges of modern war? Growing military influence in Soviet policy-making perhaps made it more difficult than ever for Russian and American negotiators to arrive at an acceptable disarmament formula at Helsinki.[86]

Although technical problems abounded, in the final analysis the success of SALT discussions would probably hinge upon the ability to resolve the *political issues* fomenting tensions and suspicion between the United States and the Soviet Union. In the absence of a foolproof system of international inspection and control (and the prospect of establishing such a system seemed altogether remote), effective disarmament depended ultimately upon the existence of mutual trust among the more powerful nations of the world. America had to be convinced that Soviet Russia genuinely desired arms control and would comply with its stipulations in good faith; and Soviet policy-makers had to believe the same thing about the United States. Without such mutual confidence, arms limitation would be difficult to achieve; and even if an accord were reached, it would probably collapse rapidly in an environment of continuing suspicion and hostility. Almost inevitably, some new scientific discovery or technological breakthrough would upset the arms balance, providing fresh impetus to renewed weapons competition. Today, as in earlier eras, the old dilemma still exists: Mutual trust is needed before disarmament is possible, but if this trust existed—if America really believed Soviet Russia planned no hostile move, and vice versa—then the level of global armaments would pose no real danger to peace and security. Participants in pervious disarmament conferences failed to resolve this dilemma. Whether negotiators at SALT discussions would be more successful was one of the crucial questions facing the international community in the 1970s.

NOTES

1. Gerald J. Mangone, *A Short History of International Organization* (New York: McGraw-Hill, 1954), pp. 67–90.
2. *Ibid.*, pp. 105–120; Inis L. Claude, *Swords into Plowshares* (New York: Random House, 1956), pp. 19–42. An incisive analysis of the theory and practice of international organization.
3. Julius W. Pratt. *A History of United States Foreign Policy* (Englewood Cliffs, N.J.: Prentice-Hall, 1955), pp. 454–460.
4. James T. Watkins and J. William Robinson, *General International Organization* (New York: Van Nostrand Reinhold, 1956), pp. 81–84. Provides historical background on the UN and its functions.
5. Mangone, *op. cit.*, pp. 132–133.
6. Pratt, *op. cit.*, pp. 527–558.
7. *Ibid.*, pp. 580–581.
8. Leland M. Goodrich and Edward Hambro, *Charter of the United Nations* (Boston: World Peace Foundation, 1949), p. 21.
9. *Ibid.*, pp. 20–21; Claude, *op. cit.*, pp. 76–77.
10. Goodrich and Hambro, *op. cit.*, p. 408.
11. For Communist China's views toward the United Nations, see the opinions of various Sinologists in Akira Iriye, *U.S. Policy Toward China* (Boston: Little, Brown, 1968), pp. 169–186; and the excerpts from Chinese sources in Senate Government Operations Committee, *Peking's Approach to Negotiation: Selected Writings*, 91st Congress, 1st Session, 1969, pp. 75–80.
12. The concept of America's "hidden veto" in the UN Security Council is discussed in John C. Stoessinger, *The United Nations and the Superpowers* (New York: Random House, 1965), pp. 3–19.
13. For discussions of America's attitude toward UN activity respecting the Vietnam War, see *The United States in World Affairs: 1967* (New York: Harper & Row, 1968), pp. 33, 55, 70–71. One American official reported a "general unwillingness" by members of the UN Security Council to involve itself with the Vietnam question (*ibid.*, p. 71). Yet, UN Secretary-General U Thant was highly active in trying to bring about a cease-fire in Southeast Asia. For numerous references to his role, see David Kraslow and Stuart H. Loory, *The Secret Search for Peace in Vietnam* (New York: Random House, 1968), *passim.*
14. H. Field Haviland, Jr., *The Political Role of the General Assembly* (New York: Carnegie Endowment for International Peace, 1951), pp. 11–18.
15. *Ibid.*, pp. 18–20.
16. *Ibid.*, p. 37.
17. Department of State, *American Foreign Policy, 1950–1955*, General Foreign Policy Series, no. 117, vol. I (1957), 187–192.
18. "The Situation in Hungary," *United Nations Review* 3 (December, 1956), 46–71, *passim.*
19. See William R. Frye, *A United Nations Peace Force* (New York: Oceana, 1957); and *The United States in World Affairs: 1956* (New York: Harper & Row, 1957), pp. 358–360.
20. For a discussion of these and other UN activities carried on under General Assembly auspices, see "Issues Before the 24th General Assembly," *International Conciliation* 574 (September, 1969), *passim*, and subsequent publications in this series.
21. See Secretary of State Dean Rusk's remarks, as reported in *The New York Times*, (January 11, 1964).
22. See *idem.*
23. *Documents on American Foreign Relations: 1961* (New York: Harper & Row, 1962), p. 491.
24. Numerous studies of voting behavior—showing the cohesiveness (or lack of it) among voting blocs in the UN—are available. See, for example, Thomas Hovet, Jr., *Bloc Politics in the United Nations* (Cambridge, Mass.: Harvard University Press, 1960), and *Africa in the United Nations* (Evanston, Ill.: Northwestern University Press, 1963); Bruce M. Russett, "Discovering Voter Groups in the United Nations," *American Political Science Review* 60 (June, 1966), 327–339; and the collection of articles on UN voting behavior in Maurice Waters, ed., *The United Nations* (New York: Macmillan, 1967), pp. 282–345.
25. See, for example, Edward R. Rowe, "The Emerging Anti-Colonial Consensus in the United Nations," in Waters, *op. cit.*, pp. 465–470; and Rupert Emerson, "Colonialism, Political Development and the UN," in Norman J. Padelford and Leland M. Goodrich, eds., *The United Nations in the Balance* (New York: Praeger), pp. 120–140.
26. See Emerson, *op. cit.*, pp. 129–136; and "Issues Before the 24th General Assembly," *op. cit.*, pp. 70–90.
27. Arthur M. Schlesinger, *A Thousand Days* (Boston: Houghton Mifflin, 1965), pp. 509–512.
28. *Ibid.*, p. 510.
29. UN activities with respect to colonial questions and the policies of Southern Rhodesia are conveniently summarized in "Issues Before the 24th General Assembly," *op. cit.*, pp. 70–90.
30. See the text of President Johnson's speech on African issues in *The New York Times* (May 27, 1966).
31. See President Nixon's comprehensive statement on American foreign policy, as reproduced in *The New York Times* (February 19, 1970).
32. The evidence and UN discussion on this issue are presented in "Issues Before the 24th Gen-

eral Assembly," *op. cit.* pp. 74–77, 107–110.
33. A detailed discussion and critique of American foreign policy toward racial problems in Africa may be found in George W. Ball, *The Discipline of Power* (Boston: Little, Brown, 1968), pp. 243–259; and for a recent appraisal of American policy in Africa by a former diplomatic official, see Charles B. Marshall, "Sub-Saharan Africa," in Abdul A. Said, *America's Role in the 1970s* (Englewood Cliffs, N.J.: Prentice-Hall, 1970), pp. 75–91. A different view—urging that the United States involve itself more actively in African problems—is presented by Ernest A. Gross, "The Coalescing Problem of Southern Africa," *Foreign Affairs* 46 (July, 1968), 743–758.
34. *The New York Times* (February 19, 1970).
35. The nonpolitical activities of the UN are discussed in detail in Marian Maury, *The Good War: The UN's Worldwide Fight Against Poverty, Disease, and Ignorance* (New York: Mac-Fadden-Bartell, 1965), *passim.*
36 See *idem;* "Issues Before the 24th General Assembly," *op. cit.*, pp. 47–68, 114–169; and the selections included in Waters, *op. cit.*, pp. 345–378, 417–465.
37. Stephen S. Goodspeed, "Political Considerations in the United Nations Economic and Social Council," in Waters, *op. cit.*, pp. 349–350.
38. Ernest B. Haas, *The Web of Interdependence: The United States and International Organizations* (Englewood Cliffs, N.J.: Prentice-Hall, 1970), pp. 61–62.
39. For discussions of EPTA and SUNFED, see Philip E. Jacob and Alexine L. Atherton, *The Dynamics of International Organization* (Homewood, Ill.: Dorsey, 1965), pp. 419–420.
40. Richard N. Gardner, *In Pursuit of World Order* (New York: Praeger, 1964), p. 120.
41. *Ibid.*, p. 123.
42. The problems confronting the developing nations as they entered the 1970s were identified and evaluated in Chapter 14. For data concerning the progress of individual countries and regions, see Lester B. Pearson, *Partners in Development: Report on the Commission on International Development* (New York: Praeger, 1969); and *The Rockefeller Report on the Americas* (Chicago: Quadrangle, 1969).
43. "Issues Before the 24th General Assembly," *op. cit.*, p. 123.
44. Quoted in Jacob and Atherton, *op. cit.*, p. 458.
45. See *The Rockefeller Report on the Americas, op. cit.*, pp. 70–80.
46. An informative and detailed discussion of the subject is "UNCTAD: North–South Encounter," *International Conciliation* 568 (May, 1968), pp. 9–14.
47. *Ibid.*, p. 13.
48. *Ibid.*, p. 23.
49. *Ibid.*, p. 27.
50. See Haas, *op. cit.*, pp. 75–76.
51. "Issues Before the 24th General Assembly," *op. cit.*, p. 91.
52. *Ibid.*, p. 95.
53. For these and other examples, see *ibid.*, pp. 90–114.
54. Jacob and Atherton, *op. cit.*, pp. 593–602.
55. See Lincoln P. Bloomfield, *The United Nations and U.S. Foreign Policy*, 2nd ed. (Boston: Little, Brown, 1967), pp. 202–211.
56. Gardner, *op. cit.*, p. 250.
57. The Kennedy administration's new concern for international human rights questions is discussed in Gardner, *op. cit.*, pp. 238–263; and in Ernest A. Gross, *The United Nations: Structure for Peace* (New York: Harper & Row, 1962), pp. 104–116.
58. Gardner, *op. cit.*, pp. 257–259.
59. Haas, *op. cit.*, p. 87.
60. See the discussion of the American government's position on human rights questions in *ibid.*, pp. 84–90.
61. See the text of President Nixon's message on American foreign policy in *The New York Times* (February 19, 1970).
62. A detailed analysis of American public opinion toward the UN may be found in Alfred O. Hero, Jr., "The American Public and the UN: 1954–1966," in Waters, *op. cit.*, pp. 505–523; and the voluminous data presented in the same author's *The Southerner and World Affairs* (Baton Rouge: Louisiana State University Press, 1965), pp. 223–247.
63. James T. Shotwell and Marina Salvin, *Lessons on Security and Disarmament from the History of the League of Nations* (New York: Columbia University Press, 1949), p. 10.
64. *The New York Times* (September 26, 1961).
65. See the text of President Nixon's message on American foreign policy in *The New York Times* (February 19, 1970).
66. For studies of disarmament negotiations prior to World War II, see Shotwell and Salvin, *op. cit., passim;* Senate Foreign Relations Committee, *Disarmament and Security: A Collection of Documents, 1919–1955,* 84th Congress, 2nd Session, 1956; Joseph H. Choate, *The Two Hague Conferences* (Princeton, N.J.: Princeton University Press, 1913); Raymond L. Buell, *The Washington Conference* (New York: Appleton-Century-Crofts, 1922).
67. See the studies released by the Institute for Strategic Studies in London and other data cited in *The New York Times* (August 18, 1969), dispatch by John L. Hess.
68. *The New York Times* (November 19, 1969), dispatch by James Reston.
69. Inis L. Claude, Jr., *Swords into Plowshares* (New York: Random House, 1956), p. 303
70. Senate Foreign Relations Committee, *A Decade of American Foreign Policy, 1940–1949,* 81st Congress, 1st Session, 1950, pp. 1076–1077.
71. *Ibid.*, pp. 1079–1087.
72. *Ibid.*, pp. 1090–1091.
73. The text may be found in *The New York Times* (July 27, 1963); and see Lawrence W. Martin, "Disarmament: An Agency in Search of a Policy," *The Reporter* 29 (July 4, 1963), 26.
74. *The New York Times* (September 26, 1961).

75. See President Nixon's views as reported in *The New York Times* (February 19, 1970).
76. *The New York Times* (July 27, 1963).
77. Senate Foreign Relations Committee, *Control and Reduction of Armaments: A Decade of Negotiations, 1946–1956*, Staff Study no. 3, 84th Congress, 2nd Session, 1956, p. 21.
78. Senate Foreign Relations Committee, *The Control and Reduction of Armaments, Hearings*, 84th Congress, 2nd Session, 1956, Part 4, p. 165.
79. *The New York Times* (September 20, 1959).
80. See, for example, the nine-point disarmament proposal advocated by the Soviet Union early in 1969, as reported in *The New York Times* (January 21, 1969).
81. For appraisals of the problems involved in banning nuclear weapons testing, consult Arthur Dean, *Test Ban and Disarmament* (New York: Harper & Row, 1966); and for discussions of the implications of an international nuclear nonproliferation agreement, see Mortan A. Kaplan, "The Nuclear Non-Proliferation Treaty: Its Rationale, Prospects, and Possible Impact on International Law," in Mortan A. Kaplan, ed., *Great Issues of International Politics* (Chicago: Aldine, 1970), pp. 156–187.
82. For discussion of these and other limited- steps toward arms control, consult William L. Tung, *International Organization Under the United Nations System* (New York: Thomas Y. Crowell, 1969), pp. 122–126.
83. Background commentary on SALT disarmament discussions is provided by Jeremy L. Stone, "When and How to Use SALT," *Foreign Affairs* 48 (January, 1970), 262–274; William C. Foster, "Prospects for Arms Control," *ibid.* 47 (April, 1969), 413–422; Harold Brown, "Security Through Limitations," *ibid.*, pp. 422–433; D. G. Brennan, "The Case for Missile Defense," *ibid.*, pp. 433–449; Robert L. Rothstein, "The ABM, Proliferation and International Stability," *ibid.*, 46 (April, 1968), 487–503; and Carl Kaysen, "Keeping the Strategic Balance," *ibid.*, 46 (July, 1968), 665–678.
84. See again the text of President Nixon's statement on American foreign policy, reproduced in *The New York Times* (February 19, 1970).
85. *The New York Times* (April 23, 1969).
86. For a lengthy treatment of military influence in Soviet policy-making and data on the Soviet armed forces, see the article in *Time Magazine* 95 (May 4, 1970), 36–47; and see *The New York Times* (October 27, 1969).

Sixteen
PHILOSOPHICAL FOUNDATIONS OF FOREIGN POLICY: The Quest for Guiding Principles

A "PHILOSOPHICAL FRAMEWORK" FOR FOREIGN AFFAIRS

Much of the controversy surrounding American foreign policy in recent years has stemmed from public and official uneasiness over a problem lying at the center of the foreign policy process. In reality, it is an extremely old problem. Statesmen debated it during the era of the Greek city-states; British, French, Russian, and other European officials deliberated about it endlessly in the the eighteenth and nineteenth centuries; academicians and policy-makers in the United States considered it in detail during the 1950s. The problem might be regarded as a kind of common denominator uniting critics of American involvement in the Vietnam War during the 1960s; and if experience is a reliable guide, it can confidently be predicted that it will be discussed during the 1970s and 1980s—indeed, as long as the United States remains a great power.

The problem to which we have alluded is: What philosophical principles and precepts ought to guide the United States in its relations with the outside world? In its dealings with the NATO allies, with the nations of sub-Saharan Africa, or with the Arab states; in its policies toward the Soviet Union and Communist China; in its diplomacy in the United Nations; in its participation in disarmament negotiations; in its postwar foreign aid programs—in these and myriad other contexts, is there not a set of "guiding principles" serving to unify literally hundreds of separate American actions and policy statements? Is it not possible to discover a cohesive *doctrine or philosophy* according to which America's policies toward NATO are rationally compatible with its diplomacy toward Latin America or its efforts to promote the progress of developing nations like India? More generally, is it not possible to define American foreign policy in *all* its separate aspects by reference to one or more logically harmonious concepts, upon which the specific actions of the United States outside its own borders are based?

To the recurrent lament of baffled citizens—"But does the United States even *have* a foreign policy?"—why is it apparently so difficult to give a relatively simple and clear answer?

The problem of the underlying philosophy of American foreign relations is incontestably important and pertinent. But, as we shall discover in this chapter, it is also extraordinarily difficult—perhaps the most difficult which the President and his principal foreign policy advisers consistently confront. For, like so many deceptively "simple" questions, the problem is in fact extremely complex; its ramifications extend into nearly every sphere of national life. The problem involves at least three major elements. First, is it possible for *any nation* to have a consistent philosophy of foreign relations? For reasons we shall identify in due course, this question presents unique difficulties for the American society. Second, if a basic philosophy of foreign affairs is possible, what are the main ingredients or concepts in it, insofar as the United States is concerned? The question itself suggests two important corollaries. Nations may have an underlying philosophy of foreign relations *because they are nations* (as distinct from colonies, city-states, or world governments). The fact of their existence—and their desire for continued existence—as nations supplies them with certain goals or aims forming part of their philosophy of foreign affairs. Thus every nation, it seems clear, desires to maintain and assure its existence. But all nations are of course to some degree *unique;* their philosophies of foreign affairs are derived in some measure from their own distinctive historical traditions, cultures, ethical value systems, political and constitutional principles, and other sources which make one nation different from another. Thus, even though the United States and Communist China are both nations, it is evident that their philosophies of foreign relations will differ radically because of unique influences shaping their approaches to the outside world. Third, the problem of establishing an applicable set of philosophical principles motivating foreign policy raises the question of the degree to which government officials actually *follow* these principles in the day-to-day conduct of foreign affairs. Frequently, as in the internal dissension over America's involvement in Southeast Asia during the 1960s and early 1970s, critics assert that *failure to adhere* to the principles supposedly guiding the nation's external behavior is the root cause of its difficulties abroad. Officials in Washington are accused having forgotten or "abandoned" or otherwise disregarded those concepts which ought to guide the United States in its relations with Southeast Asia or other regions. To many critics, America's failure to "live up to its highest ideals and traditions" in dealing with the outside world largely accounts for the inability to achieve its goals overseas. And this problem in turn raises the question of *why* policy-makers experience difficulty in adhering to a reasonably consistent and clear set of principles in their relations with other countries.

The Contribution of Philosophical Principles

Why is some kind of underlying philosophy of foreign affairs desirable? What contribution does it make to effective diplomacy? More specifically, how can deeper insight into the philosophical foundations of American foreign policy enable us to understand more clearly the nature of the cold war, or the role of the United States in NATO, or the problems of inter-American relations?

To answer such questions, we must bear in mind a point emphasized in Chapter 1: The political organization of society *is purposive.* When the Founding Fathers drafted the Constitution of the United States in 1787, for example, they sought to create a "more perfect Union" in order to achieve certain goals set forth in the Preamble. In various ways, the Constitution was expected to contribute to the betterment of American society, to advance that particular society's conception of the good life. Presumably, the acts and policies of the government established under the Consitution are conformable with this broad objective. Ideally, everything the United States government does at home and abroad contributes in some way to the attainment of this end.

A nation or a lesser form of political organization consists of a group of individuals. It can be contended that every individual operates upon some implicit or explicit philosophy which guides his behavior as a single member of society or as a member of a group. For some people (probably a small minority), this philosophy *is explicit and highly articulated.* For most individuals, it is primarily *implicit and unsystematic;* the average person would perhaps be hard pressed to present a clear and consistent philosophy of life purporting to explain his conduct in all its myriad aspects. And for still other individuals, such a philosophy is *explicitly rejected:* Some people are convinced

that it is simply not possible to construct such a system. Without entering into a detailed discourse about how or why different viewpoints on the matter exist, the point we wish to underscore here is that, irrespective of the particular category to which they belong, nearly all people operate upon the basis of *some underlying conception* of man's nature and his destiny in the scheme of things. The individual who denies that the political organization of society is purposive—who asserts that it is aimless, random, accidental, or otherwise without conscious design—presumably believes this because it conflicts with his own conception of man's nature and destiny. Such a view, for example, might stem from a denial of the possibility that the human will can prevail over environmental factors at home and abroad; the environmentalist may be convinced that America's conduct in foreign affairs is predetermined by environmental forces in the international community. But even if we accept this view for the purpose of discussion, it is clear that this avowed rejection of a conscious philosophy of foreign affairs *is itself a philosophy.* It rests upon certain metaphysical foundations and judgments about the nature and destiny of man and the impact of the environment upon him. It presupposes the existence of certain environmental forces influencing human conduct; it assumes that *the environment acts and that man reacts.* Credible or not, this conceptior permits (perhaps requires) *a highly rational* philosophical structure concerning how or why man conducts himself as he does. This is merely one possible example to illustrate the point that the explicit rejection of a conscious philosophy of life means the *implicit acceptance* of some alternative explanation of man's conduct and his potentialities. Almost no one (including those who reject the need for a systematic philosophy) regards human beings as nothing more than enlarged amoebas, whose life patterns consist of reacting instinctively to external stimuli. Man's possession of a brain, a highly developed nervous system, and the capacity for rational thought elevates him considerably above such forms of animal life. Crudely and inconsistently as they express their guiding philosophies, most people profess certain goals and aspirations; for countless citizens, these become at least one important yardstick by which the nation's policies at home and abroad are evaluated and by which the performance of government officials is measured.

The American Ethos and Philosophical Inquiry

For the student of American foreign relations, the relevant question is not *whether* the United States is guided by certain underlying principles in responding to challenges in the external environment. Rather, it is in trying to identify those principles, in endeavoring to make implicit principles more explicit, in trying to discern *why* certain principles instead of others influence national behavior abroad, and in analyzing the extent to which the principles guiding foreign policy do or do not comprise a logically compatible system. Such questions present unusually difficult problems for Americans. As we noted in Chapter 2, Americans are not a philosophically oriented people. Traditionally, the American society has not been favorable for the emergence of philosophies. Action, rather than thinking about action or endeavoring to discern the underlying reasons for action, has customarily been the hallmark of the American society. The most distinctive American philosophy—Pragmatism, in which the ultimate standard for judging among alternative courses is to ask which *works most beneficially*—was perhaps an inevitable outgrowth of American experience.* Popularized conceptions of pragmatism—the idea of dealing with "one problem at a time" or "crossing that bridge when we come to it"—infuse the American approach to internal and external issues. Justifiably or not, many Americans regard engaging in philosophical speculations and "accomplishing things" as mutually exclusive enterprises; the former in fact may be seen by many Americans as a detriment to the latter. To the American mind, the creation of elaborate philosophical systems is associated with the Old World; it is an undertaking at variance with certain cherished American virtues like hard work, the improvement of society's lot, economic expansion, and other ideas deeply woven into the fabric of the American tradition. In modern history, Americans have also perhaps tended to be repulsed from engaging in systematic philosophiz-

*The philosophy of Pragmatism, one commentator observes, "takes its name from its central teaching that any idea which gives practical results must be accepted as true; provided, of course, it does not conflict with experience." Rejecting the idea of the existence of ultimate or metaphysical truth, the Pragmatists teach "that knowledge should be sought after, not as an end in itself, but as a means for improving conditions on earth." Pragmatism was first identified with the American Charles Peirce around 1875 and was disseminated by certain philosophers in England and Europe. Its foremost spokesman was the American philosopher William James. James urged his followers to abandon logic, metaphysics, and other unsatisfactory standards and to substitute "reality, life, experience, concreteness, immediacy" as guides to human conduct. Believing that truth constantly changed, and that diversity was the prevalent condition of mankind, James favored pluralism, the free trade in ideas, and individualism. James' most noted disciple, John Dewey, is associated with the idea of *instrumentalism:* philosophies, ideologies, and the like must be looked upon as *means* for the improvement of human societies. The leading tenets of Dewey's thought—innovation, experimentation, investigation, constant testing of results, willingness to abandon old methods for new approaches—accorded well with the emerging scientific method and with the American way of life. See Edward McNall Burns, *Ideas in Conflict: The Political Theories of the Contemporary World* (New York: Norton, 1960), pp. 89–97.

ing because of the odium attached to the totalitarian philosophical systems of countries like Nazi Germany and Communist Russia. A preoccupation with ideology, many Ameicans would perhaps agree, is characteristic of a totalitarian way of life. By contrast, democracy is inescapably associated with *pluralism,* in which the construction of philosophical systems is left to the individual members of society (most of whom in fact evince little interest in such pursuits). Philosophical thought may be no less objectionable to many Americans for a different reason, symbolized by the problems afflicting modern France. French society is very philosophically oriented—as much perhaps as any society on the globe. The multiplicity of political parties in French political life reflects the many forces at work in the society, not the least of which is the premium many Frenchmen put upon philosophical inquiry and speculation; political parties and other movements are often established upon the basis of very fine philosophical distinctions, sometimes involving little more than semantic quibbling. Americans who have some knowledge of modern French history often are convinced that there is a connection between the French preoccupation with such philosophical quarrels and the *instability* which has been a conspicuous part of French political life for the past century. Put differently, the relative *absence* of internal disputes over philosophical questions would probably be cited by many students of history as a major factor contributing to the American society's relative political *stability* since 1789.

That a deep predisposition against philosophical thought exists within the American tradition can hardly be doubted. This tendency perhaps goes hand in hand with another trend—a pronounced *anti-intellectualism* in some periods of American history—turning many Americans against the idea of philosophical inquiry. The Jacksonian tradition, extolling the political acumen of the "plain people" is to some degree in conflict with the idea that the thoughts of an intellectual elite can determine the basic goals applicable to the mass of the people. If America has moved past the point at which, according to Jacksonian ideas, any citizen is qualified to hold any governmental position, this notion still forms part of the American ethos. Intellectual and other elites of course exist in the American society, but it is difficult for the democratic ideology to acknowledge their existence and to assign specific responsibilities to them. Indeed, from the experience of the Vietnam War, it appears that many members of the intellectual elite do not themselves believe in elitism: Authorities in fields like Anthropology, Chemistry, or English Literature believe themselves as competent to criticize American foreign policy in Asia as specialists in the field of foreign relations.

The nature of American society and of the country's unique traditions thus pose numerous obstacles to an analysis of the philosophy of American foreign relations. In all likelihood, only a small minority of the American people see any real necessity for a "philosophy" of foreign affairs. Perhaps not even the process of "incrementalism" by which America became deeply implicated in the affairs of Southeast Asia has had any lasting impact upon the pragmatic attitudes of the American people.* Both in domestic and foreign affairs, solving "one problem at a time" or "crossing that bridge when we get to it" remains the approach most nearly according with America's historic propensities. Yet however non-philosophical Americans may be, informed citizens and government officials cannot be oblivious to the fact that *other societies* usually attribute philosophical significance to America's conduct overseas. Foreigners draw conclusions about the American ideology or the "democratic way of life" from the way the United States conducts itself abroad and from the statements of its foreign policy-makers. This fact obligates America to see to it that its philosophical goals and values are *interpreted correctly* by societies outside its borders.

ALTERNATIVE PHILOSOPHIES OF FOREIGN AFFAIRS

Assuming then that some implicit or explicit set of philosophical principles will guide the foreign policy of the United States, what specific ideas ought to serve as the foundation of national policy? The Western philosophical heritage, offers a highly varied selection of possibilities. In the space available, let us examine three alternative approaches that might be chosen as the philosophical foundation for American foreign relations.

Balance of Power and National Interest

The first approach we shall analyze involves certain very old concepts in diplomacy. According to some authorities, the antecedents of this approach can be discovered in the experience of the Greek city-states; it served as the foundation of European statecraft during the so-called "Golden Age" of diplomacy in the eighteenth and nineteenth centuries. This is the concept of *balance of power;* and in the writings of modern-day political "Real-

ists," balance of power is frequently coupled with the idea of *national interest.* In its simplest terms, the elemental diplomatic principle which ought to guide the United States in its foreign relations can be expressed by saying: In all aspects of foreign affairs, the United States seeks to pursue its *national interest* by creating and maintaining a *balance of power* in global affairs conducive to its security and well-being. Thus, in its relations with the Soviet Union, the United States must be guided above all else by an attempt to preserve and promote its own interests as a nation; in order to do so successfully, American policy-makers must aim at bringing about, and then maintaining, an equilibrium of global power vis-à-vis Soviet Russia. National interest is the cardinal goal; balance of power becomes the means (in this view, the only truly effective means) of safeguarding and promoting America's national interest.

As we have already observed, concepts like balance of power and national interest are in reality venerable ideas in the history of international relations. For two centuries before World War I, foreign offices in all the major European capitals were thoroughly familiar with these concepts, and diplomatic dispatches and memoirs contained literally hundreds of allusions to them. More than any other country, perhaps, Great Britain openly subscribed to the ideas of balance of power and national interest in its relations with the other European powers during the era of *Pax Britannica.* Attachment to these principles meant that Britain sought to prevent any one nation (or coalition of nations) from dominating the European continent. Functioning as the "balancer" among several more or less equally powerful Western nations, Britain allied itself temporarily with the weaker side to "restore the balance" among the contestants. London avoided *permanent* alliances with the European nations in order to choose its allies according to balance-of-power considerations (a tactic which earned England the epithet of "perfidious Albion" because of its short-lived alliances and friendships with other countries). At least theoretically, ideological considerations did *not* influence British foreign policy. Only one thing counted in the calculations of the Foreign Office: What was required of Great Britain to maintain a stable balance of power in Europe? (Great Britain did not, it is important to note, follow the balance-of-power principle with regard to another major area of diplomatic and military concern: *command of the seas.* Here, London's policies dictated *naval supremacy* over any two hostile fleets that might be combined against the Royal Navy.)

Beginning in the early 1950s, a school of political Realist academicians emerged within the United Nations. Led by commentators like Professor Hans J. Morgenthau and the individual who was thought (correctly or not) to have been the

---

*The concept of incrementalism—the step-by-step process by which the United States gradually became heavily involved in the security of South Vietnam, without realizing the long-term consequences of doing so—is employed by Roger Hilsman, in his book *To Move a Nation: The Politics of Foreign Policy in the Administration of John F. Kennedy* (Garden City, N.Y.: Doubleday, 1967), pp. 413–524.

author of America's "containment policy" against Soviet Russia, the high-ranking diplomatic official George F. Kennan, this group sought to apply balance-of-power and national interest concepts to the conduct of American diplomacy.* According to proponents of this viewpoint, most of the errors, aberrations, and unsuccessful ventures in American foreign policy since World War I could be attributed to the failure of policy-makers in Washington, who were themselves frequently influenced by a politically naïve body of citizen opinion, to comprehend and apply the axiomatic truths guiding the diplomatic behavior of Western nations for two centuries or more. Time and again, American diplomatic ventures had miscarried because they were not based upon the cardinal principles of national interest and balance of power. The diplomatic experience of World War II afforded innumerable examples. To cite but one, perhaps the most crucial cold war issue fomenting tensions between the Western and Marxist nations—the political division of Germany at the end of the war—was an outgrowth of Ameri-

*More detailed presentations of the Realist school of thought concerning the principles which ought to guide American foreign policy may be found in the following: Hans J. Morgenthau, "The Mainspring of American Foreign Policy," *American Political Science Review* 44 (December, 1950), 833–849; the same author's *In Defense of the National Interest* (New York: Knopf, 1951); and most recently, his *A New Foreign Policy for the United States* (New York: Praeger, 1969); George F. Kennan, *American Diplomacy, 1900–1950* (New York: New American Library, 1952), and his *Memoirs: 1925–1950* (New York: Bantam, 1969); Hanson W. Baldwin, *Great Mistakes of the War* (New York: Harper & Row, 1950); Robert Strausz-Hupé, "U.S. Foreign Policy and the Balance of Power," *Review of Politics* 10 (January, 1948), 76–83; Ernest Lefever, *Ethics and United States Foreign Policy* (New York: Meridian, 1957); Dean Acheson, *Present at the Creation: My Years in the State Department* (New York: Norton, 1969); George W. Ball, *The Discipline of Power: Essentials of a Modern World Structure* (Boston: Atlantic–Little, Brown, 1968); Kenneth W. Thompson, *Political Realism and the Crisis of World Politics* (Princeton, N.J.: Princeton University Press, 1960); Robert W. Tucker, "Force and Foreign Policy," *Yale Review* 47 (March, 1958), 374–392; Walter Lippmann, *The Public Philosophy* (Boston: Atlantic–Little, Brown, 1955). It should not of course be assumed that the Realist approach to international relations is homogeneous. To the contrary, significant differences can often be found among commentators who might be classified as belonging to this school of thought, particularly as regards specific foreign policy issues confronting the United States. It must also be recognized that individual students of American foreign policy not infrequently change their viewpoints over the course of time. Two examples in the above group are George F. Kennan and Dean Acheson. In his *Memoirs*, for example, Kennan disclaims many of the ideas correctly or incorrectly attributed to him as the author of the "containment" strategy adopted by the Truman administration to counter Communist expansionism. Similarly, in his memoirs, *Present at the Creation*, and in his other writings after he retired as Secretary of State, Dean Acheson appears to have gravitated perceptibly toward a "hard-line" or power-oriented approach toward the Soviet Union and Red China.

ca's failure to understand and follow the classical rule motivating British foreign policy toward the European continent. Preferring to postpone "political decisions" until the end of the war, American officials thereby proved indifferent to Europe's postwar political and military future. Once the defeat of the Axis powers could be anticipated, America should have used its great military power (as Winston Churchill repeatedly recommended) *to create and maintain a stable political equilibrium* in the heart of Europe, thereby avoiding the insecurity produced by West Germany's (and especially Berlin's) acute military vulnerability after 1945. As much as any other factor, this failure was responsible for the over-all insecurity of the West throughout the postwar period. Other commentators have analyzed more recent American diplomatic experience in much the same terms. Some critics of the Vietnam War, for example, are convinced that failure to seek a stable balance of power in Asia (particularly by trying to arrive at a *détente* with Communist China) was the root cause of America's "failure" in Southeast Asia and a primary cause of the domestic turmoil about the Vietnam conflict within the American society. Successive administrations in Washington ignored or forgot that in Asia, as in other regions, the dominant goal of American foreign policy was promotion of the national interest through reliance upon a stable balance of power. In this case, critics charged, America's attempt to establish a position of *preponderant power* in Southeast Asia led it into a military and political campaign it could not possibly win.*

The "National Interest" in American Foreign Policy

Using the writings of Professor Morgenthau as the leading example of contemporary political Realism, let us take note of the main tenets of this

*This viewpoint was widespread among critics of America's involvement in the vietnam conflict. See for example the critique of American foreign policy in Roger D. Masters, *The Nation is Burdened: American Foreign Policy in a Changing World* (New York: Knopf, 1967), esp. pp. 204–246. For a more detailed presentation of this viewpoint, see Fred Greene, *U.S. Policy and the Security of Asia* (New York: McGraw-Hill, 1968). Along with commentators like Hans J. Morgenthau and George Kennan, Greene contends that ever since its earliest involvement in Asian affairs, the United States has been cognizant of the need to preserve the balance of power within this region. Although American policy was *not* based on a conscious or sophisticated avowal of the balance-of-power principle, nevertheless, "American actions did follow a course that, with all its inconsistencies, was pointed toward the maintenance of a balance in Asia." The balance-of-power concept thus is deeply rooted in the nation's diplomatic experience in Asia; and, as the United States liquidates its military commitment in Southeast Asia, Greene believes that "a balance-of-power approach can be applied fruitfully to Asia." See pp. 35–36, 40.

point of view. The first necessity for American policy-makers, Morgenthau asserted, is "to relearn the great principles of statecraft which guided the path of the republic in the first decade and—in moralistic disguise—in the first century of its existence." When they do so, American officials will realize that the United States has acted "on the international scene, as all nations must, in power-political terms," although Americans have tended to "conceive of our actions in nonpolitical, moralistic terms." Once the heavy encrustation of moralism–legalism customarily surrounding American foreign policy decisions is penetrated, it will become apparent that in their policies toward Europe, Latin America, and Asia before World War II, American policy-makers were in reality endeavoring to preserve the balance of power. America's best-known foreign policy principle— the Monroe Doctrine—was aimed at preserving "the unique position of the United States as a predominant power without rival" in the Western Hemisphere.* Toward Europe, the United States basically sought what England had sought in the nineteenth century: to preserve an *equilibrium* of power on the continent, thereby minimizing threats to the United States and its friends (such as Great Britain). In the famous Open Door policy toward China, enunciated at the end of the nineteenth century, America was pursuing the same goal: Washington sought to prevent the dominance of the Chinese mainland by a single country, thereby giving the United States equal commercial rights (and in time possibly a dominant position) in that country. Although Americans were prone for many years thereafter to regard the Open Door policy as the epitome of idealism and altruistic concern for China's

welfare, Realists believe that in fact it was nothing more than the old balance-of-power principle, camouflaged in moralistic–legalistic ideology; Americans may have been deceived about the true nature of the policy, but China and other nations were not.[1]

The period of World War I and of Wilsonian idealism was crucial in explaining how the United States "got off the track" diplomatically. President Woodrow Wilson, according to the Realist interpretation, naïvely believed that the United States could avoid "power politics" and international quarrels and conflicts, and could take the lead in creating a new order of international relations, based upon principles like those expressed in the Fourteen Points and the Covenant of the League of Nations. Wilson categorically rejected Old World concepts like balance of power and national interest; he felt that national attachment to these ideas had been in large part responsible for the holocaust of World War I. Wilsonians deceived themselves into thinking that public acceptance of concepts like "self-determination," "open covenants, openly arrived at," "making the world safe for democracy," and the like would usher in a new age of international peace and harmony. Instead, Wilsonian espousal of these ideas planted fundamental misconceptions at the center of American foreign policy; it largely vitiated American influence in world affairs for the next generation; and it contributed to the most destructive conflict the international community has experienced— World War II. Wilson's fatal error, according to Morgenthau's assessment, was that instead of seeking the "restoration of the European balance of power," he substituted for "the concrete interest of the United States the general postualte of a brave new world where the national interest of the United States, as that of all other nations, would disappear in a community of interest comprising mankind." Wilsonians of all ages, Morgenthau has contended, draw a false distinction between morality and power in the conduct of nations. George F. Kennan has deplored the "carrying over into the affairs of states of the concepts of right and wrong" or "the assumption that state behavior is a fit subject for moral judgment." There is only one "moral" policy for the United States in global affairs: to pursue its own national interests and to safeguard its own security by endeavoring to preserve a stable equilibrium of global power.[2] Such, in brief compass, is the position of the Realist school of thought concerning the philosophical basis of American foreign policy.

Political Realism: Insights and Limitations

It must be conceded frankly that there is considerable validity to the Realist approach to international relations and to its prescriptions for American foreign policy. Anyone who studies the

*As many students will have no doubt noted, Morgenthau's reference to the purpose of the Monroe Doctrine illustrates a certain ambiguity in his conception of the doctrine of balance of power, which appears to be endemic in the concept. Usually, by balance of power, Morgenthau and other writers mean an approximate *equilibrium* of power, as suggested by the familiar figure of a see-saw in a horizontal position: The weight of one person is more or less equal to the weight of the other, keeping the see-saw in balance. But balance of power can also mean a *preponderance of power* or power that is *not* in equilibrium, as when we speak of a person's "bank balance" or a "favorable balance of trade." In these instances, what is really meant is an *imbalance* favorable to one's own side. Thus, in the above discussion, by pursuing balance of power within the Western Hemisphere, the United States presumbly sought, according to Morgenthau, a *preponderance* of its power within this region; but toward Western Europe, balance of power was aimed at *preventing a preponderance of power* by any single country or coalition. The ambiguity inherent in the balance-of-power idea thus enables it often to be invoked by citizens who favor an *extension* of American power abroad (e.g., "hawks" who wanted to "win" the Vietnam War), as well as those who advocated a *retrenchment* in American power overseas (e.g., "doves" who urged the United States to withdraw from Southeast Asia).

history of the nation-state system must agree that that "power politics," wars and lesser forms of national rivalries, and clashing goals among powerful nations are recurrent themes in modern history. Nor does there appear to be any reasonable likelihood that these themes will disappear from international relationships in the near future. In Chapter 15, for example, the point was emphasized that the more powerful nations (joined in recent years even by the smaller countries) continue to build up their armed strength, endangering the future of civilization itself in the process. Soviet Russia's reliance upon overwhelming military force when it invaded Czechoslovakia in 1968; America's massive military involvement in Southeast Asia; continuing strife between India and Pakistan; the ongoing and increasingly ominous struggle between Israel and the Arab states —these are merely a few recent developments reminding us that nations still pursue their interests, relying upon force when necessary to do so.

Moreover, every nation *defines its interests for itself;* it is unwilling to leave this determination to its allies, to the United Nations, or to such forces as "world public opinion." These no doubt play a role in international relations, and in some respects their influence may be increasing. But in the last analysis, no government is willing to permit the determination of its interests by outsiders; it reserves this right for itself, regarding it as an intrinsic part of the doctrine of national sovereignty.

These considerations apply to the United States, as much as to any other country in the family of nations. Despite a deeply ingrained folklore—engendering the idea that the New World conducts its affairs differently from the Old World—Realists emphasize the idea that America shares with other great powers of history many common diplomatic goals and behavior patterns. America is no exception to the rule that all nations *have* their interests in foreign relations, and all nations— especially great powers—are prepared to defend these interests by force when necessary. The Realists insist, in effect, that the first requisite for diplomatic success is objectivity and candor in assessing the nation's goals and capabilities. The nation's diplomatic record must be examined with detachment and honesty, if diplomatic mistakes of the past are not to be repeated. Realists thus seek to foster an intellectually honest understanding of America's role in world affairs; emotionalism, sterotypes, moralistic tendencies, and self-deception have no place in the attempt by the American people and their chosen officials to deal successfully with the problems of the external environment. Much as it may offend certain widely cherished ideas in the American mythology, the fact has to be faced unequivocally that the United States *is* devoted to the pursuit of its national interest (or interests); that its own policy-makers,

relying of course upon the backing of public opinion, define these interests; and that America's interests not infrequently are at variance with those of other nations, sometimes even its closest friends and allies. Whether, in some ideal political order, this *ought* to be the case is not the main point; nor is it inconceivable that, at some point in the future, the concept of national interest may be superceded by a new doctrine (such as a universally held idea of "international interest"). But if foreign policy is to be founded upon reality and not illusion, the fact of national interest as what Professor Morgenthau calls the "mainspring of American foreign policy" cannot be seriously questioned.*

Realist thought also suffers from certain defects and logical fallacies which caution the student of American foreign policy against accepting it without serious qualifications as a satisfactory guide to relations with the outside world. Most fundamentally, perhaps, the Realist viewpoint rests upon a highly dubious assumption which human societies in the twentieth century *reject* in nearly all spheres of life. This is the idea that because the history of the nation-state system is filled with episodes of violent conflict among its members, with clashing national interests and ambitions, and with the egocentric pursuit of power politics, such behavior patterns must somehow be accepted as unalterable, as a kind of "given" of international political life that is impervious to the will of man. Realists, it must be conceded, are often more accurate than their critics in describing how nations have tended to conduct their affairs in the past. Moreover, they are on firm ground in pointing out that the policies of the United States have been

---

*As we shall see, the Realist school of thought also has certain fundamental defects, militating against its being accepted *in toto* as an adequate guide to American foreign policy. The concept of national interest, for example, suffers acutely from imprecision and ambiguity. It is one thing to assert that America and all other nations *have* diplomatic interests; it is quite another thing to *define* these interests and to gain a consensus within the United States on behalf of them. More often than not, the problem policy-makers encounter is *choosing among divergent comceptions of the national interest,* as advocated by different groups within American society. Every group routinely operates upon the premise that its proposals are synonymcus with the national interest, while measures it opposes are in conflict with it. That America has interests in Asia seems incontestable. But what precisely are these interests? Do they dictate a total American withdrawal from Southeast Asia? Do they call for a *détente* in Sino–American relations or continued hostility between the two countries? Do they perhaps ordain a Soviet–American agreement in Asia directed against Red China? America's specific interest in this instance is far from clear. One difficulty with the doctrine of national interest is that it serves more often perhaps *to legitimatize* national policy than to determine it. We may be certain that if American officials decided at some future date that a Sino–American accord were justified, that policy would be presented to the American public and to the world as in the national interest of the United States.

motivated by concepts like national interest and power politics more frequently than most Americans are aware or are prepared to admit. Nevertheless, this assertion tells us little or nothing of value about how American foreign policy *ought to be conducted*. Even in earlier periods, the purposes of the American society might well have been better promoted by some *alternative* approach (the frustrating record of America's reliance upon force and coercion in dealing with its neighbors in Latin America over the past half-century could be cited as evidence). Realists slip too easily and uncritically into a kind of "power politics determinism," reasoning that because nations have customarily based their foreign policies upon national interest, they are incapable of being guided by any other, more socially beneficial, principle. The unavoidable implication of Realist thought is that nations are destined simply to repeat the behavior patterns of the past—and that doing so is not only natural, but represents the epitome of "morality" in international political life.

Now this is a presupposition which societies are unprepared to accept in any other realm of human experience. Neither Americans nor any other people are prepared to say that poverty ought to be perpetuated because it can be demonstrated that poverty has always existed. Poverty is no longer viewed as "inevitable"; still less is the fact of its existence elevated into a moral–ethical good. For centuries, scientists and physicians have similarly rejected this premise of Realist thought with respect to the existence of disease and malnutrition. Progress in health and sanitation would have been impossible if physicians had deduced its inevitability from its existence throughout history. Admittedly, problems of ill health will never be completely eliminated from human society; as experience in recent years has shown, the prolongation of life has itself created the "problems of the aged"; as the epidemics of earlier eras have been controlled or eliminated, new physical disorders have threatened the well-being of citizens in the advanced societies. Yet none of these considerations is accepted as a legitimate reason why campaigns to elevate health and nutritional standards ought not to be waged vigorously. In nearly every sphere, progress toward the good life rests upon the assumption that *established behavior patterns and modes are not acceptable standards for present and future conduct*. Herein lies one of the most logically vulnerable points in the Realist position. Without offering any persuasive evidence why, Realists *assume* that because Europe followed a balance-of-power philosophy in the nineteenth century, America must do so in the twentieth. Among its other defects, this reasoning *fails to take cognizance of the consequences* of pursuing doctrines like national interest and the balance of power. According to many historians,

their attachment to the concept of balance of power led the nations of the world into the abyss of World War I.[3] Similarly, the impulses arising from the pursuit of "power politics" brought about an infinitely more destructive conflict— World War II. Are we to conclude that mankind has no higher destiny than to remain chained to this depressing cycle of war and conflict—fought the next time perhaps with nuclear weapons which could reduce the planet to radioactive dust? When what nations have done is elevated into a kind of "law of politics" decreeing what they *must* do, what other conclusion is possible?

Many of these same reservations apply to the concept of balance of power, which is a central tenet of the Realist approach.[4] The principal difficulty with this concept, as we have already observed, is its inherent ambiguity. Precisely what kind of "balance" should the United States seek, for example, in the Middle East? Is it trying to maintain or establish a *preponderance* of American (or, at any rate, Western) power in the region (which might dictate efforts to achieve a substantial *contraction* in Soviet power there)? Or is it instead trying to create an *equilibrium* between Western and Soviet power (which could dictate American acceptance of a massive Soviet presence in the Arab world, possibly even an *expansion* of Soviet influence in the region)?[5] Whatever the answer to this question, it is extremely difficult for a foreign policy based upon balance-of-power calculations to satisfy a twofold test. First, as we noted at length in Chapter 1, the determination of national power is per se a highly subjective and uncertain matter. Before a balance of power can be achieved, it is necessary to make some kind of decision about relative American vis-à-vis Soviet power, both in general and in specific areas like the Middle East. This may be relatively easy to do with respect to *military power* (although even in this realm, *intangible* aspects of national power often weigh heavily); it is all but impossible to do with any degree of precision with regard to other elements of power, such as the condition of civilian morale, the degree of alliance cohesion, the willingness of the Soviet or American people to make sacrifices to achieve foreign policy objectives, and a variety of other calculations necessary to arrive at a clear determination of American power relative to Soviet power.

Second, even if such a calculation of the national power of the United States vis-à-vis another country were possible (and assuming at this point that the objective were to bring about an *equilibrium* of power between them) how is the balance of power to be maintained? In Chapter 1, it was emphasized that a decisive influence affecting the power of nations is ongoing scientific and technological progress; in the main, this is *not* a process subject to rigid control by government officials. At any time, some new scientific discovery or technological development can alter the distribution of global power, upsetting what is always a highly precarious "balance" between two nations like the Soviet Union and the United States. Chapter 15, for example, called attention to the momentous impact of the new MIRV missile system upon disarmament negotiations; in the American view, MIRV's were themselves an "answer" to Soviet Russia's antiballistic missile system. Or take another major dimension of national power: economic strength. By what process is it possible to "freeze" productivity levels in the interests of ensuring that the United States does not widen its lead over the Soviet Union in the production of goods and services? Would the Soviet Union be willing to accept an arrangement preventing it from narrowing the gap between itself and its principal diplomatic rival in economic output? Or how can a balance of power be maintained throughout the zone of the emerging nations? Should (or could) the smaller nations of the Middle East, for example, be *required* to accept economic and military aid *equally* from both super-powers —or possibly be prohibited from accepting such aid from either—in order to assure continuance of a power equilibrium in global affairs?

One of the most serious challenges to the balance-of-power principle for some two centuries has been the problem of *political change*—a phenomenon which is more characteristic of the postwar era than any other period of modern history. How is it possible to preserve the balance of power in societies or regions marked by pervasive and often violent political instability? Would a successful left-wing insurrection against the government of the Philippines pose a threat to the balance of power in the Far East, for instance, by raising the prospect that a country with which America has traditionally had close relations might become more intimate with Soviet Russia or Communist China? Conversely, would a right-wing movement in the internal politics of India, possibly signaling closer relations between India and the West, jeopardize the Asian balance of power? Or what about the prospect of a resurgent Japan? Might the introduction of enhanced Japanese power in the region threaten to displace American or Soviet or Chinese influence in parts of Asia? In these and other cases, might adherence to the old balance-of-power principle require the super-powers to "intervene" in the internal affairs of smaller nations in order to preserve an equilibrium they had established by mutual agreement? Such interventionist policies, it ought not to be forgotten, were an inherent part of balance-of-power politics in nineteenth-century Europe.

Such considerations suggest why it is so difficult in practice to follow the balance-of-power idea in contemporary international relations. They demonstrate why lessons from the history of eighteenth- or nineteenth-century Europe often have little application to the present era. We need to recall that during the nineteenth century, when the balance of power presumably maintained international peace and stability with notable success, certain special conditions existed which are wholly or partially lacking today. In the main, the more powerful nations followed this doctrine *with regard to Western Europe only;* it was thus confined to a fairly narrow area. The doctrine was perhaps well suited to the existence of *several more or less equally matched nations.* The principal "actors" in international politics were the nations of Europe; the rest of the world, including the United States, played little role in global decision-making. Africa, the Middle East, and Asia were dependencies of European nations; decisions affecting their interest (such as the determination of Africa's boundaries) were routinely made in European capitals. The nations following the balance-of-power concept shared certain common traditions (they were all, for example, members of the Judeo–Christian community); for the most part, ideological disputes did not engender hostility among them. That these conditions do not exist in the second half of the twentieth century is evident, nor does there seem to be any likelihood that these conditions will ever again be reproduced in the international environment. The smaller nations of the world, for example, are simply unwilling to play the kind of passive role in global decision-making which was their lot before World War II. As the American experience in Vietnam suggests, even Western public opinion will not tolerate the kind of overtly "interventionist" diplomacy that was taken for granted in nineteenth-century Europe and was an integral part of balance-of-power politics. Although territorial and governmental changes brought about by military force are not unknown in the contemporary period, other issues—such as American and Soviet "influence" in the Middle East, or the path to modernization chosen by the developing nations, or the programs and ideologies espoused by governing elites within the new nations—are perhaps even more at the forefront of international concern today. European experience with the balance of power in the eighteenth and nineteenth centuries would seem to have little application to such novel problems.

In one sense, of course, the Realist insistence upon maintenance of the balance of power is justifiable and indeed axiomatic: The United States ought to try to prevent possible enemies like Soviet Russia and Communist China from gaining a *preponderance* of power globally or in regions like Europe and Asia. American officials were perhaps oblivious to that necessity until early 1947, when President Truman called for the Greek–Turkish Aid Program, which became the first concrete measure taken to implement the "containment" strategy adopted by the United States to counter Soviet expansionism. Yet, curiously enough, many commentators belonging to the Realist school did *not* regard the policy of containment as synonymous with the concept of balance of power, and several advocates of the latter principle were highly critical of America's commitment to the former.* By whatever name it was called, the strategy of containment *did* seek to prevent further deterioration in the balance of power; its basic objective was to thwart attempts by Soviet Russia (and later Red China) to expand its power at the expense of the non-Communist world. Similarly, proponents of the balance of power concept have been critical of another idea —the "liberation" of Eastern Europe and possibly other regions under Communist control—sometimes proposed as a diplomatic and military strategy for the United States. Concerning events in Eastern Europe in the 1950s and 1960s, and in Southeast Asia in the 1960s and early 1970s, Realists have often been at the forefront in advocating *restraint* in the use of American power, even if this meant a gain in Soviet or Chinese power in these regions.

In brief, as the viewpoints of Realists themselves toward particular diplomatic issues in the postwar period often illustrate, the balance-of-power principle seems *highly inoperable* as an underlying strategy for American foreign policy. With the possible exception of the narrow sphere of national armaments, it is extremely difficult to decide whether a balance of power exists today; it is perhaps even more difficult to determine how a new balance (in the sense of equilibrium) can be created; and most perplexing of all is the question of how such a balance, once achieved, is to be *maintained* without reliance by the United States upon the kind of overtly "interventionist" policies which Realists themselves often object to in settings like Southeast Asia.

Idealism as an Approach to Foreign Policy

Another possible approach to foreign affairs can be more or less accurately described by the term *Idealism.*† Although in many respects their view-

points tend to be complementary rather than mutually exclusive, Idealism and Realism are often regarded as opposite approaches to problems in the outside world. As we shall see at a later stage, most government officials and informed citizens actually combine elements of both Idealism and Realism in their attitudes toward external issues.

As the term implies, Idealism emphasizes the moral, ethical, spiritual, and legal content of American foreign policy. Its basic position is that American diplomatic conduct must continually be measured by *ideal standards*, derived from the Western Judeo–Christian tradition, Humanistic philosophy, and the principles (such as those enunciated in the Declaration of Independence and the Constitution of the United States) forming an integral part of the American tradition. Idealism thus rejects the premise upon which Realism is founded: that applicable norms for the conduct of American foreign policy can be derived from a study of how nations have conducted themselves in the past. For Idealists, experience in international relations may often be most useful as a guide to how nations ought *not* to conduct their affairs in the present and future—particularly when the consequences of a global conflict could be disastrous, not only for existing civilization but also for the future of the human race itself. In international relations, as in all other spheres of human endeavor, Idealists are convinced that man can and must raise the level of his performance, bringing it more closely into conformity with the requirements of the world's great religious and ethical systems. Idealists insist that true political realism demands recognition of an inescapable fact: *Ideals play a pivotal role in international political life*—not merely (as Realists sometimes suggest) because they serve to legitimatize policies actually based upon power politics, but because today more than ever in the history of the world, all governments are expected to promote the welfare of their citizens, to make progress toward creating the good life, to respond positively to the "revolution of rising expectations" or otherwise to achieve goals growing out of some ideal conception of human experience.

---

*One of the most penetrating critiques of the doctrine of containment can be found in Walter Lippmann, *The Cold War* (New York: Harper & Row, 1957); see also George F. Kennan's analysis of the weaknesses of the doctrine, which he asserts was incorrectly attributed to him, in his *Memoirs: 1925–1950* (New York: Bantam, 1969), pp. 373–388.

†For a representative selection of writings by Idealists on American foreign policy, see: Dexter Perkins, *The American Approach to Foreign Policy* (Cambridge, Mass.: Harvard University Press, 1952); Frank Tannenbaum, *The American Tradition in Foreign Policy* (Norman: University of Oklahoma Press, 1952); Livingston Merchant, "The Moral Element in Foreign Policy," *Department of State Bulletin* 37 (September 2, 1957), 374–379; Edward H. Buerig, *Woodrow Wilson and the Balance of Power* (Bloomington, Ind.: University of In-

diana Press, 1955); Arthur A. Ekrich, Jr., *Ideas, Ideals and American Diplomacy: A History of Their Growth and Interaction* (New York: Appleton-Century-Crofts, 1966); Louis Henkin, *How Nations Behave* (New York: Praeger, 1968); Charles E. Bohlen, *The Transformation of American Foreign Policy* (New York: Norton, 1969); Townsend Hoopes, *The Limits of Intervention* (New York: McKay, 1969); Richard N. Gardner, *In Pursuit of World Order* (New York: Praeger, 1964); Paul Seabury, *Power, Freedom, and Diplomacy: The Foreign Policy of the United States of America* (New York: Random House, 1963). See especially pp. 138–184 of this last title for a brief but illuminating discussion of the role of ethics in foreign affairs.

Idealism in the American Tradition

Idealism, as we observed in Chapter 2, has very deep roots in the American tradition. Proponents of this school of thought do not regard the idealistic tendencies of the American people as aberrations, as denoting a lack of political sophistication, or as indicating inexperience in resolving difficult political problems and conflicts. To the contrary, the modes of thought, hopes, and aspirations of the New World *are* in many ways unique; America does have a "mission" to elevate the standards of international political life—and in several notable respects (the history of international organizations like the United Nations affords countless examples), the influence of the United States *has* in fact had a crucial impact upon the conduct of international relations. Idealists *reject* the idea (which they view as a fatal flaw in Realist philosophy) that America can in effect lead a schizophrenic existence—following one set of moral–ethical principles at home, while engaging in Machiavellian (or amoral) behavior abroad; as many critics of the Vietnam War repeatedly asserted, sooner or later, such schizophrenia will destroy the cohesion and integrity of the nation. Idealists believe in the concept of *progress* in all realms of human experience (although they do not necessarily accept the idea of "automatic progress," in a Darwinian sense). No less than in medicine, natural science, psychology, or other fields, new truths can be learned in political life. Utilizing his intelligence, man is capable of advancing slowly out of the jungle-like existence that has characterized international relations in modern history—where today, perhaps more than in any earlier age, civilization is constantly threatened by a new Hobbesian state of nature, in which life is "nasty, brutish, and short."

To Idealists, it is self-evident that in the twentieth century moral, ethical, and spiritual aspects of foreign policy are *even more fundamental* than they were before 1900. Idealists take note of the fact that the ostensible aim of systems like Soviet and Chinese Communism is progress toward the good life. Abhorrent and ethically indefensible as the means used by such regimes may be, Communist elites routinely justify the policies of their governments by reference to idealistic (not to say utopian) goals. Similarly, the objectives of nearly all of the newly independent countries—eliminating poverty, raising standards of living, providing expanded educational and medical services to the masses, elevating the status of women—are *idealistic* programs. The attitudes of these countries toward the United States are determined in large measure by the degree to which America supports these goals and furnishes tangible assistance toward their realization. The emerging nations, that is to say, judge the United States *according to an idealistic standard.* Some of the sharpest criticisms leveled against the diplomatic conduct of the United States in the postwar period has been directed at this very point: America, it has been charged, was not living up to its own professed ideals or exhibiting the kind of conduct other nations "expected" it to follow in its relations with the outside world.

If these are some of the general tenets in Idealist thought, what are the more specific proposals and recommendations which Idealists urge upon American policy-makers? Most fundamentally, perhaps, this school of thought is identified with the idea of *political freedom;* as much as any other, this concept lies at the heart of the Idealist philosophy. The principle of "self-determination," for example, was one of the leading tenets of Wilsonianism. Although it was actually applied only to the liquidation of the Austro–Hungarian (along with a part of the Russian) empire after World War I, the concept of self-determination gave a considerable impetus to nationalist movements throughout the Afro–Asian world in the years that followed. Less than a generation later, President Franklin D. Roosevelt repeatedly called for freedom for colonial peoples; America's anticolonial position was unquestionably a force accelerating the breakup of the British, French, Dutch, and other empires after World War II. America's own revolutionary struggle, the Bill of Rights embodied in the Constitution, the speeches of Abraham Lincoln, and above all perhaps the steady democratization of the American society itself have had a momentous effect upon leaders and masses throughout the world. Some of the newly independent nations have based their own constitutional provisions upon the American model; the activities of the United Nations in the field of human rights likewise owe much to the American tradition. Sometimes to America's embarrassment, African nations in the contemporary period have based their militant campaigns against Southern Rhodesia, South Africa, and Portugal's remaining African empire upon ideas of political freedom with which the United States has long been identified, although black Africans feel, as we have seen, that the American government is unwilling to follow its own highest principles toward racial and colonial issues.

The promotion of "democracy" on a worldwide basis is another specific goal often advocated by Idealists. America is the world's oldest functioning democracy. In the face of deep skepticism on the European Continent, Americans proved the viability of democratic government; their success undoubtedly exerted a powerful attraction for European political movements, resulting in the expansion of political freedoms in that region. In the Wilsonian conception, World War I was fought to "make the world safe for democracy." During the twentieth century, Americans developed deep antipathies toward totalitarian regimes, like Hitler's Germany or Stalin's Russia, because these governments denied their citizens most of the fundamental liberties associated with democracy. Correctly or not, many Americans *believed* that this was why the United States found itself at war with the Axis powers during World War II. At any rate, after the war America played a leading role in introducing what now appear to be stable democratic systems in Germany and Japan; under American guidance and example, both countries joined the ranks of the world's leading democracies. As we observed in Chapter 12, the encouragement of democracy has been a persistent theme in American relations with Latin America for more than a century. Strengthening democratic political processes and institutions was an avowed objective of the Alliance for Progress, the ten-year program of hemispheric development inaugurated in the early 1960s.

To the minds of some Idealists, the United States has been derelict in recent years in the degree to which it has adhered to its own historic commitment to democracy. Despite examples such as the political reorganization of Germany and Japan, or the attempt to promote progress toward democracy in Latin America, numerous critics of postwar American policy are convinced that in too many instances the United States has "abandoned" or otherwise neglected this vital goal. Indeed, policy-makers in Washington have frequently been accused of "betraying" or actually opposing democracies throughout the world and of "preferring" right-wing dictatorships in Asia, in Latin America, and in other regions as part of America's "containment" strategy against Communism. This was one of the principal indictments brought by many Americans against America's massive support of the government of South Vietnam; no regime in Saigon since the mid-1950s had demonstrated respect for the principles of democracy, as judged by its actions rather than its professions. Large-scale American support for Thailand, which for many years has been governed by a military junta, exemplifies the same problem. In the Middle East, substantial numbers of Americans favor continued American assistance to Israel on the grounds, as the idea is often expressed, that it is "the only democracy in the region"; conversely, they oppose American aid to or close identification with Arab states like Egypt, Iraq, Saudi Arabia, and several others because they do not subscribe to or presumably practice Western liberal democracy. In recent years, the same problem confronted American policy-makers in Greece, where a military junta seized power in 1967 and proceeded to violate the usual canons of democracy by suspending the rights of free speech, assembly, and opposition party movements. As in other settings, the military clique governing Greece used American weapons, supplied to the country under the NATO alliance, to enforce its authority against political dissidents. Both at home and abroad, the United States was widely criticized because of its association with the Greek military dictatorship and its unwillingness or inability to oppose this new assault against democracy.

Besides a commitment to the promotion of political freedom outside America's borders, Idealists of course have advocated many other specific proposals for the guidance of policy-makers in Washington. In brief space, we can do no more than suggest some of these leading ideas. *Respect for international law* is a recurrent theme in the thought of Idealists.[6] One definition of a democracy is that it is a government founded on "the rule of law and not of men." Americans have always extolled the value of legal agreements and instruments, in domestic as well as in foreign affairs. Examples from the latter realm include American initiative in drawing up legal instruments like the Covenant of the League of Nations and the Charter of the United Nations; American support for documents like the Kellogg–Briand Pact (1928), "outlawing" war as a instrument of national policy; and the influential role played by the United States in instituting the "war crimes trials" against officials of the Axis powers after World War II. A more recent example is afforded by the Cuban missile crisis of 1962. Officials of the Kennedy administration devoted intensive efforts to the *legal aspects* of America's proposed response to this crisis; they regarded it as essential that, in the United Nations and outside it, America's "quarantine" of Cuba be consonant with existing international law.* By contrast, critics of American diplomacy during this crisis often asserted that the administration's blockade of Cuba

---

*For an illuminating analysis of the role of international law in one of the most serious diplomatic crises in the postwar era, see William P. Perberding, "International Law and the Cuban Missile Crisis," in Lawrence Scheinman and David Wilkinson, eds., *International Law and Political Crisis: An Analytic Casebook* (Boston: Little, Brown, 1968), pp. 175–211. As is so often the case with American diplomatic behavior, considerable evidence exists in this example that American foreign policy exhibits elements of both the Realist and Idealist points of view. The author of this case study shows convincingly that the United States and other countries in the international community, not excluding the Soviet Union, were keenly interested in the legal aspects of America's "quarantine" of Cuba; the legal dimensions of the crisis, for example, were prominent in UN debate over the issue. And in the main, the United States was reasonably successful in convincing the world of the legality of its action. Yet Perberding also concedes that the basic decision to blockade Cuba was based on *political and military* considerations; international law served mainly to legitimatize this decision—in part because international law generally remains obscure, uncodified, and often contradictory. Yet the fact that the international community would *not* respond favorably to the use of force solely on the grounds of "national interest" or *raison d'état* testifies to man's need for some kind of ethical justification for national action.

in fact *violated* international law relating to freedom of the seas and other concepts. The case of Cuba was but one among numerous instances illustrating America's traditional interest in the legal dimensions of international relations. Here, as in nearly all cases involving the application of international law to a particular global issue, the question may of course legitimately be raised of *why* the United States (or any other country) invoked legal principles. Was Washington really endeavoring to *follow* international law? Or was it, as Realists often suggested, seeking to invoke international law to *legitimatize* action it proposed to take on the grounds of "national interest"?

Humanitarianism is another important element in the approach of Idealists to international questions. American postwar foreign aid programs provide innumerable illustrations of the humanitarian impulse in external policies. Some American grants and loans to other countries (particularly military aid) were unquestionably designed to promote a clear military purpose related to the defense of the United States and its allies. But for most economic and technical assistance, humanitarian concern about the welfare of societies overseas was, in the Idealist view, the principal motivation for American aid. As the richest country in the history of the world, Idealists feel, the United States is obligated to provide such aid primarily because Americans are (or ought to be) genuinely concerned about the problems of global poverty, inadequate housing and medical care, and the population explosion in other countries. In the Idealist conception, America is inextricably "involved" in the destiny of societies outside its own borders. It can no more be indifferent to the global campaign against poverty, for example, than to the conidition of poverty-stricken groups at home. For if it is insensitive to the world's needs, it will betray its own highest traditions and forfeit any claim it has asserted to a position of global leadership. Consequently, Idealists have tended to deplore the decline in America's foreign aid budget during the 1960s and 1970s, viewing this tendency as a distinct retrogression in the nation's diplomatic role.

Few specific issues surpass *arms reduction* as a cause eliciting the support of Idealists. Disarmament was discussed at length in Chapter 15. We shall not reproduce that coverage here. It is sufficient merely to emphasize that, from the period of the First Hague Conference in 1899, idealistic thought has repeatedly supplied the impetus needed to renew the search for international agreement on arms control. Despite a depressing record of failures, the effort to reduce global armaments goes on. More than any other group, perhaps, Idealists have insisted that the attempt must not be abandoned as futile; and the limited gains achieved in the field of arms reduction can be attributed in no small measure to the interest

displayed by Idealists in this extremely difficult problem. As the cost of modern weapons continues to escalate, Idealists seem to be more convinced than ever that somehow governments must discover a way to divert the billions of dollars spent annually on armaments into more socially constructive channels. Man's ability to solve other problems (like the global population explosion) may well depend upon success in reaching an agreement on arms control.

Idealism: A Critique

We may summarize the Idealist approach to American foreign policy as saying that over the entire range of its relations with other countries, the United States must build its policies upon ethical and humanitarian foundations. Idealists do not deny that at times this is extremely difficult; sometimes it may be impossible, in an imperfect human society. They recognize that, under optimum conditions, a hiatus will *always* exist between America's ethical professions and its behavior. Nevertheless, Idealists assert both that the United States itself must endeavor to keep this gap as narrow as possible and that it must remain at the forefront of nations seeking to raise the moral–ethical standards of international political behavior generally. Progress in this direction may be slow, and in some periods imperceptible. But one condition is an essential prerequisite for such progress: continual awareness that man's political relationships are *capable* of being improved. Idealists thus reject the notion that norms of state behavior or immutable political "laws" can be derived from a study of bygone eras. The fact that nations *have* followed certain modes of conduct in the past may prove nothing more than that, for a variety of reasons, *they were failing to exemplify man's highest spiritual and ethical aspirations.* Far from constituting some kind of behavior norm for the future, this failure must be recognized for what it is and changed. Idealists also dismiss the idea that the nation-state possesses some kind of unique Hegelian quality, endowing it with a kind of "spirit" or moral–ethical system of its own. Idealists insist upon acceptance of a concept that lay at the heart of the prophetic tradition as elaborated in the Old Testament: Kings, rulers, governments, and elites, as well as ordinary citizens, are subject to judgment on the basis of moral–ethical values. There is no reason to suppose that the emergence of a particular kind of political unit—the nation-state—has changed that fact.

That idealism has always been a part of, and has powerfully affected, the conduct of American diplomacy seems undeniable. Americans have never freely accepted the Machiavellian idea that *raison d'état* (or "reason of state") provides a sufficient legitimacy for state action. Without constructing elaborate philosophical systems explaining why, Americans have always felt or sensed (rather perhaps than consciously believed) a concept with which classical political philosophers were always keenly concerned. This is the idea that, in the last anlaysis, the state exists *to promote beneficial human ends*. The actions of the state must, therefore, always be judged by reference to these ends. The ends for which the state exists of course vary from one society to another. For America, the idea that the republic exists to promote "life, liberty, and the pursuit of happiness" might serve as an acceptable definition, as might the goals enumerated in the Preamble of the Constitution.* But without entering into a detailed delineation of them here, the main point is that, in common with all other societies, the American republic exists to achieve *certain underlying goals* shared by the society. The actions of the government presumably contribute in some way to their realization. In the Idealist view, the state is thus *instrumental* to the fulfillment of these ends.

Idealists also insist upon the application of moral–ethical standards with regard to *the means* employed by the United States and other nations in pursuing their goals. It is not enough for the proposed goals of a nation to be derived from, or based upon, ideals. The methods a nation uses to attain these goals *must be in harmony with the professed goals themselves*. Idealists are aware (often much better than Realists) that means frequently "count" for more than goals in foreign policy: That is, the United States may be judged by other nations more by the methods its employs to achieve a particular goal than by the goal itself. Few critics of the Vietnam War, for example, really objected to the stated purposes of that involvement, such as assuring the continued freedom of small countries or containing Communist expansionism or trying to stabilize Southeast Asia. More often than not, American policy in Southeast Asia was condemned because of the *methods* used by the United States (such as bombing North Vietnam or supporting an authoritarian regime in Saigon) in behalf of these goals. Here, as in many other instances in postwar American foreign relations, the criticism was expressed that the use of certain means vitiated or rendered impossible the attainment of the ultimate goal. Indeed, in many cases, *the means become the de facto ends*, in the sense that the methods employed actually determine what the United States accomplishes (or fails to accomplish). America of course does not suffer uniquely from this possible tension between the ends and means of foreign policy; it may in fact

experience this dichotomy less than other countries such as Soviet Russia or Communist China; policy-makers in all nations must grapple with the problem of bringing the over-all objectives of policy and the means utilized to achieve them into harmony. But Idealists point to the fact that any genuine political realism is compelled to recognize the existence of the problem and to acknowledge that consistent reliance upon unethical means to acheive external goals can, in a quite literal sense, *subvert* the original goals themselves, thereby robbing the nation of any claim that its behavior has moral–ethical legitimacy. When that occurs, man has reverted to the law of the jungle in his political relationships. Even by the Realist criterion of "national interest," it may be seriously questioned whether the United States is capable of accomplishing its objectives abroad without convincing citizens in America and other countries that its policies possess *legitimacy*. *Raison d'état* is no longer acceptable as an adequate justification for state behavior, in an age when the "revolution of rising expectations" has created new visions of the good life for millions of people throughout the world.

Idealism of course is not without its limitations and imperfections as an approach to foreign policy issues. By definition, ideals are standards of conduct substantially above those normally associated with human behavior. They comprise *ultimate goals* toward which mankind ought to strive. Consequently, they can seldom serve as aims to be achieved immediately or within the near future. Policy-makers in all countries must always consider the *feasibility* of alternative courses of action; in democracies, officials must always weigh the extent to which public opinion will support a proposed course of action abroad. Idealist aims (like "general and complete disarmament" or "peace with justice" or eliminating global poverty) can seldom be regarded as policy objectives applicable to the day-to-day administration of foreign relations. Even as long-range goals, Idealists often forget, such objectives *are not self-executing*. Stating the aims of American foreign policy in idealistic pronouncements is not equivalent to achieving them; to do the latter, detailed plans and programs entailing the allocation of funds, resources, and energies over a period of many years are required. Progress is likely to be inordinately slow, and setbacks will almost certainly be experienced. Under some circumstances, policy-makers may be hard pressed to prevent *retrogressions* in America's relations with other countries. During some stages, Realists may well be correct in their contention that agreements based upon a reconciliation of diverse national interests constitute the best attainable accord.

Idealists often evince little recognition of what is the most agonizing dilemma confronting policy-

---

*According to the Preamble, the Constitution of the United States was designed "to form a more perfect Union, establish Justice, insure domestic Tranquility, provide for the common defence, promote the general Welfare, and secure the Blessings of Liberty to ourselves and our Posterity. . . ."

makers: the necessity to *choose* among several possible courses of action, any one of which is ethically defensible and legitimate. Eliminating poverty at home, for example, may have to be given priority over expanded American assistance programs to needy societies abroad. Reducing the military budget and curtailing the influence of the military–industrial complex may weaken America's ability to "protect" Israel, to lead a "confrontation" against South Africa, or to create a new basis for security in Asia. As in the most difficult legal cases coming before the Supreme Court, decisions in foreign affairs more often than not involve the conflict *between* ethically legitimate policies; the choice of one inescapably means the rejection of others.

Realists are also correct in calling attention to the fact that idealistic schemes for restructuring international politics often suffer acutely from utopianism and self-delusion. If Idealists are correct that a knowledge of how nations actually behave is not the epitome of political wisdom, such knowledge must be "the beginning of wisdom"; it must serve as the *starting point* for the construction of an adequate philosophy of foreign relations. In the resolution of Soviet–American tensions, or in the operations of the United Nations, or in disarmament negotiations, or in countless other areas, Idealists are too often prone to pin their hopes upon some spectacular diplomatic "breakthrough" that will resolve long-standing deadlocks. Toward many issues engendering international tensions and conflicts, the premise of Idealists often seems to be that by a kind of diplomatic "great leap forward," mankind can move into a new era of international peace and brotherhood, perhaps as a result of a new summit conference among heads of state (a favorite idealistic prescription for the ills afflicting global political life). Idealists tend to forget that something more is needed than merely reiterating the desirability of change, eloquently criticizing existing policies, or emphasizing the benefits to be derived from new modes of political conduct. With regard to many issues engendering international tensions, the real debate centers upon *how to achieve goals which nearly all nations share,* such as avoidance of global war, arms control, and promoting the economic advancement of the developing nations. Today, it is a rare policy-maker or informed citizen who is unaware of the manifold *problems* existing in international relations—from the danger of nuclear annihilation to the implications of the global population explosion. What policy-makers seek is insight into how such problems *are to be solved.* Yet in too many instances, the guidance provided by contemporary Idealists consists chiefly of criticism of existing policies, moralizing, emotional denunciations of decision-makers, and sometimes self-flagellation. In the process, the really difficult questions—precisely *how* policy-

makers are to use national resources in a manner best calculated to promote national developments schemes abroad; or *how* stability is to be achieved in Southeast Asia; or *how* American influence can best be used to preserve peace in the Middle East —receive altogether superficial attention from idealistic critics.

The Vietnam War period illustrated many of the deficiencies and *lacunae* characteristic of the idealistic approach to foreign policy. Critics of America's involvement in the Vietnam conflict (which, of course, Realists also sometimes condemned for different reasons) properly called attention to many valid objections to the nation's massive commitment in Southeast Asia. Without attempting a definitive list of its shortcomings (a subject which was discussed more fully in Chapter 13), it is enough simply to mention some of the more prominent contradictions apparent in American policy. The United States intervened heavily in the affairs of Indochina, ostensibly to protect the country from totalitarian Communism. Yet in doing so, Washington supported a succession of authoritarian (not to say in some respects totalitarian) political regimes in Saigon, whose policies were more often than not antithetical to the essential requirements of democracy and political justice. In order to "preserve" South Vietnam from alien control, the United States had itself become inextricably enmeshed in the affairs of the country; South Vietnam was dependent upon the United States economically and militarily—so much so that its future as an independent nation, once American power was withdrawn, was extremely dubious. America regarded Marxist revolutionary programs and violent political tactics in Southeast Asia as a threat to Western security; yet the American impact upon nearly all aspects of South Vietnamese life could only be described as *revolutionary and shattering.* Whatever might happen in this region after the American military retrenchment, this much seemed certain: Owing in large part to America's role in Southeast Asia, traditional society, long-established ways of life, customary modes of thought and values—such things would probably never be restored in Indochina. Deliberately or not, America had "subverted" the customary pattern of society in this region perhaps even more than Soviet Russia or Communist China, rendering continuation of the *status quo* impossible.

Idealists could and did draw up a convincing bill of particulars against the evils, the ethical contradictions, the human and monetary waste, and the generally nonproductive nature of the Vietnam War. In this respect, their indictment was eloquent and persuasive. But in another respect, it left much to be desired as an adequate critique of a frustrating and extraordinarily complex episode in recent American foreign relations. Idealists frequently weakened the force of their case, and generated adverse public reaction to their position, by the utopian coloration of their arguments, by the self-righteousness surrounding their criticisms, by the obvious psychological satisfaction which many critics derived from condemning America's role in Southeast Asia, and by their recurrent failure to address themselves to *concrete problems which had to be solved by policy-makers* before American forces could be evacuated from Indochina. It was one thing to bemoan America's growing commitment in Southeast Asia and to review the destressing record of how the United States got involved in this region. It was likewise not difficult to document the manifold "mistakes" of the Kennedy, Johnson, and Nixon administrations in Vietnam in recent years. Theoretically, such hindsight judgments can be extremely useful—indeed, indispensable—if mistakes are to be avoided in the future. But the point which many critics of the Vietnam conflict missed was that policy-makers are not primarily historians: They are required to do more than review the record to identify the mistakes of the past, since even an objective knowledge of this record may offer very little guidance in terms of solving the problems of the present and future. Even if policy-makers agreed with their critics (and about many aspects of the history of the Vietnam War, there was a substantial amount of agreement), this fact threw very little light upon what was possibly the hardest problem connected with the conflict by the late 1960s: How was the United States to liquidate its massive commitment in Southeast Asia *without in the process making new mistakes, engaging in no less unethical conduct, and raising problems which could demand another massive American engagement in the future?* Idealists often appeared strangely indifferent to such dilemmas, as though criticizing America's role in Vietnam afforded a new basis for security in Asia, or as though reminding the nation of its moral–ethical heritage automatically gave policy-makers answers as to how to avoid mistakes in formulating a course of action for reducing the American presence in Southeast Asia.

Much of the criticism directed by Idealists at the liquidation of America's commitment in Indochina seemed distressingly reminiscent of the kind of utopianism which surrounded American foreign policy in earlier periods. Idealists have exhibited a tendency to *personalize or objectify* the frustrations attendant upon America's role as a great power. During World War I, Wilsonians tended to identify the Kaiser's government in Germany as the embodiment of evil. Once that government was defeated and superceded by a democracy, the theory was, democracy would become worldwide and wars among nations would come to an end. Much the same idea came to be attached by Idealists to the Axis powers in World War II. The "unconditional surrender" of Germany, Italy, and Japan would make possible realization of the "Four Freedoms" throughout the world;* the concept of "great-power unanimity" would survive the war and convert the United Nations into a dynamic instrument for global peace and security; a new age of international peace and brotherhood would dawn. Idealists (much more than Realists) overlooked the prospect that new international tensions, growing out of conflicts among the wartime allies, could and did immerse the world once more into cold war and sometimes violent encounters among powerfully armed nations.

Against this background, much of the criticism surrounding America's involvement in Vietnam during the 1960s and 1970s appears depressingly familiar. Many positive gains could conceivably flow from termination of the Vietnam conflict, for the United States, for Asia, and for the world as a whole. But as in World Wars I and II, the tendency of Idealists to entertain utopian expectations about the war's termination, to greatly exaggerate what an end to armed conflict will achieve, and to anticipate revolutionary change in the nature of internal and external problems once the "horror of the war" is eliminated—such tendencies are bound to foster self-delusion among even informed citizens about what American policy-makers can and will accomplish. When these more utopian results are *not* forthcoming—when citizens discover that the evacuation of American forces from Indochina does not per se cure the problem of poverty at home or relieve them of all agonizing choices in foreign affairs—then a mood of national frustration and disillusionment will almost certainly follow. The familiar cycle in American diplomatic history—utopian schemes for correcting *all* the ills of international political life, followed by a national mood of dejection, disappointment, and apathy—is an almost inevitable

*In his message to Congress on January 6, 1941, President Franklin D. Roosevelt enumerated four freedoms designed to promote world security. These were: freedom of speech and expression; freedom of religion; freedom from want ("which, translated into world terms, means economic understandings which will secure to every nation a healthy peacetime life for its inhabitants —everywhere in the world"); and freedom from fear (which FDR interpreted as "a worldwide reduction of armaments to such a point and in such a thorough fashion that no nation will be in a position to commit an act of physical aggression against any neighbor—anywhere in the world"). Several months later, President Roosevelt and British Prime Minister Churchill issued the Atlantic Charter setting forth their "hopes for a better future for the world." Somewhat comparable to President Wilson's Fourteen Points during World War I, this document contained eight points (such as renunciation of territorial aggrandizement, self-determination, and abandonment of the use of force) proposed as the basis of a new world order. Texts in Senate Foreign Relations Committee, *A Decade of American Foreign Policy: Basic Documents, 1941–1949,* 81st Congress, 1st Session, 1950, pp. 1–2.

by-product of unrestrained Idealism. And the irony is that this kind of national attitude then makes it more difficult than ever for Idealists to accomplish the goals to which they are committed in the conduct of foreign affairs.

Syntheses of Realist and Idealist Thought

Few commentators on American foreign policy belong exclusively to the Realist or Idealist school of thought. Idealists do not accept the idea that their approach is divorced from political realities; similarly, Realists deny that they are indifferent to ideals. As our treatment thus far has indicated, both points of view offer important and useful insights into the problems of formulating and executing foreign policy. To a substantial degree, the two approaches are *complementary;* each calls attention to aspects and problems of international relations often neglected by the other. Implicitly or explictly, therefore, most informed students of foreign policy endeavor to combine elements of Idealism and Realism into a systhesis of principles for the guidance of American policymakers.

Illustrative of this approach is the thought of Professor John G. Stoessinger, whose treatment of contemporary international relations is geared to four major themes[7] First, there is the conflict between two national goals—the struggle for power and the struggle for order—characteristic of state behavior. The former is conspicuous in the viewpoint of Realists, while Idealists emphasize the latter. Second, there is the "divergence between the images that nations entertain of world affairs and of each other and the international realities as they actually are"; from their own different perspectives, Idealists and Realists alike are conscious of this disparity, although each group would perhaps account for it differently. Third, postwar international relations have obviously been preoccupied with the East–West (or, more specifically, the Soviet–American) conflict, popularly designated the cold war. Realists and Idealists alike of course acknowledge the existence of the cold war, much as they might disagree in explaining its origins and its perpetuation.* Fourth, contemporary international politics have also involved the conflict between modern nationalism and the desire of some countries to maintain their colonial empires or what Afro–Asian nationalists call a "neo-colonial" relationship.[8] One notable characteristic of Stoessinger's approach, therefore, is that it is *multidimensional.* His premise is that international relations are simply too complex, and their ramifications are too all-encompassing, to be adequately embraced within a single or unitary approach. Moreover, any satisfactory understanding of international political relationships must, in Stoessinger's view, be *interdisciplinary.*

In his assessment of one of the central concepts of international relations—the idea of *national power*—Stoessinger again adopts a position combining elements of both the Realist and Idealist philosophies. He agrees with the Realists in acknowledging the crucial importance of the concept of national power; he feels that an understanding of it is essential to any intelligent comprehension of international political life. Yet he emphasizes (much more than do most Realists) that the concept of power must be construed *broadly;* that it encompasses something more than the "capabilities" of nations; that its psychological, and other *intangible,* aspects are vitally important; and that power is *always relative* (whereas the "capabilities" of nations may not be, as least to the same degree). In fact, he observes that sometimes the *power* of a nation and its *capabilities* are, as postwar experience with Soviet–American relations has frequently indicated, *inversely correlated:* The greater the military strength of a super-power, the less able it may be to *use* that strength for diplomatic ends. After a certain point is reached, a super-power may in effect become "muscle bound"; its overwhelming strength becomes in reality a form *of weakness,* inhibiting it from playing as active and influential a role in world affairs as it might have played at an earlier stage. Stoessinger also parts company with the political Realists when it comes to the role of *geography* as the leading determinant of national power. Nor does he agree with Realists like Professor Hans J. Morgenthau that ideological influences are (as Morgenthau expresses it) nothing more than a "flattering unction" for the concealment of national expansionist tendencies. In Stoessinger's assessment, ideology is itself often a major ingredient in a nation's power. "The relationship between power and ideology seems, up to a point, to be one of mutual reinforcement." Commitment to an ideology, based upon confidence in the ultimate achievement of its goals, is per se "a source of tremendous long-range power." Yet, Stoessinger makes a key distinction between the role of ideology in the foreign policies of *totalitarian* and *democratic* states. By definition, the former are usually committed to ideologically derived programs. The latter, however, tend by nature to be *pluralistic;* they are devoted to diverse goals instead of a single unified belief system.

Stoessinger is extremely critical in his appraisal of the Realist conception of the "national interest" as the underlying principle activating the foreign policy of the United States or any other nation. Since we have already pointed out several deficiencies in this concept, here it is sufficient merely

---

*Differing evaluations of the origins and nature of the cold war were presented and assessed at length in Chapter 8.

to note that Stoessinger finds it vague, ambiguous, and at best only a partial explanation of what nations seek in their relationships abroad. The concept of national interest "is ambiguous and frequently not at all helpful when applied to a concrete situation." In Stoessinger's view, it is more enlightening to discuss the goals of nations in terms of whether they are *clearly defined* (i.e., more or less universally shared throughout the society) or *diffuse* (i.e., essentially the goals of groups within the society). Alternatively, national goals may be regarded as *static* or *dynamic.* One of the oldest themes in international relations is the tension between forces favoring the status quo and those seeking *change* in the international environment. Stoessinger is thus convinced that "There is no single concept that explains the national interest." If it is admittedly true that some nations (especially powerful ones) use their power to enhance their own influence and prestige, it is equally true that other nations use power "in the pursuit of cooperation and international order."[9]

A pivotal idea in Stoessinger's treatment of international politics is what he calls "the frequent and highly significant differences between the way nations perceive one another and the way they really are." Tensions and conflicts do not arise among nations solely on the basis of "objective realities." What he calls "imagery and illusion" also play key roles; ideology is a significant factor in creating what are often highly subjective views of the outside world. When it is said that the United States feared a certain event, the student of American foreign policy must ask *who* precisely had such fears; and this leads him in turn to an analysis of group and elite behavior in American political life. This dichotomy between national perceptions and realities exists in the foreign policy of *every* nation. Stoessinger is convinced, for example, that it has been conspicuous in the cold war between the United States and the Soviet Union.[10]

Stoessinger believes that the "greatest challenge" facing the world's statesmen "concerns the role of ethics in a world of power." He is as critical of many of the assumptions made by Wilsonians in their approach to international relations as the Realist school of thought. At the same time, he rejects the Realist–Idealist dichotomy as "too simple" and as providing an incomplete set of alternatives upon which to base foreign policy. Statesmen are neither saints nor beasts. If Idealists err in stressing *intentions* as the dominant consideration in judging an act moral or immoral, Realists are no less wrong in focusing upon the *consequences* as being its all-important aspect. Idealists fail to realize that behavior springing from the best of intentions may produce ethically objectionable results (many critics would cite America's support of right-wing dictatorships abroad as a recurrent and familiar example). Real-

ists appear oblivious of the fact that judging the validity of national action solely on the basis of its consequences is tantamount to the idea that *any means* may be employed to achieve a beneficial end. In Stoessinger's view, "power and morality are inseparable and must be so considered by the statesman."[11] This being the case, the statesman is forever engaged "in a process of continual balancing." As he weighs alternatives, the policy-maker seldom discovers "the merits in favor of one course of action to be clearly greater than the arguments for another." In numerical terms, the arguments for and against a particular line of action are almost never in the magnitudes of 90 percent in favor, 10 percent against; instead, they nearly always tend to be on the order of 55 percent in favor, 45 percent against. Small as they are, these distinctions between acceptable and unacceptable courses are often the difference "between success and failure" in foreign affairs. Expressed differently, nearly any conceivable proposal for dealing with a concrete problems in foreign relations *can be legitimately criticized;* every possible alternative has certain drawbacks —sometimes significant ones. The course finally selected may well be chosen because it has *the fewest shortcomings* or because *it does the least damage* to the diplomatic interests of the nation. Idealists can never free policy-makers of such dilemmas by urging them to apply ethical principles in America's relations with other countries; nor does the Realist invocation of the principle of "national interest" rid policy-making of such difficult choices. Stoessinger is convinced that the "statesman must act with the tragic knowledge that he cannot choose between good and evil but only among varying stages of evil." Inescapably, the policy-maker is confronted with the unpalatable alternative of becoming either "a dogmatist" (if he pushes Idealist principles too far) or a "sloppy relativist" (if he embraces Realist principles uncritically). Avoiding these polar positions poses an unending challenge to the statesman.[12]

An attempted synthesis of Realist and Idealist thought, such as Stoessinger essays, has certain advantages as well as disadvantages. Perhaps one of its principal attractions is that this approach recognizes, considerably better than Idealism or Realism alone, that a unidimensional philosophy of foreign affairs is apt to be misleadingly simplistic. For super-powers like the United States especially, international relationships are too variegated—and the circumstances confronting policy-makers are too disparate—to permit consistent adherence to a single foreign policy principle or set of principles. Neither of these philosophies alone adequately acknowledges the need for *flexibility* in foreign relations; neither gives sufficient weight to the fact that American foreign policy toward Latin America must, for a variety of good reasons, often be very different from its policy toward the Middle East or Asia. A policy which assumes widespread international agreement upon common moral, ethical, and legal principles, such as Idealists advocate, may be appropriate for nations belonging to the Western community. It is no coincidence that postwar American foreign policy toward Europe furnishes many of the examples showing the influence of ethical and humanitarian considerations upon foreign relations. Asia and the Middle East, on the other hand—regions with which the American society has very little in common in terms of traditions, philosophical systems, and moral–ethical codes—perhaps best illustrate the extent to which Realist ideas have affected American foreign policy. Such inconsistencies may also be accounted for, as Stoessinger's treatment suggests, by the differences in the *time span* over which American policy is evaluated. The Idealist approach may be, and in some instances unquestionably is, very difficult to follow *in the short run,* in the day-to-day conduct of foreign relations, particularly when cold war considerations create a threat to national security. In crisis situations, the United States and all other nations find Realist principles more applicable than those associated with Idealism. Yet *in the long run,* Idealism supplies ultimate goals and objectives for policy-makers. As the Idealists emphasize, genuine political realism may consist of *endeavoring to remove threats to the security of all nations,* by trying to engender a sense of *international community,* rather than by merely responding to such threats on the basis of a narrowly egocentric understanding of the "national interest."

Stoessinger's synthesis of Realist and Idealist thought also commends itself because it is a more accurate description of what the United States and most other nations *actually do* in the formulation of foreign affairs. The vast majority of American citizens and officials, as we have already observed, exhibit elements of both schools of thought in their attitudes toward the outside world. Almost no one (including professed Realists and Idealists themselves) adopts one approach or the other in its pure form. To cite but a single example, it is clear from the memoirs of officials like former Secretary of State Dean G. Acheson that he and most other State Department officials base their policy recommendations to the President upon *some combination* of Realist and Idealist attitudes.[13] No two Secretaries of State, to be sure, synthesize these viewpoints in quite the same way; in any individual case, Idealism may be preponderant over Realism, or the reverse. And for a particular Secretary of State, an idealist approach may seem more suitable toward certain problems confronting the United States abroad, while Realism appears more relevant to other problems. Moreover, as Stoessinger's approach emphasizes, the student of foreign relations must

continually distinguish between the underlying forces *actuating* foreign policy and the way that policy is *rationalized or explained* to the outside world. Again, the Realist approach may be more useful for one purpose, while Idealism is a more valuable point of view for the other. Stoessinger properly insists upon a point which receives inadequate attention in Realist thought: How policy is rationalized and explained is itself part of the "power" of a nation and an integral part of the foreign policy process. The failure of an administration in Washington to carry out this process skillfully and convincingly—to create and maintain a sense of "legitimacy" in behalf of American foreign policy goals—can (as President Lyndon B. Johnson discovered painfully) detract significantly from the power of the United States to achieve its objectives. Far from being an unimportant aspect of foreign policy, as Realist thought sometimes suggests, the necessity to legitimatize decisions, both to the people at home and to the outside world, has come to be a crucial realm of decision-making. Government officials must not merely *in fact* promote the interests of the nation, as policy-makers might define those interests. In the contemporary era, they must also *appear* to do so to the minds of millions of citizens within the United States and to societies overseas. If policies meet the former standard but not the latter—if they fail, that is to say, to accord with popular expectations and demands concerning what policy-makers *ought* to achieve—they will be incapable of producing a satisfactory relationship between the United States and the outside world. One of the striking defects in Realist thought is failure to acknowledge that, far more than was the case in the eighteenth or nineteenth centuries, this is one of the major limitations upon the conduct of foreign affairs in the twentieth century.

Yet, in common with Idealism, Realism, or other possible approaches to foreign policy, attempted syntheses of diverse schools of thought also have their deficiencies and limitations. Stoessinger's synthesis suffers from the same disabilities as all compromises: It satisfies no one completely. As in any attempt to achieve "the best of both worlds," the net result can be "the worst of both worlds," producing an approach which suffers from innate inconsistency, internal incompatibility of its central tenets, and a kind of built-in ambiguity which does little really to resolve the dilemmas normally confronting the policy-maker. Unidimensional philosophies of course have the virtue of simplicity and, when they are adhered to consistently, *of predictability.* Within reasonable limits, it was easy for an informed student of American foreign relations to predict how a Wilsonian Idealist would react to concrete issues like American membership in the League of Nations, the desirability of disarmament, or attempts to extend the compass of international law. (Parenthetically, we might note that it would have been much *more* difficult to predict the behavior of Wilsonians toward problems in Latin America—where, in fact, the United States carried out more overt "interventions" during President Wilson's administration than it did under the leadership of a Realist like President Theodore Roosevelt!) For good or for ill, as long as Wilsonian thought motivated American foreign policy, the attitudes and actions of the government formed a fairly consistent pattern, containing few "surprises" to citizens at home and abroad. Multidimensional philosophies, such as the one proposed by Professor Stoessinger, introduce a greater measure of doubt and uncertainty about how the United States will react to particular issues abroad. In fact, this approach advocates the idea that the United States *ought* to respond *differently* to diverse problems and to dissimilar circumstances overseas. Foreign policy officials in the United States should recognize that political developments in Africa present a very different set of problems from crises in Asia; and America's relations within the Western community are inherently dissimilar to its relations with the developing nations. Insofar as this approach reflects the disparate nature of the international environment, it has much to recommend it. Yet it also inevitably means that American foreign policy will continually be subjected to the criticism that *it lacks consistency and internal cohesion*, that the behavior of the United States in one region "contradicts" its behavior in another region, and that Americans "do not know their own mind" when it comes to their policies overseas. Other nations may, therefore, find it very difficult to anticipate how the United States is likely to respond to events abroad, thereby enhancing the danger that a miscalculation in Moscow or Peking concerning American intentions could trigger a new global conflict. One answer to this criticism is of course that the very *unpredictability* of American (or Soviet or Chinese) policy induces caution in the capitals of the world and makes all nations less prone to engage in "risky" diplomatic or military ventures abroad. There is undoubtedly some merit to the contention that this kind of calculated uncertainty serves as a deterrent to national policies likely to engender international hostilities in the nuclear age.

A substantial area of ambiguity still surrounds foreign policy decision-making in the kind of synthesis advocated by Professor Stoessinger. Even if it is conceded that American officials in fact draw from both Realist and Idealist principles in formulating national policy toward a particular region like Latin America, *why* they follow certain tenets of Realism and not others, or the specific manner in which they combine Realist and Idealist principles in a given case remains far from clear. Nor does this approach enlighten us in any

detail concerning why Idealism should be preferred over Realism, or the reverse, with respect to different areas of the world or different categories of international problems. Take a concrete issue confronting the United States in several settings throughout the world: What ought the attitude of America to be toward revolutionary change throughout the zone of the emerging nations? The Realist would answer that the guiding principle of American foreign policy toward this, as toward all other international issues, ought to be the "national interest." The United States, that is to say, ought to formulate its policies primarily in terms of what course of action best promotes American foreign policy goals, the foremost of which is national security (and, according to Realist thought, this can most effectively be safeguarded by maintenance of the balance of power). Adherence to this course of action would of course dictate differing American responses to diverse revolutionary situations abroad: It would mean opposing some revolutions, supporting others, and perhaps taking a "wait and see" attitude toward others, depending upon an over-all assessment by policy-makers in Washington as to how American interests are best served. Since the security and well-being of the United States must always be the dominant consideration, Realists would appraise revolutionary ideologies and programs in terms of how they accorded with American security interests. The extent to which a particular revolutionary movement abroad had popular support; or the desirability of revolutionary change in a given society; or the degree to which the movement sought to democratize the society—such considerations would be important only to the extent that they bore directly upon some clear American diplomatic interest affected by revolutionary change.

By contrast, Idealists would base their assessment of the problem of revolutionary movements abroad on different premises. Their appraisal might begin by emphasizing the importance of America's own revolutionary heritage: By many criteria, the American democracy has been a more truly "revolutionary" force in its effect upon modern Afro–Asian nationalist movements than has Soviet or Chinese Communism. Idealists would take note of the fact that revolutionary change appears to be ubiquitous throughout the Afro–Asian world; in many societies within this zone, radical reconstructions of society have been too long delayed; the one common denominator of political activity from South America to east Asia is mass unwillingness to accept the status quo and belief in "the revolution of rising expectations." Idealists are, therefore, convinced that the United States must "identify" with the forces of change and modernization abroad; in too many instances, it has been too closely associated with discredited incumbent regimes opposed to change and prepared to use oppressive methods to resist it. But change, Idealists are convinced, is inevitable. The only meaningful question for American policy-makers is: "How can the United States use its influence most effectively to promote change in a manner best according with the needs and desires of the societies concerned?" Failure to do so, Idealists tend to be convinced, will isolate the United States more and more from societies outside the West, leaving the Soviet Union, Communist China, and other totalitarian regimes to become the champions of "revolution" around the world. In brief, Idealists tend to interpret revolutionary movements abroad as basically desirable, as inevitable, and as phenomena which in most cases the United States ought to support.

The informed student of contemporary international politics is aware that both the Realist and the Idealist assessments of revolutions abroad have considerable merit, as well as conspicuous weaknesses. Realists are unquestionably correct that, toward this question as toward all others confronting American policy-makers, the security interests of the United States are uppermost in the minds of government officials. Realists are on sound ground also in their contention that revolution in other countries per se is neither good nor bad; history offers ample precedents to support the view that even the most idealistic revolutionary programs sometimes ultimately result in tyranny for the society concerned and, what may be more to the point, in *aggressive tendencies* threatening the security of other countries. The Realist, in other words, *rejects the idea that any revolutionary program is preferable to the status quo,* because his knowledge of history tells him that in fact revolutions are *not* always synonymous with progress or greater security for the international community. The Realist, therefore, insists that American policy-makers carefully appraise factors besides the abstract desirability of revolutionary change abroad or the announced programs offered by revolutionary groups in other countries. What are the prospects that a new regime can actually *achieve* its proclaimed revolutionary goals? In order to do so, how dependent will it have to become upon other countries, like the United States, Soviet Russia, Communist China, or the nations of Western Europe? Will the dynamics of the revolutionary program drive the new government into conflict with its neighbors, perhaps arousing apprehensions among them because of fears of expansionism or of foreign support for insurrections within their borders? Will the all too familiar cycle be repeated, by which a new regime—pledged to carrying out radical changes for the benefit of the society concerned—degenerates into elitist rule based upon repression and self-glorification?

Yet Idealists often make a persuasive case when they argue that in many regions of the world societies living in backwardness are prone to give the benefit of the doubt to any revolutionary movement capable of seizing and exercising power; conditions in many of these societies cannot perhaps become more intolerable. and they may conceivably be improved by revolutionary change. In the light of its own traditions—and of its evident desire to preserve maximum influence with countries outside its own borders—the United States must differentiate among revolutionary programs and ideologies. In the Idealist view, such determinations must be made primarily on the basis of whether the movement's goals accord with the universal desire for modernization; national development; greater political, economic, and social democracy; the creation of new opportunities for advancement for the masses; and other aims widely espoused by Afro–Asian nationalist movements. Idealists appear aware (much more than Realists) that true political stability within such societies—a prerequisite for genuine regional and global security—depends upon the degree to which governments in the modern period are responsive to such demands on the part of their citizens. At the same time, too many Idealists are perhaps inclined to believe that the statement of revolutionary goals is tantamount to achieving them; too often they are not concerned with the *actual prospects* that such programs can be, and will be, successfully carried out; still less are they prone to remember that throughout the postwar era, Afro–Asian revolutionary movements have *more often than not* in the end disappointed their supporters within the country as well as their friends abroad. Idealists often exhibit a kind of blind and undiscriminating faith in revolutionary causes overseas; nearly always, they are inclined to give any self-styled "revolution" the benefit of the doubt. In this sense, revolution tends to serve the same purpose for the Idealist that balance of power serves for the Realist: Supposedly, it is a kind of automatic guarantee of international peace, security, and well-being which the United States in principle ought always to support! Little attention can be found in the thought of many Idealists to an idea which was emphasized in Chapter 14: *Evolutionary programs* in several countries have thus far proved the most promising approach to modernization and national development. American policy-makers are *not* restricted to a choice between revolution and reaction, as Idealists sometimes suggest. Evolutionary approaches may, in some societies, offer a more favorable prospect of actually realizing idealistic goals than either radical change or adherence to the status quo. Nor are Idealists sufficiently mindful of the long-range consequences for the United States of indiscriminately supporting revolution throughout the world. As the Soviet Union has discovered in several countries, such support can and frequently does entail responsibility for (and implicit approval of) the policies of the regime in question; and when the regime begins to lose popular support, the influence of its great-power sponsor is adversely affected. In some contexts, the net result has been a significant *decline* in good will toward the great power involved and a sharp public "reaction" against its support of the incumbent government.

As the discerning reader will have already concluded, an attempt to combine or synthesize Realist and Idealist thought with respect to a single problem, like revolutionary movements abroad, by no means resolves all the dilemmas and contradictions inherent in policy-making. Admittedly, it fails to produce a "clear principle" upon which to base American foreign policy in responding to such problems. Indeed, the result of endeavoring to synthesize these two approaches may simply be to *highlight the complexities* inherent in the problem and to underscore the idea that any proposed course of action abounds with difficulties, objections, and frustrations. Whether he advocates Realism, Idealism, or some alternative approach to foreign policy, the critic of American foreign relations seldom lacks evidence to demonstrate the defects or inadequacies of existing policy. As experience during the Vietnam conflict repeatedly indicated, however, he is often extremely hard pressed to suggest alternatives to existing policies which do not involve more, or more serious, risks than the policies he condemns.

Hard and unpalatable choices thus remain the lot of policy-makers. No unidimensional or multidimensional approach frees the process of foreign policy from what the theologian might call "the existential dilemma" which humans encounter at every turn. More so perhaps in foreign affairs than in domestic policy, officials are compelled to choose among competing goals, any one of which in its own right may be desirable and beneficial. The difficulty is that frequently *they are mutually exclusive.* For America to "identify" too closely with a revolutionary regime abroad, for example, may ultimately dictate the kind of "interventionist" policies which Idealists almost uniformly deplore. Conversely, failure to support revolutionary movements in some settings could prove to be politically unrealistic, possibly ruinous for American diplomatic interests. American power is vast; but it *remains finite.* It must, so to speak, be "apportioned" more widely, and among more different kinds of situations, than in any other era of history. Moreover, after the Vietnam War, the proportion of America's total resources, time, energy, and other ingredients available to officials in foreign affairs is clearly less than in the 1950s or early 1960s. Long-neglected domestic problems claim priority over new commitments in foreign affairs. No less crucially, in that vitally important realm—the intangible components of national power—the American people and their leaders have absorbed a series of psychological shocks and frustrations as a result of the prolonged struggle in Vietnam, the net effect of which is to make them reluctant to assume commitments anywhere else in the world that are likely to escalate into massive American involvement in the affairs of another region. Whether it constitutes a "new wave of isolationism" or not, this national sentiment undoubtedly exists; and it narrows the options available to American policy-makers in regions like the Middle East and Sub-Saharan Africa. Foreign policy officials have fewer resources with which to achieve diplomatic objectives, and the means available to them are more limited. One inevitable result of this situation is that the *dilemmas of choice become sharper than ever.* The search for a satisfactory guiding principle (or principles) will go on—under circumstances virtually guaranteeing that the choice made will leave many officials and informed citizens dissatisfied. But perhaps the existence of this dissatisfaction—deriving from a conviction that America's diplomatic conduct is capable of being improved—is the real well-spring of American foreign policy.

NOTES

1. See Hans J. Morgenthau, "The Mainspring of American Foreign Policy," *American Political Science Review* 44 (December, 1950), 833–836, 844, 849; George F. Kennan, *American Diplomacy, 1900–1950* (New York: New American Library, 1952), pp. 93–94.
2. Morgenthau, *op. cit.*, pp. 840, 853–854; and the same author's "Another 'Great Debate': The National Interest of the United States," *American Political Science Review* 46 (December, 1952), 970–978; and his *In Defense of the National Interest* (New York: Knopf, 1951), pp. 34, 38–39.
3. See, for example, the criticisms of balance-of-power politics as a major cause of World War I, in Sidney B. Fay, "Balance of Power," *Encyclopedia of the Social Sciences*, vol. 2, (New York: Macmillan, 1933), pp. 396–398.
4. The literature on the concepts of power and the balance of power is voluminous. See, for example, P. H. Partridge, "Some Notes on the Concept of Power," *Political Studies* 11 (June, 1963), 107–126; this author is convinced that the concept of power remains characterized by "vagueness, indeterminateness, and generality" and that there is no "precision or uniformity in the employment of the concept." For another illuminating critique of the concept, see K. R. Minogue, "Power in Politics," *Political Studies* 7 (October, 1959), 269–289. For evaluations of the concept of the balance of power, see Ernst B. Haas, "The Balance of Power as a Guide to Policy-Making," *Journal of Politics* 15 (August, 1953), 370–399; and the same author's "The Balance of Power: Prescription, Con-

cept, or Propaganda?" *World Politics* 5 (July, 1953), 442–478. Haas focuses upon the ambiguities inherent in the concept and identifies the preconditions necessary for its successful operation, very few of which exist in the contemporary international setting. Another helpful analysis of power and the balance of power is Inis L. Claude, *Power and International Relations* (New York: Random House, 1962), *passim*, but esp. pp. 11–94.

5. The complexities involved in trying to establish and maintain a balance of power in a volatile area like the Middle East are dealt with in two helpful studies: J. C. Hurewitz, *Middle East Politics: The Military Dimension* (New York: Praeger, 1969); and Walter Laqueur, *The Struggle for the Middle East* (New York: Macmillan, 1969).

6. A forceful and persuasive appraisal of the role of international law in international politics— in which many Realist criticisms are analyzed in detail—is Louis Henkin, *How Nations Behave: Law and Foreign Policy* (New York: Praeger, 1968).

7. See John G. Stoessinger, *The Might of Nations: World Politics in Our Times*, 3rd ed. (New York: Random House, 1969). For another effort to synthesize Realist and Idealist thought, see Thomas I. Cook and Malcolm Moos, *The Realism of Idealism as a Basis for Foreign Policy* (Baltimore: John Hopkins, 1954).

8. Stoessinger, *op. cit.*, p. 5.

9. *Ibid.*, pp. 7–30.

10. *Ibid.*, pp. 390–403.

11. *Ibid.*, p. 230.

12. *Ibid.*, pp. 228–233.

13. See, for example, Dean Acheson, *Present at the Creation* (New York: Norton, 1969), *passim*.

BIBLIOGRAPHY

This bibliography is designed to supplement the list of references appearing at the end of each chapter. Normally, titles listed there have not been repeated. Instead, recent studies have been included here relating various aspects of American foreign policy to the broad international environment that forms the context within which the United States must shape its response to the outside world. For convenience and ease in utilizing both the list of references at the end of chapters and this bibliography, references have been arranged here in the same order as the subject matter of the book. A list of bibliographies and general references precedes the topical reading lists.

Bibliographies

American Political Science Review.

Beers, H. P., *Bibliographies in American History* (New York: H. W. Wilson, 1942).

Bemis, Samuel F., and Grace G. Griffin, *Guide to the Diplomatic History of the United States, 1775–1921* (Washington, D.C.: Government Printing Office, 1935).

Council on Foreign Relations, *Foreign Affairs Bibliography, 1919–1932* (New York: Harper & Row, 1933).

Council on Foreign Relations, *Foreign Affairs Bibliography, 1932–1942* (New York: Harper & Row, 1945).

Council on Foreign Relations, *Foreign Affairs Bibliography, 1942–1952* (New York: Harper & Row, 1955).

Handlin, Oscar, *et. al., Harvard Guide to American History* (Cambridge, Mass.: Belknap Press, 1954).

Library of Congress, General Reference and Bibliography Division, *American History and Civilization: A List of Guides and Annotated or Selective Bibliographies* (Washington, D.C.: 1951).

Rips, Rae E., ed., *United States Government Publications*, 3rd rev. ed. (New York: H. W. Wilson, 1949).

United Nations, Headquarters Library, *Biblio-graphical Series.* Titles listed in this series include *Latin America, 1939–1949* (1952); *A Bibliography of the Charter of the United Nations* (1955); and *Industrialization in Underdeveloped Countries* (1956).

United Nations, Headquarters Library, *Ten Years of United Nations Publications, 1945–1955.* Provides a convenient source for locating UN publications on a variety of subjects.

United Nations, Headquarters Library, *United Nations Documents Index.* This publication is indispensable in using documentary sources relating to the UN.

United States Government, *U.S. Government Publications—Monthly Catalogue* (Washington, D.C.) An invaluable guide to the use of materials published by all branches of the American government.

General References

Carnegie Endowment for International Peace, *Institutes of International Affairs* (New York: 1953). Describes organizations within the United States and abroad interested in international relations.

Council on Foreign Relations, *The United States in World Affairs* (New York: Harper & Row, 1931 to date). This annual volume provides a readable secondary treatment of the main trends in American foreign policy.

Department of State. The Department of State publishes a number of continuing series devoted to selected aspects of American foreign relations. The following would perhaps be of greatest interest to the student:

Commercial Policy
Conference
Department and Foreign Service
Documents and State Papers
European and British Commonwealth
Far Eastern
General Foreign Policy
Inter-American

International Organization
Near and Middle Eastern
United States and the United Nations

London Institute of World Affairs, *The Year Book of World Affairs* (London: Stevens and Sons, Ltd., 1946 to date). This series contains articles on aspects of international affairs.

Periodicals. The following are scholarly periodicals dealing directly or indirectly with American foreign policy:

American Political Science Review, 1907–.
Annals of the American Academy of Political and Social Science, 1890–.
Current History, 1941–.
Department of State Bulletin, 1939–.
Foreign Affairs, 1922–.
International Affairs, London, 1922–.
International Conciliation, 1907–.
International Journal, Toronto, 1946–.
International Organization, 1947–.
Journal of International Affairs, 1947–.
Journal of Politics, 1945–.
Middle East Journal, 1947–.
Pacific Affairs, 1928–.
Political Science Quarterly, 1886–.
United Nations Review, 1954–.
Virginia Quarterly Review, 1925–.
Western Political Quarterly, 1948–.
World Affairs, 1901–.
World Politics, 1948–.
Yale Review, 1911–.

Royal Institute of International Affairs, *Documents on International Affairs* (London: Oxford University Press, 1928 to date).

Savord, Ruth, and Donald Wasson, *American Agencies Interested in International Affairs* (New York: Council on Foreign Relations, 1955). Describes the activities of agencies and groups within the United States active in the sphere of foreign relations.

United Nations, *Yearbook of the United Nations* (New York: Columbia University Press). A valuable summary of proceedings in the UN, providing a guide for further exploration in documentary sources.

World Peace Foundation, *Documents on American Foreign Relations* (Boston: 1939 to date). A convenient documentary source.

Chapter One. FOUNDATIONS OF AMERICAN FOREIGN POLICY

Bailey, Richard, *Problems of the World Economy* (Baltimore: Penguin Books, 1967).

Bernstein, Peter L., *The Price of Prosperity* (New York: Random House, 1966).

Blum, John M. *The Promise of America: An His-torical Inquiry* (Baltimore: Penguin Books, 1967).

Bohlen, Charles E., *The Transformation of American Foreign Policy* (New York: Norton, 1969).

Congressional Quarterly Service, *Global Defense: U.S. Military Commitments Abroad* (Washington, D.C.: Congressional Quarterly Service, 1969).

Congressional Quarterly Service, *National Diplomacy: 1965–1970* (Washington, D.C.: Congressional Quarterly Service, 1970).

Ekirch, Arthur A., Jr., *Ideas, Ideals, and American Diplomacy: A History of Their Growth and Interaction* (New York: Appleton-Century-Crofts, 1966).

Filene, Peter G., ed., *American Views of Soviet Russia* (Homewood, Ill.: Dorsey Press, 1968).

Goodman, Paul, *New Reformation: Notes of a Neolithic Conservative* (New York: Random House, 1970).

Graebner, Norman A., *Ideas and Diplomacy: Readings in the Intellectual Tradition of American Foreign Policy* (New York: Oxford University Press, 1964).

Haas, Ernst B., *American Commitments and World Order* (Englewood Cliffs, N.J.: Prentice-Hall, 1969).

Hammond, Paul Y., *The Cold War Years: American Foreign Policy Since 1945* (New York: Harcourt Brace Jovanovich, 1969).

Hoffman, Stanley, *Gulliver's Troubles, or the Setting of American Foreign Policy* (New York: McGraw-Hill, 1968).

Horowitz, David., *The Free World Colossus: A Critique of American Foreign Policy in the Cold War* (New York: Hill & Wang, 1971).

Johnson, Harry G., ed., *New Trade Strategy for the World Economy* (Toronto: University of Toronto Press, 1969).

Kolko, Gabriel, *The Roots of American Foreign Policy* (Boston: Beacon Press, 1969).

Mendel, Douglas, *American Foreign Policy in a Polycentric World* (Belmont, Calif.: Dickinson, 1968).

Osgood, Robert E., *et. al., America and the World: From the Truman Doctrine to Vietnam* (Baltimore: Johns Hopkins Press, 1970).

Paterson, Thomas G., *Cold War Critics: Alternatives to American Foreign Policy in the Truman Years* (Chicago: Quadrangle Books, 1971).

Payne, James L., *The American Threat: The Fear of War as an Instrument of Foreign Policy* (Chicago: Markham, 1970).

Said, Abdul A., *America's World Role in the Seventies* (Englewood Cliffs, N.J.: Prentice-Hall, 1970).

Seabury, Paul, *Power, Freedom, and Diplomacy: The Foreign Policy of the United States of America* (New York: Random House, 1963).

Seabury, Paul, *The Rise and Decline of the Cold War* (New York: Basic Books, 1967).

Seabury, Paul, and Aaron Wildavsky, *U.S. Foreign Policy: Perspectives and Proposals for the 1970s* (New York: McGraw-Hill, 1969).

Shaffer, Edward M., *The Oil Import Program of the United States: An Evaluation* (New York: Praeger, 1968).

Swomley, John M., Jr., *The American Empire: The Political Ethics of Twentieth Century Conquest* (New York: Macmillan, 1970).

Whitworth, William, *Naive Questions About War and Peace* (New York: Norton, 1970).

Chapter Two. AMERICA LOOKS AT THE WORLD

Divine, Robert A., *Second Chance: The Triumph of Internationalism in America During World War II* (New York: Atheneum, 1967).

Free, Lloyd A., and Hadley Cantril, *The Political Beliefs of Americans: A Study of Public Opinion* (New Brunswick, N.J.: Rutgers University Press, 1967).

Gardner, John W., *The Recovery of Confidence* (New York: Norton, 1970).

Glad, Betty, *Charles Evans Hughes and the Illusion of Innocence: A Study in American Diplomacy* (Urbana: University of Illinois Press, 1966).

Hacker, Andrew, *The End of the America Era* (New York: Atheneum, 1970).

Hofstadter, Richard, *American Violence: A Documentary History* (New York: Knopf, 1970).

Jonas, Manfred, *Isolationism in America* (Ithaca, N.Y.: Cornell University Press, 1966).

Masters, R. D., "Lockean Tradition in American Foreign Policy," *Journal of International Affairs,* 21 (1967), 253–277.

Parenti, Michael, *The Anti-Communist Impulse* (New York: Random House, 1970).

Reich, Charles A., *The Greening of America: How the Youth Revolution Is Trying to Make America Livable* (New York: Random House, 1970).

Rieselbach, Leroy N., "The Basis of Isolationist Behavior," *Public Opinion Quarterly* XXIV (Winter 1960), 645–657.

Ways, Max, "O, Say Can You See? The Crisis in Our National Perception," *Fortune,* 78 (October 1968), 120–123.

Chapter Three. THE WHITE HOUSE AND THE STATE DEPARTMENT

Anderson, Patrick. *The Presidents' Men* (Garden City, N.Y.: Doubleday, 1968).

Barnett, Vincent M., Jr., ed., *The Representation of the United States Abroad*, rev. ed. (New York: Praeger, 1965).

Beichman, Arnold, *The "Other" State Department* (New York: Basic Books, 1968).

Bell, Jack, *The Johnson Treatment* (New York: Harper & Row, 1965).

Bell, Jack, *The Presidency: Office of Power* (Boston: Allyn & Bacon, 1967).

Berding, Andrew H., *Dulles on Diplomacy* (New York: Van Nostrand Reinhold, 1965).

Blancké, W. Wendell, *The Foreign Service of the United States* (New York: Praeger, 1969).

Briggs, Ellis, *Anatomy of Diplomacy: The Origin and Execution of American Foreign Policy* (New York: McKay, 1968).

Briggs, Ellis, *Farewell to Foggy Bottom* (New York: McKay, 1964).

"Congress, the President, and the Power to Commit Forces to Combat," *Harvard Law Review,* 81 (June 1968), 1771–1805.

Cornwell, Elmer E., Jr., *Presidential Leadership of Public Opinion* (Bloomington: Indiana University Press, 1965).

Cronin, Thomas E., and Sanford D. Greenberg, eds., *The Presidential Advisory System* (New York: Harper & Row, 1969).

Davis, James W., Jr., *The National Executive Branch: An Introduction* (New York: Free Press, 1970).

Dulles, Eleanor Lansing, *American Foreign Policy in the Making* (New York: Harper & Row, 1968).

Einstein, Lewis, *A Diplomat Looks Back* (New Haven, Conn.: Yale University Press, 1968).

Fenno, Richard F., *The President's Cabinet: An Analysis in the Period from Wilson to Eisenhower* (New York: Random House, 1959).

Ferrell, Robert H., *George C. Marshall* (New York: Cooper Square Publishers, 1966).

Flash, Edward S., Jr., *Economic Advice and Presidential Leadership: The Council of Economic Advisers* (New York: Columbia University Press, 1965).

Frankel, Charles, *High on Foggy Bottom: An Outsider's Inside View of the Government* (New York: Harper & Row, 1969).

Gerson, Louis L., *John Foster Dulles* (New York: Cooper Square Publishers, 1967).

Geyelin, Philip L., *Lyndon B. Johnson and the World* (New York: Praeger, 1966).

Gimlin, Hoyt, "State Department and Policy Making," *Editorial Research Reports* (June 26, 1968), 467–484.

Goldman, Eric F. *The Tragedy of Lyndon Johnson* (New York: Knopf, 1969).

Graff, Henry F., *The Tuesday Cabinet: Deliberation and Decision on Peace and War Under Lyndon B. Johnson* (Englewood Cliffs, N.J.: Prentice-Hall, 1970).

Hargrove, Erwin C., *Presidential Leadership: Personality and Political Style* (New York: Macmillan, 1966).

Heinrichs, Waldo H., *American Ambassador* (Boston: Little, Brown, 1967).

Heren, Louis, *No Hail, No Farewell* (New York: Harper & Row, 1970).

Hilsman, Roger, *To Move a Nation: The Politics of Foreign Policy in the Administration of John F. Kennedy* (Garden City, N.Y. Doubleday, 1967).

Hirschfield, Robert S., *The Power of the Presidency: Concepts and Controversy* (New York: Atherton, 1968).

"How the Secretary of State Apportions His Time," *The Department of State Bulletin*, LIV, no. 1400 (April 25, 1966), 651–654.

Jackson, Henry M., ed., *The Secretary of State and the Ambassador* (New York: Praeger, 1964).

James, Dorothy B., *The Contemporary Presidency* (New York: Pegasus, 1969).

Johnson, Richard A., *The Administration of American Foreign Policy* (Austin: University of Texas Press, 1971).

Kennan, George F., *Memoirs, 1925–1950* (Boston: Little, Brown, 1967).

Koenig, Louis W., *The Chief Executive*, rev. ed. (New York: Harcourt Brace Jovanovich, 1968).

Landecker, Manfred, *The President and Public Opinion: Leadership in Foreign Affairs* (Washington, D.C.: Public Affairs Press, 1968).

Leacocoa, John P., *Fires in the Basket: The ABC's of the State Department* (New York: World, 1968).

Lepper, Mary M., and John C. Walker, *Foreign Policy Formation: A Case Study of the Nuclear Test Ban Treaty of 1963* (Columbus, O.: Merrill, 1971).

McCamy, James L., *Conduct of the New Diplomacy* (New York: Harper & Row, 1964).

McLellan, D. C., "Dean Acheson and the Korean War," *Political Science Quarterly*, 83 (March 1968), 16–39.

Mann, Dean E., and W. Doig Jameson, *The Assistant Secretaries: Problems and Processes of Appointment* (Washington, D.C.: The Brookings Institution, 1965).

Mosher, Frederick C., *Programming Systems and Foreign Affairs: An Attempted Innovation* (New York: Oxford University Press, 1970).

Nicholas, H. G., "Men and Methods in American Foreign Policy," *International Affairs*, 40 (April 1965), 287–292.

Paolucci, Henry, *War, Peace, and the Presidency* (New York: McGraw-Hill, 1968).

Phillips, Cabell, *The Truman Presidency* (Baltimore: Penguin Books, 1969).

Plischke, Elmer, *Conduct of American Diplomacy*, 3rd ed. (New York: Van Nostrand Reinhold, 1967).

Plischke, Elmer "Eisenhower's Correspondence Diplomacy with the Kremlin—Case Study in Summit Diplomacy," *Journal of Politics*, 30 (February 1968), 137–159.

Plischke, Elmer, "The President's Inner Foreign Policy Team," *Review of Politics*, 60 (July 1968), 292–307.

Reedy, George E., *The Twilight of the Presidency* (New York: World, 1970).

Reston, James B., "The Press, the President and Foreign Policy," *Foreign Affairs*, 44 (July 1966), 553–573.

Rostow, W. W., *View from the Seventh Floor* (New York: Harper & Row, 1964).

Sapin, Burton M., *The Making of United States Foreign Policy* (Washington, D.C.: The Brookings Institution, 1966).

Sidey, Hugh, *A Very Personal Presidency* (New York: Atheneum, 1968).

Simpson, Smith, *Anatomy of the State Department* (Boston: Houghton Mifflin, 1967).

Villard, Henry S. *Affairs at State* (New York: Crowell, 1965).

Wise, Sidney, and Richard F. Schier, *The Presidential Office* (New York: Crowell, 1968).

Chapter Four.   NATIONAL SECURITY AND POLICY COORDINATION

Art, Robert J., *The TFX Decision: McNamara and the Military* (Boston: Little, Brown, 1968).

Art, Robert J., and Kenneth N. Waltz, eds., *The Use of Force: A Reader in International Politics* (Boston: Little, Brown, 1970).

Baldwin, Hanson W., "Slow-Down in the Pentagon," *Foreign Affairs*, 43, no. 2 (January 1965), 262–280.

Baumgartner, Stanley, *The Lonely Warriors: Case for the Military Industrial Complex* (Los Angeles: Nash Publishing, 1970).

Berkowitz, Morton, and P. G. Bock, eds., *American National Security: A Reader in Theory and Policy* (New York: Free Press, 1965).

Blackstock, Paul W., *The Strategy of Subversion: Manipulating the Politics of Other Nations* (Chicago: Quadrangle Books, 1964).

Bobrow, David B., ed., *Components of Defense Policy* (Chicago: Rand McNally, 1965).

Borklund, C. W., *Men of the Pentagon: From Forrestal to McNamara* (New York: Praeger, 1966).

Carrison, Captain Daniel J., *The United States Navy* (New York: Praeger, 1968).

Collins, F. W., "In Defense of the CIA," *Round Table*, 57, (January 1967), 115–121.

Collins, J. Lawton, *War in Peacetime: The History and Lessons of Korea* (Boston: Houghton Mifflin, 1969).

Dark, John J., *The New Economics of National Defense* (New York: Random House, 1966).

Deitchman, Seymour J., *Limited War and American Defense Policy* (Cambridge, Mass.: MIT Press, 1969).

Donovan, Col. James A., *Militarism: USA* (New York: Scribners, 1970).

Dulles, Allen, *The Craft of Intelligence* (New York: Harper & Row, 1963).

Erickson, John, ed., *The Military-Technical Revolution: Its Impact on Strategy and Foreign Policy* (New York: Praeger, 1966).

Falk, S. L., "The National Security Council Under Truman, Eisenhower and Kennedy," *Political Science Quarterly,* 79 (Summer 1964), 403–434.

Fulbright, Senator J. W., *The Pentagon Propaganda Machine* (New York: Liveright, 1970).

Gates, Thomas S., *The Report of the President's Commission On An All-Volunteer Armed Force* (New York: Macmillan, 1970).

Guttmann, Allen, *Korea and the Theory of Limited War* (Lexington, Mass.: Heath, 1967).

Halperin, Morton H., *Defense Strategies for the Seventies* (Boston: Little, Brown, 1971).

Hitch, Charles J., *Decision-Making for Defense* (Berkeley: University of California Press, 1965).

Huntington, Samuel P., ed., *Changing Patterns of Military Politics* (New York, Macmillan, 1962).

Jackson, Henry M., ed., *The National Security Council* (New York: Praeger, 1965).

Jordon, Col. Amos A., Jr., ed., *Issues of National Security in the 1970's* (New York: Praeger, 1967).

Just, Ward, *Military Men* (New York: Knopf, 1970).

Kaufmann, William W., *The McNamara Strategy* (New York: Harper & Row, 1964).

Kim, Young H., *The Central Intelligence Agency: Problems of Secrecy in a Democracy* (Lexington, Mass.: Heath, 1968).

Kirkpatrick, Lyman B., Jr., *The Real CIA* (New York: Macmillan, 1968).

Knoll, Erwin, and Judith N. McFadden, eds., *American Militarism, 1970* (New York: Viking, 1969).

Knorr, Klaus, "Failures in National Intelligence Estimates: The Case of the Cuban Missiles," *World Politics,* 16 (April 1, 1964), 455–467.

Knorr, Klaus, *Military Power and Potential* (Lexington, Mass.: Heath, 1970).

Knorr, Klaus, *On the Uses of Military Power in the Nuclear Age* (Princeton, N.J.: Princeton University Press, 1966).

Lens, Sidney, *The Military-Industrial Complex* (Philadelphia: Pilgrim Press, 1970).

Lough, T. S., "Military Liaison Missions in Germany," *Journal of Conflict Resolution,* 11 (June 1967), 258–261.

Lyons, Gene M., and Louis Morton, *Schools for Strategy: Education and Research in National Security Affairs* (New York: Praeger, 1965).

MacCloskey, General Monro, *The United States Air Force* (New York: Praeger, 1967).

McNamara, Robert S., *The Essence of Security: Reflection in Office* (New York: Harper & Row, 1968).

McNamara, Robert S., "Security in the Contemporary World," *The Department of State Bulletin,* LIV, no. 1406 (June 6, 1966), 874–881.

Millis, Walter, ed., *American Military Thought* (Indianapolis: Bobbs-Merrill, 1966).

Mollenhoff, Clark R., *The Pentagon* (New York: Putnam, 1967).

Pizer, Lt. Col. Vernon, *The United States Army* (New York: Praeger, 1967).

Posvar, Wesley W., *et. al.*, *American Defense Policy* (Baltimore: Johns Hopkins Press, 1965).

Powers, Patrick W., *A Guide to National Defense* (New York: Praeger, 1964).

Proxmire, William, *Report from Wasteland: America's Military-Industrial Complex* (New York: Praeger, 1970).

Ransom, Harry Howe, *The Intelligence Establishment* (Cambridge, Mass.: Harvard University Press, 1970).

Rodberg, Leonard, and Derek Shearer, eds., *The Pentagon Watchers* (Garden City, N.Y.: Doubleday, 1970).

Roherty, James M., *Decisions of Robert S. McNamara: A Study of the Role of the Secretary of Defense* (Coral Gables, Fla.: University of Miami Press, 1970).

Russett, Bruce M., *What Price Vigilance? The Burdens of National Defense* (New Haven, Conn.: Yale University Press, 1970).

Russett, Bruce M., "Who Pays for Defense?" *American Political Science Review,* LXIII (June 1969), 413–427.

Schiller, Herbert I., and Joseph D. Phillips, eds., *Super-State: Readings in the Military-Industrial Complex* (Urbana: University of Illinois Press, 1970).

Smith, Bruce L. R., *The Rand Corporation* (Cambridge, Mass.: Harvard University Press, 1966).

Smith, Mark E., and Claude J. Johns, eds., *American Defense Policy,* 2nd ed. (Baltimore: John Hopkins Press, 1968).

Tyrell, C. Merton, *Pentagon Partners: The New Nobility* (New York: Grossman, 1970).

Waskow, Arthur I., *The Debate over Thermonuclear Strategy* (Lexington, Mass.: Heath, 1965).

Wylie, J. C., *Military Strategy: A General Theory of Power Control* (New Brunswick, N.J.: Rutgers University Press, 1967).

Yarmolinsky, Adam, *The Military Establishment: Its Impact on American Society* (New York: Harper & Row, 1971).

Zuckerman, Sir Solly, *Scientists and War: The Impact of Science on Military and Civil Affairs* (New York: Harper & Row, 1967).

Chapter Five.   CONGRESS AND FOREIGN RELATIONS

Bailey, Stephen K., *Congress in the Seventies* (New York: St. Martin's Press, 1970).

Baldwin, D. J., "Congressional Initiative in Foreign Policy," *Journal of Politics*, **28** (November 1966), 754–774.

Barber, James D., *The Lawmakers: Recruitment and Adaptation to Legislative Life* (New Haven, Conn.: Yale University Press, 1965).

Carroll, Holbert N., *The House of Representatives and Foreign Affairs* (Boston: Little, Brown, 1966).

Coffin, Tristram, *Senator Fulbright: Portrait of a Public Philosopher* (New York: Dutton, 1966).

Dvorin, Eugene P., *The Senate's War Powers* (Chicago: Markham, 1971).

Fairlie, H., "Senators and World Power," *Encounter*, **30** (May 1968), 57–66.

Fenno, Richard F., Jr., *The Power of the Purse* (Boston: Little, Brown, 1966).

Fox, Annette B., "NATO and Congress," *Political Science Quarterly*, **80** (September 1965), 395–414.

Gallagher, Hugh G., *Advise and Obstruct* (New York: Delacorte Press, 1969).

Hitchens, H. L., "Influences on the Congressional Decision to Pass the Marshall Plan," *Western Political Quarterly*, **21** (March 1968), 51–68.

Horu, Stephen, *Unused Power: The Work of the Senate Committee on Appropriations* (Washington, D.C.: The Brookings Institution, 1970).

Huitt, Ralph K., and Robert L. Peabody, *Congress: Two Decades of Analysis* (New York: Harper & Row, 1969).

Javits, Jacob K., "The Congressional Presence in Foreign Relations," *Foreign Affairs*, **48** (January 1970), 221–235.

Jones, Charles O., *Minority Party Leadership in Congress* (Boston: Little, Brown, 1970).

Kolodzie, Edward A., "Congress and Foreign Policy: Through the Looking Glass," *Virginia Quarterly Review* **42** (Winter 1966), 12–27.

Peabody, Robert L., and Nelson W. Polsby, *New Perspectives on the House of Representatives*, 2nd ed. (Chicago: Rand McNally, 1969).

Pettit, Lawrence K., and Edward Keynes, *The Legislative Process in the United States Senate* (Chicago: Rand McNally, 1969).

Polsby, Nelson W., ed., *Congressional Behavior* (New York: Random House, 1971).

Pressmar, Jeffrey L., *House vs. Senate: Conflict in the Appropriations Process* (New Haven, Conn.: Yale University Press, 1966).

Rieselbach, Leroy N., ed., *The Congressional System* (Belmont, Calif.: Wadsworth, 1970).

Rieselbach, Leroy N., "The Demography of Congressional Vote on Foreign Aid, 1939–1958," *American Political Science Review*, **58** (September 1964), 577–589.

Ripley, Randall B., *Party Leaders in the House of Representatives* (Washington, D.C.: The Brookings Institution, 1967).

Ripley, Randall B., *Power in the Senate* (New York: St. Martin's Press, 1969).

Saloma, John S., *Congress and the New Politics* (Boston: Little, Brown, 1969).

Vinyard, Dale, *Congress* (New York: Scribners, 1968).

Westerfield, H. B., "Congress and Closed Politics in National Security Affairs," *Orbis*, **10** (Fall 1966), 737–753.

Wise, Sidney, and Richard F. Sehier, eds., *Studies on Congress* (New York: Crowell, 1969).

Chapter Six.   BIPARTISANSHIP

Aberbach, Joel D., "Alienation and Political Behavior," *American Political Science Review*, **LXIII** (March 1969), 86–100.

Amlund, Curtis Arthur, "Executive-Legislative Imbalance: Truman to Kennedy," *Western Political Quarterly*, **XVIII** (September 1965), 640–645.

Bailey, Thomas A., *Democrats vs. Republicans: The Continuing Clash* (New York: Meredith, 1968).

Caridi, Ronald J., *The Korean War and American Politics: The Republican Party as a Case Study* (Philadelphia: University of Pennsylvania Press, 1969).

Cummings, Milton C., Jr., *The National Election of 1964* (Washington: The Brookings Institution, 1966).

Dahl, Robert A., *Political Oppositions in Western Democracies* (New Haven, Conn.: Yale University Press, 1968).

DeGrazia, Alfred, *Republic in Crisis: Congress Against the Executive Force* (New York: Federal Legal Publications, 1965).

Dreyer, Richard C., and Walter A. Rosenbaum, eds., *Political Opinion and Behavior*, 2nd ed. (Belmont, Calif.: Wadsworth, 1970).

Geyelin, Philip, *Lyndon Johnson and the World* (New York: Praeger, 1966).

Grenville, John A., and George B. Young, *Politics, Strategy and American Diplomacy* (New Haven, Conn.: Yale University Press, 1966).

Handler, Edward, *The American Political Experience: What Is the Key?* (Lexington, Mass.: Heath, 1968).

Hanson, S. G., "Success of the International Coffee Agreement: How the State Department Deceived the Congress," *Inter-American Economic Affairs*, **21** (Autumn 1967), 55–79.

Holtzman, Abraham, *Legislative Liaison: Executive Leadership in Congress* (Chicago: Rand McNally, 1970).

Kaufman, Arnold S., *The Radical Liberal: New Man in American Politics* (New York: Atherton, 1968).

Livermore, Seward W., *Politics Is Adjourned: Woodrow Wilson and the War Congress, 1916–1918* (Middletown, Conn.: Wesleyan University Press, 1966).

Lubell, Samuel, *The Hidden Crisis in American Politics* (New York: Norton, 1970).

Philipps, Kevin P., *The Emerging Republican Majority* (New Rochelle, N.Y.: Arlington House, 1969).

Pipe, C. P. "Congressional Liaison: The Executive Branch Consolidates Its Relations with Congress," *Public Administration Review*, 26 (March 1966), 14–24.

Polsby, Nelson, *Congress and the Presidency* (Englewood Cliffs, N.J.: Prentice-Hall, 1964).

Rieselbach, Leroy N., *The Roots of Isolationism: Congressional Voting and Presidential Leadership in Foreign Policy* (Indianapolis: Bobbs-Merrill, 1966).

Robinson, James A., *Congress and Foreign Policy-Making* (Homewood, Ill.: Dorsey Press, 1966).

Rose, Richard, *Influencing Voters: A Study of Campaign Rationality* (New York: St. Martin's Press, 1967).

Scammon, Richard M., and Ben J. Wattenberg, *The Real Majority: An Extraordinary Examination of the American Electorate* (New York: Putnam, 1970).

Schlesinger, Arthur M., Jr., and Alfred deGrazia, *Congress and the Presidency: Their Role in Modern Times* (Washington: American Enterprises Institute, 1967).

Theoharis, Athan G., *The Yalta Myths: An Issue in American Politics, 1945–1955* (Columbia: University of Missouri Press, 1970).

Tompkins, A. David., *Senator Arthur H. Vandenberg: Evolution of a Modern Republican* (East Lansing: Michigan State University, 1971).

Chapter Seven. THE PUBLIC CONTEXT OF FOREIGN POLICY

Abt, C. C., "National Opinion and Military Security: Research Problems," *Journal of Conflict Resolution*, 9 (September 1965), 334–344.

Almond, Gabriel, *The American People and Foreign Policy* (New York: Praeger, 1960).

Aronson, James, *The Press and the Cold War* (Indianapolis: Bobbs-Merrill, 1970).

Baek, Kurt W., and Kenneth Gergen, "Public Opinion and International Relations," *Social Problems*, 11 (Summer 1963), 77–87.

Chase, S., "American Values: A Generation of Change," *Public Opinion Quarterly*, 29 (Fall 1965), 357–367.

Cohen, Bernard C., "The Military Policy Public," *Public Opinion Quarterly*, 30 (Summer 1966), 200–211.

Cohen, Bernard C., *The Press and Foreign Policy* (Princeton, N.J.: Princeton University Press, 1965).

Devine, Donald J., *The Attentive Public* (Chicago: Rand McNally, 1970).

Ellenport, S. "American Foreign Policy and Mass Democracy," *American Scholar*, 36 (Autumn 1967), 589–593.

Eulau, H., "Lobbyists: The Wasted Profession," *Public Opinion Quarterly*, XXVIII (Spring 1964), 27–38.

Franklin, John Hope, "The American Scholar and American Foreign Policy," *American Scholar*, 37 (Autumn 1968), 615–623.

Gamson, William A., "Evaluating Beliefs About International Conflict," in Roger Fisher, ed., *International Conflict and Behavioral Science*, (New York: Basic Books, 1964), pp. 27–40.

Gamson, William A., and Andre Modigliani, "Knowledge and Foreign Policy Opinions: Some Models for Consideration," *Public Opinion Quarterly*, 30 (Summer 1966), 187–199.

Gardner, C. Lloyd, *et al.*, *The Origins of the Cold War* (Waltham, Mass.: Ginn/Blaisdell, 1970).

Gronouski, John A., "The Intellectual and American Foreign Policy," *Department of State Bulletin*, 57 (October 2, 1967), 432–435.

Hero, Alfred O., Jr., "American Public and the U.N., 1954–1966," *Journal of Conflict Resolution*, 10 (December 1966), 436–475.

Hero, Alfred O., Jr., *The Southerner and World Affairs* (Baton Rouge: Louisiana State University Press, 1965).

Hohenberg, John, *Between Two Worlds: Policy, Press, and Public Opinion in Asian-American Relations*, (New York: Praeger, 1967).

Hutchins, Lavern C., *The John Birch Society and United States Foreign Policy* (New York: Pageant, 1968).

Landecker, Manfred, *The President and Public Opinion: Leadership in Foreign Affairs* (Washington: Public Affairs Press, 1968).

Lane, R. E., "Politics of Consensus in an Age of Affluence," *American Political Science Review*, 59 (December 1965), 874–895.

Lerche, Charles O., Jr., *The Uncertain South: Its Changing Patterns of Politics in Foreign Policy* (Chicago: Quadrangle Books, 1964).

Levertov, D., "Intellectuals and the War Machine," *North American Review* 5 (January 1968), 11–14.

Lipset, Seymour M., "Doves, Hawks, and Polls," *Encounter*, 27 (October 1966), 38–45.

Lipset, Seymour M., "Polls and Protests," *Foreign Affairs*, 49 (April 1971), 548–556.

Monsen, R. Joseph Jr., and Mark W. Cannon, *The Makers of Public Policy: American Power Groups and Their Ideologies,* (New York: McGraw-Hill, 1965).

Morrison, Samuel E., *Dissent in Three American Wars* (Cambridge, Mass.: Harvard University Press, 1970).

Mueller, John E., "Presidential Popularity from Truman to Johnson," *American Political Science Review,* LXIV (March 1970), 18–36.

Rivers, William L., *The Opinion Makers* (Boston: Beacon Press, 1965).

Rogers W. C., *et al.,* "Comparison of Informed and General Public Opinion on U.S. Foreign Policy," *Public Opinion Quarterly,* 31 (Summer 1967), 242–252.

Rosenau, James N., *National Leadership and Foreign Policy: A Case Study in the Mobilization of Public Support* (Princeton, N.J.: Princeton University Press, 1963).

Rosenau, James N., ed., *Domestic Sources of Foreign Policy* (New York: Free Press, 1967).

Rosenberg, M. J., S. Verba, and P. E. Converse, *Vietnam and the Silent Majority* (New York: Harper & Row, 1970).

Rostow, Eugene V., "A Certain Restlessness," *Department of State Bulletin,* 58 (March 25, 1968), 405–416.

Russett, Bruce M., "Demography, Salience, and Isolationist Behavior," *Public Opinion Quarterly,* XXIV (Winter 1960), 658–664.

Tucker, Robert W., *The Radical Left and American Foreign Policy* (Baltimore: Johns Hopkins Press, 1970).

Verba, Sidney, *et al.,* "Public Opinion and the War in Vietnam," American *Political Science Review,* 61 (June 1967), 317–333.

Veysey, Laurence, ed., *Law and Resistance: American Attitudes Toward Authority* (New York: Harper & Row, 1970).

Waltz, Kenneth N., *Foreign Policy and Democratic Politics* (Boston: Little, Brown, 1967).

White, R. K., "Conflict as Seen by Americans," *Journal of Social Issues* 22 (July 1966), 82–146.

Willis, R. H. "Ethnic and National Images: Peoples vs. Nations," *Public Opinion Quarterly,* 32 (Summer 1968), 186–301.

Windmuller, J. P., "Foreign Policy Conflict in American Labor," *Political Science Quarterly,* 82 (June 1967), 205–235.

Woodhouse, C. E. and D. S. McLellan, "American Business Leaders and Foreign Policy," *American Journal of Economics and Sociology,* 25 (July 1966), 267–280.

Chapter Eight. THE COLD WAR

Alperovitz, Gar, *Cold War Essays* (Garden City, N.Y.: Doubleday, 1969).

Dewey, Donald O., "America and Russia, 1939–1941" *Journalism Quarterly,* 44 (Spring 1967), 62–70.

Divine, Robert A., *Roosevelt and World War II* (Baltimore: Penguin Books, 1970).

Druks, Herbert, *Harry S. Truman and the Russians, 1945–1953,* (New York: Speller, 1967).

Eudin, Xenia J., and Robert M. Slusser, *Soviet Foreign Policy, 1928–1934: Documents and Materials,* (University Park: Pennsylvania State University Press. 1967).

Feis, Herbert, *From Trust to Terror: The Onset of the Cold War, 1945–1950* (New York: Norton, 1970).

Filene, Peter G., *Americans and the Soviet Experiment, 1917–1933* (Cambridge, Mass.: Harvard University Press, 1967).

Fontaine, Andre, *History of the Cold War: From the October Revolution to the Korean War, 1917–1950* and *History of the Cold War: From the Korean War to the Present* (New York: Pantheon, 1970).

Garthoff, Raymond L., *Soviet Military Policy: A Historical Analysis* (New York: Praeger, 1966).

Hamby, A. L., "Henry A. Wallace, The Liberals, and Soviet-American Relations," *Review of Politics,* 30 (April 1968), 153–169.

Jados, Stanley S., *Documents on Russian-American Relations: Washington to Eisenhower* (Washington, D.C.: Catholic University of America Press, 1965).

Knight, J., "George Frost Kennan and the Study of American Foreign Policy: Some Critical Comments," *Western Political Quarterly,* 20 (March 1967), 149–160.

Librach, Jan, *The Rise of the Soviet Empire: A Study of Soviet Foreign Policy,* rev. ed. (New York: Praeger, 1965).

McKenzie, Kermit E., *Comintern and World Revolution, 1928–1943: The Shaping of Doctrine* (New York: Columbia University Press, 1964).

Paterson, Thomas G., *Cold War Critics: Alternatives to American Foreign Policy in the Truman Years* (Chicago: Quadrangle Books, 1971).

Salisbury, Harrison E., *The Soviet Union: The Fifty Years* (New York: Harcourt Brace Jovanovich, 1967).

Seabury, Paul, and Brian Thomas, "Cold War Origins," *Journal of Contemporary History,* 3 (January 1968), 169–198.

Seabury, Paul, and Brian Thomas, *The Rise and Decline of the Cold War* (New York: Basic Books, 1967).

Smith, Gladdis, *American Diplomacy During the Second World War, 1941–1945* (New York: Wiley, 1965).

Sutton, Antony C., *Western Technology and Soviet Economic Development, 1917 to 1930* (Stanford, Calif.: Hoover Institution on War, Revolution and Peace, 1968).

Toynbee, A. J., "Russian-American Relations: The Case for Second Thoughts," *Journal of International Affairs*, 22 (No. 1, 1968), 1–4.

Welch, William, *American Images of Soviet Foreign Policy* (New Haven, Conn.: Yale University Press, 1970).

Wilson, Clifton E., *Cold War Diplomacy* (Tucson: University of Arizona, 1966).

Chapter Nine.   THE COLD WAR AFTER STALIN

Amalrik, Andrei, *Will the Soviet Union Survive Until 1984?* (New York: Harper & Row, 1970).

Aspaturian, Vernon V., *Power and Process in Soviet Foreign Policy* (Boston: Little, Brown, 1970).

Berger, Peter L., ed., *Marxism and Sociology: Views from Eastern Europe* (New York: Appleton-Century-Crofts, 1969).

Bromke, Adam, and Philip Wren, eds., *The Communist States and the West* (New York: Praeger, 1967).

Bunzel, John H., *Anti-Politics in America* (New York: Random House, 1970).

Byrnes, Robert F., ed., *The United States and Eastern Europe* (Englewood Cliffs, N.J.: Prentice-Hall, 1967).

Campbell, John C., *American Policy Toward Communist Eastern Europe: The Choices Ahead* (Minneapolis: University of Minnesota Press, 1965).

Conquest, Robert, "Stalin's Successors," *Foreign Affairs*, 48 (April 1970), 509–525.

Crozier, Brian, *Since Stalin* (New York: Coward-McCann, 1970)

DeGeorge, Richard T., *The New Marxism: Soviet and East European Marxism Since 1956* (New York: Pegasus, 1968).

Deutscher, Isaac, *Russia, China, and the West* (New York: Oxford University Press, 1970).

Deutscher, Isaac, *The Unfinished Revolution: Russia, 1917–1967* (London: Oxford University Press, 1969).

Drashkovitch, Milorad M., *Fifty Years of Communism in Russia* (University Park: Pennsylvania State University Press, 1968).

Drashkovitch, Milorad M., ed., *Marxist Ideology in the Contemporary World* (New York: Praeger, 1966).

Dulles, Eleanor W., and Robert Crane, *Détente: Cold War Strategies in Transition* (New York: Praeger, 1965).

Fainsod, Merle, "Some Reflections on Soviet-American Relations," *American Political Science Review*, 62 (December 1968), 1093–1103.

Fischer, George, *The Soviet System and Modern Society* (New York: Atherton Press, 1968).

Gilbert, Stephen, and Wynfred Joshua, *Arms for the Third World: Soviet Military Aid Diplomacy* (Baltimore: Johns Hopkins Press, 1969).

Graebner, Norman A., *The Cold War: Ideological Conflict or Power Struggle?* (Lexington, Mass.: Heath, 1963).

Griffith, William E., *Cold War and Coexistence: Russia, China, and the United States* (Englewood Cliffs, N.J.: Prentice-Hall, 1971).

Harriman W. Averell, *America and Russia in a Changing World: A Half Century of Personal Observation* (Garden City, N. Y.: Doubleday, 1971).

Hayter, Sir William, *Russia and the World: A Study of Soviet Foreign Policy* (New York: Taplinger, 1970).

Herrick, Commander Robert Waring, *Soviet Naval Strategy* (Annapolis, Md.: United States Naval Institute, 1968).

Horelick, Arnold L., and Myron Rush, *Strategic Power and Soviet Foreign Policy* (Chicago: University of Chicago Press, 1966).

Horowitz, David, *The Free World Colossus: A Critique of American Foreign Policy in the Cold War* (London: McGibbon and Kee, 1965).

Jacobs, Dan N., ed., *The New Communism* (New York: Harper & Row, 1969).

Juviler, Peter H., and Henry W. Morton, *Soviet Policy-Making: Studies of Communism in Transition* (New York: Praeger, 1967).

Kassof, Allen, ed., *Prospects for Soviet Society* (New York: Praeger, 1968).

Kinter, William R., ed., *The Nuclear Revolution in Soviet Military Affairs* (Norman: University of Oklahoma Press, 1968).

Labedz, Leopold, ed., *International Communism After Khrushchev* (Cambridge, Mass.: MIT Press, 1965).

Lengyel, Emil, *Nationalism—the Last Stage of Communism* (New York: Funk & Wagnalls, 1969).

Lerche, Charles O., Jr., *The Cold War—and After* (Englewood Cliffs, N.J.: Prentice-Hall, 1965).

Little, R. Richard, *Liberalization in the U.S.S.R.: Facade or Reality?* (Lexington, Mass.: Heath, 1968).

Lodge, Milton, *Soviet Elite Attitudes Since Stalin* (Columbus, O.: Merrill, 1969).

London, Kurt, ed., *The Soviet Union: A Half-Century of Communism* (Baltimore: Johns Hopkins Press, 1968).

Lowenthal, Richard, *World Communism: The Disintegration of a Secular Faith* (London: Oxford University Press, 1964).

MacKintosh, Malcolm, *Juggernaut! A History of the Soviet Armed Forces* (New York: Macmillan, 1967).

McLellan, David S., *The Cold War in Transition* (New York: Macmillan, 1966).

Morris, Bernard S., *International Communism*

and American Policy (New York: Atherton, 1966).

Mosely, Philip E., "Communist Policy and the Third World," *Review of Politics,* **28** (April 1966), 210–237.

Mosely, Philip E., and Marshall Shulman, *The Changing Soviet Challenge* (New York: Free Press, 1964).

Naik, J. A., *Soviet Policy Towards India: From Stalin To Brezhnev* (Delhi: Vikas Publications, 1970).

Nettl, J. P., *The Soviet Achievement* (New York: Harcourt Brace Jovanovich, 1968).

Parenti, Michael, *The Anti-Communist Impulse* (New York: Random House, 1970).

Pisar, Samuel, *Coexistence and Commerce: Guidelines for Transactions Between East and West* (New York: McGraw-Hill, 1970).

Ra'anan, Uri, *The USSR Arms The Third World* (Cambridge, Mass.: MIT Press, 1969).

Reed, Edward, ed., *Beyond Coexistence: The Requirements of Peace* (New York: Viking, 1968).

Rosser, Richard F., *An Introduction to Soviet Foreign Policy* (Englewood Cliffs, N.J.: Prentice-Hall, 1969).

Rush, Myron ed., *The International Situation and Soviet Foreign Policy: Reports of Soviet Leaders* (Columbus, O.: Merrill, 1970).

Sheldon, Charles S., *Review of the Soviet Space Program,* (New York: McGraw-Hill, 1968).

Shub, Anatole, *An Empire Loses Hope: The Return of Stalin's Ghost* (New York: Norton, 1970).

Shub, Anatole, *The New Russian Tragedy* (New York: Norton, 1970).

Shulman, M. D., "Recent Soviet Foreign Policy: Some Patterns in Retrospect," *Journal of International Affairs,* **22** (No. l, 1968), 26–47.

Spinelli, A., "Soviet Security and the West," *Atlantic Community Quarterly,* **6** (Spring 1968), 43–60.

Starr, Richard F., *Aspects of Modern Communism* (Columbia: University of South Carolina Press, 1968).

Stoessinger, John G., *Nations in Darkness: China, Russia, and America* (New York: Random House, 1971).

Tanham, George K., *Communist Revolutionary Warfare* (New York: Praeger, 1967).

Tatu, Michel, *Power in the Kremlin* (New York: Viking, 1970).

Thomas, J. R., "U.S.—East European Relations: Strategies Issues," *Orbis,* **12** (Fall 1968), 754–773.

Thornton, Thomas Perry, ed., *The Third World in Soviet Perspective* (Princeton, N.J.: Princeton University Press, 1964).

Treml, Vladimir G., and Robert Ferrell, *The Development of the Soviet Economy* (New York: Praeger, 1968).

Triska, Jan F., *Communist Party-States: Comparative and International Studies* (Indianapolis: Bobbs-Merrill, 1969).

Ulam, Adam B., *Expansion and Coexistance: The History of Soviet Foreign Policy, 1917–1967* (New York: Praeger, 1968).

Valkenier, E. K., "Changing Soviet Perspectives on the Liberation Revolution," *Orbis,* **9** (Winter 1966), 953–969.

Weeks, Albert L., *The Other Side of Coexistence* (New York: Putnam, 1970).

Weintal, Edward, and Charles Bartlett, *Facing the Brink: An Intimate Study of Crisis Diplomacy* (New York: Scribners, 1967).

Wetter, Gustav A., *Soviet Ideology Today* (New York: Praeger, 1966).

Wilber, Charles W., *The Soviet Model and Underdeveloped Countries* (Chapel Hill: University of North Carolina Press, 1969).

Wolfe, Thomas W., *Soviet Power and Europe, 1945–1970* (Baltimore: Johns Hopkins Press, 1970).

Zimmerman, William, *Soviet Perspectives on International Relations, 1956–1967* (Princeton: N.J.: Princeton University Press, 1969).

Chapter Ten.   WESTERN EUROPE

Ardach, John, *The New French Revolution* (New York: Harper & Row, 1969).

Armand, Louis, and Michel Drancourt, *The European Challenge* (New York: Atheneum, 1970).

Atlantic Institute, *The Technology Gap: U.S. and Europe* (New York: Praeger, 1970).

Barclay, G. St. John, *Commonwealth of Europe* (St. Lucia, Australia: University of Queensland Press, 1970).

Barnet, Richard J., and Marcus G. Raskin, *After 20 Years: Alternatives to the Cold War in Europe* (New York: Random House, 1965).

Baumann, Carol E., *Western Europe: What Path to Integration?* (Lexington, Mass.: Heath, 1967).

Beer, Francis A., *Integration and Disintegration in NATO* (Columbus: Ohio State University Press, 1969).

Beloff, Max, *The Future of British Foreign Policy* (New York: Taplinger, 1969),

Beugel, Ernst H. van der, *From Marshall Aid to Atlantic Partnership: European Integration as a Concern of American Foreign Policy* (New York: Elsevier, 1966).

Blackmer, Donald L. M., *Unity in Diversity: Italian Communism and the Communist World* (Cambridge, Mass.: MIT Press, 1968).

Bliss, Howard, ed., *The Political Development of the European Community: A Documentary Collection* (Waltham, Mass.: Ginn/Blaisdell, 1969).

Brinton, Crane, *The Americans and the French* (Cambridge, Mass.: Harvard University Press, 1968).

Buchan, Alstair, *Europe's Futures, Europe's Choices: Models of Western Europe in the 1970's* (London: Chatto & Windus, 1969).

Burgess, W. Randolph, and James R. Huntley, *Europe and America—the Next Ten Years* (New York: Walker, 1970).

Burks, R. V., *The Future of Communism in Europe* (Detroit, Mich.: Wayne State University Press, 1969).

Calleo, David, *The Atlantic Fantasy: The U.S., NATO, and Europe* (Baltimore: Johns Hopkins Press, 1970).

Cerny, Karl H., and Henry W. Briefs, eds., *NATO in Quest of Cohesion* (New York: Praeger, 1965).

Clark, W. Hartley, *The Politics of the Common Market* (Englewood Cliffs, N.J.: Prentice-Hall, 1967).

Cleveland, Harlan, *NATO: the Transatlantic Bargain* (New York: Harper & Row, 1970).

Coffee, J. I., "Strategy, Alliance Policy and Nuclear Proliferation," *Orbis,* 11 (Winter 1968), 375–395.

Cosgrove, Carol A., *The New International Actors: The United Nations and the European Economic Community* (New York: St. Martin's Press, 1970).

Crawford, Oliver, *Done This Day: The European Idea in Action* (New York: Taplinger, 1970).

Cromwell, William C., ed., *Political Problems of Atlantic Partnership: National Perspectives* (Bruges, Belgium: College of Europe, 1969).

Cross, Colin, *The Fall of the British Empire, 1918–1968* (New York: Coward-McCann, 1969).

Debre, Michel, "France's Global Strategy," *Foreign Affairs,* 49 (April 1971), 395–407.

De Carmoy, Guy, *The Foreign Policies of France, 1944–1968* (Chicago: University of Chicago Press, 1969).

Deutsch, Karl W., *et. al.,* France, Germany, and the Western Alliance* (New York: Scribners, 1967).

Dulles, Eleanor L., *One Germany or Two: The Struggle at the Heart of Europe* (Stanford, Calif.: Stanford University Press, 1970).

Feld, Werner, "External Relations of the Common Market and Group Leadership Attitudes in the Member States," *Orbis,* 10 (Summer 1966), 564–587.

Friedrich, Carl J., *Europe: An Emergent Nation:* (New York: Harper & Row, 1970).

Gladwyn, Lord Hubert M., *Europe After De Gaulle* (New York: Taplinger, 1969).

Grosser, Alfred, "France and Germany: Less Divergent Outlooks?" *Foreign Affairs,* 48 (January 1970), 235–245.

Hanrieder, Wolfram F., *Stable Crisis: Two Decades of German Foreign Policy* (New York: Harper & Row, 1970).

Hartmann, Frederick H., *Germany Between East and West: The Reunification Problem* (Englewood Cliffs, N.J.: Prentice-Hall, 1965).

Heath, Edward, *Old World, New Horizons: Britain, Europe, and the Atlantic Alliance* (Cambridge, Mass.: Harvard University Press, 1970).

Hogan, Willard N., *Representative Government and European Integration,* (Lincoln: University of Nebraska Press, 1967).

Holbik, Karel, and Henry A. Myers, *West German Foreign Aid, 1956–1966: Its Economic and Political Aspects* (Boston: Boston University Press, 1969).

Holborn, Hajo, *Germany and Europe* (Garden City, N.Y.: Doubleday, 1970).

Jackson, Henry M., ed., *The Atlantic Alliance* (New York: Praeger, 1967).

Kaiser, Karl, *German Foreign Policy in Transition: Bonn Between East and West* (New York: Oxford University Press, 1969).

Kaplan, Lawrence, S., *NATO and the Policy of Containment* (Lexington, Mass.: Heath, 1968).

Laqueur, Walter Z., *The Rebirth of Europe* (New York: Holt, Rinehart and Winston, 1970).

Lerche, Charles O., *Last Chance in Europe: Bases for a New American Policy* (Chicago: Quadrangle Books, 1967).

Lieber, Robert J., *British Politics and European Unity: Parties, Elites, and Pressure Groups* (Berkeley: University of California Press, 1970).

Lindberg, Leon N., and Stuart A. Scheingold, *Europe's Would Be Polity: Patterns of Change in the European Community* (Englewood Cliffs, N.J.: Prentice-Hall, 1969).

McCloy, John J., *The Atlantic Alliance: Its Origins and Its Future* (New York: Columbia University Press, 1969).

Maclean, Donald, *British Foreign Policy: The Years Since Suez, 1956–1968* (New York: Stein & Day, 1970).

McMillan, James, and Bernard Harris, *The American Take-Over of Britain* (New York: Hart, 1968).

Mayne, Richard, *The Recovery of Europe: From Devastation to Unity* (New York: Harper & Row, 1970).

Mendl, Wolf, *Deterrence and Persuasion: French Nuclear Armament in the Context of National Policy, 1945–1968* (New York: Praeger, 1970).

Merritt, Richard L., and Donald J. Puchala, *Western European Perspectives on International Affairs* (New York: Praeger, 1967).

Neustadt, Richard E. *Alliance Politics* (New York: Columbia University Press, 1970).

Orvik, N., "NATO, NAFTA and the Smaller

Allies," *Orbis,* **12** (Summer 1968), 455–464.

Osgood, Robert E., *Alliances and American Foreign Policy* (Baltimore: Johns Hopkins Press, 1968).

Parker, Geoffrey, *An Economic Geography of the Common Market* (New York: Praeger, 1969).

Pfaltzgraff, Robert L., Jr., *The Atlantic Community: A Complex Imbalance* (New York: Van Nostrand Reinhold, 1969).

Pinder, John, and Ray Pryer, *Europe After De Gaulle: Towards a United States of Europe* (Baltimore: Penguin Books, 1970).

Preeg, Ernest H., *Traders and Diplomats: An Analysis of the Kennedy Round of Negotiations Under the General Agreement on Tariffs and Trade* (Washington, D.C.: The Brookings Institution, 1969).

Richardson, James L., *Germany and the Atlantic Alliance: The Interaction of Strategy and Politics* (Cambridge, Mass.: Harvard University Press, 1966).

Roach, James R., and M. Donald Hancock, eds., *The United States and the Atlantic Community: Issues and Prospects* (Austin. University of Texas Press, 1967).

Rosecrance, R. N., *Defense of the Realm: British Strategy in the Nuclear Epoch* (New York: Columbia University Press, 1968).

Salter, Leonard M., "Toward a Supranational Law: The Common Market Experience," *American Bar Association Journal,* **53** (July 1967), 620–623.

Servan-Schreiber, J. J., *The American Challenge* (New York: Atheneum, 1968).

Stanley, Timothy W., *NATO in Transition* (New York: Praeger, 1965).

Stanley, Timothy W., and Darnell M. Whitt, *Détente Diplomacy: United States and European Security in the 1970's* (New York: Dunellen, 1970).

Stettner, Edward, A., ed., *Perspectives on Europe* (Cambridge, Mass.: Schenkman Publishing, 1970).

Stewart, Michael; "Britain, Europe and the Alliance," *Foreign Affairs,* **48** (July 1970), 648–660.

Strauss, Franz J., *The Grand Design: a European Solution to German Reunification* (New York: Praeger, 1965).

Symposium, "The Politics of Europe," *Foreign Affairs,* **49** (January 1971), 271–315.

Von Geusau, Frans A. M. Alting, *Beyond the European Community* (Leyden, Netherlands: Sijthoff, 1969).

Von Geusau, Frans A. M. Alting, ed., *Economic Relations After the Kennedy Round* (Leyden, Netherlands: Sijthoff, 1969).

Wallich, H. C., "United States and the European Economic Community: A Problem of Adjustment," *International Organization,* **22** (Autumn 1968), 841–854.

Walter, Ingo, *The European Common Market: Growth and Patterns of Trade and Production* (New York: Praeger, 1967).

Weil, Gordon L., *A Foreign Policy for Europe? The External Relations of the European Community* (Bruges, Belgium: College of Europe, 1970).

Chapter Eleven.   THE MIDDLE EAST AND AFRICA

Adu, A. L., "Post Colonial Relationships: Some Factors in the Attitudes of African States," *African Affairs,* **66** (October 1967), 295–309.

Agwani, M. S., *Communism in the Arab East* (New York: Asia Publishing House, 1970).

Andreski, Stanislav, *The African Predicament: A Study in the Pathology of Modernization* (New York: Atherton, 1969).

Arkhurst, Frederick S., *Africa in the Seventies and Eighties: Issues in Development* (New York: Praeger, 1970).

Attwood, William, *The Reds and the Blacks: A Personal Adventure* (New York: Harper & Row, 1967).

Balinger, Margaret, *From Union to Apartheid: A Trek to Isolation* (New York: Praeger, 1970).

Barnes, Leonard, *African Renaissance* (Indianapolis: Bobbs-Merrill, 1970).

Benson, Mary, *South Africa: The Struggle for a Birthright* (New York: Funk & Wagnalls, 1969).

Blair, Leon B, *Western Window in the Arab World* (Austin: University of Texas Press, 1970).

Burley, John, and Peter Tregear, eds., *African Development and Europe* (New York: Pergamon, 1970).

Busia, K. A., *Africa in Search of Democracy* (New York: Praeger, 1967).

Cartey, Wilfred, and Martin Kilson, eds., *The Africa Reader: Colonial Africa* and *The Africa Reader: Independent Africa* (New York: Random House, 1970).

Cerenka, Zdenek, *The Organization of African Unity and Its Charter* (New York: Praeger, 1969).

Childs, J. Rives, *Foreign Service Farewell: My Years in the Near East* (Charlottesville: University of Virginia Press, 1969).

Clements, Frank, *Rhodesia: A Study of the Deterioration of a White Society* (New York: Praeger, 1969).

Cohen, Aharon, *Israel and the Arab World* (New York: Funk & Wagnalls, 1970).

Cohen, Ronald, and John Middleton, *From Tribe to Nation in Africa* (San Francisco: Chandler, 1970).

Dagan, Avigdor, *Moscow and Jerusalem* (New York: Abelard-Schuman, 1970).

Davidson, Basil, *The African Genius* (Boston: Little, Brown, 1970).

Davis, John A., and James K. Baker, eds., *Southern Africa in Transition* (New York: Praeger, 1966).

Davis, John H., *The Evasive Peace: A Study of the Zionist-Arab Problem* (London: Murray, 1968).

deLosignan, Guy, *French-Speaking Africa Since Independence* (New York: Praeger, 1969).

Douglas-Home, Charles, *The Arabs and Israel: A Background Book* (Chester Springs, Pa.: Dufour Editions, 1969).

Dowse, Robert E., *Modernization in Africa and the U.S.S.R.* (New York: Humanities Press, 1969).

Duffy, James, *Portugal in Africa* (Baltimore: Penguin Books, 1963).

Dumoga, John, *Africa Between East and West* (Chester Springs, Pa.: Dufour Editions, 1969).

Dumont, Rene, *False Start in Africa* rev. ed. (New York: Praeger, 1969).

Feit, Edward, *African Opposition in South Africa: The Failure of Passive Resistance* (Stanford, Calif.: Hoover Institution on War, Revolution, and Peace, 1967).

Frady, Marshall, *Across a Darkling Plain: An America's Passage Through the Middle East* (New York: Harper's Magazine Press, 1971).

Frye, William, *In Whitest Africa: The Dynamics of Apartheid* (Englewood Cliffs, N.J.: Prentice-Hall, 1968).

Goldman, Nahum, "The Future of Israel," *Foreign Affairs*, **48** (April 1970), 443–460.

Gutteridge, William, *The Military in African Politics* (New York: Barnes and Noble, 1969).

Hance, William A., *African Economic Development* rev. ed. (New York: Praeger, 1967).

Hartshorn, J. E., *Politics and World Oil Economics* rev. ed. (New York: Praeger, 1967).

Hazelwood, Arthur, ed., *African Integration and Disintegration: Case Studies in Economic and Political Union* (New York: Oxford University Press, 1967).

Hirschmann, Ira, *Red Star Over Bethlehem* (New York: Simon and Schuster, 1971).

Hodes, Aubrey, *Dialogue With Ishmael* (New York: Funk & Wagnalls, 1969).

Hughes, A. J., *East Africa: Kenya, Tanzania, Uganda* rev. ed. (Baltimore, Penguin Books, 1970).

Hunter, Guy, "The New Africa," *Foreign Affairs*, **48** (July 1970), 712–726.

Isaacs, Harold, *American Jews in Israel* (New York: John Day, 1967).

Ismael, Tareq Y., *The U.A.R. in Africa: Egypt's Policy Under Nasser* (Evanston, Ill.: Northwestern University Press, 1971).

Jacob, Paul, *Between the Rock and the Hard Place* (New York: Random House, 1970).

July, Robert W. *The Origins of Modern African Thought* (New York: Praeger, 1968).

Kamarek, Andrew M., *The Economics of African Development* (New York: Praeger, 1967).

Kennan, George A., "Hazardous Courses in Southern Africa," *Foreign Affairs*, **49** (January 1971), 218–237.

Khadduri, Majid D., *The Arab-Israeli Impasse* (New York: McKay, 1969).

Khadduri, Majid D., *Political Trends in the Arab World: The Role of Ideas and Ideals in Politics* (Baltimore: Johns Hopkins Press, 1970).

Kimche, Jon, *The Second Arab Awakening* (New York: Holt, Rinehart and Winston, 1970).

Kleiman, Aaron S., *Soviet Russia and the Middle East* (Baltimore: Johns Hopkins Press, 1970).

Klinghoffer, A. J., *Soviet Perspectives on African Socialism* (Rutherford, N.J.: Fairleigh Dickinson Press, 1969).

Laufer, Leopold, *Israel and the Developing Countries: New Approaches to Cooperation* (New York: Twentieth Century Fund, 1967).

Lee, J. M., *African Armies and Civil Order* (New York: Praeger, 1969).

Lefever, Ernest W., *Spear and Scepter: Army, Police, and Politics in Tropical Africa* (Washington, D.C.: The Brookings Institution, 1970).

Lefever, Ernest W., "State-Building and Tropical Africa," *Orbis*, **12** (Winter 1969), 984–1003.

Legum, Colin, *Pan-Africanism: A Short Political Guide* (New York: Praeger, 1965).

Legum, Colin, and Margaret Legum *South Africa: Crisis for the West* (New York Praeger, 1964).

Legvold, Robert, "Moscow's Changing View of Africa's Revolutionary Regimes," *Africa Report*, **14** (March-April 1969), 54–58.

Legvold, Robert, *Soviet Policy in West Africa* (Cambridge, Mass.: Harvard University Press, 1970).

Markovitz, Irving L., ed., *African Politics and Society* (New York: Free Press, 1970).

Mazuri, Ali A., *Anglo-African Commonwealth* (New York: Pergamon, 1967).

Mazuri, Ali A., "Functions of Anti-Americanism in African Political Development," *Africa Report*, **14** (January 1969), 11–15.

Miller, J. D. B., *Politics of the Third World* (New York: Oxford University Press, 1967).

Mondlane, Eduardo, *The Struggle for Mozambique* (Baltimore: Penguin Books, 1969)

Nielsen, Waldemar A., *The Great Powers and Africa* (New York: Praeger, 1969).

Nove, Alec, and J. A. Newth, *The Soviet Middle East: A Communist Model for Development* (New York: Praeger, 1967).

Odell, Peter R., *Oil and World Power* (Baltimore: Penguin Books, 1970).

Okigbo, P. N., *Africa and the Common Market* (Evanston, Ill.: Northwestern University Press, 1967).

Ottaway, David, and Marina Ottaway, *Algeria: The Politics of a Socialist Revolution* (Berkeley: University of California Press, 1970).

Parkes, James, *Whose Land? A History of the Peoples of Palestine* (Baltimore: Penguin Books, 1970).

Peretz, Don, "Arab Palestine: Phoenix or Phantom?" *Foreign Affairs*, **48** (January 1970), 322–334.

Post, Ken, *The New States of West Africa* (Baltimore: Penguin Books, 1968).

Potholm, Christian, *Four African Political Systems* (Englewood Cliffs, N.J.: Prentice-Hall, 1970).

Quigg, P.W., "Changing American Views of Africa," *Africa Reports*, **14** (January 1969), 8–11.

Ramazani, Rouhollah K., *The Middle East and the European Common Market* (Charlottesville: University of Virginia Press, 1964).

Rivkin, Arnold, *Nation-Building in Africa: Problems and Prospects* (New Brunswick, N.J.: Rutgers University Press, 1970).

Robson, Peter, *Economic Integration in Africa* (Evanston, Ill.: Northwestern University Press, 1969).

Rodinson, Maxine, *Israel and the Arabs* (New York: Pantheon, 1969).

Said, Abdul A., *The African Phenomenon* (Boston: Allyn & Bacon, 1968).

Schatten, Fritz, *Communism in Africa* (New York: Praeger, 1966).

Schoenfield, Hugh H., *The Suez Canal in Peace and War, 1869–1969* (Coral Gables, Fla.: University of Miami Press, 1969).

Shepherd, George W., Jr., *Nonaligned Black Africa: An International Subsystem* (Lexington, Mass.: Heath, 1970).

Silverberg, Robert, *If I Forget Thee Oh Jerusalem: American Jews and the State of Israel* (New York: Morrow, 1970).

Stocking, George W., *Middle East Oil: A Study in Political and Economic Controversy* (Nashville, Tenn.: Vanderbilt University Press, 1970).

Taylor, Alan R, and Richard N. Tetlie, eds., *Palestine—A Search for Truth: Approaches to the Arab-Israeli Conflict* (Washington, D.C.: Public Affairs Press, 1970).

Thompson, Vincent B., *Africa and Unity: The Evolution of Pan-Americanism* (New York: Humanities Press, 1969).

Thompson, W. Scott, *Ghana's Foreign Policy, 1957–1966* (Princeton, N.J.: Princeton University Press, 1969).

Trevelyan, Humphrey, *The Middle East in Revolution* (Boston: Gambit, 1971).

Vandenbosch, Amry, *South Africa and the World: Foreign Policy and Apartheid* (Lexington: University of Kentucky Press, 1970).

Warburg, James P., *Cross-Currents in the Middle East* (New York: Atheneum, 1968).

Welch, Charles E., Jr., ed., *Soldier and State in Africa: A Comparative Analysis of Military Intervention and Political Change* (Evanston, Ill.: Northwestern University Press, 1970).

Williams, G. Mennen, *Africa for the Africans* (Grand Rapids, Mich.: Eerdmans, 1969).

Wright, Quincy, *The Middle East: Prospects for Peace* (Dobbs Ferry, N.Y.: Oceana, 1969).

Zartman, I. W., "Africa as a Subordinate State System in International Relations," *International Organization*, **21** (Summer 1967), 545–564.

Zartman, I. W., *The Politics of Trade Negotiations Between Africa and the European Economic Community* (Princeton, N.J.: Princeton University Press, 1971).

Chapter Twelve.   THE WESTERN HEMISPHERE

Abel, Elie, *The Missile Crisis* (Philadelphia: Lippincott, 1966).

Aguilar, Alonso, *Pan-Americanism From Monroe to the Present: A View From the Other Side* (New York: Monthly Review, 1969).

Aguilar, Luis E., *Marxism in Latin America* (New York: Random House, 1968).

Alba, Victor, *Alliance Without Allies: The Mythology of Progress in Latin America* (New York: Praeger, 1965).

Alba, Victor, *The Latin Americans* (New York: Praeger, 1970).

Alba, Victor, *Nationalists Without Nations: The Oligarchy Versus the People in Latin America* (New York: Praeger, 1968).

Alexander, Robert J., *Today's Latin America*, rev. ed. (New York: Praeger, 1968).

Astiz, Carlos Alberto, ed., *Latin American International Politics* (Notre Dame, Ind.: University of Notre Dame Press, 1969).

Bailey, Samuel L., ed., *Nationalism in Latin America* (New York: Knopf, 1970).

Ball, M. Margaret, *The OAS in Transition* (Durham, N.C.: Duke University Press, 1969).

Beautac, Willard L., *A Diplomat Looks at Aid to Latin America* (Carbondale, Ill.: Southern Illinois University Press, 1970).

Bernstein, Marvin, ed., *Foreign Investment in Latin America* (New York: Knopf, 1966).

Burnett, Ben G., et. al., eds., *Political Forces in Latin America: Dimensions of the Quest for Stability* 2nd ed. (Belmont, Calif.: Wadsworth, 1970).

Burr, Robert N., *Our Troubled Hemisphere: Perspectives on United States-Latin American Relations* (Washington, D.C.: The Brookings Institution, 1967).

Calvert, Peter, *Latin America: Internal Conflict and International Peace* (New York: St. Martin's Press, 1969).

Campos, Roberta de Oliveira, *Reflections on Latin American Development* (Austin: University of Texas Press, 1969).

Carlton, Robert G., ed., *Soviet Images of Latin America: A Documentary History, 1960–1968* (Austin: University of Texas Press, 1971).

Cochrane, James D., *The Politics of Regional Integration: The Central American Case* (New Orleans, La.: Tulane University Press, 1969).

Corkran, Herbert, Jr., *Patterns of International Cooperation in the Caribbean, 1942–1969* (Dallas, Tex.: Southern Methodist University Press, 1970).

Draper, Theodore, *Castroism: Theory and Practice* (New York: Praeger, 1956).

Duncan, W. Raymond, *et. al.*, eds., *The Quest for Change in Latin America* (New York: Oxford University Press, 1970).

Fagen, Richard F., and Wayne A. Cornelius, Jr., eds., *Political Power in Latin America: Seven Confrontations* (Englewood Cliffs, N.J.: Prentice-Hall, 1970).

Garcia-Amador, F. V., *The Inter-American System* (Dobbs Ferry, N.Y.: Oceana, 1966).

Geyer, George A., *The New Latins: Fateful Change in South and Central America* (Garden City, N.Y.: Doubleday, 1970).

Gil, Federico G., *Latin American-United States Relations* (New York: Harcourt Brace Jovanovich, 1971).

Gregg, Robert W., ed., *International Organization in the Western Hemisphere* (Syracuse, N.Y.: Syracuse University Press, 1968).

Hamill, Hugh M., Jr., ed., *Dictatorship in Spanish America* (New York: Knopf, 1966).

Hanson, Simon G., *Dollar Diplomacy Modern Style: Chapters in the Failure of the Alliance for Progress* (Washington, D.C.: Inter-American Affairs Press, 1970).

Hilton, Ronald, *The Movement Toward Latin American Unity* (New York: Praeger, 1969).

Horowitz, Irving L., *et. al.*, eds., *Latin American Radicalism* (New York: Random House, 1969).

Jackson, D. Bruce, *Castro, The Kremlin and Communism in Latin America* (Baltimore: Johns Hopkins Press, 1969).

Johnson, Cecil, *Communist China and Latin America, 1959–1967* (New York: Columbia University Press, 1970).

Jose, James R., *An Inter-American Peace Force Within the Framework of the Organization of American States* (Metuchen, N.J.: Scarecrow Press, 1970).

Kennedy, Robert F., *Thirteen Days: A Memoir of the Cuban Missile Crisis* (New York: Norton, 1970).

Levinson, Jerome, and Juan de Onis, *The Alliance That Lost Its Way: A Critical Report on the Alliance for Progress* (Chicago: Quadrangle Books, 1970).

Lockwood, Lee, *Castro's Cuba, Cuba's Fidel* (New York: Random House, 1969).

Lodge, George C., *Engines of Change: United States Interests and Revolution in Latin America* (New York: Knopf, 1970).

Lowenthal, Abraham F., "Alliance Rhetoric Versus Latin American Reality," *Foreign Affairs*, 48 (April 1970), 494–609.

May, Herbert K., *Problems and Prospects of the Alliance for Progress* (New York: Praeger, 1968).

Needler, Martin C., *Political Development in Latin America: Instability, Violence, and Evolutionary Change* (New York: Random House, 1968).

Nisbet, Charles T., ed., *Latin America: Problems in Economic Development* (New York: Macmillan, 1969).

Pachter, Henry M., *Collision Course: The Cuban Missile Crisis and Coexistence* (New York: Praeger, 1964).

Perloff, Harvey S., *Alliance for Progress: A Social Invention in the Making* (Baltimore: Johns Hopkins Press, 1969).

Quester, George H., "Missiles in Cuba, 1970," *Foreign Affairs*, 49 (April 1971), 493–507.

Ronning, C. Neale, *Intervention in Latin America* (New York: Knopf, 1970).

Rotberg, Robert I., *Haiti: The Politics of Squalor* (Boston: Houghton Mifflin, 1971).

Ruiz, Ramon E., *Cuba: The Making of a Revolution* (New York: Norton, 1970).

Shapiro, Samuel, ed., *Cultural Factors in Inter-American Relations* Notre Dame, Ind.: University of Notre Dame Press, 1968).

Sigmund, Paul E., ed., *Models of Political Change in Latin America* (New York: Praeger, 1970).

Slater, Jerome, *Intervention and Negotiation: The United States and the Dominican Republic* (New York: Harper & Row, 1970).

Stepan, Alfred, *The Military in Politics: Changing Patterns in Brazil* (Princeton, N.J.: Princeton University Press, 1971).

Suarez, Andres, *Cuba: Castroism and Communism, 1959–1966* (Cambridge, Mass.: MIT Press, 1969).

Symposium, "Latin America," *Foreign Affairs*, 49 (April 1971), 442–480.

Szulc, Tad, ed., *The United States and the Caribbean* (Englewood Cliffs, N.J.: Prentice-Hall, 1971).

Veliz, Claudio, ed., *Obstacles to Change in Latin America* (London: Oxford University Press, 1969).

Vernon, Raymond, ed., *How Latin America Views the U.S. Investor* (New York: Praeger, 1966).

Wagner, R. Harrison, *United States Policy Toward Latin America: A Study in Domestic and In-*

ternational Politics (Stanford, Calif.: Stanford University Press, 1970).

Wiarda, Howard J., *The Dominican Republic: Nation in Transition* (New York: Praeger, 1969).

Wilgus, A. Curtis: *The Caribbean: Its Hemispheric Role* (Gainesville: University of Florida Press, 1968).

Chapter Thirteen. ASIA

Asia Research Centre, *The Great Power Struggle in China* (Hong Kong: Hong Kong Book Centre, 1969).

Badgley, John, *Asian Development* (New York: Free Press, 1971).

Barnett, A. Doak, ed., *Chinese Communist Politics in Action* (Seattle: University of Washington Press, 1969).

Barnett, A. Doak, and Edwin W. Reischauer, eds., *The United States and China: The Next Decade* (New York: Praeger, 1970).

Basche, James, *Thailand: Land of the Free* (New York: Taplinger, 1971).

Bloodworth, Dennis, *An Eye for the Dragon: Southeast Asia Observed* (New York: Farrar, Straus & Giroux, 1970).

Boettinger, John R., ed., *Vietnam and American Foreign Policy* (Lexington, Mass.: Heath, 1968).

Bowles, Chester A., *View from New Delhi* (New Haven, Conn.: Yale University Press, 1969).

Brackman, Arnold C., *The Communist Challenge in Indonesia* (New York: Norton, 1969).

Brackman, Arnold C., *Southeast Asia's Second Front: The Power Struggle in the Malay Archipelago* (New York: Praeger, 1966).

Bulletin of the Atomic Scientists, *China and the Cultural Revolution* (New York: Random House, 1970).

Burnell, Elaine H., ed., *Asian Dilemma: United States, Japan and China* (Santa Barbara, Calif.: Center for the Study of Democratic Institutions, 1969).

Buttinger, Joseph, *Vietnam: A Political History* (New York: Praeger, 1968).

Butwell, Richard, *Southeast Asia Today—and Tomorrow: Problems of Political Development*, 2nd ed. (New York: Praeger, 1969).

Chandrasekhar, Sripati, ed., *Asia's Population Problems* (New York: Praeger, 1967).

Chaudhri, Mohammed A., *Pakistan and the Great Powers* (Karachi: Council for Pakistan Studies, 1970).

China and U.S. Far East Policy, 1945–1967, 2nd ed. (Washington, D.C.: Congressional Quarterly, 1967).

Cole, David C., and Princeton N. Lyman, *Korean Development: The Interplay of Politics and Economics* (Cambridge, Mass.: Harvard University Press, 1971).

Cooper, Chester L., *The Lost Crusade* (New York: Dodd, Mead, 1970).

Donnison, F. S. V., *Burma* (New York: Praeger, 1970).

Douglas, Bruce, and Ross Terrill, eds., *China and Ourselves* (Boston: Beacon Press, 1970).

Douglas, Stephen A., *Political Socialization and Student Activism in Indonesia* (Urbana: University of Illinois Press, 1970).

Eldridge, P. J., *The Politics of Foreign Aid in India* (New York: Schocken Books, 1970).

Elegant, Robert S., *Mao's Great Revolution* (New York: World, 1971).

Fall, Bernard B., ed. *Ho Chi Minh on Revolution: Selected Writings, 1920–1966* (New York: Praeger, 1967).

Farwell, George, *Mask of Asia: The Philippines Today* (New York: Praeger, 1967).

Fleming, D. F., *America's Role in Asia* (New York: Funk & Wagnalls, 1969).

Fryer, Donald W., *Emerging Southeast Asia: A Study in Growth and Stagnation* (New York: McGraw-Hill, 1970).

Garthoff, Raymond L., ed., *Sino-Soviet Military Relations* (New York: Praeger, 1966).

Geoffrey-Dechaume, François, *China Looks at the World* (New York: Random House, 1967).

Gerberding, W. P., "Vietnam and the Future of the United States Foreign Policy," *Virginia Quarterly Review*, 44 (Winter 1968), 19–42.

Gould, James W., *The United States and Malaysia* (Cambridge, Mass.: Harvard University Press, 1969).

Granqvist, Hans, *The Red Guard: A Report on Mao's Revolution* (New York: Praeger, 1967).

Gray, Jack, and Patrick Cavendish, *Chinese Communism in Crisis: Maoism and the Cultural Revolution* (New York: Praeger, 1968).

Guillain, Robert, *The Japanese Challenge* (Philadelphia: Lippincott, 1970).

Gurtov, Melvin, *Southeast Asia Tomorrow: Problems and Prospects for U.S. Policy* (Baltimore: Johns Hopkins Press, 1970).

Harper, Norman, ed., *Pacific Orbit: Australian-American Relations since 1942* (New York: Humanities Press, 1969).

Haviland, H. Field, Jr., *et. al.*, *Vietnam After the War: Peacekeeping and Rehabilitation* (Washington, D.C.: The Brookings Institution, 1969).

Hellman, Donald C., *Japanese Foreign Policy and Domestic Politics* (Berkeley: University of California Press, 1969).

Henderson, Gregory, *Korea: The Politics of the Vortex* (Cambridge, Mass.: Harvard University Press, 1968).

Hinton, Harold C., *China's Turbulent Quest* (New York: Macmillan, 1970).

Hslung, James C., *Ideology and Practice: The Evolution of Chinese Communism* (New York: Praeger, 1970).

Hsu, Francis L. K., *Americans and Chinese: Purpose and Fulfillment in Great Civilizations* (Garden City, N.Y.: Natural History Press, 1970).

Huck, Arthur, *The Security of China: Chinese Approaches to Problems of War and Strategy* (New York: Columbia University Press, 1970).

Kajima, Morinosuke, *Modern Japan's Foreign Policy* (Rutland, Vt.: Tuttle, 1969).

Kalb, Marvin, and Elie Abel, *Roots of Involvement: The U.S. in Asia, 1784–1971* (New York: Norton, 1970).

Kavic, Lorne J., *India's Quest for Military Security: Defense Policies, 1947–1966* (Berkeley: University of California Press, 1967).

Kitagawa, Joseph M., *Understanding Modern China* (Chicago: Quadrangle Books, 1969).

Koh, Byung C., *The Foreign Policy of North Korea* (New York: Praeger, 1969).

Lall, Arthur, *How Communist China Negotiates* (New York: Columbia University Press, 1969).

Lamb, Beatrice P., *India—A World in Transition* 3rd ed. (New York: Praeger, 1968).

Langer, Paul F., and Joseph J. Zasloff, *North Vietnam and the Pathet Lao: Partners in the Struggle for Laos* (Cambridge, Mass.: Harvard University Press, 1970).

Levi, Werner, *The Challenge of World Politics in South and Southeast Asia* (Englewood Cliffs, N.J.: Prentice-Hall, 1968).

Lifton, Robert J., *Revolutionary Immorality: Mao Tse-tung and the Chinese Cultural Revolution* (New York: Random House, 1968).

Lowenthal, Richard, ed., *Issues in the Future of Asia: Communist and Non-Communist Alternatives* (New York: Praeger, 1969).

McAlister, John T., Jr., *Viet Nam: The Origins of Revolution* (New York: Random House, 1969).

McAlister, John T., Jr., *The Vietnamese and Their Revolution* (New York: Harper & Row, 1970).

Maung, Maung, *Burma and General Ne Win* (New York: Asia Publishing House, 1969).

Melby, J. F., "Origins of the Cold War in China," *Pacific Affairs*, **41** (Spring 1968), 19–33.

Miller, J. D. B., ed., *India, Japan, Australia: Partners in Asia?* (Canberra, Australia: Australian National University Press, 1968).

Myrdal, Gunnar, *Asian Drama: An Inquiry Into the Poverty of Nations* (New York: Random House, 1968).

Myrdal, Gunnar, *China: The Revolution Continued* (New York: Pantheon, 1971).

Narayana, Gondker, *The India-China Border: A Reappraisal* (New York: Asia Publishing House, 1968).

Narayana, Gondker, *India and Southeast Asia,* (Bombay: Blatkal Books, 1968).

Nichols, H. G., "Vietnam and the Traditions of American Foreign Policy," *International Affairs*, **44** (April 1968), 189–201.

O'Connor, Richard, *Pacific Destiny: An Informal History of the U.S. in the Far East* (Boston: Little, Brown, 1969).

Oh, John K., *Korea: Democracy on Trial*, (Ithaca, N.Y.: Cornell University Press, 1968).

Ojha, Ishwer C., *Chinese Foreign Policy in an Age of Transition* (Boston: Beacon Press, 1971).

Olson, Lawrence, *Japan in Postwar Asia* (New York: Praeger, 1970).

Paul, Roland A., "Laos: Anatomy of an American Involvement," *Foreign Affairs*, **49** (April 1971), 533–548.

Pfeffer, Richard M., *No More Vietnams? The War and the Future of American Foreign Policy* (New York: Harper & Row, 1968).

Ravenal, Earl C., "The Nixon Doctrine and Our Asian Commitments," *Foreign Affairs*, **49** (January 1971), 201–218.

Reese, Trevor R., *Australia, New Zealand, and the United States* (New York: Oxford University Press, 1970).

Reischauer, Edwin O., *The United States and Japan*, rev. ed. (New York: Viking, 1962).

Rupen, Robert A., and Robert Farrell, eds., *Vietnam and the Sino-Soviet Dispute* (New York: Praeger, 1967).

Ryan, William L., and Sam Summerlin, *The China Cloud: America's Tragic Blunder and China's Rise to Nuclear Power* (Boston: Little, Brown, 1968).

Scalapino, Robert A., *The Communist Revolution in Asia: Tactics, Goals and Achievements*, 2nd ed. (Englewood Cliffs, N.J.: Prentice-Hall, 1969).

Schurmann, Franz, *Ideology and Organization in Communist China* (Berkeley: University of California Press, 1969).

Scott, Sir Robert, "China, Russia and the United States," *Foreign Affairs*, **48** (January 1970), 334–344.

Shand, R. T., ed., *Agricultural Development in Asia* (Berkeley: University of California Press, 1969).

Shaplen, Robert, *Time Out of Hand: Revolution and Reaction in Southeast Asia* (New York: Harper & Row, 1969).

Simmonds, J. D., *China's World: The Foreign Policy of a Developing State* (New York: Columbia University Press, 1971).

Simon, Sheldon W., *The Broken Triangle: Peking, Djarkarta, and the PKI* (Baltimore: Johns Hopkins Press, 1969).

Sinha, K. K., ed., *Problems of Defense of South and East Asia* (Bombay: Manaktalas, 1969).

Smith, David S., *The Next Asia: Problems for U.S. Policy* (New York: Columbia University Press, 1969).

Smith, Ralph, *Vietnam and the West* (Ithaca, N.Y.: Cornell University Press, 1971).

Stein, Arthur, *India and the Soviet Union: The*

Nehru Era (Chicago: University of Chicago Press, 1969).

Stone, P. B., *Japan Surges Ahead: The Story of an Economic Miracle* (New York: Praeger, 1969).

Symposium, "Indochina," *Foreign Affairs,* **48** (July 1970), 601–629.

Taylor, George E., *The Philippines and the United States: Problems of Partnership* (New York: Praeger, 1964).

Tilman, Robert O., ed., *Man, State, and Society in Contemporary Southeast* Asia (New York: Praeger, 1969).

Trager, Frank N., and William, Henderson, eds., *Communist China, 1949–1969: A Twenty-Year Appraisal* (New York: New York University Press, 1970).

Trumbull, Robert, ed., *This Is Communist China* (New York: McKay, 1968).

Tsou, Tang, ed., *China's Policies in Asia and America's Alternatives* (Chicago: University of Chicago Press, 1970).

Van Ness, Peter, *Revolution and Chinese Foreign Policy: Peking's Support for Wars of National Liberation* (Berkeley: University of California Press, 1970).

Weinstein, Martin E., *Japan's Postwar Defense Policy, 1947–1968* (New York: Columbia University Press, 1971).

Williams, Maslyn, *The Land in Between: The Cambodian Dilemma* (New York: Morrow, 1970).

Williams, Shelton L., *The U.S., India, and the Bomb* (Baltimore: Johns Hopkins Press, 1969).

Wilson, David A., *The United States and the Future of Thailand* (New York: Praeger, 1970).

Wilson, Dick, *Asia Awakes: A Continent in Transition* (New York: Weybright and Talley, 1970).

Woodman, Dorothy, *Himalayan Frontiers: A Political Review of British, Chinese, Indian and Russian Rivalries* (New York: Praeger, 1970).

Zablocki, Clement J., ed., *Sino-Soviet Rivalry: Implications for U.S. Policy* (New York: Praeger, 1966).

Chapter Fourteen. INFORMATIONAL AND ECONOMIC POLICY IMPLEMENTS

Amuzegar, Jahangir, *Technical Assistance in Theory and Practice: The Case of Iran* (New York: Praeger, 1966).

Andrzej, Krassowski, *The Aid Relationship* (London: Overseas Development Institute, 1968).

Asher, Robert E., *Developing Assistance in the Seventies: Alternatives for the United States* (Washington, D.C.: The Brookings Institution, 1970).

Baldwin, David A., *Economic Development and American Foreign Policy, 1943–1962*

(Chicago: University of Chicago Press, 1966).

Baldwin, David A., *Foreign Aid and American Foreign Policy* (New York: Praeger, 1966).

Bangs, Robert B., *Financing Economic Development: Fiscal Policy for Emerging Countries* (Chicago: University of Chicago Press, 1968).

Basch, Antonin, *A Pragmatic Approach to Economic Eevelopment* (New York: Vantage, 1970).

Bell, David, "The Quality of Aid," *Foreign Affairs,* **44** (July 1966), 601–608.

Benton, William, "Education as an Instrument of American Foreign Policy," *The Annals of the American Academy of Political and Social Science,* **366** (July 1966), 33–40.

Bermel, Albert, "The Split Personality of USIA," *Harper's Magazine,* **231** (September 1965), 116–125.

Bhagwati, Jagdish N., *Amount and Sharing of Aid* (Washington, D.C.: Overseas Development Council, 1970).

Black, Lloyd D., *The Strategy of Foreign Aid* (New York: Van Nostrand Reinhold, 1968).

Blum, Robert, ed., *Cultural Affairs and Foreign Relations* (Englewood Cliffs, N.J.: Prentice-Hall, 1963).

Brown, Lester R., *Seeds of Change: The Green Revolution and Development in the 1970's* (New York: Praeger, 1970).

Byrnes, Francis C., *Americans in Technical Assistance* (New York: Praeger, 1965).

Cerych, Ladislav, *Problems of Aid to Education in Developing Countries* (New York: Praeger, 1965).

Choukas, Michael, *Propaganda Comes of Age* (Washington, D.C.: Public Affairs Press, 1965).

Clews, John C., *Communist Propaganda Techniques* (New York: Praeger, 1964).

Cohen, Benjamin J., ed., *American Foreign Economic Policy* (New York: Harper & Row, 1968).

Coombs, Philip H., *The Fourth Dimension of Foreign Policy: Educational and Cultural Affairs* (New York: Harper & Row, 1964).

Cowan, Paul *The Making of an Un-American: A Dialogue With Experience* (New York: Viking, 1970).

Davison, W. Phillip, *International Political Communication* (New York: Praeger, 1965).

Domergue, Maurice, *Technical Assistance: Theory, Practice, and Politics* (New York: Praeger, 1968).

Erskine, H., "Polls: World Opinion of U.S. Racial Problems," *Public Opinion Quarterly,* **32** (Summer 1968), 299–312.

Frankel, Charles, "The Era of Educational and Cultural Relations," *Department of State Bulletin,* **LIV** (June 6, 1966), 889–897.

Frankel, Charles, *The Neglected Aspect of Foreign Affairs: American Educational and Cultural*

Policy Abroad (Washington, D.C.: The Brookings Institution, 1966).

Freeman, Orville, *World Without Hunger* (New York: Praeger, 1968).

Gardner, Richard N., *Sterling-Dollar Diplomacy: The Origins and the Prospects of Our International Economic Order:* (New York: McGraw-Hill, 1969).

Gardner, Richard N., and M. F. Millikan, eds., *The Global Partnership: International Agencies and Economic Development* (New York: Praeger, 1968).

Goldman, Marshall I., *Soviet Foreign Aid* (New York: Praeger, 1967).

Goldwin, Robert A., ed., *Why Foreign Aid?* (Chicago: Rand McNally, 1965).

Hanff, Helene, *Good Neighbors: The Peace Corps in Latin America* (New York: Grosset & Dunlap, 1966).

Hapgood, David, and Bennett Meridan, *Agents of Change: A Close Look at the Peace Corps* (Boston: Little, Brown, 1968).

Harris, Elliot, *The "Un-American" Weapon: Psychological Warfare* (New York: M. W. Lads, 1967).

Hoopes, Roy, *The Peace Corps Experience* (New York: Clarkson N. Potter, 1968).

Hoskins, Halford, "Aid and Diplomacy in the Middle East," *Current History,* 51 (July 1966), 14–19.

Hovey, Harold A., *United States Military Assistance: A Study of Policies and Practices* (New York: Praeger, 1965).

Kaplan, Jacob J., *The Challenge of Foreign Aid* (New York: Praeger, 1967).

Kock, Karin, *International Trade Policy and the GATT, 1947–1967* (Stockholm: Almavist & Wiksell (distr.), August, 1969).

Lasswell, Harold D., *et. al.,* eds., *Propaganda and Promotional Activities: An Annotated Bibliography* rev. ed. (Chicago: University of Chicago Press, 1969).

Legum, Colink ed., *The First U.N. Development Decade and Its Lessons for the 1970's* (New York: Praeger, 1970).

Linder, Staffan B., *Trade and Trade Policy for Development* (New York: Praeger, 1967).

McCamant, John F., *Development Assistance in Latin America* (New York: Praeger, 1968).

McGuire, Edna, *The Peace Corps: Kindlers of the Spark* (New York: Macmillan, 1966).

Mahajani, Usha, "Kennedy and the Strategy of Aid: The Clay Report and After," *Western Political Quarterly,* XVIII (September 1965), 656–668.

Mares, Vaclav E., "U.S. Aid to East Europe," *Current History,* 51 (July 1966), 36–44.

Mason, Edward S., *Foreign Aid and Foreign Policy* (New York: Harper & Row, 1964).

Mason, Edward S., "The Formulation of Aid Policies," *Current History,* 50 (June 1966), 328–334.

Myrdal, Gunnar, *The Challenge of World Poverty: A World Anti-Poverty Program in Outline* (New York: Pantheon, 1970).

Nathan, R.S., "Psychological Warfare: Key to Success in Viet Nam," *Orbis,* 11 (Spring 1967), 182–198.

Nelson, Joan M., *Aid, Influence, and Foreign Policy* (New York: Macmillan, 1968).

O'Leary, Michael K., *The Politics of American Foreign Aid* (New York: Atherton, 1967).

Pearson, Lester B., *The Crisis of Development* (New York: Praeger, 1970).

Pearson, Lester B., *Partners in Development* (New York: Praeger, 1969).

Romson, Moritz, *Living Poor: A Peace Corps Chronicle* (Seattle: University of Washington Press, 1970).

Rowan, Carl T., "USIA: Building Bridges of Peace in a Changing World," *Department of State Bulletin,* LI (December 28, 1964), 906–912.

Rubin, Jacob A., *Your 100 Billion Dollars: The Complete Story of American Foreign Aid* (Philadelphia: Chilton, 1964).

Rubin, Ronald I., *The Objectives of the U.S. Information Agency* (New York: Praeger, 1968).

Sawyer, Carole A., *Communist Trade With Developing Countries, 1955–65* (New York: Praeger, 1966).

Schickele, Rainer, *Agrarian Revolution and Economic Progress* (New York: Praeger, 1968).

Schwarz, H. G., "America Faces Asia: The Problem of Image Projection," *Journal of Politics,* 26 (August 1964), 532–549.

Schwarzenberger, Georg, *Foreign Investments and International Law* (New York: Praeger, 1969).

Smith, Hadley E., ed., *Problems of Foreign Aid* (London: Oxford University Press, 1965).

Sorensen, Thomas C., *Word War: The Story of American Propaganda* (New York: Harper & Row, 1968).

Spiller, Robert E., "American Studies Abroad: Culture and Foreign Policy," *The Annals of The American Academy of Political and Social Science,* 366 (July 1966), 1–16.

Stokke, Baard R., *Soviet and Eastern Europe Trade and Aid in Africa* (New York: Praeger, 1967).

Tansky, Leo, *U.S. and USSR Aid to Developing Countries: A Comparative Study of India, Turkey, and the UAR* (New York: Praeger, 1967).

Textor, Robert T., ed., *Cultural Frontiers of the Peace Corps* (Cambridge, Mass.: MIT Press, 1966).

Thompson, Charles A., and Walter H. C. Laves, *Cultural Relations and U.S. Foreign Policy* (Bloomington: Indiana University Press, 1963).

Thompson, Kenneth W., "American Education and the Developing Areas," *The Annals of the American Academy of Political and So-cial Science,* 366 (July 1966), 17–32.

Thorp, Willard L., *The Reality of Foreign Aid* (New York: Praeger, 1971).

Walters, Robert S., *American and Soviet Aid: A Comparative Analysis* (Pittsburgh, Pa.: University of Pittsburgh Press, 1970).

Westwood, Andrew F., *Foreign Aid in a Foreign Policy Framework* (Washington, D.C.: The Brookings Institution, 1966).

Wetzel, Charles J., "The Peace Corps in Our Past," *The Annals of the American Academy of Political and Social Sciences,* 365 (May 1966), 1–11.

Whitton, John B., and Arthur Larson, *Propaganda: Toward Disarmament in the War of Words* (Dobbs Ferry, N.Y.: Oceana, 1964).

Whitton, John B., ed., *Propaganda and the Cold War* (Washington, D.C.: Public Affairs Press, 1963).

"Why They Don't Like Us—A Dissection," *Atlas,* 15 (February 1968), 48–51.

Wilton, Dillon, *Gifts and Nations: The Obligation to Give, Receive and Repay* (The Hague: Mouton, 1968).

Wofford, Harris, "The Future of the Peace Corps," *The Annals of the American Academy of Political and Social Sciences,* 365 (May 1966), 12–20.

Zeitlin, Arnold, *To The Peace Corps With Love* (Garden City, N.Y.: Doubleday, 1965).

Chapter Fifteen.   INTERNATIONAL ORGANIZATION AND ARMS CONTROL

Adams, T. W., and A. J. Cottrell, "American Foreign Policy and the U.N. Peace-Keeping Force in Cypress," *Orbis,* 12 (Summer 1968), 490–503.

Andrassy, Juraj, *International Law and the Resources of the Sea* (New York: Columbia University Press, 1970).

Armacost, Michael H., *The Politics of Weapons Innovation* (New York: Columbia University Press, 1969).

Baade, H. W., ed., *The Soviet Impact on International Law* (Dobbs Ferry, N.Y.: Oceana, 1965).

Bader, William B., *The United States and the Spread of Nuclear Weapons* (New York: Pegasus, 1968).

Bailey, Sydney D., *The General Assembly of the United Nations,* rev. ed. (New York: Praeger, 1964).

Bailey, Sydney D., *The Secretariat of the United Nations* (New York: Praeger, 1964).

Bailey, Sydney D., *Voting in the Security Council* (Bloomington: University of Indiana Press, 1969).

Barker, Charles A., *et. al., Problems of World Disarmament* (Boston: Houghton Mifflin, 1963).

Barnaby, C. F., ed., *Preventing the Spread of Nuclear Weapons* (New York: Humanities Press, 1969).

Barnaby, C. F., and A. Boserup, eds., *Implications of Anti-Ballistic Missile Systems* (New York: Humanities Press, 1970).

Barnett, A. Doak, "A Nuclear China and U.S. Arms Policy," *Foreign Affairs,* 48 (April 1970), 427–443.

Beeker, Benjamin J., *Is the United Nations Dead?* (Philadelphia: Whitmore Publishing, 1969).

Berman, H. J., and P. B. Maggs, *Disarmament Inspection Under Soviet Law* (Dobbs Ferry, N. Y.: Oceana, 1967).

Bloomfield, Lincoln P., *et. al., Khrushchev and the Arms Race* (Cambridge, Mass.: MIT Press, 1966).

Boskey, Bennett, and Mason Willrich, eds., *Nuclear Proliferation: Prospects for Control* (New York: Dunellen 1970).

Bowett, D. W., *United Nations Forces: A Legal Study* (New York: Praeger, 1965).

Bull, Hedley, *The Control of the Arms Race,* 2nd ed. (New York: Praeger, 1965).

Castaneda, Jorge, *Legal Effects of United Nations Resolutions* (New York: Columbia University Press, 1970).

Chayes, Abram, and Jerome B. Wiesner, *ABM: An Evaluation of the Decision to Deploy An Anti-Ballistic Missile System* (New York: Harper & Row, 1969).

Claude, Inis L., Jr., "Collective Legitimization as a Political Function of the United Nations," *International Organization,* 20 (Summer 1966), 367–369.

Clemens, Walter C., Jr., *The Arms Race and Sino-Soviet Relations* (Stanford, Calif.: Hoover Institution on War, Revolution, and Peace, 1968).

Collins, Edward, Jr., *International Law in a Changing World* (New York: Random House, 1970).

Cosgrove, Carol A., and Kenneth J. Twitchett, *The New International Actors: The United Nations and the European Economic Community* (New York: St. Martin's Press, 1970).

Cox, Robert W., *The Politics of International Organizations* (New York: Praeger, 1970).

Coyle, David Cushman, *The U.N. and How It Works* (New York: Columbia University Press, 1970).

Dallin, Alexander, *et. al., The Soviet Union and Disarmament* (New York: Praeger, 1964).

Dan, Kenneth W., *The GATT: Law and International Economic Organization* (Chicago: University of Chicago Press, 1970).

Edwards, David V., *Arms Control in International Politics* (New York: Holt, Rinehart and Winston, 1969).

Eichelberger, Clark M., *U.N.—The First 25 Years* (New York: Harper & Row, 1970).

Englemann, Brent, *The Weapons Merchants* (New York: Crown, 1968).

Fabian, Larry L., *Soldiers Without Enemies: Preparing the United Nations for Peacekeeping* (Washington, D.C.: The Brookings Institution, 1971).

Falk, Richard A., *Legal Order in a Violent World* (Princeton, N.J.: Princeton University Press, 1968).

Falk, Richard A., and Richard J. Barnet, eds., *Security in Disarmament* (Princeton, N.J.: Princeton University Press, 1965).

Falk, Richard A., and Cyril E. Black, eds., *The Future of the International Legal Order* (Princeton, N.J.: Princeton University Press, 1969).

Finkelstein, Lawrence, ed., *The United States and International Organization in the Seventies* (Cambridge, Mass.: MIT Press, 1969).

Finkelstein, Lawrence, and Marina Finkelstein, eds., *Collective Security* (San Francisco: Chandler, 1966).

Frank, Lewis A., *The Arms Trade in International Relations* (New York: Praeger, 1969).

Gardner, Richard N., "Can the United Nations Be Revived?" *Foreign Affairs,* 48 (July 1970), 660–677.

Gardner, Richard N., ed., *The Global Partnership: International Agencies and Economic Development* (New York: Praeger, 1968).

Goodrich, Leland M., *et. al.*, *Charter of the United Nations: Commentary and Documents* (New York: Columbia University Press, 1969).

Hagras, Kamal, *United Nations Conference on Trade and Development: A Case Study in U.N. Diplomacy* (New York: Praeger, 1965).

Halderman, J. W., *The United Nations and the Rule of Law* (Dobbs Ferry, N.Y.: Oceana, 1967).

Halperin, Morton H., and Dwight H. Perkins, *Communist China and Arms Control* (New York: Praeger, 1965).

Halperin, Morton H., ed., *Sino-Soviet Relations and Arms Control* (Cambridge, Mass.: MIT Press, 1967).

Higgins, Benjamin H., *U.N. and U.S. Foreign Economic Policy* (Homewood, Ill.: Richard D. Irwin, 1962).

Higgins, Rosalyn, ed., *United Nations Peacekeeping, 1946–1967* (New York: Oxford University Press, 1970).

Holst, Johan J., and William Schneider, Jr., *Why ABM? Policy Issues in the Missile Defense Controversy* (New York: Pergamon, 1969).

James, Alan, *The Politics of Peace Keeping* (London: Chatto & Windus, 1969).

Kay, David A., "Impact of African States on the U.N." *International Organization,* 23 (Winter 1969), 20–47.

Kay, David A., *The New Nations in the United Nations, 1960–1967* (New York: Columbia University Press, 1970.

Kemp, Geoffrey, "Dilemmas of the Arms Traffic," *Foreign Affairs,* 48 (January 1970), 274–285.

Keohane, Robert O., "Political Influence in the General Assembly," *International Conciliation,* No. 556 (January 1966), 1–64.

Kirdar, Uner, *The Structure of United Nation's Economic Aid to Underdeveloped Countries* (The Hague, Netherlands: Martinus Nijhoff, 1966).

Kolkowicz, Roman, *et. al.*, *The Soviet Union and Arms Control* (Baltimore: Johns Hopkins Press, 1970).

Lande, G. R., "Effect of the Resolutions of the United Nations General Assembly," *World Politics,* 19 (October, 1966), 83–105.

Lapp, Ralph E., *Arms Beyond Doubt: The Tyranny of Weapons Technology* (New York: Cowles, 1970).

Lapp, Ralph E., *The Weapons Culture* (Baltimore: Penguin Books, 1968).

Larson, Thomas B., *Disarmament and Soviet Policy, 1964–1968* (Englewood Cliffs, N.J.: Prentice-Hall, 1969).

Lawson, Ruth C., ed., *International Regional Organizations: Constitutional Foundations* (New York: Praeger, 1964).

Luard, Evan, *The International Protection of Human Rights* (New York: Praeger, 1967).

Luard, Evan, ed., *The Evolution of International Organization* (New York: Praeger, 1966).

Manno, C. S., "Majority Decisions and Minority Responses in the U.N. General Assembly," *Journal of Conflict Resolution,* 10 (March 1966), 1–20.

Moskowitz, Moses, *The Politics and Dynamics of Human Rights* (Dobbs Ferry, N.Y.: Oceana, 1958).

Nazrui, A. A., "U.N. and Some African Political Attitudes," *International Regional Organizations* (Summer 1969), 499–520.

Nicholas, H. G., *The United Nations as a Political Institution,* 4th ed. (New York: Oxford University Press, 1971).

O'Brien, Conor C., and Feliks Topolski, *The United Nations: Sacred Drama* (New York: Simon and Schuster, 1968).

Ramundo, Lt. Col. Bernard A., *Peaceful Coexistence: International Law in the Building of Communism* (Baltimore: Johns Hopkins Press, 1967).

Rejai, M., "Communist China and the United Nations," *Orbis,* 10 (Fall 1966), 823–838.

Roberts, Chalmers M., *The Nuclear Years: The Arms Race and Arms Control, 1945–70* (New York: Praeger, 1970).

Ross, Alf, *The United Nations: Peace and Progress* (New York: Bedminster Press, 1966).

Rubinstein, Alvin Z., *The Soviets in International*

Organizations (Princeton, N.J.: Princeton University Press, 1964).

Russell, Ruth B., *The United Nations and United States Security Policy* (Washington, D.C.: The Brookings Institution, 1968).

Sen, Sudhir, *United Nations in Economic Development: Need for a New Strategy* (Dobbs Ferry, N.Y.: Oceana, 1969).

Sharma, D. N., *Afro-Asian Group in the U.N.* (Allahabad, India: Chaitanya Publishing House, 1969).

Sharp, Walker R., *The United Nations Economic and Social Council* (New York: Columbia University Press, 1969).

Sohn, Louis B., *The United Nations in Action: Ten Cases from United Nations Practice* (New York: Foundation Press, 1969).

Stroessinger, Joyn G., *The U.N. and the Superpowers*, rev. ed. (New York: Random House, 1970).

Teltsch, Kathleen, *Cross-Currents at Turtle Bay: A Quarter-Century of the United Nations* (Chicago: Quadrangle Books, 1971).

Thayer, George, *The War Business: The International Trade in Armaments* (New York: Simon and Schuster, 1969).

Townley, Ralph, *The United Nations: A View From Within* (New York: Scribners, 1969).

Tung, William L., *International Law in an Organizing World* (New York: Crowell, 1968).

Van Dyke, Vernon, *Human Rights, The United States, and World Community* (New York: Oxford University Press, 1970).

Weiggert, K.M., and R. E. Riggs, "Africa and U.N. Elections: An Aggregate Data Analysis," *International Organization*, **23** (Winter 1969), 1–19.

White, Irvin L., *Decision-Making for Space: Law and Politics in Air, Sea, and Outer Space* (West Lafayette, Ind.: Purdue University Press, 1970).

Willrich, M., "ABM and Arms Control," *International Affairs*, **44** (April 1968), 228–239.

Wilson, Thomas W., Sr., *The Great Weapons Heresy* (Boston: Houghton Mifflin, 1970).

Xydis, Stephen G., *Cyprus: Conflict and Conciliation, 1954–1958* (Columbus: Ohio State University Press, 1967).

Chapter Sixteen. PHILOSOPHICAL FOUNDATIONS OF FOREIGN POLICY

Arich, Yehoshua, *Individualism and Nationalism in American Ideology* (Baltimore: Penguin Books, 1964).

Bailey, Thomas A., *The Art of Diplomacy: The American Experience* (New York: Meredith, 1968).

Benson, Leonard G., *National Purpose: Ideology and Ambivalence in America* (Washington: Public Affairs Press, 1963).

Bloomfield, L. B., "Future Small Wars: Must the United States Intervene?" *Orbis*, **12** (Fall 1968), 669–684.

Bohlen, Charles E., *The Transformation of American Foreign Policy* (New York: Norton, 1969).

Boorstin, Daniel J., *The Decline of Radicalism: Reflections on America Today* (New York: Random House, 1969).

Brandon, Donald, *American Foreign Policy: Beyond Utopianism and Realism* (New York: Appleton-Century Crofts, 1966).

Brown, Seyom, *The Faces of Power: Constancy and Change in United States Foreign Policy from Truman to Johnson* (New York: Columbia University Press, 1968).

Brzezinski, Zbigniew, *Between Two Ages: America's Role in the Technetronic Revolution* (New York: Viking, 1970).

Chomsky, Noam, *American Power and the New Mandarins* (New York: Random House, 1969).

Cleveland, Harlan, *The Obligations of Power: American Diplomacy in the Search for Peace* (New York: Harper & Row, 1966).

Cobb, Roger W., and Charles Elder, *International Community: A Regional and Global Study* (New York: Holt, Rinehart and Winston, 1970).

Dietze, Gottfried, *America's Political Dilemma: From Limited to Unlimited Diplomacy* (Baltimore: Johns Hopkins Press, 1968).

Dolbeare, Kenneth, and Patricia Dolbeare, *American Ideologies: The Competing Political Beliefs of the 1970's* (Chicago: Markham, 1970).

Finletter, Thomas K., *Interim Report: On the Search for a Substitute for Isolation* (New York: Norton, 1968).

Frankel, Joseph, *National Interest* (New York: Praeger, 1970).

Friedman, W., "Intervention, Liberalism, and Power—Politics: The Unfinished Revolution in International Thinking," *Political Science Quarterly*, **83** (June 1968), 169–189.

Gardner, Lloyd C., *Architects of Illusion: Men and Ideas in American Foreign Policy* (Chicago: Quadrangle Press, 1970).

Gordon, Kermit, ed., *Agenda for the Nation* (Washington, D.C.: The Brookings Institution, 1968).

Gross, Bertram M., ed., *A Great Society?* (New York: Basic Books, 1968).

Haas, Ernst B., *Tangle of Hopes: American Commitments and World Order* (Englewood Cliffs, N.J.: Prentice-Hall, 1969).

Horowitz, David, *The Free World Colossus* (New York: Hill & Wang, 1965).

Houghton, Neal D., ed., *Struggle Against History: U.S. Foreign Policy in an Age of Revolution* (New York: Washington Square Press, 1968).

Howe, Irving, ed., *A Dissenter's Guide to Foreign Policy* (New York: Praeger, 1968).

Kissinger, Henry A., *American Foreign Policy: Three Essays* (New York: Norton, 1969).

Kolko, Gabriel, *The Roots of American Foreign Policy: An Analysis of Power and Purpose* (Boston: Beacon Press, 1969).

Lillibridge, George D., *The American Image* (Lexington, Mass.: Heath, 1968).

Liska, George, *Imperial America: The International Politics of Primacy* (Baltimore: Johns Hopkins Press, 1967).

McCarthy, Eugene J., *The Limits of Power: America's Role in the World* (New York: Holt, Rinehart and Winston, 1967).

Morgenthau, Hans J., *A New Foreign Policy for the United States* (New York: Praeger, 1969).

Morgenthau, Hans J., *Truth and Power: Essays of a Decade, 1960–1970* (New York: Praeger, 1970).

Morris, Richard B., *The Emerging Nations and the American Revolution* (New York: Harper & Row, 1970).

Niebuhr, Reinhold, and Paul E. Sigmund, *The Democratic Experience: Past and Prospects* (New York: Praeger, 1969).

Nichols, H. G., "Vietnam and the Traditions of American Foreign Policy," *International Affairs,* **44** (April 1968), 189–201.

Osgood, Robert E., *et. al., America and the World: From the Truman Doctrine to Vietnam* (Baltimore: Johns Hopkins Press, 1970).

Osgood, Robert E., *Ideals and Self Interest in America's Foreign Relations: The Great Transformation of the Twentieth Century* (Chicago: University of Chicago Press, 1964).

Ransom, Harry H., *Can American Democracy Survive the Cold War?* (Garden City, N.Y.: Doubleday, 1963).

de Riencourt, Amaury, *The American Empire: A Study in Reluctant Domination* (New York: Dell, 1970).

Rosenau, James N., *The Scientific Study of Foreign Policy* (New York: Free Press, 1971).

Schapsmeier, F. H., and E. L. Schapsmeier, "Walter Lippmann: Critic of American Foreign Policy," *Midwest Quarterly,* **7** (January 1966), 123–137.

Schlesinger, Arthur, Jr., *Violence: America in the Sixties* (New York: New American Library, 1968).

Schwarz, Urs, *American Strategy: A New Perspective* (Garden City, N.Y.: Doubleday, 1966).

Skolnick, Jerome H., and Elliot Currie, *Crisis in American Institutions* (Boston: Little, Brown, 1970).

Steel, Ronald, *Pax Americana* (New York: Viking, 1967).

Stillman, Edmund, and William Pfaff, *Power and Impotence: The Failure of America's Foreign Policy* (New York: Random House, 1966).

Tucker, Robert W., *Nation or Empire? The Debate Over American Foreign Policy* (Baltimore: Johns Hopkins Press, 1968).

Waltz, Kenneth N., *Foreign Policy and Democratic Politics: The American and British Experience* (Boston: Little, Brown, 1967).

Young, James P., *The Politics of Affluence: Ideology in America Since World War II* (San Francisco: Chandler, 1968).

INDEX